IMPORTANT

D0509623

HERE IS YOUR REGISTRATION CODE TO ACCESS MCGRAW-HILL
PREMIUM CONTENT AND MCGRAW-HILL ONLINE RESOURCES

For key premium online resources you need THIS CODE to
gain access. Once the code is entered, you will be able to
use the web resources for the length of your course.

Access is provided only if you have purchased a new book.

If the registration code is missing from this book, the registration screen on our
website, and within your WebCT or Blackboard course will tell you how to obtain
your new code. Your registration code can be used only once to establish access.
It is not transferable

To gain access to these online resources

1. USE your web browser to go to: **http://www.mhhe.com/etzel07**

2. CLICK on "First Time User"

3. ENTER the Registration Code printed on the tear-off bookmark on the right

4. After you have entered your registration code, click on "Register"

5. FOLLOW the instructions to setup your personal UserID and Password

6. WRITE your UserID and Password down for future reference. Keep it in a safe place.

If your course is using WebCT or Blackboard, you'll be able to use this code to
access the McGraw-Hill content within your instructor's online course.

To gain access to the McGraw-Hill content in your instructor's WebCT or
Blackboard course simply log into the course with the user ID and Password provided by your instructor. Enter the registration code exactly as it appears to the
right when prompted by the system. You will only need to use this code the first
time you click on McGraw-Hill content.

These instructions are specifically for student access. Instructors are not required
to register via the above instructions.

Thank you, and welcome to your
McGraw-Hill/Irwin Online Resources.

Etzel
Marketing, 14/e
ISBN 10: 0-07-301635-7
ISBN 13: 978-0-07-301635-1

TGAA-8Q7X-8H63-PQN

REGISTRATION CODE
REGISTRATION CODE

McGraw-Hill
Irwin

The McGraw-Hill Companies

Mc
Graw
Hill McGraw-Hill
Irwin

Marketing

14th Edition

Marketing

14th Edition

Michael J. Etzel
University of Notre Dame

Bruce J. Walker
University of Missouri–Columbia

William J. Stanton
University of Colorado–Boulder

McGraw-Hill
Irwin

Boston Burr Ridge, IL Dubuque, IA Madison, WI New York
San Francisco St. Louis Bangkok Bogotá Caracas Kuala Lumpur
Lisbon London Madrid Mexico City Milan Montreal New Delhi
Santiago Seoul Singapore Sydney Taipei Toronto

MARKETING

Published by McGraw-Hill/Irwin, a business unit of The McGraw-Hill Companies, Inc., 1221 Avenue of the Americas, New York, NY, 10020. Copyright © 2007 by The McGraw-Hill Companies, Inc. All rights reserved. No part of this publication may be reproduced or distributed in any form or by any means, or stored in a database or retrieval system, without the prior written consent of The McGraw-Hill Companies, Inc., including, but not limited to, in any network or other electronic storage or transmission, or broadcast for distance learning.

Some ancillaries, including electronic and print components, may not be available to customers outside the United States.

This book is printed on acid-free paper.

1 2 3 4 5 6 7 8 9 0 QPD/QPD 0 9 8 7 6 5

ISBN-13   978-0-07-301634-4
ISBN-10   0-07-301634-9

Editorial director: *John E. Biernat*
Publisher: *Andy Winston*
Sponsoring editor: *Barrett Koger*
Freelance developmental editor: *Joanne Butler*
Editorial coordinator: *Jill M. O'Malley*
Executive marketing manager: *Dan Silverburg*
Media producer: *Benjamin Curless*
Project manager: *Laura Griffin*
Senior production supervisor: *Rose Hepburn*
Senior designer: *Mary E. Kazak*
Photo research coordinator: *Ira C. Roberts*
Photo researcher: *Mike Hruby*
Media project manager: *Joyce J. Chappetto*
Cover design: *Sarah Dukes*
Cover image: © Getty Images/Mitchell Funk
Interior design: *Amanda Kavanagh*
Typeface: *10/12 Sabon*
Compositor: *Carlisle Communications, Ltd.*
Printer: *Quebecor World Dubuque Inc.*

Library of Congress Cataloging-in-Publication Data
Etzel, Michael J.
    Marketing/Michael J. Etzel, Bruce J. Walker, William J. Stanton.—14th ed.
        p. cm.
    Includes bibliographical references and indexes.
    ISBN-13:978-0-07-301634-4 (alk. paper)
    ISBN-10:0-07-301634-9 (alk, paper)
        1. Marketing. I. Walker, Bruce J. II. Stanton, William J.   III. Title.
    HF5415.S745 207
    658.8—dc22

                                        2005044581

www.mhhe.com

About the Authors

Michael J. Etzel received his Ph.D. in marketing from the University of Colorado. Since 1980, he has been a professor of marketing at the University of Notre Dame. He also has been on the faculties at Utah State University and the University of Kentucky. In 1990, he was a Fulbright Fellow at the University of Innsbruck, Austria. He returned to the University of Innsbruck in 2006 as a Fulbright Distinguished Chair in Social and Economic Sciences. His other overseas assignments have included directing and teaching in the University of Notre Dame's program in Fremantle, Australia, in 1994, and in Notre Dame's London MBA program in 1998. Professor Etzel has taught marketing courses from the introductory through the doctoral level. He received a Kaneb undergraduate teaching award from the University of Notre Dame in 2001. His research, primarily in marketing management and buyer behavior, has appeared in the *Journal of Marketing, Journal of Marketing Research, Journal of Consumer Research, Journal of Retailing,* and other publications. He is the coauthor of another college-level text, *Retailing Today.*

Professor Etzel has been active in many aspects of the American Marketing Association at the local and national levels. He served as chairman of AMA's board of directors in 1996–1997.

Bruce J. Walker became professor of marketing and dean of the College of Business at the University of Missouri–Columbia in 1990. Professor Walker received his undergraduate degree in economics from Seattle University and his master's and Ph.D. degrees in business from the University of Colorado.

Professor Walker was a member of the marketing faculties at the University of Kentucky and then at Arizona State University. Dr. Walker has taught a variety of courses, including principles of marketing. His research, focusing primarily on franchising, marketing channels, and survey-research methods, has been published in the *Journal of Marketing, Journal of Marketing Research,* and other periodicals. He has also coedited or coauthored conference proceedings and books, including *Retailing Today.*

Dr. Walker has been involved with the American Marketing Association, including serving as vice president of the Education Division. Currently, he is a trustee for the International Franchise Association's Education Foundation and a member of several corporate boards including Salton, Inc., an international housewares company.

William J. Stanton is professor emeritus of marketing at the University of Colorado–Boulder. He received his Ph.D. in marketing from Northwestern University, where he was elected to Beta Gamma Sigma. He has worked in business and has taught in several management development programs for marketing executives. He has served as a consultant for various business organizations and has engaged in research projects for the federal government. Professor Stanton also has lectured at universities in Europe, Asia, Mexico, and New Zealand.

A coauthor of the leading text in sales management, Professor Stanton has also published several journal articles and monographs. *Marketing* has been translated into Spanish, and separate editions have been adapted (with coauthors) for Canada, Italy, Australia, and South Africa. In a survey of marketing educators, Professor Stanton was voted one of the leaders in marketing thought. And he is listed in *Who's Who in America* and *Who's Who in the World.*

Dedication

Mike Etzel
To Jake, Eric, Nick, and Audrey

Bruce Walker
To Pam, and Walker, Nicole, Justin, Aidan, Chase, and Evangeline

Bill Stanton
To Kelley and Little Joe

Brief Contents

Contents

Part Two
Identifying and Selecting Markets

Part Three
Product

22 Marketing and the Information Economy   610

Can AMAZON Keep the Sales Flowing?   611

Preface

As we began planning this, the 14th edition of *Marketing,* we asked ourselves: How can a textbook best meet the needs of its market? We started out by defining the market as consisting of two related groups, each with a quite different role:

- One group is *students,* who would learn about marketing from the book. Many of these students are taking their first course in marketing at the college level. Some, but not all, of these students have practical marketing experience in part-time or full-time jobs. They actually buy the book.

- The other group is *professors* who choose what text their students will read in a marketing course. The professors don't actually purchase the book, but they are the decision makers. Their choice of a text influences how well their students learn and, therefore, how successful the professors are in teaching the course.

Considering students first, we examined research as well as feedback on previous editions of *Marketing* from our students and others. For the professors, we looked at where our book had been used and we sought the views of adopters and nonadopters. In brief, here's what we learned and what served as the guiding principles as we prepared this edition:

- Students tell us they definitely want a book that is readable—one that explains concepts clearly, holds their interest, and is up-to-date and relevant. They desire a book that helps them learn and also makes studying for tests efficient and effective. Most would also like a book to be as concise as possible. Finally, they want a text that is affordable.

- Professors want the same things, and more. They recognize this will be the only marketing course that many students take but that it will be the foundation for a marketing major and possibly a marketing career for other students. Thus, instructors want a full array of marketing topics covered so that both types of students can appreciate the role of marketing. In addition, they want the organization of the topics in the text and the support materials to contribute to efficient and effective teaching.

We also obtained perspectives from the business world, both directly through conversations with executives and indirectly by examining periodicals and trade journals. From these sources, we identified the people, organizations, and topics that are having the greatest impact on business and marketing today as well as those predicted to play a major role in the near future. What we discerned can be placed into four categories: technology, internationalization, the physical environment, and ethical and socially responsible behavior. As you will see as you read the book, these topics take many forms in marketing. A brief preview will indicate some of the ways we incorporated these topics in the 14th edition of *Marketing.*

Technological advances affect business in many ways, such as how people and organizations communicate. The rise, and now prevalence, of cellular phones, communication satellites, and the Internet have had dramatic impacts on business. In fact, they have even given new meaning to existing words such as *spam, cookies,* and *files* and have added new words to our vocabulary such as *instant messaging, googgling, bloggers,* and *podcasting.*

Another very significant ongoing trend is the internationalization of business. Increasingly, corporations are thinking and acting globally in selecting suppliers and seeking customers. Looking to the future, Western firms are jockeying for position in China and India, while China looks for markets in the west, and Indian firms benefit from outsourcing by many Western firms. (Of course, many more countries than China and India are key parties to the internationalization trend.) Trading alliances such as the European Union look for expansion opportunities even as the members try to settle their differences.

Then there are two areas that are gaining greater prominence. The physical environment, reflected in topics such as global warming, air and water quality, and waste disposal, influence marketing with regards to the use of natural resources, the proliferation of products, and the efficiency of how products are distributed. There also is greater interest in ethical and socially responsible behavior. Concerns in this area include health and nutrition, product safety, advertising claims, brand protection, and understandable pricing. Reports of unethical conduct, success stories of firms that make ethical choices, and the increasing use of codes of conduct indicate the growing sensitivity to fostering an ethical and socially responsible dimension in decisions.

Finally, but certainly not last in our content considerations for this edition, we recognized that ample coverage should be given to the fundamental concepts, strategies, and techniques that serve as the cornerstones of marketing programs. As you read this book, you will learn how and why organizations serve only a portion of a market, how they select the groups they choose to serve, where the information comes from for making these decisions, and the approaches to strategic decision making.

It is our belief that marketing can and should be applied to every exchange situation. As a result, it is relevant to everyone, regardless of whether a person plans on a career in business, in the government, or in a nonprofit organization. Our response to this belief and the inputs provided by students, professors, and the business community was to develop a package that will help prepare students for a challenging, dynamic, and exciting future. The features that make this possible are described next.

Overview of this Edition

In every new edition of *Marketing*, we make changes to produce a structure we believe is effective as well as student- and instructor-friendly. We seek to do that by:

- Organizing the topics around seven themes that logically build from fundamental concepts, strategies, and techniques through the major tasks associated with marketing to the strategic role of marketing in an organization.

- Bringing attention to the global nature of marketing by dedicating Chapter 3 to this important topic, integrating global examples throughout the book, and providing "A Global Perspective" box in almost every chapter.

- Emphasizing the similarities as well as the differences between consumer and business marketing by means of back-to-back coverage in Chapters 4 and 5.

- Combining demand forecasting with its logical antecedents—segmentation, targeting, and positioning—in Chapter 6.

- Covering marketing research in Chapter 7, after students have been exposed to consumer and business markets and segmentation.

- Making Services Marketing, Chapter 11, part of the product section of the book.

- Combining wholesaling and physical distribution in one chapter.

- Integrating planning, implementation, and evaluation in Chapters 20 and 21 to provide a broad strategic context after students have a grasp of what marketing entails.

- Carrying four themes throughout the book—global marketing, ethical challenges, the marketer as decision maker, and the impact of technology on marketing—with separate boxes interspersed throughout the chapters. These vignettes are intended to both inform students about noteworthy topics and issues and stimulate critical thinking on their part.

- Concluding the book with a chapter that examines the growing role that technology has—and surely will continue to have—in marketing.

Other Noteworthy Features

The changes in the 14th edition and previous editions have a singular purpose, namely to make the book an even better learning tool for students. Among the noteworthy changes are:

- Over time, the text has been shortened without reducing the number of topics covered.

- The Internet's role is properly reflected throughout the book with examples, Web addresses, and boxes.

- The chapter-opening and part-ending cases, within-chapter boxes, and Interactive Marketing Exercises at the end of each chapter are useful instruments for stimulating active learning through projects, classroom discussions, and debates.

- Two appendices, which can be found on the website for the text (www.mhhe.com/etzel07), deal with marketing math and career planning and job search. These appendices contain practical material that can be integrated into the course by instructors or used independently by students.

Chapter-Related Cases

Each chapter begins with a contemporary case that sets the stage for the upcoming material. At the conclusion of the chapter, the case is revisited and more specific information is presented about marketing-related activities associated with the organization or product that is the subject of the case. By addressing the questions following the "More about . . ." part of the case at the end of the chapter, students discover how they can apply what they have learned in the chapter to an actual marketing situation.

Some of the organizations and products that are highlighted in the cases are highly recognizable, whereas others are relatively unknown or somewhat unusual. However, we have made a special effort to select cases that students will not only find interesting but also can learn from. We have been asked, "Aren't you concerned that some of the facts in a case may become dated or firms or products may be gone by the time the case is covered in class?" Our answer is an emphatic "No." Students should be encouraged to do some research on any case they examine and focus on the concepts, strategies, and techniques highlighted in the case. Students can learn from failures as well as successes.

Chapter-opening cases involving relatively well-known organizations and products that have significant marketing opportunities and challenges include:

- Trader Joe's
- Song Airlines
- Boeing
- Dunkin' Donuts
- Cadillac
- IKEA
- Nike
- Starbucks
- Walgreens

Another group of cases address situations in which technology, including the Internet, is an important issue. This group of cases includes:

- iTunes
- Kodak
- Toys "R" Us
- NetFlix
- Amazon
- Priceline.com

Still others deal with less familiar products and situations that have substantial marketing implications. Among these cases are:

- W. W. Grainger
- ZipCar
- Imaginatik
- USDA Food Pyramid
- CDW Corporation
- Zara
- Bose

Most of the chapter-opening cases are new to this edition. Any cases carried over from the 13th edition have been thoroughly updated.

Part-Ending Cases

Each of the seven parts of the text ends with two cases. All of these cases involve real organizations and products. Rather than being comprehensive, we have focused each case on the subject matter covered in that particular part of the text in order to avoid overwhelming students with the complexity of many business problems. Included among the part-ending cases are:

- Google
- Dell
- Target
- The Gap
- Hummer
- McDonald's
- Walt Disney Co.
- Southwest Airlines
- BlackBerry

Cases we have developed that focus on competitive rivalries have been well received by both students and instructors, so we have retained this feature. Part-ending cases that illustrate the competitive battles between or among companies are:

- Sirius versus XM
- UPS versus FedEx versus DHL
- Coca-Cola Co. versus PepsiCo
- Costco versus Sam's Club
- Nintendo versus Sony versus Microsoft

Learning Aids

Given the accelerated pace of business today and the dynamic nature of marketing, we anticipate important developments related to the part-ending cases. Therefore, we will put news about major breaking developments related to the cases on the website for the 14th edition. This form of updating will keep the cases timely and interesting over the life of the edition. Students should go to the website to obtain this additional information about the organizations and products covered in the cases.

Students need to be informed about and, in turn, recognize the significance of the evolving context in which marketing is performed. We have selected three dimensions—globalization, information technology, and ethics—for special attention. Besides examples throughout the book, we have prepared boxes titled "A Global Perspective," "Marketing in the Information Economy," and "An Ethical Dilemma?" to help students understand how these important dimensions affect marketing and, more broadly, business and society.

To place students in a more active role as they learn about marketing, we have incorporated "You Make the Decision" boxes throughout the text. After actual situations faced by marketers are described briefly, students are asked how they would deal with the particular challenge or opportunity.

Each chapter concludes with three learning aids in addition to the "More about . . ." part of the chapter-opening case:

- A list of Key Terms and Concepts that reinforces important vocabulary from the chapter.

- A set of Questions and Problems that stresses the application of the text material rather than memorizing or defining terms.

- Several Interactive Marketing Exercises that require students to interact with customers and/or marketers outside the classroom. In carrying out these assignments, students will observe marketing situations, gather information firsthand, and/or utilize valuable secondary sources. The objective of these exercises is to give students a better sense of how marketing is actually carried out.

Teaching and Learning Supplements

In addition to the *Marketing* text, which serves as the primary learning instrument, several supplements facilitate the teaching and learning process. These supplements include:

- An *Instructor's Resource CD-ROM* that contains all the resources for classroom support. The CD-ROM includes the *Instructor's Manual* with additional lecture material, commentaries on the chapter-opening and part-ending cases, suggested answers to the chapter-ending Questions and Problems, and discussion material for two categories of boxes—"An Ethical Dilemma?" and "You Make the Decision." We've also prepared a *Test Bank* of over 2,500 objective questions, coded to indicate the type (definition, concept, application) and text location. Instructors will also find a complete set of *PowerPoint*® slides for each chapter.

- A *Video Program* featuring cases of real-world companies, incorporating concepts, strategies, and techniques from every chapter.

- Our *Online Learning Center* allows instructors to access the *Instructor's Manual* and PowerPoint materials as well as part-ending case commentaries, video segment notes, and links to professional resources. A link to McGraw-Hill's PageOut enables professors to create a course-specific website. For students, the two appendices—"Marketing Math" and "Careers and Marketing"—can be found at this website in addition to helpful study tools such as self-assessing quizzes and flashcards.

- A *Student CD-ROM* features an interactive online business case from Smart-Sims. The case focuses on a hypothetical company, Music2Go. This interactive simulation provides students with the opportunity and the incentive to develop strategies and make decisions related to marketing and production in a realistic, interesting business setting.

Acknowledgments

We are grateful to many people, including our teachers both in the classroom and from the world of marketing, our students, past and present colleagues, and business executives who have shared their insights and experiences with us. Although too numerous to identify by name, we wish to thank all of these people who have contributed to our professional endeavors, including this text.

Special thanks are extended to Therese Basham for preparing drafts of the part-ending cases. A number of students who assisted with research and other tasks also deserve our thanks: Steve Duran, Tim Kelly, and Merritt Noble.

Several individuals have contributed significantly to the preparation of the supplements and learning aids, and we thank them for doing so. Dr. Tom Adams, one of our long-time collaborators, prepared the *Instructor's Manual*. Two other valuable partners, Professors Betty and Tom Pritchett of Kennesaw State University developed the extensive *Test Bank*. Joanne Butler prepared the PowerPoint presentation materials.

We'd also like to recognize those professors who helped shape previous editions of *Marketing*. We want to acknowledge them by name and indicate their affiliation at the time of their involvement with our text: Bruce L. Conners, Kaskaskia College; Carol Bienstock, Valdosta State University; Charles Prohaska, Central Connecticut State University; Craig A. Hollingshead, Marshall University; Craig A. Kelley, California State University–Sacramento; Darryl W. Miller, Washburn University; Denise M. Johnson, University of Louisville; Ed Timmerman, University of Tennessee; Irving Mason, Herkimer County Community College; Jack L. Taylor, Portland State University; Jennifer Friestad, Anoka Ramsey Community College; John Phillips, University of San Francisco; Joyce H. Wood, Northern Virginia Community College; Justin Peart, Florida International University; Keith B. Murray, Bryant College; Kenneth Laird, Southern Connecticut State University; Larry Crowson, Florida Institute of Technology; Louise Smith, Towson State College; Madeline Johnson, University of Houston; Mark Mitchell, University of South Carolina–Spartanburg; Mary Lou Lockerby, College of De Page; Michael J. Swenson, Brigham Young University; Mort Ettiner, Salem State College; Robert E. Thompson, Indiana State University; Robert G. Roe, University of Wyoming; Ronald J. Adams, University of North Florida; Roy Cabaniss, Western Kentucky University; Sharon Wagner, Missouri Western State College; Stephen Goodwin, Illinois State University; Steven Engel, University of Colorado–Boulder; Thomas J. Adams, Sacramento City College; and Timothy L. Wilson, Clarion University.

We are also very grateful to the staff at McGraw-Hill/Irwin, whose talents, efforts, and patience helped to assure that this text was published. The team of professionals includes: Joanne Butler, development editor; Laura Griffin, project manager; Mike Hruby and Ira Roberts, photo research; Barrett Koger, sponsoring editor; Dan Silverburg, marketing manager, Rose Hepburn, production supervisor; Mary Kazak, designer; and Ben Curless, media producer. The individual and collective efforts of the editorial, design, and production departments at McGraw-Hill/Irwin have been vital in making this textbook an effective and attractive teaching and learning resource. We are very grateful for their assistance.

Michael J. Etzel
Bruce J. Walker
William J. Stanton

Guided Tour

Marketing, 14th edition by Etzel, Walker, and Stanton continues to be a popular softcover text for introductory marketing courses. This 14th edition has been thoroughly revised and completely updated. Current marketing issues, including customer relationship management (CRM), database management, global marketing, marketing research, supply-chain management, and integrated marketing communications are all explored in this edition of the text.

The numerous in-text and boxed examples highlight global issues, technology, ethics, and applied decision making. The chapter-opening and part-ending cases offer crucial real world applications to key concepts. These features, combined with some of the finest supplements available in this course area, provide you with everything you need for a solid introduction to the successful world of marketing in a modern business environment.

Chapter Opening Cases

Each chapter is introduced with a contemporary case highlighting the key concepts, strategies, and tactics covered in the chapter.

Chapter 2

PART 1

"Apple's main motivation for launching the online music service was to stimulate sales of its iPod."

The Dynamic Marketing Environment

Is iTunes Playing Your Song?

Just as it revolutionized the consumer market for desktop computers in the 1980s, Apple Computer Inc. is again transforming another burgeoning business. Apple's entrant in the digital-music business, the iTunes Music Store, was launched in 2003. In seeking sustained success in the competition among online music services, Apple faces several obstacles. Among them are illegal file-sharing services, many new legitimate competitors, technological challenges, and a reluctant music industry.

Like several other Internet-based enterprises, the music file-sharing industry began in a dorm room. Shawn Fanning, a student at Northwestern University, created Napster in 1999. Napster allowed individuals to exchange MP3 music files over the Internet and to download them onto their computers. Music companies such as BMG and Warner were distressed by this new peer-to-peer (PTP) model for file sharing. Believing that it infringed upon their copyrights, the companies sued to put Napster out of business. In July 2001, Napster was shut down, but by then, a number of imitators had sprung up and were offering free PTP music-sharing services. Millions of songs were being downloaded illegally. There were few legitimate alternatives because the music companies were wary of licensing their collections for Internet consumption.

Apple's iTunes Music Store was the first online service to reach an agreement with all five of the major music companies (as well as several independents). iTunes charges $.99 for each song a customer downloads.

However, because it pays $.65 to $.79 per song to the record companies, Apple earns little profit from iTunes. Apple's main motivation for launching the online music service was to stimulate sales of its iPod MP3 music player.

Apple's technology for iTunes allows customers to purchase a song, play it on up to three computers, and also copy or "burn" that song onto an iPod (but no other MP3 player) or multiple compact discs. An "album," a playlist of 10 songs, can be purchased for $9.99. Both songs and albums are encrypted to prevent them from being transferred onto free peer-to-peer sites.

iTunes' main competitors were Napster, MusicMatch, RealPlayer, and yes, even Wal-Mart. In addition to selling individual songs for $.99 each, Napster and MusicMatch also offer subscriptions that allow users to pay a monthly fee in order to "stream," which means they can listen to as many songs as they want on their computer. Rob Glaser, chief executive officer of RealNetworks (which owns RealPlayer), stated that only 13% of RealPlayer's customers were paying $.99 to download singles, whereas 72% were simply listening to music on their computer. Steve Jobs of Apple rejected that approach, saying, "The subscription services are not working. People want to own their music, not rent it."

Apple developed a slick advertising campaign that featured U2's Bono promoting both iTunes and the iPod. By September 2004, iTunes had sold more than 100 million songs and had 70% of the legal online digital-music business. Despite 60 competitors, iTunes was selling more than four times as many songs each week as its closest competitor, the legal version of Napster.[1]

What marketing considerations will be important for Apple as it tries to make iTunes a long-lasting success, especially in the face of competition from Microsoft and other online music services?

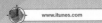
www.itunes.com

Thematic Boxes

Intended to inform and stimulate your critical thinking, these boxed examples highlight the latest marketing issues and topics to keep you abreast of current marketing trends. Found throughout the text, these boxes emphasize four themes:

A Global Perspective boxes demonstrate the global nature of marketing to you. These examples emphasize the international dimensions of virtually all industries and career paths.

You Make the Decision boxes present synopses of actual situations faced by marketers. You are given the opportunity to respond to various marketing challenges. These examples move you from passive observer to active participant in the decision-making process.

An Ethical Dilemma? boxes will raise your awareness of the nature and frequency of ethical challenges in the field of marketing. They have been written to not only present ethical issues but also to help you formulate an ethical perspective.

Marketing in the Information Economy boxes illustrate to you the pervasive impact technology continues to have on marketing and emphasizes technology's importance as a component of business progress.

Closing Case Commentaries

Companies featured in the opening chapter cases are revisited at the end of each chapter in the "More About" feature. By addressing questions posed at the end of these cases, you can apply what you've learned in the chapter to challenges you'll face in actual marketing situations.

More about **iTunes**

As 2004 drew to a close, still more digital-music services were entering the competition. Perhaps the most interesting (and potentially formidable) newcomer was the company that set off the Apple verses PC operating-system war of the 1980s—Microsoft. Just as Apple launched iTunes to increase sales of its iPod MP3 player, Microsoft introduced MSN Music to spur sales of its Windows XP operating system and Windows Media Player as well as a number of other Microsoft products. The match-up mimicked the Apple versus Microsoft desktop computer wars of the 1980s.

Similar to earlier times when Apple refused to license its Macintosh operating platform, it has resisted allowing other companies to develop products or services that work with iPods and iTunes. In contrast, Microsoft is allowing other suppliers to develop devices and services that use its new Windows Media

The original digital-music master, Shawn Fanning, also launched a new online music service in late 2004. After selling the rights to the Napster name, Fanning decided to try to legitimize the peer-to-peer (PTP) digital-music model. He envisioned his new company, Snocap, as a clearinghouse to bring together music companies and PTP file-sharing networks. Up to this point, most PTP networks operated illegally, allowing users to trade copyrighted material without paying royalties to the rights-holding music company or artist. Fanning's goal was to allow users to continue to exchange files while paying for the privilege of doing so.

A number of illegal sites were still operating and offering free PTP file sharing and, in the case of Kazaa, an enormous collection of songs from which to choose. Utilizing a network of computers rather than one main server, Kazaa was proving to be much more difficult to shut down than Napster. Whereas 67% of people over the age of 25 were legally downloading music from the Internet in late 2004, almost 70% of those between 18 and 24 years old were using unlicensed services. But, as the adage says, you get

Part-Ending Cases

These real world cases give you a glimpse into the world of marketing and offer you an opportunity to apply what you've learned to solve a problem, develop a plan, or address a marketing issue.

Cases for Part 1

CASE 1   Google

Searching for Success On the Web

As the Internet began proliferating in the mid-1990s, researchers and companies alike scrambled to develop tools that would allow Web surfers to navigate its massive stores of data in order to find specific bits of information. But it was two young graduate students, Larry Page and Sergey Brin, whose efforts yielded today's most popular Internet search engine and a highly profitable Internet company called Google. Named after the mathematical term that represents the number 10 to the hundredth power, Google is such a dominant presence on the Web, that it is now being used as a verb. Have you ever "Googled" anyone? No? Well then, read on.

Moving Out of the Dorm Room and Into the Boardroom

When they met at Stanford University, Page and Brin already had the reputation of being technical whiz kids. (Page once made a computer printer built entirely out of Legos.) Together, they decided to try to develop a process for searching the Internet, but they agreed out of necessity to do it by using a network of inexpensive personal computers instead of large-scale servers. Short of resources, they borrowed PCs from around campus, set up the data center in Page's dorm room and, in 1997, produced their first iteration of a search engine they dubbed BackRub.

Although the people who saw BackRub were impressed, Page and Brin were unsuccessful in selling the technology to other Internet companies. Undeterred, they began looking for investors, and gladly accepted a check for $100,000 from Andy Bechtolsheim, a founder of Sun Microsystems. They eventually raised almost $1 million, and Google, Inc. was born.

The company officially opened in September of 1998, and despite the fact that Google.com was still being beta tested, it was named one of the "Top 100 Web Sites and Search Engines" by *PC Magazine* in 1998. By February 1999, it was handling half a million searches each day and growing by leaps and bounds. The company expanded by hiring a number of new employees and settled into spacious office

space, nicknamed the Googleplex, in Mountain View, California. Later that year, the beta test was concluded, and clients such as America Online began signing on to use Google's search technology on their own sites.

Google became the largest search engine in the world in 2000, conducting 18 million searches each day. That number exploded to 100 million searches each day in February 2001. In addition, the Googleplex acquired the reputation of being a creative, desirable place to work and began attracting top talent. Its open floor plan encouraged communication among its employees, and its founders hired a world-renowned chef, organized roller hockey games, and held meetings each Friday that included the entire company. This collaborative environment has spawned a slew of new innovations and rapid international expansion that succeeded in attracting additional big-name clients and advertisers. But the key to Google's success has always been its underlying technology—a unique formula originally developed by Page and Brin that allows users to conduct swift and accurate searches across the World Wide Web in a matter of seconds.

Setting Its "Sites" on More Accurate Results

With the inception of the Internet, a profusion of information became available to those who were patient enough and skilled enough to sort through it. Brin and Page were determined to help those who weren't. "The perfect search engine would understand exactly what you mean and give back exactly what you want," explained Page. Other search engines already existed, and they worked by scanning through the Web, summarizing information by creating an index, and then matching the original query with pages that contained the relevant word or phrase. However, the results were often inaccurate or too voluminous to be helpful.

Brin and Page solved this by creating an algorithm called PageRank that sorts results according to their perceived importance. The algorithm starts by

Google has also gotten involved in Web shopping by introducing Google Catalog Search, a service that allows users to peruse more than a thousand catalogs that were not previously available online. It also unveiled a feature called Froogle, which enables users to compare prices for the same product available at different e-tailers.

The second most popular search site on the Web is Yahoo!, and it has actively been upgrading its capabilities in an effort to compete with Google. Yahoo! has been doing so by introducing features that allow users to customize their searches by blocking certain sites and highlighting others, and by creating their own home pages. "Historically there's been 'search the Web,' now we're creating 'search my Web,'" explained Yahoo!'s senior vice president, Jeff Weiner.

Due to Google's ever-widening scope, Yahoo! isn't the only online company that worries about competing with the Google machine. eBay is concerned that Google's AdWords will lure advertisers away. Froogle is a threat to Amazon, and in response, Amazon has developed its own search engine called A9. So has Microsoft, but its MSN Search beta proved to be less accurate than Google in a test conducted by *The Washington Post*. In addition, the many companies that offer e-mail services are keeping an eye on the performance of GMail. "Google, Yahoo!, Amazon and eBay are on a collision course," stated Bill Gross, chairman of Idealab, an Internet think tank and venture capital firm. "They're all stepping into each other's territory, and it's going to lead to interesting battles."

To stay one step ahead of the competition, Google has developed a list of "ten things it has found to be true." Each tenet is discussed in detail on its website, but four of them seem to have particularly influenced its success. The eighth item declares that "the need for information crosses all borders." Early in its history, Google addressed the fact that it was indeed a "world wide web" by allowing users to conduct searches in English and ten other languages. By 2001, its search services were available in 40 different languages, and Google even provided automated translations. The company was operating in offices in

Paris, London, Tokyo, Hamburg, and Toronto and supported 88 languages by 2003. It even announced plans to open an office on the moon in early 2004.

Another corporate truth is Google's contention that "you can make money without doing evil." By not accepting payment in order to influence search results, by excluding irrelevant pop-up ads, and by clearly delineating advertisers as "sponsors," Google has been able to maintain its integrity without selling itself out. Google has also clearly demonstrated that "democracy on the web works." Its PageRank formula takes a sophisticated tally to determine what sites most closely match the queries posed by Google users, and it does so with a high degree of accuracy.

But the first item on the list of things Google has learned is to "focus on the user and all else will follow." Google's absolute devotion to its user base has resulted in it becoming one of the top five most-visited sites on the Web. In addition, *USA Today* published a survey in December 2004 in which consumers predicted Google would continue to be a big hit in 2005. In fact it was number three on the list of projected "winning" brand names.

Are you interested in the other six things that Google has learned? Just Google it!

Questions

1. Describe the three components of the marketing concept as they apply to Google. Which is likely to provide the greatest challenge to Google's success?

2. Describe how each factor in the external macroenvironment will influence Google's marketing activities.

3. Do you agree with Google's strategy of expanding its product mix to include services other than just search capabilities? Why or why not?

 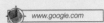 www.google.com

CASE 2   Sirius versus XM

Tuning into a New Market with Satellite Radio

A new entertainment product was launched, literally, in 2001 when XM Satellite Radio Holdings Inc. propelled its two satellites, nicknamed Rock and Roll, into outer

space. Shortly thereafter, the new company began offering premium radio services to subscribers willing to pay $120 per year, plus the cost of the necessary hardware.

Supplements

Marketing, 14th edition features some of the finest supplements available in this course area. From the free Student CD-ROM with Music2Go—a student marketing simulation program—to the interactive text website, you get all the tools you'll need to understand marketing functions within a dynamic business environment.

Online Learning Center

This text-specific site features online quizzes, flashcards, marketing math, and Internet exercises tied specifically to *Marketing*, 14th edition. The site also includes an up-to-date Careers in Marketing appendix that offers guidelines on the job search process and insights on how to apply what you've learned in the course to your career. Career opportunities in marketing are also described in detail. Go to www.mhhe.com/etzel07.

Student CD-ROM

Included free with all new copies of the text, this disc introduces an interactive online business case from SmartSims, featuring a simulated portable music player company, Music2Go. Students make the marketing decisions about one of the company's products within a simulated consumer electronics industry. The concepts of market analysis, segmentation, marketing mix, and product life cycle are all applied in this realistic case study.

Videos

Real world companies are profiled, incorporating concepts from every chapter in *Marketing* 14th edition. These video cases further demonstrate the application of marketing concepts, strategies, and techniques learned in the text to actual businesses.

Chapter 1

"Rather than trying to offer everything grocery shoppers need, Trader Joe's lures them with novel and intriguing items."

Can **Trader Joe's** Keep the Deals Coming?

Faced with full-line supermarkets such as Albertson's, Ralph's, and Kroger as well as discounters such as Wal-Mart and Target, how can a firm compete in the brutally competitive grocery business? It's not easy. As one retail consultant noted, "The grocery business is a zero-sum game." That is, any gains one firm makes must come at the expense of the other competitors in the market because total demand grows very slowly. Against these tough odds one retailer has taken the approach of redefining the customer experience.

Many view shopping for groceries as an unpleasant chore. Planning meals on the fly, coping with bored children, and juggling coupons, while trying to finish the task as quickly as possible, makes a visit to the supermarket about as attractive as a trip to the dentist. But what if a store changed grocery shopping into an adventure by offering a constantly changing variety of interesting items at attractive prices? Welcome to Trader Joe's, a curiously upscale specialty grocery store with highly competitive prices and friendly, helpful employees.

In 1967, Joe Coulombe, the owner of a grocery store in the Los Angeles area, saw problems on the horizon with the rapid expansion of convenience-store chains such as 7-Eleven. In response he revamped his operation, creating a nautical decor, adding unique gourmet and imported food items as well as discontinued merchandise purchased at deep discounts, decking out employees in Hawaiian shirts, and renaming the store Trader Joe's (TJ's). The resources of German retailer Aldi were put behind the fledgling concept through a buyout in 1979, the business model was tweaked, and today there are over 210 TJ's stores in 19 states.

What's behind TJ's success? First, they understand their customers. Rather than trying to offer everything grocery shoppers need, Trader Joe's lures them with novel and intriguing items. That means TJ's is unlikely to be a consumer's primary store. Rather shoppers visit on an occasional basis when they are looking for something special or just want to browse. To create the desired atmosphere, the stores:

- Stock over 2,000 exclusive, private label items, fully 85% of an outlet's entire offering, under such names as Trader Jose and Baker Josef.

- Offer only about 10% of the number of products found in a full-service supermarket and restrict the assortment to interesting and unusual items such as soy ice cream cookies, Thai lime and chili cashews, and sugar-free truffles.

- Keep costs down with low-rent locations, volume buying, and hard bargaining with suppliers, all to make attractive prices possible.

- Hire employees with outgoing personalities and a good sense of humor who commit to making every customer experience fun.

The result is annual revenue over $2 billion and sales per square foot twice that of a traditional supermarket.[1] What will it take for Trader Joe's to maintain this type of performance and keep consumers coming on board?

 www.traderjoes.com

Marketing and the Internet The Internet is a powerful and dynamic marketing tool. Throughout the book we have included uniform resource locators (or URLs, the technical term for Internet addresses), to help you find interesting and informative "home pages." We encourage you to explore these websites to learn more about how the Internet is currently being used and to stimulate your thinking about how it can be utilized even more effectively. Space limitations occasionally require us to break URLs into two lines; but when entering an Internet address always type it on one line.

Trader Joe's is an excellent example of both the rewards and challenges of marketing. It became a highly successful operation by identifying and meeting the needs of many consumers. However, maintaining a high level of success is difficult. So Trader Joe's, like most organizations, is faced with making adjustments in its operation that will satisfy its customers. Finding ways to satisfying customers effectively and efficiently is what marketing is all about. To understand what that means, we need to systematically examine the question, "What is marketing?"

After studying this chapter, you should be able to explain:

- The centrality of exchange to marketing.
- A definition of marketing that applies to business and nonbusiness situations.
- The way marketing has evolved in the U.S.
- The marketing concept and related issues.
- The heightened concern about ethics in marketing.
- The components of a company's marketing program.
- The many ways in which marketing affects our lives.

Nature and Scope of Marketing

Marketing can occur any time a person or organization strives to exchange something of value with another person or organization. Thus, at its core marketing is a transaction or exchange. In this broad sense, marketing consists of activities designed to generate and facilitate exchanges intended to satisfy human or organizational needs or wants.

Buying and selling industrial commodities in a futures market meets all the conditions for a market exchange. One of the world's largest is The Chicago Mercantile Exchange, which has been in existence for over 100 years. Annually over 640 million contracts valued at over $340 trillion change hands by means of eye contact, hand signals, and shouted offers and bids.

 www.cme.com

Exchange as the Focus

Exchange is just one of three ways we can satisfy our needs. If you want something, you can make it yourself, acquire it by theft or some form of coercion, or you can offer something of value (perhaps your money, your services, or another good) to a person or organization that has that desired good or service and will exchange it for what you offer. Only this last alternative is an exchange in the sense that marketing is occurring.

The following conditions must exist for a marketing exchange to take place:

- Two or more people or organizations must be involved, and each must have needs or wants to be satisfied. If you are totally self-sufficient, there is no need for an exchange.

- The parties to the exchange must be involved voluntarily.

- Each party must have something of value to contribute in the exchange, and each must believe that it will benefit from the exchange.

- The parties must communicate with each other. The communication can take many forms and may even be through a third party, but without awareness and information, there can be no exchange.

These exchange conditions introduce a number of terms that deserve some elaboration. First there are the parties involved in the exchange. On one side of the exchange is the marketer. *Marketers* take the initiative by trying to stimulate and facilitate exchanges. They develop marketing plans and programs and implement them in hopes of creating an exchange. In this respect, a retailer such as Trader Joe's, a college or university recruiting students, the American Cancer Society soliciting donors, and United Airlines seeking passengers are all marketers.

On the other side of the exchange is the *market,* which consists of people or organizations with needs to satisfy, money to spend, and the willingness to spend it. Marketing programs are directed at markets that either accept or reject the offer. Markets are made up of current and prospective *customers,* defined as any person, group, or organization with whom a marketer has an existing or potential exchange relationship.

The object of the exchange or what is being marketed is referred to generically as the *product.* It can be a good, service, idea, person, or place. All of these can be marketed, as we shall see.

We most often think of *something of value* as money. However, barter (trading one product for another) is still fairly common among small businesses and even between countries. Of course, many exchanges in the nonbusiness world, such as donating blood in exchange for the good feeling of helping others, do not involve cash.

Marketers use many forms of personal and nonpersonal *communication,* from billboards to personal selling, to inform and persuade their desired markets. Because there are so many communication methods available, selecting the most effective combination is an important marketing task.

In describing exchanges, we use the terms *needs* and *wants* interchangeably because marketing is relevant to both. Technically, needs can be viewed in a strict physiological sense (food, clothing, and shelter), with everything else defined as a want. However, from a customer's perspective, the distinction is not as clear. For example, many people consider a cellular phone or a home computer a necessity.

Definition of Marketing

This book focuses on the activities carried out by organizations to facilitate mutually beneficial exchanges. These organizations may be profit-seeking business firms, or they may have a primary objective other than profit—a university, charity, church, police department, or political party, for example. (Marketing can also be performed

Like many Midwestern communities, Red Wing, Minnesota, located on the Mississippi River, is being marketed as a regional tourism destination. One difference from rival towns is the presence in the town of the 100-year-old Red Wing Shoe Company. To call attention to its uniqueness the company has constructed an exact replica of its signature work boot—in size 638 D. The boot is 20 feet long, 16 feet high, and weighs 2,300 pounds. If Paul Bunyan stops by, they'll be ready!

www.redwingshoes.com

by individuals. As you approach graduation, you can use marketing principles to maximize the effectiveness of your job search. We have more to say about this in "Careers and Marketing" on our website www.mhhe.com/etzel07.)

Both types of organizations face essentially the same marketing challenges and opportunities. Trader Joe's, the retailer described in the chapter-opening case, must attract buyers. Initially it focused on a unique decor and carefully selected merchandise to attract attention. However, faced with increasing competition, the firm is exploring other alternatives including highly personalized service and many private-brand items unavailable in other stores. Similarly, Jacksonville, Florida, hosted the 2005 NFL Super Bowl not only to generate an immediate economic impact on the region, which was estimated at over $300 million, but also to showcase the area. With the game drawing 100,000 visitors and a television audience of 800 million, the city hopes to attract tourists as well as businesses looking for an attractive place to locate. Consequently, we need a definition of marketing to guide executives in business and nonbusiness organizations in the management of their marketing efforts, and to direct our examination of the subject.

Therefore, our definition of marketing—based on the concept of exchange and applicable in any organization—is as follows: **Marketing** is a total system of business activities designed to plan, price, promote, and distribute want-satisfying products to target markets in order to achieve organizational objectives.[2] This definition has two significant implications:

- *Focus:* The entire system of business activities should be customer-oriented. Customers' wants must be recognized and satisfied.
- *Duration:* Marketing should start with an idea about a want-satisfying product and should not end until the customers' wants are completely satisfied, which may be some time after the exchange is made.

As you will see in the discussion below, these conditions are not always met.

Evolution of Marketing

The foundations of marketing in America were laid in Colonial times, when the early settlers traded among themselves and with the Native Americans. Some settlers became retailers, wholesalers, and itinerant peddlers. However, large-scale marketing in the U.S. did not begin to take shape until the Industrial Revolution in the latter part of the 1800s. Since then, marketing thought has evolved through three successive stages of development: product orientation, sales orientation, and market orientation.

Our description links each stage with a period of time. But you should understand that these stages depict the general evolution of marketing thought and reflect states of mind as much as they do historical periods. Thus, although many firms have progressed to a market-orientation, some are still mired in a product or sales orientation, as shown in Figure 1.1.

Product-Orientation Stage

Firms with a **product orientation** typically focus on the quality and quantity of offerings while assuming that customers will seek out and buy reasonably priced, well-made products. This mindset is commonly associated with a long-ago era when the demand for goods generally exceeded the supply, and the primary focus in business was to efficiently produce large quantities of products. Finding the customers was viewed as a relatively minor function.

Manufacturers, wholesalers, and retailers operating in this stage emphasized internal operations and focused on efficiency and cost control. There wasn't much need to worry about what customers wanted because it was highly predictable. Most people spent the vast majority of their incomes on necessities. If a firm could make a good quality shoe inexpensively, for example, a market almost certainly existed.

When this was the prevailing approach to business the term *marketing* was not in use. Instead, producers had sales departments headed by executives whose primary responsibility was to supervise a sales force. The function of the sales department was simply to carry out the transaction, at a price often dictated by the cost of production. The philosophy of the Pillsbury company in the late 1800s is characteristic of this stage: "Blessed with a supply of the finest North American wheat, plenty of water power, and excellent milling machinery, we produce flour of the highest quality. Our basic function is to mill high-quality flour, and of course (and almost incidentally) we must hire salesmen to sell it, just as we hire accountants to keep our books."[3]

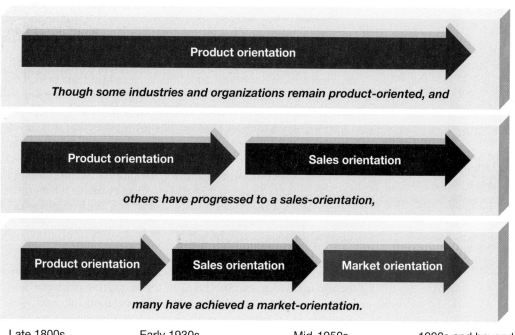

FIGURE 1.1

Marketing Evolution in the United States.

Though some industries and organizations remain product-oriented, and

others have progressed to a sales-orientation,

many have achieved a market-orientation.

Late 1800s   Early 1930s   Mid-1950s   1990s and beyond

This emphasis on products and operations dominated until the early 1930s. The approach is understandable when you consider that for generations the primary concern of business was how to produce and distribute an adequate quantity of acceptable products to meet the needs of a rapidly growing population. Despite the fact that these conditions are no longer typical, some managers still operate with a product orientation.

Sales-Orientation Stage

The world economic crisis of the late 1920s (commonly referred to as the Great Depression) changed perceptions. As the developed countries emerged from the depression it became clear that the main economic problem no longer was how to manufacture efficiently, but rather it was how to sell the resulting output. Just offering a quality product was no assurance of success. Managers began to realize that to sell their products in an environment where consumers had limited resources and numerous options required substantial postproduction effort. Thus, a **sales orientation,** characterized by a heavy reliance on promotional activity to sell the products the firm wanted to make, became common. In this stage, advertising consumed a larger share of a firm's resources, and sales executives began to gain respect and responsibility from company management.

Along with responsibility came expectations for performance. Unfortunately, these pressures resulted in some managers resorting to overly aggressive selling—the "hard sell"—and unscrupulous advertising tactics. As a result, selling developed an unsavory reputation in the eyes of many. Old habits die hard, and even now some organizations believe that they must use a hard-sell approach to prosper. In the United States the sales stage was common into the 1950s, when modern marketing began to emerge.

Market-Orientation Stage

At the end of World War II there was strong pent-up demand for consumer goods created by wartime shortages. As a result, manufacturing plants turned out tremendous quantities of goods that were quickly purchased. However, the postwar surge in consumer spending slowed down as supply caught up with demand, and many firms found that they had excess production capacity.

In an attempt to stimulate sales, firms reverted to the aggressive promotional and sales activities of a sales-orientation. However, this time consumers were less willing to be persuaded. Sellers discovered that the war years had also changed consumers. The thousands of service men and women who spent time overseas came home more sophisticated and worldly. In addition, the war effort brought many women out of the home and into the work force for the first time. Because of their experiences, consumers had become more knowledgeable, less naive, and less easily influenced. In addition, they had more choices. The technology that was developed during the war made it possible to produce a much greater variety of goods when converted to peacetime activity.

Thus the evolution of marketing continued. Many companies recognized that to put idle capacity to work they had to make available what consumers wanted to buy instead of what the businesses wanted to sell. With a **market orientation,** companies identify what customers want and tailor all the activities of the firm to satisfy those needs as efficiently as possible.

Using this approach, firms are marketing rather than merely selling. Several tasks that were once associated with other business functions became the responsibility of the top marketing executive, called the marketing manager or vice president of marketing. For instance, inventory control, warehousing, and some aspects of product planning are turned over to the head of marketing as a way to serve customers better. To increase effectiveness, input from the marketplace is sought before a product is produced not just at the end of a production cycle. In addition, marketing is included in long-term as well as short-term company planning.

A market orientation is often reflected in an executive's attitude toward marketing. Philip Knight, co-founder and until recently chairman and CEO of Nike, makes this point: "For years we thought of ourselves as a production-oriented company, meaning we put all our emphasis on designing and manufacturing the product. But now we understand that the most important thing we do is market the product."[4]

We are *not* saying that marketing is more important than other business functions. They are all essential. Nor are we suggesting that marketing executives should hold the top positions in a company. But it is necessary that everyone in an organization understand the importance of the market, that is, be *market-oriented*.

Many American business firms and not-for-profit organizations are presently in this third stage in the evolution of marketing. Others may recognize the importance of a market orientation, but have difficulty implementing it. Implementation requires accepting the notion that the wants and needs of customers, not the desires of management, direct the organization. Forty-five years ago Peter Drucker, the most influential business writer of the 20th century, observed that companies exist not to make a profit, but to create and satisfy customers. In a recent interview, he commented that the statement is even more true today because the customer has the ultimate power to choose.[5]

Fundamental to instilling a market orientation is the way an organization describes what it does. Table 1.1 shows how some well-known organizations might define their businesses under a product orientation and invites you to try your hand at defining them based on a market orientation.

Note that not every organization needs to be market-oriented to prosper. A monopolist selling a necessity is guaranteed of having customers. Therefore, its management should be much more concerned with low-cost, efficient production than with marketing. Such was the case for public utilities prior to deregulation. Now, however, many electricity and natural gas providers are scrambling to find ways to satisfy customers who have alternative sources of supply. There are also instances in which the potential customers consider the product to be so superior that they will seek it out. For example, the world's best heart surgeons or particularly popular artists find a market for their services regardless of their orientations.

The Marketing Concept

Managers who adopt a market orientation recognize that marketing is vital to the success of their organizations. This realization is reflected in a fundamental approach to doing business that gives the customer the highest priority. Called the **marketing concept,** it emphasizes customer orientation and coordination of marketing activities to achieve the organization's performance objectives.

TABLE 1.1	How Should a Business Be Defined?	
	(Try your hand at composing a market-oriented answer and then see note 6 for some possibilities.)[6]	
Company	**Product-Oriented Answer**	**Market-Oriented Answer**
Kodak	We make cameras.	We help preserve beautiful memories.
Amazon.com	We sell books and recordings.	?
Hewlett-Packard	We make computer printers.	?
McGraw-Hill	We publish books and magazines.	?
Steelcase	We make office furniture.	?
Caterpillar	We make construction machinery.	?

Nature and Rationale

The marketing concept is based on three beliefs that are illustrated in Figure 1.2:

- All planning and operations should be *customer-oriented*. That is, every department and employee should be focused on contributing to the satisfaction of customers' needs. The inspiration for the "hub and spoke" air delivery concept created by FedEx was the customer need for reliable, overnight package delivery. Making it work requires the coordination provided by sophisticated information management, state-of-the-art material handling, and dedicated customer service personnel. What seemed like an impractical idea 40 years ago is now the basis for a $25 billion business that delivers 5.5 million packages a day in over 215 countries.

- All marketing activities in an organization should be *coordinated*. This means that marketing efforts (product planning, pricing, distribution, and promotion) should be designed and combined in a coherent, consistent way, and that one executive should have overall authority and responsibility for the complete set of marketing activities. At Barnes & Noble stores, consumers discover a relaxing environment where they can enjoy a cup of coffee in a store that's big enough to offer a broad selection of books and small enough to provide local entertainment and children's story hours. The combination of carefully selected inventory, discount pricing, and inviting surroundings produces over $5.6 billion a year in sales for the firm.

- Customer-oriented, coordinated marketing is essential to achieve the *organization's performance objectives*. The ultimate objective for a business is typically measured in terms of return on investment, stock price, and market capitalization. However, the immediate objective might be something less ambitious that will move the organization closer to its ultimate goal. For example, when Procter & Gamble introduced a bevy of new products including Crest Whitestrips, Swifter mops, and improved Pampers, sales came at the expense of competitors such as Colgate-Palmolive and Kimberly-Clark. In response, these firms shifted their focus from the traditional goal of profits to one of regaining sales (or market share) in these key areas. The result was increased spending on research and development to generate new products.[7]

Sometimes the marketing concept is simply stated as a customer orientation, as expressed in these words of the late Sam Walton, founder of Wal-Mart: "There is only one boss: the customer."[8] However, it is important to keep in mind that such a comment implies the managerial activities necessary to implement it.

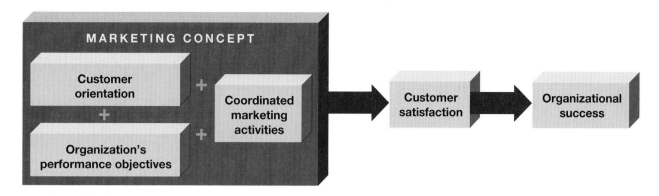

FIGURE 1.2

Components and Outcomes of the Marketing Concept.

Implementing the Marketing Concept

The marketing concept is an appealing idea, but it must be converted into specific activities to be useful for managers. Over the years it has been interpreted and applied in a number of different ways. "No questions asked" return policies to satisfy customers and automated warehouses to speed up delivery and support discounted prices are examples from the past. Today the marketing concept is being applied in a number of other ways. Several of the most important developments are introduced below.

Customer Orientation

Relationships. The value of a good relationship is not a new idea. However, it has been only fairly recently that organizations, with the benefit of extensive data, have made a concerted effort at **customer relationship management (CRM)**—establishing multidimensional connections with a customer such that the organization is seen as a partner. Data are often a key ingredient in CRM. By sorting and analyzing data supplied by customers, gathered from third parties, and collected from previous transactions, a marketer is able to better understand a customer's needs and preferences. But there is more to relationship management than data. By examining successful partnerships in business and elsewhere, marketers have discovered that enduring relationships are built on trust and mutual commitment, require a lot of time and effort to create and maintain, and are not appropriate for every exchange situation. Applying this concept to their marketing programs, many firms are dedicating much of their marketing effort to building lasting relationships with selected customers.[9]

Consider, for example, what motorcycle maker Harley-Davidson has done. The firm created a club (The Harley Owners Group or HOG) for bike owners. It offers the more than 650,000 members insurance, travel planning, roadside emergency service, the Harley-Davidson magazine, free safety lessons, safe-riding competitions, and 1,150 local chapters that hold regular meetings. The Internet, with its two-way communication capability, has made it easier for firms to build relationships with customers by personalizing their interactions. On its website, Harley-Davidson has a HOG's "members only" page where Harley owners can get specific questions answered and chat with other club members.[10]

What do Harley-Davidson and other firms that make these investments hope to get in return? A feeling of goodwill among their best customers and a sense that the firms care about more than making the next sale. That is, they are seeking a longterm relationship with their customers that will be mutually beneficial.

Mass Customization. The modern marketing system was built on identifying a need experienced by a large number of people (a mass market), and using mass production techniques and mass marketing (relying heavily on network television advertising) to satisfy that need. By producing and selling large quantities of standardized products, firms were able to keep the unit costs low and offer need-satisfying products at attractive prices. However, the market has changed. Mass marketing is being challenged by **mass customization,** that is, developing, producing, and delivering affordable products with enough variety and uniqueness that nearly every potential customer can have exactly what he or she wants. Deere & Company, maker of John Deere farm machinery, produces 45 different models of seed planters with a total of 1.7 million options in order to meet the varied needs of all types of farmers. What may be more remarkable is that they can all be built on the same assembly line in Moline, Illinois.[11]

www.johndeere.com

The movement toward mass customization is made possible by the tremendous advances in information, communications, and manufacturing technology. Firms are now able to learn a lot more about their current and prospective customers, and use that information in designing products, manufacturing, and distribution. They also can advertise to very specific audiences through cable television and via the Internet. The result is a proliferation of products in many product categories. Consider, for example, the variety of dry breakfast cereals available from General Mills and the corn-based snack alternatives offered by Frito-Lay.

Marketers are coming to realize, however, that more variety is not always better. In some areas the number of choices creates as much confusion as satisfaction. Consider, for example, the number of different pain relievers available in the drugstore. Retailers are so concerned by the explosion of new products, most of which fail, that they are charging manufacturers for shelf space to display them.[12]

Coordinated Marketing Activities

Quality. Although most firms do not ignore quality, there is a tendency to think in terms of "acceptable" levels of quality as determined by engineers and manufacturing people. However, when some firms added quality as defined by customers as a key ingredient of their strategies, it wasn't long before consumers responded. Soon the benefits of a commitment to quality became evident in the success of firms such as Sony and Honda. Thus, beginning in the 1980s improving quality became a priority for most organizations.

Some suggest that American executives became complacent about quality. However, it is more likely that American businesspeople had come to believe that quality and cost were directly related. That is, as quality is increased, costs must go up. Although that is generally true, the relationship is not as strong as first thought.

Through careful study, firms found it is possible to substantially increase quality without unacceptable cost increases by:

- Obtaining and responding to input from customers about how they define quality and what they expect in a particular product.

- Improving designs to reduce problems in manufacturing, and identifying and correcting problems early in the production process to reduce expensive reworking and waste.

- Encouraging employees to call attention to quality problems, and empowering them to initiate action to improve quality.

Concerns about quality are not limited to manufacturing and service. Every business function has a quality component. Within marketing there are quality aspects to making sales calls, answering customers' questions, preparing advertisements, and every other activity. The breadth of quality issues, along with the realization that achieving and maintaining quality depends on the efforts of employees, led to the development of **total quality management (TQM)** in the 1980s. TQM is a system for implementing organization-wide commitment to quality that involves every employee accepting responsibility for continuous quality improvement. Despite the good intentions that surrounded TQM programs, their focus on introducing change led many proponents to overlook the costs and benefits of the changes. As a result, firms are now evaluating the impact of quality proposals on customer satisfaction and treating quality improvements as investments. This refinement of TQM is known as a **return on quality (ROQ)** approach.

Value Creation.   The customer's perception of all the benefits of a product weighed against all the costs of acquiring and consuming the product is its **value.**[13] The benefits can be functional (the roominess of a minivan for a large family), aesthetic (the attractiveness of the minivan), or psychological (the peace of mind that the van is designed to withstand a collision). Besides the money paid to the seller, the costs might include learning about the product, negotiating the purchase, arranging financing, learning how to use the product, and disposal of the product when it is no longer useful.

Marketers are taking a closer look at what customers value in a product. As we have noted earlier, the heavy emphasis on mass production and mass marketing were largely driven by the desire to offer products at the lowest possible price. The focus on price overshadowed other benefits sought by customers. With better information about what customers desire and constant improvements in technology that make meeting those desires possible, marketers are engaging in **value creation** that extends beyond just offering the lowest possible prices.

Two points are important to note here. First, value means much more to the buyer than the amount of money charged for a product. For example, some consumers have found the Blackberry handheld electronic device indispensable for keeping track of appointments and phone numbers, making calls, sending and receiving e-mail, and other day-to-day activities. Second, the perception of value varies among individuals. In response to calls for more nutritious food, Taco Bell undertook a study to determine the value of a healthy burrito, one with fewer calories and more vegetables. However survey respondents rejected the proposed product and instead opted for a bigger, fattier, and more expensive "indulgent" burrito.[14]

Organizational Objectives

Performance Metrics.   Recall that one element of the marketing concept is the accomplishment of organizational goals. In the past the impact of marketing on organizational goals has been defined rather broadly. Because marketing is only one of many factors that influence how customers behave, it was assumed that a specific cause-and-effect relationship between marketing efforts and sales or profits could not be measured. As a result, marketing expenditures generally have been treated as expenses rather than investments, and managers adopted a short-term approach of trying to minimize these expenses as opposed to investing in marketing for both the short and long term. Today that thinking is changing.

Recognizing that marketing now accounts for at least 50% of all corporate costs, while manufacturing has gone from 50% to less than 30%, managers are demanding greater accountability for marketing. In response, organizations are searching for creative ways to measure marketing's effect, or the **return on the marketing investment.**

Marketers are now expected to demonstrate a link between traditional measures of marketing performance such as positive attitudes toward a brand, customer satisfaction, and customer retention and the firm's financial performance. As a result, efforts are underway in many firms to put a dollar value on their brands (referred to as brand equity) and to determine the lifetime value of a customer (referred to as customer equity).[15] Not surprisingly, these are difficult to isolate and measure. For example, estimating customer equity requires that a firm predict all future revenue from a current customer and subtract from that the marketing costs of acquiring the customer, retaining the customer, and servicing the customer.

The Societal Marketing Concept. Not long after the marketing concept became a widely accepted approach to doing business, it came under fire. For more than 40 years critics have persistently charged that marketing ignores social responsibility. That is, although the marketing concept may help an organization achieve its goals, it may at the same time encourage actions that conflict with society's best interests.

From one point of view, these charges are true. A firm may totally satisfy its customers (and in the process achieve a hefty profit), while also adversely affecting society. To illustrate, a number of firms in the fashion industry have provided their customers with attractive merchandise at low prices, but they have been accused of exploiting workers in Third World countries who are employed in sweatshops that produce the clothes.

However, this need not be the case. A firm's social responsibility can be quite compatible with the marketing concept. Compatibility depends on two things: how broadly a firm perceives its marketing goals and what the firm is willing to invest to achieve those goals. A firm that sufficiently extends the *breadth* and *commitment* dimensions of its marketing goals to fulfill its social responsibility is practicing what has become known as the **societal marketing concept.**

When the marketing concept's breadth is extended, a company recognizes that its market includes not only the buyers of its products but also anyone directly affected by its operations. In our example, the fashion retailers have several markets to satisfy, including (1) the owners or stockholders, (2) the employees who make the

For-profit firms cooperating with charitable organizations exemplify the societal marketing concept. Whirlpool Corporation has supported the home-building efforts of Habitat for Humanity since 1999, providing over 59,000 appliances and encouraging its employees to volunteer their time and skills to the construction projects. Although the short-term benefits to Whirlpool may be impossible to measure, committing to this type of effort indicates the firm has adopted a broad notion of its role in society.

www.whirlpool.com

www.habitat.org

clothing, and (3) the Third World economies that would be affected if the jobs were not available.

Extending the commitment dimension of its marketing goals means a firm must recognize that meeting the broader needs of society may require more time, technology, and skill than meeting just the needs of its immediate customers. Although these investments seem costly when they are made, they reflect a long-term view of customer satisfaction and performance objectives, rather than a focus only on today. For a company to prosper in the long run, it must satisfy its customers' social needs as well as their economic needs.

To draw attention to firms that have adopted a broad societal view, a ranking has been developed that equally weights seven performance indicators: profitability, as well as service to employees, the community, the environment, overseas stakeholders, minorities and women, and customers.[16] Firms that have ranked in the top 20 all five years that the assessments have been done are presented in Table 1.2. It is interesting to note that the top performers include both industry giants such as IBM and Procter & Gamble as well as much smaller firms.[17]

Thus the marketing concept and a company's social responsibility are compatible if management strives over the long run to (1) satisfy the wants of its product-buying customers, (2) meet the societal needs of others affected by the firm's activities, and (3) achieve the company's performance objectives.

If the marketing concept and the refinements we've just discussed direct a modern marketer's approach to the marketing task, just what is it that marketers do? In the next section we'll describe the areas of responsibility and decision making that are generally referred to as marketing management.

A Company's Marketing Program

Recall that we said a **market** consists of people or organizations with needs to satisfy, money to spend, and the willingness to spend it. For example, many people need transportation, are willing to pay for it, and have the resources to buy it. However, this large group is made up of many subgroups or segments with different transportation needs. For example, among the people who want to travel long distances by air, there are some who want low prices and efficiency, whereas others are willing

TABLE 1.2	Firms Ranked among America's 100 Best Corporate Citizens Five Years in a Row*			
Company	**Average Rank**	**Company**	**Average Rank**
Fannie Mae	1	Timberland Co.	17
Procter & Gamble	2	Cisco System	19
Intel Corp.	3	Southwest Airlines	22
St. Paul Companies	4	Motorola	24
Deere and Company	6	Cummins Inc.	27
Avon Products	7	Adolph Coors	31
Hewlett-Packard	8	Modine Manufacturing	32
Ecolab Inc.	10	Clorox	33
IBM	12	AT&T	43
Herman Miller	14	Pitney Bowes	44

Source: "100 Best Corporate Citizens," *Business Ethics* website: *www.business-ethics.com*, Feb. 2005.

*Annual ranking is based on how well firms serve seven stakeholder groups: stockholders, employees, the community, the environment, overseas stakeholders, minorities and women, and customers. Rankings from 2000 to 2004 were used to compute the five-year averages above.

to pay for luxury and privacy. These subgroups or **market segments** are consumers or organizations within the larger transportation market that share similar wants, buying preferences, or product-use behaviors. If a segment is large and sufficiently distinct, firms typically respond with a specially designed marketing program. Thus, we often see the same basic need satisfied in very different ways. For example, South-west Airlines, with low prices but no meals and no reserved seats, and NetJets Inc., which offers private jets on a time-share basis, are both successful air transportation marketers.

Ordinarily it is impractical for a firm to satisfy all or even most of the segments of a market. Instead, a company first identifies the existing segments and then selects one or more at which to target its efforts. Thus a **target market** refers to a market segment at which a firm directs a marketing program.

www.volvocars.com

Usually several firms are pursuing a particular target market at the same time, and each attempts to be viewed in a distinct and attractive way by prospective customers. That is, each firm uses strategies and tactics in an effort to establish a unique **position** in the prospects' minds. For example, Volvo's marketing strives to have its cars perceived by consumers as safe. Segmenting markets, selecting targets, and devising positioning strategies are fundamental marketing tasks.

Typically firms do a considerable amount of research to identify markets and define segments. Among the many questions market research seeks to answer, one of the most important is the sales potential of particular market segments. To determine sales potential, a firm must **forecast demand** (that is, sales) in its target markets. The results of demand forecasting will indicate whether the segments are worth pursuing, or whether alternatives need to be identified.

Next, management must design a **marketing mix**—the combination of a product, where and when it is distributed, how it is promoted, and its price. Together, these four components of strategy must satisfy the needs of the target market(s) and, at the same time, achieve the organization's marketing objectives. Some of the challenges facing marketing managers in developing a marketing mix are:

- *Product.* Strategies are needed for deciding what products to introduce, managing existing products over time, and dropping products that are no longer viable. Strategic decisions must also be made regarding branding, packaging, and other product features such as warranties.

- *Price.* Setting the base price for a product is a marketing decision. Other necessary strategies pertain to changing price, pricing related items within a product line, terms of sale, and possible discounts. An especially challenging decision is selecting the price for a new product.

- *Distribution.* Here, strategies relate to the channel(s) by which ownership of products is transferred from producer to customer and, in many cases, the means by which goods are moved from where they are produced to where they are purchased by the final customer. In addition, any middlemen, such as wholesalers and retailers, must be selected and their roles designed.

- *Promotion.* Strategies are needed to combine individual methods such as advertising, personal selling, and sales promotion into an integrated communications campaign. In addition, promotional budgets, messages, and media must be adjusted as a product moves from the early stages to the later stages of its life.

The four marketing-mix elements are interrelated; decisions in one area affect actions in another. To illustrate, design of a marketing mix is certainly affected by whether a firm chooses to compete on the basis of price *or* on one or more other elements. When a firm relies on price as its primary competitive tool, the other elements must be designed to support aggressive pricing. For example, the promotional campaign likely will be built around a theme of "low, low prices." In nonprice competition, however, product, distribution, and/or promotional strategies come to the forefront. For instance, the product must have features worthy of a higher price, and promotion must create a high-quality image for the product.

Each marketing-mix element contains countless alternatives. For instance, a producer may make and market one product or many, and the products may be related or unrelated to each other. They may be distributed through wholesalers, to retailers without the benefit of wholesalers, or even directly to final customers. Ultimately, from the multitude of alternatives, management must select a combination of elements that will satisfy target markets and achieve organizational and marketing goals.

Like many areas of business, marketers sometimes face seemingly contradictory goals. The desire to satisfy customers, for example, may seem to conflict with a particular revenue or profit objective. When this occurs, ethical predicaments may arise. Thus ethics in marketing deserves our attention.

Ethics and Marketing

Marketers are responsible to a variety of groups. Certainly their customers depend on them to satisfy their needs. Also, their employers expect them to generate sales and profits, suppliers and distributors look to them for their continued business, and society expects them to be responsible citizens. The frequently divergent interests of these groups create a wide variety of ethical challenges for marketers.

What Is Ethical Behavior?

A discussion of the philosophical underpinnings of ethics is beyond the scope of this book.[18] However, it is safe to say that there is considerable disagreement over what is and what is not ethical conduct. For example, ethics vary from society to society. Take bribery; although repugnant in most societies, it is an accepted and even necessary aspect of business behavior in many parts of the world. Thus, for our purposes it is sufficient to say that **ethics** are the standards of behavior generally accepted by a society. Note that ethics goes beyond laws, which establish the minimum rules a society agrees to follow. Thus, it is possible to behave legally but still be unethical.

The temptation to act in an ethically questionable fashion can be very strong, particularly when the behavior can be rewarding. Take, for example, a development in the drugstore business. For years it has been a common practice for suppliers to grant discounts to retailers for damaged or outdated merchandise. However, some firms appear to be taking advantage of the policy. There have been a number of mergers among retail drugstore chains, giving them substantial leverage. As suppliers have become more dependent on these chains, they charge that some chains have gotten more liberal in their interpretation of "damaged and outdated," and are taking unauthorized deductions from their invoices. Is this unethical? The suppliers think so, but others say the suppliers have had the upper hand for years. In the past they had been able to dictate terms to the retailers and now "turnabout is fair play."

Instilling an Ethical Orientation

Organizations are addressing ethical issues. For example, most firms have a code of ethics for their employees.[19] However, as long as there are conflicting goals and the opportunity for people to make judgments, ethical failures will occur. To relieve some of the pressure on employees faced with ethical challenges and perhaps to reduce the frequency and severity of ethical problems, organizations have taken several steps:

- Clearly communicating the organization's ethical standards and expectations through initial training and frequent reminders and updates.
- Ensuring that employee requirements in terms of goals, quotas, and deadlines are reasonable.

AN ETHICAL DILEMMA?

Transparency International (TI) produces an annual ranking of countries in terms of the degree to which corruption is perceived to exist. The index is a composite derived from a number of surveys of businesspeople and analysts carried out by reputable firms. Scores range from 10 (no corruption) to 0 (highly corrupt). The sampling here is from the 145 countries ranked.

Corruption comes in many forms. One of the most common in business is bribery. Are there any conditions in which bribery to obtain and/or to retain business would be ethical?

Transparency International's Corruption Perception Index

Rank	Country	Score
1	Finland	9.7
5	Singapore	9.3
11	United Kingdom	8.6
17	U.S.	7.5
35	Taiwan	5.6
42	Italy	4.8
59	Brazil	3.9
64	Mexico	3.6
90	India	2.8
129	Pakistan	2.1
145	Haiti	1.5

Source: Transparency International website: *www.transparency.org*. Students also may want to examine the text of the Foreign Corrupt Practices Act of 1977 that stipulates what U.S. businesses are permitted to do when conducting business internationally.

- Creating a senior-level position of "ethics officer" occupied by a person with the skill to provide advice as well as the authority to respond to complaints and inquiries.

- Commending extraordinary ethical behavior and dealing decisively with ethical violations.

- Heightening employee sensitivity by communicating ethical statements formulated by relevant professional organizations such as the American Marketing Association.[20]

The Benefits of Ethical Behavior

You could argue that ethical behavior should in itself be rewarding. However, there are tangible benefits as well. Business is built on relationships with suppliers, customers, employees, and other groups. The strength of those relationships is largely a function of the amount of trust the parties have in each other. Unethical behavior undermines trust and destroys relationships.

Issues related to ethics are often ambiguous. There are situations in which the behavior of a marketer might be judged inappropriate and unethical by some and totally acceptable by others. It is important for you to be aware of typical ethical challenges in marketing and to consider how you would respond to them. To help you in that regard, we have included An Ethical Dilemma? boxes throughout the book. In most, there are no absolutely right or wrong answers. That's why we call them dilemmas. We hope you find them interesting and helpful in refining your own sense of ethics.

Importance of Marketing

It would be difficult to imagine a world without marketing. But it may be equally difficult to appreciate the importance effective marketing plays in many aspects of our lives.[21] We take for granted the media that are largely supported by advertising, the vast assortment of goods distributed through stores close to our homes, and the ease with which we can make purchases. To better appreciate marketing, consider for a moment how marketing plays a major role in the global economy, in the American socioeconomic system, in any individual organization, and in your life.

Globally

Until the late 1970s, American firms had a large and secure domestic market. The only significant foreign competition was in selected industries, such as agriculture, or for relatively narrow markets, such as luxury automobiles. But this changed dramatically through the 1980s as more foreign firms developed attractive products, honed their marketing expertise, and then successfully entered the U.S. market. Imported products in some industries, such as office equipment, autos, apparel, watches, semiconductors, and consumer electronics, have been very successful. As a result, in recent years the U.S. has been importing more than it exports, creating large annual trade deficits.

In the not too distant future there will be new challenges. The dramatic changes taking place in the governments and economies of eastern Europe and growing capitalism in China and the former Soviet Union will certainly create new and stronger international competitors.

Trade agreements are also altering the global business picture. The European Union, the North American Free Trade Agreement, and the Asia-Pacific Economic Cooperation forum are reducing economic barriers and liberalizing trade between their members. However, as trade agreements increase the marketing opportunities for firms within the member countries, they often result in stiffened competition for firms from outside.

In response to these developments, more and more U.S. firms are looking abroad. They are concluding that their profit and growth objectives are most likely to be achieved through a combination of domestic and international marketing, rather than solely from domestic marketing. Table 1.3 gives you some insight into how important foreign trade is for U.S. firms.

McDonald's began opening company-owned outlets in China in the early 1990s, but recent changes in government regulations have made franchising attractive. The firm expects to have 1,000 franchised stores in China by 2008, with many of the owners trained at its company-operated Hamburger University in Hong Kong.

www.mcdonalds.com

Although we don't yet know everything that will result from these developments, one thing is certain. We live in a global economy. Most nations today—regardless of their degree of economic development or their political philosophy—recognize the importance of marketing beyond their own national borders. Indeed, economic growth in the less

TABLE 1.3

U.S. International Trade and Major Trading Partners, 2001–2003

Exports			Imports		
Destination	**$ Value (billions)**		**Source**	**$ Value (billions)**	
	2001	**2003**		**2001**	**2003**
Canada	179	170	Canada	229	222
Mexico	112	97	China	100	152
Japan	65	52	Japan	147	138
United Kingdom	42	34	Mexico	136	118
Germany	29	29	Germany	59	68
Total U.S. exports	1,066	725	Total U.S. imports	1,441	1,257

Sources: *Statistical Abstract of the United States: 2004–2005*, 124th ed., U.S. Bureau of the Census, Washington, DC, 2005; Economic Indicators, Bureau of Economic Analysis, U.S. Department of Commerce, at *www.economicindicators.gov.*

developed nations of the world depends greatly on their ability to design effective marketing systems to produce global customers for their raw materials and industrial output. We will explore these issues in more detail throughout the book.

Domestically

Aggressive, effective marketing practices have been largely responsible for the high standard of living in the United States. The efficiency of mass marketing—extensive and rapid communication with customers through a wide variety of media and a distribution system that makes products readily available—combined with mass production brought the cost of many products within reach of most consumers. Since about 1920 (except during World War II), the available supply of products in the United States has far surpassed total demand.

Now mass customization means even more products virtually tailored to individual tastes.[22] As a result, the average American enjoys things that once were considered luxuries and in many countries are still available only to people earning high incomes.

Employment and Costs We can get an idea of the significance of marketing in the U.S. economy by looking at how many of us are employed in some way in marketing and how much of what we spend covers the cost of marketing. *Between one-fourth and one-third of the U.S. civilian labor force is engaged in marketing activities.* This figure includes employees in retailing, wholesaling, transportation, warehousing, and communications industries, as well as people who work in marketing departments of manufacturers and those who work in marketing in agricultural, mining, and service industries. Furthermore, over the past century, jobs in marketing have increased at a much more rapid rate than jobs in production, reflecting marketing's expanded role in the economy. On the average, *about 50 cents of each dollar we spend as consumers goes to cover marketing costs.* The money pays for designing the products to meet our needs, making products readily available when and where we want them, and informing us about products. These activities add want-satisfying ability to products.

Creating Utility A customer purchases a product because it provides satisfaction. The want-satisfying power of a product is called its **utility,** and it comes in many forms. It is through marketing that much of a product's utility is created.

Consider eBay as an example. Pierre Omidyar and Jeff Skoll, two San Jose, California, entrepreneurs, envisioned operating a giant auction where many buyers and sellers could gather and trade goods. But an auction in San Jose was not likely to generate the kind of crowds they desired. Faced with the challenge of how to increase access to their auction, they came upon the Internet. They wondered if the Internet could transport information from sellers about their products and bids from buyers interested in making purchases. Even if the technology could be made to work, potential buyers and sellers had to be made aware of this unique auction format and informed about how to use it. Excited by the possibilities, they created eBay, Inc., and the rest, as we say, is history.

Let's see what kinds of utility have been created in this process:

- *Form utility* is associated primarily with production—the physical or chemical changes that make a product more valuable. When lumber is made into furniture, form utility is created. This is production, not marketing. However, marketing contributes to decisions on the style, size, and color of the furniture. Similarly, marketing is involved in developing almost all products whether they are goods or services. In the case of eBay, an attractive, easy-to-use website had to be designed. Visitors to the site had to be able to find goods that interested them quickly and easily. These features contribute to the product's form utility.

- *Place utility* exists when a product is readily accessible to potential customers. An auction on the Internet can increase the number of buyers and sellers, but once products are purchased they still have to be delivered quickly and in good condition. Physically moving a purchased item to a successful bidder is an essential element of its value.

- *Time utility* means having a product available when you want it. In the case of eBay, this may be one of its primary attractions. Prospective buyers can visit the eBay Internet site day or night at their convenience. There's no need to have a store open or staffed.

- *Information utility* is created by informing prospective buyers that a product exists. Unless you know about a product and where you can get it, the product has no value. Advertising that describes the eBay auction concept and provides some information about how to list an item and how to make bids creates information utility. To create awareness of eBay, it had to be advertised. *Image utility* is a special type of information utility. It is the emotional or psychological value that a person attaches to a product or brand because of its reputation or social standing. Image utility is ordinarily associated with prestige or high-status products such as designer clothes, expensive foreign automobiles, or certain residential neighborhoods. However, the image-utility value of a given product may vary considerably depending on different consumers' perceptions. Shopping on the Internet using an online auction is still a novelty for many consumers. For some it may even be a status symbol that they can tell their friends about. Thus, for some consumers using eBay also provides image utility.

- *Possession utility* is created when a customer buys the product—that is, ownership is transferred to the buyer. This is a concern for eBay because there is virtually no policing of the buyers or the sellers. It's possible for sellers to misrepresent goods and for buyers to renege on paying. Clearly this is much less of an issue in face-to-face transactions. For eBay, providing possession utility is taking on growing significance as the number and types of users of the service increases.

Organizationally

Marketing considerations should be an integral part of all short-range and long-range planning in any company. Here's why:

Extreme sports have become an important services industry. Event sponsorships and participant endorsements are a way to connect with the 19 million inline skaters, 11 million skateboarders, and 8 million snowboarders, not to mention paintballers, wall climbers, and motorcross enthusiasts. This relatively young market first attracted firms representing soft drinks, fast food, automobiles, and personal grooming products, but other industries will likely be on board soon.

- The success of any business comes from satisfying the wants of its customers, which is the social and economic basis for the existence of all organizations.

- Although many activities are essential to a company's growth, marketing is the only one that produces revenue directly.

When managers are internally focused, products are designed by designers, manufactured by manufacturing people, priced by financial managers, and then given to sales managers to sell. This approach generally won't work in today's environment of intense competition and constant change. Just making a good product will not result in sales. Two special applications, services marketing and not-for-profit marketing, are described below.

Services Marketers   The U.S. has gone from primarily a manufacturing economy to the world's first service economy. As opposed to goods, services are activities that are the object of a transaction. Examples are transportation, communications, entertainment, medical care, financial services, education, and repairs. Services account for over two-thirds of the nation's gross domestic product. Almost three-fourths of the country's nonfarm labor force is employed in services industries, and over one-half of all consumer expenditures are for the purchase of services. Projections indicate that services' share of all these categories (gross domestic product, employment, expenditures) will continue to grow.

Because the production of goods dominated our economy until fairly recently, most marketing knowledge was derived from experience with goods (such as groceries, clothing, machine tools, and automobiles) rather than from services. But progress in services has been rapid, and now some services sector firms such as FedEx, Southwest Airlines, and Marriott Corp. are generally considered to be among the most market-oriented companies in the world.

Not-for-Profit Marketers   During the 1980s and early 1990s many not-for-profit organizations realized they needed effective marketing programs to make up for shrinking government subsidies, a decrease in charitable contributions, and other unfavorable economic conditions. Colleges with declining enrollments, hospitals with empty beds, and symphony orchestras playing to vacant seats all began to understand that marketing was essential to help them turn their situations around.

Today charities, museums, and even churches—organizations that formerly rejected any thought of marketing—are embracing it as a means of growth and, for some, survival. This trend is likely to accelerate for two reasons:

- Increasing competition among nonprofit organizations. For example, the competition among colleges and universities for students is intensifying, and the search for donors has become more intense as the number of charities has increased.

- Not-for-profit organizations need to improve their images and gain greater acceptance among donors, government agencies, news media, and of course, consumers, all of which collectively determine an organization's success.

Personally

Okay, so marketing is important globally, in our economy, and in an individual organization. But what's in it for you? Why should you study marketing? There are a number of reasons:

- Consider how many marketers view you as part of their market. With people like you in mind, firms such as Nike, VISA, Microsoft, and Kellogg's have designed products, set prices, created advertisements, and chosen the best methods of making their products available to you. In response, you watch television with its commercials, buy various articles over the Internet and in stores, and sometimes complain about prices or quality. As we said at the outset of the chapter, marketing occupies a large part of your daily life. If you doubt this, just imagine for a moment what it would be like if there were no marketing institutions—no retail stores to buy from or no advertising to give you information, for example. Clearly it is important to understand such a significant part of our society.

- Studying marketing will make you a better-informed consumer. You'll have a better appreciation for why some firms are successful and other, seemingly well-run businesses, fail. More specifically, you will discover how firms go about deciding what products to offer and what prices to charge. Your exploration of marketing will help you understand the many forms of promotion and how they are used to inform and persuade consumers. And it will help you appreciate the modern miracle of efficient distribution that makes products available when and where buyers want them.

- Last, marketing probably relates—directly or indirectly—to your career aspirations. If you are thinking about a marketing major and employment in a marketing position, you can develop a feel for what marketing managers do. (For an introduction to the many career opportunities in the field, we especially suggest you read "Careers and Marketing" found on our website www.mhhe.com/etzel07) If you're planning a career in accounting, finance, or some other business field, you can learn how marketing affects managerial decision making in these areas. Finally, if you are thinking about a career in a nonbusiness field such as health care, government, music, or education, you will learn how to use marketing in these organizations.

Summary

The foundation of marketing is exchange, in which one party provides to another party something of value in return for something else of value. In a broad sense, marketing consists of all activities designed to generate or facilitate an exchange intended to satisfy human needs.

Business firms and nonprofit organizations engage in marketing. Products marketed include goods as well as services, ideas, people, and places. Marketing activities are targeted at markets consisting of potential purchasers and also individuals and groups that influence the success of an organization.

In a business context, marketing is a total system of business activities designed to plan, price, promote, and distribute want-satisfying products to target markets in order to achieve organizational objectives.

Marketing's evolution in the United States has gone through three stages: It began with a product orientation, passed through the sales orientation, and is now in a market orientation. In this third stage a company's efforts are focused on identifying and satisfying customers' needs.

Some successful organizations remain at the first or second stage, not progressing to a market-orientation, because they have monopoly power or because their products are in such great demand. Other firms have difficulty accepting a market-driven approach to business or have problems implementing a market orientation.

A business philosophy called the marketing concept was developed to aid companies with supply capabilities that exceed consumer demand. According to the marketing concept, a firm is best able to achieve its performance objectives by adopting a market or customer orientation, coordinating all of its marketing activities, and fulfilling the organization's goals. Examples of implementation of the marketing concept include relationship building, mass customization, heightened sensitivity to quality, value creation, utilizing performance metrics, and the societal marketing concept. Ethics, the standards of behavior accepted by society, are important concerns of market-oriented organizations.

Marketing management involves segmenting markets, selecting target markets, and establishing a desirable position in the minds of buyers. The primary focus of marketing is the marketing mix—the combination of a product, price, promotion, and distribution process to meet the needs of a targeted segment of a market.

Marketing is practiced today in all modern nations, regardless of their political philosophy. As international competition has heated up, the attention paid to marketing has increased. In the U.S. between one-fourth and one-third of the civilian work force is involved with marketing, and about one-half of consumer spending covers the cost of marketing. This investment in marketing is justified by the form, information, place, time, and possession utilities it creates.

Depending on circumstances, marketing can be vital to an organization's success. In recent years numerous services firms and nonprofit organizations have found marketing to be necessary and worthwhile. Marketing also is useful to individuals. Students particularly find marketing helpful in the search for career opportunities.

More about **Trader Joe's**

Trader Joe's is not the only successful specialty grocery retailer. Often mentioned in the same breath are Whole Foods, a 165-store chain, and Wild Oats, with over 100 stores. They are two leading entrants in a somewhat different category, called natural and organic foods. In fact, the *Nutrition Business Journal* reports that there are 8,200 natural and health food stores operating in the U.S. The growing popularity of organic foods as well as nutritional supplements and vitamins is attributed to an overall concern about pollution and the environment as well as publicity given to outbreaks of E. coli and fear of mad cow disease.

However, novelty or publicized health concerns are not enough to sustain a business. To compete successfully, firms must find ways to satisfy consumers and outperform the competition. Interestingly, in the grocery business where weekly newspaper ads are standard, Trader Joe's does not rely on advertising. Instead, it uses a combination of outstanding employees, carefully selected merchandise, and attractive prices to draw in shoppers.

Employees are selected as much for their attitude as their ability. The ideal employee is described as someone who is "ambitious, adventurous, enjoys smiling, and has a strong sense of values." Individual store managers (called "Captains") have considerable autonomy in deciding what their stores will stock, and individual employees are free to open any product a customer wants to taste.

All merchandise stocked in TJ's has been tasted and tested by the company's tasting panel, and store employees are encouraged to tell customers what they think of products, even ones they don't like.

At the heart of TJ's success is an upward flow of information from the customers through the store employees to the management. By formally monitoring what customers are buying and informally tapping into what they are saying to employees, TJ's constantly adapts its offerings.

The result is a localized store with the buying power of a chain that stays in touch with its customers and changes grocery shopping from a chore to a welcome experience.[23]

1. What facts would suggest that Trader Joe's has adopted a market-oriented approach to marketing?

2. In what ways has Trader Joe's management implemented the "marketing concept?"

Customer relationship management (CRM) (11)
Mass customization (12)
Total quality management (TQM) (13)
Value (13)
Value creation (13)
Return on marketing investment (14)
Societal marketing concept (14)
Market (15)
Market segments (15)
Target market (16)
Position (16)
Forecast demand (16)
Marketing mix (16)
Ethics (17)
Utility (20)

Questions and Problems

1. Explain the concept of an exchange, including the conditions that must exist for an exchange to occur, and give one example each of a business exchange that does not involve money and a nonbusiness exchange.

2. Name some companies that you believe are still in the product or sales stages in the evolution of marketing. Explain why you chose each of them.

3. Describe how each of the following could go beyond an exchange situation to establishing a relationship with customers.
   a. Online fresh-cut flower retailer
   b. CPA firm
   c. Blood bank
   d. Automobile dealership
   e. University
   f. Appliance manufacturer

4. Describe how the operation of a product-oriented shoe manufacturer might be different from the operation of a market-oriented manufacturer.

5. Explain the relationship between the three elements that constitute the marketing concept.

6. "The marketing concept does not imply that marketing executives will run the firm. The concept requires only that whoever is in top management be market-oriented." Give examples of how a production manager, company treasurer, or personnel manager can be market-oriented.

7. For each of the following organizations, describe the marketing mix.
   a. Luxor hotel and casino in Las Vegas
   b. Airline Pilots Association labor union
   c. Professor teaching a first-year chemistry course
   d. Police department in your city

8. One way to explain the utilities provided by marketing is to consider how we would live if there were no marketing facilities. Describe some of the ways in which your daily activities would be affected if there were no retail stores or advertising.

9. Name two service firms that, in your opinion, do a good marketing job. Then name some that you think do a poor marketing job. Explain your reasoning in each case.

Interactive Marketing Exercises

1. Select an organizational unit at your school (for example, food service, placement office, intramural sports, library), observe the operation, and interview an administrator and some customers to identify (a) what is being exchanged; and (b) whether the unit is product-, sales-, or market-oriented.

2. Visit the sites of two different online book retailers (for example, www.amazon.com and www.barnesandnoble. com) and request information about this book. Keep track of the length of time it takes to find the book on the site and what information the site provides about the book. Next, note what information a customer is required to provide in order to purchase the book (but don't actually order one unless you need another copy). From the perspective of a consumer seeking utility, how does the Internet search compare with visiting a bookstore?

Chapter 2

"*Apple's main motivation for launching the online music service was to stimulate sales of its iPod.*"

Is **iTunes** Playing Your Song?

Just as it revolutionized the consumer market for desktop computers in the 1980s, Apple Computer Inc. is again transforming another burgeoning business. Apple's entrant in the digital-music business, the iTunes Music Store, was launched in 2003. In seeking sustained success in the competition among online music services, Apple faces several obstacles. Among them are illegal file-sharing services, many new legitimate competitors, technological challenges, and a reluctant music industry.

Like several other Internet-based enterprises, the music file-sharing industry began in a dorm room. Shawn Fanning, a student at Northwestern University, created Napster in 1999. Napster allowed individuals to exchange MP3 music files over the Internet and to download them onto their computers. Music companies such as BMG and Warner were distressed by this new peer-to-peer (PTP) model for file sharing. Believing that it infringed upon their copyrights, the companies sued to put Napster out of business. In July 2001, Napster was shut down, but by then, a number of imitators had sprung up and were offering free PTP music-sharing services. Millions of songs were being downloaded illegally. There were few legitimate alternatives because the music companies were wary of licensing their collections for Internet consumption.

Apple's iTunes Music Store was the first online service to reach an agreement with all five of the major music companies (as well as several independents). iTunes charges $.99 for each song a customer downloads.

However, because it pays $.65 to $.79 per song to the record companies, Apple earns little profit from iTunes. Apple's main motivation for launching the online music service was to stimulate sales of its iPod MP3 music player.

Apple's technology for iTunes allows customers to purchase a song, play it on up to three computers, and also copy or "burn" that song onto an iPod (but no other MP3 player) or multiple compact discs. An "album," a playlist of 10 songs, can be purchased for $9.99. Both songs and albums are encrypted to prevent them from being transferred onto free peer-to-peer sites.

iTunes' main competitors were Napster, MusicMatch, RealPlayer, and yes, even Wal-Mart. In addition to selling individual songs for $.99 each, Napster and MusicMatch also offer subscriptions that allow users to pay a monthly fee in order to "stream," which means they can listen to as many songs as they want on their computer. Rob Glaser, chief executive officer of RealNetworks (which owns RealPlayer), stated that only 13% of RealPlayer's customers were paying $.99 to download singles, whereas 72% were simply listening to music on their computer. Steve Jobs of Apple rejected that approach, saying, "The subscription services are not working. People want to own their music, not rent it."

Apple developed a slick advertising campaign that featured U2's Bono promoting both iTunes and the iPod. By September 2004, iTunes had sold more than 100 million songs and had 70% of the legal online digital-music business. Despite 60 competitors, iTunes was selling more than four times as many songs each week as its closest competitor, the legal version of Napster.[1]

What marketing considerations will be important for Apple as it tries to make iTunes a long-lasting success, especially in the face of competition from Microsoft and other online music services?

www.itunes.com

As the iTunes situation illustrates, any organization must identify and then respond to numerous environmental forces ranging from shifting consumer tastes to advancing technology. Some of these forces are external to the firm, whereas others come from within. Management can't do much about controlling the external forces, but it generally can control the internal ones.

Many of these forces influence what can and should be done in the area of marketing. Ultimately, a firm's ability to adapt to its operating environment determines, in large part, its level of business success. Thus Apple Computer, like any organization, must manage its marketing program within its combined external and internal environment.

After studying this chapter, you should be able to explain:

- The concept of environmental monitoring.
- How external environmental forces such as demographics, economic conditions, and social and cultural trends can affect an organization's marketing.
- How external factors such as markets, as well as suppliers and intermediaries that are specific to a given firm, can influence that firm's marketing.
- How nonmarketing resources within a firm can affect its marketing

Environmental Monitoring

Environmental monitoring—also called *environmental scanning*—is the process of (1) gathering information regarding a company's external environment, (2) analyzing it, and (3) forecasting the impact of whatever trends the analysis suggests. Often the word *environment* is associated with our physical environment—air quality, water pollution, solid-waste disposal, and natural-resource conservation. However, we use the term *environment* in a much broader sense in this chapter.

An organization operates within an *external* environment that it generally *cannot* control. At the same time, marketing and nonmarketing resources exist *within* the organization that generally *can* be controlled by its executives.

There are two levels of external forces:

- *Macro* influences (so called because they affect all firms) such as demographics, economic conditions, culture, and laws.
- *Micro* influences (so called because they affect a particular firm) consist of suppliers, marketing intermediaries, and customers. Micro influences, although external, are closely related to a specific company.

Successful marketing depends largely on a company's ability to manage its marketing programs within its environment. To do this, a firm's marketing executives must determine what makes up the firm's environment and then monitor it in a systematic, ongoing fashion. They must be alert to spot environmental trends that could be opportunities or problems for their organization. According to one source, "Environmental scanning helps an organization form a strategic position from which it can address external forces over which it has little, if any, control." Noteworthy recent trends include growing interests in personal safety (no doubt magnified by fear of terrorism) and life-long learning.[2]

How important is environmental monitoring to business success? In a word, *very*. One study of about 100 large companies concluded, "Firms having advanced systems to monitor events in the external environment exhibited higher growth and greater profitability than firms that did not have such systems."[3]

External Macroenvironment

The following external forces have considerable influence on any organization's marketing opportunities and activities (see Figure 2.1). Therefore, they are *macroenvironmental forces:*

- Demographics
- Economic conditions
- Competition
- Social and cultural forces
- Political and legal forces
- Technology

A change in any one of them can cause changes in one or more of the others. Hence, they are interrelated. One thing they all have in common is that they are dynamic forces—that is, they are subject to change *and* at an increasing rate!

These forces are largely uncontrollable by management, but they are not *totally* uncontrollable. A company may be able to influence its external environment to some extent. For instance, a firm may influence its political–legal environment by

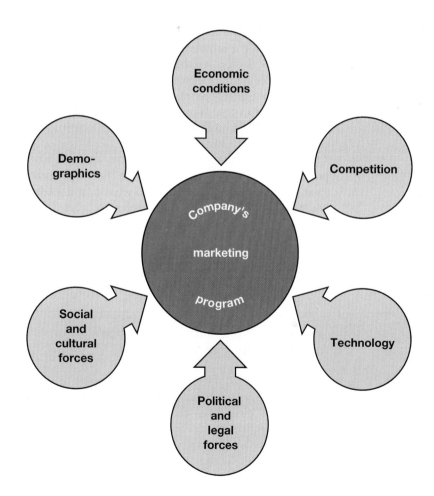

FIGURE 2.1

External Macroenvironment of a Company's Marketing Program.

Six largely uncontrollable external forces influence an organization's marketing activities.

www.nestea.com

www.purplepill.com

www.census.gov

lobbying or by contributing to a legislator's campaign fund. Or, in international marketing, a company can improve its competitive position by a joint venture with a foreign firm that markets a complementary product. Coca-Cola and Swiss-owned Nestlé, the world's largest food manufacturer, joined forces to market ready-to-drink iced Nestea in the U.S. and chocolate, coffee, and tea drinks in Europe.[4]

On the technological frontier, new-product research and development can strengthen a firm's competitive position. For instance, Nexium, a drug that treats stomach disorders, generated over $6 billion in sales for AstraZeneca during the product's first three years on the market. Clearly, technological developments have a significant impact on competition.[5]

Now let's take a look at these six external forces in more detail.

Demographics

Demographics refer to the characteristics of populations, including such factors as size, distribution, and growth. Because people constitute markets, demographics are of special interest to marketing executives. Here we'll just cover a few examples of how demographic factors influence marketing programs; some aspects of demographics related to consumer buying behavior will be considered in Chapter 4.

According to projections, there will be approximately 336 million Americans by the year 2020, an increase of about 38 million over the present total. Perhaps the most significant demographic trend at this time is the aging of the U.S. population, a shift that is expected to continue for a while. The statistics in Table 2.1 underscore how the age distribution of the population evolves over time. Changes in the age distribution are the result of many factors, including the quality of health care and nutrition. Two key factors are the number of women who are of child-bearing age and the birthrate. The number of women of child-bearing age is a function of the births that occurred some years before and thus is highly predictable. However, the birthrate at any one point in time is influenced by a wide variety of social and economic factors that are much less predictable. For example, attitudes toward careers and family size certainly affect the birthrate.

There are several noteworthy points in Table 2.1. First, peaks and valleys in the population distribution move through time. To mention one example, the relatively small growth in the age groups between 5 and 44 years old can be traced back to lower birthrates during the last several decades of the last century. Therefore, it is possible to track changes and, to the extent that behavior is related to age, anticipate

TABLE 2.1   **Projected Changes in the Distribution of the U.S. Population**

	% change	
	2000–2010	2010–2020
Under 5 years old	11.5	7.0
5–19 years old	0.8	6.7
20–44 years old	0.4	4.0
45–64 years old	29.7	3.3
65–84 years old	10.8	38.8
Over 84 years old	43.5	18.7
Total population	9.5	8.7

Source: U.S. Bureau of the Census, "U.S. Interim Projections by Age, Sex, Race, and Hispanic Origin," at *www.census.gov/ipc/www/usinterimproj/natprojtab02b.pdf*, accessed February 19, 2005.

In preparing their marketing programs, marketers in companies and also in not-for-profit organizations must recognize the shifting composition of the U.S. population. This Spanish-language ad is seeking recruits for the Air National Guard, the official reserve component of the U.S. Air Force. Although the text is in Spanish, the ad is careful to depict the ethnic and racial diversity a new recruit would find in the Guard. The ad also stresses the benefit of joining the Guard, including the opportunity to prepare for one of about 200 different careers.

www.GoANG.com

what impacts they will have. Second, even in a 10-year period, there can be quite dramatic shifts in the population. For instance, the number of people in the 65 to 84 age group will increase by nearly 40% from 2010 to 2020, which means growing markets for products such as health care and retirement communities.

The composition of households has also been changing rather dramatically. For instance, over the past 50 years, the proportion of households consisting of married couples has declined from 80% to about 50%. Further, only one-half of married-couple households have children living at home. Another noteworthy and perhaps surprising shift is that families consisting of working fathers and stay-at-home mothers represent just 10% of all households. Marketers need to consider these statistics in choosing target markets as well as in designing marketing programs.[6]

Another notable demographic trend is the rapid growth of minority markets—and their buying power. Minorities now represent about 33% of the total U.S. population; by the year 2020, the proportion is expected to increase to 39%. Between 2000 and 2020, particularly rapid growth is forecast for Asian Americans and persons of Hispanic origin (both with projected increases of 68%). In recent years, the buying power of minorities has expanded more than the size of this segment of the population did. It is projected that Hispanics' buying power will account for almost 10% of the U.S. total of $10.6 *trillion* in 2008. The respective shares for African Americans, Asian Americans, and Native Americans are 9%, 5%, and less than 1%.[7]

None of these ethnic groups is homogeneous, however. The Hispanic market, which became the largest minority group in the U.S. in 2001, includes subgroups of Cubans, Puerto Ricans, Dominicans, Mexicans, Central Americans, and South Americans. A simple product such as beans illustrates the differences among subgroups. Cubans prefer black beans, Mexicans eat refried beans, and Puerto Ricans go for red beans.[8] Many consumer-product companies realized only recently that they must target their products and advertising at each of the Hispanic subgroups.

How can a firm appeal to Generation Y?

For decades, demographers and sociologists have labeled generations for various reasons, including an effort to understand their buying behavior. Rather than grouping by income or education, these cohorts are based on age and, as a result, shared historical experiences. **Baby boomers** are Americans born in the 20 years following World War II. **Generation X** refers to about 40 million people born roughly between 1966 and 1976 who, in turn, entered the workplace during a recession. Not surprisingly, "Gen X" has been labeled as cautious and somewhat pessimistic.

Generation Y (also labeled echo boomers) represents the successors to Generation X. Gen Y is most commonly defined as those young people born between 1977 and 1994, essentially representing the children of baby boomers. (However, some experts define Gen Y differently, such as including people born through 1997.) Numbering 71 million, Gen Y is a sizable target market—three times as large as Gen X and rivaling the number of baby boomers. Growing up in the best economy ever, these young adults are also relatively affluent and materialistic. Gen Y is diverse—in fact, more diverse than previous cohorts—in that about one-third are minorities, one-quarter come from a single-parent household, and three-quarters have working mothers. This diversity also manifests itself in more acceptance of sexual and racial differences, non-traditional families, and global perspectives.

Many members of Gen Y probably have vivid memories of the O. J. Simpson case, the Bill Clinton–Monica Lewinsky scandal, the tragedy at Columbine High School, and the horror of 9/11. Although it's difficult (and sometimes dangerous) to generalize, Gen Y members tend to be optimistic and committed to enjoying life but also are concerned about their personal safety and skeptical of the media. Further, Gen Y does not look at public figures as role models. Instead, in a recent survey, 57% of college seniors listed a parent as the person they admired and respected the most. And talk shows and reality TV have reinforced beliefs that everyone deserves to be heard and involved, that there is often more than one right answer, and that differing viewpoints should be tolerated.

No group as large as Gen Y is homogeneous and receptive to a single marketing appeal, of course. Thus companies are trying various approaches to sell goods and services to Gen Y, often using media that allow specific targeting. Marketers have tried to develop messages that take into account the values, attitudes, and life experiences of Gen Y. For instance, Sprite was successful with its "Image is nothing, obey your thirst" campaign. Innovative new products with the Gen Y lifestyle in mind—such as a backpack with speakers to be used with an MP3 player—are hitting store shelves. Automobile manufacturers definitely have their sights on this consumer market. Toyota's Scion, Saturn's Ion, and Honda's Element are all targeted at Gen Y members. To reach Gen Y, Scion marketers are not relying on TV but are using so-called stealth marketing, including projecting catchy slogans such as "Ban Normality" on buildings after dark in neighborhoods that are popular with young people.

What marketing strategies would you suggest to a company that wants to appeal to Generation Y consumers? What strategies should be avoided?

www.scion.com

Sources: Michelle Koidin Jaffee, "Gen Y-ers Might Outstrip Boomers in Shaping Our Culture," *St. Louis Post-Dispatch,* Mar. 21, 2004, p. EV1; Christopher Palmieri, "Toyota's Scion: Dude, Here's Your Car," *BusinessWeek,* June 9, 2003, p. 44; Pamela Paul, "Getting Inside Gen Y," *American Demographics,* September 2001, pp. 42–49; Jim Pearse, "Gen Y Gold Mine," *Dealerscope,* September 2001, pp. 26–28; Bob Dart, "What's Your Generation?" *St. Louis Post-Dispatch,* Apr. 9, 2001, pp. G1, G3; Maricris G. Briones, "Ad Biz Faces Technology, Gen Y and Competition," *Marketing News,* Dec. 7, 1998, pp. 2, 10; and Ellen Neuborne, "Generation Y," *BusinessWeek,* Feb. 15, 1999, pp. 81–84+.

Economic Conditions

People alone do not make a market. They must have money to spend and be willing to spend it. Consequently, the **economic environment** is a significant force that affects the marketing activities of just about any organization. A marketing program is affected especially by such economic factors as the current and anticipated stage of the business cycle, as well as inflation and interest rates.

Stage of the Business Cycle
The traditional **business cycle** goes through four stages—prosperity, recession, depression, and recovery—then returns full cycle to prosperity. Economic strategies adopted by the federal government have averted the depression stage in the U.S. for about 75 years. Marketing executives need to know

which stage of the business cycle the economy currently is in, because a company's marketing programs usually must be changed from one stage of the business cycle to another.

Prosperity is a period of economic growth. During this stage, organizations tend to expand their marketing programs as they add new products and enter new markets.

A *recession* is a period of retrenchment for consumers and businesses—we tighten our economic belts. People can become discouraged, scared, and angry. Naturally, these feelings affect their buying behavior. For example, some consumers cut back on eating out and entertainment outside the home. As a result, firms catering to these needs face serious marketing challenges, and some may incur economic losses.

Recovery is the period when the economy is moving from recession to prosperity. The marketers' challenge is to determine how quickly prosperity will return and to what level. As unemployment declines and disposable income increases, companies expand their marketing efforts to improve sales and profits.

After prosperity for most of the 1990s, the U.S. economy slowed down and entered a recession in 2001. This relatively mild recession was characterized by decreased business spending, workforce reductions (especially in the technology sector), and a drop in the stock market. The domestic economy rebounded in the second half of 2003. As you read this, what stage of the business cycle do you think the U.S. economy is in currently?

Inflation A rise in the prices of goods and services represents **inflation.** When prices rise at a faster rate than personal incomes, consumer buying power declines. Inflation rates affect government policies, consumer psychology, and also marketing programs.

During the late 1970s and early 1980s, the U.S. experienced what for us was a high inflation rate—above 10%. But inflation dropped below 5% in the early 1990s and to one-half that rate since then.[9] Some countries around the world are plagued by extremely high rates of inflation—increases of 20%, 30%, or even 50% yearly.

Perhaps surprisingly, periods of declining prices—called *deflation*—or low inflation—sometimes termed *disinflation*—present challenges for marketers. In particular, it is very difficult for firms to raise prices because of consumer resistance. As a result, they need to cut their costs or else profits will evaporate. To do so, companies must take such steps as redesigning products to pare production costs and cutting back on coupons and other promotions that in effect lower prices.[10]

Interest Rates **Interest rates** are another external economic factor that influences marketing programs. When interest rates are high, for instance, consumers tend not to make long-term purchases such as housing. Marketers sometimes offer below-market interest rates (a form of price cut) as a promotional device to increase business. Auto manufacturers use this tactic occasionally.

Competition

A company's competitive environment obviously is a major influence on its marketing programs. A firm generally faces three types of competition:

www4.toysrus.com

- *Brand competition* comes from marketers of directly similar products. Despite an online partnership with Amazon.com, Toys "R" Us has suffered as a result of growing competition from discounters such as Wal-Mart and Target.[11] VISA, MasterCard, Discover, and American Express compete internationally in the credit card field. And, yes, even the authors' three schools compete with each other for charitable contributions from business firms and from alumni who hold degrees from any pair of these schools.

A number of companies have developed software that helps firms manage their relationships with customers. Competitors engage in aggressive marketing to build their brands and gain a differential advantage. Here one competitor in this field, salesforce.com, states its case against a larger competitor, Siebel Systems.

www.salesforce.com

www.lyricopera.org

www.cso.org

- *Substitute products* satisfy the same need. During winter in Chicago, for example, the Bulls professional basketball team, the Blackhawks hockey team, the Lyric Opera, the Chicago Symphony Orchestra, and stores selling or renting videos all compete for the entertainment dollar. In recent years, a growing number of homeowners have been choosing wood flooring instead of carpeting, causing carpet sales to stagnate.[12]

- In a third, more general type of competition, *every company* is a rival for the customer's limited buying power. So the competition faced by the maker of Wilson tennis rackets might be several new pairs of Levi's Docker slacks, a Nissan repair bill, or a cash contribution to some charity.

Skillful marketing executives constantly monitor all aspects of competitors' marketing activities—their products, pricing, distribution systems, and promotional programs. Any enterprise strives to gain a **differential advantage,** which is any feature of an organization or brand that is perceived to be desirable and different from those of the competition. In contrast, this same enterprise has to work hard to avoid a differential *dis*advantage. A differential advantage attracts customers, whereas a differential disadvantage drives them away.

Social and Cultural Forces

The task facing marketing executives is becoming more complex because our sociocultural patterns—lifestyles, values, and beliefs—are changing much more quickly than they used to. Here are a few changes in **social and cultural forces** that have significant marketing implications.

Concern about Natural Environment
Many Americans emphasize the *quality* of life rather than the *quantity* of goods consumed. The theme is "not more, but better." High on the list of what people consider integral to quality of life is the natural environment. Thus we hear concerns expressed about air and water pollution,

How competitive do we want to be?

The North American Free Trade Agreement (NAFTA) was established in 1994 among the U.S. and its two largest trading partners, Canada and Mexico. Its purpose is to promote trade by phasing out all tariffs on goods between these countries by 2008. (Other trade agreements, linking countries in various regions, will be described in Chapter 3.)

Without tariffs, imports and exports compete on more equal footing. And, without the burden of having their goods taxed in another country, it is expected that the "best" producers (that is, those that are most efficient or effective) will rise to the top. The proponents of free trade and NAFTA assert that businesses, workers, and consumers all benefit from this increased competitiveness and efficiency. Businesses benefit through increased trade with the participating countries. Workers benefit as more jobs are created to support the increased trade. And consumers benefit from access to a wider range of competitively priced goods.

However, there is a significant issue of contention: job loss. Critics claimed that opening up borders would result in millions of jobs moving out of the U.S. to lower-wage countries and other workers in the U.S. suffering from depressed wages because of the increased labor competitiveness.

NAFTA has been in effect for more than a decade, and the increase in trilateral trade has been dramatic, rising from $297 billion in 1993 to over $650 billion in 2003. Other specific outcomes include:

- U.S. exports to its two NAFTA partners increased 91% from 1993 to 2004.

- According to the U.S. trade representative, 900,000 jobs were created to support U.S. exports to Mexico and Canada since 1993, and the wages for these jobs were about 15% higher than the average American wage.

- Mexico's exports to the U.S. now account for 25% of its economy, almost double the pre-NAFTA level.

- About 1.75 million jobs have been created in Mexico since 1995 to support the NAFTA export boom.

- Mexico's exports to the other two NAFTA countries more than tripled from 1993 to 2003; Canada's imports to the U.S. and Mexico almost doubled during the same period.

- About 99% of the tariffs charged on goods exchanged by the three countries have been eliminated.

Of course, there are "two sides to every story," so NAFTA's critics would offer contrary statistics. In that regard, the U.S. had record trade deficits with Mexico and Canada, totaling $111 billion in 2004.

In any event, it is likely that there will be more, not fewer, trade agreements in the foreseeable future. One possibility, under consideration in early 2005, is CAFTA, which stands for the Central American Free Trade Agreement. CAFTA would be similar to NAFTA in purpose but would have a different set of participants, namely the U.S. and six nations in Central America.

Sources: Robert Batterson, "NAFTA Serves as Blueprint for New Central American Trade Pact," *St. Louis Post-Dispatch,* Mar. 6, 2005, p. E7; "2004 Highlights, Foreign Trade Statistics," U.S. Census Bureau, at *http://www. census.gov/foreign-trade/statistics/highlights/annual.html;* "U.S. Trade (Imports, Exports and Balance) by Country, Foreign Trade Statistics," U.S. Census Bureau, at *http://www.census.gov/foreign-trade/balance/,* accessed on Feb. 19, 2005; "NAFTA and Trade Flows," from *www.nafta-mexico.org/ sphp_pages/ canada/exporta/txt/nafta_mexico_fta_network.htm,* accessed on Feb. 19, 2005; Charles J. Whalen, "NAFTA's Scorecard: So Far, So Good," *BusinessWeek,* July 9, 2001, pp. 54–56; and Office of the United States Trade Representative, "NAFTA Partners Speed Up Elimination of Tariffs on $25 Billion in Trade," Jan. 9, 2001, no pages given.

---

holes in the ozone layer, acid rain, solid waste disposal, and the destruction of rainforests and other natural resources. These concerns raise the public's level of environmental consciousness.

A number of businesses noticed—and responded to—consumers' environmental consciousness. Specific efforts have focused on using resources efficiently and, in particular, conserving fossil fuels. To cite several examples:[13]

- Honda is testing a car powered by a hydrogen fuel cell, with its only emission being water vapor.

- In 2005, Procter & Gamble introduced Tide Coldwater, a new detergent that is designed to clean clothes in cold water and thus save energy.

The Procter & Gamble Company offers an extensive line of Tide detergents. One version, Tide Coldwater, is aimed especially at consumers who are environmentally conscious. P&G promotes the product as saving both energy and money by being usable with cold water. In stressing that Tide Coldwater saves money, P&G recognizes that most consumers who are interested in being environmentally friendly are also seeking other benefits such as saving some money—through smaller utility bills in this case.

 www.tide.com

• Reclamere, Inc., collects old, unwanted electronic equipment such as computers and disposes of them, recycling any hazardous materials in an environmentally sound way.

www.reclamere.com

By the mid-1990s, the proportion of consumers who bought environmentally friendly products approached one-half. However, relatively few consumers (29%, according to a recent survey) purchase a product strictly because it is environmentally friendly. A common mistake by companies is neglecting to mention the product's benefit to the consumer, not just to the environment.[14] To satisfy "green consumers," a product must also be competitive with alternatives on such factors as price, reliability, and convenience.

Many people who hold favorable attitudes toward environmentally friendly products do not purchase them. Further, and perhaps most perplexing, some products that consumers think are good for the environment—and that companies promote as being environmentally friendly—are more harmful than alternatives. For example, is a paper cup more environmentally friendly than a plastic cup? Actually, "a plastic cup takes half as much energy to make and results in 35% fewer pounds of toxic chemicals . . . than a paper cup does."[15]

Thus concern about the natural environment appears to be having a diminished impact on buying decisions in the U.S. However, environmental consciousness is greater in many other parts of the world—ranging from the European Union to Japan—than it is in the U.S.[16] As a result, a company must be environmentally sensitive in its marketing activities, especially product development, all around the world.

Changing Gender Roles For many reasons (most notably the increasing number of two-income households), male–female roles related to families, jobs, recreation, and buying behavior are changing dramatically. Now, for example, a growing number of "house husbands" are staying home and assuming primary responsibility for child care and homemaking while their wives work full-time. Further, it's increasingly common for men to shop for household necessities, particularly groceries, and for women to purchase such products as cars, mutual funds, and business travel. Seeking a stronger appeal to women, Volvo relied on an all-female group of designers to develop a new concept car.[17]

One of the most dramatic shifts in our culture has been the changing role of women. Over one-half of American women, including almost three-quarters of those in the 25 to 54 age group, are working outside the home today. According to a study by an advertising agency, women need to be segmented not just by age or employment status but also by other variables such as the father's degree of involvement in the family and the mother's interest in self-fulfillment.[18] Marketers obviously need different approaches to reach, and appeal to, women who are working full-time and/or raising children on their own versus stay-at-home mothers.

Women's attitudes toward careers, shopping, and products continue to evolve. Now, employed women are seeking a better balance between work and family. In turn, they are very interested in products that help them do that, especially by saving time. Thus working women represent a prime market for frozen and prepared food, more efficient appliances, and cleaning products and services such as house cleaning and fast food. Further, they are more likely to reward themselves by going to the beauty salon for a makeover or by buying a new CD player for their car. Seeing that, Johnson & Johnson has promoted its new Neutrogena makeup line with a "be free to spend more on yourself" theme.[19]

www.neutrogena.com

Changing gender roles have affected men as well. Some men are doing more shopping and housework only because it's demanded of them, whereas other men hold more favorable attitudes toward the shift in gender roles. Research shows that "change adapters" are younger, better educated, and more affluent than the "change opposers." Marketers should be aware that these two groups of men buy different items and shop in different ways.[20]

A Premium on Time   Many Americans are working longer hours than their parents did—almost 50 hours a week now compared to just over 40 hours several decades ago. Added work hours have been increasingly common since the early 1990s, when many large companies downsized, thereby expanding the workload for the remaining employees. Further, a substantial number of people also consider it necessary to be involved in activities such as continuing education, personal fitness, and various kinds of professional or civic endeavors. In recent years, many people have also placed more emphasis on family activities. All factors considered, it's not surprising that leisure time has fallen from 26 hours a week to 19.[21]

Time-short people seek to gain more free time, if possible, and to maximize the benefit of whatever free time they have. From a marketing standpoint, this means many people, especially two-income households, with more income but less time are more willing to pay for convenience. Thus goods and services that help consumers save time or make full use of it are increasingly popular. For example, Yoplait's drinkable yogurt, Nouriche, allows consumers to "multitask" by driving and eating at the same time.

More and more women (as well as men) are paying attention to health and physical fitness. At the same time, many women are "time challenged" as a result of their family and/or career responsibilities. In line with these trends, General Mills developed Yoplait Nouriche— a non-fat yogurt smoothie— that is packaged in a plastic bottle so it's drinkable on the go. On Yoplait Nouriche's website, the product is touted as "an excellent source of calcium, protein and fiber." General Mills also offers a light version of the product, with fewer calories, sodium, potassium, and carbohydrates.

www.yoplait.com/products_nouriche.aspx

Every phase of a company's marketing program is affected by consumers' desire for convenience:

- Product planning should consider the opportunity to provide convenience related to a myriad of factors ranging from ease of preparation (with a food product, for example) to learning time (with a new computer, for example).

- Distribution arrangements should offer convenient locations and store hours. Some convenience stores (such as 7-Eleven) and copy centers (such as Kinko's—now FedEX Kinko's) responded by remaining open 24 hours a day. More and more shoppers are using the Internet to save time in purchasing a wide variety of consumer and business products.

- Pricing policies should take into account the costs of providing the various kinds of convenience. Some convenience-conscious (or technology-challenged) travelers who do not want to book their travel online are willing to pay a special per-trip fee charged by many travel agents. These fees have become essential revenue to travel agents as airlines cut their sales commissions.

- The company's commitment to saving time for consumers is a possible basis for promotion, perhaps creating a differential advantage for the firm.

MARKETING IN THE INFORMATION ECONOMY

Will online grocery retailing ever be successful?

Online retailing now generates over $150 billion in sales, with annual growth rates above 20%. This track record is impressive, considering that total retail sales typically increase by about 2% to 4% annually. Yet, despite heavy financial backing, aggressive marketing campaigns, and sometimes strong growth, numerous online merchants (also called e-tailers) have failed. Etoys, pets.com, and drugstore.com are just a few of the high-profile e-tailers that had to shut their virtual doors. They had trouble making a profit on each order, let alone recouping the massive investments made in technology, warehouses, and other business components.

One of the more prominent casualties was Webvan, which offered next-day delivery of groceries to a consumer's home. The service appeared to be well-suited for the steadily increasing number of two-income households as well as other consumers who place a premium on free time. Webvan had many attractive features, including an easy-to-use website, extensive selection, delivery within a 30-minute timeframe, and free delivery for orders over $75. The average order was about $110.

Despite these positives, Webvan closed down after losing a whopping $830 million in just 27 months of existence. What went wrong? Evidently not enough consumers valued the service. And it had enormous overhead, including technology and warehouses to serve 26 markets. Webvan needed, but didn't reach, 4,000 orders per day per market to break even.

However, because retail sales of groceries are in the vicinity of $600 billion annually, other firms such as Peapod and FreshDirect are still trying to master online grocery retailing. In contrast to several years ago, the focus today is on gradual city-by-city expansion and on avoiding investments in trucks and warehouses. Thus it's common for supermarket chains to have an online division that draws upon its existing inventory. A recent independent entrant, FreshDirect, strives to minimize its inventory through "just-in-time" purchasing and by making prepared foods (such as vegetable quiches and roasted coffee) to fill each day's orders and no more. Another firm, Netgrocer, even uses FedEx's ground service for deliveries.

Under what circumstances, if any, could an online grocery store be successful?

Sources: Greg Saitz, "Online Shopping for Food Makes Comeback in New Jersey and Elsewhere," *The Star-Ledger of Newark*, Jan. 16, 2005, pp. 9, 14; Susan Reda, "It Clicks! Sales and Profitability Rise for On-Line Retailers," *Stores*, July 2004, p. 106; Erick Schonfeld, "The Big Cheese of Online Grocers," *Business 2.0*, January/February 2004, pp. 60–61; Linda Himelstein, "Webvan Left the Basics on the Shelf," *BusinessWeek*, July 23, 2001, p. 43; and Mylene Mangalindan, "Webvan Joins List of Dot-Com Failures," *The Wall Street Journal*, July 10, 2001, pp. A3, A6.

Physical Fitness and Health Most demographic and economic segments of our society seem to reflect an increased interest in physical fitness and health. Participation in fitness activities from aerobics to yoga (we could not think of an activity beginning with a *z*) is on the rise. Fitness centers as well as manufacturers of exercise equipment have benefited from this trend. However, with an expanding number of competitors, there is no assurance of success for an individual firm.

Paralleling the fitness phenomenon, many Americans are changing their dietary habits. The public is constantly made aware of the relationship between diet, on the one hand, and heart disease and cancer, on the other. Consequently, a large number of consumers have become more interested in diets for weight loss; foods low in salt, additives, and cholesterol; and foods high in vitamins, minerals, and fiber content. (Some habits are hard to shake, however, so some of us still consume bacon double cheeseburgers.)

Companies need to recognize and respond to the public's growing interest in health. Thus, at the retailing level, most supermarkets now stock an assortment of health foods. At the manufacturing level, Campbell Soup Co. developed and introduced Intelligent Quisine, a line of nutrient-fortified foods. However, success of new products that try to address consumer needs is not assured. For example, even though many customers raved about the health benefits of Intelligent Quisine during market tests, the product failed because of insufficient sales.[22]

Political and Legal Forces

Every company's conduct is influenced, often a great deal, by the political and legal processes in our society. The **political and legal forces** on marketing can be grouped into the following four categories:

- *Monetary and fiscal policies.* Marketing efforts are affected by the level of government spending, the money supply, and tax legislation.

- *Social legislation and regulations.* Legislation affecting the environment—antipollution laws, for example—and regulations set by the Environmental Protection Agency fall into this category.

- *Governmental relationships with industries.* Here we find subsidies in agriculture, shipbuilding, passenger rail transportation, and other industries. Tariffs and import quotas also affect specific industries. Government *deregulation* continues to have an effect on financial institutions and public utilities (such as electric and natural gas suppliers) as well as on the telecommunications and transportation industries.

- *Legislation related specifically to marketing.* Marketing executives do not have to be lawyers, but they should know something about laws affecting marketing—why they were passed, their main provisions, and current ground rules set by the courts and regulatory agencies for administering them.

The marketing-related laws, which are summarized in Table 2.2, are designed either to regulate competition or to protect consumers. Note that there has been very little new legislation affecting marketing since 1980. However, court decisions and agency rulings based on these laws are issued quite frequently. To forestall added legislation, individual companies and perhaps even entire industries sometimes respond to government signals and modify troublesome business practices.

Occasionally, a government agency alleges that a business has violated a law. Other times, companies sue each other, claiming illegal behavior. For example, Gillette Co. sued Energizer Holdings Inc., charging that Energizer's Schick Quattro razor violated Gillette's patents. According to one viewpoint, such lawsuits might be intended to delay introductions or new products.[23]

www.schiekquattro.com

Selected Legislation Affecting Marketing

TABLE 2.2

To Regulate Competition

1. Sherman Antitrust Act (1890). Prohibits monopolies and combinations in restraint of trade.
2. Federal Trade Commission (FTC) Act (1914). Prohibits unfair competition.
3. Clayton Antitrust Act (1914). Regulates several activities, notably price discrimination.
4. State Unfair Trade Practices Acts (1930s). Prohibit "loss-leader" pricing (selling below cost). Laws still in effect in about half the states.
5. Robinson-Patman Act (1936). Amends the Clayton Act by strengthening the prohibition of price discrimination. Regulates price discounts and allowances.
6. Wheeler-Lea Act (1938). Amends the FTC Act; broadens and strengthens regulation of unfair or deceptive competition.
7. Lanham Trademark Act (1946). Regulates brands and trademarks.
8. Consumer Goods Pricing Act (1975). Repeals *federal* laws supporting *state* fair-trade laws. Does away with state laws allowing manufacturers to set retail prices.
9. Various *deregulation* laws pertaining to specific industries:
   a) Natural Gas Policy Act (1978)
   b) Airline Deregulation Act (1978)
   c) Motor Carrier Act (1980)
   d) Staggers Rail Act (1980)
   e) Depository Institutions Act (1981)
   f) Drug Price Competition and Patent Restoration Act (1984)

To Protect Consumers

1. Pure Food and Drug Act (1906). Regulates labeling of food and drugs and prohibits manufacturing or marketing of adulterated food or drugs. Amended in 1938 by Food, Drug, and Cosmetics Act.
2. Automobile Information Disclosure Act (1958). Requires manufacturers to post suggested retail prices on new passenger vehicles.
3. Kefauver-Harris Drug Amendments (1962). Requires that drugs be labeled with their generic names, new drugs be pretested, and new drugs get approval of the Food and Drug Administration before being marketed.
4. National Traffic and Motor Vehicle Safety Act (1966). Provides safety standards for tires and autos.
5. Fair Packaging and Labeling Act (1966). Regulates packaging and labeling.
6. Cigarette Labeling and Advertising Acts (1966, 1969). Require manufacturers to label cigarettes as being hazardous to health and prohibit TV advertising of cigarettes.
7. Consumer Credit Protection Act (1968). The "truth in lending" law that requires full disclosure of interest rates and other financing charges on loans and credit purchases.
8. Consumer Product Safety Act (1972). Establishes the Consumer Product Safety Commission with broad powers to limit or even halt the marketing of products ruled unsafe by the commission.
9. Consumer Product Warranty Act (1975). Increases consumers' rights and sellers' responsibilities under product warranties.
10. FTC Improvement Act (1980). Limits the power of the Federal Trade Commission to set and enforce industry trade regulations. In effect, reverses the trend toward more FTC protection of consumers.
11. Nutritional Labeling and Education Act (1990). Requires that detailed nutritional information be stated on labels of most food products.
12. Children's Television Act (1990). Limits the number of minutes of advertising that can be shown on programs designed for children.
13. Can-Spam Act (2003). Allows consumers and business firms to remove themselves from mass e-mail lists and gives enforcement authority to the Federal Trade Commission.
14. Do-Not-Call Implementation Act (2003). Allows consumers to sign up for a Do-Not-Call Registry in order to prevent most, but not all, telemarketing calls.

Up to this point, our discussion of political and legal forces affecting marketing has dealt essentially with the activities of the *federal* government. However, there are also strong political and legal influences at the *state and local* levels. For instance, many firms' marketing programs are affected by zoning requirements, interest-rate regulations, state and local taxes, prohibitions against unsubstantiated environmental claims, and laws affecting door-to-door selling. All of these have been put in place by numerous states and municipalities.

Technology

Technology has a tremendous impact on our lifestyles, our consumption patterns, and our economic well-being. Just think of the effect of technological developments such as the airplane, plastics, television, computers, antibiotics, lasers, and—of course—video games. Except perhaps for the airplane, all these technologies reached their major markets in your lifetime or your parents' lifetime. Think how your life in the future might be affected by cures for the common cold, development of energy sources to replace fossil fuels, low-cost methods for making ocean water drinkable, or even commercial travel to the moon.

Technological breakthroughs can affect markets in three ways:

- By starting entirely new industries, as computers, lasers, and robots have done.
- By radically altering, or virtually destroying, existing industries. When it first came out, television crippled the radio and movie industries. And digital photography all but replaced so-called instant photography, sending Polaroid Holding Co. into bankruptcy protection in 2001.
- By stimulating markets and industries not related to the new technology. New home appliances and microwavable foods give people additional time in which to engage in other activities.

Advances in technology also affect how marketing is carried out. For example, breakthroughs in communications now permit people and organizations to transact business from almost any location at any time of the day. Since the late 1990s, the

Dean Kamen, who invented the Segway Human Transporter, also created the iBOT Mobility System, a high-tech wheelchair. Both products are single-person battery-powered transportation devices that use new technologies to address what Kamen saw as unsatisfied needs. The iBOT relies on gyroscopes and electronic sensors to keep its balance, which it does better than a human, according to its inventor. With two pairs of midsize wheels set on a swivel, the iBOT can climb curbs and stairs and move through sand and other soft surfaces. Now marketed by a division of Johnson & Johnson, the iBOT gives added mobility to people who need to use a wheelchair.

www.independencenow. com/ibot/index.html

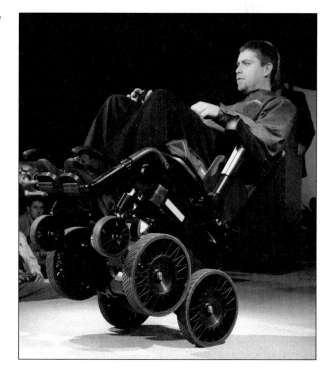

Some grains and vegetables can now be genetically modified (GM) so they are more resistant to insects and chemicals that are used to kill weeds. GM crops, with a worldwide value of about $5 billion, have been criticized by some consumer and environmental groups, including Greenpeace, as having health risks. Responding to or fearing criticism, both Gerber and Heinz banned GM corn and soybeans in its baby food. In the countries comprising the European Union, any product that contains as much as 0.9% GM ingredients must have a label stating these contents.

Other business people, however, contend that there are no harmful outcomes from ingredients that are altered in this way. Going a step further, it has been stated that GM seeds would boost agricultural pro-

ductivity in developing countries. To date, the U.S. government has rejected requests to place special labels on all food products containing genetically engineered ingredients.

Is it ethical for manufacturers to use genetically modified ingredients in food products? If they do so, must they inform consumers that the products contain genetically engineered ingredients?

 www.polaroid.com

Sources: Scott Miller, "EU's New Rules Will Shake Up Market for Bioengineering Food," *The Wall Street Journal,* Apr. 16, 2004, p. A1; and Lucette Lagnado, "Gerber Baby Food, Grilled by Greenpeace, Plans Swift Overhaul," *The Wall Street Journal,* July 30, 1999, pp. A1, A6.

Internet has had a profound effect on millions of Americans as well as countless enterprises.

We should also note that technology is a mixed blessing in some ways. A new technology may improve our lives in one area while creating environmental and social problems in other areas. Television and video games provide built-in child care, but they are criticized for reducing family discussions and reading by children. The automobile is a convenient form of personal transportation, but it also creates traffic jams and air pollution. In turn, technology is expected to solve some problems it is criticized for having caused (air pollution, for example).

External Microenvironment

Three additional environmental forces are external to an organization and affect its marketing activities. These are the firm's market, suppliers, and marketing intermediaries. They represent *microenvironmental forces* for a company (see Figure 2.2). Dealing effectively with them is critical to business success. Recognizing that, many companies are using customer relationship management software to keep track of their customers' buying activities and to communicate better with them.[24]

Although all three of these external forces are generally uncontrollable, they can be influenced in some situations. As such, they are different than the *macro*environmental forces discussed previously. A marketing organization, for example, may be able to exert pressure on its suppliers or middlemen. And, through its advertising, a firm should have some influence on its market.

The Market

The market really is what marketing is all about—how to reach it and serve it profitably and in a socially responsible manner. The market should be the focus of all marketing decisions in an organization. But just what is a market? A *market* may be defined as a place where buyers and sellers meet, goods or services are offered for sale, and transfers of ownership occur. A *market* may also be defined as the demand made by a certain group of potential buyers for a good or service. For instance, there is a farm *market* for petroleum products.

FIGURE 2.2

External Microenvironment of a Company's Marketing Program.

The arrows reflect the interrelationships—flows of products, payments, information, and influence—between the company and its external environment.

These definitions are not sufficiently precise to be useful to us here. For marketing purposes, we define a **market** as people or organizations with needs to satisfy, money to spend, and the willingness to spend it. Thus, in marketing any given good or service, three specific factors need to be considered:

- People or organizations with needs,

- Their purchasing power, *and*

- Their buying behavior.

When we consider *needs*, we do so from the perspective of the dictionary definition of need as the lack of anything that is required, desired, or useful. We do not limit needs to the physiological requirements of food, clothing, and shelter essential for survival. Recall from Chapter 1 that the words *needs* and *wants* are used interchangeably in this text.

Suppliers

A business cannot sell a product without being able to make or buy it. That's why the people or firms that supply the goods or services required by a producer to make what it sells are critical to marketing success. So too are the firms that provide the merchandise a wholesaler or retailer resells. And that's why we consider a firm's **suppliers** a vital part of its marketing environment.

Marketing executives often are not concerned enough with the supply side of marketing. However, when shortages occur, they recognize the need for cooperative relationships with suppliers. Further, as online sales rise, Internet companies are paying much more attention to sources of supply and also the methods by which orders will be processed and delivered to buyers.

Marketing Intermediaries

Marketing intermediaries are independent business organizations that directly aid in the flow of goods and services between a marketing organization and its markets. There are two types of intermediaries: (1) the firms we call *middlemen*—wholesalers and retailers, and (2) various *facilitating organizations* furnishing such services as transportation, warehousing, and financing that are needed to complete exchanges between buyers and sellers. These intermediaries operate between a company and its markets and between a company and its suppliers. Thus they are part of what we call *channels of distribution.*

In some cases, it may be more efficient for a company to not use marketing intermediaries. A producer can deal *directly* with its suppliers or sell *directly* to its customers and do its own shipping, financing, and so on. But marketing intermediaries are specialists in their respective fields. They often do a better job at a lower cost than the marketing organization can do by itself.

Collectively, the company, its suppliers, and its intermediaries (both middlemen and facilitating organizations) comprise a **value chain.** That is, all of these enterprises—each in its own way—perform activities to add value to the product that is eventually bought by an individual or an organization. It's relatively easy to comprehend the value added by a manufacturer when it combines various materials to form a finished product. But it's more difficult to detect the value added by other members of the value chain. For example, consider a financial institution that agrees to provide credit to consumers who buy vehicles from an auto dealership. This facilitating organization has added value to the product, essentially by making it easier for a prospective buyer to make a purchase.

Organization's Internal Environment

An organization's marketing effort is also shaped by *internal forces* that are controllable by management. As shown in Figure 2.3, these internal influences include a firm's production, financial, and personnel activities. If the Colgate-Palmolive Co. is considering adding a new brand of soap, for example, it must determine whether existing production facilities and expertise can be used. If the new product requires a new plant or machinery, financial capability enters the picture. Although this example involves a manufacturer, we are viewing *production* in a broad sense, referring to the various activities that create the set of products an organization offers to its markets. Therefore, all concerns—retailers, wholesalers, service firms, and not-for-profit organizations—engage in production, in this broad sense.

Other nonmarketing forces are the company's location, its research and development (R&D) strength, and the overall image the firm projects to the public. For a manufacturer, plant location often determines the geographic limits of the company's market, particularly if transportation costs are high or its products are perishable. For a middleman, location of a store (in the case of a retailer) or a warehouse (in the case of a wholesaler) affects the number of customers drawn to the firm as well as its operating expenses. Of course, online retailers may not have to worry about the loca-

FIGURE 2.3

Internal Environment Affecting a Company's Marketing Activities.

A company's internal, nonmarketing resources influence and support its marketing program.

tion of physical stores, but they still need to be concerned about the location of warehouses. The R&D factor may determine whether a firm will lead or follow in its industry. An organization's image has an impact on its ability to attract capital, employees, and customers.

Another consideration in a firm's internal environment is the need to coordinate marketing and nonmarketing activities. Sometimes this can be difficult because of conflicts in goals and executive personalities. Production people, for example, like to see long production runs of standardized items. However, marketing executives may want a variety of models, sizes, and colors to satisfy different market segments. Financial executives typically want tighter credit and expense limits than the marketing people consider necessary to be competitive.

To wrap up our discussion of the marketing environment, Figure 2.4 shows how all environmental forces combine to shape an organization's marketing program. Within the framework of these constraints, management should develop a marketing program to satisfy the needs of its markets.

FIGURE 2.4

The Entire Operating Environment for a Company's Marketing Program.

A marketing program must take into account both internal resources and external forces.

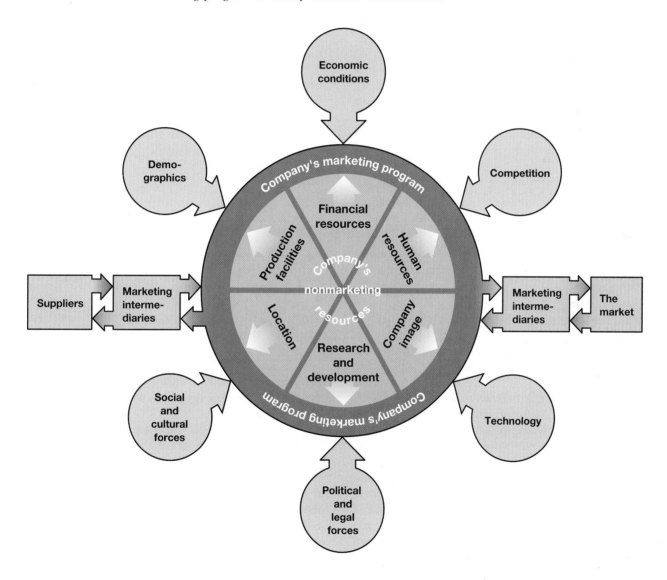

Summary

Various environmental forces influence an organization's marketing activities. Some are external to the firm and are largely uncontrollable by the organization. Other forces are within the firm and are generally controllable by management. Successful marketing requires that a company develop and implement marketing programs that take into account its environment. To start with, management should set up a system for environmental monitoring—the process of gathering and evaluating environmental information.

Six broad variables constitute the external environment that generally cannot be controlled by an organization. Demographic factors are one of these macro influences. Another is economic conditions such as the business cycle, inflation, and interest rates. Management also must be aware of the various types of competition and the competitive structure within which its firm operates. Social and cultural forces, such as changes in lifestyles, values, and beliefs, must be taken into account as marketing programs are developed. Four noteworthy sociocultural trends are the greening of America, changing gender roles, a greater premium on time, and added emphasis on physical fitness and health. Political and legal forces, ranging from monetary and fiscal policies to legislation, also affect marketing. As with the other external macroenvironmental influences, technology can present both opportunities and challenges for marketers.

Another set of environmental factors—suppliers, marketing intermediaries, and the market itself—is also external to the firm. But these forces can be controlled to some extent by the firm. Although all three of these external forces are generally uncontrollable, they can be influenced in some situations. As such, these *micro*environmental forces are different from *macro*environmental forces such as economic conditions and technology.

At the same time, a set of nonmarketing resources *within* the firm—production facilities, personnel, finances, location, research and development, and company image—affects its marketing effort. These variables generally are controllable by management.

More about iTunes

As 2004 drew to a close, still more digital-music services were entering the competition. Perhaps the most interesting (and potentially formidable) newcomer was the company that set off the Apple verses PC operating-system war of the 1980s—Microsoft. Just as Apple launched iTunes to increase sales of its iPod MP3 player, Microsoft introduced MSN Music to spur sales of its Windows XP operating system and Windows Media Player as well as a number of other Microsoft products. The match-up mimicked the Apple versus Microsoft desktop computer wars of the 1980s.

Similar to earlier times when Apple refused to license its Macintosh operating platform, it has resisted allowing other companies to develop products or services that work with iPods and iTunes. In contrast, Microsoft is allowing other suppliers to develop devices and services that use its new Windows Media Player technology. One industry analyst noted, "Apple designs things to work well together, whereas Microsoft kind of glues things all together."

The original digital-music master, Shawn Fanning, also launched a new online music service in late 2004. After selling the rights to the Napster name, Fanning decided to try to legitimize the peer-to-peer (PTP) digital-music model. He envisioned his new company, Snocap, as a clearinghouse to bring together music companies and PTP file-sharing networks. Up to this point, most PTP networks operated illegally, allowing users to trade copyrighted material without paying royalties to the rights-holding music company or artist. Fanning's goal was to allow users to continue to exchange files while paying for the privilege of doing so.

A number of illegal sites were still operating and offering free PTP file sharing and, in the case of Kazaa, an enormous collection of songs from which to choose. Utilizing a network of computers rather than one main server, Kazaa was proving to be much more difficult to shut down than Napster. Whereas 67% of people over the age of 25 were legally downloading music from the Internet in late 2004, almost 70% of those between 18 and 24 years old were using unlicensed services. But, as the adage says, you get what you pay for—and sometimes more, such as computer viruses and occasional lawsuits aimed at users downloading pirated material.

On the legal side of the competition, by January 2005, Apple was selling 90% of all songs downloaded from the Internet. And, to paraphrase the Shangri-Las, Apple Computer hopes iTunes will remain "The Leader of the Pack."

1. Other than technology, which macroenvironmental forces are particularly important to Apple's iTunes?
2. Do you think legal digital-music services will prevail over their now illegal counterparts? Why or why not?
3. Does legal digital-music downloading coincide with or run counter to major demographic, social, and cultural trends in the U.S.?

Key Terms and Concepts

Environmental monitoring (28)
Demographics (30)
Baby boomers (32)
Generation X (32)
Generation Y (32)
Economic environment (32)

Business cycle (32)
Inflation (33)
Interest rates (33)
Differential advantage (34)
Social and cultural forces (34)
Political and legal forces (39)

Technology (41)
Market (43)
Suppliers (43)
Marketing intermediaries (43)
Value chain (43)

Questions and Problems

1. In areas where the number of college-age students is still declining, what marketing measures should a school take to adjust to this trend?
2. For each of the following companies, give some examples of how its marketing program is likely to differ during periods of prosperity as contrasted with periods of recession:
   a. Schwinn bicycles
   b. Williams-Sonoma.com (the online arm of the home-furnishings retailer)
   c. General Cinema movie theaters
   d. Salvation Army
3. What would be the likely effect of high interest rates on the market for the following goods or services?
   a. Swatch watches
   b. Building materials
   c. Nursery school programs
4. Explain the three types of competition faced by a company. What marketing strategies or programs would you recommend to meet each type?
5. Name three U.S.-manufactured products you think would be highly acceptable to "green consumers" in European markets. Name three products you think would be environmentally unacceptable.

6. Give some examples of how the changing role of women has been reflected in American marketing.
7. What are some marketing implications of the increasing public interest in physical fitness and health?
8. Using examples other than those in this chapter, explain how a firm's marketing can be influenced by the environmental factor of technology.
9. Specify some external macroenvironmental forces affecting the marketing programs of:
   a. Pizza Hut
   b. Your school
   c. Drugstore.com
   d. Clairol (hair-care products)
10. Other than technology, which macroenvironmental forces are particularly important to Internet companies?
11. Explain how each of the following resources within a company might influence its marketing program:
    a. Plant or store location
    b. Company image
    c. Financial resources
    d. Personnel capabilities

Interactive Marketing Exercises

1. Identify two controversial social or cultural issues in the community where your school is located, and explain their impact on firms that market in the community.

2. After doing some "Net surfing," identify two product categories (other than those mentioned in the chapter) that you believe can be sold well over the Internet. Then identify two categories that you think will be hard to sell online.

Chapter 3

"*Like many successful businesses, IKEA is structured around a simple concept: offering a wide range of well-designed, functional home furnishing products at prices so low that many people will be able to afford them.*"

Can **IKEA** Furnish Global Decorating Needs?

If you follow business success stories, you may recognize the names Ray Kroc, Sam Walton, or Herb Kelleher. They are, respectively, the masterminds behind McDonald's, Wal-Mart, and Southwest Airlines. But what about Ingvar Kamprad? Would you believe he is purported to be the wealthiest man in the world, even richer than Bill Gates? Kamprad is the founder of IKEA, a Swedish firm and the world's largest home furnishing retailer.

Kamprad began the company in 1943, when he was only 17 years old, selling simple items such as wallets, pens, and picture frames in and around his hometown. The name of the company is a combination of Kamprad's initials and the first letters from his home (a farm called Elmtaryd near the village of Agunnaryd). By 1951, he was going door-to-door selling furniture made by local carpenters. With the growth in popularity of his merchandise, Kamprad opened his first retail store in 1958 in the town of Almhuit in southern Sweden.

Like many successful businesses, IKEA is structured around a simple concept: offering a wide range of well-designed, functional home furnishing products at prices so low that many people will be able to afford them. Also, like many successes, the key is in finding creative ways to implement the concept. For IKEA that means following a set routine. Every new item at IKEA begins with the identification of a need and the determination of a price consumers will pay to satisfy the need. Then designers come up with a product, and production methods and materials are configured with an eye on providing quality while keeping costs as low as possible. Finally, by dealing with 2,000 suppliers in 55 countries and only offering items that can be produced and sold in volume, costs are reduced even more.

IKEA has come up with many innovations in marketing home furnishings including customer self-service, "flat-pack" packaging with final assembly by the customer, and huge stores that incorporate furnished model homes displaying over 10,000 items. By blending quality and low prices through cost savings, IKEA has developed a retail system with over 200 franchised stores in 30 countries, catalogs that are distributed to over 100 million homes, and a growing Internet business. In 2004, sales exceeded $16 billion and there are plans to open a dozen new stores every year for the foreseeable future. If IKEA's business model still has legs in the 21st century it may yet make Kamprad a familiar name not only in Sweden but also around the world.[1]

How is IKEA able to successfully operate outlets in so many different countries?

www.ikea.com

IKEA's sustained international marketing performance is certainly impressive. But as the opening case indicates, even experienced firms such as IKEA face unfamiliar challenges when they venture beyond their domestic borders. Something as basic as the marketing mix—the plans for the product, along with pricing, distribution, and promotion programs—may be more difficult in a foreign market. Complicating factors such as language, culture, business practices, and government restrictions affect the process. As a result, "going international" involves many unique strategic and tactical considerations. Given the differences from domestic marketing, we need to examine international marketing in some detail.

After studying this chapter, you should be able to explain:

- The significance of international marketing to firms and countries.
- What makes foreign markets attractive.
- Challenges in designing marketing strategies for international markets.
- Alternative organizational structures for operating in foreign markets.
- Marketing-mix issues and some concepts unique to international marketing such as countertrade and gray marketing.

The Significance of International Trade

International trade is not a new phenomenon. There is evidence that it was an important part of the lives of many ancient civilizations, including the Etruscans, Egyptians, and the Chinese. The economic reasons for international trade are:

- *Access to products otherwise unavailable.* A large number of goods, including many foodstuffs, spices, and even types of wood, are available only in certain parts of the world. Without foreign trade, consumers in other regions could not experience these products.
- *Comparative advantage.* Some countries possess unique natural or human resources that give them an edge when it comes to producing particular products. This factor, for example, explains South Africa's dominance in diamonds, and the ability of developing Asian and Central American countries with low-wage rates to compete successfully in products assembled by hand. By specializing where it has a comparative advantage and trading for other products, a country maximizes its economic prosperity.

International trade also has political and social implications. In fact, historians give trade much of the credit for the peace and well-being that existed for centuries in the far-flung Roman Empire. In today's world, the interaction fostered by trade reduces social barriers and prejudices and increases tolerance.

To get an idea of how significant international marketing has become, consider that in 2002 world exports had a value of more than $6.3 *trillion*. As the total volume suggests, trade is critical to the economies of many countries. For example, each year the U.S. exports an amount equal to about 10% of what it produces, whereas Germany and France each annually export an amount equal to 30% of what they produce. In contrast, 49 of the world's least developed countries (according to the World Trade Organization) account for only 0.5% of all international trade. Trade does not have the same impact on all countries. China, with 1.3 billion people had exports of $484 billion in 2003. In the same year, Japan with less than one-tenth as many people had $100 billion more in exports.[2] The differences among countries are further illustrated in Table 3.1, which shows each country's exports and imports as a percentage of its total domestic output.

TABLE 3.1	Role of Exports and Imports in the Economies of Selected Countries		
		2003 Exports as a % of GDP	**2003 Imports as a % of GDP**
	S. Korea	38.2	35.6
	Canada	37.7	35.4
	China	33.0	32.0
	Mexico	28.4	30.1
	United Kingdom	25.0	28.4
	Brazil	16.8	13.2
	Japan	12.5	11.4
	United States	9.3	14.1

GDP = gross domestic product

Source: World Bank Development Indicators Database, September 2004. Accessed at *www.worldbank.org.*

Countries use trade to hasten their economic growth. The underdeveloped countries of the world accounted for over 25% of all exports in 2003, a far higher proportion than their share of world productivity. By engaging in trade, these countries provide jobs and income for their citizens.

What are the prospects for international business? At both the national and individual firm levels, international trade is important to the health of a nation. However, the relationship between how much a country imports and how much it exports has significant implications. To appreciate this, we need to examine the concepts of balance of payments and balance of trade, and we will use the U.S. as an example.

A country's **balance of payments** is an accounting record of all its transactions with all the other nations of the world. The major categories of expenditures and income in a country's balance of payments are military and foreign aid, investments abroad, profits returned on foreign investments, tourism, and its trade balance. These terms are self-explanatory except for a country's **trade balance,** which is the difference between what it exports and what it imports. When exports exceed imports, the balance is positive and the country is said to have a trade *surplus*. When imports exceed exports, the balance is negative and the country has a trade *deficit*.

The Huli tribe members of New Guinea had virtually no contact with the outside world until the 1940s. From this photo of a young Huli woman (in ceremonial native costume), it appears they are making up for lost time! Due to advances in communication technology and improved transportation methods, products are reaching some of the most remote locations on the planet. In today's world enterprising marketers should not limit themselves to domestic markets.

By definition, a country's balance of payments must balance. That is, the outflow of wealth must equal the inflow. So, for example, if the foreign tourism expenditures of a country's citizens (outflow) exceed the expenditures of tourists visiting the country (inflow), the difference must be made up by one of the other balance-of-payment categories. What happens if there is not enough surplus in the other categories to offset a deficit? Then the country must borrow to make up the difference, and that is where a problem lies. If a country's debt grows, it is faced with pressure to raise taxes and lower government spending.

Historically, the U.S. has had large expenditures in four areas that significantly affect the balance of payments: (1) military forces stationed overseas, (2) foreign aid, (3) oil imports, and (4) American tourist travel abroad. To offset these expenditures and maintain equilibrium in the U.S. balance of payments, American businesses had to generate a substantial trade surplus. That is, exports of goods and services had to greatly exceed imports. Up to about 1970, this was not a problem because the U.S. generally had a positive balance of trade. Then the balance declined to the point where it was not sufficient to offset the expenditures abroad.

Through most of the 1980s, the U.S. was in an unfavorable trade position with large trade deficits. The relationship between imports and exports improved in the late 1980s and early 1990s, with the deficit reaching a low of $31 billion in 1991, but the balance was consistently unfavorable. Since then the deficit has steadily increased, amounting to $520 billion in 2003, more than tripling in five years.[3] Large trade deficits have a direct negative effect on jobs, investment, and growth.

Several factors affect a country's balance of trade. In the case of the U.S., the most significant are:

- *Consumer preferences.* U.S. consumers have come to know and buy many imported products.
- *Technology.* The "technology gap" between the U.S. and other major industrial countries has narrowed significantly or has disappeared entirely, so the U.S. does not enjoy the same technology advantage it once did.
- *Trade barriers.* Some countries have barriers that severely limit, or entirely prohibit, the importation of products that might compete with their domestic output.
- *Subsidized industries.* Some foreign governments aid their export trade more than the U.S. These subsidies often enable the producers to sell their products in foreign markets at prices lower than the prices of domestic producers.
- *Tax structure.* Some countries derive substantial revenue from indirect taxes, such as a value-added tax, which are often rebated when products are exported. As a result, companies in these countries have an added incentive to seek markets abroad.
- *Relative marketing capabilities.* Firms worldwide have narrowed the gap between their marketing skills and those of the more developed nations.

The foreign trade balance in the U.S. has changed from a bright spot to a problem. Imports probably will remain high because of the factors described above. Consequently, the U.S. must continue to expand its exports by:

- Offsetting higher labor costs with improved productivity.
- Adapting marketing efforts to foreign cultures to improve the attractiveness of products.
- Investing in the future by taking a longer-range view than currently is typical among most U.S. firms.

The Attraction of International Marketing

International trade describes any type of business that firms carry out beyond their domestic borders. More specific to our interests, **international marketing** takes place when an organization actively markets its products in two or more countries. For many U.S. companies, international markets account for a substantial share of their operations. For example, IBM and Boeing regularly get about half their annual sales revenues from outside the U.S. Likewise, many non–U.S. companies, such as Sony,

Are offshore call centers working out?

If you telephone customer service at a major company, you may notice the person on the other end of the line has an unfamiliar accent. The reason may be that the company has outsourced its contact center to a firm in India, China, the Philippines, or some other country. A combination of sophisticated telecommunications technology and low labor costs have made these centers attractive. The firms relying on this alternative want to save money but they also want their customers to be satisfied. Problems have occurred when call center employees do not have the most current details on new products, price changes, or other issues and when cultural differences in how fast they speak or the tone of voice they use upsets callers. A call-monitoring software industry has emerged as a result. Firms relying on these centers now record conversations, monitor the length of calls, the frequency callers are put on hold, and even track the occurrence of key words, such as the name of a competitor.

Source: Jason Overdorf, "Outsourcing Jobs to . . . Europeans?," *Business 2.0*, January/February 2005, p. 32; Alex Ortolani, "Call-Monitoring Industry Is Booming," *The Wall Street Journal*, Nov. 29, 2004, p. A11.

Bic, Gucci, Toyota, Lipton, Shell Oil, and adidas, rely heavily on the U.S. market. International trade is not limited to large businesses. Thirteen percent of U.S. businesses employing fewer than 20 people report having made foreign sales during the most recent three years.[4]

A firm moves beyond its domestic market into international trade for several possible reasons:

www.hp.com

- *Potential demand in foreign markets.* There is a strong demand for a wide variety of products all over the world. Among the developing as well as the developed nations of the world, there is a demand for business products such as machine tools, construction equipment, and computers. As a result, firms can often take advantage of their specialized skills in manufacturing or distribution in new regions. For example, Hewlett-Packard, which began in 1938 manufacturing an electronic instrument to test sound equipment, now markets an array of technology goods and services to over a billion customers in 170 countries.

www.mcdonalds.com

- *Saturation of domestic markets.* Firms—even those without international experience—look to foreign markets when domestic demand plateaus. As attractive domestic locations became harder to find in the 1970s, McDonald's opened an increasing number of outlets overseas. Now half the firm's 30,000 restaurants are outside the U.S., and expansion plans are almost exclusively focused abroad.

www.remyinc.com

- *Customer expectations.* Often a firm follows its domestic customers abroad. For example, many U.S. banks found it necessary to establish branches in foreign countries because their customers were doing business internationally. Because Remy International, formerly Delco Remy, a U.S. supplier of automotive electrical equipment, finds it efficient to locate its manufacturing near automakers, it now has plants all over the world.

Strategic Planning for International Marketing

Firms that have been very successful in domestic marketing have no assurance whatsoever that their success will be duplicated in foreign markets. Satisfactory performance overseas is based on (1) understanding the environment of a foreign market and (2) gauging which domestic management practices and marketing-mix elements should be transferred directly to foreign markets, which ones should be modified, and which ones should not be used at all.

A **global strategy** is one in which essentially the same marketing program is employed around the world. Because it is very cost efficient, a global strategy is an ideal situation. FedEx is an example of a company that has globalized its strategy. According to a senior marketing executive, "We're the largest all-cargo carrier in the world, and as a result we've got a pretty good formula for attacking any market whether it's China or Japan or Germany, it really doesn't make any difference."[5]

In consumer product marketing, a global strategy is often more difficult to accomplish because of social and cultural differences. However, some firms have at least approached a global strategy. Dove, developed in 1957 and positioned by Unilever as a "beauty bar" rather than as a soap because it contains moisturizers, is marketed in essentially the same way in over 80 countries around the world.

www.unilever.com

When large geographic areas have much in common, but are quite distinct from other regions because of factors such as climate, custom, or taste, a firm might develop a **regional strategy**. This is what Coca-Cola has done in beverages. On its website Coca-Cola lists over 380 different beverage brands that it markets around the world. Among the most intriguing are Jolly Juice, Monsoon, Samurai, Water Salad, and Love Body!

www.cocacola.com

In some cases markets differ so much that a firm must develop customized marketing programs for each area it enters. When a firm employs a **local strategy**, there are relatively few marketing-mix dimensions that are transferred from one market to another. Surprisingly, that can be the case even for a commodity. To market its packaged flour in India, Pillsbury had to change the ingredients (for local taste), the package size and packaging material (because of the climate), the advertising (to demonstrate local uses), and the distribution (because small retail stores carry little inventory).[6] Even in countries with quite similar cultures such as the U.S. and the United Kingdom, the flour differs in texture and additives.

To develop a strategic plan, a firm must examine the operating environment that exists in a foreign market. Several of the most important dimensions of the environment are described below.

Analysis of the Environment

Throughout the world, market demand is determined by the number of people, the ability to buy, and buying behavior. Also, human wants and needs have a universal similarity. People need food, clothing, and shelter. They seek a better quality of life in terms of lighter workloads, more leisure time, and social recognition and acceptance. But at about this point, the similarities in foreign and domestic markets seem to end, and the differences in culture, the economic environment, and political and legal forces must be considered.

Social and Cultural Forces
Culture is a set of shared values passed down from generation to generation in a society. These values determine what is socially acceptable behavior. Some of the many cultural elements that can influence a company's marketing program are described below.

Family. The priorities of families and the relationships among family members with regard to purchasing and consumption vary considerably from culture to culture. In some countries a mother would always accompany a teenager shopping for clothes, whereas in other cultures shopping "with Mom" would be avoided at all costs. In China, where one-child families are the norm, parents typically spend one-third to one-half of their disposable incomes on their children. The family situations in each country may require a distinctive type of promotion, and perhaps even different types of products.

Rites are common to all cultures. In the Hispanic community, the Quinceanera is a rite of passage for a young woman. It marks her transition from childhood to adulthood. Other rites signify separation, for example, a funeral, and inclusion, such as baptism. Interestingly, many rites incorporate both a religious dimension and a festive or party activity. Even funerals often include a "wake" to celebrate the deceased's life. Because understanding the event is a must, it's common for the marketers serving the needs of consumers participating in a rite to be part of the culture.

Customs and Behavior.   Some customary behavior defies explanation. For example, when it comes to medication, red is the preferred color of pills among Americans, whereas English and Dutch consumers prefer white pills. Other differences among cultures such as in eating behavior, personal space, physical contact, the degree of formality in social and business interactions, gift giving, and the use of gestures may be easier to anticipate but may still trip up the unwary. Wal-Mart's acquisition of the Japanese supermarket group Seiyu, poses some significant cultural challenges for the firm. Japanese consumers are more sensitive than Americans to the way products are presented. Individually wrapped items and attractive packaging are much more common in Japan. As opposed to their American counterparts who eat a lot of processed foods, Japanese consumers prefer fresh food. And Japanese consumers tend to visit stores more frequently and buy in small quantities. Wal-Mart has initially made changes behind the scenes, for example in point-of-sale and inventory tracking systems to reduce inventory costs and improve the flow of goods. However, visible changes, such as where particular items are displayed in the store and increasing the proportion of generic brands, are being made more slowly so as not to upset Japanese consumers.[7] It remains to be seen what other adjustments the firm will have to make in order to duplicate its success in the U.S.

Education.   The educational level in a country affects the literacy rate, which in turn influences advertising, branding, and labeling. The brand mark may become the dominant marketing feature if potential customers cannot read and must recognize the article by the picture on the label.

Language Differences.   Language differences pose many problems in international marketing, from being one of the primary explanations for the high failure rate of cross-border mergers to making it difficult to complete customs forms. Language is often the hurdle that discourages firms from entering foreign markets. In marketing strategy, a literal translation of advertising copy or a brand name may result in ridicule of a product, or even hostility toward it. For example, Mercedes-Benz introduced its Grand Sports Tourer in Canada as the Mercedes GST, not realizing that the initials are an acronym for the country's controversial and widely disliked goods and services tax.[8]

Economic Environment   In international marketing a firm must closely examine the economic conditions in a particular country. A nation's infrastructure and stage of economic development are key economic factors that affect the attractiveness of a market and suggest what might be an appropriate marketing strategy.

Infrastructure. A country's ability to provide transportation, communications, and energy is its **infrastructure.** Depending on the product and the method of marketing, an international marketer will need certain levels of infrastructure development. For example, an Internet marketer such as Amazon.com selling a low-priced product requires a warehouse and transportation system that will permit widespread distribution. How about communications? Some firms would find it impossible to do business without the availability of newspapers in which to advertise or telephones with which to contact other businesses.

There is a danger in assuming that systems a marketer takes for granted domestically will be available elsewhere. The international marketer must recognize what infrastructure is needed and what is available. For example, in France there is one phone for every two people, whereas in India there is about 1 phone for every 35 people.

Level of Economic Development. The level of economic development of a country is a general indicator of its attractiveness as a market as well as an indicator of the types of products that are likely to be in demand. A useful criterion for assessing economic development is gross national income (GNI) per capita, a measure of the value of all goods and services produced in a country during a year, divided by its population. The average per capita GNI for all the countries in the world is $5,500, while the lowest is Ethiopia at $90 and the highest is Norway with $43,350. Using per capita GNI, countries can be grouped according to their level of development.[9]

Among the world's approximately 200 independent countries, about 55 have a per capita GNI of less than $900. These *preindustrial* countries account for about 40% of the world's population but only about 3% of its total production of goods and services. In these countries most of the population engages in subsistence farming because they lack most of the resources for industrial growth. These countries tend to rely heavily on foreign aid. Overpopulation is a common problem, and the governments are frequently unstable. Included in this category are Cambodia, Chad, Ethiopia, Haiti, Uzebekistan, Tanzania, and Vietnam. Generally these countries provide very few market opportunities; however, some are developing a small export trade by becoming the final assembly points for such things as clothing items.

At the next level are the *less developed countries* (or LDCs), with per capita GNI between $900 and $3,500. The 60 countries in this group also have about 40% of the world's population and about 12% of the GNI. Included are Bolivia, Estonia, Philippines, Romania, and Turkey. These countries are just beginning the industrialization process. They have factories that produce a variety of consumer goods for their domestic market, though they still depend on imports for many consumer items. They combine an eager work force, low wages, and reasonably stable governments to produce standardized, labor-intensive products for export. Athletic shoes for companies such as Nike and adidas are produced in LDCs. These countries are attractive markets for many consumer goods as well as basic technology that will increase productivity.

About 60 countries make up the next group that might be called *industrializing* countries. With per capita GNI between $3,500 and $9,500, these countries account for about 7% of the world's population and a like percentage of its GNI. The population in most of these countries has experienced a significant shift from agriculture to urban industrialization. The levels of literacy and education are rising, along with wages. The production of goods for export are typically an important part of the economy. These countries import technology and a wide variety of consumer luxury goods. Among the countries in this group are Chile, Hungary, Mexico, Poland, and Venezuela.

Finally, there are the *postindustrial* countries. There are about 40 countries in this group with per capita GNI over $9,500. In includes Australia, Canada, France, Japan, Singapore, and the U.S. They have well-developed infrastructures, high levels of education, constantly advancing technology, and stable governments. They are called postindustrial economies because the services sector accounts for more than 50% of output, and information and technology have become the primary resources. These countries are heavily involved in both importing and exporting. Although they are the wealthiest countries and therefore would appear to offer the most attractive markets, they are also the ones in which a foreign firm is likely to face the stiffest competition.

Note that a classification like this can be useful, but its simplicity may make it misleading. For example, Saudi Arabia, because of its oil revenues and small population, is in the highly industrialized group. However, Saudi Arabia's level of economic development is quite different from countries such as Japan and Switzerland. On the other hand, China, with a per capita GNI of only $1,100, attracts many foreign firms that see enormous potential in its huge population. Thus, when analyzing a given foreign market, management must also consider other indications of development. Common economic indicators include the (1) distribution of income, (2) rate of growth of buying power, and (3) extent of available financing. Useful noneconomic indicators are (1) infant mortality rate, (2) percent of the population that lives in urban areas, and (3) the number of daily newspapers.

Competition.   Sometimes overlooked by firms considering international opportunities are the strength and resilience of the native competition. The new entrant must have a differential advantage sufficiently strong to overcome the loyalty built up by established brands and the nationalism that may motivate buyers to support local producers.

International marketers can also expect local competitors to design strategies to protect their businesses. On discovering that a foreign competitor is entering the market, local firms often introduce new products, spruce up customer service, and increase promotion and advertising. As an alternative, the local competitor may also retaliate in the foreign competitor's home market as Kodak did by creating a Japanese subsidiary when Fuji boosted its marketing efforts in the U.S.

Political and Legal Forces

International marketers often discover regulations quite different from those experienced in domestic markets. For example, Japan regulates retail store hours, and in all of Europe advertising prescription drugs to consumers is banned. The principal political concerns of international marketers are the stability of governments and their attitudes toward free trade.

An unresolved legal issue is the global regulation of electronic commerce. The challenges are formidable. For instance, in Europe disputes over cross-border consumer purchases must be resolved in the courts of the consumer's country. Unless this is changed it is likely to have a chilling effect on a large segment of electronic commerce because one of the most attractive features of the Internet is the ability to shop for goods worldwide.

Founded in late 1995, eBay is an indication of the Internet's global impact. It now has operations in 25 countries (the Asian website is pictured here), over 147 million users, and income in 2005 exceeding $4 billion. Merchandise is organized in 12 categories, which are then subdivided into 264 "stores," all online. Ten years ago, who would have thought that today millions of consumers would be making hundreds of thousands of purchases without leaving home.

www.ebay.com

Trade Barriers. The most common legal forces affecting international marketers are barriers created by governments to restrict trade and protect domestic industries. Examples include the following:

- **Tariff**—a tax imposed on a product entering a country. Tariffs are used to protect domestic producers and/or raise revenue. To illustrate, for over 40 years the U.S. has imposed a 25% tariff on imported pickup trucks, keeping brands such as Volkswagen and Hyundai out of the market and causing other foreign manufacturers such as Toyota and Nissan to build factories in the U.S.

- **Import quota**—a limit on the amount of a particular product that can be brought into a country. Like tariffs, quotas can protect a country's domestic industry or can broaden access to its markets. For example, U.S. textile manufacturers want stiff quotas placed on imports from China, while large retailers such as JCPenney, seeking low cost goods, are strongly opposed to such quotas.

- **Local-content law**—a regulation specifying the proportion of a finished product's components and labor that must be provided by the importing country. For example, to be sold in Taiwan, Japanese cars must be at least partially assembled there. To comply with a local-content law, a firm may import most of a product's parts, buy some locally, and have the final product assembled locally. These laws are used to provide jobs and protect domestic businesses.

- **Local operating laws**—a constraint on how, when, or where retailing can be conducted. These regulations, many intended to protect small businesses, are having an impact on Internet shopping. For example, in some countries the retail price of a product has to be the same for everyone. As a result, a system like Priceline.com, where consumers propose a price for an airline seat, rental car, or hotel room and the seller decides if it is acceptable, is illegal.

- **Standards and certification**—a requirement that a product contain or exclude certain ingredients or that it be tested and certified as meeting certain restrictive standards. European countries, for example, have restricted genetically altered corn and also beef that has been fed growth hormones.

- **Boycott**—a refusal to buy products from a particular company or country. Boycotts, also called embargoes, are used by a government to punish another country for what are perceived to be unfair importation rules.

Trade Agreements. Trade agreements reduce trade barriers by giving preferential treatment to firms in the member countries. However, they may also result in member countries establishing barriers to trade with the rest of the world. Thus they have implications for all marketers. By examining several major trade agreements, we can form an impression of the role they play in international marketing. In parentheses following the abbreviation of the trade organization is the volume of all the members' merchandise exports in 2003, and the proportion of those exports that went to other members of the trade organization.[10]

www.wto.org

- **World Trade Organization (WTO).** This organization was created in 1995, as the governing body of global commerce. It has 148 member countries that account for 97% of world trade. The members participate in periodic negotiations on issues such as tariff reductions, import restrictions, local-content rules, and subsidization of industry by government. The WTO provides a forum for airing trade disputes between countries, but it does not guarantee that solutions to disagreements will be found. Recently it has addressed the issue of safeguarding intellectual property rights and public health.

  The WTO is the successor to the *General Agreement on Tariffs and Trade*, or GATT, founded in 1948. GATT negotiations resulted in the liberalization of trade in 50,000 products and a 40% reduction in tariffs around the world, significant decreases in the subsidies provide for firms engaged in exporting, and the extension of trading rules beyond just goods to include investments.

- **European Union** (EU, $2,901 billion, 62%). This political and economic alliance evolved from the Treaty of Rome in 1957 that brought together France, Italy, Belgium, West Germany (now the combined East and West Germanys), Luxembourg, and the Netherlands. It was originally called the European Common Market and later the European Community. It is now known as the European Union or EU. Over the years Denmark, Great Britain, Greece, Spain, Ireland, Portugal, Austria, Sweden, and Finland were added. Then, in 2004, they were joined by 10 more countries—Cyprus, Czech Republic, Estonia, Hungary, Latvia, Lithuania, Malta, Poland, Slovakia, and Slovenia (see Figure 3.1).

The EU's overriding objective is to liberalize trade among its members. More specifically, the goal is a single market for its members permitting the free movement of goods, services, people, and capital. In addition, the members would be governed by the same set of rules for transporting goods, regulating business,

FIGURE 3.1

The European Union Countries (green) and the European Economic Area Countries (purple) in 2004 (with population figures in millions).

www.europa.eu.int

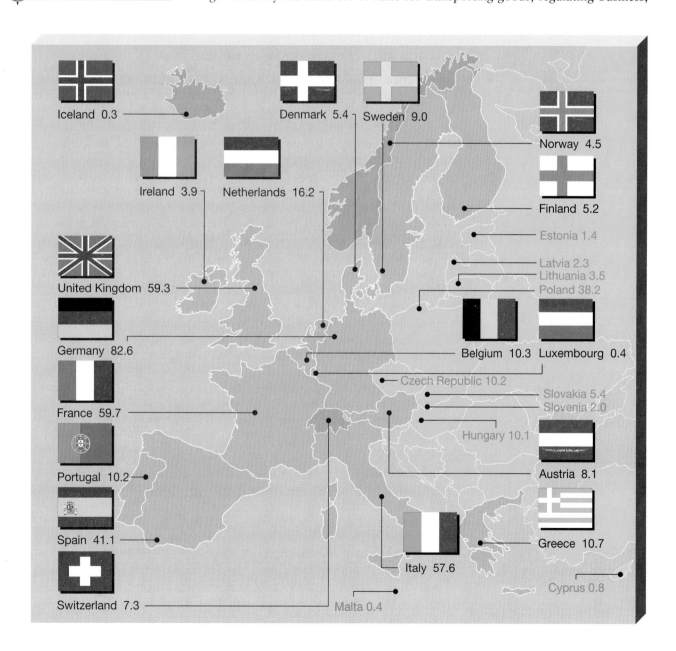

and protecting the environment. Fully accomplishing these goals entails adopting a common currency, a single central bank, and a shared foreign policy, among other things.

A major milestone was accomplished in 2002 when the full adoption of the euro as the official currency for 12 of the members was completed (Sweden, Denmark, and the United Kingdom declined to participate). Given the history of animosities and rivalries that exist among European countries, the level of cooperation has been quite remarkable. In all likelihood the EU will continue to evolve, dealing with social and cultural issues as well as economic ones.

The prospect of a market with 380 million consumers with the same regulations for product ingredients, advertising, packaging, and distribution is very appealing. However, for some American firms it is creating a new reality. In the past, if products were designed to meet U.S. regulations, it generally meant they would be acceptable anywhere in the world. But because many EU consumer protection standards are stricter than those in the U.S., items from promotional toys to air-conditioning compressors must be modified before they can be sold in Europe.

Several more central and eastern European countries are being considered for membership in the EU. These countries, which now consume very small amounts of western goods, are seen as primary growth markets.

- **North American Free Trade Agreement** (**NAFTA**, $1,162 billion, 56%). The U.S. and Canada forged a pact in 1989 that over a 10-year period phased out tariffs on goods traded between the two countries. The agreement was expanded in 1994 to include Mexico, creating a North American free-trade zone. Several other Western Hemisphere countries are interested in joining and may eventually become members (see Figure 3.2).

  Despite the fact that Canada and Mexico were major trading partners with the U.S. before NAFTA the agreement still has had a substantial impact. For example, U.S. exports to Mexico increased by 100% between 1995 and 2003, while Mexican exports to the U.S. increased by nearly 225% in the same period. This growth in trade has added to the economic stability of Mexico. However, the specialization that some analysts predicted, with assembly jobs moving from the U.S. to Mexico and technical production increasing in the U.S., has been slow to materialize.[11]

- **Asia-Pacific Economic Cooperation forum** (**APEC**, $3,136 billion, 72%). Twenty-one Pacific Rim nations participate in this trade pact—Australia, Brunei, Canada, Chile, China, Indonesia, Japan, Malaysia, Mexico, New Zealand, Papua New Guinea, the Philippines, Singapore, South Korea, Taiwan, Thailand, Peru, Russia, Taipei, Vietnam, and the U.S. The objective of the members, which account for 45% of the world's international trade, is to create a free-trade zone in the Pacific. South Asia and the Asian side of the Pacific Rim are shown in Figure 3.3. Not surprisingly, given the number of participants in APEC, progress is slow. Their representatives met for the first time in 1992, and the current goal is to have the major trade barriers substantially eliminated by 2020.

- **Association of Southeast Asian Nations** (**ASEAN**, $451 billion, 23%). This pact was established in 1967 as a free-trade zone initially consisting of Indonesia, Malaysia, the Philippines, Singapore, and Thailand. They were later joined by Brunei, Cambodia, Laos, Myanmar, and Vietnam. The ASEAN nations have a combined population of 500 million and a gross domestic product of $737 billion. The rapid growth and industrialization of these nations have led analysts to predict that their imports from the U.S. could soon reach $150 billion.

- **Common Market of the South** (**MERCOSUR**, $106 billion, 12%). Consisting of Argentina, Brazil, Paraguay, and Uruguay, and encompassing 190 million people, this pact permits 90% of the trade among these countries to occur tariff-free. The objectives of MERCOSUR are very similar to the EU, the elimination of tariffs among the members and the establishment of common external tariffs. A

www.nafta-sec-alena.org

www.apec.org

www.aseansec.org

www.mercosurinvestment.com

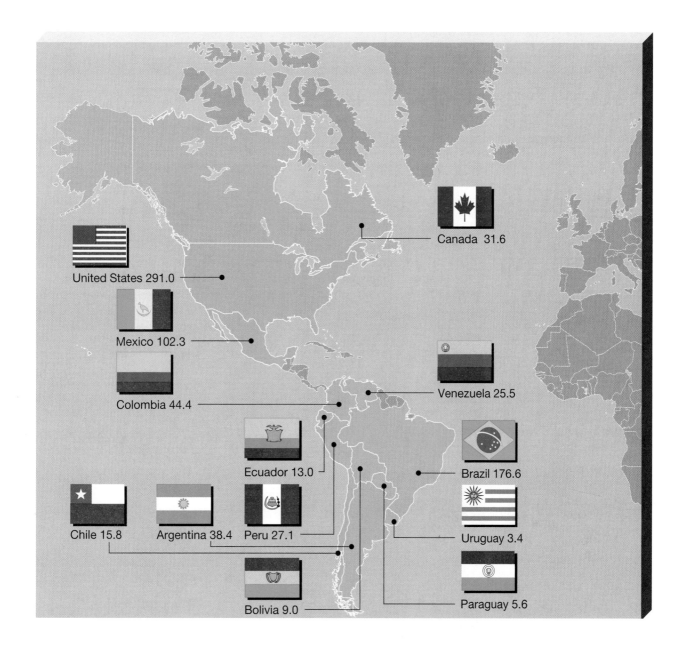

United States 291.0

Canada 31.6

Mexico 102.3

Colombia 44.4

Venezuela 25.5

Ecuador 13.0

Brazil 176.6

Chile 15.8   Argentina 38.4   Peru 27.1

Uruguay 3.4

Bolivia 9.0

Paraguay 5.6

FIGURE 3.2

The Americas (with population figures in millions).

similar agreement, called the Andean Common Market (ANCOM), has reduced trade barriers among Venezuela, Colombia, Ecuador, Peru, and Bolivia.

Other trade agreements with significant potential are too new to assess. The U.S., El Salvador, Nicaragua, Guatemala, Honduras, Costa Rica, and the Dominican Republic joined to form the Central American Free Trade Agreement (CAFTA) in 2005. Modeled after NAFTA, it is designed to remove trade barriers, facilitate investment, and strengthen intellectual property protection. And seven South Asian nations with a combined population of over a billion people have created the South Asian Association for Regional Cooperation (SAARC).

What do regional trade agreements mean for the rest of the world? Although they may eventually eliminate *internal* trade barriers among the members, trade agreements create fears that *external* barriers may restrict entry of products from outside the member countries. For example, the EU's exports to Mexico declined significantly when NAFTA opened Mexico up to U.S. and Canadian exports. Recognizing these concerns, some coalitions are undertaking efforts to build good relations with nonmember countries. For example, Mexico and the EU have reached a free-trade agreement. And the U.S. and the EU established an accord called the New

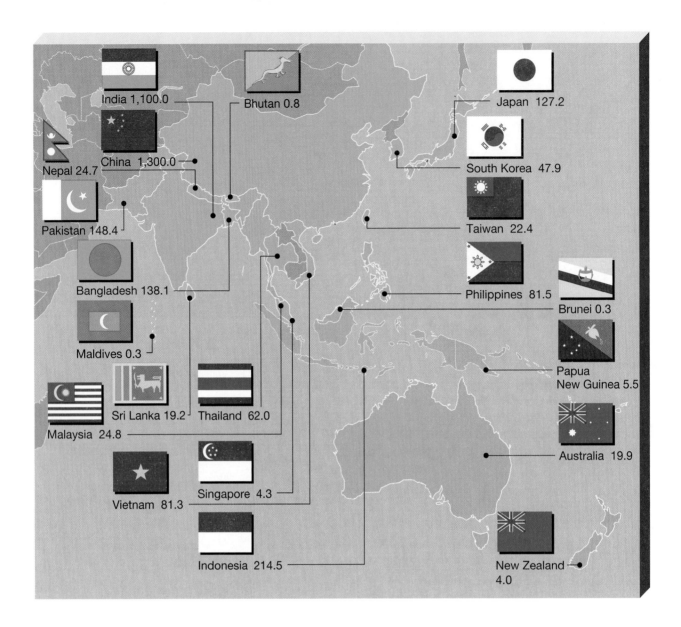

India 1,100.0
Bhutan 0.8
Japan 127.2
Nepal 24.7
China 1,300.0
South Korea 47.9
Pakistan 148.4
Taiwan 22.4
Bangladesh 138.1
Philippines 81.5
Brunei 0.3
Maldives 0.3
Papua New Guinea 5.5
Sri Lanka 19.2
Thailand 62.0
Malaysia 24.8
Australia 19.9
Vietnam 81.3
Singapore 4.3
Indonesia 214.5
New Zealand 4.0

FIGURE 3.3

South Asia and the Asian Side of the Pacific Rim (with population figures in millions).

Transatlantic Agenda that commits them to working toward establishing common product standards, agreement on standards for television programming, and many other trade-related issues.

It is impossible to generalize about the impact of trade agreements. However, the growth of regional economic trading blocs is a significant development that will create both opportunities and challenges for international marketers.

In the 21st century, perhaps the area with the greatest international marketing potential is China, with its 1.3 *billion* people. Already we have seen glimpses of these possibilities. Foreign cosmetic sales in China, unheard of a few years ago, are soaring. KFC opened its first store in China in 1987. Now the firm has over 1,000 outlets in 150 Chinese cities with average per store sales higher than in the U.S. China also has significant potential as an exporter. By 1990, the country was a major exporter of clothing. And China is using American and European investments in a quest to become a significant international exporter of automobiles, semiconductors, and telecommunications equipment.

Organizational Structures for International Markets

Having evaluated the opportunities and conditions in a foreign country, management must select an appropriate organizational structure for its marketing effort. There is a range of methods for operating in foreign markets (see Table 3.2) that represents successively greater international involvement.

Exporting

The simplest way to operate in foreign markets is by **exporting**: selling goods either directly to foreign importers or through import–export middlemen. Because it is the easiest way to get into international markets, exporting is popular with small firms. The Internet has created new export opportunities for many companies. Amazon.com, the best-known online bookseller, derived 44% of its 2004 revenue from customers in 225 countries outside the U.S.[12] However, using the Internet to sell directly to consumers in other countries presents some interesting challenges. There are issues of the language or languages to use on the site, the currency in which to quote prices, selection of the method of payment, and arrangements for reliable delivery of the goods.

www.amazon.com

In international markets, just as in domestic markets, middlemen may own the goods they deal in or simply bring buyers and sellers together. An **export merchant** is a middleman operating in the manufacturer's country that buys goods and exports them. Very little risk or investment on the part of the manufacturer is involved. Also, minimal time and effort are required on the part of the exporting producer. However, the exporter has little or no control over merchant middlemen.

An **export agent** may be located in either the manufacturer's country or in the destination country. The agent negotiates the sale of the product and may provide additional services such as arranging for international financing, shipping, and insurance on behalf of the manufacturer, but the agent does not own the goods. Greater risk is involved because the manufacturer retains title to the goods. Because they typically deal with a number of manufacturers, both types of middlemen generally are not aggressive marketers, nor do they generate a large sales volume.

To counteract some of these deficiencies, management can export through its own **company sales branches** located in foreign markets. Operating a sales branch enables a company to (1) promote its products more aggressively, (2) tailor its distribution network to the product, and (3) control its sales effort more completely. If sales people require extensive training and frequent retraining in order to provide the

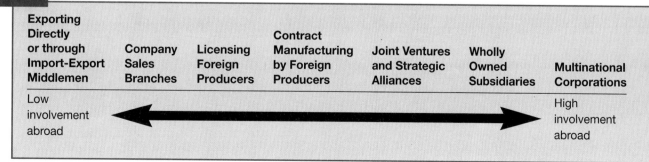

| TABLE 3.2 | The Range of Structures for Operating in Foreign Markets |

Exporting Directly or through Import-Export Middlemen	Company Sales Branches	Licensing Foreign Producers	Contract Manufacturing by Foreign Producers	Joint Ventures and Strategic Alliances	Wholly Owned Subsidiaries	Multinational Corporations
Low involvement abroad	←————————————————————————→					High involvement abroad

services customers need, as is the case with Microsoft software, sales branches in international markets are used frequently. Another situation in which sales branches may be preferable to export agents is when a firm must deal with complex local regulations as is the case for marketers of alcoholic beverages and prescription drugs.

With an international sales branch, management now has the task of managing a sales force. The difficulty is that these sales people are either employees sent from the home country who are unfamiliar with the local market, or foreign nationals who are unfamiliar with the product and the company's marketing practices.

Contracting

Contracting involves a legal relationship that allows a firm to enter a foreign market indirectly, quickly establish a market presence, and experience a limited amount of risk. Three frequently used forms of contracting are licensing, contract manufacturing, and franchising.

Licensing means a company grants to another producer—for some amount of compensation—the right to use its production process, patents, trademarks, or other assets. For example, Anheuser-Busch has licensing agreements with brewers in six countries outside the U.S. to produce Budweiser beer, including Labart's in Canada, Guiness in Ireland, and Peroni in Italy. Producers run the risk of encouraging future competition by licensing. A licensee may learn all it can from the producer and then proceed independently when the licensing agreement expires.

In **contract manufacturing**, a marketer such as Sears Roebuck contracts with a foreign producer to supply products that Sears then markets in the producer's country. For example, rather than import U.S.–made tools and hardware for its department stores in Mexico, Brazil, and Spain, Sears contracts with local manufacturers to supply many of these products.

If you have traveled outside the U.S., most likely you have seen the impact of one form of contracting firsthand. **Franchising** has allowed many U.S. retailers, such as McDonald's and KFC, to expand overseas rapidly and with minimal risk. Franchising combines a proven operating formula with local knowledge, financing, and entrepreneurial initiative.

Contracting offers companies flexibility with minimal investment. It allows a producer to enter a market that might otherwise be closed to it because of exchange restrictions, import quotas, or prohibitive tariffs.

Direct Investment

Another alternative is **direct foreign investment,** through which a company can build or acquire production or distribution facilities in a foreign country. U.S. firms have about $1,520 billion in direct investments around the world. In comparison, the foreign direct investment in the U.S. amounts to about $1,350 billion.[13] Table 3.3 indicates where U.S. firms have made the greatest amounts of foreign investments. Note that these are not sales figures; they are the value of the owned assets such as plants and equipment at a point in time.

The magnitude of foreign investments is a direct reflection of the strength and stability of a country's economy in comparison to the rest of the world. The amount invested in a particular country reflects its political and social receptivity to foreign investment as well as its economic attractiveness.

Direct investment can take the form of a joint venture or a wholly owned foreign subsidiary. A **joint venture** is a partnership arrangement in which the foreign operation is owned in part by a domestic company and in part by a foreign company. In 2005, IBM entered into a joint venture with China's Great Wall Computer that shifts manufacturing and sales of PCs to China.

When the controlling interest (more than 50%) is owned by foreign nationals, the domestic firm has no real control over the marketing or production activities.

Do you think the original Colonel (Harland) Sanders envisioned serving consumers in Kuala Lumur when he began marketing his fried chicken in 1939? These two Malaysian women, sharing a bench with a statue of the icon, have visited one of the 300 KFC franchised restaurants in their country. Worldwide the firm serves over a billion meals annually in over 80 countries. KFC, along with Taco Bell, Pizza Hut, A&W, and Long John Silver's, now make up the company called YUM! Brands.

www.yumbrands.com

However, a joint venture may be the only structure, other than licensing, through which a firm is legally permitted to enter some foreign markets. Joint ventures are frequently undertaken on a country-by-country basis. For example, in less than a year, Royal Crown Cola entered Mexico, Argentina, Syria, Portugal, Australia, and Indonesia on the basis of joint ventures.

Some major corporations have created a hybrid version of a joint venture called a strategic alliance. A **strategic alliance** is a formal, long-term agreement between firms to combine their capabilities and resources to accomplish global objectives without joint ownership. For example, DaimlerChrysler, Mitsubishi, and Hyundai have formed an alliance to develop a "small-car engine" that would power as many as a million of the companies' cars. Because an engine is one of the most expensive parts of a car and the profit margins on small cars are razor thin, this type of alliance provides savings for all the firms but still lets them compete on other product features.

TABLE 3.3 Direct Foreign Investment in the United States and Foreign Investment by U.S. Firms, Selected Countries, 2002 ($ billions)

Country	U.S. Foreign Investment	Foreign Investment in U.S.
United Kingdom	255	283
Canada	153	92
Netherlands	146	155
Switzerland	70	113
Germany	65	137
Japan	66	152
Mexico	58	9
France	44	172
Australia	36	25
Luxembourg	36	34

Source: *Statistical Abstract of the United States: 2004–2005,* 124th ed., U.S. Bureau of the Census, Washington, DC, 2004, pp. 805, 807.

Joint ventures and alliances in international marketing are particularly attractive when:

- Local laws create barriers to foreign ownership of a business. For example, the national regulations countries impose on airlines led Lufthansa, United Airlines, and other airlines to form alliances for passenger sharing and pooling maintenance facilities.

- Local knowledge is especially important. Retailing in particular requires an understanding of local customs and tastes. Even powerful firms such as Wal-Mart, in an alliance with Seiyu in Japan, recognize that much can be learned from established local firms. In contrast, many attribute French retailer Carrefour's lack of success in Japan to its attempt to enter the market alone.[14]

- A firm wants access to a market but does not want to expand its resources or expertise. If the risks of a foreign venture are too great for a firm to assume or gaining the necessary expertise would be too costly or time-consuming, a joint venture may be an option. Turner Broadcasting Services joined with Philips, a Dutch electronics firm, to gain quick access to digital communications hardware. Differences in expectations, performance, or corporate culture can undermine a joint venture. After only five years General Motors paid $2 billion to extract itself from a failed joint venture with Italian automaker Fiat.[15]

Wholly owned subsidiaries in foreign markets are foreign-based assembly or manufacturing facilities. They are commonly used by companies that have evolved to an advanced stage of international business. Nissan built Europe's most efficient auto manufacturing plant in England, where it will make a car for the European market using a design provided by Renault.

With a wholly owned foreign subsidiary, a company has maximum control over its marketing program and production operations. To ensure that the product is made and presented according to the same standards around the world, the company makes use of subsidiaries rather than licensees. For example, adidas America, a wholly owned subsidiary of adidas-Salomon AG, produces a broad range of footwear and apparel targeted at U.S. preferences and tastes. The line includes baseball and football cleats, adventure shoes, and women's workout shoes for which there are strong U.S. markets. Because it is a subsidiary, the actions of adidas America come under the scrutiny of the parent organization. Thus, it operates with the same corporate philosophy but a somewhat different strategy. For example, adidas America places greater emphasis on fashion merchandise and has higher sales volume goals than other units of the company, reflecting the greater potential in the U.S.[16] A wholly owned subsidiary requires a substantial investment of money, labor, and managerial attention.

Multinational Corporations

We've now come to the highest level of international involvement—one reached by relatively few companies. It is the truly global enterprise—the **multinational corporation**—in which both the foreign and the domestic operations are integrated and are not separately identified except possibly for legal reasons. A regional sales office in Atlanta is basically the same as one in Paris. Business opportunities abroad are viewed in the same way as those in the home country. That is, domestic opportunities are no longer automatically considered to be more attractive. From a legal point of view, a multinational has a home country. Thus, Nestlé is a Swiss firm and Shell Oil is Dutch. However, from a strategic perspective, a true multinational firm is a worldwide enterprise and does strategic marketing planning on a global basis. The result can produce some interesting management challenges, such as the ones faced by Nestlé with its 230,000 employees, operating over 500 factories in 83 countries, producing more than 8,000 different products ranging from cat food to candy bars. For example, even though it entered China in 1980 with Nescafe and was manufacturing products there by 1990, Nestlé has been outperformed in several of its major product categories by smaller, nimbler firms.[17]

Even though we have described these operating methods as distinct, it is not uncommon for a firm to use more than one of them at the same time. To illustrate, Honda Motor Company exports cars from Japan, imports minivans to Japan from its subsidiary in Canada, and manufactures cars and trucks for the U.S. market at subsidiaries in the U.S. Likewise, Hershey exports candy to Canada, is involved in a joint venture with the largest candy company in Scandinavia, and has a wholly owned subsidiary in Germany—Gubor, a boxed-chocolate company.

Designing the Marketing Mix

As in domestic marketing, the manager must design a marketing mix that will effectively meet customers' needs and accomplish the organization's objectives. However, as the following discussion suggests, domestic practices may have to be modified or entirely replaced in international marketing.

Marketing Research

The scarcity of reliable statistical data is often a major impediment in many foreign markets. Typically, the quality of the data is related directly to a country's level of economic development. However, the nature of the data varies widely. For example, most nations (including England, Japan, France, Spain, and Italy) do not even ask their citizens for income figures in their national censuses.

Another problem is a lack of uniformity among countries in how they define basic measures such as unemployment and the cost of living. As a result, comparisons across countries are often unreliable. In some parts of the world, figures on population and production may be only crude estimates. In less developed countries, studies on such things as buying habits or newspaper readership are even less likely. It was only in the 1990s that China was able to report television audience figures, even in the largest urban areas.

Other challenges arise when collecting data directly from customers and prospects. The absence of reliable lists makes it very difficult even to select a representative sample. Telephone surveys, for example, are likely to be invalid if telephone service is not available to virtually the entire population of a country. Even conducting a focus group can be very difficult. The quality of data also depends on the willingness of people to respond accurately when researchers pose questions about attitudes or buying behavior. Gathering useful data is very difficult in societies where opinion polls are relatively uncommon or strangers are viewed with suspicion.

Product Planning

A critical question in product planning concerns the extent to which a company can market the same product in several different countries. *Product extension* describes the situation in which a standard product is sold in two or more countries. For example, Gillette sells the same razor blades worldwide, and Burger King operates over 11,000 stores in 61 countries.

We can make a few broad generalizations regarding product extensions. The best bet for standardization is in the area of durable business goods. In such industries as aircraft, computers, and tractors, the worldwide market (at least among industrialized nations) is quite uniform. For example, the Boeing Company is selling its two-engine 777 airliner to both Singapore Airlines and United Airlines.

Consumer durable goods such as cameras, watches, pocket calculators, small appliances, and television sets are only slightly more difficult to extend into foreign markets virtually unchanged. The benefits and challenges of standardization are reflected in the efforts of automakers to develop "world cars"—vehicles that are fundamentally the same but produced and marketed in many parts of the world. Ford estimates that a world car could reduce its $8 billion annual product-development budget by *billions*. So far, however, the compromises necessary to meet differing standards and tastes have not produced a car acceptable to a global market.[18]

The most difficult products to standardize globally are personal products such as food, health and beauty aids, and apparel. This difficulty can be traced to national tastes and habits. For example, U.S. consumers eat four times as much dry cereal per capita as the French. This should come as no surprise, because even in large national markets such as the U.S., we often find strong regional differences in food and clothing preferences. Marketers frequently respond with a second product strategy option, *product adaptation,* or modifying a product that sells successfully in one market to suit the unique needs or requirements of other markets. Procter & Gamble modified its Max Factor line of cosmetics with brighter colors for Latin Americans, and its Vidal Sassoon shampoo with more conditioners for the Asian market.

The third alternative product strategy is *invention,* the development of an entirely new product for a foreign market. For example, Maybelline developed a high-humidity face makeup formula for the Asian Pacific market.

Marketers must study carefully the cultural and economic environment of any market—foreign or domestic—before planning products for that particular area. In Europe, for example, large refrigerators are popular in the north because consumers prefer to shop once a week. In contrast, southern Europeans enjoy shopping at open-air markets daily and therefore opt for small refrigerators. And in Europe, where washing machines are often in the kitchen, consumers prefer smaller, quieter versions than U.S. households.

Branding and labeling are other considerations in foreign marketing. Most firms would prefer to use the same brand name in domestic and foreign markets, because it provides greater overall familiarity and recognition and can also produce some economies in promotion. However, care must be taken with translating brand names. Clairol introduced a curling iron in Germany called the Mist Stick only to discover that mist is a German slang word for manure.

A concern of many marketers is **trademark infringement.** In many countries copyright laws are nonexistent or poorly enforced. As a result, local firms manufacture products with names and packaging very similar to well-known imported goods in hopes of deceiving consumers. For example, a Chinese food outlet apparently was trying to take advantage of the popularity of McDonald's and KFC when it named itself "McKentucky." Often these products are of inferior quality, so not only do they steal business from the imported brand, they also damage its reputation.

Global pirating of computer software, music, and videos—virtually anything that can be transmitted electronically—is another serous problem. In the past, firms were provided with at least some protection from pirating by domestic laws and the physical limitations of making and shipping a videotape or CD. With those constraints reduced or eliminated, it has been suggested that the makers of these electronic products will be forced to find new ways to market their products. One approach, already used by some software firms, is to give their products away via the Internet, and generate revenue by selling advertising space on the Internet site.

Pricing

Determining the price for a product is a complex and inexact task, frequently involving trial-and-error decision making. This process is often even more complex in international marketing. An exporter faces variables such as currency conversion, differences in what is included in the price (such as postsale service), and often a lack of control over middlemen's pricing.

Cost-plus pricing (setting price by adding an amount to provide a profit to the cost of manufacturing a product) is relatively common in export marketing. Because of additional physical distribution expenses, tariffs, and other export costs, foreign prices usually are considerably higher than domestic prices for the same product. For example, a Jeep Cherokee costs about 50% more in Japan than in the U.S. At the retail level, price bargaining is quite prevalent in many foreign markets—especially in Asia, Africa, and South America—and must be taken into consideration in setting the initial price.

Sometimes companies engage in a practice called **dumping**—selling products in foreign markets at prices below those charged for the same goods in their home markets. The price may be lowered to meet foreign competition or to dispose of slow-moving products. Dumping, which frequently involves selling goods below cost, is viewed as an unfair business practice by most governments, and generally results in threats of tariffs or establishment of quotas. In the U.S., dumping accusations and subsequent restrictions have been applied to imports ranging from steel to shrimp.

An issue of growing concern is the **price differential** charged for an identical brand in different, often neighboring, countries. Price differences result from the strength of demand, the complexity of the distribution structures in various countries, and differences in tax systems. With the easy flow of information across borders and increased travel by consumers, price differentials add considerable complexity to the job of middlemen, especially retailers, doing business in several countries. They also encourage **arbitrage**—the purchase and sale of a product in different markets to benefit from the unequal prices.

Prices may be quoted in the seller's currency or in the currency of the foreign buyer. Here we encounter problems of **foreign exchange** and conversion of currencies. As a general rule, a firm engaged in foreign trade—whether it is exporting or importing— prefers to have the price quoted in its own national currency. If a seller deals in a foreign currency and that currency declines in value between the signing of a contract and the receipt of the foreign currency, the seller incurs a loss. Similarly, a buyer dealing in a foreign currency would lose money if the foreign currency increased in value before payment was made. The risks from fluctuations in foreign exchange are shifted to the other party in the transaction if a firm deals in its national currency.

An alternative to currency-based pricing is **countertrade** or **barter.** Rather than buy goods with cash, some countries arrange to trade domestically made products for imported goods. PepsiCo, for example, has traded soft drinks to Poland for wooden chairs that were used in U.S. Pizza Hut stores it owned at the time. Two reasons for countertrade are:

- *Lack of hard currency.* Less developed countries may not have enough "hard" currency (the money of countries viewed in world markets as reasonably stable) to buy needed capital goods. So they trade their less-sophisticated products for equipment and technology. A Canadian firm selling steel in Indonesia was compensated in palm oil, coffee, timber, and rattan furniture.

- *Inadequate marketing structure.* Some countries do not have a marketing structure that encourages or permits international trade. Without global distribution systems, adequate promotion, or the ability to provide service, they cannot sell their domestic goods overseas. To overcome this problem, these countries may require foreign firms that import products into the country to accept local goods in total or partial payment. Both China and Romania have required that importers accept countertrade.

Agreements between manufacturers and middlemen in the same industry are tolerated to a far greater extent in many foreign countries than in the U.S. They are allowed even when the avowed purpose of the combination is to restrain trade and reduce competition. Recognizing this, Congress passed the Webb-Pomerene Act in 1918. This law allows American firms to join this type of trade combination in a foreign country without being charged with violation of American antitrust laws.

The best-known of these international marketing combinations is the cartel. A **cartel** is a group of companies that produce similar products and act collectively to restrain competition in manufacturing and marketing. Cartels exist to varying degrees in steel, aluminum, fertilizers, petroleum products, rayon, and sulfur. Probably the world's best-known cartel is OPEC, the Organization of Petroleum Exporting Countries, which has tried—with varying degrees of success—to control the price of crude oil.

Distribution Systems

The different environments in foreign markets force firms to adjust their distribution systems, because marketing institutions, such as various types of retailers, are responses to the environment. They can also provide an opportunity to experiment with new strategies. For example, as foreign retailers are allowed to expand into China's rural areas, chains such as Carrefour, Metro, and Wal-Mart will likely test new store sizes and merchandise assortments.[19]

Middlemen and Channels of Distribution   International middlemen were introduced earlier in this chapter in connection with organizational structures for international marketing. Foreign middlemen representing importers and operating within foreign countries are, in general, less aggressive and perform fewer marketing services than their counterparts selling domestically produced products. The foreign marketing situation, however, usually argues against bypassing these middlemen. Often the demand is too small to warrant establishing a sales office or branch in the foreign country. Also, in many countries, knowledge of the market may be more important than knowledge of the product, even for high-technology products. And sometimes government controls preclude the use of a firm's sales organization abroad. Thus, middlemen in foreign countries ordinarily are a part of the channel structure.

A deceptive practice employed by some middlemen is called export diversion or **gray marketing.** When a distributor buys a product made in one country and agrees to distribute it in a second country, but instead diverts the product to a third country, gray marketing is occurring. The term used to describe the practice comes from the fact that the goods are typically sold in a reputable outlet, typically at a substantial discount, and thus do not appear on the "black market." The discounts stem

As China opens its borders to Western marketing practices it must confront a number of challenges. One is deciding what is considered permissible advertising. Recently TV ads for personal hygiene products and over-the-counter medications were banned during meal times, and stations were told they can broadcast only two beer ads between 7 P.M. and 9 P.M. In addition, specific ad content has been censored. A McDonald's spot showing a man licking drippings from a chicken sandwich on a magazine page was considered undignified by authorities, as was a Nike ad featuring U.S. basketball player LeBron James defeating a cartoon kung fu master. In the Nike case, the ad was said to violate national dignity and respect for Chinese culture.

Should advertising be restricted? If so, how should the restrictions be determined?

Sources: Geoffrey A. Fowler, "China Cracks Down on Commercials," *The Wall Street Journal*, Feb. 19, 2004, p. B7; Geoffrey A. Fowler, "China Bans Nike's LeBron Ad as Offensive to Nation's Dignity," *The Wall Street Journal*, Dec. 7, 2004, p. B4.

from the fact that the gray marketer does not bear any of the promotional costs for the product, instead capitalizing on the promotional efforts of the authorized dealers, nor does the gray marketer provide the service and warranty protection of an authorized dealer. An investigation of a health scare associated with Coke bottled in Belgium led to the discovery that as much as 20% of all the soft drinks sold in Great Britain are diverted goods. One reason gray marketing occurs is because manufacturers selling their products in several countries often have more difficulty monitoring the activities of middlemen than they do in the domestic market.

Physical Distribution Various aspects of physical distribution in foreign marketing are quite different from anything found on the domestic scene. Generally, physical distribution expenses account for a much larger share of the final selling price in foreign markets than in domestic markets. Problems caused by climate, pilferage, handling, and inadequate marking must be considered in international shipments. Requirements regarding commercial shipping, insurance, and government documents complicate foreign shipping. As noted earlier, one of the primary benefits of economic alliances like the EU is the efficiency they bring to physical distribution. With the free movement of goods across European borders, distribution time and expense are drastically reduced.

Bribes, kickbacks, and sometimes even extortion payments are facts of life in international distribution. Bribery is so rooted in many cultures that it is described with special slang words. It's called *mordida* (small bite) in Latin America. The French call it *pot de vin* (jug of wine). In Italy there is *la bustarella* (the little envelope), left on a bureaucrat's desk to cut the red tape. South Koreans use *ttuk kab* (rice cake expenses).

Revelations about the amount of bribery led Congress to pass the Foreign Corrupt Practices Act in 1977. The act prohibits U.S. companies, their subsidiaries, or representatives from making payments to high-ranking foreign government officers and political parties. The law, however, does not exclude small, facilitating payments to lower-level foreign government employees who are not policymakers, because these payments are a way of life in many parts of the world.

What complicates this situation is the fact that bribery is not a sharply defined activity. Sometimes the lines are blurred among a bribe, a gift to show appreciation, a reasonable commission for services rendered, and a finder's fee to open a distribution channel. For example, businesses in South Korea make contributions to government officials to mark major holidays. According to South Korean executives, the payments are not made to obtain favors. Rather, they serve to protect a firm from punitive treatment by government bureaucrats. Realistically, in some foreign markets a seller must pay a fee or commission to an agent to get in touch with prospective buyers. Without paying such fees, there is simply no effective access to those markets.

Advertising

There are numerous advertising decisions in international marketing. The availability of media, access to consumers, choice of advertising agencies, and the design of messages are just a few examples. Rather than trying to deal with all aspects of advertising and promotion, we limit our discussion to the issue of standardizing the message to illustrate the strategic challenges faced by international marketers in communicating with customers.

In its purest form, standardization entails using the same advertisement in multiple countries. Although posed as a strategic alternative over 30 years ago, the conditions under which it is practical remains a controversial topic. In recent years, interest in standardization has been spurred by the increase in international communication and entertainment. Many TV broadcasts reach worldwide audiences through satellite and cable networks. The Internet has made it possible for consumers to instantaneously visit the websites and view the messages of firms anywhere. Magazines and newspapers are widely circulated and are also globally available on the Internet. In addition, international business and pleasure travel have become quite common.

A second factor contributing to the interest in standardization is the economies it can produce. Creating quality advertising is expensive. Substantial savings can be achieved if the same advertisement can be used effectively in various parts of the world.

Despite its attractiveness, pure standardization is not typical. Rather, there are frequently efforts by international marketers to optimize their investment in advertising by adapting the same basic theme, appeal, or message in different countries. A recent study of print ads by multinational consumer product manufacturers found only 11% utilized pure standardization. However, nearly half standardized over 80% of the content of their ads, and most (78%) standardized to some degree.[20] Firms that have used modified global appeals successfully include Gillette for its Sensor razor, Nike, Procter & Gamble, and Nestlé for Nescafe coffee. However, in each case the advertiser has customized the way the message is presented to fit the local market.

For international marketers, the issue is not whether to standardize, but how much and where it is possible. Advertising must capture attention and convey a message. Advertisements do that by using a variety of communication devices such as humor, contrast, and surprise. The difficulty in standardizing international advertising is what works in one setting might take on quite a different meaning in another. For example, firms advertising in the south of China find slapstick humor is effective, but in the northern regions clever wordplays attract attention.[21]

In 2003, McDonald's set out to identify a slogan that would say everyone is welcome, and say it in virtually any language. The result was the "I'm lovin' it" campaign, created by a German advertising agency. Within a month after it was launched in Germany, the slogan was being used in over 100 countries. Did it work? The proof is in the results: after a flat performance in 2002, sales in every region of the world increased in 2003 and again in 2004. But maybe the best indicator is that the slogan is still being used.

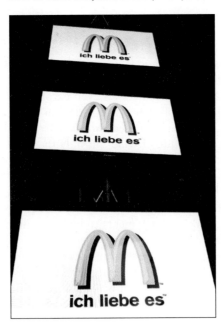

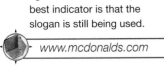

www.mcdonalds.com

The challenge of standardization comes down to balancing efficiency by minimizing the investment in advertising with its effectiveness by maximizing the fit of the ads to the particular market.

The goal of advertising is the same in any country, namely to communicate information and persuasive appeals effectively. For some products, the appeals are sufficiently universal and the markets are sufficiently homogeneous to permit the use of very similar advertising in several countries. It is only the media strategy and the details of a message that must be fine-tuned to each country's cultural, economic, and political environment. However, companies must take care to recognize when differences in national identity and characteristics will require specialized advertising in a particular country.

Our discussion has described environmental factors, organizational arrangements, and tactical issues related to the marketing mix elements of product, price, distribution, and promotion that are fundamental to designing an international marketing strategy. Certainly there are other issues that further distinguish domestic from international or global marketing. However, a primary purpose of this chapter is to make you aware of the fact that along with the opportunities, marketing beyond one's domestic borders raises new and unique strategic challenges.

Summary

Countries encourage international trade for economic, social, and political reasons. In particular, it provides access to goods and services that otherwise would be unavailable and, because of comparative advantage, it maximizes a country's economic potential. Firms engage in international marketing because of demand abroad, the saturation of domestic markets, and to serve the international needs of their domestic customers. Many companies in the U.S. and abroad derive a substantial share of their total sales and profits from their foreign marketing operations.

Although international trade can contribute to the growth of a nation's economy, a country must be concerned about the relationship between exports and imports. For the U.S., trade surpluses are needed to offset deficits in other balance-of-payment categories. In recent years, the U.S. balance of trade has been adversely affected by consumers' preferences for imported products, entry barriers, and other policies of foreign governments, as well as the growing technological and marketing capabilities of other countries.

In terms of organizational structure, the simplest way to operate in a foreign market is to export. Products can be exported directly to consumers via the Internet or through middlemen specializing in foreign trade. Another method is to export through company sales branches located in foreign countries. More involved approaches include contracting, engaging in a joint venture, or forming a wholly owned subsidiary. The most fully developed organizational structure for international marketing is the multinational corporation.

The macroenvironment faced by an international marketer in various countries will determine whether a global, regional, or local strategy is appropriate. Differences in the social and cultural environment are reflected in family values, customs, education, and language. Critical economic conditions include the infrastructure in a market and a country's stage of economic development. Political and legal forces unique to international marketing are trade barriers and international trade agreements. Organizations such as the World Trade Organization (WTO) as well as trade agreements and economic alliances in Europe (EU), North America (NAFTA), South America (MERCOSUR), Asia (ASEAN), and elsewhere in the world have implications for marketers in both member and nonmember nations.

Oftentimes operating in a foreign market entails accommodating unique conditions. Chief among these are dumping, foreign exchange, countertrade, price differentials, gray markets, cartels, and bribery.

To develop an international marketing program, a basic issue is how global or standardized the marketing can be. This is made difficult by the fact that market data may be less plentiful in many parts of the world, and conducting marketing research can be very difficult. In some cases each of the marketing-mix elements—product, price, distribution, and promotion—requires modification or adaptation.

More about IKEA

Some think there's a side benefit to IKEA's cost-cutting strategy of having consumers perform the final assembly of its furniture products. Having "built" the table or chair, the consumer forms an emotional attachment to it and the brand. Whatever the reason, IKEA has about 3.6% of the world's market for home furnishings. While that might not sound like much, consider that it is nearly three times that of its nearest competitor, and the total market is estimated at over $325 billion.

The bulk of IKEA sales are in Europe (66% of the total), with Germany leading the way. U.S. operations account for 16% of sales, while Asia is only at 3%. Thus the opportunity in the largest growth area of the world looks very promising. However, IKEA is still learning how to adapt its operation for the Chinese market. The company opened its first Chinese store in Shanghai in 1998 and quickly learned its prices were too high for the target market, so they made adjustments. There were also other miscalculations. The firm initially offered shorter than standard-size beds, but these were rejected by consumers and were quickly replaced with the larger version. And because labor costs are so low in China, Chinese consumers have been slower to accept the idea of assembling their purchases themselves.

The business formula IKEA has followed from the beginning—functionality, quality, and low price—has global appeal. However, to make it work the firm must constantly find ways to balance its goals by coming up with attractive designs, innovations in production, and cost savings. One approach is to produce products where quality standards can be met at the lowest cost. On its website, IKEA offers this simple illustration: When designers combine function with good quality, will an expensive finish on the back of a shelf or under a tabletop improve function or appearance? If not, don't do it because a product that is unaffordable is of no use to the customer. Another source of cost savings is minimizing production costs. Presently that means China, with its low labor costs, is the source of most IKEA products produced outside of Europe (19%), while within Europe, Poland is the primary source (12%).

As IKEA seeks continued growth opportunities it is expanding its offerings in two directions. One is adding product categories including lighting, rugs, cookware, tableware, and other housewares. The other is to move beyond a single, economy-focused item in a category to good/better/best versions of many products. The risk here is that IKEA is moving away from its success formula and its clear brand image may become muddled in consumers' minds.

When asked about its biggest challenges, IKEA's North American president said it is keeping each store's 40,000 to 50,000 weekly visitors happy. That means having adequate inventory on hand and keeping check-out time to a minimum. IKEA's keys to success, in his mind, are to keep the operation simple for consumers and to provide them with instant gratification by having products readily available.[22]

1. What areas of IKEA's marketing mix will most likely need modification if it seeks further expansion in Asia?

2. In what ways might IKEA consider taking advantage of its well-known brand name and positive reputation?

Key Terms and Concepts

Balance of payments (51)
Trade balance (51)
International marketing (52)
Global strategy (54)
Regional strategy (54)
Local strategy (54)
Infrastructure (56)
Tariff (58)
Import quota (58)
Local-content law (58)
Local operating laws (58)
Standards and certification (58)

Boycott (58)
World Trade Organization (WTO) (58)
European Union (EU) (59)
North American Free Trade Agreement (NAFTA) (60)
Asia-Pacific Economic Cooperation forum (APEC) (60)
Association of Southeast Asian Nations (ASEAN) (60)
Common Market of the South (MERCOSUR) (60)

Exporting (63)
Export merchant (63)
Export agent (63)
Company sales branch (63)
Contracting (64)
Licensing (64)
Contract manufacturing (64)
Franchising (64)
Direct foreign investment (64)
Joint venture (64)
Strategic alliance (65)
Wholly owned subsidiary (66)

Multinational corporation (66)   Arbitrage (69)   Cartel (70)
Trademark infringement (68)   Foreign exchange (69)   Gray marketing (70)
Dumping (69)   Countertrade or barter (69)   Bribes (71)
Price differential (69)

Questions and Problems

1. Find out which U.S. products have the largest volume of exports. (*Hint:* Check *International Financial Statistics* or *International Marketing Data and Statistics*—two publications that are likely in your school's library and on the Internet.) What explains the popularity of these products outside the U.S.?

2. What should a country such as the U.S. do to reduce its trade deficits?

3. A U.S. manufacturer of premium-quality luggage has been exporting its products to Europe. However, the firm has discovered that its luggage is often sold alongside many lower-quality products in discount stores. What approach to international marketing should the firm consider if it wants greater control over how its products are sold at retail?

4. Interview some foreign students on your campus to determine how the grocery buying behavior of people in their countries differs from yours. Consider such factors as when, where, and how people in their countries buy. What roles do various family members play in buying decisions?

5. Many countries have a low literacy rate. In what ways might a company adjust its marketing program to overcome this problem?

6. Visit the website of an international trade organization such as the EU or NAFTA. What are the major issues being addressed by the organization's governing body? Are the issues the result of the relative size of the member countries, their differing levels of industrialization, or some other factors?

7. If an American company uses foreign middlemen, it must usually stand ready to supply them with financial, technical, and promotional help. If this is the case, why is it not customary to bypass these middlemen and deal directly with the ultimate foreign buyers?

8. Examine the ads in a foreign magazine in your college or city library. Particularly note the ads for American products, and compare these with the ads for the same products in American magazines. In what respect do the foreign ads differ from the domestic ads? Are there significant similarities?

9. "Prices of American products are always higher in foreign countries than at home because of the additional risks, expenses of physical distribution, and extra middlemen involved." Discuss.

Interactive Marketing Exercises

1. Report on export marketing activities of companies in the state where your school is located. Consider such topics as the following: What products are exported? How many jobs are created by export marketing? What is the dollar value of exports? How does this figure compare with the value of foreign-made goods imported into the state?

2. Select one product—manufactured or nonmanufactured—for export, and choose the country to which you would like to export it. Examine the macroenvironmental factors described in the chapter and prepare an analysis of the market for this product in the selected country. Be sure to include the sources of information you use.

Cases for Part 1

CASE 1	Google

Searching for Success On the Web

As the Internet began proliferating in the mid-1990s, researchers and companies alike scrambled to develop tools that would allow Web surfers to navigate its massive stores of data in order to find specific bits of information. But it was two young graduate students, Larry Page and Sergey Brin, whose efforts yielded today's most popular Internet search engine and a highly profitable Internet company called Google. Named after the mathematical term that represents the number 10 to the hundredth power, Google is such a dominant presence on the Web, that it is now being used as a verb. Have you ever "Googled" anyone? No? Well then, read on.

Moving Out of the Dorm Room and Into the Boardroom

When they met at Stanford University, Page and Brin already had the reputation of being technical whiz kids. (Page once made a computer printer built entirely out of Legos.) Together, they decided to try to develop a process for searching the Internet, but they agreed out of necessity to do it by using a network of inexpensive personal computers instead of large-scale servers. Short of resources, they borrowed PCs from around campus, set up the data center in Page's dorm room and, in 1997, produced their first iteration of a search engine they dubbed BackRub.

Although the people who saw BackRub were impressed, Page and Brin were unsuccessful in selling the technology to other Internet companies. Undeterred, they began looking for investors, and gladly accepted a check for $100,000 from Andy Bechtolsheim, a founder of Sun Microsystems. They eventually raised almost $1 million, and Google, Inc. was born.

The company officially opened in September of 1998, and despite the fact that Google.com was still being beta tested, it was named one of the "Top 100 Web Sites and Search Engines" by *PC Magazine* in 1998. By February 1999, it was handling half a million searches each day and growing by leaps and bounds. The company expanded by hiring a number of new employees and settled into spacious office space, nicknamed the Googleplex, in Mountain View, California. Later that year, the beta test was concluded, and clients such as America Online began signing on to use Google's search technology on their own sites.

Google became the largest search engine in the world in 2000, conducting 18 million searches each day. That number exploded to 100 million searches each day in February 2001. In addition, the Googleplex acquired the reputation of being a creative, desirable place to work and began attracting top talent. Its open floor plan encouraged communication among its employees, and its founders hired a world-renowned chef, organized roller hockey games, and held meetings each Friday that included the entire company. This collaborative environment has spawned a slew of new innovations and rapid international expansion that succeeded in attracting additional big-name clients and advertisers. But the key to Google's success has always been its underlying technology—a unique formula originally developed by Page and Brin that allows users to conduct swift and accurate searches across the World Wide Web in a matter of seconds.

Setting Its "Sites" on More Accurate Results

With the inception of the Internet, a profusion of information became available to those who were patient enough and skilled enough to sort through it. Brin and Page were determined to help those who weren't. "The perfect search engine would understand exactly what you mean and give back exactly what you want," explained Page. Other search engines already existed, and they worked by scanning through the Web, summarizing information by creating an index, and then matching the original query with pages that contained the relevant word or phrase. However, the results were often inaccurate or too voluminous to be helpful.

Brin and Page solved this by creating an algorithm called PageRank that sorts results according to their perceived importance. The algorithm starts by assigning all of the pages that are a "hit" the same initial value. It goes on to increase the value of a page for every other relevant page with which it links. The final scores are used to rank the results in a meaningful way for the person who initiated the search, so that the page with the highest perceived relevance is displayed first, with the rest following in a descending order. While this may sound like a simple equation, it is actually much more complicated and utilizes a linear algebraic calculation to speed up the process and return results almost instantaneously.

For businesses, it is extremely beneficial to be displayed near the top of a search result. Have you ever noticed all of the "Triple-A" companies at the start of each category in the yellow pages? That's because companies know that many consumers will begin calling the first company they see, and the yellow pages are organized alphabetically. Therefore, several companies have sprung up to try to manipulate Google's search results by increasing their clients' PageRank values by creating more links to them. But the PageRank algorithm is being continually updated to foil such attempts.

While Google was able to solve some of the challenges related to Internet search engines, it didn't immediately hit upon a way to become profitable. Unlike many start-up Internet ventures however, it quickly solved that equation as well.

Ranking High on the List of Profitable Web Businesses

Google decided early on not to accept concessions from other business ventures that wanted to increase their rankings in search results, and to clearly distinguish between paid advertisements and results generated by user searches. The company generated some revenue by selling banner ads, but quickly realized it wasn't going to produce enough income to support Google's aggressive aspirations and expensive research and development costs.

As Google's search technology became widely admired, other companies began inquiring about the possibility of licensing it for their own websites. Many online publishers, like Washingtonpost.com, and other companies such as Procter & Gamble and Boeing, utilize Google's search services in one way or another, and pay for the privilege of doing so. However, Google provides free search services to a number of academic institutions around the world, perhaps in recognition of the fact that Stanford University was tremendously supportive of the early efforts of Google's founders.

In mid-2000, Google introduced AdWords, an advertising program that allows online businesses to place ads next to related search results. For instance, if a user initiates a search for "plasma television sets," ads for online companies that sell plasma TVs will pop up beside the corresponding results. The ads are ranked in descending order according to the amount paid by advertisers. However, the popularity of the ad can raise or lower its position. For instance, if users are consistently clicking on an ad that is located near the bottom of the page, it will be moved up. Conversely, a less popular ad will be moved down, even if the company that bought the ad had the highest bid for the term "plasma television set." In addition, Google made it incredibly simple for advertisers to place their bids online by allowing them to create an account for just $5 and by simply using a credit card. It further enhanced AdWords by instituting a usage-based pricing model that charges advertisers based on the number of hits their ads receive, making it affordable for small as well as large businesses.

AdWords played an integral role in Google's ability to turn a profit in 2001, an achievement that has eluded many online companies. By August 2004, Google was one of the largest private companies in the world, but that was about to change, because it was transformed into a public company when shares of its stocks were sold on the New York Stock Exchange for the first time through a very well-publicized initial public offering (IPO.) The shares were originally priced at $85 each, and by the end of the day they were worth $100. Brin and Page each cashed in $41 million in stock and held onto almost $4 billion more. And Bechtolsheim's initial $100,000 investment had ballooned into almost a third of a billion dollars.

Seeking a Competitive Edge

Not content to simply be the Internet's largest and most popular search engine, Google has rapidly been expanding its product offerings and enhancing its search capabilities in an effort to make it an indispensable, multifaceted tool for its multitude of users. It offers Google PhoneBook, an online telephone directory, Google News Headlines, a service that recaps the latest news stories, and the Google Toolbar, which users can install on their desktop, thereby eliminating the need to even visit the Google website when conducting online searches. In April 2004, Google began testing a service called GMail, which was offered to a select group of users and gives them 1,000 megabytes of storage memory and the ability to conduct searches through their stored messages.

Google has also gotten involved in Web shopping by introducing Google Catalog Search, a service that allows users to peruse more than a thousand catalogs that were not previously available online. It also unveiled a feature called Froogle, which enables users to compare prices for the same product available at different e-tailers.

The second most popular search site on the Web is Yahoo!, and it has actively been upgrading its capabilities in order to compete with Google. Yahoo! has been doing so by introducing features that allow users to customize their searches by blocking certain sites and highlighting others, and by creating their own home pages. "Historically there's been 'search the Web,' now we're creating 'search my Web,'" explained Yahoo!'s senior vice president, Jeff Weiner.

Due to Google's ever-widening scope, Yahoo! isn't the only online company that worries about competing with the Google machine. eBay is concerned that Google's AdWords will lure advertisers away. Froogle is a threat to Amazon, and in response, Amazon has developed its own search engine called A9. So has Microsoft, but its MSN Search beta proved to be less accurate than Google in a test conducted by *The Washington Post*. In addition, the many companies that offer e-mail services are keeping an eye on the performance of GMail. "Google, Yahoo!, Amazon and eBay are on a collision course," stated Bill Gross, chairman of Idealab, an Internet think tank and venture capital firm. "They're all stepping into each other's territory, and it's going to lead to interesting battles."

To stay one step ahead of the competition, Google has developed a list of "ten things it has found to be true." Each tenet is discussed in detail on its website, but four of them seem to have particularly influenced its success. The eighth item declares that "the need for information crosses all borders." Early in its history, Google addressed the fact that it was indeed a "world wide web" by allowing users to conduct searches in English and ten other languages. By 2001, its search services were available in 40 different languages, and Google even provided automated translations. The company was operating in offices in Paris, London, Tokyo, Hamburg, and Toronto and supported 88 languages by 2003. It even announced plans to open an office on the moon in early 2004.

Another corporate truth is Google's contention that "you can make money without doing evil." By not accepting payment in order to influence search results, by excluding irrelevant pop-up ads, and by clearly delineating advertisers as "sponsors," Google has been able to maintain its integrity without selling itself out. Google has also clearly demonstrated that "democracy on the web works." Its PageRank formula takes a sophisticated tally to determine what sites most closely match the queries posed by Google users, and it does so with a high degree of accuracy.

But the first item on the list of things Google has learned is to "focus on the user and all else will follow." Google's absolute devotion to its user base has resulted in it becoming one of the top five most-visited sites on the Web. In addition, *USA Today* published a survey in December 2004 in which consumers predicted Google would continue to be a big hit in 2005. In fact it was number three on the list of projected "winning" brand names.

Are you interested in the other six things that Google has learned? Just Google it!

Questions

1. Describe the three components of the marketing concept as they apply to Google. Which is likely to provide the greatest challenge to Google's success?

2. Describe how each factor in the external macroenvironment will influence Google's marketing activities.

3. Do you agree with Google's strategy of expanding its product mix to include services other than just search capabilities? Why or why not?

www.google.com

<table>
<tr><td>CASE 2</td><td>Sirius versus XM</td></tr>
</table>

Tuning into a New Market with Satellite Radio

A new entertainment product was launched, literally, in 2001 when XM Satellite Radio Holdings Inc. propelled its two satellites, nicknamed Rock and Roll, into outer space. Shortly thereafter, the new company began offering premium radio services to subscribers willing to pay $120 per year, plus the cost of the necessary hardware.

Actually, a competitor, Sirius Satellite Radio Inc., already had three satellites in orbit. Among the most powerful communications satellites ever built, they use a different band than satellite TV and maintain their signals even in bad weather. However, because of technological challenges, Sirius didn't begin programming until 2002, giving XM almost a year's head start to attract subscribers and upgrade its chip technology.

Since then, the two companies have battled fiercely for programming, paying enormous sums of money to secure popular radio personalities, such as Howard Stern, and sporting events, such as Major League Baseball (MLB) games. Neither firm expects to be profitable until 2008. As technology continues to evolve and the Internet becomes increasingly pervasive, both companies face escalating competition from other forms of entertainment.

Hitting the Airways (and the Roadways) with XM

Sirius was formed two years before XM, and was licensed by the Federal Communications Commission (FCC) and launched its satellites first. But the pioneer quickly lost its lead when development of its chipsets was delayed. A critical component in receivers, chipsets transform radio signals into sound. Sirius had to use an inferior chipset in its original receivers. Even then, it wasn't able to beat its nemesis, XM, to market.

In contrast, XM was able to design its chipsets with no major setbacks and commissioned several other companies to engineer and manufacture its receivers. By working in tandem with experienced firms like Pioneer and Sony, XM was able to launch its service in November 2001. By the end of that year, XM was boasting a customer base of 30,000 subscribers. It took Sirius another year to reach that level of subscribers.

When satellite radio was introduced, receivers were rather expensive, costing between $300 and $400. By the end of 2003, both companies offered portable receivers for about $120. These devices can be plugged into the power jack of an automobile or a home stereo system. XM's Roady was smaller than a deck of cards, whereas Sirius' Plug & Play was considerably larger. In addition, the Plug & Play unit required an additional investment of $60 to make it compatible with both a car and a home stereo.

As is true of most types of technology, satellite-radio hardware has become progressively more sophisticated. The industry leader, XM unveiled the MyFi portable player in 2004, and priced it at $350.

Similar to an MP3 player, the MyFi is about the size of a Walkman and can store several hours of content, giving users greater control over what they listen to and when. When introduced in late 2004, Sirius announced that its version of a portable player wouldn't be available for another year.

XM also developed a receiver that is compatible with a home stereo and a car stereo. The SkyFi Radio receiver costs $130 and plugs into a dock (which retails for about $70) that is attached to a car stereo. The receiver can be unplugged from the car and used in a portable "boom box" that costs an additional $100. Lagging behind XM, Sirius offered a similar product with fewer features and a higher price. XM may eventually lose its advantage in the receiver market, however, because the FCC has ordered the two companies to begin working on making their hardware compatible with one another's signals.

Consumers can purchase satellite-radio subscriptions and hardware at major electronics chains like Best Buy and Circuit City. However, there is another, far more important element of XM's and Sirius' distribution strategy: automakers. "It's nice you can walk into Circuit City and have them retrofit a receiver into your car, but what's really going to get them launched and where they need to be is the factory installation," commented Robert Taylor, the editor of *Inside Radio* magazine.

Again, XM accelerated past Sirius on this front by signing deals with several large automakers. General Motors, an early investor in XM, offered satellite radio as an option in 90% of its models by the end of 2004. Honda, Toyota, Hyundai, and Nissan also partnered with XM, as did the JetBlue and AirTran airlines and Hertz Car Rental. Sirius struck deals with DaimlerChrysler, BMW, Volkswagen, and Ford Motor. "The car is very important to radio because it's a big audience of captive listeners," explained one media analyst.

To entice drivers to consider its service, XM is providing real-time traffic reports in 20 major cities across the United States. "For the average commuter, there's no reason to have a navigation system because you travel the same routes," stated an industry analyst. "Once you add in traffic (information), it becomes much more valuable to them."

Most new cars that are equipped with satellite radio give the buyer a free trial subscription. When the trial period ends, 57% of the car owners purchase a subscription. By the end of 2004, satellite radio was available in almost 40% of 2005 models, and XM was generating one-half of its business through its automotive partners, compared to 25% for Sirius. As a result, Sirius had to spend more money on advertising and getting people into retail outlets to sign up for satellite service, resulting in a cost of $234 per new subscriber compared to $57 for XM.

"The industry can get to five million subscribers by developing the distribution channels," commented an industry consultant, "but to get to 20 or 30 million, you need something dramatically more."

Getting Sirius about Programming

Shortly after being launched, both XM and Sirius developed their own unique personalities. Sirius was pegged as more liberal because it featured several public radio channels; a channel programmed exclusively for the gay community; and Sirius Left, a liberal talk-show channel. (The company tried to appeal to all political persuasions, however, by offering Sirius Right, a talk-based channel aimed at conservatives.) By contrast, XM featured several conservative talk-show hosts, including Glenn Beck and Michael Reagan. However, XM was first to court devoted music listeners by offering several channels featuring knowledgeable disc jockeys with many years of experience in the music industry who could respond to live requests. (Both XM and Sirius also provide a plethora of channels with preprogrammed music.)

In late 2004, the first of a series of multimillion-dollar programming commitments was announced. Howard Stern decreed that he was moving his talk show from "terrestrial" (traditional) radio to join the Sirius lineup. Stern said the switch was prompted by his being fined repeatedly by the FCC for being indecent on the public airwaves (satellite radio is not regulated in this manner). Perhaps finances were also part of Stern's decision. According to its announcement, Sirius would pay Stern $100 million during a five-year contract to broadcast exclusively on its airwaves.

Sirius expects Stern to attract affluent, middle-aged listeners in order to justify his steep price tag. In a survey conducted by the Odyssey market research firm, 30% of Stern's listeners stated they were very likely to subscribe to Sirius in order to continue listening to the self-proclaimed "King of All Media." This proportion of potential buyers, combined with the fact that Stern's terrestrial show has 12 million regular listeners, represented hopeful news for Sirius.

XM has been offering the similarly controversial "Opie and Anthony Show" for quite some time, and charged its customers a premium to receive it. Similarly, XM subscribers pay an additional $2.99 per month for the Playboy channel.

A flood of new partnerships was announced following the Stern deal. In October 2004, XM paid

$650 million for the exclusive satellite rights to broadcast Major League Baseball for 11 years, starting in 2005. Sirius had already been carrying National Football League (NFL) games, and was outbid by XM for baseball. However, Sirius returned the favor when it wooed away the rights to broadcast NASCAR Racing from XM, beginning in 2007.

Sirius continued to woo big celebrities by inking deals with rappers Eminem and 50 Cent and the "domestic diva, Martha Stewart." Less than six weeks after its namesake was released from prison in early 2005, Martha Stewart Living (MSL) Omnimedia, announced it would develop a channel for Sirius that features advice regarding a variety of topics, including entertaining, cooking, wedding planning, and home décor. In return, MSL would receive $30 million from Sirius, plus advertising revenue. MSL's chief executive officer, Susan Lyne, stated, "Radio gives us an opportunity to interact (with our audience) on a very personal and immediate level." In return, Sirius' CEO, Mel Karmazin, said he hoped the new channel would contribute "both significant subscriber growth and substantial advertising revenue."

By early 2005, Sirius offered 65 channels of commercial-free music and 55 channels that feature news, sports, and talk formats, all of which have several minutes of advertising each hour. XM had 67 commercial-free music channels and 85 additional channels with ads.

Turning Up Subscription Volume

Within a few years of their inception, both companies had developed very distinct strategies for seeking subscribers. XM was trying to attract them with better technology and through new-car sales, and Sirius was tempting them with higher-profile content. "They (XM) today are the technology leaders," stated Sirius CEO Karmazin. "We are the content leader." XM's CEO, Hugh Panero, countered, "In pop culture, people come and people go."

When introduced, Sirius charged $12.95 per month, and XM offered its basic service for $9.95 per month, with an additional charge for several special channels. In early 2005, XM announced an increase to $12.95, a monthly price that included Opie and Anthony's show. (The Playboy channel still costs an additional $2.99 per month.)

Despite Sirius' push for content, XM continued to lead in number of subscribers. By March 2005, XM had 3.2 million subscribers compared to 1.24 million for Sirius. XM was also generating more revenue—$244 million in 2004 versus $67 million for Sirius. But both companies were losing large amounts—each was estimated to have lost approximately $600 million in 2004. Neither company is expected to be profitable until at least 2008. If they can stay in business that long, projections are that 40% of all American households will have satellite-radio service by 2010, bringing its total subscriber base to 32 million listeners.

Coping with Interference from Other Competition

Free, or "terrestrial," radio generates $20 billion in annual revenues in the U.S. It clearly is satellite radio's biggest competitor for now. It attracts 225 million listeners each day, compared to almost 4.5 million total satellite-radio subscribers. Besides being free, traditional radio has the benefit of being local (except for nationally syndicated programming).

According to Arbitron, 94% of Americans at least 12 years of age listen to traditional radio at least once a week. To stay profitable, radio stations have been increasing the number of commercials they broadcast up to 20 minutes per hour. This approach repels younger people who can listen to commercial-free music on MP3 players and share music files over the Internet. At this time, radio's audience is slowly tuning out. Teenagers spend 11% less time listening today compared to five years ago, and the amount of time young adults spend with an ear near a radio has decreased 8% during that same period. In response, Clear Channel, which owns 1,200 stations across the country, decreased the number of commercials allowed on its stations to 12 minutes per hour. To strike back at its satellite competition, the entire terrestrial radio industry launched a $28 million advertising campaign that proclaimed, "You hear it here first."

The traditional radio industry also began touting the benefits of HD Radio. This new technology provides unprecedented sound quality for local radio and also has storage and replay capabilities similar to those found in digital video recorders. Commenting on this development, a spokesman for the National Association of Broadcasters stated, "It's going to be a vastly improved listening experience." Clear Channel announced it would implement the new technology in 1,000 of its stations beginning in 2005. However, as of early 2005, the hardware to support HD Radio wasn't being made available in new cars, so very few people had access to it.

Satellite and terrestrial radio have other competitors. For instance, the Internet has made music available on cell phones, MP3 players, and computers. "I don't want to compete with iPods," commented Steve Blatter, who oversees music programming at Sirius.

"If we're just a jukebox, we're much more vulnerable." To counter this, both Sirius and XM have bolstered their staffs of disc jockeys and have added channels programmed by music industry experts with a built-in fan base. XM features shows produced by Quincy Jones, Tom Petty, and Snoop Dogg, while Sirius has handed one channel to Steven Van Zandt (Bruce Springsteen's guitarist) and another to an all-Elvis format.

The Internet has its own type of specialized programming, developed mostly by amateurs. Nicknamed "podcasters," these individuals develop their own "shows" and then "stream" (transmit) them over the Web. Listeners can download them onto MP3 players or computers, and listen to them at their convenience. Podcasters typically specialize in certain topics or areas of music. As of March 2005, there were approximately 3,500 podcasters. Some advertisers, such as Volvo, have even begun sponsoring podcasts.

"XM and Sirius know the Internet is coming like a freight train," said the editor of *Inside Radio*. "So satellite may look like transitional technology—it may look like the fax machine." Many industry experts believe wireless broadband will undoubtedly prove to be satellite radio's greatest threat. XM is countering with XM Radio Online, which is available to subscribers and allows them to listen to the service over the Internet. Sirius plans to sweeten its offering by providing mobile video programming as early as 2006, which could prove to be very attractive to its sports-fan subscribers who already listen to the National Basketball Association (NBA) and the National Football League (NFL) on Sirius satellite radio.

"What we increasingly have here is one big, bad digital soup" of programming, explained one industry analyst. XM and Sirius both offer 72-hour trial subscriptions with the hope that once consumers get a taste, they will want a steady diet of satellite radio.

Questions

1. Does satellite radio coincide with, or run counter to, major demographic, social, and cultural trends in the U.S.?

2. What consumer needs does satellite radio fill?

3. Which firm do you think has a differential advantage, and why?

www.sirius.com

www.xmradio.com

Sources

Case 1: Google

www.google.com, accessed on Oct. 5, 2004; Michael McCarthy, "Gadgets, Google Top Consumers' 2005 'Hot' Picks," *USA Today,* Dec. 28, 2004, p. 6B; Leslie Walker, "Microsoft's Search Falls Far Short of Google's," *The Washington Post,* Nov. 14, 2004, p. F.07; Nick Wingfield and Kevin J. Delaney, "Google Encroaches on Amazon as Rivalries Grow," *The Wall Street Journal,* Oct. 7, 2004, P. B3; Kevin J. Delaney, "Yahoo Answers Rivals with New Search Tools," *The Wall Street Journal,* Oct. 5, 2004, p. D9; Fred Vogelstein, "No Love Lost for Google," *Fortune,* Aug. 23, 2004, pp. 19–20; "How Google Works," *The Economist,* Sept. 18, 2004, p. 32; Gregory Zuckerman, "Google Shares Prove Big Winners," *The Wall Street Journal,* Aug. 20, 2004, p. C.1; Terence O'Hara, "Insiders Get Rich Through IPO," *The Washington Post,* Aug. 20, 2004, p. E.04.

Case 2: Sirius versus XM

"Martha Gets Sirius in Radio Deal," *CNN Money Online,* Apr. 18, 2005; Sarah McBride, "Two Upstarts Vie for Dominance in Satellite Radio," *The Wall Street Journal,* Mar. 30, 2005, pp. A1, A9; Gregory Lamb, "Not Your Father's Radio," *CBS News Online,* Mar. 19, 2005; Heather Green, Tom Lowry, and Catherine Yang, "The New Radio Revolution," *Business Week Online,* Mar. 3, 2005; Sarah McBride, "XM Raises Subscription Price, Matching Rival Sirius Satellite," *The Wall Street Journal,* Mar. 1, 2005, p. D4; Seth Sutel, "XM Raises Satellite Radio Prices," *USA Today Online,* Feb. 28, 2005; Kristi Swartz, "Satellite Radio's Growth Makes Some Wonder If It Will Become the Standard," *The Palm Beach Post,* Dec. 19, 2004, p. 1F; Tom Lowry, "Satellite Radio Shoots the Moon," *BusinessWeek,* Nov. 8, 2004, p. 52; John Helyar, "Radio's Stern Challenge," *Fortune,* Nov. 1, 2004, pp. 123–124+; Andy Pasztor and Stefan Fatsis, "XM Satellite Wins Baseball Deal," *The Wall Street Journal,* Oct. 20, 2004, p. B9; Andy Pasztor, "Stern's Move Could Aid Satellite-Radio Industry," *The Wall Street Journal,* Oct. 7, 2004, p. D8; David Welch, "Satellite Radio: Two for the Road," *BusinessWeek,* Nov. 24, 2003, pp. 144, 146; Adam Aston, "XM Radio: Now You Can Try It at Home," *BusinessWeek,* Jan. 27, 2003, p. 116.

Chapter 4

"A more recent development, Song Airlines, is based on the belief that the consumer market for air travel can be sliced even finer."

Consumer Markets and Buying Behavior

Is **Song** Playing the Right Tune?

Assume for a moment that you are planning a pleasure trip and there are at least two airlines that fly the desired route. How do you choose one? For some consumers the flight schedules or the airlines' on-time arrival histories might be the most important considerations. For others it could be the expected mix of fellow travelers (lots of little children?) or possibly the amenities (assigned seats, food and refreshments, entertainment?). And certainly there are some who would be most influenced by price. During the "golden" years of air travel, the established carriers such as United, American, and Delta (now commonly referred to as "legacy" airlines) all were profitable, but their offerings became increasingly similar. They focused on the business traveler, so pleasure travelers found little reason to prefer one over the others. However, the arrival of Southwest Airlines on the scene in the early 1970s, and its continued success over the years, has changed perceptions. Southwest proved an airline could serve pleasure travelers who place a very high priority on price, even at the expense of conveniences such as assigned seats. A more recent development, Song Airlines, is based on the belief that the consumer market for air travel can be sliced even finer.

Song was created by Delta as a lower-price alternative to the legacy airlines but with more amenities than the discount carriers such as Southwest, JetBlue, and Frontier. The target customer has been described as a "discount diva"—a woman, aged 35 to 54, who can afford to pay more for a ticket but is too savvy to do so. She prefers to seek out low airfares and spend the savings on a hotel upgrade or a massage at a spa. This woman goes online to do leisure travel research and is highly likely to be the one who makes her family's vacation choices.

To attract this consumer, the exterior of Song's Boeing 757s are white and lime green, and the seats are sky blue leather with two inches more leg room than a conventional 757. Features include a digital television at every seat, Internet access, 100 channels of XM Satellite Radio, streaming MP3 programming, Game Boys for kids, and numerous food choices (available for sale). Other features (also available for sale) are "sleep packs" with eye shades and ear plugs, and "exercise packs" with squeeze balls and rubber resistance bands.

By offering pleasure travelers more value through lower prices and distinctive features, Song hopes to "reglamorize" air travel. But there's more. As the first airline to specifically pursue the female head-of-the-household, Song is faced with the challenge of assembling a coordinated marketing program unlike any that has been designed in the past.[1]

Is Song's definition of the market innovative, or will it be grounded by a lack of interest?

www.flysong.com

The market, consisting of buyers and prospective buyers, is made up of consumers and businesses. In this chapter we examine consumer markets, and in Chapter 5 we will discuss business markets. To help you understand consumers, we will first describe their demographics and highlight changes that influence marketing to them. As Song's strategy suggests, these changes can profoundly impact performance. Then we will examine how consumers go about making purchase decisions, a process influenced by information, social environment, psychological forces, and situational factors.

After studying this chapter, you should be able to explain:

- The factors commonly used by marketers to describe consumer markets.
- Important consumer demographic changes.
- How consumers make purchase decisions.
- The information sources, psychological forces, social factors, and situational influences that affect consumers' decisions.

The Consumer Market

Ultimate consumers buy goods and services for their own personal or household use. In the U.S., there are over 290 million consumers, living in 111 million households. They spend over $7.3 trillion a year on goods and services. The efforts of many marketers are focused on these (or more likely a subset of these) potential customers.

The consumer market is not only large, it is dynamic. Consider that the U.S. is the fastest-growing industrialized nation, and that every hour there are 459 births, 279 deaths, 268 marriages, 135 divorces, and 121 new immigrants.[2] These statistics convert to a net change of over half a million people and 280,000 households a month in the mix of consumers. Thus, the first challenge is to gain an understanding of what this market looks like and how it is changing. To develop an appreciation of this dynamic consumer market, we will examine its geographic distribution, several demographic dimensions, and some representative behaviors.

Geographic Distribution

About 16% of the U.S. population moves to a different home every year. Marketing executives monitor current patterns and projected trends in the regional distribution of the population in order to make decisions that range from where to locate retail stores to the appropriate mix of products to offer. The largest population concentrations are in the eastern half of the country, as they always have been. However, the greatest rate of population growth over the past four decades has occurred in the Southern and Western regions. Figure 4.1 shows the states projected to grow at the fastest rates between 2000 and 2010. By the year 2010, the four most populous states will be California, Texas, New York, and Florida, in that order.

The Rural Population
Rural areas of the U.S. lost population to the cities for decades, but this trend seems to have reversed. In the 1990s nearly five times as many Americans took up residence in rural areas as in the 1980s. Rural areas, although they contain only about one-fourth the total population, are now growing at nearly the same rate as cities. There are several explanations for this development. One is the growth in employment opportunities on the outer edges of large urban areas. People can take advantage of these jobs while still living in the country. Another factor is the growing number of retirees who are leaving the cities for rural areas with smaller communities and slower-paced lifestyles.

Rather than view the increasing popularity of rural living as a temporary adjustment, some see it as a gradual deconcentration of the U.S. population. With the

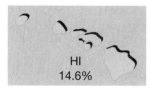

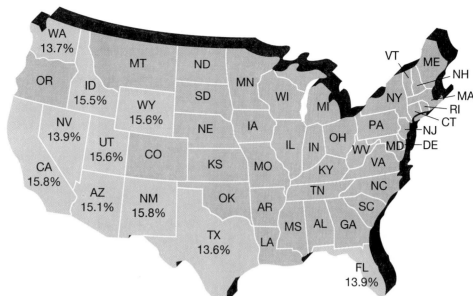

FIGURE 4.1

The Fastest Growing States in the United States.

The projected population increases between 2000 and 2010 for the 12 most rapidly growing states.

Source: *Statistical Abstract of the United States 2000,* 120th ed., U.S. Bureau of the Census, Washington, DC, 2000, p. 26.

continual growth in telecommuting (working from home), advances in communication technology, and the decline in factory jobs, the need for people to concentrate in small areas is greatly diminished. As a result, the population may be slowly moving toward a country of smaller, more widely dispersed cities and towns.

There is also a change in the mix of the rural population. In the past, young adults migrated from rural to urban areas, and the primary source of replacements was births. Now an important source of replacements for young adults leaving rural areas is older adults moving away from urban areas. Certainly these are developments to watch because changes in the size and mix of the rural population have many implications. For example, retailers such as Wal-Mart that depend on masses of customers must consider these population shifts as store locations and the assortment of merchandise are selected. On the other hand, catalog retailers and merchants using the Internet to reach customers are likely beneficiaries of this shift.

The Urban Population

About 75% of the U.S. population lives in large urban areas. Recognizing the importance of the urban population, the Census Bureau utilizes a three-part classification of metropolitan areas. Observing trends within these classifications provides marketers with a means of identifying growing and declining areas. The three categories are as follows:

- The **Metropolitan Statistical Area (MSA)** is the basic urban unit. An MSA has an urban area with at least 50,000 residents. The boundaries of an MSA are drawn along county lines and may cross state borders. But the counties must be socially and economically integrated, and virtually all employment must be nonagricultural. There are about 370 MSAs. Not suprisingly, almost all of the MSAs projected to grow the fastest are in the West and Southwest. Within MSAs that have at least 2.5 million residents, smaller economically and socially integrated groups of counties are designated *Metropolitan Divisions*. The eleven largest MSAs contain a total of 29 Metropolitan Divisions.

- A **Micropolitan Statistical Area** must have at least one urban cluster of at least 10,000 residents but less than 50,000. There are 565 of these micro areas.

- A **Combined Statistical Area (CSA)** consists of an adjacent metropolitan and micropolitan statistical area. There are 116 CSAs.

The Suburban Population

As metropolitan areas have grown, their composition has also changed. The central cities are growing very slowly, and in some cases older, established parts of the cities are actually losing population. In 1950, 60% of the people living in metropolitan areas lived in the central city. By 1990 that figure had been reversed, with over 65% of metropolitan residents living in the suburbs.

Most of the real growth in the last 25 years has occurred in the suburbs. As families moved to the suburbs to escape the congestion and turmoil in the cities, the economic, racial, and ethnic compositions of many cities (especially the core areas) changed. For example, 60% of African American households live in the central cities of large metro areas, but only 25% of African American households reside in the suburbs. More recently, the suburbs have expanded outward, creating "inner-ring" suburban communities that are more like the urban centers they encircle than the affluent suburbs. The changes in these areas have had several market implications.

First, suburbanites are more likely than city dwellers to have two cars because of the unavailability of mass transit. They also are inclined to spend more leisure time at home, so they are a big market for home entertainment and recreation.

Second, services providers typically locate close to their markets. That's why retail services firms such as banks, fast-food establishments, florists, and travel agents open branches or start new ventures in the suburbs. In addition, many investment and insurance brokers, realtors, physicians and dentists, and other professional service firms have left the central cities to pursue suburbanites.

The slow but steady migration of retailers to the suburbs created a void in many inner cities and led to the assumption that inner cities have little market potential. However, that view may be changing. The Initiative for a Competitive Inner City (ICIC) has identified several advantages inner-city locations offer businesses. Of particular interest to retailers are a ready supply of employees and underserved markets. For example, inner-city residents annually spend $85 billion, but more than 25% of that spending is done with retailers outside the inner city.[3]

Consumer Demographics

Demographics are the vital statistics that describe a population. Marketers make use of a variety of demographic characteristics including age, gender, family life cycle, education, income, and ethnicity. They are important to marketers because they are closely related to the demand for many products.

Changes in demographics signal the rise of new markets and the elimination of others. Some noteworthy demographic developments and their significance for marketers are described below.

Age

As was pointed out in Chapter 2, the U.S. population is getting older. This aging trend will continue. By 2010, there will be 23 million more consumers over the age of 50. The marketing implications are significant because this group will account for just 32% of the population, but half of all discretionary income and three-quarters of the total financial assets held by consumers. This age group spends more than younger consumers on health insurance, medical services, drugs, education (for

their children), housing, and home remodeling. Other areas likely to feel the impact are the apparel industry (older consumers buy less) and the travel industry (older consumers have the income and time to travel).

Family Life Cycle

Family life-cycle stages, the various forms

To help foster a healthy lifestyle, Fisher-Price's Baby Gymtastics line of toys is specifically designed to encourage babies to engage in more movement and physical play.

www.fisherprice.com

families can take over time, are major determinants of behavior. For example, a single-parent family (divorced, widowed, or never married) with dependent children faces social and economic challenges quite different from those of a two-parent family. Young married couples with no children typically devote large shares of their income to clothing, autos, and recreation. When children start arriving, expenditure patterns shift as many young families buy and furnish a home. Families with teenagers find larger portions of the budget going for food, clothing, and educational needs.

Researchers have identified nine distinct life-cycle stages with different buying behavior:[4]

- *Bachelor stage:* young, single people
- *Young married:* couples with no children
- *Full nest I:* young married couples with children
- *Single parents:* young or middle-aged people with dependent children
- *Divorced and alone:* divorced without dependent children
- *Middle-aged married:* middle-aged married couples without children
- *Full nest II:* middle-aged married couples with dependent children
- *Empty nest:* older married couples with no children living with them
- *Older single:* single people still working or retired

Just over 40% of adults or about 80 million people are unmarried. The living arrangements of these singles take several forms. Many live alone. For the first time the number of single-person households is greater than the number of traditional families—married couples with children. The impact that singles of either sex have on demand is demonstrated by the availability of apartments for singles; social clubs for singles; and resorts, cruises, and restaurants catering to singles. Other arrangements include single parents living with children, people living together as unmarried couples, or people sharing a house or apartment with one or more roommates.

In 2000, there were over 8 million single-parent households with children under 18, a number projected to increase to 9 million by 2010. Although they typically have less money to spend than traditional households, more purchase decisions and a greater proportion of actual purchases are made by the children in these families. As a result, advertisers that normally focus on adults are increasingly looking for ways to reach children.

The bottom line is marketers today think beyond the traditional stereotype of a household—a married couple with children—in developing marketing plans. There are two concerns in particular they must address. The first is the decision-making process in today's households. For example, it is not as apparent who are the primary decision makers and who may be the influencers. The second concern is the expected duration of the living arrangement. Young adults today are likely to have several more different household arrangements during their lives than their parents. As a result, they are likely to include the expected length of a living arrangement in the purchase decisions of durable goods such as appliances or furniture.

Education and Income   Education has a significant impact on income. A high school diploma is worth about $600,000 in additional income over a lifetime, and a college degree is worth $1.5 million. For families where both spouses work (that is, over half of all the couples in the U.S.), these earnings figures can be doubled. About 85% of Americans over 25 have completed high school, and 25% have at least a bachelor's degree. Combine these observations with the fact that 15 million Americans are enrolled in institutions of higher learning, an increase of 50% over just 25 years ago, and it suggests that the U.S. population is well educated and prosperous.

However, these figures don't represent the complete picture. In spite of the considerable increase in disposable income in the past 30 years, 35 million people (about

12.5% of the population) live below the government-defined poverty level. And the situation may get worse if high-paying, unionized manufacturing jobs for unskilled workers continue to be replaced by lower-paid, nonunion service jobs.

Knowing what is happening to incomes is important because spending patterns are influenced by a person's income level. Here are some findings from Department of Labor studies of consumer spending:[5]

- For all product categories, people in a given income bracket spend significantly more *total* dollars than those in lower brackets. However, the lower-income households devote a larger *percentage* of their total expenditures to some product categories, such as housing.

- In each successively higher-income group, the amount spent for food declines as a percentage of total expenditures.

- The percentage of total expenditures devoted to the total of housing, utilities, and home operation remains reasonably constant in the middle- and high-income brackets.

- The percentage of total expenditures for transportation, including the purchase of automobiles, tends to grow as incomes increase in low- and middle-income groups. The proportion levels off or drops a bit in higher-income brackets.

- In each successively higher-income group, a smaller percentage of total family expenditures goes for health care, but a higher percentage goes for insurance and pensions.

Race and Ethnicity   In many cities, the ethnic population is especially large. African Americans, Hispanics, and Asians constitute over 50% of the population in 25 of the nation's largest cities. These cities include Los Angeles, San Antonio, New Orleans, Miami, Atlanta, Baltimore, Washington, DC, Detroit, and Chicago. During the 1990s, ethnic minorities accounted for nearly 70% of total U.S. population growth, a trend that is expected to continue.

Segmenting markets based on ethnicity presents an interesting challenge. On one hand, a company must understand an ethnic group's buying behavior and motivation. Studies by the Bureau of Labor Statistics and private research firms show that there are some distinct differences among races. For example, on average, African American and white Americans differ in income, level of education, and the likelihood of living in urban or rural areas. And data from the 2000 population census indicate that the racial mix of most neighborhoods did not change during the 1990s. The average white person lives in a neighborhood that is 83% white. The average black person lives in a neighborhood that is 54% black.[6]

On the other hand, ethnic markets are not more homogeneous units than any other population segment consisting of 20 or 30 million people. This is reflected in the 2000 census in which, for the first time, respondents had the option of identifying themselves with more than one racial group. Given this opportunity, nearly 7 million people declared they were multiracial.[7] There is nearly as much diversity within every ethnic group as there is similarity. For example, the African American and Hispanic populations contain demographic subgroups based on income, occupation, geographic location, and life-cycle stage with differing tastes and purchase preferences. Thus, it would be a serious marketing error to be misled by aggregate figures and averages.

This broad overview of the consumer market is intended to suggest its vibrancy and diversity. It also indicates that there are many ways to describe consumers. A challenge faced by marketers, which we will discuss in detail in Chapter 6, is how to most effectively describe particular markets. But first, let's continue our examination of consumers with a look at their decision making.

Consumer Decision Making

Why is consumer marketing difficult? We've just described one reason: The mix of people in the market is constantly changing. Not only is it difficult to anticipate what marketing program will work, but what worked yesterday may not work today—or tomorrow. Another challenge is understanding how consumers make decisions. This is reflected in the chapter-opening case about Song Airlines. In recent years airlines have paid much greater attention to leisure flyers. Now Song has taken that further by recognizing the female household head as a major decision maker for family travel. However, recognition is not enough. Song, like all other marketers, must constantly improve its understanding of consumers and adapt its strategies accordingly.

Figure 4.2 brings all the dimensions of buying behavior together in a model that provides the structure for our discussion. The model features the buying-decision process and the four primary forces that influence each stage.

The Consumer Buying-Decision Process

To deal with the marketing environment and make purchases, consumers engage in a decision process. One way to look at that process is to view it as problem solving. When faced with a problem that can be resolved through a purchase ("I'm bored. How do I satisfy my need for entertainment?"), the consumer goes through a series of logical stages to arrive at a decision.

As shown in the center of Figure 4.2, the stages of the **consumer buying-decision process** are:

1. *Need recognition.* The consumer is moved to action by a need or desire.

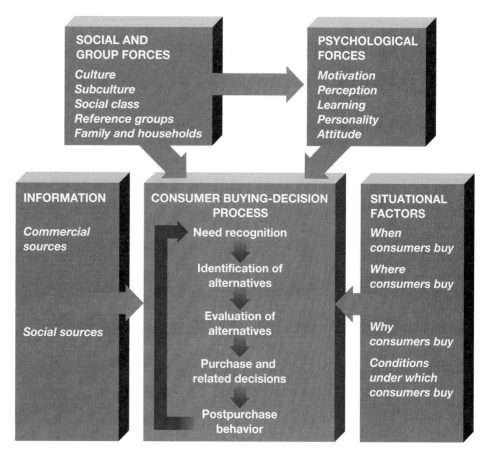

FIGURE 4.2

The Consumer Buying-Decision Process and the Factors Influencing It.

2. *Identification of alternatives.* The consumer identifies alternative products and brands and collects information about them.

3. *Evaluation of alternatives.* The consumer weighs the pros and cons of the alternatives identified.

4. *Decisions.* The consumer decides to buy or not to buy and makes other decisions related to the purchase.

5. *Postpurchase behavior.* The consumer seeks reassurance that the choice made was the correct one.

Although this model is a useful starting point for examining purchase decisions, the process is not always as straightforward as it may appear. Consider these possible variations:

- The consumer can withdraw at any stage prior to the actual purchase if the need diminishes or no satisfactory alternatives are available.
- The stages usually are of different lengths, may overlap, and some may even be skipped.
- The consumer is often involved in several different buying decisions simultaneously, and the outcome of one can affect the others.

A significant factor influencing how consumer decisions are made is the consumer's **level of involvement,** reflected in the amount of effort that is expended in satisfying a need. Some situations are *high* involvement. That is, when a need arises a consumer decides to actively collect and evaluate information about the purchase situation. These purchases entail all five stages of the buying-decision process.

Although it is risky to generalize because consumers are so different, involvement tends to be *greater* under any of the following conditions:

- The consumer lacks information about alternatives for satisfying the need.
- The consumer considers the amount of money involved to be large.
- The product has considerable social importance.
- The product is seen as having a potential for providing significant benefits.

Most buying decisions are for relatively low-priced products that have close, acceptable substitutes and therefore do not meet any of these conditions. These are *low*-involvement situations, in which the consumer either skips or moves very quickly through stages 2 and 3 of the decision process—identification of alternatives and evaluation of alternatives. Typical examples of low-involvement situations are the majority of purchases made in supermarkets, variety stores, and hardware stores.

The notion of involvement raises two important marketing issues: loyalty and impulse purchases. **Loyalty** exists when a consumer, because of past experience, is sufficiently satisfied with a particular brand or retailer that he or she buys that brand or from that retailer when the need arises without considering other alternatives. This is low-involvement purchasing because the decision does not involve gathering and analyzing information. However, the product may be very important to the consumer.

Impulse buying, or purchasing with little or no advance planning, is also a form of low-involvement decision making. A shopper waiting in the checkout line at a grocery store who notices the headline "Plane Missing since 1939 Lands at LaGuardia" on an issue of *Weekly World News* and purchases a copy to satisfy his or her curiosity is engaging in impulse buying. Self-service, open-display retailing has conditioned shoppers to do more impulse buying. Marketing researchers have found that an increasingly large proportion of purchases are unplanned. Consider, for example, how many of your purchases are unplanned (or impulsive). Because of the growth of this type of low-involvement purchasing, retailers must place greater emphasis on promotional programs such as in-store signage and videos demonstrating product

How important are the conditions faced by consumers in determining their behavior?

Procter & Gamble (P&G) invested 4 years and $10 million developing a water-purifying product suitable for Third World consumers. The product, called Pur, comes in small packets for household use. It can transform 2.5 gallons of contaminated water into drinkable water in 20 minutes. Many, including P&G's top management, consider it revolutionary. However, the company has been unable to make the product commercially successful. Why? Consumers have to carefully follow directions regarding the proper amount of water to use and the 20-minute waiting period in order for the powder to work. Second, it is priced at 10 cents a packet. A villager in the Sri Lanka tsumani region without clean water said he wouldn't pay more than the equivalent of one-half of one cent per packet. P&G has donated millions of packets to relief agencies in disaster areas, but it still hopes the product can eventually cover its costs. What is the lesson to be learned here? Regardless of how well a product meets a need, marketers must also consider the circumstances of the buyer.

Sources: Sarah Ellison and Eric Bellman, "Clean Water, No Profit," *The Wall Street Journal,* Feb. 23, 2005, p. B1+; Rick Carter, "For Tsumani Survivors and the World," *Industrial Maintenance & Plant Operation,* February 2005, p. 4.

benefits. They must also make displays and packages appealing, because they serve as silent sales people.

In the following discussion we examine the complete five-stage process that characterizes high-involvement buying decisions. However, keep in mind that the stages may have to be adjusted to fit the circumstances of a particular purchase situation. For a wealthy person, the purchase of a country club membership could be a low-involvement experience, whereas for a person with a high need for social acceptance, purchasing toothpaste might be highly involved. Thus involvement must be viewed from the perspective of the consumer, not the product.

Recognition of an Unsatisfied Need

Everyone has unsatisfied needs and wants that create discomfort. Some needs can be satisfied by acquiring and consuming goods and services. Thus the process of deciding what to buy begins when a need that can be satisfied through consumption becomes strong enough to motivate a person. This need recognition may arise internally (for example, when you are bored). Or the need may be dormant until it is aroused by an external stimulus, such as an ad or the sight of a product. The decision process can also be triggered by the depletion of an existing product (your pen runs out of ink) or dissatisfaction with a product currently being used.

Becoming aware of a need, however, is not enough to generate a purchase. As consumers we have many needs and wants, but finite amounts of time and money. Thus there is competition among our needs.

Identification of Alternatives

Once a need has been recognized, the consumer must next identify the alternatives capable of satisfying the need. Typically alternative products are identified first, and then alternative brands are identified. Product and brand identification may range from a simple memory scan of previous experiences to an extensive external search.

The search for alternatives is influenced by:

- How much information the consumer already has from past experiences and other sources.

- The consumer's confidence in that information.

- The expected value of additional information or, put another way, what more information is perceived to be worth in terms of the time and money required to get it.

Evaluation of Alternatives

When a satisfactory number of alternatives have been identified, the consumer must evaluate them before making a decision. The evaluation may involve a single criterion, or several criteria, against which the alternatives are compared. For example, you might select a frozen dinner on price alone or on price, taste, and ease of preparation. When multiple criteria are involved, they typically do not carry equal weight. For example, preparation time might be more important than price for a frozen dinner.

Because experience is often limited or dated and information from sources such as advertising or friends can be biased, evaluations can be factually incorrect. That is, a consumer may believe that the price of brand A is higher than that of brand B, when in fact the opposite is true. Marketers monitor consumers to determine what choice criteria they use, to identify any changes that may be taking place in their criteria or priorities, and to correct any unfavorable misperceptions.

Purchase and Related Decisions

After searching and evaluating, the consumer must decide whether to buy. Thus the first outcome is the decision to purchase or not to purchase the alternative evaluated as most desirable. If the decision is to buy, a series of related decisions must be made regarding product features, where and when to make the actual transaction, how to take delivery or possession, the method of payment, and other issues. So the decision to make a purchase is really the beginning of an entirely new series of decisions that may be as time-consuming and difficult as the initial one.

Alert marketers recognize that the outcome of these additional decisions affects satisfaction, so they find ways to help consumers make them as efficiently as possible. For example, car dealers have speeded up loan approval, streamlined the process of tracking down a car that meets the buyer's exact specifications, and, in the case of Saturn, made delivery of the car a "miniceremony" to make the customer feel important.

Selecting a source from which to make a purchase is one of the buying decisions. Sources can be as varied as Internet websites or manufacturers' outlets. The most common source is a retail store, and the reasons a consumer chooses to shop at a particular store are called **patronage buying motives.**

People want to feel comfortable when they shop. They want the assurance of being around people like themselves and in an environment that reflects their values. There are consumers, for example, who would feel uncomfortable shopping in an upscale store such as Saks Fifth Avenue or Neiman Marcus.

Patronage motives can range from something as simple as how easy an item is to find, to something more intangible and complex, such as the atmosphere of a restaurant. Some common patronage motives are:

- Location convenience
- Service speed
- Merchandise accessibility
- Crowding
- Prices

- Merchandise assortment
- Services offered
- Store appearance
- Sales personnel
- Mix of other shoppers

Like the criteria consumers use to choose products and brands, their patronage motives will vary depending on the purchase situation. Successful retailers evaluate their customers carefully and design their stores accordingly. For example, some shoppers might be surprised to learn that such different apparel outlets as The Gap, Old Navy, and Banana Republic are part of The Gap, Inc. A manufacturer, in turn, selects retailers with the patronage characteristics that complement its product and appeal to its market.

Firms selling on the Internet must also identify and appeal to patronage motives. For example, one of the features attributed to Internet shopping is convenience. Thus it's essential that a firm's website be easy to access and navigate. Fancy, animated graphics may be pretty, but they may not be what Internet shoppers are seeking.

Postpurchase Behavior
What a consumer learns from going through the buying process has an influence on how he or she will behave the next time the same need arises. Furthermore, the consumer has formed new opinions and beliefs and revised old ones. It's this change in the consumer that is indicated by an arrow in Figure 4.2 from the *postpurchase behavior* stage of the buying-decision process model back to the need-recognition stage.

Something else often occurs following a purchase. Have you ever gone through a careful decision process for a major purchase, selected what you thought was the best alternative, but then had doubts about your choice after the purchase? What you were experiencing is **postpurchase cognitive dissonance**—a state of anxiety brought on by the difficulty of choosing from among desirable alternatives. Unfortunately for marketers, dissonance is quite common, and if the anxiety is not relieved, the consumer may be unhappy with the chosen product even if it performs as expected!

Postpurchase cognitive dissonance occurs when each of the alternatives seriously considered by the consumer has both attractive and unattractive features. For example, in purchasing a portable music player, the one selected may be the most expensive (unattractive), but it may provide the best sound system (attractive). The brand not chosen was recommended by a friend (attractive), but it came with a very limited warranty (unattractive). After the purchase is made, the unattractive features of the product purchased grow in importance in the consumer's mind, as do the attractive features offered by the rejected alternatives. As a result, the buyer begins to doubt the wisdom of the choice and experiences anxiety over the decision. Internet shoppers may be especially prone to dissonance because they are unable to physically examine or test the product and must wait for some time after the purchase before taking possession of the product. Dissonance typically increases based on (1) the greater the importance of the purchase decision and (2) the greater the similarity between the item selected and item(s) rejected. Thus buying a house or car is likely to create more dissonance than buying a set of tires.

www.botspot.com

Consumers try to reduce their postpurchase anxieties. They avoid information (such as ads for the rejected products) that is likely to increase the dissonance. And they seek out information that supports their decision, such as reassurance from friends. For Internet shoppers, the use of electronic shopping agents, known as bots, to compare prices and find the best deals may reduce postpurchase dissonance. Also, prior to the purchase, putting more effort into evaluating alternatives can increase a consumer's confidence and reduce dissonance. Sellers can reduce the likelihood of dissonance with guarantees and liberal return policies, high-quality postsale service programs, and reassuring communications after the purchase.

With this background on the buying-decision process, we can examine what influences buying behavior. We'll begin with the sources and types of information used by consumers.

Information and Purchase Decisions

Purchase decisions require information. Until consumers know what products and brands are available, what features and benefits they offer, who sells them at what prices, and where they can be purchased, the decision process leading to a purchase can't be completed.

As shown in Figure 4.2, there are two sources of buying information—the commercial environment and the social environment. The **commercial information environment** consists of all marketing organizations and individuals that attempt to communicate with consumers. It includes manufacturers, retailers, advertisers, and sales people whenever any of them are engaged in efforts to inform or persuade.

Wal-Mart has its own TV network broadcasting into 2,600 of its stores and reaching 133 million consumers over a four-week period, or about one-third of the customers who visit the stores. According to research by A. C. Nielsen, the recall of brands advertised on Wal-Mart TV is almost three-times greater than brands advertised on in-home television. Advertisers are charged $50,000 to $300,000 per four-week period for 10-second spots, depending on how often the ad appears.

Advertising is the most familiar type of commercial information. In the U.S., $265 billion is spent every year on advertising of all types. It's estimated that on average, the typical adult is exposed to about 300 ad messages a day, or almost 10,000 per month.[8] Other commercial sources include retail store clerks, business websites, and telephone solicitors as well as consumers' physical involvement with products, such as trial product use and sampling.

The **social information environment** is comprised of family, friends, and acquaintances who directly or indirectly provide information about products. To appreciate the marketing significance of these social sources, consider how often your conversations with friends or family deal with purchases you are considering or have made.

The most common kind of social information is word-of-mouth communication—two or more people discussing a product. "Chat rooms" on the Internet have become popular places for consumers with similar interests to gather and exchange information. Other social sources include observing others using products and exposure to products in the homes of others. Recognizing the power of word-of-mouth communication, marketers actively stimulate it. For example, Ford identified trendsetters in several markets and gave them each a new Ford Focus subcompact to drive for six months. Their only duty was to give away a Ford-themed trinket to anyone showing an interest in the car. Similar tactics, aimed at getting consumers to talk about products, have been employed by the marketers of Vespa Scooters, Lee Jeans, and the Harry Potter book series.[9]

When all the different types of information are considered, it becomes apparent that there is enormous competition for the consumer's attention. Consequently, the consumer's mind has to be marvelously efficient to sort and process this barrage of information. To better understand consumer behavior, we will begin by examining the social and group forces that influence the individual's psychological makeup and also play a role in specific buying decisions.

Social Influences

The ways we think, believe, and act are determined to a great extent by social forces. And our movement through the buying decision process—including the needs we experience, the alternatives we consider, and the ways in which we evaluate them—are affected by the social forces that surround us. To reflect this dual impact, the arrows in Figure 4.2 extend from the social forces in two directions—to the psychological makeup of the individual and to the buying-decision process. Our description begins with culture, the force with the most *general* impact, and moves to the force with the most *specific* impact, the household.

Culture   As the broadest social influence, **culture** is a set of symbols and artifacts created by a society and handed down from generation to generation as determinants and regulators of human behavior. The symbols may be intangible (attitudes, beliefs, values, language) or tangible (tools, housing, products, works of art). Although culture does not include instinctive biological acts, the way people perform instinctive acts such as eating is culturally influenced. Thus, everybody gets hungry, but what, when, and how people eat vary among cultures. For example, in the Ukraine, raw pig fat is considered a delicacy.

Cultures do change over time as old patterns gradually give way to the new. During recent years in the U.S., cultural trends of far-reaching magnitude have occurred. Marketing executives must be alert to these changes so they can adjust their planning to be in step with, or even a little ahead of, the times. Some cultural trends affecting the buying behavior of U.S. consumers in recent years include the following:

- *Time has become as valuable as money.* Americans feel overcommitted, with more obligations and demands on their time than they can fulfill. This has contributed to the popularity of multitasking, the growth in time-saving services (such as home cleaning services and Internet shopping), and labor-saving products (such as prepared entrées in grocery store delis).

- *Two-income families are the norm.* When both adults in a household work outside the home, it affects not only the ability to buy but also the choice of products and the time available to buy and consume them. It has also created a demand for preschools and day-care centers.

- *Gender roles are losing their identity.* This is reflected in educational opportunities, occupations, clothing styles, sports participation, and language.

- *Youthfulness is admired.* To be thought of as younger than your chronological age (once you're over 21!) is seen by most as a compliment. To retain the vigor and healthy appearance generally associated with youth, more Americans have made exercise a regular part of their lives.

Subcultures   In any society as heterogeneous as the U.S., there are bound to be subcultures. **Subcultures** are groups in a culture that exhibit characteristic behavior patterns sufficient to distinguish them from other groups within the same culture. The behavior patterns that distinguish subcultures are based on factors such as race, nationality, religion, and urban–rural identification. Some of these were discussed earlier in the chapter in the context of demographic market forces.

A subculture takes on importance in marketing if it constitutes a significant part of the population and specific purchasing patterns can be traced to it. For example, increasing attention is being paid in the U.S. to behavioral influences stemming from racial and ethnic subcultures. Early immigrants came to America primarily from Europe. Now the principal sources are Asia and Latin America. West Coast cities have had large Chinese and Japanese populations for over a century. The new wave of Asian immigrants, however, includes people from Korea, Vietnam, and Thailand. The U.S. Census Bureau has observed that over 40 separate languages are spoken by substantial segments of the Los Angeles area population. These new subcultures bring with them different beliefs, customs, and values, not to mention languages, that must be taken into consideration by firms attempting to sell to them.

Social Class   **Social class** is a ranking within a society determined by the members of the society. Social classes exist in virtually all societies, and people's buying behavior is often strongly influenced by the class to which they belong or to which they aspire.

Without making value judgments about whether one class is superior to or happier than another, sociologists have attempted to describe class structure in a meaningful way. One scheme useful to marketing managers is the five-class model developed by Coleman and Rainwater,[10] classifying people by education, occupation, and type of residential neighborhood.

Notice that income is not one of the classification factors. Social class is not an indication of spending capability; rather, it is an indication of preferences and lifestyle. For example, a young lawyer might make the same income as a middle-aged electrician, but they probably have quite different family backgrounds, tastes, and attitudes. Although social mobility, the ability to move up from one class to another, is generally assumed to exist in the U.S., recent evidence suggests movement is difficult.[11]

In the summary of the five classes in U.S. society that follows, the emphasis is on how each behaves as consumers. The population percentages are only approximations and may vary from one geographic area to another.

- The *upper class*, about 2% of the population, includes two groups: (1) socially prominent "old families," often with inherited wealth, and (2) major corporate executives, owners of large businesses, and professionals. They live in exclusive neighborhoods and patronize fancy shops. They buy expensive goods and services, but they do not conspicuously display their wealth.

- The *upper-middle class*, about 12% of the population, is composed of moderately successful business and professional people and owners of medium-sized companies. They are well educated, have a strong desire for success, and push their children to do well. Their purchases are more conspicuous than those of the upper class. They live well, belong to private clubs, and support the arts and various social causes.

- The *lower-middle class*, about 32% of the population, consists of office workers, most sales people, teachers, technicians, and small business owners. As a group they are often referred to as white-collar workers. They strive for respectability and buy what is popular. Their homes are well cared for, and they save money to send their children to college. They are future oriented, strive to move up to the higher social classes, have self-confidence, and are willing to take risks to get ahead.

- The *upper-lower class*, about 38% of the population, is the blue-collar working class of production workers, semiskilled workers, and service personnel. These people are tied closely to family for economic and emotional support. Male-female roles are quite clearly defined. They live in smaller houses than the lower-middle class, drive larger cars, have more appliances, and watch bigger television sets. They buy American products and stay close to home on vacations. Their orientation is short term, and they are very concerned about security.

- The *lower-lower class,* about 16% of the population, is composed of unskilled workers, the chronically unemployed, unassimilated immigrants, and people frequently on welfare. They are typically poorly educated, have low incomes, and live in substandard houses and neighborhoods. They tend not to have many opportunities; hence they focus on the present. Often their purchases are not based on economic considerations. The public tends to differentiate within this class between the "working poor" and the "welfare poor."

Marketers recognize that there are substantial differences among classes with respect to buying behavior. Because of this diversity, different social classes are likely to respond differently to a seller's marketing program. Thus, it may be necessary to design marketing programs tailored to specific social classes.

Reference Groups   Each group in a society develops its own standards of behavior that then serve as guides, or frames of reference, for the members. Families and a circle of friends are such groups. Members share values and are expected to conform to the group's behavioral patterns. But a person does not have to be a member of a group to be influenced by it. There are groups we aspire to join (a campus honor society or club) and groups we admire even though membership may be impossible (a professional athletic team).[12] All of these are potential **reference groups**—groups of people who influence a person's attitudes, values, and behavior.

Studies have shown that personal advice in face-to-face groups is much more effective as a behavioral determinant than advertising. That is, in selecting products or changing brands, we are more likely to be influenced by word-of-mouth information from members of our reference groups than by ads or sales people. This is especially true when the information comes from someone we consider knowledgeable about the product and/or whom we trust. A research firm that tracks consumer trends reports that 83% of consumers considering a purchase ask for information from someone they know already owns the product.[13]

Advertisers are relying on reference-group influence when they use celebrity spokespersons. Professional athletes, musicians, actors, and others in the public eye can influence people who would like to be associated with them in some way. For example, Phil Mickelson for Callaway golf, Enrique Iglesias for Tommy Hilfiger fragrances, Miss Piggy for Pizza Hut, and deejay Aston Taylor, Jr. (better known as Funkmaster Flex) for Ford, suggest the range of targets and products.[14]

Reference-group influence in marketing is not limited to well-known personalities. Any group whose qualities a person admires can serve as a reference. For example, the physically fit, the socially conscious, and company employees have all served as reference groups in advertising.

Celebrities, in this case basketball player LeBron James, can be effective reference group influencers. Before securing the services of a celebrity, a marketer should ask two questions: Is the person a referent for the target audience, and Is the person's association with the product believable. James also appears in ads for athletic wear, basketball shoes, and Sprite. Is he the right endorser for Bubblicious gum?

www.bubblicious.com

Families and Households   A **family** is a group of two or more people related by blood, marriage, or adoption living together in a household. During their lives many people will belong to at least two families—the one into which they are born and the one they form at marriage. The birth family primarily determines core values and attitudes. The marriage family, in contrast, has a more direct influence on specific purchases. For example, family size is important in the purchase of a car.

A household is a broader concept that relates to a dwelling rather than a relationship. A **household** consists of a single person, a family, or any group of unrelated persons who occupy a housing unit. Thus an unmarried homeowner, college students sharing an off-campus apartment, and cohabiting couples are examples of households.

Average *nonfamily* household size in 2003 was 1.24 members, whereas average family size was 3.19 persons. Average household size has remained about 2.6 since 1990, but family size has been trending downward for years. This is due to more single-parent families, childless married couples, and unmarried people living together.

Sensitivity to household and family structure is important in designing marketing strategy. It affects such dimensions as product size (How large should refrigerators be?) and the design of advertising (Who might not relate to the depiction of a "traditional" family in a TV ad?).

In addition to the impact household structure has on the purchase behavior of members, it is also interesting to consider the buying behavior of the household as a unit. Marketers should treat this issue as four separate questions, because each may call for different strategies:

- Who influences the buying decision?
- Who makes the buying decision?
- Who makes the actual purchase?
- Who uses the product?

Different household members may assume these various roles, or one individual may play several roles in a particular purchase. For example, children aged 4 to 12 influence over $670 billion in family purchases and actually spend $35 billion a year of their own money.[15] There have also been changes in who does the shopping. In families, for many years the female household head did most of the day-to-day buying. However, as was described earlier, this behavior has changed as more women have entered the work force, and men and children have assumed greater household responsibility.

Psychological Factors

In discussing the psychological influences on consumer behavior, we will continue to use the model in Figure 4.2. Recall the process begins with one or more motives within a person activating goal-oriented behavior. One such behavior is perception; that is, the collection and processing of information. Other important psychological activities that play a role in buying decisions are learning, attitude formation, personality, and self-concept.

Motivation—the Starting Point

To understand why consumers behave as they do, we must first ask why a person acts at all. The answer is, "Because he or she experiences a need." All behavior starts with a need. Security, social acceptance, and prestige are examples of needs. A need must be aroused or stimulated before it becomes a motive. Thus, a **motive** is a need sufficiently stimulated to move an individual to seek satisfaction.

We have many dormant needs that do not produce behavior because they are not sufficiently intense. Hunger strong enough to impel us to search for food and fear great enough to motivate a search for security are examples of aroused needs that become motives for behavior.

The broadest classification of motives is based on the source from which a need arises:

- Needs aroused from physiological states of tension (such as the need for sleep).
- Needs aroused from psychological states of tension (such as the needs for affection and self-respect).

A refinement of this concept was formulated by the psychologist Abraham Maslow. He identified a hierarchy of five need levels, arrayed in the order in which people seek to gratify them.[16] **Maslow's needs hierarchy** is shown in Figure 4.3.

FIGURE 4.3

SELF-ACTUALIZATION
Needs for self-fulfillment

ESTEEM
Needs for self-respect,
reputation, prestige, and status

BELONGING AND LOVE
Needs for affection, belonging
to a group, and acceptance

SAFETY
Needs for security, protection, and order

PHYSIOLOGICAL
Needs for food, drink, sex, and shelter

Maslow recognized that a normal person is most likely to be working toward need satisfaction on several levels at the same time, and that rarely are all needs on a given level fully satisfied. However, the hierarchy indicates that the majority of needs on a particular level must be reasonably well satisfied before a person is motivated at the next higher level.

For marketers attempting to design appealing products, persuasive ad messages, inviting retail store layouts, and the like, Maslow's five levels may be too general. Fortunately, there are continuing efforts to describe motives more specifically. For example, one model suggests that all behavior is determined by 15 fundamental motives, and individual differences are the result of varying priorities and intensities among these motives.[17] The 15 motives are:

• Curiosity	• Food	• Honor
• Rejection	• Sex	• Physical exercise
• Order	• Independence	• Power
• Citizenship	• Pain avoidance	• Prestige
• Family	• Social contact	• Vengeance

Identifying the motive(s) for a particular action can range from simple to impossible. To illustrate, buying motives may be grouped on three different levels depending on consumers' awareness of them and their willingness to divulge them. At one level, buyers recognize, and are quite willing to talk about, their motives for buying most common, everyday products. At a second level, they are aware of their reasons for buying but will not admit them to others. For example, some people probably buy luxury cars to impress others. But when questioned about their motives, they may offer other reasons that they think will be more socially appropriate. The most difficult motives to uncover are those at the third level, where even the buyers cannot explain the factors motivating their buying actions. These are called unconscious or subconscious motives, and we will have more to say about them when we discuss personality.

To further complicate our understanding, a purchase is often the result of multiple motives. Moreover, various motives may conflict with one another. In buying a new suit, a young man may want to (1) feel comfortable, (2) please his girlfriend, and (3) spend as little as possible. Accomplishing all three objectives in one purchase may be truly difficult! Finally, a particular motive may produce different behavior at different times.

Despite the challenges, significant advances have been made in understanding buyer's needs. Some of the methods for gaining insights into motives will be described in Chapter 7 in the discussion of marketing research. However, because marketers are unable to precisely describe the needs operating in many purchase situations, more work needs to be done to identify consumption-specific motives and measure their strengths.

Perception In many purchase situations, a person gathers information before making a choice. **Perception** is the process of receiving, organizing, and assigning meaning to information or stimuli detected by our five senses. It is in this way that we interpret or understand the world around us. Perception plays a major role in the stage of the buying-decision process where alternatives are identified.

What we perceive—the meaning we give something sensed—depends on the object and our experiences. In an instant the mind is capable of receiving information, comparing it to a huge store of images in memory, and providing an interpretation. Consumers make use of all five senses. Scents, for example, are powerful behavior triggers. Who can resist the aroma of popcorn in a theater or of fresh cookies in a supermarket bakery?

Every day we come in contact with an enormous number of marketing stimuli. However, with the aid of **selective perception** techniques we are able to deal with the commercial environment.

- We pay attention by exception. That is, of all the marketing stimuli our senses are exposed to, only those with the power to capture and hold our attention have the potential of being perceived. Using a somewhat insensitive analogy, an ad executive compared consumers to roaches—"you spray them and spray them and they get immune after a while."[18] This phenomenon is called *selective attention.*

- As part of perception, new information is compared with a person's existing store of knowledge, or frame of reference. If an inconsistency is discovered, the new information will likely be distorted to conform to the established beliefs. Despite the fact that most authorities claim people are not saving enough for retirement, many consumers continue to spend all or most of their discretionary income. Why? One reason is because the advice is inconsistent with the way these consumers want to live now, so they distort the incoming information. For example, they may decide the authorities are simply being too conservative even though there is no evidence to support such a conclusion. This is called *selective distortion.*

- We retain only part of what we have selectively perceived. For example, nearly 80% of Americans cannot remember a typical TV commercial one day after seeing it. This is known as *selective retention.*

There are many communication implications in this selectivity process. For example, to grasp and hold attention, an ad must be involving enough to stimulate the consumer to seek more information. If the ad is too familiar, it will be ignored. On the other hand, if it is too complex, the ad will be judged not worth the time and effort to figure out. Thus, the goal is a mildly ambiguous first impression that heightens the consumer's interest.

Selective distortion tells us that marketers cannot assume a message, even if it is factually correct, will necessarily be accepted as fact by consumers. In designing a message, marketers must consider the distance between the audience's

People perceive selectively, and a key part of the selectivity process is the ability of a stimulus to gain attention. An advertisement for a familiar product such as M&M candy by itself would probably be ignored. So Masterfoods USA, maker of M&Ms teams up with popular movies such as *Shrek 2* and, in this case *Star Wars,* in hopes of breaking through the perceptual selectivity barrier.

www.mms.com

If sheer volume is the measuring stick, as recently as 2003, pop-ups were the preferred method of Internet advertising. According to Nielsen Research, they had a click-through rate more than 10 times better than their predecessor, banner ads. But in 2004 pop-up ads on the Internet declined by 65% from 2003. Why? Their effectiveness dropped off partly due to overuse, which caused consumers to view them as annoying rather than novel. Also, to protect subscribers, many Internet providers installed pop-up blockers. What will replace pop-ups? Our analysis of consumer behavior suggests it should be a communication that overcomes selective perception. That means something novel in order to be noticed and something of interest to the consumer so the message will be processed and retained. Some advertisers think 10- or 15-second videos may be the answer. However, if they are not directed to well-defined, target audiences they are likely to quickly go the way of banner ads and pop-ups.

Sources: Diane Anderson, "Pop-Up Ads Are No Longer as Popular with Marketers," *Brandweek,* Jan. 31, 2005, p. 13; Catherine Arnold, "Crackdown on Pop-Ups," *Marketing News,* Dec. 15, 2004, p. 13.

current belief and the position proposed by the message. If the distance is large, a moderate claim may be more believable than a dramatic claim, and therefore more effective in moving consumers in the desired direction.

Even messages received undistorted are subject to selective retention. Consequently, ads are repeated many times. The hope is that numerous exposures will etch the message into the recipient's memory. This aim partially explains why a firm with very familiar products, such as Wrigley's, spends over $400 million a year worldwide advertising candy and chewing gum.

Learning

Learning involves changes in behavior resulting from observation and experience. It excludes behavior that is attributable to instinct such as breathing or temporary states such as hunger or fatigue. Interpreting and predicting consumer learning enhances our understanding of buying behavior, because learning plays a role at every stage of the buying-decision process.

There is no universally accepted learning theory. However, one with direct application to marketing strategy is stimulus-response. According to **stimulus-response theory,** learning occurs as a person (1) responds to some stimulus by behaving in a particular way and (2) is rewarded for a correct response or penalized for an incorrect one. When the same correct response is repeated in reaction to the same stimulus, a behavior pattern, or learning, is established.

From a marketer's perspective, learning can be desirable or undesirable. As examples of desirable learning, marketers have "taught" consumers to respond to certain cues, such as:

- End-of-aisle displays in supermarkets suggest that the displayed item is on sale.
- "Sale" signs in store windows suggest that bargains can be found inside.
- Large type in newspaper grocery ads suggests that the item is a particularly good bargain.

Once a behavior pattern has been established it becomes a habit and replaces conscious, willful behavior. In terms of the purchase-decision process, this means when a habit is established the consumer skips several of the steps in the buying process, and usually goes directly from the recognized need to the purchase.

What will it take to overcome previously learned beliefs about automobile quality?

By their own admission, U.S. automakers have contributed to some undesirable consumer learning. Forty years ago three auto manufacturers—General Motors, Ford, and Chrysler (now DaimlerChrysler)—accounted for the bulk of U.S. car sales. Their quality slipped badly in the 1970s, which alienated many baby boomers who were buying their first new cars at that time. According to a Ford researcher describing that period, "We taught them that we build junk (and) the lessons learned in the 1970s will stay with baby boomers the rest of their lives." Despite substantial quality improvements in subsequent years, the Big Three automakers have had a difficult time overcoming this early learning and its generalization to their later products. However, they continue to make large investments in both "hard" quality improvements—making sure things don't break or fail—and "perceived" quality improvements—making sure things consumers can see, such as the quality of interior materials and the way parts fit together, look and feel right, because both are critical to overcoming the undesirable learning that has taken place. In addition, their advertising stresses product quality. Recently, for the first time in over 25 years, a credible independent source, *Consumer Reports,* rated U.S. cars and trucks as slightly better than competing European brands. Will that be enough to overcome the negative learning of the past?

Sources: Gregory L. White, "Battling the Inferior–Interior Complex." *The Wall Street Journal,* Dec. 3, 2001, pp. B1+; Karen Lundegaard, "Buick Beats BMW: New Car Rankings," *The Wall Street Journal,* Mar. 9, 2004, pp. D1+.

Learning is not a perfect predictor of behavior because a variety of other factors also influence a consumer. For example, a pattern of repeatedly purchasing the same brand may be disrupted by a person's desire for variety or novelty. Or a temporary situation such as being short of money or pressed for time may produce behavior different than a learned response. Thus a learned response does not necessarily occur every time a stimulus appears.

Personality   **Personality** is defined broadly as an individual's pattern of traits that influences behavioral responses. For example, we speak of people as being self-confident, domineering, introverted, flexible, and/or friendly, and as being influenced (but not controlled) by such personality traits in their responses to situations.

It is generally agreed that personality traits do influence consumers' perceptions and buying behavior. However, there is considerable disagreement as to the nature of this relationship—that is, *how* personality influences behavior. Many studies have been made of personality traits in relation to product and brand preferences in a wide variety of product categories, with mixed results. The findings generally have been too inconclusive to be of much practical value. Although we know, for example, that people's personalities frequently are reflected in the clothes they wear, the cars they drive (or whether they use a bicycle or motorcycle instead of a car), and the restaurants they eat in, researchers have not been particularly successful in predicting behavior on the basis of personality traits. The reason is simple: Many things besides personality enter into the consumer buying-decision process.

The **psychoanalytic theory** of personality, formulated by Sigmund Freud at the turn of the century and later modified by his followers and critics, has had a tremendous impact on the study of human behavior and also on marketing. Freud contended that people have subconscious drives that cannot be satisfied in socially acceptable ways. As we learn that we cannot gratify these needs in a direct manner, we develop other, more subtle means of seeking satisfaction. This results in very complex reasons for some behavior.

One significant marketing implication is that a person's real motive(s) for buying a product or shopping at a certain store may be hidden. Sometimes even we ourselves do not understand why we feel or act as we do. Psychoanalytic theory has caused marketers to realize that they must appeal to buyers' dreams, hopes, fantasies, and fears. Yet at the same time they must provide buyers with socially acceptable rationalizations for many purchases. Thus, we see ads emphasizing the practicality of $60,000 cars, the comfort of fur coats, and the permanence of diamond jewelry.

Self-concept is a marketing application of personality theory. Your **self-concept**, or *self-image*, is the way you see yourself. At the same time it is the picture you think others have of you. Psychologists distinguish between the *actual self-concept*—the way you see yourself—and the *ideal self-concept*—the way you want to be seen or would like to see yourself.

Studies of purchases show that people generally prefer brands and products that are compatible with their self-concepts. However, again there are mixed reports concerning the degree of influence that actual and ideal self-concepts have on brand and product preferences. Some researchers contend that consumption preferences correspond to a person's actual self-concept. Others disagree, holding that the ideal self-concept plays a significant role in consumers' choices.

Perhaps there is no consensus here because in real life we often switch back and forth between our actual and ideal self-concepts. A middle-aged man may buy some comfortable, but not fashionable, clothing to wear at home on a weekend, where he is reflecting his actual self-concept. But he may also buy some expensive, high-fashion clothing for public events, envisioning himself as a young, active, upwardly mobile guy (ideal self-concept).

Attitudes   An **attitude** is a learned predisposition to respond to an object or class of objects in a consistently favorable or unfavorable way.[19] In our buying-decision process model (Figure 4.2), attitudes play a major role in the evaluation of alternatives. All attitudes have the following characteristics in common:

- Attitudes are *learned*. They are formed as a result of direct experiences with a product or an idea, indirect experiences (such as reading about a product in *Consumer Reports*), and interactions with social groups. For example, the opinions expressed by a friend about a diet plus the consumer's favorable or unfavorable experience as a result of following the diet will contribute to an attitude toward the particular diet.

- Attitudes have an *object*. By definition, we can hold attitudes only toward something. The object can be general (professional sports) or specific (Chicago Cubs); it can be abstract (campus life) or concrete (the school's computer lab). In attempting to determine consumers' attitudes, the object of the attitude must be carefully defined. This is because a person might have a favorable attitude toward the general concept (exercise) but a negative attitude toward a specific dimension of the concept (jogging).

- Attitudes have *direction and intensity*. Our attitudes are either favorable or unfavorable toward the object. They cannot be neutral. In addition, they have a strength. For example, you may like this text mildly or you may like it very much (we hope!). This factor is important for marketers, because both strongly held favorable and unfavorable attitudes are difficult to change.

- Finally, attitudes tend to be *stable* and *generalizable*. Once formed, attitudes usually endure, and the longer they are held, the more resistant to change they become. People also have a tendency to generalize attitudes. For instance, a person who likes the produce section in a particular supermarket has a tendency to form a favorable attitude toward the entire store.

A consumer's attitudes do not always predict purchase behavior. A person may hold very favorable attitudes toward a product but not buy it because of some inhibiting factor. Typical inhibitors are not having enough money or discovering that your preferred brand is not available when you want to buy it. For example, the sale of french fries is declining in part because of attitudes toward fried foods, but also because many of the newer fast-food outlets such as Subway don't offer them. Under such circumstances, purchase behavior may even contradict attitudes.

Changing attitudes can be difficult or impossible. When change is accomplished, it frequently takes a long time. Consider that it took years to gain widespread acceptance of air bags in cars. They were initially ridiculed but now are demanded by car buyers. Interestingly, more recent side-impact air bags were much more quickly accepted because of the generalized favorable attitudes toward front air bags. When faced with unfavorable attitudes, and recognizing how difficult changing them will be, marketers frequently alter the product to conform to the attitudes.

Situational Influences

Often the situations in which we find ourselves play a large part in determining how we behave. Students, for example, act differently in class than they do when they are in a stadium watching a football game. The same holds true of buying behavior. On spring break you might buy a souvenir that seems very strange when you get home. This is an example of **situational influence,** a temporary force associated with the immediate purchase environment that affects behavior.

Situational influences tend to be less significant when the consumer is very loyal to a brand and when the consumer is highly involved in the purchase. However, they often play a major role in buying decisions. The four categories of situational influences are related to when, where, and how consumers buy as well as the conditions under which they buy.

The Time Dimension
In designing strategy for a product, a marketer should be able to answer at least three time-related situational questions about consumer buying:

- How is it influenced by the season, week, day, or hour?
- What impact do past and present events have on the purchase decision?
- How much time does the consumer have to make the purchase and consume the product?

Gambling casino operators are very aware of the importance of surroundings in influencing behavior. Bright lights, the jingling of coins as slot machines payoff, the absence of windows (to reduce the sense of time), and even free refreshments all contribute to the excitement and positive mood of the visitor. Under such conditions, who can resist dropping a few quarters in a machine?

www.harrahs.com

The time of day influences the demand for some products. For example, because they associate it with breakfast, Americans drink 10 times as much orange juice as the Japanese. The time dimension of buying has implications for promotion scheduling. Promotional messages must reach consumers when they are in a decision-making frame of mind. It also influences pricing decisions, as when marketers adjust prices in an attempt to even out demand. For instance, supermarkets may offer double coupons on Tuesdays, usually a slow business day.

The second question concerns the impact of past or future events. For example, the length of time since you last went out to dinner at a nice restaurant may influence a decision on whether to go to a fancy restaurant tonight. Marketers are now using consumer-specific databases about recent and planned behavior to anticipate the effects of these past and future events.

The growth and popularity of fast-food restaurants, quick-service oil-change outlets, and catalog retailers such as L. L. Bean are marketers' responses to the time pressure experienced by consumers. A factor in the growing popularity of the Internet as a place to make purchases is consumers' desire to spend less time shopping. To help consumers conserve time, marketers are making large and small changes. For example, some photoprocessing operations return the developed prints by mail to eliminate the customers' second trip to pick up the pictures. And to help customers locate specific products and therefore reduce shopping time, a number of supermarkets have electronic directories attached to their shopping carts.

The Surroundings
Physical surroundings are the features of a situation that are apparent to the senses, such as lighting, smells, weather, and sounds. Think of the importance of atmosphere in a restaurant or the sense of excitement and action created by the sights and sounds in a gambling casino. Music can be an important element in a retailer's strategy. Reseachers have found the speed at which restaurant customers eat is influenced by the tempo of the background music, and the amount diners are willing to spend is influenced by the type of music played.[20]

The social surroundings are the number, mix, and actions of other people at the purchase site. You probably would not go into a strange restaurant that has an empty parking lot at dinnertime. In a crowded store with other customers waiting, you will probably ask the clerk fewer questions and spend less time comparing products.

Terms of the Purchase
Terms and conditions of sale as well as the transaction-related activities that buyers are willing to perform affect consumer buying. For instance, for many years credit was extended only by retailers selling big-ticket items. However, today consumers can use credit cards at fast-food restaurants and grocery stores. Another transaction device, the debit card, is growing in popularity. A debit card looks like a credit card, but when it is used the payments are deducted directly from the consumer's checking account. Debit cards provide the convenience of making purchases without carrying cash or having to write a check. Also some consumers see them as a way of avoiding overspending. In a continuing shift away from cash, credit and debit cards are now used for 53% of all consumer transactions in the U.S.[21]

Marketers have also experimented with transferring functions or activities to consumers. What were once called "service stations" are now called "gas stations" because you pump your own gas and wash your own windshield. Consumers have shown a willingness to assemble products, sack their own groceries, and buy in case quantities—all in exchange for lower prices.

Consumer Moods and Motives
Sometimes consumers are in a temporary state that influences their buying decisions. When you are feeling ill or late for an appointment, you may be unwilling to wait in line or to take the time or care that a particular purchase deserves. Moods can also influence purchases. Feelings such as anger or excitement can result in purchases that otherwise would not have been made. In the atmosphere accompanying a rock concert, for example, you might pay more for a commemorative T-shirt than you would under normal circumstances. Part of the success of online auctions such as eBay and television shopping networks such as QVC can be attributed to the excitement of competing against other consumers.

www.conference-board.org

www.isr.umich.edu

Marketers must also monitor long-term situational influences. The Conference Board and the University of Michigan Survey Research Center monitor and regularly report on how consumers feel about their current and future economic situation. Uncertainty about the future can create a more cautious mood among consumers and affect their purchasing behavior.

This chapter has dealt with willingness to buy—part of our definition of marketing. We described the consumer market and examined the consumer's decision-making process. You should now appreciate why it is so challenging for marketers to identify needs and predict consumer buying behavior. In the next chapter we will examine the other category of buyers—the business market.

Summary

The dynamic nature of the consumer market is reflected in its geographic distribution and its demographic characteristics. The U.S. population is shifting toward the West and the South. Further, the mix of people in rural communities is changing as the out-migration of young people continues but an in-migration of older Americans increases.

Demographics are the vital statistics that describe a population. They are useful to marketers because they are related to behavior and they are relatively easy to gather. Demographics frequently used to describe consumers are age, gender, family life cycle, income, ethnicity, and other characteristics such as education, occupation, religion, and nationality.

The buying behavior of ultimate consumers is described as a five-stage buying-decision process, influenced by information, social and group forces, psychological forces, and situational factors.

The stages in the buying-decision process are need recognition, identification of alternatives, evaluation of alternatives, purchase and related decisions, and postpurchase behavior. Buying decisions are either high or low involvement. Low-involvement decisions include fewer stages; high-involvement decisions consist of all five stages. Low-involvement situations occur when the consumer views the decision as relatively minor, has brand and/or store loyalty, or makes an impulse purchase.

Information fuels the buying-decision process. Without it, there would be no decisions. There are two categories of information sources: commercial and social. Commercial sources include advertising, personal selling, selling by phone, and personal involvement with a product. Word of mouth, observation, and experience with a product owned by someone else are social sources.

Social and group forces are composed of culture, subculture, social class, reference groups, family, and households. Culture has the broadest and most general influence on buying behavior, whereas other household occupants have the most specific and immediate impact on an individual. Social and group forces have a direct impact on individual purchase decisions as well as on a person's psychological makeup.

Psychological forces that impact buying decisions are motivation, perception, learning, personality, and attitudes. All behavior is motivated by some aroused need. Perception is the way we interpret the world around us and is subject to three types of selectivity: attention, distortion, and retention.

Learning is a change in behavior as a result of experience. Stimulus-response learning involves drives, cues, responses, and reinforcement. Continued positive reinforcement leads to habitual buying and brand loyalty.

Personality is the sum of an individual's traits that influence behavioral responses. The Freudian psycho-analytic theory of personality has caused marketers to realize that the true motives for behavior are often hidden. The self-concept is related to personality. Because purchasing and consumption are very expressive actions, they allow us to communicate to the world our actual and ideal self-concepts.

Attitudes are learned predispositions to respond to an object or class of objects in a consistent fashion. Besides being learned, all attitudes are directed toward an object, have direction and intensity, and tend to be stable and generalizable. Strongly held attitudes are difficult to change.

Situational influences deal with when, where, how, and why consumers buy and the consumer's personal condition at the time of purchase. Situational influences are often so powerful that they can override all the other forces in the buying-decision process.

More about **Song**

Song's management has initially defined its target market as upscale female pleasure travelers going from New York to Florida. It has positioned the airline as low price but unique with more comfort, food, and media choices than either the higher- or lower-priced alternatives. How can Song provide more for less? By adjusting both the offering and controlling costs. For example, utilizing new luggage handling technology reduces the time a plane is on the ground from 90 minutes to 50 minutes; with just a single class of service the number of flight attendants on the 757 is reduced from five to four; flying point-to-point and avoiding expensive hub airports lowers gate fees; and adding 10% more seats (even with additional leg room) generates more revenue per flight. The net effect is a saving of 2 cents per seat mile as compared to its parent airline, Delta.

This is how the CEO of Song explains what's happening: "We know which way the industry is going—towards quality, low cost carriers." Though that may reflect the broad strategy, the challenge of getting it right in terms of implementation certainly remains. Adjusting for inflation, the average airfare has actually gone down by 50% from 25 years ago. As a result, firms in the industry have much less margin for error than in the past. There is also the generally poor record for discount airlines. Despite the success of Southwest, Frontier, and JetBlue, the landscape is littered with failures including United Shuttle, Delta Express, Continental Lite, and U.S. Airways' Metrojet. Finally, there's a wild card on the sidelines. Richard Branson, the founder of the many Virgin brands that have revolutionized several industries, is planning a low-fare entry in the U.S. market.[22]

1. Are mass media advertisements likely to be sufficient to inform Song's market about this new airline alternative?

2. What social or cultural factors are likely to enter into the purchase decision for airline pleasure travel?

Key Terms and Concepts

Ultimate consumers (86)
Metropolitan Statistical Area
  (MSA) (87)
Micropolitan Statistical Area (87)
Combined Statistical Area
  (CSA) (87)
Demographics (85)
Family life-cycle stages (88)
Consumer buying-decision
  process (91)
Level of involvement (92)
Loyalty (92)

Impulse buying (92)
Patronage buying motives (94)
Postpurchase cognitive
  dissonance (95)
Commercial information
  environment (95)
Social information environment (96)
Culture (97)
Subculture (98)
Social class (98)
Reference groups (99)
Family (99)

Household (99)
Motive (100)
Maslow's needs hierarchy (100)
Perception (102)
Selective perception (102)
Learning (103)
Stimulus-response theory (103)
Personality (104)
Psychoanalytic theory (104)
Self-concept (105)
Attitude (105)
Situational influence (106)

Questions and Problems

1. Give two examples of goods or services whose market demand would be particularly affected by each of the following population factors:
   a. Regional distribution
   b. Urban-rural-suburban distribution
   c. Marital status
   d. Gender
   e. Age

2. List three population trends noted in this chapter (for instance, the over-65 segment is growing). Speculate on how each of the following types of retail operations might be affected by each of the trends:
   a. Supermarket
   b. Sporting goods store
   c. Online auction
   d. Sports bar

3. Under what conditions might a relatively inexpensive purchase (under $10) be high involvement for a consumer?

4. From a consumer behavior perspective, why is it incorrect to view the European Union or the countries of Asia as single markets?

5. Provide examples of a person and a group that could serve as reference groups in the choice of the following products:
   a. Shampoo
   b. Auto tune-up
   c. Office furnishings
   d. Cellular phone service

6. What roles would you expect a husband, a wife, and their young child to play in the purchase of the following items?
   a. Preschool
   b. Choice of a fast-food outlet for dinner
   c. Personal computer
   d. Lawn-care service

7. Does the psychoanalytic theory of personality have any practical application in the marketing of cars that have a top speed of 120 mph when the speed limit on most U.S. highways is 70 mph or less?

8. Explain how self-concept might come into play in the purchase or use of the following:
   a. Eyeglasses
   b. Man's suit
   c. Online brokerage
   d. College education

9. Interview the manager of a store that sells big-ticket items (furniture, appliances, electronic equipment) about the methods, if any, the store uses to reinforce purchase decisions and to reduce the cognitive disso- nance of its customers. What additional methods can you suggest?

10. What situational influences might affect a family's choice of a motel in a strange town while on vacation?

Interactive Marketing Exercises

1. Go to the Census Bureau website (*www.census.gov*) and open the American Fact Finder page. Select a city and examine the data on the population, economy, and geography that is available. Comment on how the data could be used by a bank marketer looking for sites for new branch locations. Comment on how any differences you find may be useful to a fast-food franchisee looking for a location for a new outlet.

2. Have a friend describe a high-involvement purchase that he or she recently made. Show how each of the five stages described in the chapter is reflected in the description. Identify the primary social influences that played a part in the decision.

Chapter 5

"If you've ever taken a commercial airline flight, you've probably flown on a Boeing aircraft."

Will **Boeing** Be Flying High in the Future?

If you've ever taken a commercial airline flight, you've probably flown on a Boeing aircraft. The reason is simple: of the approximately 17,000 jetliners in service around the world, over 75% or 13,000 were built by Boeing.

It began in the early 1900s, when William Boeing became fascinated with the idea of flying. Utilizing a fortune he had amassed in the lumber industry, he moved from studying flight, to learning how to fly, and finally to starting a business designing and building planes. His first commercial order was for 50 small seaplanes used by the U.S. Navy to train pilots at the beginning of World War I. Boeing's company continued exploring applications for aviation, developing a variety of aircraft to deliver mail and other cargo, and finally building its first commercial passenger plane, an 18-seater, in 1929.

With advances in technology, the industry continued to evolve with Boeing playing a major role. By the late 1940s, the firm was concentrating solely on jet aircraft, producing models that could be adapted for either military or commercial applications. In 1955, the Boeing 707 was introduced, revolutionizing travel with its speed and efficiency.

Boeing and McDonnell Douglas merged in 1997. Eventually the line of commercial jetliners grew to consist of the 717, 737, 747, 767, and 777 families of airplanes and the Boeing Business Jet. From a humble beginning nearly 100 years before, by 2005 Boeing employed over 156,000 people in 70 countries and had annual revenues over $50 billion. However, the firm is not without challenges.

Boeing's major competitor is Airbus, owned by EADS, a European aerospace consortium. Airbus was created in 1970 because the major European countries did not want to find themselves in a situation where only one firm, Boeing, was the sole supplier of passenger aircraft. However, the lead times to build airplanes are great, and the required investments are enormous. As a result, Airbus could not survive on its own. So it was supported by the governments of Germany, France, Spain, and Britain, which subsidize up to 33% of the development costs of new model airplanes. Now, with Airbus profitable and having recently overtaken Boeing as the world's largest producer of commercial aircraft, the U.S. government, on behalf of Boeing, is protesting continuation of the subsidies.

Boeing's last significant new plane was the long-distance 777 introduced in 1990. Scheduled for service in 2008, is the Boeing 7E7, a super-efficient craft made of a lighter-weight composite material that can carry 250 passengers up to 10,000 miles. As Boeing sought commitments from airlines for the new jet, Airbus announced its A350, also a high-technology, fuel-efficient jet, which will be ready for flight in 2010. For both firms the risks are great. Boeing is working with several Japanese companies that will build a third of the 7E7. This is the first time the company has outsourced any of its production.

Meanwhile, Airbus is committing $5.3 billion to the development of the A350. What's the potential reward? Including the expected growth in the Chinese market, worldwide sales for these new planes is expected to be 3,100 units over the next 20 years.[1] The question now is what will determine which of these two companies will emerge as the highest-flyer?

 www.boeing.com

Although most people recognize large, technical equipment such as the robots used in assembling cars or the air-conditioning units used in office buildings as business products, many other products, like paper bags or bottle caps, are easily overlooked. In fact, the business market is big, dynamic, and widely diversified. It employs millions of workers in thousands of different jobs and is actually larger than the consumer market. And, as the chapter-opening case describing Boeing suggests, the high stakes and competitive intensity make marketing important.

In many ways business markets are similar to the consumer markets we examined in Chapter 4, but there are also important differences. After studying this chapter, you should be able to explain:

Chapter Goals

- The nature and scope of the business market.
- The seven categories of business buyers.
- The differentiating characteristics of business markets.
- What determines business market demand.
- The buying processes in business markets.

Nature and Scope of the Business Market

The business market consists of all individuals and organizations that buy goods and services for one or more of the following purposes:

- *To make other goods and services.* Dell buys microprocessors to make computers, and Henredon buys wood to make furniture.
- *To resell to other business users or to consumers.* Toys "R" Us buys electronic games to sell to consumers, and ReCellular, Inc., buys used cellular phones and wireless equipment to refurbish and sell to business customers.
- *To conduct the organization's operations.* Kroger buys bags to sack groceries, the University of Vermont buys office supplies and computer software for use in the registrar's office, and the Mayo Clinic buys hazardous-materials disposal services to get rid of its medical refuse.

So, any good or service purchased for a reason other than personal or household consumption is part of the **business market,** and each buyer within this market is termed a **business user.** The activity of marketing goods and services to business users, rather than to ultimate consumers, is **business marketing,** and a firm performing the activity is a **business marketer.**

The distinction of whether a good or service is a consumer or business product depends on the reason it is purchased, not on the item itself. For example, a PC purchased from Dell by a small business to keep track of its orders, inventory, and accounts receivable would be a business good. The same PC (with different software), also purchased from Dell but as a family Christmas gift for educational and entertainment use at home, would be a consumer good. This is not simply a semantic distinction because, as you will see, the marketing activities associated with these two situations are very different.

Because the business market is largely unknown to the average consumer, it is easy to underestimate its significance. Actually, it is huge in terms of total sales volume and the number of firms involved. About 50% of all manufactured products are sold to the business market. In addition, about 80% of all farm products and virtually all mineral, forest, and sea products are business goods. These are sold to firms for further processing.[2] At each step along the way the value of the product increases. This contribution, known as **value added,** is the dollar value of a firm's output minus the value of the inputs it purchased from other firms. If a manufacturer buys lumber for $40 and converts it into a table that it sells for $100, the value added by the manufacturer is $60.

The magnitude and complexity of the business market are also evident from the many transactions required to produce and market a product. Consider, for example, the business marketing transactions and total sales volume involved in getting leather workshoes to their actual users. First, cattle are sold through one or two middlemen before reaching a meatpacker. Then the hides are sold to a tanner, who in turn sells the leather to a shoe manufacturer. The shoe manufacturer may sell finished shoes to a wholesaler, who markets them to retail stores or to employers that supply shoes for their workers. Each sale in the chain is a business marketing transaction.

In addition, the shoe manufacturer buys metal eyelets, laces, thread, glue, steel safety toe plates, heels and soles, and shoe polish. Consider something as simple as the shoelaces. Other industrial firms must first buy the raw cotton. Then they must spin, weave, dye, and cut the cotton so that it becomes shoestring material. All the manufacturers involved have factories and offices with furniture, machinery, lights, and maintenance equipment and supplies required to run them—and these also are business goods that have to be produced and marketed. In short, thousands of business products and business marketing activities come into play before almost any product—consumer good or business good—reaches its final destination.

The magnitude and complexity of the business market loom even larger when we consider all the business services involved throughout our workshoe example. Each firm engaged in any stage of the production process probably uses outside accounting and law firms. Several of the producers may use advertising agencies. And all the companies will use services of various financial institutions.

Every retail store and wholesaling establishment is a business user. Every bus company, airline, and railroad is part of this market. So is every hotel, restaurant, bank, insurance company, hospital, theater, and school. In fact, the total sales volume in the business market far surpasses total sales to consumers. This difference is due to the very many business marketing transactions that take place before a product is sold to its ultimate user.

To create time and place utility for consumers, fashion retailers must make decisions about which designs will be popular far in advance of the actual selling season. In this photo of a Milan, Italy, fashion show, retail buyers are viewing spring and summer clothing and selecting items in mid-winter. This suggests that in many cases providing utility for consumers involves considerable risk for marketers.

Components of the Business Market

In the past, business markets were referred to as industrial markets. This caused many people to think the term referred only to manufacturing firms. But as you can see from what we just described, the business market is a lot more than that. Certainly manufacturers constitute a major portion of the business market, but not to be overlooked are also six other components—agriculture, reseller, government, services, nonprofit, and international.

The Agriculture Market

The large amount of income from the sale of agricultural products—over $192 billion in 2002, the most recent data available—gives the 2 million U.S. farmers, as a group, the purchasing power that makes them a highly attractive business market. Moreover, world population forecasts and food shortages in many countries undoubtedly will keep pressure on farmers to increase their output. Companies hoping to sell to the farm market must analyze it carefully and be aware of significant trends. For example, both the proportion of farmers in the total population and the number of farms have been decreasing and probably will continue to decline. Counterbalancing this has been an increase in large corporate farms. Even the remaining "family farms" are expanding in order to survive. Also, farming is becoming more automated and mechanized. These developments mean that capital investment in farming is increasing. **Agribusiness**—farming, food processing, and other large-scale farming-related businesses—is big business in every sense of the word.

Agriculture has become a modern industry. Like other business executives, farmers are looking for ways to increase their productivity, cut their expenses, and manage their cash flows. Technology is an important part of the process. For example, many of today's farmers are engaged in what is called precision agriculture—a term that describes a wide variety of technology products and processes designed to reduce costs and increase farm output. Yield monitoring, grid sampling, variable rate fertilization, self-guided machines, and disease tracking are examples of techniques and equipment that utilize computers, satellite-generated photographs, and sophisticated soil analysis to identify problems and opportunities.[3] Representatives of agricultural product firms such as John Deere and International Mineral and Chemical Company can use this information to design unique strategies for individual farms and adapt them as necessary to best serve their customers.

The Reseller Market

Intermediaries in the American marketing system—over 440,000 wholesaling middlemen and 2.8 million retail establishments—constitute the **reseller market.** The basic activity of resellers—unlike any other business market segment—is buying products from supplier organizations and reselling these items in essentially the same form to the resellers' customers. In economic terms, resellers create time, place, information, and possession utilities, rather than form utility.

Resellers are also business users, buying many goods and services for use in operating their businesses—items such as office supplies, warehouses, materials-handling equipment, legal services, electrical services, and janitorial supplies.

It is their role as buyers for resale that differentiates resellers and attracts special marketing attention from their suppliers. To resell an item, you must please your customer. Usually it is more difficult to determine what will please an outside customer than to find out what will satisfy someone within your own organization. Consider an airline that decides to redesign the uniforms of its flight crews. Management can carefully study the conditions under which the uniforms will be worn and work closely with the people who will be wearing the uniforms to get their views. As a result, the airline should be able to select a design that will be both functional and acceptable. Contrast that with a retailer trying to anticipate what clothing fashions will be popular. The Gap, Express, and Ann Taylor have all had their ups and downs as they try to predict tastes. In both cases clothing is being purchased. However, the opportunity for interaction with the users and the greater interest by those likely to be affected by the purchase make buying for internal use less difficult and less risky than buying for resale.

Especially in a large reseller's organization, buying for resale can be a complex procedure. For a supermarket chain such as Kroger or Vons, buying is frequently done by a buying committee made up of experts on demand, supply, and prices. Timing purchasing to balance obtaining good prices with optimizing the investment in inventory often plays a major role in determining a reseller's profitability.

Resellers, also called "middlemen" or "intermediaries," are the business marketers most directly affected by electronic commerce. Government data indicate that in 2002, 1.5% of retail sales (about $44 billion) and 12% of all wholesale sales (about $320 billion) were made electronically.[4] The growth of Internet-based selling is contributing to the replacement of some traditional intermediaries in a process that has become so commonplace it has a name—**disintermediation.** Only resellers that can create utility will continue to prosper.

The Government Market

The fantastically large **government market** includes over 87,000 federal, state, and local units that spend over $2.3 *trillion* a year buying for government institutions, such as schools, offices, hospitals, and military bases. Spending by the federal government alone accounts for about 20% of our gross domestic product. Spending at the state and local levels accounts for another 20%.

Government procurement processes are different from those in the private sector of the business market. A unique feature of government buying is the competitive bidding system. Much government procurement, by law, must be done on a bid basis.

The National Aeronautics and Space Administration (NASA) is one government customer. In 2004, NASA purchased over $13.5 billion in goods and services, 80% from private businesses. Small businesses accounted for 19% of NASA's 109,000 purchases. Though NASA is a highly visible prospect due to its dramatic end-products, virtually all branches and levels of government are important business markets.

www.nasa.gov

That is, the government agency advertises for bids using a standard format called a request for proposals (RFP) that states specifications for the intended purchase. Then it must accept the lowest bid that meets these specifications. However, for some purchases the lowest bid may not be the selection criterion and the government agency may negotiate a contract with a particular supplier. This marketing practice might be used, for instance, when the Department of Defense wants to have a new weapons system developed and built and there are no comparable products on which to base bidding specifications.

www.fedbizopps.gov

A glance at an issue of *FedBizOpps/Commerce Business Daily* (formerly the *Commerce Business Daily*), a publication that describes RFPs for contracts in excess of $25,000, will give you an idea of the size and variety that exists in this market. The potential is sufficiently attractive that some firms concentrate exclusively on it, and for others it can be a springboard to additional opportunities. AM General Corporation, for example, developed the HUMMER, an all-terrain vehicle, in response to a Department of Defense RFP. The firm eventually expanded its marketing effort for the vehicle to other government agencies such as the Forest Service, and business firms such as mining and oil exploration companies. Now several civilian versions of the HUMMER are being marketed by General Motors. To learn more about the HUMMER see the case at the end of Part 6.

Despite its potential, many companies make no effort to sell to the government because they are intimidated by the red tape. There is no question that dealing with the government to any significant extent usually requires specialized marketing techniques and information. Some firms, such as ZDS (Zenith Data Systems), have established special departments to deal with government markets. Also, there are information and guidelines available from agencies such as the General Services Administration and the Small Business Administration on the proper procedures for doing business with the government.

The Services Market

Currently, firms that produce services greatly outnumber firms that produce goods. That is, there are more service firms than the total of all manufacturers; mining companies; construction firms; and enterprises engaged in farming, forestry, and fishing. The **business services market** includes purchasers of marketing research and the services of ad agencies. Also operating in this market with the products they produce are trucking companies and public utilities, as well as the many financial, insurance, investment, legal, and real estate firms. Organizations that provide such diverse services as office rental, temporary help, repairs, and executive search services are also examples of services marketers.

Services marketers themselves constitute a huge market that buys goods and other services. Mirage resorts, for example, buys blankets and sheets from textile manufacturers. Hospitals buy supplies and medical equipment from Baxter Healthcare Corporation. The Chicago Cubs and other professional baseball teams buy their Louisville Slugger baseball bats from Hillerich and Bradsby. And all of these services firms buy legal, accounting, and consulting advice from other services marketers.

Brokerage firms that bring buyers and sellers together are important services marketers. With the growth of electronic commerce in recent years, their significance is growing. Business marketers are using Internet-based brokers to inform buyers about the goods they have available, and buyers are publicizing their needs electronically. For example, Ariba brings together organizations such as British Airways and Saks Fifth Avenue department stores with a broad mix of suppliers. Firms in industries as diverse as paper stock and metals are finding that Internet brokers provide more alternative sources of supply while saving them time and money.

www.ariba.com

Where can a business marketer learn about international opportunities?

Exporting has become commonplace for large firms. With the availability of the Internet it has also become an option for smaller companies. However, doing business abroad has many challenges. For U.S. firms looking for opportunities abroad and businesses in other countries considering the U.S. market, the Census Bureau provides valuable resources. At its website (*www.census.gov/foreign-trade*) the Foreign Trade Division of the Census Bureau provides a wealth of useful information on the export and import of specific products. For firms looking for market opportunities, trying to evaluate the competition, or assessing trade patterns over time, it is an excellent resource. Macro information available on the site about U.S. exporters include:

- Manufacturers make up 28% of exporters, but account for 66% of the total export value.
- Firms with 500 or more employees account for 74% of export value but less than 4% of exporters.
- Firms with less than 100 employees make up nearly 90% of exporters but only 18% of exports.
- Over 60% of exporting companies trade with only one country.
- 0.5% of exporters trade with 50 or more countries but account for one-half the total export value.
- More than twice as many companies (92,000) export to Canada as export to Mexico (39,000).

Source: *www.census.gov/foreign-trade*.

The "Nonbusiness" Business Market

In recent years some long-overdue marketing attention has been given to the multibillion-dollar market comprised of not-for-profit organizations. The **nonbusiness market** consists of organizations that do not have profit-making as a primary objective. Included are such diverse institutions as churches, colleges and universities, museums, hospitals and other health care institutions, political parties, labor unions, and charitable organizations. To prosper, each of these so-called nonbusiness organizations should think of itself as a business enterprise. In the past, however, our society (and the institutions themselves) did not perceive a museum or a charity as a business because its primary objective is something other than making a profit. And many people today still feel uncomfortable thinking of their church, school, or political party as a business. Nevertheless, these organizations do virtually all the things that businesses do—offer a product, collect money, make investments, hire employees—except having profit as one of their goals. Therefore, they require professional management.

Not-for-profit organizations also conduct marketing campaigns—albeit under different names—in an effort to attract billions of dollars in donations, grants, and contributions. In turn, they spend billions of dollars buying goods and services to run their operations and to provide for their clients.

The International Market

Annual exports of goods and services by U.S. firms amount to approximately $1.4 trillion, a figure that has increased steadily since the mid-1980s. The biggest recent growth in the **international market** has been in medical products, scientific instruments, environmental protection systems, and consumer goods.

Many small organizations are also heavily involved in the export market. These firms benefit from help from the U.S. Commerce Department with trade fairs and "matchmaking" programs, reduced language barriers as English becomes more common in global business, and greater access to markets via the Internet. The market-expanding potential of the Internet for small businesses is unprecedented.

Another dimension of international business is foreign-based subsidiaries. Although these sales do not count as exports, they are a significant part of the operations of many firms. McDonald's domestic sales are growing, but its foreign sales are growing nearly four times as fast, and now account for half the firm's total volume. A significant number of U.S. firms receive over half their total revenue from overseas subsidiaries. Included are ExxonMobil, IBM, Procter & Gamble, and Coca-Cola.

Operating overseas has several benefits for U.S. firms:

- It gains them access to countries participating in trade agreements that restrict imports from nonmembers. For example, a joint operation between Dow Chemical and Sumitomo in Japan to make high-performance plastics gives Dow greater access to the countries of the Pacific Rim than it would otherwise have.

- Manufacturing abroad allows firms to gain a better understanding of local markets and customers. Ford could have tried to export a windshield wiper to Europe that was designed for the U.S. market. Instead, through its German subsidiary, Ford learned that it had to produce a specially designed wiper to accommodate the speeds on German autobahns (where there are no speed limits).

- Foreign operations contribute to the volume of a firm's exports. About 25% of all exports by U.S. firms are sales to affiliates located overseas.

Characteristics of Business Market Demand

Four demand characteristics differentiate the business market from the consumer market. In business markets demand is derived, demand for a product tends to be inelastic, demand fluctuates, and the market is well informed.

Demand Is Derived

The demand for a business product is **derived demand**, generated from the demand for the consumer products in which that business product is used. Thus the demand for steel depends partially on consumer demand for automobiles and refrigerators, but it also depends on the demand for butter, baseball gloves, and CD players. This is because the tools, machines, and other equipment needed to make these items are made of steel. Consequently, as the demand for baseball gloves increases, Wilson Sporting Goods may buy more sewing machines with steel components and more steel filing cabinets for an expanding managerial staff.

There are two significant marketing implications in the fact that business market demand is a derived demand. First, to estimate the demand for a product, a business marketer must be very familiar with how it is used. This is fairly easy for a company like Pratt & Whitney, a maker of jet engines. But what about the manufacturer of rubber O-rings (doughnut-shaped rings of all sizes that are used to seal connections)? Considerable research may be necessary to identify specific uses and users.

Second, the producer of a business product may find it worthwhile to engage in marketing efforts to encourage the sale of its buyers' products. For example, Texas Instruments is trying to duplicate the success of the famous "Intel Inside" ad campaign with a marketing program touting the presence of its light-processing chips in flat screen television sets.[5] The idea, of course, is that increases in demand for the consumer product will, in turn, trigger an increase in derived demand for the components.

Demand Is Inelastic

Another characteristic of the business market is the demand elasticity of business products. **Elasticity of demand** refers to how responsive demand is to a change in the price of a product. (If you would like to review some economics relative to marketing, see Appendix A on the website for this text where demand elasticity and other concepts are explained.)

The industry demand for many business products is relatively inelastic, which means that the total demand for all producers of the product responds very little to changes in its price. Two situations contribute to *inelasticity:*

- *If the cost of a part or of material is a small portion of the total cost of a finished product.* For example, Boeing, the maker of passenger jet airplanes, has over 1,200 suppliers. One, Huck International, produces fasteners for aerospace applications. If the price of fasteners should suddenly rise or fall considerably, how much effect would it have on the price of Boeing jets? Despite the fact that the fasteners are critical parts, they are such a small portion of a jet's cost that the price increase would not likely change the price of the plane. As a result, demand for passenger jets would remain the same, so there would be no appreciable change in the demand for fasteners either.

  Even the cost of expensive capital equipment such as a robot used in assembling automobiles, when spread over the thousands of units it helps produce, becomes a very small part of the final price of each one. As a result, when the price of the business product changes, there is very little change in the price of the related consumer products. Because there is no appreciable shift in the demand for the consumer goods, then—by virtue of the derived-demand feature—there is no change in the demand for the business product.

- *If the part or material has no close substitute.* In the mid-1990s the cost of white bond paper increased over 50% because of a shortage of supply. Because paper is a major component of catalogs and magazines, producers of these products had no alternative but to buy it. The catalog and magazine publishers were unable to pass the increase along to their customers because it would have nearly doubled the price of their publications. As a result, they were severely affected by the price change. The bond paper manufacturers, on the other hand, sold all they could produce at the higher price. However, an interesting longer-run effect was that catalog producers and other firms dependent on paper began looking at the Internet as a communication alternative sooner than they would have if paper prices had remained stable.

From a marketing point of view, three factors can moderate the inelasticity of business demand. The quantity of a product demanded is likely to be affected by a change in price:

- *If the price change occurs in a single firm.* An industry-wide increase in the price of aerospace fasteners used in jets will have little effect on the price of planes and therefore little effect on the demand for Boeing aircraft. Consequently, it will cause minimal shift in the total demand for fasteners. The pricing policy of an individual firm, however, can substantially alter the demand for its products. If one supplier raises the price of its fasteners significantly, the increase in price may shift business to competitors. Thus, in the short run, the demand curve faced by a single firm may be quite elastic.

- *If demand is viewed from a long-run time perspective.* Much of our discussion thus far applies to short-term situations. Over the long run, the demand for a given business product is more elastic. If the price of cloth for women's suits rises, there probably will be no immediate change in the price of the finished garment. However, the increase in the cost of materials could very well be reflected in a rise in suit prices for next year. This rise could then influence the demand for suits, and thus for cloth, a year or more hence.

- *If the cost of a specific business product is a significant portion of the cost of the finished good.* We may generalize to this extent: The greater the cost of a business product as a percentage of the total price of the finished good, the greater the elasticity of demand for this business product.

Demand Fluctuates

Although the demand for many business goods does not change much in response to price changes, it does respond to other factors. In fact, market demand for most classes of business goods fluctuates considerably more than the demand for consumer products. The demand for installations—major plant equipment, factories, and so on—is especially subject to change. Substantial fluctuations also exist in the market for accessory equipment—office furniture and machinery, delivery trucks, and similar products. The fluctuating demand for finished goods tends to accentuate the swings in the demand for raw materials and fabricating parts. We can see this very clearly when changes in demand in the construction and auto industries affect suppliers of lumber, steel, and other materials and parts. Likewise, changes in the demand for raw materials impact the demand for equipment and supplies to produce them. For example, Caterpillar, a manufacturer of heavy equipment for mining, has benefited greatly from increases in worldwide demand for iron ore, copper, and coal.[6]

A major reason for these fluctuations is that individual businesses are very concerned about having a shortage of inventory when consumer demand increases or, alternatively, being caught with excess inventory should consumer demand decline. Thus they tend to overreact to signals from the economy, building inventories when they see signs of growth in the economy and working inventories down when the signs suggest a downturn. When the actions of all the individual firms are combined, the effect on their suppliers is widely fluctuating demand. This is known as the *acceleration principle*. One exception to this generalization is found in agricultural products intended for processing. Because people have to eat, there is a reasonably consistent demand for animals intended for meat products, for fruits and vegetables that will be canned or frozen, and for grains and dairy products used in cereals and baked goods.

Fluctuations in the demand for business products can influence all aspects of a marketing program. In product planning, fluctuating demand may stimulate a firm to diversify into other products to ease production and marketing problems. For example, IBM moved from concentrating on large, mainframe computers to software and consulting. Distribution strategies may also be affected. When demand declines, a manufacturer may discover that selling to some resellers is unprofitable, so they are dropped as customers. In its pricing, management may attempt to stem a decline in sales by cutting prices, hoping to attract customers away from competing firms. In a long struggle with imported steel and alternative products such as aluminum and fiberglass, Bethlehem Steel repeatedly reduced its prices, eventually resulting in the firm's bankruptcy.

Buyers Are Well Informed

Typically, business buyers are better informed about what they are buying than ultimate consumers. They know more about the relative merits of alternative sources of supply and competitive products for three reasons. First, there are relatively few alternatives for a business buyer to consider. Consumers generally have many more brands and sellers from which to choose than do business buyers. Consider, for example, how many options you would have in purchasing a TV set. However, in most business situations a buyer has only a few firms that offer the particular combination of product features and service desired. Second, the responsibility of a buyer in an organization is ordinarily limited to a few products. Unlike a consumer who buys many different things, a purchasing agent's job is to be very knowledgeable about a narrowly defined set of products. Third, for most consumer purchases, an error is only a minor inconvenience. However, in business buying the cost of a mistake may be thousands of dollars or even the decision maker's job!

The importance of information in business marketing has two significant implications. For sellers of business products, it means placing greater emphasis on personal selling than do firms that market consumer products. Business sales people must be carefully selected, properly trained, and adequately compensated. They must give effective sales presentations and furnish satisfactory service both before and after each sale is made. It is increasingly common to have sales people focus on a particular industry so they can become experts on that business. For example, an IBM representative may be an industry specialist, calling only on health care providers, financial institutions, or auto makers. Firms also identify especially important customers, called key accounts, and direct sales people to become very familiar with their businesses and give them extra attention.

For buyers and sellers, information is valuable, and the Internet has made information even more accessible. FreeMarkets, a division of Ariba, facilitates online business-to-business actions. Its service allows a buyer to consider the bids of many sellers in a short period of time. Thus, it and similar online auction services permit unprecedented comparison shopping. The Internet has also made it efficient for buyers to pool their purchasing power to get better prices. By combining their needs over an intranet and buying on the Internet, various divisions of General Electric have saved 20% on $1 billion in purchases of operating supplies.

Determinants of Business Market Demand

Recall from Chapter 4 that to analyze a consumer market a marketer would study the distribution of population and various demographics such as income, and then try to determine the consumers' buying motives and habits. Essentially the same type of analysis is used by a firm selling to the business market. The only difference, but a very important one, is the attributes selected for analysis. The factors affecting the market for business products include the number of potential business users and their purchasing power, their buying motives, and their buying habits. In the following discussion we'll identify several features common to business markets.

Describing Business Markets

Similar to consumer demographics, businesses' attributes are used to group firms.

Profile of Buyers   In the U.S. there are about 20 million business users, in contrast to about 290 million consumers divided among more than 100 million households. The business market is even more limited because most companies sell to only a small segment of the total market. For example, a firm that markets hard-rock coal mining equipment certainly is not interested in the total business market, or even in all 24,000 firms engaged in various forms of mining and quarrying. It won't even describe the 1,200 firms involved in coal mining as its market. Rather, it will focus on the 60 that extract anthracite coal. The point is, unlike most consumer marketers, business marketing executives in many industries are able to pinpoint their markets carefully by type of industry or geographic location, sometimes down to the level of individually identifying every prospect.

Amusement parks are business customers for firms supplying thrill rides, arcade games, and a variety of services from maintenance to food service, but the number of parks, and thus business customers, is relatively small compared to the number of park visitors. According to the International Association of Amusement Parks and Attractions, 328 million consumers visited amusement parks in 2004, spending $10.8 billion. Yet IAAPA, the industry's largest professional association, has only 5,000 business members.

www.iaapa.org

www/naics.html

An important resource for business marketers is the **North American Industry Classification System (NAICS),** jointly adopted by the U.S., Canada, and Mexico. Using numerical codes, NAICS divides all types of businesses into 20 industry sectors, with a range of two-digit code numbers assigned to each. Then additional numbers are used to subdivide each of the major industries into smaller segments. Specifically, the 20 NAICS sectors are subdivided into 96 three-digit subsectors, 313 four-digit industry groups, and 1,170 five- and six-digit industries. Table 5.1 lists the NAICS two-digit industry sector codes, and shows the breakdown for one industry—pagers (a segment of the wireless telecommunications industry)—within the information sector.

TABLE 5.1

NAICS Industry Sectors and the Classification of the Pager Industry

NAICS Industry Sectors	An Industry Subclassification
11 Agriculture, forestry, fishing, & hunting	
21 Mining	
22 Utilities	
23 Construction	
31–33 Manufacturing	
42 Wholesale trade	
44–45 Retail trade	513 Broadcast & telecommunications
48–49 Transportation & warehousing	↓
51 Information	5133 Telecommunications
52 Finance & insurance	↓
53 Real estate, rental, & leasing	51332 Wireless telecommunications carrier
54 Professional, scientific, & technical	↓
55 Management of companies	513321 Pagers
56 Waste management	
61 Education	
62 Health care	
71 Arts, entertainment, & recreation	
72 Accommodations & food services	
81 Other services	
92 Public administration	

Source: *North American Industry Classification System—United States, 1997,* U.S. Government Printing Office, Washington, DC, 1997.

Using the NAICS classification scheme and data from its Survey of Business, the federal government provides information on the number of establishments, number of employees, payroll, and measures of output (typically sales or the value of shipments, depending on the industry), all by geographic area. These valuable data are used by marketers to identify potential target industries and geographic markets, monitor trends in growth or decline, and benchmark the activities of other firms in an industry or area.[7]

One limitation of data reported using these codes is that a multi-product company is listed in only its largest four-digit category. Thus, the diversity of a conglomerate such as General Electric, which produces jet engines and home appliances, is hidden. Also, the government's nondisclosure rules prevent revealing information that will identify a given establishment. Consequently, four-digit detail is not available for an industry in a geographic location where this information would easily be linked to a particular company.

Prior to the establishment of NAICS, marketers relied on a method for organizing industry information called the Standard Industrial Classification (SIC) system. However, the SIC codes were too restrictive for modern industry and did not account for the anticipated growth in cross-border trade resulting from NAFTA.

Size of Business Buyers

Although the business market may be limited in the total number of buyers, it is large in purchasing power. In many industries a relatively small percentage of firms account for the greatest share of the value added to products by manufacturing.

The marketing significance of this fact is that buying power in many business markets is highly concentrated in relatively few firms. That is, a high percentage of industry sales are accounted for by a very small number of firms. That's obvious in some major industries such as automobiles, mainframe computers, and jet aircraft, but it is also true in many smaller industries. To illustrate, a firm that sells to U.S. manufacturers of lightbulbs can cover 97% of the manufacturing capacity of the industry by contacting only 39 firms. Similarly, four firms produce 78% of all lead pencils, and eight firms make 85% of household vacuum cleaners.

When industries have such a small number of firms, suppliers have the opportunity to deal with them directly. As a result, middlemen often are not as essential in business markets as they are in the consumer market.

Of course, these statements are broad generalizations covering the total business market. They do not take into account the variation in business concentration from one industry to another. In some industries—women's dresses, upholstered furniture, natural and processed cheese, and ready-mix concrete, for example—there are many producers and, therefore, a relatively low level of concentration. Nevertheless, even a so-called low-concentration industry represents far more concentration than anything in the consumer market.

Regional Concentration of Business Buyers

There is substantial regional concentration in many major industries and among business buyers as a whole. A firm that sells products used in copper mining will find the bulk of its American market in Utah and Arizona, and a large percentage of American-produced shoes come from the Southeast.

The eight states constituting the Middle Atlantic and East North Central census regions account for almost 40% of the total value added by manufacturing. Just 10 metropolitan areas (3% of all MSAs) account for about 25% of the total U.S. value added by manufacturing.

Vertical and Horizontal Business Markets

For effective marketing planning, a company should know whether the market for its products is vertical or horizontal. A **vertical business market** exists when a firm's product is usable by virtually all the firms in only one or two industries. For example, aircraft landing gear is intended only for the airplane manufacturing market, but every plane maker is a potential customer. A **horizontal business market** is one in which the firm's product is usable by many industries. Some component and business supplies, such as General Electric small motors, Pennzoil lubricating oils and greases, and Weyerhauser paper products, are examples of products with horizontal markets.

A company's marketing program ordinarily is influenced by whether its markets are vertical or horizontal. In a vertical market, a product can be tailor-made to meet the specific needs of one industry. However, the industry must buy enough to support this specialization. In addition, advertising and personal selling can be directed more effectively in vertical markets. In a horizontal market, a product is developed as an all-purpose item, to reach a larger market. Because of the larger potential market, however, the product is likely to face more competition and the seller must decide how and where to focus its marketing effort.

Buying Power of Businesses

Another determinant of business market demand is the purchasing power of business customers. This can be measured either by the expenditures of business buyers or by their sales volume. Unfortunately, such information for individual customers is typically unavailable. As a result, purchasing power is estimated indirectly using an **activity indicator of buying power**—that is, some market factor related to sales and expenditures. One important source of data is the Economic Census conducted and reported every five years (in years ending in 2 and 7) by the U.S. Census Bureau. The results of the census are published in 18 industry reports ranging from construction to health care. Following are examples of activity indicators that give some idea of the purchasing power of business buyers.

www.census.gov/epcd

Measures of Manufacturing Activity
Firms that sell to manufacturers might use as activity indicators the number of employees, the number of plants, or the dollar value added by manufacturing. One firm that sells work gloves determined the relative attractiveness of various geographic areas from the number of employees in manufacturing establishments within the areas. Another company that sells a product to control stream pollution used two indicators to estimate potential demand: (1) the number of firms processing wood products (paper mills, plywood mills, and so forth) and (2) the manufacturing value added by these firms. These types of data are gathered in the Economic Census and reported in 473 manufacturing sector reports. Yearly updates are available in the *Annual Survey of Manufactures*, a report based on a sample of 55,000 manufacturing firms.

Measures of Mining Activity
The number of mines operating, the volume of their output, and the dollar value of the product as it leaves the mine may all indicate the purchasing power of mining and mining-related firms. These data are published every five years in the mining sector reports derived from the Economic Census. This information is useful to any firm marketing business products related to extracting and processing everything from aluminum to zirconium.

Measures of Agricultural Activity
A company marketing agricultural products or equipment can estimate the buying power of its farm market by studying such indicators as cash farm income, commodity prices, acreage planted, or crop yields. A chemical producer that sells to a fertilizer manufacturer might study the same indices, because the demand for chemicals in this case derives from the demand for fertilizer. These data are in the *Census of Agriculture*, conducted by the U.S. Department of Agriculture.

Measures of Construction Activity If a business is marketing building materials, such as lumber, brick, gypsum products, or builders' hardware, its market depends on construction activity. This can be gauged by the number and value of building permits issued. Another indicator is the number of construction starts by type of structure (single-family residence, apartment, or commercial). Local data are available from county and city records, whereas regional and national statistics are found in reports from the Census Bureau's Manufacturing and Construction Division.

These sources illustrate the kinds of information available for predicting buying power of business markets. Many other public and private information sources are useful in forecasting demand. We will have more to say about forecasting in Chapter 6.

Business Buying Behavior

Business buying behavior, like consumer buying behavior, is initiated when an aroused need (a motive) is recognized. This leads to goal-oriented activity designed to satisfy the need. Once again, marketers must try to determine what motivates the buyer and then understand the buying process and buying patterns of business organizations in their markets. The actual process is very similar to consumer decision making, except the influences are different. Figure 5.1 summarizes the business buying-decision process and the primary influences.

The Importance of Business Buying

Top managers in most companies have come to realize that the buying decisions their organizations make are an important part of overall strategy. Securing the right products at the right time for the right price can play a major role in a firm's performance for at least three reasons:

- *Companies are making less and buying more.* For example, in North America alone Toyota annually buys $25 billion worth of parts, materials, and services from hundreds of suppliers for use in its production. When outside suppliers become this significant, buying becomes a prime strategic issue.

- *Firms are under intense quality and time pressures.* To reduce reworking costs and improve efficiency, firms cannot tolerate defective parts and supplies. As a result, price is only one of several decision criteria used in selecting vendors.

FIGURE 5.1

The Business Buying-Decision Process and the Factors Influencing It.

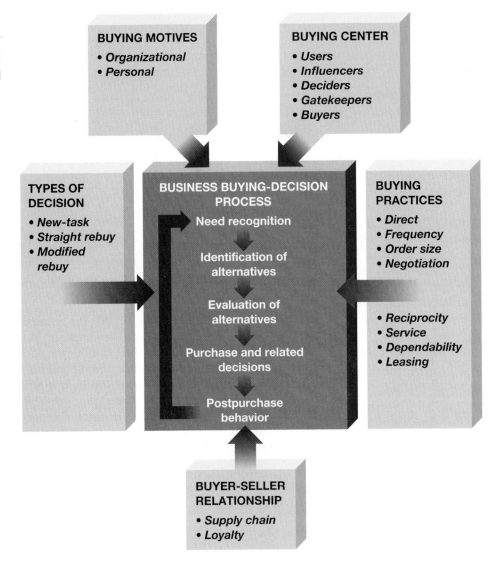

BUYING MOTIVES
- *Organizational*
- *Personal*

BUYING CENTER
- *Users*
- *Influencers*
- *Deciders*
- *Gatekeepers*
- *Buyers*

TYPES OF DECISION
- *New-task*
- *Straight rebuy*
- *Modified rebuy*

BUSINESS BUYING-DECISION PROCESS
- Need recognition
- Identification of alternatives
- Evaluation of alternatives
- Purchase and related decisions
- Postpurchase behavior

BUYING PRACTICES
- *Direct*
- *Frequency*
- *Order size*
- *Negotiation*

- *Reciprocity*
- *Service*
- *Dependability*
- *Leasing*

BUYER-SELLER RELATIONSHIP
- *Supply chain*
- *Loyalty*

- *Firms are concentrating their purchases.* To get what they need, companies are dealing with fewer suppliers but are developing long-term "partnering" relationships with them. This level of involvement extends beyond a purchase to include such things as working together to develop new products and sharing information on inventories, production schedules, and costs. For example, Maytag, the appliance maker, reduced its number of suppliers by nearly 75%, with the remaining suppliers expected to provide on-site representation at Maytag manufacturing plants, continuous cost improvements, and research and development efforts to produce new products.

Buying-Decision Process in Business

The buying-decision process in business markets is a sequence of five steps. It is depicted in the center of Figure 5.1. To illustrate the process, let's assume that Hershey Foods Corporation, responding to increased concerns about diet and nutrition, is considering introducing a line of confectionary goods using a sugar substitute:

- *Need recognition.* Hershey's marketing research has found that a growing number of consumers are concerned about sugar and calories in their diets. For some it is related to a medical condition such as diabetes. For others, it is simply a matter of trying to lose weight or avoid excess weight gains without changing their

Many major purchase decisions must be made when a city creates a mass transit system. Millions of dollars are spent on an investment expected to pay dividends in the form of efficient commuter transportation for many years. This is an example of a highly involved decision that would include all the steps in the business buying process.

lifestyle. The opportunity to produce high-quality, good-tasting confections without sugar or with fewer calories is, therefore, very attractive, but finding the right sugar substitute is the challenge.

- *Identification of alternatives.* Hershey's marketing, production, and research and development managers draw up a list of product-performance specifications for the sugar-free goods. To appeal to consumers they must taste good, be competitively priced, meet their dietary needs, and have the texture or mouth-feel of sugar-based products. To satisfy production requirements the ingredient must be easy to use, available in sufficient quantities, and reasonable in cost. The R&D staff is concerned about the stability of the finished product on the shelf, how it interacts with other ingredients, and how the human body processes it. Given the agreed-upon specifications, the purchasing department goes about identifying possible alternatives and sources of supply. Possibilities include aspartame, sucralose, neotame, malitol, and a few others. Suppliers include such firms as Merisant Co., McNeil Specialty Products (a division of Johnson & Johnson), and Monsanto.

- *Evaluation of alternatives.* The marketing, production, and research people jointly evaluate the alternatives. Suppliers that meet some preliminary qualifications are invited to make presentations, and knowledgeable sources such as university food science researchers are contacted for information. Hershey discovers that some sugar substitutes cannot withstand high temperatures, there are differences in how well they simulate the taste and texture of sugar, and the approval from the Food & Drug Administration restricts how others can be used and must be labeled. The evaluation goes beyond performance and price to consider the suppliers' abilities to meet delivery schedules and provide consistent quality.

- *Purchase decision.* Based on the evaluation, Hershey managers decide on a specific ingredient and supplier. Next, the purchasing department negotiates the contract. Because large sums of money are involved, the contract will likely include many details. For example, it might incorporate provision of marketing support for Hershey's finished product by the producer of the sugar substitute.

- *Postpurchase behavior.* Hershey managers continue to evaluate the performance of the sugar substitute and the selected supplier to ensure that both meet expectations. Future dealings with the supplier will depend on this performance evaluation and on how well the supplier handles any problems that may arise involving its product.

In the following sections we will explore several of the differences between consumer buying behavior and business buying behavior that are reflected in this scenario.

Motives of Business Buyers

Business **buying motives** are the needs that direct the purchasing behavior of business users. As shown in Figure 5.1, they fall into two broad categories—organizational and personal. Generally, business purchases are methodical and structured. Thus business buying motives are presumed to be, for the most part, practical and unemotional. Business buyers are assumed to be motivated to achieve organizational goals by securing the optimal combination of price, quality, and service in the products they buy.

An opposing view is that business buyers are human, and their business decisions are certainly influenced by their attitudes, perceptions, and values. In fact, many sales people would maintain that business buyers seem to be motivated more toward personal goals than organizational goals, and the two are often in conflict.

The truth is actually somewhere in between. Business buyers have two goals—to further their company's position (in profits, in acceptance by society) and to protect or improve their position in their firms (self-interest). Sometimes these goals are mutually consistent. For example, the firm's highest priority may be to save money, and the buyer expects to be rewarded for negotiating a low price. Obviously the more consistent the goals are, the better for both the organization and the individual, and the easier it is to make buying decisions.

However, there are often significant areas where the buyer's goals do not coincide with those of the firm, such as when the firm insists on dealing with the lowest-price supplier, but the buyer has developed a good relationship with another supplier and doesn't want to change. In these cases a seller must appeal to the buyer both on a rational "what's good for the firm" basis, and on a self-interest "what's in it for you" basis. Promotional appeals directed to the buyer's self-interest are particularly useful when two or more competing sellers are offering essentially the same products, prices, and postsale services.

Types of Buying Situations

In Chapter 4 we observed that consumer purchases can range from routine to complex buying decisions, termed low involvement and high involvement, respectively. In like manner the buying situations in business organizations vary widely in their complexity, number of people involved, and time required. Thus, not every purchase involves all five steps of the buying decision process.

To account for these different situations, Figure 5.1 depicts three classes of business buying situations. The three **buy classes** are new-task buying, straight rebuy, and modified rebuy:

- **New-task buying.** This is the most difficult and complex buying situation because it is a first-time purchase of a major product. Typically more people are involved in new-task buying than in the other two situations because the risk is great. Information needs are high and the evaluation of alternatives is difficult because the decision makers have little experience with the product. Sellers have the challenge of discovering the buyer's needs and communicating the product's ability to provide satisfaction. A hospital's first-time purchase of laser surgical equipment and a company buying robots for a factory (or buying the factory itself) are likely to be new-task buying conditions.

- **Straight rebuy.** This is a routine, low-involvement purchase with minimal information needs and little or no consideration of alternatives. Typically the buyer has had extensive, satisfactory experience with the seller, so there is no incentive to search. An example is the repeat purchase of linens and towels by a hospital. These buying decisions are made in the purchasing department, usually from a predetermined list of acceptable suppliers. If a supplier is not on this list, it may have difficulty even getting an opportunity to make a sales presentation to the buyer.

Who will be affected by haptics?

Nearly everyone is familiar with the impressive images and sounds created by computers, but what about touch? A field of technology called haptics focuses on simulating pressure to produce touch-related sensations. The name is derived from a Greek word that means "able to lay hold of." The concept has fascinated scientists and computer designers for years, but commercial applications have been more difficult to identify. One application is the use of joysticks in video games to give players the sensation of a bump in the road or the centrifugal force of cornering. A business market has developed in medical training devices. Surgery simulators give medical students the sensation of feeling, as well as seeing, what's happening inside a patient during an operation. And needle-insertion simulators create the feeling of a needle entering a vein. As the costs of computer processing power and hardware come down, other applications will likely be found. Someday, for example, a clothing buyer in New York may be able to "feel" a garment in China through her computer. What type of buying situation would be faced by a firm considering the addition of a haptic feature in its product?

Sources: Ken Brown, "New Technologies Bring the Sense of Touch to Computers," *The Wall Street Journal*, Nov. 26, 2004, pp. B1+; "Data You Can Virtually Touch," *Economist*, Sept. 18, 2004, p. 12+; David Armstrong, "Touch and Go," *Forbes*, Feb. 28, 2005, pp. 50+.

- **Modified rebuy.** This buying situation is somewhere between the other two in terms of time and people involved, information needed, and alternatives considered. For example, in selecting diagnostic equipment to test blood samples, a hospital would consider a small number of reputable suppliers and evaluate the new features added to the equipment since its last purchase. Similarly, a school district would have a committee review textbooks from a defined group of publishers in selecting a book to replace an outdated edition.

Understanding how the buyer views a buying situation is very important to a seller. The allocation of sales resources, the nature of the presentation made to the buyer, and even the prices offered should be influenced by the buyer's perception of the buying situation.

Multiple Buying Influences—the Buying Center

A **buying center** consists of all the individuals or groups involved in the process of making a decision to purchase. This includes the individuals within and outside an organization that influence the buying decision as well as the person ultimately responsible for the decision. Typically the members of a buying center are not formally identified. That is, there is no list of the buying center members to which a supplier or sales person can refer. One of the biggest challenges in business-to-business marketing is identifying the members of the buying center and their roles for a particular purchase.

Research suggests that the average size of a buying center ranges from three to five persons.[8] In other words, there are *multiple* buying influences, particularly in medium-sized and large firms. Even in small companies where the owner-managers make all major decisions, knowledgeable employees are usually consulted before certain purchases are made. The size and makeup of a buying center will vary depending on the product's cost, the complexity of the decision, and the stage of the buying process. The buying center for a straight rebuy of office supplies will be quite different from the center handling the purchase of a building or a fleet of trucks. Recognizing the existence of buying centers helps sellers appreciate that a successful sales effort seldom can be directed to a single individual.

As shown in Figure 5.1, a buying center includes the people who play any of the following **buying roles:**

- *Users*—the people who actually use the business product, perhaps a secretary, an executive, a production-line worker, or a truck driver.
- *Influencers*—the people who set the specifications and identify the acceptable suppliers in buying decisions because of their technical expertise, their organizational position, or even their political power in the firm.
- *Deciders*—the people who make the actual buying decision regarding the business product and the supplier. A purchasing agent may be the decider in a straight-rebuy situation. But someone in top management may make the decision regarding whether to buy an expensive computer system.
- *Gatekeepers*—the people who control the flow of purchasing information within the organization as well as between the firm and potential vendors. These people may be purchasing agents, secretaries, receptionists, or technical personnel.
- *Buyers*—the people who interact with the suppliers, arrange the terms of sale, and process the actual purchase orders. Typically this is the purchasing department's role. But again, if the purchase is an expensive, complex new buy, the buyer's role may be filled by someone in top management.

Several people in an organization may play the same role. For example, in the same firm, accountants and product designers use PCs for different purposes. As a result, they may prefer different brands. Or the same person may occupy more than one role. A secretary may be a user, an influencer, and a gatekeeper in the purchase of word processing software.

The variety of people contributing to any business buying decision, plus the differences among companies, present real challenges to sales people. As they try to determine who is performing each buying role in a buying situation, sales reps often call on the wrong people. Even knowing who the decision makers are is not enough, because these people may be very difficult to reach and people move into and out of the buying center as the purchase proceeds through the decision process. This, in part, explains why a sales person typically has only a few major accounts.

Certainly the challenges presented in the business buying-decision process should suggest the importance of coordinating the selling activities of the business marketer with the buying needs of the purchasing organization.

Buyer-Seller Relationships

A purchase can be looked upon as an isolated transaction or as part of a larger relationship that involves more parties than the buyer and seller and more interaction than the specific exchange. Figure 5.1 notes two dimensions of this relationship perspective—the supply chain and loyalty.

Rather than focus only on the immediate customer, many marketers approach marketing as a series of links between buyers and sellers. This **supply chain** approach considers the roles of suppliers, producers, distributors, and end users to see how each adds value to and benefits from the final product. This perspective leads to a recognition and understanding of the roles played by the entire value network in successfully bringing a product to market.

Business marketers are also placing greater emphasis on building repeat customers. Research has shown that it is as much as six times less expensive to make a repeat sale than it is to make a sale to a new customer. Repeat sales are often the result of **loyalty**—a willingness of the buyer to purchase from the seller without an extensive evaluation of alternatives. Loyalty requires a high level of trust on the part of the buyer. The time and effort necessary to build such trust is a major undertaking for both parties. For example, it typically entails sharing information about costs, processes, and plans for the future. The process of moving toward long-term, cost-effective, mutually beneficial trust with selected customers is known as relationship marketing, and its implementation is called **customer relationship management (CRM)**. Besides establishing criteria for selecting customers to do business with, CRM involves managing interactions with them. The types of interactions and the processes for effectively using them are organized into three categories:[9]

- *Operational CRM.* The objective is to make routine marketing operations such as sales calls, service programs, and customer support activities more efficient. By keeping track of a customer's purchase history, service schedule, and special requests, a firm can do a better job of anticipating the customer's needs, deciding which new products are best suited to the customer's operation, and providing preventive maintenance before problems occur.

- *Analytical CRM.* The objective is to effectively analyze all the available data about a customer. This involves merging data from internal company sources such as billing and payment histories, data generated by the customer such as average inventory amounts and reorder schedules, and data from third parties such as the government and credit bureaus. The analysis of such data helps a firm assess a customer's current and potential profitability, satisfaction, and loyalty.

www.crmguru.com

- *Collaborative CRM.* The objective is to provide mechanisms for customers to interact with the firm. Rather than the traditional one-way seller-to-buyer communication of media advertising, brochures, or printed catalogs, this is an effort to regularly tap into what the customer is thinking. Examples include incoming call centers, seller-sponsored chat rooms where customers can communicate with one another, and regular satisfaction surveys. Encouraging customer input permits a firm to identify issues before they become problems that disrupt the relationship.

The level at which CRM is conducted depends on the organization. Good sales people have always practiced some form of it, but often their efforts were informal and as a result missed important information. Today's formal CRM approaches combine sophisticated software that can link a firm with its customers, utilize the Internet to move data quickly, and employ data mining techniques that can look for patterns and meaning in databases that far exceed what the human mind can accomplish.

Several traditional business practices tend to discourage relationship building. For example, compensation plans for sales people that reward the volume of sales may result in customers' best interests being overlooked. Likewise, the common accounting practice of treating each department in a firm as a cost center may cause managers to focus on cost minimization rather than customer service. And even the procedure of setting individual department performance goals may foster an environment of competition rather than cooperation.

Building and maintaining relationships may require changing the way business is done. For example, Apple Computer, which once relied exclusively on independent dealers, recognized that many of its larger customers needed specialized service. To satisfy this segment of the market and maintain strong ties to these key customers, the computer firm now has its own sales force calling directly on about 1,000 large accounts. However, many of the orders taken by the sales force are passed along to the dealers for fulfillment to ensure that they are involved as well.

Buying Practices of Business Users

Buying practices in the business market are similar to situational influences in consumer behavior. Several are shown in Figure 5.1. These practices, which are described below, stem from the nature and use of the products and characteristics of the markets.

Business buying is often a long, drawn-out activity due to the complexity of the products and the size of the transaction. From the seller's perspective this often means investing large amounts of human and financial resources in an effort to make the sale. Salespeople invest time in building relationships and gathering information, engineers and scientists create designs to meet the buyer's specifications, prototypes may be built, and presentations made, all in the hope of securing a contract. Of course, many times these efforts are unsuccessful because the prospective buyer selects an alternative supplier or product. However, does the prospective buyer have any ethical obligations in this process? For example, is it unethical to ask a seller to bid on a project when the buyer has no intention of considering the bid but only wants to keep its current supplier from getting too comfortable with the business?

Direct Purchase In the consumer market, consumers rarely buy directly from the producer except in the case of services. In the business market, however, direct purchase by the business user from the producer is quite common even for goods. This is true especially when the order is large and the buyer needs much technical assistance. Makers of microprocessors and semiconductors, such as Intel Corp. and Micron Technology, deal directly with personal computer manufacturers because the memory technology is changing so rapidly. From a seller's point of view, direct selling in the business market is economically viable when there are relatively few potential buyers, they are geographically concentrated, and the individual purchases are large.

Frequency of Purchase In the business market, firms buy certain products very infrequently. Large installations are purchased only once in many years. Small parts and materials to be used in the manufacture of a product may be ordered on long-term contracts, thus a selling opportunity exists as seldom as once a year. Even standard operating supplies, such as office supplies or cleaning products, may be bought only once a month. Because of this buying pattern, a great burden is placed on the personal selling programs of business sellers. The sales force must call on potential customers often enough to keep them familiar with the company's products and to know when a customer is considering a purchase.

Size of Order The average business order is considerably larger than its counterpart in the consumer market. This fact, coupled with the infrequency of purchase, spotlights the significance of each sale in the business market. China Airlines, Taiwan's largest commercial carrier, is buying 12 wide-body jets that will have a purchase price of over $2 billion. Production and delivery of the planes is scheduled to take place over several years. Given the relatively small number of airlines in the world buying these big jets and the impact of each purchase on the operation of the successful seller, it's clear why winning the contract is so important to a company such as Boeing.

Length of Negotiation Period The period of negotiation in a business sale is usually much longer than in a consumer transaction. Reasons for extended negotiations include:

• The number of executives participating in the buying decision.

• The large amount of money involved.

• The customization of the product to meet the buyer's needs.

Reciprocity Arrangements   There has been a significant decline, but not elimination, of reciprocity: the practice of "I'll buy from you if you'll buy from me." This decline has occurred for two reasons, one legal and the other economic. Both the Federal Trade Commission and the Antitrust Division of the Department of Justice have forbidden the practice of reciprocity in any *systematic* manner, particularly in large companies. A firm can buy from a customer, but it must be able to prove that it is not given any special privileges regarding price, quality, or service.

From an economic point of view, reciprocity may not make sense because the price, quality, or service offered by the seller may not be competitive. In addition, when a firm fails to pursue objectives that maximize profits, morale of both the sales force and the purchasing department may suffer.

U.S. firms run into problems with reciprocity in doing business overseas. In many parts of the world, it is taken for granted that if I buy your product, you will buy mine.

Service Expectation   The user's desired level of service is a strong business buying motive that may determine buying practices. Frequently a firm's only differentiating feature is its service, because the product itself is so standardized that it can be purchased from any number of companies. Consider the choice of suppliers that provide elevators for a major office building or hotel. The installation of the elevators is no more important than keeping them operating safely and efficiently. Consequently, in its marketing efforts, a firm such as Montgomery Elevator emphasizes its maintenance service as much as its products.

Sellers must be ready to furnish services both before and after the sale. For example, suppliers such as Kraft Foods conduct a careful analysis of a supermarket's customers and sales performance and then suggest a product assortment and layout for the store's dairy department. In the case of office copiers, manufacturers train the buyers' office staffs in the use of the equipment and, after the machines have been installed, offer other services, such as repairs by specially trained technicians.

Dependability of Supply   Another business buying practice is the user's insistence on an adequate quantity of uniform-quality products. Variations in the *quality* of materials going into their finished products can cause considerable trouble for manufacturers. They may be faced with costly disruptions in their production processes if the imperfections exceed quality control limits. The emphasis on total quality has increased the significance of dependability. Because it has been established that firms can operate with virtually zero defects, buyers expect a very high standard of performance.

Adequate *quantities* are as important as good quality. A work stoppage caused by an insufficient supply of materials is just as costly as one caused by inferior quality of materials. However, firms refuse to buy well in advance of their needs, because doing so would tie up their resources in large inventories of supplies. In order for suppliers to provide sufficient quantities of a product just in time for the buyer's intended use, called just-in-time (JIT) delivery, unprecedented amounts of information must be exchanged. For example, Ford permits its automotive suppliers to have access to its detailed production schedule so that critical parts and components can be delivered exactly when they are needed.

Leasing   Many firms in the business market lease business goods instead of buying them. In the past this practice was limited to large equipment, such as computers (IBM), packaging equipment (American Can Company), and heavy construction equipment. Presently, firms are expanding leasing arrangements to include delivery trucks, automobiles used by sales people, aircraft, shipping containers, office furniture, machine tools, and almost anything else needed to operate a business.

Leasing has several merits for the lessor—the firm providing the equipment:

- Total net income—the income after charging off repairs and maintenance expenses—is often higher than it would be if the equipment were sold.
- The lessor's market may be expanded to include users who could not afford to buy the product, especially for large equipment.
- Leasing offers an effective method of getting users to try a new product. They may be more willing to rent a product than to buy it. If they are not satisfied, their expenditure is limited to a few monthly payments.

From the lessee's, or customer's, point of view, the benefits of leasing are:

- Leasing allows users to retain their investment capital for other purposes.
- Firms can enter a new business with less capital outlay than would be necessary if they had to buy equipment.
- Leased products are usually repaired and maintained by lessors, eliminating one headache associated with ownership.
- Leasing is particularly attractive to firms that need equipment seasonally or sporadically, as in food canning or construction.

The Impact of Electronic Commerce

The most important feature differentiating business from consumer marketing is the customization of products. Because of the significance of a purchase on the buyer's operation, business products often have to be adapted to the user's specific circumstances. For example, Western Star, a division of Freightliner, a truck manufacturer, works with customers to design individual trucks to meet the buyer's needs. Thus, hundreds of decisions are required, all the way from the engine type and size to the configuration of the outside mirrors. Verson, a firm that makes metal presses used by appliance manufacturers and automakers, takes up to 18 months to build a press to meet the exact needs of a buyer. As a result, in many business marketing situations there must be a close, personal working relationship between many levels and functions of buyers and sellers.

However, there are also many business purchases of standardized products. For example, the sale of commodities such as bulk plastic, diesel fuel, and steel stock require much less buyer-seller interaction. There are also many low-technology, standardized products such as office supplies, maintenance products, and many component parts that are purchased in large quantities. In some cases, these are purchased through automatic reorder systems in which the buyer's computer places an order with the seller when inventories decline to a specified level.

Electronic commerce, which involves interactions and transactions over the Internet, takes a variety of forms. Small businesses are buying supplies and equipment on eBay, and reverse auctions (in which the buyer indicates what it wants and the sellers make bids for the business) such as those conducted by FreeMarkets, are growing in popularity. Also, electronic bulletins boards (where sellers can post their offerings and prospective buyers can post their needs) are expanding rapidly. Web-based firms such as Ariba and Commerce One are giving buyers and sellers 24-hour, real-time access to each other.

www.commerceone.com

Electronic commerce will not change all business marketing. There is still a need for personalized relationships in most situations. However, the impact and growth of business transactions on the Internet is a major development that requires the attention of all business marketers. Therefore, we will describe it in detail in Chapter 22.

At this point you know what marketing is and how it fits into an organization's strategy. You also appreciate the nature of consumer and business markets, and how they function. With this background, we are now ready to examine how firms identify the particular markets they wish to serve.

Summary

The business market consists of organizations that buy goods and services to produce other goods and services, to resell to other business users or consumers, or to conduct the organization's operations. It is an extremely large and complex market spanning a wide variety of business users that buy a broad array of business goods and services. Besides manufacturing, the business market includes agriculture, reseller, government, services, nonprofit, and international components.

Business market demand generally is derived, inelastic, and widely fluctuating. Business buyers usually are well informed about what they are buying. Business market demand is analyzed by evaluating the number and kinds of business users and their buying power.

Business buying, or purchasing, has taken on greater strategic importance. Organizations are buying more and making less, under intense time and quality pressures, and developing long-term partnering relationships with suppliers.

The buying-decision process in business markets may involve as many as five stages: need recognition, identification of alternatives, evaluation of alternatives, purchase decision, and postpurchase behavior. The actual number of stages in a given purchase decision depends on a number of factors including buying motives, the type of decision, the buying center, the buyer-seller relationship, and business buying patterns.

Business buying motives are focused on achieving a firm's objectives, but the business buyer's self-interest must also be considered. The types of business buying situations are new-task buy, straight rebuy, or modified rebuy.

The concept of a buying center reflects the multiple buying influences in business purchasing decisions. In a typical buying center people play the roles of users, influencers, deciders, gatekeepers, and buyers.

Developing a buyer-seller relationship stems from recognizing the importance of the customer's supply chain and the benefits of developing loyalty. Relationships require commitment and are built on trust and sharing information.

Buying practices of business users often are quite different from buying practices in the consumer market. In the business market, direct purchases (that is, without middlemen) are more common, purchases are made less frequently, and orders are larger. The negotiation period usually is longer, and reciprocity arrangements sometimes exist. The demand for service is greater, and the dependability of supply is more critical. Finally, leasing (rather than product ownership) is quite common in business marketing.

Electronic commerce is having a major impact on business transactions involving standardized products. Even though it will not replace the need for personalized relationships in many situations, the Internet will affect nearly every aspect of business marketing.

More about Boeing

Boeing's management feels the subsidies given to Airbus by European governmental sponsors, now totaling over $15 billion, create an uneven competitive situation. On the other hand, without support it is unlikely that any organization would invest the time and money necessary to enter the airline manufacturing business. And most observers would contend that the competition between Boeing and Airbus has resulted in better products for the airlines and ultimately the flying public. The questions now seem to be how much is a reasonable subsidy and how long should subsidies be continued.

Boeing also has other challenges. Recently the firm has lost several loyal customers (airlines that were flying Boeing planes almost exclusively) to Airbus. For example, Air Berlin, Germany's second largest carrier, is replacing aging Boeing 737s with 110 Airbus jets. Critics of Boeing contend it is because the firm has not adjusted its prices to the reality of the marketplace. With excess capacity and high operating costs, many airlines are either in or on the verge of bankruptcy. As a result, they are not willing to pay a premium for new planes. After decades as the world's dominant manufacturer, Boeing management argues that buyers should consider the quality of its products and their long-term operating efficiency ahead of purchase price. Boeing's chief executive, feeling that the company's sales force had not done enough to build relationships with the airlines, fired the company's sales manager. He observed, "If you get down to where price is the only discriminator, then you lost the campaign long before (you began)."[10]

1. As the air travel industry is increasingly dominated by discount airlines, can Boeing continue to operate as a premium quality manufacturer?

2. Which of the factors that influence the business buying-decision process are likely to be most important in the sale of commercial passenger jets?

Key Terms and Concepts

Business market (114)
Business user (114)
Business marketing (114)
Business marketer (114)
Value added (114)
Agribusiness (116)
Reseller market (116)
Disintermediation (117)
Government market (117)
Business services market (118)
Nonbusiness market (119)

International market (119)
Elasticity of demand (121)
North American Industry
    Classification System
    (NAICS) (124)
Vertical business market (125)
Horizontal business market (126)
Activity indicator of buying
    power (126)
Buying motives (130)
Buy classes (130)

New-task buying (130)
Straight rebuy (130)
Modified rebuy (131)
Buying center (131)
Buying roles (132)
Supply chain (132)
Loyalty (132)
Customer relationship management
    (CRM) (133)
Electronic commerce (136)

Questions and Problems

1. What are some marketing implications in the fact that the demand for business goods:
   a. Fluctuates widely?
   b. Is inelastic?
   c. Is derived?

2. What are the marketing implications for a seller in the facts that business customers are typically geographically concentrated and limited in number?

3. What differences would you expect to find between the marketing strategies of a company that sells to horizontal business markets and those of a company that sells to vertical business markets?

4. An American manufacturer has been selling to a large oil company in Norway for 10 years. What factors might influence which of the three buy classes would best describe this buyer-seller relationship?

5. Explain how the five stages in the buying-decision process might be applied in the following buying situations:
   a. New-task buying of a conveyor belt for a soft-drink bottling plant.
   b. Straight rebuying of maintenance services for that conveyor belt.

6. How would you go about determining who occupies each of the buying-center roles in a hospital buying patient beds?

7. NCR, IBM, Xerox, and other manufacturers of office equipment make a substantial proportion of their sales directly to business users. At the same time, wholesalers of office equipment are thriving. Are these two market situations inconsistent? Explain.

Interactive Marketing Exercises

1. Find an ad for a business good or service that is directed toward the business market and another ad for the same product that is directed toward consumers (such as an ad for leasing fleets of Chevrolets and an ad for Chevrolets aimed at consumers). Discuss the buying motives appealed to in the ads.

2. Interview a purchasing agent about buying a product that would qualify as a modified rebuy. Draw a diagram that shows the purchasing agent's perceptions of (a) the stages of the decision process; (b) who was in the buying center at each stage of the decision process; and (c) what role(s) each person played at each stage of the process. Comment on how this diagram might be useful to a sales person representing the product in question.

Chapter 6

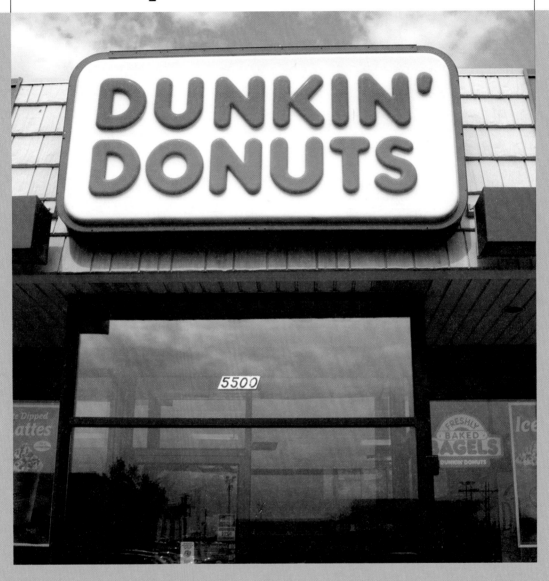

"As for Dunkin' Donuts, its customers are concerned with speed."

Market Segmentation, Targeting, and Positioning

Does the Future Hold More Coffee for **Dunkin' Donuts?**

Would you consider three retailers whose primary offerings are caffeinated drinks and pastries to be competitors? What if they are Starbuck's, Krispy Kreme, and Dunkin' Donuts? It is a question the management of Dunkin' Donuts had to answer as it set out to rejuvenate the venerable chain.

Dunkin' Donuts was begun in 1950 by Bill Rosenberg with a single shop in Quincy, Massachusetts. He began franchising additional outlets in 1955, and by 1979 there were a thousand Dunkin' Donuts outlets in the Northeast. Through a series of transactions in the 1980s and 1990s, Dunkin' Donuts, along with Baskin-Robbins (ice cream) and Togo's (sandwiches) became the quick service restaurant operation of the British firm, Allied Domecq PLC. In 2002, as Allied Domecq looked for growth opportunities, its Dunkin' Donuts (DD) business was described as a "sleeping giant" as much for its fiercely loyal clientele as its $2.8 billion in sales and more than 3,800 U.S. outlets.

In assessing the competitive landscape it would be easy to paint a dark picture. After years of stable growth as a result of providing a morning cup of coffee and a doughnut to millions of commuters, in 2002 DD was confronted with two major challenges.

Starbuck's, the Seattle-based chain, continued to grow in popularity as an increasing number of coffee drinkers shifted to espresso varieties. And at about the same time, Krispy Kreme went public, quickly opening 150 new outlets amid a flurry of media attention over record-breaking sales and celebrities praising the hot, glazed pastry.

Though concern is always warranted when firms selling similar offerings grow rapidly, a closer look at this situation suggests that these firms may be serving different markets. Krispy Kreme's major customers buy only occasionally and when they do, it's in large quantities. The Krispy Kreme marketing director describes his outlets as a "destination experience," more of a dietary splurge or a special indulgence than a regular habit. Starbuck's, on the other hand, is an upscale hangout, an escape from the everyday world, with china cups, comfortable chairs, and Internet access. Howard Shultz, the founder, says, "Starbucks' is more than a wonderful cup of coffee, it's an experience." As for Dunkin' Donuts, its customers are concerned with speed. For many it's a daily pit stop for a quick energy boost, made convenient with drive-through windows. The marketing vice-president describes a typical visit as "get 'em in, sell 'em coffee and a snack, and get 'em out." Another difference is that Starbuck's does nearly 80% of its volume in beverages, while at DD, beverages account for less than 60% of sales.

Even though Dunkin' Donuts serves over 1 billion cups of coffee a year, there's room to grow since more than 100 million Americans drink coffee every day. Growth, however, will depend on the ability of the firm to meet the needs of its customers better than its competitors.[1] Is it wise for the firm to bet that a large part of the coffee and pastry market is more interested in convenience and speed of service than dunking?

www.dunkindonuts.com

Dunkin' Donuts faces a classic marketing challenge. It has a distinctive offering that is clearly not for everyone. However, due to competitive pressure, the firm must do a better job of defining its market, selecting a target, and deciding what features, price, and promotion strategy will be most effective. In this chapter, we will see why markets are segmented and how it is done. We will also consider the alternatives a firm faces in selecting which segments or target markets it wishes to pursue. Then we will introduce the concept of positioning or how a firm makes its offering attractive to a target market. Finally, we'll examine forecasting, the process of estimating the sales potential of a market. After studying this chapter, you should be able to explain:

Chapter Goals

- The related concepts of market segmentation, target marketing, and positioning.
- The process of market segmentation, including its benefits and conditions for use.
- Bases for segmenting consumer and business markets.
- Three target-market strategies: aggregation, single-segment strategy, and multiple-segment strategy.
- The three steps in developing a positioning strategy.
- The most frequently used methods of forecasting the demand of market segments.

An Overview of Market Segments and Target Markets

In Chapter 2 we defined a market as people or organizations with (1) needs to satisfy, (2) money to spend, and (3) the willingness to spend it. However, within a total market, there is always some diversity among the buyers. Not all consumers who wear pants want to wear jeans. Some vacationers take a cruise for rest and relaxation, others look for adventure and excitement. Among businesses, not all firms that use computers want the same amount of memory or speed, and not every software buyer needs the same amount of expert advice.

What we are seeing here is that within the same general market there are groups of customers—**market segments**—with different wants, buying preferences, or product-use behavior. In some markets these differences are relatively minor, and the benefits sought by consumers can be satisfied with a single marketing mix. In other markets, some customers are unwilling to make the compromises necessitated by a single marketing mix. As a result, the firm must decide which segment or segments to pursue, a strategy called **target marketing.** For a targeted segment the firm then moves to establish a *position* in the minds of its members through the design and implementation of a marketing mix. A firm targeting only one segment would have a single marketing mix, whereas a firm pursuing several segments would have an equal number of marketing mixes.

Before positions can be defined and marketing mixes designed, however, potential target markets must be identified and described. This process is called *market segmentation.*

Market Segmentation

The variation in customers' responses to a marketing mix can be traced to differences in buying habits, in ways in which the good or service is used, or in motives for buying. Customer-oriented marketers take these differences into consideration, but they usually cannot afford to design a different marketing mix for every customer. Consequently, most marketers operate between the extremes of one marketing mix for all and a different one for each customer. To do so involves **market segmentation,** a process of dividing the total market for a good or service into several smaller, internally homogeneous groups. The essence of segmentation is that the members of each group are similar with respect to the factors that influence demand. A major element in a company's success is the ability to segment its market effectively.

Benefits of Market Segmentation

Market segmentation is customer-oriented, and thus it is consistent with the marketing concept. In segmenting, we first identify the wants of customers within a submarket and then decide if it is practical to develop a marketing mix to satisfy those wants.

By tailoring marketing programs to individual market segments, any company can do a better marketing job and make more efficient use of its marketing resources. Focus is especially important for a small firm with limited resources. Such a firm might compete very effectively in one or two small market segments; however, it would likely be overwhelmed by the competition if it aimed for a major segment. For example, The Hain Celestial Group, Inc., is focusing on various segments of the U.S. and international markets for organic and natural foods. Under one of its brands, Celestial Seasonings, the firm markets specialty teas. After water, tea is the most heavily consumed drink in the world, and Hain Celestial is developing new market and distribution strategies to support new tea flavors for many different market segments.

www.hain-celestial.com

By developing strong positions in specialized market segments, medium-sized firms can grow rapidly. For example, the Oshkosh Truck Corporation has become the world's largest producer of fire and rescue trucks for airports.

Even very large companies with the resources to engage in mass marketing supported by expensive national advertising campaigns are abandoning mass-market strategies. These companies embrace market segmentation as a more effective strategy to reach the fragments that once constituted a mass, or homogeneous, market in the U.S.

Of the 60 million U.S. households with pets, some need services such as boarding when the family members are traveling. However, not all kennels are alike. In fact, some prefer to be called pet hotels and offer all sorts of special amenities including day care and birthday parties for pets. How would you go about segmenting the market of pet owners for a service such as the one described on this website?

 www.theloveddog.com

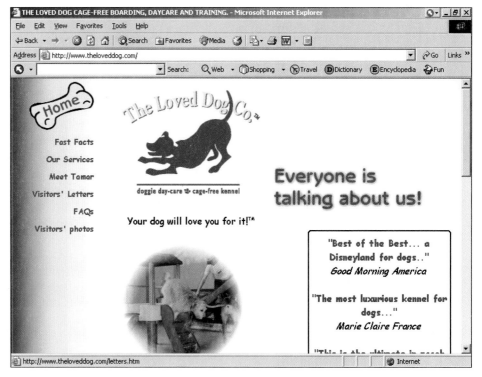

The marketing of many consumer products illustrates this approach. The typical supermarket stocks about 40,000 items, twice the number of a few years ago. Many are very similar. For example, there are 19 different types of Pert shampoos and conditioners, each purporting to offer distinctive benefits such as "deep moisturizing" or "volume." Similarly, P&G offers 14 versions of Crest toothpaste and 72 varieties of Pantene hair-care treatments, and Kellogg's has 16 flavors of Eggo waffles.

This proliferation of alternatives has a potential downside. Consumers can become frustrated by the complex decision making that is required for even a simple purchase when many similar products are available. As a result, marketers should seek a balance between meeting the specialized needs of consumers and overwhelming them with choices.

The Process of Market Segmentation

Markets are sometimes segmented intuitively; that is, a marketer relies on experience and judgment to make a decision about the segments that exist in a market and how much potential each offers. Others follow the lead of competitors or earlier market entrants. For example, Gatorade was invented by University of Florida scientists to rapidly replenish the body fluids of the school's football players. When it was later introduced as a consumer product, it met the needs of a group of beverage consumers that became known as the "sports drink" segment. As Gatorade's popularity grew, imitators such as Powerade from Coca-Cola and All Sport from Pepsi were introduced. Each has taken a small share of the market, but they did not unseat Gatorade as the brand with the largest share. And the future may get even rougher for these imitators now that Gatorade has been acquired by Pepsi, and will benefit from even broader distribution.

Another alternative is to perform a structured analysis, usually supported by some market research, in order to identify segments and measure their potential. This approach, even if done with a small budget, often produces insights and opportunities that would be overlooked otherwise.

The steps involved in segmenting a market in an organized fashion are:

1. *Identify the current and potential wants that exist within a market.* The marketer carefully examines the market to determine the specific needs being satisfied by current offerings, the needs current offerings fail to adequately satisfy, and the needs that may not yet be recognized. This step may involve interviewing and/or observing consumers or firms to determine their behavior, levels of satisfaction, and frustrations. Within the market for wristwatches there is a common desire among all customers to know the time, and certainly all watches must accurately tell time. But there are also customers who variously want a watch to be a fashion accessory, a status symbol, an exercise timer, or an appointment reminder. There might be others who would like a watch to function as a computer, a voice recorder, a pulse monitor, a television receiver, or a telephone. These wants individually or in some combination represent potential market segments within the wristwatch market.

2. *Identify characteristics that distinguish among the segments.* In this step the focus is on what prospects who share a particular want have in common to distinguish them from other segments in the market that have different wants. Among business firms it could be a physical feature (like size or location). Among consumers it might be an attitude or a behavior pattern. From the results of this step, potential marketing mixes (including product ideas) for the various segments can be designed. These alternatives can then be further analyzed.

3. *Determine the potential of the segments and how well they are being satisfied.* The final step is to estimate the size (or potential sales) of each segment, the

urgency of the need, and the strength of the competition. These forecasts will determine which segments are worth pursuing. American Express launched an Internet banking service that allows customers to make deposits, purchase certificates of deposit, obtain loans, and pay bills online. Despite the fact that online competition from conventional banks and other credit card companies is fierce, American Express' existing cardholders make up an attractive initial market segment.

A group that shares a want distinguishable from the rest of the market is a market segment. However, to be useful to marketers, results of a segmentation effort must also meet some conditions:

- The bases for segmenting—that is, the characteristics used to describe what segments customers fall into—must be *measurable,* and data describing the characteristics must be *obtainable.* The age of customers is both measurable and obtainable. On the other hand, the "desire for environmentally friendly products" may be a factor useful in segmenting the market for mulching lawn mowers. But this characteristic is not easily measured, nor can the data be easily obtained.

- The market segment should be *accessible* through existing marketing institutions—middlemen, advertising media, the company's sales force—with a minimum of cost and wasted effort. To increase the benefits of segmentation, most national magazines such as *Time* and *Sports Illustrated* and large metropolitan newspapers such as the *Chicago Tribune* publish separate geographic editions. This allows an advertiser to run a magazine ad aimed at, say, a Southern segment of the market or a newspaper ad for particular suburbs, without having to pay for exposure in other, nontargeted areas.

- Each segment should be *large enough* to be profitable. Procter & Gamble found a segment of candy consumers that wants a low-calorie product. However, it is too small to justify the investment a line of confections would require. In concept, management could treat each single customer as a separate segment. Actually, this situation, called **micromarketing**, is becoming more common in consumer markets and is quite common in some business markets, as when Freightliner custom-designs a long-haul truck for a customer, or when Citibank makes a loan to the government of Mexico or Argentina. Micromarketing occurs in selected consumer markets such as custom-designed homes. But in segmenting most consumer markets, a firm must not develop too broad an array of styles, colors, sizes, and prices, because the production and inventory costs would make it unprofitable.

Ultimate Consumers and Business Users—the First Cut

As we shall see, a company can segment its market in many different ways, and the bases for segmentation vary from one market to another. Often the first step is to divide a potential market into two broad categories: ultimate consumers and business users. Black & Decker does this, offering the DeWalt line of power tools for professionals, the Quantum line for the do-it-yourself segment, and the Black & Decker brand for the consumer who takes on occasional small tasks.

The sole criterion for this first cut at segmenting a market is the customer's reason for buying. Recall from Chapter 4 that ultimate consumers buy goods or services for their own personal or household use and are satisfying strictly nonbusiness wants. They constitute the consumer market. Business users, described in Chapter 5, are business, industrial, or institutional organizations that buy goods or services to

When you consider the cost of creating three marketing programs, as Black & Decker (B&D) has done for its power tools, it suggests how important segmentation is to the success of a company and its products. DeWalt, Quantum, and the Black & Decker brand each has distinct product features, prices, packaging, advertising, and distribution.

 www.bdk.com

use in their organizations, to resell, or to make other products. Black & Decker recognized that professionals who earn their living in the building trades need durable tools that perform precisely. Do-it-yourselfers, on the other hand, use their tools less often, typically take on less complicated projects, and are satisfied with less powerful equipment. These segments were judged to be so different that each requires a separate marketing mix.

Segmenting a market into these two groups—consumers and businesses—is extremely significant from a marketing point of view because the two segments buy differently. Consequently, the composition of a seller's marketing mix will depend on whether it is directed toward the consumer market or the business market.

Segmenting Consumer Markets

Dividing a total market into ultimate consumers and business users results in segments that are still too broad and varied for most products. We need to identify some characteristics within each of these segments that will enable us to divide them further into more specific targets.

As shown in Table 6.1, there are a number of ways the consumer market can be segmented. The bases for segmentation include many of the characteristics used to describe the consumer market in Chapter 4, as well as some psychological and behavioral dimensions. To illustrate, we will discuss four bases for segmenting consumer markets that are used separately or in combination: geographic, demographic, psychographic, and behavioral.

Geographic Segmentation

Subdividing markets into segments based on location—the regions, counties, cities, and towns where people live and work—is **geographic segmentation.** The reason for this is simply that consumers' wants and product usage often are related to one or more of these subcategories. Geographic characteristics are also measurable and accessible—two of the conditions for effective segmentation. Let's consider how the geographic distribution of population may serve as a basis for segmentation.

Regional Population Distribution
Many firms market their products in a limited number of geographic regions, or they may market nationally but prepare a

TABLE
6.1

Segmentation Bases for Consumer Markets

Segmentation Basis	Possible Market Segments
Geographic	
Region	New England, Middle Atlantic, and other census regions
City or metro-area size	Population under 25,000; 25,000–100,000; 100,001–500,000; 500,001–1,000,000; etc.
Urban–rural	Urban, suburban, rural
Climate	Hot, cold, sunny, rainy, cloudy
Demographic	
Income	Under $25,000; $25,000–$50,000; $50,001–$75,000; $75,001–$100,000; over $100,000
Age	Under 6, 6–12, 13–19, 20–34, 35–49, 50–64, 65 and over
Gender	Male, female
Family life cycle	Young, single; young, married, no children; etc.
Social class	Upper class, upper-middle, lower-middle, upper-lower, etc.
Education	Grade school only, high school graduate, college graduate
Occupation	Professional, manager, clerical, sales, student, homemaker, unemployed, etc.
Ethnic background	African, Asian, European, Hispanic, Middle Eastern, etc.
Psychographic	
Personality	Ambitious, self-confident, aggressive, introverted, extroverted, sociable, etc.
Lifestyle	Activities (golf, travel); interests (politics, modern art); opinions (conservation, capitalism)
Values	Values and lifestyles (VALS2), list of values (LOV)
Behavioral	
Benefits desired	Examples vary widely depending on product: appliance—cost, quality, operating life; toothpaste—no cavities, plaque control, bright teeth, good taste, low price
Usage rate	Nonuser, light user, heavy user

separate marketing mix for each region. The regional distribution of population is important to marketers because people *within* a given region generally tend to share similar values, attitudes, and style preferences. However, significant differences often exist *among* regions because of differences in climate, social customs, and other factors. For example, Campbell Soup Company has altered the spiciness of some of its soup and bean recipes to suit regional tastes, and Friday's, with over 525 restaurants nationwide, allows each outlet to offer up to 30 regional items on its menu.

Many organizations segment their markets on the basis of city size or population concentration; that is, they utilize an urban-suburban-rural distribution. You may find it surprising that Wal-Mart's initial strategy was to locate only in towns of *less* than 35,000 people in order to minimize the amount of competition.

A popular reference source used for geographic segmentation is *Sales & Marketing Management* magazine's annual "Survey of Buying Power." This two-part report provides information on population, income, and spending behavior by state, county, major metropolitan area, television market, and newspaper market. With these data, a marketer can compare spending power and purchasing behavior across geographic areas.

Demographic Segmentation

Demographics are also a common basis for segmenting consumer markets. They are frequently used because they are often strongly related to demand and are relatively easy to measure. Recall that several demographic variables were discussed in Chapter 4 in descriptions of the consumer market. The most popular characteristics, used alone or in combination, for **demographic segmentation** are age, gender, occupation, income, and education. For example, Pepsi-Cola successfully targeted its Sierra Mist lemon-lime soft drink at 18- to 34-year-olds because they were largely being ignored by the marketers of Sprite and 7Up.[2] Examples of demographic segmentation characteristics are shown in Table 6.1.

It is important to note that there are no rules for the number or breadth of categories used in a segmentation effort. The market and the need being satisfied should dictate the choices. For example, there may be a certain symmetry in an age category that includes all teenagers (and data may be available on "teens"), but the purchase behavior and motivations of 13- and 14-year-olds in a particular market may be quite different from 18- and 19-year-olds.

Social class, a measure indicative of a person's social position made up of several demographic dimensions, and family life cycle, describing stages parents and their children go through, illustrate this approach to segmenting a market. The most commonly used indicator of social class includes level of education, type of occupation, and the type of neighborhood a person lives in. Many consider social class a "richer" indicator than income or any of the individual social class components taken separately. They would argue that a lawyer and a plumber, for example, might have the same income but be members of different social classes. Because a person's social class—be it upper class or blue-collar working class—has a considerable influence on that person's choices in many product categories, companies frequently select one or two social classes as target markets and then develop a product and marketing mix to reach those segments.[3]

The ways in which segmentation bases can be combined is limited only by the imagination of the marketer and the availability of data. For example, an approach called geodemographic clustering is based on ZIP codes, demographic data available from the U.S. Census, and household data collected by the research firm Claritas. The trade name for the procedure is PRIZM (short for Potential Rating Index for ZIP Markets). Using Census data on education, income, occupation, housing, ethnicity, urbanization, and other variables, Claritas grouped the 36,000 U.S. ZIP codes into 15 groups and 66 similar clusters or segments. Each cluster then was further examined for similarities in lifestyles and consumption behavior, and given descriptive names such as "kids and cul-de-sacs," "gray power," and "shotguns and pickups." Marketers use this information to identify ZIP codes for direct-mail promotions, to select locations for retail outlets, and to determine the best mix of products and brands to offer in particular stores.

www.claritas.com

Psychographic Segmentation

Demographics are used to segment markets because these data are related to behavior and because they are relatively easy to gather. However, demographics are not in themselves the causes of behavior. Consumers don't buy windsurfing equipment because they are young. They buy it because they enjoy an active, outdoor lifestyle, and it so happens that such people are also typically younger. Thus demographics often correlate with behavior, but they do not explain it.

Marketers often go beyond demographic attributes in an effort to better understand why consumers behave as they do. They engage in what is called **psychographic segmentation,** which involves examining attributes related to how a person thinks, feels, and behaves. Frequently included in a psychographic segmentation effort are personality dimensions, life-style characteristics, and consumer values.

Personality Characteristics An individual's **personality** is usually described in terms of traits that influence behavior. Intuitively, they would seem to be a good basis for segmenting markets. Our experience suggests that compulsive people buy differently from cautious consumers, and quiet introverts do not buy the same things or in the same way as gregarious, outgoing people.

AN ETHICAL DILEMMA?

However, personality characteristics pose problems that limit their usefulness in practical market segmentation. First, the presence and strength of these characteristics in the general population are virtually impossible to measure. For example, how would you go about measuring the number of people in the U.S. who could be classified as aggressive? Another problem is associated with the accessibility condition of segmentation. There is no advertising medium that provides unique access to a particular personality type; that is, television reaches introverts as well as extroverts, aggressive people as well as timid people. So one of the major goals of segmentation, to avoid wasted marketing effort, is not likely to be accomplished using personality.

Nevertheless, firms often tailor their advertising messages to appeal to personality traits. Even though the importance of the personality dimension in a particular decision may be unmeasurable, the seller believes that it does play an influential role. Thus, for years Hallmark promoted its greeting cards by suggesting to consumers, "When you care enough to send the very best," and L'Oréal models used the company's products "Because I'm worth it."

Lifestyle A person's activities, interests, and opinions (AIO) reflects their **lifestyle.** To marketers, your lifestyle represents how you spend your time and what your beliefs are on various social, economic, and political issues. It is a broad concept that overlaps what some consider to be personality characteristics.

People's lifestyles undoubtedly affect what products they buy and what brands they prefer. Marketers are aware of this and often design their strategies based on life-style segments. Ads for Polo clearly portray a life-style image. And the firm's website describes the strategy in the words of Ralph Lauren:[4]

www.polo.com

> Polo has always been about selling a quality product by creating worlds and inviting our customers to be part of our dream. We were the first to create lifestyle advertisements that tell a story. We were the first to create stores that encourage customers to participate in that lifestyle.

Although it is a valuable marketing tool, life-style segmentation has some of the same limitations as segmentation based on personality characteristics. For example, it is difficult to accurately measure the size of life-style segments in the population. For example, how many people want to reflect the "Polo lifestyle" in what they wear? Another problem is that a given life-style segment might not be accessible at a reasonable cost through a firm's usual distribution system or promotional program.

The Smart Car, produced by DaimlerChrysler, is only 8 feet long and goes 57 miles on a gallon of gas. With a price tag of around $9,000 it has proven to be quite popular in Europe and Asia. Despite its obvious advantages of low operating cost, maneuverability, and ease of parking, there are questions about how well the Smart Car would fit American car buyers' lifestyles and values. The success of SUVs and minivans in the U.S. suggests that capacity, comfort, and safety concerns may drive automobile purchases. What demographic and psychographic features should DaimlerChrysler examine in searching for a U.S. Smart Car market segment?

 www.smart.com

Values   According to psychologists, **values** are a reflection of our needs adjusted for the realities of the world in which we live. Researchers at the Survey Research Center at the University of Michigan have identified nine basic values that relate to purchase behavior. The nine, which they call the list of values (LOV), are:

- Self-respect
- Security
- Excitement
- Fun and enjoyment in life
- Having warm relationships
- Self-fulfillment
- Sense of belonging
- Sense of accomplishment
- Being well respected

Although almost everyone would view all these values as desirable, their relative importance differs among people, and their relative importance affects behavior. For example, people who place a high value on fun and enjoyment are more likely to enjoy skiing, dancing, bicycling, and backpacking, whereas people who have high value for warm relationships tend to give gifts for no particular reason. Thus, the relative strength of values could be the basis for segmenting a market.

Behavioral Segmentation

Some marketers regularly attempt to segment their markets on the basis of product-related behavior—they utilize **behavioral segmentation.** In this section we briefly consider two of these approaches: the benefits desired from a product and the rate at which the consumer uses the product.

Benefits Desired   From a customer-oriented perspective, the ideal method for segmenting a market is on the basis of customers' desired benefits. Certainly, using benefits to segment a market is consistent with the idea that a company should be marketing benefits and not simply the attributes of a product. After all, a carpenter wants a smooth surface (benefit), not a Black & Decker electric sander (the product). In many cases, however, benefits desired by customers do not meet the first condition of segmentation described above. That is, they are not easily measured because customers are unwilling or unable to reveal them. For example, what benefits do people derive from clothing that has the label on the outside? Conversely, why do others refuse to wear such clothing?

Performing benefit segmentation is a multistep process. First, the specific benefits consumers are seeking must be identified. This typically involves several research steps, beginning with the identification of all possible benefits related to a particular product or behavior through brainstorming, observing consumers, and listening to group discussions. Then more research is conducted to screen out unlikely or unrealistic benefits and to amplify and clarify the remaining possibilities. Finally, largescale surveys are conducted to determine how important the benefits are and how many consumers seek each one.

To illustrate, with the growth of the Internet, bankers saw an opportunity to shift consumers to electronic banking. They developed the technology, closed branch banks, and promoted the idea heavily. However, when the effort was met with consumer resistance, the banks' research uncovered the benefits of personalized service. For many financial transactions consumers simply want to deal with a person. As a result, between 2000 and 2004 the six largest banks in the U.S. have reestablished or opened over 1,500 branches.[5]

Usage Rate   Another basis for market segmentation is the rate at which people consume a product. A popular categorization of usage rates is nonusers, light users, medium users, and heavy users. Normally a company is most interested in the heavy users of its product because fewer than 50% of all users of a product typically account for 80% to 90% of the total purchases. These heavy users are often referred to in an industry as the "heavy half" of the market. Many marketers aim their marketing efforts at retaining the consumers who make up the heavy half for their brand, and encouraging the heavy-half users of competitors' brands to switch. For example, Best Buy, the consumer-electronics retailer, uses demographic data, sales records, and other databases to categorize customers as "angels" or "devils." Angels, who are about 20% of the chain's customers and generate the bulk of its profits, buy high-margin items such as high-definition televisions and new CDs without the benefit of rebates or markdowns. Devils, on the other hand, are a drain on profits because they shop for bargains, utilize rebates, and frequently return merchandise. Best Buy employees are trained to identify angels and give them special attention.[6]

Sometimes a marketer will select as a target market the nonuser or light user, intending to woo these customers into higher usage. Or light users may constitute an appealing niche for a seller simply because they are being ignored by firms that are targeting heavy users. Once the characteristics of these light users have been identified, management can go to them directly with an attractive positioning to increase usage, for example by (1) describing new uses for a product (baking soda as a refrigerator deodorizer, chewing gum as an alternative to cigarettes); (2) suggesting new times or places for use (soup as an after-school snack, air fresheners in school lockers); or (3) offering multiple-unit packaging (a 12-pack of soft drinks).

MARKETING IN THE INFORMATION ECONOMY

Can technology benefit grocery shoppers?

Albertsons, a grocery and drugstore retailer, combines convenience for its most loyal customers with electronic data gathering. Customers who have registered in Albertsons' preferred shopper program can use handheld scanner devices as they move through the store. Using the scanners, they tally and bag their items as they shop. The device provides a running total of selected items and suggests complementary items such as buns to go along with hot dogs. It also provides coupons and discount offers on selected items. Customers can remove items or add items until they arrive at the pay station, where all the information is electronically downloaded into a register, and they pay.

The information from the devices used by the customers is also downloaded into a database which is analyzed by Albertsons to identify customer preferences and shopping trends. According to the company's management, customers who use the device have doubled the amount they buy on each store visit because they can keep track of exactly how much they are spending.

Sources: Beth Bachelor, "Scanning for Groceries," *InformationWeek*, Apr. 12, 2004, p. 28; Carol Hymowitz, "CEOs Use Technology to Gather Information, Build Customer Loyalty," *The Wall Street Journal*, Oct. 26, 2004, p. B1.

Segmenting Business Markets

Even though the number of buyers in a business market may be relatively few compared to a consumer market, segmentation remains important. The reason is quite simple—a highly focused marketing effort directed at meeting the specific needs of a group of similar customers is both more efficient and more likely to be successful.

In Table 6.2 (below) examples of business market segmentation bases are grouped by customer location, customer type, and transaction conditions. Notice that many of the bases are similar to ones used for segmenting consumer markets. To provide a feel for business market segmentation, several of these bases are described in more detail.

Customer Location

Business markets are frequently segmented on a geographic basis. Some industries are geographically concentrated. For example, businesses that process natural resources locate close to the source to minimize shipping costs. Other industries are geographically concentrated simply because newer firms either spun off from or chose to locate near the industry pioneers. For example, several brands of recreational vehicles, including Skyline and Monaco Coach are manufactured in northern Indiana. Some firms that sell to this industry, such as Patrick Industries (cabinets and paneling) and LaSalle-Bristol (floor covering), have chosen to locate nearby and focus their efforts geographically.

Companies also segment international markets geographically. In considering developing countries, for example, a firm might consider the reliability of public utilities, the quality of the transportation system, and the sophistication of the distribution structure in deciding where to expand its operation.

Customer Type

Industry   Any firm that sells to business customers in a variety of industries may want to segment its market on the basis of industry. For example, a company that sells small electric motors would have a broad potential market among many different industries. However, this firm will do better by segmenting its potential market

TABLE 6.2

Segmentation Bases for Business Markets

Segmentation Basis	Possible Market Segments
Customer Location	
Region	Southeast Asia, Central America, Upper Midwest, Atlantic Seaboard
Locations	Single buying site, multiple buying sites
Customer Type	
Industry	Selected NAICS codes
Size	Sales volume, number of employees
Organization structure	Centralized or decentralized, group or individual decision
Purchase criteria	Quality, price, durability, lead time
Transaction Conditions	
Buying situation	Straight rebuy, modified rebuy, new buy
Usage rate	Nonuser, light user, heavy user
Purchasing procedure	Competitive bidding, lease, service contracts
Order size	Small, medium, large
Service requirements	Light, moderate, heavy

by type of customer and then specializing in order to more completely meet the needs of organizations in a limited number of these segments. The NAICS codes, described in Chapter 5, are particularly useful for this purpose because information published by the government and industry on such factors as the number of firms, their size, and their location is often organized according to this scheme.

Size   Business customer size can be estimated using such factors as sales volume, number of employees, number of production facilities, and number of sales offices. Many sellers divide their potential market into large and small accounts, using separate distribution channels to reach each segment. The seller's sales force may contact large-volume accounts directly, but to reach the smaller accounts, the seller may use a middleman or rely on the Internet or telemarketing.

Organization Structure   Firms approach buying in different ways. Some rely heavily on their purchasing departments to control the inflow of information, reduce the number of potential alternatives, and conduct negotiations. Selling to such companies would require a strong personal selling effort directed specifically at purchasing executives. It would also need excellent supporting materials if the product exceeded the technical expertise of the purchasing managers.

Other buyers opt for greater involvement in the purchase process by the people who will be directly affected by the purchase. These buyers tend to include many people in their decisions, hold meetings over a long period of time, and engage in a lot of internal communication. Government agencies are especially known for lengthy purchase decisions. For example, because of the extensive approval processes, obtaining an order to sell supplies to a federal prison often takes two or three years. Selling to a market segment such as this requires many, varied contacts, and often involves several people from the selling firm.

Purchase Criteria   All buyers want good quality, low prices, and on-time delivery. However, within a market there are groups for which one of these or some other purchase criterion is particularly significant. Consider the automotive business. General Motors buys over $90 *billion* in components, machinery, and equipment a year. In selecting suppliers GM has a formal process that takes into account a prospect's technical capabilities, defect rates, and delivery schedule among other criteria.

Transaction Conditions

The circumstances of the transaction can also be a basis for segmenting a market. Sellers may have to modify their marketing efforts to deal with different buying situations, usage rates, purchasing procedures, order sizes, or service requirements. To illustrate, three of these transaction conditions are described below.

Buying Situation   When Singapore Airlines was faced with the decision of whether or not to buy Boeing's 7E7 Dreamliner, a plane that would replace its existing 747s, it was making a new buy. The decision is quite different from the modified rebuy that occurs when United purchases additional 737s, a plane it has flown successfully for years. These buying situations, along with the straight rebuy, are sufficiently unique that a business seller might well segment its market into these three buy-class categories. Or the seller could at least set up two segments by combining new buy and modified rebuy into one segment. Different marketing programs would be developed to reach each of these two or three segments.

Usage Rate   Markets for most products can be divided into heavy users, light users, and nonusers (prospects). Heavy users appear to be the most attractive because of the volume they purchase, but they also generate the most competition. As an alternative to pursuing heavy users, some firms have found it profitable to avoid the competition by concentrating on light users.

Purchase Procedure   Products can be leased, financed, or purchased outright. A price can be simply stated, negotiated, or submitted in a sealed bid. Consider how a bidding system affects a seller. Government agencies often buy on the basis of sealed bids; that is, each prospective seller submits a confidential bid in response to a detailed description of what the agency wants to buy. When the bids are opened, the agency is typically bound by law to accept the lowest bid unless it is clearly inappropriate. How is this different from a negotiated price? For one thing, the seller has only one chance to propose a price. Also, to compete in a sealed-bid market, it is essential to have low costs. And good industry knowledge is important in order to accurately predict what other firms will bid. These differences might cause a firm to treat the government as a distinct segment.

Segmentation identifies the opportunities that exist in a market. The next step is for a firm to decide which of those opportunities to target with a marketing effort.

Target-Market Strategies

A specific market segment (people or organizations) on which a seller focuses its efforts is called a **target market**. The alterntive strategies are market aggregation, single-segment concentration, or multiple-segment targeting.

Aggregation Strategy

By adopting a **market-aggregation strategy**—also known as a *mass-market strategy* or an *undifferentiated-market strategy*—a seller treats its total market as a single segment. An aggregate market's members are considered to be alike with respect to demand for the product. That is, customers are willing to make some compromises on less important dimensions in order to enjoy the primary benefit the product offers. In this situation, the total market is the firm's target. Therefore, management can develop a single marketing mix and reach most of the customers in the entire market. The company offers a single product for this mass audience; it designs one pricing structure and one distribution system for its product; and it uses a single promotional program aimed at the entire market. This is sometimes described as a "shotgun" approach (one program to reach a broad target).

When is an organization likely to adopt a market-aggregation strategy? In reality, the notion of an aggregate market is relatively uncommon. Even a commodity such as gasoline is provided at different octane levels, with or without ethanol, and with a variety of other additives. The total market for most types of products is too varied—too heterogeneous—to be considered a single, uniform entity. To speak of a market for vitamin pills, for example, is to ignore the existence of submarkets that differ significantly from one another. Because of these differences, One-A-Day vitamins are offered in *19* variations including the well-known regular formula for adults, a special women's formula, the Scooby-Doo children's formula, and also separate formulations for energy, memory, tension and mood, as well as several others.

Generally an aggregation strategy is selected after the firm has examined a market for segments and concluded that regardless of their differences, the majority of customers in the total market are likely to respond in very similar fashion to one marketing mix. This strategy may be appropriate for firms that are marketing an undifferentiated, staple product such as salt or sugar. In the eyes of many people, sugar is sugar, regardless of the brand, and all brands of table salt are pretty much alike.

The strength of a market aggregation strategy is cost minimization. It enables a company to produce, distribute, and promote its products very efficiently. Producing and marketing one product for the entire market means longer production runs at lower unit costs. Inventory costs are minimized when there is no (or a very limited) variety of colors and sizes of products. Warehousing and transportation are most efficient when one product is going to one market. Promotion costs are minimized when the same message is transmitted to all customers.

The strategy of market aggregation typically is accompanied by the strategy of product differentiation in a company's marketing program. **Product differentiation** occurs when, in the eyes of customers, one firm distinguishes its product from competitive brands offered to the same aggregate market. Through differentiation an organization creates the perception that its product is better than the competitors' brands, as when C&H Sugar advertises its product as "pure cane sugar."[7] In addition to creating a preference among consumers for the seller's brand, successful product differentiation can also reduce price competition.

A seller differentiates its product either by (1) creating a distinctive appearance with the package or product shape, for example, or (2) using a promotional appeal that features a differentiating claim. For example, various brands of aspirin claim to be the most effective in relieving pain, although they all contain essentially the same ingredients.

Single-Segment Strategy

A **single-segment strategy,** also called a *concentration strategy,* involves selecting one segment from within the total market as the target market. One marketing mix is developed to reach this single segment. A company may choose this strategy to avoid directly taking on many competitors in the broader market.

When manufacturers of foreign automobiles first entered the U.S. market, they typically targeted a single segment. The original Volkswagen Beetle was intended for the low-price, small-car market, and Mercedes-Benz targeted the high-income market. Today, of course, most of the established foreign car marketers have moved into a multisegment strategy. Consider, for example, the Volkswagen product line. Only a few, such as Rolls-Royce and Ferrari, continue to concentrate on their original single segment.

A single-segment strategy enables a seller to penetrate one market in depth and to acquire a reputation as a specialist or an expert in this limited market. Firms that pursue single segments are often referred to as **niche marketers** and their targeted segments as **niche markets.** Niche markets are often, but not always, relatively small. Two firms recently included in a list of fast-growing companies and their niches are Brass Eagle, an outfitter for the sport of paintball, and Ahead, a manufacturer of golf caps.

A company can initiate a single-segment strategy with limited resources. As long as the single segment remains a small market, large competitors are likely to leave it alone. However, if the small market should show signs of significant growth, the larger firms may jump in.

The risk and limitation of a single-segment strategy is that the seller has "all its eggs in one basket." If the market potential of that single segment declines, the seller can suffer considerably. Also, a seller with a strong name and reputation in one segment may find it very difficult to expand into another segment. For example, General Motors decided to eliminate the Oldsmobile brand when it was unable to attract a younger segment of the car-buying market.

Multiple-Segment Strategy

Under a **multiple-segment strategy,** two or more different groups of potential customers are identified as target markets. A separate marketing mix is developed to reach each targeted segment. For example, Bayer offers nine variations of aspirin as well as Aleve among its pain relief products, each with its own marketing program.

www.bayer.com

Can a building supply retailer target both men and women?

Home Depot, a retailer of tools and supplies for building projects, has always targeted men. Management positioned the stores for male do-it-yourselfers and professional contractors; that is until they did some research on all their customers. They found women are tackling more major remodeling projects alone, and in many households husbands and wives are taking on renovation projects as equal partners. The challenge for Home Depot was to make its stores more female-friendly without offending its male customers. Changes included moving shelves down and making them shallower so women can more easily see the merchandise, providing aisle markers like the ones found in grocery stores, polishing the concrete floors to produce a tidier appearance, and adding decorating ideas to its catalog to increase the appeal to women. A major program involves "Do-It-Herself" workshops in the stores with the topics determined by female customers. One thing Home Depot hasn't done is change its product mix. It found women don't want dainty tools just for them, rather they want to learn how to use "real" tools.

With professional contractors accounting for 35% of its nearly $60 billion in sales, and its core do-it-yourself customers being male, is Home Depot overreaching by pursuing a female target as well?

Sources: Fara Warner, "Yes, Women Spend (and Saw and Sand)," *New York Times*, Feb. 29, 2004, p. 3; Sarah Dobson, "Skeptical Consumers," *Marketing Magazine*, Oct. 25, 2004, p. 3; Walter E. Johnson, "The Evolving DYI Consumer," *Chain Store Age*, October 2004, p. 60.

In a multiple-segment strategy, a seller frequently will develop a different version of the basic product for each segment. For example, Harley-Davidson's V-rod line of high-performance motorcycles with liquid-cooled engines is viewed by Harley purists as nontraditional and therefore unappealing. This new line is faster and lighter than the familiar Harley heavyweight touring bikes and is designed to attract a younger segment of the market.[8] However, market segmentation can also be accomplished with no change in the product, but rather with separate distribution channels or promotional appeals, each tailored to a given market segment. Wrigley's, for example, targets smokers by promoting chewing gum as an alternative in situations where smoking is unwelcome. And Evian bottled water is attempting to broaden its market beyond athletes and fitness-oriented consumers with advertising aimed at other groups, including pregnant women and environmentalists.

A multiple-segment strategy normally results in a greater sales volume than a single-segment strategy. It also may be useful for a company facing seasonal demand. Because of lower summer enrollments, many universities market their empty dormitory space to tourists—another market segment. A firm with excess production capacity may well seek additional market segments to absorb this capacity.

Multiple segments can provide benefits to an organization, but the strategy has some drawbacks with respect to costs and market coverage. In the first place, marketing to multiple segments can be expensive in both the production and marketing of products. Even with today's advances in production technology, it is obviously less expensive to produce mass quantities of one model and one color than it is to produce a variety of models, colors, and sizes. And a multiple-segment strategy increases marketing expenses in several ways. Total inventory costs grow because adequate inventories of each style, color, and the like must be maintained. Advertising costs go up because different ads may be required for each market segment. Distribution costs are likely to increase as efforts are made to make products available to various segments. Finally, general administrative expenses go up when management must plan and implement several different marketing programs. A leading marketing research firm contends that a nationally distributed, packaged-good line extension, for example a new version of Crest toothpaste, must generate $100 million in annual sales to be considered successful.[9]

Before selecting a strategy, management must determine the desirability of each of the segments it has identified. Some guidelines that are helpful in making that evaluation are discussed next.

Guidelines in Selecting a Target Market

Four guidelines govern how to determine whether a segment should be chosen as a target market. First, a target market should be compatible with the organization's goals and image. For years many manufacturers resisted distributing their products through Wal-Mart because of the chain's discount image. However, as Wal-Mart achieved a high level of acceptability with consumers, image concerns seemed to disappear.

A second guideline is to match the market opportunity represented by the target market with the company's resources. In examining the power tool and appliance markets, Black & Decker considered several options and chose as one of its targets the do-it-yourself home-improvement segment because of the marketing economies that could be achieved. The parent firm's name was well known to consumers, and the products could be sold through the retail outlets already selling Black & Decker products. Thus, entering this market was much less expensive than entering a market in which Black & Decker was inexperienced.

Over the long run, a business must generate a profit to survive. This rather obvious statement translates into our third market selection guideline. That is, an organization should seek markets that will generate sufficient sales volume at a low enough cost to result in a profit that justifies the required investment. Surprisingly, companies often have overlooked profit in their quest for high-volume markets. Their mistake is going after sales volume, not *profitable* sales volume. When the online grocery delivery service Webvan went bankrupt, costing investors hundreds of millions of dollars, it became apparent that the firm had vastly overestimated the size of the potential market. Its business model required huge, automated warehouses to stock groceries and large fleets of trucks to deliver them. But there were simply not enough consumers willing to buy groceries online to support the infrastructure.

Fourth, a company ordinarily should seek a market where competitors are few and/or weak. A seller should not enter a market that is already saturated with competition unless it has some overriding advantage that will enable it to take customers from existing firms. Charter schools provide an interesting example. The schools are designed to appeal to families that are dissatisfied with public schools but are unable to afford fancy private schools. The objective is to provide a solid education without many of the constraints associated with the public school system. The purported advantage of these schools over traditional public schools is greater flexibility. Despite these differences, charter schools have had difficulty in a market with many established competitors, notably public schools.[10]

Positioning

Having identified the potential segments and selected one or more to target, the marketer must next decide what position to pursue. A **position** is the way a firm's product, brand, or organization is viewed relative to the competition by current and prospective customers. To establish itself in a market that was dominated by fast-food firms appealing primarily to the preferences of children, Wendy's positioned its burgers as "hot and juicy," and therefore primarily for adults. If a position is how a product is viewed, then **positioning** is a firm's use of all the elements at its disposal to create and maintain in the minds of a target market a particular image relative to competing products.

When positioning a product, the marketer wants to convey the benefit(s) most desired by the target market. A classic example of successful positioning is the original Head and Shoulders shampoo. As the first shampoo positioned as a dandruff

How would you describe the typical Harley-Davidson motorcycle owner? The position the firm has fostered for years depicts its products as contributing to an image of an owner who is slightly rebellious and ruggedly individualistic. However, it may be time for some adjustment. The average Harley owner is now 46 years old, up almost ten years from 1990. As the company looks to the future, younger prospects appear to be more interested in product performance than rider stereotypes. As a result, Harley has responded with a lower-priced, lighter weight line of motorcycles called the V-Rod. Could that confuse consumers about Harley-Davidson's position?

www.harleydavidson.com

remedy, the product's name implied the benefit, the medicinal fragrance suggested its potency, and the color (blue-green) and consistency (a paste rather than a liquid) indicated that it wasn't an ordinary shampoo. As other dandruff-control products entered the market, the positioning for Head and Shoulders has been modified with changes in the appearance of the product and claims of additional benefits.

To simplify their decision making, consumers formulate mental positions for products, brands, and organizations. Often these positions are based on a single attribute and/or limited experience because consumers are seldom willing to invest much time and effort in the process. Because a product's position is critical to its evaluation, firms go to great lengths to influence how positions are formed.

There are three steps in a positioning strategy:

1. *Select the positioning concept.* To position a product or an organization, a marketer needs to first determine what is important to the target market. Marketers can then conduct positioning studies to see how members of a target market view competing products or stores on the important attributes. The results of this research can be portrayed in a **perceptual map** that locates the brand or organization relative to alternatives on dimensions reflecting the attributes. A hypothetical example for jeans is shown in Figure 6.1. The length of each line (or vector) indicates the relative importance of the attribute, and the position of a brand relative to a vector indicates how closely the brand is associated with the attribute. For example, Calvin Klein jeans are perceived as more expensive than Gap jeans but not as comfortable, whereas Wranglers are seen as durable but low in status. This map suggests that a brand offering comfort and durability at a reasonable price would have little competition from these other brands. Thus it might be an attractive option if a substantial segment of the market finds these attributes desirable.

2. *Design the dimension or feature that most effectively conveys the position.* A position can be communicated with a brand name, a slogan, the appearance or other features of the product, the place where it is sold, the appearance of employees, and in many other ways. However, some features are more effective than others. It is important to not overlook details. According to a consultant, chairs for customers are vital in upscale retail environments because they signal that the seller "cares." Because the marketer has limited resources, decisions have to be made on how best to convey the desired positioning concept.

FIGURE 6.1

A Hypothetical Perceptual Map for Jeans.

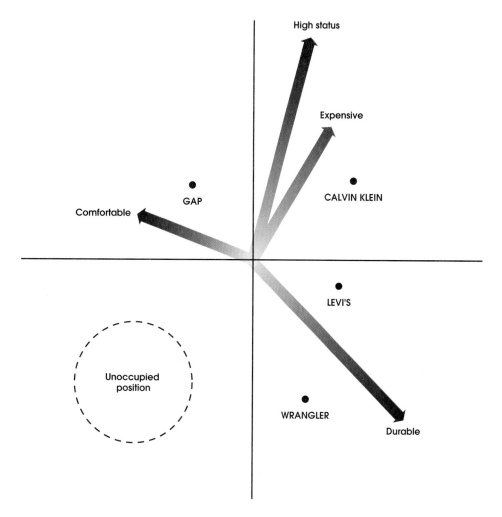

3. *Coordinate the marketing mix components to convey a consistent position.* Even though one or two dimensions may be the primary position communicators, all the elements of the marketing mix—the product, price, promotion, and distribution—should complement the intended position. Many product failures are the result of inconsistent positioning that confuses consumers. For example, Tetley Instant Iced Tea (in Britain, where the people take great pride in brewing tea) flopped.

Over time a position may erode because of lack of attention, become less attractive to the market as needs or tastes change, or be usurped by a competitor. Hence positions must be regularly monitored and sometimes adjusted. For example, Quality Inns, Comfort Suites, and Sleep Inns, all brands of Choice Hotels, Inc., were losing ground and sales to competitors such as Hampton Inn and Holiday Inn. An evaluation of their position in the minds of consumers suggested they had become dated and less desirable relative to the competition. In response the firm upgraded the facilities at many of its locations and signaled the revised position with new logos and signs as well as a major ad campaign.

When its position has eroded, and a firm attempts to reestablish its attractiveness, it is engaging in **repositioning.** When it discovered that "oil" had a negative connotation for younger women evaluating beauty products, Procter & Gamble repositioned its venerable Oil of Olay brand with a simple name change to "Olay." The 50-year-old brand, which is not oily, generates $50 million in sales of skin-care and cosmetics products around the world. To avoid alienating existing customers, P&G did not publicize the name change. Rather, it simply introduced it with a new logo and other packaging changes.

Forecasting Market Demand

Recall that one condition for useful segmentation is that the resulting segments be large enough to produce a profit. The potential of a segment is determined by forecasting how much it will buy. The process of forecasting demand is discussed next.

Demand forecasting estimates sales of a product during some defined future period. Forecasting is done to make various kinds of predictions. For example, a forecast can refer to an entire industry (such as apparel), an industry category (such as jeans), one firm's product line (Levi casual wear), or an individual brand (Levi 501 jeans). Thus, for a forecast to be understood, it is important to make very clear what it describes.

Basic Forecasting Terms

In this section we'll explain some concepts so our discussion will be easier to follow.

Market Share   A term used frequently in business as a performance measure, **market share** is the proportion of total sales of a product during a stated period in a specific market that is captured by a single firm. If Almega Corp. sold $210 million worth of turbine engines in 2005, and total industry sales of turbine engines that year were $7 billion, Almega's market share was 3%.

The base for calculating market share can refer to entire industries (aircraft), segments of industries (single-engine business jets), or particular geographic areas (Pacific Rim), and can also apply to past, present, or future periods. For example, the steel industry, which has a 95% market share for canned-food containers, is working to prevent a recurrence of the inroads in food packaging that were made by aluminum makers in the market for beverage cans. So awareness of the base and time period used in computing market share is essential to correctly interpreting the statistic.

Market Factor   A **market factor** is something that (1) exists in a market, (2) is measurable, and (3) is related to the demand for a product in a known way. To illustrate, the "number of cars three years old and older" is a market factor related to the demand for replacement tires. It's a market factor because the number of replacement tires that can be sold changes as the number of older cars changes.

In segmenting world markets geographically, McDonald's at one time used population, per capita income, and the number of people per store in the U.S. as market factors to obtain a rough forecast of the number of stores a country could support. The formula looked like this:

$$\frac{\text{population of the country}}{\text{\# of people per McDonald's in U.S.}} \times \frac{\text{per capita income of the country}}{\text{per capita income of U.S.}} = \frac{\text{the number of stores the country can support}}{}$$

The result was a preliminary estimate that was adjusted for factors such as eating habits and competition.

Market Potential, Sales Potential, and Sales Forecast

Market potential is the total sales volume that *all organizations* selling a product during a stated period of time in a specific market could expect to achieve under ideal conditions. **Sales potential** is the portion of market potential that a *specific company* could expect to achieve under ideal conditions. For example, market potential applies to all refrigerators, but sales potential refers only to a single brand of refrigerators (such as Whirlpool).

With either of these measures of potential, the market may encompass whatever group or area interests the forecaster. It could be the world, one country, or a smaller market defined by income or some other basis. For example, Whirlpool may consider the market potential for refrigerators in the New England states, or the sales potential for Whirlpool refrigerators in households with incomes of $25,000 to $50,000.

The term *potential* refers to a maximum level of sales assuming that (1) all marketing plans are sound and effectively implemented and (2) all prospective customers with the desire and ability to buy do so. Of course, few industries or companies achieve their full potential. Therefore, potential should not be the final outcome of demand forecasting. It is an intermediate step. We must move from *potential* sales to *probable* sales, which are estimated by preparing sales forecasts.

A **sales forecast** is an estimate of probable sales for one company's brand of a product during a stated period in a specific market, assuming a defined marketing plan is used. Like measures of potential, a sales forecast can be expressed in dollars or product units. However, whereas market potential and sales potential are estimated on the basis of general factors and market assumptions, a sales forecast is made on the basis of a specific marketing plan for the product.

A sales forecast is best prepared after market potential and sales potential have been estimated. Sales forecasts typically cover a one-year period, although many firms review and revise their forecasts quarterly or even monthly. Forecasts of less than a year may be desirable when activity in the firm's industry is so volatile that it is not feasible to look ahead an entire year. As a case in point, many retailers and producers in the fashion industry prepare forecasts for only one fashion season at a time. Hence, they prepare three or four forecasts a year.

A sales forecast is made assuming a particular marketing budget and program. However, once a sales forecast has been prepared, it affects all departments in a company. Planning the necessary amount of working capital, plant utilization, and warehousing facilities is accomplished on the basis of anticipated sales. Additionally, scheduling production, hiring production workers, and purchasing raw materials depend on the sales forecast.

Methods of Forecasting Sales

There are many methods of forecasting sales. Several of the more commonly used methods are described below.

Market-Factor Analysis   In many situations, future demand for a product is related to the behavior of certain market factors. When this is true, we can forecast future sales by studying the behavior of these market factors. Basically, **market-factor analysis** entails determining what the related factors are and then measuring their relationship to sales activity.

Using market-factor analysis successfully requires that the analyst (1) select the best market factors and (2) minimize the number of market factors. The best factors are ones that vary in a consistent way with the demand for the product being forecast. Fewer factors are preferable in order to simplify the data collection and analyses.

We can translate market-factor behavior into a demand forecast with the **direct-derivation method.** To illustrate, suppose a producer of automobile tires wants to know the market potential for replacement tires in the U.S. in 2008. The primary market factor is the number and age of automobiles on the road. The first step is to estimate how many cars are prospects for new tires.

Assume that the producer's studies show (1) the average car is driven 10,000 miles per year and (2) the average driver gets 30,000 miles of use from a set of tires. This means that all cars that become three years old or multiples of three years old in 2008 can be considered as comprising the potential market for replacement tires during that year. From state and county auto license agencies as well as private organizations, the producer can obtain a reasonably accurate count of the number of cars that were sold in the U.S. in 2005 and therefore will be three years old in 2008. In addition, with a little digging the producer can determine how many cars will become 6, 9, and 12 years old and still be on the road in 2008, and therefore would also be ready for another set of tires.

The number of cars in these age brackets multiplied by four (tires per car) should give the approximate market potential for replacement tires in 2008. Of course, we are dealing in averages. Not all drivers will get 30,000 miles from their tires, and not all cars will be driven 10,000 miles per year.

The direct-derivation method is simple, inexpensive, and requires little statistical analysis. Executives who are not statisticians can understand it and interpret its results. This method's main limitation is that it can be used only when it is possible to identify an easily measured market factor that affects the product's demand in a stable way.

Correlation analysis is a statistical refinement of the direct-derivation method. It is a measure of the association between potential sales of the product and the market factor affecting its sales. Detailed explanation of this statistical technique is beyond the scope of this text. However, in general, a correlation analysis measures, on a scale of 0 (no association) to 1 (perfect association), the variation between two data series. For example, one data series might be the number of residential housing starts (from government statistics), and the other the wholesale furniture sales (from industry sources) in the corresponding years. If there is a reasonably strong historical relationship between these two series, a marketer might use current housing starts to predict the demand for furniture.

Correlation analysis gives a more precise estimate of how well the market factor predicts market demand than does direct derivation. That's because in direct derivation, the association is assumed to be 1.0 (that is, perfect). But rarely is there a perfect association between a market factor and the demand for a product. Using a more sophisticated form of correlation analysis called **multiple correlation,** it is possible to include more than one market factor in the calculation.

Correlation analysis has two major limitations. First, it can be used only when both of the following are available: (1) a sales history of the industry or firm consisting of at least 20 consecutive time periods, and (2) a corresponding history of the market factor being used to forecast demand. Second, correlation analysis depends on the assumptions, which can be quite unrealistic, that approximately the same relationship has existed between sales and the key market factor(s) during the entire period, and that this relationship will continue in the sales period being predicted.

Survey of Buyer Intentions

A **survey of buyer intentions** involves asking a sample of current or potential customers how much of a particular product they would buy at a given price during a specified future period. Some firms ask a sample of consumers from the target segment about their buying intentions and then extrapolate the result to the entire segment.

Selecting a representative sample of potential buyers can be a problem. For many consumer products, a large sample is needed because many groups with different buying patterns make up the market. Thus gathering the required data can be costly in terms of both money and time. This method has another serious limitation. Because it is one thing for prospects to *intend* to buy a product but quite another for them to *actually* buy it, surveys of buying intentions often show an inflated measure of market potential. Such surveys are probably most accurate in forecasting demand when (1) there are relatively few current or potential buyers, (2) the buyers are willing to express their buying intentions, and (3) their past records show a consistent relationship between their actual buying behavior and their stated intentions. These conditions are most likely to exist in a business market.

Test Marketing

In **test marketing** to forecast demand, a firm markets a new product in a limited geographic area, measures sales, and then—from this sample—projects the product's sales over a larger area. Test marketing is often used to determine whether there is sufficient demand for a new product to be viable. It also serves as a basis for evaluating new-product features and alternative marketing strategies. More details about test marketing, including its benefits and drawbacks, are presented in Chapter 7.

Past Sales and Trend Analysis

A popular method of forecasting is based entirely on past sales. Small retailers whose main goal is to "beat last year's figures" frequently use this technique. In **past sales analysis,** the demand forecast is simply a flat percentage change applied to the volume achieved last year or to the average volume of the past few years.

This technique is simple and inexpensive. For a firm operating in a stable market where its market share has remained constant for a period of years, past sales alone can be used to predict future volume. However, few companies operate in unchanging environments, making this method potentially unreliable.

Trend analysis examines past sales data to calculate the rate of change in sales volume and uses it to forecast future sales. One type of trend analysis is a long-term projection of sales, usually computed with a statistical technique called regression. However, the statistical sophistication of long-term trend analysis does not offset the inherent weakness of basing future estimates only on past sales activity. A second type of trend analysis entails a short-term projection using a seasonal index of sales covering several months. Short-term trend analysis may be acceptable if a firm's sales follow a reliable seasonal pattern. For example, assume that the second quarter of the year historically produces sales about 50% higher than the first quarter. Hence, if sales reach 10,000 units in the first quarter, we can reasonably forecast sales of 15,000 units for the second quarter.

Sales-Force Composite

In sales forecasting, a **sales-force composite** consists of collecting from all sales people estimates of sales for their territories during the future period of interest. The total of all these estimates is the company's sales forecast.

A sales-force composite method can produce an accurate forecast if the firm has competent, well-informed sales people. Its strength is that it takes advantage of sales people's specialized knowledge of their own markets. Furthermore, it should make sales people more willing to accept their assigned sales quotas, because they participated in the process that produced the forecasts that serve as the basis for their quotas. A sales-force composite is most useful for firms selling to a market composed primarily of a few large customers where sales people work closely with them and are well informed about their plans. Thus this method would be more applicable to sales of large electrical generators to energy utilities than to sales of small general-use motors to many thousands of firms.

This method also has limitations. A sales force may not have the time or the experience to do the research needed for sales forecasting, and managers must guard against sales people who overestimate or underestimate future sales, depending on circumstances. For instance, sales people are by nature optimistic and therefore may overestimate future possibilities. Or, if compensation is based on meeting or exceeding sales quotas, sales people may intentionally underestimate future sales.

Executive Judgment Basically, **executive judgment** involves obtaining opinions from one or more executives regarding future sales. If these are well-informed opinions, based on valid measures such as market-factor analysis, then executive judgment can produce accurate forecasts. However, forecasting by executive opinion alone is risky, because such opinions are sometimes simply intuition or guesswork. Many Internet businesses were initiated in the 1990s on the basis of executives' guesses about potential sales and failed a year or two later when the forecasts proved to be overly optimistic.

One specialized form of executive judgment is the **Delphi method**, named after the location of an oracle in ancient Greece. Developed by the Rand Corporation for use in environmental forecasting, this technique can also be applied to sales forecasting. It is especially applicable to products that are truly innovative or are significant technological breakthroughs.

The Delphi method begins with a group of knowledgeable individuals anonymously estimating future sales. Each person makes a prediction without knowing how others in the group have responded. These estimates are summarized, and the resulting average and range of forecasts are fed back to the participants. Now, knowing how the other group members responded, they are asked to make another prediction on the same issue. Participants may change or stick to their original estimates. This process of estimates and feedback is continued for several rounds. In some cases—and usually in sales forecasting—the final round involves face-to-face discussions among the participants to produce a consensus sales forecast.

An advantage of the Delphi method is that the anonymity in the early rounds prevents one individual (for example, a marketing vice president) from influencing others (regional sales managers). And it permits each participant to consider the combined judgment of the group. If an individual's forecast is widely divergent from the group's average, the individual can justify or modify it in the next round. A potential disadvantage of the Delphi method—and of any executive judgment method—is that participants may lack the necessary information on which to base their judgments.

No method of sales forecasting is perfect. An executive's challenge is to choose an approach that is likely to produce the most accurate estimate of sales given the firm's particular circumstances. Because all techniques have limitations, frequently companies employ a combination of forecasting methods and then reconcile any differences that are produced.

Summary

A market consists of people or organizations with wants, money to spend, and the willingness to spend it. However, within most markets the buyers' needs are not identical. Therefore, a single marketing program for an entire market is unlikely to be successful. A sound marketing program starts with identifying the differences that exist within a market, a process called market segmentation, deciding which segments will be pursued as target markets, and selecting a competitive position that will be conveyed to customers through the marketing mix.

Most marketers adopt some form of market segmentation as a compromise between the extremes of a strategy that treats the market as an aggregate, undifferentiated whole, and a strategy that views each customer as a different market. Market segmentation enables a company to make efficient use of its marketing resources. Also, it allows a small company to compete effectively by concentrating on one or two segments. The apparent drawback of market segmentation is that it will result in higher production and marketing costs than a one-product, mass-market strategy. However, if the market is correctly segmented, a better fit with customers' needs will actually result in greater efficiency. For segmentation to be effective: (1) the bases for segmentation must be measurable with obtainable data, (2) the segments identified must be accessible through existing marketing institutions, and (3) the segments must be large enough to be potentially profitable.

At the broadest level, most markets may be divided into two segments: ultimate consumers and business users. The four major bases used for further segmenting the consumer market are geographic, demographic, psychographic, and behavioral. The business market may be segmented on the basis of customer location, customer type, and transaction conditions. Normally, in either the consumer or business market, a seller will use a combination of two or more segmentation bases.

The three alternative strategies for selecting a target market are market aggregation and single-segment and multiple-segment strategies. Market-aggregation strategy involves using one marketing mix to reach a mass, undifferentiated market. With a single-segment strategy, a company still uses only one marketing mix, but it is directed at only one segment of the total market. A multiple-segment strategy entails selecting two or more segments and developing a separate marketing mix to reach each segment. The guidelines for selecting segments to target are compatibility with the firm's goals, fit with the firm's resources, profit potential, and the strength of the competition.

When targets have been selected, the organization must decide how to position the offering. Position is the way a brand or organization is viewed relative to the competition by current and prospective customers. A positioning effort should convey the benefits most desired by the target market. The three steps in positioning are (1) selecting the positioning concept, (2) designing the feature to convey the position, and (3) coordinating the marketing mix to consistently communicate the desired position.

Forecasting is essential in evaluating possible target segments. It involves estimating the demand of a market. Management usually estimates the total sales that could be expected under ideal conditions for all firms comprising the industry—market potential—and for its particular product—sales potential. The final step in estimating demand is a sales forecast, indicating probable sales for the company's brand of a particular product in a future time period and with a specified marketing program. The forecast normally covers one year.

Specific methods used to forecast sales are market-factor analysis, survey of buyer intentions, test marketing, past sales and trend analysis, sales-force composite, and executive judgment. Management's challenge is to select the techniques that are appropriate in a particular situation.

More about **Dunkin' Donuts**

When Jon Luther took over as CEO in 2003, he recognized that satisfying Dunkin' Donuts' market required some fundamental changes. First, there was a wide disparity in the appearance of the outlets, with many having become run-down. To deal with the problem, franchisees were asked to undertake some improvements, and those who did not were asked to leave the system.

Next he considered the competition. Luther engaged in an informal perceptual mapping exercise, drawing a circle representing Dunkin' Donuts, and then adding slightly overlapping circles for Starbuck's, McDonald's, Tim Horton's, and even convenience stores. Interestingly, he placed Krispy Kreme off by itself because, he explained, "It's not really in the coffee business."

In examining eating behavior, Luther has concluded that the quick-service restaurant business has made a fundamental mistake. Rather than try to replace one of America's three daily meals, Luther thinks consumers should be viewed as snackers, not meal eaters. The average lunch "hour" is now 19 minutes. He sees consumers grabbing five or six quick snacks a day rather than consuming real meals. To that end, he has defined a visit to DD as a "ritual that revives," and he is changing the menu to provide for three dimensions important to his customers: wellness, mobility, and portability.

Other changes are being made in the operations. Super-fast, mistake-proof espresso machines are being installed in prime locations to appeal to younger consumers who have developed a taste for the newer coffee drinks but don't want to pay the price or take the time typical of a Starbuck's visit. Another move is to transfer doughnut production out of the stores to centralized kitchens that can serve a number of shops. The benefits are consistent quality, standardized freshness, and less waste.

What's next? Under consideration are additions to the menu, more high-margin drinks, and combination outlets that will offer Dunkin' Donuts and Baskin-Robbins or Togo sandwiches.[11] As the strategy unfolds and the target market votes with its dollars, we'll see if DD's mission of offering "rituals that revive" is accomplished.

1. Should Dunkin' Donuts' pursue a single-segment or multiple-segment strategy?

2. Given Dunkin' Donuts' positioning, what types of firms should be considered competitors?

Key Terms and Concepts

Market segments (142)
Market segmentation (143)
Micromarketing (145)
Geographic segmentation (146)
Demographic segmentation (148))
Psychographic segmentation (148)
Personality (148)
Lifestyle (149)
Values (150)
Behavioral segmentation (150)
Target market (154)
Market-aggregation strategy (154)
Product differentiation (155)

Single-segment strategy (155)
Niche marketers (155)
Niche markets (155)
Multiple-segment (155)
Position (157)
Positioning (157)
Perceptual map (158)
Repositioning (159)
Demand forecasting (160)
Market share (160)
Market factor (160)
Market potential (161)
Sales potential (161)

Sales forecast (161)
Market-factor analysis (162)
Direct-derivation method (162)
Correlation analysis (162)
Multiple correlation (162)
Survey of buyer intentions (163)
Test marketing (163)
Past sales analysis (163)
Trend analysis (163)
Sales-force composite (163)
Executive judgment (164)
Delphi method (164)

Questions and Problems

1. Give two examples of goods or services whose market demand would be particularly affected by each of the following population factors:
   a. Regional distribution
   b. Marital status
   c. Gender
   d. Age
   e. Urban-rural-suburban distribution

2. From the most recent "Survey of Buying Power" (from *Sales & Marketing Management* magazine), record the available data for the county in which you live and another county with which you are familiar (maybe the one in which your school is located). Comment on how differences you find may be useful to a fast-food franchisee seeking a location for a new outlet.

3. Using the psychographic bases discussed in this chapter, describe the segment appropriate to investigate as a market for:
   a. Ski resorts
   b. Online auto sales
   c. Power hand tools
   d. Donations to United Way
   e. PC that includes Internet access

4. What user benefits in advertising for each of the following three products might lead you to conclude that the marketer is trying to appeal to each of these three market segments?

Product	Market
a. DVD player	a. Young singles
b. Toothpaste	b. Retired people
c. 10-day Caribbean cruise	c. Empty-nest couples

5. What demographic characteristics would you think are likely to describe heavy users of the following?
   a. Online investment advice and stock trading
   b. Ready-to-eat cereal
   c. Videocassette recorders
   d. Laptop computers

6. How would you segment the market for Xerox copying machines?

7. How might the following organizations implement the strategy of market segmentation?
   a. Manufacturer of personal computers
   b. American Heart Association
   c. Universal Studios (Hollywood movies)
   d. Internet-only retail banking service

8. Find a magazine advertisement that communicates the position for a product in each of the following categories:
   a. Household appliance
   b. Cellular phone service
   c. Airline
   d. Hotel or motel chain

9. What market factors might you use in estimating the market potential for each of the following products?
   a. Central home air-conditioning
   b. Electric milking machines
   c. First-class airline travel
   d. Printers to accompany personal computers

10. How would you determine (a) market potential and (b) a sales forecast for a textbook for an introductory marketing course?

Interactive Marketing Excercises

1. Interview three friends or acquaintances who all own athletic shoes but differ on some demographic dimension (for example, education or age). Using the criteria of demographics, psychological variables, and behavioral variables, describe in as much detail as possible the market segment each represents.

2. Examine the annual reports (available in your library) of two consumer product marketers and two business product marketers to determine what target markets they are currently serving.

Chapter 7

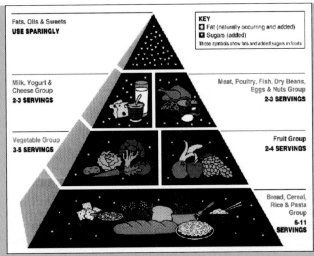

(Old–1992)

(New–2005)

"There is a lot at stake for the $500 billion food industry in this revision of the food pyramid."

How Difficult is Building a **Pyramid?**

The federal government, through the Department of Agriculture (USDA), has long been concerned about the dietary habits of consumers. To assist consumers in making healthy choices the USDA provides dietary guidelines. The guidelines are also used in the design of public school lunch programs. In 1992, a "food pyramid" was developed to supplement the guidelines. The purpose of the pyramid was to provide a simple visual aid for use in classrooms as an educational tool and generally to indicate for consumers the proper mix of various food groups appropriate for a healthy lifestyle.

The dietary guidelines are revised every five years based on the current scientific evidence. The most recent revision was issued at the beginning of 2005. At the same time, the USDA decided to update the pyramid, which had remained unchanged since it was introduced in 1992.

The 1992 U.S. pyramid format allocates the base, and therefore the greatest amount of space, to bread, cereal, rice, and pasta. Moving up the pyramid, there are fruits and vegetables, dairy products, meat, poultry, and fish, and at the top of the pyramid, with the least amount of space, are fats, oils, and sweets. Several other countries utilize similar visual devices, but with shapes other than a pyramid. Korea and China use something that resembles a pagoda, while most European governments use a pie chart. The Canadian government uses what it calls a dietary rainbow.

Any revision in the guidelines as well as how they are communicated are very important to the $500 billion food industry. For example, prior to 1992, the USDA recommended 4 daily servings of bread, cereal, rice, and pasta. Then in 1992,

the recommendation was increased to 6 to 11 servings. One result was double-digit growth for many bread products. If changes in the pyramid reduce the impression that these products are the foundation of a healthy diet, grain-based industries will suffer.

In developing the new pyramid, the USDA invited input. Lobbyists from virtually all the concerned industries provided research results and testimony. Among those offering advice were the U.S. Potato Board, National Cattlemen's Beef Association, Chocolate Manufacturers Association, and the California Walnut Commission. Comments from the public also produced suggestions. Some offered ideas on what the new visual should look like, including a tree with the food groups drawn into the leaves, a steering wheel to remind consumers that they should "steer (their) way to good health," and an hourglass.

With nearly 65% of U.S. adults overweight, obesity among children reaching epidemic proportions, and weight-related illnesses such as diabetes increasing, there is a lot at stake in educating consumers about diet. The revised pyramid is intended to help consumers make good decisions. A key to its value is how effective it is at attracting the attention of consumers and conveying meaningful and accurate information.[1]

Is there a role for marketing research in educating consumers about a healthy diet?

www.usda.gov

There are many ways to make a decision. Faced with revising the food pyramid and marketing it to the American public, the managers at the U.S. Department of Agriculture could rely on their experience, the advice of the many special interests, or, as a last resort, the flip of a coin. Another alternative is to use research to produce managerially useful information. If properly planned and conducted, research can provide insights and accurate information about consumer and business questions.

In this chapter we will examine how information essential to marketing is obtained and utilized.

After studying this chapter, you should be able to explain:

Chapter Goals

- What marketing research is, the need for it, and the variety of forms it takes.
- How information systems increase the usefulness of data.
- The growing role of technology in marketing research.
- The appropriate way to conduct a marketing research project.
- How firms gather and use information about competitors.
- How ethics enters into the performance of marketing research.
- Some threats to the future of marketing research.

The Marketing Research Function

Marketing research is needed before a product is introduced to the market and on a regular basis throughout its life. Research is not limited to products; it is conducted to answer questions about potential market segments, entire stores, brand names, advertising, prices, and every other aspect of marketing. The challenges in every research project are to correctly define the issue to be studied, gather the appropriate data, and transform the raw data into useful information. To see how to do this, we will begin by briefly discussing where organizations use research. Then we will focus our attention on how research is performed and managed.

Uses of Marketing Research

Competitive pressure, the cost of making a strategic mistake, and the complexity of both domestic and foreign markets dictate that a firm must have access to timely information. Consider some of the marketing issues that are frequently researched:

- *Markets and market segments.* Experienced managers often suspect that a need exists in the market, but intuition is usually not sufficient to justify a decision that may require the investment of millions of dollars. Research can be used to clarify the need, identify and describe exactly who has it, and determine the strength of the need in various segments.
- *Marketing mix.* Even when a marketer is confident that a need exists, it is not always clear what form a product should take to satisfy the need, at what price it will sell, how prospects should be informed about it, or in what fashion it should be distributed. Consider that several firms are designing and testing personal delivery units that are necessary if electronic shopping is to grow. These units are storage boxes that permit deliveries to a home or office when no one is present to personally accept the merchandise. The boxes must be accessible yet secure, large enough to hold a variety of different deliveries but not obtrusive, reasonably attractive, and easy to install. Having consumers evaluate alternative designs and react to possible prices will help the makers. Then there's the question of how best to inform and persuade potential customers about a product like this. What message and media will reach the intended audience, attract their attention, and convey the desired message about a storage box? Finally, where should they be sold? Would a home improvement retail store be a better distri-

bution route than direct sales over the Internet? These and other marketing-mix questions are addressed with marketing research.

- *Competition.* Finding out what current and potential competitors are doing and how it may affect a firm's strategy, called competitive intelligence, is an increasingly important dimension of marketing research.

- *Expectations and satisfaction.* It is important to know what customers expect, which is influenced by what marketers have promised, and how well those expectations are being satisfied. Surprisingly few customers volunteer information to a firm. For example, it's frequently suggested that as few as 10% of dissatisfied customers formally complain to the company responsible. However, what they do is tell their friends and take their business elsewhere. Firms need research to quickly identify problems and solve them before they result in lost business.

This is just a sample of the many topics of marketing research. The 50 largest U.S. marketing research firms are paid over $11.5 *billion* a year by their clients from around the world for information to improve the quality of decision making.[2] Unaccounted for in this figure is the research done internally by firms and the hundreds of smaller marketing research companies. Obviously, research is an important part of marketing!

What Is Marketing Research?

Marketing research consists of all the activities that enable an organization to obtain the information it needs to make decisions about its environment, marketing mix, and present or potential customers. More specifically, **marketing research** is the development, interpretation, and communication of decision-oriented information to be used in all phases of the marketing process.

This definition has two important implications:

- Research plays a role in all three phases of the marketing management process: planning, implementation, and evaluation.

- It recognizes the researcher's responsibility to develop information, which includes defining problems, gathering and analyzing data, interpreting results, and presenting the information in such a way that it is useful to managers.

Scope of Marketing Research Activities

Depending on their needs and level of sophistication, marketing managers make use of four main sources of information. One is regularly scheduled reports that are produced and sold by research firms. These are called *syndicated services* because they are developed without a particular client in mind but are sold to anyone interested. An example is ACNielsen's Retail Measurement Services. The firm gathers data at the retail store level on product movement, market share, and prices across a wide variety of consumer packaged goods in over 80 countries. Subscribing to this service allows a marketer to regularly monitor retail sales of its own and competitors' products by type of outlet and geographic area.

The second source is a *marketing information system,* an internally coordinated activity that provides continuous, scheduled, or on-demand standardized reports. Most marketing information systems rely heavily on internal data such as sales reports, inventory amounts, and production schedules, but they also often include information purchased from research firms or trade associations. An MkIS is used by both managers and sales people. For example, a sales person sitting in a customer's office can use a laptop computer and an MkIS to check on the availability of current inventory and the schedule for producing more. Other frequent applications include tracking the sales performance of products and monitoring changing consumer tastes.

acnielsen.com/services/ retail

A *decision support system* is the third source. It is also internal, but it is interactive. It permits a decision maker to interact directly with data through a personal computer to answer specific questions. A manager, for example, might have a decision support system that will estimate the impact of various levels of advertising on sales of a product when given specific assumptions.

The fourth source is a nonrecurring, proprietary *marketing research project,* conducted by a company's own staff or by an independent research firm to answer a specific question. For example, Toro, a manufacturer of lawn mowers, might conduct a survey of retail dealers, consumers, or both to identify the most common problems customers have with power mowers.

There are many providers of syndicated research, the first source of information mentioned above. In fact, they account for about 40% of the total amount spent on research in the U.S.[3] However, detailing the topics and varied research methods of syndicated researchers goes beyond the scope of this discussion. (For more information and more examples of syndicated research services, see the websites of Information Resources, Inc., and Market Facts, Inc.) Now, we will concentrate our discussion on the other three sources.

www.infores.com

www.marketfacts.com

Marketing Information Systems

As computers became common business tools, firms were able to collect, store, and manipulate larger amounts of data to aid marketing decision makers. Out of this capability developed the **marketing information system (MkIS)**—an ongoing, organized procedure to generate, analyze, disseminate, store, and retrieve information for use in making marketing decisions. Figure 7.1 illustrates the characteristics and operation of an MkIS.

The ideal MkIS:

- Includes real-time data.

- Generates regular reports and recurring studies as needed.

- Analyzes data using statistical analysis and mathematical models that represent the real world.

- Integrates old and new data to provide information updates and identify trends.

Designing a Marketing Information System

To build an effective MkIS, marketing managers must identify the information that will help them make better decisions. Working with researchers and systems analysts, managers then determine whether the data needed are available within the organization or must be procured, how the data should be organized, the form in which the data should be reported, and the schedule according to which the data will be delivered.

For example, the brand manager at Procter & Gamble who is responsible for Tide wants to know the retail sales of all detergent brands by geographic area on a weekly basis. The same manager may want monthly reports on the prices that com-

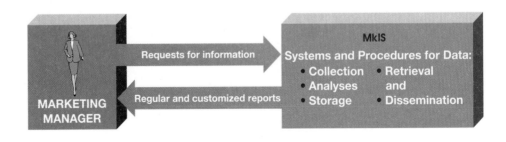

FIGURE 7.1

The Structure and Function of a Marketing Information System.

petitors are charging and how much advertising they are doing. Less frequently, possibly once a year, this manager needs to know about developments in the marketplace such as demographic changes that might affect Tide in the long term. In addition to these (and probably other) regular reports, the manager may periodically request special reports that can be compiled from existing data. For example, while contemplating a proposal to introduce another version of Tide, the manager may want to see what share of the total market each detergent brand had by quarter over the last five years and a projection of how each is likely to perform over the next three years.

A well-designed MkIS can provide a continuous flow of this type of information for decision making. Collecting data on consumer purchases has been greatly facilitated by electronic cash registers and computer systems that connect retailers directly with their suppliers. The storage and retrieval dimensions of an MkIS allow a manager to examine data for trends and patterns over time. With this capability, managers can continually monitor the performance of products, markets, sales people, and even individual business customers.

An MkIS is of obvious value in a large company, where information is likely to get lost or distorted as it becomes widely dispersed. However, experience shows that even relatively simple information systems can upgrade management's decision making in small and medium-sized firms. For example, a small manufacturer of electric motors that tracks sales by customer over time can use the information to divide its customers into good, better, and best categories, and allocate the effort of salespeople accordingly.

How well an MkIS functions depends on three factors:

- The nature and quality of the data available.

- The ways in which the data are processed and presented to provide usable information.

- The ability of the operators of the MkIS and the managers who use the output to work together.

Global Marketing Information Systems

As firms expand their operations beyond national borders, their needs for information also grow. Centrally managed international organizations must be informed about what is happening around the world. Thus, many companies maintain global marketing information systems. However, establishing worldwide agreement on the types and forms of information to be maintained can be challenging. For example, to maintain its prominence in food as well as home and personal-care products, Unilever keeps 90,000 of its employees in over 150 countries linked through an information system. Besides sharing information on new product research and innovation, this company with brands such as Slim-Fast, Lipton, Ragu, Dove, Vaseline, and Breyers ice cream, gathers and distributes information on product performance and best marketing practices by various units. In a typical day, Unilever employees respond to over a million electronic messages.

Clearly, designing and operating a global MkIS can be more complex than developing one at the domestic level. It requires convincing each unit of the value of timely and accurate information, accommodating differences in the operational definitions of terms, and adjusting for the use of different currencies and measures in reporting data.

The original features of an MkIS—a focus on preplanned, structured reports and centralized control over the information by computer specialists—resulted from the skills required to operate computers. Now, personal computers with greatly enlarged capacity and user-friendly software have reduced that dependency and led to the development of decision support systems.

Gillette, now merged with Procter & Gamble, has worldwide sales of $10.5 billion. It has 31 manufacturing operations in 14 countries and nearly 29,000 employees worldwide. To coordinate these far-flung operations, share information, and benefit from the scale economies of marketing the same products in many countries, Gillette has invested heavily in a sophisticated global information system.

Decision Support Systems

A **decision support system (DSS)** is a computer-based procedure that allows a manager to directly interact with data using various methods of analysis to integrate, analyze, and interpret information. Like an MkIS, the heart of a DSS is data—different types of data from a wide variety of sources. Typically, a DSS contains data describing the market, customers, competitors, economic and social trends, and the organization's performance. Also, like an MkIS, the DSS has methods for analyzing data. These methods range from simple procedures such as computing ratios or drawing graphs to sophisticated statistical techniques and mathematical models.

Where the MkIS and DSS differ is in the extent to which they permit managers to interact directly with the data. By combining personal computers and user-friendly software, the DSS allows managers to independently retrieve data, examine relationships, and even create unique reports to meet their specific needs. This interactive capability makes it possible for managers to react to what they see in a set of data by asking questions and getting immediate answers. Figure 7.2 depicts the relationships in a DSS.

FIGURE 7.2

The Structure and Function of a Decision Support System.

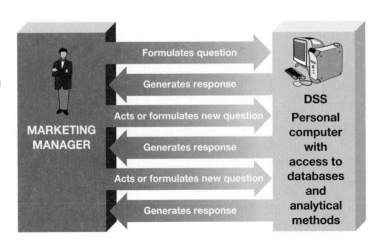

Consider this example: Midway through the month, the brand manager for Sunshine brand of frozen lemonade wants to check on the performance of the product. Sitting down at her computer, she calls up the monthly forecast and the actual sales figures to date. Discovering that sales are slightly below the rate necessary to achieve the month's forecast, she commands the system to provide similar data for each of the four different package sizes of the product. Finding that three of the sizes are on target, she concludes that there is a problem with only one. Next, she asks the system to break down the total sales figure by geographic areas and discovers that the poor sales results occurred in only two of seven regions.

Suspecting competitive activity, she then has the system retrieve and compare couponing activity, advertising levels, and prices of Sunshine lemonade and competing brands in the markets where sales forecasts were achieved and where they weren't. Finding nothing out of the ordinary, she decides to examine distribution in the territories. Requesting data on stock-outs for all package sizes of the lemonade, she finds that in the two regions where sales have slipped the frequency of stockouts is higher than elsewhere. Next, she checks production figures and warehouse inventory levels and finds the problem is not due to internal shortages. Thus she concludes there must be a problem in the distribution of the product to the retail stores. As a result, she decides to investigate the performance of distributors in the problem regions.

Notice that, with an adequate DSS, this entire task was done in a short time by simply formulating a question, requesting information, analyzing the information, and moving on to another question suggested by the analysis. Note also that to function optimally the system requires current, accurate data that can be both costly and difficult to assemble and maintain.

The DSS adds speed and flexibility to the MkIS by making the manager an active part of the research process. The increased use of desktop computers, user-friendly software, and the willingness of suppliers and customers to link their computer systems (networking) have greatly enhanced the potential of DSS.

Databases, Data Warehouses, and Data Mining

An MkIS or a DSS uses data from a variety of sources both within the organization and from outside suppliers. Typically these data are organized, stored, and updated in a computer. The assembled data pertinent to a particular topic—customers, market segments, competitors, or industry trends, for example—are called a **database.**

Marketers probe databases with specific questions to uncover useful relationships and developments. For example, with a system now in place, the manager of an Albertsons retail supermarket can identify how often a member of its preferred customer group buys a particular product. The information is used to target particular customers with promotions and to track store inventories to avoid stock-outs.[4] By having the computer sort through the electronic records of all completed transactions, this information can be compiled quickly. At the division or corporate level, the resulting tallies can be used to customize each store's layout and improve customer convenience. Databases are not new. For years managers have been monitoring their customers and the environment. Computers, with their speed and capacity, have simply made the process more manageable, efficient, and accurate.

Analyzing databases has enabled marketers to better understand marketplace behavior and, as a result, address their customers' needs more specifically. Some believe that through the management of data, marketers will eventually reach the ultimate level of personalized marketing—targeting individuals. Some large banks, for example, are moving in that direction. By comparing an individual customer's transaction pattern to a database of many customers' transactions, customers that are showing signs of closing their accounts are "red flagged." The bank managers investigate the causes and, when possible, develop individually tailored programs to solve the problem and retain the customer.

Some organizations move beyond databases to create large and complex data repositories. Acknowledging that they are more than simply a "base" of data, these collections are called data warehouses. A **data warehouse** is an enormous collection of data, from a variety of internal and external sources, compiled by a firm for its own use or for use by its clients. For example, American Express has the history of every transaction made with an American Express card—over 500 billion bits of data.

Data warehouses can be analyzed in the same way as databases, searching for predetermined patterns in the data. However, because of their size, it would be a slow and cumbersome process. Fortunately, more advanced statistical and artificial intelligence techniques are now being applied to data warehouses. Called **data mining,** these techniques have the capability to identify patterns and meaningful relationships in masses of data that would be overlooked or unrecognizable to researchers. Harrah's Entertainment, owner of over two dozen casinos, is especially interested in getting a larger share of its existing customers' gambling dollars. By combining a customer identification card (a plastic card with a magnetic strip the customer voluntarily inserts into the gaming machine while gambling) with a network that links its 40,000 machines in 12 states, the company is able to collect a vast amount of data about individual customers regardless of which Harrah's casinos they visit. From the data Harrah's develops a profile of a person's gambling behavior and a profit projection that determines what promotional incentives are likely to be most effective. Harrah's data mining effort has isolated 90 demographic segments with different marketing strategies directed to each.[5]

Grocery self scanning is frequently used by consumers who typically have not enrolled in frequent shopper programs, buy a small number of items during a store visit, and purchase ready-to-consume products. These customers constitute an important market segment that could be easily overlooked. A database collected from the self-scanning equipment includes what they buy, the quantities they purchase, and the prices they pay. This information allows the retailer to make informed decisions about inventories of convenience items, where to place products for easy access, and what prices are acceptable.

Major Data Sources

The data used by researchers and managers in databases and data warehouses are gathered from many sources. Internally, data can come from the sales force, marketing, manufacturing, and accounting. Externally, information is available from hundreds of research suppliers. Companies such as Information Resources, Inc. (IRI), have developed computer systems to take the data captured from supermarket checkout systems to provide information on how well specific coupons work in various neighborhoods and which in-store displays are the most effective in generating sales.

Some sources provide a continuous flow—as when all transaction data for a retailer are fed into the system—whereas others are occasional or periodic providers—as when new demographic information on the population is released by the government.

Probably the most important data source for consumer databases is **retail scanners,** the electronic devices at retail checkouts that read the bar code on each item purchased. Scanners were originally intended to speed up checkout and reduce errors in supermarkets. By matching an item's unique code with price information stored in a computer, the scanner eliminated the need for clerks to memorize prices and reduced mistakes caused by hitting the wrong cash register key. However, retailers quickly discovered scanners could also produce information on purchases that could be used to improve decisions about how much of a product to keep in inventory and the appropriate amount of shelf space to allocate to each product.

Many retailers, including Kroger and Safeway, have taken scanning a step further by adding the customer's identity to the record of their purchases in what are called frequent shopper programs. Participants in the stores' frequent shopper programs are given discounts if they permit the cashier to run their membership card through a reader when they check out. This allows the store to combine data stored on the card about household demographics and lifestyle with the shopper's scanned purchases. The store is then able to relate product choices to household characteristics and adjust the product assortment and store layout to make it more appealing.

Linking household information to product purchases is even more valuable if you know what advertising the purchasers have been exposed to and the coupons they have used. IRI has created a database to provide this information. The firm maintains a sample of cooperating households for which it:

- Maintains an extensive demographic profile.
- Monitors television viewing electronically.
- Tracks the use of coupons.
- Records grocery purchases.

The result is that household demographics can be correlated to television advertising exposure, coupon usage, and product purchases. The output is called **single-source data** because all the information can be traced to individual households, providing a single source for the data.

An alternative to bar coding is **Radio Frequency Identification (RFID),** which involves placing a tag in or on an object that emits a signal that can be read and interpreted by a receiver. These tags can store more information than a bar code, can be read much faster without direct contact, and cannot be interfered with by dirt, paint, or other substances. RFID can be passive, functioning much like a bar code, or active. An active RFID can accept as well as send information. So, for example, an active tag might indicate the necessary servicing a product requires and when it should be performed. When the service is completed the tag would be automatically updated. A current application is in monitoring and tracking inventory. However, it has been suggested that RFID tags will some day be so small and inexpensive that they will be placed in virtually all products. When that day comes, you may walk into a store and the retailer will instantly know when and where you bought every item you are wearing as well as how much you paid for it![6]

Can research identify needed adjustments?

Although many products sold around the world have much in common, there are situations in which adapting to a local market is the difference between success and failure. Japanese auto manufacturers have used several types of consumer research to discover the need for important features or modifications to existing features to satisfy the North American market. For example:

- Honda didn't add a third row of seats to its sports utility vehicle to be sold in the U.S. until observation convinced management that "soccer moms" frequently do haul the entire team and the family's pet dog as well!

- Toyota's Sienna minivan was initially much less successful than Honda's Previa. To help close the gap, Toyota tested its vehicle over many different conditions in the U.S. Among other things, the research found the vehicle was too noisy on many rough Western roads, too unstable in Midwestern high winds, and too easily dented on crowded Eastern city streets. The result was modifications in the undercarriage to reduce twisting, the exterior to cut down on wind resistance, and the bumpers to reduce damage in minor collisions.

- Nissan conducted focus groups with 8- to 15-year-olds to find out how many cup holders they want in its minivan, among other things.

- After disappointing sales for its small T100 pickup truck in the U.S., Toyota's post-performance research indicated that for many American pickup buyers image is as important as function. The result was the full-sized Toyota Tundra pickup with enough room for the passengers to wear 10-gallon hats.

- Honda found that while Japanese consumers associate a quiet car with luxury and power, American consumers feel a deep, throaty exhaust noise indicates those features. As a result, the exhaust system for luxury Hondas marketed in the U.S. was modified to create the right sound.

Sources: Norihiko Shirouzu, "Tailoring World's Cars to U.S. Tastes," *The Wall Street Journal,* Jan. 15, 2001, pp. B1+; Jonathan Fahey, "53,000 Miles of Market Research," *Forbes,* Feb. 17, 2003, p. 56.

Marketing Research Projects

Before MkIS and DSS, much of what was called marketing research consisted of projects to answer specific managerial questions. Projects, some that are nonrecurring and others that are repeated periodically, are still an important part of marketing research. The results of a project may be used to make a particular decision. They could also become part of a database to be used in an MkIS or a DSS. Examples of marketing research projects are described briefly in Table 7.1.

Well-designed marketing research projects follow the procedure outlined in Figure 7.3. Let's examine what goes into conducting such a project.

TABLE 7.1

Typical Marketing Research Projects

Project	Objective
Concept test	To determine if a new-product idea is attractive to potential customers
Copy test	To determine if the intended message in an advertisement is being communicated effectively
Price responsiveness	To gauge the effect a price change would have on demand for a brand
Market-share analysis	To determine a firm's proportion of the total sales of a product
Segmentation studies	To identify distinct groups within the total market for a particular product
Customer satisfaction studies	To monitor how customers feel about an organization and its products

FIGURE 7.3

**Marketing Research
Procedure.**

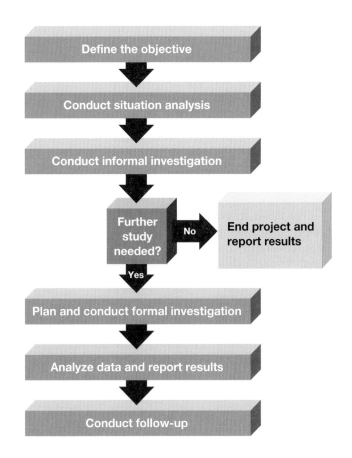

Define the Objective

Research is often conducted by someone other than the marketing manager who will be using it. Therefore, it is essential that a clear idea of what is to be learned—the **research objective**—is specified. Usually the objective is to solve a problem, but this is not always so. Often the objective is to better understand or *define* a problem or opportunity.

Sometimes the objective is simply to determine if there is a problem. To illustrate, a manufacturer of commercial air-conditioning equipment had been enjoying a steady increase in sales volume over a period of years. Management decided to conduct a sales analysis. This research project uncovered the fact that, although the company's volume had been increasing, its share of the market had declined because the industry was growing even faster. In this instance, marketing research uncovered a problem that management did not know existed. After specifying the objective, the researcher is ready for the second step—the situation analysis.

Conduct a Situation Analysis

Next, the researchers try to get a feel for the situation surrounding the problem. They analyze the company, its market, its competition, and the industry in general. The **situation analysis** is a background investigation that helps refine the research problem. This step involves obtaining information about the company and its business environment by means of library research and possibly conversations with company officials.

In the situation analysis, researchers also try to refine the problem definition and develop hypotheses for testing. A research **hypothesis** is a tentative supposition that, if supported, would suggest a possible solution to a problem. An example of a testable hypothesis is: More women than men use the Internet. If research supports this hypothesis, it would likely lead to changes in large Internet portals such as Yahoo! and MSN to make sure their entry sites and banner ads are appealing to the correct audiences. The project then turns to generating data that can be used to test the correctness of the hypotheses.

Conduct an Informal Investigation

Having developed a feel for the problem, the researchers are now ready to collect some preliminary data. This **informal investigation** consists of gathering readily available information from relevant people inside and outside the company—middlemen, competitors, advertising agencies, and consumers.

The informal investigation is a critical step in a research project because it will determine whether further study is necessary. Decisions can frequently be made with information gathered in the informal investigation. For example, hotels hire professional "mystery shoppers" to check in and act like typical guests when in fact they are evaluating the hotel's service. For as little as $1,500, a hotel can have its operation completely examined. And the examinations are thorough! For example, one hotel-rating company evaluates 50 items between a hotel's front door and the completion of check-in. If the results of such a test are very positive, a hotel might decide that additional research is not needed. Alternatively, a poor result may dictate some immediate changes or more research.[7]

Plan and Conduct a Formal Investigation

If the project warrants continued investigation, the researcher must determine what additional information is needed and how to gather it.

Select Sources of Information
Primary data, secondary data, or both can be used in an investigation. **Primary data** are new data gathered specifically for the project at hand. When researchers at a midwestern supermarket chain watched 1,600 shoppers move through the store and discovered that 80% of the traffic was in 20% of the store (the produce, dairy, and meat sections), they were collecting primary data. **Secondary data** are available data, already gathered for some other purpose. For example, the data in a study by the Food Marketing Institute, an industry trade group, that reported the differences in food preference and shopping behavior of men and women, are secondary data.

One of the biggest mistakes made in marketing research is to collect primary data before exhausting what can be learned from information available in secondary sources. Ordinarily, secondary information can be gathered much faster and at far less expense than primary data. This is especially true today with so much data available over the Internet. For example, the U.S. Census Bureau has created the American FactFinder website to assist researchers in locating population data down to the community level. Statistics on housing, income, transportation, employment, and education are readily accessible at this site.

www.census.gov

Sources of Secondary Data. Excellent sources of secondary information are available to marketing researchers. One source is the many records and reports *inside* the firm itself. For example, the daily call reports completed by sales people are used primarily to keep track of how they are spending their time. However, if they are examined over several months or years, they can provide a firm with important information on how its mix of customers is changing. Similarly, a contest with mail-in entries might be a good promotional tool. It also can be a source of information. Consumers who enter contests have indicated by their behavior that they are interested in particular products. Examining the geographic origins of these responses might indicate where the best potential markets are.

The U.S. Census Bureau is introducing the nation to its new American Community Survey, a rolling, random sample of 3 million U.S. households a year (about 250,000 each month). It replaces the "long form" of the decennial census. By gathering data on topics such as educational attainment, home value, commuting time, and languages spoken continuously rather than once every ten years, the Bureau will be able to report much more timely and accurate information that business can use to identify markets.

www.census.gov/acs/
www

Outside the firm there are also a number of excellent secondary data sources. The federal government is the largest provider of demographic market information. For example, the American Community Survey (ACS) being developed by the U.S. Census Bureau for nationwide implementation will provide annual demographic, economic, and housing data on all communities in the country. Rather than rely on the decennial (once every 10 years) census of the population, community planners, businesspeople, and government officials will have current data on which to base decisions. Other sources include the websites of firms and trade and professional organizations, private research firms, universities, business publications, and, of course, any good library. Some useful Web sources are described in Table 7.2.

Researchers must be aware that there is risk associated with using secondary data. Because the users have no control over how, when, by whom, or why the data were collected, they may not meet the objectives of the research. For example, some projects are undertaken to prove a preconceived point. The results of this so-called advocacy research often get considerable publicity, but may in fact be quite misleading. Thus researchers should check the source, motivation for the study, and definitions of key terms before relying on secondary data.

Sources of Primary Data.   After exhausting all the available secondary sources considered pertinent, researchers may still lack sufficient data. If so, they must turn to primary sources and gather or purchase the information. In a company's research project, for instance, a researcher may interview the firm's sales people, middlemen, or customers to obtain the market information needed.

Select a Primary Data-Gathering Method
There are three widely used methods of gathering primary data: observation, survey, and experimentation. Because each method has strengths and weaknesses, more than one may be used at different stages of a project. For example, observation may be used to develop hypotheses about shoppers' behavior and a survey may then be conducted to test those hypotheses. However, in many situations the researcher must select from among them. The choice of which to use depends on the nature of the problem, but it will also be influenced by how much time and money are available for the project.[8]

Observation Method.   The **observation method** involves collecting data by observing the actions of a person. In observation research there is no direct interaction with the subjects being studied.

Information may be gathered by *personal observation* or *mechanical observation*. In one kind of personal observation, the researcher poses as a customer. This technique is used by retailers, for example, to get information about the performance of sales people or to determine what brands the sales people emphasize. Mechanical

TABLE
7.2

Print and Electronic Sources of Secondary Data

Business and marketing publications and directories

Sales & Marketing Management magazine: <www.salesandmarketing.com>

Advertising Age magazine: <www.adage.com>

Quirk's Marketing Research Review: <www.quirks.com>

The New York Times Business section: <www.nytimes.com/pages/business>

Brandweek's list of top American brands: <www.brandweek.com> click on Superbrands

Executive Gateway to the Internet: <www.ceoexpress.com>

Marketing and research company websites

Gallup Poll: <www.gallup.com>

Nielsen Retail Index: <www.acnielsen.com>

Yankelovich Monitor: <www.yankelovich.com>

Fuld & Co.: <www.fuld.com> Click on Internet Intelligence Index for over 600 competitive intelligence-related sites

Government agencies and publications

Directory to all government agencies: <www.house.gov/house/govsites.html>

U.S. Census Bureau: <www.census.gov>

Statistical Abstract of the U.S.: <www.census.gov/statab/www>

CIA World Factbook: <www.odci.gov/cia/publications/factbook/index.html>

Fed Stats—statistics from over 100 federal government agencies: <www.fedstats.gov>

Federal Trade Commission: <www.ftc.gov>

Marketing roundtables, discussion groups, and other resources

Web Digest for Marketers: <www.wdfm.com>

Marketing Tracks—sources and commentary: <www.nsns.com/MouseTracks>

Web Marketing Today Info Center: <www.wilsonweb.com/marketing>

Professional association sources

American Marketing Association: <www.ama.org>

Direct Marketing Association: <www.the-dma.org>

Sales and Marketing Executives International: <www.smei.org>

observation takes many forms. One, described earlier, is the scanner used in retail stores to record purchases. Other, more dramatic forms are eye cameras that measure pupil dilation to record a person's response to a visual stimulus such as an ad, and brain wave monitors to test whether reactions to an object, such as a commercial, are primarily emotional or logical.

Internet "cookies" permit a special kind of observation. In Web jargon, a **cookie** is an inactive data file placed on a person's computer hard drive when that person visits a particular website. A cookie can record the visitor's activities while connected to the site. For example, it can keep track of which pages on the site are opened, how long the visitor remains at the site, the links the visitor makes to other sites, and the site from which the visitor came. If the site offers products for sale, purchases can also be recorded on a cookie. The cookie also allows the visitor (or more accurately, the visitor's computer) to be identified. All the information stored in the cookie is transferred to the host the next time the person connects to its website. The information from a cookie is used, for example, to develop a profile of an individual so that on subsequent visits to the host site the visitor can be greeted by name or offered particular products based on past purchases. Through the cookies it places on visitors' computers Amazon.com individually tracks millions of shoppers and book-buying customers and offers suggestions about titles they might enjoy based on what they have considered or purchased on past visits.

The observation method has several merits. It can provide highly accurate data about behavior in given situations. Usually the parties being observed are unaware that they are being observed, so presumably they behave in a normal fashion. Thus the observation technique eliminates bias resulting from the intrusion of the research process into the situation. Also, because there is no direct interaction with the subject, there is no limit to how many times or for how long a subject can be observed. However, observation provides only information about *what* happens, it cannot tell *why*. Observation cannot delve into motives, attitudes, or opinions. To illustrate, what might explain why the ratio of shoppers' visits to purchases is much higher for the bakery department than for any other department in a supermarket? Interviews would be necessary to test your possible explanations.

Survey Method. A **survey** consists of gathering data by interviewing people. Surveys can be conducted in person, by telephone, by mail, or via the Internet. The advantage of a survey is that information comes directly from the people you are interested in. In fact, it may be the only way to determine the opinions or buying plans of a group. Surveys have several potential limitations:

- There are opportunities for error in the construction of the survey questionnaire and in the interviewing process.

- Surveys can be expensive and time-consuming.

- Desired respondents sometimes refuse to participate, and those who do respond often cannot or will not give true answers.

As we will see below, careful design and execution of a survey can reduce the effects of these limitations.

Face-to-face interviews are more flexible than phone or mail interviews because interviewers can probe more deeply if an answer is incomplete. Ordinarily, more information can be obtained by personal interviews than by other survey methods.

Teenage Research Unlimited, a Chicago research firm, tracks teenage trends through a variety of techniques including focus groups and face-to-face interviews. By completing drawings, such as the one shown here, teens provide clues that are useful to marketers. Interpreting the data is the challenge. Is there a recent trend reflected in this actual example?

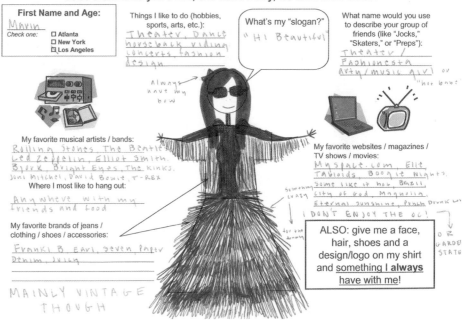

They also have the advantage of being able to use various stimuli such as products, packages, and ads. Rising costs and other problems associated with door-to-door interviewing have prompted many market researchers to conduct surveys in locations that attract large numbers of people, such as shopping centers, airports, and parks. Because this approach was first used in shopping centers, it is generally called a *mall intercept* interview. However, there is growing concern about whether or not people interviewed in these settings are "typical" consumers.

In addition to their high cost and time-consuming nature, personal interviews also face the possible limitation of interviewer bias. An interviewer's appearance, style in asking questions, and body language can all influence a respondent's answers.

Another popular face-to-face type of personal interview is the **focus group.** In a focus group, a moderator leads 6 to 12 people in a discussion. Typically the participants are strangers before the session. They are contacted, screened for suitability, and invited to attend. Because focus group sessions require that participants gather at a particular time and place, and often last for two to three hours, participants are usually rewarded with cash or merchandise. General questions are posed by the moderator to prompt participants into freely discussing the topic of interest.

The strength of focus groups is found in the interaction of the participants. A comment by one person triggers thoughts and ideas in others, and the ensuing interaction can produce valuable insights. Focus groups generate ideas and hypotheses that can be tested using other research methods. However, when several independent focus group sessions conducted on the same topic produce a common theme, managers will sometimes act on the information without additional validation.

Telephone surveys can usually be conducted more rapidly than either personal or mail surveys. Because a few interviewers can make many calls from a central location, this method is easy to administer. A telephone survey can also be timely. For instance, to determine the impact of a particular TV commercial, viewers are contacted by phone within hours of the commercial's appearance, while the experience is still fresh. Telephone surveys have been used successfully with executives at work. When preceded by a letter introducing the study and a short call to make an appointment for the actual interview, these surveys can elicit a high cooperation rate.

One limitation of telephone surveys is that the interview must be short or the respondent becomes impatient. Also, about 30% of households have unlisted numbers, have moved since the latest directory was printed, or have no telephone. To lower the cost of telephone interviewing and reduce the problems of unlisted numbers and outdated directories, some surveys are done with the aid of computers. To ensure that all telephone owners, even those with unlisted numbers, have an equal chance of being called, researchers use a method called *random digit dialing* in which computers randomly select and dial numbers.

A **mail survey** involves sending a questionnaire to potential respondents, asking them to complete it, and having them return it. Traditionally mail surveys have used the post office to deliver and return questionnaires; however, e-mail is growing in popularity as a distribution method. Because interviewers are not used, this type of survey is not hampered by interviewer bias or problems connected with managing a team of interviewers. In addition, because there is no interviewer present, the respondent can remain anonymous. As a result, answers are more likely to be frank and honest.

A major problem with mail surveys is the compilation of an appropriate mailing list. In some cases lists are readily available. However, many studies require a sample for which there is no readily available mailing list. For example, if Toys "R" Us wants to survey a nationwide sample of parents expecting the birth of their first child, it might have a difficult time compiling an up-to-date list. Fortunately, there are businesses called list brokers that develop and maintain mailing lists. Another problem is the reliability of the information in the completed questionnaires. In a mail survey, researchers have no control over who actually completes the questionnaire or how carefully it is done.

One more problem is that a mail survey usually gets a low response rate, often less than 30% of those contacted. This is more than a numbers problem. If the respondents have characteristics that differentiate them from nonrespondents on important dimensions of the survey, the results will be invalid. For example, in a community survey about interest in the local PBS television station, the people willing to take the time to respond are likely to be highly interested in public television and therefore not representative of the entire community. Techniques for improving mail response rates include prenotification by phone, offering a reward, duplicate mailings and postcard reminders, and keeping the survey short and the questions simple.

Increasingly the Internet is being used to conduct research. In an **Internet survey**, questionnaires can be posted on a firm's website or e-mailed to prospective respondents. Everything from short surveys to lengthy focus groups are being tried online. Two of the most important advantages of this tool are speed and cost. An Internet survey can be done more quickly than any other method, and because all transmissions are electronic, there are significant personnel and material savings. However, the primary advantage is the flexibility of a multimedia environment. Online surveys can include images that can be manipulated, streaming video, sounds, and other features that would be impractical with alternative data collection methods.

Internet surveys have many of the same disadvantages as mail surveys, namely, it is not possible to verify the identity of the respondent, good lists from which samples can be drawn are often difficult to find, and it is difficult to provide an incentive to encourage response because there is not yet a reliable method of electronic delivery. Until Internet usage becomes more widespread, probably the greatest single concern in using the Internet for surveys is how well users represent the general population.

Experimental Method. An **experiment** is a method of gathering primary data in which the researcher is able to observe the results of changing one variable in a situation while holding all other conditions constant. Experiments are conducted in laboratory settings or in the field. In marketing research, a "laboratory" is an environment in which the researcher has control over all the relevant conditions.

Consider this example: A small group of consumers is assembled and presented with a brief product description (called a *product concept*) and proposed package for a new breakfast cereal. After they examine the package, the people are asked whether they would buy the cereal, and their responses are recorded. Next, a similar group of consumers is brought together and presented with the identical package and product information, except that a nutritional claim for the cereal is printed on the package. Members of this group are also asked if they would buy the product. The researcher has complete control over the test environment, and the only thing changed is the nutritional claim on the package. Therefore, any difference in buying intentions between the groups can be attributed to the claim.

Laboratory experiments can be used to test many components of marketing strategy. For example, ads can be tested to determine how well the intended message is understood and various bundles of product features can be compared to see which is preferred. However, recognize that the laboratory setting is not an actual purchase, so consumers' responses may be influenced by the situation. To overcome this problem, some experiments are conducted outside the controlled conditions of the lab, or in the field. A *field experiment* is similar to a laboratory experiment but is conducted under more realistic conditions. For example, the owner of a chain of retail stores might try a traffic-building promotional program in one or two stores and then compare sales results with results in similar stores without the promotion. Certainly not everything in the stores can be controlled. However, if researchers believe all relevant conditions in the stores remained similar, any differences in sales can be credited to the promotion.

A common type of field experiment is test marketing. In **test marketing** the researcher duplicates real market conditions in a limited geographic area to measure consumers' responses to a strategy before committing to a major marketing effort. Test marketing is undertaken to forecast sales for a particular marketing mix or to compare the performance of different marketing mixes. For example, McDonald's test-marketed pizza in selected areas for over two years before deciding not to add it to the menu of their traditional outlets.

The advantage of test marketing over a survey or a lab experiment is that it informs marketers how many people *actually buy* a product, instead of how many say they *intend to buy* it. However, duplicating the entire marketing effort on a small scale has several disadvantages. Test marketing is expensive; spending $500,000 to $1 million is not uncommon. It is also time-consuming. Testing frequently lasts 9 to 12 months. Lever Bros. kept Lever 2000 deodorant soap in test for two years before going national. Another problem is the researcher's inability to control the situation. Tests are impossible to keep secret from competitors, who may intentionally disrupt the test by temporarily changing their marketing mixes. When Pepsi tested Mountain Dew Sport drink in Minneapolis, Quaker Oats, the maker of Gatorade, flooded the market with coupons and advertising. (Apparently, however, Pepsi learned quite a lot because it subsequently purchased Quaker Oats to obtain the Gatorade brand!)

International marketers sometimes use a few countries as a test market for a continent or even the world. Colgate-Palmolive introduced Palmolive Optims shampoo and conditioner in the Philippines, Australia, Mexico, and Hong Kong. When sales proved satisfactory, distribution was expanded to large portions of Europe, Asia, Latin America, and Africa.

Because of the inherent limitations of the kind of test marketing just described, researchers have tried to find faster, less visible alternatives. One of these is called a *simulated test market*. It combines surveys, product trial, and an extensive database to forecast sales. It works like this. A group of selected volunteers is shown ads and possibly other information about the new product, including the proposed price. They are then asked a number of questions about how well they like it, whether or not they'd buy it, and if it seems like a good value. Some of the consumers who indicate they like the product are given samples to test and are interviewed again. Finally,

www.bases.com

the researcher takes all this information, combines it with the marketer's planned strategy for distribution and promotion, and compares it to information on similar, previously marketed products that are stored in a database. Using a statistical model, the researcher then forecasts sales for the new product. Probably the best known of these procedures is called Bases by the research firm ACNielsen.

The potential benefits of such a simulated test market include:

- Results can be produced quickly, often in as little as eight weeks.
- The tests can be done secretly, without competitor knowledge or interference.
- The cost may be lower than using a traditional test market.

The drawbacks are:

- The procedure is suitable only for consumer packaged goods and some over-the-counter pharmaceuticals.
- Because the forecasting models are based on historical sales of similar products, it may not be appropriate for unique new products.
- It is expensive, and testing alternative marketing mixes adds to the cost.

Sometimes this approach is used to refine a marketing strategy that is then followed by traditional test marketing. The time, effort, and expense that go into researching new products indicate how important they are and how difficult it is to anticipate how consumers will respond to a marketing effort.

Prepare Forms for Gathering Data

Whether interviewing or observing subjects, researchers use a questionnaire or form that contains instructions and spaces to record observations and responses. It is not easy to design a data-gathering form that elicits precisely the information needed. Here are several fundamental considerations:

- *Question wording.* If a question is misunderstood, the data it produces are worthless. Questions should be written with the potential respondent's vocabulary, reading level, and familiarity with jargon in mind.
- *Response format.* Questions are designed for either check mark responses (such as yes-no, multiple-choice, agree-disagree scales) or open-ended replies. Open-ended questions are often easier to write and frequently produce richer answers, but they require more effort from the respondent and therefore lower the level of cooperation.
- *Questionnaire layout.* The normal procedure is to begin with easier questions and move to the more difficult or complicated questions. Possibly sensitive topics (for example, personal hygiene) or private matters (age, income) are normally placed at the very end of a questionnaire.
- *Pretesting.* All questionnaires should be pretested using a group of individuals similar to the intended respondents to identify problems and make corrections and refinements prior to the actual study.

Complete books are available on questionnaire design. Extreme care and skill are needed to produce a questionnaire that maximizes the likelihood of getting a response while minimizing bias, misunderstanding, and respondent irritation.

Plan the Sample

It is unnecessary to survey or observe every person who could shed light on a research problem. It is sufficient to collect data from a sample if it is *representative* of the entire group. We all make use of sampling. For example, we often form opinions of people based on a few interactions. However, if the interactions include only one aspect of a person's life, for example work interactions, and ignore home life or recreation, they may not be representative. The key in these personal issues *and* in marketing research is whether the sample provides an accurate representation. Representativeness has been an issue in using the Internet to collect data. As attractive as it is for data collection, many researchers are concerned about how well Internet users represent the general population.

The fundamental idea underlying sampling is that a small number of items—a sample—if properly selected from a larger number of items—a universe—will have the same characteristics and in about the same proportion as the larger number. Obtaining reliable data with this method requires the right technique in selecting the sample.

Improper sampling is a source of error in many studies. One firm, for example, selected a sample of calls from all the calls made to its 800 number and used the information to make generalizations about its customers. Would you be comfortable saying these callers are representative of all the firm's customers or even all the dissatisfied ones? Although numerous sampling techniques are available, only by using a random sample can a researcher confidently make generalizations about a universe. A *random sample* is selected in such a way that every member of the universe has an equal chance of being included.

All other (nonrandom) samples are known as *convenience samples*. Convenience samples are quite common in marketing research for two reasons. First, random samples are very difficult to get. Even though the researcher may *select* the subjects in a random fashion, there is no guarantee that they all will participate. Some will be unavailable and others will refuse to cooperate. As a result, researchers often resort to carefully designed convenience samples that reflect the characteristics of the universe as closely as possible. Second, not all research is done with the objective of generalizing to a universe. For example, to confirm the judgment of the advertising department, a researcher may be satisfied with the finding that a small group of respondents all take a similar message away from an ad.

A common question regarding sampling is: How large should a sample be? With random methods, a sample must be large enough to be truly representative of the universe. Thus the size will depend on the diversity of characteristics within the universe. All basic statistics books contain general formulas for calculating sample size. In the case of nonrandom samples, because the objective is not to make generalizations, researchers can select any size sample they and the managers using the data feel comfortable with.

Collect the Data   Collecting primary data by interviewing, observation, or both can be done by people or machines. Unfortunately, it is often the weakest link in the research process. A research project can be designed with great care, but the fruits of these labors may be lost if the data gathering is inadequately conducted.

It is often difficult to motivate people who collect data. Because they frequently are part-time workers doing what is often a monotonous task for relatively low pay, proper training and supervision are essential to avoid problems. For instance, poorly trained data gatherers may fail to establish rapport with respondents or may change the wording of questions. In extreme cases, there have even been instances where interviewers faked the responses and filled out the questionnaires themselves!

Mechanical data collection includes such devices as retail scanners (described earlier), video cameras, audiotapes, and computer terminals (often found in malls, airport terminals, and hotel lobbies). The human element of the data collector is eliminated with these devices, but there are new issues that can affect data quality such as equipment reliability, how participants' responses and behavior are affected by the mechanical device, and the conversion of the raw data into useable form.

Analyze the Data and Present a Report

The value of research is determined by its results. And because data cannot speak for themselves, analysis and interpretation are key components of any project. Computers allow researchers to tabulate and process masses of data quickly and inexpensively. This tool can be abused, however. Managers have little use for reams of computer printouts. Researchers must be able to identify pivotal relationships, spot trends, and find patterns—that's what transforms data into useful information.

The end product of the investigation is the researcher's conclusions and recommendations. Most projects require a written report, often accompanied by an oral presentation to management. Here communication skill becomes a factor. Not only must researchers be able to write and speak effectively, they must adopt the perspective of the manager in presenting research results.

Conduct a Follow-up

Researchers should follow up their studies to determine whether their results and recommendations are being used. Management may choose not to use a study's findings for several reasons. The problem that generated the research may have been misdefined, become less urgent, or even disappeared. Or the research may have been completed too late to be useful. Without a follow-up, the researcher has no way of knowing if the project was on target and met management's needs or if it fell short. As a result, an important source of information for improving research in the future would be ignored.

Competitive Intelligence

A research area that is receiving increased attention is competitive intelligence. U.S. marketers have learned from their foreign counterparts that closely monitoring competitors can be extremely useful. Japanese firms in particular have made a science out of watching and learning from their rivals.

According to a survey of its members, the Society of Competitive Intelligence Professionals reported the most common types of projects undertaken are competitor profiles, financial analysis of competitors, and analyses of alternative strategy scenarios.

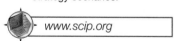
www.scip.org

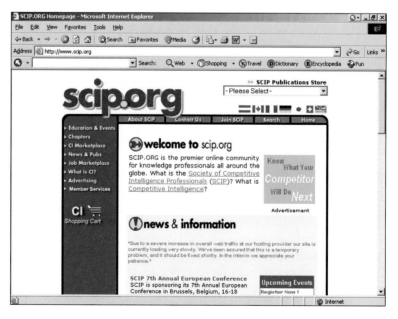

Although it sounds intriguing, **competitive intelligence** is simply the process of gathering and analyzing available public information about the activities and plans of competitors. About two-thirds of U.S. firms have organized intelligence gathering systems on which they spend $2 billion a year.[9]

The data used to study competitors come from a variety of internal and external sources. The most common are databases created and sold by research firms. The simplest of these are newspaper and magazine clipping services that monitor a large number of publications for articles on particular industries or companies. There are several thousand of these competitive database services available today.

Another source is government reports, produced and made available by U.S. and foreign government agencies. For example, the Japan Center for Information and Cultural Affairs provides government documents, statistics on Japan, and information on various Japanese industries. Along the same line, the European Union provides competitive and financial information on European commerce.

Employees, particularly sales people, are the primary internal source of competitive data. It has become a standard practice for firms to incorporate space for competitive information in the reporting forms used by sales people. Other employees, such as engineers, service personnel, and purchasing agents, can pick up and report helpful information—if they are trained to be alert.

It is relatively common to use various observation techniques to collect competitive information. For example, representatives of consumer product manufacturers regularly shop retail stores to monitor competitors' prices and promotions. And it is not uncommon for a firm to buy a competitor's new product and take it apart in order to examine and test it—a procedure called *reverse engineering.*

One of the newest sources of competitive intelligence is the Internet. In an attempt to please current or potential customers, firms put information on their websites that a few years ago would have been considered highly proprietary. Price lists, suppliers' and distributors' names, plans for the future, and new-product information are commonly posted. Other website information may be less direct but still valuable. For example, firms that are proud of their research and development efforts often list research papers produced by their technical people. These papers can provide insights into the direction the firm is headed.

Clearly there is the potential for legal and ethical abuses in gathering competitive intelligence. Incidents of sifting through trash, electronic eavesdropping, and hiring competitors' employees to learn their plans are unfortunately not uncommon. Despite trade secret laws that make it illegal to acquire data through "improper means" such as theft, there are many unclear situations. Based on court opinions, attempts to get information when a competitor is taking reasonable care to conceal it from public exposure are unethical and may be illegal.

Many firms take elaborate precautions to protect the security of confidential information, referred to as *counter intelligence*. Common techniques include the use of paper shredders, alerting employees to the importance of discretion, and limiting the circulation of sensitive documents. Of particular concern is the ease with which a thief can extract information from a careless employee's misplaced briefcase or personal computer. The potential for damage is so great, firms are hiring consultants to develop programs to protect information and sensitize employees.[10]

Ethical Issues in Marketing Research

As the desire for better information grows and the technology for gathering data improves, marketers are faced with an increasing variety of ethical issues related to the collection and use of research information. Typical of the growing concerns are the following:

www.ftc.gov

- *Privacy in data collection.* It is possible to observe people with hidden cameras, identify an individual's purchase behavior by combining scanner data and credit card or check-cashing records, and track Internet activity with cookies. At what point does data collection became an invasion of privacy? The Federal Trade Commission is the primary government agency charged with consumer protection. From the number of issues it is addressing—including the conditions under which firms can share credit histories and purchasing information of customers, the disposition of medical records, and the protection of the privacy of children on the Internet—it's apparent this is a growing concern. Unfortunately, the temptation to misuse access to private information has proven too strong for some managers to resist.

- *Privacy in data use.* In the routine process of business, firms often gather a considerable amount of information about their customers. This information, if linked to an individual's name and address, could be highly valuable to other businesses. For example, airlines have information about travel behavior that a travel magazine publisher would find useful. Does the airline have the right to sell that information?

- *Intrusiveness.* All marketers want information. The problem is that gathering that information can be annoying and inconvenient for the respondent. Telephone surveys conducted around dinnertime, extraneous (to the transaction) data collected at the time of a purchase, and questionnaires sent to people at work can all be intrusive. The issue here is this: At what point does requesting information become excessively intrusive?

- *Deceptive implementation.* On occasion, researchers use deception to gather data. For example, phoning a business and falsely representing oneself as a

www.casro.org

AN ETHICAL DILEMMA?

Advocacy research supports a particular position. Rather than simply stating a viewpoint or prediction, a person or organization reports findings from a survey or other research to bolster an argument. Some recent examples of advocacy research in the business press include:

- By 2008, the U.S. will be the world's leading wine-drinking nation.

- Only 39% of firms responded to e-mail messages from prospective customers within 24 hours and, of those responding, three-fourths were not helpful.

- The average American gains seven pounds between Thanksgiving and Christmas, and nearly 40% make losing weight a New Year's resolution.

- Only 11% of discarded computers and 5% of discarded cell phones are recycled worldwide.

Advocacy research is frequently reported as factual. However, its validity is often suspect because of the methods used to produce the results. Some warning signs include research that reports only percentages or percentage changes, does not describe the sample or respondents to a survey, or does not identify the sponsor of the project.

Is it unethical to design research to produce a desired result?

Sources: Dan Seilgman, "New Crisis—Junk Statistics," *Forbes*, Oct. 18, 2004, pp. 118+; Andy Reinhardt and Rachel Tipaldy, "Europe Says: Let's Get the Lead Out," *BusinessWeek*, Feb. 7, 2005, p. 12; Rachel Tipaldy, "America the Bibulous," *BusinessWeek*, Feb. 28, 2005, p. 14; Linda Stern, "Mailbox Manners," *Newsweek*, Nov. 29, 2004, p. E4; Olga Kharif, "Plug In, Turn On, Fight Fat," *BusinessWeek*, Jan. 24, 2005, p. 14.

potential customer in order to collect data, or intentionally misleading respondents about the sponsor or objective of the research are deceptions. Some researchers intentionally don't disclose to respondents that they are research subjects participating in a study. For example, a researcher in a grocery store pretending to be a shopper and asking fellow shoppers their opinions of products or brands is nondisclosure. In most cases, these deceptions are harmless and are actually viewed by researchers as essential to gathering candid responses. However, at what point is extracting information from a person under false or misleading pretenses inappropriate?

- *False representation.* Practices called "sugging" (selling under the guise of research) and "frugging" (fund raising under the guise of research) are unfortunately so common that they are negatively affecting the ability of legitimate researchers to gain respondents' cooperation. Practitioners of these techniques use the ruse that they are researchers conducting a survey. After securing the cooperation of the unsuspecting consumer and posing a few questions, they attempt a sale or ask for a donation. Some argue that research and selling or fund raising should never be combined in the same presentation. Others contend that the issue is whether the consumer is misled, not what is presented.

There have been several reactions to practices such as these. One is efforts by professional associations such as the American Marketing Association and the Council of American Survey Research Organizations (CASRO) to discourage such practices among their members and other practitioners.

Status of Marketing Research

Significant advances have been made in both quantitative and qualitative research methodology, and researchers are making effective use of the behavioral sciences, mathematics, and statistics. Still, many companies invest very little in determining market opportunities for their products. Several factors account for the less-than-universal acceptance of marketing research:

- *Predicting behavior is inexact.* Because of the many variables involved, marketing research often cannot predict future market behavior accurately. The difficulty in developing a helpful food pyramid, described in the chapter-opening case, indicates some of the challenges and opportunities in conducting consumer research. When dealing with consumer behavior, the researcher may be hard pressed to determine present attitudes or motives (for reasons that were explained in Chapter 4), much less what they will be next year.

- *Conflicting objectives between researchers and managers.* The manager is frequently required to make quick decisions in the face of uncertainty, often with incomplete information. Researchers, on the other hand, are prone to approach problems in a cautious, scientific manner. This leads to disagreements about the research that should be conducted, how long it should take, and the way in which the results should be presented.

- *A project orientation to research.* Many managers do not treat marketing research as a continuous process. Too often marketing research is viewed in a fragmented, one-project-at-a-time manner. It is used only when management realizes that it has a marketing problem. The growth in the use of MkIS, DSS, and data mining will likely improve this situation.

Making research more "actionable"—that is, on target and of value to managers—is a challenge. However, it is far from impossible. In examining the issue in interviews with both researchers and managers, communications proved to be the key. When managers and researchers communicate continuously and consistently at every stage of the research process, research is more likely to lead to effective action.

Summary

Competitive pressure, the cost of making a mistake, and the complexity of both domestic and foreign markets all contribute to the need for marketing research. For a company to operate successfully today, management must engage in marketing research: the development, interpretation, and communication of decision-oriented information. Three tools used in research are marketing information systems, decision support systems, and research projects.

A marketing information system (MkIS) is an ongoing set of procedures designed to generate, analyze, disseminate, store, and retrieve information for use in making marketing decisions. An MkIS provides a manager with a regularly scheduled flow of information and reports. As firms develop global MkISs, they are faced with problems of timing, accuracy of data, and terminology and measurement differences. A decision support system (DSS) differs from an MkIS in that the manager, using a personal computer, can interact directly with data. The DSS adds speed and flexibility to the MkIS but requires considerable investment to create and maintain.

Data used in an MkIS or DSS come from databases, which are organized sets of data pertinent to a particular topic stored and updated in a computer.

Retail scanners are major sources of data that go into databases.

When data sets grow beyond simply a "base" of information, they are referred to as data warehouses. These enormous collections of data are probed for patterns and meaningful relationships in a process called data mining.

A marketing research project is undertaken to help resolve a specific marketing problem. The problem must first be clearly defined. Then a researcher conducts a situation analysis and an informal investigation. If a formal investigation is needed, the researcher decides which secondary and primary sources of information to use. Secondary data already exist. Primary data are gathered for the problem at hand. Primary data are gathered using observation, surveys, or experiments.

Observation is unintrusive but cannot provide explanations for the behavior observed. Surveys are conducted in person, by phone, or through the mail. The Internet and e-mail are growing in popularity as tools for conducting surveys. The challenges in survey research are selecting a sample, designing a questionnaire, and generating an adequate response. The research project is completed when data are analyzed and the results reported. Follow-up provides information for improving future research.

Researchers have recently developed a stronger interest in competitive intelligence, or finding out what competitors are currently doing and forecasting what they are likely to do in the future. The news media, government, the Internet, and a company's own sales people are important sources of competitive intelligence information.

Among the ethical issues in marketing research are protecting the privacy of respondents when collecting and using data, being overly intrusive, deceiving respondents, and selling or fund raising under the guise of research.

Some managers are not highly supportive of research because its task—predicting behavior—is inexact and very difficult to accomplish, researchers and managers often operate with different objectives, and research is conducted sporadically. These problems can be reduced and research made actionable if researchers and managers remain in close contact.

More about the USDA's food pyramid

The U.S. Department of Agriculture's Center for Nutrition Policy and Promotion may have decided that discretion was the better part of valor when it outsourced the dietary guide project. It issued a request for proposals (RFP) inviting public relations firms to bid on the development of a new pictorial food guide and communicate it to the public through the media. The contract, won by Porter Novelli, was for three years with the first year budget set at $1.6 million.

The design, which was announced in mid-2005 and ultimately cost $2.5 million, is also a pyramid. However, instead of being divided horizontally, it is divided vertically much like a fan. Each blade represents a food group, with the width of the blades indicating the recommended proportions for a healthy diet. With the food groups depicted this way, none is given the prime spot at the base of the pyramid. The "winners," with recommended increases in consumption, are whole grains, fruits and vegetables, and low-fat dairy products. Not surprisingly, the "losers" were products high in fat, sugar, and sodium. The pyramid also incorporates a stickman climbing stairs to indicate the importance of regular exercise in achieving good health.

The final result is actually 12 versions of the pyramid. By entering their age, gender, and activity level on the website mypyramid.gov, consumers are presented with an adjusted pyramid and recommendation for eating and exercise. On its first day, the website received over 15 million hits.

In developing the pyramid input was received from the food industry, health and nutrition interest groups, and even members of the U.S. Congress from states with a vested interest in certain food products. However, there are several reasons to believe the pyramid and accompanying recommendations will have little impact on eating behavior:

- The success of fad diets suggests that American consumers are searching for a "quick fix" for losing or maintaining weight rather than a healthy regimen of eating and exercise.

- A survey in 2000 found that most consumers were aware of the old pyramid but only 10% actually followed its recommendations.

- Consumers have voted with their dollars for taste over nutrition. According to a research firm that monitors food products, 3,730 low-carbohydrate products introduced in 2003 and 2004 are experiencing sales lower than expected.

Some critics of the pyramid concept have called for stronger measures even including government regulations to remove unhealthy food products from the market. Others are equally critical of the pyramid but for different reasons. They feel there is enough information available about what is and isn't healthy eating, and consumers should assume responsibility for their behavior without government involvement.

Can this or any other proposed design be effective in changing the eating behavior of consumers? Ultimately this is an issue of marketing an idea. For it to be successful, consumers must act on the belief that a healthy diet and exercise will provide greater benefit than the alternative. However, before that happens, many questions must be addressed that marketing research can help answer. By following the guidelines for conducting a marketing research project it may be possible to move toward the desired result with more enlightenment and less heat.

1. What are some objectives that should be addressed in research on consumer nutrition and eating?

2. What groups of consumers should be involved in research investigating changing eating behavior?

3. What roles might focus groups, in-depth interviews, and experiments play in the research for a food pyramid replacement?

 www.mypyramid.gov

Key Terms and Concepts

Marketing research (171)
Marketing information system (MkIS) (172)
Decision support system (DSS) (174)
Database (175)
Data warehouse (176)
Data mining (176)
Retail scanners (177)
Single-source data (177)

Radio Frequency Identification (RFID) (177)
Research objective (179)
Situation analysis (179)
Hypothesis (179)
Informal investigation (180)
Primary data (180)
Secondary data (180)
Observation method (181)
Cookie (182)

Survey (183)
Face-to-face interviews (183)
Focus group (184)
Telephone survey (184)
Mail survey (185)
Internet survey (185)
Experiment (185)
Test marketing (186)
Competitive intelligence (190)

Questions and Problems

1. Explain how a marketing information system (MkIS) differs from a decision support system (DSS).

2. Should the task of marketing research go beyond providing data to marketing managers?

3. Evaluate surveys, observation, and experimentation as methods of gathering primary data in the following projects:
   a. A sporting goods retailer wants to determine college students' brand preferences for skis, tennis rackets, and golf clubs.
   b. A supermarket chain wants to determine shoppers' preferences for the physical layout of fixtures and traffic patterns, particularly around checkout counters.
   c. A manufacturer of conveyor belts wants to know who makes buying decisions for his product among present and prospective users.

4. Using the steps in the research process from the text, describe how you would go about investigating the feasibility of opening a copy shop adjacent to your campus.

5. Examine the procedure that the Consumers Union uses in formulating the evaluations of automobiles presented in *Consumer Reports*. (The method is described in the magazine.) Based on the discussion of sampling in the chapter, comment on the procedure.

6. Shortly after a patient used a credit card to pay a bill at a dentist's office, she received a direct mail solicitation for dental insurance. This suggests that the credit card company is developing a database using the specific purchasing activity of cardholders and selling it. Does this raise an issue of invasion of privacy?

7. If you were designing an academic program for the marketing researcher of the future, what areas of study would you include?

Interactive Marketing Exercises

1. Assume you work for a manufacturer of a liquid glass cleaner that competes with Windex and Glass Wax. Your manager wants to estimate the amount of product that can be sold throughout the country. To help the manager in this project, prepare a report that shows the following information for your state and, if possible, your home city or county. Carefully identify the sources you use for this information.
   a. Number of households or families.
   b. Income or buying power per family or per household.
   c. Total retail sales in the most recent year for which you can find reliable data.
   d. Total annual sales of food stores, hardware stores, and drug stores.
   e. Total number of food stores.

2. Interview the manager of the bookstore that serves your school about the marketing information system it uses (keep in mind that it may be a very informal system).
   a. What are the data sources?
   b. What are the data collected?
   c. What reports are received and on what schedule?
   d. What problems arise with the MkIS?
   e. How could the MkIS be improved?

Cases for Part 2

The Gap

Fashioning a New Target-Market Strategy

When businesses all across America began allowing their employees to wear "business-casual" clothes in the 1990s, Gap was well positioned to capitalize on the new fashion trend. Its Chief Executive Officer (CEO) at the time, Millard "Mickey" Drexler, was famous for his uncanny ability to accurately predict the whims of fickle shoppers, and the Gap's classic line of khaki pants and button-down shirts were the epitome of the updated office dress code. As a result, Gap quickly became the nation's largest specialty apparel retailer. Its sales rose dramatically from $1.93 billion in 1990 to $11.64 billion in 1999 as the number of Gap stores around the United States (and the rest of the world) grew.

But other retailers soon followed Gap's example of offering simple lines of casual clothes and, in 2000, Gap's sales (and profits) began declining as the company was unable to sustain its momentum. In response, Gap tried to change its fortunes by offering trendier fare, but it wound up alienating its core customer base of 20- to 30-year-olds. This uncharacteristic misstep caused Drexler to muse that, "We probably got a little bored at being consistent and simple. Big mistake." Same-store sales started a steady, precipitous decline, culminating with an $8 million loss in 2001. Gap's founder, Donald Fisher, reflected that "it took us 30 years to get to $1 billion in profits and two years to get to nothing."

In 2002, a new CEO, Paul Pressler, was brought in to help Gap achieve profitability once again, and he implemented a new direction that relied more on market research than gut instinct. A former Disney executive, Pressler became the first person from outside the Gap organization to take its helm, leaving employees and stockholders alike to wonder whether he was the right person to keep Gap from losing its proverbial shirt.

Designing a Retail Success Story

Donald Fisher founded Gap in 1969, when he became frustrated by a store that would not allow him to return a pair of Levi jeans that were too short. He located his first Gap store in San Francisco and stocked it with Levi's in a wide variety of sizes. Gap quickly expanded across the country, supported by a fixed 50% markup that Levi Strauss required of all retailers selling its merchandise. However, the Federal Trade Commission ruled that manufacturers such as Levi Strauss could not fix retail prices for their products, and jeans became a discounted product overnight.

The Gap responded by adopting a back-to-basics merchandise strategy, stocking its stores with all-cotton apparel in a wide assortment of colors. Gap acquired Banana Republic in 1983, a chain of stores featuring safari styles that were popularized by a number of successful movies, such as the *Indiana Jones* series. That trend had waned by 1988, however, and the Banana Republic chain was repositioned as an upscale Gap with more adventurous fashions. Gap branched out even more when it introduced GapKids in 1986 and babyGap fashions in 1990. The company tried to further expand its customer base in 1994 with Old Navy Clothing Co., a chain that carries specially designed apparel and accessories targeted at consumers with incomes of $20,000 to $50,000. Its wide selection offers a department-store style assortment of items for men, women, children, and babies and is priced 20% to 25% below Gap's merchandise. Along the way, Gap also became a publicly traded company, making the Fisher family extremely wealthy.

Falling into the Gap

Mickey Drexler was appointed president of Gap Inc. in 1987 and later promoted to CEO. He was credited with anticipating the khaki craze of the 1990s and successfully guided Gap's merchandising strategy for many years. As sales at Gap stores took off in the early 1990s, Drexler made plans for aggressive expansion, more than doubling the number of company stores between 1996 and 2001. By October 2001, Gap boasted 2,759 stores, followed by Old Navy with 732, and Banana Republic with 422. Gap also introduced its first website, *www.gap.com*, in 1997, followed by *www.gapkids.com* and *www.babygap.com* in 1998. Banana Republic and Old Navy went online in 2000.

However, Gap's sales growth began to depend on new store openings because sales at existing stores were not increasing. In 2000, Gap posted revenue of $13.67 billion and profits of $877 million. Sales were barely higher in 2001 ($13.8 billion) but the company lost $7.8 million. That was because sales at stores open at least one year began falling in mid-2000, dropping 5% for the year, and declining 11% in 2001. Even so, Gap continued expanding by adding more stores. "Who in their right mind would have expanded like Gap in the face of such terrible results?", asked one retail consultant.

Several factors were responsible for Gap's problems, including a weak economy and more intense competition. Discounters such as Target, Wal-Mart, and Kohl's were particularly successful in luring loyal customers from Gap and Old Navy. In a disastrous attempt to increase sales by attracting a new market segment, Gap began offering trendier fashions to appeal to the country's 31.3 million teens, while still targeting its core 20- to 30-year-old market. As a result, Gap found itself competing with a new array of specialty retail chains, including American Eagle, Deb Shops, and Rave. But the teen market is a fickle one, and predicting what they will purchase at any given time is a gamble. They are also extremely price sensitive and will sacrifice quality for economy. Not only did Gap's new fashions fail to attract teen shoppers, they alienated its older client base. Drexler conceded that "We changed too much, too quickly in ways that weren't consistent with our brands."

Tightening Its Belt

In 2001, Gap management began taking steps to get the company back on track. It laid off 1,040 employees in July and announced it would reduce its capital spending to $400 million in 2002, down from $1 billion in 2001. Some of this reduction was realized by closing 51 under-performing Gap stores. Drexler also announced that Gap would once again return to its roots and begin emphasizing classic lines, such as khakis.

But the damage was done, and in May of 2002, Drexler announced his resignation. By the time Pressler came on board, however, Gap was showing signs of improvement. It posted profits of $477 million in 2002, but that didn't stop Pressler from implementing several significant changes. He began by working in Gap stores to better understand the company's logistics, operations, and customers. This led to his dictate that store managers better utilize software to assist them in making merchandising decisions regarding markdowns in order to boost sales margins. He also interviewed each of Gap's 50 highest-ranking executives to determine what most needed to be done. What he learned was that "They'd been relying on sales numbers and anecdotal evidence. All that tells you is what people bought, not what they need."

Pressler's next step was to hire the advertising firm of Leo Burnett to perform brand-segmentation studies using focus groups and surveys to provide added insight into Gap's customers. These have led to the development of separate ad campaigns for men and women, a first for Gap. He has also continued closing more domestic stores, although he professes a desire to continue international expansion. Stores outside the United States contributed 12% of Gap's total sales in 2003. "Our styling is absolutely relevant around the world," he stated.

Gap made headlines worldwide when it refused to continue to do business with more than 130 factories in China, Africa, India, and Central and South America because of a number of labor issues having to do with wages, health, and safety. With unprecedented honesty, the company published a "social-responsibility report" that listed a number of problems it had encountered with its vendors, including physical abuse of employees, inadequate safety equipment, and more. While many retailers have been accused of covering up such allegations, Gap was uncharacteristically open regarding its findings, and many industry analysts applauded their efforts, hoping it would spur important changes across the industry.

Making Over Gap Stores

Pressler's most pressing challenge is to once again define each of Gap's retail chains. In the spring of 2003, Gap went back to basics and introduced a line of stretch khakis to try to recapture the attention of 20- and 30-somethings. Banana Republic, which had been offering mostly basics up to that point, sought to differentiate itself from Gap by being more fashionable. Toward that end, it hired a designer from Nautica, unveiled its fall 2004 line at the Chelsea Art Museum in New York, and succeeded in having its clothes photographed for several top fashion magazines. Banana Republic was also one of the main sponsors of a reality television show called "Project Runway" that sought to discover the next big American designer. The winner was awarded a one-year mentorship opportunity with Banana Republic's design department, and one of the show's winning designs was sold in select stores throughout the country. (It sold out almost immediately.) Relying on the results of the market research he commissioned, Pressler also ordered that Banana Republic carry more petite sizes to meet the needs of its customers.

Cases for Part 2   **197**

Old Navy, which now accounts for 41% of Gap's total business, began targeting families in 2003, instead of just teens. "Teenagers are a narrow and fickle segment," explained Old Navy president Jenny Ming. "We realized we're too big to focus on them." Old Navy also began offering maternity wear, infant items, socks, and underwear in an effort to become a one-stop shopping destination and be able to meet the needs of an entire family. Ming hopes the new lines will increase sales and profit margins. Pressler's research indicated that Old Navy could further improve its shoppers' experience by adding color-coded tags to its hangers to make finding the correct size easier, and indicated that Old Navy customers wanted more elastic waistbands. The resulting changes contributed to an 8% increase in sales in 2003.

Taking Fashion Forward

In 1996, Gap introduced GapBody, a line of lingerie, sleepwear, lotions, and potions that is sold in select Gap stores and a few stand-alone locations. "GapBody offers women their first layer of fashion which helps them feel special and confident from the inside out," stated Margot McShane, Brand Director of GapBody. By 2005, GapBody products were available in 200 different stores across the United States, the majority of which were existing Gap stores.

In late 2004, Gap also announced plans to open a new chain of stores targeting women over the age of 35. Women between the ages of 35 and 54 spent $30.7 billion between August 2003 and July 2004, compared to the $11.85 billion spent by teens between the ages of 13 and 17 during that same period. "This is a group we still have an opportunity to service," explained a Gap spokesperson. Gap isn't the only clothing company embracing this more mature market. Gymboree, a leading baby and children's clothing store, opened a new chain called Janeville in ten locations. Teen clothier Abercrombie & Fitch also developed a new store called Ruehl. Meanwhile, department stores have been switching their focus from teens to older shoppers by offering more fashions from Oscar de la Renta, Michael Kohrs, and other big-name designers. Always admired for its cutting-edge style, Target hired fashion icon Isaac Mizrahi to design a chic new line of women's clothing.

Gap began assessing the new concept, named Forth & Towne, by opening five stores in the second half of 2005. "Up until recently, this has been an underserved market," commented one industry analyst. "Very shortly, you are going to see a saturated market." Chico's, a clothing store that targets women over the age of 45 has already opened and closed a chain called Pazo that was meant to bring in a slightly younger audience.

"We'll start with these test stores and see where it goes," observed Pressler. "When we think about growth strategies, we are looking for opportunities that are going to meaningfully add to our growth, given the size of our company." No doubt Pressler will continue to rely heavily on research findings when he makes decisions about this and other new directions for Gap Inc. Only time will tell whether this new, buttoned-up approach makes sense for the $15.9 billion company.

Questions

1. What social influences in consumer behavior are likely to have an effect on Gap's future marketing strategy?

2. How would you segment the markets for Gap, Banana Republic, Old Navy, and the new, as yet unnamed chain?

3. Is it possible to define four distinct target markets for these chains?

4. How would you identify underserved target markets and unfilled positions Gap might consider?

www.gap.com

UPS versus FedEx versus DHL

Delivering More Services for Their Customers

Jim Casey began United Parcel Service (UPS) in 1907 with $100 he borrowed from a friend to start a parcel-delivery and messenger service. Hired to deliver packages from Seattle, Washington, department stores to shoppers' homes, UPS's early "fleet" of delivery vehicles included a Model T and a few motorcycles. As UPS approaches its centennial, it now boasts a fleet of more than 88,000 vehicles and over 265 company-owned jet aircraft, supplemented by almost 300 chartered aircraft. UPS serves every address in North America and Europe, and is expanding across the globe. On one particular day in December 2004, UPS delivered more than 20 million packages, an impressive performance for anyone, with the possible exception of Santa Claus. And while Santa keeps track of who's been naughty and nice, UPS allowed a record number of customers (16 million) to track their deliveries online that day.

UPS had very little private-sector competition in the package delivery market until Frederick Smith started Federal Express (now FedEx) in 1971. Smith originally outlined his idea for FedEx in a term paper while a student at Yale University. Despite the fact that his paper didn't receive a very high grade, Smith was undeterred. "I knew the idea was profound," he stated. At the time UPS was known for its reliable, albeit somewhat slow, delivery of parcels via ground transportation. In contrast, FedEx invested in an extensive fleet of planes in order to "absolutely, positively" deliver its clients' documents and parcels overnight. Although FedEx charged a premium for its speedy service and sophisticated tracking system, businesses large and small willingly paid for this previously unavailable expedience. By 2004, FedEx was overseeing a fleet of more than 71,000 trucks and 645 aircraft, in order to deliver an average of 5.5 million shipments each day.

By the 1980s the positions of the two firms were firmly established in the U.S. commercial and residential markets. UPS was the favored choice for less expensive delivery via slower, ground transportation when some tracking capabilities were required. FedEx was most often used for critical documents and packages that had to be received the next day. Since then, a variety of factors have dramatically changed the parcel-delivery business. Globalization and advancements in technology, including the Internet, have created new opportunities and challenges for shipping suppliers as well as their customers. Thus, in order to remain competitive, UPS and FedEx have been forced to rethink their core businesses and have begun offering directly competing services. Additionally, they are facing competition from a new source that will test both companies on their home turf, as well as abroad.

Boxing Up the Competition

Just as it was in 1907, UPS's primary business is ground transportation. No other company, or even the United States Postal Service, is as adept, reliable, and economical at moving packages to any address, residential or commercial. UPS moves more than 3.6 billion packages each year, and the vast majority of

those are via ground transportation. But Big Brown, as the company is often called, has also expanded its air express business to compete head-to-head with FedEx, often performing the task in a more efficient and less costly manner than its competitor. For example, UPS utilizes trucks instead of airplanes to deliver packages up to 500 miles overnight. This translated into an average cost per package of $6.65, compared to $11.89 for FedEx in 2001. The differences in operations are reflected in the firms' performance. For the 2004 fiscal year, UPS reported net income of over $3.3 billion on revenue (sales volume) of more than $36.5 billion. By comparison, FedEx had revenues of $24.7 billion and net income of $838 million. In the air express portion of the shipping business, FedEx held a leading share of the market with 44% in late 2004, but UPS was right behind with 32%.

To further compete with FedEx's overnight delivery service, UPS upgraded its own tracking system so that as a customer signs to accept a delivery, the information is immediately transmitted to UPS's computers. Senders can go online to receive real-time status reports about their shipments, including the time of delivery. UPS now delivers over 2 million air express packages each day, compared to almost 3.2 million for FedEx.

UPS spends about $1 billion each year on technological improvements, and its core business also received an upgrade in late 2003. A new system that assists truck loaders and drivers was implemented to streamline operations. Prior to its installation, UPS employees had to memorize street addresses and zip codes and then load trucks according to when each delivery should be made. One mistake and a driver would have to double back and retrace his route to deliver a misplaced package. The new computer system automatically assigns a shelf on a truck for each package, then prints a corresponding label that indicates where each package should be placed. It also generates route assignments that optimize each driver's time. The company estimated the new system would result in its trucks driving 100 million fewer miles each year, thereby saving 14 million gallons of fuel.

Such advancements enhance UPS's reputation as the leading supplier of delivery services for online firms. For example, the Web spawned many electronic retailers that require a means for shipping their goods to customers. With its dominance in ground shipping, UPS was well positioned to establish itself in this market. By 2001, the company was responsible for 55% of online sales shipments. By comparison, FedEx had 10% of the business.

Besides shipping packages for e-tailing enterprises, UPS has begun to help these same clients streamline their operations by handling a variety of their physical distribution tasks. UPS's former chief executive officer stated, "We're becoming a logistics company because we have many customers who don't want to do certain things themselves any longer, customers who are saying, 'I want to produce a product, and after that I want you to take care of it.' " This UPS division offers warehousing, order picking and packing, product repair, and customer service.

Trucking into Ground Delivery

In retaliation, FedEx is challenging UPS on the ground. Between 1999 and 2001, FedEx spent about $4 billion on the purchase and upgrade of delivery companies with trucking operations. And unlike UPS, which utilizes union labor, FedEx Ground's 14,000 drivers are independent contractors who own their trucks. They are paid according to how many deliveries they make and are responsible for their own schedules, a flexibility appreciated by customers. The CEO of a small business remarked that his FedEx Ground driver "not only did two Saturday pickups, but he said, 'I don't usually pick up on Sunday, but I live nearby and can bring my truck by.' That blew me away." Such outstanding service is helping FedEx to slowly chip away at UPS's ground business, and by late 2004, FedEx's share of the market was 16%, compared to 75% for UPS. Perhaps more revealing is the fact that revenue in this area has grown at a brisk 26% rate annually for FedEx, while UPS's only rose by 0.2% in 2002.

In an attempt to become even more grounded, FedEx acquired two different freight companies and began competing in the less-than-truckload (LTL) category with a division called FedEx Freight. LTL is a lucrative business that accommodates equipment too heavy or bulky for traditional ground delivery service. FedEx Freight became the first company to offer LTL shippers an on-time delivery guarantee, prompting one company executive to state "FedEx brought certainty to an industry that never had it." UPS entered the LTL business in 2005 when it acquired Overnite Corp. for $1.25 billion, prompting a FedEx spokesperson to comment that, "UPS is recognizing the value of the portfolio we have been offering for nearly five years now. Their job is to catch up."

The companies seem to be locked in a fierce game of chess, constantly making moves to outmaneuver and keep up with one another. In 2001, UPS purchased Mail Boxes Etc. (MBE), a retail chain that provides a convenient storefront for consumers and small businesses to ship their packages, and also access a variety of related services, such as faxing and copying. UPS changed the name of most of the 4,300 outlets to "The UPS Store." FedEx followed suit by purchasing the Kinko's chain in early 2003 for $2.4 billion. FedEx hopes to increase the services provided by Kinko's in order to compete with the likes of Xerox and serve large corporations as well as small businesses. To that end, FedEx has invested in more than 700,000 hours of employee training, and has found the task of running a retail chain quite challenging. "Every time you move away from the core, the odds of success go down," commented one industry analyst.

But as more and more people utilize e-mail for sensitive documents and move away from shipping them overnight, FedEx must continue to find ways to increase revenues and decrease costs. By moving into document production with its Kinko's enterprise and freight delivery with FedEx Freight, it is able to provide more services to its corporate clients who enjoy interacting with just one FedEx sales team. Its reputation for innovation and high levels of customer service earned it the sixth spot on *Fortune* magazine's list of America's Most Admired Companies. In the same poll UPS received an honorable mention for its commitment to social responsibility. But both companies are being targeted by another shipping enterprise looking to make a name in the U.S. market.

Packaging Its Services Domestically

DHL was founded by Adrian Dalsey, Larry Hillblom, and Robert Lynn in 1969. Originally its role was to expedite paperwork for ocean shipments between the U.S. West Coast and Hawaii so that when the ships arrived, the freight they carried wouldn't sit on board while their "bills of lading" were being processed. Eventually, the company initiated package delivery services to Asia and Australia, and then to Europe as well. It was the first air express company to operate in Europe's Eastern Bloc and China, and currently serves more than 220 countries. In 2003, the company merged with a Swiss company called Danzas that specializes in forwarding freight and providing logistics services, and more significantly, with the German post office, Deutsche Post AG. The express delivery arm of Deutsche Post serves all of Europe as well as Germany, giving the new DHL an enviable and established distribution network for ground as well as air deliveries.

In 2004, Deutsche Post World Net, the parent company of DHL, had revenues of $50 billion, with DHL contributing more than $30 billion. Its fleet of 75,000 vehicles and 250 aircraft are well-known internationally, and DHL hopes that will soon become the case in the U.S. as well. Its $1.05 billion acquisition of Airborne Inc. announced the company's intention to compete with FedEx and UPS, both in the air and on the ground in the $48 billion U.S. package delivery business. Despite the fact that Airborne held only a 6% share of the U.S. market, the move prompted FedEx and UPS to file an appeal with the Department of Transportation on the grounds that foreign-owned airlines cannot operate within the U.S.

The appeal failed, the merger went through, and DHL lost no time repainting Airborne's trucks and drop boxes and redesigning packaging materials and employee uniforms in its own corporate colors of red and yellow. In 2004, it launched an aggressive ad campaign that announced, "The Roman Empire, the British Empire, the FedEx Empire. Nothing lasts forever." Other ads in the $150 million branding campaign mentioned UPS as well, prompting DHL's vice president of advertising and brand management to comment, "The campaign is designed to create awareness for DHL and an understanding that there's now a third choice." The strategy worked. Prior to the campaign, DHL registered a brand recognition of only 6%; after the campaign, that number more than quadrupled. To further establish itself within the U.S. market, DHL has set up shipping centers within Office Max locations throughout the country.

DHL plans to attack FedEx and UPS by providing better service at lower rates. One company that has traditionally shipped its products from South Korea to California via DHL gave the company a try for U.S. ground delivery as well. "We did a test on ground freight with DHL. They moved the goods one day faster and then cut the price," explained the company's president. "They basically told us they would do whatever it takes." While popular with customers, this approach has resulted in losses of $350 million a year in North and South America, but the operation is expected to break even in 2005.

Parceling Up a New Market

While DHL is trying to move overseas into the U.S., FedEx and UPS are attempting to do the opposite. Deliveries between the U.S. and China are expected to grow between 10% and 25% each year until 2014, and both companies are scrambling to position themselves in the burgeoning Far Eastern marketplace. In 2005, UPS was awarded a number of new routes that would triple the company's activity in and out of China, and will no doubt help UPS increase its current 28% share of the express market between the U.S. and China. UPS has also been aggressively marketing its logistics offerings in Asia. China alone represents an $84 billion opportunity for such services, and UPS

manages in excess of 1 million square feet of warehouse space around the industrial city of Shanghai to handle clients' inventories. "It makes perfect sense," explained an executive for UPS's Supply Chain Solutions unit. "Nobody wants to own more square footage than they need."

FedEx's founder and CEO, Fred Smith, anticipated the importance of the Far Eastern market when he purchased several Asian air routes in 1989. That same year he established a major hub in Anchorage, Alaska, the perfect stopping point between the U.S. and Asia. By 2004, FedEx had more than 600 flights to and from Asian markets each week and boasted 39% of the express market between the U.S. and China. In 2005, FedEx was allowed to double its number of flights in and out of China, and FedEx has also ventured into supply chain management and logistics, both in Asia and elsewhere. "We knew (the Asian business) would take off, but frankly I don't think anyone could have predicted the level of explosive growth we are seeing now," commented Smith.

"But nobody knows Asia like we do," countered DHL's executive in charge of the U.S. DHL is the second largest player in the U.S.-China air express market with a 29% share, and has the advantage of being more established in the Asian market than either UPS or FedEx. Deere & Co., a tractor manufacturer based in Illinois, has been a long-time customer of DHL. "DHL is our partner of choice in China. They have the best connections with all levels of government," stated the manager of Deere's global transportation division. In a recent survey conducted in Asia, DHL ranked first among express delivery and logistics companies in eight major cities, and DHL continues to invest in its Asian operations. It spent $100 million on a state-of-the-art cargo facility in Hong Kong to support its express business and operates an additional five hubs throughout the Far East.

Exhibiting a willingness to do everything from transporting documents, packages, or freight to taking over a company's physical distribution function, these three companies are evolving to meet the needs of their customers in today's multinational, fast-moving business environment. Though each has established a leadership position in a specific market, in order to grow they must continue to explore other opportunities.

Questions

1. Explain how the characteristics of business market demand will impact these three companies.
2. a. Would the purchase of delivery services for letters and packages always be the same buy class for a large company?

b. How would buy class affect the buying-decision process for this particular product?

3. How, if at all, would the motives and decision processes used in selecting delivery services for letters and packages differ between individual consumers and business users?

4. What type(s) of target-marketing strategies are being used by UPS, FedEx, and DHL?

Sources

Case 1: Gap, Inc.   *www.bravotv.com*, March 2005; *www.gap.com*, January 2005; Sarah Duxbury, "New GapBody Chain Ready to Flex Muscles," *San Francisco Business Times*, Jan. 28, 2005; "Gap Inc. to Bow New Retail Concept in 2nd Half of 2005," *DSN Retailing Today*, Oct. 11, 2004, pp. 48–50; Amy Merrick, "Gap's Greatest Generation?," *The Wall Street Journal*, Sept. 15, 2004, p. B1; Cheryl Dahle, "Gap's New Look: The See-Through," *Fast Company*, September 2004, p. 69; Anne D'Innocenzio, "Wooing Thirty Somethings," *The Washington Times*, Sept. 28, 2004, accessed at www.washtimes.com; Louise Lee, "Yes, We Have a New Banana," *BusinessWeek*, May 31, 2004, p. 70; Louise Lee, "The Gap Has Reason to Dance Again," *BusinessWeek*, Apr. 19, 2004, p. 42; Patricia Sellers, "Gap's New Guy Upstairs," *Fortune*, Apr. 14, 2003, pp. 110–116.

Case 2: UPS versus FedEx versus DHL
www.ups.com, accessed May 27, 2005; *www.fedex.com*, accessed May 27, 2005; *www.dhl.com*, accessed May 27, 2005; Daniel Machalaba, "UPS Deal Lifts Stakes in FedEx War," *The Wall Street Journal*, May 17, 2005, p. A3; Jerry Useem, "America's Most Admired Companies," *Fortune*, Mar. 7, 2005, pp. 67–69; Bruce Stanley, "Express Delivery Firms Expand Their Logistics Services in China," *The Wall Street Journal*, Nov. 29, 2004, p. A16; Matthew Boyle, "Why FedEx Is Flying High," *Fortune*, Nov. 1, 2004, pp. 145–150; "Best Creative Integrated Campaign," *BtoB*, Oct. 25, 2004, pp. 28–29; Deborah Orr, "Delivering America," *Forbes*, Oct. 4, 2004, pp. 78–80; Dean Foust, "No Overnight Success," *BusinessWeek*, Sept. 20, 2004, p. 18; Rick Brooks, "DHL Plans to Spend $1.2 Billion in Challenge of FedEx and UPS," *The Wall Street Journal*, June 25, 2004, p. B2; Chuck Salter, "Not Going the Extra Mile," *Fast Company Web Exclusives*, January 2004; Kevin Kelleher, "Why FedEx Is Gaining Ground," *Business 2.0*, October 2003, pp. 56–57.

Chapter 8

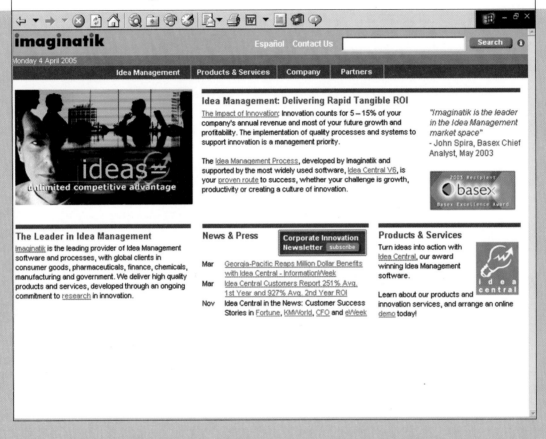

"A company that is able to take advantage of the ideas from its employees, customers, and partners and turn them into valuable business opportunities is a company that is built to survive and thrive."

Can **Imaginatik** Stimulate Practical, Profitable Ideas?

Great ideas are a cornerstone of business success. If they are feasible, creative ideas can lead to improved production processes and customer service, cost savings, and better products.

According to a study by PricewaterhouseCoopers, just over one-half of plausible business ideas come from customers, competitors, and suppliers. The rest, almost one-half, are offered by a company's employees, ranging from R&D staff members to salespeople. The two-fold challenge for firms is first, to stimulate employees to make suggestions about business opportunities and solutions and second, to sort through the submissions in order to identify promising ideas.

A suggestion box, whether it's wooden or electronic, ordinarily is ignored by employees. Even if submissions are plentiful, they can be difficult to discern (or even read, if handwritten) or challenging to compile in order to take further action.

Imaginatik, a relatively young and small company, has created a technology-based program that not only generates ideas but also can help take them from concept to either the wastebasket or the drawing board. The company was founded in London in 1994 by two researchers working on the kitchen table of the soon-to-be CEO, Mark Turrell. Now based in Boston, Imaginatik specializes in "innovation and idea management." According to Imaginatik, "A company that is able to take advantage of the ideas from its employees, customers, and partners and turn them into valuable business opportunities is a company that is built to survive and thrive."

Imaginatik's main product, Idea Central, is an electronic suggestion box—and much more. True, it requests ideas about a particular topic, such as possible new products or cost savings, from a defined group of employees. But then the software allows the participants to interact online to discuss and evaluate the submissions and to further develop the more promising ideas. For instance, several ideas that can't stand alone might be combined into one that has profit potential. Because it's car-

ried out online, employees in widespread locations can participate in the process.

Idea Central is being used by a growing number of companies in wide-ranging industries, including Georgia-Pacific in forest products, Sun Life in financial services, Goodyear in tires and rubber products, and Bristol-Myers Squibb in consumer packaged goods. Grace Performance Chemicals, a division of W. R. Grace, turned to Idea Central because, in the words of a vice president, "We weren't getting enough good ideas into the front end of the system." Grace has used Idea Central about three dozen times, generating almost 2,700 suggestions from employees. More importantly, following evaluations, refinements, and development, the outcome has been 76 new products as well as 67 process improvements. W. R. Grace's director of innovation stated, "Before we started doing this in 2001, we had no systematic way of developing new ideas."

Another company in a totally different setting—Belgacom, a large telecommunications firm in Belgium—has also tried Idea Central. According to an executive, "Belgacom wanted to develop a corporate culture of innovation where anyone in any job function—sales, support, field service, administration—can share their ideas and help shape the future of the company." Idea Central Global, the international version of the program, can be used with many languages. That was essential for Belgacom, so that all of its employees could participate despite language differences. One of Belgacom's first Idea Central processes generated 180 suggestions. Following review by an evaluation team, 20 ideas were judged to have revenue potential and thus were put forward for development.[1]

Is Idea Central a good way of obtaining ideas for new products? Are there other ways?

 www.imaginatik.com

Four important factors are suggested by the Imaginatik case. First, both relatively young enterprises and well-established companies need to develop new products in order to attain success in the marketplace. Second, the nature of new products is as extensive as our imagination. Third, as illustrated by the Imaginatik case, steps can be taken to stimuate the flow of new-product ideas. And fourth, success with new products is not guaranteed, as numerous failures (including costly flops such as the Edsel automobile, the Premier "smokeless" cigarette, and Corfam artificial leather) indicate.

This chapter will provide you with insights regarding each of these important issues. Specifically, after studying this chapter, you should be able to explain:

| Chapter Goals |

- The meaning of the word *product* in its fullest sense.
- What a "new" product is.
- The classification of consumer and business products.
- The relevance of these product classifications to marketing strategy.
- The importance of product innovation.
- The stages in the new-product development process.
- Criteria for adding a product to a company's line.
- Adoption and diffusion processes for new products.
- Organizational structures for product planning and development.

The Meaning of Product

In a *narrow* sense, a product is a set of basic attributes assembled in an identifiable form. Each product is identified by a commonly understood descriptive (or generic) name, such as steel, insurance, tennis rackets, or entertainment. Features such as brand name and postsale service that appeal to consumer emotions or add value play no part in this narrow interpretation. According to this interpretation, an Apple and a Dell would be the same good—a personal computer. And Disney World and Six Flags would be equivalent—both are amusement parks.

In marketing we need a broader definition of product to indicate that customers are not really buying a set of attributes, but rather benefits that satisfy their needs. Thus users don't want sandpaper; they really want a smooth surface. To develop a sufficiently broad definition, let's start with *product* as an umbrella term covering goods, services, places, persons, and ideas. Throughout this book, when we speak of products, we are using this broad connotation.

Thus a product that provides benefits can be something other than a tangible *good*. Red Roof Inn's product is a *service* that provides the benefit of a comfortable night's rest at a reasonable price. The Hawaii Visitors Bureau's product is a *place* that provides sun and sand, relaxation, romance, cross-cultural experiences, and other benefits. In a political campaign, the Democratic or Republican Party's product is a *person* (candidate) whom the party wants you to buy (vote for). The American Cancer Society is selling an *idea* and the benefits of not smoking. In Chapter 11 we discuss in more detail the marketing of intangible products such as services and ideas.

www.visit.hawaii.org

www.aol.com

www.msn.com

To further expand our definition, we treat each *brand* as a separate product. In this sense, two Internet service providers, America Online and MSN, for example, are different products. Squibb's aspirin and Bayer aspirin are also separate products, even though the only physical difference may be the brand name on the tablet. But the brand name suggests a product difference to the consumer, and this brings the concept of want-satisfaction into the definition. Going a step further, some consumers prefer one brand (Squibb's) and others favor a different brand (Bayer) of a similar product.

Any change in a feature (design, color, size, packaging), however minor, creates another product. Each such change provides the seller with an opportunity to use a new set of appeals to reach what essentially may be a new market. Pain relievers (Tylenol, Ascriptin) in capsule form are a different product from the same brand in tablet form, even though the chemical contents of the tablet and the capsule are identical. Seemingly minor product changes can be the key to success (or failure). On the minus side, what seemed like a relatively small change in the formula for Coke in 1985 turned out to be a huge mistake. On the plus side, after the Arby's sandwich chain reworked its "BLT" by adding more bacon and switching to honey wheat bread, stores that sold this item enjoyed a 6% sales increase.[2]

We can broaden this interpretation still further. A Sony big-screen TV bought at a discount store on a cash-and-carry basis is a different product than the identical model purchased from a consumer-electronics chain store. In the electronics store, the customer may pay a higher price for the TV but buys it on credit, has it delivered free of charge, and receives other store services. Our concept of a product now includes the services that accompany it when purchased. A prime example is the warranty that assures a buyer of free replacement or repair of a defective product during a specified period of time.

We're now ready for a definition that is useful to marketers. As shown in Figure 8.1, a **product** is a set of tangible and intangible attributes, which may include packaging, color, price, quality, and brand, plus the seller's services and reputation. A product may be a good, service, place, person, or idea. In essence, then, customers are buying much more than a set of attributes when they buy a product. They are buying want-satisfaction in the form of the benefits they expect to receive from the product.

FIGURE 8.1

The Attributes Comprising a Product.

A product—in this case, the Treo brand of personal digital assistant—is much more than a set of physical attributes.

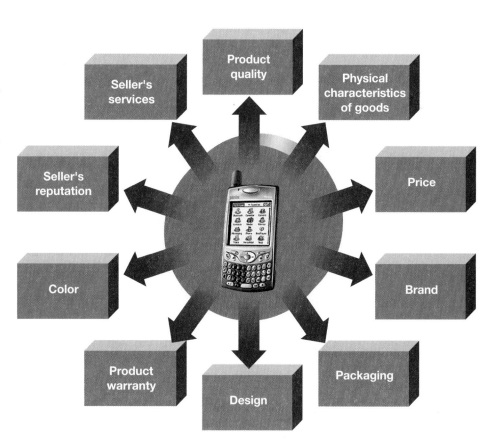

Classifications of Products

To design effective marketing programs, organizations need to know what kinds of products they are offering to potential customers. Thus it's helpful to separate *products* into homogeneous categories. First we will divide all products into two categories—consumer products and business products—that parallel our description of the total market. Then we will subdivide each category.

Consumer and Business Products

Consumer products are intended for personal consumption by households. **Business products** are intended for resale, for use in producing other products, or for providing services in an organization. Thus the two types of products are distinguished on the basis of *who will use them* and *how they will be used*.

The position of a product in its distribution channel has no bearing on its classification. Kellogg's cornflakes are categorized as consumer products, even if they are in the manufacturer's warehouses, in a freight line's trucks, or on retailers' shelves, *if ultimately they will be used in their present form by households*. However, Kellogg's cornflakes sold to restaurants and other institutions are categorized as business products no matter where they are in the distribution system.

Often it is not possible to place a product in only one class or the other. Seats on a United Airlines flight from Chicago to Phoenix may be considered a consumer product if purchased by students or a family going on vacation. But a seat on the same flight bought by a sales rep on a work-related trip is categorized as a business product. United Airlines, or any other company in a similar situation, recognizes that its product falls into both categories and therefore develops separate marketing programs for each market.

These distinctions may seem like "splitting hairs," but they are necessary for the strategic planning of marketing programs. Each major category of products ultimately goes to a distinctive type of market and thus requires different marketing methods.[3]

Classification of Consumer Goods

For marketing purposes, distinguishing consumer goods from business goods is helpful but only a first step. The range of consumer goods is still too broad to be useful. Consequently, as shown in Table 8.1, they are further classified as convenience goods, shopping goods, and specialty goods, and also as unsought goods (not in table). This classification is not based on intrinsic differences in the products themselves. Rather, it is based on how consumers go about buying a particular product. Depending on the buying behavior of different consumers, a single product—such as wine or software—can fall into more than one of the four categories.

Convenience Goods
A tangible product that the consumer feels comfotable purchasing without gathering additional information and then actually buys with a minimum of effort is termed a **convenience good.** Normally the advantages resulting from shopping around to compare price and quality are not considered worth the required time and effort. A consumer is willing to accept any of several brands and thus will buy the one that is most accessible. For most buyers, convenience goods include many food items, inexpensive candy, drug sundries such as aspirin and toothpaste, and staple hardware items such as light bulbs and batteries.

Convenience goods typically have a low unit price, are not bulky, and are not greatly affected by fad and fashion. They usually are purchased frequently, although this is not a necessary characteristic. Items such as Christmas tree lights or Mother's Day cards are convenience goods for most people, even though they may be bought only once a year.

TABLE 8.1

Categories of Consumer Goods: Characteristics and Marketing Considerations

	Type of Product*		
	Convenience	**Shopping**	**Specialty**
Examples	Canned fruit	Furniture	Expensive suits
Characteristics			
Time and effort devoted by consumer to shopping	Very little	Considerable	As much as necessary to find desired brand
Time spent planning the purchase	Very little	Considerable	Considerable
How soon want is satisfied after it arises	Immediately	Relatively long time	Relatively long time
Are price and quality compared?	No	Yes	No
Price	Usually low	Usually high	Usually high
Purchase frequency	Usually frequent	Infrequent	Infrequent
Marketing Considerations			
Length of channel	Long	Short	Short to very short
Retailer	Relatively unimportant	Important	Very important
Number of outlets	As many as possible	Few	Few; often only one in a market
Stock turnover	High	Lower	Lower
Gross margin	Low	High	High
Responsibility for advertising	Producer's	Joint responsibility	Joint responsibility
Point-of-purchaser display	Very important	Less important	Less important
Brand or store name	Brand name	Store name	Both
Packaging	Very important	Less important	Less important

*Unsought products are not included. See text explanation.

Because a convenience good must be readily accessible when consumer demand arises, a manufacturer must be prepared to distribute it widely and rapidly. However, because most retail stores sell only a small volume of the total output of a convenience good (such as a particular brand of candy bar), it is not economical for the manufacturer to sell directly to all retail outlets. Instead the producer relies on wholesalers to sell the product to selected retailers.

Retailers usually carry several brands of the same type of convenience item, because consumers frequently have a brand preference (even though they will accept a substitute). However, retail outlets are not inclined to advertise convenience goods because many other stores carry the same brands (such as General Electric and Sylvania light bulbs). Thus any advertising by one retailer would help its competitors. As a result, much of the advertising burden is shifted to the manufacturer.

Shopping Goods   A tangible product for which a consumer wants to compare quality, price, and perhaps style in several stores before making a purchase is considered a **shopping good.** Examples of shopping goods—at least for most consumers—are fashionable apparel, furniture, major appliances, and automobiles. The process of searching and comparing continues as long as the customer believes that the potential benefits from more information are worth the additional time and effort spent shopping. A *better* purchase might be saving several hundred dollars on the purchase of a new car or finally finding a software package that prepares financial statements in the manner that the buyer desires.

With shopping goods, buying habits affect the distribution and promotion strategies of both manufacturers and middlemen (such as retail stores). Shopping-goods manufacturers require fewer retail outlets because consumers are willing to look around for what they want. To facilitate comparison shopping, manufacturers often try to place their products in stores located near other stores carrying competing items. Similarly, department stores and other retailers that carry primarily shopping goods like to be near each other. Further, many retailers carry several brands of the same shopping good to allow shoppers to make in-store comparisons.

Manufacturers usually work closely with retailers in marketing shopping goods. Because manufacturers use fewer retail outlets, they are more dependent on those they do select. Retail stores typically buy shopping goods in large quantities, and it's common for manufacturers to distribute directly to retailers. To buyers of a shopping good, the reputations of the stores carrying the product often are more important than the images of the manufacturers. For example, a consumer may be more loyal to a Circuit City store than to various brands of audio and video equipment, such as JVC and Sanyo.

Specialty Goods   A tangible product for which a consumer has a strong brand preference and is willing to expend substantial time and effort locating the desired brand is called a **specialty good**. The consumer is willing to forgo more accessible substitutes to search for and purchase the desired brand. Examples of products usually categorized as specialty goods include expensive men's suits, stereo sound equipment, health foods, photographic equipment, and, for many people, new automobiles and certain home appliances. Various brands, such as Armani, Nikon, and BMW, have achieved specialty-good status in the minds of some consumers.

Because consumers *insist* on a particular brand and are willing to expend considerable effort to find it, manufacturers can use few retail outlets. Ordinarily the manufacturer deals directly with these retailers. The retailers are extremely important, particularly if the manufacturer uses only one in each geographic area. And where the opportunity to handle the product is highly valued, the retailer may be quite willing to abide by the producer's policies regarding the amount of inventory that needs to be maintained, how the product should be advertised, or other marketing factors.

www.giorgioarmani.com

Attaining specialty-good standing in consumers' minds, as Cole Haan has done, is highly desirable. Shoppers exert added effort to locate a specialty good, and they tend to be less concerned about price than other features of this type of product. Of course, becoming a specialty good requires not just outstanding quality or value but also large expenditures on advertising to build a distinctive brand image.

www.colehaan.com

Because relatively few outlets are used *and* the product's brand name is important to buyers, both manufacturer and retailer advertise the product extensively. Often the manufacturer pays a portion of the retailer's advertising costs, and the name of the store carrying the specialty good frequently appears in the manufacturer's ads.

Unsought Goods   There's one more, quite different category of goods. In fact, it's so unlike the other three categories that we have not included it in Table 8.1. Nevertheless, because some firms sell unsought goods, this category deserves brief discussion.

An **unsought good** is a new product that the consumer is not yet aware of *or* a product that the consumer is aware of but does not want right now. A battery-powered one-person scooter, now available in the form of the Segway Human Transporter, might be an unsought good for most people either because they are unaware of it or do not want one after learning about it. Bathroom tissue made strictly from cotton fiber, including the Cottonelle brand, would seem to be an unsought good. Despite a commercial in which a roll of tissues says, "I've got a silk gentle touch you can actually feel," few consumers know about the product and fewer still seek it out at the store.[4] Other unwanted products might include gravestones for those who have not lost a loved one and snow tires in the summer.

As the name suggests, a firm faces a very difficult, perhaps impossible, advertising and personal selling job when trying to market unsought goods. The best approach may be to make consumers aware of the product and continue to remind them of it, so they will buy the advertised brand when the need arises. Marketers of unsought goods try to build familiarity with their offerings by placing ads on bus stop benches or in church bulletins.

Classification of Business Goods

As with consumer goods, the general category of *business goods* is too broad to use in developing a marketing program. Consequently, as shown in Table 8.2, we separate business goods into five categories: raw materials, fabricating materials and parts, installations, accessory equipment, and operating supplies. This classification is based on the product's broad *uses*. For example, a business good may be used in producing other products, in operating an organization, and in other ways we will discuss.

Raw Materials   Business goods that become part of another tangible product prior to being processed in any way (except as necessary to assist in handling the product) are considered **raw materials.** Raw materials include:

- Goods found in their natural state, such as minerals, land, and products of the forests and the seas.

- Agricultural products, such as cotton, fruits, livestock, and animal products, including eggs and raw milk.

Because of their distinctive attributes, these two groups of raw materials usually are marketed differently. For instance, the supply of raw materials in their natural state is limited, cannot be substantially increased, and often involves only a few large producers. Further, such products generally are of a commodity nature, must be carefully graded, and, consequently, are highly standardized. Consider coal as an example; it is extracted in great quantities and then is graded by hardness and sulfur content.

The characteristics of raw materials in their natural state affect how they are marketed. For example:

- Prices are normally set by supply and demand, approximating the conditions of perfect competition. As a result, individual producers have little or no control over the prevailing market price.

TABLE
8.2

Categories of Business Goods: Characteristics and Marketing Considerations

	Type of Product				
	Raw Materials	**Fabricating Materials and Parts**	**Installations**	**Accessory Equipment**	**Operating Supplies**
Examples	Iron ore	Engine blocks	Blast furnaces	Storage racks	Paper clips
Characteristics					
Unit price	Very low	Low	Very high	Medium	Low
Length of life	Very short	Depends on final product	Very long	Long	Short
Quantities purchased	Large	Large	Very small	Small	Small
Frequency of purchase	Frequent delivery; long-term purchase contract	Infrequent purchase, but frequent delivery	Very infrequent	Medium frequency	Frequent
Standardization of competitive products	Very much; grading is important	Very much	Very little; custom-made	Little	Much
Quantity of supply	Limited; supply can be increased slowly or not at all	Usually no problem	No problem	Usually no problem	Usually no problem
Marketing Considerations					
Nature of channel	Short; no middlemen	Short; middlemen only for small buyers	Short; no middlemen	Middlemen used	Middlemen used
Negotiation period	Hard to generalize	Medium	Long	Medium	Short
Price competition	Important	Important	Varies in importance	Not main factor	Important
Presale/postsale service	Not important	Important	Very important	Important	Very little
Promotional activity	Relatively little	Moderate	Sales people very important	Important	Not too important
Brand preference	None	Generally low	High	High	Low
Advance buying contract	Important; long-term contracts	Important long-term contracts	Not usual	Not usual	Not usual

- Because of their great bulk, low unit value, and the long distances between producer and business user, transportation is an important consideration for natural raw materials.

- As a result of the same factors, natural raw materials frequently are marketed directly from producer to business user with a minimum of physical handling.

- Not much effort is expended on product differentiation for this type of product. It is tough, for example, to distinguish one producer's coal from another producer's. However, some producers have been successful in developing and promoting their own brands of agricultural products (such as the famous Chiquita bananas).

Agricultural products are supplied by small producers as well as larger corporate farms, typically located some distance from their markets. The supply is largely controllable by producers, but it cannot be increased or decreased rapidly. The product is perishable and is not produced at a uniform rate throughout the year. Most citrus fruits, for example, ripen in late winter and thus are readily available at that time of year and become less available in subsequent months. Standardization and grading are commonplace for agricultural products. Also, transportation costs are likely to be high relative to the product's unit value.

Middlemen are ordinarily needed to market agricultural products because many producers are small and numerous and markets are distant. Transportation and warehousing greatly influence effectiveness *and* efficiency of distribution. Typically, there is relatively little promotional activity with agricultural products, as compared to other types of business goods.

Fabricating Materials and Parts

Business goods that become part of the finished product after having been processed to some extent fit into the category of fabricating materials and parts. The fact that they have been processed distinguishes them from raw materials. **Fabricating materials** undergo further processing; examples include pig iron going into steel, yarn being woven into cloth, and flour becoming part of bread. **Fabricating parts** are assembled with no further change in form; they include such products as zippers in clothing and semiconductor chips in computers.

Fabricating materials and parts are usually purchased in large quantities. Normally, buying decisions are based on the price and the service provided by the seller. To ensure an adequate, timely supply, a buyer may place an order a year or more in advance. Because consumers are concerned about price, service, and reliability of supply, most fabricating products are marketed directly from producer to user. Middlemen are used most often when the buyers are small in size and/or when buyers have small fill-in orders (after the large initial order) requiring rapid delivery.

Branding fabricating materials and parts is generally unimportant. However, some firms have successfully pulled their business goods out of obscurity by branding them. Talon zippers and the NutraSweet brand of sweeteners are examples.

www.nutrasweet.com

Installations

Manufactured products that are an organization's major, expensive, and long-lived equipment are termed **installations.** Examples are large generators in a dam, a factory building, diesel engines for a railroad, and blast furnaces for a steel mill. The characteristic of installations that differentiates them from other categories of business goods is that they directly affect the scale of operations in an organization producing goods or services. Adding 12 new Steelcase desks will not

Some products, including Talon zippers, are purchased by both business and consumer markets. For apparel makers, zippers are a fabricating part in a clothing item. Most consumers view a zipper as a convenience good, purchased as easily as possible. However, consumers who sew their own clothes may view a Talon zipper as a specialty good and, if so, will expend extra effort to locate and buy Talon rather than accepting another brand.

ONE OF THE FEW THINGS TALON DOESN'T MAKE A ZIPPER FOR.

www.boeing.com/
commercial/777family

affect the scale of operations at American Airlines, but adding 12 Boeing 777 jet aircraft certainly will. Therefore, jet aircraft are categorized as installations, but desks normally are not.

The marketing of installations presents a real challenge, because each unit sold represents a large dollar amount. Often each unit is made to the buyer's detailed specifications. Also, much presale and postsale servicing is essential. For example, an elevator or an escalator requires installation, maintenance, and—inevitably—repair service. Sales are usually made directly from producer to business user; no middlemen are involved. Because installations are technical in nature, a high-caliber, well-trained sales force is needed to market installations. Because installations require careful, detailed explanation, promotion emphasizes personal selling.

Accessory Equipment   Tangible products that have substantial value and are used in an organization's operations are called **accessory equipment.** This category of business goods neither becomes an actual part of a finished product nor has a significant impact on the organization's scale of operations. The life of accessory equipment is shorter than that of installations but longer than that of operating supplies. Some examples are point-of-sale terminals in a retail store, small power tools, forklift trucks, and office desks.

It is difficult to generalize about how accessory equipment should be marketed. For example, for some products in this category, it is suitable for a manufacturer to sell directly to a final customer. This is true particularly when an order is for several units or when each unit is worth a lot of money. A manufacturer of forklift trucks may sell directly to customers because the price of a single unit is large enough to make this form of distribution profitable. Normally, however, manufacturers of accessory equipment use middlemen—for example, office equipment distributors—because typically, the market is geographically dispersed, there are many different types of potential users, and individual orders may be relatively small.

Operating Supplies   Business goods that are characterized by low dollar value per unit and a short life and that contribute to an organization's operations without becoming part of the finished product are called **operating supplies.** Examples are lubricating oils, pencils and stationery, and heating fuel. Purchasers want to buy operating supplies with fairly little effort. Thus operating supplies are the convenience goods of the business sector.

As with the other categories of goods, the characteristics of operating supplies influence how they should be marketed. Because they are low in unit value and are bought by many different organizations, operating supplies—like consumer convenience goods—are distributed widely. Thus, the producing firm uses wholesaling middlemen extensively. Also, because competing products are quite standardized and there is little brand insistence, price competition is normally stiff.

Importance of Product Innovation

A business exists to satisfy customers while making a profit. Fundamentally, a company fulfills this dual purpose through its products. New-product planning and development are vital to an organization's success. This is particularly true now, given (1) rapid technological changes, which can make existing products obsolete, and (2) the practice of many competitors to copy a successful product, which can neutralize an innovative product's advantage. Thus, as emphasized by a former head of Procter & Gamble, "The core business is innovation. If we innovate well, we will win."[5] Of course, new products must be satisfying to customers and profitable for the firm.

For many years, Procter & Gamble (P&G) dominated the toothpaste market with Crest as its bellwether brand. But then, Colgate-Palmolive (C-P) came up with Total, which had a distinctive, appealing attribute. Total was the first toothpaste to gain approval from the federal Food and Drug Administration to state that it fights gum disease. This product catapulted C-P ahead of P&G in terms of toothpaste market share.

www.colgate.com/app/
ColgateTotal/US/Home.
cvsp

Requirement for Growth

Sooner or later, many product categories and individual brands become outdated. Their sales volume and market shares drop because of changing consumer desires and/or superior competing products. Once successful products for which there is now little, if any, demand include videocassette recorders (VCRs), 35-millimeter cameras, and electric typewriters. Some brands that no longer exist or have been relegated to remote locations in stores include Munsingwear shirts, Sony personal digital assistants (PDAs), Oldsmobile and Plymouth autos, and Royal Crown Cola.[6]

Thus a guideline for management is "innovate or die." For many companies a substantial portion of this year's sales volume and net profit will come from products that did not exist 5 to 10 years ago. Introducing a new product at the right time can help sustain a firm. In fact, companies that are leaders in terms of profitability and sales growth obtain 39% of their revenues from products introduced during the preceding 5 years; the corresponding figure for the least successful companies is 23%.[7]

Some firms that were successful innovators for long periods—familiar names such as Rubbermaid, McDonald's, H. J. Heinz, Kraft, and Jaguar (a division of Ford Motor Company)—haven't maintained a steady flow of new products in recent years. Some of their competitors have been more successful. For example, General Motors has revitalized its Cadillac brand, with largely favorable results.[8]

www.cadillac.com

High Failure Rates

For many years, the "rule of thumb" has been that about 80% of new products fail. However, because of dissimilar definitions of *new product* and *failure*, the statistics often vary from one study to another. According to one study, even the best companies suffer 35% mortality for new products. An examination of 11,000 new goods and services discovered that 56% are still on the market five years after being introduced. Of course, some of those products still on the market undoubtedly are on the brink of failure whereas others are hugely successful.[9]

Why do new products fail? The most common problem is not being different than existing products. Among the numerous examples are Heinz Bite Me frozen snacks, Cracker Jack Cereal, and Miller colorless beer. A new product is also likely

Some products are significant, perhaps even revolutionary, innovations. Perhaps that's true with the Segway Human Transporter, a battery-powered one-person scooter with a target price of $3,000 to $5,000. The product is aimed at commercial customers, such as the U.S. Postal Service and police forces, as well as consumers. Acceptance has been limited, underscoring that even a truly innovative product must satisfy needs and desires.

www.segway.com

to fail if it does not deliver on its promise. Beech Aircraft's Starship plane was supposed to perform like a jet at the price of a propeller plane. Instead, the finished product wound up performing like a propeller plane (indeed it was a turboprop) at the price of a jet![10]

Further, a product is subject to failure if it is perceived as providing too few benefits in relation to its price. Priced at $4 to $7 apiece, the General Foods Culinova refrigerated dinners did not pass consumers' value tests. Other factors that can undermine new products include poor positioning and lack of marketing support.

Considering how vital new products are to a company's growth, the large number of new-product introductions, and the high failure rates, product innovation deserves special attention. Given that a product introduction by a large company often costs from $20 million to $100 million,[11] firms that are inattentive to their new products may face financial ruin because of the high cost of product failure. Organizations that effectively manage product innovation can expect to reap a variety of benefits—differential advantage, higher sales and profits, and a solid foundation for the future.

Development of New Products

It's often said that nothing happens until somebody sells something. This is not entirely true. First there must be something to sell—a good, service, person, place, or idea. And that "something" must be developed.

What Is a "New" Product?

Just what is a "new" product? Are annual models of autos new products? Would a guided tour on an audio CD for use in your car (Tour Guide USA) qualify as new in your view? Or, how about square-bottom taco shells? Does an online auction of

Can a new product create both pleasure and pain?

For years, actually decades, people recorded television shows using a videocassette recorder (VCR). But that was before TiVo!

Now a substantial segment of TV viewers consider TiVo the greatest invention since the television itself. In 1997, TiVo Inc. pioneered a recording device that did not require videotapes. Compared to the standard VCR, the new digital video recorder (DVR) is more user-friendly and has more features. Also, a user can select shows to record by name rather having to enter the date, time, and channel of the designated show. Then, once a program is recorded, a viewer can pause and then catch up to the current point in a live TV program and can skip over commercials. With these features, consumers can now watch TV shows more quickly and when they choose to.

The pleasure of DVRs has been for consumers who value their time and seek convenience. The pain associated with them has been for TV networks, cable operators, and satellite-TV firms. With DVRs, viewers can ignore advertising. In that way, devices such as TiVo harm distributors of TV programming by reducing the audience for commercials—a major source of revenue for businesses that transmit TV programming to consumers.

However, there's more pain . . . for TiVo Inc. itself. As with many successful pioneers, TiVo faces new, cheaper competition. Cable operators, for example, are offering their own DVRs, rather than partnering with TiVo. The pioneering firm is countering with technological advances, one of which will permit TiVo subscribers to download and store movies from the Internet. It is also considering an alliance with another pioneer, Netflix Inc., which rents DVDs that are delivered by mail.

Typically, an innovative product such as TiVo is new for just a short period. After that, it needs to enhance its product or other elements of the marketing mix in order to retain a differential advantage.

 www.tivo.com

Sources: Cliff Edwards, "TiVo: Going, Going . . . Pause," *BusinessWeek*, Mar. 14, 2005, p. 84; Nick Wingfield, "TiVo Setbacks Raise Doubts about Its Future," *The Wall Street Journal*, Feb. 2, 2005, pp. B1, B3; and Greg Tarr, "TiVo's Ramsay Outlines Enhanced Services," *TWICE*, Jan. 17, 2005, p. 6.

 www.monster.com

 www.garmin.com

prospective employees run by Monster.com qualify as new?[12] Or must a product be revolutionary, never before seen, before we can class it as *new*? Does this last description apply to the Segway HT scooter? Or to a GPS (global positioning system) device that pinpoints the user's location? How new a product is affects how it should be marketed.

There are numerous connotations of "new product," but we will focus our attention on three distinct categories of **new products:**

- Products that are *really innovative*—truly unique. Notable innovations during the 20th century range from the zipper to the photocopy machine and, of course, the computer. A recent example is a security device that electronically compares a photo of a person's face against a security database to assure proper identification; a similar product uses fingerprints.[13] Still-to-be-developed products in this category would be a cancer cure and, easily, inexpensively repaired automobiles. Any new product in this category satisfies a real need that is not being satisfied at the time it is introduced.

- Replacements that are *significantly different* from existing products in terms of form, function, and—most important—benefits provided. Notable successes from the past century include cellophane, sterile bandage strips, and ballpoint pens. Disposable contact lenses, digital cameras, and some low-fat foods are replacing predecessors because the newer products deliver new or added benefits desired by buyers.

- *Imitative* products that are new to a particular company but not new to the market. Usually, annual models of autos and new versions of cereals are appropriately placed in this category. In another situation, a firm may simply want to

In many product categories, there are numerous slightly different variations of the basic product. Companies use this costly approach in order to attract more customers and to keep competitors from gaining an edge. This photo depicts samples of the assortments of the Robitussin and Advil cold and cough remedies.

capture part of an existing market with a "me too" product. To maximize company-wide sales, makers of cold and cough remedies routinely introduce imitative products, some of which compete with a nearly identical product *from the same company*. That's the case with Robitussin Severe Congestion, Robitussin Multi-Sympton Cold and Flu, Advil Cold and Sinus, and Advil Flu and Body Ache, all put out by Wyeth Consumer Healthcare.

Ultimately, of course, whether or not a product is new depends on how the intended market perceives it. If buyers consider it to be significantly different from competitive products in some relevant characteristic (such as appearance or performance), then it is indeed a new product. Lately, marketers have found that anything labeled *digital* is especially appealing to numerous consumers. Thus "digital" has been attached not just to telephones and televisions, but also to lights, music, and even a KitchenAid toaster priced at $89.99. Even though not all of these products are technically digital, many buyers prefer them to regular or analog versions.[14] As in other situations, *perception is reality!*

New-Product Strategy

To achieve strong sales and healthy profits, every producer of business goods or consumer goods should have an explicit strategy with respect to developing and evaluating new products. This strategy should guide every step in the process of developing a new product.

A **new-product strategy** is a statement identifying the role a new product is expected to play in achieving corporate and marketing goals. For example, a new product might be designed to protect market share, meet a specific return-on-investment goal, or establish a position in a new market. Or a new product's role might be to maintain the company's reputation for innovation or social responsibility. The last outcome appears to have been a primary aim of General Motors when it introduced the EV1 electric vehicle. Although EV1 may have helped GM rebut criticism about not being environmentally sensitive, it failed because it did not achieve sufficient sales.[15]

A new product's intended role also will influence the *type* of product to be developed. To illustrate:

Company Goal		Product Strategy		Recent Examples
To defend market share	→	Introduce an addition to an existing product line or revise an existing product	→	Pizza Hut's Dippin' Strips and 4forALL pizzas
To strengthen a reputation as an innovator	→	Introduce a *really* new product, not just an extension of an existing one	→	Digital cameras offered by Sony, Canon, and other firms

A new-product strategy can also help a firm avoid the problem of having numerous products under development but few actually ready for the market.[16] The priorities in the strategy can be used to determine which prospective products should receive special attention, which should go on the "back burner," and which should be scrapped. Only in recent years have many companies consciously identified new-product strategies. The process of developing new products has become more efficient *and* more effective for firms with strategies because they have a better sense of what they are trying to accomplish.

Stages in the Development Process

Guided by a company's new-product strategy, a new product is best developed through a series of six stages, as shown in Figure 8.2. Compared to unstructured development, the formal development of new products provides benefits such as improved teamwork, less rework, earlier failure detection, shorter development times, and—most important—higher success rates.[17]

At each stage, management must decide whether to proceed to the next stage, abandon the product, or seek additional information.[18] Here's a brief description of what should happen at each stage of the **new-product development process:**

1. *Generating new-product ideas.* New-product development starts with an idea. A system must be designed for stimulating new ideas within an organization and then reviewing them promptly. In one study, 80% of companies pointed to customers as their best source for new-product ideas. A growing number of manufacturers are encouraging—in some cases, requiring—suppliers to propose innovations. And franchise systems frequently turn their owner–managers' ideas into highly successful products, such as the Egg McMuffin sandwich at McDonald's and annual club memberships at MotoPhoto film-processing shops.[19]

2. *Screening ideas.* At this stage, new-product ideas are evaluated to determine which ones warrant further study.[20] Typically, a management team relies on its experience and judgment, rather than on market or competitive data, to screen the pool of ideas.

3. *Business analysis.* A surviving idea is expanded into a concrete business proposal. During the stage of **business analysis,** management (a) identifies product features; (b) estimates market demand, competition, and the product's profitability; (c) establishes a program to develop the product; and (d) assigns responsibility for further study of the product's feasibility.

4. *Prototype development.* If the results of the business analysis are favorable, then a prototype (or trial model) of the product is developed. In the case of services, the facilities and procedures necessary to produce and deliver the new product are designed and tested. That certainly is a necessary step in developing a new roller-coaster ride for an amusement park!

   In the case of goods, a small quantity of the trial model is manufactured to designated specifications. Technical evaluations are carried out to determine whether it is practical to produce the product. A firm may construct a prototype and subject it to lab tests in order to judge whether the proposed product will endure normal—even abnormal—usage. Apple Computer puts new models through various durability tests that range from pouring a soft drink onto the computer to subjecting the screen to over 100 pounds of pressure.[21]

FIGURE 8.2

Major Stages in the New-Product Development Process.

Seeking added sales and perhaps a differential advantage, a growing legion of companies are scanning foreign markets for new-product ideas. Various products introduced in the U.S.—including Whiskas cat food from Mars Inc., the Symphony chocolate bar from Hershey Foods, and Colgate Fresh Confidence toothpaste from Colgate-Palmolive—originated in foreign markets.

Several factors prompt U.S. companies to look abroad for new-product ideas:

- Bored with mere imitations, consumers are willing to accept novel products.

- Truly innovative products, even potential breakthroughs, might be uncovered in foreign markets where problems are approached from a different perspective. For instance, Shaman Pharmaceuticals of San Francisco tapped the knowledge of "medicine men" in Ecuador to identify tropical plants and trees that may contain curative compounds. This approach helped the company develop several drugs.

- Buying the rights to a foreign product can be much cheaper than starting the development process from scratch. With that in mind, Prince, the sporting goods company, acquired the U.S. distribution rights for a high-tech tennis ball machine that can fire 10 types of shots at 8 degrees of difficulty.

- An existing foreign product may be the best way of satisfying an ethnic market segment in the home country. When chips it developed weren't very pleasing to Hispanic consumers in the U.S., Frito-Lay turned to four successful brands of chips from its subsidiary in Mexico. The imported brands, such as Sabritones chile and lime puffed wheat snacks, quickly surpassed $100 million in sales.

An established foreign product is not guaranteed success here. The following guidelines can help:

- Stick to products that coincide with American trends. A greater interest in healthful foods helped Kellogg's achieve success in the U.S. with Mueslix, a cereal combining grains, nuts, and fruits that was invented in Switzerland.

- Don't just rely on the product's newness, but ensure it has a significant benefit.

- Concentrate on products that have achieved widespread success in foreign markets. Häagen-Dazs successfully brought a very sweet, butterscotch-like flavor from Buenos Aires to the U.S.

Some products introduced recently in other countries are likely to find their way to the U.S., perhaps in a slightly adapted form or carrying a different brand. Do you see promise in "functional" beverages that are intended to erase bad breath and/or alleviate the effects of hangovers for Asian consumers? Or how about a product from the United Kingdom, the Sushi Made Easy kit that contains all the necessities except the fresh fish?

Sources: Normandy Madden, "Coke Likely to Import Asian Innovations to U.S." *Advertising Age,* Apr. 25, 2005, p. 49; Diane Brady, "A Thousand and One Noshes," *BusinessWeek,* June 14, 2004, pp. 54, 56; Nanette Byrnes, "Brands in a Bind," *BusinessWeek,* Aug. 28, 2000, p. 236; Allyson L. Stewart-Allen, "Innovative Products Introduced in Europe," *Marketing News,* Apr. 10; 2000, p. 19; David Leonhardt, "It Was a Hit in Buenos Aires—So Why Not Boise?" *BusinessWeek,* Sept. 7, 1998, pp. 56, 58; Frederick C. Klein, "New Aussie Giant Serves Up Aces; Our Man Is Bushed," *The Wall Street Journal,* May 26, 1995, p. B8; and Thomas M. Burton, "Drug Company Looks to 'Witch Doctors' to Conjure Products," *The Wall Street Journal,* July 7, 1994, p. A1.

5. *Market tests.* Unlike the internal tests conducted during prototype development, **market tests** involve actual consumers. A new tangible product may be given to a sample of people for use in their households (in the case of a consumer good) or their organizations (a business good). Following the trial, users are asked to evaluate the product.

This stage in new-product development often entails test marketing, in which the product is placed on sale in a limited geographic area. Market-test findings, including total sales and repeat purchases by the same customers, are monitored by the company that developed the product (and perhaps by competitors as well). Some companies seek to interrogate shoppers as they examine a product in a store. Quaker State, for instance, used that approach to gauge purchase likelihood and other factors during a test market for a Slick 50 engine-treatment product.[22]

www.slick50.com

Virtually all products, ranging from Barbie dolls to Goodyear tires, undergo various tests before and also after being introduced to the market. Some producers do the testing themselves; others outsource the testing to specialized firms. Here, a new Goodyear tire is tested under simulated conditions in a laboratory.

www.goodyear.com

The product's design and production plans may be adjusted as a result of test findings. Following market tests, management must make a final "go–no go" decision about introducing the product.

6. *Commercialization.* In this stage, full-scale production and marketing programs are planned and then implemented. Up to this point in development, management has virtually complete control over the product. However, once the product is "born" and made available for purchase, the external competitive environment becomes a major determinant of its destiny.

Note that the overall new-product strategy guides the first two stages—idea generation and screening. This strategy can provide a focus for generating new-product ideas *and* a basis for evaluating them.

In the six-stage process, the first three stages are particularly critical because they deal with ideas and, as such, are the least expensive.[23] More important, many products fail because the idea or the timing is wrong—and the first three stages are intended to identify such situations. Each subsequent stage becomes more costly in terms of the dollars and human resources necessary to carry out the required tasks.

New-product development can be a lengthy process, taking almost a year for minor revisions and more than three years to complete the process for a major breakthrough. Even with a mandate for rapid development, it took a team of 7-Eleven and Frito-Lay employees more than a year to develop a new "Frito pie" to the point where it was ready for test marketing.[24]

Because of such factors as intense competition and rapid technological change, organizations are trying to complete the new-product development process in months rather than years. In order to bring new products to market faster and faster, some companies skip stages in the development process. The most common omission is the fifth stage, market tests. Without this stage, however, the company lacks the

www.fritolay.com

Many, perhaps more than 50, firms in the U.S. tell inventors they will help them refine their ideas for new products, prepare patent applications and business plans, develop prototypes, and line up business deals with manufacturers and other producers. Typically, an inventor pays the "matchmaker" a total fee that can exceed $10,000, including $1,000 or more at the outset. Thousands of people have signed up with these invention-promotion firms. It's possible that the firm can satisfy its contractual obligation by submitting the inventor's product design to a single manufacturer.

Is it ethical for invention-promotion firms to charge substantial up-front fees? Would your opinion about whether or not this practice is ethical be changed if the invention-promotion firm received its fee later in the new-product development process?

Sources: Thuy-Doan Le, "Inventors Must Be Wary of Promotional Scam Artists Seeking Quick Buck," *The Sacramento Bee,* Dec. 12, 2004, p. D2; and Stephen Gregory, "Patently Dishonest?" *Los Angeles Times,* Nov. 18, 1998, p. C1.

most telling reactions to the proposed product. Ford Motor Co. sought to cut the time needed to move a new model through the process from 32 to 24 months. Rather than skipping stages, the automaker reorganized its development group based on four distinct structural designs underlying all of its models.[25]

Historically, the marketing of goods has received more attention than the marketing of services. Thus it is not surprising that the new-product development process is not as advanced in services fields as it is in goods industries.[26] Thus service firms can (oftentimes, must) devise a new-product development process that suits their distinctive circumstances.

Producer's Criteria for New Products

When should a company add a new product to its current assortment of products? Here are guidelines that some producers use in answering this question:

- There must be *adequate market demand*. Too often management begins with the wrong question, such as, "Can we use our present sales force?" or "Will the new item fit into our production system?" The necessary first question is, "Do enough people really want this product?" A product is destined to fail if it fills a need that isn't important to consumers or doesn't even exist.

- The product must *satisfy key financial criteria*. At least three questions should be asked: "Is adequate financing available?" "Will the new item reduce seasonal and cyclical fluctuations in the company's sales?" And most critical, "Can we make a sufficient profit with the product?"

- The product must be *compatible with environmental standards*. Key questions include "Does the production process avoid polluting the air or water?" "Will the finished product, including its packaging, be friendly to the environment?" And, "After being used, does the product have recycling potential?"

- The product must *fit into the company's present marketing structure*. The Donna Karan brand that features women's clothing probably could be applied to a new line of designer sheets and towels, whereas the Sherwin Williams paint company would likely find it more difficult to add sheets and towels to its product mix. Specific questions related to whether or not a new product will fit the company's marketing expertise and experience include "Can the existing sales force be used?" "Can the present channels of distribution be used?"

Besides these four issues, a proposed product must satisfy other criteria. For instance, it must be in keeping with the company's objectives and image. The product also must be compatible with the firm's production capabilities. And it must satisfy any pertinent legal requirements.

Middleman's Criteria for New Products

In considering whether to buy a new product for resale, middlemen such as retailers and wholesalers should apply all the preceding criteria except those related to production. In addition, a middleman should apply the following guidelines:

- The middleman must have *a good working relationship with the producer.* By distributing a new product, a middleman should stand to benefit from (a) the producer's reputation, (b) the possibility of getting the right to be the only company to sell the product in a given territory, and/or (c) the promotional and financial help given by the producer.

- The producer and middleman must have *compatible distribution policies and practices.* Pertinent questions include "What kind of selling effort is required for the new product?" "How does the proposed product fit with the middleman's policies regarding repair service, alterations (for clothing), credit, and delivery?" "Does the product complement existing products?"

- As in the case of producers, the product must *satisfy key financial criteria.* One question is especially pertinent to middlemen: "If adding a new product necessitates eliminating another product because of a shortage of shelf or storage space, will the result be a net gain in sales?" And the fundamental question always is: "Can we make a sufficient profit with the product?"

New-Product Adoption and Diffusion

The likelihood of achieving success with a new product, especially a really innovative product, is increased if management understands the adoption and diffusion processes for that product. Once again, we stress that organizations need to understand how prospective customers behave. The **adoption process** is the set of successive decisions an *individual person or organization* makes before accepting an innovation. **Diffusion** of a new product is the process by which an innovation spreads throughout a *social system* over time.[27]

By understanding these processes, an organization can gain insight into how a product is or is not accepted by prospective customers and which groups are likely to buy a product soon after it is introduced, later on, or never. This knowledge of buying behavior can be valuable in designing an effective marketing program.

Stages in the Adoption Process

A prospective buyer goes through six **stages in the adoption process**—deciding whether to purchase something that is really new:

Stage	Activity in That Stage
Awareness	Individual is exposed to the innovation; becomes a prospect.
Interest	Prospect is interested enough to seek information.
Evaluation	Prospect judges the advantages and disadvantages of a product and compares it to alternatives.
Trial	Prospect adopts the innovation on a limited basis. A consumer tries a sample, if the product can be sampled.
Adoption	Prospect decides whether to use the innovation on a full-scale basis.
Confirmation	After adopting the innovation, prospect becomes a user who immediately seeks assurances that the decision to purchase the product was correct.

Adopter Categories

Some people will adopt an innovation soon after it is introduced. Others will delay before accepting a new product, and still others may never adopt it. Research has identified five **innovation adopter categories,** based on when in the life of a product individuals adopt a given innovation. In addition, some people reject or disregard a new product and thus fall into the category of nonadopters. Characteristics of early and late adopters are summarized in Table 8.3.

We should add that it's unlikely an individual will be in the same category, such as early adopter, for all products. It's possible a person may fall in one category for a specific product (like audio equipment) but go into another category for a much different product (like clothing).

Furthermore, adoption of a new product refers to a first-time purchase. Subsequently, because of dissatisfaction with the initial experience or other reasons, such as cost, a buyer may decide to not purchase the product (e.g., a teeth-whitening product or service) on an ongoing basis. Thus there is no assurance that first-time buyers will become loyal or even repeat customers.

Innovators Representing about 3% of the market, **innovators** are venturesome consumers who are the first to adopt an innovation. For example, some consumers buy the newest electronic products before they are introduced in the U.S. They do this by ordering from one of two online vendors that offer Japanese products that have not yet been exported by their manufacturers.[28]

www.dynamism.com

In relation to later adopters, innovators are likely to be younger, have higher social status, and be in better financial shape. Innovators also tend to have broad social relationships involving various groups of people in more than one community. They are likely to rely more on nonpersonal sources of information, such as advertising, rather than on sales people or other personal sources.

Early Adopters Comprising about 13% of the market, **early adopters** purchase a new product after innovators but sooner than other consumers. Unlike innovators, who have broad involvements *outside* a local community, early adopters tend to be

---

TABLE 8.3

Characteristics of Early and Late Adopters of Innovations

	Early Adopters	Late Adopters
Key Characteristics		
Venturesome	Innovators	
Respected	Early adopters	
Deliberate	Early majority	
Skeptical		Late majority
Tradition-bound		Laggards
Other Characteristics		
Age	Younger	Older
Education	Well educated	Less educated
Income	Higher	Lower
Social relationships: within or outside community	Innovators: outside Others: within	Totally local
Social status	Higher	Lower
Information sources	Wide variety; many media	Limited media exposure; limited reliance on outside media; reliance on local peer groups

involved socially *within* a local community. Early adopters are greatly respected in their social system; in fact, other people are interested in and influenced by their opinions. Thus the early adopter category includes more opinion leaders than any other adopter group. Sales people are probably used more as information sources by early adopters than by any other category.

www.wherifywireless.com

In the process of diffusion, a **change agent** is a person who seeks to accelerate the spread of a given innovation. In business, the person responsible for introducing an innovative new product must be a change agent. Consider a new security device that combines global-positioning and digital-wireless technologies in a three-ounce bracelet. When worn by a child, the bracelet allows a parent to monitor a child's location by Internet or phone. Marketers of this device must be effective change agents, convincing consumers that it is worthwhile to spend about $400 to purchase the bracelet and then about $30 per month in service fees for this type of added safety.[29]

A change agent focuses the initial persuasive efforts, notably targeted advertising campaigns, on people who fit the demographic profile of early adopters. Other consumers respect—often request—the opinions of early adopters and eventually will emulate their behavior. Thus, if a firm can get early adopters to buy its innovative product and they are satisfied by it, then they will say good things about the new offering. This is called *word-of-mouth communication.* In turn, the broader market eventually will accept the product as well. Of course, unlike advertising that is controlled by the firm, word of mouth can be influenced through advertising but is still largely uncontrolled. And sometimes, it turns out to be unfavorable and harmful rather than favorable and helpful.[30]

Early Majority
The **early majority,** representing about 34% of the market, includes more deliberate consumers who accept an innovation just before the "average" adopter in a social system. This group is a bit above average in social and economic measures. Consumers in the early majority group rely quite a bit on ads, sales people, and contact with early adopters.

Late Majority
The **late majority,** another 34% of the market, is a skeptical group of consumers who usually adopt an innovation to save money or in response to social pressure from their peers. They rely on members of the early and late majorities as sources of information. Advertising and personal selling are less effective with this group than is word-of-mouth communication.

Laggards
Laggards are consumers who are bound by tradition and, hence, are last to adopt an innovation. They comprise about 16% of the market. Laggards are suspicious of innovations and innovators; they wonder why anyone would pay a lot for a new kind of safety device, for example. By the time laggards adopt something new, it may already have been discarded by the innovators in favor of a newer concept. Laggards typically are older and usually are at the low end of the social and economic scales.

We are discussing only *adopters* of an innovation. For most innovations, there are many people who are *not* included in our percentages. They are **nonadopters;** they never adopt the innovation.

Characteristics Affecting Adoption Rate

The speed or ease with which a new product is adopted is termed its **adoption rate.** Five characteristics affect the adoption rate, especially in the case of truly innovative products:[31]

- *Relative advantage:* the degree to which an innovation is superior to currently available products. Relative advantage may be reflected in lower cost, greater safety, easier use, or some other relevant benefit. Safest Stripper, a paint and

Malden Mills has developed a jacket that can heat up to 114 degrees. The jacket's technology relies on ultra-thin stainless-steel fibers that conduct heat and can survive normal washing. Two light-weight rechargeable batteries heat the jacket for up to five hours. Considering the five characteristics that affect the pace at which a new product is adopted, is this new product likely to get off to a hot start?

varnish remover introduced by 3M, has several advantages and thus scores high on this characteristic. The product contains no harmful chemicals, has no odor, and allows the user to refinish furniture indoors rather than having to work outdoors.

- *Compatibility:* the degree to which an innovation coincides with the values and lifestyles of prospective adopters. Because many consumers want to save time *and* satisfy their desires now rather than later, microwave popcorn certainly satisfies this characteristic.

- *Complexity:* the degree of difficulty in understanding or using an innovation. The more complex an innovation is, the more slowly it will be adopted—if it is adopted at all. Combined shampoo and conditioners certainly are simple to use, so adoption of them was not impeded by complexity. However, some consumer electronics products and various services on the Internet have problems with this characteristic.

- *Trialability:* the degree to which an innovation may be sampled on some limited basis. Setting aside the other characteristics, the greater the trialability, the faster the adoption rate. For instance, a central home air-conditioning system is likely to have a slower adoption rate than a new seed or fertilizer, which may be tried on a small plot of ground. In general, because of this characteristic, costly products will be adopted more slowly than will inexpensive products. Likewise, many services, such as insurance, are difficult to use on a trial basis, so they tend to be adopted rather slowly.

- *Observability:* the degree to which an innovation actually can be demonstrated to be effective. In general, the greater the observability, the faster the adoption rate. For example, a new weed killer that works on existing weeds probably will be accepted sooner than a product that prevents weeds from sprouting. The reason? The latter product, even if highly effective, produces no dead weeds to show to prospective buyers!

A company would like an innovative product to satisfy all five characteristics as previously discussed. But few do. One-time cameras come close, however. Procter &

Gamble hopes that a kit for dry cleaning clothes at home also does.[32] A moist cleaning cloth from the Dryel kit and the dirty clothes are placed in a nylon bag, then run through a heated cycle in the clothes dryer, a process that minimizes *complexity*. Considering that it can be used at home at any time, time-short consumers probably would give the product high marks for *compatibility*. Dryel and Fresh Care, a competing brand, cost about $10, a price level that contributes to *trialability*. Each manufacturer claims that its brand produces clean clothes at a fraction of the cost of so-called professional dry cleaning. If so, home dry-cleaning kits also possess *relative advantage* and *observability*, the final two characteristics that accelerate the adoption rate for new products.

Organizing for Product Innovation

For new-product programs to be successful, they must be supported by a strong, long-term commitment from top management. This commitment must be maintained even when some new products fail. To implement this commitment to innovation effectively, new-product efforts must be soundly organized.

Types of Organization

There is no "one best" organizational structure for product planning and development. Many companies use more than one structure to manage these activities. Some widely used organizational structures for planning and developing new products are:

- **Product-planning committee.** Members include executives from major departments—marketing, production, finance, engineering, and research. In small firms, the president and/or another top-level executive often serve on the committee.
- **New-product department or team.** These units are small, consisting of five or fewer people. The head of the group typically reports to the company president. In a large firm, this may be the president of a division.
- **Brand manager.** This individual is responsible for planning new products as well as managing established products. A large company may have many brand managers who report to higher marketing executives.

Product innovation is too important of an activity to handle in an unorganized, nonchalant fashion, figuring that somehow the job will get done. What's critical is to make sure that some person or group has the specific responsibility for new-product development and is backed by top management.

As the new product is completed, responsibility for marketing it usually is shifted either to an existing department or to a new department established just for this new product. In some cases the team that developed the product may continue as the management nucleus of the new unit.

Integrating new products into departments that are already marketing established products carries two risks, however. First, executives who are involved with ongoing products may have a short-term outlook as they deal with day-to-day problems of existing products. Consequently, they may not recognize the long-term importance of new products and, as a result, may neglect them. Second, managers of successful existing products often are reluctant to assume the risks inherent in marketing new products.

Shifting Arrangements

Beginning in the 1950s, many companies—Procter & Gamble, Pillsbury, and General Foods, to name a few—assigned the responsibility for planning new products as well as coordinating the marketing efforts for established ones to a brand manager.

Essentially, a brand manager, sometimes called a *product manager,* plans the complete marketing program for a brand or group of products. Specific tasks include setting marketing goals, preparing budgets, and drafting plans for advertising and personal selling activities. Developing new products along with improving established products may also be part of the job description.

The biggest drawback of this structure is that a company often saddles brand managers with great responsibility but provides them with little authority. For instance, brand managers are expected to develop the plan by which the sales force will market the product to wholesalers and retailers, but they have no real authority over the sales force. Their effectiveness depends largely on their ability to influence other executives to cooperate with their plans.

The pace of technological change since the early 1990s has placed a premium on rapid decision making. For this reason and others, such as lack of authority, one observer went so far as to state that brand managers were an "endangered species." Over time, the brand manager structure was modified in some companies. For instance, Ford turned to brand managers, General Motors dropped them, and Procter & Gamble added *category managers* who oversee the activities of a related group of brand managers.[33]

Despite these prominent examples, many firms are now relying on team efforts—such as the product-planning committee discussed earlier—to develop new products. Typically, these are *cross-functional* teams, consisting of representatives from not only market research and marketing but also product design, engineering, and manufacturing. The rationale has been explained as follows, "Cross-functional teams offer the benefits of different perspectives and skill sets, and . . . a functionally diverse team can improve the quality of products developed and reduce the cycle time necessary to launch new products."[34]

Summary

The first commandment in marketing is "Know thy customer," and the second is "Know thy product." The relative number and success of a company's new products are a prime determinant of its sales, growth rate, and profits. A firm can best serve its customers by producing and marketing want-satisfying goods or services.

To manage its products effectively, a firm's marketers must understand the full meaning of *product,* which stresses that customers are buying want satisfaction. Products can be classified into two basic categories—consumer products and business products. Each category is then subdivided, because a different marketing program is required for each distinct group of products.

There are many views as to what constitutes a *new* product. For marketing purposes, three categories of new products need to be recognized—innovative, significantly different, and imitative.

A clear statement of the firm's new-product strategy serves as a solid foundation for the six-stage development process for new products. At each stage, a firm needs to decide whether to proceed to the next stage or to halt the project. The early stages in this process are especially important. If a firm can make an early *and correct* decision to stop the development of a proposed product, a lot of money and labor can be saved.

In deciding whether or not to add a new product, a producer or middleman should consider whether there is adequate market demand for it. The product also should fit in with the firm's marketing, production, and financial resources.

Management needs to understand the adoption and diffusion processes for a new product. A prospective user goes through six stages in deciding whether or not to adopt a new product. Adopters of an innovation can be divided into five categories, depending on how quickly they accept an innovation such as a new product. These categories are innovators, early adopters, early majority, late majority, and laggards. In addition, there usually is a group of nonadopters. Five characteristics of an innovation seem to influence its adoption rate: relative advantage, compatibility, complexity, trialability, and observability.

Successful product planning and development require long-term commitment and strong support from top management. Furthermore, new-product programs must be soundly organized. Most firms use one of three organizational structures for new-product development: product-planning committee or team, new-product department, or brand manager.

Recently, the trend has been away from brand managers and toward team efforts for developing new products.

More about Imaginatik

Imaginatik's idea management system is intended to stimulate ideas from a company's employees. However, it can also solicit and capture suggestions from another valuable source, namely customers.

One approach for doing so is indirect; for instance, employees can be asked to watch customers and submit these observations. Using the indirect approach, Grace Performance Systems requested that its sales representatives report on the unintended ways in which customers use the division's products. The notion was that new products might be created or existing products might be modified to suit these applications. The 134 reports submitted by the reps included the use of Grace waterproofing materials to repair boots and tents and, especially surprising, to soundproof vehicles. But these sometimes "oddball" uses of Grace's products produced seven promising concepts that could yield millions of dollars in sales for the division.

Wanting to allow its clients to obtain ideas directly from customers (and undoubtedly desiring to build its own sales and profits in so doing), Imaginatik developed a variation on Idea Central. The newer product, Idea Chain, is designed to solicit and compile ideas from various external groups, including suppliers and customers. Although similar to Idea Central, it has added features that address potential issues, such as managing intellectual property rights, which may arise when ideas are submitted to a firm by parties who are not employees. Besides generating useful ideas, a side benefit of Idea Chain is building stronger relationships with other members of a company's value chain (such as suppliers and middlemen) and also with key customers.

Of course, Imaginatik does not give away its idea management systems. The actual cost that a client incurs depends on many factors, ranging from number of users within the company to how many, if any, add-on modules (for example, idea warehouse) a client purchases. In round numbers, the Idea Central software costs about $75,000 for a firm that will have 1,000 users of the program.[35]

1. Which step(s) in the new-product development process would Idea Central or Idea Chain take care of, and which would still need to be carried out following the use of one of these programs?

2. What are the potential drawbacks of using an "idea management system" such as Idea Central or Idea Chain?

3. Could a company justify the cost of using one of Imaginatik's programs?

Key Terms and Concepts

Product (207)
Consumer products (208)
Business products (208)
Convenience good (208)
Shopping good (209)
Specialty good (210)
Unsought good (211)
Raw materials (211)
Fabricating materials (213)
Fabricating parts (213)
Installations (213)
Accessory equipment (214)

Operating supplies (214)
New products (217)
New-product strategy (218)
New-product development
    process (220)
Business analysis (220)
Market tests (220)
Adoption process (223)
Diffusion (223)
Stages in the adoption process (223)
Innovation adopter categories (224)
Innovators (224)

Early adopters (224)
Change agent (225)
Early majority (225)
Late majority (225)
Laggards (225)
Nonadopters (225)
Adoption rate (225)
Product-planning committee (227)
New-product department or
    team (227)
Brand manager (227)

Questions and Problems

1. In what respects are the products different in each of the following cases?
   a. A Whirlpool refrigerator sold at an appliance store and a similar refrigerator sold by Sears under its Kenmore brand name. Assume that Whirlpool makes both refrigerators.
   b. A CD by the singer Jewel purchased online from Amazon.com and the same CD sold by a Blockbuster store.
   c. An airline ticket purchased through a travel agent and an identical ticket purchased directly from the airline via the Internet.

2. a. Explain the various interpretations of the term *new product*.
   b. Give some examples, other than those cited in this chapter, of products in each of the three new-product categories.

3. "Because brand preferences are well established with regard to many items of women's clothing, these items—traditionally considered shopping goods—will move into the specialty-goods category. At the same time, however, other items of women's clothing can be found in supermarkets and variety stores, thus indicating that some items are convenience goods."
   a. Explain the reasoning in these statements.
   b. Do you agree that women's clothing is shifting away from the shopping-goods classification? Explain.

4. Compare the elements of a producer's marketing mix for a convenience good with those of the mix for a specialty good.

5. In which of the five categories of business goods should each of the following be included? And which products may belong in more than one category?
   a. Trucks
   b. Medical X-ray equipment
   c. Typing paper
   d. Copper wire
   e. Printing presses
   f. Nuts and bolts
   g. Paper clips
   h. Land

6. In developing new products, how can a firm make sure that it is being socially responsible with regard to scarce resources and our environment?

7. Assume that the following organizations are considering additions to their product lines. In each case, does the proposed product meet the criteria for adding a new product? Explain your decisions.
   a. McDonald's—salad bar
   b. Safeway supermarkets—automobile tires
   c. Exxon—personal computers
   d. Banks—life insurance
   e. Amazon.com—life insurance

8. Several new products from foreign countries are described in the Global Perspective box. In your opinion, which ones will enjoy the greatest success in the U.S.? Explain your choices.

9. Describe the kinds of people who are most likely to be found in (a) the innovator category of adopters and (b) the late-majority category.

10. Why are many firms relying more on cross-functional teams and less on product managers for new-product development?

Interactive Marketing Exercises

1. Arrange a meeting with the manager of a large retail outlet in your community. Discuss two topics with the manager:
   a. What recently introduced product has been a failure or appears destined to fail?
   b. Did this product, in retrospect, satisfy the criteria for adding a new product? (Remember to consider not just the middleman's criteria but also applicable producer's criteria.)

2. Design, either in words or drawings, a new product that fits into one of the first two categories of newness—that is, it is a really innovative product or a significant replacement, not just an imitative product. Then evaluate how your proposed product rates with respect to the five characteristics of an innovation that influence the adoption rate.

Chapter 9

Eastman Kodak faced challenges that threatened the future prosperity, perhaps the existence, of the business.

Product-Mix Strategies

Can KODAK Create a Different Image for Its Future?

It's not an overstatement to say that George Eastman created a new industry. In 1879, he obtained a patent that was the basis for photography involving film in rolls. Less than 10 years later, his fledgling firm started producing and marketing Kodak cameras for amateur photographers. By 1896, the Eastman Kodak Co. had sold 100,000 cameras.

Eastman's enterprise embraced a philosophy emphasizing customer needs, mass production to lower costs, widespread (international) distribution, and extensive promotion. Guided by this philosophy, the company introduced the Brownie camera in 1900 at a price of $1. As a result of Kodak's film and cameras, a growing number of consumers decided to take photos themselves rather than relying on professionals.

Over time, Kodak products became available in almost every country in the world, and the firm's sales exceeded $13 billion. The Kodak brand was highly respected worldwide.

Eventually, Eastman Kodak faced challenges that threatened the future prosperity, perhaps the existence, of the business. What happened? First, serious competition. Next, disruptive new technologies.

As the market leader, Kodak attracted a wide array of firms offering alternative films and cameras. The most heated battle occurred in the film business. To build market share in the U.S., Fuji Photo Film sought to match the breadth and quality of Kodak's products. In addition, the Japanese firm was quite willing to undercut Kodak's film prices and spend substantial amounts on promotion.

Eventually, both Kodak and Fuji faced a bigger issue than their own heated competition. For decades, images were recorded on film. But then, following a technological breakthrough, images could be stored in a digital format (that is, on microchips). As a result, sales of traditional film declined, from a peak of 800 million rolls in 1999 to 300 million rolls in 2005. Clearly, a mature product went into a rapid, sharp decline.

Facing facts, the Eastman Kodak Co. announced in late 2003 that it would de-emphasize traditional film and related products and would instead focus on digital technologies and allied offerings. It now sought to be "the leader in helping people take, share, print, and view images—for memories, for information, or for entertainment."

Eastman Kodak has had mixed results in the digital photography arena, lagging in printing pictures but leading in camera sales. Consumers who use filmless cameras can print their pictures at a self-serve kiosk, through an online service, with a home printer, or at a retail store. Kodak is in good position with the first two options; however, analysts don't believe these methods have strong long-term potential. Eastman Kodak is marketing home printers; unfortunately, so are many other firms. Over time, analysts believe that a growing proportion of consumers will let retail outlets do the printing. In this method, expensive all-in-one machines produce 2,000 prints an hour from the digital media turned in by consumers. Fuji is way ahead of Kodak in placing these minilabs in retail stores.

Eastman Kodak has moved to the head of the pack in digital-camera sales. In terms of units sold, Kodak had a 22% share in 2004, followed by Sony, Canon, and Hewlett-Packard. On average, Kodak's digital cameras cost less than other brands, so Eastman Kodak doesn't command as large a share in terms of dollar volume of sales.

Digital cameras in all price ranges are now outselling film cameras by a ratio of four-to-one, perhaps five-to-one. As a result, the proportion of American households that have a digital camera has grown from 8% in 2000 to over 40%, perhaps 50%, at present. Clearly, for Kodak and its competitors, the future is digital—at least, until a technological advance yields a better way of capturing, storing, and sharing images.[1]

Has Kodak's transition from film to filmless cameras positioned the company for future success in the rapidly growing area of digital photography?

 www.kodak.com

Eastman Kodak Co., like most firms, faces the challenges of protecting its competitive position as well as building sales and profits with new products as a market evolves. This case illustrates that, over time, a company must make numerous decisions about its array of products. Whether the correct decisions are made—and made at the right time—greatly affects a company's degree of success, not just for a single year but for many years to come.

At any given time, a firm may be marketing some new products and some old ones while others are being planned and developed. This chapter covers a number of strategic decisions pertaining to an organization's assortment of products. After studying this chapter, you should be able to explain:

Chapter Goals

- The difference between product mix and product line.
- Major product-mix strategies—positioning, expansion, alteration, and contraction.
- Trading up and trading down.
- Managing a product throughout a life cycle.
- Planned obsolescence.
- Style and fashion.
- The fashion-adoption process.

Product Mix and Product Line

www.carma-labs.com

Red Hat Inc. markets only Linux software, and Carma Laboratories, Inc. sells just lip balm (and one other item). These examples notwithstanding, few firms rely on a single product; instead, most sell many products. A **product mix** is the set of all products offered for sale by a company. The structure of a product mix has both breadth and depth. Its **breadth** is measured by the number of product lines carried, its **depth** by the variety of sizes, colors, and models offered within each product line. A product-mix structure is illustrated in Figure 9.1.

A broad group of products, intended for essentially similar uses and having similar physical characteristics, constitutes a **product line.** Firms may delineate a product line in different ways. For Wyeth Consumer Healthcare, its various forms of Robitussin cough remedies (such as Pediatric and Maximum Strength syrups and cherry-flavored drops) represent a product line. However, for a large drugstore or supermarket, all brands of cough suppressants—not just Robitussin products—comprise one of the store's many product lines.

FIGURE 9.1

Product Mix—Breadth and Depth in a Lawn and Garden Store.

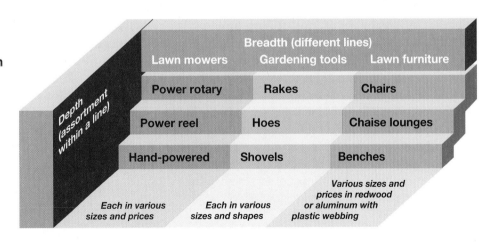

Product-Mix Strategies

At one time, Anheuser-Busch Companies offered snack foods, baked goods, adventure park entertainment, and about 20 brands of beer to consumers. Did this diverse assortment of products develop by accident? No—it reflected a planned strategy, as did the company's subsequent decision to dispose of the snack foods and baked goods divisions. To be successful in marketing, producers and middlemen need carefully planned strategies for managing their product mixes, as we'll see next.

Positioning the Product

Management's ability to bring attention to a product and to differentiate it in a favorable way from similar products goes a long way toward determining that product's revenues. Thus management needs to engage in *positioning*. Recall from the discussion in Chapter 6 that positioning entails developing the image that a product projects in relation to competitive products and to the firm's other products.

Regardless of which positioning strategy is used, the needs of the target market always must be considered. For example, InterContinental Hotels Group has developed multiple (too many?) offerings to satisfy diverse target markets. Thus the lodging firm now has Holiday Inn full-service, Express, Select, Garden Court, Nickelodeon Family Suites, and SunSpree Resort properties as well as Staybridge Suites, Candlewood Suites, and InterContinental and Crowne Plaza hotels and resorts. Likewise, to satisfy different consumers' desires, Anheuser-Busch has both regular and light beers at multiple price levels, several brands of nonalcoholic brews, and now a beer that is low in carbohydrates.[2]

Marketing executives can choose from a variety of positioning strategies. Sometimes they decide to use more than one for a particular product. Here are several major positioning strategies.

Positioning in Relation to a Competitor

For some products the best position is directly against the competition. This strategy is especially suitable for a firm that already has a solid differential advantage or is trying to solidify such an advantage. After nine years of relying on a single (but successful) model, General Motors' Saturn division finally brought out larger models. The L (for "larger") series was intended, but failed, to attract customers from Saturn's primary competitors, Honda and Toyota. Saturn is trying again with the Aura sedan and Sky roadster. To fend off rival makers of microprocessors, Intel Corp. has used the slogan, "Intel Inside," and a long-running advertising campaign to convince buyers that its product is superior to competitors'.[3]

For other products, head-to-head positioning is exactly what *not* to do, especially when a competitor has a strong market position. In women's professional basketball, the American Basketball League and the Women's National Basketball Association competed directly against each other, including overlapping seasons. Ultimately, the ABL lost out to the WNBA, which has the financial backing of the men's NBA.[4]

One view is that underdogs should try to be the opposite of—or at least much different than—the market leader. Southwest Airlines positioned itself effectively as the low-fare alternative to full-service airlines. In fact, larger competitors as well as more recent entrants, such as JetBlue and Frontier, have been trying to emulate Southwest's practices, which satisfy a sizable segment of travelers and generate profits.[5]

Positioning in Relation to a Product Class or Attribute

Sometimes a company's positioning strategy entails associating its product with (or distancing it from) a product class or attribute. For example, some companies try to place their products in a desirable class, such as "Made in the USA."

Marriott International, Inc. positions its brands by price and quality *and* in relation to competition. Marriott's array of hotels and resorts, with variations in price point and range of amenities, are intended to attract different target markets. Facing widespread competition, Marriott has added brands such as Spring Hill Suites to assure that its product mix satisfies its targeted customers.

www.marriott.com/
corporateinfo/default.mi

BE HERE FASTER

Marriott
R E W A R D S.

BE HERE 30% FASTER THAN WITH OTHER HOTEL PROGRAMS*
With Marriott Rewards,' you need fewer points to get to your dream destination than with other leading hotel programs. And with more than 2,400 hotels participating, we offer more resorts, spas, and golf locations than any other hotel program. What more could you dream of?

Curaçao Marriott Beach Resort & Emerald Casino

Other firms promote their wares as having an attractive attribute, such as "low energy consumption" or "environmentally friendly." This strategy is widely used now for food products. Libby's, Campbell Soup, Kellogg's, and competing companies, for instance, have introduced lines of foods with one common denominator—they contain no or very little salt. These items are positioned against products that are packed with the conventional amounts of salt. Sometimes what's in, rather than what's left out of, the product is emphasized. That's the case with Volvo, which constructed a steel frame around the passenger compartment in order to be positioned as *the* safe automobile.

Positioning by Price and Quality

Certain producers and retailers are known for their high-quality products and high prices. In the retailing field, Saks Fifth Avenue and Neiman Marcus are positioned at one end of the price–quality continuum. Discount stores such as Wal-Mart and Dollar General are at the other end. We're not saying that discounters ignore quality; rather, they stress low prices.

In recent years, both Ford and General Motors have sold large numbers of sport-utility vehicles (SUVs). Now, virtually every automaker has introduced its own SUV, most of which feature four-wheel drive and other high-quality, but expensive amenities. In a market filled with dozens of models of SUVs, ranging from the familiar Ford Explorer and Chevy Suburban to the obscure Kia Sorento and Buick Rainier, producers are struggling to differentiate their particular model from all the others. Without differentiation, particularly with respect to positioning on the price–quality continuum, some models are likely to fail.

Product-Mix Expansion

Product-mix expansion is accomplished by increasing the depth within a particular line and/or the number of lines a firm offers to customers. Let's look at these options.

When a company adds a similar item to an existing product line with the same brand name, this is termed a **line extension.** For illustrations, pull the coupons out of your Sunday newspaper. You'll probably see examples such as Pillsbury promoting about 10 variations of its well-known biscuits and rolls, L'Oréal announcing new versions of its kids' shampoos, and Uncle Ben's plugging several different kinds of rice.

The line-extension strategy is also used by organizations in services fields. For example, some years ago the Roman Catholic Church broadened its line of religious services by adding Saturday and Sunday evening masses, and universities offer programs to appeal to prospective older students.

There are many reasons for line extensions. The main one is that a firm wants to appeal to more market segments by offering a wider range of choices for a particular product. Line extensions have been one of the more prominent—and debatable—practices during the past 15 or so years. As discussed in the "You Make the Decision" box, line extensions have become so common that it raises questions about their effectiveness.

Another way to expand the product mix, referred to as **mix extension,** is to add a new product line to the company's present assortment. Jell-O pudding pops and Bic disposable lighters, both successes, and Bic pantyhose and adidas colognes, both failures, are examples of mix extension. The maker of Swatch watches went so far afield in creating the very small and inexpensive Smart Car that eventually Daimler (the maker of Mercedes Benz autos) took the project over.

Johnson & Johnson's products illustrate the distinction between mix extension and line extension. When J&J introduced a line of Acuvue disposable contact lenses, that's *mix* extension because it added another product to the company's product mix. In contrast, line extension adds more items within the same product line. When J&J adds new versions of Tylenol pain reliever, that's *line* extension.

www.jnj.com

Under a mix-extension strategy, the new line may be related or unrelated to current products. Furthermore, it may carry one of the company's existing brand names or may be given an entirely new name.

Typically, the new line is related to the existing product mix because the company wants to capitalize on its strengths and experience. Given the success of Reese's peanut butter cups, Hershey's thinks the brand says "peanut butter" to consumers, so it introduced a line of Reese's peanut butters. Hunt-Wesson holds a similar view about its Swiss Miss brand and chocolate, so it developed Swiss Miss puddings in chocolate and other flavors. In both cases, the new lines carry one of the company's popular brands to benefit from consumers' familiarity with and good feelings toward that brand. We'll consider this approach in more detail when *brand equity* is discussed in the next chapter.

In order to gain a competitive advantage, generate more sales, and build customer satisfaction, Kimberly-Clark Corp. has extended its line of diapers in several ways. For example, as shown in the ad, the company not only offers a line of training pants under the Pull-Ups brand, but it also has separate versions for boys and girls.

www.pull-ups.com

Clothes make the man, but underpants make the kid.

Nothing makes a little kid feel like a big kid quite like a pair of real underpants. Which is why Pull-Ups® training pants have fun designs that make them look just like underwear. There are even blue sides for boys and pink for girls. Pull-Ups training pants. When your child feels like a big kid, he'll stay dry like one.

Pull-Ups® TRAINING PANTS I'm a Big Kid Now.®

Visit Parentstages.com – the best of the web for every parenting stage. Powered by Pull-Ups.com

In a typical year, more than 30,000 new products (the term *new* is used loosely) are placed in front of consumers. In fact, the annual flow of introductions has almost doubled in the last 10 years. Just in the category of beverages, which ranges from carbonated soft drinks to alcoholic beverages, there are over 3,500 new entries annually. Seeking a larger share of the carbonated-beverages market, which generates over $65 billion in revenues annually, PepsiCo came out with a reformulated Pepsi One in early 2005. Coca-Cola followed suit with a version of Diet Coke that is sweetened with Splenda as well as with the new Coca-Cola Zero.

In the auto industry, the number of "nameplates" exploded from fewer than 50 to more than 250 in the past 55 years or so. There's even a proliferation of nameplates in the sports-car submarket, where marketers of about 20 different models compete for just 200,000 purchases yearly.

Does this flow of new offerings benefit consumers and retailers as well as manufacturers? A variety of evidence says "no." Many consumers cannot differentiate across the numerous alternatives, and they get frustrated or angry in the process. Really, do you know the differences among the following remedies—Tylenol Flu, Tylenol Cold, Tylenol Sinus, and Tylenol Allergy Sinus, not to mention their different forms (tablets, caplets, and gel caps)?

The basic problem may be that almost three-quarters of so-called new products are line extensions within an existing product category, in which the new entry represents a different form or promises an added benefit. Only about one-quarter of new products are a mix or line extension outside the company's current category, and only 6% have truly new features.

Supermarkets lack shelf space to add all or even most of the new products. According to a study conducted for the Food Marketing Institute, a trade association, the number of separate items carried by a supermarket can be reduced by 5% to 25% without reducing sales or causing consumers to think that the store offers a poor assortment of products.

Further, with so many branded products (sometimes too similar), manufacturers spend so much money designing new variations that they don't benefit from the economies of scale that come with long production runs. Typically, their funds are also spread too thin to carry out forceful marketing programs for their brands.

How should a manufacturer decide what number of separate items in a product line will best serve the interests of consumers, retailers, and itself?

Sources: Chad Terhune, "Coke, Pepsi Launch New Diet Drinks," *The Wall Street Journal*, Mar. 22, 2005, p. A6; Thomas Lee, "Why Foods Fail," *Star Tribune* (Minneapolis, MN), Aug. 30, 2004, p. 1D; Jerry Flint, "267 Flavors," *Forbes*, Aug. 16, 2004, p. 88; "The Best New Products," *Beverage Industry*, February 2002, pp. 35–37; and Ira Teinowitz and Jennifer Lawrence, "Brand Proliferation Attacked," *Advertising Age*, May 10, 1993, pp. 11+.

Alteration of Existing Products

Rather than developing a completely new product, management might do well to take a fresh look at the organization's existing products. Often, improving an established product, termed **product alteration,** can be more profitable and less risky than developing a completely new one. The substitution of NutraSweet for saccharin in diet sodas increased sales of those drinks. Redesigning the product itself can sustain its appeal or even initiate its renaissance. For example, Kimberly-Clark redesigned its disposable diapers so that they are less bulky and also come in separate styles for girls and boys.

Product alteration is not without risks, however. When the Coca-Cola Co. modified the formula for its leading product and changed its name to New Coke, sales plunged. As a result, the old formula was brought back three months later under the Coca-Cola Classic name.

Alternatively, especially for consumer goods, the product itself is not changed but its packaging is altered. For example, Pillsbury developed a unifying background for the package of most of its dessert mixes, a royal blue field with small white polka dots.[6] To gain a small differential advantage, companies are offering a variety of food products (such as sliced and shredded cheeses) in packages that reseal using zipper-like devices. Thus packages can be altered to enhance appearance or to improve the product's usability.

Product-Mix Contraction

Another strategy, **product-mix contraction,** is carried out either by eliminating an entire line or by simplifying the assortment within a line. Thinner and/or shorter product lines or mixes can weed out low-profit and unprofitable products. The intended result of product-mix contraction is higher profits from fewer products. General Mills (Wheaties, Betty Crocker, Gold Medal flour) decided to concentrate on its food business and, consequently, sold its interest in Izod (the "alligator" apparel maker) and its lines of children's toys and games. In services fields, some travel agencies have shifted from selling all modes of travel to concentrate on specialized tours and trips to exotic places. And, to reduce their liability risks and insurance costs, many physicians have stopped offering obstetrical services.

During the early 1990s, most companies expanded—rather than contracted—their product portfolios. Numerous line extensions document this trend. Lately, some firms that wound up with an unmanageable number of products or multiple unprofitable items or lines engaged in product-mix pruning. As a result, many organizations now have fewer product lines, and the remaining lines are thinner and shorter. There are myriad examples of product-mix contraction, sometimes involving well-known firms. For example, Procter & Gamble pruned its food business by selling the Jif brand of peanut butter and the Crisco brand of cooking oils to J. M. Smucker Co. and then its Sunny Delight and Punica brands of beverages to a private firm. More recently, P&G engaged in significant mix extension by acquiring The Gillette Company and its stable of razors, blades, batteries, and other product lines. Eventually, P&G may contract its mix again by shedding any of Gillette's brands that do not meet the firm's aim of "building big brands in core categories."[7]

www.smucker.com

This image shows how a company, Giorgio Armani in this case, can develop a separate and somewhat lower-price offering in order to appeal to a new segment of the market. As such, Armani Exchange is a good example of the marketing practice called trading down.

www.armaniexchange.com

www.swatch.com

www.westelm.com

Trading Up and Trading Down

The product strategies of trading up and trading down involve a change in product positioning *and* an expansion of the product line. **Trading up** means adding a higher-price product to a line in order to attract a broader market. Also, the seller intends that the new product's prestige will help the sale of its existing lower-price products.

Consider some examples of trading up. To its line of inexpensive sport watches, Swatch added a $70 Chrono stopwatch and other upgraded watches. Home-improvement retailers, including both Home Depot and Lowe's, are now offering more expensive products, all the way up to $39,500 chandeliers.[8] And even pet food manufacturers have traded up to "superpremium" lines, as illustrated by Pedigree from Kal Kan and Purina ONE from Nestlé.

Trading down means adding a lower-price product to a company's product line. The firm expects that people who cannot afford the original higher-price product or who see it as too expensive will buy the new lower-price one. The reason: The lower-price product carries some of the status and some of the other more substantive benefits (such as performance) of the higher-price item.

The Marriott Corp. followed a trading-down strategy when it started (1) Courtyard by Marriott hotels, targeted at the midprice market long dominated by chains such as Holiday Inn and Ramada Inn, and (2) Fairfield Inns, to compete in the economy-price market. Even some designers of highly fashionable women's clothing, such as Donna Karan and Bill Blass, are trading down by introducing lower-price lines. The new lines are priced between $100 and $900 per item, typically less than one-half the price of their top lines. Apple Computer did likewise, introducing lower-priced Mac personal computers and iPod music players in 2005.[9]

Trading up and trading down are perilous strategies because the new products may confuse buyers, resulting in negligible net gain. It is equally undesirable if sales of the new item or line are generated at the expense of the established products. When *trading down*, the new offering may permanently hurt the firm's reputation and that of its established high-quality product. To reduce this possibility, new lower-price products may be given brand names unlike the established brands. That's why Hewlett-Packard Co. established a separate Apollo label for a new line of low-price printers, and Williams-Sonoma Inc. chose West Elm as the label for its lower-price furniture catalog.[10] With this approach, a company forfeits the benefits of a well-known brand name but still can capitalize on its experience in distributing and promoting the successful product.

In *trading up*, on the other hand, the problem depends on whether the new product or line carries the established brand or is given a new name. If the same name is used, the firm must change its image enough so that new customers will accept the higher-priced product. At the same time, the seller does not want to lose its present customers. The new offering may cloud the established image, not attracting new

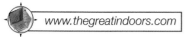
customers but driving away existing customers. To avoid that problem, Sears used the Great Indoors name for a new chain of stores that sells comparatively expensive brands that are not found in Sears' traditional stores.[11]

If a different brand name is used, either for trading down or trading up, the company must create awareness for it. Of course, promotion and other steps must be taken to stimulate consumers to buy the new product or to shop at the new store.

The Product Life Cycle

As we saw in Chapter 8, a product's life cycle can have a direct bearing on a company's survival. The life cycle of a product consists of four stages: introduction, growth, maturity, and decline. The concept of product life *applies to a generic category of product* (microwave ovens and microprocessors, for example) and not to specific brands (Sharp and Intel, respectively). A **product life cycle** consists of the aggregate demand over an extended period of time for all brands comprising a generic product category.

A life cycle can be graphed by plotting aggregate sales volume for a product category over time, usually years. It is also worthwhile to accompany the sales volume curve with the corresponding profit curve for the product category, as shown in Figure 9.2. After all, a business is interested ultimately in profitability, not just sales.

The *shapes* of these two curves vary from one product category to another. Still, for most categories, the basic shapes and the relationship between the sales and the profit curves are as illustrated in Figure 9.2. In this typical life cycle, the profit curve for most new products is negative, signifying a loss, through much of the introductory stage. In the latter part of the growth stage, the profit curve starts to decline while sales volume is still rising. Profits decline because the companies in an industry usually must increase their advertising and selling efforts and/or cut their prices to sustain sales growth in the face of intensifying competition during the maturity stage.

Introducing a new product at the proper time will help maintain a company's desired level of profit. Striving to maintain its dominant position in the wet-shaving market, the Gillette Company faces that challenge often. A while back, a large French firm cut into Gillette's market share by introducing the highly successful Bic disposable razors. After considerable research and development, Gillette counterattacked with the Sensor razor, featuring independently suspended blades. The strategy

FIGURE 9.2

Typical Life Cycle of a Product Category.

During the introduction stage of a life cycle, a product category—and virtually all brands within it—is unprofitable. Total profits for the product category are healthy during the growth stage but then start to decline while a product's sales volume is still increasing.

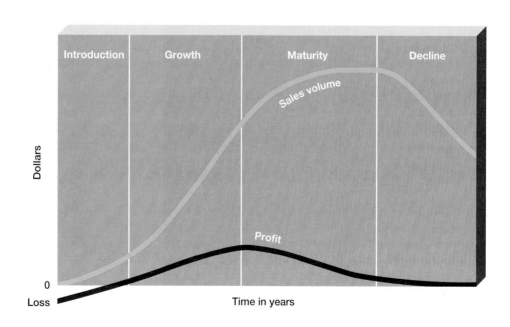

worked, as many consumers left the convenience of low-price disposable razors in favor of the better shaves provided by the higher-price Sensor razor. Gillette then traded up again, introducing the triple-blade Mach3 razor, priced about 35% higher than the Sensor.[12]

If a new product lacks competition and is particularly appealing to consumers, a firm can charge a fairly high price and achieve strong profits. That was the case with Mach3, so Gillette was able to reap healthy profits from the wet-shaving market soon after the new product was introduced. Intel Corp. sought a measure of control over prices by introducing new generations of microprocessors only two or three years apart, even while demand was still growing for its current version. Eventually, though, the company had to rely more on price cuts to maintain its share of the market for "chips" used in personal computers. Now Intel is seeking to avoid direct price competition by combining microprocessors and software to create platforms that perform specific tasks (for example, preventing viruses on business computers).[13]

The product life-cycle concept has been criticized as lacking empirical support and being too general to be useful in specific cases.[14] Admittedly, the product life cycle is not perfect and it must be adapted to fit different circumstances. Nevertheless, it is both straightforward and powerful. A company's marketing success can be affected considerably by its ability to determine and adapt to the life cycles for each of its product categories.

Characteristics of Each Stage

Management must be able to recognize what part of the life cycle its product is in at any given time. The competitive environment and marketing strategies that should be used ordinarily depend on the particular life-cycle stage. Table 9.1 contains a synopsis of all four stages. Each stage is highlighted below.

TABLE 9.1

Characteristics and Implications of Different Product Life-Cycle Stages

	Stage			
	Introduction	**Growth**	**Maturity**	**Decline**
Characteristics				
Customers	Innovators	Mass market	Mass market	Loyal customers
Competition	Little, if any	Increasing	Intense	Decreasing
Sales	Low levels, then rising	Rapid growth	Slow/no annual growth	Declining
Profits	None	Strong, then at a peak	Declining annually	Low/none
Marketing Implications				
Overall strategy	Market development	Market penetration	Defensive positioning	Efficiency or exit
Costs	High per unit	Declining	Stable or increasing	Low
Product strategy	Undifferentiated	Improved items	Differentiated	Pruned line
Pricing strategy	Most likely high	Lower over time	Lowest	Increasing
Distribution strategy	Scattered	Intensive	Intensive	Selective
Promotion strategy	Category awareness	Brand preference	Brand loyalty	Reinforcement

Source: Adapted from material provided by Professor David Appel, University of Notre Dame.

Introduction During the **introduction stage,** sometimes called the *pioneering stage,* a product is launched into the market in a full-scale marketing program. It has gone through product development, including idea screening, prototype, and market tests. The entire product may be new, such as the zipper, the videocassette recorder, and the fat substitute for prepared foods. Or it may be well-known but have a significant novel feature that, in effect, creates a new-product category; microwave ovens and in-line skates are examples.

www.zenith.com

For really new products, normally there is very little direct competition. However, if the product has tremendous promise, numerous companies may enter the industry early on. That occurred with digital TV, introduced in 1998. Although only about one-fifth of TV sets currently sold each year are digital rather than analog, the category is viewed as having enormous potential because of the product's enhanced picture quality. Consequently, major producers such as Zenith and Sony are placing more and more emphasis on digital TVs (high definition being the most common type). Mitsubishi's American division, in fact, stopped producing analog TVs to concentrate entirely on digital sets. Growth in this product category also depends on high-definition programming becoming more widespread.[15]

Because consumers are unfamiliar with the innovative product or feature, a pioneering firm's promotional program is designed to stimulate demand for the entire product category rather than a single brand. Introduction is the most risky and expensive stage because substantial dollars must be spent not only to develop the product but also to seek consumer acceptance of the offering. Many, perhaps most, new products are not accepted by a sufficient number of consumers and fail at this stage.

Growth In the **growth stage,** or *market-acceptance stage,* sales and profits rise, frequently at a rapid rate. Competitors enter the market, often in large numbers if the profit outlook is particularly attractive. Mostly as a result of competition, profits start to decline near the end of the growth stage.

As part of firms' efforts to build sales and, in turn, market share, prices typically decline gradually during this stage. In high-tech fields, such as microprocessors, prices tend to fall sharply even as the industry is growing rapidly. According to a top executive at Eastman Kodak, "The only thing that matters is if the exponential growth of your market is faster than the exponential decline of your prices."[16] Appropriate marketing strategies for this stage, as well as the other three, are summarized in Table 9.1.

Maturity During the first part of the **maturity stage,** sales continue to increase, but at a decreasing rate. When sales level off, profits of both producers and middlemen decline. The primary reason: intense price competition.

Seeking to differentiate themselves, some firms extend their product lines with new models; others come up with a "new and improved" version of their primary brand. During this stage, the pressure is greatest on those brands that trail the #1 and #2 brands. During the latter part of this stage, marginal producers, those with high costs or no differential advantage, drop out of the market. They do so because they lack sufficient customers and/or profits.

Decline For most products, a **decline stage,** as gauged by sales volume for the total category, is inevitable for one of the following reasons:

- A better or less expensive product is developed to fill the same need. Microprocessors made possible many replacement products such as handheld calculators (which made slide rules obsolete) and video games (which may have pushed the category of board games, such as Monopoly and Clue, into their decline stage).

- The need for the product disappears, often because of another product development. For example, the broad appeal of frozen orange juice virtually eliminated the market for in-home mechanical or electrical fruit squeezers. (However, renewed interest in fresh foods has recently boosted sales of fruit squeezers.)

- People simply grow tired of a product (a clothing style, for instance), so it disappears from the market.

Seeing little opportunity for revitalized sales or profits, most competitors abandon the market during this stage. However, a few firms may be able to develop a small market niche and remain moderately successful in the decline stage. Some manufacturers of wood-burning stoves have been able to do this.

Length of Product Life Cycle

The total length of the life cycle—from the start of the introduction stage to the end of the decline stage—varies across product categories. It ranges from a few weeks or a short season (for a clothing fashion) to many decades (for autos or telephones). And it varies because of differences in the length of individual stages from one product category to the next. Furthermore, although Figure 9.2 suggests that all four life-cycle stages cover nearly equal periods of time, the stages in any given product's life cycle usually last for different periods.

Three variations on the typical life cycle are shown in Figure 9.3:

- In one, the product gains widespread consumer acceptance only after an extended introductory period (see part *a*). Fat substitutes, such as Olestra, can be used in making foods ranging from potato chips to ice cream. However, this product category appears to be stuck in the introduction stage of its life cycle, perhaps because of shifts in consumer attitudes regarding fat in foods and/or concerns about possible side effects such as abdominal cramps.[17]

- In another variation, the entire life cycle begins and ends in a relatively short period of time (part *b*). This variation depicts the life cycle for a **fad,** a product or style that becomes immensely popular nearly overnight and then falls out of favor with consumers almost as quickly. Hula hoops and lava lamps are examples of past fads. Nasal dilators (such as Breathe Right strips) and silicon rubber wristbands (now available in any one of a rainbow of colors) may be classified as fads from the past 10 years. Over 50 million yellow LIVESTRONG bands have been sold by the Lance Armstrong Foundation, with proceeds supporting cancer research and aid. Nevertheless, history repeats itself, at some point the strong demand will drop quickly and sharply.[18]

www.laf.org

FIGURE 9.3

Product Life-Cycle Variations.

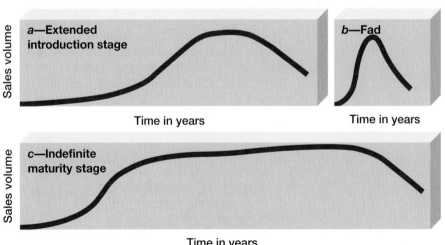

Some types of products are like shooting stars. That is, they are brilliant in terms of surging sales for a short period of time and then they burn out as sales go into a free fall. In 2004 and 2005, silicon rubber wristbands were being purchased at the rate of more than 100,000 per day in support of a wide variety of causes and organizations. At one point eBay had listings for over 600 different wristbands. Are wristbands a fad or an enduring product category?

- In a third variation, the product's mature stage lasts almost indefinitely (part *c*). This life cycle is illustrated by canned, carbonated soft drinks, portable stereos (such as the Walkman and now MP3 players),[19] and also the automobile with a gasoline-powered, internal-combustion engine. Electric- and hybrid-powered cars have been introduced, but the automobile as we know it remains dominant.

Setting aside fads, which represent a special case, product life cycles are generally getting shorter. If competitors can quickly introduce a "me too" version of a popular product, it may move swiftly into the maturity stage. Or, as described in the chapter-opening case about Kodak, rapid changes in technology can make a product completely or nearly obsolete virtually overnight. Some said that would occur in the audio field, with digital audiotapes replacing compact discs (CDs), but that didn't happen. Later forecasts were that even newer formats, notably DVD-audio and direct download from the Internet, would turn the CD into a dinosaur. Thus far, direct downloads (first through illegal and now through legal means) are surging, but the DVD-audio format is languishing.[20]

Moreover, a number of product categories do not make it through all four stages of the life cycle. Some fail in the introductory stage. That occurred a while back with a product that played laser discs rather than videotapes. The product suffered from several shortcomings (such as limited storage capacity), never caught on, and was superseded by the digital versatile disc (DVD) player.

Also, because the life cycle refers to product categories rather than individual brands, not every brand proceeds through all four life-cycle stages. For instance, some brands fail early in the cycle. That's what happened with Cord and LaSalle, both of which failed during the introduction stage of the life cycle for automobiles. Other brands are not introduced until the market is in the growth or maturity stage. The Saturn is a very successful example in the automotive field.

Life Cycle Is Related to a Market

When we say a product is in a specific stage of its life cycle, implicitly we are referring to a specific market. A product may be well accepted (growth or maturity stage) in some markets but still be striving for acceptance in other markets. At the time Ortho Pharmaceuticals introduced Retin-A as a treatment for acne, existing products already served this purpose. Thus the acne-treatment category probably was in the maturity stage. However, it was discovered that Retin-A might be effective in reducing facial wrinkles. In effect, it created a new product category. Hence, Retin-A fit into both the acne-treatment category that was in the maturity stage among teenagers, and into the wrinkle-remover category that was in the introductory or perhaps early growth stage among middle-aged people.

In terms of geographic markets, a product may be in its maturity stage in one country and its introductory stage or perhaps even unknown in another country. For example, steel-belted radial tires were in their maturity stage in western Europe well before they were available across the U.S. In contrast, so-called fast foods are a mature product category in America, but are less common in some other parts of the world. And finally, chilled coffee in cans and bottles is widely accepted in Japan—at least $8 *billion* in annual sales. Yet sales of this beverage in the U.S. are paltry—less than 10% of the level in Japan. However, seeing growth potential for this product in North America, PepsiCo and Starbucks Coffee are collaborating to market chilled coffeebased beverages. Frappuccino, a product of the joint venture, has been very well received by consumers, commanding an 80% market share in this still small category.[21]

Life-Cycle Management

To some degree, the collective actions of firms offering competing products in the same category affect the shape of the sales and profit curves over the course of a life cycle. Even single companies can have an impact. A giant firm may be able to shorten the introductory stage by broadening the distribution or increasing the promotional effort supporting the new product.

Generally, however, companies cannot substantially affect the sales and profit curves for a product category. Thus their task is to determine how best to achieve success within the life cycle for a category. For an individual firm, successful life-cycle management depends on (1) predicting the shape of the proposed product's cycle even before it is introduced and (2) successfully adapting marketing strategies at each stage of the life cycle.

Entry Strategies
A firm entering a new market must decide whether to plunge in during the introductory stage. Or, it can wait and make its entry during the early part of the growth stage, after innovating companies have proven there is a viable market.

The strategy of entering during the introductory stage is prompted by the desire to build a dominant market position right away, and thus lessen the interest of potential competitors and the effectiveness of actual competitors. This strategy worked for Sony with the Walkman, Amana and Litton with microwave ovens, and recently USRobotics (now Palm, Inc.) with personal digital assistants (PDAs), Intuit with Quicken financial software, and eBay with online auctions.

www.intuit.com

According to one line of thinking, there is a benefit, called a **first-mover advantage** (or *pioneer advantage*), to getting a head start in marketing a new type of product. The premise is that the company that introduces a new product can target the highest potential market segments and can determine how to produce the good or service at lower and lower costs, to mention just a couple of specific benefits. However, pioneering requires a large investment, and the risks are great—as demonstrated by the high failure rate among new products. In fact, in the PDA category, Apple's Newton was the pioneer, but soon failed. Many dot-com failures, such as eToys, Kozmo, and Garden.com, were pioneers in their categories, but failed nevertheless—raising doubts about whether there really is a first-mover advantage.[22]

Large companies with the marketing resources to overwhelm smaller innovating firms are most likely to be successful with a delayed-entry strategy. In one such case, Coca-Cola introduced Tab and then Diet Coke, and Pepsi-Cola introduced Diet Pepsi, and the two giants surpassed Kirsch's No-Cal Cola, the pioneer.

A study of 50 product categories concluded that the first-mover advantage is temporary, not lasting. The pioneer remains the market leader in only four of the categories (cola soft drink, color television, shortening, and telephone). In contrast, delaying entry until the market is proven can sometimes pay off. According to this same study, being an "early leader" can be advantageous over the long run. An early leader, which is a firm that enters a product category many years after the first mover but then gains market leadership during the growth stage of the cycle, is the current leader in more than one-half of the 50 product categories.[23]

Managing on the Rise

When sales are growing strongly and profits are robust in a product category, you might think marketing managers have little to do except tally up their anticipated bonuses. That's not the case. Decisions made during the growth stage influence (1) how many competitors enter the market and (2) how well the company's brand within a product category does both in the near and distant future.

During the growth stage of the life cycle, a company has to devise the right strategies for its brand(s) in that product category. Target markets have to be confirmed or, if necessary, adjusted. Product improvements must be formulated, prices assessed and perhaps revised, distribution expanded, and promotion enhanced.

Home video games were introduced in the 1970s, but the more captivating (perhaps addictive) Nintendo brand, in effect, created a new product category in the 1980s. As described in a case following this part of the text, this product appeared to be in the growth stage of its life cycle as the 1990s began. However, video game sales stagnated in the mid-1990s. Since then, to stimulate sales, Nintendo, Sony, and now Microsoft have been engaged in "technological leap frog." That is, the three competitors are constantly striving to gain a differential advantage, even if only temporary, by building more video, audio, and graphics capabilities into their systems, while controlling prices.[24]

Managing during Maturity

Common strategies to maintain or boost sales of a product during the maturity stage of its life cycle include not just implementing line extension, but also modifying the product, designing new promotion, and devising new uses for the product.[25] Such steps may lead to added purchases by present customers and/or may attract new customers.

www.sikids.com

To reach a new market, Time Inc. extended its *Sports Illustrated* line, introducing separate editions for women (publication halted at end of 2000) and kids. As sales flattened out, some cruise lines modified their services by adding new destinations and ports of call and offering special theme cruises (sometimes in conjunction

One responsibility of the United States Mint is to sell proof and uncirculated coins, commemorative coins, and medals to the public. To sustain interest in the country's coinage, with a side benefit of recounting aspects of American history, the Mint puts new coins into circulation and promotes them on its website.

www.usmint.gov

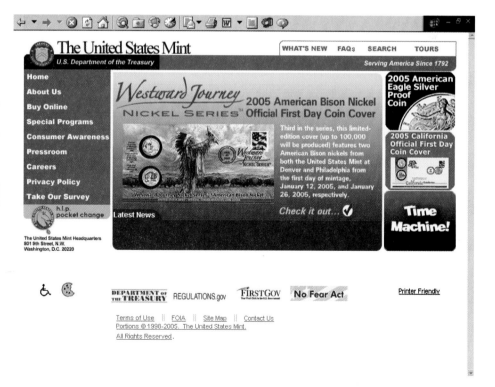

with a professional sports team). In the public sector, the U.S. Mint put out a nickel with a more modern image of Thomas Jefferson and is introducing 50 new quarters, one design for each of the 50 states.[26]

The DuPont Co. appears to be particularly adept at sustaining mature products, such as Teflon protective coating and Lycra fiber. Lycra is a brand of spandex, a fiber DuPont invented in 1959. DuPont's primary strategy to generate continuing interest in Lycra has been to develop improved versions of it. The product now is used in a variety of clothing, ranging from hosiery to women's and men's fashions to cycling shorts. DuPont also backs Lycra with aggressive promotion, such as a $40 million global ad campaign stressing that clothes made with Lycra help consumers "look better, feel better."[27]

www.eaglebrand.com

Surviving the Decline Stage   Perhaps it is in the decline stage that a company finds its greatest challenges in life-cycle management. For instance, condensed milk was developed prior to the Civil War when there was no electrical refrigeration to prevent food from spoiling. Now, with refrigerators in almost all U.S. homes, this product is in its decline stage. Borden sold its brand of condensed milk to Eagle Family Foods, which is trying to reinvigorate the product. Eagle launched a "Make Magic in Minutes" campaign to show consumers that condensed milk can help them make various food treats, easily and year-round.[28]

When sales are declining, management has the following alternatives:

- Ensure that marketing and production programs are as efficient as possible.

- Prune unprofitable sizes and models. Frequently this tactic will *decrease* sales but *increase* profits.

- "Run out" the product; that is, cut all costs to the bare minimum to maximize profitability over the limited remaining life of the product.

- Best (and toughest) of all, improve the product in a functional sense, or revitalize it in some manner. Some publishers are working hard to maintain the appeal of the dictionary. St. Martin's Press, for instance, introduced a printed dictionary that includes workplace slang and also bios of celebrities. As part of a collaboration with Microsoft, the dictionary is available in either CD or DVD format for use on personal computers.[29]

If one of these alternatives doesn't work, management will have to consider **product abandonment.** The expense of carrying profitless products goes beyond what shows up on financial statements. For example, there is a very real cost to the managerial time and effort that is diverted to terminally ill products. Management often is reluctant to discard a product, however, partly because it becomes attached to the product over the years. Knowing when and how to abandon products successfully may be as important as knowing when and how to introduce new ones.

www.fluke.com

Either before or after abandoning a declining product, a company may redefine its mission to concentrate on a more promising venture. That's what Fluke Manufacturing did when its traditional test and measurement devices started to become obsolete because of computing technology. Thus it was no fluke that the company came up with the following mission statement: "To be the leader in compact professional electronic test tools."[30]

Planned Obsolescence and Fashion

American consumers seem to be constantly searching for "what's new" but not "*too new.*" They want newness—new products, new styles, new colors. However, they want to be moved gently out of their habitual patterns, not shocked out of them. Consequently, many manufacturers use a product strategy of planned obsolescence. The intent of this strategy is to make an existing product out of date and thus increase the market for replacement products. Consumers often satisfy their thirst for newness through fashion. And producers of fashions rely heavily on planned obsolescence, as we'll see.

Nature of Planned Obsolescence

The term **planned obsolescence** is used to refer to either of two developments:

- **Technological obsolescence.** Significant technical improvements result in a more effective product. For instance, cassette tapes made vinyl phonograph records outmoded, and then compact discs rendered cassettes virtually obsolete. This type of obsolescence is generally considered to be socially and economically desirable, because the replacement product offers more benefits and/or a lower cost.
- **Style obsolescence.** Superficial characteristics of a product are altered so that the new model is easily differentiated from the previous model. Style obsolescence, sometimes called "psychological" or "fashion" obsolescence, is intended to make people feel out-of-date if they continue to use old models. Products subject to this type of obsolescence include clothing, furniture, and automobiles.

Normally, when people criticize planned obsolescence, they mean style obsolescence. Still, technological (or functional) obsolescence is sometimes criticized. For example, Microsoft has been chided for its periodic revisions of Windows and related products. As one critic said sarcastically, "New versions of software are often little more than 'bug fixes,'. . . and you're given the privilege of paying for those fixes."[31] In our discussion, when we speak of planned obsolescence, we will mean *only* style obsolescence, unless otherwise stated.

Nature of Style and Fashion

Although the words *style* and *fashion* are often used interchangeably, there is a clear distinction. A **style** is a distinctive manner of construction or presentation in any art, product, or endeavor (singing, playing, behaving). Thus we have styles in automobiles (sedans, station wagons), in bathing suits (one-piece, bikini), in furniture (early American, French provincial), and in music (jazz, rap).

A **fashion** is any style that is popularly accepted or purchased by successive groups of people over a reasonably long period of time. Not every style becomes a fashion. To be considered a fashion, or to be called "fashionable," a style must be accepted by many people. All styles listed in the preceding paragraph, except perhaps rap music, qualify as fashions. All past societies, including ancient Egypt and medieval Europe, had fashions and so does contemporary America.

Fashion is rooted in sociological and psychological factors. Basically, most of us are conformists. At the same time, we yearn to look and act a *little* different from others. We probably are not in revolt against custom; we simply wish to be a bit distinctive but not be accused of having bad taste or disregarding norms. Fashion furnishes the opportunity for self-expression.

Fashion-Adoption Process

The fashion-adoption process reflects the concepts of (1) cultural, social-class, and reference-group influences on consumer buying behavior, as discussed in Chapter 4, and (2) the diffusion of innovation, as explained in Chapter 8. People usually try to imitate others at the same or the next higher socioeconomic level. One way of doing this is to purchase a product that is fashionable in the group you want to be like.

Thus the **fashion-adoption process** is a series of buying waves that arise as a particular style is popularly accepted in one group, then another group, and another, until it finally falls out of fashion. This movement, representing the introduction, rise, popular culmination, and decline of the market's acceptance of a style, is referred to as the **fashion cycle.** A case can be made that synthetic fibers such as polyester in clothing and the convertible model of automobile are two products that have run the full fashion cycle.

There are three theories of fashion adoption, as depicted in Figure 9.4:

- **Trickle-down,** where a given fashion cycle flows *downward* through several socioeconomic levels.
- **Trickle-across,** where the cycle moves *horizontally* and *simultaneously within* several socioeconomic levels.
- **Trickle-up,** where a style first becomes popular at lower socioeconomic levels and then flows *upward* to become popular among higher levels.

Traditionally, the *trickle-down* theory has been used to explain the fashion-adoption process. As an example, designers of women's apparel first introduce a style to opinion leaders in the upper socioeconomic groups. If they accept the style, it quickly appears in leading fashion stores. Soon the middle-income and then the lower-income markets want to emulate the leaders, and the style is mass marketed. As its popularity wanes, the style appears in bargain-price stores and finally is no longer considered fashionable.

The *trickle-up* process also explains some product-adoption processes. Consider how styles of music such as jazz and rap became popular. Also look at blue denim pants and jackets, athletic footwear, even pasta in the 1990s, and so-called urban clothing in recent years.[32] They all have one thing in common: They were popular first with lower socioeconomic groups, and later their popularity "trickled up" to higher-income markets.

Today the *trickle-across* theory best explains the adoption process for most fashions. It's true that there is some flow downward, and obviously there is an upward flow. But, by means of modern production, communication, and transportation, companies can disseminate style information and products so rapidly that all social levels can be reached at about the same time.

Recognizing this accelerated adoption process, most apparel manufacturers produce a wide *variety* of essentially one style. They also produce distinct *qualities* of the same basic style so as to appeal to different income groups.[33] For example, within a

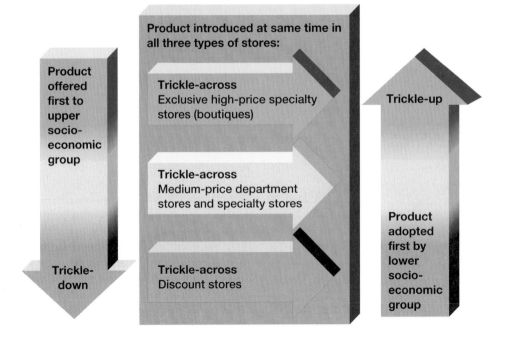

FIGURE 9.4

Fashion-Adoption Processes.

few weeks of the beginning of the fall season, the same style of dress (but at different quality levels) appears in (1) small, exclusive dress shops appealing to the upper social class, (2) large department stores aiming at the middle class, and (3) discount houses and low-price women's ready-to-wear chain stores, where the target is the portion of the lower class that has some disposable income.

Within each class, the dresses are purchased early in the season by the opinion leaders—the innovators. If the style is accepted, its sales curve rises as it becomes popular with the early adopters and then with the late adopters. Eventually, sales decline as the style loses popularity. This cycle is a horizontal movement, occurring virtually simultaneously within each of several socioeconomic levels.

Marketing Considerations in Fashion

Accurate forecasting is critical to success in fashion merchandising. This is extremely difficult, however, because the forecaster must deal with complex sociological and psychological factors. On-target forecasting—indeed, effective marketing—has become increasingly difficult in the clothing industry in recent years. One reason: Smaller numbers of female consumers are responding to annual style changes; many women are simply buying fewer clothes. Another reason: The trend in which firms allowed—even encouraged—casual dress by workers has slowed, perhaps reversed. In fact, sales of business suits and other tailored clothing have had double-digit annual increases in recent years. Several factors probably underlie the increased interest in "dressing up," including consumers' weariness with casual wear and a desire by businesspeople and other professionals to be taken seriously during a period when there is still economic uncertainty.[34]

When a firm's products are subject to the fashion cycle, management must know what stage the cycle is in at all times. Managers must decide at what point to get into the cycle and when to get out. Frequently a manufacturer or a retailer of fashionable items operates largely on intuition and inspiration, tempered by considerable experience.

Ordinarily a retailer cannot participate successfully in all stages of the fashion cycle at the same time. Thus a specialty apparel store—whose stocks are displayed in limited numbers without price tags—should get in at the start of a fashion trend. And a department store appealing to the middle-income market should plan to enter the cycle in time to mass-market the style as it is climbing to its peak of popularity. For example, given its middle-income target market, Sears has strived to have its clothing stay within one year of the latest styles. Fundamentally, retail executives must keep in mind the product's target market in deciding at which stage(s) of the life cycle its stores should offer fashionable apparel.[35]

Summary

Many strategic decisions must be made to manage a company's assortment of products effectively. To start, a firm must select strategies regarding its product mix. One decision is how to position the product relative to competing products and other products sold by the firm.

Another strategic decision is whether or how to expand the product mix by adding items to a line and/or introducing new lines. Altering the design, packaging, or other features of existing products is still another option among the strategies of selecting the best mix. The product mix also can be changed by eliminating an entire line or by simplifying the assortment within a line. Alternatively, management may elect to trade up or trade down relative to existing products.

Executives need to understand the concept of a product life cycle, which reflects the total sales volume for a generic product category. Each of the cycle's four stages—introduction, growth, maturity, and decline—has distinctive characteristics that have implications for marketing. Managing a product as it moves through its life cycle presents a number of challenges and opportunities. Eventually, a product category may lack adequate acceptance; at that point, all or most companies should abandon their versions of this product.

Planned obsolescence is a controversial product strategy, built around the concepts of style, fashion, and the fashion cycle. Fashion—essentially a sociological and psychological phenomenon—follows a reasonably predictable pattern. With advances in communications and production, the fashion-adoption process has moved away from the traditional trickle-down pattern. Today the process is better described as trickle-across. There also are examples of fashions trickling up. Managing a product, such as expensive apparel, through a fashion cycle may be even more challenging than adjusting another type of product's strategies during its life cycle.

More about KODAK

The Eastman Kodak Co. is best known for its ubiquitous yellow film packages. However, even when film photography was dominant, Kodak generated substantial revenues from other product lines. Now, with the shift to digital imaging, these product lines are critical to the firm's plan to not only solidify its future vitality but also regain its stellar worldwide reputation.

Eastman Kodak's product mix includes an array of product lines focused on four areas:

- Digital and film imaging, not just for amateurs, but also for professionals and cinematographers;
- Health imaging, especially products for the medical and dental fields;
- Graphic communications, spanning an array of printing and scanning applications; and
- Displays and components, concentrating on leading-edge display devices.

In 2003, Eastman Kodak decided to emphasize nonphotographic areas in the future. It wants to be a major player in the market for printers, from inexpensive ink-jet models for consumers to very expensive digital machines for large organizations. These product spaces are already crowded, with consumers able to choose among various brands including Epson, Canon, and Hewlett-Packard, and business buyers having multiple options such as Xerox and HP. Eastman Kodak is acquiring firms that will allow it to be a more formidable competitor in the high-end digital-printer market.

Eastman Kodak has other successful lines that do not have much public exposure. For example, the year after X-ray technology was invented, Kodak began selling a type of paper that was designed specifically for capturing X-ray images. Now Eastman Kodak is a leader in health imaging, offering various complex products such as digital radiography systems and picture archiving and communications systems.

Also since 1896, Eastman Kodak has sold specially coated film that is used in making theatrical movies. In fact, *all* of the movies that have won the Oscar for "Best Picture" were recorded on Kodak film. Introduced in 2002, Kodak Vision2 film is intended to work well with digital technologies used in the postproduction phase of making a movie ready for commercial audiences.

In the future, Eastman Kodak intends to be a leader in "infoimaging," which the company describes as "the use of technology to combine images and information—creating the potential to profoundly change how people and businesses communicate." Applications related to infoimaging include means for printing images captured by mobile phones and brighter, more energy-efficient displays for digital cameras, cell phones, and other electronic devices. Clearly, as demand for the yellow boxes of film has shrunk, Eastman Kodak has had to "think outside of the box" in developing a product mix that will give it a good chance for success in the future.[36]

1a. Has Eastman Kodak relied on product-mix expansion, alteration of existing products, or product-mix contraction in the past five years?

1b. Which of these three product-mix strategies will Kodak need to follow in the next five years?

2. How well has Kodak managed its key product lines in relation to their life cycles?

Key Terms and Concepts

Product mix (234)
Breadth (234)
Depth (234)
Product line (234)
Product-mix expansion (237)
Line extension (237)
Mix extension (237)
Product alteration (238)
Product-mix contraction (239)
Trading up (240)

Trading down (240)
Product life cycle (241)
Introduction stage (243)
Growth stage (243)
Maturity stage (243)
Decline stage (243)
Fad (244)
First-mover advantage (246)
Product abandonment (248)
Planned obsolescence (249)

Technological obsolescence (249)
Style obsolescence (249)
Style (249)
Fashion (249)
Fashion-adoption process (249)
Fashion cycle (250)
Trickle-down theory (250)
Trickle-across theory (250)
Trickle-up theory (250)

Questions and Problems

1. "It is inconsistent for management to follow concurrently the product-line strategies of *expanding* its product mix and *contracting* its product mix." Discuss.

2. "Trading up and trading down are product strategies closely related to the business cycle. Firms trade up during periods of prosperity and trade down during recessions." Do you agree? Why?

3. Name one category of goods and one category of services you believe are in the introductory stage of their life cycles. For each product, identify what market would consider your examples to be truly new.

4. Does the Internet accelerate or delay the movement of a new product category through the introduction stage and into later stages of its life cycle?

5. What are two products that are in the decline stage of the life cycle? In each case, point out whether you think the decline is permanent. What recommendations do you have for rejuvenating the demand for either of these products?

6. How might a company's advertising strategies differ, depending on whether its brand of a product is in the introduction stage or the maturity stage of its life cycle?

7. What products, other than apparel and automobiles, stress fashion and style in marketing? Do styles exist among business products?

8. Is the trickle-across theory applicable to the fashion-adoption process in product lines other than women's apparel? Explain, using examples.

9. Planned obsolescence is criticized as a social and economic waste because we are urged to buy things we do not like and do not need. What is your opinion? If you object to planned obsolescence, what are your recommendations for correcting the situation?

Interactive Marketing Exercises

1. Select a product category in which you are interested. Go to either the Internet or the library and identify the national or state trade association for this product category. Then obtain from the association sales figures for this product over its history and other information that will allow you to plot the life cycle for this product. What stage of the life cycle is this product in? Explain.

2. Arrange a meeting with a supermarket manager or a department manager in a supermarket. Discuss how the manager handles the challenge of line extensions. In which product category are line extensions most common? When new items are added to the line, how does the manager find space for the new entries—by giving more space to this category, dropping other items carrying this same brand, pruning other brands in this category, or some other means? What criteria are used in making this decision?

Chapter 10

Realistically, could General Motors reverse the fortunes of its fading Cadillac brand?

Brands, Packaging, and Other Product Features

Has CADILLAC Been Revitalized?

About four decades ago, the Cadillac brand signified luxury and status to automobile buyers. Although Cadillacs were among the highest priced cars on the market, demand from successful and relatively wealthy consumers was strong.

By the late 1990s, however, the Cadillac brand had lost much of its luster as well as significant market share. The problem was that Cadillac autos came to be viewed as "geriatric-friendly land yachts." Equally bad, too many car buyers considered the Cadillac to be an ordinary vehicle with a high price, which translates to poor value. Some people, including industry analysts, thought that Cadillac was doomed to the junk yard of failed products.

What a humiliating ending that would have been for a once-dominant brand. Founded in 1902 as the Cadillac Automobile Company, the firm was renowned for innovations. For instance, Cadillac produced the first step-in fully enclosed car design and V-8 engine.

For more than three-quarters of a century, Cadillac has been integral to the stable of brands marketed by the General Motors Corp. Chevrolet drew in the mass market of car buyers; Buick, Oldsmobile, and Pontiac appealed to the middle market; and Cadillac attracted the high-end market. In the 1950s, Cadillac accounted for 80% of all luxury cars purchased in the U.S. Although Cadillac had a relatively small sales volume, as measured by units, the brand was very profitable for GM.

Over time, even though its domestic competition diminished with the demise of the Packard and the Chrysler Imperial, Cadillac faced increasingly stiff competition from foreign brands. Luxury automobiles from Europe and Asia—most notably BMW, Mercedes Benz, Lexus, and Jaguar—gained at Cadillac's expense. Numerous car buyers perceived the imports to be more stylish, better equipped, and/or superior values compared to the Cadillac and the Lincoln brand from Ford Motor Co.

Realistically, could General Motors reverse the fortunes of its fading Cadillac brand? GM is not above abandoning brands, as it did in 2004 with Oldsmobile. However, the automaker recognized that consumers 50 years of age and older buy more than one-half of all autos in the U.S. In contrast, the 30-and-under segment, normally viewed as a highly desirable target for marketers of consumer goods, makes just one-eighth of all car purchases.

Thus GM decided to try to turn around its most prestigious brand, Cadillac, by focusing on baby boomers. In a period of four years, GM spent over $4 *billion* on this effort. The cornerstone of the new strategy for Cadillac is a series of distinctive designs, a more powerful engine, upbeat, rock-themed television commercials, and complementary promotion. In 2001, Cadillac took the first step by showing off its new CTS model, featuring a distinctive design. Subsequently the Escalade sport-utility vehicle and the STS sedan were introduced. All of the new models featured angular exterior styling and interiors with numerous "creature comforts."

Thus far, the efforts have produced some favorable results. In 2004, GM's high-end brand ranked #1 in the U.S. in sales of luxury vehicles. Cadillac sold over 180,000 units, placing it more than 25,000 units ahead of Mercedes Benz. Also, Cadillac moved in front of Lexus in the much-watched quality ratings compiled by J. D. Power. Equally important, the typical Cadillac buyer is now 59 years old (or young), down from 64 before the turnaround.

Cadillac's revitalization is not complete, however. For example, only about one-quarter of CTS buyers traded in an import. Thus Cadillac is not doing as much competitive damage to foreign-owned luxury brands as it would like to. Still, in contrast to the 1990s, Cadillac's rejuvenation has been receiving good press. One article went so far as to say, "Cadillac is cool again."[1] Is the Cadillac turnaround typical or exceptional with regards to companies' efforts to revitalize fading or failing brands?

www.cadillac.com

As the Cadillac case illustrates, a brand can be very important for many products. Otherwise, how do you account for some consumers wanting Bayer aspirin and others preferring or at least accepting Walgreen's brand, when both are physically and chemically the identical product? Other consumers' choices are influenced not only by the brand but also by the package, design, or another product feature. Because these product features are important elements in a marketing program, we devote this chapter to them. After studying this chapter, you should be able to explain:

Chapter Goals

- The nature and importance of brands.
- Characteristics of a good brand name.
- Branding strategies of producers and middlemen.
- Why and how a growing number of firms are building and using brand equity.
- The nature and importance of packaging and labeling.
- Major packaging strategies.
- The marketing implications of other product features—design, color, and quality—that can satisfy consumers' wants.

Brands

The word *brand* is comprehensive; it encompasses other narrower terms. A **brand** is a name and/or mark intended to identify the product of one seller or group of sellers and to differentiate the product from competing products. *Brand* is also used, not really correctly, to refer to a specific product, as in "sales of the brand."[2]

A **brand name** consists of words, letters, and/or numbers that can be vocalized. A **brand mark** is the part of the brand that appears in the form of a symbol, design, or distinctive color or lettering. A brand mark is recognized by sight but cannot be expressed when a person pronounces the brand name. Crest, FUBU, and Bearing Point (formerly KPMG Consulting) are brand names. Brand marks are the U.S. Postal Service's stylized eagle's head inside a trapezoid and the Nike "swoosh." Green Giant (canned and frozen vegetable products) and Arm & Hammer (baking soda) are both brand names and brand marks. Sometimes the term *logo* (short for *logotype*) is used interchangeably with brand mark or even brand name, especially if the name is written in a distinctive, stylized fashion.

www.fubu.com

A **trademark** is a brand that has been adopted by a seller and given legal protection. (A trademark for a service has come to be called, not surprisingly, a *service mark*. Our use of *trademark* also covers *service mark*.) A trademark includes not just the brand mark, as many people believe, but also the brand name. The Lanham Act of 1946 permits firms to register trademarks with the federal government to protect them from use or misuse by other companies. The Trademark Law Revision Act, which took effect in 1989, is intended to strengthen the registration system to the benefit of U.S. firms. Recently, officials of the U.S. and Japanese governments as well as the European Union entered into an agreement that should expedite trademark registration in these countries.[3]

Companies strive vigorously, even filing lawsuits, to protect their trademarks. Recent instances include Gateway, the computer maker, filing suit against a company for imitating its black-and-white cow pattern on another product. Also, the World Wrestling Federation and the World Wildlife Fund grappled over the initials WWF. Eventually, a court ruled in favor of the wildlife group; subsequently, the wrestling enterprise changed its initials to WWE, with "E" representing Entertainment.[4]

www.worldwildlife.org

One method of classifying brands is on the basis of who owns them. Thus we have **producers' brands** and **middlemen's brands,** the latter being owned by retailers or wholesalers. Florsheim (shoes), Prozac (Eli Lilly & Company's antidepressant drug), Courtyard by Marriott (lodging), and Qantas (an Australian airline) are pro-

A company trying to establish a global brand may find another firm using the same brand in some countries. For example, Anheuser-Busch Companies (A-B), the St. Louis–based brewery, isn't the only company placing the Budweiser brand on beer. A century-old brewery in the Czech Republic, Budejovicky Budvar, sells a Budweiser brew in parts of eastern Europe as well as Germany. The American brand is sold throughout most of the rest of the world. Further, the Czech brand is called "the beer of kings," and the American brand "the king of beers."

What's the problem? Essentially, both brewers lay claim to the Budweiser trademark. A-B began making Budweiser beer in the U.S. in 1876. Then in 1895, Czechs in a community called Budweis started a brewery to make and sell its own Budweiser beer. When the two enterprises began to expand into other countries, the dispute over the Budweiser trademark erupted.

Eventually, in 1939, the two competitors agreed to divide up the world market with respect to where each concern could use the Budweiser brand. Thus A-B affixes various names on its product in European countries—the well-known Budweiser in some, but Bud, American Bud, and Anheuser-Busch B in others. The only area in which both brewers use the Budweiser brand is Great Britain.

Wanting to develop its version of Budweiser as a global brand, A-B persisted in seeking an agreement with Budvar. In late 1995, A-B offered to pay the Czech brewery $200 million for the worldwide rights to the Budweiser name. Because the name is so well known, the Czech brewery saw added sales potential for its own Budweiser brand and, consequently, rejected A-B's proposal. Now the Czech beer is available in some parts of the U.S. under the Czechvar brand.

In early 2005, a court in Brussels decided that the Czech brewer could use both the Budvar and Budweiser brands in Belgium, Luxembourg, and the Netherlands. More recently, the World Trade Organization issued a ruling in A-B's favor, essentially thwarting Budvar's attempt to remove A-B's exclusive trademark rights in some European Union countries. This "cold war" continues as the brewing companies battle over their brand names in at least 40 countries.

 www.budvar.cz

Sources: Gregory Cancelada, "A-B Wins a Round over Budvar in WTO Ruling on Budweiser," *St. Louis Post-Dispatch,* Mar. 17, 2005, pp. D1, D8; "Czech Brewery Claims Victory over Anheuser-Busch in Benelux," *Associated Press Worldstream,* Jan. 27, 2005, no pages given; Katka Krosnar, "Brewers Go Head to Head in Battle of the Buds," *Agence France Presse,* Oct. 24, 2004, no pages given; and Roger Thurow, "The King of Beers and Beer of Kings Are at Lagerheads," *The Wall Street Journal,* Apr. 3, 1992, p. A1.

ducers' brands; Lucerne (Safeway), Craftsman (Sears), and St. John's Bay (JCPenney) are middlemen's brands.

The terms *national* and *private* have been used to describe producer and middleman brand ownership, respectively. However, marketing people prefer the *producer–middleman* terminology. To say that a brand of poultry feed marketed in three states by a small Birmingham, Alabama, manufacturer is a *national* brand, or that the brands of Wal-Mart and Sears are *private* brands, stretches the meaning of these two terms.

Reasons for Branding

For consumers, brands make it easy to identify goods or services. They aid shoppers in moving quickly through a supermarket, discount outlet, or other retail store and in making purchase decisions. Brands also help assure consumers that they will get consistent quality when they reorder.

For sellers, brands can be promoted. They are easily recognized when displayed in a store or included in advertising. Branding reduces price comparisons. That is, because brands are another factor to be considered in comparing different products, branding reduces the likelihood of purchase decisions that are based solely on price. The reputation of a brand also influences customer loyalty among buyers of services as well as business and consumer goods. Finally, branding can differentiate commodities (Sunkist oranges, Morton salt, and Domino sugar, for example). A wholesaler has even established a Hearts on Fire brand for diamonds.[5]

 www.hearts-on-fire.com

Not all brands are widely and favorably recognized by their target markets. And among those that are, many are unable to maintain a position of prominence. However, as a result of such activities as aggressive promotion and careful quality control, a few brands (Chevrolet autos and Fidelity mutual funds) retain their leadership positions over a long time. Consequently, enormous amounts of money are spent to acquire companies that have widely recognized brands. Italy's Gucci Group bought another firm in order to acquire several well-known brands, including Yves Saint Laurent (luxury fashion accessories) and Van Cleef & Arpels (fragrances); later, another firm bought the Gucci Group and its assortment of high-end brands. Recently, the Procter & Gamble Co. agreed to pay more than $50 *billion* to purchase the Gillette Co., acquiring not only the famous Gillette name but also other popular brands such as Oral-B, Braun, and Duracell.[6]

Reasons for Not Branding

Two responsibilities come with brand ownership: (1) promoting the brand and (2) maintaining a consistent quality of output. Many firms do not brand their products because they are unable or unwilling to assume these responsibilities.

Some items remain unbranded because they cannot be physically differentiated from other firms' products. Clothespins, nails, and raw materials (coal, cotton, wheat) are examples of goods for which product differentiation, including branding, is generally unknown. The perishable nature of products such as fresh fruits and vegetables works against branding. However, well-known brands such as Dole pineapples and Chiquita bananas demonstrate that even agricultural products can be branded successfully.

Selecting a Good Brand Name

Some brand names are so good that they contribute to the success of products. Consider, for example, DieHard batteries and the Roach Motel (which is a pest-eradication device, not a discount motel). But it takes more than a clever brand name to ensure success in the marketplace. Witness Trans World Airlines, the aptly named airline that eventually faltered and was acquired by a competitor. Other brand names are so poor that they are a factor in product failures. Occasionally products achieve success despite poor brand names—consider Exxon (now part of ExxonMobil), which had no meaning when it was first introduced.

Despite the difficulty of differentiating a commodity, Morton International succeeded in creating a well-known, favored brand of salt. Some Morton ads, including this one, have been aimed at reinforcing the brand name; others promote new uses for the product.

www.mortonsalt.com

Choosing a name for a product may appear trivial, but it's not. One consultant went so far (perhaps too far) as to say, "The most important element in a marketing program—and the one over which marketing managers can exert the most control—is the naming of a product."[7]

The Challenge

Nowadays, selecting a good brand name for a new product is especially challenging. The reason? We're running out of possibilities. On the one hand, about 10,000 new products are launched annually; on the other hand, only 50,000 words comprise the standard desk-size dictionary. Further, many words either already adorn products (such as Pert Plus, Cascade, and Veryfine) or are unsuitable as brand names (such as obnoxious, hypocrite, and deceased). Following the late-2004 natural disaster in the area of the Indian Ocean, tsunami became an undesirable name for some brands and companies.[8]

web.net2phone.com

www.ameritrade.com

One solution is to combine numbers with words, numbers, and/or letters to form a brand name. Examples include Net2Phone (an Internet telecommunications service), Formula 409 (household cleaner), WD-40 (lubricant and protectant), and Lotus 1-2-3 (software). Another possibility is to create a brand name that isn't part of the English language. Examples of so-called *morphemes* include Ameritrade stock brokerage, Lexus autos, Google search engine, and Compaq computers.[9]

Desirable Characteristics

Various characteristics determine the desirability of a brand name for either a good or a service.[10] It's difficult to find a brand name that rates well on every attribute. Still, a brand name should have as many of the following five characteristics as possible:

- *Suggest something about the product, particularly its benefits and use.* Names connoting benefits include Beautyrest, Mr. Goodwrench, and Minute Rice. Product use is suggested by Dustbuster, Ticketron, and La-Z-Boy chairs.

Ralston Purina devised the brand name of Beneful for a line of dog food. Does this brand pass the test of suggesting what the product's benefits or uses are? If you think "beneficial" or "benefit" when you see Beneful, then it certainly does. Also, the ad's last line is "Healthful. Flavorful. Beneful," placing a thought in consumers' minds about the last part of the name. Does the brand have the other four characteristics of a desirable brand name?

www.beneful.com

- *Be easy to pronounce, spell, and remember.* Simple, short, one-syllable names such as Tide, Ban, Aim, and Surf are helpful. However, even some short names, such as Aetna and Inacom, aren't easily pronounced by some consumers. Other brands that may not meet this criterion, at least not in the U.S., include Frusen-Glädje (ice cream), Au Bon Pain (bakeries), and Asahi (beer).

www.aubonpain.com

- *Be distinctive.* Brands with names like National, Star, Ideal, United, Allied, or Standard fail on this point. Many services firms begin their brand names with adjectives connoting strength and then add a description of the business, creating brands such as Allied Van Lines and United Parcel Service. But are these really distinctive?

- *Be adaptable to additions to the product line.* A family name such as Kellogg, Lipton, or Ford may serve the purpose better than a highly distinctive name suggesting product benefits. When fast-food restaurants added breakfasts to their menus, McDonald's name fit better than Burger King or Pizza Hut. Likewise, names like Alaska Airlines and Southwest Airlines may inhibit geographic expansion more than a name such as United Airlines.

- *Be capable of registration and legal protection.* Brand names are covered under the Lanham Act, its 1989 revision, and other laws.

The naming process isn't cheap, costing $25,000 and up for the name itself. Then an organization typically has to spend much more than that to promote the new brand.

To protect its famous brand name, Xerox ran humorous ads to make a serious point, namely that Xerox is a brand name. The ads stressed that Xerox is neither a verb nor a common noun. Also note that the ad indicated that "Xerox" should be used in conjunction with a noun, such as "copier."

www.xerox.com

"But Mr. Carruthers, you said you needed forty Xeroxes."

Mr. Carruthers used our name incorrectly. That's why he got 40 Xerox copiers, when what he really wanted was 40 copies made on his Xerox copier.

He didn't know that Xerox, as a trademark of Xerox Corporation, should be followed by the descriptive word for the particular product, such as "Xerox duplicator" or "Xerox copier."

And should only be used as a noun when referring to the corporation itself.

If Mr. Carruthers had asked for 40 copies or 40 photocopies made on his Xerox copier, he would have gotten exactly what he wanted.

And if you use Xerox properly, you'll get exactly what you want, too.

P.S. You're welcome to make 40 copies or 40 photocopies of this ad. Preferably on your Xerox copier.

XEROX

Should a company try to thwart counterfeit products?

According to a "guesstimate" by the World Customs Organization, fake versions of branded products account for 5% to 7%, perhaps $500 billion, of global merchandise trade. Knockoffs can be found in virtually every category of goods, such as ink-jet cartridges, golf clubs, power tools, computer chips, and motorcycles. Occasionally, fake components are incorporated into authentic products (such as a phony battery in a Kyocera cell phone). Perhaps most frightening, the World Health Organization estimates that as much as 10% of medicines are not real. That is, they are not made by the company that owns the brand on the package and, in some cases, do not contain any or all of the vital ingredients.

Why and how do companies make phony products? The primary reason is the same motive as for the rest of commerce, namely profitable revenues. Professional, rather than amateur, methods such as the following are commonly used to make phony products:

- Counterfeiters employ high-tech devices, including three-dimension design software, to "reverse engineer" (that is, figure out how to copy) well-known products.

- Relying on digital technology, the pirating firms can produce packaging that is almost a replica of what is used by the authentic brand.

- The counterfeiting companies have figured out how to imitate security devices, such as holograms, that are intended to distinguish real from fake products.

The most popular location for counterfeiters is China, which accounts for about two-thirds of bogus goods. The U.S. government is very troubled by this situation. Seeking assistance in efforts to curb counterfeiting, the Commerce Secretary demanded that the Chinese government police the widespread violations vigorously. Now that China-based firms are knocking off popular Chinese brands, enforcement is expected to increase.

Counterfeiters can't be eliminated, but companies can take the following steps to battle knockoffs:

- Businesses need to watch carefully for counterfeit goods carrying one of their brands.

- Producers—particularly through their trade associations—can offer cash rewards for information about piracy.

- When knockoffs are detected, legal action should be taken against the violators.

- Companies can take preventative measures, such as using new radio-frequency ID tags (more about these in Chapter 16) to monitor the identity and location of an authentic product at all times.

Some companies persist in battling counterfeiters. In that vein, Lego, the Danish toy maker, won a judgment against a Chinese firm that was producing and selling an imitation of the famous building blocks. In a case involving the sale of counterfeit information-security software, Papa B Enterprises agreed to pay $3.2 million to Symantec Corp. and to stop producing and selling fake Symantec products.

Of course, discovering knockoffs is difficult and sometimes occurs almost by chance. Further, the preventative measures and legal battles to reduce the flow of counterfeit products can be very costly. Symantec has its own "director of corporate security and the brand protection task force." Most small companies cannot afford such specialists or the fees incurred in a costly legal battle that may yield a favorable but hollow judgment (i.e., the counterfeiting firm is outside U.S. legal jurisdiction and thus does not make restitution).

Sources: Frederick Balfour, "Fakes!" *BusinessWeek*, Feb. 7, 2005, pp. 54–58+; Dan Neel, "Symantec Settles Suit," *CRN*, June 28, 2004, p. 32; Geoffrey A. Fowler, "Copies 'R' Us," *The Wall Street Journal*, Jan. 31, 2003, p. B1; and Russell E. Brooks and Gila E. Gellman, "Combating Counterfeiting," *Marketing Management*, vol. 2, no. 3, 1993, pp. 49–51.

Protecting a Brand Name

A firm with a well-known, successful brand name needs to actively safeguard it. Otherwise, this valuable asset can be damaged—or even lost entirely—in either of two ways.

Product Counterfeiting
Some unscrupulous manufacturers engage in **product counterfeiting** by placing a highly regarded brand on their offering, disregarding the basic fact that they do not own the rights to the brand. If you have ever been to

In China, product piracy grew to be a big business, with little policing. As a result, the counterfeiters became very bold in promoting their wares. Here, a seller in Shanghai uses a catalog to show the array of imitation purses and watches that are available for purchase in a nearby store.

New York City, you probably have been offered "genuine" Rolex or Gucci watches for $10 to $20 by a street vendor. Counterfeiting can be found in many categories, including leather goods, athletic footwear, software, toys, video games, and automobile replacement parts.

According to the latest estimates, imitation products cost American companies as much as $250 *billion* annually. One study concluded that over 100,000 jobs in the U.S. were lost as a result of piracy in a single category, namely software. Because it's relatively easy to do, and because law enforcement agencies do not vigorously pursue violators, a top FBI official called product counterfeiting "the crime of the 21st century."[11]

Generic Usage Over a period of years, some brand names become so well accepted that they are commonly used instead of the generic names of the particular product categories.[12] Examples follow:

Generic Terms That Formerly Were Brand Names

aspirin	escalator	linoleum	thermos
brassiere	harmonica	nylon	yo-yo
cellophane	kerosene	shredded wheat	zipper

Originally these names were trademarks that could be used only by the owner. What happened? Well, a brand name can become generic in two primary ways:

- There is no simple generic name available, so the public uses the brand name as a generic name. This occurred with shredded wheat, nylon, and cellophane. The Formica Corporation wages an ongoing struggle, thus far successful, to retain the legal status of its Formica brand of decorative laminate.[13]

www.formica.com

- As contradictory as it appears, sometimes a firm is too effective in promoting a brand name. Although not yet legally generic, names such as Band-Aid, Scotch Tape, Kleenex, and TiVo are on the borderline. These brand names have been promoted so heavily and so successfully that many people use them generically. To illustrate, which terms do you use in conversation—facial tissue or Kleenex, Internet search or Google? We suspect the latter in both cases.

There are various means to prevent the generic use of a brand name:

- Right after the brand name, place the ® symbol (if the brand is a registered trademark for a good), TM (if it is not registered), or SM (for a service).

- Better yet, use the brand name together with the generic name—Dacron brand polyester, for instance.

- Call attention to and challenge improper use of your brand name. Rollerblade Inc. has gone so far as to sue competitors who use "rollerblade" as a generic word. Google Inc. took the preventative step of contacting an individual to request that he remove the verb "google" from the online dictionary he edits.[14]

Branding Strategies

Both producers and middlemen face strategic decisions regarding the branding of their goods or services.

Producers' Strategies

Producers must decide whether to brand their products and whether to sell any or all of their output under middlemen's brands.

Marketing Entire Output under Producer's Own Brands
Companies that rely strictly on their own brands usually are very large, well financed, and well managed. Maytag and IBM, for example, have broad product lines, well-established distribution systems, and large shares of the market. The reasons why a producer relies strictly on its own brands were covered in the earlier section of this chapter on the importance of branding to the seller.

A small proportion of manufacturers rely strictly on this strategy, refusing to produce items to be sold as retailers' or wholesalers' brands. Gillette is one such company. The firm's top executive said that manufacturing so-called private-label products would be "a sign of weakness." A company vice president was more blunt, "If any manager did that, he should be shot by the shareholders."[15] This stubbornness will not eliminate competition from middlemen, however. Many middlemen want to market under their own brands. If one manufacturer refuses to sell to them, they simply go to another.

It's particularly difficult for a new firm to produce only for its own brands. Only a minority of manufacturers employ this strategy, and the number seems to be decreasing. A primary reason is that there are lots of opportunities to make products to which middlemen apply their own brands.

Intel Corporation produces processors that are an integral fabricating part in computers. The company has used an "Intel Inside" branding strategy and extensive advertising to convince numerous manufacturers and buyers of computers that its processor to competing products. In this ad, Intel promotes its centrino mobile technology, a processor and additional components that are used in laptop computers.

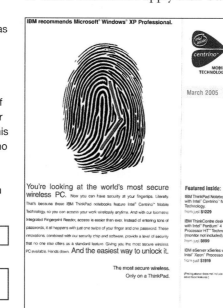

Branding of Fabricating Materials and Parts
Some producers use a strategy of *branding fabricating materials and parts* (manufactured goods that become part of another product following subsequent manufacturing).[16] This strategy is used in marketing Splenda artificial sweetener, Dan River cottons, Acrilan fabrics, and many automotive parts such as spark plugs, batteries, and oil filters. For many years, DuPont and now INVISTA have consistently and successfully used this strategy with Lycra spandex fiber and Stainmaster stain repellant for carpets.

With this strategy, the seller seeks to develop a market preference for its branded parts or materials. Dolby Labs seeks to create a market situation in which buyers insist that a stereo sound system include a Dolby noise-reduction component. This firm wants to convince manufacturers that their stereo sound systems will sell better if they contain Dolby noise-reduction units.

This strategy is most likely to be effective when the particular type of fabricating parts or materials has two characteristics:

- The product is also a consumer good that is bought for replacement purposes—Champion spark plugs and Delco batteries, for example.

- The item is a key part of the finished product—an integral part of an automobile, for instance. Johnson Controls and General Motors are trying to build recognition for, respectively, the HomeLink control pad and the OnStar navigation system. Other manufacturers are likely to follow suit, considering that 44% of consumers said they will take branded auto parts into account when choosing the next brand and model of car they will buy.[17]

www.homelink.com

www.onstar.com

Marketing under Middlemen's Brands   A widespread strategy among manufacturers is to sell part or all of their output to middlemen for branding by these customers. Firms such as Borden, Keebler, and Reynolds Metals have their own well-known brands, and they also produce goods for branding by middlemen.

This approach allows a manufacturer to "hedge its bets." A company employing this strategy hopes its own brands will appeal to some loyal customers, whereas middlemen's brands are of interest to other, perhaps more cost-conscious shoppers. Moreover, for a manufacturer, the output produced for middlemen's brands ordinarily represents additional sales. This strategy also helps a manufacturer fully utilize its plant capacity.

One drawback of this strategy is that the manufacturer may lose some customers for its own brands. Another drawback to marketing under middlemen's brands is that the producer's revenues depend on the strength of the middleman's marketing campaign for that brand. This problem grows as the proportion of a producer's output going to middlemen's brands increases.

Middlemen's Strategies

Middlemen must also answer the question of whether to brand.

Carry Only Producers' Brands   Most retailers and wholesalers carry only producers' brands. Why? They do not have the finances or other resources to promote a brand and maintain its quality.

Carry Both Producers' and Middlemen's Brands   Many large retailers and some large wholesalers stock popular producers' brands and also have their own labels. Sears, for instance, offers an assortment of manufacturers' brands such as Healthtex children's clothing and Bridgestone tires as well as its own brands such as Kenmore appliances and Craftsman tools.

Middlemen may find it advantageous to market their own brands in place of or in addition to producers' brands, because it increases their control over their target markets. A retailer's brand can differentiate its products. If customers prefer a given retailer's brand, sometimes called a *store brand*, they can get it only from that retailer. Examples include:

www.nordstrom.com

Some Retailers' Brands
Nordstrom: Classiques Entier, Caslon
Target: Archer Farms, Michael Graves
Wal-Mart: Ol' Roy, George, Sam's Choice

Traditionally, a retailer's own brand was the lowest price point in each product category. Now, many merchants realize that store brands represent one of their best opportunities to create and offer distinctive merchandise *and* to boost their profit margins. In this case, Macy's displays its Hotel Collection by Charter Club, an assortment of luxurious bedding with prices ranging up to $1,350 for an Italian-made duvet.

Prices on producers' brands sometimes are cut drastically when retail stores carrying these brands compete with each other. For an extended time, clothing carrying the labels of designers such as Ralph Lauren and Liz Claiborne was subject to price cutting. A retailer might avoid at least some of this price competition by establishing its own appealing brands. Department stores, ranging from Famous-Barr to JCPenney, are placing more emphasis on store brands. One consultant estimated that store brands will soon account for about 35% of department stores' volume, compared to about 12% 10 years ago.[18]

Furthermore, middlemen usually can sell their brands at prices below those of producers' brands and still earn higher gross margins. For example, in dry cereals, a store brand may provide up to twice as much gross profits as a producer's brand.[19] This is possible because middlemen often can acquire merchandise carrying their own brands at lower costs than similar merchandise carrying producers' brands. Costs may be lower because manufacturers have to pay to advertise and sell their own brands, but these expenses are not included in the prices of products sold for branding by middlemen. In some cases, but fewer than in the past, costs may be lower because the quality of the products carrying middlemen's brands is lower than the quality of competing products bearing producers' brands. Also, producers may offer good prices in this situation because they are anxious to get the extra business.

Middlemen have to be careful in pricing their own brands. According to one study, if store brands of groceries are not priced at least 10% below producers' brands, many consumers will not buy them. However, if the store brand is more than 20% lower in price, some consumers become suspicious about quality. In contrast, another study concluded that other factors such as relative quality are more important than price level in determining the success of middlemen's brands versus producers' brands.[20]

Middlemen's brands have had their greatest impact in the marketing of consumer packaged goods, such as groceries and personal care products. The Safeway supermarket chain has long relied on Lucerne and other brands it owns. Loblaw's, the largest supermarket chain in Canada, has found great success with its President's Choice (PC) brand. According to one source, upwards of 40% of Wal-Mart's sales comes from its own brands. Wal-Mart's Great Value brand, which is on such products as bread and cereal, rings up $5 *billion* annually. And Ol' Roy is the top-selling brand of dog food, outpacing Nestlé's Purina brand.[21]

Middlemen's brands are now on about one of every five items sold in supermarkets, drug stores, and discount outlets in the U.S. The outlook for middlemen's brands is strong, with one study indicating that 60% of retailers plan to place more emphasis on middlemen's brands. According to one estimate, the private-brand food business accounts for $100 billion in volume in North America, which is about three times the volume for private brands *in all product categories* just 10 years earlier. Clearly, retailers are relying more and more on store brands, and enjoying considerable success with them.[22]

To counter middlemen's brands, some large manufacturers cut their prices. For most, that was a short-lived strategy because it harmed profit margins and didn't build consumer loyalty. Other manufacturers, including Gillette, concentrate on convincing consumers of the superiority of their brands in relation to private brands. Still others are pruning their product mixes and lines. The resources are being shifted to efforts to build "superbrands." P&G has that vision for Pamper diapers and Iams dog food.

All factors considered, neither producers' brands nor middlemen's brands have demonstrated a convincing competitive superiority over the other in the marketplace. Consequently, the "battle of the brands" shows every indication of remaining intense.[23]

Strategies Common to Producers and Middlemen

Producers and middlemen alike must choose strategies with respect to branding their product mixes, branding for market saturation, and joint branding activity with another company.

Branding within a Product Mix

At least three different strategies are used by firms that sell more than one product:

- *A separate name for each product.* This strategy is employed by Lever Brothers and Procter & Gamble. Citigroup, the largest financial services firm in the U.S., still emphasizes some of its individual brands (such as Smith Barney and Diners Club) while also using the "Citi" part of its corporate identity in other brand names (such as Citibank and Citimortgage). To reduce brand confusion, Inter-Continental Hotels Group removed the Holiday Inn name from its upscale Crowne Plaza establishments.[24]

- *The company name combined with a product name.* Examples include Johnson's Pledge and Johnson's Glo-Coat, and Kellogg's Rice Krispies and Kellogg's Corn Pops.

- *The company name alone.* Today few companies rely exclusively on this policy. However, it is followed for the most part by Heinz and Libby in the food field as well as by General Electric in various industries.

www.armorall.com/
prodcat

Using the company name for branding purposes, often termed **family branding,** makes it simpler and less expensive to introduce new, related products to a line.[25] Also, the prestige of a brand can be spread more easily if it appears on several products rather than on only one. Armor All Products took advantage of the smashing success of Armor All Protectant by adding other car care products, such as Armor All Auto Glass Cleaner and Armor All Spray On Car Polish. The company name is best suited for marketing products that are related in quality, in use, or in some other manner.

Branding with the company name places a greater burden on the firm to maintain consistent quality among all products. One bad item can reflect unfavorably, even disastrously, on all other products carrying the same brand. For this reason, many companies prefer to let each individual product succeed or fail on its own—the first branding strategy in the list above.

Branding for Market Saturation

With increasing frequency, firms are employing a **multiple-brand strategy** to increase their total sales in a market. They have more than one brand of essentially the same product, aimed either at the same target market or at distinct target markets. Suppose, for example, that a company has built one type of sales appeal around a given brand. To reach other segments of the market, the company may use other appeals with other brands. Two Procter & Gamble detergents, Tide and Dreft, illustrate this point. Some people feel that if Tide is strong enough to clean soiled work clothes, it should not be used on lingerie and other fine clothing. For these people P&G has Dreft, a detergent promoted as being gentler than Tide.

Not surprisingly, ConAgra Foods, Inc. is interested in capitalizing on the widespread recognition of its Healthy Choice brand. As indicated by this insert distributed in Sunday newspapers, the Healthy Choice has been applied to soups and ice cream products in addition to frozen dinners.

www.healthychoice.com

Sometimes, multiple brands are necessary to penetrate separate target markets. For instance, Black & Decker (B&D) tools have strong appeal to do-it-yourselfers but not to professional tradespeople. Hence, B&D removed its company name from power tools aimed at tradespeople and switched to DeWalt, the name of a maker of high-quality stationary saws that was acquired by Black & Decker years ago.[26]

Cobranding More and more often, two separate companies or two divisions within the same company agree to place both of their respective brands on a particular product or enterprise. This arrangement is termed **cobranding,** or *dual branding.*

Cobranding is evident in the food products field and also in franchising. Boxes of Betty Crocker cake mix proclaim that the product contains Hershey's fudge. Sunkist lemons, Knott's Berry Farm cherries, and Ocean Spray cranberries are ingredients of other products, such as Betty Crocker's Sunkist Lemon Bars mix. In franchising, cobranding occurs when two or more companies—often in the restaurant field—agree to share the same or adjacent retail space. As one example involving divisions of the same company, Yum! Brands sometimes pairs two of its restaurants (A&W, KFC, Long John Silver's, Pizza Hut, and Taco Bell) in the same location. Such cobranding is intended to maximize drawing power and space efficiency.[27]

As with any marketing strategy or tactic, cobranding has potential benefits and drawbacks. This form of cooperation can result in a differential advantage over competitors. Cobranding can provide added revenues for one or both of the participating firms. When two franchises cooperate, they may ring up greater combined sales than if they were in separate locations. The biggest potential drawbacks to cobranding are possible overexposure of a brand name and, even more significant, the risk of damaging a brand's reputation if the cooperative endeavor fails.

Building and Using Brand Equity

In the minds of many consumers, just having a brand name such as Verizon, Nabisco, Hilton, or Hallmark adds value to a product. In particular, brands like these connote favorable attributes (such as quality or economy). What we're talking about is **brand equity,** which is the value a brand adds to a product.[28]

The leading brands, according to three different studies, are shown in Table 10.1. The Harris poll reported in the left column asked consumers which brands they "consider the best." In contrast, the Interbrand-*Business Week* project judged the worth of a brand to be the present value of future earnings that can be attributed to the brand itself. The other Harris poll, called EquiTrend, focuses more on specific products rather than on wide-ranging brands that are sometimes corporate names. To gauge brand equity, EquiTrend takes into account familiarity, quality, purchase intent, brand expectations, and distinctiveness.

TABLE 10.1　The Leading Brands—Based on Different Criteria

Rank	Harris Interactive— Best Brands	Interbrand-*BusinessWeek* Brand Value	Harris Interactive— Brand Equity
1.	Sony	Coca-Cola	Reynolds Wrap aluminum foil
2.	Coca-Cola	Microsoft	Hershey's milk chocolate candy bars
3.	Dell	IBM	Ziploc food bags
4.	Kraft	GE	Heinz ketchup
5.	Toyota	Intel	Duracell batteries
6.	Ford	Nokia	WD-40 spray lubricant
7.	Honda	Disney	Kleenex facial tissues
8.	Procter & Gamble	McDonald's	Kraft
9.	General Electric	Toyota	Clorox bleach
10.	General Motors	Marlboro	Oreo cookies

Sources: "Sony Tops the List in Annual 'Best Brands' Survey for Fifth Consecutive Year," *www.harrisinteractive.com/harris%5Fpoll/index.asp?PID=479,* accessed Feb. 19, 2005; "The 100 Top Brands," *BusinessWeek,* Aug. 1, 2005, pp. 90–92, 94; and "Reynolds Wrap Aluminum Foil Ranks #1 in OVERALL Brand Equity," *www.harrisinteractive.com/news/allnewsbydate.asp?NewsID=818,* accessed Feb. 19, 2005.

There is little overlap across the top-10 lists. In fact, no brand was on all three lists, and only four were on two. Also note that only two services—Disney and McDonald's—were on any of the lists. Finally, and not surprising considering that two of the studies polled only American consumers, just four of the leading brands—Sony, Toyota, Honda, and Nokia—originated outside the U.S.

Brands, however they are judged or ranked, are very important assets for a company. The former head of Quaker's food business stated it this way: "If this company were to split up, I would give you the property, plant and equipment and I would take the brands and the trademarks, and I would fare far better than you."[29]

If you're not convinced that a brand name by itself can have much value, consider some research results. In one study, the proportion of subjects choosing corn flakes cereal jumped from 47% when the brand was not known to 59% when the brand was identified as Kellogg's. In another study, when samples of computer buyers were asked how much more or less they would pay for particular brands rather than a relatively unknown brand, there was a range of $339. Brands commanding a premium—that is, possessing substantial equity—included IBM, Compaq, Hewlett-Packard, and Dell.[30]

We tend to think of brand equity as a positive aspect of a product. Occasionally a brand will have negative equity. In such a situation, a brand creates unfavorable impressions about a product in a consumer's mind. For example, after Bridgestone/Firestone Inc. had to recall millions of defective tires, one analyst stated, "You have a serious risk of the Firestone brand imploding." In the services field, Trans World Airlines was plagued by financial problems and uneven customer service for many years. As a result, in the minds of many air travelers, the TWA brand had negative equity. Trans World eventually agreed to be acquired by American Airlines, which eliminated the TWA name.[31]

Building a brand's equity consists of developing a favorable, memorable, and consistent image, which is no easy task.[32] Product quality and advertising play vital roles in this endeavor. However, if substantial brand equity can be achieved, the organization that owns the brand can benefit in several ways:

- The brand itself can become an edge over competition, what we call a *differential advantage,* influencing consumers to buy a particular product. Examples

include Craftsman (Sears' brand for hand tools and gardening equipment), BMW, and Häagen-Dazs.

- Because it is expensive and time-consuming to build brand equity, it creates a barrier for companies that want to enter the market with a similar product.

- The widespread recognition and favorable attitudes surrounding a brand with substantial brand equity can facilitate international expansion. For example, a top executive at McDonald's described what happens when the company brings the Golden Arches to a new country: "It is a huge event. It is a happening. . . . We time and again set new sales records."[33]

- Brand equity can help a product survive changes in the operating environment, such as a business crisis or a shift in consumer tastes.

Brand equity is often used to expand a product mix, especially by extending a product line. Examples include Ocean Spray drinks in flavors other than the original cranberry, and Wesson olive and canola oils. Similarly, all or part of a strong brand name can be applied to a new product line. For instance, there are now Olay cosmetics, Ann Taylor personal care products, Starbucks ice cream, Courtyard by Marriott motels, and Marquis by Waterford crystal ware.[34] The rationale for using an existing, strong brand name on a new item or line is that the brand's equity will convey a favorable impression of the product and increase the likelihood that consumers will at least try it.

If a brand has abundant equity, that does not necessarily mean it should be applied to other products. Procter & Gamble decided its hugely successful Crest name should be used on different kinds of toothpaste but not on other product categories such as mouthwash. In developing a spaghetti sauce, Campbell determined its popular brand name would not convey an Italian image, so it selected Prego as the name for its new sauce. Also, strong equity does not guarantee success for new items or lines using the well-regarded brands. Even with their famous brand names, Harley-Davidson cigarettes, Levi's tailored men's clothing, Dunkin' Donuts cereal, and Swatch clothing did not pass the test of continuing consumer acceptance.

Trademark Licensing

Products with considerable brand equity have strong potential for **trademark licensing,** also called *brand licensing*. For example, Polo/Ralph Lauren licenses its popular brand to numerous companies for their use on various items of apparel. Under a licensing arrangement, the owner of a trademark grants permission (a license) to other firms to use its brand name and brand mark on their products. A licensee, which is the company that receives a license, ordinarily pays a royalty of about 5% to 10% of the wholesale price of each item bearing the licensed trademark. The royalty percentage varies depending on the amount of equity connected with the brand offered by a licensor, which is the company that owns it.

This branding strategy accounted for under $20 billion in retail sales in the early 1980s and now racks up about $100 *billion* in annual volume in the U.S. However, sales of licensed merchandise fluctuate from year to year, primarily as a result of economic conditions. Likewise, the characters that are the basis for licensing agreements tend to come and go rather quickly, from Harry Potter several years ago to SpongeBob SquarePants more recently. One popular area for licensing is toys, but the biggest category of licensed merchandise is apparel. Recognizing that women account for the majority of purchases of licensed items, some manufacturers are designing licensed sports apparel to suit female sizes and tastes. Even New York City decided to expand its licensing program, seeking fees for the use of the trademarks of the city and its agencies such as the New York Fire Department.[35]

Strategic decisions must be made by both the licensor and the licensee. For instance, a licensor such as Pierre Cardin must ask, "Should we allow other firms to use our designer label?" In turn, a potential licensee such as a manufacturer of eyeglass frames must ask, "Do we want to put out a line of high-fashion frames under the Pierre Cardin name?"

Owners of well-known brands are interested in licensing their trademarks for various reasons:

- *It can be very profitable.* There is little expense for the licensor. However, to protect the reputation of its trademark, the licensor must set criteria for granting licenses and monitoring licensing arrangements.

- *There is a promotional benefit.* The licensor's name gets circulation far beyond the original trademarked item. As phrased by the licensing director at Timberland Co., licensing generates both "cash and cachet."[36]

Licensing also offers promise to potential licensees. Specific reasons for acquiring a trademark license are:

- *The likelihood of new-product success may be improved.* It's a lot easier for an unknown firm to get both middlemen and consumers to accept its product if it features a well-known trademark.

- *Marketing costs may be reduced.* One licensee explained that licensing is "a way of taking a name with brand recognition and applying it to your merchandise without having to do the advertising and brand building that is so expensive."[37] Any savings may exceed the royalty fees paid to the licensor.

Packaging and Labeling

Even after a product is developed and branded, strategies must still be devised for other product-related aspects of the marketing mix. One such product feature, and a critical one for some products, is packaging. Closely related to packaging, labeling is another aspect of a product that requires managerial attention.

Purposes and Importance of Packaging

Packaging consists of all the activities of designing and producing the container or wrapper for a product. Packaging is intended to serve several vital purposes:

- *Protect the product on its way to the consumer.* A package protects a product during shipment. Furthermore, it can prevent tampering with products, notably medications and food products, in the warehouse or the retail store. The design and size of a package can also help deter shoplifting. That's why small items, such as compact discs, come in larger-than-needed packages.

- *Protect the product after it is purchased.* Compared with bulk (that is, unpackaged) items, packaged goods generally are more convenient, cleaner, and less susceptible to losses from evaporation, spilling, and spoilage. Also, "childproof" closures thwart children (and sometimes adults) from opening containers of medications and other potentially harmful products.

- *Help persuade middlemen to accept the product.* A product must be packaged to meet the needs of wholesaling and retailing middlemen. For instance, a package's size and shape must be suitable for displaying and stacking the product in the store. An odd-shaped package might attract shoppers' attention, but if it doesn't stack well, the retailer is unlikely to purchase the product.

- *Help persuade consumers to buy the product.* Packaging can help get customers to notice a product. Here's why that is important: "The average shopper spends 20 minutes in the store, viewing 20 products a second."[38] At the point of purchase—such as a supermarket aisle—the package can serve as a "silent sales person." In the case of middlemen's brands, which typically are not advertised heavily, packaging must serve as the means of communicating with shoppers.

When shopping in a supermarket or a discount store, have you ever noticed how similar the packages of some products are to the packages of their direct competitors? That's no coincidence. In fact, it's a common practice for retail chains to use "copycat" packaging. Essentially, the chains put their own brands of products, such as shampoos and liquid window cleaners, in packages with virtually identical shapes and colors to those used by the leading brands, such as Pert Plus and Windex. Middlemen hope that by having virtually identical packaging, the favorable attributes of the leading brand will carry over to the private brand, boosting its sales.

Is it acceptable behavior for chains to imitate the packaging of leading brands?

Sources: "It's a Wrap," *The Grocer*, Feb. 5, 2005, p. 38; and Justin Martin, "Is It Mr. Clean or Captain Shine?" *Fortune*, July 7, 1997, p. 206.

Historically, packaging was intended primarily to provide protection. Today, with its marketing significance fully recognized, packaging is a major factor in gaining distribution and customers. For example, seeking an edge over competing brands of paints, Dutch Boy switched its packaging from the traditional metal can with a wire handle to a plastic container with a side handle and a pouring spout. Women, in particular, reacted favorably to the new Twist and Pour packaging, which is important considering that more women than men purchase interior paints.[39] In the cases of convenience goods and operating supplies, most buyers consider one well-known brand about as good as another. Thus these types of products might be differentiated by a package feature—no-drip spout, reusable jar, or self-contained applicator (liquid shoe polish and glue, for example).

Ultimately, a package may become a product's differential advantage, or at least a significant part of it. That was certainly true with Coca-Cola and its distinctive contour glass bottle, so much so that the firm replicated the contour shape in bottles made of other materials, such as plastic. The Wolfgang Puck brand of canned coffee hopes for similar success. After the consumer pushes a plastic button on the package, the beverage heats itself (through a chemical reaction) to 145 degrees in about seven minutes. According to one recent survey, 47% of marketers think that packaging will be a "key differentiator of products in the near future."[40]

Packaging Strategies

In managing the packaging of a product, executives must make the following strategic decisions.[41]

Packaging the Product Line

A company must decide whether to develop a family resemblance when packaging related products. **Family packaging** uses either highly similar packages for all products or packages with a common and clearly noticeable feature. Campbell's Soup, for instance, uses visually similar packaging for all of its condensed-soup cans, although minor changes (such as adding pictures of the prepared product) are made in the labels occasionally. When new products are added to a line, recognition and images associated with established products extend to the new ones. Family packaging makes sense when the products are of similar quality and have a similar use.

Multiple Packaging

For many years there has been a trend toward **multiple packaging,** the practice of placing several units of the same product in one container.

A package with an attractive appearance and a useful function can boost a product's sales, as Dean Foods' "chug" container has shown. The single-serving package is used for pints of various milk products and even orange juice in different sizes. The package has helped make milk "cool" to some teenagers, which is critical to the dairy industry in its constant battle with carbonated beverages, juices, and bottled water.

 www.deanfoods.com

Dehydrated soups, motor oil, beer, golf balls, building hardware, candy bars, towels, and countless other products are packaged in multiple units.

Test after test has proved that multiple packaging increases total sales of a product. Several years ago, Coca-Cola introduced the Fridge Pack, a carton that holds 12 cans, has an opening in the front for access, and fits nicely on a shelf in most refrigerators. This seemingly small packaging improvement boosted Coke sales in markets where the Fridge Pack was introduced, essentially because it allows consumers to keep more soft drinks cold.[42]

Changing the Package   When detected, a company needs to correct a poor feature in an existing package, of course. Unless a problem was spotted, firms stayed with a package design for many years. Now, for competitive reasons, packaging strategies and tactics are reviewed annually along with the rest of the marketing mix.[43]

Firms need to monitor—and consider—continuing developments, such as new packaging materials, uncommon shapes, innovative closures, and other new features (measured portions, metered flow). All are intended to provide benefits to middlemen and/or consumers and, as a result, are selling points for marketers.

To increase sales volume, many companies find it costs much less to redesign a package than to conduct an expensive advertising campaign. To attract the teen market, Dean Foods Co. introduced a new single-serving "chug" container that can be resealed and fits in a car's drink holder. Although milk consumption didn't get a boost from the familiar "milk mustache" advertising campaign, milk sales jumped markedly following the introduction of the chug container.[44]

Redesign of packaging is neither easy nor inexpensive, however. This task can cost from $20,000 for a simple, single product to $250,000 for a project that entails a product line and requires consumer research and testing. And these figures do not include the expense of promoting the new package design.[45]

Criticisms of Packaging

Packaging is in the public eye today largely because of environmental issues. Specific concerns are:

- *Packaging that depletes natural resources.* This problem is magnified by firms that prefer larger-than-necessary containers. This criticism has been partially addressed through the use of recycled materials in packaging. A point in favor of packaging is that it minimizes spoilage, thereby reducing a different type of resource waste.

- *Forms of packaging that are health hazards.* Government regulations banned several suspect packaging materials, notably aerosol cans that used chlorofluorocarbons as propellants. Just as important, a growing number of companies are switching from aerosol to pump dispensers.

- *Disposal of used packages.* Consumers' desire for convenience in the form of throwaway containers conflicts with their stated desire for a clean environment. Some discarded packages wind up as litter, others add to solid waste in landfills. This problem can be eased by using biodegradable materials in packaging.

- *Deceptive packaging.* A common problem is that the package size conveys the impression of containing more than the actual contents. Government regulations plus greater integrity on the part of business firms regarding packaging have alleviated this concern to some extent.

- *Expensive packaging.* Even in seemingly simple packaging, such as for soft drinks, as much as one-half the production cost is for the container. Still, effective packaging reduces transportation costs and spoilage losses.

Marketing executives are challenged to address these criticisms. At the same time, they must retain or even enhance the positive features of packaging, such as product protection, consumer convenience, and marketing support.

Labeling

A **label** is the part of a product that carries information about the product and the seller. A label may be part of a package, or it may be a tag attached to the product. Obviously there is a close relationship among labeling, packaging, and branding.

Types of Labels   There are three primary kinds of labels:

- A **brand label** is simply the brand alone applied to the product or package. Some oranges are stamped Sunkist or Blue Goose, and some clothes carry the brand label Sanforized.

- A **descriptive label** gives objective information about the product's use, construction, care, performance, and/or other pertinent features. On a descriptive label for a can of corn, there will be statements concerning the type of corn (golden sweet), style (creamed or in niblet kernels), can size, number of servings, other ingredients, and nutritional contents.

- A **grade label** identifies the product's judged quality with a letter, number, or word. Canned peaches are grade-labeled A, B, and C, and corn and wheat are grade-labeled 1 and 2.

Brand labeling is an acceptable form of labeling, but it does not supply sufficient information to a buyer. Descriptive labels provide more product information but not necessarily all that is needed or desired by a consumer in making a purchase decision.

Statutory Labeling Requirements   Labeling has received its share of criticism. Consumers have charged, for example, that labels contained incomplete or misleading

information and there were a confusing number of sizes and shapes of packages for a given product.

The public's complaints about false or deceptive labeling and packaging have led to a number of federal labeling laws. The Fair Packaging and Labeling Act of 1966 provides for (1) *mandatory* labeling requirements; (2) an opportunity for business to *voluntarily* adopt packaging standards that can limit the proliferation of the same product in different weights and measures; and (3) administrative agencies, notably the Food and Drug Administration and the Federal Trade Commission, with the *discretionary* power to set packaging regulations.

More recently, the Nutrition Labeling and Education Act (NLEA), which was enacted in 1994, established a set of **nutrition labeling** standards for processed foods. The intent of this law is to ensure full disclosure of foods' nutritional contents. Labels must clearly state the amount of calories, fat, cholesterol, sodium, carbohydrates, and protein contained in the package's contents. In addition, the amounts must be stated as a percentage of a daily intake of 2,000 calories. Vitamin and mineral content also must be expressed as a percentage of the recommended daily allowance.[46]

As part of the NLEA, the Food and Drug Administration issued standard definitions for key terms used in labeling, such as *light, lean,* and *good source.* To be labeled *light,* for example, a brand ordinarily has to contain one-half the fat or one-third fewer calories than standard products in this category. The NLEA allows firms to include on labels some health claims, such as fiber's value in preventing heart disease. And companies are permitted to list on labels endorsements of their products from health organizations such as the American Heart Association.

The nutrition labeling changes mandated by the NLEA apply to about 200,000 packaged foods, including meat and poultry products. Supporters of this law argue that the labeling requirements promote improved nutrition, thereby reducing health care costs. Of course, these savings occur only if consumers read the labels and use the information in choosing foods. The results of one study suggest that shoppers obtained and understood more nutrition information following the introduction of nutrition labeling.[47]

Recently, as so-called organic foods grew to about $10 billion in sales, the U.S. Department of Agriculture decided it was necessary to define what qualified as *organic.* For example, animals that are the sources of organic meat, eggs, and dairy products cannot have had any growth hormones or antibiotics. Products certified as organic can display a green-and-white USDA label on their packages.[48]

An amendment to the Fair Packaging and Labeling Act that was implemented in 1994 mandates that metric weights and measures along with traditional American weights and measures (such as inches, pounds, and pints) be shown on the labels of selected products. Rather than replacing the American system, as many companies feared, the metric information is supplementary.[49]

Design, Color, and Quality

A well-rounded program for product planning and development will include strategies and policies on several additional product features. Design, color, and quality are covered in this chapter. Two more features, warranties and postsale service, are covered in Chapter 21 because they closely relate to the implementation of a company's marketing program.

Design

One way to satisfy customers and gain a differential advantage is through **product design,** which refers to the arrangement of elements that collectively form a good or service. Good design can improve the marketability of a product by making it easier to operate, upgrading its quality, improving its appearance, and/or reducing production

Here, designers with Samsung Electronics Co. consider alternative formats for a new product. Samsung is now placing as much emphasis on design as on technology in creating new products, ranging from MP3 players to liquid-crystal displays, for both consumer and business markets.

www.samsung.com

costs. For instance, computer programmers are supposed to assure that any new software is very user-friendly.

According to an IBM executive, design is "a strategic marketing tool."[50] Design is receiving more and more attention for several reasons:

- Rapidly advancing technologies are generating not only new products (such as desktop computer cameras for videoconferencing) that need attractive, yet functional designs, but also new materials that can enhance design capabilities.

- A growing number of firms have turned to low prices as a competitive tool. In turn, designers have been asked to rework some of their companies' products and lower the costs of making them as one way of maintaining profit margins.

- A distinctive design may be the only feature that significantly differentiates a product. Perhaps with that in mind, Samsung appears to be paying particular attention to product design—with excellent results. In 2004, no corporation won more Industrial Design Excellence Awards (IDEA) than Samsung. Its IDEA winners in recent years ranged from a DVD player that is less than 1 inch thick to the "Smart Cooker," a cooking pad with a sensor that measures cholesterol and other attributes of foods so a chef or homemaker can adjust recipes as desired.[51]

Companies are also being called upon to design products that are more socially responsible. Two approaches that are being used are:[52]

- **Universal design.** In this method, the intent is to design products so they can be easily used by all consumers, including disabled individuals, the burgeoning number of senior citizens, and others needing special considerations. As one example, the Kohler Co. designed a bathtub with a door, eliminating the danger of having to climb into the tub.

- **C2C design.** This method, "cradle to cradle," seeks to recycle parts and components as much as possible. It is markedly different from the traditional "cradle-to-grave" approach in which discarded products wind up in landfills. As one example of C2C, 99% of the parts in Steelcase Inc.'s new Think model of chair can be recycled when the product is broken or no longer wanted.

For most consumer and business goods, ranging from furniture to electronic equipment, design has long been recognized as important. According to estimates, design accounts for only 2% of the total cost of producing and marketing a product. As a result, a design that's a hit with consumers can produce a giant return on investment for a firm. Consider, for example, Volkswagen's Beetle. Decades ago, the car's odd shape generated a great deal of attention and attracted many buyers. It eventually fell out of favor, largely because of safety and environmental reasons. In 1998, Volkswagen of America introduced the New Beetle, featuring a familiar design including a front end that resembles a "happy face." This time around, a variety of new technology was added to complement the Beetle's appealing design.[53]

Color

Like design, **product color** often is the determining factor in a customer's acceptance or rejection of a product, whether it is a dress, a table, or an automobile. In fact, color is so important that the U.S. Supreme Court confirmed in 1995 that the color of a product or its packaging can be registered as part of a trademark under the Lanham Act. Color by itself can qualify for trademark status when, according to the Court's ruling, it "identifies and distinguishes a particular brand, and thus indicates its source." The case under review involved greenish-gold dry-cleaning press pads manufactured by the Qualitex Company. Other distinctive colors that help identify specific brands are Owens-Corning's pink insulation and UPS' brown trucks and uniforms.[54]

As with other marketing-mix elements, a differential advantage might be gained by identifying the most pleasing color and in knowing when to change colors. Apple Computer often offers its products in multiple colors, the miniature version of its iPod music player being a recent example. Apple's color decisions for its iMac PC were backed by a survey indicating that over one-half of consumers disdained drab colors for high-tech products.[55]

Designers of fashionable clothing and home furnishings face the challenge (or maybe opportunity) of selecting the "in" colors at least annually. For fall 2005, the hot colors for women's clothing were supposed to be deep blue and rich browns. Are these colors still popular, or have they been supplanted by others? Of course, new hot colors typically mean added sales for fashion marketers. Poor color choices can result in a differential *dis*advantage and lost sales.[56]

Color can be extremely important for packaging as well as for the product itself. Color specialists say it's no coincidence that Nabisco, Marlboro, Coca-Cola, Campbell, and Budweiser are all top-selling brands. In each case, red is the primary color of their packaging or logo. Red may be appealing because it "evokes feelings of warmth, passion and sensuality."[57]

In the first years of the 21st century, blue was the color of choice for many companies' brand names and/or brand marks. You've probably heard of JetBlue Airways,

For some products, such as clothing and autos, color is a critical ingredient. For many others, it would seem to be less important. Recently, however, rainbow colors have proved to be an appealing feature for a variety of other products, ranging from personal computers to household appliances, including Apple Computer's iPod mini digital music player.

but how about two start-up airlines overseas—Blue Fox and Virgin Blue? Why is blue so pervasive? The color can be seen by everyone, including those who suffer from color blindness, and it conveys stability. Maybe that's why it's part of the name of so many fledgling information technology firms, such as BlueKite, Bluetooth, Blue Squirrel, and Bluesocket, to mention several examples. However, it takes more than a color to make a product successful. For example, Pepsi Blue, which was blue in both brand name and product color, failed despite massive promotion.[58]

Quality

There's no agreement on a definition of product quality, even though it is universally recognized as significant. One professional society defines **product quality** as the set of features and characteristics of a good or service that determine its ability to satisfy needs.[59] Despite what appears to be a straightforward definition, consumers frequently disagree on what constitutes quality in a product, whether it is a cut of meat or a performance by a rock musician. Personal tastes are deeply involved; what you like, another person may dislike. It is important to recognize, therefore, that quality (like beauty) is to a large extent "in the eyes of the beholder."

Besides personal tastes, individual expectations also affect judgments of quality. That is, a consumer brings certain expectations to a purchase situation. Sometimes you have high expectations, as with a movie about which you read rave reviews. Other times you have modest expectations, as with a course for next semester that is described by a current student as "not too boring." Your evaluation of a product's quality depends on whether the actual experience with the good or service exceeds, meets, or falls short of your expectations.

For some companies, *optimal* quality means that the product provides the consumer with an experience that meets, but does not exceed, expectations. The rationale is that there's no sense in incurring added costs to provide what amounts to *excessive* quality. Some firms that adopt this viewpoint supplement adequate product quality with superior customer service. According to one survey of personal computer users, this approach can be effective in generating repeat customers.[60] Other businesses, however, strive to exceed consumers' expectations in order to produce high levels of customer satisfaction and, in turn, brand loyalty.

For many years, there was substantial room for improved quality in many American-made products. For instance, German and Japanese automakers beat their American competitors by turning out better-performing, more-reliable cars. Hence, since the 1980s, U.S. industry has paid more and more attention to product quality. According to the latest ratings from *Consumer Reports*, domestic automakers have eliminated the quality gap in relation to European brands, but they still trail Japanese brands of cars and trucks.[61] As will be discussed in Chapter 11, product quality should be a primary consideration not only for manufacturers of goods but also for producers of services.

Recently, quality was called "the single most critical factor for businesses to survive in the ever expanding and competitive global market place." For instance, General Motors discovered that Chinese consumers thought that products made in their own country were inferior to imports. Hence, GM's advertising in China stressed the high quality of Buicks that were made in Shanghai. At first, the cars sold as fast as GM could make them, but then sales slowed to the point that the GM–Chinese joint venture decided to introduce new models and cut prices.[62]

Because it is not easily duplicated, many organizations seek to boost product quality to gain a differential advantage. At the least, an enterprise needs to avoid a differential *dis*advantage related to product quality.

To seize an advantage or avert a disadvantage, a number of businesses, government agencies, and nonprofit entities have implemented **total quality management (TQM)** programs. Implemented in 14% of U.S. manufacturing plants, TQM entails not just specific policies and practices, but a philosophy that commits the organization to continuous quality improvement in all its activities. TQM has received some criticism for not improving financial performance as much as would be expected given the necessary investment of time and effort. However, according to one study, 40% of firms practicing TQM improved their inventory turnover over three years, and 48% reduced their manufacturing costs.[63]

www.iso.org

Another noteworthy quality-related development is called **ISO 9000** (pronounced ICE-o). ISO 9000, a set of related standards of quality management, has been adopted by more than 150 countries, including the U.S. Companies that meet ISO 9000 standards are awarded a certificate, which often puts them in a favorable position with large customers. Worldwide, over 600,000 companies have earned ISO 9000 certification. Now some firms are attaining ISO 14001 certification, demonstrating implementation of an environmental management system. Beginning in mid-2006, all products marketed in European Union countries must meet ISO 14001 standards.[64]

Some critics say that the standards place too much emphasis on documenting what a producer is doing and pay too little attention to whether what's being done results in satisfactory products. As one skeptic observed, "You can certify a manufacturer that makes life jackets from concrete, as long as those jackets are made according to the documented procedures." Perhaps with such criticism in mind, new ISO 9001:2000 standards emphasize customer-related processes as well as ongoing improvement.[65]

Summary

Effective product management involves developing and then monitoring the various features of a product—its brand, packaging, labeling, design color, quality, warranty, and postsale service. A consumer's purchase decision may take into account not just the basic good or service, but also the brand and perhaps one or more of the other want-satisfying product features.

A brand is a means of identifying and differentiating the products of an organization. Branding aids sellers in managing their promotional and pricing activities. The dual responsibilities of brand ownership are to promote the brand and to maintain a consistent level of quality. Selecting a good brand name—and there are relatively few really good ones—is difficult. Once a brand becomes well known, the owner may have to protect it from product counterfeiting and from becoming a generic term.

Manufacturers must decide whether to brand their products and/or sell under a middleman's brand. Middlemen must decide whether to carry only producers' brands or to establish their own brands as well. Both producers and middlemen must set policies regarding branding groups of products and branding for market saturation. The use of cobranding, placing two brands on a product or an enterprise, is growing.

An increasing number of companies are recognizing that the brands they own are or can be among their most valuable assets. They are building brand equity—the added value that a brand brings to a product. Although it's difficult to build brand equity, doing so successfully can be the basis for expanding a product mix. Products with abundant brand equity also lend themselves to trademark licensing, a popular marketing arrangement.

Packaging is becoming increasingly important as sellers recognize the problems, as well as the marketing opportunities, associated with it. Companies must choose among strategies such as family packaging, multiple packaging, and changing the package. Labeling, a related activity, provides information about the product and the seller. Many consumer criticisms of marketing relate to packaging and labeling. As a result, there are several federal laws regulating these activities.

Companies are now recognizing the marketing value of both product design and quality. Good design can improve the marketability of a product; it may be the only feature that differentiates a product. Projecting the appropriate quality image and then delivering the level of quality desired by customers are essential to marketing success. In many cases, firms need to enhance product quality to eliminate a differential disadvantage; in others, firms seek to build quality as a way of gaining a differential advantage.

More about CADILLAC

Since the start of the new century, General Motors has worked hard and effectively to improve Cadillac's standing in the U.S. But to what extent is the rest of the world important to GM, and what if anything is the automaker doing with Cadillac in foreign markets?

GM definitely wants to build its sales volume around the world, particularly in Europe and Asia. The automaker is starting from a very small base of fewer than 10,000 Cadillacs sold outside North America in 2005. Cadillac's marketing in other countries faces significant challenges, such as American cars having a reputation for poor quality in Japan and the brand being relatively unknown in China.

How does General Motors intend to boost sales of Cadillacs in foreign markets? One important step for GM in Japan is to add more dealerships that will sell the Chevrolet Corvette as well as several Cadillac models. The aim is not just to build distribution efficiency by selling two brands through the same network, but also to combine the drawing power of two brands in order to bring prospective buyers into showrooms.

Cadillac's director of international marketing believes that steady sales growth in Europe is critical to worldwide success. However, according to another Cadillac executive, GM has entered a "lions' den" in Europe, referring to entrenched competition. Cadillac's progress in Europe depends on building brand awareness and then a favorable image among prospective customers, most of whom are quite familiar with the brands of cars produced in the region but know little about Cadillac. To create "buzz" and bring shoppers to showrooms, Cadillac is introducing a new model in 2006. The BLS, designed specifically for the European market, is a front-wheel-drive, turbo-charged sedan. Cadillac will produce the new model in Europe.

In China, Cadillac is striving to have at least 100 showrooms and dealerships in place in the next several years. The advertising theme for GM's luxury brand in China is "Dare to be first."

The market potential in China is gigantic. There are only eight cars per 1,000 people in China, compared to 940 in the U.S., so demand is expected to surge as buying power continues to improve. By 2011, it is expected that China will move ahead of Japan to become the second largest market for automobile sales, ranking behind only the U.S. Thus it's not surprising that Cadillac intends to switch as quickly as possible from exporting new cars to China to assembling them in Chinese facilities.[66]

1. What differences does Cadillac face in marketing its brand of vehicles in foreign countries compared to its home market?

2. How much brand equity does Cadillac have in Europe? In China? In Japan?

3. Will the design and quality of Cadillac automobiles be more important in foreign markets or in the U.S.?

Key Terms and Concepts

Brand (258)
Brand name (258)
Brand mark (258)
Trademark (258)
Producer's brand (258)
Middleman's brand (258)
Product counterfeiting (263)
Family branding (268)
Multiple-brand strategy (268)
Cobranding (269)

Brand equity (269)
Trademark licensing (271)
Packaging (272)
Family packaging (273)
Multiple packaging (273)
Label (275)
Brand label (275)
Descriptive label (275)
Grade label (275)

Nutrition labeling (276)
Product design (276)
Universal design (277)
C2C design (277)
Product color (278)
Product quality (279)
Total quality management (TQM) (279)
ISO 9000 (280)

Questions and Problems

1. Evaluate each of the brand names in Table 10.1 in relation to the characteristics of a good brand, indicating the strong and weak points of each name.

2. Do the following e-commerce brands possess the characteristics of a good brand?
   a. Fogdog Sports (sporting goods)
   b. CareerBuilder.com (job search and employee recruiting)
   c. Peapod, Webvan, and HomeGrocer.com (all of which are or were grocery shopping and delivery services)
   d. HotBot (search engine for the Web)
   e. FreeRealTime.com (stock quotes and financial information at no charge)

3. Identify one brand that is on the verge of becoming generic.
   a. Why should a company protect the separate identity of its brand?
   b. What course of action should a company take to do so?

4. In which of the following cases should the company use its name as part of the product's brand name?
   a. A manufacturer of men's underwear introduces women's underwear.
   b. A manufacturer of hair care products introduces a line of portable electric hair dryers.

5. A manufacturer of snow skis sold under a brand that has built up substantial equity acquires a company that markets ski boots carrying a brand that enjoys about the same amount of equity. What branding strategy should the acquiring organization adopt? Should all products (skis and boots) now carry the ski brand? The boot brand? Is there some other alternative that you think would be better?

6. Why do some firms sell identical products under more than one of their own brands?

7. Assume that a large department store chain proposed to the manufacturers of Maytag washing machines that Maytag supply the department store with machines carrying the store's brand. What factors should Maytag's management consider in making a decision? If the situation instead involved a supermarket chain and General Foods' Jell-O, to what extent should different factors be considered?

8. An American manufacturer plans to introduce its line of camping equipment (stoves, lanterns, ice chests) in several European Union countries. Should management select the same brand for all countries or use a different brand in each country? What factors should influence the decision? How should brand equity enter into the decision?

9. Select one product and indicate how you would improve its design.

10. Give examples of products for which the careful use of color has increased sales. Can you cite examples to show that poor use of color may hurt a product's salability?

Interactive Marketing Exercises

1. Visit a large local supermarket and:
   a. Obtain the store manager's opinions regarding which products are excellently packaged and which are poorly packaged. Ask the manager for reasons.
   b. Walk around the store and compile your own list of excellent and poor packages. What factors did you use to judge quality of packaging?

2. Ask five students who are not taking this course to evaluate the following names for a proposed expensive perfume: Entice, Nitespark, At Risk, and Foreglow. For evaluation purposes, share with the students the characteristics of a good brand name. Also ask them to suggest a better name for the new perfume.

Chapter 11

zipcar.com

"Cars were available around the city,
and subscribers to a service could rent
them by the hour."

Who Will Be Next to Find **Zipcar** the Way to Go?

Have you ever thought it would be nice to have temporary access to a car for a quick outing or an errand? On a trip to Europe in 1999, Robin Chase witnessed just such a service in Berlin. Cars were available around the city, and subscribers to a service could rent them by the hour. On her return to Cambridge, Massachusetts, she figured out a way to combine rental cars with the Internet and launched Zipcar, a self-service, on-demand, car-sharing business that has proven attractive to a variety of customers.

Here's how it works. Zipcar has over 400 cars strategically placed in large urban areas such as Boston, Washington, and New York. Prospective renters apply and have their driving records checked. Once approved, the customer receives a membership card that doubles as a key that can be used with any Zipcar vehicle.

To reserve a car, the member logs in to the Zipcar website and provides the date and time of the desired rental. In response, the service provides a list of the five nearest cars, their assigned parking spaces, and their rental rates. When the reservation is confirmed, the information is transmitted electronically to a receiver in the designated car. At the specified time a swipe of the member's card provides access to the vehicle.

Rental rates range from $8.50 to $12.50 an hour, depending on the type of vehicle, and include gas and insurance.

In return, members are required, among other things, to return the car to the designated parking spot at the agreed upon time, make sure it is left with more than one-quarter of a tank of gas, refrain from smoking or otherwise defacing the car, and pay any traffic or parking fines incurred. In general members are expected to treat the car as if it were their own, except, of course, for any maintenance or repairs.

The initial target consisted of city dwellers who had only an occasional need for a car and would be willing to pay a $25 application fee and a $100 refundable membership deposit (to cover the initial cost of setting up a personal page and credit card billing arrangement on the website). However, several other segments have been identified. Corporations and local government agencies whose employees need to attend meetings or visit clients in major metropolitan areas have found Zipcar to be an attractive alternative to taxis and traditional rentals. Also, over 20 urban colleges and universities including MIT, Harvard, Tufts, and Wellesley have programs with Zipcar that make vehicles available on campus to students who enroll as members. Most recently a number of transit authorities have forged partnerships with Zipcar to have cars available in train and subway station lots so shoppers can get from a station to a mall or shopping center. Staring with 19 cars and 250 members in 1999, Zipcar had over 400 cars and 30,000 members that provided $7 million in revenue in 2004.[1]

Is it possible that one of American's most cherished possessions, the automobile, will be replaced with a service?

www.zipcar.com

Zipcar is marketing a service—use of a vehicle. Recall that our definition of a product in Chapter 8 includes goods *and* services. This distinction is much more than a matter of semantics. Services are fundamentally different from goods in ways that affect their marketing. Recognizing what those differences are and understanding their implications are essential in developing effective services.

After studying this chapter, you should be able to explain:

Chapter Goals

- The importance of services in advanced economies.
- The special situation of nonbusiness services marketing.
- The characteristics of services and their marketing implications.
- How a services marketing mix is designed.
- The challenge of managing services quality.
- The productivity and performance challenges faced by services marketers.

Nature and Importance of Services

The U.S. has moved beyond the stage where goods production is its main economic activity to the stage where it has become the world's largest services economy. Services account for over two-thirds of the nation's gross domestic product (GDP), and just over one-half of all consumer expenditures are for services. Projections indicate that services will attract an even larger share of consumer spending in the future.

Services are also the major source of employment. More than 80% of the non-farm labor force is employed in services industries. According to U.S. Department of Labor predictions, virtually all the fastest-growing occupations between 1996 and 2008 are in services. The industries in which job growth will be the fastest are data and information management, institutional and in-home health care, education, and financial services.[2]

That services account for over one-half of consumer expenditures is impressive, but it still grossly understates the economic importance of services. These figures do not include the vast amounts spent for business services. And by all indications, spending for business services will continue to grow. As commerce has become increasingly complex and competitive, managers have found that calling on specialized service providers is effective and efficient. The result is that many tasks formerly performed by regular employees, from research and training to advertising and distribution, are increasingly being "outsourced" to specialists.

Definition of Services

What should be classified as a service? The answer isn't always apparent because invariably services are marketed in conjunction with goods. Virtually all services require supporting goods (you need an airplane to provide air transportation service), and goods require supporting services (to sell even a shirt or a can of beans calls for at least a cashier's service). Furthermore, a company may sell a combination of goods and services. Thus, along with repair service for your car, you might buy a battery or an oil filter. Therefore, it may be helpful to think of every product as a mix of goods and services located on a continuum ranging from mostly goods to mostly services, as shown in Figure 11.1.

For marketing purposes, it is useful to separate services into two categories. In the first are services that are the main *purpose or object* of a transaction. Suppose you rent a car from Enterprise. The company makes a car available (a tangible good), but what you are purchasing is accessibility to transportation (a service). Because you are buying the use of the car, not the car itself, this is a service transaction. In the

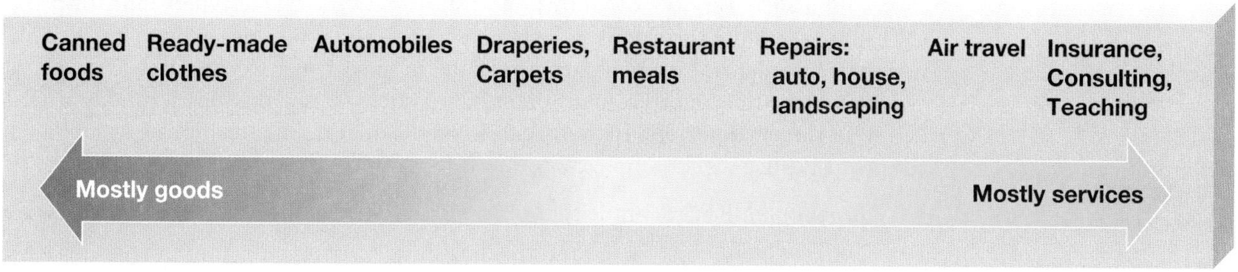

| Canned foods | Ready-made clothes | Automobiles | Draperies, Carpets | Restaurant meals | Repairs: auto, house, landscaping | Air travel | Insurance, Consulting, Teaching |

Mostly goods ← ————————————————————————————————————— → **Mostly services**

FIGURE 11.1

A Goods-Services Continuum.

second category are services that *support or facilitate* the sale of a good or another service. Thus, when you rent the car from Enterprise, you can also obtain collision insurance, the use of a cellular phone, and an electronic navigational device. These are called supplementary or support services because you obtain them only in conjunction with renting the car.

Considering these distinctions, we define **services** as identifiable, intangible activities that are the main object of a transaction designed to provide want-satisfaction to customers. This definition excludes supplementary services that support the sale of goods or other services. Even though we are excluding supplementary services from our discussion, we don't want to underestimate their importance. In industries where there are few differences among the primary products of competitors, supplementary services can be the basis for a differential advantage.

Scope of Services

Using a broad definition of transactions and customers, it is appropriate to recognize both for-profit and nonbusiness services organizations. **For-profit services firms** sell to consumers or other businesses with profitable operations as a primary goal. This category is reflected in the following examples, grouped by industry:

- *Housing and other structures:* Rental of offices, warehouses, hotels, motels, apartments, houses, and farms.
- *Household operations:* House maintenance and repairs, security, landscaping, and household cleaning.
- *Recreation and entertainment:* Theaters, spectator sports, amusement parks, participation sports, restaurant meals, and resorts.
- *Personal care:* Laundry, dry cleaning, personal grooming care, and spas.
- *Medical and health care:* Physical and mental medical services, dental, nursing, hospitalization, optometry, and physical therapy.
- *Private education:* Vocational schools, nursery schools, charter schools, and some continuing education programs.
- *Professional business services:* Legal, accounting, advertising, marketing research, public relations, and management consulting.
- *Financial services:* Personal and business insurance, banking, credit and loan service, brokerage service, and investment counseling.
- *Transportation:* Freight and passenger service on common carriers, automobile repairs and rentals, and express package delivery.
- *Communications:* Broadcasting, telephone, fax, computer, and Internet services.

These groups are not separated into business and consumer services as we did with goods because most of these services are purchased by both market groups.

Nonbusiness services organizations are of two types. One type is **not-for-profit (N-F-P) services organizations,** which have a profit goal because growth and continued existence depend on generating revenue in excess of its costs. However, profit (which may be referred to by a different name, such as "surplus") is secondary to the N-F-P's primary objective. In many cases N-F-Ps operate in a fashion very similar to for-profit businesses. Examples, organized by primary focus, include:

- *Educational:* Private grade schools, high schools, colleges, and universities.
- *Cultural:* Museums, opera and theater groups, zoos, and symphony orchestras.
- *Religious:* Churches, synagogues, temples, and mosques.
- *Charitable and philanthropic:* Charities, service organizations (Salvation Army, Red Cross), research foundations, and fund-raising groups (United Way).
- *Social concerns:* Organizations dealing with family planning, civil rights, termination of smoking, environmental concerns, the homeless, those for or against abortion, or those for or against nuclear energy.
- *Professional and trade:* Labor unions, certification groups, professional associations (American Marketing Association, American Medical Association), trade associations, and lobbying groups.
- *Social:* Fraternal organizations, civic clubs, special interest clubs.
- *Health care:* Hospitals, nursing homes, health research organizations (American Cancer Society, American Heart Association), health maintenance organizations.
- *Political:* Political parties, individual politicians.

You may note some overlap in the preceding two lists. For example, private education appears on both lists because some educational institutions are profit seeking, whereas others are not-for-profit. Also, most museums and hospitals are not-for-profit, but some are profit seeking.

Finally, the scope of services is further broadened by including a second type of nonbusiness organization. A **nonprofit organization** provides services but does not have a profit or surplus objective. Federal, state, and local government agencies fall into this category. They provide services, often charging for them, and may even operate in competition with for-profit businesses. For example, the U.S. National Park Service competes with private forms of outdoor recreation.

www.usps.com

Many nonprofit organizations are heavily involved in some form of marketing. For example, the U.S. Postal Service has a marketing staff of over 500 and annually spends over $100 million on advertising aimed at consumers and businesses that includes television, radio, and print media as well as direct mail and point-of-purchase materials. The agency paid $25 million over four years to sponsor the pro cycling team that included multiple Tour de France winner, Lance Armstrong.[3]

If nonbusiness organizations do an ineffective marketing job, the costs are high. Empty beds in hospitals and empty classrooms constitute a waste of resources a society can ill afford. There are additional social and economic costs of ineffective nonbusiness marketing. If the death rate from smoking rises because the American Cancer Society and similar organizations cannot persuade people that smoking is harmful, we all lose. When antilitter organizations fail to convince people to control their solid-waste disposal, society suffers. Thus, marketing by nonbusiness organizations should be treated as a serious undertaking with important consequences.

All three types of services—for profit, N-F-P, and nonprofit—continue to grow in importance. To illustrate, between 1990 and 2003, employment in U.S. goods-producing industries declined by 8%. At the same time, employment in services providing industries grew by 26%, and government employment increased by 17%. Today nearly six times as many people are employed by services firms than by goods-producing organizations.

The Development of Services Marketing

Traditionally, many services industries—both business and nonbusiness—have not been market-oriented. There are several reasons why they lagged behind sellers of goods in accepting the marketing concept and in adopting marketing techniques.

Some services providers enjoy monopoly status. Until very recently most public utilities (telephone, electricity, water, natural gas) were operated as geographic monopolies under the supervision of government agencies. Quite naturally, when an organization is the only supplier of a necessity in a market, the focus of attention is on production and efficient operations, not marketing.

In some cases marketing activities are externally constrained. A number of large services industries are subject to substantial restrictions by federal and state governments or professional associations. Until recently, for example, all major forms of interstate transportation services were severely restricted in marketing practices such as pricing, distribution, market expansion, and product introduction. In the fields of law, accounting, and health care, various state laws and professional-association regulations prevented and, to varying degrees, still prevent their members from engaging in advertising, price competition, and other marketing activities.

Many nonbusiness services providers are uncomfortable with a business image. These organizations attempt to distance themselves from business and its profit objective. As a result, they do not employ many business techniques, including marketing. In some professional-service industries, tradition suggests that the focus should be on producing the service, not on marketing it. Proud of their abilities to conduct an orchestra, diagnose an illness, or give legal advice, these professionals historically have not considered themselves businesspeople.

More recently, several developments have contributed to a growing awareness of marketing among services organizations:

- The success of services companies such as Marriott hotels and FedEx are examples of the power of good marketing.

- Consumer protests, changes in laws, and court decisions have removed many of the governmental and professional-association restrictions on marketing in some services industries. These changes, along with increased competition, have generated a growing awareness of marketing challenges and opportunities.

- Reductions in federal aid, tax law changes that discourage gift giving, competition for funds from a new generation of social causes, and a slowdown in corporate contributions have squeezed the budgets of many nonbusiness services organizations. Consequently, many have begun to adopt modern business techniques, including marketing with a customer orientation.

Designing a Services Marketing Program

Marketing business and nonbusiness services includes the same basic elements as marketing goods. Whether its focus is goods or services, every organization should first define and analyze its markets, identify segments, and select targets. Then the organization should turn its attention to designing a coordinated marketing mix—the goods or services offering, the price structure, the distribution system, and the promotional activities—around a differential advantage that will create the position it desires. However, some important differences between goods and services influence these marketing decisions. The most important differences are described below.

Characteristics of Services

The four characteristics that differentiate services from goods—**intangibility, inseparability, heterogeneity,** and **perishability**—are major factors driving the differences between goods and services marketing.

Intangibility   Because services do not exist until they are consumed, it is impossible for prospective customers to sample—feel, see, hear, taste, or smell—the specific service they are buying before they buy it. For example, until a Chicago White Sox game is actually played, you cannot tell if it will be exciting, with many hits and close plays, or slow and boring. Consequently, a company's promotional program must be explicit about the benefits to be derived from the service, rather than emphasizing the service itself. Four promotional strategies that may be used to suggest service benefits and reduce the effect of intangibility are:[4]

www.carnival.com

- *Visualization.* For example, Carnival Cruise Lines depicts the benefits of its cruises with ads that show happy people dancing, dining, playing deck games, and visiting exotic places.

www.merrillynch.com

- *Association.* By connecting the service with a tangible good, person, object, or place, a particular image can be created. Professional sports teams are linked with cities or regions to give them an identity. Prudential Insurance suggests stability and security with its Rock of Gibraltar. Merrill Lynch uses the symbol of a bull to imply strength and leadership.

www.unitedway.org

- *Physical representation.* American Express uses color—gold or platinum—for its credit card services to symbolize wealth and prestige. Enterprise, the auto rental firm, depicts a car wrapped as a package in its TV ads to emphasize its unique delivery feature. The United Way depicts its role with a helping hand and a rainbow—symbols of support and a brighter future.

- *Documentation.* There are two forms of documentation—*past performance* and *future capability.* A hospital can document its past performance, for example, by pointing out in its ads how many babies have been born and cared for in its obstetrics department. Another hospital might choose to stress its capability by highlighting the specialized equipment it has available should an emergency arise during the delivery of a baby.

Websites are a valuable tool in reducing the intangibility of services. They make it possible for marketers to present extensive information, use animation and sound, and answer a site visitor's specific questions via e-mail. By expanding the marketer's communications arsenal, the Web increases the quantity and quality of available information and thereby improves the customer's understanding of the service. An example is Royal Caribbean Cruise Line.

www.rccl.com

To counteract the intangibility of their products, service firms such as insurance companies use familiar symbols that suggest security or protection. Can you identify the companies associated with these brand marks?

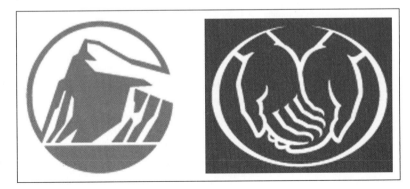

Inseparability   Services typically cannot be separated from the creator–seller of the service. Moreover, many services are created, dispensed, and consumed simultaneously. For example, dentists create and dispense almost all their services at the same time, *and* they require the presence of the consumer for the services to be performed. The same is true of a fast-food drive-up window employee, a physical therapist, and even an automatic teller machine.

A service's inseparability means that services providers are involved concurrently in the production and the marketing efforts. One physician can treat only so many medical patients in a day. This characteristic limits the scale of operation in a services firm. And the customers receive and sometimes consume the services at the production site—in the firm's "factory," so to speak. Consequently, customers' opinions regarding a service frequently are formed through contacts with the production-sales personnel and impressions of the physical surroundings in the "factory." In the case of education, this would be the teacher and the classroom.

From a marketing standpoint, inseparability limits distribution. It frequently means that direct sale is the only possible channel of distribution, and an individual seller's services can be sold only where direct contact is possible.

There is an exception to the inseparability feature. Some services are sold by a person who is representing the creator–seller. A travel agent, insurance broker, or rental agent, for instance, represents, promotes, and sells services that will be provided at a later time by the institutions producing them. In these situations, the customer's opinion of the service can be influenced by the intermediary's appearance and behavior. Thus services marketers should be particularly careful in selecting agents and brokers.

Heterogeneity   It is difficult if not impossible for a service firm, or even an individual seller of services, to standardize output. Each unit of the service is somewhat different from every other unit of the same service because of the human factor in production and delivery. Regardless of its efforts, Delta Airlines does not provide the same experience on every flight or even to each passenger on the same flight. All performances of the Boston Pops Orchestra or all haircuts you get are not the same.

For the buyer this condition means it is difficult to forecast quality in advance of consumption. You pay a fixed amount to attend a concert without knowing if the performers will be at their best or having an off night. For some services it may even be difficult to judge the quality after it has been received, such as when you receive a diagnosis from a physician or get advice from a minister or rabbi.

To offset heterogeneity, services companies should pay special attention to the product-planning and implementation stages of their marketing programs. From the beginning, management must do all it can to ensure consistent quality and to maintain high levels of quality control. Service quality will be given special attention later in this chapter.

Unused services capacity, such as these empty chairlift seats, is lost forever. In response to this perishability feature, services marketers develop strategies, such as offering discounts during slow periods, to balance supply and demand.

Perishability   Services are highly perishable because the existing capacity cannot be stored or inventoried for future use. A cruise ship that sails with unoccupied staterooms, empty seats at a church service, and idle house painters represent available supply that is lost forever. Perishability creates potential imbalances in supply and demand. Furthermore, the demand for many services fluctuates considerably by season, by day of the week, and by hour of the day. Ski lifts can sit idle all summer, whereas golf courses in some areas go unused in the winter. The ridership of city buses fluctuates greatly during the day.

Perishability and the resulting difficulty of balancing supply with fluctuating demand poses promotion, product-planning, scheduling, and pricing challenges to services executives. Some organizations have developed new uses for idle capacity during off-seasons. During the summer, ski resorts operate their ski lifts for hikers and sightseers. Advertising and creative pricing are also used to stimulate demand during slack periods. Marriott Hotels, for example, offer lower prices and family packages on weekends, when there are fewer business travelers.

The Services Customer

Like goods marketers, services businesses should define a target market consisting of present and potential customers. They then direct their marketing only towards these prospective buyers.

In contrast, nonbusiness services organizations must aim at two markets. One is the **provider market**—the contributors of money, labor, materials, or other resources to the organization. The second is the **client market**—the recipients of money or services from the organization. This recipient market is much like the customer market for a business. However, nonbusiness institutions such as churches, hospitals, or universities don't refer to their clients as customers. Instead, they call them parishioners, patients, or students. Because a nonbusiness organization must deal with two different markets, it must develop two different marketing programs—one directed at its resource providers, the other aimed at its clients.

Selecting Target Markets

Selecting target markets is essentially the same whether a firm is marketing goods or services. From Chapters 4 through 6, we know that services marketers need to understand how geographic and demographic factors of the market affect the demand for a service. Marketers also must try to determine their customers' buying behavior—their buying motives and patterns. In the absence of a physical product to evaluate, customers must rely on feelings and beliefs to make a decision. Thus, the psychological determinants of buying behavior—motivation, perceptions, attitudes, personality—become more important when marketing services rather than goods. For the same reasons, the sociological factors of social-class structure and reference groups are significant determinants of buying behavior in services markets.

In the course of selecting target markets, the concept of market segmentation has been adopted by many services marketers. There are apartment complexes for students, and others for the over-55 crowd. Some car-repair shops target owners of foreign cars. Limited-service motel chains (Motel 6, Days Inn) cater to the economy-minded segment. Hotels providing only suites (Embassy Suites, Residence Inn) seek to attract families and business travelers who prefer a "home away from home."

Segmentation strategies are also useful for nonbusiness marketers. Remember, they have two quite separate markets to analyze—resource providers and clients. Each of these two markets usually needs to be further segmented in some detail. A broad (nonsegmented) appeal to the provider market is likely to produce poor results. Likewise, trying to be all things to all people in the client market may mean being "nothing to anybody" and going broke in the process.

Many nonbusiness organizations segment their client markets, although they probably do not consider it market segmentation. For instance, community recreation departments develop different programs for golfers, tennis players, swimmers, and card players. Symphony orchestras design special programs for children, and arrange bus transportation and matinee performances for senior citizens.

AN ETHICAL DILEMMA?

Many food marketers, chief among them the fast food firms, are criticized for offering unhealthy items that taste good but contain ingredients or are prepared in such a way that they are not good for consumers. Responses by the fast food industry have come on two fronts: efforts to reduce the unhealthy nature of many products, and attempts to make existing products appear healthier. For example, the major fast food outlets now offer salads as a menu option, kids meals with milk instead of soft drinks, and fruit instead of fries. In some cases this is misleading. For example, Wendy's Chicken BLT salad has more sodium, cholesterol, and fat than its burger. They have also discovered adding certain code words such as "slow-roasted," "spicy," and "fresh-cut" to describe items causes consumers to believe the food is healthier even when it isn't.

Why haven't the fast food marketers simply replaced the unhealthy items with more nutritious food? Because consumers say they want healthier foods but they continuously reject those alternatives in favor of the unhealthy items.

Should the marketer provide consumers with what they say they want or what they vote for with their dollars? On the other hand, is it responsible for consumers to demand healthy food but then reject it in favor of unhealthy items when they buy?

Sources: Alex Laracy, "Convenience Still Beats Health," *Convenience Store News*, Jan. 10, 2005, p. 8; Matthew Boyle, "Can You Really Make Fast Food Healthy?," *Fortune*, Aug. 9, 2004, pp. 134–139; Wendy Melilo, "Ahead of the Law," *Adweek*, Jan. 17, 2005, p. 16.

Product Planning

The planning and development of goods has its counterpart in the marketing of services—by both business and nonbusiness organizations. The nonbusiness institution, however, requires one product-planning program for its provider market and one for its client market. Intangibility, inseparability, and high perishability present significant product-planning challenges in services marketing. In terms of product planning, a marketer of services must make strategic decisions concerning:

- What services to offer.
- What product-mix strategies to adopt.
- What features, such as branding and support service, to provide.

Services Offering

Many service firms have become successful by identifying—and then satisfying—a previously unrecognized or unsatisfied consumer want. Consider the cellular phone producers that have entered the expanding market for immediate access to communications. These firms provide a familiar service but overcome the constraint of the fixed-base telephone. In the process they had to create a signal transfer infrastructure and an easy-to-use, highly portable cellular phone.

Like goods marketers, service firms seek ways to *differentiate* their offerings. This is particularly important for services because of the intangibility characteristic. In the absence of physical differences, competing services may appear very similar to the customer. One option is to expand the product, preferably by adding attractive, promotable features. For example, in the highly competitive financial services industry, banks are trying to lure new retail customers. For example, J. P. Morgan Chase has greeters meet customers as they enter the bank and escort them to the area they wish to visit, and banks in some areas are opening branches in grocery and other retail stores. Other banks are opening their branches on Sundays. Ideally, added features should be ones that cannot be easily duplicated by competitors or they will be quickly neutralized. In the case of banks, opening branches on Sunday, for example, is easily copied. On the other hand, improving the customer interaction skills of bank employees would likely produce a more durable difference. The lesson here is that service features should be added with caution.

In most nonprofit organizations the "product" offered to *clients* typically is a service (education, health care, religion, culture), a person (in politics), a cause (stop smoking or don't do drugs), or a cash grant (research foundation). Some nonprofits offer goods such as food and clothing to clients, but usually these goods are incidental to the main services provided by the organization.

For an organization, the keys to selecting the services to offer are deciding (1) what "business" it is in and (2) what client markets it wants to reach. If a church views its mission only as providing religious services, its assortment will be limited. If this church views its mission broadly—as providing fellowship, spirituality, and personal development—it will offer more services to more markets. The church may then offer family counseling services, day-care services, religious education courses, and social activities for single adults.

Planning the services offering to the *provider* market is more difficult. An organization asks people to contribute money, time, skills, or other resources to a cause. The contribution is the price paid in order to make the organization's services available. But what is the contributor getting for this price? What are the contributors buying with their donations? In the case of donations, the donors can receive an assortment of benefits that may include:

- Feeling good about themselves or relieving guilt.

- Helping a worthwhile organization provide services to others.

- Receiving a tax deduction.

- Contributing to their social status.

- Supporting their social or religious beliefs.

The challenge for the marketer is to understand what particular benefits motivate a potential provider, communicate those benefits, and ensure that the provider actually receives them following the donation.

Product-Mix Strategies Several of the product-mix strategies discussed in Chapter 9 can be employed by services marketers. Consider the strategy of *expand-*

MARKETING IN THE INFORMATION ECONOMY

Is the Internet replacing local newspapers?

One of the Internet's attractions is its ability to transcend distances. Customers are able to contact sellers, both businesses and individuals, miles or even continents away. As a result it provides buyers with access to many more options. However, some consumers are uneasy conducting business at such distances. More than half of all consumers who gather information from the Web say they prefer to make actual purchases offline. The growing concern about fraud in Internet transactions adds credence to their fears.

Now websites such as StepUp, ShopLocal, and Cairo have been created to help buyers and sellers in the same community or area find each other so they can do business face-to-face. Established in 1995 in San Francisco, Craigslist was the first of these services. It operates in over 100 cities worldwide and receives more than 1 billion page views a month. Interestingly these localized sites contradict what is often seen as one on the major strengths attributed to the Internet, and their success is a threat to local newspaper classified advertising.

Sources: Mylene Mangalindan, "Internet Shopping . . . in Person," *The Wall Street Journal*, Nov. 11, 2004, pp. D1+; Daniel Askt, "For Putting the Free in Free Markets," *Inc.* April 2005, p. 83; Steven Levy, "Looking for Something?," *Newsweek*, Dec. 27, 2004, p. 94.

www.disney.com

ing the line. Disney added parks in Paris and Tokyo and is developing a theme park in Hong Kong, following on its success in the U.S. Although not identical, the parks will be sufficiently similar to benefit greatly from the worldwide recognition of the Disney name.

In the nonprofit field, symphony orchestras expand their line by offering children's concerts and pop concerts for teenagers and college students. Universities have added adult night classes, distance learning utilizing the Internet, and concentrated between-semester courses.

Carnival Cruise Lines *contracted its services mix* by selling a casino hotel in the Bahamas—part of a series of moves designed to get the cruise ship company out of the resort business. Because of the high cost of malpractice insurance, some physicians have contracted their product mix by discontinuing the practice of obstetrics.

In response to the growing success of discount brokerage firms, Merrill Lynch, the largest full-service securities firm in the U.S., *altered its services offering*. The firm introduced online trading for its 5 million customers, a dramatic change for a firm that takes great pride in the personal attention provided by its brokers.

Managing the life cycle of a service is another strategy. Recognizing that the credit card industry is in the maturity stage, VISA sought ways to maintain its growth. The answer was new uses for the card, rather than issuing cards to more people. For starters, VISA targeted dentists, physicians, supermarkets, theaters, and even fast-food outlets, trying to get them to encourage their customers to pay with a VISA card. Likewise, amusement parks such as Knott's Berry Farm in California, Six Flags, and Universal Studios' Islands of Adventure have avoided the sales-decline stage of the life cycle by periodically adding new attractions.

Product Features

The emphasis in product planning is different for services than for goods. For example, packaging is nonexistent in services marketing. However, other features—branding and quality management, for instance—present greater challenges for services industries.

Branding a service is a problem because maintaining consistent quality, a responsibility of brand ownership, is difficult. Also, the intangibility characteristic means a brand cannot be physically attached to the service itself. Some service firms use devices such as employee uniforms to create an identity, and one, UPS, even built an ad campaign, "What can Brown do for you?," around its distinguishing color scheme.

A services marketer's goal should be to create an effective brand image. The strategy to reach this goal is to develop a total theme that includes more than just a

Having accomplished its original mission, the virtual eradication of polio, the March of Dimes could have declared victory and disappeared. However, that would have wasted its recognized brand, established organization, and solid base of providers or donors. So, the agency has redefined its "product" as protecting children in many different ways.

www.marchofdimes.com

good brand name. To implement this strategy, the following tactics frequently are employed:

- Use a *tangible object* to communicate the brand image or difference. The "gift-wrapped" car of Enterprise and the permanence and stability of Prudential's "rock" symbolize what these firms feel make them stand out.
- Develop a *memorable slogan* to accompany the brand. "We'll leave the light on for you" by Motel 6 and the Yellow Pages' "Let your fingers do the walking" are appealing and easily remembered slogans.
- Use a *distinctive color scheme* on all tangible aspects of the brand. JetBlue's planes and Hertz's black and gold office décor, shuttle vans, and uniforms are highly recognizable.

Nonbusiness organizations have been slow to exploit branding. The little that has been done suggests that brands can provide effective marketing support. Colleges not only use nicknames (a form of brand name) primarily for their athletic teams, but also to identify their students and alumni. Most universities have school colors—another feature that helps increase the market's recognition of the school. Among health research organizations, the Lung Association has registered as a trademark its double-barred Christmas Seal cross. Likewise, the trademarks of the American Red Cross and the YMCA, prominently displayed on their websites, are readily recognized by many people.

www.redcross.org

www.ymca.net

Pricing Structure

In services marketing there is a great need for managerial skill in pricing. Because services are perishable, they cannot be stored, and demand for them often fluctuates considerably. Each of these features has significant pricing implications. To further complicate pricing, customers often have a "do-it-yourself" alternative, as in auto or home repairs. There are two tasks in designing a *pricing structure:* Determine the base price and select strategies to adjust the base price.

Price Determination in For-Profit Firms

Services marketers set their prices by adding a markup to their costs (called cost plus) or by estimating what target customers are willing to pay, with cost treated only as a minimum constraint that must be covered. Electric power and telephone companies, for example, use a cost basis to set prices that will generate a predetermined rate of return on investment. Painters, plumbers, and electricians frequently price their services on a cost-plus basis. Airlines, on the other hand, tend to meet competitors' prices, especially on routes served by two or more airlines.

The perishability characteristic of services suggests that the demand for a service should influence its price. Sellers often do recognize situations of strong demand and limited supply. For example, ticket prices are raised significantly for the farewell tours of popular musical groups, and hotels located near sports stadiums raise their room rates for the dates of championship events. Perishability also influences the opposite situation, excess supply, producing an industry on the Internet. Firms such as Priceline allow a buyer to specify a price he or she is willing to pay for a service such as a plane ticket on a particular day. If an airline flying the route is willing to sell a seat at that price, they have a deal. Other services offered on Priceline include hotel rooms, cars, home mortgages, and long-distance phone service.

www.priceline.com

Price Determination by Nonprofits

Pricing in nonbusiness organizations is different from pricing in a for-profit firm. In the first place, pricing becomes less important when profit making is not a goal. Also, a nonbusiness organization is faced with special forms of pricing in the provider market and in the client market.

In the *provider* market, nonbusiness organizations do not set the price—the amount of the resource contributed. That price is set by contributors when they decide how much they are willing to pay (donate) for the benefits they expect to receive. However, a price is often suggested—for example, donate one day's pay or volunteer for one day a month. And the suggested price is often translated into a client benefit (for example, the amount of food or clothing $100 will provide in an underdeveloped country) to provide the donor with a basis for valuing the contribution.

In the *client* market, some nonbusiness organizations face the same pricing situation, and can use the same methods, as profit-seeking firms. Museums and opera companies, for example, must decide on admission prices; fraternal organizations must set a dues schedule; and colleges must determine how much to charge for tuition. But most nonbusiness organizations cannot use the same pricing methods employed by business firms. These nonbusiness organizations know that they cannot cover their costs with prices charged to clients. The gap between anticipated revenues and costs must be made up by contributions. As yet, there simply are no real guidelines for nonbusiness pricing.

Also, some nonbusiness groups tend to believe there are no pricing considerations with regard to clients because there is no monetary charge to the client. Actually, the goods or services received by clients rarely are free—that is, without a price of some kind. The client almost always pays a price—possibly in the form of travel or waiting time and, perhaps, embarrassment or humiliation—that a money-paying client would not have to pay.

Pricing Strategies   Several common pricing strategies are applicable in services marketing—in both profit-seeking and nonbusiness organizations. *Discounts,* for example, are widely used in marketing services. A season pass for the Metropolitan Opera or the Los Angeles Philharmonic Orchestra costs less per performance than tickets purchased for individual performances. Daily rates charged by Hertz or Avis are lower if you rent a car for a week or a month at a time. These are forms of quantity discount.

A *flexible-price* strategy is used by many services organizations. Museums and movie theaters offer lower prices for children and senior citizens. In some cities, bus transportation costs less during off-peak hours. The University of Colorado charges a higher tuition in its business and engineering colleges than in arts and sciences. On the other hand, the University of Notre Dame and many other universities typically follow a *one-price* strategy. That is, all students pay the same tuition for a full load of course work.

Databases that allow a company to examine an individual's purchase history, can be combined with real-time supply information that indicates how much of a service remains unsold. Using this information a firm can engage in *dynamic pricing,* or adjusting price to meet individual circumstances. For example, an airline can calculate the value of each of its customers based on their individual purchase histories. It can also compute the likelihood of selling the remaining inventory of seats on a particular flight at any time, using historical data. Combining these two pieces of information, an airline can offer an individual a price that considers the value of retaining the person's loyalty, maximizes the probability of a ticket being purchased, and optimizes the revenue from the flight.

Price competition among services providers varies by industry. Where it has become more common, the use of price competition seems to exist at three levels:

- Price is rarely mentioned as organizations attempt to compete on other dimensions. For example, a health maintenance organization (HMO) will run an ad explaining its services, but will not dwell much on price.
- The seller uses a segmentation strategy and targets a given market at a specific price. A law firm, for example, may prominently advertise its low prices for divorce proceedings or the preparation of a will.

- Intense price competition occurs as firms stress comparative prices in their advertising. Credit card companies and cellular phone service providers have engaged extensively in advertising that compares their prices with those of competitors.

Price competition is particularly intense in services industries where the products are viewed as highly interchangeable, such as fast food. Interestingly, in areas where the products should be fairly easy to differentiate, such as professional services, price competition seems to be increasing. This would suggest that professional services marketers are not effectively using the other components of the marketing mix to differentiate their offerings.

Distribution System

Designing a distribution system for a service (whether in the for-profit or nonbusiness context) involves two tasks. One is to select the parties through which ownership will pass (called the channel of distribution), and the other is to provide facilities for physically distributing the service.

Channels of Distribution
The ownership channel for most services is short and quite simple because of the inseparability characteristic. That is, a service usually cannot be separated from its producer.

Short channels usually mean more control on the part of the seller. With direct distribution or only a single middleman, it would seem that service marketers should be able to reduce the heterogeneity or variance in the service from one transaction to another. However, because the service creator is also distributing the service, a single firm may operate a large number of virtually identical short channels. For example, McDonald's has over 30,000 outlets in 121 countries, all producing and distributing the product. Thus, the control problems are in the *number* of middlemen to be managed, not the length of the channel.

The only other frequently used channel includes one agent middleman. For example, an agent or broker often is used when marketing securities, travel arrangements, or housing rentals.

Distribution Facilities
A good location is essential when the distribution of a service requires personal interaction between producer and consumer, especially today because consumers are so convenience-oriented. Some services marketers have broadened their distribution by extending their accessibility, thus offsetting to some extent the limitations imposed by the inseparability factor. Zoots, a dry-cleaning chain with operations in five eastern states, is using technology to improve distribution convenience. In addition to home or office pick-up and delivery service, Zoots has drive-through locations. By providing customers with bar-coded garment bags, soiled clothing can be dropped off at one of its outlets, cleaned, and picked up by the customer at any time from lockers outside the store. Preapproved charges are made to the customer's credit card and the customer is sent an itemized statement monthly. By eliminating all personal interaction, Zoots makes the transaction more convenient.

www.zoots.com

The Internet has greatly broadened the distribution of some services, making it easier for buyers and sellers to establish contact. Bank One and other U.S. banks are faced with competition from Canadian banks that can offer consumers Internet-based accounts virtually anywhere in North America that the banking laws permit. Like Bank One, all services retailers need to examine how the Internet impacts the inseparability characteristic of their businesses.

Not-for-profit organizations try to provide arrangements to make donor contributions easy and convenient. Besides cash and checks, charities use payroll deductions, installment plans, and credit cards. If you are contributing used goods, the Disabled American Veterans may collect them at your residence.

Is there a downside to cause-related marketing?

The websites of almost every major firm in the U.S. include pages describing philanthropic activity. One of the most common forms is cause marketing—an alliance between a for-profit business and a not-for-profit organization that generates publicity and good will for the firm and resources for the cause. One of the most successful cause marketing efforts links firms with breast cancer. Avon, Ford, Estee Lauder, Revlon, Lee Jeans, Polo Ralph Lauren, Yoplait, Saks, BMW, American Express, Kitchen Aid, J. C. Penney, Loew's (theatres), American Airlines, Eureka (vacuum cleaners), Wilson Sporting Goods, and Dryer's (ice cream) are just some of the firms that have been or are currently linked with providing support for this cause. Activities range from sponsoring events (Avon's walks) to linking sales of a product to donations (Yoplait yogurt lids). Critics contend that the marketing objectives of participating firms play too great a role in how the cause is portrayed and funds are raised. For example, it's been suggested that the complexity of the cause gets oversimplified in the mind of the public because the allied firms do not want it to overshadow their marketing message. Others argue that equally important causes are overlooked as firms concentrate on the few with the strongest emotional appeals to their target customers. On the other hand, advocates suggest that regardless of where the funds raised go, it is money that would not be donated without the corporate connections.

Sources: Susanna Hammer, "LiveStrong Wristband," *Business 2.0*, April 2005, p. 91; Susan Orenstein, "The Selling of Breast Cancer," *Business 2.0*, February 2003, pp. 88–94.

Location is also critical when dealing with nonbusiness client markets. Libraries have branches; blood banks conduct blood drives on location in factories and schools; Goodwill Industries locates its stores in low-income neighborhoods; and big-city museums arrange for portable exhibits to be taken to small towns.

Promotional Program

Several types of promotion are used extensively in services marketing—in both profit-seeking and nonprofit organizations. In fact, promotion is the one part of the marketing mix with which services marketers are most familiar and adept. Unfortunately, many services firms, especially nonbusiness organizations, believe that promotion is marketing and overlook the other mix elements.

Personal Selling   Because of the inseparability characteristic, personal selling plays a pivotal role in promotional programs for most services. Face-to-face contact between buyer and seller is required in order to make a transaction. Thus, it is important that a service employee be skilled at customer relations as well as capable of providing a quality service.

Personal selling is frequently employed by not-for-profit organizations in soliciting donations. Potentially large donors may be approached by fundraisers (sales people). Many nonprofit organizations also use personal selling to reach their clients. For example, all branches of the military make use of recruiters. For centuries, religious missionaries recruited new members by personal contact. Colleges send admissions officers, alumni, and current students to talk to high school students, their parents, and their counselors. These representatives may not be called sales people, but that is exactly what they are.

Whether they realize it or not, all employees of a service provider who come in contact with a customer are, in effect, part of that organization's sales force. In addition to a regular sales force, customer-contact personnel might include airline counter attendants, law office receptionists, package delivery people, bank tellers, ticket takers, and ushers at ballparks or theaters.

The term **service encounter** is used to describe a customer's interaction with any service employee or with any tangible element such as a service's physical surroundings (bank, theatre, medical office). A large part of a customer's evaluation of an organization and its service is made on the basis of service encounters. Consequently, management must prepare its contact personnel and physical surroundings. The approach to this preparation is often called *internal marketing* to emphasize the idea that a services organization should view its employees as customers to whom it markets customer-contact jobs. When an organization adopts this perspective, it will go to great lengths to select the right people for these jobs, train them, and make the jobs interesting and fulfilling. The objective is to create satisfying service encounters for customers and success for the organization. Unfortunately, many service organizations do not think in these terms and, as a result, have not developed the orientation necessary to produce outstanding customer-contact employees.[5]

Advertising   For years, advertising has been used extensively in many service fields—transportation, recreation, and insurance, for example. At one time, advertising by professional-services providers including attorneys, physicians, and accountants was prohibited by their professional associations on the grounds that it was unethical. However, the Supreme Court has ruled that prohibiting a professional firm from advertising is restraint of trade and thus a violation of antitrust laws. Some associations still try to impose constraints on advertising, but the restrictions continue to be eased.

Nonbusiness organizations use advertising extensively to reach their donor markets. Mass media (newspapers, television, radio) frequently are used in annual fund-raising drives. Direct-mail and telephone solicitation can be especially effective in reaching particular donor-market segments, such as cash contributors, religious or ethnic group members, or college alumni. However, telephone contact is coming under fire under the broad heading of telemarketing. Because some firms have abused this form of communication, several states have passed laws allowing consumers to place themselves on "no-call" lists, with organizations that ignore the lists risking severe penalties. The relatively low cost of a website on the Internet has provided nonprofits such as colleges and universities, and organizations like the Special Olympics and Mothers Against Drunk Driving (MADD) with an opportunity to communicate more information than was possible in the past.

www.madd.org

Forming an alliance with a for-profit organization can be another valuable source of promotion for nonbusiness organizations. Called **cause-related marketing,** it involves developing a relationship that generates sales for the firm and publicity (along with donations) for the nonprofit organization. A survey of young people found that two-thirds consider the causes that may be affected when they shop for clothing and other items. And more than one-half say they would switch to a brand or retailer that is associated with a good cause if price and quality are equal.[6] An example of cause-related marketing is the Avon Breast Cancer Crusade, begun by the firm in 1993. Its stated mission is funding access to care and finding a cure for breast cancer. Through its various activities the firm has raised over $350 million in 50 countries.

www.avon.com/women

Large and small nonbusiness groups also can communicate with client markets through advertising. The military branches are heavy users of marketing, with the U.S. Army alone spending over $200 million annually. Utilizing what it describes as a "corporate" model, the Pentagon is reducing its reliance on traditional, network television ads and is moving toward alternatives. For example, short spots on youth-oriented cable channels and information booths at NASCAR events are part of today's recruitment advertising. Another promotional tool, a video game that can be downloaded from the Internet is called America's Army and is aimed at 13- to 24-year-olds.[7] In another kind of recruiting, a Midwestern women's religious order with a budget of less than $200,000, developed a marketing plan and is using advertising to help attract prospective members.[8]

www.usmilitary.com

www.americasarmy.com

www.adriansisters.org

Some for-profit, nonprofit, and not-for-profit organizations have identified ways to work together to achieve their individual goals. For example, once a year law enforcement officials become celebrity servers in Red Lobster restaurants, talking to guests about Special Olympics and accepting donations. Recently, the program called "Cops & Lobsters" raised more than $1.2 million for the Special Olympics' cause.

www.redlobster.com/fun/
cops.asp

Other Promotional Methods   Various forms of sales promotion are frequently used by services marketers. Laundry and dry-cleaning firms, opticians, and auto-repair shops include reduced-price offers in telephone directories and coupon books mailed periodically to local households. Travel agents, ski resorts, and landscaping services have displays at sports shows or home shows. These displays show the beneficial results of using the service.

Other promotional tools used by not-for-profit organizations include front-end premiums (a gift or incentive such as sheets of personalized return address labels that accompany direct-mail solicitations), back-end premiums (gifts such as mugs, T-shirts, CDs, or videos offered for donations of various amounts), and virtual incentives (coupons that can be redeemed at online retailers).

Many service firms, especially in the recreation and entertainment fields, benefit considerably from free publicity. Sports coverage by newspapers, radio, and television provides publicity, as do newspaper reviews of movies, plays, and concerts. Travel sections in newspapers help sell transportation, housing, and other services related to the travel industry.

Managing Service Quality

In Chapter 10, we noted the elusiveness of product quality. Service quality is particularly difficult to define, measure, control, and communicate. Yet in services marketing, the quality of the service is critical to a firm's success. Two airlines each fly Boeing 737s and charge the same fare; two auto-repair shops each use factory-authorized parts and charge the same price; and two banks make home mortgage loans at identical interest rates. Assuming similar times and locations, quality of the service is the only factor that differentiates what is offered by these firms.[9]

Services providers must understand two attributes of **service quality**: First, quality is defined by the customer, not by the producer-seller. Your hairstylist may be delighted with the job done on your hair, but if you think your hair looks terrible, then the service quality is poor. Second, customers assess service quality by comparing their expectations to their perceptions of how the service is performed. In this process, there is no guarantee that expectations will be reasonable, nor is there any assurance that a customer's perception of performance will be based on more than a single experience.

Consequently, to effectively manage quality, a services firm should:

1. Help customers formulate expectations.
2. Measure the expectation level of its target market.
3. Strive to maintain consistent service quality at or above the expectations level.

Expectations are based on information from personal and commercial sources, promises made by the service provider, and experience with the particular service as well as other similar services. Firms have an opportunity through their formal and informal communications to influence customers' expectations. Because of the intangibility of services, some providers tend to exaggerate performance. Extravagant claims for education programs, weight-loss regimens, and vacation packages that contribute to unrealistic expectations are unfortunately too commonplace.

A services firm must conduct research to measure expectations. Gathering data on the target market's past behavior, existing perceptions and beliefs, and exposure to information can provide the basis for estimating expectations.

With the desired level of service keyed to expectations, the next challenge is standardizing service performance—that is, maintaining consistency in service output. Service performance typically varies even within the same organization. This is true in such diverse fields as opera, legal services, landscaping, baseball, hospital care, and marketing courses. The reason is simple: Services are most often performed by people and their behavior is very difficult to standardize.

As part of managing service quality, an organization should design and operate an ongoing quality assessment and improvement program. The foundation of quality improvement is monitoring the level and consistency of service quality. Holding to the idea that service quality is defined by customers, a firm must regularly measure customer satisfaction—that is, customers' perceptions of the quality of an organization's services. The Ritz-Carlton hotel chain, a two-time winner of the Malcolm Baldrige National Quality Award, emphasizes employee training and measuring customer satisfaction.

www.ritzcarlton.com

One proposal for standardizing the quality of service delivery is to substitute machines for people whenever possible. At least in theory, an ATM machine or a website on the Internet treats every interaction in the same fashion. Although it's a fact that a machine will not suffer from fatigue, forgetfulness, or stress, this argument ignores the variability on the customer side of the exchange. If a consumer is not adept at surfing the Internet, forgets the required ATM personal identification number, or gets impatient with the branching process on a recorded telephone answering system, the quality of the service encounter is likely to be inconsistent. This possible shortcoming, despite the standardization and reliability of machines, is one factor that may explain why Internet shopping accounts for less than 2% of total retail sales.[10]

To standardize the quality of their local operations, some nonbusiness organizations are copying the operating structures used by commercial franchise systems. For example, Camp Fire Girls and Boys and United Way provide local units with managerial expertise, performance evaluation, marketing guidance, and purchasing assistance in exchange for a fee. This arrangement provides the local unit with policies to achieve consistency in all its operations, a high level of managerial expertise, and valuable operating economies.

The Future of Services Marketing

Until recently, many services industries enjoyed growth, supported by government and professional-association regulations, the absence of significant foreign competition, and a strong economy. But the environment is changing, bringing with it a focus on increasing productivity and customer-satisfying performance.

There are interesting global services growth opportunities in several areas, including tourism by the Chinese and medical services outsourced to India. However, a development with services applications in many industries seems ready for take-off. The U.S. Department of Defense made its global positioning system (GPS) signals available for commercial use in 1993. Since then, the market for location-linked services has grown to nearly $5 billion. It already has been applied in agriculture, transportation, navigation, and consumer safety, and in 2005 the U.S. government began adding new, more powerful satellites to the system. As a result, the applications seem almost endless and sometimes a little frightening. For example:

- UPS is equipping its 100,000 drivers around the globe with GPS handheld devices to help them find destinations more efficiently.

- Zingo, a taxicab service in Great Britain, can pinpoint the location of a customer who calls on a cell phone for a cab.

- Outfitted tractors can be steered by signals from the satellite, and the amount of pesticides and fertilizers can be controlled using images of the fields being worked.

- Trucking companies, rental car firms, and insurance providers can track the whereabouts and driving behavior of their employees and customers.

- Most cell phones are designed so emergency personnel can determine the location of a caller in case of an accident.

The momentum of GPS-related services is expected to increase with applications creating a $10 billion industry by 2010.

Sources: Matthew Maier, "Finding Profits in the GPS Economy," *Business 2.0,* April 2005, pp. 21+; Bob Deierlein, "Is The 'Eye-in-the-Sky' Good or Bad?," *Beverage World,* Mar. 15, 2005, p. 44; Anne Kandra, "Watch Out for Spies with Friendly Faces," *PC World,* April 2005, pp. 39+.

The Impact of Technology

Technology has dramatically changed some services industries and created others. The most immediate impact is being felt by firms that act as agents or brokers for services providers. The Internet offers firms in the travel, accommodations, recreation, and insurance industries a cost-effective way to bypass intermediaries. As a result, travel agents, insurance brokers, and other types of middlemen are being confronted with a new type of competition. In another industry, interactive telecommunications technology has created a distance learning capability that is changing the way training and education are distributed. These and other developments on the horizon will force many services firms to redefine what they do. For example, facsimile machines have diminished the need for overnight delivery of documents, causing FedEx to reinvent itself as a supply-chain management company rather than a delivery service.

Need for Increased Productivity

The changing services environment has exposed inefficiency and poor management in many services industries, demonstrating a need for restructuring. At the same time, inefficiency provides competent services firms with a tremendous opportunity to increase productivity. This opportunity is being seized by services chains and franchise systems that are replacing small-scale services firms and independent professionals in many fields. Examples include Kaiser Permanente and Humana in health care; Midas Muffler and Jiffy Lube in auto repairs and maintenance; Pearle Vision and LensCrafters in vision improvement; and Re/Max and Century 21 in real estate.

However, there are concerns that attempts to increase services productivity utilizing a manufacturing-based approach are misdirected. The most widely adopted technology is some form of computer-based information system that increases operating efficiency. For example, Burger King and McDonald's adopted assembly line techniques and increased their output per worker for a time.

The basic premise of the manufacturing model is that machines and technology are the primary keys to increased productivity and that the people who deliver the services are not as important. But this premise is no longer accepted in the services environment. Instead, a model that combines the benefits of technology with human interaction skills and designs the business operations around the needs of the customer is viewed as more desirable.

Performance Measurement

Profit-seeking service firms can evaluate their performances by using quantitative measures such as profitability, market share, or return on investment and then can compare these figures with industry averages and trends. However, for most nonbusiness organizations, because their objectives are so varied, there are few generally accepted performance measures. Consequently, measuring marketing performance in the nonbusiness sector requires some imagination and creativity.

Nonbusiness organizations can quantify the contributions they receive, but the result reflects only their fund-raising abilities. It does not measure the services rendered to their clients. How do you quantitatively evaluate the performance of, say, the Red Cross? Perhaps by the number of people the organization houses and feeds after a hurricane or some other natural disaster. Or by the number of people trained in first aid and life-saving techniques. Churches, museums, and YMCAs can count their attendance, but how do they measure the quality of the services and benefits they provide to their clients?

The analysis and management of customer complaints is an evaluation tool that can be used by both nonbusiness and profit-seeking organizations. The complaint-management process involves keeping track of (1) customer complaints, (2) how they are resolved, and (3) whether the complaint handling was satisfactory, so the complaining customer ends up as a returning customer.

Prospects for Growth

Services will continue to take an increasing share of the consumer dollar, just as they have done over the past 40 years. Time pressure, individual priorities, and the increasing complexity of many tasks are all contributing factors. This forecast seems reasonable even for periods of economic decline. History shows that the demand for services is less sensitive to economic fluctuations than the demand for goods.

The demand for commercial services should also continue to expand as business becomes more complex and as management further recognizes its need for specialized support services and the value of outsourcing. In professional services especially, the use of marketing programs is expected to continue growing. This expansion will occur as physicians, lawyers, and other professionals come to understand the economic benefits they can derive from an effective marketing program.

The significance of nonbusiness marketing will also increase as the people in these organizations understand what marketing is and what it can do for them. As noted earlier in this chapter, many nonbusiness organizations engage in exchange stimulating efforts (usually some form of promotion), but have a limited concept of marketing and its full potential. The marketing activities they do perform often are not well coordinated, and the people in charge of them usually have other duties and titles. In a university, for example, personal selling may be managed by the director of admissions, fund raising coordinated by a director of development, and advertising done through an office of public information. For a more effective marketing job, most nonbusinesses need a more formal, recognizable marketing structure.

Summary

The scope of services marketing is enormous. About 50% of what consumers spend goes for services, and more than 80% of nonfarm jobs are in services industries. Services purchased by businesses constitute another major segment of the economy. The nonbusiness services field includes thousands of organizations spanning educational, cultural, religious, charitable, social, health care, and political activities. Services marketers can be divided into for-profit businesses and nonbusiness organizations, made up of not-for-profits and nonprofits. The not-for-profit organizations have a profit (or surplus) objective, but it is secondary to some other goal. Nonprofits do not have a profit objective.

Most product offerings are a mix of tangibles (goods) and intangibles (services), somewhere between pure goods and pure services. To distinguish between goods and services, we define services as separately identifiable, intangible activities that are the main object of a transaction designed to provide want-satisfaction.

Services are intangible, usually inseparable from the seller, heterogeneous, highly perishable, and widely fluctuating in demand. These characteristics that differentiate services from goods have several marketing implications.

The growth in services has not been matched by service management's application of the marketing concept. Monopoly status, external constraints, and a nonbusiness orientation have caused many services marketers to be slow in adopting marketing techniques that, in goods marketing, have brought satisfaction to consumers and profits to producers and middlemen. However, that is changing as constraints and restrictions are removed, and service producers observe the benefits of effective marketing.

Developing a program for marketing services is much the same as for goods, but it takes into account the characteristics of services. Management first identifies its target market, making use of market segmentation strategies, and then designs a marketing mix around a differential advantage to provide want-satisfaction for the market.

Many nonbusiness services organizations must deal with two markets: donors, the contributors to the organization; and clients, the recipients of the organization's money or services. Consequently, a nonbusiness organization must develop two separate marketing programs: one to attract resources from donors and one to provide services to clients.

In the product-planning stage, services enterprises use various product-mix strategies, and they should try to brand their services. Service firms must determine base prices and select appropriate pricing strategies. Pricing in nonbusiness organizations often is quite different from pricing in profit-seeking businesses.

Channels of distribution are quite simple in services marketing, and middlemen are not often used. The main physical distribution challenge is to locate the services organization where it can most effectively serve its markets. Regarding promotion, services firms often use personal selling and advertising extensively and quite effectively. These organizations are recognizing the importance of service encounters and the need to engage in internal marketing directed at customer-contact personnel.

Consistently maintaining a level of quality that the customer expects is critical to a company's success. Managing customers' expectations is an important services issue.

The expanding services arena has exposed inefficiency in services industries. Key issues in improving services marketing are the effective use of technology, the need to increase productivity, and the development of useful performance measures.

More about **Zipcar**

As attractive as Zipcar sounds for providing the convenience of a car while overcoming congestion and reducing pollution in cities, it is faced with some formidable challenges. For example, how can the company ensure that cars are always in good shape and clean? Zipcar has progressed from mostly VW "bugs" to over 20 makes and models ranging from pickups to convertibles. How can it have the right vehicles in the right places to satisfy customers? And then there's the challenge of time of day, day of the week, and season. An unrented Zipcar is money lost, but demand that exceeds supply means unhappy members. How can the company adapt to fluctuating demand? Then there's the question of competition. A similar business, Flexcar, is based in Seattle and is operating in Los Angeles, and Portland as well. Zipcar would like to become a national chain with operations in 25 urban areas by 2010, but its basic business model appears quite easy to copy.[11]

Questions

1. Like all services, Zipcar must adapt to the characteristics of intangibility, inseparability, heterogeneity, and perishability.
   a. Which of these elements pose the greatest threats to Zipcar's future?
   b. What could Zipcar do to better adapt to these characteristics?

2. What other market segments should Zipcar consider pursuing in order to grow its business? To reduce the peaks and valleys of demand?

Key Terms and Concepts

Service (287)
For-profit services firms (287)
Not-for-profit (N-F-P) services organizations (288)
Nonprofit organization (288)

Intangibility (290)
Inseparability (290)
Heterogeneity (290)
Perishability (290)
Provider market (292)

Client market (292)
Service encounter (299)
Cause-related marketing (300)
Service quality (301)

Questions and Problems

1. Collect several pieces of letterhead stationery from different departments at your school and business cards from administrators and professors. Are the colors, logos, symbols, type styles, and other layouts identical or different? Make the same comparison for the websites of several units of the school. Which of the four characteristics of services do your findings support or contradict?

2. Services are highly perishable and are often subject to fluctuations in demand. In marketing an amusement park, how can a company offset these factors?

3. Cite some examples of large service firms that seem to be customer-oriented, and describe what these firms have done to create this impression. (A good resource is *www.fastcompany.com/themes.*)

4. Identify three segments of your school's donor market and the benefits offered to them in return for their donations.

5. Present a brief analysis of the market for each of the following service firms. Make use of the components of a market discussed in Chapters 4 and 5, and the concepts of market segmentation in Chapter 6.
   a. Hospital in your city
   b. Hotel near a large airport
   c. Indoor tennis club
   d. Regional airline

6. What are some ways in which each of the following services firms might expand its product mix?
   a. Certified public accountant (CPA)
   b. Hairstyling salon
   c. Bank

7. A financial consultant for a private university suggested a change in the school's pricing methods. He recommended that the school discontinue its present one-price policy, under which all full-time students pay the same tuition. Instead, he recommended that the tuition vary by departments within the university. Thus, students majoring in high-cost fields of study, such as engineering or a laboratory science, would pay higher tuition than students in lower-cost fields, such as English or history. Should the school adopt this recommendation?

8. Explain how the components of the marketing mix (product, price, distribution, promotion) are applicable to marketing the following social causes:
   a. The use of returnable bottles, instead of the throwaway type
   b. The prevention of heart ailments
   c. A campaign against smoking
   d. Obeying the speed limit

9. "When used by consumers for making purchases, the Internet seems to offset the service characteristics of inseparability and heterogeneity." Explain whether or not that statement is true.

10. How would you measure the marketing performance of each of the following?
    a. adidas website
    b. Your school
    c. The Republican Party
    d. A group in favor of gun control

Interactive Marketing Exercises

1. Grade the marketing performance of a sample of five profit-seeking services firms in your college community by asking 10 of your friends to rate each of them on a scale of 10 (excellent performer) to 1 (very poor performer). Compute an average "performance score" for each firm. On the basis of your survey, identify those firms that are doing a good marketing job and those that are not. In your report, explain briefly the reasons that contribute to the ratings of the best and worst performers.

2. Examine the websites of three nonbusiness services organizations (for example, a charity, a college or university, and a professional or trade association). Report the evidence you find that indicates the organizations are focused on a need, have identified a target market, and have developed a complete marketing mix.

Cases for Part 3

<table>
<tr><td>CASE
1</td><td>The Walt Disney Company</td></tr>
</table>

Riding Its Theme Parks into Tomorrowland

When Michael Eisner became chairman and chief executive officer of The Walt Disney Company in 1984, the much-beloved firm was best known for its revolutionary animated movies, U.S. amusement parks, and children's television programming. During the next two decades, Eisner expanded the company's holdings by building more theme parks; adding a cruise line and a chain of retail stores; and acquiring movie production companies, special-effects firms, cable and network television stations, and sports teams.

Eventually, the House of Mouse became overextended, and in 2003 sold several of its high-profile enterprises. In addition, a power struggle ensued between Eisner and Walt Disney's nephew, Roy Disney. Ultimately, in January 2005, Eisner announced that he would step down from his executive posts in September of that year.

Despite these problems, the year 2005 looked promising for the venerable corporation. Disney's net income was on the rise, up 85% in 2004 compared to 2003. Also, the company was preparing to celebrate the 50th anniversary of its first theme park, Disneyland, in 2005. A new theme park was scheduled to open in Hong Kong late in the year. And the ABC television network was being revitalized by a bunch of *Desperate Housewives* and a group of travelers who became *Lost*.

Opening the First House of Mouse

The first Disney park was conceived and funded by the company's namesake. Walt Disney purchased 182 acres of land in Anaheim, California, and transformed the site into Disneyland, which opened in 1955. Later, the company bought 28,000 acres in Orlando, Florida. The Magic Kingdom at Walt Disney World opened in 1971, followed by Epcot in 1982, and Disney-MGM Studios in 1989. Disney acquired another 55 acres of land in Anaheim, and Disney's California Adventure debuted in 2001.

The California complex now has more of the resortlike feel of its Florida counterpart, albeit on a much smaller scale. With three hotels and a shopping and restaurant area known as Downtown Disney, the company hopes that visitors will stay longer and spend more money at the California property. Shortly after California Adventure opened, patrons complained about the paucity of activities for small children. To remedy the problem, a new kids' area was developed and a thrill ride was added. Still, although attendance at California Adventure was up 6% in 2004, the $5.6 million profit level didn't meet the company's expectations.

Walt Disney World has also been seeking more visitors. It continues to add attractions: most recently Disney's Animal Kingdom in 1998, followed by the spectacular Animal Kingdom Lodge. However, it is also trying another approach. "Many people perceived that we were just for families," explained a marketing executive for the company. "We're reinventing the brand by making it relevant to various life stages." Four markets are being targeted: younger couples, older couples with grown children, families with young children, and families with teens. By emphasizing its golf courses, Pleasure Island (a nightclub-type setting located in Downtown Disney), and fine dining options, Disney World is trying to attract everyone from honeymooners to retirees, with the latter group hopefully bringing their grandchildren.

With a variety of attractions, more than 26,000 hotel rooms, and a reputation as "the happiest place on earth," Disney World continues to be the most popular vacation spot in the U.S. Unfortunately, the tragedy of September 11, 2001, depressed attendance at virtually all tourist destinations in America, including Disney's two theme parks. The industry finally rebounded in 2004, and Walt Disney World and Disneyland had 15.1 million and 13.3 million guests, respectively.

Spreading the Magic Overseas

The Walt Disney Company entered into a licensing agreement with a Japanese company called Oriental Land and opened Tokyo Disneyland in 1983. In exchange for an initial investment of $20 million, Disney receives between 5% and 10% of the park's revenues. The park was a huge success, drawing 13.2 million guests in 2004. One Japanese professor referred to it as "the greatest cultural event in Japan."

Tokyo DisneySea opened in 2001. Much like its California Adventure counterpart, this complementary attraction was intended to boost attendance at Tokyo Disneyland—perhaps from 17 million to 25 million a year. DisneySea is targeting a slightly older crowd with wilder rides, a full-service spa, and alcoholic beverages. Disney's operations in Tokyo face stiff competition from Universal Studios, which opened its own theme park in Osaka in 2001.

The second park that Disney built outside the U.S. was Euro Disney, which opened for business in 1992. Located outside Paris, the park initially had to deal with criticism from some people and apathy from many others. In stark contrast to Japanese enthusiasm about Disney parks, some French intellectuals characterized Euro Disney as a cultural wasteland. The park lost hundreds of millions of dollars in its first several years of operation.

Disney executives threatened to close Euro Disney unless costs were slashed and revenues increased. Financing was rearranged, ticket prices were cut, and attractions were added. The park also changed its name to Disneyland Paris. Attendance jumped 21% from 1994 to 1995, up to 10.7 million visitors; hotel occupancy increased as well. Perhaps more important, the park turned a profit of $23 million in 1995.

Disneyland Paris is now the number one tourist attraction in France—drawing more visitors than the Louvre and the Eiffel Tower combined—and is a major tourist destination for all of Europe. In 2002, it attracted 13.1 million visitors. Optimistic Disney executives approved the construction of a second park to attract even more guests. Walt Disney Studios Paris replicates many of the most successful attractions at its sister park, MGM Studios in Orlando, but it also features a variety of rides and shows that have a distinct European flavor. It too faces competition, this time from Warner Brothers, which has its own parks in Germany and Spain.

It was hoped that Walt Disney Studios Paris would draw eight million visitors its first year, and help increase attendance at Disneyland Paris to 16 million visitors by 2004. That didn't occur; the two parks' combined attendance was 12.2 million visitors in 2004. Euro Disney reported a loss of $190 million for the 2004 fiscal year. Analysts agreed that the war in Iraq, uncharacteristically hot weather, and a weak economy all dampened demand. Nevertheless, the French government rallied to support the enterprise by securing more financing from local institutions and working out a deal with Disney (which owns 41% of the Paris complex) to defer debts and forgive loans.

On the other side of the globe, Disney hosted a groundbreaking ceremony for a new theme park in Hong Kong. Eisner referred to this Chinese site as "a beach-head for the Disney brand in the most populous nation on earth." Disney reportedly provided $314 million toward the park's construction, giving it a 43% stake, with the Chinese government spending an additional $416 million. Hong Kong Disneyland, slated to open in September 2005, is being modeled after Disneyland in Anaheim, with two hotels, a number of retail stores, and several restaurants.

In mid-2002, the *Hong Kong Economic Times* reported that Disney intended to open a second park in China, this one in Shanghai. According to some observers, the two parks would compete for the same customers. Not surprisingly, Disney had a different view, namely that China's population (over 1.3 billion) was more than large enough to support two parks. Still, Disney postponed the opening of the new park until 2010, partly to give the Hong Kong park sufficient time to grow and flourish. Disney's decision was welcome news to Universal, which planned to open a theme park in Shanghai in 2006.

Consolidating and Strengthening Mickey's Holdings

Disney's theme parks are interrelated with the rest of the firm's holdings. In the parks, for example, you will find a wealth of Disney merchandise as well as shows that promote its network and cable programs, such as popular Disney Channel cartoons. Radio Disney hubs and Internet kiosks that feature Disney websites are also highly visible. And the ESPN Zone restaurant, located within several parks, is especially popular on game days.

The man responsible for The Walt Disney Company's broad holdings is Eisner. He judged that long-term success required diversification as well as expansion into fast-growing international markets. Thus Disney started a chain of retail stores in the 1990s, but sagging sales caused the company to rethink its retail strategy. In October 2004, Disney announced the sales of its stores to Children's Place Retail Stores Inc., a chain that specializes in fashions for babies and kids.

Two of Disney's higher-profile enterprises were Major League Baseball's Anaheim Angels and the National Hockey League's Mighty Ducks of Anaheim. The two-fold rationale for purchasing the teams was to allow cross-promotion of Disney's other properties in the area and to keep tourists in Anaheim for a longer period of time. However, the results didn't justify the expense, so Disney sold the Angels in 2003 and the Ducks in 2005.

In contrast, Disney's 1995 purchase of ESPN, the successful TV channel, has produced huge returns. As of 2004, largely because it commanded the industry's highest subscriber fees, ESPN was generating more than $1 billion worth of profits each year. ESPN's success was a key factor in Comcast's decision to try to purchase the Walt Disney Co. in 2004. To Comcast, one benefit of the acquisition would be avoiding the $2-per-subscriber fee it was paying each month in order to have the right to include the ESPN channel among its cable offerings.

Trying to Keep the Kingdom Magical

Comcast's takeover bid eventually failed, but shareholders of The Walt Disney Company were upset by the attempt. Eisner also received criticism for allegedly alienating several people who did business with the company, including Steve Jobs, founder of Pixar, the revolutionary animation studio that created *Toy Story* and *Finding Nemo* for Disney. Jobs said he would not consider renegotiating Pixar's contract with Disney so long as Eisner was in charge. The dissenting faction, led by Roy Disney and Stanley Gold, another former Disney director, called for Eisner's ouster.

Disney's 2004 stockholders' meeting was contentious, with Eisner announcing that he would cede control of the company sooner rather than later. Despite a difficult time toward the end of his tenure, Disney's market value rose from $1.8 billion when Eisner moved into his leadership position to more than $57 billion in 2004.

In early 2005, Disney's board selected Robert Iger, Disney's president and chief operating officer, as Eisner's successor effective September 2005.

To some extent, the dissension surrounding Eisner overshadowed Disney's good performance. After reporting a loss in 2001, the company posted a net income of more than $1 billion in 2002 and 2003. The House of Mouse improved in fiscal 2004, with a net income of more than $2 billion on revenues topping $30 billion. How did that occur? Besides the steady success of ESPN, ABC experienced a ratings surge during its 2004 to 2005 season. The upswing for Disney's broadcast network was largely fueled by two hit shows, *Lost* and *Desperate Housewives*, which attracted new viewers, some of whom stay

tuned to other ABC programs. In addition, theme-park attendance was up.

Another Disney product, the Disney Channel, had successfully carved out a niche with the "tween" market (kids between the ages of 8 and 14). In 2003, the Disney Channel contributed one-half of the $1.1 billion in profit generated by the company's cable networks, despite the fact that it only recorded one-fifth of its revenues. One industry analyst stated, "The Disney Channel is probably the best run of all the businesses at Disney." It had perfected the concept of the "tween" sitcom, with *Lizzie McGuire* being the prime example. Starring Hillary Duff, *Lizzie McGuire* began airing on the Disney channel in 2000 and then made its debut in ABC's Saturday morning lineup in 2001. Its success was further leveraged when Disney released the show's soundtrack in 2002, followed by *The Lizzie McGuire Movie* and that movie's soundtrack. Namesake merchandise such as books, clothes, toys, and home furnishings followed. Soon, Lizzie McGuire had become a major franchise for Disney.

Walt himself surely would have approved of seeing Lizzie McGuire jeans and Lizzie McGuire pillows, because he wholeheartedly believed in leveraging his beloved characters by licensing their images for a plethora of products. "He created a brand that stood for clean, wholesome family entertainment, using synergy before there was even a word for it," stated a former executive for Columbia Pictures.

In looking at the future of The Walt Disney Company, Iger asserted, "Our mission is to create more high-quality entertainment for more people to consume in more places more often . . . we begin with a great asset base, a strong set of executives, a great set of characters, brands and creativity, and that should go a long way." No doubt Walt would approve.

Questions

1. How does Disney address the unique challenges and opportunities posed by the four distinguishing characteristics of a service?

2. How has Disney attempted to increase the brand equity associated with its Disney World resort?

3. What product-mix strategy is Disney pursuing with the development of the new park in Hong Kong? What product-mix strategy is it pursuing with Walt Disney Studio Paris, Tokyo DisneySea, and California Adventure?

Nintendo versus Sony versus Microsoft

Positioning Their Products for a Big Score

A new product category was born in 1976 when Fairchild invented the Video Entertainment System. The product featured 21 different video games that could be played using a television as the monitor. The most popular game was *Pong,* which was really just video ping pong. But millions of users found it to be addictive, and the video game market took off. Enthusiasm for home video games soared in 1977, when Atari introduced the Video Computer System. By 1978, hardware and software sales totaled $200 million.

Today, home video games represent a $30 *billion* market worldwide. However, the enormity of this market could not save the industry's pioneers, Fairchild and Atari, which succumbed as a result of intense competition. Recently, another hardware manufacturer (Sega) was forced out of the game. In order to win or retain the favor of "gamers," both serious and casual players, the leading firms in this field must continuously strive to improve the capabilities of their equipment.

Jockeying for Position

The rise of personal computers in the mid-1980s spurred interest in computer games, which caused a crash in stand-alone video game consoles. Eventually, a number of different companies developed hardware consoles that provided graphics superior to the capabilities of computer games.

By 1990, the Nintendo Entertainment System dominated the product category with a 90% market share, only to be usurped by Sega when it introduced its Genesis system. By 1993, Sega commanded almost 60% of the U.S. video game market, and was one of the most recognized brand names among American kids. Sega's success was short-lived, however. In 1995, it launched a new, 32-bit system. (Bit, as you probably know, is a unit of computer memory.) The Saturn was a dismal failure for several reasons, including manufacturing delays, Sega's unwillingness to allow nonemployees to design compatible games, and a relatively high price.

Nintendo and Sony benefited greatly from Saturn's missteps. Unveiled late in 1994, Sony's PlayStation was used in 70 million homes worldwide by the end of 1999. Its "open design" encouraged the efforts of outside developers, resulting in a vast array of games—almost 3,000 in all—that were compatible with the PlayStation. It too featured 32-bit graphics, which appealed to an older audience. As a result, at one time, more than 30% of PlayStation owners were over 30 years old.

Introduced in 1996, Nintendo 64 and its eye-popping 64-bit graphics could be found in more than 28 million homes by 1999. Its primary users were between the ages of 6 and 13, a result of Nintendo's efforts to limit violent and adult-oriented material featured on games that can be played on its systems. Because the company exercises tight control over software development, Nintendo 64 had only one-tenth the number of compatible games as PlayStation did.

By 1999, Sony commanded 56% of the console market, followed by Nintendo with 42%. Sega, hanging onto its last 1% of market share, introduced the Sega Dreamcast in September 1999. Initial sales were promising, but the Dreamcast didn't deliver all the functionality Sega had promised. The company stopped manufacturing hardware in 2001.

Making Room for a New Player

Sony and Nintendo each released a new console in 1999. Nintendo's Neptune and Sony's PlayStation 2 (PS2) were both built on a DVD (digital versatile disc) platform and featured a 128-bit processor. Analysts applauded the move to DVD because it is less expensive to produce and allows more storage than CDs. It also gives purchasers the ability to use the machines to play music CDs and video (movie) DVDs.

In addition, the PS2 is able to play games developed for its predecessor, which utilized CDs. This "backward compatibility" gave the PS2 an enormous advantage in the number of game titles that could be played on it. Further enhancing the PS2's appeal is its high-speed modem, which allows users to access the Internet through digital cable as well as telephone lines. However, some prospective customers were put off by the console's initial price of $360.

Shortly after the Neptune was introduced, Nintendo switched strategies and announced the impending release of a different console, the GameCube. Unlike the Neptune, the GameCube doesn't run on a DVD platform, nor does it offer any online capabilities. However, Nintendo sought to offset the limited features with an attractive initial price of $199. A marketing vice president for Nintendo of America explained the company's change of direction, "We're the only competitor whose only business is video games. We want to create the best gaming system."

Nintendo also learned from past mistakes and made the GameCube friendly for outside game developers. Best known for its monstrous successes with games aimed at younger kids, such as *Donkey Kong, Super Mario Bros.*, and *Pokemon,* the company tried to appeal to an adult audience by adding different types of games, such as sports titles. Anticipating stiff competition during the holiday shopping season, both from Sony and a newcomer to the industry, Nintendo budgeted $450 million to market its new product.

Because of strong brand loyalty and high product-development costs, it is exceedingly difficult to break into the video games hardware market. One company with "very deep pockets" was undeterred, however. Microsoft began selling its new Xbox in November 2001, three days before the GameCube made its debut. Like the PS2, the Xbox was built on a DVD platform; it was priced at $299. Its open design allowed Microsoft to develop the Xbox in just two years and gave software developers the option of using standard PC tools for creating compatible games.

Further differentiating the Xbox from the GameCube was Microsoft's online strategy. Whereas Nintendo had no immediate plans for Web-based play, the Xbox came equipped with an Ethernet port for broadband access to the Internet. Microsoft announced its own Web-based network, dubbed Xbox Live, on which gamers can compete online in head-to-head play as well as in tournaments. Subscribers to this service pay a small monthly fee and must have high-speed access to the Internet (which was available in one-half of all American households in May 2005). "The online experience, the ability to create virtual communities online, is going to be a much bigger part of the industry going forward," explained a Microsoft executive.

In contrast, Sony promoted an open network that allows software developers to manage their own games, including fees charged to gamers. Although it would require a significant investment for them to manage their own servers on the Sony-based network, and they would have to pay Sony royalty fees, game companies were concerned about ceding online control to Microsoft. The promise of more flexibility and control, as well as a larger built-in audience, eventually won out. Thus Electronic Arts (EA), the world's largest game developer, announced in 2003 that it would make its biggest titles available online exclusively for Sony PS2 users for at least one year before it would consider putting them on Xbox Live. This new endeavor, dubbed EA Sports Nation, allows players to come together online to play John Madden Football, Tiger Woods Golf, and a number of other virtual sports.

Nintendo eventually went online in fall 2002, allowing GameCube users to play a subset of its games over the Internet. However, it did not make online gaming a cornerstone of its strategy going forward. "The profitable part of the online business is very likely several years away," commented Nintendo's director of corporate planning.

Shooting for More Functionality

At the same time that Sony, Microsoft, and finally Nintendo were promoting their online capabilities to gain new players, each was also attempting to squeeze remaining revenues out of their mature consoles by regularly cutting prices. In March 2004, Microsoft halved the original price of the Xbox to $149. Sony, which had reduced the price of the PS2 to $179 in 2003, then matched Microsoft's move. In September 2003, Nintendo began pricing the GameCube at $99.

By May 2005, Sony had sold 87 million PlayStation 2 units, and Nintendo and Microsoft had each sold 20 million of their consoles. Sony had amassed 68% of the market, and Nintendo and Microsoft both hovered around 15%. About that same time, all three companies began whetting the appetites of their loyal gamers by promoting next-generation consoles.

After getting trounced by Sony's PlayStation 2, which had a 20-month head start on the Xbox, Microsoft vowed to be first to market with its next console. The huge software company announced it would begin selling the Xbox 360 in fall 2005. With more than $2 billion in operating losses since entering the video games field, Microsoft wanted and expected the Xbox 360 to be a massive success.

To that end, Microsoft partnered with International Business Machines (IBM) to develop the console's chip. It also hired a sculptor to redesign the physical console, which had been criticized for being too "clunky" and "menacing." The new console features a fresh, sleek design with an interchangeable face plate, similar to those on cell phones. The games themselves will have a new feel as well, since they will all be in Dolby 5.1 digital surround sound and will have a high-definition, wide-screen format. In addition, the Xbox 360 is backward compatible with all of the Xbox's existing games, and comes with a basic level of access to Xbox Live.

But Microsoft doesn't want users to buy the Xbox 360 just for its ability to play video games. The new console can utilize a television set to display digital photos, play CDs and DVDs, or access other types of digital files by connecting wirelessly to PCs running Microsoft Windows XP. It can burn songs from CDs or copy pictures from digital cameras and save them to an optional 20-gigabyte hard drive. Quite simply, Microsoft wants the Xbox 360 to be the digital platform for all of a consumer's entertainment needs.

Being first to market doesn't necessarily guarantee success. Sega launched the Dreamcast a year before the PS2 hit the market, but the PS2 proved to be a better product and eventually rendered the Dreamcast obsolete. The PlayStation 3 (PS3), due in stores in spring 2006, is touted as being 35 times faster than the PS2 and being able to support high-definition, high-resolution video. Sony has been working with IBM and Toshiba Corporation to develop a superfast microprocessor, nicknamed "The Cell," for the PS3. Like the Xbox, the PS3 will be able to download music and movies, and will be backward compatible to allow users to play titles they originally purchased for the PlayStation or PS2.

Like Microsoft, its competitor, Sony envisions its console as being an all-encompassing entertainment unit, not just a video game machine. The Cell technology will allow the PS3 to communicate with other devices. According to an executive VP at Sony, "The battle is over entertainment. Period." He added, "If you don't have that vision, you are forever going to be a niche player."

Staying Serious about Games

This strategy of cramming more functionality into video game consoles has produced mixed results. After the PS2 was introduced in Japan in 2000, it became the country's best selling DVD player. Buoyed by this success, Sony launched the PSX, a combined video game platform and DVD recorder, in Japan in late 2003. Sales were disappointing, probably because the dual-function was difficult to market and confusing to consumers.

Nintendo remains single-minded, focused on video game consoles. "We're not looking to become TiVo or other things," insisted a senior vice president for Nintendo's U.S. division. Instead, Nintendo plans to release a new console, dubbed the "Revolution," in spring 2006. Nintendo will continue to focus on its successful video game franchises, such as *The Smash Brothers*. Thus the Revolution won't have the capability of playing DVDs unless users purchase an additional component. According to the Nintendo VP, "If someone buys a DVD and watches it on the Nintendo GameCube, we wouldn't receive any revenue from that. We'd rather have them play our games."

Another major component of Nintendo's focus on gaming is its hand-held GameBoy unit. By 2003, the GameBoy was responsible for 70% of the company's profits and maintained a dominant 98% share of the hand-held market. In August 2003, there were 150 million GameBoys in circulation worldwide and more than 1,200 compatible games available.

But two companies were set to challenge Nintendo's leadership position. Nokia, the world's number-one mobile phone manufacturer, introduced the N-Gage in late 2003. In addition to being a phone, the N-Gage has a full-color screen, 3-D graphics, and a powerful processor that allows users to play sophisticated video games. It also has a built-in FM radio and an MP-3 player. However, initial reviews faulted the N-Gage for being a bit awkward to use and too expensive at $299.

Nintendo retaliated with the Nintendo DS (which stands for dual screen). True to the company's convictions, the DS is simply a video game machine, albeit a very good one. It went on sale in fall 2004, with an attractive price of $150. Its two screens provide even more information for the player, and the bottom screen is similar to a touchpad, usable with a stylus. The DS includes voice-recognition capabilities, and up to 16 users can compete wirelessly or chat and send instant messages to each other. It is also backward compatible with GameBoy Advance games. Nintendo found itself in a good news–bad news situation when it couldn't keep up with demand and its initial 800,000 unit shipment sold out before Thanksgiving.

Not to be outdone, Sony launched the PlayStation Portable (PSP) in spring 2005 and began touting it as the Walkman of the Digital Age. With its 4.3-inch color LCD display and wireless networking capabilities, the PSP has won rave reviews as a game player. It can also play music and movies and display photos, but it is unclear whether that functionality will compel people to pay $250 for a very small movie screen with a limited library of compatible titles. Sony insists it will continue to produce more movies for the PSP. However, PSP owners who want to view that movie on a television set will have to acquire the movie on DVD, because the PSP has no "video out" connectors.

So Sony is gunning for Nintendo in the hand-held market, and Microsoft has set its sights on Sony with its newest console. What remains to be seen is whether these three companies can keep their names on the industry's list of "high scorers."

Questions

1. Where is the video game console with regards to the product life cycle?
   a. How about online gaming?
   b. What are the implications of each product's life-cycle stage?

2. Should video game companies:

   a. Continue to alter their products to include functions besides games? Or do you agree with Nintendo's pure gaming strategy?

   b. Move aggressively into online gaming?

3. Does Microsoft's Xbox have the desired attributes of a brand name?

Sources

Case 1: Walt Disney Co. *disney.go.com,* accessed Apr. 15, 2005; "Disney's New CEO Reflects on His Style," *Forbes.com,* Mar. 18, 2005; Edward Jay Epstein, "In Praise of Michael Eisner," *The Wall Street Journal,* Mar. 18, 2005, p. A12; Ronald Grover and Tom Lowry, "Disney Crowns a Familiar Head," *BusinessWeek Online,* Mar. 14, 2005; Merissa Marr, Mylene Mangalindan, and Joann Lublin, "Disney Turns to Insider Iger to Take CEO Reins from Eisner," Mar. 14, 2005, p. A1; Krysten Crawford, "Disney Profits Are Up, But Image is Down," *CNN Money Online,* Feb. 1, 2005; Jo Wrighton and Bruce Orwall, "Despite Losses and Bailouts, France Stays Devoted to Disney," *The Wall Street Journal,* Jan. 26, 2005, p. A1; "Michael Eisner," *BusinessWeek,* Jan. 10, 2005, p. 76; Suzanne Vranica and Bruce Orwall, "Disney's Ailing Parks to Get Global Ad Boost," *The Wall Street Journal,* Dec. 29, 2004, p. B1; "Attendance at Theme Parks Increases," *MSNBC.com,* Dec. 14, 2004; Robert Niles, "2004 Theme Park Attendance Estimates Announced," *Theme Park Insider,* Dec. 13, 2004; Michael McCarthy, "ABC Cashes in on 'Desperate Housewives,' " *USA Today Online,* Dec. 12, 2004; "Disney to Sell 313 Stores to Children's Place," *The Wall Street Journal,* Oct. 21, 2004, p. B8; Ronald Grover, "He Built a Better Mouse," *BusinessWeek,* May 17, 2004, p. 20; "Moreno Agrees to Buy for Just Over $180 Million," *ESPN Online,* Apr. 16, 2004; Joe Flint, "Why Comcast Covets ESPN," *The Wall Street Journal,* Feb. 13, 2004, p. B1; Bruce Orwall and Emily Nelson, "Hidden Wall Shields Disney's Kingdom: 80 Years of Culture," *The Wall Street Journal,* Feb. 13, 2004, p. A1; Carol Matlack, "Euro Disney: Looking Euro Dismal," *BusinessWeek,* Dec. 8, 2003, p. 14; Julia Boorstin, "Disney's 'Tween Machine," *Fortune,* Sept. 29, 2003, pp. 111–114; Jamey Keaten, "Debt, Dwindling Tourism Pinch Euro Disney," *St. Louis Post-Dispatch,* Aug. 2, 2003, p. BIZ3; "Disney Execs Break Ground on Hong Kong Theme Park," *Columbia Daily Tribune,* Jan. 13, 2003, p. 3B; Ben Dolven and Bruce Orwall, "Disney Will Slow Theme-Park Drive into China," *The Wall Street Journal,* Dec. 9, 2002, p. B4; "Disney to Focus on Hong Kong Theme Park," *Columbia Daily Tribune,* Dec. 9, 2002, p. 2B; "The Best Managers: Ken Kutaragi," *BusinessWeek,* Jan. 13, 2003, p. 64; Eryn Brown, "Sony's Big Bazooka," *Fortune,* Dec. 30, 2002, pp. 111, 112, and 114; Bruce Orwall and Karby

Leggett, "Disney Signs Letter of Intent to Build Shanghai Theme Park," *The Wall Street Journal,* July 22, 2002, p. A3; Matthew Benz, "Disney Assets Ready to Shine in 2002," *Amusement Business,* Jan. 14, 2002, p. 8; Juliana Koranteng, "Euro Disney Preparing to Unwrap $600 Mil Walt Disney Studio Park," *Amusement Business,* Dec. 17, 2001, p. 12; Johnnie Roberts, "Disney's Lost Magic," *Newsweek,* Dec. 10, 2001, p. 52; Erika Rasmusson, "Brand New World," *Sales & Marketing Management,* December 2001, p. 56; "Now Playing at Disney: Twofers," *BusinessWeek,* Nov. 19, 2001, p. 50; Chester Dawson, "Will Tokyo Embrace Another Mouse?" *BusinessWeek,* Sept. 10, 2001, p. 65; and Ronald Grover, "Now Disneyland Won't Seem So Mickey Mouse," *BusinessWeek,* Jan. 29, 2001, pp. 56–58.

Case 2: Nintendo versus Sony versus Microsoft *www.nintendo.com,* accessed May 30, 2005; Robert Guth, "New Xbox Aim for Microsoft: Profitability," *The Wall Street Journal,* May 24, 2005, p. C1; Lev Grossman, "Out of the Xbox," *Time,* May 23, 2005, pp. 44–53; Nick Wingfield, Rob Guth, and Phred Dvorak, "A Buyer's Guide to the New Gameboxes," *The Wall Street Journal,* May 18, 2005, p. D1; Byron Acohido, "Microsoft Angles to Be Lord of the Game Consoles," *USA Today,* May 10, 2005, p. 3B; Robert Guth, Nick Wingfield, and Phred Dvorak, "It's Xbox 360 Vs. PlayStation 3, and War Is About to Begin," *The Wall Street Journal,* May 9, 2005, p. B1; Peter Lewis, "It's Fun and Games Again at Sony," *Fortune,* Apr. 4, 2005, p. 40; Phred Dvorak, "Videogame Whiz Reprograms Sony after 10-Year Funk," *The Wall Street Journal,* Sept. 2, 2004, p. A1; Robert Guth, "Game Gambit: Microsoft to Cut Xbox Price," *The Wall Street Journal,* Mar. 19, 2004, p. B1; Joseph Pereira and Phred Dvorak, "Nintendo's DS Player Emerges as Tickle Me Elmo of 2004," *The Wall Street Journal,* Dec. 13, 2004, p. B1; Andy Reinhardt, Eric Sylvers, and Irene Kunii, "Nokia's Big Leap," *BusinessWeek,* Oct. 13, 2003, pp. 50–52; Peter Lewis, "The Biggest Game in Town," *Fortune,* Sept. 15, 2003, pp. 132–142; Geoff Keighley, "Is Nintendo Playing the Wrong Game?" *Business 2.0,* August 2003, pp. 110–115; Robert Guth, "Videogame Giant Links with Sony, Snubbing Microsoft," *The Wall Street Journal,* May 12, 2003, p. A1; Rebecca Buckman, Khanh Tran, and Robert Guth, "Secret Project at Microsoft Features Xbox with Extras," *The Wall Street Journal,* July 1, 2001, p. B1; Byron Acohido, "Will Microsoft's Xbox Hit the Spot?" *USA Today,* June 4, 2002, p. 1B; Khanh Tran, "U.S. Vidogame Industry Posts Record Sales," *The Wall Street Journal,* Feb. 7, 2002, p. B5; Kenneth Hein, "Nintendo Grows Up," *Brandweek,* Jan. 7, 2002, pp. 12–15; Steve Hamm and Jay Greene, "In This Game, Microsoft Is More David than Goliath," *BusinessWeek,* Nov. 19, 2001, p. 46; Khanh Tran, "How Microsoft Hopes to Win with Xbox," *The Wall Street Journal,* Jan. 31, 2001, p. B1; Steven Levy, "Here Comes PlayStation 2," *Newsweek,* Mar. 6, 2000, pp. 54–59; Ben Pappas, "From Pong to Kingpin," *Forbes,* May 31, 1999, p. 54; Maryanne Murray Buechner, "The Battle Has Just Begun," *Time Digital,* Apr. 12, 1999, pp. 28–31; Benjamin Fulford, "Killer Sequel," *Forbes,* Apr. 5, 1999, pp. 52–53; and "The Interactive Digital Software Association Report on Video and Computer Game Software," *Billboard,* Apr. 4, 1998, p. 56.

Chapter 12

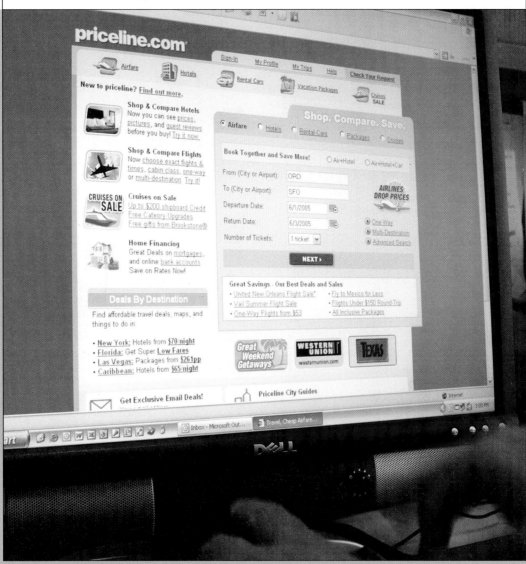

"According to founder Jay Walker,
Priceline.com's approach to pricing . . .
is 'absolutely revolutionary.'"

Price Determination

Should **Priceline.com** Offer Low Prices or More Choices in Travel?

Priceline.com was launched during the dot-com boom in the late 1990s. The "name your own price" website focused on air travel by consumers who were flexible with regards to departure and arrival dates and times as well as choice of airline. Shortly after the company's first public stock offering, Priceline.com's market value was $23 *billion,* on paper. Soon thereafter, the stock price plunged, which was not surprising considering that the firm's sales were in the tens of millions and it was unprofitable.

Priceline.com built brand awareness through a series of ads in which William Shatner, the former star of *Star Trek,* urged consumers to "name your own price" for airline tickets, car rentals, home mortgages, and other products. According to founder Jay Walker, Priceline.com's approach to pricing and selling these products is "absolutely revolutionary."

Under Priceline's patented process, a consumer who went to the firm's website filled out a form specifying desired departure and arrival cities and travel dates as well as the maximum acceptable ticket price. A bidder agreed to accept any departure time between 6 A.M. and 10 P.M. on the stipulated date. Required by the airlines, the restrictions sought to ensure that the tickets were sold to people, typically leisure travelers, who probably would not purchase an airline ticket without a special inducement. If there was a match (that is, the desired travel dates and cities at a mutually acceptable price), the traveler had to purchase the ticket, and no refund was allowed.

In Priceline.com's first year, only 7% of the requests submitted by prospective travelers wound up in a match, largely because only TWA (subsequently bought by American Airlines) and America West agreed to participate. To build a solid base of customers, Priceline subsidized many of the bids and wound up losing about $30 on each ticket it sold. Eventually, traffic levels and match rates grew, and Priceline recorded its first-ever profit in the second quarter of 2001.

The terrorist attacks of September 11, 2001, hit the entire travel industry very hard. Industry analysts wondered whether or not Priceline was well equipped to survive an extended slowdown in travel at the same time that it battled other services such as Travelocity and Expedia. Priceline.com's CEO at the time asserted, "People's desire to save money is, if anything, higher as they step up their level of travel."

In 2004, Priceline garnered 7% of the sales made by online travel services, a small share compared to the 41% claimed by industry leader Expedia. Several factors were working against Priceline's business model:

- Many, perhaps most, consumers are reluctant to buy air travel without added information such as departure time and airline to be flown.

- As a result of industry consolidation and rebounding demand for air travel, there are fewer unsold seats that airlines make available to a discount operation such as Priceline.

- Many airlines are relying on their own websites to sell discounted tickets to travelers.

In 2005, Priceline adapted its business model to give prospective customers more choice. It will compete more directly with Expedia, Orbitz, and Travelocity by showing a list of travel products (hotel and car rentals besides air travel) that meet the dimensions (e.g., range of acceptable departure times).

Priceline thinks that the new approach will attract more travelers who will purchase not just flights, using either option, but also other travel products. The company expects that its profitable revenues will be from the complementary products.[1]

Can Priceline.com appeal to both price-conscious and information-sensitive travelers effectively? Do you think Priceline's expanded business model will allow it to prosper (generate profits), not just survive?

www.priceline.com

"How much should we charge for airline seats?" "How does price fit into our marketing mix?" Airlines—in fact, all organizations—face these questions constantly. These kinds of questions are asked any time an enterprise introduces a new product or considers changing the price on an existing one.

In this chapter we cover the role of price in the marketing mix—what price is, how it can be used, and how it is set relative to such factors as product costs, market demand, and competitors' prices. After studying this chapter, you should be able to explain:

Chapter Goals

- The meaning of price.
- The significance of price in our economy, in a consumer's mind, and to an individual firm.
- The concept of value and how it relates to price.
- Major pricing objectives.
- Key factors influencing price.
- The types of costs incurred in producing and marketing a product.
- Approaches to determining prices, including cost-plus pricing, marginal analysis, and setting prices in relation only to other prices in the market.
- Break-even analysis.

In this chapter we will discuss major methods used to determine a price. Before being concerned with actual price determination, however, executives—and you—should understand the meaning and importance of price.

Meaning of Price

Some pricing difficulties occur because of confusion about the meaning of *price*, even though the concept is easy to define in familiar terms. Simply, **price** is the amount of money and/or other items with utility needed to acquire a product. Recall that *utility* is an attribute with the potential to satisfy wants.

Thus price may involve more than money. To illustrate, the price of a rare Alex Rodriquez baseball card may be (1) $500; (2) the rookie cards for 10 players, including Albert Pujols and Roger Clemens; or (3) some combination of dollars and baseball cards. Exchanging goods and/or services for other products is termed **barter**. Because our economy is not geared to a slow, ponderous barter system, we typically state price in monetary terms and use money as our medium of exchange.

Based in Connecticut, Barter Business Unlimited (BBU) brings together organizations that want to barter. BBU clients use trade dollars, rather than cash, to make a transaction. For example, if a hotel that is a BBU client trades 10 hotel rooms worth $1,000, the hotel earns that amount of trade dollars for use in acquiring needed goods and/or services from other BBU clients.

www.bbu.com

In socially undesirable situations, there are prices called blackmail, ransom, and bribery. Here are prices under various names and the products with which they are associated in normal situations:[2]

Price Is What You Pay . . .		For What You Get
Tuition	→	Education
Interest	→	Use of money
Rent	→	Use of living quarters or a piece of equipment for a period of time
Fare	→	Taxi ride or airline flight
Fee	→	Services of a physician or lawyer
Retainer	→	Lawyer's or consultant's services over a period of time
Toll	→	Long-distance phone call or travel on some highways
Salary	→	Services of an executive or other white-collar worker
Wage	→	Services of a blue-collar worker
Commission	→	Sales person's services
Dues	→	Membership in a union or a club

Practical problems arise when we try to state simply the price of a product. Suppose you paid $395 for a desk, but your instructor paid only $295 for one of similar size. At first glance, it looks as if the instructor taught the student a lesson! But consider this: Your desk—which has a beautiful finish—was delivered to your apartment, and you had a year to pay for it. The instructor, a do-it-yourself buff, bought a partially assembled, unfinished desk that had to be put together and then stained and varnished. The seller provided neither delivery nor credit. Now, even with the differences in price, who got the better deal? The answer is not as easy as it first appeared.

This example indicates that the definition depends on determining exactly what is being sold. A seller usually is pricing a combination of (1) the specific good or service that is the object of the transaction, (2) several supplementary services (such as a warranty), and (3) in a very real sense, the want-satisfying benefits provided by the product. Sometimes it is difficult even to define the price of the predominant good or service itself. On one model of automobile, a stated price may include radio, power steering, and power brakes. For another model of the same brand, these three items may be priced separately. So, to know the real price of a product, you need to look at the identifiable components that make up that product.

Importance of Price

Price is significant in our economy, in the consumer's mind, and in an individual firm. Let's consider each situation.

In the Economy

A product's price influences wages, rent, interest, and profits. Price is a basic regulator of the economic system because it influences the allocation of the factors of production: labor, land, and capital. High wages attract labor, high interest rates attract capital, and so on. As an allocator of resources, price determines what will be produced (supply) and who will get the goods and services produced (demand).

Criticism of the American system of reasonably free enterprise and, in turn, public demand for added restraints on the system are often triggered by negative reactions to prices or pricing policies. To reduce the risk of government intervention, businesses need to establish prices in a manner and at a level that consumers and government officials consider socially responsible.

In the Customer's Mind

Some prospective customers are interested primarily in low prices, whereas another segment is more concerned with other factors, such as service, quality, value, and brand image. It's safe to say that few, if any, customers are attentive to price alone *or* are entirely oblivious to price. One study identified four distinct segments of shoppers: *brand loyals* (relatively uninterested in price), *system beaters* (prefer certain brands but try to buy them at reduced prices), *deal shoppers* (driven by low prices), and *uninvolveds* (seemingly not motivated by either brand preferences or low prices).[3]

An important question is whether consumer price sensitivity can be predicted. There is no clear-cut answer. The four shopper segments mentioned above are not distinguished by demographic factors. Rather, according to the study's results, the segments' differing degrees of price sensitivity are more likely to be related to psychographic factors, such as lifestyle, or to which product categories are involved. In contrast, a major study of sales data for 18 product categories in a chain of 83 supermarkets concluded that consumers' relative interest in price does vary across demographic groups. According to this research, consumers with particular attributes—such as low income level, small house, or large family—are likely to be price sensitive.[4]

Another consideration, supported by recent research, is that some consumers' perceptions of product quality vary directly with price. Typically, the higher the price, the better the quality is perceived to be. In the words of an engineering consultant, "Many consultants have told me that when they raised their prices, their sales went up." The explanation was that with higher prices, clients felt more comfortable regarding the quality of the advice.[5]

Haven't you been concerned about product quality—such as when you are looking at ads for DVD players—if the price is unexpectedly low? Or, at the other extreme, have you selected a restaurant for a special dinner because you heard it was fairly high priced so you expected it to be very nice? Consumers' perceptions of quality may be influenced not just by price but also by such factors as store reputation and advertising.

Price is also important as a component of value. In recent years customers, both in consumer and business markets, have come to expect—and have sought—better value in the goods and services they purchase. **Value** is the ratio of perceived benefits to price and any other incurred costs. Examples of *other incurred costs* for consumers include time associated with shopping for the product, gasoline used traveling to the place of purchase, and perhaps the aggravation involved in assembling the product. Online shopping can reduce some of these other costs, such as the effort of traveling from one store to another; however, it may increase some costs, such as the perceived risk of buying a product without seeing it in person.

When we say a product has ample value, we don't necessarily mean it is inexpensive or has a very low price. Rather, good value indicates that a particular product has the kinds and amounts of potential benefits—such as quality, image, and purchase convenience—consumers expect at a particular price level.

Many businesses are responding to calls for more value by devising new products. For instance, during the past

In this ad, the Xerox Corp. stresses this machine's multiple functions—notably printing, copying, and scanning. In addition, Xerox emphasizes that the Work Centre Pro 2128 produces color prints at a low cost per page.

www.xerox.com

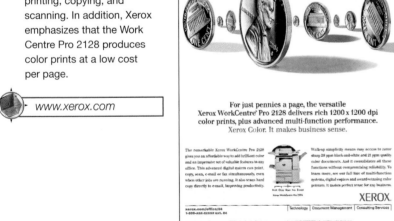

For just pennies a page, the versatile
Xerox WorkCentre Pro 2128 delivers rich 1200 x 1200 dpi
color prints, plus advanced multi-function performance.
Xerox Color. It makes business sense.

www.extstay.com

10 years, extended-stay hotel chains, such as Residence Inn by Marriott, Candlewood Suites, and InTown Suites, have grown dramatically by emphasizing value. The target market for this product consists of people who need or want to stay in the same locale for several days, weeks, or even months. Extended-stay hotels offer value by providing relatively low rates as well as amenities that are important to longer-term guests, such as spacious rooms, kitchenettes, and free buffet breakfasts. In the words of one executive in this segment of the lodging industry, "What makes us attractive for business travelers is that they're not asked to pay for all the extras the way they would in a full-service transient business hotel." To pare expenses, this type of hotel reduces or eliminates less important amenities, such as room service and daily housekeeping.[6]

www.abb.com

Other businesses are striving for better value with existing products. ABB Ltd., a manufacturer of power transformers and other large, expensive equipment, has worked hard to enhance product quality *and* pare production costs. With lower costs, the urge to increase prices in order to maintain profits is lessened. Another avenue to enhanced value is to give customers more at the same price. Although they are dissimilar in many respects, both Little Caesar's and California Pizza Kitchen used that approach by providing larger portions and holding the line on prices.[7]

Attention to value was certainly heightened by the recessions of the early 1990s and the start of the new century. However, the increased emphasis on value probably reflects a more fundamental shift in attitudes. Consumers' greater interest in the ratio of benefits to price has created a new approach to pricing, not surprisingly called "value pricing," which we will discuss in Chapter 13.

In the Individual Firm

A product's price is a major determinant of the market demand for it. Through prices, money comes into an organization. Thus price affects a firm's competitive position, revenues, and net profits. According to a McKinsey consultant, "Pricing is extremely important because small changes in price can translate into huge improvements in profitability." In fact, in a study of 1,000 companies, the McKinsey firm found that a 1% increase in price would improve profits by 7%, assuming no change in sales volume.[8]

Some businesses use higher prices to convey an image of superior quality. This approach will have a positive impact only on consumers who consider quality important. It's most likely to work well in the case of services and certain goods for which consumers have difficulty judging quality on an objective basis. To be highly effective in signaling superior quality, the high price should be combined with other conspicuous elements of the marketing mix, such as a compelling advertising message and an appealing package design.[9]

Prices are important to a company most of the time, but not always. Several factors can limit how much effect pricing has on a company's marketing program. Differentiated product features, a favorite brand, high quality, convenience, or some combination of these and other factors may be more important to consumers than price. As we saw in Chapter 10, one object of branding is to *decrease* the effect of price on the demand for a product. Thus we need to put the role of pricing in a company's marketing program in its proper perspective: It is only one of four marketing-mix elements that must be skillfully combined—and then adapted over time—to achieve business success.

Pricing Objectives

Every marketing activity—including pricing—should be directed toward a goal. Thus management should decide on its pricing objective before determining the price itself.[10] Yet, as logical as this may sound, few firms consciously establish a pricing objective.

To be useful, the pricing objective management selects must be compatible with the overall goals set by the firm and the goals for its marketing program. Let's assume that a *company's goal* is to increase return on investment from its present level of 15% to 20% within three years. It follows that the primary *pricing goal* during this period should be to achieve some stated percentage return on investment. It would be questionable, in this case, to adopt a primary pricing goal of maintaining the company's market share or of stabilizing prices.

We will discuss the following **pricing objectives:**

- Profit-oriented:
  - —To achieve a target return
  - —To maximize profit
- Sales-oriented:
  - —To increase sales volume
  - —To maintain or increase market share
- Status quo–oriented:
  - —To stabilize prices
  - —To meet competition

Recognize that all these objectives can be sought—and hopefully attained—through pricing that is coordinated with other marketing activities such as product design and distribution channels. And all these objectives are ultimately aimed at satisfactory performance over the long run. For a business, that requires ample profits.

Profit-Oriented Goals

Profit goals may be set for the short or long term. A company may select one of two profit-oriented goals for its pricing policy.

Achieve a Target Return
A firm may price its product to *achieve a target return*—a specified percentage return on its *sales* or on its *investment*. Many retailers and wholesalers use a target return *on sales* as a pricing objective for short periods such as a year or a fashion season. They add an amount to the cost of the product, called a *markup,* to cover anticipated operating expenses *and* provide a desired profit for the period. Safeway or Kroger's, for example, may price to earn a net profit of 1% on a store's sales. A chain of men's clothing stores may have a target profit of 6% of sales, and price its products accordingly. (Markup and other operating ratios are discussed fully in Appendix A, which can be found at the website for this text.)

www.mhhe.com/etzel/07

Achieving a target return *on investment* is measured in relation to a firm's net worth (its assets minus its liabilities). This pricing goal is often selected by the leading firm in an industry. Target-return pricing is used by industry leaders such as DuPont, Alcoa, and ExxonMobil because they can set their pricing goals more independently of competition than smaller firms in the industry. The leaders may price so that they earn a net profit that is 15% or 20% of the firm's net worth.

Maximize Profits
The pricing objective of making as much money as possible is probably followed more than any other goal. The trouble with this goal is that to some people, *profit maximization* has an ugly connotation, suggesting profiteering, high prices, and monopoly. Where prices are unduly high and entry into the field is severely limited, public criticism can be expected. If market conditions and public opinion do not bring about reasonable prices, government may intervene.

In both economic theory and business practice, however, there is nothing wrong with profit maximization. Theoretically, if profits become high in an industry because supply is short in relation to demand, new capital will be attracted to increase production capacity. This will increase supply and eventually reduce profits.

Virtually all supermarket chains seek to build an image of having competitive prices. Thus Kroger promotes its low prices in this newspaper ad. Although the chain may not make much profit on these advertised items, it seeks to achieve its target return by having higher (and more profitable) prices on numerous items that are not subject to extensive comparisons by shoppers.

www.kroger.com

In the marketplace it is difficult to find many situations where profiteering has existed over an extended period of time. Substitute products are available, purchases are postponable, and competition can increase to keep prices at a reasonable level.

A profit-maximization goal is likely to be far more beneficial to a company if it is pursued over the *long term*. To do this, however, firms may have to accept modest profits or even losses over the short term. For example, a company entering a new geographic market or introducing a new product frequently does best by initially setting low prices to build a large clientele. Repeat purchases from this large group of customers may allow the firm to maximize its profits over the long term.

The goal should be to maximize profits on *total output* rather than on each single product. In fact, a company may maximize total profit by setting low, relatively unprofitable prices on some products in order to stimulate sales of others. For instance, Salton, Inc. has a relatively low suggested retail price for its single-cup coffee maker. The firm hopes that once consumers acquire its Melitta One:One product, they will become loyal customers for its brand of coffee pods, which generate healthy profits for the company. The same would appear to be true for Hewlett-Packard with regards to its printers and, in turn, print cartridges.

www.saltoninc.com/
brands/melitta.html

Sales-Oriented Goals

In some companies, management's pricing is focused on sales volume. The pricing goal may be to increase sales volume or to maintain or increase the firm's market share.

Increase Sales Volume
This pricing goal of *increasing sales volume* is typically adopted to achieve rapid growth or to discourage other firms from entering a

Pharmaceutical companies have introduced various drugs to fights AIDS or the HIV virus. Typically, the firms have been criticized for charging excessive prices for these drugs—prices that are beyond the means of the majority of those infected with HIV or AIDS. Recently, for example, Abbott Laboratories drew angry complaints when it raised the price of a daily dosage of HIV treatment Norvir from $1.75 to $8.57. Drug companies have responded to the criticism by saying that high prices are necessary in order to recover the enormous costs of developing the complex drugs. Several years ago, to offset criticism, Merck announced that its prices for two HIV-suppressing drugs in impoverished parts of the world, such as sub-Saharan Africa, would be about one-tenth of the price charged in the U.S.

Is it ethical to charge a seemingly high price for a product that could be a life or death necessity?

Sources: Bruce Japsen, "Abbott Defends Pricing Practices of HIV Drugs," *Chicago Tribune,* Apr. 24, 2004, p. 2; John Carey and Amy Barrett, "Drug Prices: What's Fair?" *BusinessWeek,* Dec. 10, 2001, pp. 60–64+; and Lori Hinnant, "Merck Slashes AIDS Drug Prices for the World's Poor," *Pittsburgh Post-Gazette,* Mar. 19, 2001, p. D4.

market. The goal is usually stated as a percentage increase in sales volume over some period, say, one year or three years.

Management may seek higher sales revenues by discounting or by some other aggressive pricing strategy. Periodically, the Monsanto Co. has lowered the prices of its popular Roundup brand of herbicide. For some time, the intent of these price cuts seemingly was to stimulate more farmers to use the product, and on more acres of land. Following the expiration of the U.S. patent on Roundup, ongoing price reductions have been necessary to fend off generic competitors.[11]

Occasionally companies are willing to incur a loss *in the short run* to expand sales volume or meet sales objectives. Clothing stores run end-of-season sales, and auto dealers offer rebates and below-market loan rates on new cars. Many vacation spots, such as golf courses and resorts, reduce prices during off-seasons to increase sales volume.

Maintain or Increase Market Share In some companies, both large and small, the pricing objective is to *maintain or increase market share.* Why is market share protected or pursued so vigorously? In growing fields, such as computers and other technology-based products, companies want large shares in order to gain added clout with vendors, drive down production costs, and/or project a dominant appearance to consumers. In order to gain a foothold in the marketplace, many electronic-commerce firms emphasized market share or sales volume over profits, at least in the short run. Perhaps that's one reason why so many of these dot-coms went out of business.[12]

Some industries are not growing much, if at all, *and* have excess production capacity. Many firms need added sales to utilize their capacity more fully and, in turn, gain economies of scale and better profits. Because the size of the "pie" isn't growing in most cases, businesses that need added volume have to grab a bigger "slice of the pie"—that is, greater market share. The U.S. auto and retail grocery industries illustrate these situations.

In the mid-1990s, the Japanese yen rose considerably in relation to the American dollar, making Japanese products more expensive in American dollars. To maintain their market shares, Toyota, Nissan, and Honda accepted smaller profit margins and reduced their costs so that they could lower the selling prices of their autos in the U.S. The situation changed when the yen weakened in the first years of the new century. American automakers charge that Japanese government officials manipulate the yen in order to gain unfair price advantages for their exports, including motor vehicles.[13]

Status Quo Goals

Two closely related goals—*stabilizing prices* and *meeting competition*—are the least aggressive of all pricing goals. They are intended simply to maintain the firm's current situation—that is, the status quo. With either of these goals, a firm seeks to avoid price competition.

www.phelpsdodge.com

Price stabilization often is the goal in industries where (1) the product is highly standardized (such as steel or bulk chemicals) *and* (2) one large firm, such as Phelps Dodge in the copper industry, historically has acted as a leader in setting prices. Smaller firms in these industries tend to "follow the leader" when setting their prices. What is the reason for such pricing behavior? A price cut by any one firm is likely to be matched by all other firms in order to remain competitive; therefore, no individual firm gains, but all may suffer smaller profits. Conversely, a price boost is unlikely to be matched. But the price-boosting firm faces a differential disadvantage, because other elements of a standardized product such as gasoline are perceived to be fairly similar.

Even in industries where there are no price leaders, countless firms deliberately price their products to meet the prevailing market price. This pricing policy gives management an easy means of avoiding difficult pricing decisions.

Firms that adopt status quo pricing goals to avoid price competition are not necessarily passive in their marketing. Quite the contrary! Typically these companies compete aggressively using other marketing-mix elements—product, distribution, and especially promotion. This approach, called *nonprice competition,* will be discussed in Chapter 13.

Factors Influencing Price Determination

Knowing its pricing objective, a company can move to the heart of price management: determining the base price of a product. **Base price,** or *list price,* refers to the price of one unit of the product at its point of production or resale. This price does not reflect discounts, freight charges, or any other modifications such as leader pricing, all of which will be discussed in the next chapter.

The same procedure is followed in pricing both new and established products. Pricing an established product usually is less difficult than pricing a new product, however, because the exact price or a narrow range of prices may be dictated by the market.[14]

According to one consultant, failing to consider the various interrelated factors that affect pricing is "the most common mistake made by small businesses."[15] Thus other factors, besides objectives, that influence price determination are discussed next.

Estimated Demand

In pricing, a company must estimate the total demand for the product. This is easier to do for an established product than for a new one. The steps in estimating demand are: (1) determine whether there is a price the market expects and (2) estimate what the sales volume might be at different prices.

The **expected price** of a product is the price at which customers consciously or unconsciously value it—what they think the product is worth. Expected price usually is expressed as a *range* of prices rather than as a specific amount. Thus the expected price might be "between $250 and $300" or, for another product, "not over $20."

A producer must also consider a middleman's reaction to price. Middlemen are more likely to promote a product if they approve its price. Sometimes they don't. For instance, last decade, Wal-Mart and other retailers complained when Rubbermaid Inc. tried to raise prices. The manufacturer thought it needed to, after the cost of resin (a major ingredient in its various plastic housewares and toys) more than doubled. However, rather than antagonize retailers, Rubbermaid settled for smaller increases, which hurt the company's profits. Losing this battle over wholesale prices contributed to a severe financial decline for Rubbermaid.[16]

It's possible to set a price too low. If the price is much lower than what the market expects, sales may be lost. For example, it probably would be a mistake for L'Oreal, a well-known cosmetics maker, to put a $1.49 price tag on its lipstick or to price its imported perfume at $3.49 an ounce. In all likelihood, shoppers would be suspicious about product quality, or their self-concept would not let them buy such low-priced products.

After raising a product's price, some organizations have experienced a considerable increase in sales. When this occurs, it indicates that customers infer better quality from the higher prices. This situation is called **inverse demand**—the higher the price, the greater the unit sales. Inverse demand usually exists only within a given price range and only at low price levels. At some point (see Figure 12.1), inverse demand ends and the usual-shaped curve is evident. That is, demand declines as prices rise.

How do sellers determine expected prices? One restaurant in London, rather than putting prices in its menus, lets patrons decide how much to pay after they have completed their meals. With this unconventional approach, customers pay an amount they think is equal to the value received from the dining experience. The restaurant owner claims that patrons pay about 20% more than he would charge![17]

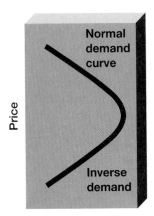

FIGURE 12.1

Inverse Demand.

Typically, to gauge expected prices, sellers may submit products to experienced retailers or wholesalers to gauge the selling price the market will accept for a particular item. Or they may go to customers. A business goods manufacturer, for instance, might get price estimates by showing models or blueprints to engineers working for prospective customers. Another alternative is to ask a sample of consumers what they would expect to pay for the product, or which item in a list of alternatives with known prices is most similar to the test product. Using such methods, a seller can determine a reasonable range of prices.

It is extremely helpful to estimate what the sales volume will be at several different prices. By doing this, the seller is, in effect, determining the demand curve for the product. Moreover, the seller is gauging *price elasticity of demand,* which refers to the responsiveness of quantity demanded to price changes. (Price elasticity of demand is covered in more detail in Appendix A on this book's website.)

Sellers can choose from several methods to estimate sales at various prices. Recall some of the demand-forecasting methods discussed in Chapter 6—survey of buyer intentions, test marketing, executive judgment, and sales-force composite, for example. These methods can be used in this situation as well.[18]

Competitive Reactions

Competition greatly influences base price. A new product is distinctive only until competition arrives, which is inevitable. The threat of potential competition is greatest when the field is easy to enter *and* profit prospects are encouraging. Competition can come from these sources:

- *Directly similar products:* Nike versus adidas or New Balance running shoes.
- *Available substitutes:* DHL air express versus Schneider National truck shipping or Union Pacific rail freight.
- *Unrelated products seeking the same consumer dollar:* DVD (digital versatile disc) player versus a bicycle or a weekend vacation.

For directly similar products, it is important to learn what consumers think about competing products. Thus a marketer at DuPont stressed, "Understanding

customer perceptions of the organization's and competitors' offerings is the first step in developing good pricing decisions."[19]

For similar or substitute products, a competitor may adjust its prices. In turn, other firms have to decide what price adjustments, if any, are necessary to retain their customers. In the air travel industry, for instance, Southwest Airlines and now other discount carriers such as JetBlue lower prices whenever possible to build or sustain market share. In turn, tradition-bound airlines such as Delta and United had to cut prices and slash costs in order to remain somewhat competitive and not become any more unprofitable. As Delta reduced its prices in several different ways in early 2005, the airline tried to squeeze up to $5 *billion* out of its cost structure. One cost-cutting step was to eliminate a hub, Dallas/Ft. Worth, meaning that Delta passengers will have to connect with other flights through one of three remaining hubs.[20]

www.delta.com

Other Marketing-Mix Elements

A product's base price is influenced considerably by the other ingredients in the marketing mix.

Product   We've already observed that a product's price is affected by whether it is a new item or an established one. Over the course of a life cycle, price changes are necessary to keep the product competitive. A product's price is also influenced by whether (1) it may be leased as well as purchased outright, (2) a trade-in is involved, and (3) it may be returned by the customer to the seller for a refund or an exchange. For example, a firm that has a liberal return policy may compensate by having higher initial prices.

The end use of the product must also be considered. For instance, there is little price competition among manufacturers of packaging materials or producers of industrial gases, so their price structure is stable. These business products are only an incidental part of the final article, so customers will buy the least expensive product consistent with the required quality.

Distribution Channels The channels and types of middlemen selected will influence a producer's pricing. A firm selling both through wholesalers and directly to retailers often sets a different factory price for these classes of customers. The price to wholesalers is lower because they perform services that the producer would have to perform, such as providing storage, granting credit to retailers, and selling to small retailers.

Promotion The extent to which the product is promoted by the producer or middlemen and the methods used are added considerations in pricing. If major promotional responsibility is placed on retailers, they ordinarily will be charged a lower price for a product than if the producer advertises it heavily. Even when a producer promotes heavily, it may want retailers to use local advertising to tie in with national advertising. Such a decision must be reflected in the producer's price to retailers.

Cost of a Product

Pricing of a product also should consider its cost. A product's total unit cost is made up of several types of costs, each reacting differently to changes in the quantity produced. In many industries, especially those based on leading-edge technologies, such as microprocessors and optic fibers, a product's costs are viewed—and treated—in much different ways than they were just a decade or so ago.

Consider a couple of examples. In the software field, there are substantial upfront research and development costs, but the costs of producing each unit of the finished product are relatively small. Thus some software developers give away hundreds of thousands of copies of their product when it is introduced in order to gain favorable word-of-mouth publicity and, in turn, sales of related software and future upgrades of this product. Red Hat Inc. essentially gives away Linux operating-systems software but then sells technical support services to Linux users. In another industry, Teleport Communications (a provider of local network services that is now part of AT&T Corp.) installed more optic fibers than a customer requested and did so without additional charge. Why? As technology surely advances, the customer will want more capacity. Therefore, the company installed more capacity than was needed because the cost of extra fibers is far less than the cost of labor to do the job again in the future.[21]

The following cost concepts are fundamental to our discussion of pricing:

www.redhat.com

Various Kinds of Costs

- A **fixed cost,** such as rent, executive salaries, or property tax, remains constant regardless of how many items are produced. Such a cost continues even if production stops completely. It is called a fixed cost because it is difficult to change in the short run (but not in the long run).
- **Total fixed cost** is the sum of all fixed costs.
- **Average fixed cost** is the total fixed cost divided by the number of units produced.
- A **variable cost,** such as labor or materials, is directly related to production. Variable costs can be controlled in the short run simply by changing the level of production. When production stops, for example, all variable production costs become zero.
- **Total variable cost** is the sum of all variable costs. The more units produced, the higher this cost is.

- **Average variable cost** is the total variable cost divided by the number of units produced. Average variable cost is usually high for the first few units produced. And it decreases as production increases because of such things as quantity discounts on materials and more efficient use of labor. Beyond some optimum output, it increases because of such factors as crowding of production facilities and overtime pay.
- **Total cost** is the sum of total fixed cost and total variable cost for a specific quantity produced.
- **Average total cost** is total cost divided by the number of units produced.
- **Marginal cost** is the cost of producing and selling one more unit. Usually the marginal cost of the last unit is the same as that unit's variable cost.

These concepts and their interrelationships are illustrated in Table 12.1 and Figure 12.2. The interrelationship among the various *average costs per unit* from the table is displayed graphically in the figure. It may be explained briefly as follows:

- The **average fixed cost curve** declines as output increases, because the total of the fixed costs is spread over an increasing number of units.

- The **average variable cost curve** usually is U-shaped. It starts high because average variable costs for the first few units of output are high. Variable costs per unit then decline as the company realizes efficiencies in production. Eventually the average variable cost curve reaches its lowest point, reflecting optimum output with respect to variable costs (not total costs). In Figure 12.2 this point is at three units of output. Beyond that point the average variable cost rises, reflecting the increase in unit variable costs caused by overcrowded facilities and other inefficiencies. If the variable costs per unit were constant, then the average variable cost curve would be a horizontal line at the level of the constant unit variable cost.

- The **average total cost curve** is the sum of the first two curves—average fixed cost and average variable cost. It starts high, reflecting the fact that total *fixed* costs are spread over so few units of output. As output increases, the average total cost curve declines because unit fixed cost and unit variable cost are decreasing. Eventually the point of lowest total cost per unit is reached (four units of output in the figure). Beyond that optimum point, diminishing returns set in and average total cost rises.

TABLE 12.1 An Example of Costs for an Individual Firm

Total fixed costs do not change in the short run, despite increases in quantity produced. Variable costs are the costs of inputs—materials and labor, for example. Total variable costs increase as production quantity rises. Total cost is the sum of all fixed and variable costs. The other measures in the table are simply methods of looking at costs per unit; they always involve dividing a cost by the number of units produced.

(1) Quantity Produced	(2) Total Fixed Costs	(3) Total Variable Costs	(4) Total Costs (2) + (3)	(5) Marginal Cost per Unit	(6) Average Fixed Cost (2) ÷ (1)	(7) Average Variable Cost (3) ÷ (1)	(8) Average Total Cost (4) ÷ (1)
0	$256	$ 0	$256		Infinity	Infinity	Infinity
1	256	84	340	$ 84	$256.00	$84	$340.00
2	256	112	368	28	128.00	56	184.00
3	256	144	400	32	85.33	48	133.33
4	256	224	480	80	64.00	56	120.00
5	256	400	656	176	51.20	80	131.20

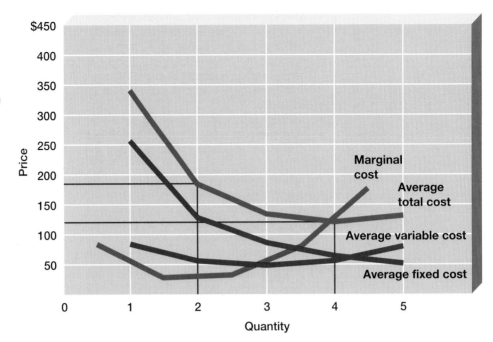

FIGURE 12.2

Unit Cost Curves for an Individual Firm.

This figure is based on data in Table 12.1. Here we see how *unit* costs change as quantity increases. Using cost-plus pricing, two units of output would be priced at $184 each, whereas four units would sell for $120 each.

- The **marginal cost curve** has a more pronounced U-shape than the other curves in Figure 12.2. The marginal cost curve slopes downward until the second unit of output, at which point the marginal costs start to increase.

  Note the relationship between the average total cost curve and the marginal cost curve. The average total cost curve slopes downward *as long as the marginal cost is less than the average total cost.* Even though marginal cost increases after the second unit, the average total cost curve continues to slope downward until the fourth unit. This occurs because marginal cost—even when going up—is still less than average total cost.

  The two curves—marginal cost and average total cost—intersect at the lowest point of the average total cost curve. Beyond that point (the fourth unit in the example), the cost of producing and selling the next unit is higher than the average cost of all units. The data in Table 12.1 show that producing the fifth unit reduces the average fixed cost by $12.80 (from $64 to $51.20) but causes the average variable cost to increase by $24. From then on, the average total cost rises because the average variable cost is increasing faster than the average fixed cost is decreasing.

Cost-Plus Pricing

We are now at the point in price determination to talk about setting a *specific* selling price. Most companies establish their prices based on:

- *Total cost plus a desired profit,*
- *Marginal analysis*—a consideration of both market demand and supply, and/or
- *Competitive market conditions.*

According to a survey that examined the approaches used to price new products, 9% of companies "guesstimate" what the base price for a new product should be, whereas 37% match what competitors charge for similar offerings. One-half the responding firms charge what the market will bear, if conditions allow. The most common approach, used by 52% of the companies, is to choose a price that is intended to cover costs and provide a fair profit. Because the total is more than 100%, evidently most firms use more than one approach. That's true, according to a survey by the Professional Pricing Society, which found that the majority of companies use a combination of methods to set price.[22]

Let's first discuss the most popular method, **cost-plus pricing**, which means setting the price of one unit of a product equal to the total cost of the unit plus the desired profit on the unit. Suppose that King's Kastles, a contractor, figures the labor and materials required to build and sell 10 condominiums will cost $1,100,000, and other expenses (office rent, depreciation on equipment, management salaries, and so on) will be $200,000. The contractor wants to earn a profit of 10% on the total cost of $1,300,000. This makes cost plus desired profit $1,430,000. So, using the cost-plus method, each of the 10 condos is priced at $143,000.

Although it is an easily applied method, cost-plus pricing has limitations. One is that it does not recognize various types of costs or the fact that these costs are affected differently by changes in level of output. In our housing example, suppose that King's Kastles built and sold only eight condos at the cost-plus price of $143,000 each. As shown in Table 12.2, total sales would then be $1,144,000. Labor and materials chargeable to the eight condos would total $880,000 ($110,000 per unit). Because the contractor would still incur the full $200,000 in overhead expenses, the total cost would be $1,080,000. This would leave a profit of $64,000, or $8,000 per condominium instead of the anticipated $13,000. On a percentage basis, profit would be only 5.9% of total cost rather than the desired 10%.

A second limitation of this pricing approach is that market demand is ignored. That is, cost-plus pricing assumes that cost determines the value of a product, or what customers are willing to pay for it. But what if the same number of units could be sold at a higher price? Using cost-plus pricing, the seller would forgo some revenues. Conversely, if fewer units are produced, each would have to sell for a higher price to cover all costs and show a profit. But if business is slack and output must be cut, it's not wise to raise the unit price. Another limitation of this method is that it doesn't recognize that total unit cost changes as output expands or contracts. However, a more sophisticated approach to cost-plus pricing can consider such changes.

Prices Based on Marginal Costs Only

Another approach to cost-plus pricing is to set *prices based on marginal costs only*, not total costs. Refer again to the cost schedules shown in Table 12.1 and Figure 12.2, and assume that a firm is operating at an output level of three units. Under marginal cost pricing, this firm could accept an order for one more unit at $80 or above, instead of the total unit cost of $120. The revenue from a unit sold at $80 would

TABLE 12.2	King's Kastles: An Example of Cost-Plus Pricing

Actual results often differ from planned outcomes because various types of costs react differently to changes in output.

| King's Kastles' Costs, Selling Price, and Profit | Number of Condominiums Built and Sold by King's Kastles | |
	Planned = 10	Actual = 8
Labor and materials costs ($110,000 per condo)	$1,100,000	$880,000
Overhead (fixed) costs	200,000	200,000
Total costs	$1,300,000	$1,080,000
Total sales at $143,000 per condo	1,430,000	1,144,000
Profit: Total	$ 130,000	$ 64,000
Per condo	$ 13,000	$ 8,000
As percent of cost	10%	5.9%

cover its variable costs. However, if the firm can sell for a price above $80—say, $85 or $90—the balance contributes to the payment of fixed costs.

Not all orders can be priced to cover only variable costs. Marginal cost pricing may be feasible, however, if management wants to keep its labor force employed during a slack season. It may also be used when one product is expected to attract business for another. Thus a department store may price meals in its café at a level that covers only the marginal costs. The reasoning is that the café will bring shoppers to the store, where they will buy other, more profitable products.

Pricing by Middlemen

At first glance, cost-plus pricing appears to be widely used by retailing and wholesaling middlemen. A retailer, for example, pays a given amount to buy products and have them delivered to the store. Then the merchant adds an amount, called a markup, to the acquisition cost. This markup is estimated to be sufficient to cover the store's expenses and provide a reasonable profit. Thus a building materials outlet may buy a power drill for $30 including freight, and price the item at $50. The $50 price reflects a markup of 40% based on the selling price, or 66 ⅔% based on the merchandise cost. Of course, in setting prices, middlemen also should take into account the expectations of their customers.

Various types of retailers require different percentage markups because of the nature of the products handled and the services offered. A self-service supermarket has lower costs and thus can have a lower average markup than a full-service delicatessen. Figure 12.3 shows examples of markup pricing by middlemen. (Markups are discussed in more detail in Appendix A.)

Is cost-plus pricing really used by middlemen? For the following reasons, it's safe to say that cost-plus pricing is *not* used widely by middlemen:

- Most retail prices are really just offers. If customers accept the offer, the price is fine. If they reject it, the price usually will be changed quickly, or the product may even be withdrawn from the market. Prices thus are always on trial.

- Many retailers don't use the same markup on all the products they carry. A supermarket, for instance, may have a markup of 10% to 15% on sugar and soap products, 15% to 25% on canned fruit and vegetables, and 10% to 45% on fresh meats and produce, depending on the particular item. These different markups for distinctive products reflect competitive considerations and other aspects of market demand.

- A middleman usually doesn't actually set a base price but only adds a percentage to the price already set by the producer. The producer's price is set to allow each middleman to add a reasonable markup and still sell at a competitive retail

FIGURE 12.3

Examples of Markup Pricing by Retailers and Wholesalers.

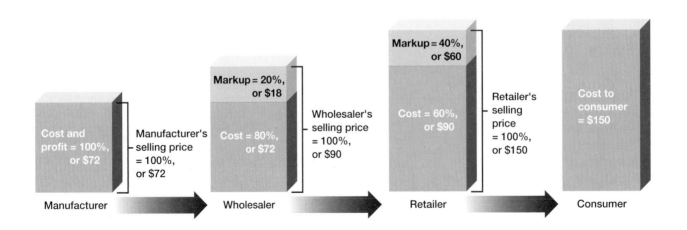

price. The key price is set by the producer, with an eye on the final market. Thus what seems to be cost-plus pricing by middlemen is usually market-influenced pricing.

Evaluation of Cost-Plus Pricing

If a firm should be market-oriented and cater to consumers' wants, why are we considering cost-plus pricing? Simply, cost-plus pricing must be understood because it is straightforward, easy to explain, and as a result, used by numerous firms. In fact, although it is not commonplace among traditional middlemen, a recent study found that cost plus is the most common pricing method among *e-commerce companies*.[23]

The traditional perspective has been that costs should be a determinant of prices, but not the only one. Costs are a floor for a company's prices. If goods are priced below this floor for a long time, the firm will be forced out of business.

In recent years, inflation has diminished and firms have had great difficulty raising prices. As a result, a new perspective is that price should determine costs. That is, a firm may not have much flexibility in setting its price so costs must be reduced if profits are to be realized. If this perspective is accepted, production processes and marketing activities must be revamped to squeeze out costs wherever possible. After cutting prices in its battle with Fuji, Eastman Kodak started a major effort to cut costs by about $750 million.[24] The appropriate conclusion is that used by itself, cost-plus pricing is a weak and unrealistic method because it ignores market conditions (notably demand) and new competition (notably digital cameras).

Break-Even Analysis

One way to consider both market demand and costs in price determination is using **break-even analysis** to calculate break-even points. A **break-even point** is that quantity of output at which total revenue equals total costs, *assuming a certain selling price*. There is a different break-even point for every selling price. Sales exceeding the break-even point result in a profit on each additional unit. The more sales are above the break-even point, the larger the total and unit profits will be. Sales below the break-even point result in a loss to the seller.

Determining the Break-Even Point

The method of determining a break-even point is illustrated in Table 12.3 (below) and Figure 12.4 on the next page. In our example, Futon Factory's fixed costs are

TABLE 12.3	**Futon Factory: Computation of Break-Even Point**

At each of several prices, we wish to find out how many units must be sold to cover all costs. At a unit price of $100, the sale of each unit contributes $70 to cover overhead expenses. The Futon Factory must sell about 357 units to cover its $25,000 in fixed costs. See Figure 12.4 for a depiction of the data in this table.

(1) Unit Price	(2) Unit Variable Costs	(3) Contribution to Overhead (1) − (2)	(4) Overhead (Total Fixed Costs)	(5) Break-even Point (Rounded) (4) ÷ (3)
$ 60	$30	$ 30	$25,000	833 units
80	30	50	$25,000	500 units
100	30	70	$25,000	357 units
150	30	120	$25,000	208 units

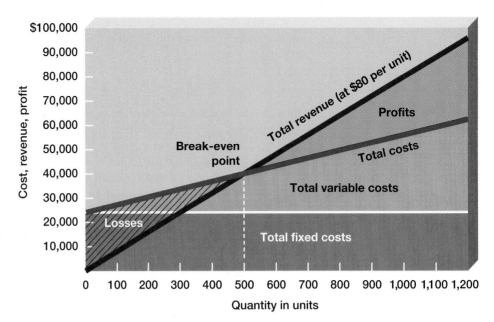

FIGURE 12.4

Break-Even Chart for Futon Factory with an $80 Selling Price.

If this company sells 500 units, total costs are $40,000 (variable cost of 500 × $30, or $15,000, plus fixed costs of $25,000). At a selling price of $80, the sale of 500 units will yield $40,000 revenue, and costs and revenue will equal each other. At the same price, the sale of each unit above 500 will yield a profit.

$25,000, and variable costs are constant at $30 per unit. In our earlier example (Table 12.1 and Figure 12.2), we assumed that unit variable costs are *not* constant but fluctuate. To simplify our break-even analysis, we now assume that variable costs *are* constant.

The total cost of producing one unit is $25,030—Futon Factory obviously needs more volume to absorb its fixed costs! For 400 units, the total cost is $37,000 ($30 multiplied by 400, plus $25,000). In Figure 12.4 the selling price is $80 a unit and variable costs of $30 per unit are incurred in producing each unit. Consequently, any revenue over $30 contributes to covering fixed costs (sometimes termed *overhead*). When the price is $80, that would be $50 per unit. At a price of $80, the break-even point is 500 units, because a $50 per-unit contribution will just cover overhead of $25,000.

Stated another way, variable costs for 500 units are $15,000 and fixed costs are $25,000, for a total cost of $40,000. This amount equals the revenue from 500 units sold at $80 each. So, at an $80 selling price, the break-even volume is 500 units. Figure 12.4 shows a break-even point for an $80 price. However, it is highly desirable to calculate break-even points for several different selling prices.

The break-even point may be found with this formula:

$$\text{Break-even point in units} = \frac{\text{total fixed costs}}{\text{unit contribution to overhead}}$$

Because unit contribution to overhead equals selling price less the average variable cost, the working formula becomes:

$$\text{Break-even point in units} = \frac{\text{total fixed costs}}{\text{selling price} - \text{average variable cost}}$$

Evaluation of Break-Even Analysis

A drawback of break-even analysis is that it cannot tell us whether or not we *can* actually sell at the break-even amount. Table 12.3, for example, shows what revenue will be at the different prices *if* the given number of units can be sold at these prices. The amount the market will buy at a given price could be below the break-even point. If that happens, the firm will not break even—it will show a loss.

Two basic assumptions underlie simple break-even analysis: (1) Total fixed costs are constant, and (2) variable costs remain constant per unit of output. Actually, fixed costs may change (although usually not in the short term) and average variable costs normally fluctuate.

Despite these limitations, management should not dismiss break-even analysis as a pricing tool. Even in its simplest form, break-even analysis is helpful because in the short run many firms experience reasonably stable cost and demand structures.[25]

Prices Based on Marginal Analysis

Another pricing method, marginal analysis, also takes into account both demand and costs to determine the best price for profit maximization. Firms with other pricing goals might use *prices based on marginal analysis* to compare prices determined by different means.

Determining the Price

To use marginal analysis, the price setter must understand the concepts of average and marginal revenue as well as average and marginal cost. **Marginal revenue** is the income derived from the sale of the last unit. **Average revenue** is the unit price at a given level of unit sales; it is calculated by dividing total revenue by the number of units sold.

Referring to the hypothetical demand schedule in Table 12.4, we see that Limos for Lease can sell one unit (that is, lease one limousine for a five-hour period on a weekend night) for $200. Planning a night on the town, a group of students asks for a discount if it rents at least four limos. Limos for Lease tells the group that the price would be $180 apiece for two vehicles, $159 for three, and $133 for four. As shown in the table, the company receives an added $160 (marginal revenue) by renting a second unit. Before the paperwork is signed, the students' negotiator (a finance major) calls Limos and proposes rates of $105 and $82.50 apiece for five and six units, respectively. In examining the table, the entrepreneur sees that after the fourth unit, total revenue declines each time the unit price is lowered in order to sell an additional unit. To avoid negative marginal revenue, Limos indicates it can rent no more than four vehicles to the group under these terms.

Marginal analysis is illustrated in Figure 12.5. We assume that a company—a services firm, like Limos for Lease, or a manufacturer—will continue to produce and sell its product as long as revenue from the last unit sold exceeds the cost of producing this last unit. That is, output continues to increase as long as marginal revenue

TABLE 12.4	**Limos for Lease: Demand Schedule for an Individual Firm**

At each market price a certain quantity of the product—in this example, a five-hour rental of a limousine on a weekend night—will be demanded. Marginal revenue is simply the amount of additional money gained by selling one more unit. Limos for Lease gains no additional marginal revenue after it has rented its fourth limo at a price of $133.

Units Sold (Limos Leased)	Unit Price (Average Revenue)	Total Revenue	Marginal Revenue
1	$200	$200	
2	180	360	$160
3	159	477	117
4	133	532	55
5	105	525	−7
6	82.50	495	−30

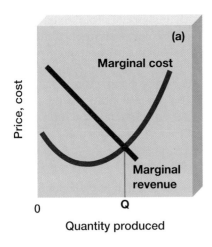
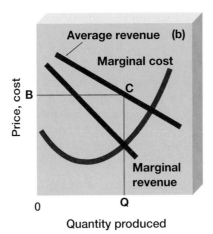
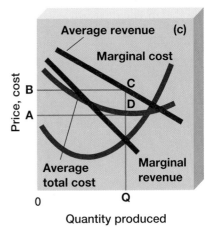

FIGURE 12.5

Price Setting and Profit Maximization through Marginal Analysis.

exceeds marginal cost. At the point where they meet, production theoretically should cease. Ordinarily a company will not want to sell a unit at a price less than its out-of-pocket (variable) costs of producing it. The optimum volume of output is the quantity level at which *marginal cost equals marginal revenue,* or quantity Q in Figure 12.5a.

Thus the unit price is determined by locating the point on the average revenue curve that represents an output of quantity Q—the level at which marginal cost equals marginal revenue. Remember that average revenue represents the unit price. Referring to Figure 12.5b, in which the average revenue curve has been added, the unit price at which to sell quantity Q is represented by point C—that is, price B.

The average total cost curve has been added in Figure 12.5c. It shows that for output quantity Q, the average unit cost is represented by point D—that is, unit cost A. Thus, with a price of B and an average unit cost of A, the company enjoys a unit profit given by B minus A in the figure. Total profit is quantity Q times the unit profit.

Evaluation of Marginal Analysis Pricing

Marginal analysis has been used sparsely as a basis for price setting. According to businesspeople, it can be a help in studying past price movements. However, many managers think marginal analysis *cannot* serve as a practical basis for setting prices unless accurate, reliable data can be obtained for plotting the curves.

On the brighter side, management's knowledge of costs and demand is improving. Computerized databases are bringing more complete and detailed information to management's attention all the time. And experienced management can do a fairly accurate job of estimating marginal and average costs and revenues.

Prices Set in Relation to Market Alone

Cost-plus pricing is one extreme among pricing methods. At the other extreme is *prices set in relation to the market alone.* The seller's price may be set right at the market price to meet the competition, or it may be set above or below the market price.

Pricing to Meet Competition

Pricing to meet competition is simple to carry out. In a situation with multiple suppliers, a firm should ascertain what the prevailing market price is and, after allowing for customary markups for middlemen, should arrive at its own selling price. To illustrate, a manufacturer of women's shoes knows that retailers want to sell the shoes for $70 a pair and have an average markup of 40% of their selling price. Consequently, after allowing $28 for the retailer's markup, the producer's price is $42. This manufacturer then has to decide whether $42 is enough to cover costs and provide a reasonable profit. Sometimes a producer faces a real squeeze if its costs are rising but the market price is holding firm.

One situation in which management might price a product right at the market level is when competition is keen and the firm's product is not differentiated significantly from competing products.[26] To some extent, this pricing method reflects the market conditions of **perfect competition.** That is, product differentiation is absent, buyers and sellers are well informed, and the seller has no discernible control over the selling price. Most producers of agricultural products and small firms marketing well-known, standardized products use this pricing method. As explained in the Marketing in the Information Economy box, the Internet is moving some industries toward perfect competition.

The sharp drop in revenue occurring when the price is raised above the prevailing market level indicates that the individual seller faces a **kinked demand** (see

MARKETING IN THE INFORMATION ECONOMY

Who gets a price advantage from the Internet?

The Internet facilitates **dynamic pricing,** in which prices are adjusted instantly and frequently in line with what the market will bear. Dynamic pricing is evident in various forms of electronic commerce. The most popular, or at least the most visible, is online auctions. The auction can be initiated by a seller, who offers a product for sale online, or by a buyer, who announces the desire to purchase a particular good or service online. Ariba, Bluefly, eBay, and Priceline.com are examples of online auctions, each being distinctive in one or more respects.

It's believed that dynamic pricing will result in lower prices. However, one study concluded that the prices of three online booksellers were virtually identical for over one-half of the items examined. In contrast, a late-1990s research project determined that prices for the two products examined, books and music CDs, were 9% to 16% lower online than at conventional retailers. A more recent study concluded that prices for term life insurance dropped as Internet usage grew.

What are the reasons for these lower prices? First, comparison shopping is easier on the Internet, helped greatly by "shopping robots" (more on this type of electronic search engine in the next chapter). In addition, online buyers may be able to design a product to meet their particular needs, thereby assuring maximum value from the purchase. Dell Computer stressed that advantage in order to build its online sales volume.

However, the Internet also should benefit sellers' pricing activities. Why? For one thing, it's much easier for a seller to change prices online than to retag every item in an actual retail store. In addition, because shoppers have to provide various information to make an online purchase and their transactions can be compiled and analyzed, e-commerce firms can tailor special offerings for individual customers. For example, if a consumer purchases several decorating accessories at PotteryBarn.com that were all related to the living room, the company could provide the customer with a special incentive (such as a 25% discount) for a purchase related to a different room in the home.

In a real sense, the Internet fosters conditions approaching perfect competition. Thus the Internet has had—and probably will continue to have—a tremendous impact on pricing, perhaps affecting this element of marketing more than any other element.

Slowly but surely, dynamic pricing is making its way to bricks-and-mortar retailers. They are trying newly developed methods such as electronic shelf labels and tiered loyalty programs. The ultimate goal is, of course, one-to-one pricing in which there is a new price for every buying situation and prospective customer.

Sources: Ted Kemp, "The Road to One-to-One Pricing," *Fairchild's Executive Technology,* May 2004, p. 36; David P. Hamilton, "The Price Isn't Right," *The Wall Street Journal,* Feb. 12, 2001, pp. R8, R10; Gene Koretz, "E-Commerce: The Buyer Wins," *BusinessWeek,* Jan. 8, 2001, p. 30; Robert D. Hof, "Going, Going, Gone," *BusinessWeek,* Apr. 12, 1999, pp. 30–32; and Amy E. Cortese, "Good-Bye to Fixed Pricing?" *BusinessWeek,* May 4, 1998, pp. 71–73+.

FIGURE 12.6

Kinked Demand Curve.

This type of curve faces firms selling well-known, standardized products as well as individual firms in an oligopolistic market structure. The kink occurs at the point representing the prevailing price, A. At prices above A, demand declines rapidly. A price set below A results in very little increase in volume, so revenue is lost; that is, marginal revenue is negative.

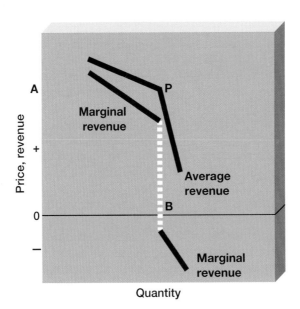

Figure 12.6). The prevailing price is at A. Adjusting this price is not beneficial to the seller for the following reasons:

- Above the prevailing price, demand for the product drops sharply, as indicated by the fairly flat average revenue curve beyond point P. Above price A, demand is highly elastic and, as a result, total revenue declines.

- Below price A, demand for the product increases very little, as shown by the steeply sloping average revenue curve and the negative marginal revenue curve below point P. Demand is highly inelastic and, as a result, total revenue still declines.

In the case of kinked demand, total revenue decreases each time the price is adjusted from the prevailing price, A in Figure 12.6. The prevailing price is well established. Consequently, when a single firm reduces its price, its unit sales will not increase very much—certainly not enough to offset the loss in average revenue.

So far in our discussion of pricing to meet competition, we have observed market situations that involve *many* sellers. Oddly enough, this same pricing method is often used when the market is dominated by a *few* firms, each marketing similar products. This type of market structure, called an **oligopoly**, exists in such industries as copper, aluminum, soft drinks, breakfast cereals, auto tires, and even among barber shops and grocery stores in a small community. When the demand curve is kinked, as in Figure 12.6, oligopolists should simply set prices at a competitive level and leave them there. Typically they do.

Pricing below Competition

A variation of market-based pricing is to set a price *below* the level of your main competitors. **Pricing below competition** is done by discount retailers, such as Wal-Mart, Costco, and Target, which stress low markup, high volume, and few customer services (including sales people). They price heavily advertised, well-known brands 10% to 30% below the suggested list price, which is normally charged by full-service retailers. Aldi, a groceries retailer with stores across Europe as well as in Australia and the U.S., offsets very low prices by focusing on a limited assortment of products, primarily middlemen's brands. Even retailers that offer an assortment of customer services may price below the competitive level by eliminating some services.

The risk in pricing below the competition is that consumers begin to view the product (or an entire retail store) as an undifferentiated commodity, such as coal and

www.aldi.com

bulk salt, with the entire focus on price differences. If that happens, and some would say it already has for products such as personal computers and flat-panel televisions, then consumers choose the brand with the lowest price. In turn, competing firms are likely to wind up in a price war that diminishes or eliminates profits. One observer asked a question that applies to any industry in which firms rely on price as a way to gain an edge over competitors: "How can restaurant chains ever expect to charge top dollar again after relentlessly pushing . . . [low] prices?"[27]

Pricing above Competition

Producers or retailers sometimes set their prices *above* the prevailing market level. Usually, **pricing above competition** works only when the product is distinctive or when the seller has acquired prestige in its field. Most communities have an elite clothing boutique and a prestigious jewelry store where prices are noticeably above the level set by other stores with seemingly similar products. However, a gas station

TAG Heuer SA positions its watches as both high quality and stylish. The watchmaker uses celebrities, including golfer Tiger Woods, to promote its watches. Here, Shahrukh Khan, a movie star in India, shows off his TAG Heuer watch in front of an oversized print ad for this brand of watch. TAG Heuer is seeking a strong market position as demand for luxury watches grows in India.

www.tagheuer.com

that has a strong advantage based on a superior location (perhaps the only such station for many miles on an interstate highway) may also be able to use above-market pricing.

www.waterford.com

www.patekphilippe.com

Above-market pricing often is employed by manufacturers of prestige brands of high-cost goods such as autos (Ferrari, Bentley), crystal (Waterford), leather products (Gucci, Fendi), and watches (Breguet, Rolex). Patek Philippe, a Swiss firm, makes only about 30,000 watches per year, but they are priced from about $9,000 to over $1 million per watch! Above-market pricing also is used for business goods. Sometimes it can be effective for relatively low-cost goods. Premier Industrial, for example, prices its fasteners and tubing at least 10% higher and occasionally much higher than competing products. Premier, an industrial distributor, can do this because, unlike competitors, it accepts small orders and ships an order within 24 hours.[28]

Some service providers also price above their competitors. In the hotel industry, the Ritz Carlton and Fairmont chains have used this approach successfully. Consider an example of pricing above competition from the personal services field, specifically

golf instruction. Most of the teaching pros in *Golf Magazine*'s annual "top 100" list charge $100 to $250 per hour for their services. However, a handful who have worked with stars such as Tiger Woods and Vijay Singh command much more—$5,000 per half day and even higher. Of course, such lofty prices curtail demand, which is fine with some of these elite instructors.[29]

Summary

In our economy, price influences the allocation of resources. In individual companies, price is one significant factor in achieving marketing success. And in many purchase situations, price can be of great importance to consumers. However, it is difficult to define price. A general definition is: Price is the amount of money and/or other items with utility needed to acquire a product.

Before setting a product's base price, management should identify its pricing objective. Major pricing objectives are to (1) earn a target return on investment or on net sales, (2) maximize profits, (3) increase sales, (4) hold or gain a target market share, (5) stabilize prices, and (6) meet competition's prices.

Besides the firm's pricing objective, other key factors that influence price setting are: (1) demand for the product, (2) competitive reactions, (3) strategies planned for other marketing-mix elements, and (4) cost of the product. The concept of elasticity refers to the effect that unit-price changes have on the number of units sold and on total revenue.

Three major methods used to determine the base price are cost-plus pricing, marginal analysis, and setting the price only in relation to the market. For cost-plus pricing to be effective, a seller must consider several types of costs and their reactions to changes in the quantity produced. A producer usually sets a price to cover total cost. In some cases, however, the best policy may be to set a price that covers marginal cost only. The main weakness in cost-plus pricing is that it completely ignores market demand. To partially offset this weakness, a company may use break-even analysis as a tool in price setting.

In actual business situations, price setting is influenced by market conditions. Hence, marginal analysis, which takes into account both demand and costs to determine a suitable price for the product, is helpful in understanding the forces affecting price. Price and output level are set at the point where marginal cost equals marginal revenue. The effectiveness of marginal analysis in setting prices depends on obtaining reliable cost data.

For many products, price setting is relatively easy because management simply sets the price at the level of competition. Pricing at prevailing market levels makes sense for firms selling well-known, standardized products and sometimes for individual firms in an oligopoly. Two variations of market-level pricing are to price below or above the levels of primary competitors.

More about **Priceline.com**

After establishing its website as a place to bid on airline tickets, Priceline.com had much bigger ambitions. According to the company's founder, Jay Walker, "There is no [product] category we won't be in." Regarding the first area of expansion, Walker explained, "Until now, hotels have been faced with the worst of two possible worlds. If they lower prices for some rooms, they risk angering guests who paid higher prices. If they keep prices static, there is the opportunity risk, where rooms go unsold."

By allowing consumers to name their own price, Priceline does business with travelers who otherwise would not book rooms with the participating hotel chains. In October 1998, just months after its launch, Priceline was booking more than 4,000 rooms per month; by mid-2001, the level of transactions rose to 50,000 room nights monthly. Demand grew to over 7.5 million room nights in 2004, compared to Priceline's corresponding figures of 2.8 million airline tickets booked and about 5 million car rental days.

Seeking other areas of expansion, the company moved into groceries and gasoline, unsuccessfully as it turned out. In a venture called WebHouse Club Inc., Priceline sought to entice shoppers to buy cereal, soft drinks, and other groceries online instead of at a "bricks and mortar" supermarket. Shoppers specified the prices they would pay for items in 149 different categories. A $3 monthly fee entitled consumers to make bids and instantly find out whether or not the products' manufacturers accepted them. The customer paid online, and then went to one of the participating local supermarkets, walked the aisles, and picked out the items purchased. To counter criticism that the process was time-consuming, Priceline's management stated that many shoppers already spend time clipping and organizing manufacturers' coupons on groceries.

Basically, many large consumer product companies refused to participate, leaving WebHouse to subsidize the discounts it had promised shoppers. Firms like Kimberly-Clark were reluctant to give discounts to WebHouse because they did not want to endanger their brands or other distribution channels.

For this reason and others, the "name your own price" groceries website failed. The gasoline online venture flopped for similar reasons. Large petroleum distributors balked because WebHouse refused to tell retailers which of their competitors had joined the program. Also, as one marketer pointed out, "Gasoline is partly a convenience purchase. People don't want to search across town to save $2 a month."

Undaunted but perhaps wiser, Priceline.com Inc. is forging ahead in the area of travel products. For example, the online service reached an agreement to sell discounted hotel rooms from some well-known chains at its Lowestfare.com website. In announcing the arrangement in 2003, Priceline said the participating chains were Marriott, Hilton, Hyatt, Six Continents (now InterContinental), and Starwood.[30]

1. What issues did Priceline's WebHouse venture overlook in attempting to apply the name-your-own-price concept to groceries?

2. What other product categories might be suitable for Priceline's business model?

Key Terms and Concepts

Price (318)	Total variable cost (328)	Break-even point (333)
Barter (318)	Average variable cost (329)	Marginal revenue (335)
Value (320)	Total cost (329)	Average revenue (335)
Pricing objectives (322)	Average total cost (329)	Pricing to meet competition (336)
Base price (list price) (325)	Marginal cost (329)	Dynamic pricing (337)
Expected price (325)	Average fixed cost curve (329)	Perfect competition (337)
Inverse demand (326)	Average variable cost curve (329)	Kinked demand (337)
Fixed cost (328)	Average total cost curve (329)	Oligopoly (338)
Total fixed cost (328)	Marginal cost curve (330)	Pricing below competition (338)
Average fixed cost (328)	Cost-plus pricing (331)	Pricing above competition (339)
Variable cost (328)	Break-even analysis (333)	

Questions and Problems

1. a. Explain how a firm's pricing objective may influence the promotional program for a product.
   b. Which of the six pricing goals involves the largest, most aggressive promotional campaign?

2. What marketing conditions might logically lead a company to set "meeting competition" as a pricing objective?

3. What is your expected price for each of the following articles? How did you arrive at your estimate in each instance?
   a. An Internet service that would send you, via e-mail, daily news from two cities of your choosing (for example, your hometown and a city where you might like to live in the future).

   b. A new type of cola beverage that holds its carbonation long after it has been opened; packaged in 12-ounce (355-milliliter) and 2-liter bottles.
   c. A nuclear-powered 23-inch table-model television set, guaranteed to run for 10 years without replacement of the original power-generating component; requires no battery or electric wires.

4. Name three products, including at least one service, for which you think an inverse demand exists. For each product, within which price range does this inverse demand exist?

5. In Figure 12.2, what is the significance of the point where the marginal cost curve intersects the average total cost curve? Explain why the average total cost

curve is declining (slightly) to the left of the intersection point and rising (again, slightly) beyond it. Explain how the marginal cost curve can be rising while the average total cost curve is still declining.

6. What are the merits and limitations of the cost-plus method of setting a base price?

7. In a break-even chart, is the total *fixed* cost line always horizontal? Is the total *variable* cost line always straight? Explain.

8. Referring to Table 12.3 and Figure 12.4, what would be Futon Factory's break-even points at prices of $50 and $90, if variable costs are $40 per unit and fixed costs remain at $25,000?

9. A small manufacturer sold ballpoint pens to retailers at $8.40 per dozen. The manufacturing cost was 50 cents for each pen. Expenses, including all selling and administrative costs except advertising, were $19,200. How many dozen must the manufacturer sell to cover these expenses and pay for an advertising campaign costing $6,000?

10. In Figure 12.5, why would the firm normally stop producing at quantity Q? Why is the price set at B rather than at D or A?

Interactive Marketing Exercises

1. Select three goods (new or used nonfood items in the price range of $10 to $100) that you are considering buying. Determine the price of each of these items in your local community by checking with one or more retail outlets. Then go to an online auction site such as eBay.com or Amazon.com, and check the prices of each of these items. Which are cheaper—the online or in-store prices? Where would you buy each item? What reasons underlie your decisions?

2. Identify one store in your community that generally prices *below* the levels of most other firms and one that prices *above* prevailing market levels. Arrange an interview with the manager of each store. Ask both managers to explain the rationale and procedures associated with their pricing approaches. Also ask the manager of the store with below-market prices how profits are achieved with such low prices. Ask the manager of the store with above-market prices how customers are attracted and satisfied with such high prices.

Chapter 13

PART 4

"Bose then committed to achieving a contradiction: 'big sound from a small speaker.'"

Pricing Strategies

Can **Bose** Stay on the Crest of the Wave?

How can a combined radio and single-CD player sell well at a price of $499? What would cause consumers to commit over $1,000 for an upgraded system with a five-CD changer? The perhaps overly simple answer is that the Bose Corporation offers superior products based on extensive research.

The Bose Corp. was founded in 1964 by a Massachusetts Institute of Technology professor, Dr. Amar Bose after he was disappointed by the quality of sound produced by a stereo system he purchased. The company's first product, the 2201 speaker, created excellent sound but was large.

Bose then committed to achieving "big sound from a small speaker." The 901 Direct/Reflecting Speaker, launched in 1968, did that. By reflecting 89% of the sound off walls, the product replicated a live concert as much as possible. However, the 901 speaker was not well received initially. According to Bose, "It did everything that was considered wrong." That is, the speaker was small, did not have woofers or tweeters, and had 4″ speakers pointed in nontraditional directions.

Following 14 years of research, Bose introduced new products based on "acoustic waveguide speaker technology." This technology is the basis *and* justification for Bose's relatively high-price radios, radio/CD players, and so-called music systems.

According to Bose, its new Wave Music System reproduces musical notes one-half octave lower than its predecessor. Improved, lower-price products can "cannibalize" sales of higher-price (and presumably more profitable) offerings. The company's founder isn't worried, saying that enterprises "should never be afraid of outdating products with their own (new and better) products."

Bose offers its products through multiple distribution channels. The company sells directly to consumers who see its ads in various media or go to its website. In addition, it has a large network of retailers. Another method is a set of 115 "showcase stores" in the U.S. and over 25 in other countries. Here, an interested consumer can listen to the quality of sound produced by Bose products in realistic settings.

The 3·2·1 product typifies the company's marketing strategies, at least for its consumer products:

- The 3·2·1 is aimed at households that don't have surround sound, because they have too little space for the normal set of five speakers or believe this product is too complex or doesn't provide good value.

- The 3·2·1 delivers benefits not found in competing products. It provides full surround sound from two speakers and delivers a larger area in which people can enjoy surround sound than earlier two-speaker setups.

- The 3·2·1 is sold by a wide variety of retailers, including major chains such as Tweeter and Best Buy, and also through Bose-controlled channels.

- Bose's products, including the 3·2·1, are heavily promoted, especially through print media (ranging from lifestyle magazines to newspapers) and in-store displays.

- When introduced in 2001, the product's retail price of $999 was noticeably higher than competing products. Nevertheless, the 3·2·1 became the top-selling home-theater system.

The Bose Corporation is privately held and thus does not need to disclose its actual sales or profits. A competitor speculated that the Massachusetts-based company sells a total of about 1 million units of its two basic products, the Wave music system and the Wave radio, annually.

Bose's philosophy is that through research "yesterday's fiction becomes tomorrow's reality." Thus the cornerstone for the company's marketing is offering a superior product. If that occurs, relatively high prices are possible because many consumers conclude that Bose products provide exceptional value.[1]

What are the advantages and disadvantages of Bose's use of relatively high prices?

 www.bose.com

Fundamentally, in managing the price element of a company's marketing mix, management of a firm—whether it is a manufacturer such as Bose, a services firm such as Accenture consulting, a retailer such as Macy's, or an online firm such as Bluefly—first must decide on its pricing goal and then set the base price for a good or service. The final task, as shown in Figure 13.1, is to design pricing strategies that are compatible with the rest of the marketing mix. Many strategic questions related to price must be answered—not just by Bose as in the preceding case, but by all firms. These questions include: Will our company compete primarily on the basis of price, or on other factors? What kind of discount schedule should be adopted? Will we occasionally absorb shipping costs? Are our approaches to pricing ethical and legal?

In this chapter we primarily discuss ways in which a firm adjusts a product's base price to coincide with its overall marketing program. After studying this chapter, you should be able to explain:

Chapter Goals

- Price competition, notably value pricing, and nonprice competition.
- Pricing strategies for entering a market, especially market skimming and market penetration.
- Price discounts and allowances.
- Geographic pricing strategies.
- Special pricing situations, notably one-price and flexible-price approaches, leader pricing, everyday low pricing and high-low pricing, and reactive and proactive changes.
- Legal issues associated with pricing.

We will use the term *strategy* frequently in this chapter, so let's explain its meaning. A **strategy** is a broad plan of action by which an organization intends to reach a particular goal. To illustrate, a company may adopt a strategy of offering quantity discounts to achieve the goal of a 10% increase in sales this year.

Price versus Nonprice Competition

In developing a marketing program, management has to decide whether to compete primarily on the basis of price or the nonprice elements of the marketing mix. This choice obviously affects other parts of the firm's marketing program.

FIGURE 13.1

The Price-Determination Process.

The first two steps were discussed in Chapter 12. The third step is the subject of this chapter.

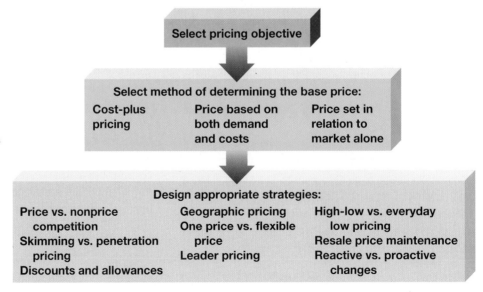

Select pricing objective

Select method of determining the base price:
Cost-plus pricing — Price based on both demand and costs — Price set in relation to market alone

Design appropriate strategies:
Price vs. nonprice competition — Geographic pricing — High-low vs. everyday low pricing
Skimming vs. penetration pricing — One price vs. flexible price — Resale price maintenance
Discounts and allowances — Leader pricing — Reactive vs. proactive changes

Price Competition

A company engages in **price competition** by regularly offering products priced as low as possible and typically accompanied by few, if any, services. Consumer electronics, computers, and air travel are among the myriad industries characterized by rigorous price competition at the present time. New airlines promoting discount fares have intensified price competiton in both the U.S. and Europe recently.[2]

In the retail sector, large discount chains, including Wal-Mart and Kmart, compete largely on the basis of price. Smaller chains, such as Dollar General and Family Dollar Stores, offer so-called deep discounts and thus depend even more on low prices. Deep discounters have been expanding rapidly by "enticing consumers with a wide range of food and household products in clean, well-organized and heavily stocked stores."[3]

Price competition has been spreading to other parts of the world as well. For example, price reductions are becoming more common throughout Europe. This switch in competitive strategy was due to the elimination of various trade barriers and, more recently, the introduction of a common currency, the euro. Some online retailers, both in the U.S. and abroad, have used price competition in their efforts to lure buyers and establish a foothold in the market.

In Chapter 12 we discussed how more and more consumers are seeking better value in their purchases. In response, many companies are using what's called **value pricing**. This form of price competition aims to improve a product's value—that is, the ratio of its benefits to its price and related costs. To implement value pricing, a firm typically (1) offers products with lower prices but the same, or perhaps added, benefits and, at the same time, (2) seeks ways to slash expenses so profits do not suffer.

Value also can be improved by introducing a much better product with a somewhat higher price than competing entries. Gillette's M3Power razor, Intel's Xeon microprocessor chip, and Goodyear's Eagle F1 tire all illustrate this approach.[4] Despite these notable examples, this approach is not commonly used today.

Since the early 1990s, value pricing has been a pivotal marketing strategy in diverse fields, ranging from personal computers to fast food. Consider an example.

Dollar Tree Stores, Inc., which has over 2,800 outlets under the Dollar Tree and other banners, sells all of its merchandise for $1 per item. To make a profit, "deep discounters" such as Dollar Tree must control both operating expenses and cost of goods sold. One approach is finding suppliers willing to sell closeout merchandise and excess inventory at very low costs.

Does the Wal-Mart way work around the globe?

In becoming the world's largest enterprise, Wal-Mart adhered to a basic formula—selling consumables (such as health and beauty aids), soft goods (such as apparel), and hard goods (such as gas-powered outdoor grills) at sharply discounted prices. The formula, emphasizing price competition, has been phenomenally effective in the U.S. However, the company is, relatively speaking, a novice internationally. Its initial foray into a foreign country did not occur until 1991 when Wal-Mart established a partnership with Cifra SA, a discount retail chain in Mexico. The first joint effort, a Sam's Club, was hugely successful from the outset.

Despite its first triumph in Mexico, Wal-Mart has found it difficult to attain success, much less blockbuster performance, outside the U.S. In every new country, the American chain has encountered cultural differences and/or unfamiliar regulations; the company has also made some mistakes. In China, for example, Wal-Mart tried to sell items (such as extension ladders) that wouldn't fit into the residents' tiny apartments. In Germany, the firm underestimated the resolve of trade unions and more than a dozen well-entrenched competitors. In fact, the arrival of Wal-Mart precipitated a price war (*preiskreig* in German).

Wal-Mart's top management has "learned by doing" in the international arena. For example, it determined that giving local managers ample authority with regards to merchandising decisions is preferable to centralized buying. The American retailer also outlasted a regulation in Germany prohibiting prices that are "too low."

Many consumers in the countries that Wal-Mart enters are pleased about the broad collections of low-price merchandise in the newcomer's stores. But some consumers, executives, and government officials are not enthralled with the invader from America. For example, a common refrain in Europe has been that Wal-Mart's arrival will force small retailers out of business as a result of stepped-up price competition.

Wal-Mart now has over 1,500 stores in nine foreign countries, ranging from Argentina to China. It also has a minority share in a prominent Japanese retail chain and is the largest retailer in both Canada and Mexico. The retail behemoth is opening more than 125 stores outside the U.S. annually. Wal-Mart's sales outside the U.S. are about $50 billion—to go along with around $250 billion in sales in its home market!

Of course, Wal-Mart's ultimate success outside the U.S. is far from assured. For example, in China's $600 billion retail market, the retailer has opened just 50 stores. In Germany, Wal-Mart has had to close unsuccessful stores and is struggling to be profitable. However, given its huge size and winning track record, the company founded by Sam Walton probably has a better chance for worldwide success, if not domination, than any other foreign invader.

www.walmartstores.com

Sources: *www.walmartstores.com*, accessed Feb. 16, 2005; Jack Ewing, "Wal-Mart: Local Pipsqueak," *BusinessWeek*, Apr. 11, 2005, p. 54; Alex Ortolani, "China Opens Its Doors to the World's Retailers," *The Wall Street Journal*, Dec. 14, 2004, p. A13; David Luchnow, "How NAFTA Helped Wal-Mart Reshape the Mexican Market," *The Wall Street Journal*, Aug. 31, 2001, pp. A1, A2; Barbara Thau, "Wal-Mart Takes On the World," *HFN*, Sept. 3, 2001, p. 8; and Ernest Beck and Emily Nelson, "As Wal-Mart Invades Europe, Rivals Rush to Match Its Formula," *The Wall Street Journal*, Oct. 6, 1999, pp. A1, A6.

After trying but then dropping cheaper snack-size items, Taco Bell introduced a Big Bell Value menu featuring larger portions such as extra–beef and double-decker tacos. Equally important, the chain attacked its cost structure, particularly labor costs. Its employees "assemble" tacos and other items from meats and vegetables cooked, sliced, and otherwise prepared by outside suppliers and delivered to the outlets.[5]

Value pricing certainly emphasizes the price element of the marketing mix. But that's not enough. A top executive of a computer company stated it in this way: "If all you have to offer is price, I don't think it's a successful long-term strategy."[6] Consequently, value pricing depends on creatively combining all elements of the marketing mix in order to maximize benefits in relation to price and other costs.

With a value-pricing strategy, products often have to be redesigned to expand benefits and/or pare costs. Relationships with customers have to be strengthened to generate repeat sales. Steps toward this end include frequent-buyer programs, toll-free customer service lines, and hassle-free warranties. And advertising has to be revamped to provide more facts and fewer emotional appeals. Finally, firms that desire to stress value need to negotiate aggressively with suppliers. What was said about one deep discounter applies rather well to all firms relying on value pricing, ". . . to sell merchandise at Family Dollar's low price points, you had to first buy it at the right price."[7]

Nonprice Competition

In **nonprice competition,** sellers maintain stable prices and attempt to improve their market positions by emphasizing other aspects of their marketing programs. Of course, competitors' prices still must be taken into consideration, and price changes will occur over time. Nevertheless, in nonprice competition, the emphasis is on something other than price.

Using terms familiar in economic theory, we can differentiate price and nonprice competition. In *price* competition, sellers attempt to move up or down their individual demand curves by changing prices. In *nonprice* competition, sellers attempt to shift their demand curves to the right by means of product differentiation, promotional activities, or some other technique. In Figure 13.2, the demand curve faced by the producer of a given model of skis is DD. At a price of $350, the producer can sell 35,000 pairs a year in the European market. On the basis of price competition alone, sales can be increased to 55,000 if the producer is willing to reduce the price to $330. The demand curve is still DD. However, the producer is interested in boosting sales without any decrease in selling price. Consequently, the firm embarks on a fresh promotional program—a form of nonprice competition. Suppose that enough new customers are persuaded to buy at the original $350 price that unit sales increase to 55,000 pairs a year. In effect, the firm's entire demand curve has been shifted to position D'D'.

With price competition, many consumers "learn" to buy a brand only as long as it has the lowest price. There is little customer loyalty when price is the only feature differentiating products from each other. As one consultant advised retailers, "Long-term price competition can take a devastating toll on profits."[8] With nonprice competition, however, a seller retains some advantage through its differentiation on other features (such as stylish design), even when another company decides to undersell it. Thus many firms stress nonprice competition, and others would like to rely on it rather than price competition. Wanting to be masters of their own destinies, companies believe they have more control in nonprice competition.

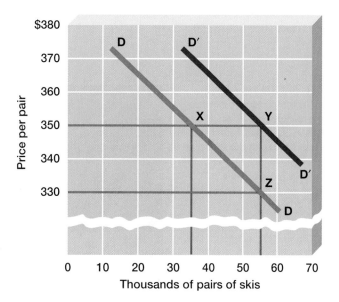

The best approach in nonprice competition is to build strong—if possible, unassailable—brand equity for the firm's products. Two methods of accomplishing this are to develop distinctive, hopefully unique, products and to create a novel, appealing promotional program. In that vein, Gap introduced $98 jeans featuring a higher grade of denim, special stitching, and fashionable prefaded look. In addition, some firms emphasize the variety and quality of the supplementary services they offer to customers.[9]

Market-Entry Strategies

In preparing to enter the market with a new product, management must decide whether to adopt a skimming or a penetration pricing strategy.

Market-Skimming Pricing

Setting a relatively high initial price for a new product is referred to as **market-skimming pricing.** Ordinarily the price is high in relation to the target market's range of expected prices. That is, the price is set at the highest possible level that the most interested consumers will pay for the new product. For example, Procter & Gamble used this strategy in introducing SK-II to the U.S. after the product earned "star" status in Asia. A suggested retail price of $130 was placed on the facial treatment essence.[10]

Market-skimming pricing has several purposes. Because it should provide healthy profit margins, it is intended primarily to recover research and development costs as quickly as possible. Lofty prices can be used to connote high quality. Market-skimming pricing is likely to curtail demand to levels that do not outstrip the firm's production capacities. Finally, it provides the firm with flexibility, because it is much easier to lower an initial price that meets with consumer resistance than it is to raise an initial price that has proven to be too low to cover costs. Even though the price may be lowered gradually, the high initial prices associated with market skimming are subject to criticism from consumers and government officials.

Market-skimming pricing is suitable under the following conditions:

- The new product has distinctive features strongly desired by consumers.
- Demand is fairly inelastic, most likely the case in the early stages of a product's life cycle. Under this condition, lower prices are unlikely to produce greater total revenues.
- The new product is protected from competition through one or more entry barriers such as a patent.

MGM Mirage owns and operates 24 hotels and casinos in Michigan, Mississippi, and Nevada. In order to serve various segments of the tourism and gaming markets, MGM Mirage has more than ten different properties in Las Vegas, including the Bellagio, Circus Circus, MGM Grand, Mirage, New York-New York, and Mandalay Bay. The Bellagio targets high-end consumers who desire luxury and special amenities (the Bellagio has its own art gallery) and thus has used market-skimming pricing.

www.fourseasons.com

Market skimming is used for various products, notably in pricing new technological goods such as flat-panel high-definition TVs. Some new hotels and resorts, such as the Four Seasons Hotels, use market-skimming pricing. And in a much different industry, the original price of the LASIK vision-correction procedure was more than $2,000 per eye. As a result of growing competition, LASIK prices started dropping, however.[11]

Market-Penetration Pricing

www.pg.com

In **market-penetration pricing,** a relatively low initial price is established for a new product. The price is low in relation to the target market's range of expected prices. The primary aim of this strategy is to penetrate the mass market immediately and, in so doing, to generate substantial sales volume and a large market share. At the same time, starting with a low price is intended to discourage other firms from introducing competing products. When it launched the SpinBrush, a battery-powered toothbrush, Procter & Gamble chose penetration pricing for these reasons. However, P&G's entry was so successful that despite the low price, directly competing products such as Gillette's Oral-B CrossAction Power have been introduced.[12]

Market-penetration pricing makes the most sense under the following conditions:

- A large market exists for the product.

- Demand is highly elastic, typically in the later stages of the life cycle for a product category.

- Substantial reductions in unit costs can be achieved through large-scale operations. In other words, economies of scale are possible.

- Fierce competition already exists in the market for this product or can be expected soon after the product is introduced.

www.trendmicro.com

Some software companies have used the ultimate in penetration pricing—giving away their products for a limited time or up to a stipulated quantity. Trend Micro, for example, gave users of "smart" mobile phones free access to its new Mobile Security Version 1.0 anti-virus software for up to six months. What motivates such a giveaway? Some firms want to create favorable word-of-mouth communication to motivate later buyers and to stimulate purchases of upgrades and complementary software by the recipients of the giveaways. Others intend to generate revenue from such sources as training, technical support, and even advertising at their websites for various firms.[13]

Referring to penetration pricing, two consultants stated, "Extended use of this offensive tactic inevitably leads to kamikaze pricing and calamity in markets as competitors respond, cost savings disappear, and customers learn to ignore value."[14] Thus, to avoid triggering intense price competition that erodes profits, firms typically need to use penetration pricing selectively.

In an extreme case, penetration pricing might violate federal antitrust laws. If a company gives away its products or charges a price that is below its cost and plans to raise prices later on in order to recoup earlier losses, such **predatory pricing** is likely to be illegal. Microsoft was charged with this practice when it gave away its Web browser, Internet Explorer, allegedly to obtain a dominant position in the market. Critics charge that predatory pricing can drive firms out of a market, thereby reducing competition, in which case the surviving firm(s) can raise prices substantially. Other observers say that low prices, whatever the seller's purpose, benefit buyers. In any event, following an early-1990s Supreme Court decision that rejected a charge of harmfully low prices, it has become very difficult to prove predatory pricing in a court case.[15]

Discounts and Allowances

Discounts and allowances result in a deduction from the base (or list) price. The deduction may be in the form of a reduced price or some other concession, such as free merchandise or advertising allowances. Discounts and allowances are common in business dealings.

Quantity Discounts

Quantity discounts are deductions from a seller's list price intended to encourage customers to buy in larger amounts or to buy most of what they need from the seller offering the deduction. Discounts are based on the size of the purchase, either in dollars or in units.

A **noncumulative discount** is based on the size of an *individual order* of one or more products. A retailer may sell golf balls at $2 each or at three for $5. A manufacturer or wholesaler may set up a quantity discount schedule such as the following, used by a manufacturer of industrial adhesives:

Boxes Purchased in a Single Order	% Discount from List Price
1–5	None
6–12	2.0
13–25	3.5
Over 25	5.0

Noncumulative quantity discounts are intended to encourage large orders. Many expenses, such as billing, order filling, and salaries of sales people, are about the same whether the seller receives an order totaling $10 or one totaling $500. Consequently, selling expense as a percentage of sales decreases as orders grow in size. With a noncumulative discount, a seller shares such savings with a purchaser of large quantities.

A **cumulative discount** is based on the total volume purchased *over a specified period*. This type of discount is advantageous to a seller because it ties customers closely to that firm. The more total business a buyer gives a seller, the greater the discount.

The Monsanto Co. used this off-beat ad to draw attention to one of its products, Posilac. To build customer loyalty, Monsanto offered a cumulative discount to customers. A noncumulative discount encouraged a single large purchase, but a cumulative discount built loyalty by giving customers another reason (besides satisfaction with the product) to purchase a good or service on a consistent basis.

www.monsanto.com

Cumulative discounts can be found in many industries. Airline frequent-flyer and hotel frequent-guest programs are one example. For some time, Monsanto Co. offered a form of cumulative discount in order to gain more purchases of Posilac, a drug that stimulates milk production in cows. To qualify for the discount, farmers had to agree to purchase the drug for at least six months.[16] Cumulative discounts also are common in selling perishable products. These discounts encourage customers to buy fresh supplies frequently so that the buyer's merchandise will not become stale.

Quantity discounts can help a producer achieve real economies in production as well as in selling. On the one hand, large orders (motivated by a noncumulative discount) can result in lower production and transportation costs. On the other hand, frequent orders from a single customer motivated by a cumulative discount can enable the producer to make much more effective use of production capacity. Thus the producer might benefit even though individual orders are small and do not generate savings in marketing costs.

Trade Discounts

Trade discounts, sometimes called *functional discounts,* are reductions from the list price offered to buyers in payment for marketing functions the buyers will perform. Storing, promoting, and selling the product are examples of these functions. A manufacturer may quote a retail price of $400 with trade discounts of 40% and 10%. The retailer pays the wholesaler $240 ($400 less 40%), and the wholesaler pays the manufacturer $216 ($240 less 10%). The wholesaler is given the 40% and 10% discounts. The wholesaler is expected to keep the 10% to cover costs of wholesaling functions and pass on the 40% discount to retailers. Sometimes, however, wholesalers keep more than the 10%, and it's not illegal for them to do so.

Note that the 40% and 10% discounts do not constitute a total discount of 50% off list price. They are not additive because the second discount (in this case, 10%) is computed on the amount remaining after the preceding discount (40%) has been deducted.

Cash Discounts

A **cash discount** is a deduction granted to buyers for paying their bills within a specified time. The discount is computed on the net amount due after first deducting trade and quantity discounts from the base price. Every cash discount includes three elements, as indicated in Figure 13.3:

- The percentage discount.
- The period during which the discount may be taken.
- The time when the bill becomes overdue.

Let's say a buyer owes $360 after other discounts have been granted and is offered terms of 2/10, n/30 on an invoice dated October 8. This means the buyer may deduct a discount of 2% ($7.20) if the bill is paid within 10 days of the invoice date—by October 18. Otherwise the entire (net) bill of $360 must be paid in 30 days—by November 7.

There are almost as many different cash discounts as there are industries. For example, in women's fashions, large discounts and short payment periods have been common; thus a cash discount of 5/5, n/15 would not be surprising. Such differences persist not so much for business reasons but because of tradition in various industries.

Most buyers are eager to pay bills in time to earn cash discounts. The discount in a 2/10, n/30 situation may not seem like very much. But this 2% is earned just for paying 20 days in advance of the date the entire bill is due. If buyers fail to take the cash discount in a 2/10, n/30 situation, they are, in effect, borrowing money at a 36%

FIGURE 13.3

Parts of a Cash Discount.

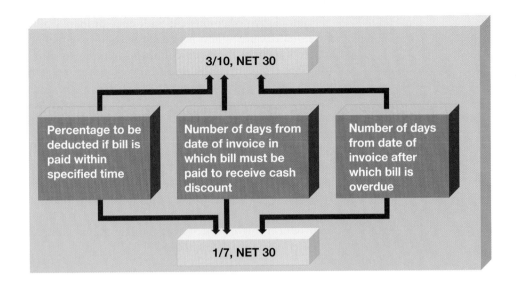

annual rate of interest. Here's how we arrived at that rate: In a 360-day business year, there are 18 periods of 20 days. Paying 2% for one of these 20-day periods is equivalent to paying 36% for an entire year.

Other Discounts and Allowances

To stimulate sales, some sellers offer rebates to prospective customers. A **rebate** is a discount on a product that a customer obtains by submitting a form or certificate provided by the seller. There are two kinds of rebates:

- A *coupon*, which is a small printed certificate that the customer presents when purchasing the product in order to obtain a discount equal to the value shown on the certificate. In 2004, about 250 million coupons were distributed as part of free-standing inserts in newspapers, making it the most popular method. Coupons are distributed in other ways, ranging from being part of an ad to being available in a store. According to one estimate, about 1% of coupons are redeemed, and 77% of American shoppers use coupons at least once in awhile, saving over $3 billion on purchases annually.[17]

- A *mail-in rebate*, in which the customer fills out a short form, encloses proof of the purchase, and sends the paperwork to a specified address. If all goes well, a rebate check arrives in the mail a short while later. Estimates of redemption rates vary greatly, from 10% to 80%. As you would expect, large rebates, such as $100, have the highest rates of redemption.[18]

It appears that use of mail-in rebates has been growing more rapidly than the distribution of *printed* coupons. But a relatively new technique, called e-coupons or virtual coupons, is emerging. A company places an e-coupon on its website *or* sends a coupon to a consumer via e-mail. A shopper can redeem this kind of coupon in cyberspace and/or at a physical store that sells the firm's products, depending on the conditions attached to the offer. Using brand new technology, firms (such as restaurants) can send a text-message coupon to the cell phones of willing recipients (such as students).[19]

The intent of **price customization** is to establish various prices on the basis of how much value is attached to a product by different people. It's important, though, to build a "fence" to keep customers who value a product highly from taking advantage of low prices. Quantity discounts are one fencing mechanism that can be used in conjunction with price customization. Others include multiperson pricing (such as "companion fares" offered by airlines) and a less expensive alternative (which involves developing a lower-price line of products).[20]

A manufacturer of goods such as air conditioners or toys purchased on a seasonal basis may consider granting a **seasonal discount**. This discount of, say, 5%, 10%, or 20% is given to a customer who places an order during the slack season. Off-season orders enable manufacturers to better use their production facilities and/or avoid inventory-carrying costs. Many services firms also offer seasonal discounts. For example, Club Med and other vacation resorts lower their prices during the off-season.

A **promotional allowance** is a price reduction granted by a seller as payment for promotional services performed by buyers. To illustrate, a producer of builders' hardware gives a certain quantity of free goods to dealers who prominently display its line. Or a clothing manufacturer pays one-half the cost of a retailer's ad featuring its product.

The Robinson-Patman Act and Price Discrimination

The discounts and allowances discussed here may result in various prices for different customers. Such price differentials represent **price discrimination.** In certain situations price discrimination is prohibited by the Robinson-Patman Act, one of the most important federal laws affecting a company's marketing program. (Any federal law regulating pricing is applicable only in cases where there is *interstate* trade. However, many states have pricing statutes that cover sales *within* the state—that is, *intrastate* trade.)

Main Provisions of the Act

The **Robinson-Patman Act,** passed in 1936, was intended to curb price discrimination by large retailers. It was written in very general terms, so over the years it has also become applicable to manufacturers.

Not all price differentials are illegal under the act. Price discrimination is unlawful only when the effect *may be* to substantially injure competition. In other words, a price difference is allowed if it does not substantially reduce competition. This law does *not* apply to sales to ultimate household consumers, because presumably they are not in business competition with each other.

Defenses and Exceptions

Price discrimination is legal in response to changing conditions that affect the marketability of products. For instance, differentials are allowed in cases of seasonal obsolescence (for products such as Christmas decorations), physical deterioration (fruits and vegetables), and going-out-of-business sales. Competitive considerations also are relevant. Typically a price differential is allowable if it is needed to meet competitors' prices.

Price differentials also are permissible if they do not exceed differences in the cost of manufacture, sale, or delivery of the product (see Figure 13.4). Cost differences may result from (1) variations in the quantity sold or (2) various methods of sale or delivery of the product. Thus, if selling a large quantity of a product directly to Safeway is more efficient than selling a small quantity through wholesalers to a neighborhood grocery store, the producer can legally offer Safeway a lower price per unit of the product. Such differentials are allowable even though there is a reasonable probability of injuring competition.

Under the Robinson-Patman Act, a buyer is as guilty as the seller if the buyer *knowingly* induces or receives an unlawful price differential. This provision is intended to restrain large buyers from demanding discriminatory prices. To illustrate, a group of independent auto-parts retailers and distributors filed a lawsuit alleging that large retailers such as Autozone, Pep Boys, and Wal-Mart receive unjustified allowances and rebates from parts manufacturers, making their purchase prices less than those of the plaintiffs on essentially similar items. The jury did not see illegal price discrimination and thus found in favor of the defendants. The persistent plaintiffs subsequently filed another similar lawsuit, this time targeting both large retailers and parts manufacturers.[21]

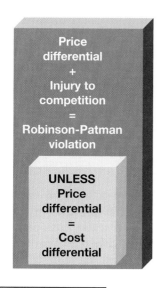

FIGURE 13.4

The Robinson-Patman Act.

Quantity discounts result in different prices to various customers. Consequently, these discriminatory prices could be illegal under the Robinson-Patman Act if it is shown that they injure competition. To justify price differentials stemming from its quantity discount schedule, a firm must rely on the cost defense provided in the act. In a nutshell, quantity discounts are legal if the resulting price differentials do not exceed differences in the cost of manufacturing, selling, or delivering the product.

Trade discounts are not addressed in the Robinson-Patman Act or in its predecessor, the Clayton Act. However, court cases many years ago established that separate discounts could be given to distinct classes of buyers. That is, one discount could be granted to wholesalers and another to retailers, as long as all buyers within a given group were offered the same discount.

Various types of promotional allowances are lawful *only* if they are offered to all competing customers on proportionally equal terms. For example, assume that a large chain receives promotional support valued at $15,000 when it purchases $750,000 of goods from a manufacturer. Another retailer should not expect the same dollar amount of support on a much smaller (say, $40,000) order. However, the second retailer is entitled to the same percentage amount of support as given to the large chain, 2% in this case. The $40,000 order should yield promotional services and materials valued at $800. Despite the straightforward math, disputes frequently arise over what is meant by "proportionally equal terms."

Geographic Pricing Strategies

In pricing, a seller must consider the costs of shipping goods to the buyer. These costs grow in importance as freight becomes a larger part of total variable costs. Pricing policies may be established whereby the buyer pays the entire freight expense, the seller bears the whole burden, or the seller and buyer share this expense. The strategy chosen can influence the geographic limits of a firm's market, locations of its production facilities, sources of its raw materials, and its competitive strength in various geographic markets.

Point-of-Production Pricing

In a widely used geographic pricing strategy, the seller quotes the selling price at the point of production, and the buyer selects the mode of transportation and pays all freight costs. **FOB factory pricing** (or *FOB mill pricing*) is the only geographic pricing strategy in which the seller does not pay any of the freight costs. The seller pays only for loading the shipment aboard the freight carrier—hence the term *FOB*, which stands for *free on board*.

Under FOB factory pricing, the seller nets the same amount on each sale of similar quantities. The delivered price to the buyer varies according to the freight costs. In purchasing goods from a manufacturer in Columbia, Missouri, differences in freight costs surely will provide a customer in St. Louis with a lower delivered price than a customer in Pittsburgh.

The Federal Trade Commission has considered FOB factory pricing to be legal. However, this pricing strategy has serious marketing and financial implications. In effect, FOB factory pricing makes a given seller more attractive to nearby customers and much less attractive to distant customers. Why? Because the customers bear the freight costs, they prefer to deal with suppliers located close to them, rather than far away. Thus the firm in Pittsburgh mentioned above probably would seek suppliers in Pennsylvania or nearby Ohio and West Virginia as alternatives to the supplier in Missouri. Of course, this assumes that alternative suppliers are comparable with respect to other important factors, such as product quality.

Uniform Delivered Pricing

Under **uniform delivered pricing,** the same delivered price is quoted to all buyers regardless of their locations. This strategy is sometimes referred to as *postage stamp pricing* because of its similarity to the pricing of first-class mail service. Of course, just like first-class mail, freight costs go up as weight of the shipment increases. Using our same example, if the Missouri-based manufacturer adopted uniform delivered pricing, the delivered cost of goods would be the same for the businesses in Pittsburgh, St. Louis, and elsewhere across the country, assuming of course that the shipments weigh the same amounts.

Uniform delivered pricing is typically used where freight costs are a small part of the seller's total costs. This strategy is also used by many retailers who believe "free" delivery is an additional service that strengthens their market position.

With a uniform delivered price, the net revenue to the seller varies depending on the freight cost involved in each sale. In effect, buyers located near the seller's factory pay some of the costs of shipping to more distant locations. Critics of FOB factory pricing usually favor a uniform delivered price. They maintain that the freight cost should not be charged separately to customers any more than other single marketing or production expenses.

Zone-Delivered Pricing

Zone-delivered pricing divides a seller's market into a limited number of broad geographic zones and then sets a uniform delivered price for each zone. The freight charge built into the delivered price is an average of the charges to all points within a zone. An eastern firm that quotes a price and then says "Slightly higher west of the Rockies" is using a two-zone pricing system. Zone-delivered pricing is similar to the *distance-based pricing* used by package-delivery services, notably UPS and Federal Express. In switching from flat-rate to distance-based prices, FedEx divided the continental U.S. into eight zones.[22] Of course, even with zone-delivered pricing, freight costs vary on the basis of the weight of the shipment.

When using this strategy, a seller must be careful to avoid charges of illegal price discrimination. Under a strict interpretation, the zones must be drawn so that all buyers who compete for a particular market are in the same zone. This condition is almost impossible to meet in densely populated areas, such as the East, which means that zone-delivered pricing is not practical everywhere.

For many years, FedEx charged the same flat rate for shippping a particular weight of package in the mainland U.S., irrespective of whether the destination was nearby or far away. Now FedEx uses geographic zones as the basis for charging different rates. This approach, in contrast to uniform delivered pricing, relates the shipping fee to the anticipated expense of moving the package to the intended destination.

www.fedex.com/us/
rates/zone

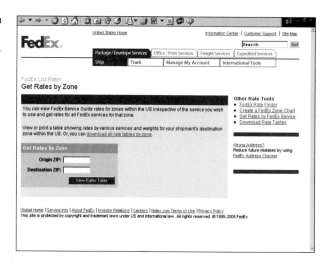

Freight-Absorption Pricing

To penetrate distant markets, a seller may be willing to pay part of the freight cost. Thus, under **freight-absorption pricing,** a manufacturer quotes to the customer a delivered price equal to its factory price *plus* the shipping costs that would be charged by a competitive seller located near that customer. In our continuing example, let's assume the manufacturing firm in Missouri agreed to freight absorption. Then the customer in Pittsburgh would not be charged full freight costs, but only the costs that would be charged by a competing supplier located close to the customer—say, in Youngstown, Ohio.

A freight-absorption strategy is adopted to offset competitive disadvantages of FOB factory pricing. With an FOB factory price, a firm is at a price disadvantage when trying to sell to buyers located in markets near competitors' plants. The reason? Because buyers pay the shipping costs under FOB factory pricing, these charges will grow as the distance between supplier and customer increases. A nearby supplier has an advantage over more distant suppliers, at least with respect to shipping costs. Freight absorption erases any price advantages that are due to differences in shipping costs.

A seller can continue to expand its geographic market as long as its net revenue after freight absorption is larger than its marginal cost for units sold. If a manufacturer's cost of producing, selling, and shipping one more unit—that is, its marginal cost—is $75, then freight-absorption pricing makes sense so long as the revenue received by the manufacturer exceeds $75. The firm's revenue would consist of the selling price of the product plus any freight costs charged to the buyer.

Freight absorption is particularly useful to a firm that has (1) excess capacity, (2) high fixed costs, and (3) low variable costs per unit of product. In these cases, management must constantly seek ways to cover fixed costs. Freight-absorption pricing is one means of generating additional sales volume to do that.

Freight absorption is legal if it is used independently and not in collusion with other firms. Also, it must be used only to meet competition. In fact, if it is practiced properly, freight absorption can strengthen competition by breaking down geographic monopolies.

Special Pricing Strategies and Situations

To be effective in setting initial prices, evaluating existing prices, and adjusting them as necessary, a firm needs to be aware of a variety of special pricing strategies and situations.[23]

One-Price and Flexible-Price Strategies

Early in its pricing deliberations, management should decide whether to adopt a one-price or a flexible-price strategy. Under a **one-price strategy,** a seller charges the *same* price to all similar customers who buy identical quantities of a product. Under a **flexible-price strategy,** also called a *variable-price strategy*, similar customers may pay *different* prices when buying identical quantities of a product. Although you may think otherwise, this practice is normally legal.

In the U.S., most organizations follow a one-price policy. This strategy shifts the focus from price to other factors, such as product quality. A one-price strategy can build customer confidence in a seller—whether at the manufacturing, wholesaling, or retailing level—because the buyer does not have to worry that other customers paid lower prices. Thus, with a one-price strategy, weak bargainers need not think they are at a disadvantage.

Several airlines, Continental and US Airways for example, have used aggressive flexible pricing to enter new markets and to increase their market shares on existing routes. (However, this strategy hasn't produced consistent profits for either enterprise.) Their new business comes from two sources—passengers now flying on other airlines and passengers who would not fly at higher prices. Especially in the second group, demand for air travel is highly elastic. The trick is to keep apart the segment of pleasure travelers (in which demand tends to be elastic) and the segment of business travelers (in which demand is typically inelastic). Airlines separate these segments by placing restrictions on lower-price tickets—requiring advance purchase and a Saturday night stay in the destination city, for example. Flexible pricing is also used in many other fields.

A variable-price strategy abounds in buying situations involving trade-ins. With flexible pricing, buyer-seller bargaining often determines the final price.[24] Both factors, trade-ins and bargaining, are common in automobile retailing. Thus, even though window-sticker prices may suggest a one-price policy, variable pricing has been the norm in selling cars.

www.saturn.com

In launching the Saturn model about 20 years ago, General Motors urged its dealers to set fixed prices so as to minimize haggling between consumer and sales person. That pricing approach set Saturn apart from other brands, with car shoppers responding favorably to Saturn's one-price approach. Of course, as independent firms, dealers can decide whether to use a one-price ("no-haggle") strategy or a variable-price ("let's make a deal") strategy. In the same industry, used-car superstores such as AutoNation and CarMax chose a one-price strategy.[25]

Flat-rate pricing, a variation of the one-price strategy, received some attention lately. Under such an arrangement, a purchaser pays a stipulated single price and then can consume as little or as much of the product as desired. An example of highly successful flat-rate pricing is the single admission fee charged by the Walt Disney Co. at its amusement parks. Some years ago, America Online switched to a flat rate of $19.95 per month (later raised to $23.90) for unlimited time online. Flat-rate pricing should be used only for products with a low marginal cost and, as one writer stated, "for which there's a natural limit to demand—like all-you-can-eat salad. Or bus trips."[26]

www.aol.com

A **single-price strategy** is an extreme variation of the one-price strategy. Not only are all customers charged the same price, but all items sold by the firm carry a single price! This approach, which originated many decades ago, involves offering frugal shoppers a variety of merchandise ranging from grocery items to cosmetics at a single price of $1.

Typically a store that adopts a single-price strategy purchases discontinued products as well as production overruns from a variety of sources at a small fraction of their original costs. Low prices cannot sell unappealing merchandise for long; therefore, single-price stores cannot get by with merchandise that is outdated and/or shoddy. Several single-price chains, including 99¢ Only, are growing rapidly because they provide shoppers with exceptional values.[27]

www.99only.com

Price Lining

Price lining involves selecting a limited number of prices at which a business will sell related products. It is used extensively by retailers of apparel. The Athletic Store, for instance, sells several styles of shoes at $39.88 a pair, another group at $59.95, and a third assortment at $79.99.

For the consumer, the main benefit of price lining is that it simplifies buying decisions. For the retailer, price lining helps in planning purchases. The buyer for The Athletic Store can go to market looking for shoes that can be sold at one of its three price points.

Rising costs can put a real squeeze on price lines. That's because a company hesitates to change its price line every time its costs go up. But if costs rise and prices are not increased accordingly, profit margins shrink and the retailer may be forced to seek products with lower costs.

Odd Pricing

Earlier, we briefly discussed pricing strategies that might be called *psychological* pricing: pricing above competitive levels, raising an unsuitably low price to increase sales, and price lining. All these strategies are intended to convey desirable images about products.

Odd pricing, another psychological strategy, is commonly used in retailing. **Odd pricing** sets prices at uneven (or odd) amounts, such as 49 cents or $19.95, rather than at even amounts. Autos are priced at $13,995 rather than $14,000, and houses sell for $119,500 instead of $120,000. Odd pricing is often avoided in prestige stores or on higher-priced items. Expensive men's suits, for example, are priced at $750, not $749.95.

The rationale for odd pricing is that it suggests lower prices and, as a result, yields greater sales than even pricing. According to this reasoning, a price of 98 cents will bring in greater revenue than a $1 price for the same product. Research has indicated that odd pricing can be an effective strategy for a firm that emphasizes low prices. According to another study, many consumers look only at the first two digits in a price. If so, companies should choose a price such as $1.99, rather than $1.95 or $2.09, in order to maximize sales and profits for a particular product.[28]

Leader Pricing and Unfair-Practices Acts

Many firms, primarily retailers, temporarily cut prices on a few items to attract customers. This strategy is called **leader pricing.** The items on which prices are cut are termed **leaders;** if the leader is priced below the store's cost, it's a **loss leader.**

www.bestbuy.com

Leaders should be well-known, heavily advertised products that are purchased frequently. Thus supermarkets as well as discount and drug stores promote popular brands of soft drinks and paper towels at low prices. Best Buy uses DVDs of popular movies as leaders, typically loss leaders. The giant chain is willing to lose money on this item in order to build store traffic, expecting that the added shoppers will buy other products—ranging from other DVDs to an expensive flat-panel TV—that generate profits.[29]

More than 20 states have **unfair-practices acts,** sometimes called *unfair-sales acts,* to regulate leader pricing. Typically, these laws prohibit a retailer or wholesaler from selling an item below invoice cost *plus* some stipulated amount. Varying from state to state, "cost plus" is usually defined as either a markup of several percent or the firm's cost of doing business.

In a widely publicized test of this type of law, three Arkansas drugstores charged that Wal-Mart's pharmacies sold some prescription drugs below cost in order to drive small competitors out of business. The giant discounter admitted it sold some products below cost but did so to provide value to customers rather than to destroy competitors. Ultimately, the Arkansas Supreme Court sided with Wal-Mart, stating, "Drugstores are far from destroyed. There is simply enhanced competition in the area." More recently, Wal-Mart was not as fortunate; these state laws prevented the chain from selling gasoline at the "everyday low prices" it had in mind."[30]

According to their supporters, unfair-practices acts eliminate price cutting intended to drive other products or companies out of business. However, such laws permit firms to use leaders—if their price is *above* the stipulated minimum. According to critics, these laws reduce retailers' freedom to set prices. Going a step further, the purpose of a business is to make a profit on the *total* enterprise, not necessarily on each transaction. Thus unfair-practices acts limit retailers' ability to determine

The first product category that Amazon.com, Inc. sold over the Internet was books. Ever since, the online retailer has used best-selling books as leaders to draw shoppers to its website. The company believes that these shoppers will also buy other products, hopefully some that are not discounted.

www.amazon.com

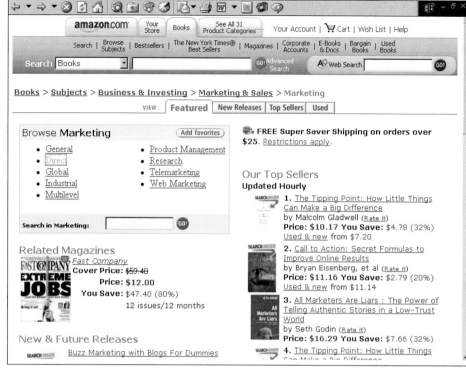

how best to generate profits. Also, the minimum prices stipulated by these laws may result in higher prices, which hurt consumers' pocketbooks. In some states these laws have been declared unconstitutional.

High-Low Pricing and Everyday Low Pricing

Many retailers, especially supermarkets and department stores, that want to engage in price competition rely on **high-low pricing.** This strategy entails alternating between regular and "sale" prices on the most visible products offered by a retail firm. Frequent price reductions are combined with aggressive promotion to convey an image of low prices. By starting with relatively high prices, retailers can boost their profits through sales to the segment of shoppers that really wants the product and is not very price sensitive. Then prices can be cut by various amounts on the basis of remaining inventory. The practice of high-low pricing is common; according to one study, over 60% of transactions in department stores involved "sale" (lower than original) prices.[31] JCPenney is a prime example of a retailer that relies on high-low pricing.

Given the need to change prices frequently, high-low pricing can be costly. It also may cause some consumers to not purchase products at regular prices but always to wait for reduced prices. Some consumer advocates have criticized high-low pricing, asserting that it misleads shoppers. The concern is that most transactions are made at decreased prices, which means that the so-called low prices are normal rather than real bargains.[32]

For a retailer that intends to compete on the basis of price, the alternative to high-low pricing is everyday low pricing (EDLP). Basically, **everyday low pricing** involves consistently low prices and few, if any, temporary price reductions. This strategy is featured by some large discounters, such as Wal-Mart and Family Dollar, and warehouse clubs, such as Costco. "Jeden Tag Tefpreise!" signs proclaiming everyday low prices were hung in German retail outlets that were acquired by Wal-Mart. EDLP has also been adopted by numerous other retailers, including such diverse chains as Linens 'n Things, Stein Mart, and Men's Wearhouse.[33]

Costco Wholesale, a chain of warehouse clubs, uses everyday low pricing (EDLP) on all of its offerings, including the variety of office products being purchased here. EDLP is also used by Sam's Club, which is Costco's most significant competitor. The battle between these two huge chains is described in a case following Part 5 in this text.

www.costco.com

Retailers expect (or at least hope) that EDLP will improve their profit margins because the average sales price will be higher than would be the case with high-low pricing. Further, retailers can point to their use of EDLP when negotiating lower purchase prices from suppliers. And operating expenses should be lessened, because of lower levels of advertising.[34]

All channel members, not just retailers, must choose between high-low and EDLP pricing. When a manufacturer gives retailers various discounts and allowances to stock and promote its particular brands, that's high-low pricing. So too is providing short-term "special deals" involving large deductions and/or free merchandise. The alternative is EDLP, in which a manufacturer or a wholesaler attaches consistently low prices to its goods. Procter & Gamble tried this approach in the 1990s. When P&G lost market share, it abandoned EDLP and reverted to high-low pricing.[35]

Which is better—EDLP or high-low pricing? A controlled experiment compared the effects of the pricing strategies on 26 product categories in a chain of grocery stores. EDLP increased sales, whereas high-low pricing resulted in slightly lower volume. More important, profits fell 18% with EDLP but jumped almost as much with high-low pricing. In a separate assessment, researchers concluded that the choice between the two strategies depends largely on issues associated with a retailer's assortment of merchandise. They recommended the use of high-low pricing by furniture stores, fast-food restaurants, supermarkets, traditional department stores, consumer electronics chains, and car dealers. In contrast, they thought that EDLP was preferable for high-end department stores, specialty stores, home-improvement chains, discount stores, and warehouse clubs.[36]

Resale Price Maintenance

Some manufacturers want to control the prices at which middlemen resell their products; this is termed **resale price maintenance.** Manufacturers seek to do this to pro-

AN ETHICAL DILEMMA?

Most, perhaps nearly all, retailers use electronic systems in which a checkout clerk scans bar codes on products to automatically ring up prices. Now, some stores are experimenting with similar self-scanning systems that allow shoppers to check out on their own.

Both systems have the potential for ethical problems, but let's focus here on store-controlled (rather than self-scanning) electronic systems. According to a tabulation of mid-1990s pricing-accuracy studies in nine states, the price charged for 3.9% of the almost 150,000 items examined was in error. However, perhaps surprisingly, undercharges outnumbered overcharges by a ratio of almost 3 to 2. The error rate was much lower in grocery stores (2.7%) than in other retail outlets (6%).

Retailers say any mispricing is due to human error, specifically clerks failing to put price reductions into the scanning system's computer. Some consumers and their advocates charge that retailers put price increases into the system before price decreases. That means the store is in an advantageous position compared to consumers when price changes are made.

Is it ethical for retail chains to use electronic checkout scanning systems?

Sources: Richard Clodfelter, "An Examination of Pricing Accuracy at Retail Stores That Use Scanners," *Journal of Product & Brand Management,*" Vol. 13, No. 4, 2004, pp. 269–278; and Catherine Yang. "Maybe They Should Call Them 'Scammers,' " *BusinessWeek*, Jan. 16, 1995, pp. 32, 33.

tect the brand's image. Publicly, they state that their control of prices—and avoidance of discounted prices—provides middlemen with ample profit margins. In turn, consumers should be able to expect sales help and other services when they buy the manufacturers' products from middlemen. Critics, however, claim that control over prices leads to inflated prices and excessive profits.

One way in which producers can gain a bit of control, and perhaps provide guidance to retailers, is with a **suggested list price.** This price is set by a manufacturer at a level that provides retailers with their normal markups. To illustrate, a producer sells to, say, a hardware store a certain product for $6 a unit. It recommends a retail price of $9.95, which would furnish the store with its normal markup of 40% of selling price. This is only a *suggested* retail price. Retailers have the right to sell the product for less or more than the suggested price.

Other manufacturers try even harder to control their products' retail prices. Such effort is worthwhile only for a producer selling to relatively few retailers that want very much to carry the product. A manufacturer may even threaten to stop shipment of products to retailers that price products substantially below suggested list prices.

Is it legal to act aggressively in order to control retail prices? From about 1930 to 1975, a set of state and federal laws permitted manufacturers to set minimum retail prices for their products. The state laws became known as *fair-trade laws.* However, such price controls were prohibited by the federal Consumer Goods Pricing Act of 1975. According to this law, a producer no longer can set resale prices and impose them on resellers.[37]

The struggle over resale price maintenance never seems to end, however. Recently, the focus has been on whether or not a supplier can set a *maximum* price without violating antitrust laws. In what turned out to be a significant case, the owner of a Unocal 76 gas station charged that the supplier stipulated the maximum retail price, thereby limiting the station owner's ability to compete and be profitable. After hearing this case, the U.S. Supreme Court ruled that a supplier's setting maximum prices was not automatically illegal but had to be considered on a case-by-case basis. The key issue is whether or not fixing a maximum price enhances or inhibits competition.[38] This ruling did not affect the fixing of *minimum* prices, a practice that remains automatically illegal.

Sometimes manufacturers are charged with violating antitrust laws as a result of their efforts to control resale prices. For example, Nine West Group Inc., a large women's shoe company, was charged by the Federal Trade Commission with taking actions to restrict competition among shoe retailers, in order to obtain higher prices for its shoe brands. Eventually Nine West agreed to cease the controversial practices and made a $34 million payment to put the matter to rest, thereby averting future legal action.[39]

Reactive and Proactive Changes

After an initial price is set, a number of situations may prompt a firm to change its price. As costs increase, for instance, management may decide that raising price is preferable to maintaining price and either cutting quality or promoting the product aggressively. According to a pricing consultant, "Small companies are more reluctant to raise prices than their large counterparts."[40] Obviously, it's wise to raise prices gradually and with little fanfare. The "art" of raising pricing is discussed further in the You Make the Decision box on the next page.

Temporary price cuts may be used to sell excess inventory or to introduce a new product. Also, if a company's market share is declining because of strong competition, its executives may react initially by reducing price. Small firms' price cuts typically are not matched by large competitors, unless they significantly diminish the larger firm's sales. Decreasing price makes the most sense when enough new customers are attracted to offset the smaller profit margin per sale.[41] Nevertheless, for many products, a better long-term alternative to a price reduction is improving the overall marketing program.

Any firm can safely assume that its competitors will change their prices—sooner or later. Consequently, every firm should have guidelines on how it will react. If a competitor *boosts* price, a short delay in reacting probably will not be perilous. However, if a competing firm *reduces* price, a prompt response normally is required to avoid losing customers.

In the absence of collusion, occasional price reductions occur even in an oligopoly with relatively few firms, because the actions of all sellers cannot be controlled. Every so often some firm will cut its price, especially if sales are flat. From a seller's standpoint, the big disadvantage in price cutting is that competitors will retaliate—and not let up. A **price war** may begin when one firm decreases its price in an effort to increase its sales volume and/or market share. The battle is on if other firms retaliate, reducing prices on their competing products. Additional price decreases by the original price cutter and/or its competitors are likely to follow until one of the firms decides it can endure no further damage to its profits. Most businesses would like to avoid price wars.

Always part of business, price wars have been even more common since the early 1990s. Low prices often are the primary weapon in numerous disparate fields, such as computer microprocessors, cigarettes, air travel, and ready-to-eat cereals. Even ski resorts compete intensely through low prices by offering "buddy passes" and other discounts. Fast-food chains began competitive price-cutting in 2002. More recently, Yahoo! may have set off a price war when it moved into the digital-music field in 2005. The new entrant's introductory subscription fee of $7-per-month was about one-half of what competitors such as RealNetworks charge. According to one consultant, price wars often are "over-reactions to threats that either aren't there at all or are not as big as they seem."[42]

Price wars can be harmful to a firm, especially one that is financially weak. One article listed the damages as follows: "Customer loyalty? Dead. Profits? Imploding. Planning? Up in smoke." After extended price wars, companies in various industries, including groceries, personal computers, and music retailing, have gone out of business.[43]

music.yahoo.com

www.real.com/rhapsody

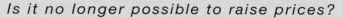

YOU MAKE THE DECISION

Is it no longer possible to raise prices?

Outright price increases are less common now than they were in the 1990s. Instead, Broadway theaters add a $1.25 "renovation fee" to the price of a ticket, a Florida resort adds a daily fee of $12 to cover amenities ranging from local calls to housekeeping, and a telecommunications provider charges long-distance customers a 99¢-per-month "regulatory assessment fee." (Whatever that is, it represents upwards of $400 million in annual revenues for the firm.) Even Microsoft, the software giant, established a subscriptionlike plan that included automatic software upgrades and that, according to some disgruntled customers, increased the cost of Microsoft products.

Why are firms taking such disguised or circular measures rather than simply raising prices across the board or at least selectively? Four factors, in particular, are reducing marketers' pricing flexibility:

- During a soft economy, which has characterized the U.S. since the late 1990s, consumers are particularly price sensitive. Further, they are willing to spend extra time searching for "good deals," with price receiving the most scrutiny. Under these circumstances, businesses keep their base prices (typically the figure that is advertised and otherwise communicated to consumers) as low as possible.

- American firms that produce goods in the U.S. face stiff competition from manufacturing plants in China. Often, the cost differential is 30% to 50%, which means that a U.S. manufacturer normally has to cut prices rather than raise them.

- It's particularly difficult to boost prices when inflation is very low, the situation during the first part of

the new century. Rather, firms must build or maintain profits by cost-cutting and economies of scale.

- The Internet has also affected pricing for products sold online as well as those sold in more traditional ways. Essentially, a growing number of consumers are using search engines to make price comparisons and identify the lowest available price for a product. These search engines tend to focus on base prices rather than on a total price that includes any special fees. (We'll discuss these *shopping robots* more in Chapter 15.)

Decisions about the frequency and amount of price increases, whether hidden or visible, ordinarily are based on several factors. Among the factors are likely reactions of the target market and the degree to which executives are comfortable taking risks (such as losing customers alienated by a price hike). Although it may be difficult to do at this time, companies may still attempt periodic price increases in order to augment or maintain profit margins.

When are visible, rather than hidden, price increases worth the risk of lost customers?

Sources: Pete Engardio and Dexter Roberts, "'The China Price,'" *Business-Week*, Dec. 6, 2004, pp. 102–105+; Emily Thornton, "Fees! Fees! Fees!" *BusinessWeek*, Sept. 29, 2003, pp. 98–102+; Rebecca Buckman, "New Microsoft Pricing Looms," *The Wall Street Journal*, June 24, 2002, p. B8; Barbara Hagenbaugh, "Low Inflation Has Officials Worried," *USA Today*, May 10, 2002, p. B6; and Lisa Gubernick, "The Little Extras That Count (Up)," *The Wall Street Journal*, July 12, 2001, pp. B1, B4.

In the short term, consumers benefit from price wars through sharply lower prices. But over the longer term, the net effects on consumers are not clear-cut. Ultimately, a smaller number of competing firms might translate to fewer product choices and/or higher prices for consumers.

Summary

After deciding on pricing goals and setting the base (or list) price, marketers must establish pricing strategies that are compatible with the rest of the marketing mix. A basic decision facing management is whether to engage primarily in price or nonprice competition. Price competition establishes price as the primary, perhaps the sole, basis for attracting and retaining customers. A growing number of businesses are adopting value pricing to improve the ratio of benefits to price and, in turn, lure customers from competitors.

In nonprice competition, sellers maintain stable prices and seek a differential advantage through other aspects of their marketing mixes. Common methods of nonprice competition include offering distinctive and appealing products, promotion, and/or customer services.

When a firm is launching a new product, it must choose a market-skimming or a market-penetration pricing strategy. Market skimming uses a relatively high initial price, market penetration a low one.

Strategies also must be devised for discounts and allowances—deductions from the list price. Management has the option of offering quantity discounts, trade discounts, cash discounts, and/or other types of deductions. Decisions on discounts and allowances must conform to the Robinson-Patman Act, a federal law regulating price discrimination.

Freight costs must be considered in pricing. A producer can require the buyer to pay all freight costs (FOB factory pricing), or a producer can absorb all freight costs (uniform delivered pricing). Alternatively, the two parties can share the freight costs (freight absorption).

Management also should decide whether to charge the same price to all similar buyers of identical quantities of a product (a one-price strategy) or to set different prices (a flexible-price strategy). Many organizations, especially retailers, use at least some of the following special strategies: price lining—selecting a limited number of prices at which to sell related products; odd pricing—setting prices at uneven (or odd) amounts; and leader pricing—temporarily cutting prices on a few items to attract customers. Some forms of leader pricing are illegal in a number of states. A company must also choose between everyday low pricing, which relies on consistently low prices and few if any temporary price reductions, and high-low pricing, which involves alternating between regular and "sale" prices on the most visible products offered by a firm.

Many manufacturers are concerned about resale price maintenance, which means controlling the prices at which middlemen resell products. Some approaches to resale price maintenance are more effective than others; moreover, some methods may be illegal.

Market opportunities and/or competitive forces may motivate companies to initiate price changes or, in different situations, to react to other firms' price changes. A series of successive price cuts by competing firms creates a price war, which can harm the profits of all participating companies.

More about **Bose**

Besides tabletop audio products aimed at consumers, the Bose Corporation sells other items to consumers, businesses, and different types of organizations (even museums and churches). Bose's other products, listed from earliest to latest introductions, include:

- The Bose Acoustic Noise Canceling Headset, for use by pilots and ground crews.

- A Lifestyle line of products that are intended to provide top-quality sound for home-theater systems, with suggested retail prices of $2,999 and up.

- The Auditioner, a remarkable product that somehow simulates what a Bose system will sound like in a building before it's even constructed.

- The SoundDock system, which provides top-quality sound for music stored on Apple's iPod or iPod mini devices and, at the same time, charges an iPod.

There are similarities in how Bose markets various products. Bose's sound system for automobiles, which was brought to market in 1982, exemplifies the company's proven approach to marketing products aimed at business markets. This high-quality product has become a desirable branded component for many upper-end automobiles. The fact that car buyers consider a Bose sound system to be a "plus" in a new automobile gives Bose more pricing power in its dealings with auto manufacturers.

Bose is also working to improve auto suspension systems, an area that seems far away from its core competency in audio products. However, the suspension system Bose is developing uses "power amplification switching" technology that the company pioneered for audio speakers. According to one assessment, the ultimate outcome of this research project—more than 20 years in duration—"has the potential to transform the auto industry." Thus far, Bose has not tried to sell the product to a carmaker.

These wide-ranging products illustrate how the Bose Corporation fulfills its mission of enhancing existing products to improve people's lives. If a company can accomplish this in the form of a truly superior product, then it can command prices that otherwise would seems unjustifiably high.[44]

1. Compared to selling its products to consumers through retail stores, does Bose have to approach pricing differently for business markets (for example, when one of its products is used in a new or renovated educational, religious, or athletic facility)?

2. For Bose, is price the most or least important element of the marketing mix?

Key Terms and Concepts

Strategy (346)
Price competition (347)
Value pricing (347)
Nonprice competition (349)
Market-skimming pricing (350)
Market-penetration pricing (351)
Predatory pricing (351)
Quantity discount (352)
Noncumulative discount (352)
Cumulative discount (352)
Trade (functional) discount (353)
Cash discount (353)
Rebate (354)

Price customization (354)
Seasonal discount (355)
Promotional allowance (355)
Price discrimination (355)
Robinson-Patman Act (355)
FOB factory (mill) pricing (356)
Uniform delivered pricing (357)
Zone-delivered pricing (357)
Freight-absorption pricing (358)
One-price strategy (358)
Flexible-price (variable-price) strategy (358)
Flat-rate pricing (359)

Single-price strategy (359)
Price lining (359)
Odd pricing (360)
Leader pricing (360)
Leaders (360)
Loss leader (360)
Unfair-practices (unfair-sales) acts (360)
High-low pricing (361)
Everyday low pricing (361)
Resale price maintenance (362)
Suggested list price (363)
Price war (364)

Questions and Problems

1. For each of the following products, should the seller adopt a market-skimming or a market-penetration pricing strategy? Support your decision in each instance.
   a. High-fashion dresses styled and manufactured by Yves St. Laurent
   b. An exterior house paint that lasts twice as long as any competitive brand
   c. A subscription website that sends you daily e-mails containing information about up to five topics of your choosing
   d. A tablet that converts a gallon of water into a gallon of automotive fuel

2. As economic unification was attained and trade barriers were removed throughout the multination European Union (EU), numerous companies deliberated on how best to achieve sales and profits in all or part of this huge market. Name two U.S. brands that might benefit from adopting a market-skimming pricing strategy in the EU and two others that should use a market-penetration strategy.

3. Carefully distinguish between cumulative and noncumulative quantity discounts. Which type of quantity discount has the greater economic and social justification? Why?

4. A manufacturer of appliances quotes a list price of $800 per unit for a certain model of refrigerator and grants trade discounts of 35%, 20%, and 5%. What is the manufacturer's selling price? Who might get these various discounts?

5. The Craig Charles Company (CCC) sells to all its customers at the same published price. One of its sales managers discerns that Jamaican Enterprises is offering to sell to one of CCC's customers, Rocky Mountain Sports, at a lower price. CCC then cuts its price to Rocky Mountain Sports but maintains the original price for all other customers. Is CCC's price cut a violation of the Robinson-Patman Act?

6. "An FOB point-of-production price system is the only geographic price system that is fair to buyers." Discuss.

7. An eastern firm wants to compete in western markets, where it is at a significant disadvantage with respect to freight costs. What pricing alternatives can it adopt to overcome the freight differential?

8. Under what conditions is a company likely to use a variable-price strategy? Can you name firms that employ this strategy other than when a trade-in is involved?

9. On the basis of the topics covered in this chapter, establish a set of price strategies for the manufacturer of a new glass cleaner that is sold through middlemen to supermarkets. The manufacturer sells the cleaner at $15 for a case of a dozen 16-ounce bottles.

10. Friends of yours are entering the world of electronic commerce, intent on selling college-related merchandise and memorabilia on the Internet. On the basis of reading this chapter, what three points of advice would you offer them about pricing strategies?

Interactive Marketing Exercises

1. Talk to the owner or a top executive of a firm in your community regarding whether this company emphasizes price or nonprice competition and the reasons for following this course. Also ask whether its approach is similar to or dissimilar from the normal approach used by competitors to market the primary product sold by this firm.

2. Identify a firm in your community that is selling products online. Arrange an interview with the person who directs the company's marketing. Ask the executive which of the following pricing strategies the online firm is using and the rationale for the choices:
   a. Price or nonprice competition
   b. Market-skimming or market-penetration pricing
   c. Noncumulative or cumulative discounts
   d. One-price or flexible-price strategy
   e. Everyday low pricing or high-low pricing

Cases for Part 4

CASE 1 Southwest Airlines

Staying on Course through Turbulent Times

At the end of 2004, Southwest Airlines Co. announced its 32nd consecutive year of profitability—a remarkable feat for any business, much less an American airline. Southwest has adhered to a basic strategy of providing no-frills service at low fares on relatively short flights. It also expanded by moving into new markets. Its carefully designed and well-executed strategies have helped Southwest maintain its position as the leading low-cost airline in the U.S. and the fourth largest airline overall.

All established airlines, even Southwest, have encountered bumpy flying in recent years, however. The entire industry had to deal with the reduced demand for air travel following the terrorist attacks on September 11, 2001. In addition, a number of low-cost carriers entered the market. To remain competitive, the big network airlines (such as United and American) had to lower their fares and then work frantically, and continually, to pare their operating expenses. The intensely competitive environment also put pressure on Southwest to keep both its fares and its costs low, and even prompted the airline to reconsider some of its core strategies.

Getting off the Ground

The groundwork for Southwest Airlines was laid in 1966 when Herb Kelleher outlined his plans for a low-fare airline on the back of a cocktail napkin. Southwest officially took off in 1971, with three planes serving three Texas cities. Eventually, Southwest spread its wings to serve 60 airports in 31 states, and it now boasts almost 10% of U.S. air traffic. At the end of 2004, Southwest reported net profit of $313 million for the year. By comparison, the other eight largest U.S. airlines reported a combined loss of $2.3 *billion* in the fourth quarter of 2004 alone.

Much of Southwest's success has been attributed to Kelleher and his quest to provide low fares and excellent customer service. His vision has been fulfilled because Southwest consistently ranks among the "most admired companies" in *Fortune* magazine's annual ranking. Southwest is the only airline to earn such accolades.

Flying in the Wake of Terror

Its reputation notwithstanding, all of Southwest Airlines' skill and resolve were tested by the tragic events of September 11, 2001. As soon as flights were allowed to resume, the entire industry, including Southwest, experienced sharp drops in passenger traffic. However, unlike the other major carriers, Southwest did not cut the number of its flights or lay off any of its employees; in fact, it has never resorted to layoffs.

Southwest's employees worked hard to keep costs low and satisfy customers in order to fill the airline's empty seats during the difficult times that followed the attack. For several weeks after September 11, Southwest's passenger load was about one-third of its normal level. The company launched a major advertising campaign on September 19, featuring employees who vowed to help get America flying again. Southwest then relied on its favorite marketing strategy by announcing lower fares. By November, industry capacity had fallen 16% from the previous year, but Southwest's had grown by 7%.

The employee unity demonstrated in Southwest's post-September 11 ads was real. Southwest has enjoyed a relatively good working relationship with its 32,000 employees, due in a large part to Kelleher, who made them a priority above all else. In 1973, he initiated a profit-sharing initiative, and a stock-purchase plan was added in 1984. Kelleher encouraged employees to have a good time at work and to inject humor into their daily activities. He believed that high employee morale means low turnover, which in turn helps maintain low costs.

Adjusting to a New Crew in the Cockpit

Kelleher retired as chief executive officer (CEO) in June 2001 and was replaced by Jim Parker, formerly the company's legal counsel. Three months later, Parker had to deal with the repercussions from the terrorist attacks. Specifically, Southwest's employees were worn out by working extra hard to keep the airline flying high following 9/11. As a result, it was difficult to sustain superior customer service. In addition, the employees' stock options weren't worth quite as much, since the company's net income fell from $511 million in 2001 to $241 million in 2002, which caused the firm's stock price to decline.

In its early days, Southwest's compensation levels were lower than those of the larger airlines. The company lured workers with its unique culture, promise of job stability, and profit-sharing plan. As the company grew and its work force matured, labor costs increased. When some of the network airlines began to fail and entered into bankruptcy proceedings, they were able to negotiate significant wage concessions with their unions. By 2004, Southwest pilots earned an average of $170,000 per year, 30% more than United Airline's pilots were paid. That same year, Parker sought, but was unable to obtain, wage concessions from the flight attendants' union. He handed the negotiations over to Kelleher (who was still involved with the company), but the resulting agreement included a 31% pay raise. Not long after, Parker resigned as CEO.

Parker was replaced by Gary Kelly, the company's chief financial officer and the architect of an innovative fuel hedging program. Several years ago, Kelly wisely began purchasing oil futures. As the cost of jet fuel began to rise, Southwest benefited by paying the prices locked in by Kelly. As a result, the company had enormous savings, more than $450 million in 2004 alone.

Fueling the Competition

Southwest has always been more innovative than the network airlines with regards to offering low fares and controlling costs. But a group of new discount airlines is challenging Southwest on both fronts. In addition, several of them have eschewed Southwest's no-frills approach and are offering extra amenities and services in order to attract passengers. For example, since its inception in 2000, JetBlue Airways has equipped its planes with leather seats and live satellite TV. America West, a network airline that has worked to transformed itself into a discount carrier, has business-class cabins and assigned seating. In spring 2005, America West and US Airways joined forces through a merger.

The low-fare approach is starting to catch on in international markets. Ryanair, an Irish airline, offers cheap tickets to compete with Europe's state-owned, high-price carriers. Michael O'Leary, the company's CEO, declared Kelleher a genius. "Kelleher was the one who brought air travel within the pockets of average people," O'Leary observed. But the service on Ryanair makes a Southwest flight seem like first class. Not only does it not offer food or a frequent-flyer program, its planes have been stripped of reclining seats, window blinds, and seat pockets.

On the other side of the globe, AirAsia has been so successful at controlling costs that it has offered one-way tickets for as low as $10 each. In fact, in mid-2004 it boasted an operating cost per available seat mile (ASM) of only four cents. At that same time, Jet Blue's cost per ASM was 5.9 cents and Southwest's had risen above 8 cents. Like Southwest in its infancy, Jet Blue operates newer planes that require less maintenance and have younger employees who earn lower wages and have fewer medical expenses.

Traditional network carriers now compete with discount airlines on more than 70% of their routes within the U.S., shrinking fares across the board. "The low-cost carriers are now dictating pricing in our business," an American Airlines executive admitted. As discounters add more flights, the big network airlines follow suit in an attempt to hang onto market share. The cumulative effect of this approach is an industry-wide glut of capacity and, to the delight of passengers, low fares even as oil prices continue to increase. Average "leisure" and business fares were 10% and 8% lower, respectively, at the end of 2004 than they were the year before.

The "Big Six" airlines (American, United, Delta, Continental, US Airways, and Northwest) had to take an even harder look at their own costs. Their most effective expense-controlling method has been to enter or threaten bankruptcy and use it as a bargaining tool when renegotiating contracts with labor unions. Several have also resorted to slashing or eliminating pension plans. US Airways is saddled with the highest cost per ASM in the industry, just over 11 cents. Continental initiated aggressive cost-cutting initiatives, but was able to reduce ASM no lower than 9.4 cents.

The Internet enables customers to compare prices and hunt for the best deals in a fairly short amount of time. Thus the Big Six are also making an effort to simplify their fare structures. Delta responded with a program called SimpliFares that cut prices by as much as 50% and capped its highest one-way fare at $499. It also eliminated the annoying Saturday-night stay requirement that was mandatory in order to secure Delta's lowest rates. Southwest, however, never charges in excess of $299 for a one-way unrestricted ticket.

Two of the major airlines decided that "if you can't beat 'em, join 'em." Hence, Delta launched Song Airlines in 2003, and United got Ted Airlines off the ground in 2004. Both are offering fares that are competitive with Southwest's, but are taking a cue from

JetBlue by providing some added amenities. Song gives passengers the option of purchasing meals, and both Song and Ted provide individual in-flight entertainment units.

Continuing to Spread Its Wings

Southwest has not allowed itself to get stuck in a "holding pattern." Instead, the airline committed to replace its fabric seats with leather ones, and is considering the addition of in-flight entertainment. "We are trying to keep in step with customer needs and also competitive changes," explained Kelly. But the airline is ever mindful of the need to control costs. It offers cheaper snacks than most other airlines; doesn't provide assigned seats; and operates a single type of aircraft, the Boeing 737, to reduce employee training costs and spare parts inventories. By turning its planes around in 20 to 25 minutes from the time they arrive at the airport gate to the time they back away with a new load of passengers, Southwest keeps its aircraft in the air for an average of 11 hours per day, compared to 8 hours for the major airlines.

Southwest was also one of the first airlines to use the Internet to save money, when they began selling tickets online in 1996. By 2004, the carrier was generating 60% of its revenue from its website, and thus closed three of its nine reservations centers.

Southwest is rethinking aspects of its core strategy, however. In the past, Southwest's basic approach revolved around short-flight, domestic routes. Over time, though, the airline has stretched the average length of its trips from 521 miles in 1994 to 753 miles in 2005.

In addition, Southwest traditionally served smaller airports that are readily accessible, but it has recently moved into several large, crowded international airports. In May 2004, it began service to Philadelphia, a long-time beachhead of US Airways. Prior to Southwest's arrival, US Air charged $938 for an unrestricted round-trip ticket between Philadelphia and Providence. Southwest began charging only $177 for the same ticket and just $39 for a restricted, one-way fare. US Air was forced to match the $177 price, and soon found itself back in bankruptcy court. It later abandoned Pittsburgh as a hub, and Southwest was quick to begin operating there as well.

Southwest expanded its operations still further when it entered into an agreement with ATA Airlines, a discount carrier caught in bankruptcy proceedings. It paid ATA $40 million for six gates at Chicago's Midway Airport, giving Southwest a commanding presence with 25 total gates at the airport. In addition, the airlines entered into a code-sharing agreement, which means that each carrier can sell seats on the other's flights. This gives Southwest access to ATA's operations at New York's La Guardia Airport and Washington's Reagan National Airport. The collaboration with ATA also allows Southwest to add Hawaii to its list of destinations. Thus Southwest's frequent flyers can redeem their Rapid Rewards vouchers for a "trip to paradise."

In the past, Southwest was successful by maintaining a disciplined approach to its operations. But it is no longer a young, upstart airline. Now a mature company with older airplanes and a well-paid corps of employees, Southwest must expand its operations in order to decrease its unit costs and keep fares low. "We think the driving factor in choosing an airline is the fare," declared Kelly. This approach has worked for Southwest for several decades. However, with many other airlines following the same approach now, Southwest will be hard pressed to maintain its standing as the nation's premier airline in terms of growth and profits.

Questions

1. What pricing strategies does Southwest Airlines employ to compete against other airlines?

2. What types of costs must airlines control to remain competitive? Are they fixed or variable costs?

3. Do you agree with the possibility of Southwest's altering some of its fundamental strategies, such as adding in-flight entertainment services, codesharing with ATA, and moving into larger, more crowded airports?

Dell

Keeping Prices as Low as Dell

Most college students just want to pass their midterms. Michael Dell wanted to take on IBM. That's a pretty ambitious goal for a student selling made-to-order personal computers (PCs) over the phone out of his dorm room at the University of Texas in Austin. In 1984, Dell decided to pursue this quest full-time, so he dropped out of school even though he had only $1,000 in seed money.

Only 12 years later, Dell Inc.'s share of the domestic PC market was larger than IBM's. By 2004, Dell was *the* leader with over 33%, surpassing Hewlett-Packard (just under 20%), Gateway (5%), and Dell's original target, IBM (almost 5%). In March 2004, Michael Dell decided to transfer the role of chief executive officer (CEO) to the firm's president, but Dell remains chairman of the board of directors. Having amassed a personal net worth of $10 billion, he is one of the wealthiest people in the world.

Dell Inc.'s climb to the top revolutionized a significant industry. Instead of focusing on product innovation, the customary strategy for computer firms, Dell created a new business model. In order to keep prices low and delivery times short, Dell purchases components directly from manufacturers, assembles them to meet a customer's specifications, and then ships the finished product to a customer very soon after the order is received.

Instead of selling through traditional retail outlets, Dell Inc. relies on a direct-sales approach, as well as catalogs. In addition, the industry leader has embraced the Internet like no other company. By 2000, Dell was selling over $50 million of computer equipment via the Web *every day*.

Once it became dominant in the PC market, Dell chose a pricing tactic (lowering prices) that is contrary to what would normally be expected in a mature industry. Furthermore, the giant company's attention has now expanded to other products, where it is attempting to replicate the success it has had with PCs.

Booting Up a New Computer Company

By adopting a direct-sales model, Dell Inc. was able to eliminate middlemen, keep prices low, and deliver products more quickly than its competitors. In 1988, the company achieved annual revenues of $159 million and began selling its stock publicly. By 1993, Dell had captured 4% of the U.S. market for PCs and had become one of the top five PC manufacturers in the world.

One of the first companies to make a serious effort to sell over the Internet, Dell Inc. introduced www.dell.com in 1996. Meanwhile, Dell continued to expand into foreign markets, such as China and Central America, and introduced new products, such as workstations and network servers. Dell became the top seller of PCs in 2001. The company now has revenues exceeding $49 billion.

The rise of the Internet facilitated Dell's direct-sales approach by giving it another means for interacting with clients and suppliers. Dell uses the Web not only to promote and sell its products, but also to order components and parts from numerous suppliers—sometimes placing orders on an hourly basis. Using the Internet for procurement helps Dell keep its inventory low and deliver custom-made PCs with preloaded software in as little as three days. Because computers are made to order, customers receive what they want and Dell isn't stuck with unwanted computers that were built according to imperfect sales forecasts. By contrast, HP custom builds only 20% of the PCs it sells.

Dell Inc.'s inventory levels are very low compared to the rest of the PC industry. Dell maintains stock for just four days of operations; by comparison, HP carries 28 days of stock. This difference represents an enormous financial advantage for Dell. Because it can deliver finished products so quickly to customers, Dell typically collects payment from clients long before it pays suppliers. In other words, the company would make money as a result of its positive cash cycle, even if it didn't turn a profit on its product sales.

But Dell Inc. does earn a profit from its PC sales. As a Dell executive explained, "Michael focuses relentlessly on driving low-cost material from the supplier through the supply chain to our customers." As a small example from some years ago, when Michael Dell noticed that one supplier had brought pastries to a meeting, he complained, "Take those back and let's knock the price off the next shipment of materials you bring in." By maintaining close contact with suppliers, Dell is also able to pass along cost savings to customers in as little as one day—something its competitors simply cannot match. In order for HP to adjust its prices, it must notify all of its retailers, who must then place ads in newspapers and circulars, a process that can take weeks.

Deleting the Competition

In an attempt to gain more market share, Dell Inc. decided to leverage its cost advantage and initiate aggressive price competition in late 2000. The market leader slashed prices up to 20%, forcing competitors either to follow suit or lose sales. Several computer makers matched Dell's prices at the outset, but could not afford to continue the battle beyond a few months. Most of the competitors were forced to lay off employees. By late 2001, the market shares of Compaq, HP, and Gateway had eroded, whereas Dell's share increased by almost one-third.

Prior to the price war, Compaq was the market leader and had been aggressively cutting prices as well as reducing its inventory and increasing its direct-sales efforts. Unable to keep up with Dell, Compaq was acquired by HP in September 2001. "We're in for a round of consolidation, and only the fittest will survive," observed an HP executive.

After returning to profitability in 2001 by focusing on higher-margin products, Gateway decided to aggressively pursue the market share it had lost in the PC sector. Thus, in early 2002, Gateway announced another round of price cuts on its brand of PCs. The underdog sold more units but because of the lower prices, generated less revenue, and in turn, suffered big losses. By 2005, its stock was worth a paltry $4 per share, a fraction of its $80 selling price in 2000.

HP and IBM originally declared the price war "irrational," electing to concede market share rather than lower prices and harm profitability. However, HP changed its tune when it dropped prices two years later in an attempt to win back market share. "We think the PC business is strategic (essential)," stated HP's CEO at that time. In other words, HP was willing to concede profits on PCs in order to sell peripheral equipment, such as printers. Its PC profit margins hovered around 1%, compared to a remarkable 8% for Dell.

Kevin Rollins, the successor to Michael Dell as CEO, complained that HP's tactics were going to result in "unprofitable growth in an unsustainable effort to protect tangentially related businesses." Industry-wide PC prices fell by 9% in the first nine months of 2003—twice as much as a year before. HP briefly managed to sell more PCs than Dell in late 2003 but quickly relinquished the lead again in 2004. And IBM exited the desktop and notebook PC business, selling the large majority of its operations to a Chinese firm, Lenovo.

By 2005, Dell Inc. was selling one-third of all of the PCs, notebooks, and servers in the U.S. and one-sixth of all those sold globally. In *Fortune* magazine's compilation of the "most admired companies" that same year, Dell was #1 in America and #3 worldwide.

Taking a Byte Out of Profit Margins

Although Dell Inc. fared better than its competitors during the price war over market share, the leader's profitability suffered. Profit margins fell to less than 6% of sales for Dell; competitors that tried to match Dell's prices experienced sharper declines. But in July 2004, Dell quietly began raising the prices on its PCs. A price comparison conducted in October 2004 revealed that compared to HP, Dell's prices were from 5% to 37% higher on comparable PCs in the consumer segment of the market. Raising prices is an unusual move for a product that appears to be in the maturity stage of its life cycle; most companies choose to lower prices in order to increase sales once its products reach this stage. Although this tactic reduced demand for Dell's PCs, the company's revenues rose 20%.

Significant product innovations would be one way to spur sales of an aging product line. HP's research and development (R&D) spending totals 6% of total revenues; Dell traditionally spends just over 1% of revenues on R&D. Competing executives contend that this number reflects the fact that Dell cares little about innovation and instead relies on other companies to make important product advancements. Microsoft and Intel, Dell's two key suppliers of PC components, continue to put substantial dollars into R&D (21% of revenue for Microsoft), and Dell benefits from their investments. Michael Dell takes issue with the characterization that Dell isn't an innovator, saying, "Let's see, innovation: Business process, supply chain, change in industry, customer value totally different, change the whole cycle in which technology is brought to market—well, there may be a few innovations there."

Keying In on New Product Opportunities

As the PC business continued to mature, Dell Inc. moved into other product lines to spur growth. In 2003, it set the ambitious goal of achieving $60 billion in revenues by the year 2006—twice its sales in 2001. That same year, it eliminated the word Computer from its name.

Dell Inc. has been jump-starting its entry into new product lines by putting its own brand on other company's products. For instance, it partnered with EMC to offer storage units. After a period of time, Dell began manufacturing several of the lower-end servers itself and cut production costs by 25%.

Dell Inc. is careful about selecting its new products. For example, after extensive evaluation, Dell decided not to enter the market for handheld computers (previously called personal digital assistants or PDAs). Dell was concerned that there are no clearly defined standards for this product, and it judged the market potential to be insufficient. However, in late 2002, Dell Inc. changed its mind and announced a move into this product category. Within six months, Dell's U.S. market share was almost 40%.

HP faced an assault when Dell entered the $50 billion printer business. HP's share of this market was a dominant 60% in 2003, and it garnered 70% of its operating profit from the sale of printers. If Dell is successful in this area, it would represent a severe blow to HP. By selling printers, a company ensures future revenues from the sale of high-margin ink cartridges, comparable to selling razors and blades. Dell began by partnering with Lexmark International Inc., but then started selling six of its own models in 2003. By late 2004, HP's market share had slipped to just over 45%, and Dell's had approximately 15%.

According to Michael Dell, "Our goal this past year was to sell five million printers, and we did that." He added, "That suggests to me that five or ten years from now this is going to be a very significant business for us in terms of revenues and profits." He also indicated that Dell's color laser printers were one-half the price of HP's. At that time, HP was selling its inkjet printers for about $90 apiece, compared to $70 for Dell. Once again, Dell will sell its printers directly, via its website and catalogs. It has also figured out how to simplify the process of purchasing refill cartridges. As a Dell printer begins to run out of ink, it alerts the user who simply clicks to reorder a new one, which is then shipped directly.

Dell Inc. is now getting into consumer electronics with flat-panel TVs—a product category that Rollins categorizes as "a transition technology with a new profit pool." Each successful foray into a new product line brings Dell closer to its 2006 revenue goal of $60 billion. In fact, Dell decided it had been too conservative when setting that objective and recently increased it to $80 billion—pretty impressive for a company widely known for its low prices. In fact, it's as ambitious as Dell.

Questions

1. a. Which pricing objectives is Dell Inc. pursuing?

   b. What type of long-term impact will Dell's pricing strategy have on the computer industry?

2. How are Dell's prices influenced by the other elements in its marketing mix?

3. When entering new markets, what type of pricing strategy does Dell Inc. employ?

www.dell.com

Sources

Case 1: Southwest Airlines *www.southwest.com* and *www.flysong.com*, both accessed June 6, 2005; Barney Gimbel, "Southwest's New Flight Plan," *Fortune*, May 16, 2005, pp. 93–98; Susan Warren and Melanie Trottman, "Southwest's Dallas Duel," *The Wall Street Journal*, May 10, 2005, p. B1; Perry Flint, "Southwest Keeps It Simple," *Air Transport World*, April 2005, p. 26; Jerry Useem, "America's Most Admired Companies," *Fortune*, Mar. 7, 2005, pp. 67+; Wendy Zellner, "Dressed to Kill . . . Competitors," *BusinessWeek*, Feb. 21, 2005, pp. 60–61; Brad Foss, "High Fuel Prices Send Airline Profits into Tailspin," *Chicago Sun-Times*, Jan. 14, 2005, p. 66; Melanie Trottman, "Southwest Will Fill US Airways' Pittsburgh Gap," *The Wall Street Journal*, Jan. 6, 2005, p. D9; Scott McCartney, "Southwest Airlines Set to Crack Hawaii Market," *The Wall Street Journal*, Jan. 4, 2005, p. D5; Melanie Trottman, "Southwest Air Considers Shift in Its Approach," *The Wall Street Journal*, Dec. 23, 2003, p. B1; Susan Carey and Scott McCartney, "How Airlines Resisted Change for 25 Years, and Finally Lost," *The Wall Street Journal*, Oct. 5, 2004, p. A1; Scott McCartney, "How Discount Airlines Profited from Their Bigger Rivals' Woes," *The Wall Street Journal*, Aug. 12, 2004, p. A1; S. Jayasankaran and Cris Prystay, "Upstart Shakes Up the Clubby World of Asian Flying," *The Wall Street Journal*, July 20, 2004, p. A1; Dan Reed, "Southwest's Bold Entry into Philly Has Rivals Quaking," *USA Today*, May 6, 2004, p. 1B; Thomas Wagner, "Europe's Budget Airlines Take No-Frills Flying a Few Steps Further," *St. Louis Post-Dispatch*, Feb. 29, 2004, p. E3; Melanie Trottman, "Inside Southwest Airlines, Storied Culture Feels Strains," *The Wall Street Journal*, July 11, 2003, p. A1; and Daniel Michaels, "No-Frills Irish Airline Flies High," *The Wall Street Journal*, Sept. 6, 2000, p. B1.

Case 2: Dell *www.dell.com*, accessed June 8, 2005; Andy Serwer, "The Education of Michael Dell," *Fortune*, Mar.7, 2005, pp. 72–82; Adam Lashinsky, "Where Dell Is Going Next," *Fortune*, Oct. 18, 2004, pp. 115–120; Andrew Park and Lauren Young, "Dell Outfoxes Its Rivals," *BusinessWeek*, Sept. 6, 2004, p. 54; David Bank and Gary McWilliams, "Picking a Big Fight with Dell, H-P Cuts PC Profits Razor-Thin," *The Wall Street Journal*, May 12, 2004, p. A1; Andrew Park and Peter Burrows, "What You Don't Know About Dell," *BusinessWeek*, Nov. 3, 2003, pp. 76–84; Gary McWilliams, "Dell Plans to Peddle PCs inside Sears, Other Large Chains," *The Wall Street Journal*, Jan. 30, 2003, pp. B1, B3; "The Best Managers: Michael Dell," *BusinessWeek*, Jan. 13, 2003, p. 62; David Kirkpatrick, "The PC's New Tricks," *Fortune*, Oct. 28, 2002, pp. 88–90+; Arlene Weintraub, "Gateway: Picking Fights It Just Might Lose," *BusinessWeek*, Sept. 9, 2002, p. 52; Gary McWilliams, "In About Face, Dell Will Sell PCs to Dealers," *The Wall Street Journal*, Aug. 20, 2002, p. B1; Andrew Park, "Whose Lunch Will Dell Eat Next?" *BusinessWeek*, Aug. 12, 2002, pp. 66–67; Tom Mainelli, "Gateway Country Goes to War," *Network World*, Feb. 8, 2002, no pages given; Andy Serwer, "Dell Does Domination," *Fortune*, Jan. 21, 2002, pp. 70–75; Aliza Pilar Sherman, "The Idol Life," *Entrepreneur*, January 2002, pp. 55–56; "Dell, the Conqueror," *BusinessWeek*, Sept. 24, 2001, p. 92; "The Mother of All Price Wars," *BusinessWeek*, July 30, 2001, p. 32; J. William Gurley, "Why Dell's War Isn't Dumb," *Fortune*, July 9, 2001, p. 134; Gary McWilliams, "How Dell Fine-Tunes Its Pricing to Gain Edge in a Slow Market," *The Wall Street Journal*, June 8, 2001, p. A1; Bob Brewin, "Dell Declares PC Price War," *Computerworld*, May 28, 2001, p. 8; Janice Revell, "The Price Is Not Always Right," *Fortune*, May 14, 2001, p. 240; and "How Dell Keeps from Stumbling," *BusinessWeek*, May 14, 2001, p. 38B.

Chapter 14

Toy manufacturers . . . feared that a key channel involving Toys "R" Us and other merchants that concentrate on toys could disappear.

Channels of Distribution

Can **Toys "R" Us** Survive to Play Another Day?

Charles Lazarus is credited with founding not only the world's largest retail toy chain, but also a new type of retail outlet the *category killer*. During the 1980s, chains of category killers sprang up in areas such as sports equipment, pet supplies, and home improvement items.

Founded in 1978, Lazarus' chain, Toys "R" Us (TRU), expanded at a phenomenal pace, averaging 30% growth per year. TRU's two primary competitors, Child World and Kiddie City, went into bankruptcy.

Eventually though, TRU's stores became run down, and customer service eroded. To complicate matters, eToys, started selling toys online in 1997. Defensively, TRU launched its own website in 1998. Like many other dot-com enterprises, eToys failed as a result of enormous expenses.

However, the tide-turning development for TRU was Wal-Mart's and Target's growing interest in this product category. Both chains, especially Wal-Mart, decided to expand their toy selections and, worse yet for TRU, to slash prices on toys so that customers would be drawn to their stores.

TRU, as well as other retailers that focused on toys, lost many customers and substantial revenues to the discount chains. From the late 1980s to the late 1990s, TRU's market share fell from 25% to 17%, and its stock lost more than one-half of its value. Wal-Mart overtook TRU in 1998 as the retailer that sold the largest volume of toys in the U.S.

Toys "R" Us was forced to reevaluate its overall strategy. In 1999, TRU committed over $300 million to renovate its stores, increase the assortment in each store from 10,000 items to approximately 17,000 items, and revamp its supply chain to reduce inventory. These efforts did little to stem the rising tide of Wal-Mart and Target in the retailing of toys.

Toy manufacturers—including Hasbro Inc., Mattel Inc., Lego AG, and Leap Frog Enterprises Inc.—feared that a key channel involving Toys "R" Us and other merchants that concentrate on toys could disappear. If that occurred, another channel and the key members in it—discounters Target and Wal-Mart—would have more clout. For toymakers, the potential outcomes of this scenario were undesirable: smaller profit margins because of pressure from the discount chains for lower wholesale prices; reduced sales outside the holiday season; and toys becoming a price-dominated "commodity" with manufacturers' brand names having less cachet.

Anxious to maintain a variety of viable channels for their wares, some manufacturers reduced the flow of "hot" toys to Wal-Mart, at least early in a product's sales cycle. (Of course, this action could anger a retailer such as Wal-Mart that may account for a substantial proportion of a producer's sales.) Some toymakers offered Toys "R" Us an exclusive launch of selected offerings. For example, Aquapets from Wild Planet Toys were available only at TRU stores in early 2004. A few toymakers gave TRU exclusive distribution rights for a number of toys for an entire holiday season and underwrote the cost of ads to promote them.

The toy industry has stalled, with total retail sales hovering around $20 billion. In 2004, TRU's company-wide sales of just over $11 billion were 2% lower than in 2003, but profits quadrupled to $250 million. In the eyes of its CEO, the toy chain "was competitive on price with the major discounters."

The turmoil in the distribution of toys is mirrored in other categories that have attracted the attention of giant discounters. In fact, Toys "R" Us, parent company found it could not compete effectively in the sale of clothing and other items for children. Thus it shut down its Kids "R" Us division, closing more than 140 stores. The scorecard for Toys "R" Us Inc. retail operations reads as follows: one success (baby products), one failure (children's merchandise), and one big problem with its fate still to be determined (toys).[1]

Are chains of category-killer stores, such as Toys "R" Us, essential and desirable in the distribution of toys?

 www1.toysrus.com

Even before a product is ready for market, management should determine what methods and routes will be used to get it there. This means establishing strategies for the product's distribution channels and physical distribution. Then, as illustrated by Toys "R" Us' situation, distribution activities and relationships need to be monitored and adjusted over time by both producers and middlemen.

The area of distribution is in a state of flux, perhaps even transformation, in large part because of the widespread usage of the Internet, the growth of electronic commerce, and the resulting competition and conflict among channels and members of supply chains. Consider, for instance, the titles of two articles: "Merrill Lynch Shakes Up Industry by Going Online" and "How to Erase the Middleman in One Easy Lesson."[2] Given the dynamic—some would say chaotic—situation in distribution, this element of the marketing mix should command substantial attention from business owners and executives.

Managing a distribution channel often begins with a producer. Therefore, we will discuss channels largely from a producer's vantage point. As you will see, however, the problems and opportunities that middlemen face in managing their channels are similar to those faced by producers. After studying this chapter, you should be able to explain:

www.ml.com

Chapter Goals

- The nature and importance of middlemen and distribution channels.
- The sequence of decisions involved in designing a channel.
- The major channels for goods and services.
- Vertical marketing systems.
- How to choose specific channels and middlemen.
- Intensity of distribution.
- The nature of conflict and control within distribution channels.
- Legal considerations in channels.

Middlemen and Distribution Channels

Ownership of a product has to be transferred somehow from the individual or organization that makes it to the consumer who needs and buys it. Goods also must be physically transported from where they are produced to where they are needed. Services ordinarily cannot be shipped but rather are produced and consumed in the same place. As explained in Chapter 2, the companies that add value to a product that is eventually bought by an individual or an organization comprise a *value chain*. In this chapter and the following two, we pay special attention to the role of middlemen and selected other facilitating organizations as members of the value chain.

Distribution's role within a marketing mix is getting the product to its target market. The first critical activity in getting a product to market is arranging for its sale and the transfer of title from producer to final customer. Other common activities (or functions) are promoting the product, storing it, and assuming some of the financial risk during the distribution process.

A producer can carry out these functions in exchange for an order—and payment—from a customer. Or producer and customer can share these activities. Typically, however, firms called middlemen perform some of these activities on behalf of the producer or the customer.

A **middleman** is a business firm that renders services related *directly* to the sale and/or purchase of a product as it flows from producer to consumer. (Note that in business, *middleman* is an accepted, gender-neutral term.) A middleman either owns

Timepieces International relies on direct sales through this website and also through ads that promote purchases by mail or by phone. Note that the firm says it can offer high-quality watches at low prices by not using middlemen. What activities does Timepieces International have to perform or forgo if it doesn't use middlemen?

www.timepiecesusa.com/
catalog/powerstore.cgi

the product at some point or actively aids in the transfer of ownership. Often, but not always, a middleman takes physical possession of the product.

Middlemen are commonly classified on the basis of whether or not they take title to the products being distributed. **Merchant middlemen** take title to the products they help to market. The two groups of merchant middlemen are wholesalers and retailers. **Agent middlemen** never own the products, but they do arrange the transfer of title. Real estate brokers, manufacturers' agents, and travel agents are examples of agent middlemen.

How Important Are Middlemen?

Critics say prices are high because there are too many middlemen performing unnecessary or redundant functions. Some manufacturers draw this conclusion, especially during a recession, and seek to cut costs by eliminating wholesaling middlemen. Although middlemen can be eliminated from channels, a practice called **disintermediation,** lower costs may not always be achieved.[3] The outcome is not predictable because of a basic axiom of marketing: *You can eliminate middlemen, but you cannot eliminate the essential distribution activities they perform.*

Activities such as creating assortments and storing products can be shifted from one party to another in an effort to improve efficiency and/or effectiveness. However, someone has to perform the various activities—if not a middleman, then the producer or the final customer.[4] It is usually not practical for a producer to deal directly with ultimate consumers. Think for a moment how inconvenient your life would be if there were no retail middlemen—no supermarkets, gas stations, or ticket sales outlets, for instance.

Middlemen may be able to carry out distribution activities better or more cheaply than producers, consumers, or even other middlemen. Huge firms sometimes conclude that using middlemen is better than a "do-it-yourself" approach to distribution. Thus such large retailers as Albertson's, Safeway, and 7-Eleven franchisees are among the customers of Core-Mark International, a wholesaler of food

www.coremark.com

products and related merchandise. Potential benefits that retailers seek in dealing with Core-Mark are better grocery assortments, reduced labor costs, and lower wholesale prices.[5]

Middlemen act as sales specialists for their suppliers. Conversely, they serve as purchasing agents for their consumers. Consider the sales role performed by Lotus Light Enterprises, a distributor that represents about 500 vendors and their 14,000 different teas, herbal products, and related items. According to a Lotus Light manager, "Our most important service is providing a forum for our customers' products. We show their products to retailers and exhibit them at trade shows."[6] As illustrated in Figure 14.1, middlemen also provide financial services for both suppliers and customers. And their storage services, capability to divide large shipments into smaller ones for resale, and market knowledge benefit suppliers and customers alike.

www.lotuslight.com

What Is a Distribution Channel?

A **distribution channel** consists of the set of people and firms involved in the transfer of title to a product as the product moves from producer to ultimate consumer or business user. A channel of distribution always includes both the producer and the final customer for the product in its present form as well as any middlemen such as retailers and wholesalers.

The channel for a product extends only to the last person or organization that buys it without making any significant change in its form. When its form is altered and another product emerges, a new channel is started. When lumber is milled and then made into furniture, two separate channels are involved. The channel for the *lumber* might be lumber mill → broker → furniture manufacturer. The channel for the *finished furniture* might be furniture manufacturer → retail furniture store → consumer.

Besides producer, middlemen, and final customer, other institutions aid the distribution process. Among these *intermediaries* are banks, insurance companies, stor-

FIGURE 14.1

Typical Activities of a Middleman.

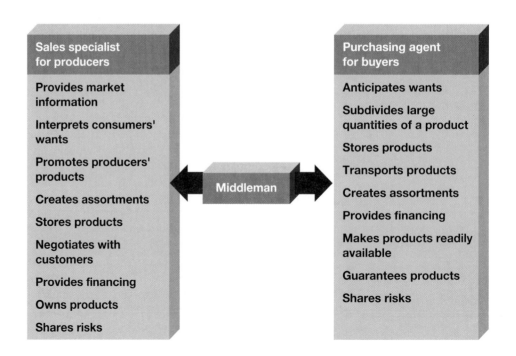

Sales specialist for producers

Provides market information

Interprets consumers' wants

Promotes producers' products

Creates assortments

Stores products

Negotiates with customers

Provides financing

Owns products

Shares risks

Middleman

Purchasing agent for buyers

Anticipates wants

Subdivides large quantities of a product

Stores products

Transports products

Creates assortments

Provides financing

Makes products readily available

Guarantees products

Shares risks

age firms, and transportation companies. However, because they do not take title to the products and are not actively involved in purchase or sales activities, these intermediaries are not formally included in the distribution channel.

This chapter focuses on the flow (or transfer) of *ownership* for a product, whereas part of Chapter 16 examines the *physical* flow of goods. These flows are distinct; consequently, different institutions may carry them out. For example, a contractor might order roofing shingles from a local distributor of building materials. To minimize freight and handling costs, the product might be shipped directly—that is, shingles manufacturer → contractor. But the channel for transfer of ownership would be manufacturer → distributor → contractor.

Designing Distribution Channels

Similar firms often have dissimilar channels of distribution. For instance, large sellers of insurance use different channels. To reach prospective customers, Aetna relies on independent agents who typically sell several brands of insurance. In contrast, State Farm markets through agents who sell only its brand of insurance products. Like virtually all firms, insurance providers have tried to determine whether or how to incorporate the Internet into their distribution strategies. Some have proceeded slowly for fear of alienating long-time middlemen. State Farm, for example, started by quoting rates online and then allowing insurance purchases via the Internet in several states. Now online purchases of State Farm insurance are possible in about two-thirds of the states where the firm operates. In other states, prospective customers must deal with a local agent.[7]

A company wants a distribution channel that not only meets customers' needs but also provides a differential advantage. With that in mind, Caterpillar uses construction equipment dealers that provide customers with many valued services, ranging from rapid order fulfillment for repair parts to advice about equipment financing. In another industry, an auto-parts distributor sought an advantage by employing former mechanics to provide expert advice to parts managers or mechanics at dealerships or repair shops who called to place orders or ask questions about a particular part.[8]

Many insurance companies sell their products through agents that offer multiple brands. Some insurance providers use agents that sell just a single brand. And a limited number sell only online. Which approach is best? That depends on company-specific factors, including the needs and desires of the firm's target markets as well as the role of distribution within the complete marketing mix.

To design channels that satisfy customers and outdo competition, an organized approach is required. As shown in Figure 14.2, we suggest a sequence of four decisions:

1. *Specify the role of distribution.* A channel strategy should be designed within the context of the entire marketing mix. First, the firm's marketing objectives are reviewed. Next, the roles assigned to product, price, and promotion are specified. Each element may have a distinct role, or two elements may share an assignment. For example, a manufacturer of pressure gauges may use middlemen, direct-mail advertising, and website announcements to convince prospective customers that it is committed to servicing the product following the sale.

2. *Select the type of channel.* Once distribution's role in the overall marketing

FIGURE 14.2

Sequence of Decisions to Design a Distribution Channel.

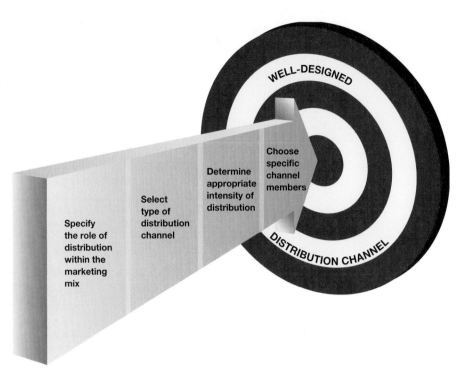

program has been agreed on, the most suitable type of channel for the company's product must be determined. At this point in the sequence, a firm needs to decide whether middlemen will be used in its channel and, if so, which types of middlemen.[9]

To illustrate the wide array of institutions available, as well as the difficulty of channel selection, consider a manufacturer of DVD (digital versatile disc) players. If the firm decides to use middlemen, it must choose among many different types. At the retail level, the range of institutions includes consumer electronics outlets, department and discount stores, mail-order firms, and e-tailers.

3. *Determine intensity of distribution.* The next decision relates to intensity of distribution—that is, the number of middlemen used at the wholesale and retail levels in a particular territory. As we will see later, the target market's buying behavior and the product's nature have a direct bearing on this decision. Because of the desires of prospective customers, Goodyear found it necessary to extend its distribution beyond its own stores and, as a result, now sells most of its tire lines through Sears and various discount outlets.

4. *Choose specific channel members.* The last decision concerns the selection of specific firms to distribute the product. Sometimes, a company—often a small one trying to market a new product—has little choice regarding which channel members to use. In this case, the company has to go with those middlemen that are willing (and hopefully able) to distribute the product. Typically, though, a company that is designing a channel has various companies from which to choose for each type of institution that will form the channel.

   Assume that the manufacturer of DVD players prefers two types of middlemen: department stores and specialty outlets. If the DVD players will be sold in Chicago, the producer must decide which department stores—Marshall Field's and/or Sears—will be asked to distribute its product line. Also, one or more consumer electronics chains—from a group including Tweeter and Circuit City—might be selected. Similar decisions must be made for each territory in the firm's market.

www.tweeter.com

When selecting specific firms to be part of a channel, a producer should consider whether the middleman sells to the customers that the manufacturer wants to reach and whether the middleman's product mix, pricing structure, promotion, and customer service are all compatible with the manufacturer's needs.

In this design sequence, the first decision relates to broad marketing strategy, the second and third to channel strategies, and the last to specific tactics. In the next two major sections, we cover these channel strategies in more detail. First we will look at the major channels traditionally used by producers and at two special channels. Then factors that most influence a company's choice of channels can be discussed. After that, we will consider how many middlemen should be used by a firm.

Selecting the Type of Channel

Firms may rely on existing channels, or they may devise new channels to better serve current customers and to reach new prospects. A small company named New Pig (its real name) decided not to use conventional middlemen such as supermarkets and

A GLOBAL PERSPECTIVE

Why do gray markets give producers and middlemen gray hair?

Occasionally items are sold through distribution channels that are not authorized by the manufacturer. It's estimated that this practice, called **gray marketing** or *export diversion,* may account for about $10 billion in sales annually in the U.S.

Gray marketing usually involves products made in one country and destined for sale in another country. Cameras, computer disk drives or entire PCs, perfumes, cars, and liquor are among the diverse products sold through gray markets. Some brands of hair-care products such as Redken and Nexxus are intended for sale only in beauty salons. However, the combination of diverted and counterfeit products may account for nearly $1 billion, or almost 3%, of annual sales volume for this product category.

Ordinarily, gray marketing arises when a product with a well-known brand name carries different prices under different circumstances. For example, wholesale price may vary depending on the country in which it is sold. In one form of gray marketing, a wholesaling middleman purchases a product made in Country A and agrees to distribute it in Country B, but instead diverts the product to Country C (often the U.S.). Because the product typically is sold in Country C at a discount in a reputable outlet, not on the "black market" or from the trunks of cars, it isn't apparent that normal distribution was not used.

According to manufacturers, gray marketing disrupts their distribution and pricing strategies. Also, after spending time and money to promote the product, authorized distributors lose sales to the gray market.

Still, some parties see benefits. Unauthorized distributors are able to sell products they normally cannot acquire. To sell excess output, some manufacturers allow gray marketing. Consumers pay lower prices for popular products and may also find them at more outlets. Based on a rationale of potentially lower prices for consumers, the European Union enacted a law to prohibit automakers from restricting gray market sales.

Some manufacturers have concluded that it's too difficult and costly to fight gray marketing. But other producers try to thwart it. General Motors, for example, won't honor warranties on new vehicles intended for the Canadian market that are diverted to the U.S. The automaker has also told its dealers that involvement in gray marketing will subject them to fines or reduced supply of new cars. Further, some law enforcement agencies, at least in the U.S., continue to prosecute gray marketing participants.

Because it continues, gray marketing represents one more challenge for both producers and wholesaling middlemen as they seek to manage the distribution of their products.

Sources: Ann Therese Palmer, "Will They Get the Gray Out?" *BusinessWeek,* Dec. 27, 2004, p. 13; Peter Brieger, "GM Fights Grey-Market Sales: To Void Car Warranties," *National Post,* July 18, 2002, p. FP3; "Car Makers Lose Power to Stop Gray Market," *Canada News Wire,* July 17, 2002, no pages given; and Amy Borrus, "Exports That Aren't Going Anywhere," *BusinessWeek,* Dec. 4, 1995, pp. 121, 124.

hardware stores to sell a dust cloth with special dirt-attracting properties. Instead, to reach a primarily female target market, this firm chose to distribute its product through beauty salons.[10] Of course, many manufacturers are using the Internet to sell their wares directly to customers. For instance, besides selling through various types of retailers, Clinique Laboratories, Inc., is selling its cosmetics and hair-care products online to American consumers.

www.clinique.com

Most distribution channels include middlemen, but some do not. A channel consisting only of producer and final customer, with no middlemen providing assistance, is called **direct distribution.** ServiceMaster uses a direct approach to sell its cleaning services to both residential and commercial customers. Pfizer Inc., the world's largest pharmaceuticals manufacturer, announced that it would start selling directly to pharmacies and hospitals in Spain. One reason for the switch was to prevent gray marketing by distributors.[11]

A channel of producer, final customer, and at least one level of middlemen represents **indirect distribution.** Marshall amplifiers, which have been used by legendary guitarists including Eric Clapton and Jimi Hendrix, are distributed indirectly. Specifically, this manufacturer uses a legion of distributors located in over 75 countries.[12]

www.marshallamps.com

One level of middlemen—retailers but no wholesaling middlemen, for example—or multiple levels may participate in an indirect channel. (For consumer goods, sometimes a channel in which wholesalers are bypassed but retailers are used is incorrectly termed *direct,* rather than indirect, distribution.) With indirect distribution a producer must determine the type(s) of middlemen that will best serve its needs. The range of options at the wholesale and retail levels will be described in the next two chapters.

Major Channels of Distribution

Diverse distribution channels exist today. The most common channels for consumer goods, business goods, and services are described next and summarized in Figure 14.3.

Distribution of Consumer Goods   Five channels are widely used in marketing tangible products to ultimate consumers:

- *Producer → consumer.* The shortest, simplest distribution channel for consumer goods involves no middlemen. The producer may sell from door to door or by mail. For instance, the Southwestern Company uses college students to market its books on a house-to-house basis.

- *Producer → retailer → consumer.* Many large retailers buy directly from manufacturers and agricultural producers. To the chagrin of various wholesaling middlemen, Wal-Mart has increased its direct dealings with producers.

- *Producer → wholesaler → retailer → consumer.* If there is a traditional channel for consumer goods, this is it. Small retailers and manufacturers by the thousands find this channel the only economically feasible choice.

- *Producer → agent → retailer → consumer.* Instead of using wholesalers, many producers prefer to rely on agent middlemen to reach the retail market, especially *large-scale* retailers. For example, The Clorox Company uses a sales and marketing agency (such as Acosta) to reach retailers (such as Dillon's and Schnucks, both large grocery chains), which in turn sell Clorox's cleaning products to consumers.

www.acosta.com

- *Producer → agent → wholesaler → retailer → consumer.* To reach *small* retailers, producers often use agent middlemen, who in turn call on wholesalers that sell to large retail chains and/or small retail stores. Working as an agent on behalf of various grocery products manufacturers, Acosta sells to some wholesalers (such as SUPERVALU) that distribute a wide range of products to retailers (such as Dierberg's, a supermarket chain in the St. Louis area). In turn, Dierberg's offers its assortment of products to final consumers.

FIGURE 14.3

**Major Channels of
Distribution for
Different Categories
of Products.**

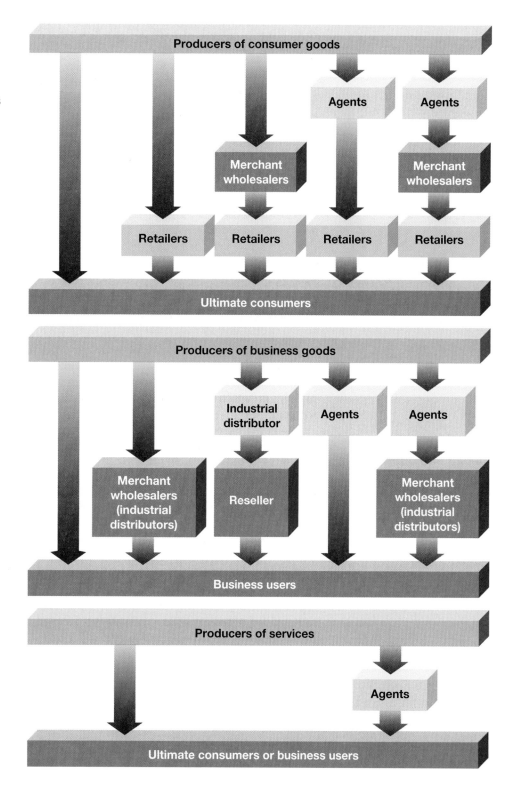

Distribution of Business Goods A variety of channels is available to reach organizations that incorporate the products into their manufacturing process or use them in their operations.[13] In the distribution of business goods, the terms *industrial distributor* and *merchant wholesaler* are synonymous. The five common channels for distributing business goods are:

- *Producer → user.* This direct channel accounts for a greater *dollar* volume of business products than any other distribution structure. Large installations, such

as jet engines, helicopters, and elevators (all of which are made by divisions of United Technologies), are usually sold directly to users.

- *Producer → industrial distributor → user.* Producers of operating supplies and small accessory equipment frequently use industrial distributors to reach their markets. Manufacturers of building materials and air-conditioning equipment are two examples of industries that make heavy use of industrial distributors.

- *Producer → industrial distributor → reseller → user.* This channel has been common for computer products and related high-tech items. Distributors, which usually are large, national companies, buy various products from manufacturers and then bundle them with related products for resale. Resellers, which usually are smaller, local firms, work closely with end users to meet the buyers' needs. With direct distribution growing, particularly sales through the Internet, distributors and resellers are seeking new ways to add value through their roles. Resellers of computer products, for example, are offering technology solutions such as network installation.[14]

- *Producer → agent → user.* Firms without their own sales departments find this channel desirable. Also, a company that wants to introduce a new product or enter a new market may prefer to use agents rather than its own sales force.

- *Producer → agent → industrial distributor → user.* This channel is similar to the preceding one. It is used when, for some reason, it is not feasible to sell through agents directly to the business user. For example, the order size may be too small to justify direct selling. Or decentralized inventory may be needed to supply users rapidly, in which case the storage services of an industrial distributor are required.

Distribution of Services   The intangible nature of services creates special distribution requirements. There are only two common channels for services:[15]

- *Producer → consumer.* Because a service is intangible, the production process and/or sales activity often require personal contact between producer and customer. Thus a direct channel is used. Direct distribution is typical for many professional services, such as health care and legal advice, and personal services, such as weight-loss counseling and hair cutting. However, other services, including travel and insurance, may also be sold and distributed directly.

- *Producer → agent → consumer.* Although direct distribution often is necessary for the performance of a service, producer–customer contact may not be required for distribution activities. Agents frequently assist a services producer with transfer of ownership (the sales task). Many services, notably travel, lodging, advertising media, entertainment, and insurance, are sold through agents. However, various advances in computing and communications technologies have made it easier for customers to deal directly with service providers, thereby threatening the role of agents.[16]

Multiple Distribution Channels

Many, perhaps most, producers are not content with only a single distribution channel. Instead, for reasons such as reaching two or more target markets or avoiding total dependence on a single arrangement, they employ **multiple distribution channels.** For example, Sherwin-Williams paints and Goodyear tires are distributed through wholesalers, independent retailers, large retail chains, and the manufacturers' own stores. Thus far, neither firm has added the Internet as another channel. (Similarly, many companies establish multiple *supply* channels to ensure that they have products when needed.)

Use of multiple channels occurs in several distinct situations.[17] A manufacturer is likely to use multiple channels to reach *different types of markets* when selling:

- The same product (for example, sporting goods or insurance) to both consumer and business markets.[18]
- Relatively unrelated products (education and consulting; rubber products and plastics).

Multiple channels are also used to reach different segments within a single market when:

- Size of the buyers varies greatly. An airline may sell directly to travel departments in large corporations but rely on travel agents to reach small businesses and ultimate consumers.
- Geographic concentration differs across parts of the market. A manufacturer of industrial machinery may use its own sales force to sell directly to customers that are located close together, but may employ agents in sparsely populated markets.

A significant trend involves selling the *same brand to a single market* through channels that compete with each other; this is sometimes called *dual distribution*. Many independent insurance agents are concerned, even angry, because insurance companies (including Allstate Corp.) are arranging for banks to sell their products and/or are experimenting with Internet selling.[19] When they are not satisfied with the market coverage provided by existing retail outlets, producers may open their own stores, thereby creating dual distribution. Or they may establish their own stores primarily as testing grounds for new products and marketing techniques.

Although multiple distribution channels provide benefits to the producer, they can aggravate middlemen. Avon's independent sales reps were upset when the company began to distribute its cosmetics through department-store chains and to accept orders directly from interested consumers. In another industry, many owners of franchised Carvel Ice Cream Stores rebelled when faced with multiple channels. The franchisees (who are middlemen) claimed their marketing efforts were undermined and sales and profits reduced when the producer decided to sell its ice cream in supermarkets as well as in franchised stores.[20]

www.carvel.com/index.asp?page=0

Many independent dealers that sell Goodyear tires are upset with the manufacturer for various reasons. A common complaint is that the Goodyear Tire and Rubber Co. sells its products through multiple channels, some of which include giant retailers such as Sears and Wal-Mart that emphasize low prices. As a result, the dealers face severe price competition. In one article, a trade magazine altered a photo to indicate how Goodyear's dealers feel.

Sometimes multiple channels can be arranged in such a way that a firm's middlemen do not get upset. One approach, which is difficult to achieve, is to develop separate marketing strategies for each channel. For example, the Scotts Company sells some of its lawn-care products to large discount chains but reserves other products only for smaller stores.[21]

Vertical Marketing Systems

Historically, distribution channels stressed the independence of individual members. That is, a producer used various middlemen to achieve its distribution objectives. However, the producer typically was not concerned with middlemen's needs. Conversely, wholesalers and retailers were more interested in preserving their freedom than in coordinating their activities with a producer. These priorities of conventional distribution channels provided an opportunity for a new type of channel.

During the past several decades, the vertical marketing system (VMS) has become *the* dominant form of distribution channel. A **vertical marketing system** is a tightly coordinated distribution channel designed specifically to improve operating efficiency and marketing effectiveness. A VMS illustrates the concept of function shifting that was discussed earlier in this chapter. In a VMS, no marketing function is sacred to a particular level or firm in the channel. Instead, each function is performed at the most advantageous position in the channel.

The high degree of coordination or control characterizing a VMS is achieved through one of three means: common ownership of successive levels of a channel, contracts between channel members, or the market power of one or more members. Table 14.1 shows these three distinct forms of vertical marketing systems.

In a **corporate vertical marketing system,** a firm at one level of a channel owns the firms at the next level or owns the entire channel. Nike (athletic shoes and sports wear) and Swatch (watches), for example, own retail outlets. Of course, there's no assurance that a corporate system, or any other channel, will work out well. At the end of the last decade, automakers (notably General Motors and Ford) started buy-

TABLE 14.1 **Types of Vertical Marketing Systems**

Type of System	Control Maintained by	Examples
Corporate	Ownership	Singer (sewing machines), Goodyear (tires), Tandy Corp. (electronics)
Contractual:		
Wholesaler-sponsored voluntary chain	Contract	IGA stores
Retailer-owned cooperative	Stock ownership by retailers	True Value hardware stores
Franchise systems:	Contract	
Manufacturer-sponsored retailers		Ford, DaimlerChrysler, and other auto dealers
Manufacturer-sponsored wholesalers		Coca-Cola and other soft drink bottlers
Marketers of services		Wendy's, Midas Muffler, Holiday Inn, National car rentals
Administered	Economic power	Hartman luggage, General Electric, Kraft foods

ing back and operating some of their previously franchised dealerships. However, the new arrangement evidently didn't improve efficiency or effectiveness and thus was abandoned. "It's a costly lesson for us, but nevertheless I think we have learned that our dealers are our partners for life," explained a Ford Division manager.[22]

Middlemen may also engage in this type of vertical integration. For example, Kroger's and many other grocery chains own food-processing facilities, such as dairies, which supply their stores. And various large retailers, including Sears, own all or part of manufacturing facilities that supply their stores with many products.

In a **contractual vertical marketing system**, independent producers, wholesalers, and retailers operate under contracts specifying how they will try to improve the effectiveness and efficiency of their distribution. Three kinds of contractual systems have developed: wholesaler-sponsored voluntary chains (for example, SUPERVALU grocery stores), retailer-owned cooperatives (Ace hardware stores), and franchise systems (Domino's pizza and Midas automotive maintenance and repairs). All will be discussed in Chapter 15.

An **administered vertical marketing system** coordinates distribution activities through (1) the market and/or economic power of one channel member or (2) the willing cooperation of channel members. Sometimes the brand equity possessed by a manufacturer's product is strong enough to secure the cooperation of retailers in matters such as inventory levels, advertising, and store display. Manufacturers such as KitchenAid in home appliances, Rolex in watches, and Kraft in food products typically are able to coordinate various aspects of the channels they use. For instance, given Kraft's strong brands and large marketing budgets, some grocery chains allow the manufacturer to decide which products are placed where on retail shelves—not just Kraft items, but also competitors' products.[23]

It's important to note that retailers, especially giant ones, are more likely to dominate channel relationships now than in prior years. Thus, even a huge manufacturer such as Procter & Gamble decided some years ago that one step toward satisfying Wal-Mart was to establish an office in Bentonville, Arkansas, the location of the largest retailer's headquarters. More than 600 other manufacturers have now set up outposts in Bentonville.[24]

In the distant past, competition in distribution usually involved two different conventional channels. For instance, two producer → retailer → consumer channels tended to compete with each other. Eventually, competition pitted a conventional channel against some form of VMS. Thus a traditional producer → retailer → consumer channel, such as Van Heusen shirts sold through various department stores, battled an administered VMS for business, such as cooperative merchandising efforts between Polo Ralph Lauren and a specific chain of department stores.

Now the most common competitive battles are between different forms of vertical marketing systems. For example, a corporate system (stores owned by Goodyear) competes with a contractual system (Firestone's franchised dealers). Considering the potential benefits of vertical marketing systems with respect to both marketing effectiveness and operating efficiencies, they should continue to grow in number and importance.

Factors Affecting Choice of Channels

If a firm is customer-oriented—and it should be if it hopes to prosper—its channels are determined by consumer buying patterns. As stated in a study about the insurance industry, "It's time to stop battling about distribution channels and listen to what the customer wants."[25] Thus the nature of the market should be the key factor in management's distribution decisions. Other considerations are the product, the middlemen, and the company itself.

Market Considerations A logical starting point is to consider the target market—its needs, structure, and buying behavior:

- *Type of market.* Because ultimate consumers behave differently than business users, they are reached through different distribution channels. Retailers, by definition, serve ultimate consumers, so they are not in channels for business goods.

- *Number of potential customers.* A manufacturer with few potential customers (firms or industries) may use its own sales force to sell directly to ultimate consumers or business users. Boeing uses this approach in selling its jet aircraft. Conversely, a manufacturer with many prospects would likely use middlemen. Reebok relies on numerous middlemen, notably retailers, to reach the millions of consumers in the market for athletic footwear. A firm that uses middlemen does not need as large a sales force as a company, such as Avon, that depends primarily on direct sales to final consumers.

- *Geographic concentration of the market.* When most of a firm's prospective customers are concentrated in a few geographic areas, direct sale is practical. This situation is found in the textile and garment manufacturing industries. When customers are geographically dispersed, direct sale is likely to be impractical because of high travel costs. Instead, sellers may establish sales branches in densely populated markets and use middlemen in less concentrated markets. Some small American manufacturers turn to specialized middlemen, called *trade intermediaries,* to crack foreign markets. Manufacturers sell their goods to these firms at lower-than-normal wholesale prices in exchange for the intermediaries' ability to secure distribution in markets around the globe.[26]

- *Order size.* When either order size or total volume of business is large, direct distribution is economical. Thus a food products manufacturer would sell directly to large supermarket chains. The same manufacturer, however, would use wholesalers to reach small grocery stores whose orders are too small to justify direct sale.[27]

Product Considerations Although there are numerous product-related factors to consider, we will highlight three:

- *Unit value.* The price attached to each unit of a product affects the amount of funds available for distribution. For example, a company can afford to use its own employee to sell a printing-press part that costs more than $10,000. But it would not make sense for a company sales person to call on a household or a business firm to sell a $2 ballpoint pen. Thus the 3M Company avoided online sales because the typically low unit value and small quantity ordered made the transaction unprofitable for the firm.[28] Products with low unit values usually are distributed through one or more levels of middlemen. There are exceptions, however. For instance, if order size is large because the customer buys many units of a product at the same time from the company, then a direct channel may be economically feasible.

www.3m.com/us/index.jhtml

- *Perishability.* Some goods, including many agricultural products, physically deteriorate fairly quickly. Other goods, such as clothing, perish in a fashion sense. As discussed in Chapter 11, services are perishable because they cannot be held in inventory. Perishable products require direct or very short channels.

- *Technical nature.* A highly technical *business* product is often distributed directly to business users. The producer's sales force must provide considerable presale and postsale service; wholesalers normally cannot do this. *Consumer* products of a technical nature pose a real distribution challenge. Ordinarily, because of other factors discussed in this section, producers cannot sell highly technical products directly to the consumer. As much as possible, they sell them directly to retailers, in which case product servicing often poses problems.

For a variety of technical products, such as golf clubs (which, believe it or not, are technical because of the myriad sizes, materials, grips, and features), some consumers do preliminary shopping in "bricks and mortar" stores. Then they go to the Internet to seek the lowest price for the specific brand and model they want. The purchase might be made online or from the store, often depending on whether the store is willing to match an online vendor's lower price.

Middlemen Considerations

Here we begin to see that a company may not be able to arrange exactly the channels it desires:

- *Services provided by middlemen.* Each producer should select middlemen offering those marketing services that the producer either is unable to provide or cannot economically perform. For instance, firms from other countries seeking to penetrate business markets in the U.S. commonly utilize industrial distributors. This kind of middleman furnishes needed capabilities such as market coverage, sales contacts, and storage of inventories.[29]

- *Availability of desired middlemen.* The middlemen preferred by a producer may not be available. They may carry competing products and, as a result, not want to add another line. Years ago, Wally Amos wanted to expand the distribution for his Famous Amos Chocolate Chip Cookies, but he was unable to get the product on the shelves of a sufficient number of supermarket chains. Hence, Amos' company relied on alternative middlemen—warehouse clubs, vending machines, and even fast-food restaurants. Now owned by the Kellogg Company, Famous Amos cookies are sold through more conventional channels, including supermarkets.[30]

- *Producer's and middleman's policies.* When middlemen are unwilling to join a channel because they consider a producer's policies to be unacceptable, the producer has fewer channel options. Some retailers or wholesalers, for example, will carry a producer's line only if they receive assurance that no competing middlemen will carry the line in the same territory. A growing number of small manufacturers have become very frustrated with the demands for lower prices and other concessions that are placed on them by giant retailers such as Wal-Mart and Home Depot. Thus makers of various products ranging from children's clothing to garden products decided, very reluctantly, to not do business with these retailers.[31]

Company Considerations

Before choosing a distribution channel for a product, a company should consider its own situation:

- *Desire for channel control.* Some producers establish direct channels because they want to control their product's distribution, even though a direct arrangement may be more costly than an indirect one. By controlling the channel, producers can achieve more aggressive promotion, assure the freshness of merchandise stocks, and set their products' retail prices. To manage its assortment of store-brand dress shirts, J.C. Penney Corp. deals directly with TAL Apparel, Ltd., in Hong Kong. The supplier compiles point-of-sale information directly from JCPenney stores, then uses a computer model to determine how many more shirts to produce and ship directly to each store. This arrangement has allowed J.C. Penney to reduce its inventory of shirts dramatically.[32]

www.talgroup.com

- *Services provided by seller.* Some producers make decisions about their channels based on the distribution functions desired (and occasionally demanded) by middlemen. For instance, numerous retail chains will not stock a product unless it is presold through heavy advertising by the producer.

MARKETING IN THE INFORMATION ECONOMY
Will the growth of the Internet be the demise of middlemen?

Many producers of diverse goods and services reach customers through the Internet. Dell Computer, Merrill Lynch, Tupperware, and all American air carriers are among the legion of firms that have established websites as one more way to sell their products.

Will direct contact between producers and ultimate consumers or end users eliminate middlemen in many industries? The potential benefits of bypassing middlemen and perhaps even a company's own sales force through online selling can be captivating. According to one estimate, selling through a website can cut expenses related to sales commissions and paperwork by as much as 15%. In addition, there may be savings from reducing or eliminating middlemen's markups.

Some companies, such as Amazon.com, locate on the Internet to gain a differential advantage. Others, such as Merrill Lynch, go online to avoid a disadvantage which for Merrill Lynch would be an inability to serve customers online. And still other firms, such as Tupperware and Avon, add the Internet as a channel in order to reach new customers.

But even in this Internet era, most companies continue to use middlemen. For one thing, few manufacturers are geared up to ship very small quantities to numerous buyers, whereas middlemen are. Further, many consumers and end users still want to see the actual product, or at least talk with a real person, prior to making a purchase. Various types of wholesaling middlemen and retailers offer these services to prospective customers. Auto dealers provide face-to-face contact as well as test drives. Thus automakers have concluded (at least for now) that they should not be selling cars directly to consumers.

Most firms that establish an Internet presence don't discard middlemen but instead strive to maintain a good working relationship with them. Thus some companies have limited their online activities by providing information only (Scotts in lawn-care products) or just a limited assortment (Tupperware) on their websites. Going a step further, numerous organizations are incorporating middlemen into their Internet activities. A common arrangement is for manufacturers to provide middlemen with a share of the revenues from Internet sales.

It's quite possible that middlemen will benefit, rather than suffer, from the move to online sales. They may be called upon to provide the services that producers with online enterprises either cannot or do not want to provide. Consider a prominent example. Most large "bricks and mortar" bookstores use a publisher → retailer → consumer channel. In contrast, Amazon.com tends to rely on a longer channel of publisher → wholesaler → retailer → consumer.

The Internet has even spurred the creation of new middlemen. For example, some consumers who want to sell merchandise through online auctions such as eBay lack computer skills or don't want to spend the time to place an item up for bid online. Several firms, such as iSoldIt and Auction Drop, will do this for consumers who bring their merchandise to the new middlemen's outlet.

Sources: Joan Verdon, "Intimidated by Selling Online? Experts Do Heavy Lifting for You," *Knight Ridder Tribune Business News*, Feb. 20, 2005, p. 1; Philip Smith, "The Web Cuts in the Middleman," *Revolution*, Oct. 20, 2004, pp. 42+; Dana Hedgpeth, "Out of the Picture?" *The Washington Post*, May 19, 2002, p. H1; Andrea Isabel Flores, "Tupperware to Launch Online Sales, Creating Rival to Own Representatives," *The Wall Street Journal*, Aug. 10, 1999, p. B8; "Merrill Lynch Shakes Up Industry by Going Online, *St. Louis Post-Dispatch*, June 2, 1999, pp. C1, C2; and George Anders, "Some Big Companies Long to Embrace Web but Settle for Flirtation," *The Wall Street Journal*, Nov. 4, 1998, pp. A1, A14.

- *Ability of management.* The marketing experience and managerial capabilities of a producer influence decisions about which channel to use. Many companies lacking marketing know-how turn the distribution job over to middlemen.

- *Financial resources.* A business with adequate finances can establish its own sales force, grant credit to its customers, and/or store its own products. A financially weak firm uses middlemen to provide these services.

In a few cases, virtually all factors point to a particular length and type of channel. However, there often is not a single "best" channel. In most cases, the guiding factors send mixed signals. If a company with an unproven product having low profit potential cannot place its product with middlemen, it may have no other option but to try to distribute the product directly to its target market.

Determining Intensity of Distribution

At this point in designing a channel, a firm knows what role has been assigned to distribution within the marketing mix, and which types of middlemen will be used (assuming indirect distribution is appropriate). Next the company must decide on the **intensity of distribution**—that is, how many middlemen will be used at the wholesale and retail levels in a particular territory. Optimal intensity, from the standpoint of a producer, is just enough middlemen to meet the desires of the target market. Extra intensity boosts the producer's marketing expenses, but does not really help the firm. Of course, like so many tasks in marketing (and life), achieving this optimum is easier said than done.[33]

There are many degrees of intensity. As shown in Figure 14.4, we will consider the three major categories—ranging from *intensive* to *selective* to *exclusive*. Distribution intensity ordinarily is thought to be a single decision. However, if the channel has more than one level of middlemen (wholesaler and retailer, for example) or the firm is using multiple channels, the appropriate intensity must be selected for each level and channel.

Different degrees of intensity may be appropriate at successive levels of distribution. A manufacturer can often achieve intensive retail coverage with selective, rather than intensive, wholesale distribution. Or selective intensity at the retail level may be gained through exclusive intensity at the wholesale level. Of course, the wholesaling firm(s) will determine which retail outlets actually receive the product. Despite this lack of control, a producer should plan the levels of intensity needed at both the wholesale and retail levels.

Intensive Distribution

Under **intensive distribution,** a producer sells its product through every available outlet in a market where a consumer might reasonably look for it. Ultimate consumers demand immediate satisfaction from convenience goods and will not defer purchases to find a particular brand. Thus intensive distribution is often used by manufacturers of this category of product. For example, some ice cream makers such as Häagen-Dazs eventually decided they needed intensive, rather than selective, distribution; as such, they supplemented their own outlets with distribution through grocery chains. Likewise, shortly after acquiring the Iams brand of pet food, Procter & Gamble concluded that sales were being lost by relying only on veterinary clinics and pet store chains at the retail level of the channel. As a result, P&G added supermarkets and discount stores to its retail channel members. The added intensity paid off; among the numerous brands of dog food, Iams moved from #5 to #1 with regards to annual sales.[34]

Retailers often control whether a strategy of intensive distribution actually can be implemented. For example, a new manufacturer of toothpaste or a small producer of potato chips may want distribution in all supermarkets, but these retailers may limit their assortments to proven fast-selling brands.

FIGURE 14.4

The Intensity-of-Distribution Continuum.

Intensive — Distribution through every reasonable outlet in a market

Selective — Distribution through multiple, but not all, reasonable outlets in a market

Exclusive — Distribution through a single wholesaling middleman and/or retailer in a market

Except when they want to promote low prices, retailers are reluctant to pay to advertise a product that is sold by competitors. Therefore, intensive distribution places much, or perhaps most, of the advertising and promotion burden on the producer. Many producers offer cooperative advertising, in which they reimburse middlemen for part of the cost of ads featuring the producer's product.

Selective Distribution

In **selective distribution,** a producer sells its product through multiple, but not all possible, wholesalers and retailers in a market where a consumer might reasonably look for it. Selective distribution is appropriate for consumer shopping goods, such as various types of clothing and appliances, and for business accessory equipment, such as office equipment and handheld tools. The relative ease of online selling has prompted firms in many industries to shift from selective to more intensive distribution.

In contrast, a company may choose to be more selective after some experience with intensive distribution. The decision to change usually hinges on the high cost of intensive distribution or the unsatisfactory performance of middlemen. Some middlemen always order in small, unprofitable amounts; others may be poor credit risks. Eliminating such marginal channel members may reduce the number of outlets *but* increase a company's sales volume. Many companies have found this to be the case simply because they were able to do more thorough selling with a smaller number of accounts.

A firm may move toward more selective distribution to enhance the image of its products, strengthen customer service, improve quality control, and/or maintain some influence over its prices. For instance, the Step2 Company, a manufacturer of large, plastic toys, decided its products would not be distributed through discount stores. Instead, the firm reached consumers through other retailers as well as a Step2 Direct page on its website. Eventually, Step2 relented and extended its distribution coverage by selling its product through Wal-Mart and Target chains.[35]

Exclusive Distribution

Under **exclusive distribution,** the supplier agrees to sell its product only to a single wholesaling middleman and/or retailer in a given market. At the wholesale level, such an arrangement is normally termed an exclusive *distributorship* and, at the retail level, an exclusive *dealership*. A manufacturer may prohibit a middleman that holds an exclusive distributorship or dealership from handling a directly competing product line. However, that type of restriction is becoming less common. Thus, even under an exclusive distributorship, many middlemen handle directly or, at least, indirectly competing products (for example, high-price and economy-price power mowers).

Producers often adopt an exclusive distribution strategy when it is essential that the retailer carry a large inventory. Thus exclusive dealerships are frequently used in marketing consumer specialty products such as expensive suits. This strategy is also desirable when the dealer or distributor must furnish installation and repair service. For this reason, manufacturers of farm machinery and large construction equipment grant exclusive distributorships.

Exclusive distribution helps a manufacturer control the last level of middleman before the final customer. A middleman with exclusive rights is usually willing to promote the product vigorously. Why? Interested customers will have to purchase the product from this middleman because no other outlets in the area carry the same brand. However, a producer suffers if its exclusive middlemen in various markets do not serve customers well. Essentially a manufacturer has "all its eggs in one basket."

An exclusive dealer or distributor has the opportunity to reap all the benefits of the producer's marketing activities in a particular area. However, under exclusive distribution, a middleman may become too dependent on the manufacturer. If the manufacturer fails, the middleman also fails (at least for that product). Another risk is that once sales volume has been built up in a market, the producer may add other dealers or, worse yet, drop all dealers and establish its own sales force.

Conflict and Control in Channels

Distribution should be, and often is, characterized by goals shared by suppliers and customers and by cooperative actions. But conflicts as well as struggles for control are increasingly common in this Internet age. To manage distribution channels effectively requires an understanding of both conflict and control, including techniques to (1) decrease conflict, or at least its negative effects, and (2) increase a firm's control within a channel.

Channel conflict exists when one channel member perceives another channel member to be acting in a way that prevents the first member from achieving its distribution objectives. Firms in one channel often compete vigorously with firms in other channels; this represents horizontal conflict. Even within the same channel, firms disagree about operating practices and try to gain control over other members' actions; this illustrates vertical conflict.

A by-product of the rise of the Internet has been added channel conflict, both horizontal and vertical in nature. For example, at one time, Home Depot decreed that its suppliers should not sell their products online. A letter from the chain to suppliers stated, "We, too, have the right to be selective in regard to vendors we select, and . . . a company may be hesitant to do business with its competitors." Perhaps trying to win favor with these same vendors, Lowe's encouraged its suppliers to go online. Lowe's stated its interest in linking websites and maybe even sharing revenues with its suppliers.[36]

Another practice, chargebacks by middlemen, has created severe vertical conflict in many channels. A **chargeback** is a penalty that a retailer or wholesaler assesses to a vendor that actually or allegedly violates an agreed-upon distribution policy or procedure. The bases for chargebacks are wide-ranging, including improperly boxed merchandise, mistimed shipments, and damaged merchandise. Producers say the charges are excessive with respect to frequency or amount and, worse yet, often are without justification. Very upset by chargebacks, an executive with a home-furnishings manufacturer described retailers as follows, "They are all cheaters and are stealing from us." In 2005, government officials began an investigation of possible illegal practices by the Saks Fifth Avenue department store chain. The focus is on chargebacks as well as allowances for markdowns. Middlemen defend chargebacks as legitimate assessments for noncompliance with reasonable policies and procedures. What is undeniable is that chargebacks have created serious tension and ill will in some channels.[37]

Horizontal Conflict

Horizontal conflict occurs among firms on the same level of distribution—for example, Toys "R" us versus Wal-Mart, as in the chapter-opening case. The cellular telephone field provides another excellent example. Cell phone equipment and services can be bought seemingly everywhere. Consider the range of competitors: office-supply outlets, department stores, warehouse clubs, and consumer electronics retailers as well as the telecommunications providers (such as Sprint) with their own outlets, toll-free telephone lines, and websites.

Basically, horizontal conflict is a form of business competition. It may occur among:

- *Middlemen of the same type:* Maryvale Hardware (an independent retailer) versus Fred's Friendly Hardware (another independent retailer), for example.

- *Different types of middlemen on the same level:* Fred's Friendly Hardware (an independent retailer) versus Dunn-Edwards Paint (one unit in a large chain) versus Lowe's paints area (a single department in a store within a giant chain).

www.dunnedwards.com/oz.html

A primary source of horizontal conflict is **scrambled merchandising,** in which middlemen diversify by adding product lines not traditionally carried by their type

Some large retail chains in Europe engage in scrambled merchandising to the point of offering autos for sale. Here, a sales representative talks to prospective customers in a Géant hypermarket (akin to a Wal-Mart supercenter) in France.

of business. Supermarkets, for instance, expanded beyond groceries by adding health and beauty aids, small appliances, snack bars, and various services. Retailers that originally sold these lines became irritated both at supermarkets for diversifying and at producers for using multiple distribution channels. Banks selling insurance, mutual funds, and trust services is another example of scrambled merchandising in the previously tradition-bound world of financial services.

Scrambled merchandising and the resulting horizontal competition may stem from consumers, middlemen, or producers. Many *consumers* prefer convenient, one-stop shopping, so stores broaden their assortments to satisfy this desire. *Middlemen* constantly strive for higher gross margins and more customer traffic, so they increase the number of lines they carry. Perhaps with that in mind, a supermarket chain in France began to sell Korean-made Daewoo autos at discount prices in its stores, much to the chagrin of regular Daewoo dealers.[38] *Producers* seek to expand their market coverage and to reduce unit production costs through economies of scale, so they add new means of distribution. Such diversification intensifies horizontal conflict.

Vertical Conflict

Perhaps the most severe conflicts in distribution involve firms at different levels of the same channel. **Vertical conflict** typically occurs between producer and wholesaler or between producer and retailer.

Producer versus Wholesaler
A producer and a wholesaler may disagree about aspects of their relationship. For instance, Anheuser-Busch (A-B) instituted a set of incentives to encourage its wholesalers to stock only A-B products and, conversely, to drop other brands. Channel friction is likely to develop between A-B and any wholesaler that desires to carry other profitable brands but does not want to miss out on the financial incentives that are part of A-B's "100% share of mind" program.[39]

Why do conflicts arise? Basically, manufacturers and wholesalers have differing points of view. On the one hand, manufacturers think that wholesalers neither promote products aggressively nor hold sufficient inventories. And they contend that wholesalers' services cost too much. On the other hand, wholesalers believe that producers either expect too much, such as requiring an extensive inventory of the product, or do not understand the wholesaler's primary obligation to customers.

Channel conflict sometimes stems from a manufacturer's attempts to bypass wholesalers and deal directly with retailers or consumers. Direct sales occur because either producers or customers are dissatisfied with wholesalers' services or because market conditions invite or require this approach. With the rise of the Internet, battles about direct sales are increasingly common.

Given its successful history and substantial brand equity, Avon Products, Inc. decided to expand its distribution by selling some of its products in retail outlets as well as through independent reps. This photo depicts an Avon display in a retail store in Shanghai, China.

www.avon.com

To bypass wholesalers, a producer has two alternatives:

- *Sell directly to consumers.* Producers may employ door-to-door, mail-order, or online selling. They may also establish their own distribution centers in various areas or even their own retail stores in major markets. Many clothing and shoe manufacturers, such as Phillips-Van Heusen and adidas America, own and operate numerous factory outlets. The Coleman Company uses factory outlets to sell products that are not yet available elsewhere as well as discontinued, excess, and reconditioned merchandise at reduced prices (more on factory outlets in the next chapter).[40] With few exceptions, manufacturers use this approach as a supplementary, rather than sole, form of distribution.

www.luxottica.com

- *Sell directly to retailers.* Under certain market and product conditions, selling directly to retailers is feasible and advisable. An ideal retail market for this option consists of retailers that buy large quantities of a limited line of products. Luxottica Group of Italy, which makes more eyeglass frames than any other company, eliminated most of its wholesale distributors (and also bought two retail chains that sell eyeglasses and sunglasses). According to the firm, a shorter channel not only boosted its profit margins but also improved service to optical shops that buy frames from Luxottica for resale.[41]

  Direct distribution—a short channel—places a financial and managerial burden on the producer. The manufacturer must operate its own sales force and handle physical distribution of its products. Further, a direct-selling manufacturer faces competition from its former wholesalers, which no doubt will begin distributing competitive products.

To avoid being bypassed in channels or to respond when they are bypassed, wholesalers need to improve their competitive positions. Their options include:

- *Improve internal performance.* Many wholesalers have modernized their operations. Functional, single-story warehouses have been built outside congested downtown areas, and mechanized materials-handling equipment has been installed. Computers have improved order processing, inventory control, and billing.

- *Provide management assistance to customers.* Wholesalers have realized that improving customers' operations benefits all parties. Thus many of them offer programs to assist their customers in areas such as layout, merchandise selection, promotion, and inventory control. For instance, Graybar Electric, a distributor with annual sales exceeding $4 billion, decided to spend $90 million on a new system for storing and analyzing sales data and to provide the reports to both suppliers and customers.[42]

Relatively small retailers may seek strength through membership in either a voluntary chain or a retailer cooperative. IGA is an example of this type of alliance. Founded in 1926, more than 4,000 retail grocers (1,750 in the U.S.) are part of the IGA organization.

www.iga.com/aboutGA/
about.asp

- *Form a voluntary chain.* In this form of vertical marketing system, a wholesaler contractually agrees to furnish management services and volume buying power to a group of retailers. In turn, the retailers promise to buy all, or almost all, their merchandise from the wholesale distributor. Wholesaler-sponsored voluntary chains are prevalent in the groceries field (IGA and SUPERVALU), but there are few, if any, such chains in other industries.

- *Develop middlemen's brands.* Some large wholesalers have successfully established their own brands. SUPERVALU has developed its Flavorite brand for groceries and Super Chill for soft drinks. A voluntary chain of retailers provides a built-in market for the wholesaler's brands.

Producer versus Retailer Conflict between manufacturers and retailers—in fact, between any two parties—is likely to intensify during tough economic times. Conflict is also bound to occur when producers compete with retailers by selling through producer-owned stores or over the Internet. A number of apparel makers, including Polo, have opened retail outlets. Doing so can aggravate department stores and specialty retailers that carry the manufacturers' brands. After increasing its distribution intensity by adding Sears, Wal-Mart, and other retailers, "Goodyear took its eye off independent dealers," stated the editor of a tire-industry magazine. Long the mainstay of Goodyear's distribution, the dealers were particularly upset by what they saw as unfair pricing and unreliable fulfillment of orders submitted to the tire manufacturer.[43]

Producer and retailer may also disagree about terms of sale or conditions of the relationship between the two parties. In recent years large retail chains have demanded not only lower prices but also more service from suppliers. Producers sometimes find it costly, if not nearly impossible, to comply with the retailers' new policies. The policies cover the gamut, including larger contributions to advertising and other promotion expenses and even the quality of hangers on which apparel is hung (so that the retailer doesn't have to pay for hangers and rehang the merchandise when it is received at the store).[44]

Conflict also has occurred as some large retailers, especially in the grocery field, have demanded a so-called **slotting fee** (also called a *slotting allowance*) to place a manufacturer's product on store shelves. An examination by a federal agency indi-

In exchange for shelf space in their stores, many supermarket chains require manufacturers to pay slotting fees (as discussed in the text). Part or all of the revenues a chain receives from this policy might be passed on to consumers in the form of lower prices. Or the chain can retain these revenues to cover added labor costs associated with shelving new products and/or to boost profits.

Critics claim that such charges stifle the introduction of new products, particularly those developed by small producers lacking the resources to pay the mandated fees. For instance, an entrepreneur who developed a novelty ice cream product was frozen out of supermarkets after being unable to afford slotting fees of $7,000 to $50,000.

Assume that you are a supermarket-chain vice president who is responsible for establishing policies regarding supply chain management. Is it ethical for your chain to demand slotting fees from manufacturers?

Sources: Brendan I. Koerner, "Pass the Ketchup, Er, Raspberry Sauce," *The New York Times,* Feb. 20, 2005, p. 2; and Paul N. Bloom, Gregory T. Gundlach, and Joseph P. Cannon, "Slotting Allowances and Fees: Schools of Thought and the Views of Practicing Managers," *Journal of Marketing,* April 2000, pp. 98–108.

cated that a typical fee is as much as $5,000 per store for each version of the product. Manufacturers with popular brands can often negotiate lower fees. According to one estimate, the slotting allowances paid by manufacturers total to about $9 billion annually. Because profit margins on grocery products are small at the retail level, these fees represent a significant share, perhaps one-quarter or more, of supermarket chains' profits. Given the controversy (see the Ethical Dilemma box), the Federal Trade Commission conducted an extensive study of slotting allowances but did not recommend any regulatory actions.[45]

Both producers and retailers have methods to gain more control. Manufacturers can:

- *Build strong consumer brand loyalty.* Meeting and surpassing customers' expectations is a key in creating such loyalty.

- *Establish one or more forms of a vertical marketing system.* Procter & Gamble uses the administered type of VMS whenever possible.

- *Refuse to sell to uncooperative retailers.* This tactic may not be defensible from a legal standpoint.

- *Arrange alternative retailers.* Squeezed by large retail chains, some producers are building their distribution strategy around smaller specialty stores. Although risky, a number of apparel makers have taken this course of action.

Effective marketing weapons are also available to retailers. They can:

- *Develop store loyalty among consumers.* Skillful advertising and strong store brands are means of creating loyal customers.

- *Improve computerized information systems.* Information is power. Knowing what sells and how fast it sells is useful in negotiating with suppliers.

- *Form a retailer cooperative.* In this type of vertical marketing system, a group of relatively small retailers bands together to establish and operate a wholesale warehouse. The primary intent is to obtain lower costs on merchandise and supplies through volume buying power. For example, the owner of Rapid Transmissions in Escondido, California, formed a cooperative with other auto repair shops to secure better prices from parts suppliers.[46]

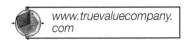
www.truevaluecompany.
com

Of course, no approach assures that a producer, wholesaler, or retailer will remain competitive. Any of these paths can become rocky. For instance, the TruServ (now True Value) cooperative suffered financial problems in the late 1990s that harmed its ability to serve its member hardware stores. As a result, some members fled TruServ and joined other cooperatives. True Value is striving to improve and grow again.[47]

Who Controls Channels?

Every firm would like to regulate the behavior of the other members in its distribution channel. A company that is able to do this has **channel control.** In many situations, including distribution channels, power is a prerequisite for control. **Channel power** is the ability to influence or determine the behavior of another channel member.

There are various sources of power in distribution channels. They include:

- *Expertise*—for example, possessing vital technical knowledge about the product or valuable information about customers.
- *Rewards*—providing financial benefits to cooperative channel members.
- *Sanctions*—penalizing uncooperative firms or even removing them from the channel.

Interestingly, power doesn't have to be exercised to provide control. A firm might be able to gain control just by making other channel members aware that it has, for example, sanctioning power. Not surprisingly, the types of power used to influence distributors have a strong effect on their levels of satisfaction.[48]

Historically, manufacturers were viewed as controlling channels; that is, they made the decisions regarding types and number of outlets, participation of individual middlemen, and business practices to be followed by a channel. Considering the enormous size and strong customer loyalty that some middlemen—particularly retailers—now possess, this point of view is one-sided and outdated.

Middlemen now control many channels. Certainly the names Safeway, Target, and Nordstrom mean more to consumers than the names of many producers' brands sold in these stores. Large retailers are challenging manufacturers for channel control, just as many manufacturers seized control from wholesalers years ago. Not surprisingly, powerful retail chains—most notably Wal-Mart—squeeze low prices and other forms of support from producers. Even small retailers can be influential in local markets because their reputations may be stronger than their suppliers' prestige.

Manufacturers contend they should assume the channel leader's role because they create the new products and need greater sales volume to benefit from economies of scale. Retailers also stake a claim for leadership, because they are closest to ultimate consumers and, as a result, are best able to know consumers' wants and to design and oversee channels to satisfy them. Various factors contributed to retailers' growing ability to control channels. Perhaps most notably, many retailers implemented electronic scanning devices, giving them access to more accurate, timely information about sales trends of individual products than manufacturers have.[49]

A Channel Viewed as a Partnership

It is myopic to see a channel as a fragmented collection of independent, competing firms. Instead, suppliers and middlemen should view a channel as a partnership aimed at satisfying end users' needs rather than as something they command or dominate. Perhaps in that vein, Wal-Mart has eased the pressure on some suppliers, even absorbing price increases in a number of cases. The head of Sutter Home Winery attributes the company's success to its good distributors and cooperative working relationship with them: "I have always felt it was a real partnership."[50]

In a distribution channel, a partnership can entail a variety of cooperative activities that benefit both parties. For instance, a supplier may be asked to get involved in a customer's new-product development efforts. A division of ABB Automation that makes control systems for large manufacturing plants even allowed one of its suppliers, Arrow Electronics, to have a warehouse at Bailey's factory.

An increasingly common occurrence is for a firm to provide a supplier with information about past or projected sales and/or existing inventory levels so the supplier can better schedule its production and fill the customer's orders in a timely manner. For example, Wal-Mart decided to allow each of its thousands of suppliers to examine two years of sales figures for that vendor's products across the giant retail chain.[51] In Chapter 16, we'll discuss *collaborative planning, forecasting, and replenishment*, which emphasizes this type of data sharing in a channel.

There are various potential benefits of partnering. Lower inventory and operating costs, improved quality of products and service, and more rapid filling of orders are all possible but by no means assured. There are risks as well. A close working relationship often requires sharing sensitive information, which may be misused by the other party; worse yet, it may wind up in a competitor's hands. Because firms entering a partnership often reduce the number of other suppliers or customers with which they do business, they may have few options if the relationship doesn't work out.[52]

To increase coordination and facilitate partnerships within channels, many large firms have pared the number of suppliers with which they do business. Some observers suggest, however, that the resulting "preferred vendor" lists are a means for sizable customers to dominate relatively small suppliers. As implied, channel partners are not necessarily equals. Still, given the potential sales volume that comes with being a preferred vendor, most suppliers are willing to meet the demands of powerful customers.[53]

Another growing practice that fosters partnerships is **category management**, in which a retailer allows a large supplier to manage an entire product category (such as carbonated beverages in a supermarket). For its stores, Borders Books & Music chose HarperCollins Publisher to oversee the cookbooks section. Under category management, the supplier designated as "captain" decides which items will be placed on a retailer's shelves and in what quantities and locations. Advocates contend that category management boosts sales and pares expenses for retailers; opponents state that retailers are giving up opportunities for autonomy and differentiation.[54]

Many channel partnerships really are part of a broader, significant trend called *relationship marketing* (introduced in Chapter 1). In the context of distribution channels, relationship marketing refers to a concerted effort by a company not only to work closely with customers to better understand and satisfy their needs but also to develop long-term, mutually beneficial relationships with them. Conversely, customers can seek to engage in relationship marketing with their suppliers.[55]

Legal Considerations in Managing Channels

Attempts to control distribution are subject to legal constraints. The legal aspects of four control methods that are sometimes employed by suppliers, usually manufacturers, warrant consideration. Each method is limited by the Clayton Antitrust Act, Sherman Antitrust Act, or Federal Trade Commission Act. None of the four methods is automatically illegal. Distribution control becomes unlawful when it is judged to (1) substantially lessen competition, (2) create a monopoly, or (3) restrain trade.

Exclusive Dealing

A manufacturer that prohibits its dealers from carrying products offered by the producer's competitors is engaged in **exclusive dealing.** If a manufacturer stipulates that any store carrying its Perfecto Gas Grill *not* carry competing brands of outdoor barbecue grills, this is exclusive dealing. Such an arrangement is likely to be *illegal* when:

- The manufacturer's sales volume is a substantial portion of total volume in a given market. Competitors are thus excluded from a major part of the market.
- The contract is between a large manufacturer and a much smaller middleman. Given the size imbalance, the supplier's power may be considered inherently coercive and thus in restraint of trade.

However, some court decisions have held that exclusive dealing is *permissible* when:

- Equivalent products are available in a market *or* the manufacturer's competitors have access to equivalent dealers. Exclusive dealing may be legal in these cases if competition is not lessened to any large degree.
- A manufacturer is entering a market *or* its total market share is so small as to be negligible. An exclusive-dealing agreement may actually strengthen the producer's competitive position if the middlemen decide to back the product with a strong marketing effort.

Likewise, a middleman that uses its clout to force a manufacturer to stop selling products to another middleman may be guilty of illegal exclusive dealing. In fact, two department store chains, Federated and May (then separate, now merged), were accused by the New York Attorney General of trying to discourage two tableware manufacturers, Waterford Wedgwood and Lenox Inc., from selling products to retailer Bed Bath & Beyond (BB&B). The renowned brands were going to be featured in BB&B's new tableware department. The four participants eventually agreed to pay almost $3 million in penalties but admitted no wrongdoing.[56]

Tying Contracts

When a supplier sells a product to a middleman only under the condition that the middleman buy another (possibly unwanted) product from the supplier, the two companies have entered into a **tying contract.** If Paramount Products requires middlemen to purchase unpopular, old models of compact disc players in order to be able to buy popular, new models of DVD players, that's a tying contract.

A manufacturer pushes for a tying agreement in several situations. When there are shortages of a popular product, a supplier may see an opportunity to unload other, less desired products. When a supplier relies on exclusive dealers or distributors (in appliances, for example), it may want them to carry a full line of its products. Or when a company grants a franchise (as in fast foods), it may see the franchisees as captive buyers of all the equipment and supplies needed to operate the business.

In general, tying contracts are considered a violation of antitrust laws. There are exceptions, however. Tying contracts may be *legal* when:

- A new company is trying to enter a market.
- An exclusive dealer or distributor is required to carry the manufacturer's full product line, but is not prohibited from carrying competing products.

According to a lawsuit filed by some Domino's franchisees, their franchise rights were tied to a requirement that they make purchases only from the parent company or approved vendors. The franchisees claimed that as a result of a tying contract, they paid excessive prices for products that were essential to their operations. However, an appeals court ultimately decided that a tying contract was not harmful in the context of franchising.[57]

Refusal to Deal

To select and perhaps control its channels, a producer may refuse to sell to certain middlemen. This practice is called **refusal to deal.** A 1919 court case established that manufacturers can select the middlemen to whom they will sell, so long as there is no intent to create a monopoly. In the mid-1990s, a federal jury decided that Eastman Kodak Co. illegally refused to sell parts for its photocopiers to independent service companies. Under the verdict, the 11 companies were awarded more than $70 million in damages from Kodak. In contrast, perhaps desiring to protect its brand image or avoid ongoing price competition, Colgate-Palmolive Co. declines to sell its Hill's Science Diet pet food to Costco and Wal-Mart. This type of refusal to deal is legal.[58]

A manufacturer's decision to end or diminish a relationship with a wholesaler or retailer may not be legal. Generally it is *illegal* to drop or withhold products from a middleman for (1) carrying competitors' products, (2) resisting a tying contract, or (3) setting prices lower than desired by the manufacturer. Some years ago, the New York attorney general charged that Stride Rite Corp. held back Keds shoes from retailers that did not abide by the manufacturer's "suggested" retail prices. Eventually, Stride Rite agreed to pay over $7 million to resolve the claim.[59]

Exclusive-Territory Policy

Under an **exclusive-territory policy,** a producer requires each middleman to sell *only* to customers located within an assigned territory. In several court cases, exclusive (also called *closed*) sales territories were ruled unlawful because they lessened competition and restrained trade. The courts sought to encourage competition among middlemen handling the *same* brand.

Exclusive territories may be *permitted* when:

- A company is small *or* is a newcomer in the market.
- A producer establishes a corporate vertical marketing system and retains ownership of the product until it reaches the final buyer.
- A producer uses independent middlemen to distribute the product under consignment, in which a middleman does not pay the supplier until after the merchandise is sold.

As you can see, these conditions certainly are subject to interpretation. Thus it is not uncommon for conflicts to be settled by the courts.

Summary

The role of distribution is to get a product to its target market. A distribution channel carries out this assignment, with middlemen performing some tasks. A middleman is a business firm that renders services directly related to the purchase and/or sale of a product as it flows from producer to consumer. Middlemen can be eliminated from a channel, but some organization or individual still has to carry out their essential functions.

A distribution channel is the set of people and firms involved in the flow of title to a product as it moves from producer to ultimate consumer or business user. A channel includes producer, final customer, and any middlemen that participate in the process.

Designing a channel of distribution for a product occurs through a sequence of four decisions: (1) delineating the role of distribution within the marketing mix, (2) selecting the appropriate type of distribution channel, (3) determining the suitable intensity of distribution, and (4) choosing specific channel members.

A variety of channels are used to distribute consumer goods, business goods, and services. Firms often employ multiple channels to achieve broad market coverage, although this strategy can alienate some middlemen. Vertical marketing systems, which are tightly coordinated channels, have become widespread in distribution. There are three forms of vertical marketing systems: corporate, contractual, and administered.

Numerous factors need to be considered in selecting a distribution channel. The primary consideration is the nature of the target market. Other considerations relate to the product, the middlemen, and the company itself.

Distribution intensity refers to the number of middlemen a producer uses at the wholesale and retail levels in a particular territory. To increase distribution intensity, which ranges from intensive to selective to exclusive, some channel members have set up Internet sites that sell products to current and/or new customers.

Firms that distribute goods and services sometimes clash. There are two types of conflict: horizontal (between firms at the same level of distribution) and vertical (between firms at different levels of the same channel). Scrambled merchandising is a prime cause of horizontal conflict. Vertical conflict typically pits producer against wholesaler or retailer. Manufacturers' attempts to bypass middlemen, perhaps through online selling, are a prime cause of vertical conflict.

Channel members frequently strive for some control over one another. Depending on the circumstances, either producers or middlemen can achieve the dominant position in a channel. Members of a channel are served best if they all view their particular network as a partnership requiring coordination of distribution activities. Channel partnerships are part of a significant trend called relationship marketing.

Attempts to control distribution may be subject to legal constraints. In fact, some practices, such as exclusive dealing and tying contracts, may be ruled illegal.

More about **Toys "R" Us**

Since the mid-1990s, Toys "R" Us (TRU) has struggled to build sales, earn a profit, curb the rise of Wal-Mart and Target in toy retailing, maintain some power in the distribution channels for toys, and sustain working relationships with its suppliers. Other toy chains have also suffered from the intense price competition but with even worse fates. KB Toys, which at one time had over 1,200 stores, filed for Chapter 11 bankruptcy protection. So did the parent company of the FAO Schwarz and Zany Brainy chains.

In early 2005, three private-equity firms stated that they would jointly acquire TRU—both the toy and baby divisions. The announced price was $6.6 *billion*.

What might TRU look like in the future? One observer surmised, "It's likely that Toys 'R' Us and KB will reinvent themselves." In particular, they will need to take steps to avoid head-to-head price competition with Target and Wal-Mart, to the extent that's possible. Chains competing with these gigantic enterprises must seek a nonprice advantage, such as broad assortments throughout the year, not just during the holiday season; exclusive merchandise; and turning shopping into a truly enjoyable experience.

One option for TRU is the so-called interactive format that allows children to participate in an onsite activity involving toys. The emphasis in this environment is on entertainment, thereby avoiding (or trying to avoid) direct price competition. Build-a-Bear and American Girl are successful examples of the interactive format. Whatever strategies are adopted, the consensus appears to be that TRU will be smaller, with about 25% of its 700 domestic stores sold off or transferred to the Babies "R" Us division.

It's expected that the new owners of Toys "R" Us Inc. will place more emphasis on the baby-products retail division. Two significant advantages Babies "R" Us has over its sibling division are (1) steadier year-round sales and (2) relatively little direct competition with the huge discount chains (although this could change shortly). For now, Babies "R" Us has a more powerful position in the distribution channels for its products than Toys "R" Us does in its field. The new owners of the TRU division can use the steady cash flows generated by Babies "R" Us to not only expand that division but also to re-engineer the TRU division.[60]

1. How much channel power does Toys "R" Us possess?
2. Which kind of channel conflict—horizontal or vertical—has plagued TRU for the past 10 years?
3. In terms of marketing strategy, what else might TRU do to be viable in the distribution of toys?

Key Terms and Concepts

Questions and Problems

1. Which of the following institutions are middlemen? Explain.
   a. Girl Scout cookie seller
   b. Electrical wholesaler
   c. Real estate broker
   d. Railroad
   e. Advertising agency
   f. Grocery store
   g. Online stockbroker
   h. Internet bank

2. Which of the channels illustrated in Figure 14.3 is most apt to be used for each of the following products? Justify your choice in each case.
   a. Fire insurance
   b. Single-family residences
   c. Farm hay balers
   d. Washing machines
   e. Hair spray
   f. An ocean cruise

3. "The great majority of business sales are made directly from producer to business user." Explain why this occurs, first in terms of the nature of the market, and then in terms of the product.

4. "You can eliminate middlemen, but you cannot eliminate essential distribution activities." Discuss how this statement is supported or refuted by vertical marketing systems.

5. A small manufacturer of fishing lures is faced with the problem of selecting its channel of distribution. What reasonable alternatives does it have? Consider particularly the nature of its product and the nature of its market.

6. Is a policy of intensive distribution consistent with consumer buying habits for convenience goods? For shopping goods? Is intensive distribution normally used in marketing any type of business goods?

7. From a producer's viewpoint, what are the competitive advantages of exclusive distribution?

8. A manufacturer of a well-known brand of men's clothing has been selling directly to one retailer in a Southern city for many years. For some time the market has been large enough to support two retailers very profitably. Yet the retailer with the exclusive arrangement objects strongly when the manufacturer suggests adding another outlet. What alternatives does the manufacturer have in this situation? What course of action would you recommend?

9. "Manufacturers should always strive to select the lowest-cost channel of distribution." Do you agree? Should they always try to use the middlemen with the lowest operating costs? Why or why not?

10. A new company is designing and making stylish—in fact, very trendy—women's clothing. Should the firm establish a website to sell its products?

Interactive Marketing Exercises

1. Arrange an interview with either the owner or a top-level manager of a small manufacturing firm. Inquire about (a) the distribution channel(s) the company uses for its primary product, (b) the factors that were the greatest influences in arriving at the channel(s), (c) whether the company would prefer some other channel, and (d) the firm's strategy regarding online selling.

2. Visit with either a supermarket manager or a buyer for a supermarket chain to learn more about slotting fees and any other charges they levy on manufacturers. Inquire whether such charges have led to channel conflict and how the supermarket chain is handling this type of situation. Also ask whether any grocery products manufacturers refuse to pay slotting fees and whether the chain ever waives the fees.

Chapter 15

Walgreens' primary appeal is based on convenience, especially nearby locations and ease of purchase.

Does **Walgreens** Have the Prescription for Long-Term Success?

How does a company go from a single pharmacy, founded by Charles Walgreen, Sr., in Chicago in 1901, to a chain of over 5,000 Walgreens drugstores? How can a firm increase its sales and profits for 30 successive years, reaching $40 billion in sales and more than $1 billion in profits annually? And can Walgreens sustain its leading position, meeting its projection of having 7,000 outlets by 2010?

The seeds of Walgreens' success were planted in its first unit. As a pharmacy employee, Charles Walgreen listened to customers. He used this information to make changes in the pharmacy when he purchased it. For example, Walgreen widened the store's aisles and added items not previously sold in a pharmacy (for example, pots and pans for 15¢ apiece). Prices were intended to be sensible and competitive.

Walgreens began to serve hot foods at the soda-fountain counters that were common in pharmacies in the early 20th century. In so doing, it generated revenues from space that previously was unproductive during cold months. (Food service was phased out in the 1980s.) The chain grew dramatically during the 1920s, from 20 outlets to 525.

In 1931, Walgreens recorded another first for drugstores by advertising on the radio in order to complement its newspaper ads. In the 1950s, Walgreens joined the move to self-service retailing. Walgreens reached the 1,000-store milestone in 1984. By mid-2005, the firm had over 4,800 outlets in 44 states and Puerto Rico.

Over three-fifths of the chain's revenues come from its pharmacy area. Demand for prescription drugs will rise steadily as the sizable cohort of baby boomers ages. The remainder of Walgreen's revenues is derived from over-the-counter medications and its "front end" comprising general merchandise, foods and beverages, and services. Walgreens offers extra features, such as being the only drugstore chain to have cosmetics specialists in each store.

Prescription drugs have relatively small margins. One way that Walgreens has boosted the profitability of its pharmacies is by switching patients to generic drugs. Compared to prescription drugs, generics cost consumers less but are more profitable for a drugstore. At the same time, the chain strives to have an appealing assortment of nondrug products for shoppers.

Walgreens invests significant sums of money to refine its distribution methods, inventory-control systems, merchandising techniques, and pricing. Walgreens also understands the importance of differences across local markets—hence, its "my Walgreens" program. To appeal to a 70% Latino population in Corpus Christi, Texas, the chain introduced a tailored Mexican-American approach in six stores.

Walgreens' primary appeal is based on convenience, especially nearby locations and ease of purchase. Almost one-half of the U.S. population has to travel under two miles to reach a Walgreens store. The chain's executives have referred to the potential for 12,000 stores in the U.S. Another convenience factor is enabling customers to renew prescriptions by phone or online. Walgreens also recognized the desire of many consumers to process their digital photos at a store rather than at home. Thus the industry leader invested about $400 million in new digital photo-lab equipment.

Walgreens will need and will be able to afford added stores only if it maintains a strong appeal to consumers who need to fill their prescriptions. As covered in the chapter-ending part of this case, several formidable competitors (notably CVS, Rite Aid, and, yes, Wal-Mart) want to put an end to Walgreens' string of annual records for sales and profits.[1]

How is Walgreens substantially different from other retailers, including competing chains of drugstores?

 www.walgreens.com

Distribution of consumer products begins with the producer and ends with the ultimate consumer. Between the two, there is usually at least one middleman—a retailer such as Walgreens. The many types of retail institutions and their marketing activities are the subjects of this chapter.

You have abundant experience with retailing—as a consumer. And perhaps you also have worked in retailing. This chapter builds on that experience and provides insights about retail markets, different types of retailers, and key strategies and trends in retailing, notably the growing volume of retail sales through the Internet. After studying this chapter, you should be able to explain:

Chapter Goals

- The nature of retailing.
- What a retailer is.
- Types of retailers classified by form of ownership.
- Types of retailers classified by marketing strategies.
- Forms of nonstore retailing, including online sales to final consumers.
- Trends in retailing.

Nature and Importance of Retailing

www.crateandbarrel.com/
aboutus/default.aspx

For every successful large retailer like Publix supermarkets, Crate & Barrel stores, and of course Wal-Mart, thousands of tiny retailers serve consumers in very small areas. Despite their differences, all have two common features: They link producers and ultimate consumers, and they perform valuable services for both. In all likelihood, all of these firms are retailers, but not all of their activities may qualify as retailing. Let's see how that can be.

Retailing and Retailers

If a Winn-Dixie supermarket sells floor wax to a gift shop operator to polish the shop's floor, is this a retail sale? Can a wholesaler or manufacturer engage in retailing? When a service such as Aamco transmission repair is sold to an ultimate consumer, is this retailing? Obviously, we need to define some terms, particularly *retailing* and *retailer,* to answer these questions and to avoid misunderstandings later.

Retailing (or *retail trade*) consists of the sale, and all activities directly related to the sale, of goods and services to ultimate consumers for personal, nonbusiness use. Although most retailing occurs through retail stores, it may be done by any institution. A Tupperware rep selling plastic containers at lunchtime meetings at a factory is engaged in retailing, as is a farmer selling vegetables at a roadside stand.

Any firm—manufacturer, wholesaler, or retailer—that sells something to ultimate consumers for their nonbusiness use is making a retail sale. This is true regardless of *how* the product is sold (in person, online, or by telephone, mail, or vending machine) or *where* it is sold (in a store, at the consumer's home, at another physical location, or on the Internet). However, a firm engaged *primarily* in retailing is called a **retailer.** In this chapter we will concentrate on retailers rather than on other types of businesses that make only occasional retail sales.

In the past few years, it has become common to differentiate *bricks-and-mortar* retailers (that is, those with physical stores) from *clicks-and-modem* retailers (those that operate online). The latter type, also referred to as *e-tailers,* is covered at various places in the chapter. Further, although this chapter focuses primarily on retailers of *goods,* much of what is said, particularly regarding marketing strategies, also applies to retailers of *services* (as covered in Chapter 11).

Economic Justification for Retailing

As discussed in Chapter 14, all middlemen basically serve as purchasing agents for their customers and as sales specialists for their suppliers. To carry out these roles, retailers perform many activities, including anticipating customers' wants, developing assortments of products, acquiring market information, and financing.

It is relatively easy to become a retailer. No large investment in production equipment is required, merchandise can often be purchased on credit, and store space can be leased with no down payment or a simple website can be set up at a modest cost. Considering these factors, perhaps it's not surprising that there are just over 1.1 million retail firms in the U.S. (excluding those that do not have employees).[2] This large number of companies, many of which are trying to serve and satisfy the same market segments, results in fierce competition and better values for shoppers.

www.neimanmarcus.com

To enter retailing is easy; to fail is even easier! To survive in retailing, a firm must do a satisfactory job in its primary role of catering to consumers. Stanley Marcus, the former chairman of Neiman Marcus, described a successful retailer as "a merchant who sells goods that won't come back to customers who will."[3] Of course, a retail firm also must fulfill its other role of serving producers and wholesalers. This dual role is both the justification for retailing and the key to success in retailing.

Size of Market and Firms

Retail sales in 2004 (the most recent year for which this figure is available) totaled over $3.5 *trillion* (see Figure 15.1). The increase in total sales volume has been tremendous—more than sevenfold from the early 1970s to 2004. Even adjusting for the rise in prices, total retail sales and per capita retail sales have gone up considerably.

There is a high degree of concentration in retailing. As depicted in Figure 15.2, more than three-quarters of retail firms have fewer than 10 employees. These small merchants ring up about one-eighth of all sales to consumers. Conversely, a small number of companies account for a large share of retail trade. Just 0.3% of all retailers had 500 or more employees, but these firms accounted for about 45% of total retail sales.

FIGURE 15.1

Total Retail Trade in the United States.

Retail sales have increased steadily over the past three decades, partly as a result of inflation.

Sources: Annual Benchmark Report for Retail Trade and Food Services: January 1992 through February 2005, U.S. Census Bureau, Washington, DC, 2005, pp. 4, 5; and corresponding censuses from prior years.

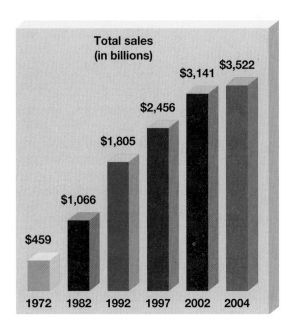

Total sales (in billions)

1972	1982	1992	1997	2002	2004
$459	$1,066	$1,805	$2,456	$3,141	$3,522

FIGURE 15.2

Distribution of Retail Stores and Sales by Number of Employees.

Sources: Statistical Abstract of the United States: 2004–2005, 124th edition, U.S. Bureau of the Census, Washington, DC, 2004, p. 494; and *Statistical Abstract of the United States: 1999,* 119th edition, U.S. Bureau of the Census, Washington, DC, 1999, p. 556.

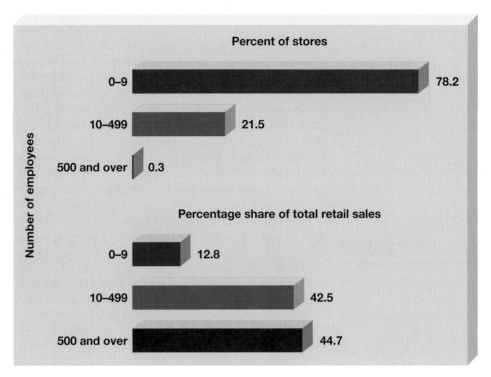

Figure 15.2 does not tell the full story of large-scale retailing because it represents a tabulation of individual *store* sales and not *company* sales volume. A single company may own many stores, as in the case of chains. When retail sales are analyzed by companies, the high degree of concentration becomes even more evident. As shown in Table 15.1, the sales of the 10 largest retailers summed to almost $700 billion in 2004, which comprised about 20% of total retail trade.

Stores of different sizes face distinct challenges and opportunities. Buying, promotion, staffing, and expense control are influenced significantly by whether a store's sales volume is large or small. The size of a retail business creates certain advantages and disadvantages, several of which are described in Table 15.2. Considering these factors, large stores ordinarily, but not always, have a competitive advantage over small stores.

Small retailers face a variety of difficulties, and many fail. Even relatively large retailers struggle, and some succumb. Notable recent failures include Tower Records, KB Toys, and Snyder's Drug Stores. Other large merchants, such as Kmart, seek Chapter 11 bankruptcy protection and survive—at least for the time being. Many factors, ranging from the relative health of the economy to the intensity of competition, influence the number of retail failures over time.[4]

How do small retailers succeed? They understand their target markets very well. Then, in seeking to satisfy their consumers, they need to differentiate themselves from large retailers.[5] Here are several possible avenues not just to survival but to success:

- Serving a segment of consumers whose desires—say, very convenient location or abundant personal service—can be met by a relatively small firm. Small outlets located near residential areas offer a form of convenience that causes some shoppers to overlook somewhat higher prices. A member of the Hopi Nation encourages visitors to her art gallery in Tucson, Arizona, to browse a little longer by providing them with home-prepared Native American finger foods.

- Offering highly distinctive and, if possible, exclusive merchandise.

TABLE 15.1 · Total Sales of 10 Largest Retailers Based in the United States

Retailer	2004 Sales (billions)	% Change in Sales, 2003–2004	2004 Net Profit as % of Sales
1. Wal-Mart	$288	+ 11	3.6
2. Home Depot	73	+ 13	6.8
3. Kroger	56	+ 5	(0.2)
4. Costco	47	+ 11	1.9
5. Target	47	−3	6.8
6. Albertsons	40	+14	1.1
7. Walgreens	38	+15	3.6
8. Lowe's	36	+18	6.0
9. Sears	36	−12	(1.4)
10. Safeway	36	+ 1	1.6
Total	$697		
Average for top 10 firms		+ 7.3	3.0

Note: In some cases, total sales may include nonretail revenues. In 2004, both Kroger and Sears had a loss rather than a profit. In 2004, Sears was acquired by Kmart, and Target sold its Marshall Field's and Mervyn's divisions.

Source: "Top 100 Retailers," *Stores,* July 2005, p. S5.

TABLE 15.2 · Competitive Positions of Large and Small Retailers

Selected Bases for Evaluation	Who Has the Advantage?
Division of labor and specialization of management	Large-scale retailers—their biggest advantage.
Flexibility of operations—merchandise selection, services offered, store design, reflection of owner's personality	Small retailers—their biggest advantage.
Buying power	Large retailers buy in bigger quantities and thus get lower wholesale prices.
Access to desirable merchandise	Large retailers promise suppliers access to large numbers of customers, whereas a single small retailer may be viewed as insignificant.
Development and promotion of retailer's own brand	Large retailers.
Efficient use of advertising, especially in citywide media	Large retailers' markets match better with media circulation.
Ability to provide top-quality personal service	Small retailers, if owners pay personal attention to customers and also to selecting and supervising sales staff.
Opportunity to experiment with new products and selling methods	Large retailers can better afford the risks.
Financial strength	Large retailers have resources to gain some of the advantages noted above (such as private brands and experimentation).
Public image	Small retailers enjoy public support and sympathy. However, the public often votes with its wallet by shopping at big stores.

- Trying different forms of promotion, ranging from e-mails to in-store receptions, to determine the best way to reach the store's target market in a cost-effective manner.
- Forming or joining a contractual vertical marketing system to gain some of the advantages of large stores, such as specialized management, buying power, and a well-known name.

Operating Expenses and Profits

According to the latest available data, total operating expenses for retailers are about 28% of retail sales. In comparison, wholesaling expenses run about 11% of *wholesale* sales or 8% of *retail* sales.[6] Thus, roughly speaking, retailing costs are about 2½ times the costs of wholesaling when both are stated as a percentage of the sales of the specific type of middleman.

Higher retailing costs are the result of dealing directly with ultimate consumers—answering their questions, showing them different products, and so on. Compared to wholesale customers, ultimate consumers typically expect more convenient locations with nicer décor, both of which drive up retailers' costs. Also, relative to wholesalers, retailers typically have lower total sales and lower rates of merchandise turnover. Retailers buy smaller quantities of merchandise, again compared to wholesalers, so their overhead costs are spread over a smaller base of operations. Furthermore, retail sales people often cannot be used efficiently because customers do not come into stores at a steady rate.

Retailers' costs and profits vary depending on their type of operation and major product line. Assorted kinds of retailers earn wide-ranging gross margins—the difference between net sales and cost of goods sold. For instance, gross margins for auto dealers and gasoline service stations are in the vicinity of 15%, whereas margins for retailers of clothing, shoes, and jewelry are around 40%.

Healthy gross margins do not necessarily translate into high levels of net profits. Some retailers have large gross margins but incur heavy operating expenses, resulting in meager profits. Conversely, other retailers with small gross margins are able to serve customers well with low operating expenses, thereby winding up with substantial net profits. For example, e-tailers have substituted new technology for physical stores and, to a large extent, for retail sales people. As a result, online stores should have lower operating expenses compared to traditional stores, if they can (1) reach a point where they do not have to advertise very heavily in order to attract customers and (2) handle the fulfillment of orders in an efficient manner.

Just as retail firms' gross margins range widely, so do their net profits. Supermarkets typically earn a profit of about 1% of sales, compared to as much as 10% for some specialized retailers. In general, retailers' net profits average 2% to 3% of sales. This modest figure may surprise people who suspect that retailers make enormous profits.

Physical Facilities

Later in this chapter we will classify retailers according to their product assortments, price strategies, and promotional methods. Here, we'll look at **physical facilities**, which represent the distribution element of a retailer's marketing mix.

Some firms engage in *nonstore* retailing by selling through catalogs or online, for example, but many more firms rely on retail *stores*. Retailers that operate physical (or bricks-and-mortar) stores must consider four aspects of physical facilities:

- *Location.* It is frequently stated that there are three keys to success in retailing: location, location, and location! Although overstated, this axiom does underscore that a store's site should be the first decision made about facilities. Considerations such as surrounding population, traffic, and cost determine where a store should be located.

www.7-eleven.com

- *Size.* This factor refers to the total square footage of the physical store, not the magnitude of the firm operating it. A firm may be quite large with respect to total sales, but each of its outlets may be only several thousand square feet in size. Even though a 7-Eleven store is quite small, the more than 21,000 of them around the globe ring up over $40 billion in annual sales.[7]
- *Design.* This factor refers to a store's appearance, both exterior and interior. As with the other aspects of facilities, there are guidelines for effective design, including clear sight lines, visual attractions to draw shoppers into and around the store, and bold, informative signage.[8]
- *Layout.* The amount of space allocated to various product lines, specific locations of products, and a floor plan of display tables and racks comprise the store's layout.

As would be expected, the location, size, design, and layout of retail stores are based on where consumers live and how they like to go about their shopping. Consequently, the bulk of retail sales occur in urban, rather than rural, areas. And in urban areas, suburban shopping areas have become dominant, whereas many downtown areas have declined.

Shopping centers are the principal type of retail location in most suburban areas. A **shopping center** consists of a planned grouping of retail stores that lease space in a structure that is typically owned by a single organization. Shopping centers can be classified by such attributes as size, market served, and types of tenants. In order of increasing size, there is the *convenience center, neighborhood center, lifestyle center, power center,* and *regional center.*

ww5.williams-sonoma.com

A life-style center combines the feel of a village square with fountains and extensive landscaping and a collection of retail stores (such as Talbots and Williams-Sonoma) that are well known and appeal to upscale shoppers. The number of lifestyle centers is growing steadily. The distinguishing attribute of a power center is a tenant mix that includes several large, popular limited-line stores that stress value (such as Circuit City, Home Depot, and Toys "R" Us), and now sometimes a department store. The rise of power centers began in the early 1990s, subsided at the end of the decade, and has now picked up again.[9]

The largest kind of shopping center, a regional center, is anchored by one or more department stores and complemented by many smaller retail outlets. Typically, regional shopping centers are enclosed, climate-controlled, and huge. The biggest, the Mall of America in suburban Minneapolis, opened in 1992. Under one roof, it combines over 500 retail stores with several entertainment areas, two lakes, 50 restaurants, and more than a dozen movie screens—all adjacent to 12,500 free parking spaces. This "megamall" draws over 40 million shoppers and tourists annually, and most retailers with stores there are generating satisfactory levels of sales. A $1 billion expansion of the Mall, nearly doubling its size with more stores and restaurants and perhaps a casino, is targeted for a late-2007 completion.[10]

Starting in the mid-1950s, regional centers became the hub of shopping and social activities in many communities. Eventually, though, many shoppers grew too time conscious for extended shopping or socializing at a huge mall. From the early 1980s to the start of the new century, the average amount of time consumers spent in malls on a monthly basis dropped from 10 hours to under 4 hours.[11]

According to one estimate, regional malls' proportion of total retail sales has dropped from 40% in the early 1990s to 20% now. Some observers are pessimistic about the future of regional centers, especially those that are several decades old. A representative of the International Council of Shopping Centers admitted that the number of malls could fall from 1,200 to 900 over a period of several years. Older regional centers that are of medium size (400,000 to 800,000 square feet) and are located closer to downtown rather than in the suburbs are in the greatest jeopardy.[12]

Best Buy Co., the largest retailer of consumer electronics in the U.S., is known for its "big box" stores. In order to have a stronger appeal to certain market segments, it is experimenting with much smaller outlets, about 4,000 square feet. Studio D stores are intended to appeal to women who purchase cameras, music players, and personal computers. Escape outlets, sample pictured here, are intended to draw consumers who are interested in consumer electronics technology.

 www.bestbuy.com

With such forecasts, it's understandable that relatively few regional centers are being built now. Instead, to enhance their appeal to shoppers, an emerging trend is to add space or use space abandoned by failed retailers such as Montgomery Ward for an open-air area. The mall owners seek to fill this space with the up-scale retailers that are "drawing cards" for life-style centers. Also, a number of successful large retailers that have relied on stand-alone locations or sites in power centers are opening stores either in or adjacent to enclosed malls. Target, Urban Outfitters, and even Costco are among the chains that are beginning to appear in regional centers. Other enclosed malls and often the space surrounding them are being revamped for mixed uses, combining retail stores, office space, and/or residential units.[13]

The growth of suburban shopping led to vacant stores and decreased retail sales in many downtown areas. Now some retail firms see opportunities in the urban core. For example, Ace Hardware, Sterling Optical, and Athlete's Foot have opened non-mall locations in urban neighborhoods. Some cities have worked to revitalize their downtown shopping districts. Enclosed shopping centers featuring distinctive designs, including Water Tower Place in Chicago, and new mixed-use projects, including Mizner Park in Boca Raton, Florida, are successful in some downtown areas.[14]

 www.shopwatertower. com

Wherever they are located, most retail stores grew larger and larger, perhaps because the overhead of operating a store doesn't vary much on the basis of size. Many outlets such as Sports Authority, Lowe's, and Best Buy are called "big boxes," alluding to their enormous sizes as well as their rather plain designs. Because some consumers do not want to devote the necessary time and energy to shop at very large stores, some chains are experimenting with smaller formats. For example, Wal-Mart has opened dozens of Neighborhood Markets, each about 43,000 square feet—approximately one-quarter the size of the chain's supercenters. Home Depot is also trying out a smaller format that is located in and merchandised for urban neighborhoods. Best Buy and Sony are experimenting with small boutiques, named Studio D and Sony Style stores, respectively.[15]

Classification of Retailers

We will classify retailers on two bases: form of ownership and marketing strategies. Any retail firm can be classified according to both bases. For example, Sears is a corporate chain of department stores with broad, relatively deep assortments, moderate prices, and levels of personal service that vary across departments. In contrast, a neighborhood paint store operates as an independent limited-line store that has narrow, relatively deep assortments, tries to avoid price competition, and provides extensive personal service.

Retailers Classified by Form of Ownership

The major forms of ownership in retailing are corporate chain, independent, and contractual vertical marketing system (VMS). The VMS category includes several different types.

Corporate Chains

A **corporate chain** is an organization of two or more centrally owned and centrally managed stores that generally handle the same lines of products. Three factors differentiate a chain from an independent store and the contractual form of VMS:

- Technically, two or more stores constitute a chain. Many small merchants that open several stores in shopping centers and newly populated areas do not think of themselves as chains, however. Perhaps with that in mind, the U.S. Bureau of the Census considers 11 stores to be the minimum size for a chain.

- A corporate chain has central ownership; as we'll see soon, a contractual VMS does not.

- Because of centralized management, individual units in a chain typically have little autonomy. Strategic decisions are made at headquarters, and operations typically are standardized for all the units in a chain. Standardization assures consistency, but it often results in inflexibility. And that means a chain sometimes cannot adjust rapidly to local market conditions.

Corporate chains are tremendously significant in retailing, accounting for about 40% of total retail trade. Chains are especially prevalent in the department store business, but are less common among auto and home supply stores or eating places.[16] Essentially, chains are large-scale retail institutions. As such, they possess the comparative strengths and weaknesses outlined in Table 15.2.

Independent Stores

An **independent retailer** is a company with a single store that is not affiliated with a contractual vertical marketing system. Most retailers are independents, and most independents are quite small. Independents usually have the characteristics of small retailers presented in Table 15.2.

Independent retailers typically are viewed as having higher prices than chain stores. However, because of differences in merchandise and services, it is difficult to compare the prices of chains and independents directly. For instance, chains often have their own private brands that are not sold by independents. Also, independents and chain stores frequently provide customers with different levels, and perhaps quality, of services. Many customers are willing to pay extra for services they consider valuable, such as credit, delivery, alterations, installation, a liberal return policy, and friendly, knowledgeable personal service.

Contractual Vertical Marketing Systems

In a **contractual vertical marketing system,** independently owned firms join together under a contract specifying how they will operate. The three types of contractual VMS are discussed below.

Retailer Cooperatives and Voluntary Chains
The main difference between these two types of systems is who organizes them. A **retailer cooperative** is formed by a group of small retailers that agree to establish and operate a wholesale

warehouse. In contrast, a **voluntary chain** is sponsored by a wholesaler that enters into a contract with interested retailers.

Historically these two forms of contractual VMS have been organized for defensive reasons—to enable independent retailers to compete effectively with large, strong chains. They do this by providing their retail members with volume buying power and management assistance in store layout, employee and management training programs, promotion, accounting, and inventory control systems.

Retailer cooperatives have large representatives in groceries (Certified Grocers) and hardware (True Value and Ace). Voluntary chains are prevalent only in the grocery field (IGA, SUPERVALU).

www.iga.com/aboutIGA/international.asp

Franchise Systems **Franchising** involves a continuing relationship in which a parent company provides management assistance and the right to use its trademark in return for payments from the owner of the individual business unit. The parent company is called a *franchisor*, whereas the owner of the unit is called a *franchisee*. The combination of franchisor and franchisees comprises a *franchise system*.

This type of contractual VMS is growing steadily, generating an estimated $1 *trillion* in annual sales and accounting for as much as two-fifths of all retail sales in the U.S. According to the International Franchise Association, about 320,000 retail units are affiliated with over 1,000 franchise systems.[17]

There are two kinds of franchising:

www.franchise.org

- **Product and trade name franchising.** Historically the dominant kind of product and trade name franchising is prevalent in the automobile (Ford, Honda) and

YOU MAKE THE DECISION

Would you buy a retail franchise?

Many products reach consumer markets through franchised retail outlets. Consider these examples:

Product Category	Sample Franchises
Fast food and other prepared food	McDonald's, Domino's, Subway, Popeyes.
Automotive repairs	Midas, Maaco, Mr. Transmission.
Clothing and footwear	Printwear Xpress, The Athlete's Foot.
Hair care	Fantastic Sams, Supercuts.
Groceries and other food products	7-Eleven, Candy Bouquet, Heavenly Ham.
Education programs	Sylvan Learning Center, Computertots.
Home decorating	Decorating Den, Stained Glass Overlay, Furniture Medic.

The total cost of buying a franchise varies greatly. As the following samples illustrate, some are inexpensive and others are steep. Of course, total start-up costs for "bricks-and-mortar" enterprises can vary widely depending upon whether or not the franchisee owns the physical facility.

Brand Name	Type of Franchise	Approximate Up-Front Franchise Fee	Approximate Total Start-Up Costs
Mr. Goodcents	Sandwiches and pasta	$12,500	$72,000–$183,000
A & W	Fast-food restaurant	$20,000–$50,000	$212,000–$1.4 million
Mr. Rooter	Sewer and drain cleaning	$22,500	$46,000–$120,000
Rainbow International	Indoor restoration and cleaning	Varies	$39,900–$90,300

Most, but certainly not all, franchise systems are successful. And, typically, franchisees work long hours to build sales and contain expenses in order to earn a reasonable profit.

If you were going to open a retail business, would you do it as an independent or would you purchase a franchise?

Sources: Financial data are drawn from www.franchiseadvantage.com and www.entrepreneur.com/franzone, both accesed on March 31, 2005.

petroleum (Chevron, Texaco) industries. It is a distribution agreement under which a supplier authorizes a dealer to sell a product line, using the parent company's trade name for promotional purposes. The franchisee agrees to buy from the franchisor and also to abide by specified policies. The focus in product and trade name franchising is on *what is sold*.

- **Business format franchising.** Much of franchising's growth and publicity over the past four decades has involved the business format kind (used by firms such as Taco Bell, Midas, and H&R Block). This kind of franchising covers an entire method (or format) for operating a business. A successful retail business sells the right to operate the same business in another geographic area. The franchisee expects to receive from the parent company a proven method of operating a business; in return, the franchisor receives from each business owner payments and also conformance to policies and standards. The focus here is on *how the business is run*.

Selling franchises can be attractive to a successful retail business that wants to expand. The advantages include:

www.berlitz.us/
aboutberlitz/franchising

- Rapid expansion is expedited, because franchisees provide capital when they purchase franchises. Ambitious, successful retailers and service firms, such as Berlitz in language training, are employing franchising as an offensive tool.
- Because they have an investment at risk, franchisees typically are highly motivated to work hard and adhere to the parent company's proven format.

Buying a franchise can offer protection to a prospective new retail store or to an independent store that faces stiff competition from chains. The benefits include:

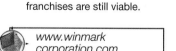
www.nestlecafe.com/
information

- Franchisees can use the parent company's well-known trade name, which should help attract customers. Nestlé's franchised cookie outlets should have good name recognition.
- Various forms of management assistance—including site-selection and store-layout guidance, technical and management training, promotional programs, and inventory control systems—are provided to franchisees prior to as well as after opening the business. Because of such aids, franchising has been referred to as "entrepreneurship with a safety net."[18]

Franchising is not without problems. Some franchisees criticize franchisors for practices such as the following: (1) not providing franchisees with the promised levels of business support; (2) locating too many of the company's outlets in the same market; or (3) unjustifiably terminating or not renewing the franchise agreement.

This franchisor, Winmark Corp., has applied its business format to the retailing of five different types of used goods. Computer Renaissance, which sold used computer equipment, is no longer offered by Winmark, but the other four franchises are still viable.

www.winmark
corporation.com

Some franchisees work long hours but do not earn an adequate return on their personal efforts or their financial investment. Even worse, a number of franchises that were based on poor products or unsound business practices have failed. Franchisors have their own complaints, notably that some franchisees deviate from the system's policies and practices.[19]

Despite some challenges, continued growth in franchising is expected. For one thing, 92% of existing franchisees consider themselves successful, a statistic that is widely publicized by franchisors. (Of course, this statistic ignores franchisees that fail.) Further, some franchisors are working more closely with their franchisees. GNC, for instance, accepted a franchisee's suggestion that smoothie bars be added to the vitamin and nutrition stores.[20]

Numerous products, especially services, lend themselves to franchising. Growth areas in franchising often coincide with demographic and social trends. At this time, therefore, services designed to aid either an aging population or time-starved individuals and families have potential as franchises. One such franchise is Home Instead, which provides companionship and assistance to senior citizens; another is House Doctors Handyman Service, which takes care of minor home repairs.[21]

www.homeinstead.com/
franchise_opp.asp

Retailers Classified by Marketing Strategies

Whatever its form of ownership, a retailer must develop marketing-mix strategies to succeed in its chosen target markets. In retailing, the marketing mix emphasizes product assortment, price, location, promotion, and customer services designed to aid in the sale of a product. Such services include credit, delivery, gift wrapping, product installation, merchandise returns, store hours, parking, and—very important—personal assistance.

Table 15.3 classifies retail stores on the basis of three elements of the marketing mix:

- Breadth and depth of product assortment.

TABLE 15.3 **Retail Stores Classified by Key Marketing Strategies**

Type of Store	Breadth and Depth of Assortment	Price Level	Amount of Customer Services
Department store	Very broad, deep	Avoids price competition	Wide array
Discount store	Broad, shallow	Emphasizes low prices	Relatively few
Limited-line store	Narrow, deep	Traditional types avoid price competition; new kinds emphasize low prices	Varies by type
Specialty store	Very narrow, deep	Avoids price competition	At least standard; extensive in some
Off-price retailer	Narrow, deep	Emphasizes low prices	Few
Category-killer store	Narrow, very deep	Emphasizes low prices	Few to moderate
Supermarket	Broad, deep	Some emphasize low prices; others avoid price competition	Few
Convenience store	Narrow, shallow	High prices	Few
Warehouse club	Very broad, very shallow	Emphasizes very low prices	Few (open only to members)

- Price level.
- Amount of customer services.

We will now consider, in very brief fashion, key factors associated with each type of retail store. There are examples of highly successful operations within each of these store types (none more successful than Wal-Mart in the category of discount stores). Likewise, other chains (Circuit City, for example) and some store types (department stores, for instance) are under severe competitive pressures and, as such, are modifying some strategies. You will see that certain retailers are similar to others because new or modified institutions have filled the "strategic gaps" that once separated different types of institutions.

Department Stores

www.fds.com/retail/index_macys.asp

Long a mainstay of retailing in the U.S., a **department store** seeks a differential advantage through a combination of distinctive, appealing merchandise and numerous customer services, such as alterations, credit plans, and bridal registry. Familiar department store names include Dillard's, Macy's, Sears, and JCPenney. Stores names that have disappeared or are likely to disappear in the near future for one reason or another are Bon Marche, Burdines, Rich's, Dayton's, Famous-Barr, Foley's, Hudson's, Lazarus, and perhaps Kmart.[22]

Some department store chains, notably Montgomery Ward, have gone out of business in recent years. There have also been significant consolidations and divestitures by department store chains. For instance, Kmart acquired Sears, Federated bought May, and Target sold two divisions (Marshall Field's and Mervyn's) in order to concentrate on its successful discount chain. The surviving chains face serious challenges. Because of their prime locations and abundant customer services, their operating expenses are considerably higher than most other retailers. Many producers' brands that used to be available exclusively through department stores are now widely distributed and available at discounted prices. And the quantity and sometimes the quality of sales help have diminished in many department stores.[23]

Other retail institutions, such as discount chains and category-killer stores, are aggressively trying to lure shoppers away from department stores by offering lower prices. The convenience of buying from catalogs or online represents still more competition. Department stores have been losing ground. For example, their share of apparel sales has been halved to 35% since the late 1980s.[24]

Striving to gain an advantage or at least remain competitive, many department stores are adjusting their strategies. Foremost, they want to differentiate themselves from both direct and indirect competitors. Typically that means offering more of their own store brands as well as some items that well-known manufacturers (e.g., Tommy Hilfiger) provide to a particular chain on an exclusive basis. Documenting this shift, JCPenney stores derive 40% of total sales from their brands.[25]

Despite their problems, department stores as a group still account for a huge amount of retail sales. Moreover, this type of institution has success stories, perhaps none more prominent than Kohl's. This rapidly growing chain is attracting customers through a combination of leading brands, convenient nonmall locations, customer-friendly store layout, relatively low prices, and very tight inventory control.[26]

www.kohls.com

Discount Stores

Discount retailing involves comparatively low prices as a major selling point combined with reduced costs of doing business. Several institutions, including off-price retailers and warehouse clubs, rely on discount retailing as their main marketing strategy.

The prime example of discount retailing is the **discount store**, a large-scale retail institution that normally carries a broad assortment of soft goods (particularly apparel)

Various manufacturers and retailers, ranging from Nike to Tommy Hilfiger, have opened huge "flagship" stores. This photo shows the interior of the 110,000-square-foot Toys "R" Us store in downtown New York that has, among other features, a 60-foot Ferris wheel. The toy retailer expects the store to generate favorable public relations *and* to be profitable. However, perhaps because of how costly they are to construct and operate, the success of retailers' flagship stores has been mixed.

  www.toysrus.com

and hard goods (including popular brands of appliances and home furnishings). Wal-Mart and Target are the largest discount chains. Kmart, the #3 discounter, has struggled mightily to develop a strong appeal to customers, so much so that hundreds of its outlets may wind up as Sears stores. In recent years, other discount chains with smaller stores, including Dollar General and Family Dollar, have been growing rapidly. Discount stores have had a major impact on retailing, causing many merchants to lower their prices.[27]

Wal-Mart and, to a lesser extent, Target are also committing substantial resources to a much expanded discount store, called a **supercenter**. Basically, it is a combined discount store and grocery store. Wal-Mart's more than 1,600 supercenters are different than discount stores in several noteworthy ways: larger size, wider aisles, more attractive decor, broader assortment of merchandise, and added customer services. A company executive surmised that all or most regular Wal-Mart stores could be supercenters in the future.[28]

Limited-Line Stores

Much of the "action" in retailing in recent years has been in **limited-line stores**, which typically sell products such as clothing, baked goods, and furniture and seek to maintain full, or nondiscounted, prices. New types of limited-line retailers have gained a foothold by emphasizing low prices.

The breadth of assortment varies somewhat across limited-line stores. A store may choose to concentrate on several related product lines (shoes, sportswear, and accessories), a single product line (shoes), or part of one product line (athletic footwear).

We identify limited-line stores by the name of the primary product line—furniture store, hardware store, or clothing store, for example. Some retailers such as grocery stores and drugstores that used to be limited-line stores now carry much broader assortments because of scrambled merchandising, a strategy described in the preceding chapter.

Specialty Stores

A **specialty store** concentrates on a particular product line (baked goods) or even part of a product line (cinnamon rolls). Examples of specialty stores are athletic footwear stores, meat markets, and dress shops. (Specialty *stores* should not be confused with specialty *goods*. In a sense, specialty stores are misnamed, because they may carry not just specialty goods but any of the categories of consumer goods that were discussed in Chapter 8.)

Most specialty stores strive to maintain manufacturers' suggested prices, although they may offer their own store brands at lower prices. The prosperity of specialty stores depends on their ability to attract and then satisfy consumers who especially want deep assortments and perhaps extensive, top-quality services as well.

www.batteriesplus.com/
aboutus.html

Successful specialty store chains include Discovery Channel Stores, which offer products that "help you explore your world and entertain your brain"; Batteries Plus, which specializes in various types of batteries; and the Old Navy clothing chain. Sunglass Hut International, which squeezes hundreds of different pairs of sunglasses into its tiny outlets, decided to add a complementary assortment of watches.[29]

www.containerstore.com

Forecasts for specialty stores are mixed. Many in malls are coping with a shrinking number of shoppers drawn to shopping centers. However, some theme-oriented specialty chains are prospering. For example, the Container Store's 30+ outlets are attracting numerous consumers who want to have "a place for everything."[30]

Off-Price Retailers

When some discount stores started to trade up during the 1980s, **off-price retailers** positioned themselves below discount stores with lower prices on selected product lines. Off-price retailers are most common in the areas of apparel (Ross Dress for Less, for example) and footwear (Payless ShoeSource).

www.payless.com/en-us/
corporate/company/
about.htm

To the extent possible, off-price retailers concentrate on well-known producers' brands. They often buy manufacturers' excess output, inventory remaining at the end of a fashion season, or irregular merchandise (called *seconds*) at lower-than-normal wholesale costs.

Factory outlets are a special type of off-price retailer. They usually sell a single company's merchandise. This type of institution gives manufacturers another channel for their products—one over which they have complete control. Many popular brands, such as Polo Ralph Lauren, Nike, Crate & Barrel, and Dansk, are featured in factory outlets.

A few of these stores are located adjacent to a company's manufacturing facility—hence, the name. However, typically they are grouped together in *outlet centers*, usually some distance from major malls and downtown shopping areas. Outlet centers grew rapidly from the inception of the concept in the early 1980s until the mid-1990s. At that time, some shoppers retreated from outlets because a growing number of retailers in regional shopping centers turned to value pricing. In the past 10 years, the number of outlet centers in the U.S. shrunk from 325 to about 225. Recently, some developers altered their outlet center strategies by adding more upscale brands (such as Prada and Chanel) as well as various amenities (such as valet parking and spacious restrooms) in order to attract more affluent consumers.[31]

Category-Killer Stores

A phenomenon of the 1980s, a **category-killer store** aims to capture a large portion of sales in a specific product category and, in so doing, "kill" the competition. What distinguishes a category killer is the combination of low prices *and* many different sizes, models, styles, and colors of the products. For example, a Borders or a Barnes & Noble bookstore ordinarily carries over 100,000 titles, perhaps 10 times the assortment of the typical mall bookstore.[32]

www.ikea-usa.com

Successful category killers include IKEA in home furnishings, Best Buy in consumer electronics, Home Depot and Lowe's in building supplies, and Bed Bath & Beyond in soft goods for the home. Other product areas with category killers are housewares, recorded music, and sporting goods. Category-killer stores take sales and customers away from long-standing retailers, especially specialty stores and department stores. The format has been extended to other products. For example, CarMax and AutoNation established "megastores" featuring very large inventories of used cars and trucks. However, AutoNation eventually closed its used-car megastores. Other category-killer chains have also stumbled; for instance, Jumbo Sports wound up in bankruptcy.[33]

Seeing the problems experienced by some category killers, one executive predicted that category killers "will be a diminishing force," mainly as a result of the size and effectiveness of large discount chains. Wal-Mart, in particular, is expanding its presence in various product categories where category killers have enjoyed success. Still, the combination of deep assortments and low prices offered by category killers is appealing to many consumers.[34]

Supermarkets

As with *discount*, the word *supermarket* can be used to describe a method of retailing *and* a type of institution. As a method, **supermarket retailing** features several related product lines, a high degree of self-service, largely centralized checkout, and competitive prices. Supermarket retailing is used to sell various kinds of merchandise, including building materials, office products, and especially groceries.

As a type of institution, a **supermarket** offers a moderately broad, moderately deep product assortment spanning groceries and some nonfood lines. Some supermarkets use price *offensively*, featuring low prices to attract customers. Others use price *defensively*, relying on leader pricing to avoid a price disadvantage. Having very thin gross margins, supermarkets need high levels of inventory turnover to achieve satisfactory returns on invested capital.

www.albertsons.com/
abs_aboutalbertsons

A grocery shopper can choose among not only many brands of supermarkets (Publix, Safeway, Albertson's, and Kroger, to name several), but also various types of institutions (warehouse clubs, meat and fish markets, and convenience stores). Competition has intensified further, as Wal-Mart and, less so, Target have made major moves into grocery retailing, opening supercenters and/or regular-size supermarkets.[35]

Reacting to competitive pressures, some supermarkets cut costs and stressed low prices, offering more private brands and few customer services. Others expanded their store size and added more nonfood lines and groceries (ethnic foods, for example) attuned to a particular market area. They also added various service departments, including video rentals, delicatessens, financial institutions, and pharmacies. Loblaw dominates grocery retailing in Canada, with one differential advantage being wide-ranging supplementary services—to the point of putting a fitness club in one of its supermarkets.[36]

www.loblaws.com/en/
about_us.asp

Convenience Stores

To satisfy consumers' increasing desire for convenience, particularly in suburban areas, the **convenience store** emerged in the latter half of the past century. Besides selected groceries and nonfoods (especially beverages, snacks, and cigarettes), gasoline, fast foods, and selected services (such as car washes and automated teller machines) can be found in many convenience stores. Its label reflects the institution's appeal and explains how its higher prices are justified. Examples of convenience store chains are 7-Eleven, Circle K, and Convenient Food Mart.

Convenience stores compete to some extent with both supermarkets and fast-food restaurants. Furthermore, petroleum companies have modified most of their service stations by phasing out auto repairs and adding a convenience section and

www.circlek.com/
circlek/aboutus

The owner of a small independent bookstore runs short of best-sellers during the peak Christmas season. Obtaining more inventory from the store's normal supplier, a wholesaler in another city, takes several days. In the meanwhile, thousands of dollars of sales could be lost. A warehouse club about 5 miles from the bookstore carries a limited selection of books, and they are priced at about the bookstore's wholesale cost. By buying best sellers at the warehouse club, substituting new price stickers, and getting the books on the store's shelves within a couple of hours rather than several days, the independent bookstore builds sales during this critical selling period *and* satisfies its customers.

Considering that customers do not know the bookstore acquired some of its best-sellers from a warehouse club and then resold them, is this ethical business behavior on the part of the bookstore owner?

perhaps a fast-food counter as well. To mention a few examples, Arco has AM PM stores, Texaco has Star Marts, and Mobil is partnering with Blimpie Subs & Salads.

To boost their competitiveness, convenience stores have adjusted their marketing mixes. For example, the 7-Eleven chain added fresh foods, notably sandwiches, and has experimented with in-store kiosks for financial services and limited online purchases. Given the name of the institution, it's logical that convenience stores are trying to open outlets wherever consumers work, reside, or travel. Thus 7-Eleven's half-size stores are appearing in large office buildings, airports, and on campuses.[37]

Warehouse Clubs

An institution that has mushroomed since the mid-1980s, the **warehouse club,** is a combined retailing and wholesaling operation. Warehouse clubs are open only to members who pay an annual fee of about $25 to $50. Their target markets are small businesses (some purchasing merchandise for resale) and individual consumers.

A warehouse club carries about the same breadth of assortment as a large discount store, but in much less depth. It is housed in a warehouse-type building with tall metal display and storage racks. The primary advantage of a warehouse club is its extremely low prices. (Prices for household consumers typically are about 5% higher than prices offered to business members.) This institution has some drawbacks. To mention a couple, the clubs' assortments are limited and skewed toward large quantities and huge packages, and customers ordinarily must load their purchases in their vehicles.

www.bjs.com

The leading warehouse clubs are Costco, Sam's Club (owned by Wal-Mart), and BJ's Wholesale. As with other retail institutions, warehouse clubs continue to modify and refine their strategies. For example, Costco added "big ticket" items such as diamond engagement rings and its own Kirkland brand of appliances. In the words of a Costco executive, "We want to surprise people at every turn. Even if you don't buy the Waterford crystal, it makes an impact on you." Not surprisingly, Sam's followed suit, even offering fine wines.[38] (For an in-depth look at the competition among warehouse clubs, see the "Costco versus Sam's Club" case following Chapter 16.)

Nonstore Retailing

A large majority, about 80%, of retail transactions are made in stores. However, a growing volume of sales is taking place away from stores. Retailing activities resulting in transactions that occur away from a physical store is called **nonstore retailing.** It is estimated that sales volume through nonstore retailing is in the vicinity of

$700 billion annually.[39] On the basis of this figure, nonstore sales account for almost one-fifth of total retail trade.

We will consider five types of nonstore retailing: direct selling, telemarketing, automatic vending, online retailing, and direct marketing. (Rather than worrying about the confusing names, we suggest that you focus on the features and competition across the five types.) Each type may be used not just by retailers, but by other types of organizations as well.

Direct Selling

In the context of retailing, **direct selling** is defined as personal contact between a sales person and a consumer away from a store that results in a sale. Annual volume of retail direct selling in the U.S. is about $30 billion. These transactions were rung up by about 13 million independent sales people, only 10% of whom devote full time to direct selling. Direct selling is also widespread in Japan, which accounts for 29% of the worldwide volume of this form of nonstore retailing. The U.S. represents 32% of the total, and all other countries the rest.[40]

The two kinds of direct selling are door to door and party plan. This channel is particularly well suited for products that require extensive demonstration. Home/family care (such as cookware and cleaning products) and personal care (such as cosmetics and jewelry) account for the largest volumes of direct selling.[41] With so many women—more than one-half—now working outside the home, reps of direct-selling firms call on employees in the workplace or give sales parties at lunchtime in offices. However, some employers take a dim view of such selling in the workplace.

www.creativememories.
com/profile.asp

Many well-known companies, including Mary Kay, Amway, Shaklee, Pampered Chef, Creative Memories, and Longaberger, market diverse products through direct selling. Sometimes their ambitions prompt them to add other channels. Thus direct-selling veterans Avon and Tupperware decided to distribute their goods through retailers. However, the sales results were disappointing, so both Avon and Tupperware retreated from these channels, deciding to concentrate on direct selling instead.[42]

Direct selling has drawbacks. Commissions, paid when a sale is made, run as high as 50% of the retail price. Recruiting, training, motivating, and retaining sales people are difficult tasks. To counter occasional problems with high-pressure sales

The Pampered Chef, Ltd., markets a wide variety of kitchen tools using party-plan selling. Each year, independent sales reps hold over 1 million Pampered Chef "kitchen shows" in the homes of friends and neighbors to present the company's line of products, such as a measuring cup that has a built-in plunger to remove the contents. Using only direct selling, Pampered Chef rings up over $700 million in annual sales.

www.pamperedchef.com

tactics, nearly all states have "cooling off" laws that permit consumers to nullify a party-plan or door-to-door sale within several days of the transaction.

Direct selling also offers significant benefits. Consumers can buy at home or at another convenient nonstore location that provides the opportunity for personal contact with a sales person. For the seller, direct selling represents the boldest method of trying to persuade ultimate consumers to make a purchase.

Telemarketing

Sometimes called *telephone selling,* **telemarketing** refers to a sales person initiating contact with a prospective customer and closing a sale over the telephone. Products that can be bought without being seen are suitable for telemarketing. Examples are pest-control services, magazine subscriptions, credit cards, and athletic club memberships. One estimate places the total annual volume of telemarketing in the retail sector at about $275 billion.[43]

Telemarketing is not problem free. Often encountering hostile people on the other end of the line and experiencing many more rejections than closed sales, most telephone sales reps last just a short while in the job. Further, some telemarketers rely on questionable and/or unethical practices, such as implying that the call is for other than selling purposes. In addition, some telemarketing involves outright fraud—for example, attempts to obtain a person's credit card number for illegal use. It's estimated that such fraud costs consumers $40 *billion* annually.[44]

www.donotcall.gov

Both states and federal agencies have enacted rules to constrain telemarketers' activities. One rule, for instance, bans calls before 8 A.M. and after 9 P.M. Also, over 40 states have passed laws that prohibit many, but not all, telemarketers from calling residents who sign up for a "no-call" list. The Federal Trade Commission established a national no-call list, and more than 85 million consumers have registered since the opening date of June 27, 2003. These rules also empower government officials to seek stiff fines against violators. The Federal Trade Commission is pursuing and penalizing violators, such as a telemarketing firm and the two timeshare companies it represented.[45]

Despite these problems, telemarketing sales have increased in recent years. Fundamentally, some people appreciate the convenience of making a purchase by phone. The future of telemarketing is sure to be affected by the degree to which the problems are dealt with *and* by the surge of online retailing.

Automatic Vending

The sale of products through a machine with no personal contact between buyer and seller is called **automatic vending.** The appeal of vending is convenient purchase. Products sold by automatic vending are usually well-known brands of foods and beverages with a high rate of turnover. It's estimated that vending rings up approximately $40 billion in annual sales, which represents just over 1% of all retail trade.[46]

Vending machines can expand a firm's market by reaching customers where and when they cannot come to a store. Thus vending equipment is found almost everywhere. Automatic vending has high operating costs because of the need to replenish inventories frequently. The machines also require maintenance and repairs. These difficulties may hinder future growth.

Vending innovations give reason for some optimism, however. For starters, there is a continuing flow of new products for vending machines, including movie soundtracks (sold in theater lobbies), freshly squeezed orange juice, heatable diet dinners, office supplies, and even live bait for fishing. Vending machines that accept credit or debit cards or even charge a purchase to the customer's cell phone account are now in use. Technological advances also allow operators to monitor vending machines from a distance, thereby reducing the number (and lost revenues) of out-of-stock or out-of-order machines. The SmartMart, a convenience store that is fully automated (no sales staff), may be the ultimate vending machine. A customer can purchase gasoline and, using a color touch screen at the gas pump, buy any of 1,500 items normally found in a convenience store.[47]

Online Retailing

When an enterprise uses its website to offer products for sale and then individuals or organizations use their computers to make purchases from this company, the parties have engaged in *electronic transactions* (also called *online selling* or *Internet marketing*). Many electronic transactions involve two businesses, but this chapter focuses on sales by firms to ultimate consumers. Thus we are interested in **online retailing,** which consists of electronic transactions in which the purchaser is an ultimate consumer.

www.fogdog.com

Online retailing has attracted numerous new enterprises, such as Fogdog Sports, Buy.com, and Blue Nile. It has also drawn existing retailers, such as Nordstrom, Crate and Barrel, and PETsMART, into operating either on their own or in alliances with Internet firms. Not all retailers have embraced online selling, however. According to a study several years ago, only 45% of the leading bricks-and-mortar merchants allow shoppers to make online purchases. The overriding reason why some retailers do not add a clicks-and-modem option are the high costs of establishing a secure e-commerce site and then processing and shipping the orders.[48]

Some websites, especially those launched by general-merchandise retailers such as Wal-Mart and Target, feature broad assortments. Other Internet-only firms, notably Amazon.com, are using various methods to broaden their offerings. However, most e-tailers concentrate on one or two product categories that are often reflected in their names; wine.com, 1-800-flowers.com, and Furniture.com are several examples.

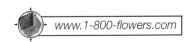
www.1-800-flowers.com

Whatever their differences, e-tailers are likely to share an attribute: They are not very profitable or, worse, are unprofitable. Gradually, the situation is improving. According to the latest available data, 70% of firms engaged in online retailing are generating a profit. However, the results vary based on the extent of online activities. Merchants that have other retail operations, such as catalogs or physical stores, are most likely to be profitable. Pure e-tailers (that is, online only) are unprofitable as a group. Of course, there are substantial costs in establishing an online operation. Aggressive efforts to attract shoppers and retain customers through extensive advertising and low prices are also expensive. Compared to five years ago, investors now expect e-tailers to deliver profits in the near term.[49]

Online retailing registered sales in the vicinity of $170 billion in 2005; travel purchased via the Internet accounts for more than one-third of the total. Online sales represented less than 1% of retail spending in 1999, but have climbed to somewhere between 3% (excluding travel) and 5% (including travel) now. Annual growth rates have been in the range of 20% to 50% for the past several years. Despite various challenges, this form of nonstore retailing is expected to grow rapidly and significantly for the foreseeable future.[50]

Which product categories are consumers most likely to buy on the Internet in the future? The categories in which online retailing accounts for the largest portions of total retail volume include books, music and videos, computer hardware and software, travel, toys, and consumer electronics. Of course, given that change on the Internet occurs at warp speed, these categories soon may be surpassed by others—perhaps health and beauty aids, auto parts, pet supplies, or even groceries.[51]

Direct Marketing

There is no consensus on the exact nature of direct marketing. In effect, it comprises all types of nonstore retailing other than direct selling, telemarketing, automatic vending, and online retailing. In the context of retailing, we define **direct marketing**

Have "bots" changed shopping and pricing on the Internet?

Many, probably most, consumers engage in comparison shopping—that is, searching for the lowest price on a particular item. Before the Internet, such comparisons required a store-to-store search or a series of price-checking telephone calls. With the advent of e-commerce, price comparisons became much easier. Still, moving from website to website and then locating the desired item and its price was somewhat time-consuming.

Online price comparisons became much easier when comparison-shopping engines made their debut in 1995. These shopping robots, nicknamed "bots," search the Web for a particular item and then furnish the interested consumer with a list of merchants who offer it, including the prices they charge. For example, within seconds, Shopzilla.com can examine several million products and a couple of thousand online merchants and furnish a shopper with a list of the best prices offered by reputable Internet firms for a specific item.

Bots are becoming increasingly popular and widespread. According to one survey, 85% of American shoppers use a bot at least some of the time they shop online; 8% use one every time. There are many competing bots now: PriceGrabber.com, mySimon, PriceScan.com, and Froogle (part of Google Inc.), to name several. Shopping robots are also increasingly common in other parts of the world. Examples include BuyCentral and Kelkoo (a Yahoo! company) in Europe.

Nothing's perfect, so shopping robots have some shortcomings:

- They don't automatically have access to every online merchant's prices. Some e-tailers have blocked bots from their sites because they are concerned about being forced into a price war with competitors.

- A few online merchants don't disclose hidden costs, such as shipping and handling, which are not always detected by a bot.

- To generate revenues, some bots give preferential, top-of-the-list placement to online merchants that pay a fee. Hence, the results may not be listed strictly according to price levels.

Shopping robots are important not just for e-tailers but also for physical stores. According to a consultant, "Seventy-five percent of American shoppers research a product online before purchasing offline." An AOL executive, commented, "We're now seeing sophisticated shoppers using . . . shopping search engines to find the best deals—whether that's online or off."

All factors considered, it appears that bots (and other factors) are forcing e-tailers and also traditional retailers to monitor and adjust their prices more frequently. As a professor stated, "After all, fixed prices have been around only for a couple hundred years."

Sources: Kavita Daswan, "E-tailing Strategies Still in Infancy," *WWD*, Mar. 9, 2005, p. 17B; Peter Lewis, "Holiday Shopping Beyond Compare," *Fortune*, Dec. 13, 2004, pp. 72+; "Online Holiday Spending Taking Bigger Share of Shrinking Budgets, America Online Survey Finds," *Business Wire*, Nov. 23, 2004, no page given; "According to BizRate.com, Comparison Shopping Bots Are Coming of Age," *Business Wire*, Mar. 14, 2002, no pages given; and Chris Taylor, "Bot till You Drop," *Time*, Oct. 11, 1999, pp. 52–53.

---

as using advertising to contact consumers who, in turn, buy products without visiting a retail store. (Be careful to distinguish among the terms direct *marketing*, direct *selling*, and direct *distribution*!) As denoted by the preceding section, we have chosen to treat online retailing, which involves computer contact, as a separate type of nonstore retailing.

Direct marketers reach consumers through one or more of the following media: radio, TV, newspapers, magazines, catalogs, and mailings (direct mail). Consumers order by telephone or mail. Some direct marketers offer a wide variety of product lines; others carry only one or two lines such as books or fresh fruit. Direct marketing is big business, accounting for over $200 billion in annual retail sales![52]

Under the broad definition, the many forms of direct marketing include:

- *Direct mail,* in which firms mail letters, brochures, and even product samples to consumers, and ask them to purchase by mail or telephone. This approach works best for selling various services, such as credit cards and athletic club memberships, and well-known goods, such as magazines and recorded music. The restrictions on telemarketing have given a boost to direct mail. Some small retailers use direct mail in creative ways. For example, Zane's Cycles, in Branford, Connecticut, sends postcards to selected customers offering a special price on a child's bike. This promotion is directed at customers who, according to the firm's database, purchased a baby seat for a bicycle three years earlier.[53]

- *Catalog retailing*, in which companies mail catalogs to consumers or make them available at retail stores. After expanding at an annual rate of 10% during the 1980s, the growth of catalog retailing flattened out during the first half of the 1990s but then picked up again. The number of catalogs distributed in the U.S. nearly doubled between 1980 and 2000, to about 15 *billion* each year, and now has leveled off at 17.5 billion. Recently, some companies have cut back on their assortment of catalogs, reduced the number of copies of each catalog they distribute, or even exited this field. An encouraging factor for catalog firms, however, is that some of their competencies, such as maintaining large customer databases and shipping small orders, transfer very well to online retailing.[54]

- *Televised shopping*, in which various categories of products are promoted on dedicated TV channels and through infomercials, which are TV commercials that run for 30 minutes or even longer on an entertainment channel. The leading shopping channels, QVC and the Home Shopping Network, sell jewelry, consumer electronics, home décor, and other products at relatively low prices. Infomercials have been used to sell various items, including cutlery and home-based businesses. Televised shopping burgeoned during the 1980s, but has slowed down in recent years as a result of the inroads made by online retailing. Thus it's not surprising that the two large shopping channels have established websites for consumer shopping and purchases.[55]

Direct marketing has drawbacks. Consumers must place orders without viewing or touching the actual merchandise (although they may see a picture of it). To offset this, direct marketers must offer liberal return policies. Furthermore, catalogs and, to some extent, direct-mail pieces are costly and must be prepared long before they are issued. Price changes and new products can be announced only through supplementary catalogs or brochures.

On the plus side, like other types of nonstore retailing, direct marketing provides shopping convenience. In addition, direct marketers enjoy comparatively low operating expenses because they do not have the overhead of physical stores. Direct marketing's future is difficult to forecast, given the rise of the Internet. The issue is whether or not firms relying on direct marketing can achieve and sustain a differential advantage in a growing competition with online enterprises.

Institutional Change in Retailing

As consumers change, so do forms of retailing. Executives would like to anticipate major changes before they occur. When the change is as revolutionary as the sudden, dramatic emergence of online retailing, that's difficult to do. However, evolutionary changes in retailing often follow a pattern in which an established institution trades up to attract a broader market and achieve higher margins. Sooner or later, high costs and, ultimately, high prices (as perceived by its target markets) make the institution vulnerable to new retail types, most likely a low-cost, low-price store.[56]

To illustrate, discount stores have been trading up recently. Target has been successful in becoming, as contradictory as it sounds, an "upscale discounter." If trading up by discount stores is pervasive, an opening may be created for a new low-cost, low-price institution. Maybe that's already here, in the form of "deep" discounters such as Save-a-Lot (groceries) or Dollar General. Perhaps the gap is being filled by e-tailers such as Amazon.com, which continues to broaden its offerings while empha-

Are all retailers moving into foreign countries?

Considering that the large majority of retail firms are tiny, the simple answer is no. Most retailers are doing well to prosper in their own community, without thinking about global success.

Nevertheless, numerous firms based in the U.S. have expanded their retail operations into other countries. For instance, Tupperware's biggest market is Europe. Perhaps surprisingly, Wal-Mart has a relatively small international presence (nine nations) but grand global plans. The world's largest retailer and many other merchants from various countries have a keen interest in China, which is expected to have a $2.5 *trillion* retail market by 2010.

Conversely, many merchants from elsewhere have significant operations in the U.S. To mention two, Ahold, a Netherlands-based company, owns several American grocery chains (including Giant and Stop & Shop) and IKEA, a Swedish firm, has ambitious plans to expand its furniture outlets in this country. And 7-Eleven, the majority of which is owned by a Japanese firm, has over 5,000 stores in the U.S. and 22,000 more in other nations.

Of course, merchants can expand geographically without leaving their home base by engaging in e-tailing on the Internet. Thus, as retailers consider how to compete effectively against other retail types (department stores against category killers, for instance), what to do online, and what institutional changes are likely to occur, they also need to be aware of global challenges and opportunities.

Sources: *www.7-eleven.com/about/history.asp*, accessed on June 5, 2005; Clay Chandler, "The Great Wal-Mart of China," *Fortune*, July 25, 2005, pp. 104+. Dexter Roberts, "Let the Retail Wars Begin," *BusinessWeek*, Jan. 17, 2005, pp. 44–45; "Wal-Mart to Expand Its Presence in China with Store Openings," *The Wall Street Journal*, Nov. 3, 2004, p. B3; Andy Reinhardt, "E-Commerce Starts to Click," *BusinessWeek*, Aug. 26, 2002, p. 56; and Delbert Ellerton, "Joining the Party," *St. Louis Post-Dispatch*, July 21, 2002, pp. G20–G21.

sizing low prices, or Woot.com, which sells one product per day (from another firm's excess inventory) at a cut-rate price.[57]

How will retail institutions or, more broadly, retailing change during the next several years? Some analysts think that retailers have overbuilt and that a "shake-out" is likely to occur. Under this scenario, some large chains and numerous small independents would fail, and other retailers would be acquired by stronger firms. It has also been suggested that there will be further blending of physical stores and online retailing, a practice that is labeled "bricks and clicks." Many, perhaps most, conventional retail businesses are establishing their own websites as another avenue for sales. Further, some stores have installed or are experimenting with Internet-linked kiosks that allow shoppers to obtain more information about desired products or to order out-of-stock items.[58]

A clear trend is retailers using multiple methods to entice consumers. Merchants with physical stores are mailing out catalogs and adding transaction-capable websites. An Internet presence can be valuable even if a sale is not made. For instance, according to a Gartner Inc. study, a visit to the J. Crew website markedly increased the likelihood of the consumer going to a J. Crew physical store. Similarly, online enterprises are using catalogs and even telephone selling in addition to their Internet sites.[59]

Retail firms must identify and respond to significant trends that affect retailing. According to one study, six major trends (for instance, the growing number of households with nontraditional composition and the added information available to shoppers) have changed the nature of the consumer market. Retailers need to recognize and understand these trends and adapt their strategies in order to satisfy shoppers. In particular, companies in the retail arena will have to provide consumers with substantial value that takes into account not just price, but also the quality of products and the shopping experience.[60]

Summary

Retailing is the sale of goods and services to ultimate consumers for personal, nonbusiness use. Any institution (even a manufacturer) may engage in retailing, but a firm engaged primarily in retailing is called a retailer. Retailers serve as purchasing agents for consumers and as sales specialists for producers and wholesaling middlemen. They perform many specific activities, such as anticipating customers' wants, developing product assortments, and financing.

There are about 1.1 million retail firms in the U.S.; collectively they generated almost $3.5 trillion in sales during 2004. Most retail firms are small—either single stores or several stores under common ownership. Small retailers can survive, and even prosper, if they remain flexible and pay careful attention to personally serving customers' needs. Retailers' profits are usually a tiny fraction of sales, generally about 3%.

Besides making decisions about product, price, promotion, and customer services, retailers also must devise strategies related to physical facilities. Specific decisions concern location, size, design, and layout of the store. Downtown shopping areas declined as suburban shopping centers grew. Now regional shopping centers are feeling competitive pressures from many sources, including Internet firms.

Retailers can be classified by (1) form of ownership, including corporate chain, independent store, and various kinds of contractual vertical marketing systems (notably franchising), and (2) key marketing strategies. Types of retailers, distinguished according to product assortment, price levels, and customer service levels, include department stores, discount stores, limited-line stores (notably specialty stores, off-price retailers, and category-killer stores), supermarkets, convenience stores, and warehouse clubs. Mature institutions such as department stores and supermarkets face strong challenges from new competitors, particularly discount chains, category-killer stores in various product categories, and online retailers.

Although the large majority of retail sales are made in physical stores, as much as 20% occur away from stores. And this proportion is growing steadily. Five major forms of nonstore retailing are direct selling, telemarketing, automatic vending, online retailing, and direct marketing. Each type has advantages as well as drawbacks. Online retailing, in particular, is surging dramatically.

Retail owners and executives must try to anticipate changes in retail institutions. Often, evolutionary change begins when one type of institution begins to trade up. To succeed, retailers need to identify significant trends and ensure that they develop marketing strategies to satisfy consumers.

More about **Walgreens**

The Walgreen Company faces, and must deal with, three distinct forms of competition:

- *Other drugstore chains.* In fact, following its purchase of more than 1,250 Eckerd stores, CVS tops Walgreens in number of stores (but not annual sales) in the U.S. The two firms are head-to-head with regards to adding locations near their customers. Rite Aid, with over 3,000 stores, is rebounding from a difficult period, including an accounting scandal.

- *Mail-order pharmacies.* Some large employers' health plans require employees to purchase their so-called maintenance medications (e.g., cholesterol-reducing drugs) from mail-order suppliers. Given its size (and hence economic power), Walgreens may be able to reduce the impact of this threat, perhaps as a result of its legion of loyal customers demanding that they be able to fill their prescriptions for maintenance drugs at Walgreens.

- *The giant discount chains.* According to one industry analyst, "Their (Walgreens') biggest threat is Wal-Mart and Target stores." At last report, Wal-Mart's more than 3,100 pharmacies had climbed to #4 in terms of total pharmacy volume. As in most other product categories, it's a threatening presence.

Walgreens' chief executive, David Bernauer, believes (or hopes) that growing demand will offset the effect of competition, at least to some extent. In his words, "U.S. prescription sales are projected to more than double in just nine years." He also explained that pharmacy revenues are expected to double, from $200 billion to $400 billion in yearly sales, between 2003 and 2012. Thus Bernauer stated,

"Yes, mail service is growing. . . . But the reality is, there's plenty of business for both of us to grow."

Besides counting on a growing market, Walgreens is taking strategic steps of its own. For instance, the industry-leading chain has its own mail-order business, which generates annual sales of $1 billion. Further, Walgreens has introduced Advantage90, which allows customers to purchase a 90-day supply of maintenance prescriptions. This program has been well received by many health-plan sponsors, which have added it as an alternative to mail service.

To deal with competitors that rely on physical stores, Walgreens will continue to add stores at a rapid pace. Its efforts will concentrate on building market share in states where it already has a strong presence, notably California, Florida, Georgia, Illinois, and Texas. Can Walgreens continue to add stores at the rate of one per day? The firm's CEO pointed out, "In the past seven years, our nearest competitor has opened 300 net new stores. Walgreen Co. has opened up 2,400." And only two have had to close as a result of poor sales![61]

1. Taking into account assortment, price level, and amount of customer service, what type of store is Walgreens?
2. In relation to its competition:
   a. What is Walgreens' differential advantage?
   b. Does it have a differential *dis*advantage?
3. From a marketing standpoint, what else can/should Walgreens do to assure that its sales and profits continue to grow?

Key Terms and Concepts

Retailing (retail trade) (408)
Retailer (408)
Physical facilities (412)
Shopping center (413)
Corporate chain (415)
Independent retailer (415)
Contractual vertical marketing system (415)
Retailer cooperative (415)
Voluntary chain (416)
Franchising (416)

Product and trade name franchising (416)
Business format franchising (417)
Department store (419)
Discount retailing (419)
Discount store (419)
Supercenter (420)
Limited-line store (420)
Specialty store (421)
Off-price retailer (421)
Category-killer store (421)

Supermarket retailing (422)
Supermarket (422)
Convenience store (422)
Warehouse club (423)
Nonstore retailing (423)
Direct selling (424)
Telemarketing (425)
Automatic vending (425)
Online retailing (426)
Direct marketing (426)

Questions and Problems

1. In each of the following situations, is the seller a *retailer* and is the transaction a *retail sale*?
   a. Independent contractor selling lawn-care services door to door.
   b. Farmer selling produce door to door.
   c. Farmer selling produce at a roadside stand.
   d. Sporting goods store selling uniforms to a professional baseball team.
   e. Fogdog Sports selling running shoes online to a college student.
2. What recommendations would you offer to a department store chain for reducing retailing costs? What would you recommend to discount stores in this regard?

3. Support or refute the following statements, using facts and statistics where appropriate:
   a. "Retailing is typically small-scale business."
   b. "There is a high degree of concentration in retailing today; the giants control the field."
4. The ease of entry into retailing undoubtedly contributes to the high failure rate among retailers, which, in the view of some, creates economic waste. Should entry into retailing be restricted? If so, how could this be done?
5. Do you agree that there are three keys to success in retailing—location, location, and location? How do you reconcile this perspective with the fact that there is so much price competition in retailing at the present time?

6. What can specialty stores do to strengthen their competitive positions?

7. "The supermarket, with its operating expense ratio of 20%, is the most efficient institution in retailing today." Do you agree with this statement? In what ways might supermarkets further reduce their expenses?

8. "Direct selling is the most efficient form of retailing because it eliminates wholesalers and retail stores." Discuss.

9. What new retail institutions might we see in the future?

10. Of the types of retail stores discussed in the chapter, which ones do you think have been or would be most successful in foreign countries? Which ones have been or would be unsuccessful in other countries? Explain your answers.

Interactive Marketing Exercises

1. Arrange an interview with a small retailer. Discuss with this merchant the general competitive positions of small and large retailers, as covered in this chapter. Which, if any, of these points does the small retailer disagree with, and why? Also ask what courses of action this merchant takes to achieve or maintain a viable competitive position. Interview a second small retailer, ask the same questions, and compare your answers.

2. Choose two retail franchise systems, and send a letter or an e-mail to their headquarters requesting information that is provided to prospective purchasers of a franchise. (Local units of the franchise systems should be able to supply you with the headquarters' mailing addresses, or go to the International Franchise Association website, *www.franchise.org*, to obtain franchisors' names and addresses.) Once you have received the information, evaluate whether you would like to own either of these franchises. What criteria did you use in making this evaluation?

Chapter 16

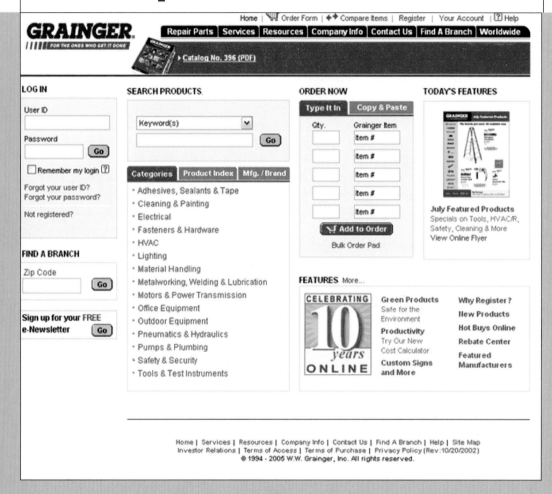

Wholesaling and Physical Distribution

Can **W. W. Grainger** Gain Share in a Fragmented Industry?

In 1927, Chicago businessman William Grainger saw that when a firm needed a replacement electric motor, the only option was to order one and wait days or even weeks for delivery. To solve the problem, Grainger started a wholesale business that stocked motors of different sizes. To advertise the motors, he distributed an eight-page catalog.

Now, W. W. Grainger, Inc., is a full-service wholesaler with a product mix of over 500,000 supplies and 2.5 million repair parts, 15,000 employees, 1.6 million customers, and annual revenues of $5 billion. The company has nine highly automated distribution centers and more than 400 branches that puts its products within 20 minutes of 70% of U.S. businesses.

Grainger has a narrow but deep product assortment, stocking 14 categories of maintenance, repair, and operations (MRO) products and reselling them to eight types of businesses and public-sector institutions. Its inventory includes hand and power tools, cleaning equipment, light bulbs, fasteners, and almost anything else that would be used to keep an organization running. Its customers range from factories to military bases to schools.

W. W. Grainger, Inc. is the largest wholesaler of MRO products, conducting almost 100,000 transactions a day. Grainger's value proposition is powerful: It reduces the search and processing costs for MRO items, allowing companies to order multiple items from a single distributor and pay one invoice.

Grainger's differential advantage has multiple dimensions, including an extensive assortment of products, availability of products at local facilities, a very efficient supply chain, and stellar customer service. To meet customers' expectations, Grainger created a "no excuses" guarantee. "It's the service that builds our brand and our national presence," said the company's head of marketing. "And that's why we've invested so heavily in multiple channels."

Grainger's channels (actually, methods of learning about the company's products and then placing orders) include:

- Telephone, which accounts for more than one-half of Grainger's orders.

- About 400 branch offices around the country.

- The Internet, which allows customers to search the company's website to locate thousands of items by product category, description, or manufacturer.

- A massive catalog, available in printed (3,700-page) format and on CD-ROM, which shows nearly 100,000 items.

Grainger's sales slipped during the recent economic slowdown. Now, with rising revenues again, the company has a tremendous opportunity in the MRO market, which represents $100 *billion* in annual volume. About 100,000 relatively small firms sell MRO products. According to Grainger's chief executive, "We have a small share of a large, fragmented market and more going for us than any of our competitors."

To build its market share, Grainger launched a four-year expansion program in the top 25 metropolitan areas in the U.S. To showcase seasonal and impulse-purchase items, larger branches are being opened in major cities ranging from Seattle to Miami. The initial impact will be adverse because of expansion costs; however, Grainger expects the augmented network of branches to improve profit by $30 million annually by 2008.

W. W. Grainger, Inc. is not ignoring international opportunities. In fact, the firm serves customers in over 125 countries, including around 170 branches in Mexico and Canada. And the wholesaler is beginning to move into China, where the market potential for MRO products is about $30 *billion* annually.[1]

What else should Grainger do in the area of distribution in order to protect its position as a leading full-service wholesaler?

 www.grainger.com

Although consumers shop regularly at the stores of retailers, they rarely see the establishments of wholesaling middlemen such as W. W. Grainger. Beyond noticing transportation carriers such as trucks and trains, consumers have little exposure to how products actually are moved from the point of production to the point of final sale. As a result, wholesaling and physical distribution are too often ignored or misunderstood by consumers.

Nevertheless, wholesaling middlemen can be essential members of a distribution channel, and physical distribution is an integral aspect of marketing most goods. And with the rise of the Internet, all aspects of distribution are receiving more attention as online enterprises try to figure out how to procure merchandise for sale and then deliver it to customers after it is sold. This chapter will provide you with insight into how wholesale markets, wholesaling institutions, and physical distribution activities relate to marketing. After studying this chapter, you should be able to explain:

	Chapter Goals

- The nature and economic justification of wholesaling.
- The role of wholesaling middlemen in the distribution process.
- Differences across three categories of wholesaling middlemen.
- The services rendered by major types of merchant wholesalers, agent wholesaling middlemen, and manufacturers' sales facilities.
- The nature and purpose of physical distribution.
- The systems approach to physical distribution.
- How physical distribution can strengthen a marketing program and reduce marketing costs.
- The five subsystems within physical distribution: order processing, inventory control, inventory location and warehousing, materials handling, and transportation.

Nature and Importance of Wholesaling

Wholesaling and retailing enable what is produced to be purchased for consumption. We already know that retailing involves sales to ultimate consumers for their personal use. Now we'll examine the role of wholesaling in the marketing system.

Wholesaling and Wholesaling Middlemen

Wholesaling (or *wholesale trade*) is the sale, and all activities directly related to the sale, of goods and services to businesses and other organizations for (1) resale, (2) use in producing other goods or services, or (3) operating an organization. When a business firm sells shirts and blouses to a clothing store that intends to resell them to final consumers, this is wholesaling. When a mill sells flour to a large bakery for making bread and pastries, this is also a wholesale transaction. And when a firm sells uniforms to an organization for its employees to wear in carrying out their duties, this is wholesaling as well.

Sales made by one producer to another are wholesale transactions, and the selling producer is engaged in wholesaling. Likewise, a discount store is involved in wholesaling when it sells calculators and office supplies to a business firm. Thus wholesaling includes sales by any firm to any customer *except* an ultimate consumer who is buying for personal, nonbusiness use. From this perspective, all sales are either wholesale or retail transactions—distinguished only by the purchaser's intended use of the good or service.

In this chapter we will focus on firms engaged *primarily* in wholesaling. This type of company is called a **wholesaling middleman.** We will not focus on either retailers involved in occasional wholesale transactions or on manufacturers and farmers because they are engaged primarily in production rather than wholesaling. Keep in mind, then, that *wholesaling* is a business *activity* that can be carried out by various types of firms, whereas a *wholesaling middleman* is a business *institution* that concentrates on wholesaling.

Economic Justification for Wholesaling

Most manufacturers are small and specialized. They don't have the capital to maintain a sales force to contact the many retailers or final users that are or could be their customers. Even for manufacturers with sufficient capital, some products or lines generate such a small volume of sales that it would not be cost-effective to establish a sales force to sell them.

At the other end of the distribution channel, most retailers and final users buy in small quantities and have limited knowledge of the market and sources of supply. Thus there is often a gap between the seller (producer) and the buyer (retailer or final user).

A wholesaling middleman can fill this gap by providing services of value to manufacturers and/or retailers. For example, this type of middleman pools the orders of many retailers and/or final users, thereby creating a market for the small producer. At the same time, a wholesaling middleman selects various items from among many alternatives to form its product mix, thereby acting as a buying service for retailers and final users. Essentially, the activities of a wholesaling middleman create time, place, and/or possession utility.

www.pleion.com

Let's look at two situations, one specific and the other broad, to see how wholesaling middlemen serve producers and retailers. A manufacturer of modular office dividers, Pleion Corp., replaced most of its sales force with independent dealers. The switch allowed Pleion to expand into new regions quicker and halved the company's marketing expenses. Taking a broader perspective, there were numerous predictions that the rise of electronic commerce would harm distributors, perhaps even eliminate many of them. Thus far, many wholesaling middlemen are thriving by furnishing needed services to online enterprises. For instance, many e-tailers rely upon distributors to fulfill customers' orders.[2]

From a broad point of view, wholesaling brings to the distribution system the economies of skill, scale, and transactions:

- Wholesaling *skills* are efficiently concentrated in a relatively few hands. This saves the duplication of effort that would occur if many producers had to perform wholesaling functions themselves. For example, one wholesaler's warehouse in Memphis, Tennessee, saves many manufacturers from having to build their own warehouses to provide speedy service to customers in this area.

- Economies of *scale* result from the specialization of wholesaling middlemen performing functions that might otherwise require several small departments run by producing firms. Wholesalers typically can perform wholesaling functions more efficiently than can most manufacturers.

- *Transaction* economies come into play when retailers and/or wholesaling middlemen are situated between producers and their customers. Assume that four manufacturers want to sell to six retailers. As shown in Figure 16.1, *without* a middleman, there are 24 transactions; *with* one wholesaling middleman, the number of transactions is cut to 10. Four transactions occur when all the producers sell to the middleman, and another six occur when the middleman sells to all the retailers.

Size of the Wholesale Market

The total annual sales volume of wholesaling middlemen was nearly $4.4 *trillion* in 2002 (the year of the last published national census of wholesale trade). As shown in

FIGURE 16.1

**The Economy
of Transactions
in Wholesaling.**

Four producers each sell directly to six retailers, resulting in 24 transactions:

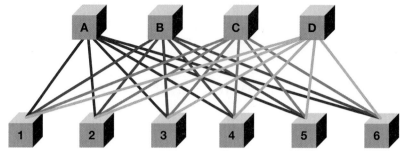

Four producers use the same wholesaling middleman, reducing the number of transactions to 10:

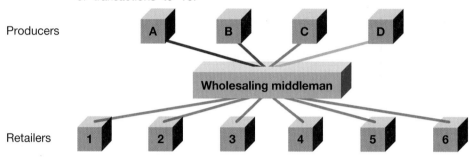

TABLE 16.1

Total Wholesale Trade versus Total Retail Trade in the United States

Total wholesale sales (in current dollars) increased only 8% between 1997 and 2002, and the number of wholesaling middlemen declined further. Compare these figures with the growth in retail sales over the same period.

Year	Number of Wholesaling Middlemen	Wholesale Sales (billions)	Retail Sales (billions)
2002	442,000	$4,379	$3,141
1997	453,000	4,060	2,456
1987	470,000	2,525	1,540
1977	383,000	1,258	723
1967	311,000	459	310

Sources: *Statistical Abstract of the United States: 2004–2005,* 124th ed., U.S. Bureau of the Census, Washington, DC, 2004, p. 654, *Annual Benchmark Report for Retail Trade and Food Services: January 1992 through February 2005,* U.S. Census Bureau, Washington, DC, 2005, pp. 4–5; *1997 Economic Census,* Retail Trade—Geographic Area Series, U.S. Census Bureau, Washington, DC, 2000, p. United States 7, *www.census.gov/prod/ec97/97r44-US.pdf;* and corresponding censuses from prior years.

Table 16.1 (above), this level of sales represents an increase of just 8% over 1997, which reflects the sluggish economy, but 850% over 1967. Even if the effects of inflation are taken into account, these figures still reflect a major increase in wholesale trade over the past several decades.

You might be surprised that total wholesale trade exceeds total retail trade by a wide margin. How can this be, especially considering that a product's retail price is higher than its wholesale price? We can find an explanation by considering the customers of wholesaling middlemen. About 75% of the sales of wholesaling middlemen are made to organizations *other than* retailers.[3] For example, some products sold to nonretailers are *business* goods (such as large printing presses or iron ore) that, by definition, are never sold at retail. Others may be *consumer* goods (such as groceries or toys) that are sold more than once at the wholesale level, with all such transactions counted as part of total wholesale trade. Thus total wholesale trade is greater than total retail trade because wholesale trade includes sales of business goods and successive sales of consumer goods at the wholesale level.

At last count, 442,000 wholesaling middlemen were conducting business in the U.S. According to Table 16.1, the number of such establishments rose substantially—by one-half, between 1967 and 1987 but has declined slightly since then. Despite the drop, these statistics document that wholesaling middlemen remain viable members of distribution channels.

Profile of Wholesaling Middlemen

A producer or a retailer considering the use of wholesaling middlemen must know what options are available, whom these middlemen serve, and how they operate.

Major Categories Wholesaling middlemen vary greatly in products carried, markets served, and methods of operation. We will discuss about 10 different types that fit into three categories developed by the U.S. Bureau of the Census (see Figure 16.2). Brief descriptions follow, with more details presented later in the chapter:

- A **merchant wholesaler** is an independently owned firm that engages primarily in wholesaling and takes title to (that is, owns) the products being distributed. Sometimes these firms are referred to simply as *wholesalers, jobbers,* or *industrial distributors.*[4] Merchant wholesalers form the largest segment of wholesaling firms when measured by either number of establishments or sales volume.

- An **agent wholesaling middleman** is an independently owned firm that engages primarily in wholesaling by actively negotiating the sale or purchase of products on behalf of other firms but that does *not* take title to the products being distributed.

- A **manufacturer's sales facility** is an establishment that engages primarily in wholesaling and is owned and operated by a manufacturer but is physically separated from manufacturing plants.[5] These facilities are common in fields ranging from major appliances to plumbing equipment to electrical supplies. The two major types are similar except in one important respect. A **manufacturer's sales**

FIGURE 16.2

Types of Wholesaling Institutions.

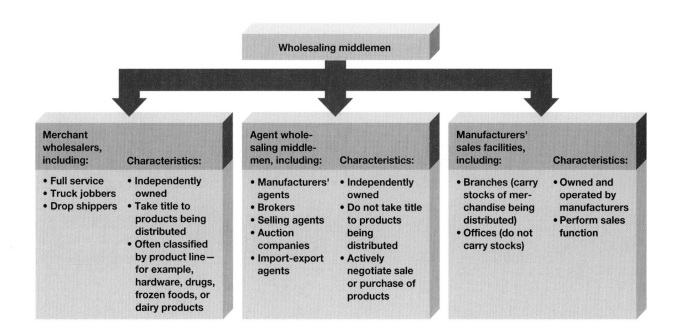

branch carries an inventory of the product being sold, but a **manufacturer's sales office** does not.

Although wholesaling middlemen are not part of every distribution channel, they are present in most. According to one survey, 32% of business goods manufacturers rely on merchant wholesalers. Another 42% use agent wholesaling middlemen, and the remaining 26% distribute their products directly (perhaps using sales branches or offices) to final customers.[6]

The statistics in Figure 16.3 (the latest available census data) indicate that merchant wholesalers account for the majority of sales made through wholesaling middlemen. Between 1967 and 1987, merchant wholesalers continually increased their share of wholesale trade, whereas the other two categories declined. Since then, agent wholesaling middlemen have taken a small amount of market share from merchant wholesalers.[7]

Operating Expenses and Profits

Total operating expenses for wholesaling middlemen average about 11% of *wholesale* sales; expenses for retailers run about 28% of *retail* sales. Therefore, generally speaking, the expenses of wholesaling middlemen take about 8% of the ultimate consumer's dollar.[8]

Operating expenses vary widely across categories of wholesaling middlemen:

- Merchant wholesalers have the highest average expenses, at 14% of sales. However, the range is wide. For example, expenses for wholesalers of a complete assortment of grocery products typically are below 10% of sales, compared with as much as 30% for office equipment wholesalers.

- Agent wholesaling middlemen have fairly low costs, around 4.5% of sales, largely because they do not have to carry inventories.

- The two types of manufacturers' sales facilities generally have much different cost structures. Sales offices' operating expenses are about 4% of sales; sales branches' expenses are around 11%, because of the costs incurred in storing merchandise.

We should not conclude that agent wholesaling middlemen are highly efficient and merchant wholesalers inefficient because of the disparity in their expenses. The differences in costs are partially traceable to differences in the services they provide. Also, because of factors such as perishability, value in relation to bulk, and special storage requirements, there are tremendous variations in the expenses connected with wholesaling various products. For example, jewelry has much higher value in relation to bulk than furniture, so this factor means lower storage costs for jewelry as a percentage of value. However, any savings on this factor might be offset by the added expenses of providing adequate security for jewelry in inventory.

Net operating profit expressed as a percent of net sales is rather modest for wholesaling middlemen and is considerably lower than for retailers (except for large grocery stores). On average, wholesaling profits are 1.5% of sales.[9]

Share of Wholesale Trade, by Category of Institution.

Sources: *1997 Economic Census,* Wholesale Trade, Geographic Area Series, U.S. Census Bureau, Washington, DC, 2000, p. United States 7, *www.census.gov/ prod/ec97/97w42.US.pdf*; and corresponding censuses from prior years.

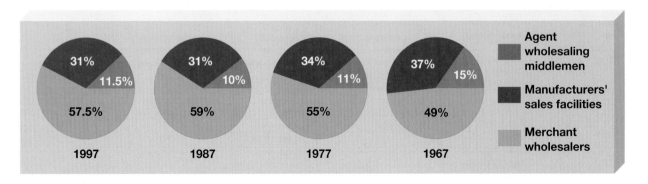

Merchant Wholesalers

Wholesaling middlemen that take title to products—that is, merchant wholesalers—are common in the marketing of both consumer goods and business goods. We'll examine several types next.

Full-Service Wholesalers

An independent merchant middleman that performs a full range of wholesaling functions is a **full-service wholesaler.** This type of middleman may handle consumer and/or business products that may be manufactured or nonmanufactured (such as grown or extracted) and are imported, exported, or made and sold domestically. W. W. Grainger, the subject of the chapter-opening case, is a prime example of a full-service wholesaler.

The forms of assistance offered by full-service wholesalers are summarized in Table 16.2. SUPERVALU Inc. illustrates how a full-service wholesaler operates. As the largest wholesaler of groceries and related products in the U.S., SUPERVALU helps independent grocery stores remain viable by providing them with the business tools that large grocery chains have. Supervalu's services include construction, design, and equipment services for grocery stores, advertising support, and three tiers of private brands.[10]

Manufacturers in various industries distribute their products directly, thereby eliminating wholesalers in their channels. Amana Refrigeration, a maker of home appliances, decided to deal directly with appliance retailers. Obviously, this action displeased many wholesalers that had carried the Amana line. On the international front, DTAC, a mobile phone company in Thailand, decided to reduce the number of wholesalers it used by 80% in order to communicate better with retailers and gain greater brand loyalty at the retail level.[11]

To remain competitive and boost profits, full-service wholesalers are striving to improve their operations. Three common avenues are enhanced quality, advanced technology, and value-added services. Distributors of semiconductor chips and related

www.supervalu.com

TABLE 16.2

Full-Service Wholesalers' Typical Services to Customers and to Producers

Service	Description
Buying	Act as purchasing agent for customers.
Creating assortments	Buy from many suppliers to develop an inventory that matches customers' needs.
Subdividing	Buy in large quantities (such as a truckload) and then resell in smaller quantities (such as a dozen).
Selling	Provide a sales force for producers to reach small retailers and other businesses at a lower cost than producers would incur by having their own sales forces.
Transportation	Make quick, frequent deliveries to customers, reducing customers' risks and investment in inventory.
Warehousing	Store products in facilities that are nearer customers' locations than are manufacturing plants.
Financing	Grant credit to customers, reducing their capital requirements. Aid producers by ordering and paying for products before purchase by customers.
Risk taking	Reduce a producer's risk by taking title to products.
Market information	Supply information to customers about new products and producers' special offers and to producer–suppliers about customers' needs and competitors' activities.
Management assistance	Assist customers, especially small retailers, in areas such as inventory control, allocation of shelf space, and financial management.

products, for example, assist manufacturers by doing some product assembly and providing inventory management and rapid delivery of orders.[12]

Partnerships between wholesalers and either producers or customers are increasingly common. Ordinarily, these arrangements represent the administered type of vertical marketing system (discussed in Chapter 14). To cite one example, Nabisco formed a partnership with a major customer, Wegmans Food Markets. Instead of Nabisco estimating the amount of, say, Planters cashews the grocery chain will need in an upcoming period, the two firms exchange sales forecasts via the Internet and then agree on a suitable order.[13]

Full-service wholesalers have held their own in competitive struggles with other forms of indirect distribution, including manufacturers' sales facilities and agent middlemen. As in many other industries, there is a strong belief that size matters. That is, a growing number of distributors believe they need to be bigger to maintain their competitive edge. Smaller wholesalers will have to decide whether they intend to acquire a competitor or a complementary firm, be acquired, or somehow insulate themselves from this trend, perhaps by serving small market niches.

Other Merchant Wholesalers

Two types of merchant wholesalers with distinctive operations also warrant brief description:

- A **truck jobber,** also called a *truck distributor,* carries a limited line of perishable products (such as candies, dairy products, or potato chips), and delivers them by truck to stores. Jobbers furnish fresh products so frequently that retailers can buy perishable goods in small amounts to minimize the risk of loss.

- A **drop shipper,** also known as a *desk jobber,* sells merchandise for delivery directly from the producer to the customer but does not physically handle the

On one hand, some retailers create tension in their distribution channels (and generate added revenues) by charging their suppliers fees for shelf space. On the other hand, retailers and their suppliers, such as Nabisco, often cooperate to feature and boost sales of certain items. The means of doing so range from special displays, shown here, to cooperative advertising.

 www.nabisco.com

product. Drop shippers are common in a few product categories, including coal, lumber, and building materials, that are typically sold in very large quantities and that have high freight costs in relation to their unit value.

Agent Wholesaling Middlemen

As distinguished from merchant wholesalers, agent wholesaling middlemen (1) do *not* take title to products and (2) typically perform fewer services. As shown in Table 16.3, product characteristics and market conditions determine whether a distribution channel should include agent or merchant wholesaling middlemen. For their assistance, agent middlemen receive a commission, which is a percentage of sales volume, to cover their expenses and to (hopefully) provide a profit. Commission rates vary from about 1% to 10%, depending mainly on the nature of the product and the services performed.

Agent wholesaling middlemen lost one-third of their share of wholesale trade between 1967 and 1987. In the case of agricultural products, agent middlemen were replaced by merchant wholesalers or by direct sales to food-processing companies and grocery stores. Likewise, for manufactured goods, agent middlemen were supplanted by merchant wholesalers or direct distribution. Since then, agents have fought back. In fact, their share of total wholesale trade grew between 1987 and 1997, the most recent year for which final census statistics are available.[14]

On the basis of sales volume, the most significant types of agent wholesaling middlemen are manufacturers' agents and brokers. Each is described next.

Manufacturers' Agents

www.rephunter.net

An independent agent wholesaling middleman that sells part or all of a manufacturer's product mix in an assigned geographic territory is a **manufacturers' agent**, or *manufacturers' representative*. According to census data, just under 30,000 manufacturers' reps operate in the U.S.[15] Agents are not employees of the manufacturers; they are independent business firms. Although technically independent, agents have little or no control over prices and terms of sale, which are established by the manufacturers they represent.

| TABLE 16.3 | **Factors Suggesting Suitable Type of Wholesaling Middlemen** | |

Factors	Favoring Agent Wholesaling Middlemen	Favoring Merchant Wholesalers
Nature of product	Nonstandard, perhaps made to order	Standard
Technicality of product	Simple	Complex
Product's gross margin	Small	Relatively large
Number of customers	Few	Many
Concentration of customers	Concentrated geographically and in a few industries	Dispersed geographically and in many industries
Frequency of ordering	Relatively infrequently	Frequently
Time between order and receipt of shipment	Customer satisfied with relatively long lead time	Customer requires or desires shorter lead time

Source: Adapted from Donald M. Jackson and Michael F. d'Amico, "Products and Markets Served by Distributors and Agents," *Industrial Marketing Management,* February 1989, pp. 27–33.

www.pioneer-research.com

Manufacturers' agents are used extensively in distributing many types of consumer and business goods, ranging from sporting goods to heating and air-conditioning vents and ductwork. Because a manufacturers' agent sells in a limited territory, each producer uses multiple agents to cover its total market. For example, Pioneer Research Inc., a New Jersey-based company that designs and markets binoculars and underwater cameras, uses 20 independent firms that give it a total of 60 sales reps.[16]

Manufacturers' agents have year-round relationships with the companies (often called *principals*) they represent. Each agent usually serves several noncompeting manufacturers of related products. For instance, a rep may specialize in toys and carry an assortment of noncompeting lines in dolls, learning materials, and outdoor play equipment.

Because a manufacturers' agent does not carry nearly as many lines as a full-service wholesaler, an agent can be expected to provide knowledgeable, aggressive selling. Manufacturers' agents are most helpful to:

- A small firm that has a limited number of products and no sales force.
- A business that wants to add a new, possibly unrelated line to its existing product mix, but its present sales force lacks familiarity with either the new line or the new market.
- A firm that wants to enter a new market that is not sufficiently developed to warrant the use of its own sales force.

www.manaonline.org

A manufacturers' agent can be cost-effective because its major expenses such as travel and lodging are spread over a number of manufacturers' lines. Also, because producers pay them a commission, reps are paid only for what they actually sell. Some agents operate on a commission as low as 2% of net sales, whereas others earn as much as 20%; the average is about 5%. Depending on how difficult the product is to sell and whether it is stocked by the agent, operating expenses of reps can vary greatly.[17]

There are limitations to what manufacturers' agents do. Agents *usually* do not carry an inventory of merchandise, do not install equipment, and are not equipped to furnish customers with repair service. However, to remain viable, manufacturers' reps are adding new services. Because they have direct contact with customers, some are able to assist their principals in developing new products. Others offer telemarketing and direct-mail programs. Perhaps most important, manufacturers' agents are the "eyes and ears" in local markets for their principals.[18]

Brokers

A **broker** is an independent agent wholesaling middleman that brings buyers and sellers together and provides market information to one party or the other. It furnishes information about many topics, including prices, products, and general market conditions. Some brokers do not physically handle the products being distributed; others provide warehousing services to the sellers they represent. In recent years, manufacturers' agents and brokers have become more similar with respect to attributes and services. In fact, in the groceries industry, what used to be a food broker is now referred to as a sales and marketing agency.

www.fsmaonline.com

Most brokers work for sellers, although some represent buyers. Brokers are used in selling real estate and securities, but they are most prevalent in the food field. For example, a seafood broker handles the output from a salmon cannery, which operates only about three months each year. The canner employs a broker to find buyers among retail stores, wholesalers, and other institutions such as government agencies.

Brokers have no authority to set prices. They simply negotiate a sale and leave it up to the seller to accept or reject the buyer's offer. Brokers receive relatively small commissions, with the average being 3.5%.[19]

Established by leading retailers around the world, GlobalNetXchange (GNX) is an electronic marketplace. Through a Web browser, GNX facilitates transactions between retailers and suppliers; GNX also provides support services, such as promotion management software. Recognizing global opportunities, the GNX website offers eight language options, with this version being in Spanish.

www.gnx.com

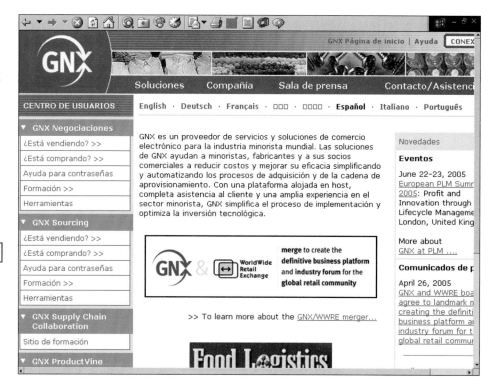

Other Agent Wholesaling Middlemen

Three additional types of agent wholesaling middlemen account for small shares of wholesale trade. Nevertheless, they are very important for certain products and in specific markets. These middlemen are:

- A **selling agent** essentially substitutes for a marketing department by marketing a manufacturer's entire output. Selling agents play a key role in distributing textile products and coal and, to a lesser extent, apparel, food, lumber, and metal products.

- An **auction company** helps assembled buyers and sellers complete their transactions. Traditional auction companies provide auctioneers who do the selling, and physical facilities for displaying the sellers' products. This type of auction company is extremely important in the wholesaling of used cars and certain agricultural products such as tobacco, livestock, and fruit. In the mid-1990s, Internet-based auction companies started to appear, providing a website at which sellers offer products for sale and both consumers and organizations search for bargains or rare products. Now, according to one source, there are 2,500 Internet-based auction sites, including Liquidation.com, DoveBid, Alibaba.com, and others focused on business markets.[20]

www.dovebid.com

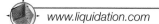

www.liquidation.com

- An **import-export agent** brings together sellers and buyers from different countries. Export agents work in the country in which the product is made; import agents are based in the country where the product will be sold.

Nature and Importance of Physical Distribution

After a company establishes its channels of distribution, it must arrange for actually moving its tangible products through these channels. **Physical distribution,** which we use synonymously with *logistics*, consists of all activities involved in moving the right amount of the right products to the right place at the right time. According to various estimates, total annual spending on logistics is about $1 *trillion* in the U.S.; worldwide, the total is approximately $2 trillion. For an individual firm, the cost of logistics can be equivalent to 10% to 15% of sales.[21]

In its full scope, physical distribution for manufacturers includes the flow of *raw materials* from their sources of supply to the production line *and* the movement of *finished goods* from the end of the production line to the final users' locations. Middlemen manage the flows of goods *onto* their shelves as well as *from* their shelves to customers' homes, stores, or other places of business.

The activities comprising physical distribution are order processing, inventory control, inventory location and warehousing, materials handling, and transportation. A decision regarding any one of these activities affects all the others. Location of a warehouse influences the selection of transportation methods and carriers; the choice of a carrier influences the optimum size of shipments.

Increasing Attention to Physical Distribution

As described in one article, "Virtually the entire economy depends on the arcane and complex science of logistics to get billions of parts and supplies into U.S. manufacturing plants on time and to distribute finished products efficiently to consumers."[22] Without effective logistics, a business is likely to have mismatches such as an out-of-stock part that shuts down an assembly line *or* a warehouse full of patio furniture in Atlanta but unsatisfied customers in New Orleans. These examples underscore that the appropriate assortment of products must be in the right place at the right time to maximize the opportunity for profitable sales. Further, the movement of goods from one place to another must be accomplished in a cost-effective manner.

Physical distribution is one area of marketing with substantial opportunities for cost cutting. And the potential savings are great. For some products, such as furniture and building materials, physical distribution represents the largest operating expense. Profits are paper-thin for many businesses, so any savings are appreciated. A supermarket, for instance, typically earns a net profit of about 1% of sales. Thus every $1 a supermarket saves in physical distribution costs has the same effect on profit as a $100 increase in sales!

Effective logistics also can be the basis by which a firm gains and sustains a differential advantage. On-time delivery, which requires competent physical distribution, can provide an edge. With that in mind, Sun Microsystems' unit in Asia is able to deliver replacement parts on time for 99.7% of all orders.[23]

MARKETING IN THE INFORMATION ECONOMY

Can the locations of over 63,000 truck tractors and trailers be pinpointed?

In years past, freight carriers often didn't know the locations of their equipment (trucks, railcars). As a result, carriers either could not inform customers about the status of their shipments or, at best, could do so only sometimes.

That has changed. Most transportation firms can pinpoint the locations of their equipment, and many monitor shipments on a real-time basis. Schneider National, based in Green Bay, Wisconsin, started this movement. Today Schneider, the largest trucking company, knows within 100 feet where all of its over 15,000 tractors (the front part of the truck that contains the engine) are at any time.

How is this done? A number of carriers have equipped their tractors with tracking devices and onboard computers that permit two-way communication between truck and company office through a satellite. Recently, Schneider decided to add similar devices to its 48,000 trailers. By doing so, it knows where they are even when they are not tethered to a tractor—in trailer staging areas or on railcars, for example. Tracking systems are also used by railroads and other modes of transportation.

Real-time monitoring pleases customers because they can know not only the precise location of a shipment but also its expected arrival time. A carrier benefits too. For instance, a tracking system helps a trucking company reroute rigs to avoid delays and locate empty trailers when extra capacity is needed. Such steps increase the efficiency of expensive transportation equipment. As a Schneider executive commented, "Most of the payback will come from greater asset utilization." Tracking both tractors and trailers could produce annual savings of $5 billion, according to one transportation consultant.

The investments in technology help in another important way. Drivers like having two-way communication capabilities in their rigs. In this time of driver shortages, trucking companies are competing not just to gain customers but also to attract and please prospective drivers.

Sources: Steve Timko, "Short-Staffed for the Long Haul," *Reno Gazette-Journal*, Feb. 22, 2005, no page given; Jim Mele, "And They're Off," *Fleet Owner*, January 2005, p. 6; "Schneider Buys Trailer-Tracking System," *Transport Topics*, Oct. 11, 2004, p. 57; and Wendy Leavitt, "Relocating the Edge," *Fleet Owner*, July 1999, p. 110.

www.landair.com

Opportunities to better satisfy customers, cut costs, and/or gain a competitive edge expanded greatly in 1980. During that year, two new federal laws (the Motor Carrier Act and the Staggers Act) completed the deregulation of marketing activities related to *interstate* transportation. Previously, pricing by railroads, airlines, and trucking companies had been subject to restrictive regulations. By the beginning of 1995, *intrastate* trucking was basically deregulated as well.

Following deregulation, transportation firms could decide which rates (prices) and levels of service would best satisfy their target markets. For example, Landair Transport Inc. gained recognition by promising ontime deliveries; in fact, 99% of its shipments arrived within 15 minutes of the scheduled time.[24] Deregulation also benefited shippers, who could shop around for rates and service levels that met their needs.

In the past several years, the surge of electronic commerce has underscored the importance of physical distribution. The challenge relates to **fulfillment,** which entails having the merchandise that is ordered by a customer in stock and then packing and shipping it in an efficient, timely manner. Manufacturers typically are adept at filling large orders for a small number of customers, and conventional retailers are used to shoppers coming to their bricks-and-mortar stores and then carrying home their purchases. However, many manufacturers and retailers that engage in e-commerce are encountering difficulties in filling and shipping small orders for a large number of customers.

Even purely Internet retailers "are discovering that if they don't control their own warehouses and shipping, their reliability ratings with customers can turn dismal." If there are problems with fulfillment, the likelihood of repeat purchases drops sharply. Some firms engaged in electronic commerce are doing their own fulfillment, but many—perhaps most—are outsourcing the fulfillment task to firms such as Lenmar and New Roads. Other distributors, such as Alliance Entertainment and GSI Commerce, serve as an **online category manager** by handling e-commerce fulfillment in a particular product area for manufacturers and conventional retailers.[25]

www.gsicommerce.com

Supply Chain Management

Occasionally we have referred to marketing as a *total system* of business activities rather than a series of fragmented operations. **Supply chain management** represents a total system perspective of distribution, combining distribution channels and physical distribution. The core of supply chain management (SCM) is coordinated logistics.

Traditionally, logistics activities were fragmented and, in many firms, they still are. If you ask, "Who's in charge of physical distribution?" the answer should not be "No one." Moreover, responsibility for it should not be delegated to units with conflicting goals. The production department, for instance, is interested primarily in long production runs to minimize unit manufacturing costs, even though the result may be high inventory costs. In contrast, the finance department wants a minimum of funds tied up in inventories. At the same time, the sales department wants to have a wide assortment of products available at locations near customers.

Uncoordinated conditions like these hamper a flow of products that satisfies the firm's goals. To alleviate this problem, a number of firms have established separate departments responsible for all logistics activities. Even when this occurs in large firms, physical distribution usually is separated from the marketing department. This separation causes problems when a company is trying to formulate and implement coordinated marketing strategies, including logistics. With supply chain management, individual logistics activities are brought together in a unified way. More and more, the Internet is being used to allow supply chain members to monitor—on a real-time bases—key factors such as the status of orders and inventory levels.[26]

The **total cost concept** is integral to effective supply chain management. A company should determine the set of activities that produces the best relationship between costs and profit for the *entire* physical distribution system. This approach is superior to focusing strictly on the separate costs of individual logistics activities.

Sometimes a company attempts to minimize the cost of only one aspect of physical distribution—transportation, for example. Management might be upset by the high fees for air freight. But the expense of this mode of transportation may be more than offset by savings from (1) lower inventory costs, (2) less insurance and interest expense, (3) lower crating costs, and (4) fewer lost sales because of out-of-stock conditions. The point is not that air freight is the best mode of transportation; which mode is best varies with the situation. The key point is that physical distribution should be viewed as a *total system,* with all related costs being analyzed.

Effective supply chain management can improve several aspects of performance. A consultant estimated that superior SCM can (1) improve on-time deliveries by about 20%, (2) reduce necessary inventory levels by about 50%, and (3) boost the firm's profits by an amount equal to 3% to 6% of sales. To cite a specific example, Autoliv, a Swedish company that produces auto-safety equipment, was able to reduce the hours needed to oversee vendors and to pare its inventory by 75% when it turned to Web-based management of its supply chain.[27]

www.chrobinson.com

As part of supply chain management, some companies are contracting out, or *outsourcing,* all or part their physical distribution function. According to a survey of executives involved in supply chain activities in 11 countries, over 75% of companies are outsourcing some of their physical distribution tasks. The growth of

Recognizing companies'
willingness to outsource
various logistics-related
activities, CNF Inc.
established Menlo Worldwide
in 2001. By offering contract
logistics and a variety of
other services such as order
fulfillment, packaging
assistance, and shipping
services, Menlo Worldwide
seeks to help its customers
attain operational excellence
and efficiency across their
global supply chains.

www.menloworldwide.
com

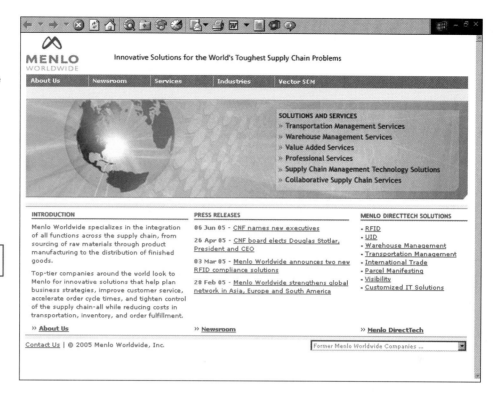

www.iwla.com

www.vector.
menloworldwide.com

contract logistics, also called *third-party logistics* or simply *3PL,* reflects a broad trend in the U.S. whereby firms are outsourcing various business tasks ranging from payroll to public relations. An independent firm that contracts to manage another company's entire supply chain is being called a *4PL,* which signifies it does even more than a 3PL provider.[28]

Contract logistics comprises at least an $80 billion business in the U.S. annually—five times its size in 1994—and has been on a steep growth curve. The logistics activities that are most often outsourced include management of warehouses and distribution centers, Web-based communications related to physical distribution, and transportation management.[29]

The scope of contract logistics becomes evident in the examination of a single industry, automobiles. In early 2000, Ford Motor Co. hired UPS to oversee movement of new cars from the end of the assembly line to dealer showrooms. General Motors Corp. went a big step further, forming a joint venture with CNF Inc., a transportation company, to handle all of GM's logistics activities.[30]

Companies are turning to contract logistics for essentially the same reasons they outsource other business tasks. Basically, by delegating one or more physical distribution tasks to a third party, a firm can concentrate on its core business (for example, producing power hand tools or fine lingerie). Further, it expects to be more effective (as indicated by greater customer satisfaction) and/or more efficient (as indicated by lower costs and greater return on investment) in the area of logistics.[31]

Strategic Use of Physical Distribution

Viewing and using physical distribution strategically may enable a company to strengthen its competitive position. The management of physical distribution can also affect a firm's marketing mix—particularly distribution channels. Each opportunity is described below.

Improve Customer Service
A well-run logistics system can improve the service a firm provides its customers, whether they are middlemen or ultimate users.

Further, the level of customer service directly affects demand. This is true especially in marketing undifferentiated products, such as chemicals and most building materials, where effective service may be a company's only differential advantage. For example, Batesville Casket is committed to delivering any one of 300 models to its funeral home customers within 48 hours.[32]

To ensure reliable customer service, management should set standards of performance for each subsystem of physical distribution. These standards should be quantitatively measurable. The goal of Fairchild Semiconductor, for instance, is to deliver 95% of its products directly from factories to customers within two days and 99% within three days.[33] Here are other hypothetical examples:

- *Sporting goods wholesaler:* Fill 99.5% of orders accurately, without increasing the size of the order-fulfillment staff.
- *Industrial distributor:* Fulfill at least 85% of orders received from inventory on hand, but maintain an inventory turnover ratio of 12 times per year.

Reduce Distribution Costs   Many avenues to cost reductions may be available through effective physical distribution management. For example, inventories—and their attendant carrying costs and capital investment—can be reduced through more accurate forecasting of demand for various goods. According to one report, a company with accurate demand forecasts can expect 5% higher profit margins and 15% less inventory than its competitors.[34]

When National Semiconductor applied the total cost concept, it committed to a major investment, building a distribution center in Singapore. The company decided that all computer chips assembled in East Asia would be shipped to this facility, sorted there, and then sent by air freight to customers around the world. National Semiconductor contracted with FedEx Corp. to manage this distribution process. Over a two-year period, logistics costs shrank from 2.6% to 1.9% of sales. On a sales base of a couple of *billion* dollars, that's a considerable savings.[35]

Create Time and Place Utilities   Storage, which is part of warehousing, creates *time utility* by correcting imbalances in the timing of production and consumption. An imbalance can occur when there is *year-round consumption* but only *seasonal production,* as in the case of agricultural products. For instance, time utility is created and value is added when apples are harvested and stored in the fall for sale and consumption months later. In other situations, warehousing helps adjust *year-round production* to *seasonal consumption.* A manufacturer may produce lawn mowers on a year-round basis; during the fall and winter, the mowers are stored for sale in the spring and summer.

Transportation adds value to products by creating *place utility*. A fine suit hanging on a manufacturer's rack in Hong Kong has less value than an identical suit ready for sale in a retailer's store in Baltimore. Transporting the suit from Hong Kong to Baltimore creates place utility and adds value to it.

Stabilize Prices   Careful management of warehousing and transportation can help stabilize prices for an individual firm or for an entire industry. If a market is temporarily glutted with a product, sellers can store it until supply and demand conditions are better balanced. This use of storage is common in the marketing of agricultural products and other seasonally produced goods.

The judicious movement of products from one market to another may enable a seller to (1) avoid a market with depressed prices or (2) take advantage of a market that has a supply shortfall and/or higher prices. If demand for heating oil is stronger in Akron, Ohio, than in Des Moines, Iowa, a producer should be able to achieve greater revenues by shifting some shipments from Des Moines to Akron.

Influence Channel Decisions

Decisions regarding inventory management have a direct bearing on a producer's selection of channels and the location of middlemen. Logistical considerations may become critical, for example, when a company decides to decentralize its inventory. In this case, management must determine (1) how many sites to establish and (2) whether to use wholesalers, the company's own warehouses, or public warehouses. One producer may select merchant wholesalers that perform storage and other warehousing services. Another may prefer to use a combination of manufacturers' agents for aggressive selling and public warehouses for assembling and shipping orders.

Control Shipping Costs

Managers with shipping responsibilities need to ensure that their companies enjoy the best combination of delivery times *and* shipping rates for whatever methods of transportation they deem to use. The pricing of transportation services is one of the most complicated parts of American business. The rate (or tariff) schedule is the carrier's price list; typically it is complex. To cite one example, shipping rates vary for different types of goods, depending on many factors including not only distance to the destination but also the bulk and weight of the products. Therefore, being able to interpret a tariff schedule properly is a money-saving skill for a manager with shipping responsibilities.

Tasks in Physical Distribution Management

Physical distribution refers to the actual physical flow of products. In contrast, **physical distribution management** is the development and operation of processes resulting in the effective and efficient physical flow of products.

Irrespective of whether a firm handles physical distribution on its own or partners with one or more other firms to carry out this function, effective physical distribution management requires careful attention to five interrelated activities:

- Order processing
- Inventory control
- Inventory location and warehousing
- Materials handling
- Transportation

Each of these activities must be carefully coordinated with the others.

Order Processing

The starting point in a physical distribution system is *order processing*, which is a set of procedures for receiving, handling, and filling orders promptly and accurately. This activity should include provisions for billing, granting credit, preparing invoices, and collecting past-due accounts. Customer ill will results if a company makes mistakes or is slow in filling orders. In addition, inefficient order processing can lead to excessive inventories. That's why virtually all firms rely on computers to execute most of their order-processing activities. At the same time, some suppliers provide customers with computer technology to use in placing orders.

There have been various technology-facilitated advances in order processing. One of the more notable is **electronic data interchange (EDI)**, in which orders, invoices, and perhaps other business information are transmitted by computer rather than by mail. As such, EDI speeds up the process and markedly reduces paperwork.

Originally, EDI required a direct computer link between supplier and customer. Now EDI is being conducted via the Internet, which has lowered the costs of the process and, in turn, expanded the number of firms that can transmit orders and other information electronically. For instance, many small retailers are using e-mail to place orders with suppliers. At the other end of the size spectrum, Wal-Mart has stipulated that all of its suppliers use the Internet for EDI.[36]

Some of the largest manufacturers, led by automakers, want to use the Internet for virtually all of their purchasing. In 2000, several automakers established an Internet-based enterprise named Covisint for parts procurement, supply chain management, and other purposes. However, suppliers to the automotive industry saw Covisint as a device for driving down prices and thus resisted using it.[37]

Electronic data interchange can trim the cost of order processing significantly, which in turn may reduce purchase prices. Companies can create their own EDI systems, or they can turn to companies such as Global Exchange Services or Perfect Commerce for EDI software and support. Data exchanges can occur in the original manner, namely through private computer networks, or via the Internet (with appropriate security measures). Despite predictions that it was a dinosaur headed toward extinction, EDI in modified form is growing in usage.[38]

Inventory Control

Managing the size and composition of inventories, which represent a sizable investment for most companies, is essential to any physical distribution system. The goal of *inventory control* is to satisfy the order-fulfillment expectations of customers while minimizing both the investment and fluctuations in inventories.

Customer-Service Requirements

Inventory size is determined by balancing costs and desired levels of customer service. Different customers have varying needs regarding order fulfillment. In today's acutely competitive environment, most individuals or organizations expect the order to be filled, accurately and completely, almost immediately. The rare customer is one who is less demanding and will accept an occasional out-of-stock item or a slight delay in receiving an order. Management must identify and respond to differences in expected levels of customer service.

When a company knows its customers' expectations regarding order fulfillment, it then must decide what percentage of orders it intends to fill promptly from inventory on hand. Out-of-stock conditions result in lost sales, erosion of goodwill, even departure of customers. Yet to be able to fill 100% of orders promptly may require a large and costly inventory, which ties up more of the company's financial resources.

Economic Order Quantity

Management must establish the optimal quantity for reorder when it is time to replenish inventory. The **economic order quantity (EOQ)** is the volume at which the sum of inventory-carrying costs and order-processing costs are at a minimum. Typically, as order size increases, (1) inventory-carrying cost goes up because the average inventory is larger and (2) order-processing cost declines because there are fewer orders.

In Figure 16.4, point EOQ represents the order quantity having the lowest total cost. Actually, the order quantity that a firm considers best (or optimal) often is larger than the EOQ. That's because management must try to balance the sometimes conflicting goals of low inventory costs and responsive customer service. For various reasons, such as gaining a differential advantage, a firm may place a higher priority on customer service than on inventory costs. To completely fill orders in a timely manner may well call for a larger order quantity than the EOQ—for example, quantity X in Figure 16.4.

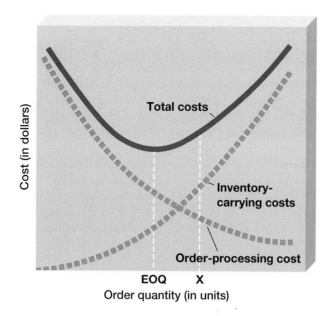

FIGURE 16.4

Economic Order Quantity.

Just-in-Time   First widely used in Japan, **just-in-time** (**JIT**) combines inventory control, purchasing, and production scheduling. Applying JIT, a firm buys in small quantities that arrive *just in time* for production and then it produces in quantities *just in time* for sale. When effectively implemented, the just-in-time concept has many benefits:

- By purchasing in small quantities and maintaining low inventory levels of parts and finished goods, a company can achieve dramatic cost savings because fewer items are stolen, damaged, or otherwise unusable.

- Production and delivery schedules can be shortened and made more flexible and reliable.

- When order quantities are relatively small and deliveries are frequent, a company can quickly spot and correct a quality problem in the products received.[39]

During the 1980s, the JIT philosophy was adopted in the American auto industry and then was implemented gradually by other leading firms such as IBM, Xerox, and General Electric. Many companies employ the philosophy, if not all of the practices, of just-in-time inventory control. For example, in a completely renovated factory in Toledo, Ohio, DaimlerChrysler is using various methods including JIT to boost efficiency in auto manufacturing. Key suppliers are supposed to deliver auto parts "not only just in time but also exactly in production line sequence."[40]

An organization that relies on JIT tends to use fewer suppliers because a high level of coordination is needed. JIT puts pressure on a supplier to meet a manufacturer's needs in a very timely fashion. As with any business practice, there are potential problems with JIT, such as friction between vendor and customer. Hence, some companies are using JIT, whereas others are not convinced the improvements in customer service and the reductions in inventory levels are sufficient to offset the added coordination and possible channel tension.[41]

Market-Response Systems   JIT's focus tends to be on production and the relationship between a producer and its suppliers. There's a parallel trend, however, involving producers or wholesalers of finished goods and their customers. Several labels have been used to describe this practice; we prefer **market-response system.** The central premise is that expected or actual purchases by final customers—those who intend to consume the product—should activate a process to produce and

Will RFID replace bar codes?

Most products contain bar codes that are read by scanners for purposes of transactions and inventory control. Now after more than 30 years in which bar codes have been paramount, a new technology has arrived. A **radio-frequency identification (RFID)** tag consists of a tiny memory chip equipped with a minuscule radio antenna. The promise of RFID is that the tags allow constant monitoring of the whereabouts of products in various locations, including manufacturing plants, warehouses, and retail storerooms and selling floors. Eventually, RFID technology will provide capabilities for in-store promotions tailored to individual shoppers and perhaps allow automated checkout and payment. At the time of a transaction, an RFID tag could also trigger automatic replenishment.

Currently, RFID tags are fairly expensive—about 25 to 50 cents apiece. Hence, they don't make sense for lower-cost items found in retail outlets. In addition, the underlying technology is still being perfected to overcome limitations such as radio waves not being able to go through some metals and liquids.

Costs and challenges notwithstanding, RFID is here to stay. Annual expenditures involving this technology already top $1 billion and are expected to approach $5 billion as early as 2007.

Wal-Mart Stores anticipates that RFID will yield substantial benefits in supply chain management. One industry analyst even speculated that widespread use of RFID could save the giant retailer upwards of $8 *billion* by 2007! With that "pot of gold" in sight, the chain asked its largest suppliers to begin using RFID tags in 2005, with widespread implementation to follow soon. Suppliers have grave concerns because the "800-pound gorilla" expects them to bear the costs of RFID.

Other retailers, such as Albertsons, Best Buy, and Target as well as the U.S. Defense Department, are also requesting RFID usage by key suppliers. Given the per-tag cost, RFID is likely to be used only on large crates and full pallets of merchandise and on high-value products in the near term. As the cost of this technology drops, broad-based usage is anticipated.

Is it possible that RFID tags will be on all merchandise in the future?

Sources: James A. Cooke, "Slow but Steady," *Logistics Management (2002)*, February 2005, pp. 30+; Rachel Melcer, "ID Chips Make Fact of Science Fiction," *St. Louis Post-Dispatch*, Nov. 19, 2004, pp. C1, C15; Susan Warren, "Suppliers Struggle with Wal-Mart ID-Tag Plan," *The Wall Street Journal*, Nov. 18, 2004, pp. B4, B5; Sandra Ward, "Attention Retail Shoppers: Here Come Radio Tags," *St. Louis Post-Dispatch*, June 6, 2004, p. E6; and Gerry Khermouch and Heather Green, "Bar Codes Better Watch Their Backs," *BusinessWeek*, July 14, 2003, p. 42.

deliver replacement items. In this way, a product is pulled through a channel on the basis of demand rather than on short-term price reductions or other inducements that often result in excess inventories.

The intent of a market-response system is similar to that of JIT, namely to have just the right amount of goods in stock to satisfy demand and then to replenish exhausted stocks rapidly. By minimizing the quantity of inventory that languishes in middlemen's warehouses, a market-response system can shrink the funds that channel members tie up in inventory. Consumer prices may also drop, or at least not rise much.

Essentially, with a market-response system, a retailer's computer knows when a product is sold and, in turn, notifies the supplier's computer that a replacement is needed. Numerous retailers, including e-tailers, have adopted some kind of market-response system. For example, various retailers, including Penney's and Wal-Mart, have their computers linked to those of VF Corp., an apparel maker based in Greensboro, North Carolina. Each night a store's computer sends to VF's computer precise information about which of the manufacturer's products, including Lee and Wrangler jeans and Vanity Fair women's underwear, were sold that day. Then VF ships replacements, either from existing inventory or as soon as they are produced. Store shelves are replenished as soon as two days later.[42]

More recently, the scope of market-response systems has expanded beyond automatic replenishment. **Collaborative planning, forecasting, and replenishment (CPFR)**

www.vfc.com

Many companies, both manufacturers and middlemen, rely on huge distribution centers as a key element of their logistics management. A top priority in designing and operating a distribution center is to curtail labor expenses. With that in mind, such features as one-story layouts, conveyor belts, various forms of automation, and even inventory pickers on inline skates are increasingly common in distribution centers.

is a method by which a producer or a wholesaler and a customer, ordinarily a retail chain, jointly develop sales forecasts through a shared website and also design marketing plans. Thus the outcomes of CPFR are not just decision rules related to replenishment but also a full program for marketing a specific product. CPFR requires sharing of confidential information between the participating channel members, so it depends on trust in the relationship.[43]

An early test of CPFR involving Warner-Lambert, Inc., which makes Listerine mouthwash, and Wal-Mart produced very promising results. Of particular interest was a 25% decrease in inventories of Listerine. Subsequent collaborations, involving other firms, have generated sales gains, fewer out-of-stock situations, and/or inventory reductions. Through CPFR, Heineken was able to reduce the time that elapsed between an order being received and the shipment arriving at the distributor's storage facility from 3 months to 4 weeks. Encouraged by such results, more and more pairs of channel members are using CPFR. According to two different surveys of executives, about 20% to 25% of firms have implemented CPFR.[44]

CPFR is very much related to company-wide initiatives that are intended to integrate by means of computer programs the various business functions of an organization. The functions include sales, manufacturing, purchasing, distribution, financial management, and human resources. These efforts are commonly called **enterprise resource planning systems,** or simply *ERP* or *enterprise software.* As ERP has evolved, increased attention is being given to what has been labeled *supply chain optimization* and *customer relationship management,* both of which are directly linked to distribution.[45]

Inventory Location and Warehousing

Management must make critical decisions about the size, location, and transportation of inventories. These areas are interrelated, often in complex ways. The number and locations of inventory sites, for example, influence inventory size and transportation methods. One key consideration in managing inventories is *warehousing,* which embraces a range of functions, such as assembling, dividing, and storing products and preparing them for reshipping. The importance of this function is underscored by the fact that the part of supply chain management receiving the largest share of information technology expenditures in a recent year was warehouse management systems.[46]

Types of Warehouses   Any producer, wholesaler, or retailer has the option of operating its own private warehouse or using the services of a public warehouse. A **private warehouse** is more likely to be an advantage if (1) a company moves a large volume of products through a warehouse, (2) there is very little, if any, seasonal fluctuation in this flow, and (3) the goods have special handling or storage requirements.

A **public warehouse** offers storage and handling facilities to individuals or companies. Public warehousing costs are a variable expense. Customers pay only for the space they use, and just when they use it. Public warehouses can also provide office and product display space, and accept and fill orders for sellers.

Distribution Centers
An effective inventory-location strategy may involve the establishment of one or more **distribution centers.** This type of facility, typically very large in size, is planned around markets rather than transportation requirements. The idea is to develop under one roof an efficient, fully integrated system for the flow of products—taking orders, filling them, and preparing them for delivery to customers. It appears that some firms, including Cardinal Health, Procter & Gamble, Rockwell Automation, and Unilever, are opting for fewer, but even larger distribution centers.[47]

Distribution centers have been established by many, perhaps most, large firms that supply numerous customers. W. W. Grainger, the wholesaler profiled at the beginning of the chapter, has invested $200 million to replace or completely refurbish its distribution centers in order to reduce the number of shipments the branches have to make and to improve customer service. In an entirely different industry, Nintendo of America has a 380,000-square-foot distribution center in North Bend, Washington, where products are received in large, sealed containers from Japan. From there, video games and accessories are shipped to 10,000 stores nationally. Orders are filled with an accuracy rate that translates to less than one item misshipped per every 10,000 shipped.[48]

At the start of the new century, ambitious e-commerce firms such as Amazon, eToys, and Webvan spent very large sums to construct distribution centers at carefully selected locations. Amazon, for example, established centers in Kansas, Kentucky, and Nevada to serve as the hubs of its physical distribution system. The other two firms, however, were among the many e-tailers that went out of business as a result of insufficient sales and/or exorbitant expenses.[49]

Distribution centers can cut costs by reducing the number of warehouses, pruning excessive inventories, and eliminating out-of-stock conditions. Companies are in business to sell goods, not to store or ship them, so warehousing and delivery times must be cut to a minimum. Distribution centers can help in this regard as well.

Materials Handling

Selecting the proper equipment to physically handle products, including the warehouse building itself, is the *materials handling* subsystem of physical distribution management. Equipment that is well matched to the task can minimize losses from breakage, spoilage, and theft. Efficient equipment can reduce handling costs as well as time required for handling.

Modern warehouses typically are huge one-story structures located in outlying areas where land is less expensive and loading platforms are easily accessed by trucks and trains. Conveyor belts, forklift trucks, and other mechanized equipment are used to move merchandise. In some warehouses the order fillers are even outfitted with in-line skates!

Containerization is a cargo-handling system that has become standard practice in physical distribution. Shipments of products are enclosed in large metal or wood containers. A container is transported and remains unopened from the shipper's facility (such as a manufacturer's plant) to its destination (such as a wholesaler's warehouse).

Containerization minimizes physical handling, thereby reducing damage, lessening the risk of theft, and allowing for more efficient transportation. In this post-9/11

How large can container ships become?

Containerization is prevalent in shipping merchandise across an ocean. Container ships navigate the Pacific Ocean between Asia and the U.S., traveling at up to 25 knots per hour. They also move between Asia and Europe by way of the Suez Canal.

Container ships are huge. Imagine three football fields laid end to end, and that's roughly the surface area of a container ship. Typically, the containers used in international transit are about 40 feet long. A few years ago, about 2,200 containers would fit on a ship. This scale of vessel was labeled *Panamax* because it was the maximum size that would fit through the Panama Canal.

Recently a global shipping firm launched *post-Panamax* ships that can haul almost 4,000 containers. Placed end to end, this quantity of containers would stretch for more than 30 miles. One projection even envisions 25% larger vessels at the start of the next decade.

Why are container ships getting bigger and bigger? The answer lies in economies of scale. Operating expenses, such as fuel and labor, do not go up in direct proportion to capacity. Thus larger ship size means that it costs less to transport a single container overseas. According to one estimate, this generation of post-Panamax vessels is about 20% more efficient than the smaller Panamax container ships.

Of course, at some point, "bigger is not better" for various reasons such as ships being too large to enter some ports. Therefore, another company is taking a different approach, testing the premise that some shippers will pay more for faster deliveries of containers.

FastShip Inc. is working on a vessel that would cut the transit time for a container ship in half (from seven days down to three or four days, for example). Of course, the ships will be more costly (perhaps $250 million apiece), and they will have much higher operating expenses. Thus shipping fees will be substantially above those charged by companies such as Maersk Sealand that rely on huge ships.

FastShip is generating some excitement. According to a professor, the speedier container ship could "do for ocean service what Federal Express has done for package delivery." Of course, the unanswered question is whether there are sufficient customers willing to pay a premium for more rapid delivery of containers.

- www.maerskselaand.com

- www.fastshipatlantic.com

Sources: Andrea MacDonald, "Ocean Liners: Does Size Really Matter?" *World Trade*, May 2004, pp. 36+; "Business: How to Shrink the World; Fast Container Ships," *The Economist*, Aug. 4, 2001, p. 51; Philip Siekman, "The New Wave in Giant Ships," *Fortune*, Nov. 12, 2001, pp. l182[l]+; and Daniel Machalaba, "Is This Boat the FedEx of the Seas?" *The Wall Street Journal*, Mar. 15, 2000, p. B1.

era, containers raise security concerns. To combat theft as well as terrorism, work is underway on a "smart box" that would be attached to a container. The device would be able to detect a sealed container being opened and transmit that information to a monitoring station, perhaps in the shipper's office. A smart box is also likely to have more advanced technologies, such as being able to detect radiation or biological agents.[50]

Transportation

A major function of the physical distribution system in many companies is *transportation*—shipping products to customers. Management must decide on both the mode of transportation and the particular carriers. In this discussion we will focus on *intercity* shipments.

Major Modes   Railroads, trucks, pipelines, water vessels, and airplanes are the leading modes of transportation. In Table 16.4 these five methods are compared on the basis of criteria likely to be used by physical distribution managers in selecting a mode of transportation. Of course, the ratings of alternative modes of transportation

TABLE 16.4 Comparison of Transportation Methods

Selection Criteria	Transportation Method				
	Rail	Water	Highway	Pipeline	Air
Speed (door-to-door time)	Medium	Slowest	Fast	Slow	**Fastest**
Cost of transportation	Medium	**Lowest**	High	Low	Highest
Reliability in meeting delivery schedules	Medium	Poor	Good	**Excellent**	Good
Variety of products carried	**Widest**	**Widest**	Medium	Very limited	Somewhat limited
Number of geographic locations served	Very many	Limited	**Unlimited**	Very limited	Many
Most suitable products	Long hauls of carload quantities of bulky products, when freight costs are high in relation to product's value	Bulky, low-value nonperishables	Short hauls of high-value goods	Oil, natural gas, slurried products	High-value perishables, where speed of delivery is all-important

TABLE 16.5 Distribution of Intercity Freight Traffic in the U.S. Based on Ton-Miles and Revenue

Specific Mode	% of Total Ton-Miles				% of Total Revenue
	2001	1990	1970	1950	2001
Railroads	42	38	40	56	10
Trucks	28	25	21	16	80
Pipelines	17	20	22	12	2
Water vessels	13	16	17	15	1
Other	n/a	n/a	n/a	n/a	7"
Total	100	100	100	100	100

Notes: The Other row refers primarily to air freight in the case of ton-miles and freight forwarders and air freight in the case of revenue. These data (the latest available) do not cover *intracity* freight traffic or ocean coastal traffic between U.S. ports. A *ton-mile* refers to 1 ton of freight being transported 1 mile. Air freight accounts for less than 0.5% of total intercity shipping, as measured in ton-miles. The 1950 and 1990 columns do not total to 100% due to rounding.

Source: Data from the Eno Transportation Foundation, as reported in "Overview of U.S. Freight Railroads," Association of American Railroads, February 2005, *www.aar.org/PubCommon/Documents/AboutTheIndustry/Overview.pdf*; and *Railroad Facts*, 1999 edition, Association of American Railroads, Washington, DC, 1999, p. 32.

can vary from one manager in a buying center to the next manager, even within the same organization.[51]

Virtually all *intracity* shipping is done by motor truck. The relative use of four of the major modes, along with trends for *intercity* shipping, are shown in Table 16.5 (above). (Airplanes are not included in the table inasmuch as air freight comprises less than 1% of the total.) By the way, virtually all *intracity* shipping is done by motor truck. As indicated in the table, the use of trucks has expanded greatly since 1950. Even as the relative position of railroads slipped between 1950 and 1970, the absolute amount of rail freight increased considerably. The railroads' position has stabilized since 1970.

The far right column in Table 16.5 presents a different story. Railroads account for the largest share of ton-miles, but trucking companies dominate with regards to a more important measure—revenue. Because of greater flexibility and perhaps reliability, trucking firms command substantially higher rates than other modes of transportation.

Demand for transportation services rose as the economy rebounded in recent years. Both trucking companies and railroads have had difficulty handling the added demand. Ground-transportation providers are having trouble recruiting a sufficient number of drivers, whereas rail capacity is limited by having only a single track in many areas. The two major modes also compete on the basis of service quality. Plagued by a reputation of freight sitting in rail yards for days on end, railroads are striving to catch up with trucks in terms of speed and dependability. One approach is coast-to-coast service in about 63 hours—almost as fast as team-driven trucks— and fast enough that United Parcel Service has tried it out.[52]

Intermodal Transportation Using two or more modes of transportation to move freight is termed **intermodal transportation.** This approach is intended to seize the advantages of multiple forms of transportation. Continued strong growth is forecast for intermodal transportation, largely because of the ongoing globalization of business, stimulated by compacts such as the North American Free Trade Agreement. In fact, intermodal has overtaken coal as the largest single revenue source for railroads.[53]

So-called *piggyback service* involves carrying truck trailers on railroad flatcars. For example, a shipment of auto glass is loaded on J. B. Hunt Transport trucks at the Pilkington Libbey-Owens-Ford plant near Toledo, Ohio. The truck trailers are placed on a Burlington Northern Santa Fe train in Chicago for a trip to Los Angeles. There, Hunt trucks take the glass to its destination in Fontana, California. This intermodal arrangement provides (1) more flexibility than railroads alone can offer, (2) lower freight costs than trucks alone, and (3) less handling of goods. Another form of intermodal transportation, *fishyback service,* combines ships or barges with either railroads or trucks, or both.

With the trend toward intermodal methods, more companies that have goods to move are interested in **one-stop shipping,** which consists of one transportation firm offering multiple modes of transportation to customers. Typically, the carrier owns the various modes (such as a truck line, cargo ships, and even airplanes); sometimes, however, they will turn to an outside firm if they need to use a mode of transportation they don't own.[54]

www.jbhunt.com

From this network operations center at the headquarters of the BNSF Railway Co. in Ft. Worth, Texas, over 100 dispatchers oversee assigned areas of the firm's rail system. Weather data and information about key customers' shipments are shown on the giant screens. Wireless technologies allow key measurement (such as speed and braking) to be transmitted from each freight train to the operations center. Dispatchers and engineers talk with each other over BNSF's private telecommunications network.

www.bnsf.com

Seeking economies of scale, container ships that carry goods across oceans have been getting larger and larger. A giant ship such as this one can cross the Pacific Ocean—often between Hong Kong, China, and Long Beach, California—in about 10 to 12 days at a speed of approximately 25 knots (29 miles) per hour. To accommodate the giant container ships, some ports have had to enlarge width and/or depth of the channel from the ocean to the terminal and to augment the cranes and computer systems to handle the larger flow of freight.

www.jesforwarding.com

Freight Forwarders A specialized intermediary serving firms that ship in less-than-full-load quantities is called a **freight forwarder.** Its main function is to consolidate less-than-carload or less-than-truckload shipments from several shippers into full-load quantities. The complexities of foreign shipments have prompted many companies to rely on forwarders.

A freight forwarder picks up the merchandise at the shipper's place of business and arranges for delivery at the buyer's door. A small shipper benefits from the speed and minimum handling associated with large shipments. It may also cost less to use a freight forwarder than to deal directly with a carrier because of the volume discounts that forwarders obtain from airlines, railroads, and other carriers. A freight forwarder also provides its customers with traffic management services, such as selecting the best transportation mode(s) and route(s).

www.dhl-usa.com

Package-Delivery Firms For more than 30 years, **package-delivery firms** have been on the rise. These companies deliver shipments of small packages and high-priority mail. In contrast to freight forwarders, which do not own their own transportation equipment, package-delivery firms do. Companies such as DHL International and United Parcel Service (UPS), in effect, use intermodal transportation. In the case of FedEx, for example, a package is picked up by truck, shipped intercity or overseas by plane, and delivered locally by truck. The surge in both just-in-time purchasing and electronic commerce, particularly where the shipment is headed to a consumer, has contributed to the continuing growth of this type of transportation company.

Package-delivery firms compete vigorously not only among themselves but also with the U.S. Postal Service. The competition is particularly intense in the overnight-delivery market, where FedEx and UPS go head-to-head. Since introducing ground-only services, FedEx has gained market share on UPS. Each giant tries to surpass the other with respect to delivery times, technology that helps customers prepare and then track their shipments, and, of course, low prices. Now most transportation firms view each other as adversaries. In the words of the head of Yellow Roadway Corp., the country's biggest trucking firm, "Our competitors today are the UPSs and the FedExs of the world."[55]

Summary

Wholesaling consists of the sale, and all activities directly related to the sale, of goods and services for resale, use in making other products, or operation of an organization. Firms engaged primarily in wholesaling, called wholesaling middlemen, provide economies of skill, scale, and transactions to other firms involved in distribution.

Three categories of wholesaling middlemen are merchant wholesalers, agent wholesaling middlemen, and manufacturers' sales facilities. The first two are independent firms; the third is owned by a manufacturer. Merchant wholesalers take title to products being distributed; agent wholesaling middlemen do not. In recent years, the shares of total wholesale trade captured by the three categories have stabilized, with merchant wholesalers accounting for the majority share.

Merchant wholesalers, which account for the majority of wholesale trade, include both full-service and limited-service wholesalers. Of the three major categories of wholesaling middlemen, merchant wholesalers offer the widest range of services and thus incur the highest operating expenses.

Agent wholesaling middlemen lost ground to merchant wholesalers for at least a couple of decades, but have rebounded in recent years. The main types of agent middlemen are manufacturers' agents and brokers. Because they perform more limited services, agent middlemen's expenses tend to be lower than merchant wholesalers'.

Physical distribution is the flow of products from supply sources to a firm and then from that firm to its customers. The goal of physical distribution is to move the right amount of the right products to the right place at the right time. The costs of trying to do this are a substantial part of total operating costs in many firms. Conversely, physical distribution is a potential source of substantial cost reductions in many companies.

Physical distribution activities are still fragmented operationally and organizationally in many firms. To overcome these shortcomings, supply chain management takes a total system perspective of distribution. The total cost concept should be applied to physical distribution. That is, management should strive *not* for the lowest total cost of a single physical distribution activity, but for the best balance between customer service and total cost. Effective management of physical distribution can help a company gain an advantage over competitors through better customer service and/or lower operating costs. To improve their physical distribution, more and more firms are turning to contract logistics.

The operation of a physical distribution system requires management's attention and decision making in five areas: order processing, inventory control, inventory location and warehousing, materials handling, and transportation. They should not be treated as individual activities but as interrelated components within a physical distribution system. Effective management of these five activities requires an understanding of electronic data interchange; economic order quantity; just-in-time processes; market-response systems such as collaborative planning, forecasting, and replenishment (CPFR); distribution centers; and intermodal transportation.

More about W. W. Grainger

With about 90,000 relatively small transactions per day (average transaction of $170), W. W. Grainger, Inc. must have a very efficient supply chain in order to be profitable. Products purchased by Grainger are transported by suppliers to one of its nine distribution centers. As Grainger receives orders, the products are shipped either to a Grainger branch to replenish its inventory or directly to a customer, usually the same day an order is placed.

Two keys to Grainger's logistics activities are automated distribution centers and advanced technologies. In 2004, the wholesaler completed an overhaul of its logistics network, which is built around five new and four renovated distribution centers. The "new and improved" network allowed Grainger to reduce its inventory levels by $115 million and improve its operating profits by $10 million without harming service. In fact, Grainger can fulfill 99% of orders on a next-day basis.

In the words of Grainger's chairman, "Technology is . . . at the very heart of our business." Given that conviction, it's not surprising that the company took to the Internet wholeheartedly and early in 1996. At one point, the firm had an array of online ventures, including:

- Grainger.com—the company's primary e-commerce method, through which customers can access 200,000 products.

- MROverstocks.com—an online auction site for discontinued and surplus supplies.

- FindMRO.com—a sourcing venture for hard-to-find items.

- Total MRO.com—a website designed to aggregate the catalogs of many suppliers, including Grainger's competitors.

However, with the exception of Grainger.com, these Internet-based selling methods failed to generate sufficient revenues and thus were closed. Grainger redirected its efforts to enhancing grainger.com. For example, a new feature on the website enables comparisons across alternative products in order to help customers save time and money.

W. W. Grainger has also invested in electronic data interchange with customers. Further, the firm has been implementing the SAP brand of enterprise resource planning (ERP) system across all of its branches. Grainger's very significant investments in technology—tens of millions of dollars annually—carry the dual expectations of better customer service and greater operating efficiency.[56]

1. Are distribution centers very important for a company such as W. W. Grainger, which has so many (almost 400) branches spread across the country?

2. As a wholesaler, is it desirable or even vital for Grainger to have Internet-based selling methods?

Key Terms And Concepts

Wholesaling (436)
Wholesaling middleman (436)
Merchant wholesaler (439)
Agent wholesaling middleman (439)
Manufacturer's sales facility (439)
Manufacturer's sales branch (439)
Manufacturer's sales office (440)
Full-service wholesaler (441)
Truck jobber (442)
Drop shipper (442)
Manufacturers' agent (443)
Broker (444)
Selling agent (445)
Auction company (445)
Import-export agent (445)

Physical distribution (445)
Fulfillment (447)
Online category manager (448)
Supply chain management (448)
Total cost concept (448)
Contract logistics (449)
Physical distribution
   management (451)
Electronic data interchange
   (EDI) (451)
Economic order quantity
   (EOQ) (452)
Just-in-time (JIT) (454)
Radio frequency identificaiton
   (RFID) (454)

Market-response system (454)
Collaborative planning, forecasting,
   and replenishment (CPFR) (454)
Enterprise resource planning (ERP)
   systems (455)
Private warehouse (455)
Public warehouse (456)
Distribution center (456)
Containerization (456)
Intermodal transportation (459)
One-stop shipping (459)
Freight forwarder (460)
Package-delivery firms (460)

Questions and Problems

1. Which of the following are wholesaling transactions?
   a. Color Tile sells wallpaper to an apartment building contractor and also to the contractor's wife for her home.
   b. General Electric sells motors to Whirlpool for its washing machines.

   c. A shrimp "farmer" sells fresh shrimp to a local restaurant.
   d. A family orders carpet from a friend, who is a home decorating consultant, at 50% off the suggested retail price. The carpet is delivered directly to the home.

2. As shown in Figure 16.3, agent wholesaling middlemen and manufacturers' sales facilities lost part of their share of wholesale trade to merchant wholesalers over time. But then this erosion stopped. What could the two types of wholesaling middlemen do to combat merchant wholesalers in the future?

3. Why is it that manufacturers' agents often can penetrate a market faster and at a lower cost than a manufacturer's sales force?

4. Which type of wholesaling middleman, if any, is most likely to be used by each of the following firms? Explain your choice in each instance.
   a. A small manufacturer of a liquid glass cleaner to be sold through supermarkets.
   b. A small canner in Vermont packing a high-quality, unbranded fruit product.
   c. A small-tools manufacturing firm that has its own sales force selling to the business market and now wants to add backyard barbecue equipment to its product mix.
   d. A textile mill in Malaysia producing unbranded towels, sheets, pillowcases, and blankets.

5. Looking to the future, which types of wholesaling middlemen do you think will increase in importance, and which ones will decline? Explain.

6. "The goal of a modern physical distribution system in a firm should be to operate at the lowest possible *total* costs." Do you agree?

7. Name some products for which you think the cost of physical distribution constitutes at least one-half the total price of the goods at the wholesale level. Can you suggest ways of decreasing the physical distribution cost of these products?

8. "A manufacturer follows an inventory-location strategy of concentration rather than dispersion. This company's inventory size will be smaller, but its transportation and warehousing expenses will be larger than if its inventory were dispersed." Do you agree? Explain.

9. "The use of public warehouse facilities makes it possible for manufacturers to bypass wholesalers in their channels of distribution." Explain.

10. For each of the following products, determine the best transportation method for shipment to a distribution center in the community where your school is located. In each case the buyer (not the seller) will pay all freight charges, and, unless specifically noted, time is not important. The distribution center has a rail siding and a dock for loading and unloading trucks.
    a. Disposable diapers from Wisconsin. Total shipment weight is 112,000 pounds.
    b. A replacement memory card for your computer, which is now inoperative. Weight of shipment is under 1 pound and you need this card in a hurry.
    c. Blank payroll checks for your company. (There is a sufficient number of checks on hand for the next two weekly paydays.) Shipment weight is 100 pounds.
    d. Ice cream from St. Louis. Total shipment weight is 42,000 pounds.

Interactive Marketing Exercises

1. Interview the owner or a manager at a firm that is a type of merchant wholesaler (such as a full-service wholesaler). Ask the owner or manager to describe the firm's activities, its differential advantage or disadvantage at the present time, and the company's prospects for the future. Conduct a similar interview with the owner or a manager of a firm that is a type of agent wholesaling middleman (such as a broker). How do you explain any discrepancies between the interview results and the content of this chapter (other than saying that the chapter must be wrong)?

2. A manufacturer of precision lenses used in medical and hospital equipment wants to ship a 5-pound box of these lenses from your college town to a laboratory in Stockholm, Sweden. The lab wants delivery in five days or less. The manufacturer wants to use a package-delivery service but is undecided as to which shipper to choose. Compile and compare the types of services provided and prices charged by FedEx, United Parcel Service, and one other package-delivery firm.

Cases for Part 5

CASE 1 | **Target**

Hitting the Bull's-Eye in Discount Retailing

For many years after its first discount store opened in 1962, what is now the Target Corporation proceeded cautiously. It followed a plan for modest growth, locating new stores throughout the Midwest. But when Bob Ulrich was appointed Target's new chief executive officer (CEO) in 1994, he had bigger plans for the company. He envisioned nationwide expansion, with Target becoming a powerful brand, similar to renowned names such as Disney and Apple.

Target's top management needed an effective strategy in order to fulfill this vision. "We had three strategic choices. . . . To specialize, to become the low-cost producer, or to differentiate ourselves," said Target's vice chairman. Wal-Mart was already the recognized low-cost leader in discount retailing, and specialization was deemed too narrow an approach. So Target decided to differentiate itself within the industry by blending *fashion* with *frugality.*

To execute this strategy, the chain hired successful designers, such as Michael Graves, Mossimo Giannulli, and Isaac Mizrahi, to develop economically priced lines of housewares and fashions that would be sold only in Target stores. And Target's top executives made difficult decisions to divest the company of underperforming divisions to allow it to concentrate on being the nation's premier discount retailer.

Missing the Mark with Marshall Field's and Mervyn's

In 1902, George Dayton opened Goodfellows, a large department store in downtown Minneapolis. By 1910, the retailer had become The Dayton Company. Over time, new stores were opened throughout the Midwest, including an outlet in the world's first enclosed, two-story shopping mall in suburban Minneapolis in 1956. Six years later, Target made its debut in Roseville, Minnesota, and was promoted as "a new idea in discount stores."

In 1969, The Dayton Company merged with the J. L. Hudson Company, another Midwestern merchant. The outcome was The Dayton Hudson Corporation (DHC). In 1978, DHC purchased Mervyn's, a West Coast chain of mid-price stores, thereby becoming the nation's seventh-largest retailer.

By 1979, Target was contributing more revenues to DHC than any of its other entities. Total corporate sales exceeded $10 billion in 1987. Given its size, DHC was able to acquire the prestigious, Chicago-based Marshall Field's department store chain in 1990.

After Ulrich took the helm, all of DHC's department stores were renamed Marshall Field's. An even more significant name change took place in January 2000 when DHC became Target Corporation. The change was understandable considering that the Target unit accounted for 80% of the entire firm's revenues at that time. As Mervyn's and Marshall Field's struggled to achieve sales growth, Target's dominance within the enterprise increased, to the point that the discount chain was responsible for 86% of the corporation's revenues of almost $44 billion in 2003.

Investors and analysts began to question whether one company could adequately address the distinctive demands of three disparate chains. Thus, in June 2004, Target sold all 62 of its Marshall Field's stores and nine Mervyn's locations to May Department Stores for $3.24 billion. One month later, several private-investment firms paid Target $1.65 billion to buy the remaining Mervyn's stores and four distribution centers. Unburdened, the Target Corp. could concentrate on its namesake chain of discount stores.

Focusing on Fashion

Target's strategies to become the designer discount chain include brightly lit, clutter-free store interiors and edgy advertising campaigns that feature the merchant's ubiquitous bull's-eye logo. But merchandise is what distinguishes Target from its rivals, and the company employs a number of strategies for developing a desirable merchandise mix.

First, big-name designers are employed to give mundane objects and apparel a designer look for budget-minded consumers. Michael Graves' signature line has transformed various products—as disparate as tea kettles, spatulas, and poker chips—into attractive merchandise, often with an "art deco" look. In a much different product category, Liz Lange was commissioned to add flair to maternity wear, which is notorious for being unfashionable.

Target also breathed new life into fading brands, such as the Mossimo line of adult apparel. The new approach is to incorporate the latest trends in this line of clothing basics (shirts, blouses, pants). However, no other brand has experienced as great a turnaround as that of Isaac Mizrahi. Once a star in the fashion industry, Mizrahi's couture clothing business failed in 1998; he then became an actor in a one-man show and host of a quirky TV show. Target offered Mizrahi a licensing agreement in 2002. Although some friends counseled him to not partner with Target, Mizrahi jumped at the opportunity. "It's not like it was Kohl's or J. C. Penney," Mizrahi commented. "Target has an image—a humor and a freedom that is more cutting-edge than anywhere. You're not selling out. You're reaching out."

Mizrahi's association with Target has actually elevated his stature in the fashion industry. "Target just enhances Isaac's cool factor," explained another designer. Mizrahi is again designing high-end clothing. Recently, Target hosted a fashion show that mixed Mizrahi fashions priced around $5,000 with inexpensive items from his Target line, some priced at less than $25.

In the past, Target's clothing lines seemed to have the most appeal for younger women, but the addition of Mizrahi's line is one facet of Target's plan to attract a broader base of customers. For instance, Target's new private label, Linden Hill, is targeted at a slightly older group of women. This line features designs that are casual and relaxed but at the same time are a bit more sophisticated and thus appropriate for office settings.

Target has also become proficient at relatively unknown product lines and turning them into power-house brands. In 2002, Target discovered Method, a small manufacturer of environmentally friendly cleaning products that is based in San Francisco. Target began to stock and promote the company's products, and they sold very well. According to Method's CEO, "We've gone from about two to ten product lines."

At various price points, Target has been adept at distinctive merchandising. It has set up "The 1 Spot" near its store entrances to sell small gift items, all priced at $1 each. In addition, the Global Bazaar made its debut in January 2005 to take advantage of space that is normally dedicated to seasonal merchandise, such as Christmas gift wrap and decorations. It features home décor items with an international flair and includes some larger pieces that are priced up to $300.

Targeting Wal-Mart and Other Discounters

Whereas Wal-Mart touts its low prices and Target promotes its fashion sense, Kmart has been unable to develop and maintain a consistent and effective appeal to shoppers. Forced into bankruptcy, many Kmart stores fell into disarray, with erratic inventory levels and outdated layouts and appearance. In contrast, Target stores are clean and uniform in appearance, with 12-foot aisles and no boxes of unshelved merchandise in sight. Target's expansion into the northeast portion of the country was especially threatening to Kmart. On Long Island, New York, for instance, a Kmart saw its sales decrease by 25% when a new Target opened in the same area.

Like Kmart, Sears grew rapidly after World War II, but it failed to adapt as Wal-Mart and Target expanded across the country. "Wal-Mart came along with its great service and low prices, [and] other retailers started to innovate more with products and service. Sears and Kmart simply trudged along and thought that was good enough," observed a marketing professor at the University of Pennsylvania.

In November 2004, Kmart announced it was purchasing Sears, Roebuck & Co. for $11 billion. The merged company, Sears Holdings, has a total of 3,500 stores in malls and also off-mall locations. Sears Holdings immediately announced it would begin transforming several hundred Kmart locations into Sears stores.

The Kmart-Sears merger dropped Target from the #2 to the #3 position in terms of size among general-merchandise retailers. In the first quarter of 2005, Target tallied revenues of $11.5 billion, up 13% over the previous year's first quarter. The company also recorded net income of almost a half billion dollars. During that same period, the new Sears Holdings Corporation estimated its new combined revenues to be $12.75 billion, but it recorded a net loss of $78 million. By comparison, Wal-Mart's revenues (including its Sam's Club division) totaled almost $72 billion, with net income just under $2.5 billion.

Even though Target Corp. is a huge enterprise, it is still relatively small compared to Wal-Mart, which is the largest company in the world as measured by sales volume. Thus Target avoids head-to-head clashes with its Arkansas-headquartered competitor by stressing fashion and using promotional discounts. In contrast, Wal-Mart emphasizes a mix of well-known producers' brands and its own brands, all with everyday low prices. But Target is intent on matching Wal-Mart's prices when they compete directly in the same market. However, Target rounds its prices up to the nearest 99 cents (for example,

$18.99), whereas Wal-Mart doesn't (for example, $18.76).

Sometimes competition plays out in unusual ways. During the 2003 holiday season, bell-ringing volunteers collected almost $9 million for the Salvation Army outside Target stores. But in 2004, Target decided to enforce its corporate policy restricting charitable solicitations on its property. Thus the chain banned Salvation Army bell ringers from the front of its stores. In response, Wal-Mart quickly announced that it would match its customers' donations to the Salvation Army, up to $1 million. Even though Target donates an average of $2 million each week to support schools, social services, and the arts, the ban on the Salvation Army's activities generated quite a bit of unfavorable publicity for Target Corporation.

Target intends to expand aggressively in the near future. It already has stores in 47 states, although its major markets remain in the Midwest. The corporate goal is to grow from 1,400 stores in late 2004 to more than 2,000 stores by the year 2010. Toward that end, Target made progress by adding 83 new stores, including 18 supercenters, in 2004.

Taking a Shot at New Formats

Wal-Mart originally developed the supercenter format as a way to get people into its stores on a more regular basis. Eventually, Target saw the huge potential of the hybrid stores. "Consumer preferences were changing, with folks being pressed for time. . . . The combination of general merchandise and food was growing in popularity," said Target's president. Thus the first SuperTarget opened in Omaha, Nebraska, in 1995, offering typical Target merchandise plus groceries. By early 2004, 136 SuperTargets had been opened, compared to 1,671 Wal-Mart Super Centers.

Adding groceries to the merchandise mix dramatically increases the complexity of a store's operations, and the profit margins are significantly smaller on food than on nonfood items. In addition, Target's image as the "classier" discount retailer might actually hurt the company's efforts to sell groceries. According to an industry analyst with the A. G. Edwards brokerage firm, consumers have the perception that Target's prices are typically higher than Wal-Mart's. In fact, when *Fortune* conducted an informal, unscientific poll to compare 17 identical items at each chain's supercenter, the magazine concluded that Target's prices were slightly lower than Wal-Mart's. Despite the fact that the two stores may have comparable prices, Wal-Mart's ownership of more than 25 grocery warehouses throughout the U.S. gives it a significant cost advantage over Target.

But Target is relying on its success with its general merchandise stores to compete effectively with Wal-Mart. Specifically, Target is developing several more brands that will be sold exclusively at Super-Targets, such as celebrity chef Ming Tsai's Blue Ginger line of cooking accessories and food items. "We have chosen to build the SuperTarget concept off of our core Target brand by showing we have surprising, innovative food concepts that you won't find somewhere else," explained Target's executive vice president of marketing.

It appears that the company's strategy is still right on target.

Questions

1. Besides other discount chains such as Wal-Mart and Kmart, what types of retailers represent serious competition for Target?

2. What else can Target do to differentiate itself from Wal-Mart?

3. What are the advantages and disadvantages to Target of operating supercenters?

www.targetcorp.com

CASE 2

Costco versus Sam's Club

Making Sure Membership Has Its Privileges

In 1977, Sol Price opened his first store in San Diego and named it the Price Club. His last name was the perfect choice for this outlet. The first warehouse club offered individuals and small businesses the opportunity to purchase a variety of merchandise at sharply reduced prices.

Buying in bulk directly from manufacturers, keeping the stores as simple as possible, and charging a small annual membership fee allowed Price Club to charge prices that were just above wholesale prices. In fact, although the majority of warehouse clubs' transactions are with consumers, a substantial portion of their annual sales volume comes from organizations that are making purchases for resale or for use in their own enterprises. Thus, although classified as retailers, warehouse clubs really are a hybrid retail–wholesale operation.

Seeing Price Club's success, other retail firms decided to develop their own brand of warehouse club. Wal-Mart opened its first three Sam's Clubs in 1983, and Costco Wholesale Corporation started the same year. Kmart tried to keep pace with, of course, the Pace chain. Soon the market became crowded, resulting in a number of store closings and acquisitions. Sam's bought Pace, and later Costco took over the Price Club organization. Before long, these two retailers—Sam's and Costco—accounted for more than 90% of the volume rung up by warehouse clubs. BJ's Wholesale Club is a distant number three.

For a time, the two chains remained separated to a large degree by geography. But as they continued to expand, Costco and Sam's began to compete directly against each other more frequently. And while Sam's parent company, Wal-Mart, dominates the landscape of discount retailing, it has struggled to match that success in the arena of warehouse clubs. With only 449 stores, Costco achieved revenues (not including membership fees) of $47.1 billion in 2004. With about 550 stores, Sam's Club had $10 billion less revenue than Costco in the same year. And Sam's has had five different chief executive officers during the past 10 years, each of them trying to improve Sam's standing compared to its warehouse rival, Costco.

Keeping Prices Low

The basic premise of a warehouse club is simple. As described by the head of Costco, James Sinegal, "Costco is able to offer lower prices and better values by eliminating virtually all the frills and costs historically associated with conventional wholesalers and retailers, including sales people, fancy buildings, delivery, billing, and accounts receivable. We run a tight operation with extremely low overhead which enables us to pass on dramatic savings to our members." The same description applies to Sam's Club.

Both chains target two groups for membership:

- Budget-minded individuals who want to buy groceries and other product categories at deep discounts.
- Small- and medium-size businesses that often resell items purchased at warehouse clubs or use them in their day-to-day operation.

Membership fees are fairly consistent across the industry. As of 2005, Costco charged $45 annually for both groups, whereas Sam's fees were $35 for individuals and $30 for organizations. Both clubs offer a premier membership level that provides added benefits in exchange for a $100 fee. And since both chains primarily derive their profits from membership sales, keeping membership rates as high as possible is absolutely imperative to being successful.

Keeping prices low is another priority. Sinegal never allows his stores' merchandise to be marked up by more than 14%. One of Costco's senior executives stated, "The members count on us to deliver the best deal. Jim (Sinegal) doesn't cheat on that." In fact, the chain's buyers are sometimes reprimanded for doing *too* well. "Our margin goal is 10%, and there better be a very good reason you did better than that," explained one Costco buyer. "Otherwise Jim will say, 'Well, why didn't you lower prices?'"

Costco has another method for keeping prices low: It partners with vendors to avoid out-of-stock situations. For example, Kimberly-Clark receives data each day from every Costco store in the country regarding its supply of, say, Huggies diapers. It is Kimberly-Clark's responsibility to monitor the data to ensure that each store has just enough diapers so it doesn't run out of stock. A larger supply would take up scarce space and reduce the funds available for other merchandise.

Kimberly-Clark, which manages inventory for a number of different retailers, says it has been able to save $200 million in two years and benefits by keeping its clients happy. Ultimately, these savings (or at least a part of the savings) are passed on to consumers.

Bulking Up on Higher-End Goods

Costco chose to differentiate itself from other warehouse clubs by offering some upscale merchandise in addition to multiple-unit packages of batteries, paper towels, and cereal. Throughout the aisles of Costco stores, shoppers can find "treasures" ranging from TaylorMade golf clubs to Prada and Coach purses. Renowned for its selection of wines, Costco sells more wine than any other U.S. retailer, in excess of a half billion dollars annually. In 2004, it also sold more than 67,000 carats of diamonds, including a $190,000 diamond ring.

The Costco chain carries everything from artwork by Picasso to general merchandise from Nautica, Kitchen Aid, and Ralph Lauren. Oprah Winfrey featured Costco on one of her TV shows and extolled the benefits of the club's cashmere sweaters ($50) and chicken pot pie ($12.50). Sometimes referred to as "the Oprah effect," the store's stock price surged following the favorable publicity.

Not to be outdone, Sam's has also added more expensive items to its merchandise mix. In early 2005, it announced it was offering a one-of-a-kind pink diamond pendant, valued at $813,000 for only $560,000. From a case of Courvoisier cognac with custom-designed labels to a 10-foot-tall Remington statue, each with a price of about $10,000, Sam's has been working to noticeably upgrade its merchandise.

But Costco doesn't appear worried. An executive stated, "You don't bring in a pallet of fancy merchandise and think you can cultivate a certain customer. They might bring in a pallet of Ralph Lauren shirts for $37. But while our customers will buy five of them, their customers won't spend $37 on a shirt." Perhaps this is a reference to Sam's parent company being Wal-Mart, a retailer that appeals to consumers with moderate incomes. Sam's connection to Wal-Mart does have its advantages, however. As part of the Wal-Mart corporate organization, Sam's has access to employee training seminars and other support programs. Both companies' buyers work together to secure good deals, thereby reducing purchasing costs and ensuring the lowest ultimate prices possible.

Introducing a Pallet of New Services

High-quality merchandise at low prices isn't the only appeal that warehouse clubs have for shoppers. Both Sam's and Costco offer an array of services, including pharmacies, optical shops, food courts, and photo processing, that are available to all of their members. In addition, both clubs sell more expensive memberships that provide even more benefits. For instance, Costco Executive Gold Star members who pay $100 annually earn rewards of up to 2% on most Costco purchases and receive extra benefits on member services, such as lower fees for check printing, automobile financing, and long-distance telephone service.

Both clubs also feature services that are attractive to small business owners. Sam's, for example, provides access to direct mail and marketing services, merchant credit card processing, small business loans, payroll processing, and even retirement plans. "A lot of our business members have 10 employees or less, so the cost for them to enroll in a traditional 401K plan is prohibitive," said a Costco executive.

These services differentiate warehouse clubs from other types of competitors, such as Target and Wal-Mart, and build customer loyalty. Both companies enjoy a membership renewal rate of about 85%.

Sam's and Costco continue to add services as they expand aggressively and compete directly with one another with increasing frequency.

Giving Its Employees a Good Deal

Reflecting its higher-price merchandise, Costco's sales-per-store figure was significantly higher than Sam's in 2004. Whereas Sam's reported $516 sales per square foot, Costco had almost $800. And with annual revenues in the neighborhood of $50 billion, Costco is the nation's fifth-largest retailer.

Despite its obvious success, Costco has been criticized for some of its policies. It has acquired the reputation of being a generous employer, paying higher-than-average wages, and providing very attractive benefits, especially compared to its competitors in the retail sector. New hires make more than $10 per hour. Cashiers can earn $40,000 annually within 3½ years. In addition, Costco covers more than 82% of its employees' healthcare costs, compared to only 47% for Sam's Club.

Many industry analysts have questioned Costco's strategy. "From the perspective of investors, Costco's benefits are overly generous," explained a retail analyst with Deutsche Bank Securities. "Public companies need to care for shareholders first. Costco runs its business like it is a private company."

"The last thing I want people to believe is that I don't care about the shareholder," countered Sinegal, who owns more than 3 million shares of Costco stock. "But I happen to believe that in order to reward the shareholder in the long term, you have to please your customers and workers." Costco's results support Sinegal's viewpoint. The chain's annual employee turnover is only 24%, versus 50% a year for Sam's. Considering that it costs about $2,500 to train new employees, relatively low turnover translates into big savings for Costco.

In addition, Costco's work force is tremendously loyal. "Employees are willing to do whatever it takes to get the job done," commented Julie Molina, a longtime Costco worker. Costco's employees generate per-person profits of $13,500 each year, compared to only $11,000 for Sam's. "Paying higher wages translates into more efficiency," explained Costco's chief financial officer. Costco employees often generate cost-savings ideas that are implemented throughout the entire company. For instance, in response to one employee's suggestion, pneumatic tubes are now being utilized in most Costco locations to carry cash directly from registers to the store's offices.

Whereas Costco has been disparaged for its benevolence, Sam's parent company, Wal-Mart, faces the opposite criticism. The largest retailer has been accused of paying relatively low wages and providing minimal benefits in order to maintain its position as the industry's low-cost leader.

Shopping for a Competitive Advantage

To increase per-store sales, Wal-Mart's warehouse club division is trying to devise other ways besides its low prices to differentiate itself. Sam's has decided to actively target small businesses, and has adopted the tag line, "We are in business for small business." With this in mind, Sam's has begun to reformulate its strategy to provide more merchandise that appeals to small business owners. In particular, it is targeting foods service companies, convenience stores, daycare centers, and vending machine operators. For instance, it has gotten rid of seasonal impulse items such as Halloween socks, and has bulked up on everyday office necessities such as file cabinets and memory upgrades for computers.

Recognizing that grocery items account for almost one-third of its sales, Sam's is returning to more bulk packaging, such as 50-pound bags of sugar, in order to appeal to restaurants. It also promotes its bakeries' ability to place company logos and slogans on its cakes and cupcakes. Sam's is also trying to bring in more small business owners by allowing them to fax their orders or to transmit them via the Internet for pick up later at the warehouse.

Costco also caters to small-business owners, partly by seeking their personal purchases as well as their business purchases. "Our customers don't drive 15 miles to save on a jar of peanut butter," stated Sinegal. "They come for the treasure hunt." In fact, according to A. C. Nielsen, more than 50% of the shoppers who frequent warehouse clubs can be described as being "affluent."

And the "treasure hunt" philosophy seems to be working for Costco. While members search for that special find, they also place staples (such as paper towels, cleaning supplies, and, yes, peanut butter) into their carts. Costco's strategy entices members to visit their warehouses about 11 times a year, spending an average of $94 each time. By comparison, members of Sam's Club visit 8.5 times per year, and pay about $78 per visit.

In addition to providing customers with the thrill of the hunt, Costco favors them in other ways as well. They are able to return items with no questions asked,

except for computers, which can be refunded within six months. And Costco has expanded its operations to include another retail venture. The corporation has opened two Costco Home outlets—one near its headquarters in the Seattle suburb of Kirkwood, Washington, and the other in the Phoenix suburb of Tempe, Arizona. Available to Costco members only, these stores feature high-end home furnishings. Although the new formats have been successful, the company's short-term plans include just a couple more Costco Home stores.

Instead, Costco plans to aggressively expand its network of warehouse clubs. The expansion schedule includes 20 openings in 2005, 30 more in 2006, and an additional 35 in 2007. In some cases, aggressive expansion has taken both Sam's and Costco out of their comfort zones. For instance, although Sam's has been the dominant warehouse club in Texas for many years, Costco added 10 new locations in the Lone Star State in a two-year period.

Analysts worry about saturating the domestic market. A Sam's vice president is less concerned, "We don't necessarily see, looking into the future, that saturation will occur. We just continue to see good growth and markets for this format."

Setting up Shop Overseas

Neither chain is overlooking the international arena—and all of its unique challenges and opportunities. There are currently more than 100 Costco locations outside the U.S.; the majority are in Canada with others located in the United Kingdom, Mexico, and Asia. Sam's operates 80 clubs in five countries besides the U.S. Both firms have had to adjust to foreign tastes and shopping styles.

Costco believes that the warehouse club concept is viable for any country. But it was surprised by how consumers' preferences varied across countries. For instance, shoppers in the United Kingdom snapped up cranberry juice, a beverage previously unavailable to them. Olive oil, basketball hoops, and doughnuts proved to be wildly popular in Japan.

At the same time, both warehouse club chains were still selling plenty of those items in the U.S. As of 2005, warehouse clubs represented a $90 billion industry domestically, with Costco and Sam's growing their sales by about 10% each year. However, warehouse clubs currently account for only 4% of the domestic retail sector, leaving plenty of room for growth. Thus the spirited competition between Costco and Sam's Club will continue—and perhaps intensify.

Questions

1. What are the pros and cons of operating a retail–wholesale outlet that requires shoppers to be members?

2. What is Costco's differential advantage in relation to Sam's? How about Sam's compared to Costco's?

3. In what ways, if any, do warehouse clubs have to deal differently with ultimate consumers than with wholesale buyers?

4. Should a warehouse club add new services that might increase its costs and, in turn, its prices in order to attract new members? Or should it seek to identify possible cost savings in order to maintain or even lower prices? Explain.

www.costco.com

www.samsclub.com

Sources

Case 1: Target *www.target.com,* accessed June 24, 2005; *www.kmart.com,* accessed June 24, 2005; Ann Zimmerman and Amy Merrick, "Wal-Mart, Target Lift Profits, But Outlooks Reveal Two Tales," *The Wall Street Journal,* May 13, 2005, p. A3; Laura Heller, "Innovative Thinking Permeates Entire Business Model," *DSN Retailing Today,* Apr. 11, 2005, p. 40; Teri Agins, "Style & Substance: The Lessons of Isaac," *The Wall Street Journal,* Feb. 7, 2005, p. B1; Ann Zimmerman, "Salvation for Ringers: Target's Charity Ban Is a Boon to Wal-Mart," *The Wall Street Journal,* Dec. 17, 2004, p. B1; Amy Merrick, Gary McWilliams, Ellen Byron, and Kortney Stringer, "Targeting Wal-Mart," *The Wall Street Journal,* Dec. 1, 2004, p. B1; Parija Bhatnagar, "The Kmart-Sears Deal," *CNN/Money,* Nov. 17, 2004 no pages given; Julie Schlosser, "How Target Does It," *Fortune,* Oct. 18, 2004, pp. 100–101+; Amy Merrick, "Target Will Sell Mervyn's to Group for $1.65 Billion," *The Wall Street Journal,* July 30, 2004, p. B3; Emily Scardino, "Target and Isaac Aiming for the Bullseye Again," *DSN Retailing Today,* July 5, 2004, p. 4; Laura Heller, "May Buys Field's from Target," *DSN Retailing Today,* June 21, 2004, pp. 1+; Emily Scardino, "Target Assortment Taps into Wider Demographics," *DSN Retailing Today,* Apr. 5, 2004, pp. 19+; Kemp Powers, "Kitchen-Sink Retailing," *Forbes,* Sept. 2, 2002, p. 78; "Target: 40 Years of Retailing," *Home Textiles Today,* May 27, 2002, pp. 16–17; "On Target," *The Economist,* May 5, 2001, p. 6; Susan Chandler, "Target Corp. Makes Field's Day," *Chicago Tribune,* Jan. 13, 2001, sec. 2, p. 1; and Gerry Khermouch, "Target Hits Bullseye," *Brandweek,* June 5, 1995, pp. 22–26.

Case 2: Costco versus Sam's Club *www.samsclub.com* and *www.costco.com,* both accessed June 26, 2005; Barbara Thau, "Costco Posts Sales, Earnings Increases," *HFN,* Mar. 7, 2005, p. 48; "Costco Cites Home As Strong Area," *Home Textiles Today,* Mar. 7, 2005, p. 6; Kortney Stringer, "Costco's Deep Discounts Don't Extend to Its Share Price," *The Wall Street Journal,* Feb. 22, 2005, p. C1; Analisa Nazareno, "Upscale But Cheap, Costco May Be the Only Retailer Wal-Mart Fears,'" *San Antonio Express-News,* Jan. 1, 2005, p. 9H; Debbie Howell and Mike Duff, "Small Business Focus Pays Off for Sam's," *DSN Retailing Today,* Oct. 11, 2004, pp. F1+; Stanley Holmes and Wendy Zellner, "The Costco Way," *BusinessWeek,* Apr. 12, 2004, pp. 76–77; Ann Zimmerman, "Costco's Dilemma: Be Kind to Its Workers, or Wall Street?" *The Wall Street Journal,* Mar. 26, 2004, p. B1; John Helyar, "The Only Company Wal-Mart Fears," *Fortune,* Nov. 24, 2003, pp. 158+; Nanette Byrnes, "The Bargain Hunter," *BusinessWeek,* Sept. 23, 2002, p. 82; Suzanne Woolley, "Costco? More Like Costgrow," *Money,* August 2002, pp. 44–46; Mike Duff, "Clubs Look to Build on Successful Initiatives," *DSN Retailing Today,* May 20, 2002, p. S5; Doug Desjardins, "Costco Forges Ahead with Clubs No. 3 and 4," *DSN Retailing Today,* May 6, 2002, pp. 4, 23; Doug Desjardins, "Clubs Benefit by Adding New Member Perks," *DSN Retailing Today,* Apr. 22, 2002, pp. 5, 29; Ken Clark, "Two Strategies, One Popular Segment," *Chain Store Age,* November 2001, pp. 56–58; Ann Zimmerman, "Taking Aim at Costco, Sam's Club Marshals Diamonds and Pearls," *The Wall Street Journal,* Aug. 9, 2001, pp. A1, A4; and Emily Nelson and Ann Zimmerman, "Kimberly-Clark Keeps Costco in Diapers, Absorbing Costs Itself," *The Wall Street Journal,* Sept. 7, 2001, pp. A1, A12.

Chapter 17

"As for promotion, Netflix has engaged in more activities than its competitors to reach prospective subscribers because it is the only major player without retail stores."

Can Netflix Create a Real-World Message for Fantasy-Minded Consumers?

In 2000, Netflix looked like it might follow in the footsteps of many other Internet-based business failures. The business plan was to duplicate the retail video rental model but without retail stores. Netflix offered consumers the opportunity to rent videos via the Internet and have them delivered by mail. Like the video stores, there was a rental charge and a late fee for videos not returned promptly. When the first year's volume was disappointing, the firm tried lowering the rental fee and extending the rental period, but neither seemed to help. Faced with the reality that the idea was unworkable, founder Reed Hastings and his top managers came up with a new business model—monthly subscription fees with no limit on the number of movies a subscriber could check out.

Initially Netflix charged $19.95 per month, which allowed a customer an unlimited number of DVDs as long as no more than three were out at a time, no limit on how long a film could be kept, and no late fee. Early advertising used banner ads on the Internet. The ads combined with word-of-mouth communication among consumers led to rapid growth for Netflix. By July 2003, with 1 million subscribers and 300,000 DVDs shipped each day, Netflix raised its subscription price to $21.99.

The success of Netflix attracted attention. Wal-Mart began an online video rental operation in 2002 for $18.76 per month, and Blockbuster, with 40% of the total video rental market, entered the online fray in August 2004 with a $19.99 subscription fee. Netflix has some advantages over its rivals. With 30 distribution centers around the country, it can get DVDs to subscribers in one day, and with 30,000 titles, it has the broadest selection of movies to choose from.

Netflix and the other video rental firms must increase subscriptions in order to grow and to account for "churn," the 3% to 5% of subscribers that drop out monthly. The tactics they have chosen to stimulate growth are price cuts and promotion. All three have lowered their prices (At the beginning of 2005, Netflix was at $17.99, Blockbuster was at $14.99, and Wal-Mart was at $17.36). As for promotion, Netflix has engaged in more activities than its competitors to reach prospective subscribers because it is the only major player without retail stores. Its primary efforts include:

- TV commercials.
- In-store promotions with cooperating retailers such as Best Buy.
- Promotions included in the packaging of new DVD players.
- Banner ads on the Internet.
- Free introductory trials of the service.

In addition, Netflix has developed some creative tools, including one it calls "Friends." Subscribers can, without charge, inform a designated list of their subscriber-friends what videos they have watched and provide a rating. The idea is to offer a convenient way for subscribers to share information and, of course, to stimulate word-of-mouth communication about Netflix. A second tool is "Affiliates." Anyone with an approved website can direct subscribers to Netfllix and be paid a $9 referral fee for each new member. In effect, these affiliates become sales agents for Netflix.[1]

What objectives does Netflix appear to be pursuing with this combination of promotional tools?

www.netflix.com

Like all marketers, Netflix is faced with deciding how much and what types of promotion to undertake. These decisions are complicated by the fact that there are many forms of promotion and no two marketing situations are exactly alike. This chapter will help you understand what promotion can accomplish and how the various forms of promotion can be brought together in an integrated marketing communications effort that contributes to a firm's total marketing program. After studying this chapter, you should be able to explain:

- The role of promotion.
- The forms promotion can take.
- The concept of integrated marketing communications.
- How the process of communicating relates to effective promotion.
- Key considerations in developing a promotion mix.
- Alternative promotional budgeting methods.
- The major types of promotion regulation.

The Role of Promotion in Marketing

A feature of a free-market system is the right to use communication as a tool to persuade as well as inform. In the U.S. socioeconomic system, that freedom is reflected in the promotional efforts by businesses to affect the awareness, feelings, beliefs, and behavior of prospective customers. To begin our examination of promotion, let's consider how it works from an economic perspective and from a marketing perspective.

Promotion and Imperfect Competition

The American marketplace operates under conditions of imperfect competition, characterized by incomplete market information, product differentiation, and emotional buying behavior. In recognition of these conditions, companies use promotion to provide information for the decision maker's buying-decision process, to assist in differentiating their products, and to persuade potential buyers.

In economic terms, the role of promotion is to change the location and shape of the demand (revenue) curve for a company's product. (See Figure 17.1 and recall the discussion of nonprice competition in Chapter 13.) Simply stated, promotion is intended to make a product more attractive to prospective buyers. Through promo-

FIGURE 17.1

The Goals of Promotion.

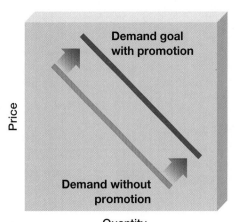

a. A shift in the demand curve to the right.

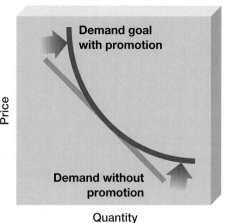

b. Changing the shape (or elasticity) of the demand curve.

How do marketers reach younger consumers who tend to avoid traditional media and advertising? BMW's solution is to go where they are and offer them entertainment. From 2001 through 2003, the auto company created 8 action films each five- to ten-minutes in length starring British actor Clive Owen and featuring its cars in exciting chases. The films can be seen on the Internet. Over 75 million visitors had logged on and watched. As a follow-up, BMW has produced a series of 6 comic books with the same hero driving BMW concept cars.

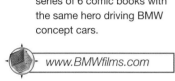

www.BMWfilms.com

tion a company strives to increase its product's sales volume at any given price (Figure 17.1a); that is, the firm seeks to shift its demand curve to the right.

A firm also hopes that promotion will affect the demand elasticity for its product (Figure 17.1b). The intent is to make the demand more inelastic when price increases and more elastic when price decreases. In other words, management wants promotion to increase the attractiveness of a product so the quantity demanded will decline very little if price goes up (inelastic demand), and sales will increase considerably if price goes down (elastic demand).

Promotion and Marketing

From a marketing perspective promotion is intended to further the objectives of an organization. It makes use of various tools to perform three essential promotional roles—informing, persuading, and reminding target audiences. The relative importance of these roles depends on the circumstances faced by the firm. Let's consider each of them separately.

The most useful product will be a failure if no one knows it exists, so the first task of promotion is to *inform*. Beyond simply being aware of a product or brand, customers must understand what benefits it provides, how it works, and how to get it. These are just a few examples of the information promotion provides channel members and consumers. In the electronic appliance industry, for example, Palm uses advertising to educate the market about the operation and features of each new generation of handhelds.

Another purpose of promotion is *persuasion*. Competition among firms puts pressure on the promotional programs of sellers to draw attention to and differentiate their offerings. In an economy with an abundant supply of products, consumers have many alternative ways of satisfying even basic physiological needs. As a result, persuasive promotion is essential. Campbell Soup Company has been marketing condensed soup for over 100 years, and accounts for 80% of all soup sales in the U.S. It is one of the most recognized brands and packages in the country. Studies show that virtually every household has some Campbell's soup in the pantry. Yet the firm spends over $100 million a year advertising soup. Why? Partly because it regularly introduces new flavors but also, more important, because its primary products are

Promotion takes many forms. Hormel's three SPAMMOBILES are replicas of a SPAM can. They travel 120,000 miles a year, appearing at retail stores, concerts, sporting events, and festivals, serving over 1.5 million miniature sandwiches made from . . . you guessed it. Are you aware of other firms that use similar promotional devices? For a start, think tires, film, and hot dogs.

www.spammobile.com

condensed soups that require some minimal preparation. And as one industry analyst quipped, "If you're under 70 years old, you buy ready-to-serve soup."[2] Thus, Campbell's, faced with intense competition from alternative easier-to-prepare foods, uses promotion to suggest alternative benefits such as nutrition and better taste in order to persuade soup buyers.

Consumers also must be *reminded* about a product's availability and its potential to satisfy. Sellers bombard the marketplace with thousands of messages every day in hopes of attracting new consumers and establishing markets for new products. Given the intense competition for consumers' attention, even an established firm must constantly remind people about its brand to retain a place in their minds. It is unlikely that a day goes by, for example, in which you don't see some form of promotion (an in-store display, counter sign, vending machine, billboard, or imprinted T-shirt) for Coca-Cola. In fact, soft drink companies spend over $375 million a year on prime-time television advertising alone.[3] Because there is little new to inform consumers about Coke, much of this promotion is intended simply to offset competitors' marketing activities by keeping the various brands in front of the consumer.

Recognizing that it is both important and varied, we define **promotion** as all personal and impersonal efforts by a seller or the seller's representative to inform, persuade, or remind a target audience.

Promotion Methods

Promotion, to whomever it is directed, is an attempt to influence. There are four forms of promotion: personal selling, advertising, sales promotion, and public relations. Each has distinct features that determine the role it can play in a promotion program:

- **Personal selling** is the direct presentation of a product to a prospective customer by a representative of the organization selling it. Personal selling takes place face-to-face or over the phone, and it may be directed to a business person or a final consumer. We list it first because, across all organizations, more money is spent on personal selling than on any other form of promotion.

- **Advertising** is nonpersonal communication paid for by a clearly identified sponsor promoting ideas, organizations, or products. The most familiar outlets for ads are the broadcast (TV and radio) and print (newspapers and magazines) media. However, there are many other advertising vehicles, from billboards to T-shirts and, more recently, the Internet.

- **Sales promotion** is sponsor-funded, demand-stimulating activity designed to supplement advertising and facilitate personal selling. It frequently consists of a temporary incentive to encourage a sale or purchase. Many sales promotions are directed at consumers. The premiums offered by fast-food outlets in conjunction with popular movies are examples. The majority, however, are designed to encourage the company's sales force or other members of a distribution channel to sell products more aggressively. When sales promotion is directed to the members of the distribution channel, it is called *trade promotion*. Included in sales promotion are a wide spectrum of activities, such as event sponsorships, frequency programs, contests, trade shows, in-store displays, rebates, samples, premiums, discounts, and coupons.

- **Public relations** encompasses a wide variety of communication efforts to contribute to generally favorable attitudes and opinions toward an organization and its products. Unlike most advertising and personal selling, it does not include a specific sales message. The targets may be customers, stockholders, a government agency, or a special-interest group. Public relations can take many forms, including newsletters, annual reports, lobbying, and support of charitable or civic events. The Fuji and Goodyear blimps and the Oscar Mayer Wienermobiles are familiar examples of public relations devices. *Publicity* is a special form of public relations that involves news stories about an organization or its products. Like advertising, it consists of an impersonal message that reaches a mass audience through the media. But several features distinguish publicity from advertising: Placement is not paid for, the organization that is the subject of the publicity has little or no control over it, and it appears as news and therefore has greater credibility than advertising. Organizations actively seek good publicity and frequently provide the material for it in the form of news releases, press conferences, and photographs. When a picture of a company's CEO appears on the cover of a business publication and is accompanied by a flattering article in the magazine, it is often attributable to the efforts of the firm's public relations department. There also is, of course, bad publicity, which organizations try to avoid or deflect.

www.goodyear.com/us/blimp

www.oscarmayer.com

YOU MAKE THE DECISION

When should a marketer go beyond the traditional modes of communication?

In a simpler time marketers had many fewer options for conveying their messages to prospects. The primary media consisted of network television, radio, magazines, newspapers, direct mail, and billboards. However, the development of cable television channels, satellite radio, and the Internet greatly expanded these options. As a result, marketers can target audiences more specifically, but they are also faced with making many more decisions. In recent years advertising seems to be appearing everywhere. It may have begun with brands and ad slogans printed on clothing (Is it possible to get a plain, white T-shirt anymore?), and now it includes print ads in public restrooms, on airport luggage carousels, on the walls of parking garages, and in the bottom of golf holes. Video ads are showing up in movies, on ATM screens, on gas pumps, in doctors' waiting rooms, and in elevators. One recent development is advergames—custom-published video games available online or via consoles that involve a high level of interaction with a product or brand. Forrester Research estimates that marketers spent $1 billion on advergames in 2005. Advergame users include Disney, BMW, GlaxoSmithKline marketing oral healthcare products, Chrysler promoting the launch of new vehicles, and Nabisco marketing various snack foods. The decision to use "alternative" media can consume a large part of a firm's promotion budget (advergames can cost from $20,000 to $150,000 to produce, depending on the sophistication) and most have yet to develop measures of effectiveness.

What criteria should be used in evaluating nontraditional modes of reaching a market with promotional messages?

Sources: Clare Goff, "Pushing the Right Buttons," *New Media Age,* Mar. 24, 2005, pp. 21+; Catherine Arnold, "Just Press Play," *Marketing News,* May 15, 2004, pp. 1+; Karen Moltenbrey, "Adver-Driving," *Computer Graphics World,* June 2004, pp. 30+.

Integrated Marketing Communication

Marketers have a variety of promotional tools at their disposal. To make effective use of them, a company's personal selling, advertising, and other promotional activities should form a coordinated promotional program within its total marketing plan. However, these activities are fragmented in many firms, with potentially damaging consequences. For example, advertising directors and sales-force managers may come into conflict over resources, or the sales force may not be adequately informed about the details of a particular sales promotion effort. This wouldn't happen if the elements comprising promotion were part of an **integrated marketing communication (IMC)** effort, a strategic business process used to plan, develop, execute, and evaluate coordinated, measurable, persuasive communications with an organization's internal and external audiences.[4]

IMC begins with a strategic planning effort designed to coordinate promotion with product planning, pricing, and distribution—the other marketing-mix elements. Promotion is influenced, for instance, by how distinctive a product is and whether its planned price is above or below the competition. A manufacturer or middleman must also consider its promotional links with other firms in the distribution channel. For example, Toyota recognizes that its success is closely tied to the performance of its independent dealers. Therefore, in addition to advertising its automobiles directly to consumers, the firm asks recent Toyota purchasers to complete an extensive questionnaire on dealer performance that includes everything from how promptly they were greeted on the first visit to the showroom to how well the new car's features were explained at delivery. A dealership's results on the survey influence its subsequent allocation of the most popular Toyota models.

An Audience Perspective

An IMC approach adopts the position that a customer or prospect is exposed to many bits and pieces of information about a company or brand. Certainly some of these are designed and presented by the marketer, but many, possibly the majority, come from other sources. These sources can include personal experiences, the opinions of friends, and comparisons made by competitors in their advertising. On the basis of all this information, an individual makes an evaluation and forms a judgment. With so little control over the information an audience uses, or how the information is used, a marketer's promotional efforts must be highly coordinated and complementary to have an impact. That means anticipating the opportunities when the target audience will be exposed to information about the company or brand, and effectively communicating the appropriate message in those "windows of opportunity." Usually this involves utilizing several promotional methods and requires a high degree of coordination.

IMC Elements

The use of an IMC approach to promotion is reflected in how managers think about the information needs of the message recipients. Organizations that have adopted an IMC philosophy tend to share several characteristics, notably:

- An awareness of the target audience's information sources, as well as their media habits and preferences.
- An understanding of what the audience knows and believes that relates to the desired response.
- The use of a mix of promotional tools, each with specific objectives but all contributing to a common goal.

- A coordinated promotional effort in which personal selling, advertising, sales promotion, and public relations communicate a consistent message tailored to the audience's information needs.

Implementing IMC

By definition, IMC embraces the entire promotional program. In developing integrated communications, a company coordinates its advertising, personal selling, sales promotion, public relations, and direct marketing to accomplish specific objectives. Today, about half of the movies released in the U.S. have promotional tie-ins with brands. IMC frequently comes into play in these partnerships. For example, when Spider-Man 2 became available on DVD, Orville Redenbacher offered a $5 mail-in rebate with the purchase of its popcorn; Embassy Suites created a Spider-Man gift package it promoted with TV, print, online, and direct mail advertising; and Energizer offered a gift with the purchase of a battery pack that it promoted with billboards. In Europe, where movie tie-ins are less common, Nestlé partnered with Shrek 2's release to promote Nesquik with Web-based games and prizes aimed at children in 21 countries, on-package promotions, and media advertising aimed at parents.[5] Because these promotional efforts must coincide with a movie's release and typically last just a few weeks, timing is critical. Printing special packages, designing games and prizes, preparing and placing advertisements, arranging retail displays, and numerous other tasks require the coordinated efforts of many internal and external departments and functions.

An IMC program may incorporate several different promotional campaigns, with some even running concurrently. Depending on objectives and available funds, a firm may undertake simultaneous local, regional, national, and international programs. Moreover, a firm may have one campaign aimed at consumers and another aimed at wholesalers and retailers.

Evaluating IMC

The last step in an IMC program is evaluation. A program can be evaluated in a number of ways. One approach is to examine how it is implemented. For example, if the promotion by a large manufacturer of consumer goods is being carried out in a manner consistent with the notion of IMC, we would expect to find:

- An advertising program consisting of a series of related, well-timed, carefully placed ads that reinforce personal selling and sales promotion efforts.
- A personal selling effort that is coordinated with the advertising program. The firm's sales force would be fully informed about the advertising portion of the campaign—the theme, media used, and the schedule for the appearance of ads. The sales people would be able to explain and demonstrate the product benefits stressed in the ads and would be prepared to transmit the promotional message and supporting material to middlemen so they can take part in the campaign.
- Sales promotional devices, such as point-of-purchase display materials, that are coordinated with other aspects of the program. Incentives for middlemen would be clearly communicated and understood. Retailers would be briefed about consumer promotions and adequate inventories would be in place.
- Public relations efforts scheduled to coincide with the other mix components and emphasizing the same theme.

More rigorous evaluation examines the results of the program. The outcome of each promotional component is compared with the objectives set for it to determine

To call attention to the success of Crest toothpaste on the brand's 50th anniversary, Procter & Gamble developed an IMC campaign. The first element was a nationwide search for a "Crest kid." Enya Martinez a five-year-old Miami girl, was selected from over 3,000 applicants. The company then featured her in print ads, retail point-of-purchase displays, and a public relations program in conjunction with dentists to encourage good oral health behavior among children.

www.crest.com

www.army.mil

"Look Mom, I'm the new Crest Kid!"

In celebration of Crest's 50th birthday, we introduce Enya Martinez, winner of a nationwide search for the new Crest Kid.

if the effort was successful. Listed below are some typical promotion objectives and some common measures associated with each of them:

- *Awareness of a company or a brand:* Brand name recognition and recall studies, focus groups with distributors at trade shows, and number of website "hits."

- *Knowledge about a company or a brand:* Perceptions of competitive brand positioning, familiarity with brand features and benefits.

- *Interest in a product or brand:* Number of brochures or other company publications distributed, attendance at company-sponsored seminars, and website traffic on specific pages.

- *Action:* Usage of sales support tools by distributors and retailers, responses to direct mail, participation in contests and drawings, customer inquiries or store visits, and sales.

To be meaningful, most of these measures need to be taken before and after the promotional effort, with the difference between the two measures indicating its effect. For example, the U.S. Army uses a number of promotional tools in its recruiting efforts including mass-media advertising, a website, and sponsorships. Included among the sponsorships are Arena Football, National Association for Stock Car Auto Racing (NASCAR), and the National Hot Rod Association (NHRA). To assess the value of its NHRA sponsorship, the Army tracks the number of leads generated from visitors to its booths at drag-racing events, and the proportion of those leads that actually become recruits. By comparing the relative productivity of these promotional tools over time, the Army can maximize the productivity of its resources.

Barriers to IMC

Despite its intuitive attractiveness, an IMC approach to promotion is not universally supported. In some organizations the promotional functions are in different departments. For example, the sales force may be in a unit apart from where advertising decisions are made. As a result, there is a lack of internal communication and coordination. In other companies there is a belief that promotion is such an imprecise activity that efforts to carefully design objectives and coordinate efforts would be unproductive. In still other firms there is a history of relying on a particular form of promotion and a resistance to consider alternatives.

Fully utilizing an IMC approach would likely require a firm to make several changes. One involves restructuring internal communication to ensure that all relevant parties involved in promotion are working together. Some firms have approached this by creating a marketing communications (or marcom) manager who oversees the planning and coordination of promotional efforts. A second change entails conducting research to gather the necessary information about the target audience. Firms utilize extensive customer databases for this purpose, but they are costly to create and expensive to maintain. Finally, and most important, top management must support the effort to integrate promotion. Strong leadership is essential in order to gain commitment from the entire organization.

Next we'll examine how communication, the core of promotion, actually works. Then we'll move to the key managerial issues in a promotion program.

The Communication Process and Promotion

Communication is the verbal or nonverbal transmission of information between someone wanting to express an idea and someone else expected or expecting to get that idea. Because promotion is a form of communication, much can be learned about structuring effective promotion by examining the communication process.

Fundamentally, communication requires only four elements: a message, a source of the message, a communication channel, and a receiver. In practice, however, important additional components come into play. Figure 17.2 illustrates these components of a communication process, and relates them to promotion activities.

Consider this example of what happens when a teenager sees an ad for adidas.

- The information the sender wants to share must first be *encoded* into a transmittable form. In the case of a recent adidas campaign this means converting an idea ("Everyone should strive to be the best they can be") into words and pictures. Thus, the adidas campaign "Impossible Is Nothing" depicts current and past athletes accomplishing remarkable achievements.

- Once the message is transmitted through a communication channel, in this case television, the symbols must be *decoded* or given meaning by the recipient. The *message as received* may be what the sender intended (Everyone is capable of exceeding his or her own highest personal expectations) or something else that is possibly less desirable (only exceptional people accomplish exceptional things), depending on the recipient's frame of reference.

FIGURE 17.2

The Communication Process in Promotion.

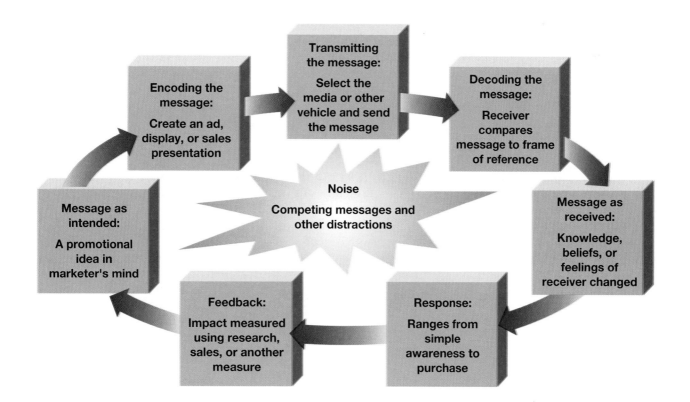

- If the message is transmitted as intended, there is some change in the receiver's knowledge, beliefs, or feelings. As a result of this change, the receiver formulates a *response*. The response could be internal (I should set my goals higher) or could involve some action (Read the biography of one of the athletes featured to see what clues it contains to becoming successful).

- The response serves as *feedback*, informing the sender whether the message was received and how it was perceived by the recipient. Through feedback, the sender can learn what a communication accomplished. Because corporate or institutional advertising such as the "Impossible Is Nothing" campaign doesn't call for a specific action, its effect is difficult to assess. An organization may have to conduct consumer research, possibly a survey, to determine what, if any, message was communicated.

- All stages of the process are affected by *noise*—any factor external to the sender or receiver that interferes with successful communication. Any distraction that undermines or competes for the recipient's attention while the message is transmitted serves as noise. Leaving the room to get a snack, picking up a newspaper, or zipping through the ad would be examples of noise.

What does the communication process tell us about promotion? First, the act of encoding reminds us that messages can take many forms. Messages can be physical (a sample, a premium) or symbolic (verbal, visual), and there are a myriad of options within each of these categories. For example, the form of a verbal message can be factual, humorous, or even threatening.

Second, the number of channels or methods of transmitting a message are limited only by the imagination and creativity of the sender. Consider that promotional messages are transmitted by the voice of a sales person, the airwaves of radio, the mail, the side of a bus, a website on the Internet, messages on a billboard, the lead-in to a feature in a movie theater, and dozens of other methods. Each channel has its own characteristics in terms of audience reach, flexibility, permanence, credibility, and cost. In selecting a channel, a marketer must have clearly defined objectives and a familiarity with the features of the many alternatives. For example, how would you promote a new energy drink? The creator of Red Bull, Dietrich Mateschitz, was faced with introducing a new beverage that doesn't taste especially good, is twice the price of an equivalent amount of Coca-Cola or Pepsi, and includes some strange sounding

Can an office products' catalog get the attention of key decision makers even when they are not actively placing orders? Boise Cascade marketers tried an unconventional interactive device that generated a large number of responses and won a promotion award. Prospects were invited to complete and submit a self-administered personality-typing questionnaire. In return, these potential customers received feedback (including this color compatibility wheel) that provided them with a little insight about themselves and their co-workers, had some fun, and were exposed to Boise Cascade and its office-products line.

ingredients such as taurine. Convinced that traditional advertising would not reach his target audience, Mateschitz chose instead to focus on sponsorships of youth-oriented events. He began with wacky contests, such as seeing who could fly the farthest in homemade flying machines, and then moved on to extreme sports events. More recently the company has added sponsorship of a Formula One auto racing team along with over 500 events around the world from rock music concerts to sky diving. As a result, Red Bull has certainly caught the eye of consumers. In 1987, its first year, the company sold 1 million cans. In 2004, it sold 1.9 *billion* cans.[6]

www.redbull.com

Third, how the message is decoded or interpreted depends on its form (encoding and transmission) and the capability and interest of the recipient. In designing and sending messages, marketers must be sensitive to the audience. What is their vocabulary and level of verbal sophistication? What other messages have they received? What experiences have they had? What will get and hold their attention?

Finally, every promotional activity should have a measurable objective. The response and feedback provided by the recipients can be used to determine if the objective is accomplished. Feedback may be collected in many forms—changes in sales, recall of advertising messages, more favorable attitudes, increased awareness of a product or an organization—depending on the objective of the promotion. For some promotional activities the objective may be modest—for example, an increase in the audience's awareness of a brand. For others, such as a direct-mail solicitation, the objective may be a particular level of sales. Without quantifiable objectives, there is no way of evaluating the effectiveness of a message.

Determining the Promotion Mix

A **promotion mix** is an organization's combination of personal selling, advertising, sales promotion, and public relations. Product differentiation, positioning, trading up, trading down, and branding all require effective promotion. Designing an effective promotion mix involves strategic decisions about five factors: (1) target audience, (2) objective of the promotion effort, (3) nature of the product, (4) stage in the product's life cycle, and (5) amount of money available for promotion.

Target Audience

As is true for most areas of marketing, decisions on the promotional mix will be greatly influenced by the target audience. The target may be final consumers, who could be further defined as existing customers or new prospects. Some marketers (notably toy and fast-food firms) direct much of their efforts at decision makers, who are likely to be children, rather than at the actual purchasers. In some cases the target consists of middlemen in order to gain their support in distributing a product, or in the case of a company about to make a stock offering, the investment community.

Final consumers and middlemen sometimes buy the same product, but they require different promotion. To illustrate, 3M Company sells its blank CDs to final consumers through computer and office-supply stores. Promotion to dealers includes sharing the cost of yellow pages ads and advertising in specialized business magazines such as *Office Products Dealer*. Different ads aimed at final consumers are run in magazines such as *Personal Computing, Fortune,* and *BusinessWeek.*

A promotion aimed at middlemen is called a **push strategy,** and a promotion directed at end users is called a **pull strategy.** Figure 17.3 contrasts these two strategies.

Using a push strategy means a channel member directs its promotion primarily at the middlemen that are the next link forward in the distribution channel. In effect, the product is "pushed" through the channel. Take the case of a hardware producer that sells its tools and replacement parts to household consumers through wholesalers and retailers such as Ace and True Value. The producer will promote heavily to wholesalers, which then also use a push strategy to retailers. In turn, the retailers promote to consumers. A push strategy usually involves a lot of personal selling and sales promotion, including contests for sales people and displays at trade shows. This promotional strategy is appropriate for many manufacturers of business products, as well as for consumer goods that are undifferentiated or do not have a strong brand identity.

With a pull strategy, promotion is directed at end users—usually ultimate consumers. The intention is to motivate them to ask retailers for the product. The retailers, in turn, will request the product from wholesalers, and wholesalers will order it from the producer. Promotion to consumers is designed to "pull" the product through the channel. This strategy relies on heavy advertising and consumer sales promotion such as premiums, samples, or in-store demonstrations.

FIGURE 17.3

Push and Pull Promotional Strategies.

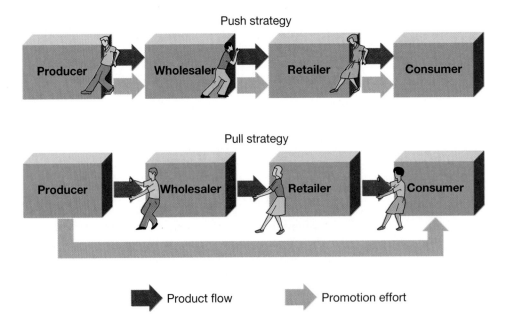

The Internet has made it possible for firms to direct carefully crafted messages to specific audiences while allowing the site visitors control over the amount and type of exposure. For example, at its website Volkswagen offers television commercials, simulated test drives, and specially created mini video dramas for each of its models. The result is strong, unobtrusive selling messages.

www.vw.com

The new Jetta

Retailers have little incentive to provide shelf space for minor variations of existing brands unless they are confident the products will sell. So manufacturers of consumer packaged goods often use a pull strategy to get new products stocked on supermarket shelves. For example, when Dr. Pepper introduced Red Fusion, the first new flavor addition in the company's 117-year history, it employed television, radio, outdoor, and Internet advertising in addition to point-of-sale materials and in-store sampling. In the crowded soft drink category, this type of pull strategy gives retailers needed reassurance that the brand has a reasonable chance of success.

Promotion Objective

A target audience can be in any one of six stages of buying readiness. These stages—awareness, knowledge, liking, preference, conviction, and purchase—are called the **hierarchy of effects** because they represent stages a buyer goes through in moving toward a purchase, with each also describing a possible goal or effect of promotion. The objective of promotion is to get the prospect to the final, or purchase stage, but in most cases that is not possible until the person has moved through the earlier stages. Thus, a promotion effort may have what appears to be a modest but essential objective, such as creating knowledge about a product's advantages.

www.grapplefruits.com

Awareness   At the *awareness* stage the seller's task is to let the buyers know that the product or brand exists. Here the objective is to build familiarity with the product and association with the brand name. Get Fit Foods has introduced the Grapple, a Fuji apple bathed in Concord grape juice. Based on tests the producers know kids like the taste, but they hope that parents also will see the product as a way to introduce their children to healthier eating. However, before consumers buy it, they will have to be made aware that it exists and the benefit it provides.[7]

www.southafrica.net

Knowledge   *Knowledge* goes beyond awareness to learning about a product's features. Recognizing that many potential visitors know very little about their country, South Africa's tourism office has produced a 45-minute 3-D Imax film for showing in the U.S., Europe, and Asia.[8] The film takes viewers on a big game safari in which they will see elephants, rhinos, leopards, lions, and Cape buffalo at close range. Because the film is more extensive than an advertisement, it can provide a considerable amount of information and answer many basic questions for prospective visitors.

Liking   *Liking* refers to how the market feels about the product. Promotion can be used to move a knowledgeable audience from being indifferent to liking a brand. A common technique is to associate the item with an attractive symbol or person. The sporting goods company, adidas, has partnering relationships with the athletic programs of seven universities including Arizona State, Northwestern, University of Tennessee, the University of Notre Dame, and the University of Nebraska. By providing uniforms and equipment to the players and coaches that include its company's logo, adidas hopes to create a favorable impression on the fans of these teams.

Preference Creating *preference* involves distinguishing among brands so that the market finds your brand more attractive than alternatives. It is not uncommon for customers to like several brands of the same product but to be unable make a decision until they prefer one brand over the alternatives. Ads that make a comparison with the competition are intended to create a preference. In the auto-rental business, Avis has made a not-so-subtle comparison for over 40 years with the ad slogan "We Try Harder." Another comparison ad campaign that created quite a stir is pizza maker Papa John's slogan "Better Ingredients, Better Pizza."[9]

Conviction *Conviction* entails the actual decision or commitment to purchase. A student may prefer the IBM PC over a clone but may not yet be convinced to buy a computer. The promotion objective here is to increase the strength of the buyer's need. Radio Shack recognizes that with electronic products many consumers are interested but uncertain. Since trying a product and experiencing its benefits are very effective in strengthening a customer's conviction to own it, Radio Shack's biggest hurdle is getting customers into the store. Thus the slogan, "You've got questions, we've got answers," encourages consumers to visit Radio Shack stores without feeling uncomfortable about their lack of knowledge.

Purchase *Purchase* can be delayed or postponed indefinitely, even for customers who are convinced they should buy a product. The inhibitor might be a situational factor such as not having enough money at the moment, or a natural resistance to change. Action may be triggered through a temporary price reduction or the offer of additional incentives. Firms distribute nearly 260 *billion* coupons annually to stimulate purchases.[10]

Promotional efforts are also aimed at obtaining repeat purchases or building loyalty among customers who have purchased a product. A credit card company's database that indicates a cardholder has not made a purchase using the credit card for an unusual length of time might trigger a direct-mail piece or a personal phone call.

Nature of the Product

Several product attributes influence the promotion mix. We will consider three that are especially significant: unit value, customization, and service requirements.

Unit Value A product with low unit value is usually relatively uncomplicated, involves little risk for the buyer, and must appeal to a mass market to survive. As a result, advertising would be the primary promotional tool. In contrast, high-unit value products often are complex and expensive. These features suggest the need for personal selling. BMW dealers are being encouraged to have sales people get out of the showroom and call on prospects. By increasing the personal selling effort through techniques such as delivering cars to potential customers for test-drives, BMW hopes to stimulate U.S. sales.

Degree of Customization The benefits of most standardized products can be effectively communicated with advertising. However, if a product must be adapted to the individual customer's needs, personal selling is typically necessary. Thus you would expect to find an emphasis on personal selling in the promotion mix for something like home remodeling or an expensive suit of clothing.

Although the principle of relying on advertising for standard products and personal selling for customized items holds in most instances, it is being challenged by firms searching for efficient ways to implement mass customization. For example Lands' End allows a consumer to design a pair of chinos using interactive systems on its website.

Presale and Postsale Service Products that must be demonstrated, for which there are trade-ins, or that require frequent servicing to stay in good working order lend themselves to personal selling. Typical examples are automobiles, riding lawn mowers, and pleasure boats.

Stage in the Product Life Cycle

Promotion strategies are influenced by a product's life-cycle stage. When a new product is introduced, prospective buyers must be informed about its existence and its benefits, and middlemen must be convinced to carry it. Thus both advertising (to consumers) and personal selling (to middlemen) are critical in a product's introductory stage. At introduction a new product also may be something of a novelty, offering excellent opportunities for publicity. Later, if a product becomes successful, competition intensifies and more emphasis is placed on persuasive advertising. Table 17.1

TABLE 17.1

Promotional Strategies for Different Product Life-Cycle Stages

Market Situation and Promotional Goals	Promotional Strategy
Introduction Stage	
Customers are not aware of the product's features, nor do they understand how it will benefit them. In this stage, a seller must stimulate primary demand—the demand for a type of product—as contrasted with selective demand—the demand for a particular brand.	Inform and educate potential customers that the product exists, how it might be used, and what want-satisfying benefits it provides. For example, producers had to sell consumers on the value of compact discs in general before they considered it feasible to promote a particular brand. Exhibits at trade shows often are used to give a new product broad exposure to many middlemen. Manufacturers rely heavily on personal selling to attract middlemen to handle a new product.
Growth Stage	
Customers are aware of the product's benefits. The product is selling well, and middlemen want to handle it. In this stage, a seller must stimulate selective (brand) demand as competition grows.	Increase emphasis on advertising to differentiate the product. Sales promotion tools (coupons, samples) are used to gain trial customers. Middlemen share more of the total promotional effort.
Maturity Stage	
Competition intensifies and sales level off. Advertising is used more to persuade prospects rather than only to provide information.	Intense competition forces sellers to devote larger sums to advertising and thus contributes to the declining profits experienced in this stage.
Decline Stage	
Sales and profits are declining. New and better products are coming into the market. The focus moves to reminding remaining customers.	All promotional efforts are cut back substantially.

What are the limits of permission marketing?

The text-messaging capability of cell phones has created a new medium for advertisers. According to research by Pew Internet, of the estimated 134 million U.S. consumers who have cell phones, over 25%, or 34 million, used the text-messaging feature during a three-week measurement period. Of that group, over 9.5 million received unsolicited commercial text messages on their phones.

Text campaigns have been run for Snapple, Reebok, and Time Warner in the U.S. Coca-Cola and British Airways have used the method in Europe and Asia. Snapple's effort, alerting consumers to a contest that involved numbers on beverage bottle caps, resulted in sales to a third of the respondents, and nearly 15% forwarded the message to friends. However, many marketers have discovered that consumers resent being bombarded with text messages just because they are inexpensive for the sender. In an effort to protect its subscribers, Verizon Wireless recently filed a federal lawsuit against a number of firms, claiming they sent over 4 million unapproved messages to cell phone users.

This type of backlash has led savvy marketers to more closely track the interests of their audiences. In many cases, they seek the consumer's permission before sending information about promotions, new products, or special offers. Now questions are arising about how far that permission should extend. If a consumer expresses an interest in a portable music player, does that firm have permission to notify the consumer about all of its entertainment equipment offerings?

This is the beginning of a new era in marketing communication. In a world where communication has been essentially one-way and communicators have tried to be intrusive we are moving to instantly interactive communication and seeking permission before sending a message.

Sources: Tatiana Serafin, "Opportunity Rings," *Forbes*, Oct. 18, 2004, p. 62; Josh Linkner, "Please Remove Your Sneakers," *Brandweek*, Apr. 18, 2005, p. 28; "Consumers Provide More Data to Trusted Companies," *Promo Xtra*, Jan. 12, 2005, on the Promo Magazine website (*www.promomagazine.com*).

shows how promotional goals and strategies change as a product moves through its life cycle.

Funds Available

Regardless of the most desirable promotional mix, the amount of money available for promotion is often the ultimate determinant of the mix. A business with ample funds can make more effective use of advertising than a firm with limited financial resources. For example, television advertising can carry a particular promotional message to far more people and at a lower cost per person than most other media. Yet a firm may have to rely on less expensive options, such as yellow pages advertising or a website.

One low-budget approach is only limited by the imagination of the marketer. Called **viral marketing** it involves creating a situation in which consumers spread information about a company or brand to other people. Viral marketing differs from word-of-mouth advertising only in that the company intentionally stimulates the communication flow. An example of viral marketing is the electronic greetings Blue Mountain Arts allows its website visitors to send to anyone with an Internet connection.

www.bluemountain.com

Firms also are using **weblogs** or blogs, personalized websites that are frequently updated and linked to other sites, to conduct electronic viral marketing. In some cases firms have authorized employees to maintain blogs and in others they have made use of consumers' blogs. For example, to introduce a milk-based product called Raging Cow, Dr. Pepper invited six bloggers in their late teens and early twenties to try the product and post their reactions.[11]

The Promotion Budget

Establishing promotion budgets is extremely challenging because management lacks reliable standards to determine how much to spend altogether on advertising, personal selling, and the remainder of the promotion mix, or how much of the total budget to allocate to each mix component. A firm may have the alternative of adding three sales people or increasing its trade show budget by $200,000 a year, but it cannot determine precisely what increase in sales or profits to expect from either expenditure.

Promotional activities generally are budgeted as current operating expenses, implying that their benefits are used up immediately. However, it's been suggested that advertising (and presumably other promotional efforts) should be thought of as a capital investment, even if it must be treated as an expense for accounting purposes. The reason is that the benefits and returns on promotional expenditures are like investments, often not immediately evident, but instead accruing over several years. For example, several advertising slogans including "The ultimate driving machine" (BMW), "Finger lickin' good" (KFC), and "Because I'm worth it" (L'Oreal) were recently inducted into the Advertising Slogan Hall of Fame because of their enduring impact. Regularly repeating messages such as these build awareness and familiarity, sometimes for years, before actual sales are produced. Taking a longer-term, investment perspective on promotion would likely lead to greater consistency in the amounts spent, and the manner in which the budget is allocated across the types of promotion.

www.adslogans.co.uk

Rather than one generally accepted approach to promotion budgeting, there are four common **promotional budgeting methods:** percentage of sales, all available funds, following the competition, and budgeting by task or objective. These methods are frequently discussed in connection with the advertising budget, but they may be applied to any promotional activity as well as being used to determine the total promotional budget.

Percentage of Sales

The promotional budget may be related in some way to company income, as a percentage of either past or anticipated sales. A common approach for determining the sales base is to compute an average between the previous year's actual sales and expected sales for the coming year. Some businesses prefer to budget a fixed amount of money per unit of past or expected future sales. Manufacturers of products with a high unit value and a low rate of turnover (automobiles or appliances, for example) frequently use the unit method.

Because the percentage-of-sales method is simple to calculate, it is probably the most widely used budgeting method. Moreover, it sets the cost of promotion in relation to sales income, making it a variable rather than a fixed expense.

There is an important flaw in basing promotional expenditures on past sales. Management is effectively making promotion a result of sales when, in fact, it is a cause of sales. As a result, using the percentage-of-past-sales method reduces promotional expenditures when sales are declining, just when promotion usually is most needed, and increases it when sales are growing.

All Available Funds

A new company or a firm introducing a new product frequently plows all available funds into its promotional program. The objective is to build sales and market share as rapidly as possible during those early, critical years. After a time, management generally finds it necessary to invest in other things, such as new equipment, expanded production capacity, or warehouses and distribution centers (as many Internet marketing firms are doing), so the method of setting the promotional budget is changed.

Following Competition

A weak method of determining the promotional budget, but one that is used occasionally, is to match the promotional expenditures of competitors or to spend in proportion to market share. Sometimes only one competitor is followed. In other cases, if management has access to industry average expenditures on promotion through a trade association, these become company benchmarks.

There are at least two problems with this approach. First, a firm's competitors may be just as much in the dark regarding how to set a promotional budget. Second, a company's promotional goals may be quite different from its competitors' because of differences in strategic marketing planning.

Task or Objective

The best approach for establishing the promotional budget is to determine the tasks or objectives the promotional program must accomplish and then decide what they will cost. The task method forces management to realistically define the goals of its promotional program and view them outside the confines of a defined budgetary period.

This is often called the *buildup method* because of the way the budget is constructed. For example, a company may elect to enter a new geographic market. Management determines this venture will require five additional sales people. Compensation and expenses of these people will cost a total of $350,000 per year. Salary for an additional sales supervisor and expenses for an extra office and administrative needs will cost $80,000. Thus in the personal selling part of the promotional mix, an extra $430,000 must be budgeted. Similar estimates can be made for the anticipated costs of advertising, sales promotion, and other promotional tools. The promotional budget is built up by summing the costs of the individual promotional tasks needed to reach the goal of entering the new territory.

Regulation of Promotion

Because a primary objective of promotion is to sell something through persuasion, the potential for abuse always exists. As a result, some firms must be discouraged or prevented from intentional or unintentional misrepresentation. In addition, some consumers, because they lack particular knowledge or skills, need protection from being misled. Thus, there is a need for regulation to discourage the occurrence of abuses and to correct those that do occur.

Regulations have been established by the federal government and most state and local governments in response to public demand. In addition, professional associations and individual businesses have established promotion guidelines.

Federal Regulation

www.ftc.gov

Federal regulation of promotional activities applies to firms engaged in interstate commerce. It is authorized by three major pieces of legislation: the Federal Trade Commission Act and the Robinson-Patman Act, both administered by the Federal Trade Commission (FTC), and the Lanham Trademark Act.

The measure that has the broadest influence on promotional messages is the **Federal Trade Commission Act.** The act prohibits unfair methods of competition. And, according to FTC and federal-court decisions, one area of unfair competition is false, misleading, or deceptive advertising.

Under the original Federal Trade Commission Act, false or misleading advertising had to injure a competitor before a violation could be charged. This loophole led to the enactment of the **Wheeler-Lea Amendment** to the FTC Act in 1938. This amendment considerably strengthened the original act by specifying that an unfair competitive act violates the law if it injures the public, regardless of the effect it may have on a competitor. Thus, consumer protection also became a concern of the FTC.

The FTC has plenty of clout, particularly in the case of ads or other promotional activities deemed false or deceptive. For example, the commission may require a company to substantiate its advertising claims by submitting test results or other supporting evidence. If the commission concludes that an ad is, in fact, deceptive it can have it removed from circulation with a consent decree or a cease and desist order. In extreme cases, if the commission concludes that a firm's deceptive ads have created an incorrect impression on the public, it can order the firm to run corrective advertising to offset the misinformation.

Some other areas of consumer protection that have drawn the attention of the FTC include lending and credit granting practices, privacy and identity theft, telemarketing, and franchising. The Internet, as an emerging tool of communication and selling, is attracting special attention. Recently, for example, the FTC notified the operators of online search engines that they must disclose if sites they list have paid to be suggested to consumers.

The **Robinson-Patman Act,** which is best known for outlawing price discrimination, has two sections relating to promotional allowances offered to wholesalers and retailers. These sections state that a seller must offer promotional services or payments for them on a proportionally equal basis to all competing wholesalers or retailers. Thus, if a manufacturer wants to furnish in-store demonstrators, advertising support, or any other type of promotional assistance, it must make it available proportionally to all firms competing in the resale of the product. "Proportionally equal" has sometimes been hard to define. Generally the courts have accepted the amount of the product purchased as a basis for allocation. Say, for example, that Martin's, a regional supermarket chain, buys $150,000 worth of merchandise per year from a grocery wholesaler, and Hank's, a neighborhood grocery store, purchases $15,000 worth from the same wholesale firm. The wholesaler may legally offer Martin's promotional allowances valued at 10 times those offered to Hank's.

The 1946 **Lanham Trademark Act** made making false claims about a company's own products illegal. It was broadened in 1988 by the **Trademark Law Revision Act** to encompass comparisons made in promotional activity. This law regulates claims about where a product is manufactured, for example, use of the phrase "Made in the U.S.A.," and it also protects firms from false comparisons made by competitors.

www.fcc.gov

Several other federal agencies are involved in the regulation of promotion. The Federal Communications Commission (FCC) licenses radio and television stations. Its mandate, to ensure that public interest is considered, combined with its authority to remove or deny the renewal of licenses, gives the FCC considerable power over the content of advertising. In addition, the FCC oversees the telephone industry and enforces the **Telephone Consumer Protection Act** of 1991. Among other things, this law requires telemarketers to keep a "do-not-call" list of consumers who request that they not receive telephone solicitations, and it restricts the indiscriminant use of automatic telephone dialing systems.

www.fda.gov

The Food and Drug Administration (FDA) is responsible for regulating the ingredients, labeling, packaging, branding, and advertising of packaged food, cosmetic, and drug products. The FDA is also responsible for warning labels that appear on food and drug packages and in advertising. Recently the agency forbade the sale of water containing nicotine without federal approval, ruling that it qualifies as a drug. The FDA is the agency that established the legal definitions for terms such as "natural," "light," and "low fat" when they are used in advertising or promotion.

The U.S. Postal Service regulates advertising done through the mail. Of particular concern is the use of the mail to commit fraud or distribute obscene material. The Postal Service also oversees sales promotions such as premiums, contests, coupons, and samples that are sent through the mail.

In its guidelines for advertisers, the Children's Advertising Review Unit (CARU) of the National Advertising Review Council (NARC), an advertising industry self-regulation body, makes it clear that personalities associated with programs or editorial content should not be used in promotions adjacent to the program or in the same publications. The reason is simply that personalities can have a strong influence on children, who are unable to distinguish between efforts to educate or entertain them and efforts to persuade them to buy products. However, advertising to adults makes no such distinction, and the lines between content and advertising are becoming increasingly blurred. For example, Enhancement, a private-label perfume co-branded by Wal-Mart and the soap opera All My Children, is featured on several episodes of the TV show. In the print media, *Country Living* magazine placed an eight-page Home Depot advertising insert facing a feature story describing how remodeling help from Home Depot can improve a kitchen. Then there's *The Apprentice,* a TV show in which executive wannabes, try their hand at developing new products for advertisers Burger King and Office Depot.

Should there be any distinction between the entertainment content of the media and the products advertised?

Sources: *www.caru.org;* Brian Steinberg and James Bandler, "Blurring the Lines?" *The Wall Street Journal,* Aug. 9, 2004, pp. B1+; Becky Ebenkamp and Todd Wasserman, "Wal-Mart Sells Enhancement: The Simpsons Get Cheesy," *Brandweek,* Sept. 13, 2004, p. 8.

Regulation of the Internet is spread across several agencies. The FTC is the most active, dealing with broad issues such as "junk" e-mail or SPAM and consumer privacy. When a particular product or service is involved, the agency charged with regulating it takes an active role. For example, the FDA is concerned with the sale of medical products and prescription drugs via the Internet, and the Federal Deposit Insurance Corporation (FDIC) deals with online banking issues.

Many other agencies and commissions exist to protect consumers and regulate businesses. Among the most active are the Environmental Protection Agency (EPA), the National Highway Traffic Safety Commission (NHTSC), and the Consumer Product Safety Commission (CPSC). Currently there are about 200 agencies listed in the federal government's directory (*www.consumer.gov*).

State and Local Regulation

Legislation at the state level is intended to regulate promotional activities in intrastate commerce. Most of these state statutes are patterned after a model developed by *Printers' Ink* magazine in 1911 to establish truth in advertising. Today 44 states have what are known as **Printers' Ink statutes** to punish "untrue, deceptive, or misleading" advertising. Several states have established separate state agencies to handle consumer protection, and some states' attorneys general have taken a very proactive stance in regulating promotional activity of tobacco and alcoholic beverages as well as telemarketing.

A general type of local legislation that affects personal selling is the so-called **Green River ordinance** (so named because Green River, Wyoming, was one of the first towns to enact such a law). Green River ordinances restrict sales people who represent firms located outside the affected city and who sell door-to-door or call on business establishments. To operate in a community with a Green River ordinance, a sales person is typically required to register locally and purchase a license. Supposedly passed to protect local citizens from fraudulent operators, the measures also serve to insulate local businesses from outside competition.

Regulation by Private Organizations

Numerous private organizations exert considerable control over the promotional practices of business. For example, the Council of Better Business Bureaus and several advertising trade associations joined forces to create a self-regulation process. Two agencies have come out of this collaboration: the Council's National Advertising Division (NAD) and its Children's Advertising Review Unit (CARU).[12] Both investigate complaints of false and misleading advertising brought by competitors, consumers, and local Better Business Bureaus. If NAD or CARU find an ad unsatisfactory, they negotiate with the advertiser to discontinue or modify the ad. Despite the fact that neither NAD nor CARU can force compliance or sanction an advertiser in any way, they have been very successful in getting objectionable ads changed or dropped.

The media also serve a regulatory role. Virtually all publications and broadcasters have established standards for acceptable advertising. For example, in ads directed at children, the three major networks have specified that the words "just" and "only" cannot be used in reference to price. Standards in the print media tend to vary by the size and type of publication. Some are quite strict. For example, *Good Housekeeping* and *Parent* magazines test products to substantiate the claims before ads are accepted. Finally, some professional associations have established codes of ethics that include standards for communications. For example, the American Marketing Association specifies that the promotional efforts of its members avoid using false or misleading advertising, high-pressure or misleading sales tactics, and sales promotions that use deception or manipulation.

Summary

Promotion is the fourth component of a company's total marketing mix. In economic terms, the role of promotion is to change a firm's demand curve—either shifting it to the right or changing its shape to make demand inelastic when prices increase and elastic when prices decrease. In marketing terms it means informing, persuading, and reminding existing or prospective customers. The primary methods of promotion are personal selling, advertising, sales promotion, and public relations.

Integrated marketing communication (IMC) describes a coordinated promotional effort that includes planning, developing, executing, and evaluating communication with an organization's publics. An IMC approach to promotion adopts a customer perspective, selects from the alternative promotional tools to produce a defined response, coordinates all promotional efforts, and evaluates the effectiveness of promotion activity.

Promotion is communication. Fundamentally, the communication process consists of a source sending a message through a channel to a receiver. The success of communication depends on how well the message is encoded, how easily and clearly it can be decoded, and

whether any noise interferes with its transmission. Feedback, the response created by a message, is a measure of how effective a communication has been.

When deciding on the promotional mix (the combination of advertising, personal selling, and other promotional tools), management should consider (1) the target audience, (2) the objective of the promotion effort, (3) the nature of the product, (4) the stage of the product's life cycle, and (5) the funds available for promotion.

There are several methods involved in setting a total promotional budget. The most common method is to set the budget as a percentage of past or anticipated sales. Other methods include using all available funds and following the competition. The best approach is to set the budget by establishing the promotional objectives and then estimating how much it will cost to achieve them.

In response to the desire to protect consumers and curb abuses, there are a number of federal laws and agencies regulating promotion. Promotional practices also are regulated by state and local legislation, by private organizations, and by industry.

More about **Netflix**

The mail is a rather cumbersome method for distributing videos, requiring extensive handling of DVDs by Netflix and its customers as well as the expense of operating distribution centers and the constant threat of increasing postal rates. An alternative is offered by a partnership of Netflix and TiVo. Subscribers to both services can download films from Netflix's inventory over the Internet directly into their TiVo boxes instead of receiving DVDs by mail. This joint effort gives TiVo more content and Netflix a simpler method of distributing videos. It also provides both firms with cross-promotional opportunities to expand their subscriber bases.

Securing a new subscriber costs Netflix nearly $40. Subscriptions are unprofitable during the first 4 months because subscribers check out lots of videos. After that, as the novelty wears off and subscribers request fewer films, they become profitable. However, the average subscriber keeps the service for just 21 months. Going forward, a challenge for Netflix is to not only develop promotional tools that attract new subscribers but also to find ways to retain existing subscribers.[13]

1. Competition from Blockbuster and Wal-Mart forced Netflix to not only expand its promotion efforts. Now as the video distribution business model continues to evolve, should the Netflix promotion mix also change?

2. For promotional purposes, should prospective subscribers and existing subscribers be viewed as separate targets?

Key Terms and Concepts

Promotion (476)
Personal selling (476)
Advertising (476)
Sales promotion (476)
Public relations (477)
Integrated marketing communication (IMC) (478)
Communication (481)
Promotion mix (483)

Push strategy (484)
Pull strategy (484)
Hierarchy of effects (485)
Viral marketing (488)
Weblogs (488)
Promotional budgeting methods (489)
Federal Trade Commission Act (490)

Wheeler-Lea Amendment (490)
Robinson-Patman Act (491)
Lanham Trademark Act (491)
Trademark Law Revision Act (491)
Telephone Consumer Protection Act (491)
Printers' Ink statutes (492)
Green River ordinance (492)

Questions and Problems

1. Integrated marketing communications is just another way to say, "Keep everyone informed about what is going on." Comment.

2. Relate each of the components of the communication process model to the following situations:
   a. A college student trying to convince her father to buy her a used car.
   b. A sales person describing the same car to the college student.

3. How might the message on a company's website differ from the message it would use in a magazine advertisement?

4. The promotional budget for many products would be divided between a push strategy and a pull strategy. For the products below, give an example of who might be in the push strategy audience and who might be in the pull strategy audience:
   a. Contact lenses
   b. Golf balls
   c. Home insulation
   d. Personal computers
   e. Frozen pizza

5. Would it be appropriate for a firm to use advertising to create awareness of its brand at the same time that it uses sales promotion to stimulate purchase? Explain using an Internet portal such as America Online as an example.

6. Explain how the nature of the following products would likely affect a company's promotion mix.
   a. Automobile tires
   b. Use of a tanning salon
   c. Light bulbs
   d. Ten-minute automobile oil changes
   e. College education
   f. Individual Retirement Account (IRA)

7. How does the life-cycle stage of the automobile industry explain the promotional efforts carried out on behalf of most brands?

8. Assume you are marketing a liquid that removes creosote (and the danger of fire) from chimneys in home fireplaces. Briefly describe the roles you would assign to advertising, personal selling, sales promotion, and direct marketing in your promotional campaign.

9. Do you think additional legislation is needed to regulate advertising? To regulate personal selling? If so, explain what you would recommend.

Interactive Marketing Exercises

1. An ad should have a particular objective that should be apparent to a careful observer. For each of the following promotional objectives, find an example of a print ad:
   a. Primarily designed to inform.
   b. Primarily designed to persuade.
   c. Primarily designed to remind.

2. An integrated promotional program is a coordinated series of promotional efforts built around a single theme and designed to reach a predetermined goal. It often includes several of the promotional methods described in the chapter. For an important event at your school (such as a homecoming, the recruitment of new students, or a fund-raising effort), describe the promotional tools used and evaluate their appropriateness based on the criteria for designing a promotion mix in the chapter.

Chapter 18

Can CDW Use Relationships to Differentiate Its Sales Force?

It may seem that computer equipment selling by middlemen would be based primarily on price. After all, a server from Hewlett-Packard or a desktop computer from Apple are identical regardless of where they are purchased. And make no mistake about it, prices are important. But one company, CDW Corporation seems to have found a way through its sales and sales support activities to create relationships with customers that reduce the importance of price.

CDW was begun by Michael Krasny in 1984. Today it has approximately 4,000 employees and does nearly $5.7 billion in 2004 annual sales. CDW is a wholesaler. It buys over 80,000 computer-related products from companies such as Microsoft, Sony, and IBM, and its 2,200 sales people sell them to businesses, schools, and government agencies. CDW's customers could buy directly from the original equipment manufacturers, but the reason they don't is summed up in a company motto: In buying from a manufacturer, you get the best that manufacturer has to offer. In buying from CDW, you get the best the industry has to offer.

The company's success stems from four factors. The first, as noted above, is the broad selection of products it offers in order to meet each customer's unique needs. The second is delivery speed. Over 90% of orders are shipped the same day they are received (and the company's goal is 97%). The third is expertise. CDW's account managers and technicians are thoroughly trained so they can provide guidance to over 400,000 customers in the fast-changing world of high technology equipment. But a fourth factor, a relationship selling strategy, is what most distinguishes CDW from its competitors. CDW's simple sales philosophy is that people will do business with individuals they like and trust. Liking comes from taking the time to get to know each individual customer as a person. Trust derives from putting the customer's well-being first. According to the CDW's chief marketing officer that means being willing to "do whatever it takes to make a customer happy."

Implementing the sales philosophy begins with selecting the right people for sales positions. Then, continuous training reinforces the traits of enthusiasm, empathy, and responsiveness identified in the hiring process. In addition, the firm stresses the value of a personal touch. Rather than giving sales people scripts or "canned" presentations, CDW allows them to adapt the content and pace of the sales interaction with each customer and even to adjust prices if conditions warrant. Account managers are expected to take a long-term partnership perspective by focusing on the needs of the customers rather than the quick sale. The goal of the company is to have every customer describe his or her account manager the way the director of operations at one firm does: "Kelly is my CDW sales rep, but he's also my friend."

Although many companies talk about building relationships with customers through their sales forces, few combine the words with the action necessary to make it happen. Based on the success achieved by CDW, the results appear to be worth the effort.[1]

What would a business need to do in order to establish a culture like the one at CDW?

www.cdw.com

The importance of personal selling and the need for its integration with marketing can seldom be overstated. The atmosphere fostered at CDW and the success it has produced certainly support this position. Another indication is the number of businesses that are using CDW's relationship approach as a model for their own sales operations.

After studying this chapter, you should be able to explain:

| **Chapter Goals** |

- The role of personal selling in a promotional program.
- When a firm is likely to utilize personal selling.
- The forms of personal selling and the variety of personal selling jobs.
- Important developments in how personal selling is performed.
- The personal selling process.
- The strategic role of sales-force management.
- The challenges in staffing, operating, and evaluating a sales force.

Nature of Personal Selling

Personal selling is involved when a student buys a Honda motorcycle or an Ann Taylor store sells a dress to a businesswoman. But you should recognize that some personal selling also occurs when (1) Target Corporation recruits a graduating senior who majored in marketing or, conversely, a student tries to convince Target to hire her; (2) a minister talks to a group of students to encourage them to attend church services; (3) a lawyer tries to convince a jury that her client is innocent; or even (4) a boy persuades his mother to buy him something from Toys "R" Us. The point is that a form of personal selling occurs in nearly every human interaction.

The goal of all marketing efforts is to increase profitable sales by providing want-satisfaction to consumers over the long run. Therefore, in a business context **personal selling** is the personal communication of information to persuade somebody to buy something. By any measure, it is the major promotional method used to reach this goal. To illustrate, the number of people employed in advertising is below 500 *thousand*. In personal selling, the number is close to 16 *million*.[2] In many companies, personal selling is the largest single operating expense, often equaling 8% to 15% of sales. In contrast, advertising costs average 1% to 3% of sales.

Personal Selling as a Form of Promotion

Personal selling is the direct, *personal* communication of information, in contrast to the indirect, *impersonal* communication of advertising, sales promotion, and other promotional tools. This means that personal selling can be more flexible than these other tools. Sales people can tailor their presentations to fit the needs and behavior of individual customers. They can see their customers' reactions to a particular sales approach and make adjustments on the spot.

Also, personal selling can be focused on individuals or firms that are known to be prospective customers if an organization has done an adequate job of segmenting and targeting its market. Advertising messages are often wasted on people who are not realistic prospects, but personal selling minimizes wasted effort.

Another advantage of personal selling is that its goal is to actually make a sale. Advertising usually has a less ambitious goal. It is often designed to attract attention, provide information, and arouse desire, but it seldom stimulates buying action or completes the transfer of title from seller to buyer.

On the other hand, a full-fledged personal selling effort is costly. Even though personal selling can minimize wasted effort, the cost of developing and operating a sales force is high. Another disadvantage is that a company may find it difficult to attract the quality of people needed to do the job. At the retail level, many firms have abandoned their sales forces and shifted to self-service for this very reason.

In Chapter 17 we discussed five factors that influence an organization's promotional mix—the target market, the objective, the product, the product's life-cycle stage, and the money available for promotion. Referring to those five factors and its nature, personal selling is likely to be a major part of the promotional effort when:

- The market is concentrated geographically in a few industries or in several large customers.
- The value of the product is not readily apparent to the prospect.
- The product has a high unit cost, is quite technical in nature, or requires a demonstration.
- The product must be fitted to an individual customer's need, as in the case of securities or insurance.
- The product is in the introductory stage of its life cycle.
- The organization does not have enough money to sustain an adequate advertising campaign.

Types of Personal Selling

In business situations, there are two types of personal selling, as shown in Figure 18.1. One is where the customers come to the sales people. Called **inside selling,** this primarily involves retail sales. In this group, we include the sales people in stores and the sales people at catalog retailers such as Lands' End or L. L. Bean, who take telephone orders. Also included are the telephone order takers at manufacturers and wholesalers, most of whom take existing customers' routine orders over the telephone. By far, most sales people in the U.S. fall into this first category, but some are being replaced by purchasing done over the Internet.

In the other kind of personal selling, known as **outside selling,** sales people go to the customer. They make contact by telephone or in person. Most outside sales forces usually represent producers or wholesaling middlemen, selling to business users and not to household consumers. However, in our definition of an outside sales force, we also include (1) producers whose representatives sell directly to household consumers—for example, insurance companies such as State Farm or Northwestern

FIGURE 18.1

Scope of Personal Selling.

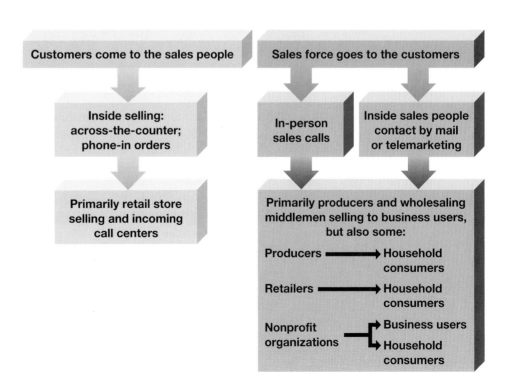

Mutual and in-home sellers such as Kirby Vacuum cleaner distributors; (2) representatives of retail organizations who go to consumers' homes to demonstrate a product, give advice, or provide an estimate, such as sales people for some furniture stores and home heating and air-conditioning retailers; and (3) representatives of nonprofit organizations—for example, charity fund raisers, religious missionaries, and workers for political candidates.

Wide Variety of Sales Jobs

The types of sales jobs and the activities involved in them cover a wide range. Consider the job of a Coca-Cola driver–sales person who calls routinely on a group of retail stores. That job is quite different from the IBM rep who sells a computer system for managing reservations to Delta Airlines. Similarly, a sales rep for Avon Products selling door to door in Japan or China has a job only remotely related to that of a Cessna airplane rep who sells executive-type aircraft to Dow Chemical and other large firms in the U.S.

A typical sales job includes three activities: order taking, customer support, and order getting. The relative emphasis on these functions is what distinguishes one sales job from another. The range of sales jobs is represented by the following six categories:

- *Delivery–sales person.* In this job the sales person primarily delivers the product—for example, soft drinks or fuel oil—and services the account. The order-getting responsibilities are secondary, although most of these sales people are authorized to and rewarded for finding opportunities to increase sales to existing accounts.

- *Inside order taker.* This is a position in which the sales person takes orders and assists customers at the seller's place of business—for example, a retail clerk on the sales floor at a JCPenney store or a telephone representative at a catalog retailer such as Eddie Bauer or Norm Thompson. Many customers have already decided to buy. The sales person's job is to answer customers' questions, serve them efficiently, and engage in suggestion selling.

- *Outside order taker.* In this position the sales person, representing a manufacturer or wholesaler, goes to the customer in the field and requests an order. An example is a John Deere sales person calling on a farm equipment dealer, or a sales rep for a radio station selling advertising time to local businesses. The majority of these sales are repeat orders to established customers, and much of the sales person's time is devoted to support activities such as assisting the distributors with promotion and training their sales people. Typically outside order takers also are assigned goals that require them to seek new customers and introduce new products to existing customers.

- *Missionary sales person.* This type of sales person is expected to provide information and other services for existing or potential customers, perform promotional activities, and build goodwill. A missionary sales person does not solicit orders. An example of this job is a detail sales person for a pharmaceutical firm such as Merck or Eli Lilly.

- *Sales engineer.* In this position the major emphasis is on the person's ability to explain the product to a prospective customer, and also to adapt the product to the customer's particular needs. The products involved here typically are complex, technically sophisticated items. As technical experts, sales engineers frequently assist regular sales reps with a particular problem or opportunity on an "as-needed" basis.

- *Consultative sales person.* This involves the creative selling of goods and services. This category contains the most complex, difficult selling jobs—especially the creative selling of services, because a customer can't see, touch, taste, or smell them. Customers often are not aware of their need for a seller's product. Or they may not realize how that product can satisfy their wants better than the product they are now using. Consultative selling requires the sales person to establish a

How far should retailers go in replacing people with machines? Increasingly frustrated by their inability to hire and retain qualified employees, merchants are turning to self-service alternatives such as those provided by Netkey. Stand-alone intranet kiosks that permit shoppers to perform traditional retail-employee tasks are appearing more often. Shoppers can request purchase suggestions, check product inventories, obtain help in locating items, and even finalize transactions without human interaction. However, each retailer must ask the question: Is this in the best interests of my customers?.

 www.netkey.com

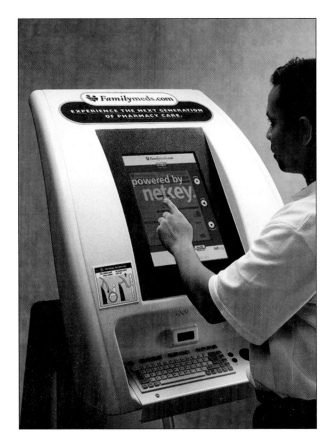

relationship of trust with the customer. It often involves designing a system to fit the needs of a particular customer to get an order.

A classification with several categories of jobs helps dispel the notion that all sales jobs are alike. However, it is worth noting that some richness is lost in the creation of any classification. In fact, there is considerable diversity in sales because firms design jobs to fit their particular situations. A study in the 1980s identified over 120 specific and reasonably exclusive tasks performed by at least some sales people.[3] A more recent study identified nearly 50 more tasks, many associated with the use of technology in selling.[4] So even though it is possible to classify sales jobs in a general way, it's important to note that specific sales jobs are tailored to the needs of the market and the sales organization.

The Professional Sales Person   As suggested by the opening case, the business-to-business sales job of today is quite different from the stereotype of the past. The images of high pressure, false friendship, and glibness are largely outdated, as is the notion of a price-cutting order chaser. Even the stereotype of the sales *man* is much less evident as more women enter selling.

The sales rep that has emerged is a professional. Today these reps are fully responsible for a designated market, which may be a geographic area or a category of customers. They frequently engage in a total selling job identifying prospects, servicing their customers, building goodwill, selling their products, and training their customers' employees. Professional reps act as a mirror of the market by relaying market information back to the firm. They organize much of their own time and effort. They often take part in recruiting new sales people, sales planning in their territories, and other managerial activities.

Greater sales professionalism also is more commonplace among retailers who view personal selling as a major component of their promotion strategy. Sales people are carefully selected to ensure they have the proper aptitude and are thoroughly trained to instill the necessary skills. Consumer electronics retailer, Best Buy, schools its sales people in a four-step personal selling process—Contact, Ask, Recommend, and Encourage. They fully understand the products they are selling and are well versed in providing customer service.[5]

The Cost of Personal Selling   The cost of a sales call depends on the sales approach used. Several years ago an authoritative source put the cost for firms selling commodities and emphasizing price at about $85. On the other hand, when the sales approach is to identify and design solutions for customers' problems, the cost of a call is $190.[6] Certainly these figures are higher today. Add to this the fact that it typically takes from three to six calls to make a sale to a new customer, and it becomes apparent that personal selling is expensive.

The Uniqueness of Sales Jobs   Several features differentiate sales jobs from other jobs in an organization:

- The sales force is largely responsible *for coordinating a firm's trade promotion with its marketing strategies.*

- Sales people are typically the most *visible representatives of their company* to customers and to society in general. Many sales jobs require the rep to socialize with customers who frequently are upper-level executives in their companies. Opinions of the firm and its products are formed on the basis of impressions made by sales people in their work and in outside activities. The public ordinarily does not judge a company by its factory or office workers, and customers can't judge products until after they are purchased and used.

- Sales reps operate with *limited direct supervision.* For success in selling, a sales rep must work hard physically and mentally, be creative and persistent, and show considerable initiative. This combination requires a high degree of self-motivation.

- By the nature of the job, sales people *have more rejections than acceptances;* that is, more prospects choose not to buy than to buy. A sales person who internalizes the rejection will quickly become discouraged.

- Sales jobs frequently involve considerable *traveling and time away from home.* To reduce sales travel time, some firms redesign sales territories, route sales trips better, and rely more on telemarketing and electronic ordering. Nevertheless, being in the field, sales people deal with a seemingly endless variety of people and situations.

- In the final analysis, it's the sales reps who *generate the revenues* that are the life-blood of an organization.

Changing Patterns in Personal Selling

Traditionally, personal selling was a face-to-face, one-on-one situation between a sales person and a prospective buyer. This situation existed both in retail sales involving ultimate consumers and also in business-to-business transactions. In recent years, however, some very different selling patterns have emerged. These new patterns reflect a growing purchasing expertise among consumers and business buyers, which, in turn, have fostered more sophistication in personal selling. Several of these patterns are described next.

A GLOBAL PERSPECTIVE

How important is situational sensitivity in personal selling?

As firms increasingly achieve a global presence, sales people are expected to function in many different cultures. By paying attention and showing sensitivity to a foreign culture, a sales person demonstrates respect and is much more likely to build a positive relationship. Some examples of cultural preferences include:

Introductions

- In the U.S., a casual handshake and smile are sufficient.
- In Japan a bow and a handshake, are typically followed by a formal exchange of business cards.
- In India a slight bow with both hands in the classic praying position is common.
- In Latin America it's not unusual to receive an "air kiss" on the cheek.

Gift giving

- In Japan a small gift to a business associate is customary.

- In Malaysia a gift of any size may be viewed as a bribe.
- In China a clock as a gift is bad luck; in South Korea it is a sign of good luck.
- In Europe flowers are an expected hostess gift but would have romantic connotations in other parts of the world.

Conversation

- Americans like to get right down to business.
- Italians expect to do business with top officials, so titles are important.
- French like to do business over a long lunch, usually with wine.
- Germans use job and academic titles in addressing business people.

Sources: Aliza Pilar Sherman, "Going Global," *Entrepreneur,* December 2004, p. 34; Michael Wynne, "Shake, Hug or Kiss?" *Global Cosmetic Industry,* May 2004, pp. 26+; "Beware the Business Culture Shock," *Management Services,* April 2004, p. 5.

Selling Centers

To match the expertise of the buying center (described in Chapter 5) in business markets, an increasing number of firms on the selling side have adopted the organizational concept of a **selling center.** A selling center is a group of people representing a sales department as well as other functional areas in a firm, such as finance, production, and research and development, brought together to meet the needs of a particular customer. This is sometimes called a *sales team* or *team selling.*

Team selling is expensive, and is therefore usually restricted to accounts that have a potential for high sales volume and profit. Due to its enormous sales volume, for example, almost all major consumer packaged-goods manufacturers have selling teams assigned to Wal-Mart. When AT&T sells to a large multinational firm such as Nestlé, AT&T will send a separate selling team to deal with each of Nestlé's major divisions.

Most sales teams are ad hoc groups, assembled to deal with a particular opportunity. Except for the sales person, the team members have other responsibilities in the firm. This creates several managerial issues. For example, who directs a team—the most senior person involved, the sales person who organizes the team, or the most experienced member? What happens if the buying center decides it prefers to work with a senior manager on the team or the technical expert who "speaks their language" rather than the sales person? Also, how should team members be evaluated and compensated? Despite these challenges, the increasing complexity of sales has made team selling increasingly popular.

Systems Selling

The concept of **systems selling** means selling a total package of related goods and services—a system—to solve a customer's problem. The idea is that the system will satisfy the buyer's needs more effectively than selling individual products separately. Xerox, for example, originally sold individual products, using a separate sales force for each major product line. Today, using a systems-selling approach, Xerox studies a customer's office information and operating problems and then provides a total automated system of machines and accompanying services to solve that customer's problems.

System selling has several benefits. The most obvious is that it produces a larger initial sale because a system rather than a product is purchased. Second, it reduces compatibility problems because all parts of the system come from the same supplier. Third, it often means that the supplier is also retained to service the system because of the supplier's familiarity with it. Finally, if the system performs effectively, the system provider is in an excellent position to propose upgrades as they are needed.

Systems selling is not right for every situation. For example, the components that make up some systems are so specialized or complex that they require the expertise of several firms.

Global Sales Teams

As companies expand their operations to far-flung corners of the globe, they expect their suppliers to do the same. Having products readily available, understanding local conditions, and providing quick service are essential to maintaining global customers. To service their largest and most profitable global customers, sellers are forming **global sales teams.** Such a unit is responsible for all of a company's sales to an account anywhere in the world. For example, IBM, with annual sales of $96 billion, supplies information technology products and services using global sales teams that are organized by industry.

By focusing on a specific industry such as aerospace, automotive, or petroleum, team members develop specialized expertise. A senior sales executive usually serves as team manager and is located at or very close to the customer's headquarters. As a result, the teams are prepared to deal with issues and opportunities on short notice wherever they may occur.

Relationship Selling

Developing a mutually beneficial relationship with selected customers over time is **relationship selling.** It may be an extension of team selling, or it may be developed by individual sales reps in their dealings with customers. In relationship selling, a seller discontinues the traditional practice of concentrating on maximizing the number and size of individual transactions. Instead, the seller attempts to develop a deeper, longer-lasting relationship built on trust with key customers—usually larger accounts.[7]

Unfortunately, often there is little trust found in buyer–seller relationships, either in retailer–consumer selling or in business-to-business selling. In fact, in some circles selling is viewed as adversarial, with one side winning and the other side losing. For example, a buyer may try to squeeze the last penny out of the seller in price negotiations, even with the knowledge that the agreed-on price may make it difficult for the seller to perform adequately.

How do sellers build trust? First and foremost, there must be a customer orientation. The seller must place the customers' needs and interests on a par with its own. This will create a shared vision of success, an expanded time horizon that looks beyond the immediate sale, and a perspective that the parties to a transaction are partners not adversaries.

Sales relationships take years to develop and are dependent on certain conditions and behaviors. They typically require the parties to:

- Share information such as forecasts, product development and termination plans, and cost information that has historically been treated as confidential.

Selling centers in sales organizations are the complement of buying centers in buying organizations. The major difference is the members of a selling center are formally designated to serve as part of the group. Otherwise the groups have much in common—they tend to be ad hoc, small, and represent various interests in the firm. The challenge for a sales person is to direct a group that typically represents various functional areas, often includes individuals higher-up in the organization, may not be familiar with the customer's business, and has a full-time job in some other part of the organization.

- Avoid opportunism, on using shared information for individual gain.
- Have similar organizational cultures when it comes to objectives such as short-term profits versus long-term growth.

Most large companies—Procter & Gamble, Hyatt Hotels, and Kraft Foods to name just a few—have realigned their sales forces to engage in relationship selling.

Telemarketing

Telemarketing is the innovative use of telecommunications equipment and systems as part of the "going to the customer" category of personal selling. Under certain conditions, telemarketing is attractive to both buyers and sellers. Buyers placing routine reorders or new orders for standardized products by telephone use less of their time than with in-person sales calls.

Many sellers find that telemarketing increases selling efficiency. With the high costs of keeping sales people on the road, telemarketing reduces the time they spend on routine order taking. Redirecting routine reorders to telemarketing allows the field sales force to devote more time to creative selling, major account selling, and other more profitable selling activities.

Here are examples of selling activities that lend themselves nicely to a telemarketing program:

- Processing orders for standardized products. Cryovac, a firm that produces packaging material for food processors and supermarkets among other things, operates an inbound call center that allows customers to place routine orders without having to contact a sales rep.
- Dealing with small-order customers, especially where the seller would lose money if field sales calls were used. Red Wing Shoe Company, a manufacturer known for its work boots and outdoor footwear, sells to many retailers all over the country. The company cannot afford to have sales reps visit small retailers

Telemarketing in many B-2-B organizations has become the standard method of handling routine, repeat purchases such as replenishing inventories of standardized products. In B-2-C marketing, however, telemarketing has been severely curtailed by federal and state Do Not Call regulations.

more than once or twice a year in, for example, Idaho mining towns or farming communities in Arkansas. Between visits these small stores are encouraged via telemarketing to replenish their inventories.

- Improving relations with middlemen. Manufacturers use telemarketing to answer dealers' questions about inventory management, service, and replacement parts. This gives the dealers an immediate source for assistance, saving them the time and effort of trying to track down a sales person.

Internet Selling

www.baxter.com

Most sales efforts over the Internet would not be considered personal, and therefore would not be part of a discussion about *personal* selling. For example, Baxter International (a seller of hospital supplies) makes it very easy for customers to place routine orders through its website, creating many impersonal transactions. In fact, the impersonal nature of the process is one of its strengths, because it speeds up purchasing and reduces the frequency of errors. However, one category of **Internet selling,** the business-to-business auction, qualifies as personal selling because of its interactive nature.

Using the traditional auction format, a seller (working through an online intermediary that provides the linking technology) notifies potential bidders of a product available for sale. Typically the item for sale is a discontinued model of a product or excess inventory of some raw material. According to a predetermined schedule, bids are submitted electronically in round-robin fashion in real time. Both the seller and all the bidders see each bid and have the opportunity to respond.

Another version is called a reverse auction. The prospective buyer notifies prequalified potential sellers of its willingness to purchase a specified product and an online auction is held to select a seller. In both auction formats, there is an interchange of information between buyers and sellers, negotiation of terms, and intense price competition.

Internet auctions began selling commodities or standardized goods. For example, a state bought salt for use on icy roads, and a computer memory chip maker sold microprocessors. However, as the technology improved Internet auctions have been more broadly applied. The business-to-business electronic auction format attracted a great deal of attention because it was credited with producing significant price concessions. The transparency of the procedure (buyers and sellers are made aware of the bids during the auction) caused price to be the primary focus. However, firms using auctions often discovered "hidden" costs such as poor quality products, late deliveries, supplier nonperformance, and post-auction attempts to renegotiate prices.[8]

Sales-Force Automation

In recent years organizations have equipped their sales people with an increasing array of electronic tools. Pagers, laptop computers, fax machines, and cellular phones allow sales people access to the Internet, e-mail, and various company databases. They also allow sales people to electronically communicate with their managers, marketers, and others in their organization by providing such things as market intelligence, call reports, credit applications, and customer questions.

Today organizations are moving beyond using these tools only for communication to integrating them with software that allows a sales person to create customized reports for customers; develop proposals with prices, discounts, delivery dates, and other information critical to making a sale; estimate costs for particular orders; and develop forecasts for customers and territories. This capability of using electronic tools to combine company and client information in real time to enhance the sales function is known as **sales force automation (SFA).**

SFA has the potential to create better-informed sales people who can more effectively respond to the needs of customers. According to a sales executive at Owens Corning, with SFA "They (sales people) become the real managers of their own business and their own territories."[9]

Automating a sales force is an expensive proposition that is likely to require frequent upgrades as new, more sophisticated tools become available. The experience of firms indicates that successful SFA implementation involves designing a user-friendly system and gaining the cooperation of the sales force so they incorporate the technology in their jobs.

Automation results have been mixed as firms sort out what works and what doesn't. Typical problems include unrealistic expectations by management because of the large investments required, attempting to implement too much at once instead of phasing in a program, and resistance by sales people. The results of a recent survey in which about half of the responding companies indicated plans to upgrade their systems, down from 83% a few years ago, suggests firms are experiencing varying levels of success.[10]

MARKETING IN THE INFORMATION ECONOMY

Can sales force technology be counterproductive?

Just a few years ago organizations were concerned about how to get their sales people to make greater use of electronic technology. Tools including customer relationship management (CRM) software, laptops, the Internet, e-mail, voice mail, text messaging, intranet, customer databases, personal digital assistants (PDAs), and cell phones became available but many sales people were reluctant to change the way they operated. It seems that today the opposite may be occurring. Many sales organizations are concerned that sales people are becoming slaves to technology. Some question the around-the-clock accessibility created by electronic devices, and others wonder if electronic tools are reducing the personal contact essential to many selling situations.

Sources: Beth Snyder Bulik, "Hiding Out," *Sales & Marketing Management,* June 2004, pp. 24–29; Jennifer Gilbert, "Get 'Em Hooked," *Sales & Marketing Management,* October 2002, pp. 23–24.

The Personal Selling Process

The **personal selling process**, depicted in Figure 18.2, is a logical sequence of four steps that a sales person takes in dealing with a prospective buyer. This process is designed to produce some desired customer action and ends with a follow-up to ensure customer satisfaction. The desired action usually is a purchase by the customer.

Prospecting

The first step in the personal selling process is really two related steps. Prospecting consists of identifying possible customers and then qualifying them—that is, determining whether they have the necessary potential to buy. They are combined as a single step because they are typically done at the same time.

Identifying Prospective Customers
The identification process is an application of market segmentation. First, a list of potential customers can be constructed using suggestions from current customers, trade associations and industry directories, the customer lists of related but noncompeting businesses, and mail-in or telephone responses to ads. A little thought also will suggest logical candidates. Homestead House (a furniture store chain) and AT&T find prospects in lists of building permits issued. Insurance companies (Northwestern Mutual or Prudential), real estate firms (Re/Max, Century 21), and even local diaper services use marriage and birth announcements in newspapers as sources.

Then, by analyzing the firm's database of past and current customers, a sales rep should be able to determine characteristics of an attractive prospect. Comparing this profile to the list of potential customers will produce a set of prospects.

Qualifying Prospects
As part of identifying prospective customers, a seller should qualify them—that is, determine whether they have the necessary willingness, purchasing power, and authority to buy. To determine willingness to buy, a seller can seek information about any changes in the prospect's situation. For example, a business firm or a household consumer may have had a recent problem with an insurance provider. In this case there may be an opportunity for a sales person from a competing insurer to get that prospect's business.

www.dnb.com

To determine a prospect's financial ability to pay, a seller can refer to creditrating services such as Dun & Bradstreet. For household consumers or small businesses in an area, a seller can get credit information from a local credit bureau. Identifying who has the authority to buy in a business or a household can be difficult, as we saw in Chapters 4 and 5. In a business, the buying authority may rest with a committee or an executive in a distant location. Besides determining the buying authority, a

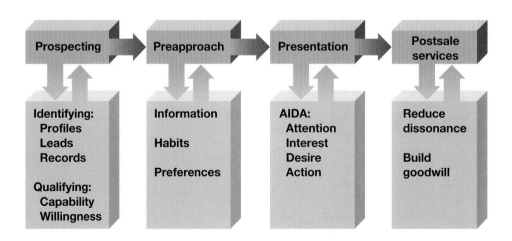

FIGURE 18.2

The Personal Selling Process.

seller also should identify who influences the buying decision, since a successful sales effort will most likely have to include them. A purchasing agent may have buying authority, but what he or she buys may depend on the recommendation of an office secretary, a factory engineer, or a vice president.

Preapproach to Individual Prospects

Before calling on prospects, sales people should conduct a preapproach—learning all they can about the persons or companies to whom they hope to sell. This might include finding out what products the prospects have used in the past, what they are now using, and their reactions to these products. In business-to-business selling, a sales person or selling team should find out how buying decisions are made in the customer's organization. A sales rep can target the right people if he or she knows who is the gatekeeper, who influences and/or makes the buying decision, and who actually makes the purchase. Here again customer databases and customer relationship management (CRM) software can be valuable in gathering, processing, and retrieving information.[11]

Finding out something about the prospect's personal life—interests, activities, and habits—as well as gathering some insights into the preferred business practices of the prospect can be useful. Sales people should try to get all the information they can, so they will be able to tailor their presentations to individual buyers.

Presenting the Sales Message

With the appropriate preapproach information, a sales person can design a sales presentation that will attract the prospect's attention. The sales person will then try to hold the prospect's interest while building a desire for the product and, when the time is right, will attempt to stimulate action by closing the sale. This approach, called **AIDA** (an acronym formed by the first letters of Attention, Interest, Desire, and Action), is used by many organizations.

Attract Attention—the Approach

The first task in a sales presentation is to attract the prospect's attention and to generate curiosity. In cases where the prospect is aware of a need and is seeking a solution, simply stating the seller's company and product may be enough. However, more creativity often is required.

For instance, if the sales person was referred to the prospect by a customer, the right approach might be to start out by mentioning this common acquaintance. Or a sales person might suggest the product benefits by making some startling statement. One sales training consultant suggests greeting a prospect with the question, "If I can cut your selling costs in half, and at the same time double your sales volume, are you interested?"

Hold Interest and Arouse Desire

After attracting the prospect's attention, the challenge for the sales rep is to hold it and stimulate a desire for the product with a sales presentation. There is no universal format here, but the presentation should be a combination of listening and speaking, with an emphasis on listening. A key component of any sales effort is clearly understanding the prospect's need and adapting to it.

Some companies train their sales people to use a canned sales talk—a memorized presentation designed to cover all points determined by management to be important. Companies engaging in telemarketing typically use scripted sales talks. They may be appropriate if the sales person is inexperienced or knows very little about the customer, but a presentation with more flexibility can be personalized and tailored to individual customers' needs. Whatever format is followed in the presentation, the sales person must always show how the product will benefit the prospect.

Meet Objections and Close the Sale   After explaining the product and its benefits, a sales person should try to close the sale—that is, obtain action on the customer's part. Periodically in a presentation, the sales person may venture a trial close to test the prospect's willingness to buy. One method is posing an "either-or" question that presumes the prospect has decided to buy. For example, "Would you prefer that the installation be done immediately or would it be better to have it done next week?"

The trial close tends to uncover the buyer's objections. The toughest objections to answer are those that are unspoken. Thus, a sales person should encourage buyers to state their objections. Then the sales person has an opportunity to meet the objections and bring out additional product benefits or reemphasize previously stated points.

Postsale Services

An effective selling job does not end when the order is written up. The final stage of a selling process is a series of postsale activities that can build customer goodwill and lay the groundwork for future business. An alert sales person will follow up sales to ensure that no problems occur in delivery, financing, installation, employee training, and other areas that are important to customer satisfaction.

Postsale service reduces the customer's postpurchase cognitive dissonance—the anxiety that commonly occurs after a person makes a significant buying decision (discussed in Chapter 4). In this final stage of the selling process, a sales person can minimize the customer's dissonance by (1) summarizing the product's benefits after the purchase, (2) repeating why the product is better than alternatives not chosen, (3) describing how satisfied other buyers have been with the product, and (4) emphasizing how satisfied the customer will be with the product.

Strategic Sales-Force Management

Managing the personal selling function is a matter of applying the three-stage management process (planning, implementation, and evaluation) to a sales force and its activities. Sales executives begin by setting sales goals and planning sales-force activities. This involves forecasting sales, preparing sales budgets, establishing sales territories, and setting sales quotas. Then a sales force must be organized, staffed, and operated to implement the strategic plans and reach the goals that were set. The final stage involves evaluating the performance of individual sales people as well as appraising the total sales performance.

Effective sales-force management starts with a qualified sales manager. Finding the right person for this job is not easy. In many organizations the common practice when a sales management position becomes available is to reward the most productive sales person with a promotion. The assumption is that, as a manager, an effective sales person will be able to impart the necessary wisdom to make others equally successful. However, this reasoning may be flawed.

The qualities that lead to effective sales management are often the opposite of the attributes of a successful sales person. Probably the biggest differences in the positions are that sales people need to be more self-motivated and self-reliant. They often work independently, receiving all the credit or blame for their successes or failures. In contrast, sales managers must work through and depend on others, and must be prepared to give recognition rather than receive it.

On the other hand, it is an unusual person who can be a successful sales manager without previous selling experience. To be effective, a sales manager must understand customers, appreciate the role of the sales person, and have the respect of the sales force. These attributes can best be acquired by spending time in sales. The resolution may come in not using the sales management position as a reward for outstanding sales performance. Rather, the criteria for sales management should be respectable sales performance coupled with the necessary attributes of management.

Staffing and Operating a Sales Force

Because most sales executives spend the bulk of their time in staffing and operating their sales forces, we will discuss these activities in some detail. Figure 18.3 shows what's involved.

Recruitment and Selection

Selecting personnel is the most important management activity in any organization. This is true whether the organization is an athletic team, a college faculty, or a sales force. No matter what the caliber of sales management, if a sales force is distinctly inferior to that of a competitor's, the rival firm will win.

Sales-force selection involves three tasks:

1. Determining the type of people needed by preparing a written job description.

2. Recruiting an adequate number of applicants.

3. Selecting the most qualified persons from among the applicants.

Determining Hiring Specifications There have been many attempts to identify a general set of personality attributes that explain selling success.[12] However, these lists tend to be of little practical value because they consist of common sense characteristics such as assertiveness and empathy, don't account for motivation, and fail to recognize the differences in sales jobs.

Some companies analyze the personal histories of their existing sales representatives in an effort to determine the traits common to successful (and unsuccessful) performers. Even when a firm thinks it knows what the important attributes are, measuring the degree to which each quality should be present or the extent an abundance of one can offset the lack of another is difficult.

A better approach is to identify the specifications for the particular job, just as if the company were purchasing equipment or supplies rather than labor. This calls for a detailed job analysis and a written job description. The description then becomes the basis for identifying the aptitude and skills a person needs to perform the job. Later, this written description will be invaluable in training, compensation, and supervision.

Recruiting Applicants A planned system for recruiting a sufficient number of applicants is the next step in selection. A good recruiting system:

- Operates continuously, not only when sales-force vacancies occur.
- Is systematic in reaching all appropriate sources of applicants.
- Provides a flow of more qualified applicants than is needed.

To identify recruits, large organizations often use placement services on college campuses or professional employment agencies. Smaller firms that need fewer new

FIGURE 18.3

Staffing and Operating a Sales Force.

sales people may place classified ads in trade publications and daily newspapers. Many firms solicit recommendations from company employees, customers, or suppliers.

Matching Applicants with Hiring Specifications Sales managers use a variety of techniques—including application forms, interviews, references, credit reports, psychological tests, aptitude tests, and physical examinations—to determine which applicants possess the desired qualifications. Virtually all companies ask candidates to fill out application forms. In addition to providing basic screening information, the application indicates areas that should be explored in an interview.

No sales person should be hired without at least one personal interview. And it is usually desirable to have several interviews conducted by different people in different physical settings. Pooling the opinions of a number of people increases the likelihood of discovering any undesirable characteristics and reduces the effects of one interviewer's possible bias.

Increasingly firms are asking finalists for sales positions to spend a day in the field with a sales person. Called "reality dosing," this is most useful when the candidate has little or no previous experience. Besides giving the applicant a sense of the routine, the host sales person can assess the candidate's reactions to the job.

The individuals involved in the selection process need to be aware of the laws against discrimination in order to avoid inadvertent violations. For example, it is illegal to ask on an application or in an interview a person's age or marital status. Testing for intelligence, attributes, or personality, although legal under the proper conditions, is somewhat controversial. Some companies avoid testing for fear that they will be accused of discrimination. However, employment tests are legitimate selection tools as long as the attributes measured can be shown to predict job performance.

Assimilating New Sales People

After sales people are hired, management should integrate them into the company. Because selling by its nature involves a considerable amount of rejection by prospects, the new sales person needs support in order to avoid becoming discouraged. A wise sales manager will recognize that the new people must be made comfortable with the details of the job, their fellow workers, and their status in the firm if they are to be successful.

Training a Sales Force

Virtually all companies put new and inexperienced sales people through an orientation and sales training program, often lasting weeks or months. Training needs vary depending on a sales person's experience, the type of sales position, and the nature of the product being sold. To keep it fresh and effective, organizations must develop creative approaches. Recognizing that the recent college graduates hired into its sales force are unlikely to have much experience with its appliances, Whirlpool Corporation had them spend two months living in a house together. After using the company's products to cook, clean, and wash their clothes, the trainees had the experience and confidence to go out into the field and teach retail sales clerks how to sell Whirlpool appliances. Texas Instruments hired a video-production company to produce a film of the company's clients providing highly critical feedback which it uses to sensitize executives and sales people to the need for training. Other training topics include the importance of body language and proper business etiquette.[13]

Even experienced sales people need continual training to improve their selling skills, learn about new products, and improve their time- and territory-management practices. A recent survey found that 70% of executives rank sales in the top three of their companies' most important functions, but only 47% believe their sales forces outperform their competitors.[14] One of the primary training areas for experienced sales people is in the use of sales-force automation tools described earlier in the chapter.

Today's professional salespeople have many tools at their disposal. Among the most important are customer databases accessible through laptop computers. Before the salesmen pictured here make a sales call, they review up-to-the minute information on the customer's inventories; recent purchases, returns, and unfilled orders; prices paid; status with regard to trial of new products; promotional support; and any recent problems or concerns as well as their resolutions. With this type of information at hand, they are seldom surprised. More important, they are prepared to identify and deal with the customer's needs.

Motivating a Sales Force

Sales people, especially outside sales forces, require a high degree of motivation. Think back to our earlier discussion about the uniqueness of sales jobs—how sales people often work with little or no direct supervision and guidance from management, and how they must deal with frequent rejection by customers. In addition, outside sales people work most of the time away from the support and comfort of home office surroundings.

Consequently, management faces a challenge in motivating sales people. One key is to determine what motivates the sales reps. Is it a need for money, status, control, accomplishment, or something else? People differ in what motivates them, and the motivations change over a person's life. A young sales person is more likely to be motivated by money, whereas an older sales person may be more interested in recognition.

Sales executives can draw from a wide assortment of specific motivational tools. Financial incentives—compensation plans, expense accounts, fringe benefits—serve as basic motivators, but they don't always push people to exceptional performance. Nonfinancial rewards—job enrichment, praise from management, recognition and honor awards (pin, trophy, certificate)—may stimulate some reps. Sales meetings and sales contests are often-used alternatives. Many firms provide cruises, resort trips, and other travel incentives as rewards to top-performing sales reps. The importance of finding ways to motivate sales people is reflected in the attention it receives in the sales management literature.[15]

Compensating a Sales Force

Financial rewards are by far the most widely used tool for motivating sales people. Consequently, designing and administering an effective sales compensation plan is a big part of a sales manager's job. Financial rewards may be direct monetary payments (salary, commission) or indirect monetary compensation (paid vacations, pensions, insurance plans).

Establishing a compensation system calls for decisions concerning the level of compensation as well as the method of compensation. The level refers to the total dollar income that a sales person earns over a period of time. Level is influenced by

YOU MAKE THE DECISION

How important is the design of an incentive?

Regardless of the compensation method used, many organizations also offer additional incentives to motivate sales people. These incentives are typically cash or some other type of reward (merchandise or travel) over and above normal compensation for meeting a defined goal in a specified period of time. Is it better to offer a few large sales incentives that can be won by only a few members of the sales force or a larger number of small incentives with many winners?

Large incentives (for example, a family cruise or a trip to Hawaii)

Pros:

- Big rewards can be linked to big increases in performance.

- Because of the attractiveness of the prize, everyone is likely to improve performance, even if there are only one or two winners.

- A sales person's family provides support and encouragement because they will benefit as well.

Cons:

- Since most companies have a few star performers, everyone knows the winners are almost certainly going to come from that group.

- Big contests take too long to complete—often six months or a year—and many sales people lose interest long before the end.

Smaller incentives (for example, shopping gift cards, consumer electronics, event tickets)

Pros:

- Can be used to stimulate specific activities such as introducing a new line or improving customer service.

- Because many different performance activities can be incentivized, everyone has a chance to win and the entire sales force is motivated.

Con:

- Small rewards may not be very appealing to sales people who make good incomes.

Sources: Sara Calabro, "Meaningful Rewards," *Sales & Marketing Management,* March 2005, p. 26; Julia Chang, "Where Everyone's a Winner," *Sales & Marketing Management,* January 2005, pp. 43–46; Julia Chang, "Trophy Value," *Sales & Marketing Management,* October 2004, pp. 24–29; Ian Mount, "Out of Control," *Business 2.0,* August 2002, pp. 38–44.

the type of person required for the job and the competitive rate of pay for similar positions. The method is the system or plan by which the sales person will reach the intended level.

The three widely used **methods of sales-force compensation** are straight salary, straight commission, and a combination plan. A *salary* is a fixed payment for a period of time during which the sales person is working. A *salary-only plan* (called a straight salary) provides security and stability of earnings for a sales rep. This plan gives management control over a rep's time, and as a result, the reps are likely to invest in nonselling activities that cater to the customer's best interests. The main drawback of a straight salary is that it does not offer an incentive for sales people to increase their sales volume. Also, a straight salary is a fixed cost for the firm, unrelated to sales volume or gross margin.

Straight-salary plans typically are used:

- While a new hire is getting established.

- To compensate missionary sales people.

- When opening new territories.

- To sell a technical product that requires a lengthy period of negotiation.

A *commission* is a payment tied to a specific unit of accomplishment. Thus a rep may be paid 5% of every dollar of sales or 8% on each dollar of gross margin. A

A competitor has offered a successful sales person a job that involves greater responsibility, a chance to advance more quickly, and better pay. The only condition is the new employer wants her to bring along her two best clients. The products of the two firms are very similar, so a switch would not affect the clients' operations. And, as a result of the effort the sales person has invested in building a relationship with the clients, she feels she is best suited to serve them. On the other hand, her current employer gave her a chance by hiring her five years ago when no one else offered her a sales position.

Is it unethical for a sales person to change jobs and shift clients to the new employer?

Sources: Jessalynn Brinkmeyer, "Close Contact," *Sales & Marketing Management,* March 2005, p. 14; Betsy Cummings, "Stopping a Client Exodus," *Sales & Marketing Management,* June 2004, p. 10.

straight-commission plan (commission only) tends to have just the opposite merits and limitations of a straight salary. A straight commission provides considerable incentive for sales people to sell, and it is a variable cost related directly to a rep's sales volume or gross margin. On the other hand, it is difficult to get straight-commission people to perform tasks for which no commission is paid.

Straight-commission plans may work well when:

- A strong incentive is needed to generate sales.
- Very little nonselling work is required, such as setting up displays in retail stores.
- The company is financially weak and must relate its compensation expenses directly to sales or gross margins.

A heavy emphasis on commissions can cause employees to lose sight of the importance of the customer. Kirby Company, for example, has sold vacuum cleaners door to door for 70 years using distributors paid on straight commission. The company is highly successful, selling about $1 billion worth of machines a year. Its long history suggests that most of its distributors are ethical. However, over 1,000 consumer complaints nationwide suggest the lure of commissions has caused some distributors to take advantage of elderly and disadvantaged consumers.[16]

The ideal method of compensation is a *combination plan* that has the best features of both the straight-salary and the straight-commission plans, with as few of their drawbacks as possible. To reach this ideal, a combination plan must be tailored to a particular firm, product, market, and type of selling. Today about three-quarters of the firms in the U.S. use some kind of combination plan.[17]

Supervising a Sales Force

Supervising a sales force is difficult because sales people often work independently at far-flung locations where they cannot be continually observed. And yet supervision serves both as a means of ongoing training and as a device to ensure that company policies are being carried out.

An issue that management must resolve is how closely to supervise. If management supervises too closely, it can unduly constrain the sales person. One of the attractions of selling is the freedom it affords sales people to develop creative solutions to customers' problems. Close supervision can stifle that sense of independence. Conversely, too little supervision can contribute to a lack of direction. Sales people who are not closely supervised may not understand what their supervisors and companies expect of them. They may not know, for example, how much time to spend servicing existing accounts and how much to spend developing new business.

The most effective supervisory method is personal observation in the field. Typically, at least half a sales manager's time is spent traveling with sales people. Other supervisory tools are reports, e-mail, and sales meetings.

Evaluating a Sales Person's Performance

Managing a sales force includes evaluating the performance of sales people. Sales executives must know what the sales force is doing in order to reward them or make constructive proposals for improvement. By establishing specific performance goals and studying sales people's activities, managers can develop new training programs to upgrade the sales force's efforts. And, of course, performance evaluation should be the basis for compensation decisions and other rewards.

Performance evaluation can also help sales people identify opportunities for improving their efforts. Employees with poor sales records know they are doing something wrong. However, they may not know what the problem is if they lack objective standards by which to measure their performance.

Both quantitative and qualitative measures should be used to formulate a complete picture of performance. **Quantitative evaluation bases** generally have the advantage of being specific and objective. **Qualitative evaluation bases** often reflect broader dimensions of behavior but are limited by the subjective judgment of the evaluators. For either type of appraisal, management faces the difficult task of setting standards against which a rep's performance can be measured.

Quantitative Bases

Sales performance should be evaluated in terms of inputs (efforts) and outputs (results). Together, inputs, such as number of sales calls per day or direct selling expenses, and outputs, such as sales volume or gross margin, provide a measure of selling effectiveness.

Useful quantitative input measures include:

- Call rate—number of calls per day or week.
- Number of formal proposals presented.
- Sales-support activities—number of promotion displays set up or training sessions held with distributors or dealers.

Some quantitative output measures useful as evaluation criteria are:

- Sales volume by product, customer group, and territory.
- Sales volume as a percentage of quota or territory potential.
- Gross margin by product line, customer group, and territory.
- Share of customer's business in a product category.
- Orders—number and average dollar amount.
- Closing rate—number of orders divided by number of calls.
- Accounts—percentage of existing accounts retained and number of new accounts opened.

An increasing number of firms, among them IBM and Hallmark, are using customer satisfaction as a sales-force performance indicator. Satisfaction is measured in a number of different ways, from detailed questionnaires that customers complete to counting the number of complaints received from customers.

By assessing satisfaction, companies recognize that there is more to selling than making a sale. Firms have discovered that finding a new customer is much more difficult and expensive than keeping an existing one. As a result, they have shifted their emphasis from a single-minded focus on sales volume to a combination of sales volume and customer satisfaction. This allows a sales person to nurture a small account with considerable potential rather than to always go for the big order. And it discourages sales people from engaging in detrimental actions such as loading up customers with unneeded inventory in order to meet a sales quota.

Qualitative Bases

In some respects, performance evaluation would be much easier if it could be based only on quantitative criteria. The standards would be absolute, and the positive and negative deviations from the standard could be measured precisely. Quantitative measures would also minimize the subjectivity and personal bias of the evaluators. However, many qualitative factors must be considered because they influence a sales person's performance. Some commonly used factors are:

- Knowledge of products, company policies, and competitors.
- Time management and preparation for sales calls.
- Quality of reports.
- Customer relations.
- Personal appearance.
- Continuing education.

A successful evaluation program will appraise a sales person on all the factors related to performance. Otherwise management may be misled. A high daily call rate may look good, but it tells nothing about how many orders are being written up. A high closing rate may be camouflaging a low average order size or a high sales volume on low-profit items.[18]

Summary

Personal selling is the main promotional method used in American business, regardless of whether it is measured by number of people employed, total expenditures, or expenses as a percentage of sales. The total field of personal selling comprises two broad types. One covers selling activities where the customers come to the sales people—primarily retail store or retail catalog selling, but also the order takers at manufacturers and wholesalers. The other includes all selling situations where the sales people go to the customer—primarily outside sales forces.

Sales jobs today range from order takers through support sales people (missionary sellers, sales engineers) to order getters (consultative sellers). The sales job has evolved. A new type of sales rep—a professional sales person—has been developing over the past few decades. But this new breed of sales rep still faces the unique characteristics of selling: implementing the firm's marketing strategy, representing the company, little direct supervision, frequent rejection by prospects, and considerable travel.

Some changing patterns in personal selling have emerged in recent years, including selling centers (team selling), systems selling, global sales teams, relationship selling, telemarketing, Internet selling, and sales force automation.

The personal selling process consists of four steps, starting with prospecting for potential buyers and then preapproaching each prospect. The third step is the sales presentation, which includes attracting attention, arousing buyer interest and desire, meeting objections, and then hopefully closing the sale. Finally, postsale activities involve follow-up services to ensure customer satisfaction and reduce dissonance regarding the purchase.

The sales management process involves planning, implementing, and evaluating sales-force activities within the guidelines set by the company's strategic marketing plan. The tasks of staffing and operating a sales force present managerial challenges in several areas. The key to successful sales-force management is to do a good job in selecting sales people. Then these new people must be assimilated into the company and trained. Management must set up programs to motivate, compensate, and supervise a sales force.

The final stage in sales-force management is to evaluate the performance of the individual sales people.

More about CDW

CDW sounds like a good place to work, and it must be. *Fortune* magazine rated it one of the "100 Best Companies to Work For" seven years in a row. It adheres to a philosophy that a happy worker will work hard and be dedicated to providing superior customer service. To create the desired atmosphere, CDW offers employee stock options, subsidized child care, tuition reimbursement, paid time off for community service, matching charitable donations, and even special benefits for adoptive parents. In return, the company has high expectations for its account managers. Even though they "own" their accounts, sales people have specific short- and long-term performance goals, and they are expected to be knowledgeable enough about

their products and the customer's business to act as business partners. This was illustrated by a CDW sales person in Ohio who spent three years courting an electric utility technology manager, all the while proving he could solve problems and reliably fill small orders. Eventually he replaced all the utilities' computer equipment vendors and now is rewarded with hundreds of thousands of dollars of sales every year.

CDW supports its sales people with extensive training (The company also recently won a *Training* magazine award for having one of the top 100 training and development programs in the country.) and multi-media advertising to open doors (The annual advertising budget exceeds $20 million).[19]

What evidence is there that CDW's sales organization and its marketing department are working together toward a common goal?

Key Terms and Concepts

Personal selling (498)
Inside selling (499)
Outside selling (499)
Selling center (503)
Systems selling (503)
Global sales teams (504)

Relationship selling (504)
Telemarketing (505)
Internet selling (506)
Sales force automation (SFA) (507)
Personal selling process (508)

AIDA (509)
Methods of sales-force
   compensation (514)
Quantitative evaluation bases (516)
Qualitative evaluation bases (516)

Questions and Problems

1. The cost of a two-page, four-color advertising spread in one issue of *Sports Illustrated* magazine is more than the cost of employing two sales people for a full year. A sales-force executive is urging her company to eliminate a few of these ads and, instead, to hire more sales people. This executive believes that for the same cost, a single good sales person working for an entire year can sell more than one ad in an issue of *Sports Illustrated*. How would you respond?

2. Would systems selling make more sense for a soft drink bottler or a plumbing supplies distributor? Why?

3. Refer to the classification of sales jobs from delivery–sales person to creative seller and answer the following questions:
   a. In which types of jobs are sales people most likely to be free from close supervision?
   b. Which types are likely to be the highest paid?
   c. For which types of jobs is the highest degree of self-motivation necessary?

4. What type of business should consider replacing inside telephone sales people with an Internet-based ordering system?

5. What are some sources you might use to acquire a list of potential customers for the following products?
   a. Bank accounts for new area residents.
   b. Dental X-ray equipment.
   c. Laptop computers.
   d. Contributors to the United Way.
   e. Baby furniture and clothes.

6. If you were preparing a sales presentation for the following products, what information about a prospect would you seek as part of your preparation?
   a. Two-bedroom condominium.
   b. New automobile.
   c. Carpeting for a home redecorating project.

7. What sources should be used to recruit sales applicants in each of the following firms? Explain your choice in each case.
   a. A Marriott Hotel that wants companies to use the hotel for conventions.
   b. IBM, for sales of software to manage parts inventories for automakers.
   c. CDW

8. Describe a sales job for which each of the following compensation plans would be most effective:
   a. Straight-salary.
   b. Straight-commission.
   c. Combination plan.

9. How might a firm determine whether a sales person is using high-pressure selling tactics that might damage customer satisfaction?

10. How can a sales manager evaluate the performance of sales people in getting new business?

Interactive Marketing Exercises

1. Review your activities of the past few days and identify those in which:
   a. You did some personal selling.
   b. People tried to sell something to you.
      Select one situation in each category where you thought the selling was particularly effective, and explain why.

2. Interview three students from your school who recently have gone through the job interviewing process conducted by companies using your school's placement office. Use the personal selling process described in the chapter to evaluate the students' sales efforts. Prepare a report covering your findings.

Chapter 19

"Their choice of Nike, the ancient Greek goddess of victory, as a name for their company now seems prophetic."

Advertising, Sales Promotion, and Public Relations

Can Nike Run Up Even Bigger Results?

It began in 1962 with a collegiate track coach (Bill Bowerman) and one of his former athletes (Phil Knight) trying to create a better performing running shoe. Their choice of Nike, the ancient Greek goddess of victory, as a name for their company now seems prophetic. In the ensuing 40 years Nike has developed into one of the world's best-known global brands with annual sales of over $12 billion.

Many factors have contributed to Nike's success. Early on the firm benefited from American consumers' increased concern about fitness. Internally, the firm has a history of investing heavily in research and development, producing numerous innovative products. And management broadened its appeal by shifting from a single-minded focus on product performance to combining performance with appearance, style, and image. More recently, Nike has paid greater attention to supply-chain management in order to better control inventories and shorten the time from product design to introduction. Also high on the list of success factors is Nike's use of promotion. Though not the first to recognize the value of endorsements by famous athletes, the firm has been the most successful at using them. Beginning in the 1980s, with stars such as Michael Jordan, John McEnroe, and Carl Lewis, Nike developed a stable of high profile endorsers. Now over 50 of the world's most prominent male and female athletes appear in Nike ads. By recently signing basketball's newest superstar, LeBron James, to a $90 million contract, Nike has signaled that it will continue to use this form of promotion.

Nike has been consistent in its use of traditional media advertising and branding. The company paid a graphic design student $35 to develop the "swoosh" logo in 1971 and has used it ever since. Today it is one of the most recognizable brand symbols in the world. Likewise, since 1988 Nike has appealed to the athlete in everyone with ad campaigns built around the theme "Just Do It." In 2004, Nike spent over $300 million advertising its products and brand.

Nike also has been heavily involved in promotional sponsorships. Appreciating the value of fans associating the Nike brand with their favorite team, the firm supplies the uniforms and equipment for the athletic teams of several colleges and a number of professional organizations, including the New York Yankees and Manchester United. In addition, it seeks goodwill by sponsoring sports events such as track meets, basketball and soccer tournaments, and even community and youth athletic events.

Not surprisingly for a company as big as Nike, it has had some missteps. For example it was slow to capitalize on several market opportunities, including extreme sports and specialized equipment for female athletes. Promotion has played a significant role in the firm's response. For example, among other things, Nike sponsors a professional skateboarding team and has added a line of women's basketball shoes—Air Swoopes—endorsed by professional player, Sheryl Swoopes.

Nike became a true global company when its 2003 international sales exceeded U.S. sales for the first time. If the firm is to reach its annual percentage sales growth targets in the high single digits and its profit goals of 15% per year, promotion will certainly continue to play a major role.[1]

How can promotion continue to be as important in Nike's future as it has been in its past?

 www.nike.com

Advertising, sales promotion, and public relations are the mass-communication tools available to marketers. As the name suggests, *mass* communication uses the same message for everyone in an audience. The mass communicator trades off the advantage of personal selling, the opportunity to deliver a tailored message in person, for the advantage of reaching many people at a lower cost per contact.

The term mass communication does not imply indiscriminate efforts to reach large audiences. As we saw with Nike in the opening case, marketers are constantly seeking refinements that will allow them to present their messages to more specifically defined target audiences.

This chapter examines *nonpersonal*, mass-communication promotional tools—advertising, sales promotion, and public relations. After studying this chapter, you should be able to explain:

- The nature and scope of advertising, sales promotion, and public relations.
- Characteristics of the major types of these mass communication tools.
- How advertising campaigns are developed and advertising media are selected.
- The alternative ways firms organize their advertising efforts.
- How sales promotion is managed to maximize its effectiveness.
- The role of public relations in the promotional mix.

Nature and Scope of Advertising

All advertisements (ads, for short) have four features:

- A verbal and/or visual nonpersonal message.
- An identified sponsor.
- Delivery through one or more media.
- Payment by the sponsor to the medium carrying the message.

Advertising, then, consists of all the activities involved in presenting through the media a nonpersonal, sponsor-identified, paid-for message about a product or organization.

Advertising in one form or another is used by most organizations. The significance of advertising is indicated by the amount of money spent on it. In 2004, total U.S. advertising expenditures were over $264 *billion*—more than twice the amount spent in 1990. A slightly smaller amount, $258 *billion*, was spent in the rest of the world during 2004. Table 19.1 shows the relative importance of the major U.S. advertising media over the past 35 years. Until 1999, newspapers were the most widely used medium, based on total advertising dollars spent. However, television is now the most heavily used medium. As newspapers' share has declined, the proportions accounted for by direct-mail advertising and the relative newcomer, the Internet, have increased.

Advertising as a Percentage of Sales

The amount of advertising that businesses do seems daunting. For example, Procter & Gamble spends more than $5.8 *billion* a year worldwide.[2] However, it's important to put the expenditure in context. When you consider that Procter & Gamble has 250 brands that it sells in more than 140 countries and that those brands are targeted at more than 5 billion consumers, the cost to get its message out (about $1 per prospect per year) seems more reasonable. Table 19.2 shows the 10 companies with the largest dollar expenditures for advertising in the U.S. Not surprisingly, these are companies with which we are all familiar.

TABLE 19.1

Advertising Expenditures in the United States by Medium

Following a decline in spending in 2001, which was attributed to the failure of many Internet companies that spent lavishly on advertising in 1999 and 2000, the dollar amount of advertising in measured media is again trending upward.

Medium	2004 Expenditures $ (in billions)	2004 Expenditures (%)	2000 (%)	1990 (%)	1980 (%)	1970 (%)
Television	62	23.0	24	22	21	18
Direct mail	52	20.0	18	18	14	14
Newspapers	47	18.0	20	25	28	29
Radio	20	7.5	8	7	7	7
Yellow pages	14	5.3	5	7	—	—
Magazines	12	4.6	5	5	6	7
Internet	7	2.7	3	—	—	—
Other*	50	19.0	17	15	24	25
Total percentage†		100	100	100	100	100
Total dollars (in billions)	$264		$247	$128	$55	$20

*Before 1988 this category included yellow pages. It also includes outdoor advertising, transportation advertising, weekly newspapers, regional farm publications, and point-of-sale advertising.

†Percentages have been rounded.

Sources: Robert J. Coen, "McCann's Insider's Report," Universal McCann Erickson, Dec. 6, 1999; Robert J. Coen, "More Gains Forseen for '95 Ad Spending," *Advertising Age,* May 8, 1995, p. 36; 1980 figures from *Advertising Age,* Mar. 22, 1982, p. 66; others adapted from *Advertising Age,* Nov. 17, 1975, p. 40; "Bob Coen's Insider Report," McCann-Erickson World Group, *www.mccann.com,* accessed on Sept. 1, 2002; "Insider's Report, Robert Coen Presentation on Advertising Expenditures, December, 2004," accessed at *www.universalmccann.com/ourview/html.,* May, 2005.

Industry averages can be misleading. How much an individual firm spends on advertising is influenced by its resources and objectives more than by what other firms in the industry are doing. In the U.S., Ford Motor Co. spends 2.5% of its sales on advertising, whereas Mitsubishi's U.S. ad budget is 9% of its sales. Despite this proportional difference, Ford spends about $6.50 on advertising for every dollar spent by Mitsubishi.[3]

TABLE 19.2

Top Ten National Advertisers in 2004, Based on Total U.S. Expenditures

Company	Ad $ (in billions)	As % of U.S. Sales
1. General Motors	4.00	2.97
2. Procter & Gamble	3.92	16.55
3. Time Warner	3.28	9.78
4. Pfizer	2.96	10.01
5. SBC Communications	2.69	6.58
6. DaimlerChrysler	2.46	3.07
7. Ford Motor Co.	2.46	2.45
8. Walt Disney	2.24	9.34
9. Verizon Communications	2.20	3.17
10. Johnson & Johnson	2.18	7.84

Source: R. Craig Endicott, "100 Leading National Advertisers," *Advertising Age,* June 27, 2005, pp. S1+.

Advertising Cost versus Personal Selling Cost

Although there are no accurate figures for the cost of personal selling, we do know it far surpasses advertising expenditures. Only a few manufacturing industries, such as drugs, toiletries, cleaning products, tobacco, and beverages, spend more on advertising than on personal selling. Advertising runs 1% to 3% of net sales in many firms, whereas the expenses of recruiting and operating a sales force are typically 8% to 15% of sales.

At the wholesale level, advertising costs are very low. Personal selling expenses for wholesalers, however, may run 10 to 15 times more than their expenditures for advertising. Even among many retailers, including some with self-service operations, the total cost of their customer-contact employees is substantially higher than what they spend on advertising.

Types of Advertising

Advertising can be classified according to (1) the target audience—either consumers or businesses, (2) the objective sought—the stimulation of primary or selective demand, and (3) what is being advertised—a product versus an institution. To fully appreciate the scope and types of advertising, it is essential to understand these three classifications.

The Target: Consumer or Business

An ad is directed at consumers or businesses; thus it is either **business-to-consumer advertising** or **business-to-business advertising.** Retailers by definition sell only to consumers; therefore, they are the only type of business not faced with this decision. On the other hand, many manufacturers and distributors must divide their advertising between business customers and consumers. For example, DaimlerChrysler advertises to fleet buyers such as the car rental companies and to final consumers; similarly, Marriott Corp. advertises its resorts and hotels to corporate clients and to households.

The Type of Demand: Primary or Selective

Primary-demand advertising is designed to stimulate demand for a generic category of a product such as coffee, electricity, or garments made from cotton. In contrast, **selective-demand advertising** is intended to stimulate demand for individual brands such as Folgers coffee, American Electric Power electricity, and Isaac Mizrahi sportswear.

Primary-demand advertising is used in either of two situations. The first is when the product is in the introductory stage of its life cycle. This is called *pioneering advertising*. Even though the brand may be mentioned, the primary objective of pioneering advertising is to inform the target market about the product. Recall from Chapter 4 that a prospect must first be made aware of a product before becoming interested in or desiring it. For example, consumers had to understand the concept of a hybrid car or a handheld computer before they could begin considering particular brands.

The other use of primary-demand advertising occurs throughout the product life cycle and therefore is considered *demand-sustaining advertising*. It is usually done by trade associations trying to stimulate or sustain demand for their industry's product. Thus, the National Fluid Milk Processor Promotion Board encourages us to consume more milk with its campaign depicting celebrities with milk "mustaches."

Selective-demand advertising is essentially competitive advertising. It pits one brand against the rest of the market. This type of advertising is employed when a product is beyond the introductory life-cycle stage and is competing for market share with several other brands. Selective-demand advertising emphasizes a brand's special features and benefits—its differential advantage.

A special case of selective-demand advertising that makes reference to one or more competitors is called **comparison advertising.** In this kind of advertising, the advertiser either directly, by naming the rival brand, or indirectly, through inferences, claims some point of superiority over the rival. Recent examples include Chevrolet, Dodge, and Ford, comparing their pickup trucks and Miller Brewing Company comparing its Miller Lite beer with Budweiser Light. Comparison advertising is encouraged by the Federal Trade Commission as a means of stimulating competition and disseminating useful information to customers. Advertisers must be careful that any comparative claims can be substantiated.

The Message: Product or Institutional

All selective advertising may be classified as product or institutional. **Product advertising** focuses on a particular product or brand. It is subdivided into direct-action and indirect-action product advertising.

- *Direct-action* advertising seeks a quick response. For instance, a magazine ad containing a coupon or an 800 number may urge the reader to send or call immediately for a free sample, or a supermarket ad in a local newspaper stresses specials available for only a few days.
- *Indirect-action* advertising is designed to stimulate demand over a longer period of time. It is intended to inform or remind consumers that the product exists and to point out its benefits. The "lonely repairman" who has appeared in television and print ads for Maytag appliances for over 35 years is an example. Most network television advertising is indirect action, whereas much local television advertising is direct action.

Institutional advertising presents information about the advertiser's business or tries to create a favorable attitude—that is, build goodwill—toward the organization. In contrast to product advertising, institutional advertising is not intended to sell a specific product. Its objective is to create a particular image for a company or brand. Examples include McDonald's global "I'm Lovin' It" campaign and General Mills' "Breakfast of Champions" campaign for Wheaties cereal that has been running for over 75 years.

The Source: Commercial or Social

The focus here is on commercial messages but the most valued form of endorsement is social, for instance, when a trusted friend or relative recommends a product. Commonly referred to as *word-of-mouth advertising*, technically it doesn't fit our definition of advertising. In fact, the very reasons that it doesn't conform to the definition are what make it so prized. That is, the message is delivered personally and the recommender is not paid. Word-of-mouth recommendations are highly credible because the recommender has only the best interests of the recipient as the motivation for sharing an opinion. So despite the fact that it is not strictly a type of advertising, word of mouth deserves our consideration.

Firms try to *stimulate* word-of-mouth endorsements. Probably the most successful word-of-mouth endorsement in history was a program created by MCI called "Friends and Family." It offered a person and a group of specified individuals reduced rates when they called each other if they all subscribed to the long-distance calling plan. In advertising circles this is referred to as "creating buzz." Alternatively, some firms try to *simulate* word-of-mouth endorsements. For example, Sony Erickson got consumers to try its mobile phone that doubles as a digital camera by having trained actors visit tourism attractions, pretending to be tourists and asking strangers to take their pictures with the phone/camera. The ensuing conversation often ended in an endorsement of the product by the actor. Not surprisingly, consumer activists object to what they consider a deceptive practice.[4]

The Internet has generated increasing interest in personalized messages. Though they are transferred electronically and not by "word of mouth," they can have the same effect. And because messages can move rapidly through an ever-expanding

Advertisers are always on the lookout for new ways to reach consumers with messages. A piece of equipment towed behind a tractor that creates imprints in beach sand is just one example. In considering this and similar non-traditional options a firm should consider not only how many people will be exposed to the message, but also how they are likely to react to it.

network of Internet users, the benefits of a positive message (and the damage of a negative one) can be very substantial. In the electronic setting, the term word of mouth has been replaced by *viral marketing,* depicting how a message is passed from one person to another through a social system. Viral marketing has the same advantages as word-of-mouth endorsements. First, it frequently has no direct cost because the message originates with a customer. Second, a person's social network is quite homogeneous, so the message likely reaches members of the target market. Finally, because it arrives as a message from a friend or acquaintance it is usually read by the recipient unlike much advertising, which is simply ignored.

As noted in Chapter 17, many individuals have moved beyond simply sharing their views via e-mail to creating their own personalized websites, called weblogs or blogs for short. Bloggers manage their sites and attract visitors by posting their own information and comments, comments of others, and links to other sites. Seeing the potential to reach audiences in a new way, many businesses are providing information to bloggers and even creating websites that have the appearance of blogs.[5]

An audio version of a weblog, called a podcast, allows individuals to record and distribute audio files via the Internet. The recordings can be downloaded to computers or digital music players and listened to any time. Podcasting is relatively easy and inexpensive, requiring only a computer, a microphone, and access to the Internet. As a result, it is a fast growing form of viral marketing.

Developing an Advertising Campaign

An **advertising campaign** consists of all the tasks involved in transforming a theme into a coordinated advertising program to accomplish a specific goal for a product or brand. Typically a campaign involves several different advertising messages, presented over an extended period of time, using a variety of media. For example, UPS had considerable success with its awareness-building campaign designed around the theme, "What can Brown do for you?" Subsequently, UPS launched a campaign called "Deliver More" to emphasize its global capabilities beyond package delivery. The campaign includes television, print, outdoor, and Internet advertising in 104 countries.

An advertising campaign is planned within the framework of the overall strategic marketing plan and as part of a broader promotional program. The framework is established when management:

- Identifies the target audience.
- Establishes the overall promotional goals.
- Sets the total promotional budget.
- Determines the overall promotional theme.

With these tasks completed, the firm can begin formulating an advertising campaign. The steps in conducting a campaign are defining objectives, establishing a budget, creating a message, selecting media, and evaluating effectiveness.

Defining Objectives

The purpose of advertising is to sell something—a good, service, idea, person, or place—either now or later. This goal is reached by setting specific objectives that are reflected in individual ads incorporated into an advertising campaign.

Typical advertising objectives are to:

- *Support personal selling.* Advertising may be used to acquaint prospects with the seller's company and products, easing the way for the sales force, as Avon is doing.
- *Improve dealer relations.* Wholesalers and retailers like to see a manufacturer support its products with advertising.
- *Introduce and position a new product.* Consumers need to be informed even about line extensions that make use of familiar brand names.
- *Expand the use of a product.* Advertising may be used to lengthen the season for a product (as Lipton did for iced tea), increase the frequency of replacement (as Fram did for oil filters), or increase the variety of product uses (as Arm & Hammer did for baking soda).
- *Reposition an existing product.* Advertising can be used to change the perception of a product (as Buick is attempting with Tiger Woods as a spokesperson).
- *Counteract substitution.* Advertising reinforces the decisions of existing customers and reduces the likelihood that they will switch to alternative brands.

Establishing a Budget

Once a promotional budget has been established (discussed in Chapter 17), it must be allocated among the various activities comprising the overall promotional program. In the case of a particular brand, a firm may wish to have several ads, as well as sales promotion and public relations activities, directed at different target audiences all at the same time. For example, at the same time it was running traditional product advertising, Avon had professional tennis players Venus and Serena Williams under contract to appear in ads, launched a "Kiss Goodbye to Breast Cancer" campaign that included a donation to breast cancer research for purchases of certain products, sponsored a charity concert and a fund-raising auction of celebrities' dresses, and continued to support launches of new products tailored to specific ethnic and demographic markets around the world. Because all these efforts must be paid for from the promotional budget, the potential value of each must be weighed and allocations made accordingly.

One method that firms use to extend their budgets is **cooperative advertising,** which is a joint effort by two or more firms intended to benefit each of the participants. There are two types of cooperative ads—vertical and horizontal. *Vertical*

www.avon.com

Have you visited Burger King's award winning "subservient chicken" website? To position its chicken sandwich (chicken any way you like it), Burger King designed a campaign that combined three 30-second television commercials featuring a chicken-costumed actor responding to verbal commands with a website where viewers could direct the chicken to carry out any of 400 actions. In the first week, the site received 20 million hits, and in less than a year the site had over 396 million hits from 14 million unique visitors.

www.subservientchicken. com

cooperative advertising involves firms on different levels of distribution. For example, a manufacturer and a retailer share the cost of the retailer's advertising of that manufacturer's product. Frequently the manufacturer prepares the actual ad, leaving space for the retailer's name and address. Then the manufacturer and retailer share the media cost of placing the ad. Many local retail ads in newspapers, radios, and on television involve co-op funds.[6]

Another type of vertical cooperation is an *advertising allowance,* or cash discount offered by a manufacturer to a retailer, to encourage the retailer to advertise or prominently display a product. In cooperative advertising the manufacturer has control over how the money is actually spent, but that is not the case with an advertising allowance.

Cooperative arrangements benefit retailers by providing them with extra funds for promotion. Manufacturers also benefit because cooperative advertising provides them with local identification for their products. In addition, a manufacturer's ad dollars go further because rates charged by local media (such as a daily newspaper) are typically lower for ads placed by local firms than for ads placed by national advertisers.

Horizontal cooperative advertising is joint advertising in which two or more firms on the same level of distribution, such as a group of retailers, share the costs. Ads for a product category, for example those reminding consumers that beef is healthy or that orange juice is not just a breakfast drink, are typically placed by a trade or professional association and paid for by the members. The principal benefit is that by pooling their funds, the firms achieve greater exposure or impact than if they advertised individually.

www.beef.org

www.floridajuice.com

Creating a Message

Whatever the objective of an advertising campaign, to be successful the individual ads must get and hold the *attention* of the intended audience, and *influence* that audience in the desired way. Attention can be achieved in many ways. (Recall our discussion of perception in Chapter 4.) Television makes possible special visual effects such as the flying cans in the Mountain Dew ads. Radio can use listeners' imaginations to create mental images that would be impossible to actually produce. Surprising, shocking, amusing, and arousing curiosity are all common techniques used to

AN ETHICAL DILEMMA?

Experts in consumer electronics, fashion, food preparation, and toys are frequently invited to review products on local television news shows and national network talk shows. These segments are often used around holidays when consumers are looking for gift-giving ideas. They are also broadcast in conjunction with major trade shows where new products are introduced. For a producer, having its product favorably mentioned in this noncommercial fashion is highly desirable. For example, the publicity value of appearing on a network show such as *Today* with over 6 million viewers is estimated to be $250,000. What the audience doesn't know is that the experts are frequently paid by the manufacturers to include their products and give them favorable reviews.

Is it ethical to broadcast a review of a product as news without acknowledging that the reviewer is being paid by the product's maker?

Sources: James Bandler, "How Companies Pay Experts for On-Air Product Mentions," *The Wall Street Journal*, Apr. 19, 2005, pp. A1+; "News Is No Place for Shady Shills," *Advertising Age*, Apr. 25, 2005, p. 32; Kelly Crow, "Food: the Sponsored Chef," *The Wall Street Journal*, Apr. 22, 2005, pp. W1+.

gain attention. Thus a print ad might be mostly white space, or a billboard might show the product in an unusual setting.

If the ad succeeds in getting the audience's attention, the advertiser has a few seconds to communicate a message intended to influence beliefs and/or behavior. The message has two elements—the *appeal* and the *execution*. The appeal in an ad is the reason or justification for believing or behaving. It is the benefit that the individual will receive as a result of accepting the message.

Some advertisers mistakenly focus their appeal on product features or attributes. They either confuse attributes with benefits, or assume that if they present the product's attributes, the audience will infer the correct benefits. Telling consumers that a breakfast cereal contains fiber (an attribute) is much less meaningful than telling them that because it contains fiber, consuming it reduces the likelihood of colon cancer (the benefit).

Execution is combining in a convincing, compatible way the feature or device that gets attention with the appeal. There are many examples of attention-getting devices that complement advertising appeals. Consider, for example, the many characters advertisers have created to get messages across—the Pillsbury Doughboy, the Green Giant, Eveready's Energizer Bunny, the Michelin man, Ronald McDonald, and Kellogg's Tony the Tiger. Great care must be taken to ensure that in the execution, the attention getting device doesn't overwhelm the appeal. Taco Bell developed an execution that featured a Chihuahua obsessed with the company's products. After a two-year campaign and $200 million of advertising, the company decided to reduce the dog's role in its ads and focus more on the food. According to a Taco Bell franchisee, the dog, which had become a pop-culture icon, appearing on the cover of *TV Guide* magazine and in a music video, became the focus. Meanwhile, the food was receiving too little attention. The evidence was in the results. Although many people were familiar with the Chihuahua, Taco Bell sales increased only 2% during the campaign.[7]

Selecting Media

In describing the steps involved in developing an advertising campaign, we discussed the creation of an advertising message before selection of the **advertising media** in which to place the ad. In actuality these decisions are usually made simultaneously. Both the message and the choice of media are determined by the nature of the appeal and the intended target audience.

Advertisers need to make decisions at each of three successive levels in selecting the specific advertising medium to use:

1. Which *type(s)* will be used—newspaper, television, radio, magazine, or direct mail? What about the less prominent media of billboards, the Internet, and yellow pages?

2. Which *category of the selected medium* will be used? Television has network and cable; magazines include general-interest (*Newsweek, People*) and special-interest (*Popular Mechanics, Runner's World*) categories; there are national as well as local newspapers; and the Internet offers portals as well as individual websites.

3. Which *specific media vehicles* will be used? An advertiser that decides first on radio and then on local stations must determine which stations to use in each city.

Here are some general factors that will influence media choice:

- *Objectives of the ad.* The purpose of a particular ad and the goals of the entire campaign influence which media to use. For example, if the campaign goal is to generate appointments for sales people, the company may rely on direct mail. If an advertiser has a short lead time, local newspaper or radio may be the medium to use.

- *Audience coverage.* The audience reached by the medium should match the geographic area in which the product is distributed. Furthermore, the selected medium should reach the desired prospects with a minimum of wasted coverage—that is, it should not reach people who are outside of the target market. Many media, even national and other large-market media, allow advertisers to target small, specialized market segments. For example, *Time* magazine publishes regional editions with different ads in the East, Midwest, and West and *Sports Illustrated* has a special edition for subscribers who have indicated an interest in golf. Large metropolitan newspapers publish suburban editions as well as regional editions within the city.

- *Requirements of the message.* The medium should fit the message. For example, magazines provide high-quality visual reproductions that attract attention along with printed messages that can be carefully read and evaluated. As a result, they are well suited to business-to-business advertising.

- *Time and location of the buying decision.* If the objective is to stimulate a purchase, the medium should reach prospective customers when and where they are about to make their buying decisions. This factor highlights one of the strengths of point-of-purchase advertising (such as ads placed on shopping carts and on in-store, closed circuit television), which reaches consumers at the actual time of purchase.

- *Media cost.* The cost of each medium should be considered in relation to the amount of funds available to pay for it and its reach or circulation. For example, the cost of network television exceeds the available funds of many advertisers. To compare various media, advertisers use a measure called **cost per thousand (CPM)**, which is the cost of reaching a thousand people, one time each, with a particular ad.

Beyond these general factors, management must evaluate the advertising characteristics of each medium it is considering. We have carefully chosen the term *characteristics,* instead of advantages and disadvantages, because a medium that works well for one product is not necessarily the best choice for another product. To illustrate, a characteristic of radio is that it makes its impressions through sound and imagination. The roar of a crowd, the rumbling of thunder, or screeching tires can be used to create mental images quickly and easily. But radio will not do the job for products that require a specific visual image. Let's examine the characteristics of the major media.

Television Virtually every U.S. household has a television, and on average viewers watch more than 18 hours per week.[8] Television combines motion, sound, and special visual effects, and products can be demonstrated as well as described on TV. It offers wide geographic coverage and flexibility in when the message can be presented. However, TV ads lack permanence, so they must be seen and understood immediately. As a result, TV does not lend itself to complicated messages.

Television can appear to be a relatively expensive medium, but it has the potential to reach a large audience. For example, a single 30-second spot on the 2005 Super Bowl telecast cost $2.4 million to reach an audience of 90 million viewers. Table 19.3 shows how the cost of a network ad in prime time has changed. The decrease in recent years is the result of a decline in the size of network audiences due to cable television, the popularity of other entertainment sources such as video games, and the growth of the Internet. The share of the television audience in prime time that is held by the networks has declined from 90% in 1980 to about 35% today. Over 65% of American homes (80% with household incomes over $50,000) have cable, with an average of 62 stations per household.[9] The result is more fragmented markets and specialized programming, making it difficult to reach a mass market. On the positive side, the specialization of cable channels such as MTV, CNBC, and ESPN offers an advertiser a more homogeneous group of viewers at a lower price (because the audience is smaller) than broadcast networks. Television ads are also expensive to produce. It's not unusual for a firm to spend $500,000 to create a 30-second commercial. As a result, fewer ads are being made, and they are being kept on the air longer.

Advertisers are also using *place-based* television to reach attractive target audiences—young professionals, teenagers, working women—who have become less

TABLE 19.3 The Cost of a 30-Second Prime-Time Advertising Spot on Network Television

Year	Program	Cost
1980	*M*A*S*H*	$150,000
	Dallas	145,000
1992	*Murphy Brown*	310,000
	Roseanne	290,000
1995	*Seinfeld*	490,000
	Home Improvement	475,000
1999	*Ally McBeal*	450,000
	ER	750,000
2000	*Will & Grace*	480,000
	Friends	540,000
2002	*Survivor*	420,000
	Everybody Loves Raymond	300,000
2005	*Desperate Housewives*	255,000
	Lost	220,000

Sources: "50 Years of TV Advertising: The Buying and Selling," *Advertising Age,* Spring 1995, p. 29; Joe Mandese, "Seinfeld Is NBC's $ 1M/Minute Man," *Advertising Age,* Sept. 18, 1995, p. 11; Joe Mandese, "'ER' Tops Price Chart, Regis Wears the Crown," *Advertising Age,* Oct. 2, 2000, pp. 1+; David Goetzl and Wayne Friedman, "'Friends' Tops Ad Price List," *Advertising Age,* Sept. 30, 2002, pp. 1+; John M. Higgins, "ABC's Upfront Payoff," *Broadcasting & Cable,* Oct. 18, 2004, p 6; and personal contacts.

accessible through traditional media. Firms such as Whittle Communications and CNN put TVs in classrooms, waiting rooms, supermarkets, airports, health clubs, and other places where "captive audiences" are likely to gather.

Direct Mail Over 60 *billion* pieces of direct-mail advertising are distributed in the U.S. each year.[10] It can be sent in the traditional fashion, using the Postal Service or an overnight delivery, or electronically by fax or e-mail.

Direct mail has the potential of being the most personal and selective of all media. Highly specialized direct-mail lists can be developed from a firm's own customer database or purchased from list suppliers (among the thousands available are lists of air traffic controllers, wig dealers, college professors, pregnant women, and disc jockeys). Because direct mail goes only to the people the advertiser wishes to contact, there is almost no wasted coverage. However, even with carefully selected mailing lists, a direct-mail effort with a response rate of 1% to 2% is often viewed as successful.[11] Traditional direct mail also allows for the distribution of product samples. Printing and postage fees make the cost per thousand of direct mail quite high compared with other media.

www.the-dma.org

The technological alternative, electronic direct mail or e-mail, is less expensive to send. However, the low cost has led to indiscriminate distribution of unsolicited commercial e-mail (called spamming). It has become so commonplace and annoying that a number of public agencies and private groups are seeking ways to regulate it.

Reaching the prospect does not ensure that the message is communicated. Direct mail is pure advertising. It is not accompanied by editorial matter (unless the advertiser provides it). Therefore, a direct-mail ad must attract its own readers. This is critical when you consider that the average American home receives more than 10 direct-mail pieces a week, and that half of all direct-mail pieces are discarded unopened.

Newspapers As an advertising medium, newspapers are flexible and timely. Ads can be inserted or canceled on very short notice and can vary in size from small classifieds to multiple pages. Pages can be added or dropped, so the space in newspapers is not limited in the way time is constrained on TV and radio. Newspapers can be used to reach an entire city or, where regional editions are offered, selected areas. Cost per thousand is relatively low.

www.naa.org

On the other hand, the life of newspapers is very short. Typically, they are discarded soon after being read. A metropolitan newspaper provides coverage of about one-half the households in a local market. However, in many large cities, circulation of daily newspapers is decreasing. Also, the growth of the Internet has created a new source of competition for newspapers. Especially hard hit is classified advertising, which accounts for about 40% of newspaper ad revenue.[12] Finally, because newspapers don't offer much format variety, it is difficult to design ads that stand out.

Radio When interest in television soared after World War II, radio audiences (especially for network radio) declined so dramatically that some people predicted radio's demise. However, radio has enjoyed a rebirth as an advertising and cultural medium, with the number of stations increasing at a steady rate. Today there are over 11,000 stations in the U.S.

Radio is a low-cost per thousand medium because of its broad reach. Nearly 75% of Americans listen to the radio daily, and on average, adults 18 year of age and over listen more than 20 hours a week.[13] With programming ranging from all-talk to sports to country music, certain target markets can be pinpointed quite effectively. Radio commercials can be produced in less than a week, at a cost far below television commercials.

www.rab.com

Because radio makes only an audio impression, it relies entirely on the listener's ability to retain information heard and not seen. Also, audience attention is often at a low level, because radio is frequently used as background for working, studying (Is your radio on now?), or some other activity.

Yellow Pages A printed directory of local business names and phone numbers organized by type of product, the yellow pages has been around since the late 1800s. The breakup of the Bell System telephone monopoly in 1983 led to an increase in the number of yellow pages directories. Today there are over 6,000 in the U.S., with large metropolitan areas commonly having four or five competing directories.[14] The yellow pages are a source of information with which most consumers are familiar. And they are used by consumers at or very near the buying decision. On the negative side, yellow page ads are difficult to differentiate, and an advertiser's message is surrounded by the messages of competitors. In addition, traditional printed yellow pages directories are receiving competition from electronic yellow pages on the Internet.

www.admworks.org

Magazines Magazines are the medium to use when high-quality printing and color are desired in an ad. Magazines can reach a national market at a relatively low cost per reader. In recent years, the rapid increase in special-interest magazines and regional editions of general-interest magazines has made it possible for advertisers to reach a selected audience with a minimum of wasted circulation. Business and trade magazines, many of which are given away to readers, can be effective in reaching specialized industry audiences. The number of different magazines in the U.S. has increased from just over 14,000 in 1993 to nearly 18,000 today.[15]

People usually read magazines in a leisurely fashion, in contrast to the haste in which they read other print media. This feature is especially valuable to the advertiser with a lengthy or complicated message. A variety of production innovations have made it possible to enliven magazine ads. Over-sized, foldouts, pullout sections, and poly-wrapped samples are becoming common. Magazines have a relatively long life, anywhere from a week to a month, and a high pass-along readership.

In recent years, many magazines have experienced declines in circulation so their reach has diminished. With less flexible production schedules than newspapers, magazines require that ads be submitted several weeks before publication. In addition, because they are published weekly or monthly, it is difficult to use timely messages. People often read magazines at times or in places—on planes or in doctors' offices, for instance—when they are far removed from where they can act on a buying impulse.

Out-of-Home Advertising Spending on out-of-home advertising is growing at about 10% a year, amounting to over $5 billion today.[16] At one time the category was dominated by billboards, and was called outdoor advertising. However, *out-of-home* is more descriptive today because billboards now are in malls, arenas, airports, and other indoor locations as well as outdoors.

There have been other changes in billboards as well. One is the computer-painting technology that makes it possible to create high-quality visual reproductions. Another development is the capability built into the boards themselves, including three-dimensional structures, special lighting effects, digital tickers, and continuous motion. Low cost per thousand is the chief advantage of out-of-home media, although prices vary by the volume of traffic passing a site.

www.oaaa.org

Most out-of-home advertising is for local businesses, but it is increasingly being used for national brand-building ads. Because it is seen by people "on the go," billboard advertising is appropriate only for brief messages. The rule of thumb is six words or less.

Billboards can provide intense market coverage within an area. However, unless the advertised product is a widely used good or service, considerable wasted circulation will occur, because many of the passersby will not be prospects. Finally, the landscape-defacing criticism of outdoor advertising may be a consideration for some advertisers.

Interactive Media Interactivity refers to a feature that permits the advertising message recipient to respond immediately using the same medium. For example, a person receiving an e-mail message can reply with the click of a mouse. The fastest-growing interactive medium is the World Wide Web, which gives millions of organizations and individuals direct, electronic access to one another.

The opportunity the Web has created has not been lost on marketers. The two primary ad formats are display ads and search-results ads. Both utilize search engines such as Google, Yahoo!, and MSN from Microsoft. *Display ads* contain graphics and may utilize animation and sound. They run atop or alongside a Web page. For example, a CNN story about travel accessed through Google might be accompanied by an ad for a cruise line. *Search-results ads* are text messages displayed in response to a keyword search. For example, if a visitor to Google types in "automobiles" several listings will appear for companies advertising cars for sale.

This medium requires the recipient to take the initiative and tap into the advertiser's message. Once the connection is established, the recipient controls the flow of information, selecting with mouse clicks the pages to examine and how long to remain connected. For example, a consumer interested in buying a car might begin by using the Web to find out which companies make minivans. From there, the consumer could move on to information about performance, safety features, technical specifications, and prices of specific makes. The next step might be to locate a page that identifies dealers in the area, their respective inventories, and financing alternatives.

www.iab.net

As an advertising medium, the Internet is particularly popular with companies selling products that involve extensive decision making. Ford Motor Co. shifted a significant portion of its national magazine advertising budget to interactive media, including the Internet. The company's primary site (www.ford.com) provides information about all the brands and directs customers to other sites including one where they can shop for a car and another where Ford owners can receive service reminders as well as recall information. The websites produce over a half million leads for Ford dealers a year, with some dealers claiming that 30% of their sales are initiated on the Internet.[17]

www.grillparts.com

Some small companies with limited promotional budgets have discovered that the Internet allows them to reach a broader geographic market. For example, Barbecue Renew, a Kirkland, Washington, retailer of barbecue-grill replacement parts, turned to the Internet after local newspaper ads proved unsuccessful. It now generates sales from all over the U.S. from its website.

Initially access to the Web required a personal computer. Now "Internet appliances" are available. Less sophisticated (and less expensive) than a PC, Internet appliances provide only the capability to traverse the Internet and to exchange e-mail messages. In addition, wireless devices such as the Palm Pilot and BlackBerry give consumers and advertisers more convenient access. These devices are likely to contribute to an even faster diffusion of the Internet as an advertising medium.

Interactivity creates a very different environment for advertisers. On the plus side, the audience has demonstrated its interest by logging on, and the technology makes it easy to track the number of visitors to the site, how long they stay connected, and what areas of the site they visit. On the other hand, using this medium requires the participants to have some proficiency with the technology. Also, with hundreds of thousands of websites only a mouse click away, holding a visitor's attention is difficult.

Media decision makers abroad are faced with different conditions that require local knowledge. For example, the move toward greater democracy has created new media options in some eastern European countries, where private radio and television stations now can run up to four times as much advertising as was permitted on state-owned stations. On the other hand, print media in most of the world cannot offer the special editions and narrowly targeted audiences available in highly developed countries.

Evaluating the Advertising Effort

Top executives want proof that advertising is worthwhile. They want to know whether dollars spent on advertising are producing as many sales as could be reaped from the same dollars spent on other marketing activities. On the other hand, advertisers promise only that a certain number of people will be exposed to an ad. They

For its Venus razor for women, Gillette supported traditional media advertising with several other promotional tools. To introduce the product, trucks such as the one shown here, visited spring break sites, where female visitors were invited to enter a sweepstakes and send electronic greeting cards to friends. Other promotions included a contest to find the best looking legs in America and a two-day "legsexperience" promotion in New York's Times Square featuring Black Eyed Peas singer Stacey Ferguson.

www.gillettevenus.com

do not guarantee a certain level of sales and, in most instances, would even find it impossible to indicate the portion of sales that are attributable to advertising.

Difficulty of Evaluation

It is hard to measure the sales effectiveness of advertising. By the very nature of the marketing mix, all elements, including advertising, are so intertwined that it is nearly impossible to measure the effect of any one by itself. Factors that make measuring the sales impact of advertising difficult are:

- *Different objectives.* Although all advertising is ultimately intended to increase sales, individual ads may not be aimed at producing immediate results. For example, some ads simply announce new store hours or service policies, and others are designed to build corporate goodwill or contribute to a brand's position.

- *Effects over time.* Even an ad designed to have an immediate sales impact may produce results weeks or months after it appears. An ad may plant in the prospect's mind a seed that doesn't blossom into a sale for several weeks.

- *Measurement problems.* Consumers cannot usually say when or if a specific ad influenced their behavior, let alone if it caused them to buy. Human motivation is too complicated to be explained by a single factor.

YOU MAKE THE DECISION

Should advertising and promotion be treated as an expense or an investment?

As promotional expenditures continue to increase (Procter & Gamble spends nearly $4 billion a year on advertising alone), firms are demanding greater accountability. Putting it in the terms used for other expenditures, CEOs want to know what the advertising return on investment is. On the other hand, marketers have argued there are too many variables involved in a buying decision over too long a period to accurately measure the contribution of a single ad or campaign.

Traditional television advertising has come under increasing pressure to produce measures of its value. In particular, CEOs are questioning the value of institutional ad campaigns built around themes such as McDonald's "I'm Lovin' It" or Coca-Cola's "Make It Real." As a result, companies are using promotional dollars to sponsor events where names and contact information of prospects can be collected and tracked or for direct marketing and online advertising where the number and types of responses can be measured.

Can sales results be connected directly to advertising expenditures?

Sources: Karen Benezra, "Spending Freely Again," *Brandweek*, Feb. 14, 2005, pp. 20–24; Tomas Kellner, "Reengineering that Ad," *Forbes*, May 23, 2005, pp. 89–90; Joe Mandese, "P&G Review Could Be Far-Reaching," *TelevisionWeek*, Apr. 15, 2004, p. 55.

Advertising, Sales Promotion, and Public Relations   **535**

Notice the yellow tabs on this print ad. They are Starch Readership scores for a sample of consumers who were able to recall seeing all or part of this ad while they were reading a magazine in which it appeared. The readership scores represent different levels of involvement with the ad, from simply noticing it to reading most of the copy. Advertisers use these scores to compare how well a particular ad format performs relative to other formats or how their ads do relative to ads for competing products. Visit the GFK website to learn more about measuring ad effectiveness.

www.gfkamerica.com

In spite of these problems, advertisers try to measure advertising effectiveness because they must, and some knowledge is better than none. An ad's effectiveness may be tested before it is presented to the target audience, while it is being presented, or after it has completed its run.

Methods Used to Measure Effectiveness

Ad effectiveness measures are either direct or indirect. **Direct tests,** which compile the responses to an ad or a campaign, can be used only with a few types of ads. Tabulating the number of redemptions of a reduced-price coupon incorporated in an ad, for example, will indicate its effectiveness. Coupons frequently are coded so they can also be traced to the publications in which they were run. Another direct test of an ad's effectiveness is the number of inquiries received from an ad that offers additional information to prospects who call or write in.

Most other measures are **indirect tests** of effectiveness, or measures of something other than actual behavior. One of the most frequently used measures is advertising recall. Recall tests are based on the premise that an ad can have an effect only if it is perceived and remembered. Three common recall tests are:

- *Recognition*—showing people an ad and asking if they have seen it before.

- *Aided recall*—asking people if they can recall seeing any ads for a particular brand.

- *Unaided recall*—asking people if they can remember seeing any ads within an identified product category.

Refinements are constantly being made in advertising testing. See the "Marketing in the Information Economy" box in this chapter for a description of a new approach to measuring television audiences. Other developments such as laboratory test markets and computer simulations hold promise for the future. However, the complexity of decision making, combined with the multitude of influences on the buyer, will continue to make measuring the effectiveness of advertising a difficult task.

Is improving the precision in TV audience size measurement enough?

The amount charged for media time or space is determined by the size and mix of the audience. For example, a 30-second spot on a television show with a large audience of young adults is much more expensive than one with a smaller audience made up of children.

For many years the accepted measure of television audience size and composition has been provided by Nielsen Media Research. The firm long relied on consumer panels and paper-and-pencil diaries to measure audiences. As viewing behavior and technology changed, Nielsen made adjustments in its data collection for multiple television sets in a household, channel "surfing" with the remote, and recording shows for later viewing.

In recent years there have been concerns that audience estimates are understated because the measures do not include viewers on college campuses or in bars, hotels, military housing, and other out-of-home locations. In response, Nielsen is testing clip-on electronic devices that can identify a television program a panel member is exposed to regardless of the location. In addition, researchers are not only attempting to measure viewing but also attentiveness to advertising. They have found that dramatic shows and those with complicated plots produce greater ad recall than news or contest shows. Thus, even a more precise measure of the size of the audience may not be the best indicator of a television show's advertising value.

Sources: Brooks Barnes, "Where's the Ratings, Dude?," *The Wall Street Journal,* Mar. 7, 2005, pp. B1+; Brian Steinberg, "A Network's Dream? TV Viewers Who Recall Commercials," *The Wall Street Journal,* May 11, 2005, pp. B1+.

Organizing for Advertising

There are three ways a firm can manage its advertising:

- Develop an internal advertising department.
- Use an outside advertising agency.
- Use a combination of an internal department and an outside advertising agency.

Regardless of which alternative is selected, generally the same specialized skills are necessary to do the advertising job. Creative people are needed to prepare the copy, generate audio and/or video material, and design the formats. Media experts are required to select the appropriate media, buy the time or space, and arrange for the scheduled appearance of the ads. And managerial skills are essential to plan and administer the entire advertising program.

Internal Departments

All these advertising tasks, some of them, or just overall direction can be performed by an internal department. A company whose advertising is a substantial part of its marketing mix will usually have its own advertising department. Large retailers, for example, have their own advertising departments, and many do not use advertising agencies at all. If a company has adopted the marketing concept, the advertising department head will report to the organization's top marketing executive.

Advertising Agencies

Many companies, especially producers, use advertising agencies to carry out some or all of their advertising activities. An **advertising agency** is an independent company that provides specialized advertising services. Many large agencies have expanded the services they offer to include sales promotion, public relations, and even broader marketing assistance. As a result, they are frequently called upon to assist in strategic

What determines how a medium can be used?

The adoption and diffusion of cell phones has occurred very differently in Japan and the U.S. In Japan the adoption was spurred by young women with a desire for privacy but without access to a personal telephone. In the U.S., it was initially seen as a means of keeping in touch with the office. It was treated as an inferior, emergency means of communications used for business purposes. The environments also differed. In Asia there initially were few regulations on sending unsolicited messages, while in the U.S. the Federal Communications Commission prohibited marketers from sending such messages. As cell phones have diffused, the perceptions and applications have broadened. However, the initial positioning continues to have an impact. In Asia, cell phones are a primary source of information and entertainment. In the U.S., cell phones remain largely a device for contacting another person. As a result of these market differences, how advertisers use cell phones has moved in quite distinct directions in Japan and the U.S.:

- Many more Japanese than U.S. cell phone users have signed up to receive regularly scheduled promotional messages from advertisers.

- Specially designed entertainment content has been developed for Japanese cell phone users by firms such as MTV, while U.S. cell phone users have limited access to nonconversational content. As a result, Japanese consumers see many more ads and promotions on their phones.

- In Japan, where cell phones are seen as unnecessary, talking on a cell phone in public is considered rude. As a result, text messaging is much more prevalent in Japan. This has spawned much more interactivity between Japanese consumers and marketers than occurs in the U.S.

- Live television on cell phones is a reality in Japan with an anticipated steep growth curve. In the U.S., it is predicted that by 2009, only 5% of cell phones sold will incorporate a TV receiver even though programming will be available.

Sources: Geoffrey A. Fowler, "Asia's Mobile Ads," *The Wall Street Journal,* Apr. 25, 2005, pp. B1+; Geoff Long, "Big Plans for the Small Screen," *Wireless Asia,* January/February, 2005, pp. 26+; Erika Brown, "Coming Soon to a Tiny Screen Near You," *Forbes,* May 23, 2005, pp. 64–76.

planning, marketing research, new-product development, package design, and selection of product names.

Advertising agencies plan and execute entire advertising campaigns. They employ more advertising specialists than their clients do, because they spread the cost over many accounts. A client company can benefit from the experience an agency gains from other products and campaigns.

Inside Department and Outside Agency

Many firms have their own advertising department and also use an advertising agency. The internal department acts as a liaison with the agency, giving the company greater control over this major expenditure. The advertising department approves the agency's plans and ads, is responsible for preparing and administering the advertising budget, and coordinates advertising with personal selling. It may also handle direct marketing, dealer displays, and other promotional activities if they are not handled by the agency.

Sales Promotion

Sales promotion is one of the most loosely used terms in the marketing vocabulary. We define **sales promotion** as demand-stimulating devices designed to supplement advertising and facilitate personal selling. Examples of sales promotion devices are coupons, premiums, in-store displays, sponsorships, trade shows, samples, in-store demonstrations, and contests.

Sales promotions are conducted by producers and middlemen. The target for producers' sales promotions may be middlemen, end users—households or business users—or the producers' own sales forces. Middlemen direct sales promotion at their sales people or prospects further down the channel of distribution.

Nature and Scope

Sales promotion is distinct from advertising or personal selling, but these three forms of promotion are often used together in an integrated fashion. For example, prospective customers may be generated from people who enter a contest to win a copier at the Canon website and at a Canon exhibit at an office equipment trade show. These prospects might be sent some direct-mail and e-mail advertising and then be contacted by a sales person.

There are two categories of sales promotion: *trade promotions*, directed to the members of the distribution channel, and *consumer promotions*, aimed at consumers. It may surprise you to learn that consumer packaged-goods manufacturers as a group spend about half of their total promotion budgets on trade promotion, about one-fourth on consumer promotions, and one-fourth on advertising.[18]

The magnitude of sales promotion activities is mind-boggling. Although no statistics are available on total expenditures, the trade publication *PROMO Magazine*, placed the figure at about $100 *billion* in 2001, an increase of about 100% since 1990.[19]

Several factors in the marketing environment contribute to the popularity of sales promotion:

- *Short-term results.* Sales promotions such as couponing and trade allowances produce quicker, more measurable sales results than brand-building advertising.

- *Competitive pressure.* If competitors offer buyers price reductions, contests, or other incentives, a firm may feel forced to retaliate with its own sales promotions.

- *Buyers' expectations.* Once they are offered purchase incentives, consumers and channel members get used to them and soon begin expecting them.

- *Low quality of retail selling.* Many retailers use inadequately trained sales clerks or have switched to self-service. For these outlets, sales promotion devices such as product displays and samples often are the only effective promotional tools available at the point of purchase.

One problem management faces is that many sales promotion techniques are short-run, tactical actions. Coupons, premiums, and contests, for example, are designed to produce immediate (but short-lived) responses. As a result, they tend to be used as stopgap measures to reverse unexpected sales declines rather than as parts of an integrated marketing program.

Sales promotion should be included in a company's promotion plans, along with advertising and personal selling. This means setting sales promotion objectives and strategies, determining a sales promotion budget, and selecting appropriate sales promotion techniques.

Determining Objectives and Strategies Three broad objectives of sales promotion were suggested when the term was introduced in Chapter 17:

- Stimulating business user or household demand for a product.

- Improving the marketing performance of middlemen and sales people.

- Supplementing advertising and facilitating personal selling.

A single sales promotion technique may accomplish one or two—but probably not all—of these objectives.

Determining Budgets

The sales promotion budget should be established as a specific part of the budget for the total promotional mix. If sales promotion is included in an advertising or public relations budget, it may be overlooked or poorly integrated with the other components of promotion. Setting a separate budget for sales promotion forces a company to recognize and manage it.

Within the concept of developing an integrated marketing communications strategy, the amount budgeted for sales promotion should be determined by the task or objective method. This forces management to identify specific objectives and the sales promotion techniques that will be used to accomplish them.

Directing the Sales Promotion Effort

Many marketers plan and implement their sales promotion efforts internally. Others rely on specialized agencies. Sales promotion agencies fall into two primary categories. The first category is called *promotional service agencies*. They specialize in executing sales promotion programs such as sampling and couponing.

The other type of organization, called a *promotional marketing agency*, provides management advice and strategic planning of sales promotion as well as execution of the resulting program. As the use of sales promotion has increased, more organizations have turned to promotional marketing agencies for guidance. Rather than treat sales promotion as a periodic, single-shot sales stimulator, more firms are now integrating it into a planned strategy with long-term goals.

Selecting the Appropriate Techniques

A key step in sales promotion management is deciding which devices will help the organization reach its promotional goals. Factors that influence the choice of promotional devices include:

- *Nature of the target audience.* Is the target group loyal to a competing brand? If so, a high-value incentive or coupon may be necessary to disrupt customers' purchase patterns. Is the product bought on impulse? If so, an eye-catching point-of-sale display may be enough to generate sales.
- *Nature of the product.* Does the product lend itself to sampling, demonstration, or multiple-item purchases?
- *Cost of the device.* Sampling to a large market may be prohibitively expensive.
- *Current economic conditions.* Coupons, premiums, and rebates are good options during periods of recession or inflation, when consumers are particularly price conscious.

Common sales promotion techniques are shown in Table 19.4, where they are divided into three categories based on the target audience: business users or households, middlemen, and producers' sales forces. To illustrate the significance of sales promotion, several of these techniques are described below.

Sampling. Sampling is the only sure way of getting a product in the hands of potential customers. And it would seem to be a powerful motivator. In a national survey of consumers, 89% of the respondents said they "feel better" about purchasing a product after sampling it, and 69% believed samples and demonstrations influence their purchase decisions more than radio or television ads.[20]

Sampling is not a new technique. A New Jersey promotions firm has been assembling samples of relevant products and distributing them to new mothers for over 45 years. However, in order to get the product in the right hands, creativity has

TABLE 19.4 — Major Sales Promotion Devices, Grouped by Target Audience

Business Users or Households	Middlemen and Their Sales Forces	Producers' Own Sales Forces
Coupons	Trade shows and exhibitions	Sales contests/incentives
Cash rebates	Point-of-purchase displays	Demonstration model of product
Premiums (gifts)	Free goods	Sample of product
Free samples	Advertising allowances	
Contests and sweepstakes	Contests for sales people	
Point-of-purchase displays	Training middlemen's sales forces	
Product demonstrations	Product demonstrations	
Trade shows and exhibitions	Advertising specialties	
Advertising specialties		
Product placements		
Event sponsorship		

www.popai.org

increased. For example, marketers have discovered that spring break is an excellent time to expose young people to their products since nearly 65% of the 18- to 25-year-olds who receive a sample at a spring break destination later buy the product. [21] S. C. Johnson, the maker of Off! insect repellent, placed samples of its product in a million new Sunbeam barbecue grills. And snack food makers have joined with Blockbuster to give video renters samples of new products.

Sampling is most commonly done through the mail. Other methods include newspaper inserts and direct person-to-person handouts on the street or in stores or malls. Some firms are experimenting with sampling through their websites on the Internet or at *pop-up stores*—store fronts in retail areas opened for only a few days or weeks and heavily advertised in which samples of a new product are distributed. Meow Mix gave away 14,000 samples of a new cat food in a 12-day period in a Manhattan New York pop-up store.[22] The advantage is that people visiting a website or pop-up store to request a sample are most likely very interested in the product.

The cost per thousand of sampling is much higher than advertising. However, the conversion rate (the proportion of people exposed who buy the product) is typically around 10% for sampling, which is considerably better than advertising.

Couponing. The volume of manufacturers' coupons directed to consumers is staggering. The largest category is free standing inserts (FSI) included in newspapers. In 2004, 251 *billion* FSIs were distributed. Although the average FSI value was more than $1, fewer than 2% were redeemed.[23]

Other methods of coupon distribution are direct mail, in magazines, and coupons packaged in or on products. An increasing number of coupons are being distributed in retail stores. One technique is to offer coupons in a dispenser attached to the retail shelf where a product is displayed. The rationale is that consumers, at the point of purchase, may be influenced to select a particular brand if a coupon is readily available. Not surprisingly, these coupons have redemption rates as much as nine times higher than coupons included in newspapers. Another method growing in popularity is to electronically dispense coupons at the checkout counter on the basis of the items a consumer purchases. Thus, when a shopper buys a particular brand of a product, a coupon might be issued for a competing alternative. This approach is designed to encourage brand switching on the consumer's next shopping trip. Also, consumers who are members of retailers' frequent-shopper programs are given coupons when they make purchases.

Most product placements involve incorporating a product in the plot of a movie or television show. However, Home Depot, a retailer of do-it-yourself products and tools, stretched the concept by playing an active role in several recent TV reality series including *The Apprentice* (shown here), *Survivor,* and *The Contender.* Measuring the impact of product placements, comparing their value to alternative promotion methods, and determining the appropriate fees are ongoing challenges for the advertisers and the media.

www.itvx.net

www.coolsavings.com

A small but growing number of coupons are being distributed on the Internet. Combining the Internet and coupons provides access to hard-to-reach audiences. For example, college students can log onto coolsavings.com, become registered members, and download coupons for redemption at campus-area restaurants and retail stores.

Although most coupons are for frequently purchased convenience items, they are used by marketers of other products as well. General Motors has mailed millions of U.S. consumers coupons worth $500 toward the purchase of new cars.

Critics of coupons point out that they are expensive in terms of distribution, wasted coverage, and reduced margins to the seller when they are redeemed. Another problem is that they may undermine brand loyalty. Coupons may teach consumers to seek out the best bargains rather than consistently select a particular brand. Finally, some marketers are discouraged by the low redemption rate. Procter & Gamble discontinued couponing for its Luvs disposable diapers after only 5 million were redeemed out of 500 million distributed. The company explained on its website (www.luvs.com/faqs) that rather than spend money on coupons it was going to lower the everyday price of the diapers. However, after receiving numerous complaints from mothers, the company reinstated coupons but only for consumers who registered online to receive them.

Couponing has increased in other parts of the world, but the methods of distribution are different from those in the U.S. Whereas the bulk of coupons in the U.S. are FSIs, in Canada, coupons are most often included as a part of print ads. Spanish and Italian marketers place coupons in or on packages. And in several other European countries, coupons are distributed door to door.

Sponsorships and Event Marketing. Corporate sponsorship of events has become a major promotional activity. Worldwide expenditures exceed $28 billion, with over $11 billion of the total spent in North America.[24] The leaders in obtaining corporate sponsors are sports events, with auto racing attracting the greatest amount, and entertainment tours. The remainder goes primarily to festivals and fairs, and the arts. Considering that there are over 50,000 festivals and fairs in the U.S. each year, the range of sponsorship opportunities is almost unlimited.

Sponsorship is typically viewed as a long-range image-building activity; for example, the U.S. Postal Service sponsors a bicycle racing team and its star, Lance Armstrong, a multiple winner of the Tour de France.

The principal difficulty in justifying sponsorship expenditures is measuring their effectiveness. Because sales are usually not the primary objective, the value of a sponsorship is frequently determined by the amount of publicity it generates for the sponsor (and comparison of that to the cost of an equivalent amount of advertising). An alternative approach is a survey of attendees before and after an event to determine awareness and brand preference.

www.ussponsorship.com

Trade Shows. Associations in industries as diverse as computers, sporting goods, food, and broadcasting sponsor trade shows. There are 5,000 trade shows a year in Canada and the U.S. alone. About half restrict attendance to business representatives, whereas the remainder allow consumers to attend.

The appeal of a trade show is efficiency. In one place and in a compressed amount of time, trade shows allow buyers and sellers to see and interact with many of their counterparts.

On the other hand, trade shows are expensive for exhibitors. In addition to the cost of the booth and the living expenses of the company representatives during the show, transporting equipment and display material is costly. As a result, firms are selective about the trade shows they attend, often requiring the sponsors to provide demographic profiles of the attendees.

The trade show industry is on track to continue growing. Much of the growth has come from offshoots of existing broad-based events. Like advertising, trade shows are seeking out narrower market segments and offering more specialized topics.

Product Placements. For many years products have appeared as props in movies and television shows. Among the most notable movie product placements are *Back to the Future* (for the sheer number of placements), *E.T.* (for the impact placement had on the sales of Reese's Pieces), and *Cast Away* (for the prominence of the product, Federal Express, in the movie). Recent television examples include Coca-Cola on *American Idol*, McDonald's on *Sex and the City*, Crest toothpaste on *The Apprentice*, and Leatherman tools on *Alias*. Other examples of product placements are shown in Table 19.5. Product placements also occur in novels and video games.

Placements have proved very beneficial to some products, taking them from virtual obscurity to national prominence. You may have noticed product placements, but if you're like most consumers, these props simply added to the realism of the experience, and that is the strength of a product placement. It displays the product in a noncommercial way, sometimes linking it with the show's characters and creating a positive association for the audience.

www.upp.net

Product placement has increased dramatically in recent years as marketers respond to the use of personal video recorders that allow television viewers to screen out advertisements. The total value of placements in 2004 was $3.5 billion, an increase of nearly 300% since 1994, with the fastest growth occurring on television.[25] The leader in product placements is Coca-Cola Classic appearing in 99 telecasts with 2,186 occurrences during 4 months of 2005.[26]

As noted earlier, technology has made "virtual product placement" in films possible. This greatly increases opportunities for product placements. For example, newer products can replace older ones or simply be added to remakes of movies or syndicated television shows. Or different brands can be displayed in a show broadcast in different parts of the country or the world.

TABLE
19.5

Examples of Product Placements

Movie	Brand
The Italian Job	MiniCooper
The Contender	Everlast
The Jacket	Volkswagen
Be Cool	Honda
Star Trek	Apple Computers
I Robot	Audi, FedEx, Nike
Shrek 2	Baskin-Robbins

Live Theatre	
Saturday Night Fever	Kellogg, Heinz, Daz detergent
LaBoheme	Montblanc pens

Television	
King of Queens	Blur Marlin clothing
One Tree Hill	Polaroid
Desperate Housewives	Buick
Arrested Development	Burger King
The Apprentice	Levi, Domino's, Pepsi Edge
Extreme Makeover	Sears, Roebuck, Ford
All My Children	Wal-Mart perfume

Internet and Video Games	
Tiger Woods PGA Tour 2005	Nike
NBA Live	Nike
NFL Street 2	Reebok

Sources: *www.upp.net/hall-of-fame.html;* Robert Guy Mathews, "London Stage Hosts U.S. Marketers," *The Wall Street Journal,* Feb. 18, 2005, p. B3; Brooks Barnes, "A Good Soap Includes Love, Tears, and Frosted Flakes," *The Wall Street Journal,* Jan. 17, 2005, p. A1+; Suzanne Vranica and Brian Steinberg, "The Robot Wore Converses," *The Wall Street Journal,* Sept. 2, 2004, p. B1.

Public Relations

www.instituteforpr.com

Public relations is a management tool designed to favorably influence attitudes toward an organization, its products, and its policies. It is an often overlooked form of promotion. In most organizations this promotional tool is typically a stepchild, relegated far behind personal selling, advertising, and sales promotion. There are several reasons for management's lack of attention to public relations:

- *Organizational structure.* In most companies, public relations is not the responsibility of the marketing department. If there is an organized effort, it is usually handled by a small public relations department that reports directly to top management.

- *Inadequate definitions.* The term public relations is used loosely by both businesses and the public. There are no generally accepted definitions of the term. As a result, what actually constitutes an organized public relations effort often is not clearly defined.

- *Unrecognized benefits.* Only recently have many organizations come to appreciate the value of good public relations. As the cost of promotion has gone up, firms are realizing that positive exposure through the media or as a result of community involvement can produce a high return on the investment of time and effort.

Nature and Scope

Public relations activities typically are designed to build or maintain a favorable image for an organization with its various publics—customers, prospects, stockholders, employees, labor unions, the local community, and the government. We're aware that this description is quite similar to our definition of institutional advertising. However, unlike advertising, public relations need not use the media to communicate its message. For example, Whirlpool Corporation supports Habitat for Humanity by providing appliances for the homes that are built.

Good public relations can be achieved in many ways. Some examples are supporting charitable projects (by supplying volunteer labor or other resources); participating in community service events; sponsoring nonprofessional athletic teams; funding the arts; producing an employee or customer newsletter; and disseminating information through exhibits, displays, and tours. Major firms such as ExxonMobil and Archer Daniels Midland sponsor shows on public television (PBS) as part of their public relations effort.

Publicity as a Form of Public Relations

Publicity is any communication about an organization, its products, or policies through the media not paid for by the organization. Publicity usually takes the form of a news story appearing in the media or an endorsement provided by an individual, either informally or in a speech or interview. This is good publicity.

There is also, of course, bad publicity—a negative story about a firm or its product appearing in the media. In a society that is increasingly sensitive about the environment and in which news media are quick to report mistakes, organizations tend to focus on this negative dimension of publicity. As a result, managers are so concerned with avoiding bad publicity that they overlook the potential of good publicity.

There are three means for gaining good publicity:

- *Prepare and distribute a story* (called a *news release*) *to the media.* The intention is for the selected newspapers, television stations, or other media to report the information as news.
- *Personal communication with a group.* A press conference will draw media representatives if they think the subject or speaker has news value. Company tours and speeches to civic or professional groups are other forms of individual-to-group communications.
- *One-on-one personal communication, often called lobbying.* Companies lobby legislators or other powerful people in an attempt to influence their opinions, and subsequently their decisions.

Publicity can help accomplish any communication objective. It can be used to announce new products, publicize new policies, recognize employees, describe research breakthroughs, or report financial performance. But to receive coverage, the message, person, group, or event being publicized must be viewed by the media as newsworthy. This is what distinguishes publicity from advertising—publicity is not "forced" on the audience. This is also the source of its primary benefit. The credibility of publicity typically is much higher than advertising. If an organization tells you its product is great, you may well be skeptical. But if an independent, objective third party says on the evening news that the product is great, you are more likely to believe it.

Other benefits of publicity are:

- *Lower cost.* Publicity usually costs less than advertising or personal selling because there are no media space or time costs for conveying the message and no sales people to support.

- *Increased attention.* Many consumers are conditioned to ignore advertising or at least pay it scant attention. Publicity is presented as editorial material or news, so it is more likely to be watched, listened to, or get read.

- *More information.* Because it is presented as editorial material, publicity can contain greater detail than the usual ad. More information and persuasive content can be included in the message.

- *Timeliness.* A company can put out a news release very quickly when some unexpected event occurs.

Of course, publicity has limitations:

- *Loss of control over the message.* An organization has no guarantee that a news release will appear in the media. In addition, there is no way to control how much or what portion of a story the media will print or broadcast.

- *Limited exposure.* The media will typically use news releases to fill space when there is a lack of other news and only use them once. If the target audience misses the message when it is presented, there is no second or third chance.

- *Publicity is not free.* Even though there are no media time and space costs, there are expenses in generating ideas for publicity and in preparing and disseminating news releases.

 www.prsa.org

Recognizing the value of publicity, some organizations have one or more staff members who generate news releases. These stories are sent to the media and are typically made available to anyone via the company's website.

Summary

Advertising, sales promotion, and public relations are the nonpersonal, mass-communications components of a company's promotional mix. Advertising consists of all the activities involved in presenting to an audience a nonpersonal, sponsor-identified, paid-for message about a product or organization. The total advertising expenditure in a firm is typically 1% to 3% of sales, which is considerably less than the average cost of personal selling. Most advertising dollars are spent on television, newspapers, and direct mail. Other frequently used media are radio, magazines, yellow pages, and out-of-home displays. The Internet is increasing in importance as an ad medium.

Advertising can be directed to consumers or businesses. Ads are classified according to whether they are intended to stimulate primary or selective demand. Primary demand is demand for a generic category of a product. Primary demand ads are used to introduce new products and to sustain demand for a product throughout its life cycle. Selective-demand ads emphasize a particular brand or company. They are divided into product ads, which focus on a brand, or institutional ads, which focus on an organization. Product ads are further subdivided into direct action ads, which call for immediate action, and indirect-action ads, which are intended to stimulate demand over a longer period of time. A selective-demand ad that makes reference to one or more competitors is called a comparative ad. Finally, ad messages are transmitted through commercial or social sources. Although not strictly advertising, social sources are very effective when they can be stimulated or simulated by advertisers.

An advertising campaign involves transforming a theme into a coordinated advertising program. Designing a campaign includes defining objectives, establishing a budget, creating new messages, selecting media, and evaluating the effort. Objectives can range from creating awareness of a brand to generating sales. Advertising budgets can be extended through vertical and horizontal cooperative arrangements. An advertising message—consisting of the appeal and the execution of the ad—is influenced by the target audience and the media used.

A major task in developing a campaign is to select the advertising media—the general type, the particular category, and the specific vehicle. The choice should be based on the characteristics of the medium, which determine how effectively it conveys the message, and its ability to reach the target audience. Each of the media that carry advertising have characteristics that make them more or less suitable for a particular advertising objective.

A difficult task in advertising management is evaluating the effectiveness of the advertising effort—

both the entire campaign and the individual ads. Some methods of advertising allow for direct measures of effect, but most can only be evaluated indirectly. A commonly used technique measures recall of an ad. To carry out an advertising program, a firm may rely on its own advertising department, an advertising agency, or a combination of the two.

Sales promotion consists of demand-stimulating devices designed to supplement advertising and facilitate personal selling. The amount of sales promotion increased considerably in the past two decades as management sought measurable, short-term sales results.

Sales promotion should receive the same strategic attention that a company gives to advertising and personal selling, including setting objectives and establishing a budget. Sales promotion can be directed toward final consumers, middlemen, or a company's own employees. Management can choose from a variety of sales promotion devices. Some of the most common are samples, coupons, sponsorships, trade shows, and product placements. Like advertising, sales promotion performance should be evaluated.

Public relations is a management tool designed to favorably influence attitudes toward an organization, its products, and its policies. It is a frequently overlooked form of promotion. Publicity, a part of public relations, is any communication about an organization, its products, or policies through the media that is not paid for by the organization. Typically these two activities are handled in a department separate from the marketing department in a firm. Nevertheless, the management process of planning, implementation, and evaluation should be applied to these activities in the same way it is applied to advertising, sales promotion, and personal selling.

More about **Nike**

Nike utilizes a wide variety of promotional tools. In the past it made use of guerilla marketing. For example, at the 1996 Atlanta Olympics spectators at the basketball venue and the television audience saw Nike Swoosh signs in the arena even though Champion paid to sponsor the event. More recently, Nike has capitalized on the capability of the Internet to reach the youth market. On its site visitors can view ads, customize products, and learn more about the company and its activities. In 2005, Nike produced its first print catalog. The 56-page, four-color document includes action photos as well as product shots to reinforce the Nike lifestyle.

As a result of its sustained efforts, Nike is "actively advocated" to other consumers by 38% of its customers worldwide. According to a global study by NOP World, a marketing research firm, only nine other firms have a higher percentage of brand advocates, and none is in the apparel or athletic equipment fields. Credit for this is certainly due to the quality of its products, but Nike's ability to build a brand image through sustained and consistent promotional efforts is also a major factor.[27]

1. Should Nike reduce its advertising now that it has such a high level of brand recognition?
2. What mix of advertising media would be the most effective for introducing a new Nike athletic shoe?

Key Terms and Concepts

Advertising (522)
Business-to-consumer advertising (524)
Business-to-business advertising (524)
Primary-demand advertising (524)
Selective-demand advertising (524)
Comparison advertising (524)

Product advertising (525)
Institutional advertising (525)
Advertising campaign (526)
Cooperative advertising (527)
Advertising media (529)
Cost per thousand (CPM) (530)

Direct tests (536)
Indirect tests (536)
Advertising agency (537)
Sales promotion (538)
Public relations (544)
Publicity (545)

Questions and Problems

1. How do you account for the variation in advertising expenditures as a percentage of sales among the different companies in Table 19.2?

2. Select a general type of advertising medium for each of the following products and explain your choice.
   a. Internet-based investment service
   b. Avon cosmetics
   c. Tax-preparation service
   d. Mortuary
   e. Toys for young children
   f. Plastic clothespins

3. Many grocery product and candy manufacturers earmark a good portion of their advertising budgets for use in magazines. In contrast, department stores use newspapers more than local radio stations as an advertising medium. Are these media choices wise for these industries and firms? Explain.

4. Why is it worthwhile to pretest ads before they appear in the media? How could a test market be used to pretest an ad? (You may want to refresh your memory with a review of test marketing in Chapter 7.)

5. What procedures can a firm use to determine how many sales dollars resulted from a direct-mail ad?

6. What type of sales promotion would be effective for selling expensive consumer products such as houses, automobiles, or cruise trips? How about expensive business products?

7. What advantage would sampling have over advertising for a new brand of sunscreen lotion?

8. Should virtual product placement raise any ethical concerns for the media?

9. Bring to class an article from a daily newspaper that appears to be the result of a firm's publicity efforts. Summarize the points made in the article that may benefit the firm. Could advertising create the same benefits?

Interactive Marketing Exercises

1. Common appeals or benefits and examples of product categories in which they are frequently used include:
   - Physical well-being (food, nonprescription drugs)
   - Social acceptance (cosmetics, health and beauty aids)
   - Material success (automobiles, investments)
   - Recognition and status (clothing, jewelry)
   - Sensory pleasure (movies, candy)
   - Time savings (websites)
   - Peace of mind (insurance, tires)

   Find print ads that make use of five of these appeals. Comment on the effectiveness of the execution (the compatability of the appeal and the method of gaining attention).

2. Visit a supermarket, drugstore, or hardware store, and make a list of all the sales promotion tools you observe. Describe how each one relates to the sales promotion objectives described in the chapter. Which do you think are particularly effective? Why?

Cases for Part 6

<table>
<tr><td>CASE
1</td><td>The Hummer</td></tr>
</table>

Steering the Promotional Strategy of the Civilian Hummers

When the first civilian Hummer, known as H1, was launched by AM General in 1992, it was something of a novelty. It generated a great deal of interest during the Gulf War, and so AM General decided to offer a consumer version to the public. However, AM General put very little muscle into promoting the vehicle, only spending about half a million dollars on advertising in the year 2000. This limited promotional effort, combined with a high sticker price, kept sales figures for the H1 well below 1,000 units on an annual basis.

Hoping to improve sales of the civilian Hummer, AM General entered into an agreement with General Motors (GM) to develop a new, less expensive version. The H2 was introduced in 2002, accompanied by a sleek well-funded advertising campaign that declared it was "Like nothing else." Demand for the new vehicle was impressive, leading to plans for a truck like version and an even more affordably priced H3.

Getting the New Civilian Hummer on the Road

In 1979, the U.S. Army developed specifications for a High Mobility Multi-purpose Wheeled Vehicle (HMMWV) that could forge its way through unforgiving terrain while carrying troops and a wide variety of military equipment and hardware. AM General was ultimately chosen to manufacture 55,000 vehicles for the Army, and the company simplified the name to Humvee. The vehicle proved successful enough that the Army ordered another 48,000 units, but AM General realized that the U.S. military market would soon be saturated, and it began exploring additional alternatives. "Although AM General is first and foremost a defense contractor," explained the company's Chief Executive Officer, "the defense industry is now changing and defense contractors must respond by looking for applications for existing products and reinvesting in new businesses."

When Arnold Schwarzenegger watched news footage from the Gulf War in the early 1990s, he saw the U.S. Army's tough-as-nails Humvee (it eventually became known as the Hummer) and he wanted to own one. He contacted AM General and custom ordered the first civilian Hummer. That started the wheels turning for a new version of the Hummer, targeted at the consumer market.

Basically the same as the military version, the civilian H1 was 6 feet tall and 7 feet wide, with a diesel V-8 engine and 16 inches of ground clearance. It had the same drivetrain, chassis, engine, and body as the military version but had been adapted with exterior lighting and markings to comply with federal highway standards. Off the highway, it could still get over rocks that were almost 2 feet high and make its way through 40 inches of water. So how much was this unique vehicle? Well, as they say, if you had to ask you probably couldn't afford a price tag that could easily exceed $100,000.

About 50 dealers throughout the U.S. were granted franchises to sell the H1. These dealers had existing car or truck dealerships and were interested in adding the Hummer as a noncompeting extension of their current product lines. They received an 18% gross margin on the selling price of each vehicle. The franchise agreement specified that the dealership's service manager and two mechanics be factory-trained by AM General and required the purchase of special factory tools and a modest inventory of spare parts.

Despite the fact that it never sold more than 1,000 units in a year, the Hummer became a popular novelty. A minimal amount of money was invested in promoting the H1, although there were some print and television ads produced that described it as the "world's most serious 4 × 4."

In 1998, General Motors decided to introduce its own heavy-duty, sport-utility vehicle (SUV) and approached AM General to see if the manufacturer of the H1 would consider selling the Hummer brand name to GM while continuing to build and assemble Hummers at its facility near South Bend, Indiana. AM General quickly agreed to the alliance, and a prototype of the new vehicle, the H2, was unveiled at the Detroit Auto Show in 2000.

Shifting Into High Gear with a New Advertising Campaign

That same year, GM decided to find a new advertising agency to handle the account, and chose Modernista!, a small ad agency in Boston. Liz Vanzura was appointed GM's advertising director for the Hummer, perhaps because she had previously been responsible for the 1998 launch of Volkswagon's restyled Beetle. "I feel lucky," she said. "It's the second time I get to work on a cool brand."

Vanzura and Modernista! wasted no time in developing a new brand image and advertising campaign for the Hummer. They started with a "bridge" campaign for the H1 in order to raise awareness of the Hummer line prior to the introduction of the H2. One analyst explained that the "Hummer has to overcome some of its military heritage. They have to go into upscale SUV territory to capture more units."

To accomplish this goal, several television spots were created, all with a tagline that declared Hummers to be "Like Nothing Else." For example, one ad proclaimed, "When the asteroid hits and civilization crumbles, you'll be ready." Another stated, "Threaten the men in your office a whole new way." Vanzura hoped they would strike a chord with "rugged individualists." "Do they get that yacht? Do they get the vacation house in Aspen?" she asked. She went on to explain, "This is what we're competing with: people's time and what they do with their money. We're really not competing in an automotive category." The new ads began appearing in August of 2001, less than one year before the H2 would make its debut.

Lining Up to Kick the H2's Tires

GM funded the construction of a new plant to accommodate the manufacture of the H2 SUV and began assembling test models in January 2002. Although it retains the flattened, boxy shape of the H1, the H2 is about half a foot longer, but not as tall (by 6 inches). It will still climb 16-inch rocks and cross water that is almost 2 feet deep, however. And the H2 is much quieter than the H1, although it will achieve only about 11 or 12 miles per gallon of gas. Whereas the H1 was designed to seat four people, the H2 can accommodate five and offers an optional third row that provides space for a sixth person as long as he or she doesn't mind sharing the space with a very large spare tire.

With a starting price of $48,800, GM hoped consumers would view the H2 as comparably priced to other luxury SUVs. Initial demand for the H2 was encouraging, and almost 35,000 vehicles were sold in 2003. To further increase the H2's visibility, GM places ads in more than 50 different magazines, each with the same basic message that was tweaked to appeal to that periodical's target audience. For example, one wine magazine featured a Hummer print ad that declared, "Same Vintage. New Grapes." "Magazines have always helped us by being highly targeted and delivering an individualized message," stated Carolyn Stocking, associate media director at GM Planworks. "It was a case of marrying the medium with the message." These ads achieved their goal by increasing consumer awareness and recall regarding the H2, according to market research conducted by Modernista!.

Buoyed by the initial success, GM demanded that all of its Hummer dealers build expensive new showrooms according to very rigid specifications it felt reflected Hummer's rugged image. "There's no way you are building anything like that around here," was what Jim Lynch was told when he presented his plans for a new dealership in Chesterfield, Missouri. In particular, the authorities objected to the enormous "H" that was standing sentry at the front of the building. Reluctantly, GM granted some flexibility to several dealers who were facing roadblocks regarding their new showroom's designs. Even so, several dealers still balked at the enormous investment of several million dollars, refused to comply with GM's demands, and risked their franchise rights by doing so.

These dealers were obviously influenced by declining sales in 2004. In the first quarter, Hummers sat on the lot for 62 days, compared to 15 the year before. In addition, H1 sales decreased by 65% between January and October of 2004, and H2 sales dropped 27%. As a result, GM cut production and began offering incentives, such as rebates and attractive financing packages, and also started leasing Hummers for the first time. One industry analyst explained that, "It had its moment in the sun when everyone had to have one. And now, that's it. It's done." The same thing happened to the new Volkswagon Beetle and other vehicles that sparked high initial interest. However, the entire SUV industry was experiencing a decline. In addition, rising gas prices highlighted the H2's fuel inefficiency, making it an easy target for environmental groups. The Sierra Club even created a web site, www.hummerdinger.com, to poke fun at its gas guzzling tendencies. (It suggested as the Hummer's theme song Jackson Brown's "Running on Empty.") However, as one potential buyer pointed out, "If gas was $5 a gallon, I'd probably forget about the Hummer, but if it was $3 a gallon, I'd buy the Hummer. It's not a major issue for me."

Revving Up the Hummer Brand

In an attempt to broaden the appeal of its brand and increase sales, GM made plans to introduce two new Hummers: the H2 Sport Utility Truck (SUT) and the H3. While industry SUV sales were falling in 2004, demand for pickup trucks was growing stronger, and sales increased more than 24% in September, compared to 2003. GM hoped to capitalize on this with its H2 SUT, which retailed for about $53,000. Looking very much like a regular H2 in the front, the SUT features a small pickup bed in the back and boasts the same offroad capabilities as its sister vehicle.

While the H2 competes in the luxury SUV category, the H3 is GM's entry into the midsize SUV class, a market that represents sales of more than 1.7 million units each year—ten times as many as luxury SUVs. "We're going to reach customers who aspired to Hummer, but the price was not within their reach," explained Susan Docherty, Hummer's general manager. Based on GM's Chevy Colorado, the H3 is 16 inches shorter than the H2 and 6 inches narrower, making it easier to park. And it can still climb 16-inch rocks and make its way through shallow streams. The H3 is also touted as being capable of achieving 20 miles per gallon on the highway.

To promote its new vehicle, GM doubled its annual marketing budget for the Hummer line to $50 million. "We need to get out the price message that not all Hummers are $50,000-plus, and that we have a smaller and more fuel-efficient Hummer," commented Docherty. She went on to say that much of the advertising money would be spent on sponsorships and events. On October 25, 2004, GM invited more than one thousand Hummer owners to a Black Eyed Peas concert in order to unveil the H3, one day prior to the start of the California Auto Show.

For GM, the H3 is more of a risk than the H2. While AM General continues to build the H1 and H2 in Indiana, the H3 is manufactured by union workers in a plant owned by GM in Louisiana. GM can no longer counter slower sales by telling AM General to decrease production. The union workers have contracts that guarantee they will receive 90% of their salary even if they are not working. Therefore, GM is more likely to offer attractive incentives to move vehicles off of sales lots than it is to decrease production of the H3.

The strategy of introducing more moderately priced vehicles is not new. It has worked for other luxury automakers including Mercedes and Cadillac. But some industry experts remain skeptical about the H3's sales prospects. "There are a fair number of people who will look at a smaller Hummer," stated Art Spinella, president of CNW Marketing Research. "But that segment saturates very quickly. Then you might have to offer massive incentives to make the pool big enough to at least hit some sort of sales target." Docherty disagrees and insists that the H3 will be a viable brand extension for GM, but concedes that "there are lots of things, particularly car-based vehicles, that would violate the brand's integrity." She cited minivans and compact cars as examples of vehicle types that would almost certainly put off potential Hummer buyers who are attracted to the brand's rugged image. "We don't want growth at all costs. You can't stretch a brand from $100,000 to $10,000."

The question is, can you stretch it from $100,000 to $30,000?

	2000	2001	2002	2003	Jan.–Oct. 2004
H1	875	768	720	730	365
H2	0	0	18,861	34,529	20,516
H2 SUT	0	0	0	0	1,957
Total Hummer Sales	875	768	19,581	35,259	22,838

Questions

1. Why would GM want the Hummer brand name when it already has an established line of SUVs?

2. GM made a decision to downplay Hummer's military heritage in its promotion strategy. Do you feel this is the correct decision? Why or why not?

3. Do you agree with GM's decision to continue introducing smaller, less expensive versions of the original Hummer? Why or why not?

4. Do you agree with GM's decision to move away from television and print ads and spend more of its marketing budget on nontraditional promotions, such as sponsorships?

www.hummer.com

Coca-Cola Co. versus PepsiCo

Thirsting for New Advertising Strategies

For many years, the term "cola wars" has been used to describe the hard-fought battle for market share that has been waged by Coca-Cola Co. and PepsiCo. Each company has an arsenal of advertising campaigns it has used to strategically position itself throughout the years, from Coke's "The pause that refreshes" (1929) to "It's the real thing" (1970) and its rival's "Pepsi-Cola hits the spot" (1940s) to "The Pepsi generation" (1964.) When *Advertising Age* named the top 100 Advertising Campaigns of the previous century, these four iconic efforts were prominently listed. But the two companies have struggled in recent years to develop memorable advertising campaigns, in particular for their flagship products, Coke and Pepsi.

Fizzling Soda Sales

There is no brand in the world more valuable or better known than Coca-Cola. It ranks ahead of the likes of Microsoft, IBM, and General Electric, and the brand itself has been valued at over $67 billion. During the 1980s and most of the 1990s, Coca-Cola's performance was excellent. Except for the embarrassing failure of "New Coke," a reformulation of its flagship cola's flavor in 1985, the company's strategy was right on target. During that period, Coca-Cola had annual earnings increases that averaged at least 15%, and its stock rose a dazzling 3,500%. But by 2001, the company experienced its third consecutive year of flat or declining market share in the U.S. In addition, earnings were declining, and Coke was facing serious threats on several fronts, not the least of which was from its perennial challenger, Pepsi.

After losing market share in the 1990s, Pepsi began to make small gains on Coke's share of the domestic cola market. The company began aggressively fighting with Coke for every vending machine, restaurant contract, and supermarket shelf that became available. In 2004, Coke Classic commanded 18% of the U.S. market, followed by 11.5% for Pepsi-Cola. However, both brands slipped in market share, with Coke Classic falling by .7% and Pepsi-Cola by .4%. In terms of overall carbonated soft drink sales, Coca-Cola Co.'s market share slid by .9% to 43.1% and Pepsi-Cola Co.'s stayed relatively steady at 31.7%.

Fueling this trend of decreasing domestic carbonated soda sales is an increasing concern with health issues that has Americans reaching for a plethora of beverages besides just sodas. The categories are endless and include bottled water (some with flavors and vitamin enhancements,) sports drinks, energy drinks, fruit juices, coffee drinks, juice-flavored drinks (such as Fruitopia and SoBe), and yogurt drinks. PepsiCo and Coca-Cola Co. have responded by adding brands in all of these categories to stay competitive. For instance, drinkable yogurts experienced sales of $460 million in 2003, compared to just $22 million in 1998. Both Danone (the maker of Dannon and Stonyfield Farms yogurt products) and General Mills (the manufacturer of Yoplait) have launched drinkable yogurts, positioning them as healthy alternatives to carbonated sodas. "It's been a very hot product for us. We're extremely happy with it," commented the president of Yoplait. In 2001, Pepsi introduced Tropicana Smoothies, which contain juice and yogurt, and Coke responded with a fruit-flavored milk-based drink called Swerve in 2003.

In addition to facing competition from new types of beverages, there are other compelling reasons for Coke and Pepsi's declining sales. After some school districts banned all soda products, Coke developed its own guidelines for in-school placement. It agreed not to sell soda in elementary schools during the day, and removed them from cafeterias (but not vending machines) in middle and high schools. Pepsi has similar guidelines in place regarding school soda sales. Although schools only comprise 1% of Coke's total North American sales volume, they have traditionally been seen as an important placement opportunity in the bid to develop brand loyalty among children and teens.

A variety of issues has also begun to plague worldwide sales of Coke and Pepsi. Both are iconic American brands, and the United States' invasion of Iraq in 2003 caused protestors in predominantly Muslim countries to boycott the companies' soda products. Mecca-Cola was launched in Paris in late-2002 by a Muslim lawyer intent on providing alternatives to Coke and Pepsi. By the end of 2003, Mecca-Cola was being distributed in 54 countries, and 10% of its profits were being donated to Palestinian children's groups and other local charities. Mecca-Cola sported a tagline that read: "No more drinking stupid. Drink with commitment!" Very little money was spent on advertising because media outlets throughout the world reported on the upstart cola, thereby boosting demand for it. Other sodas, such as Iran's Zamzam Cola and the United Kingdom's Qibla-Cola, have also recently benefited from anti-American sentiment.

Trying to Hit the Spot with Carbonated Sodas

In recent years, Coke and Pepsi have enjoyed rapid growth in China and India. With 2.3 billion people between them and growing middle class segments, they present many consumer package-goods companies with enormous opportunities. Coke has invested more than $1 billion in its Chinese operations since 1979 and began its march into India in 1993. It targeted large cities in both countries and experienced double-digit growth throughout most of the 1990s. When growth slowed, Coke began marketing its soda in smaller cities and rural areas. The strategy has paid off, with sales increasing by 16% in China in 2003 and by 22% in India. Meanwhile, Pepsi has continued to focus its efforts on urban areas, replicating its U.S. approach by trying to appeal to younger people.

Besides casting a wider net in an effort to attract additional international customers, Coke has been rethinking its domestic strategy. This has proven to be difficult in the wake of a series of management changes. The company lost its long-time and highly regarded Chief Executive Officer (CEO) in 1997 when Robert Goizueta died of cancer. The two subsequent CEO's both suffered in his shadow. It was Goizueta, after all, who guided Coke through its glory years of the 1980s and most of the 1990s, leading to perennially unrealistic expectations by shareholders. Coke may have been a victim of its own success. It became so reliant on its carbonated drinks that it was slow to react when the public began developing a thirst for new types of beverages. One of Coke's CEO's did try to purchase Quaker Oats Co. in late 2000 in order to acquire the successful Gatorade brand, but he was overruled by Coke's board of directors who didn't approve the merger. That proved to be a costly mistake, as Pepsi acquired the brand and with it a dominating 81% of the sports drink market, compared to 17% for Coke's Powerade. E. Neville Isdell, a former Coke executive, came out of retirement in May, 2004 to take the helm of the company and was faced with a number of challenges, including low company morale that resulted from an ever-changing management team.

In an effort to respond to the demand for healthier alternatives and encouraged by the fact that Diet Coke's share of the soda market increased by .3% in 2004, Isdell decided to focus a great deal of effort on extending Coke's line of diet products. By March of 2005, Coke's diet lineup consisted of regular Diet Coke, four additional flavors of Diet Coke (lemon, lime, vanilla, and cherry), and Diet Coke with Splenda. That month, the company announced it would introduce a new no-calorie soda called Coca-Cola Zero during the upcoming summer. While Diet Coke is flavored with Nutrasweet, the latest iteration would contain a combination of Splenda and ace-k and would be targeted at males between the ages of 18 and 25. This led some to wonder how many different types of Diet Cokes were necessary, and whether the products would simply cannibalize one another. In addition, Coke had introduced a lower-calorie soda called C2 in 2004 in an attempt to lure low-carb dieters. It was the company's most significant product launch since the original Diet Coke in 1982, and Coke had high hopes for it. Sales were softer than originally anticipated, however, in part because consumers were unwilling to pay a 50% to 60% premium for it.

While Coke has added many noncarbonated beverages to its lineup, such as Dasani bottled water, Minute Maid orange juice, and Planet Java coffee drinks just to name a few, sodas continue to comprise 82% of its total sales. "The whole Coke model needs to be rethought," stated one industry consultant. "The carbonated soft-drink model is 30 years old and out of date." Coke CEO, E. Neville Isdell, disagrees. "Regardless of what the skeptics might think, I know carbonated soft drinks can grow," he stated. "We are a growth company for the future in what is a growth industry."

Spicing Up Pepsi's Product Mix

The philosophy at PepsiCo (the parent company of Pepsi-Cola) is quite different. Boosting the company's overall health is its fast-growing snack foods division, Frito-Lay International, which comprises about 60% of the company's sales. Perhaps anticipating the slow-down in soda sales, Pepsi also asserted its desire to become a "total beverage company" in the early 1990s and began rapidly expanding its product mix to include bottled water, juices, and much more. This plan has paid off as consumers have become increasingly concerned about the health risks associated with caffeine, sugar, and artificial sweeteners. "Being outside carbonated (soft drinks) makes sure we're growing in the same areas where there is growth," explained PepsiCo's CEO.

While Coke has its four main brands, Coca-Cola, Diet Coke, Sprite, and Fanta, PepsiCo boasts 16 disparate brands with annual sales exceeding $1 billion, including Gatorade, Tropicana juice, and Aquafina bottled water. PepsiCo's total company sales averaged $27 billion per year between 1999 and 2004, compared to $21 billion for Coke. This translated into earnings growth of 12% per year for PepsiCo versus only 4% for Coke. As a result, Coke's stock price fell by 40% during this time period, while Pepsi's rose by 38%.

Always an innovator, Pepsi created the industry's first brand extension in 1964 when it introduced Diet Pepsi. It added snacks to its mix in 1965 when it merged with Frito-Lay, and then anticipated the public's growing concern regarding its health by acquiring Tropicana and Quaker Oats in 1998 and 2001. PepsiCo remains focused on providing snacks and beverage alternatives, prompting one analyst to state that, "They have been early to see trends, and aggressive in targeting them." To this end, Frito-Lay has removed all trans fats from its products and has developed low-fat and low-carb versions of its main sellers, including Baked Lays, Baked Tostitos, and low-carb Cheetos. The company is also adept at adapting its products to satisfy local tastes. Its Mexican subsidiary, Sabritas, markets a brand of chips that nets more than $1 billion in sales each year, and has been so successful that four of its products are now being sold within the U.S, targeting Hispanic consumers. Lay's Mediterraneas chips are a hit in southern Europe and Latin America, Nori Seaweed chips fly off the shelves in Thailand, and Cool Lemon potato chips are hot sellers in China.

Experimenting with New Flavors of Advertising

Although Pepsi has been rapidly expanding its product mix beyond its traditional carbonated beverages, the company recognizes that 12- to 24-year-olds drink the most soda. Pepsi hopes to attract them with splashy ad campaigns. This harkens back to its breakthrough "Pepsi Generation" campaign of the 1960s, and Pepsi has been targeting younger people ever since. "As far as Pepsi's concerned, we like to consider ourselves the younger, hipper cola out there, so we tend to go toward a teen and young adult audience," explained a company spokesperson. Long a proponent of celebrity-based ads, Pepsi developed upbeat spots starring pop-culture princess Britney Spears in 2001. As personal MP3 players became more prevalent in the early 2000s, Pepsi also sponsored a promotion that gave away 100 million songs on Apple's iTunes website.

In 2004, Pepsi proclaimed "It's the cola" in ads on which it spent $133 million. The company's media budget for Diet Pepsi that same year was $36 million,

and featured "Light. Crisp. Refreshing." spots. "Heavy diet advertising and promotions will be a part of every single season for many years to come," commented the editor of *Beverage Digest*. That isn't surprising when you consider that diet soda sales rose a whopping 7.5% in 2004. Pepsi committed to spend $70 million advertising its diet products in 2005, primarily focusing on Diet Pepsi.

In 2004, PepsiCo also announced plans to start putting a "Smart Spot" emblem on products it considers to be healthy. More than 200 cereals, snacks, and beverages will feature the symbol, including Baked Lay's potato chips and Tropicana orange juice. PepsiCo promoted the Smart Spots with an ad campaign that cost between $10 million and $20 million, with the slogan, "Smart choice. Enjoy life." The company hopes that the Pepsi logo on all of the associated advertising and Smart Spot products will convince consumers that Pepsi really cares about their health.

Coke also pledged to double its advertising spending on its diet brands in 2005, taking the number up to $60 million. It committed $300 million for Coca-Cola, including some new ads that sport the tagline, "Make it real." Isdell announced that his corporation would increase its worldwide marketing budget by $300 million to $400 million in 2005, with a majority of the incremental spending going toward international efforts, which he predicted would comprise almost all of the company's growth in the near future.

But the company recognized it needed help reaching the all-important 12- to 24-year-old audience. "If they lose kids, they'll lose them for life," mused one company executive. To try to prevent that from happening, Coke advertised heavily on the wildly popular television show "American Idol" and has been testing the effectiveness of Coke Red Lounges in select malls. These outlets feature comfortable seating, music, movies, and video games, as well as futuristic-looking Coke vending machines.

Such targeted efforts are important these days. Television viewers using digital video recorders deftly skip through commercials, and the proliferation of advertising opportunities due to cable and satellite television, paid programming, the Internet, and satellite radio (just to name a few) make it difficult to reach a mass audience with a single, well-intentioned ad. As a result, Coke has struggled in recent years to come up with a meaningful slogan. In 2000, it used, "Always," followed by "Life Tastes Good" in 2002, and "Real" in 2003. "They've changed their slogan almost every year," complained one industry consultant. "A complete inconsistency of message leads to no message. Now they don't really stand for anything."

That's a concern for Coke, as it has slowly been losing market share to Pepsi, despite the fact that it regularly outspends its nemesis on marketing. Time and effective strategy will tell whether Pepsi will be able to capitalize on Coke's lack of direction, and eventually emerge the victor in the infamous cola wars.

Questions

1. In terms of the challenges both companies face, what can an effective advertising campaign accomplish?

2. Why is it important for Coke and Pepsi to develop institutional advertising campaigns that promote the corporations and individual campaigns that feature specific products?

3. What pressures do more products (both line extensions and new products) put on the brand equity of Coke and Pepsi, as well as their resources for advertising and promotion? Their bottlers? Their distributors?

www.cocacola.com

www.pepsico.com

Sources

Case 1: Hummer Dan Lienert, "For 'the Baby Hummer,' It's All Relative," *www.msnbc.com*, accessed Nov. 5, 2004; Jim Flammang, "2005 Hummer," *www.cars.com*, accessed Nov. 2, 2004; Kathy Jackson, "Hummer to Budget Big for H3 Push, Expecting Women Buyers," *www.autoweek.com*, Oct. 28, 2004, accessed May 12, 2005; Brian Corbett, "The Midsize H3 SUV Will Arrive at Dealerships in the Spring,"

www.wardsauto.com, accessed Oct. 27, 2004; Mark Phelan, "Honey, I Shrunk the Hummer," *Detroit Free Press*, Oct. 27, 2004; Lee Hawkins Jr., "The Hummer Gets Downsized," *The Wall Street Journal*, Oct. 21, 2004, p. D6; Michelle Higgins, "Navistar One-Ups the H2 with a Larger Pickup," *The Wall Street Journal*, Oct. 21, 2004, p. D1; "Rolling over the Competition," *Brandweek*, Sept. 13, 2004, unnumbered advertising supplement; Richard Truett, "Design of Hummer Stores Causes Roadblocks," *Automotive News*, Sept. 6, 2004, p. 31; Lee Hawkins Jr., "General Motors Slows Production of Hummer H2," *The Wall Street Journal*, Aug. 25, 2004, p. B8; Danny Hakim, "Hummer Shows Signs of Losing Its Swagger," *The New York Times*, May 17, 2004; Michael McCarthy, "Ad Track: Hummer H2 Makes Impression Despite SUV Backsplash," *USA Today*, Dec. 26, 2002, p. 7B; "Hummer Launches Edgy Campaign," Associated Press Online, July 1, 2002; James Healey, "If You're Driving, Hummer 2 is a Humdinger," *USA Today*, June 14, 2002.

Case 2: Coca-Cola Co. versus PepsiCo

www.pepsi.com, accessed May 12, 2005; *www.cocacola.com*, accessed May 12, 2005; *www.adage.com*, accessed May 12, 2004; *www.beverage-digest.com*, accessed May 12, 2005; Kenneth Hein, "Soft Drinks," *Brandweek*, Apr. 25, 2005, p. S-3; Kenneth Hein, "Fruit: Coke Must Talk Same Brand 'Language,' " *Brandweek*, Jan. 31, 2005, p. 9; Jennifer Korolishin, "2005 Beverage Advertising Preview," *Beverage Industry*, January 2005, p. 38; Nanette Byrnes, "Gone Flat," *BusinessWeek*, Dec. 20, 2004, pp. 76–82; Kate MacArtur, "Coke Commits $400M to Fix It," *Advertising Age*, Nov. 15, 2004, p. 1; Kenneth Hein, "Coke Seeks a Return to Top of Pop Charts," *Brandweek*, Nov. 15, 2004, p. 7; Kenneth Hein, "Pepsi Fattens Diet Brands with $70M," *Brandweek*, Nov. 1, 2004, p. 10; Chad Terhune, "Coca-Cola's Low-Carb Soda Loses Its Fizz," *The Wall Street Journal*, Oct. 20, 2004, p. B1; Chad Terhune, "CEO Says Things Aren't Going Better with Coke," *The Wall Street Journal*, Sept. 16, 2004, p. A1; Kate MacArthur, "Making Coke Iconic Again," *Advertising Age*, Sept. 13, 2004, p. 1; Leslie Chang, Chad Terhune and Betsy McKay, "Coke's Big Gamble in Asia: Digging Deeper in China, India," *The Wall Street Journal*, Aug. 11, 2004, p. A1; Chad Terhune, "PepsiCo to Identify, Promote Its More-Healthful Products," *The Wall Street Journal*, July 30, 2004, p. B3; Diane Brady, "A Thousand and One Noshes," *BusinessWeek*, June 14, 2004; Betsy McKay and Chad Terhune, "Coke Pulls TV Ad After Some Call It the Pits," *The Wall Street Journal*, June 8, 2004, p. B1; "The Brand King's Challenge," *Fortune*, Apr. 5, 2005, p. 192; Kate MacArthur, "Sweet Nothings?" *Advertising Age*, Mar. 28, 2004, p. 3; Deborah Ball and Janet Adamy, "Culture of Competition," *The Wall Street Journal*, Mar. 9, 2004, p. B3; Dean Foust and Brian Grow, "Coke: Wooing the TiVo Generation," *BusinessWeek*, Mar. 1, 2004, pp. 77–80; Arundhati Parmar, "Drink Politics," *Marketing News*, Feb. 15, 2004, p. 1; Chad Terhune, "Coke's Guidelines for Soft Drinks in Schools Faces Some Criticism," *The Wall Street Journal*, Nov. 17, 2003, p. AL.

Chapter 20

*"The chain wants to be the most recognized
and respected brand in the world."*

Strategic Marketing Planning

Does **STARBUCKS** Have a Whale of a Plan for Growth?

Seattle, long known for its rainy weather, is acclaimed as the home of the most successful chain of coffee houses in the U.S., the Starbucks Corporation. Founded in 1971 and named after the first mate in *Moby Dick,* the firm expanded to five retail outlets, a roasting plant, and a local wholesaling business within 10 years. Starbucks' growth in the past 10 years has been nothing short of phenomenal.

Starbucks stores feature a variety of coffees, including blends of the day, lattés, mochas, and cappuccinos. The coffee can be iced or flavored with syrups, whatever suits the customer. The company's mission is "to establish Starbucks as the premier purveyor of the finest coffee in the world while maintaining our uncompromising principles while we grow." Those principles relate to high standards for its coffee, a great work environment, diversity, satisfied customers, profitability, and giving back to the community and the environment.

The architect of the growth plan was chief executive Howard Schultz, now the firm's chairman and chief global strategist. Some years ago, Schultz explained the company's marketing strategy: "Our goal is to make our coffee available where people shop, travel, play, and work so it bursts into the national consciousness." Starbucks is doing that, with more than 8,500 company-owned and licensed outlets by the end of 2004. More than 6,000 are in the U.S., and nearly 2,500 are located in three dozen other countries.

Starbucks opened its first foreign location in Tokyo in 1996. Despite initial resistance to Starbucks' outlet in Beijing's Forbidden City, the president of Starbucks Coffee International said, "We've been embraced everywhere we've gone without exception." Recently Starbucks entered France, a daunting task considering political tensions between the two countries and a disdain for American-style coffee. One Frenchman said it is too watery, and thus is *jus de chaussette,* which translates to "sock juice." Starbucks has struggled to be profitable overseas.

Starbucks Corp. recognizes that besides more stores, growth in revenues depends on serving more customers per store. With that in mind, Starbucks is emphasizing two strategies:

- *A broader product mix.* Beverages account for more than three-quarters of sales volume, with the remainder coming from food, whole-bean coffee, coffee-making equipment, and compact discs. Starbucks is constantly introducing beverages, such as Chantico, a drinking chocolate. Food is becoming more important in many stores, especially in other countries. Efforts in the U.S. have focused on desserts and breakfast sandwiches.

- *Faster service.* Starbucks created a "swipeable" prepaid card that cuts the time to pay for a purchase. Also, a team of industrial engineers determined how seconds can be saved in preparing beverages. Automatic espresso machines and requiring signatures only on credit-card purchases over $25 are also helping to speed service.

The chain has been expanding so rapidly that *The Onion* ran a satirical headline stating, "A New Starbucks Opens in Restroom of Existing Starbucks." The firm's sales surpassed $5 billion worldwide during the 2004 fiscal year.

Starbucks' competitors in the U.S. and beyond are striving to either expand their sales of coffee-based beverages or defend their positions. Starbucks' competition includes giant enterprises such as Dunkin' Donuts and McDonald's as well as small chains and independent coffee houses in foreign countries. The National Federation of Coffee Growers of Columbia is getting into the fray, with plans to open 300 Juan Valdez cafés.

Despite such competition, Starbucks is among the fastest-growing global brands. The chain wants to be the most recognized and respected brand in the world. Thus, Starbucks Corp. plans to develop new products and channels that capitalize on its substantial brand equity and to open many more stores all over the world (about 1,500 per year).[1]

Over the years, has the Starbucks Corporation developed sound and consistent plans?

 www.starbucks.com

In this chapter we'll examine how a company, including Starbucks, plans its total marketing program. After studying this chapter, you should be able to explain:

- The nature and scope of planning and how it fits within the management process.
- Similarities and differences among mission, objectives, strategies, and tactics.
- How strategic company planning differs from strategic marketing planning.
- The steps comprising strategic marketing planning.
- The purpose and contents of an annual marketing plan.
- Similarities and differences as well as weaknesses and strengths across several models used in strategic planning.

As the Starbucks case suggests, success for any organization requires skillful marketing management. The *marketing* part of the term *marketing management* was defined in Chapter 1, but what about the *management* part? **Management** is the process of planning, implementing, and evaluating the efforts of a group of people working toward a common goal. In this chapter we provide an overview of the management process and examine planning in some detail. In the next chapter, we will cover implementation and evaluation, the other two steps in management.

Planning as Part of Management

The management process, as applied to marketing, consists basically of (1) planning a marketing program, (2) implementing it, and (3) evaluating its performance. This process is depicted in Figure 20.1.

The *planning* stage includes setting goals and developing both strategies and tactics to reach these goals. The *implementation* stage entails designing and staffing the marketing organization and then directing the actual operation of the organization according to the plan. The *evaluation* stage consists of analyzing past performance in relation to organizational goals.[2] This third stage indicates the interrelated, ongoing nature of the management process. That is, the results of this stage are used in *planning* goals and strategies for future periods. So the cycle continues.

The Nature of Planning

"If you don't know where you're going, any road will get you there." The point of this axiom is that all organizations need both general and specific plans to fulfill their purposes. Management should first decide what it intends to accomplish as a total organization and develop a strategic plan to achieve these results. Based on this overall plan, each division of the organization should determine what its own plans will be. Of course, the role of marketing in these plans needs to be considered.

FIGURE 20.1

The Management Process in Marketing.

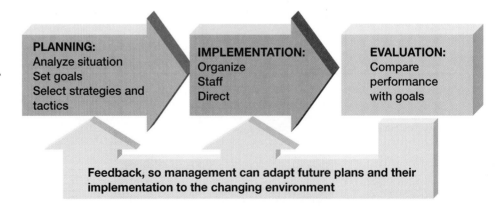

For decades, a small firm, Idus-Howard Inc., used advertising and personal selling to market custom logo merchandise. It received orders by phone and fax. But then the company changed its name and approach. Now, as eCompanyStore, it focuses on larger accounts and sells online. The firm seeks to "help our customers manage and procure their promotional products and uniforms with unprecedented speed and accuracy."

www.ecompanystore.
com

If planning is so important, exactly what is it? Simply, **planning** is deciding now what to do later, including how and when to do it. Without a plan, we cannot get anything done effectively and efficiently, because we don't know what needs to be done or how to do it.

In **strategic planning**, managers match an organization's resources with its market opportunities over the long run. A long-run perspective does not mean that plans can be developed or executed in a sluggish manner. The term **strategic window** describes the limited amount of time in which a firm's resources coincide with a particular market opportunity.[3] Typically, the "window" is open only for a relatively short period. Thus a firm must move rapidly and decisively when a strategic window opens.

Idus-Howard Inc. saw a strategic window in which it could multiply its sales volume. The firm, which sells promotional products such as clothing and glassware with company logos imprinted on them, switched from traditional methods to a reliance on online selling and adopted a more descriptive company name. To concentrate on large customers, eCompanyStore even made the painful decision to not serve its existing small customers. In two years, the firm secured 30 relatively large customers for which it built customized websites that each customer uses to purchase from eCompanyStore various promotional products displaying its own organization's logo.[4]

Essential Planning Concepts

You need to be familiar with not only the terms already introduced but also other basic terms used in discussing marketing management, especially in the planning phase.

Mission   An organization's **mission** states what customers it serves, what needs it satisfies, and what types of products it offers. A mission statement indicates, in general terms, the boundaries for an organization's activities.

Lennox International Inc. was founded more than 100 years ago in Iowa by a machine-shop operator who invented a new type of coal-fired furnace. Over the years, the company added new product lines and brands. With annual sales of about $3 billion, Lennox aims to ". . . make you feel more comfortable."

www.lennox.com

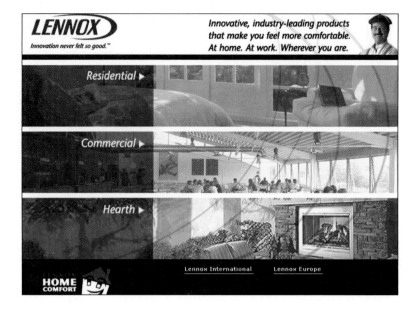

To be useful, a mission statement cannot be either too broad and vague or too narrow and specific. To say that a firm's mission is "to benefit American consumers" is vague; to state that its purpose is "to make tennis balls" is overly narrow. Neither statement outlines meaningful benefits for customers or provides much guidance to management. Unless the firm's purpose is clear to executives, strategic planning is likely to result in disagreement and confusion.

In the past, companies tended to state their missions in product-oriented terms, such as "We make furnaces" (or telephones, or golf clubs). Today, a firm abiding by the marketing concept expresses its mission in customer-oriented terms that reflect the needs it is striving to satisfy and the benefits it is providing. Thus, instead of "We make copiers, printers, and other document-management equipment," Xerox Corporation's mission is "to help people find better ways to do great work—by constantly leading in document technologies, products and services that improve our customers' work processes and business results."[5]

www.xerox.com

Objectives and Goals   Although they are sometimes differentiated, we treat *objectives* and *goals* as synonyms. An **objective** is simply a desired outcome. Effective planning must begin with a set of objectives that are to be achieved by carrying out plans. To be worthwhile and workable, objectives should be:

- Clear and specific.
- Stated in writing.
- Ambitious, but realistic.
- Consistent with one another.
- Quantitatively measurable when possible.
- Tied to a particular time period.

Consider these examples:

Weak (too general)		Workable
Increase our market share.	→	Increase our market share to 22% next year from its present 20% level.
Improve our company's image.	→	Receive favorable recognition awards next year from at least two consumer or environmental groups.

Strategies and Tactics

The term *strategy* was originally associated with military operations. In business, a **strategy** is a broad plan of action by which an organization intends to reach its objectives and, in turn, to fulfill its mission. In marketing, the relationship between objectives and strategies may be illustrated as follows:

Objective		Possible Strategies
Increase sales next year by 10% over this year's figure.	→	1. Intensify marketing efforts in domestic markets.
		2. Expand into new foreign markets.

Two organizations might have the same objective but use contrasting strategies to reach it. For instance, both firms might aim to increase their market shares by 20% over the next three years. To do that, one firm in, say, the packaged-foods industry might intensify its efforts in household markets; a competing firm might concentrate on expanding into institutional markets (for example, food-service organizations). Conversely, two organizations might have different objectives but select the identical strategy to reach them.

A **tactic** is a means by which a strategy is implemented. A tactic is a more specific, detailed course of action than a strategy. Moreover, tactics generally cover shorter time periods than strategies. Here's an illustration:

Strategy		Tactics
Direct our promotion to males, ages 25 to 40.	→	1. Advertise in magazines read by this market segment.
		2. Sponsor events attended in person and/or watched on TV by this segment.

www.planethollywood. com

To be effective, a tactic must coincide with and support the strategy with which it is related. That's sometimes difficult to do, as Planet Hollywood found out. A key strategy for the restaurant chain was a theme built around celebrities, many of whom were investors in the business. A related tactic was frequent appearances at the restaurants by stars and other well-known personalities. However, most celebrities didn't want to interact with the public. Equally damaging, the restaurants' food was generally poor. As a result, Planet Hollywood has filed for Chapter 11 bankruptcy protection twice and is in danger of disappearing from this planet as the chain has shrunk from 80 restaurants to 22.[6]

Key Questions for an Organization

The concepts of mission, objectives, strategies, and tactics raise important questions that must be answered by an organization seeking success in business or, more specifically, in marketing. These questions can be summarized as follows:

Concept		Question
Mission	→	What business are we in?
Objectives	→	What do we want to accomplish?
Strategies	→	In *general* terms, how are we going to get the job done?
Tactics	→	In *specific* terms, how are we going to get the job done?

Scope of Planning

Planning may cover long or short periods. Strategic planning is usually long range, spanning three, five, or even more years. It requires the participation of top management and often involves a planning staff.

Long-range planning deals with company-wide issues such as expanding or contracting production, markets, and product lines. For example, all firms in the home appliance industry must look ahead for perhaps as long as a decade to identify key markets, plan new products, and update production technologies.

Short-range planning typically covers one year or less and is the responsibility of middle- and lower-level managers. For example, on an annual basis, the Maytag Corporation needs to consider such issues as which target markets it will concentrate on and whether its marketing mixes for each of these markets need to be changed. Naturally, short-range plans must be compatible with the organization's long-range intentions.

www.maytag.com

Planning a firm's marketing strategies should be conducted on three different levels:

- *Strategic company planning.* At this level management defines an organization's mission, sets long-range goals, and formulates broad strategies to achieve the goals. Company-wide goals and strategies then become the framework for planning in the firm's different functional areas, such as production, finance, human resources, research and development, *and* marketing.

- *Strategic marketing planning.* The top marketing executives set goals and strategies for an organization's marketing effort. Strategic *marketing* planning obviously should be coordinated with *company-wide* planning.

- *Annual marketing planning.* Covering a specific period, usually one year, an annual marketing plan is based on the firm's strategic marketing planning.

Attitudes toward strategic planning seem to run in cycles. During the 1970s, strategic planning was highly valued in large corporations. Then, during the 1980s and most of the 1990s, the focus shifted to implementation and evaluation—especially efforts to boost efficiency and profitability. Strategic planning seems to be back in favor, particularly as it relates to global expansion. In fact, according to one survey, 27% of high-level corporate executives ranked strategic planning as the most important business function. Only product development, placed on top by 29% of the participants, ranked higher.[7]

Now one expert is urging executives to adjust their thinking about strategic planning. A basic premise, according to this new perspective, is that the macroenvironment can be influenced in some respects, such as by establishing new business models. Fairly recent start-ups, including eBay, E*Trade, and Amazon.com, have done this.[8]

us.etrade.com

Strategic Company Planning

Strategic company planning consists of four essential steps:

1. Define the organizational mission.
2. Analyze the situation.
3. Set organizational objectives.
4. Select strategies to achieve these objectives.

The process is shown in the top part of Figure 20.2.[9] The first step, *defining the organizational mission*, influences subsequent planning. For some firms, all that needs to be done is to review the existing mission statement and confirm that it is still suitable. However, this straightforward step is too often ignored.

Conducting a situation analysis, the second step, is vital because strategic planning is influenced by many factors beyond and within an organization. A **situation analysis** consists of gathering and studying information pertaining to one or more specified aspects of an organization. We'll talk more about conducting a situation analysis in an upcoming section.

The third step in strategic company planning, *deciding on a set of objectives*, guides the organization in fulfilling its mission. Objectives also provide standards for evaluating performance.

FIGURE 20.2

Three Levels of Organizational Planning.

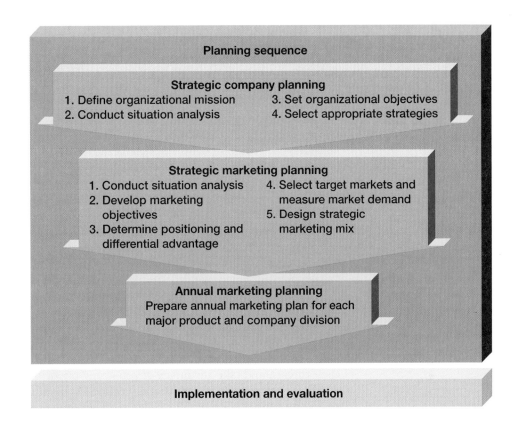

Planning sequence

Strategic company planning
1. Define organizational mission
2. Conduct situation analysis
3. Set organizational objectives
4. Select appropriate strategies

Strategic marketing planning
1. Conduct situation analysis
2. Develop marketing objectives
3. Determine positioning and differential advantage
4. Select target markets and measure market demand
5. Design strategic marketing mix

Annual marketing planning
Prepare annual marketing plan for each major product and company division

Implementation and evaluation

By this point, the organization has determined where it wants to go. The fourth step, *selecting appropriate strategies,* indicates how the firm is going to get there. **Organizational strategies** represent broad plans of action by which an enterprise intends to fulfill its mission and achieve its goals. Strategies are selected either for the entire company if it is small and/or has only a single product *or* for each division if the company is large and/or has multiple products.

Do companies actually engage in strategic planning and then prepare a written plan? The results of one survey indicated that almost 70% of firms had strategic plans in place; among them, nearly 90% believed their strategic plans had been effective. However, according to more recent data, only 12% of relatively small firms (defined as those with fewer than 500 employees) had a long-range plan in writing. In fact, almost 60% of these companies had no written plans.[10]

Strategic Marketing Planning

After planning for the organization as a whole, management needs to lay plans for each major functional area, including marketing. Of course, planning for each function should be guided by the organization-wide mission and objectives.

Strategic marketing planning is a five-step process:

1. Conduct a situation analysis.
2. Develop marketing objectives.
3. Determine positioning and differential advantage.
4. Select target markets and measure market demand.
5. Design a strategic marketing mix.

These five steps are shown in the middle of Figure 20.2, indicating how they relate to the four steps of strategic company planning. Each step is discussed below.

Situation Analysis

The first step, **situation analysis,** involves analyzing where the company's marketing program has been, how it has been doing, and what it is likely to face in the years ahead. The results of this activity enable management to determine if it is necessary to revise the old plans or devise new ones to achieve the company's objectives.

Situation analysis normally covers external environmental forces and internal nonmarketing resources that were discussed in Chapter 2. A situation analysis also considers the groups of consumers served by the company, the strategies used to satisfy them, and key measures of marketing performance. Due attention should be given to assessing competitors that are serving the same markets. Also, as stressed by two consultants, it's important to "get out of the box"—that is, to develop new perspectives on the organization's core activities and to question assumptions about how it does business (assumptions such as "we must offer competitive prices").[11]

Situation analysis is critical, but it can be costly, time-consuming, and frustrating. For example, it is usually difficult to extract timely, accurate information from the "mountains" of data compiled during a situation analysis. Moreover, some valuable information, such as sales or market-share figures for competitors, is often unavailable.

As part of a situation analysis, many organizations perform a **SWOT assessment.** In this activity, a firm identifies and evaluates its most significant *s*trengths, *w*eaknesses, *o*pportunities, and *t*hreats. To fulfill its mission, an organization needs to capitalize on its key strengths, overcome or alleviate its major weaknesses, avoid significant threats, and take advantage of promising opportunities.[12]

We're referring to strengths and weaknesses in an organization's own capabilities. For example, a strength of Federated Department Stores is its large size, which gives it—among other things—clout in dealing with suppliers. However, a weakness is its comparatively high operating expenses, which makes it difficult for Federated to offer competitive prices and to earn a healthy profit.

Opportunities and threats often originate outside the organization. According to RadioShack's chief executive, advances in computing and telecommunications technologies presented the chain with the opportunity to "demystify technology in every neighborhood in America." With nearly 7,000 stores, RadioShack Corp. intends to be the "most trusted specialty retailer" of various high-tech products and also provide installation and support services. But a threat is the variety of competitors, ranging from competing chains such as CompUSA to telecommunications giants such as SBC Communications that to some degree have similar intentions.[13]

Marketing Objectives

The next step in strategic marketing planning is to *determine marketing objectives.* Marketing goals should be closely related to company-wide goals and strategies. In fact, a *company strategy* often translates into a *marketing goal.* For example, to reach an organizational objective of a 20% return on investment next year, one organizational strategy might be to boost marketing efficiency by 10%. This company strategy could become a marketing goal. In turn, a strategy of converting all sales people from salaried compensation to a commission basis might be adopted to achieve this marketing goal.

We already know that strategic planning involves matching an organization's resources with its market opportunities. With this in mind, each marketing objective should be assigned a priority on the basis of its urgency and its potential impact on an area of focus and, in turn, the organization. Then resources should be allocated in line with these priorities.[14]

Positioning and Differential Advantage

The third step in strategic marketing planning actually entails two complementary decisions: *how to position a product in the marketplace* and *how to distinguish it*

In contrast to huge cruise ships, Windjammer Barefoot Cruises positions its product as a more informal, less crowded vacation. Windjammer's "tall ships," each with a long, unique history, accommodate fewer than 250 vacationers. The ships meander throughout the Caribbean sea, sailing primarily at night and stopping at various islands in the region during the day.

www.windjammer.com

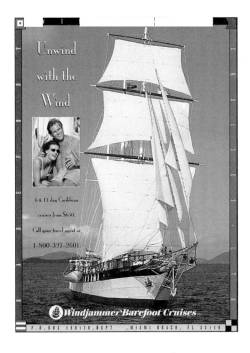

www.buckleys.com

from competitors. As described in Chapters 6 and 9, **positioning** refers to a product's image in relation to competing products as well as other products marketed by the same company. For example, a Canadian company tries to win over U.S. consumers by promoting the dreadful taste of its cough syrup! Because Buckley's Mixture doesn't use sugar or alcohol to overcome the chemical taste, the product's slogan is: "It tastes awful. And it works."[15]

After the product is positioned, a viable differential advantage has to be identified. **Differential advantage** refers to any feature of an organization or brand perceived by customers to be desirable and different from those of the competition. Some dry cleaning outlets have sought an advantage by using petroleum-based solvents rather than the traditional cleaning agent, which may cause cancer.[16]

Besides striving for an advantage, a company has to avoid a **differential disadvantage** for its product. Returning to the dry cleaning example, the outlets using the "new and improved" cleaning agents still need to offer competitive prices. Otherwise, they risk having a price *dis*advantage, which could negate the advantage gained by using an alternative cleaning method.

www.nordstrom.com

The concepts of differential advantage and differential disadvantage apply to both goods and services and, in areas such as retailing, to entire firms. One consultant believes that retailers can gain a differential advantage by developing one or more of four *est* dimensions—the low*est* prices, the bigg*est* assortments, the hott*est* (most fashionable) merchandise, and the easi*est* store to shop in. Nordstrom, a specialty fashion retailer with about 100 stores in the U.S., doesn't compete on the basis of low prices but has excelled in the other three areas. Conversely, a firm risks a differential *dis*advantage if it is only average or "pretty good" on these four dimensions.[17]

Target Markets and Market Demand

Selecting target markets is the fourth step in marketing planning. As covered in earlier chapters, a **market** consists of people or organizations with needs to satisfy, money to spend, and the willingness to spend it. For example, many people favor air travel *and* are both able and willing to pay for it. However, this large group is made up of a number of segments (that is, parts of markets) with various preferences. Because an organization typically cannot satisfy all segments with different needs, it is wise to concentrate on one or more of these segments.

Since 1980, the per capita consumption of beef has dropped from almost 80 pounds to about 65 pounds annually. How did beef fare in relation to other meats? Demand for pork also declined from almost 60 pounds per person per year to about 52 pounds. During the same period, consumption of chicken skyrocketed from under 50 pounds to 82 pounds. In fact, the demand for chicken has more than doubled since 1970. The consumption of another bird, turkey, has experienced a similar rise, with per–capita annual consumption now at 17 pounds.

Clearly, beef and pork producers face marketing challenges. In the 1980s, following extensive consumer research, pork producers decided to reposition their product as "the other white meat." The campaign successfully positioned pork closer to chicken, which has a healthful image in the minds of consumers, and further away from beef, which is perceived less favorably. The only problem was that the campaign didn't give much of a boost to pork consumption. So, in a subsequent campaign, pork producers promoted pork's tastiness. Now Smithfield Foods, a large hog producer and pork processor, has introduced a tastier and thus slightly fattier line of fresh pork.

Coming up with a real differential advantage for beef has been difficult. Several years ago, convenience and nutrition were emphasized, backed by a $30 million marketing campaign. The beef industry has also been in the test kitchen working on new easy-to-prepare products. Much attention is being given to reducing preparation time—an important consideration for time-conscious consumers. One promising avenue is precooking meat at a processing plant, which means it can be ready for the kitchen table after a short time in a microwave oven.

On a different front, both producers and supermarket chains are striving to attach brands to red meat as a first step in building greater customer loyalty. After Tyson Foods Inc. acquired IBP Inc., the king of chicken substituted its own Tyson brand for many of IBP's regional brands of beef and pork products. Another widely promoted producer's brand is Certified Angus Beef. Supermarket chains are doing their own branding, such as Albertsons' Blue Ribbon and Safeway's Rancher's Reserve beef.

Beef prices also rose, beginning in 2003, forcing producers to seek more affordable cuts of beef. Based on an extensive study, the beef industry came up with more economical steaks from the shoulder and hind quarters of a cow. For example, the "beef shoulder petite tender" cut is being positioned to compete with the boneless, skinless chicken breast.

What is, or could be, beef's differential advantage in relation to pork and chicken?

Sources: "Overview of U.S. Meat and Poultry Production and Consumption" fact sheet from the American Meat Institute, March 2005, www.meatami.com/content/presscenter/factsheets_infokits/factsheetmeatproductionandconsumption.pdf; Katy McLaughlin, "New Steaks Shoulder Their Way Onto the Grill," The Wall Street Journal, June 30, 2005, pp. D1, D4; Chris Flores, "Smithfield Breeds Fattier Line of Pork Fit for Low-Carb Dieters," Daily Press (Newport News, VA), Jan. 14, 2005, p. A1; Ed Murrieta, "Beef Suppliers Specialize to Encourage Brand Loyalty," The News Tribune (Tacoma, WA), Sept. 22, 2004, p. E1; Wendy Zellner, "Tyson: Is There Life Outside the Chicken Coop?" BusinessWeek, Mar. 10, 2003, p. 77. Scott Kilman, "Branding Beef: A Roast Is a Roast?" The Wall Street Journal, Feb. 20, 2002, p. A1; Howard Riell, "Convenience & Nutrition," Supermarket Business, Dec. 15, 1999, p. 90; and Daniel Rosenberg, "Pork Is Tasty, Say National Ads That Shift Focus from Nutrition," The Wall Street Journal, Aug. 13, 1997, p. B5.

A **target market** refers to a group of people or organizations at which a firm directs a marketing program. To choose one or more target markets, a firm must forecast demand (that is, sales) in market segments that appear promising. As discussed in Chapter 6, the results of demand forecasting represent valuable information in deciding whether a specific segment is worth pursuing, or whether alternative segments need to be considered.

Marketing Mix

For each target market, management must design a **marketing mix,** which is the combination of multiple aspects of the following four elements: a product, how it is distributed and promoted, and its price. These four elements, which were covered in detail in Chapters 8 through 19, are intended to please the target market(s) and, equally important, to achieve the organization's marketing objectives.

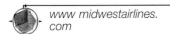
Each marketing-mix element contains numerous options. Further, decisions regarding one element affect the others. Marketing decision makers need to consider these options and relationships when designing a marketing mix for a particular target market. Here's an illustration of a customer–satisfying marketing mix. Seeking to provide "the best care in the air," Midwest Airlines offers several enhancements, including leather seats, added leg and seat room on many flights, and fresh-baked chocolate chip cookies on afternoon flights. Midwest uses the industry's standard methods for promoting and distributing its service, and it strives to have competitive coach fares, while providing what amounts to business-class service. Even with a customer-pleasing and award-winning marketing mix, Midwest Airlines' parent company has struggled to be profitable in the face of stiff price competition and rising fuel prices.[18]

Annual Marketing Planning

Besides strategic planning for several years ahead, more specific, shorter-term planning is also vital. Thus, as shown in the bottom part of Figure 20.2, preparation of an annual plan follows planning of a strategic nature. An **annual marketing plan** is the blueprint for a year's marketing activity for a specified organizational division or major product. It should be a written document, not just kept in mind.

A separate plan normally should be prepared for each major product and company division. Sometimes separate plans are even developed for key brands and important target markets. As the name implies, this type of plan usually covers one year. There are exceptions, however. Because of the seasonal nature of some products or markets, it may be advisable to prepare plans for shorter time periods. For fashionable clothing, plans are made for each season, lasting just several months. The planning horizon is even shorter in today's information economy. As noted in one article, "On the Internet, companies have to be ready to change goals or strategies virtually overnight."[19]

Purposes and Responsibilities

An annual marketing plan serves several purposes:

*   It summarizes the marketing strategies and tactics that will be used to achieve specified objectives in the upcoming year. Thus it becomes the "how-to-do-it" guide for executives and other employees involved in marketing.

AN ETHICAL DILEMMA?

Assume you are the product manager responsible for a line of cellular telephones. In the past year, your brand has fallen from second to third in terms of sales. You attribute the decline to an unfair comparative advertising campaign run by the new second-place firm. The company used ads that pointed to alleged shortcomings in your cell phones.

Unexpectedly, you are presented with an opportunity to regain the upper hand when one of your sales people brings you a copy of that competitor's marketing plan for next year. The sales person found it on a chair following a seminar attended by representatives from a number of companies that make cell phones and related products. After studying this document, you could adjust your plans to counter the other firm's strategies.

Even though you didn't buy or steal the plan, is it ethical to read and use it?

Sources: Mary Ellen Bates, "What Makes Information Public?" *Online*, November/December 2004, p. 64; and Skip Kaltenheuser, "Working the Crowd," *Across the Board*, July/August 2002, pp. 50+.

- The plan also points to what needs to be done with respect to the other steps in the management process—implementation and evaluation of the marketing program.
- Moreover, the plan should outline who is responsible for which activities, when they are to be carried out, and how much time and money can be spent.

The executive responsible for the division or product covered by the plan typically prepares it or asks one or more key staff members to do so. Preparation may begin six months or more before the start of the period covered by the plan. Early work includes necessary research and arranging other information sources. The bulk of the work occurs one to three months prior to the plan's starting date. The last steps are to have the plan reviewed and approved by upper management. Revision may be necessary before final approval is granted. The finished version of the plan, or relevant parts of it, should be shared with all employees who will be involved in implementing the agreed-upon strategies and tactics.

Recommended Contents

Annual marketing planning follows a sequence similar to strategic marketing planning. However, annual planning has a shorter time frame and is more specific with respect to the plans laid. Still, as shown in Table 20.1, the major sections in an annual plan give due attention to topics covered in strategic marketing planning.[20]

In an annual plan, more attention is devoted to tactical details than in other levels of planning. As an example, strategic marketing planning might stress personal selling within the marketing mix. If so, the annual plan might recommend increased college recruiting as a source of additional sales people.

An annual blueprint actually relates to all three steps of the management process, not just planning. Sections 5 through 7 of Table 20.1 deal with implementation, and

TABLE 20.1 **Contents of an Annual Marketing Plan**

1. *Executive Summary.* In this one- or two-page section, the thrust of the plan is described and explained for executives who need not be knowledgeable about the details.
2. *Situation Analysis.* Essentially, the marketing program for a major division of a company (called a strategic business unit) or product covered by the plan is examined within the context of pertinent past, present, and future conditions. Much of this section might be derived from the results of strategic marketing planning. Additional information of particular relevance to a one-year planning period should be included in this section.
3. *Objectives.* The objectives in an annual plan are more specific than those produced by strategic marketing planning. However, annual objectives must help achieve organizational goals and strategic marketing goals.
4. *Strategies.* As in strategic marketing planning, the strategies in an annual plan should indicate which target markets are going to be satisfied through a combination of product, price, distribution, and promotion.
5. *Tactics.* Specific activities, sometimes called action plans, are devised for carrying out each major strategy in the preceding section. For ease of understanding, strategies and tactics may be covered together. Tactics specifically answer the question of *what, who,* and *how* for the company's marketing efforts.
6. *Financial Schedules.* This section normally includes two kinds of financial information: projected sales, expenses, and profits in what's called a pro forma financial statement and the amounts of resources dedicated to different activities in one or more budgets.
7. *Timetable.* This section, often including a diagram, answers the question of *when* various marketing activities will be carried out during the upcoming year.
8. *Evaluation Procedures.* This section addresses the questions of *what, who, how,* and *when* connected with measuring performance against goals, both during and at the end of the year. The results of evaluations during the year may lead to adjustments in the plan's strategies, tactics, or even the objectives to be achieved.

section 8 is concerned with evaluation. To increase the likelihood of careful review, some firms limit annual plans to a specified length, such as 20 pages.

Selected Planning Models

For more than three decades, a number of frameworks or tools—we'll call them *models*—have been designed to assist with strategic planning. Most of these models can be used with both strategic company planning *and* strategic marketing planning. In this section, we briefly discuss several planning models that have received ample attention. First, however, you need to be familiar with a form of organization, the strategic business unit, that is integral to both planning and organizational structure in companies.

Strategic Business Units

www.altria.com/about_altria

Most large and medium-sized companies—and even some smaller firms—consist of multiple units and market numerous products. In such firms, company-wide planning cannot serve as an effective guide for executives who oversee the organization's various divisions. The Altria Group, Inc. provides an example. The mission, objectives, and strategies in its tobacco division are—and must be—quite different from those in its packaged foods division.

Consequently, for more effective planning and operations, a multidivision or multiproduct organization should be divided according to its major markets or products. Each such entity is called a **strategic business unit** (**SBU**). Each SBU may be a major division in an organization, a group of related products, or even a single major product or brand. To be considered an SBU, an entity should be a separately identi-

The McGraw-Hill Companies "provide essential information and insight that help individuals, markets, and societies perform to their potential." The firm does so through three strategic business units: information and media services (including *BusinessWeek* magazine); education (including publishing of textbooks such as this one); and financial services (including Standard & Poor's, as promoted in this ad).

www.mcgraw-hill.com

fiable business, have a distinct mission, have its own competitors, and have its own executive team with profit responsibility.

One challenge in setting up SBUs in an organization is to arrive at the *optimum* number. Too many can bog down top management in details associated with planning, operating, and reporting. Too few SBUs can result in each one covering too broad an area for meaningful planning.

SBUs for a giant corporation and a nonprofit organization are as follows:

- *The Boeing Company:* commercial airplanes, integrated defense systems, financing solutions, and Connexion by Boeing (Internet service for in-flight aircraft).

- *Your university or college:* different schools (such as business and engineering) *or* different delivery systems (such as on-campus curricula and distance learning).

  Let's now consider several well-known planning models.

Product-Market Growth Matrix

Most organizations want or need to get bigger and, therefore, objectives often focus on growth—that is, a desire to increase revenues and profits. In seeking growth, a company has to consider *both* its markets and its products. Then an enterprise has to decide whether to sustain, and perhaps enhance, what it is now doing *or* to establish new ventures. The **product-market growth matrix** depicts these options.[21]

As shown in Figure 20.3, there are four fundamental product-market growth strategies:

- *Market penetration:* A company tries to sell more of its present products to its present markets. Supporting tactics might include greater spending on advertising or personal selling. For example, the Wm. Wrigley Jr. Co. relies on this strategy, encouraging smokers to chew gum where smoking is prohibited. Or a company tries to become a single source of supply by offering preferential treatment to customers who will concentrate all of their purchases with that company.

- *Market development:* A firm continues to sell its present products, but to a new market. Firms that depend to a large degree on just a few customers often engage in market development to spread their risk. Exline Inc., a machine shop in Salina, Kansas, was forced to do that when Enron Corp. and other big customers in the energy industry imploded. In the context of consumer products, cruise lines such as Carnival and Royal Caribbean have been concentrating their marketing efforts on the almost 90% of Americans who have never taken a cruise.[22]

- *Product development:* An organization develops new products to sell to its existing markets. Some ski resorts, for example, built steep, dangerous slopes in order to appeal to thrill-seeking "extreme" customers; the Walt Disney Co. has added more "thrill rides" at its theme parks for the same reason. Wrigley also used this strategy by introducing mint-flavored gum aimed at teenagers. Medical Center Pharmacy in Scottsbluff, Nebraska, expanded by offering new product lines— first, wheelchairs and hospital beds for in-home use and, subsequently, on-site

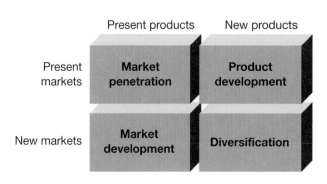

FIGURE 20.3

Product-Market Growth Matrix.

Is expansion into China a desirable growth strategy?

One of the four product-market growth strategies is to offer the firm's goods and services for sale in new markets. In this context, the additional market could be a demographic group, type of organization, or region of the world not served by the company.

Numerous North American and European firms have chosen China as a desirable market for expansion. They have experienced wide-ranging degrees of success. On the minus side, a Dutch supermarket chain, Ahold, pulled out of China. Nestlé has been marketing in China for about 25 years. However, the Swiss company has struggled to gain dominant positions in various categories, including candy and chocolate, baby formula, and bottled water. In China, Nestlé faces competition from both domestic and Taiwanese firms. In addition, it has to battle multinational enterprises that focus on specific categories; for instance, Group Danone has done well selling bottled water.

On the plus side, Coca-Cola has over 30,000 employees and 33 bottling plants after just two decades of operation in China. The most successful foreign businesses in China may be operators of giant discount stores such as Carrefour from France and Wal-Mart. In order to compete with cheaper domestic brands, L'Oreal, a French firm, has used Chinese celebrities to extol the virtues of its cosmetics. And to give credit where it's due, Nestlé has gained the #1 position in the instant-coffee category.

Here are some aspects of the Chinese market that are likely to dictate strategic adjustments:

- Chinese consumers in major urban areas like Western goods and the convenience of giant stores that allow one-stop shopping.

- Getting products to rural areas is made difficult by the immense distances and the poor roads.

- Local Chinese brands are entrenched in rural areas. When P&G entered China in 1988, there were only 30 hair-care brands in the entire country. Having witnessed P&G's success, more than 1,800 local brands have sprung up, many of them knockoffs of P&G products.

- Obtaining economies of scale is particularly important in China because operating costs, especially physical distribution, are much higher than in most Western countries. That's another reason why 100,000-square-foot "hypermarkets" have done well in urban areas.

Of course, given the enormous magnitude of the Chinese market, a steady stream of companies ranging from fashion retailer Mango to brewer SAB Miller has entered the world's most populated country. New entrants should take notice of the observation made by an employee of a giant British retailer, "Our business in China works very differently to anywhere else in the world. Because of vast regional differences we focus heavily on local markets in terms of our offer to the customers and we employ a huge army of regional buyers."

Sources: "Western Brands Vie to Fulfill Eastern Promise," *Marketing Week,* Apr. 21, 2005, p. 24; Leslie T. Chang, "Nestlé Stumbles in China's Evolving Market," *The Wall Street Journal,* Dec. 8, 2004, p. A10; "Coca-Cola Starts Profiting 10 Years after Re-entering China," *SinoCast China Business Daily News,* Nov. 10, 2004, p. 1; Brian Caulfield and Ting Shi, "Getting a Leg Up in China," *Business 2.0,* January/February 2004, pp. 69–70; Vasantha Ganesan, "Royal Ahold Leaving Malaysia's Retail Scene?" *Business Times,* Apr. 2, 2003, p. 1; and "Not So Fuzzy," *The Economist,* Feb. 23, 2002, pp. 66+.

repair and even custom building of these products. Such moves are intended to better satisfy, and generate more revenues from, existing customers.[23]

- *Diversification:* A company develops new products to sell to new markets. To cite one example, at various points in its history, The Boeing Company moved far away from aircraft to market other vehicles (light rail systems, hydrofoils) and disparate services (urban planning, desalination of water supplies). This approach is risky because it doesn't rely on either the company's successful products or its established position in one or more markets. Sometimes it works, but often it doesn't. According to research conducted by the Bain & Co. consulting firm, diversified enterprises do not perform as well financially as relatively focused organizations.[24]

Nike Inc. wanted to boost sales of its athletic shoes through broader distribution. To do so, Nike bought the Starter brand but chose to not place the famous "swoosh" symbol on these shoes. Wal-Mart Stores Inc. agreed to distribute Starter shoes, with a retail price of under $40. The marketing strategies chosen for the Starter brand are intended to avoid taking sales away from Nike's higher-price shoes.

www.nike.com/nikebiz

www.lizclaiborne.com

As market conditions change over time, a company may shift product-market growth strategies. For example, when its present market is fully saturated, an organization may have no choice other than to pursue new markets. That's the path followed by Liz Claiborne Inc., which earned a reputation for making stylish clothing for women engaged in professional careers. Eventually, the apparel firm added new brands in order to serve a variety of target markets, especially economy-minded female shoppers. Today, Claiborne labels, such as Villager and Crazy Horse, can be found in a wide range of retail outlets, including Kohl's and JCPenney.[25]

In pursuing one or more product-market growth strategies, a company seeks to build its sales and profits, of course. However, in the case of product development, it's possible that revenues rung up by new products may come at the expense of other products sold by that firm. This situation is called **cannibalization.** Eastman Kodak Co. realized that sales of its traditional films would suffer when it introduced digital-imaging products. The Claiborne clothing firm, discussed above, accepted some degree of cannibalization. Wal-Mart realizes that its new supercenters take sales away from the chain's existing stores but believes the benefits such as added market share and greater distribution efficiency outweigh this cost. Realizing that cannibalization of its flagship brands will occur, the Coca-Cola Company still introduced no- or low-calorie colas (e.g., Coca-Cola Zero, C2) in order to keep consumers away from bottled water and fruit-based beverages.[26]

Why does a company take actions that could result in cannibalization? Very simply, if it doesn't introduce new products or channels to better serve existing customers, one or more competitors almost surely will. If that occurs, the passive firm will lose customers and, in turn, revenues. A study that focused on high-tech industries cast a favorable light on cannibalization, concluding that success with truly innovative new products requires a willingness to cannibalize in order to achieve substantial gains in the future.[27]

BCG Matrix

Developed by a management consulting firm, the Boston Consulting Group, the **BCG matrix** dates back over 30 years.[28] Using this model, an organization classifies each of its SBUs (and, sometimes, major products) according to two factors: its market share relative to competitors *and* the growth rate of the industry in which the SBU operates. When the factors are divided simply into high and low categories, a 2 × 2 grid is created, as displayed in Figure 20.4.

Does the Internet foster cannibalization?

With the surge of the Internet, more and more companies face the issue of cannibalization. Online selling can result in cannibalization, taking sales away from other channels. For example, PETsMART.com surely pulls at least some shoppers away from the namesake physical stores. However, PETsMART's Web-based selling may have other benefits, such as lower operating expenses and attracting customers who are not located near one of the chain's physical stores.

Cannibalization becomes more controversial when the new efforts, online or otherwise, are taking or might take sales away from independent channel members. For example, Avon's independent sales reps expressed concern that the company's addition of a website (and other channels) would take sales away from them, thus reducing their incomes. Car and truck dealerships reacted in much the same way to the Internet forays launched—and now abandoned—by the auto manufacturers.

If added sales and profits from new products more than offset reductions experienced by existing products, then cannibalization can be beneficial. One business writer concluded, "Traditional retailers have realized that the benefits of joining the dot-com community far outweigh any potentially competitive cannibalization." With that in mind, Krause's Furniture, based in southern California, has added a website featuring an extensive electronic catalog as another channel for its merchandise.

Another perspective is that a degree of cannibalization is preferable to losing customers to competitors. With that in mind, Ameritrade came up with iZone, a lower-price, no-frills version of its brokerage service. This service, available online or by touch-tone phone to experienced investors who presumably don't need access to Ameritrade's research and live price quotes, cuts the per-trade commission in half.

For firms facing online competition, cannibalization is essential. According to one observer, "Companies that learn to cannibalize themselves today will rule tomorrow's business jungle. Those that don't will find themselves in someone else's pot."

Sources: Jed Horowitz, "Ameritrade Offers $5 Stock Trade As Brokers' Price War Heats Up," *The Wall Street Journal*, Jan. 11, 2005, p. D3; Connie Robbins Gentry, "When Worlds Collaborate," *Chain Store Age*, April 2001, pp. 101+; and Jerry Useem, "Internet Defense Strategy: Cannibalize Yourself," *Fortune*, Sept. 6, 1999, pp. 121–122+.

In turn, the four quadrants in the grid represent distinct categories of SBUs or major products. The categories differ with respect to not only market share and industry growth rate but also cash needs and appropriate strategies:

- *Stars*. High market shares and high industry growth rates typify SBUs in this category. However, an SBU with these attributes poses a challenge for companies because it requires a lot of cash to remain competitive in growing markets. Aggressive marketing strategies are imperative for stars to maintain or even build

FIGURE 20.4

The BCG Matrix.

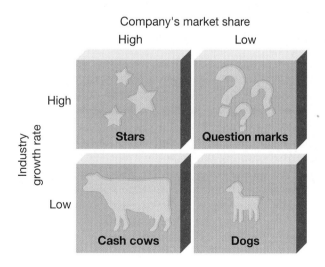

market share. The leading brands of "luxury" autos, such as BMW and Lexus, are currently viewed as stars. Although neither of these brands has a commanding market share on an absolute basis, each is doing relatively well in an expanding segment of the new-car market.[29]

www.gillette.com/
products

- *Cash cows.* These SBUs have high market shares and do business in mature (low-growth) industries. When an industry's growth diminishes, stars move into this category. Because most of their customers have been with them for some time and are still loyal, a cash cow's marketing costs are not high. Consequently, it generates more cash than can be reinvested profitably in its own operations. As a result, cash cows can be "milked" to support other SBUs that need more resources. Marketing strategies for cash cows seek to defend market share, largely by reinforcing customer loyalty. As examples, consider Campbell's efforts to rebuild sales of its canned soups and Gillette's ongoing push for its "3 B's," namely blades for razors, brushes for teeth, and batteries.[30]

- *Question marks* (sometimes called *problem children*). SBUs characterized by low market shares but high industry growth rates fit in this category. A question mark has not achieved a foothold in an expanding, but highly competitive, market. The question surrounding this type of endeavor is whether it can gain adequate market share and be profitable. If management answers "no," then the SBU should be sold off or liquidated. If management instead answers "yes," the firm must come up with the cash to build market share—more cash than the typical question mark generates from its own profits. Appropriate marketing strategies for problem children focus on establishing a strong differential advantage and, thereby, building customer support. Blockbuster Inc. is using the proceeds from its longstanding but faltering cash cow—video and now DVD rentals—to enter two growing areas—the sale of movies and games on DVDs. However, these efforts are question marks because of the presence of larger, entrenched competitors. In DVD sales, Wal-Mart prices DVDs very low to generate store traffic. Blockbuster believes its advantages lie in rewarding DVD purchasers with a free rental and in allowing DVD rental customers to buy a copy of the movie. In online rentals, Netflix has substantial brand equity and 3 million subscribers—at least two times the size of Blockbuster's roster of subscribers.[31]

www.blockbuster.com/
corporate/display
AboutBlockbuster.action

- *Dogs.* These SBUs have low market shares and operate in industries with low growth rates. A company normally would be unwise to invest substantial funds in SBUs in this category. Marketing strategies for dogs are intended to maximize any potential profits by minimizing expenditures *or* to promote a differential advantage to build market share. The company can say "Enough's enough!" and divest or liquidate a dog. Even Wal-Mart has had to deal with some dogs, selling its Deep Discount Store and Helen's Arts and Craft divisions. General Motors eventually shut down its Oldsmobile division and has been assessing whether Pontiac and/or Buick are also dogs that should be discontinued.[32]

The portfolios of most organizations with numerous SBUs or major products include a mix of stars, cash cows, question marks, and dogs. Consider one company's situation. The flagship brands of PepsiCo Inc.—Lay's, Fritos, Quaker, Pepsi-Cola, Mountain Dew, Gatorade, and Tropicana—can be described as cash cows. The company hopes that its Aquafina bottled water is another star. Recently, PepsiCo (as well as Coca-Cola and other competitors) introduced flavored bottled waters, such as Aquafina Sparkling and FlavorSplash, all of which started as question marks. Finally, Pepsi has had some dogs, such as Crystal, a clear cola, and Pepsi Blue, a berry-infused cola; both attracted too few customers and thus failed.[33]

www.pepsico.com/
company/brands/shtml

In the financial arena, an investor needs a balanced portfolio with respect to likely risks and potential returns. Likewise, a company should seek a balanced portfolio of SBUs. Certainly, cash cows are necessary, perhaps indispensable. Stars and question marks are also integral to a balanced portfolio, because products in growing markets determine a firm's long-term performance. Although dogs are undesirable, it's a rare company that doesn't have at least one.

A single firm typically cannot affect the growth rate for an entire industry. (An exception might be the dominant firm in a fairly new, rapidly growing industry. Recent examples include Microsoft in operating-systems software, and Rollerblade, Inc., in in-line skates.) If growth rate cannot be influenced, companies must turn to the other factor in the BCG matrix—market share. Hence, strategies based on the BCG matrix tend to concentrate on building or maintaining market share, depending on which of the four SBU categories is involved. Various strategies require differing amounts of cash, which means that management must continually allocate the firm's limited resources (notably cash) to separate marketing endeavors.

GE Business Screen

On the surface, the **GE business screen** appears to be very similar to the BCG matrix. This planning model, developed by General Electric with the assistance of the McKinsey consulting firm, also involves two factors and results in a grid.[34] But, as we shall see, the two models are different in significant respects.

Management can use the GE business screen to classify SBUs or major products on the basis of two factors: market attractiveness and business position. Each factor is rated according to several criteria. *Market attractiveness* should be judged with respect to market growth rate (similar to the BCG matrix), market size, degree of difficulty in entering the market, number and types of competitors, technological requirements, and profit margins, among other criteria. *Business position* encompasses market share (as in the BCG matrix), SBU size, strength of differential advantage, research and development capabilities, production capacity, cost controls, and strength of management, among others.

The criteria used to rate market attractiveness and business position are assigned different weights because some criteria are more important than others. Then each SBU or, if desired, major product is rated with respect to all criteria. Finally, overall ratings for both factors, usually numerical scores, are calculated for each SBU. On the basis of these ratings, each SBU is labeled as high, medium, or low with respect to (1) market attractiveness and (2) business position. For example, an SBU may be judged as having high market attractiveness but medium business position.

Following the ratings, an organization's SBUs are plotted on a 3 × 3 grid, as depicted in Figure 20.5. The best location for an SBU is the upper left cell because it points to (1) the most attractive market opportunity and (2) the best business position to seize that opportunity. The worst location is the lower right cell, for the opposite

FIGURE 20.5

The GE Business Screen.

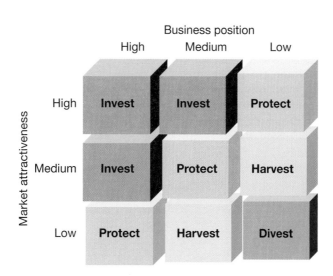

reasons. The nine cells have implications with respect to how resources are allocated and, in turn, what marketing strategies are suitable.

Every organization has to make decisions aimed at using its limited resources most effectively. That's where planning models can help—determining which SBUs or major products should be stimulated for growth, which ones maintained in their present market positions, and which ones eliminated. An SBU's evaluation, as indicated by its location on the GE business screen, suggests how it should be treated:

- *Invest strategy.* SBUs in the three cells in the upper left of the grid should receive ample resources. To strengthen or at least sustain such SBUs, bold, well-financed marketing efforts are needed. Several years ago, Silicon Graphics, Inc. announced that it would concentrate on producing powerful server computers that can handle challenging technical and Internet applications. The firm's decision seemed to be based on an assessment indicating high market attractiveness and a midrange business position. Xerox Corp. is following this strategy with respect to high-end digital copiers, as are several competitors.[35]

- *Protect strategy.* Resources should be allocated selectively to SBUs along the diagonal running from the lower left to the upper right of the grid. This somewhat defensive approach helps an SBU maintain its present market position while it generates cash needed by other SBUs. For example, the firm that makes Precious Moments, small porcelain figurines of children, suffered when demand for collectibles declined. The Enesco Group took several actions, including (a) selling inexpensive Precious Moments trinkets at discount stores in order to promote the brand and (b) distributing the figurines through different channels, including in-home parties.[36]

- *Harvest strategy.* Because they lack an attractive market and a strong business position, SBUs in the two cells just below the three-cell diagonal do not warrant substantial new resources. Instead, expenditures should be curtailed to maximize any remaining profits. An alternative is to sell these SBUs. A case can be made that the Hewlett-Packard Co. is following this strategy with regards to lower-price printers. With growth slowing and profit margins shrinking in this category, H-P is shifting resources from basic printers to higher-growth areas, including digital publishing and multipurpose printer-based machines.[37]

- *Divest strategy.* SBUs in the lower right cell do not have much going for them. Hence, an SBU in this location should not receive any resources. The best approach probably is to eliminate it from the organization's portfolio by selling it or, failing that, shutting it down. When the McDonald's Corp. assessed its portfolio several years ago, the firm decided to divest its Fazoli's and Donatos Pizzeria divisions and keep two "promising concepts," Chipotle Mexican Grill and Boston Markets, in addition to its famous namesake division.[38]

Firms typically employ more than one of these four strategies and adjust them over time. To illustrate, after assessing its portfolio, Kraft Foods Inc. employed a *harvest* strategy by selling some divisions, such as specialty oils and food service, that had small profit margins and/or did not fit into the firm's core activities. A Kraft executive labeled the divested businesses "hippopotamuses" rather than its preferred "greyhounds." The funds derived from the transactions were used to support a *protect* strategy for key brands such as Maxwell House, Oscar Mayer, and Jell-O. More recently, Kraft followed an *invest* strategy by acquiring Nabisco and its stable of strong brands and by expanding its presence in the frozen-pizza area with brands such as Jack's and DiGiorno.[39]

Assessment of the Planning Models

These planning models have been praised and criticized.[40] Although each model is somewhat distinctive, all share some limitations:

- One evident limitation is oversimplification. The models base the assessment of market opportunities and subsequent decisions on only two or three key factors. In this regard, the GE business screen, which uses multiple criteria for assessing market attractiveness and business position, is preferable to the BCG matrix. Still, the GE model lacks precision, in that what constitutes *high, medium,* and *low* for each of the two factors is largely a matter of judgment.

- There is also the possibility of placing an SBU or major product on a grid or choosing a strategy without relevant, reliable information. For example, whether market share is critical to a product's profitability is still debated.

- Another potential limitation is that the results from a planning model might be used to override the critical business judgments made by line managers such as a marketing vice president. A better approach to decision making is to take into account the results from the model *and* the judgments of executives who are well informed about the particular situation.

However, these models also produce noteworthy benefits:

- Most important, they encourage careful, consistent assessment of market and product opportunities, allocation of resources, and formulation of strategies. Without planning models, these activities might be haphazard—for example, using one set of criteria this month and, with no good reason, another set next month.

- Another benefit is straightforward classification. Each model permits an organization to examine its entire portfolio of SBUs or major products in relation to criteria that are thought to influence business performance.

- The models can also point to attractive business opportunities and suggest ventures to avoid.

The search for helpful planning aids is ongoing. A while back, for instance, two consultants urged firms to develop their organizational strategies in terms of *value disciplines*. According to this framework, a firm must increase the value offered to customers by cutting prices, improving products, or enhancing service. Doing so requires choosing and effectively implementing one of three value disciplines: *operational excellence, product leadership,* or *customer intimacy.*[41]

Dell Computer and Wal-Mart exemplify operational excellence. Illustrations of *product leadership* include Nike (footwear and sporting goods, such as golf balls) and Juniper Networks (top-of-the-line routers for directing Internet traffic, as well as other information-technology products). Customer intimacy emphasizes delivering precisely what specific customers really want and cannot find elsewhere. It appears that Amazon.com is trying to do this, as it provides customers with their own "store" (a record of their shopping experiences and additional recommendations related to a recent purchase) as well as allowing hopeful consumers to post "wish lists" that can be accessed by friends and family members.[42]

Overall, we believe planning models can help management allocate resources and also develop sound business and marketing strategies. Of course, any planning model should supplement, rather than replace or override, managers' judgments and decisions.

Summary

The management process consists of planning, implementation, and evaluation. Planning provides direction to an organization by deciding now what it is going to do later, including when and how it is going to do it. Strategic planning is intended to match an organization's resources with its market opportunities over the long run.

In any organization, there should be three levels of planning: strategic company planning, strategic marketing planning, and annual marketing planning. In strategic company planning, management defines the organization's mission, assesses its operating environment, sets long-range goals, and formulates broad strategies to achieve the goals. This level of planning guides planning in different functional areas, including marketing.

Strategic marketing planning entails five steps: conduct a situation analysis, develop marketing objectives, determine positioning and differential advantage, select target markets and measure market demand, and design a marketing mix. On the basis of strategic marketing plans, an annual marketing plan lays out a year's marketing activities for each major product and division of an organization. An annual plan includes tactics as well as strategies. It is typically prepared by the executive responsible for the division or product.

Management can rely on one or more of the following models for assistance with strategic planning: the product-market growth matrix, the BCG matrix, and the GE business screen. In seeking growth through new products, an organization may need to deal with the matter of cannibalization. A planning model helps management see how best to allocate its resources and to select effective marketing strategies.

More about **Starbucks**

Of the over $5 billion in total sales recorded annually by the Starbucks Corporation, about 84% is rung up at 8,500+ company-operated stores. The rest, representing almost $1 billion in yearly revenue, comes from what Starbucks calls "specialty operations."

The coffee purveyor's new CEO, Jim Donald, intends to grow all of Starbucks' specialty operations:

- Licensing arrangements covering over 3,300 outlets. In many cases, the chain finds it advantageous to allow another firm to operate a Starbucks store according to stringent procedures.

- Agreements through which manufacturers place the well-known brand on selected food products. Starbucks' partners and the products covered by these alliances include: Kraft, packaged coffee; Dreyer's, ice cream; PepsiCo, coffee-based beverages such as Frappuccino, a bottled iced coffee, and DoubleShot, canned espresso with a touch of cream.

- Sale of Starbucks products to food-service companies, which service restaurants, airlines, healthcare institutions, and other customers. Starbucks has entered into an agreement with SYSCO Corporation, a nationwide wholesaler, to manage and expand the coffee chain's food-service accounts.

- Other initiatives, including the company's website. At www.starbucks.com, patrons can find the nearest Starbucks, purchase CDs and coffee, and sign up for a Starbucks smart card.

Not all of Starbucks' nonstore endeavors have been successful. The list of failures includes *Joe*, a coffee-house magazine; Starbucks Cafés; an ambitious Internet enterprise intended to sell kitchen products and other items; and, occasionally, even a new beverage.

The stores side of the company also seeks bold new ventures. Lately, Starbucks has put a lot of effort into music-related initiatives. The chain has its own channel on XM Satellite Radio that is played in most Starbucks stores in the U.S. It has also attained some success (but not much profit) in co-producing and selling albums, the most visible being Ray Charles' *Genius Loves Company*.

To encourage consumers to visit, and linger, at its stores, Starbucks offers wireless Internet access at thousands of Starbucks outlets in the U.S. and Europe. In a somewhat similar vein, the company has been testing Hear Music areas in which customers can download music and burn CDs at Starbucks stores. A related venture is Hear Music Coffee Houses that sell music and, secondarily, coffee and other beverages. The early results of both ventures have been far less robust than a cup of Starbucks' renowned product.

Starbucks expects its green-and-white logo to be on 30,000 outlets and dozens of products in hundreds of thousands of retail outlets around the world. For that to happen, and for the chain to remain as famous as the first mate in *Moby Dick*, Schultz, Donald, and their team need to devise plans to build the core business still more and add growth opportunities.[43]

1. Where in the product-market growth matrix does Starbucks' expansion into grocery stores fall?

What about Frappuccino and DoubleShot? Expansion around the globe?

2. Which of the above ventures is/are in line with Starbucks' mission statement: "to establish Starbucks as the premier purveyor of the finest coffee in the world while maintaining our uncompromising principles as we grow"?

3. What strategies should Starbucks use in seeking success in countries such as Italy and France that have long-established traditions of independent coffee bars? What about in Asian countries that have long-standing tea-drinking traditions?

Key Terms and Concepts

Management (558)
Planning (559)
Strategic planning (559)
Strategic window (559)
Mission (560)
Objective (560)
Strategy (561)
Tactic (561)
Strategic company planning (562)

Situation analysis (562)
Organizational strategies (563)
Strategic marketing planning (563)
Situation analysis (564)
SWOT assessment (564)
Positioning (565)
Differential advantage (565)
Differential disadvantage (565)
Market (565)

Target market (566)
Marketing mix (566)
Annual marketing plan (567)
Strategic business unit (SBU) (569)
Product-market growth matrix (570)
Cannibalization (572)
BCG matrix (572)
GE business screen (575)

Questions and Problems

1. Should a small firm (a producer, a traditional retailer, or an online enterprise) engage in formal strategic planning? Why or why not?

2. Every organization needs to define its mission. Using a customer-oriented approach (benefits provided or wants satisfied), answer the question "What business are we in?" for each of the following companies:
   a. Holiday Inns (which is part of the InterContinental Hotels Group)
   b. Amazon.com
   c. Dell Computer
   d. Universal (movie) Studios
   e. Goodyear Tire and Rubber Co.

3. In the situation-analysis step of strategic marketing planning, what specific external environmental factors should be analyzed by a firm that manufactures equipment used for backpacking in the wilderness?

4. Can a product have a differential advantage and a differential disadvantage at the same time?

5. Identify and explain the differential advantage or disadvantage for the primary product for one of the following organizations:
   a. United Airlines
   b. Your university or college
   c. Victoria's Secret
   d. The United Way in your community
   e. Major-league baseball
   f. eBay

6. For one of the six organizations listed immediately above, describe its target market(s).

7. Use an example to explain the concept of a strategic business unit.

8. a. What's the basic difference between the BCG matrix and the GE business screen?
   b. Which do you think is better, and why?

9. If you were the vice president of marketing for a large airline, which of the three planning models would you find most useful? Why?

10. "The European Union (EU), which has a goal of the economic unification of Europe, means absolute chaos for American firms targeting consumers in countries that belong to the EU. For a number of years, the situation will be so dynamic that U.S. executives should not waste their time on formal strategic planning related to European markets." Do you agree with this statement?

Interactive Marketing Exercises

1. Either go online or to your school's library and obtain a copy of an annual report for a major corporation. On the basis of your examination of the year-end review, which of the following product-market growth strategies is being used by this company: market penetration, market development, product development, and/or diversification?

2. Talk with the owner or manager of a local firm about its marketing strategies. Considering the information you have obtained, determine the differential advantage or disadvantage for the firm's primary product. Then indicate how the advantage could be strengthened or how the disadvantage could be alleviated.

Chapter 21

". . . no fashion-focused firm executes rapidly better than Zara."

How Does **Zara** Move So Fast in Fashion Marketing?

Zara is a rapidly growing retailer of moderately priced, stylish women's clothing, referred to as "cheap chic" fashions. In an industry where fads are the norm, swift implementation of plans is necessary in order to survive. And no fashion-focused firm executes rapidly better than Zara.

The first Zara store opened in 1975 in La Coruña, Spain. The Zara chain has grown to over 750 stores in more than 50 countries. With annual sales exceeding $5 billion, it is the largest unit of Inditex, a privately held Spanish firm. The parent company also includes seven smaller chains selling such lines as lingerie, teen styles, and upscale men's clothing.

Zara's high-speed design, production, and distribution methods, along with a high degree of vertical integration allow the firm to bring new merchandise to market in just two to three weeks. Most competitors need six months or more. Instead of making changes once or twice a season, Zara delivers new styles to its outlets at least twice a week and carries no style for over a month. In this way, Zara responds to customers' changing tastes during a fashion season.

Zara's designers take real-time information from store managers to create about 11,000 new items each year. In this way, the clothing chain offers abundant variety that brings customers back to see what's new. Any merchandising mistakes don't last long enough to hurt sales, and markdowns and clearance sales do not plague Zara as they do most retailers.

Once Zara decided to make responsiveness to shoppers speed in implementation its hallmarks, its overall strategy fell into place. For example, most of its products are made in Spain whereas competitors typically use producers in developing countries in order to obtain lower costs. As Inditex's CEO explains, "The fashion world is in constant flux and is driven not by supply but by customer demand. We need to give consumers what they want, and if I go to South America or Asia to make clothes, I simply can't move fast enough."

The same rationale guides operations at the company's 5-million-square-foot warehouse (the size of about 90 football fields). This enormous space is connected to over a dozen Zara factories by tunnels that carry merchandise on rails and cables to separate staging areas for each store. To aid distribution, a new, large warehouse has opened in Zaragoza, northeast of Madrid.

Managers and technical specialists monitor the physical distribution system constantly, considering details such as the sequence and size of deliveries, departure times, and shipping routes. According to Inditex's logistics director, "We are always fine-tuning things, with the same objectives: flexibility and speed."

Deliveries are scheduled by time zone; orders for the Americas and Asia are packed and shipped in the morning, and orders for Europe in the afternoon. The aim is to deliver merchandise to stores before they open, when trucks can easily cope with downtown traffic and store managers can readily accept and process the deliveries.

Zara does almost no advertising or other promotion. Its infrequent ads announce new stores or remind customers about a new fashion season. None of Inditex's chains, including Zara, sells through the Internet or catalogs. "The center of it all is the store," explains the group's managing director.

Referring to Inditex and its largest division, Zara, an analyst stated, "No one can replicate their model." Other firms evidently are not convinced because competition in the area of "fast fashion" continues to intensify. Among the retail chains going head to head with Zara in various countries are Mango, another Spanish enterprise, and H&M, based in Sweden. Directly or indirectly, Zara also competes with American-owned mid-price fashion chains ranging from Polo Ralph Lauren's Club Monaco to Liz Claiborne's European Mexx division. And the competition continues . . . at a very fast pace.[1]

What does Zara do especially well in implementing its marketing strategies? What aspects of its implementation might be improved?

www.zara.com

The Zara case illustrates not just an imaginative strategic plan but also ongoing implementation of strategies and tactics and periodic evaluation of results. In Chapter 20 we defined the management process in marketing as planning, implementing, and evaluating marketing in an organization. Most of this book has dealt with **planning** a marketing program. For example, we discussed how to select one or more target markets and how to design an integrated marketing program that satisfies the desires of a particular market.

Now in this chapter we discuss the implementation and evaluation of a marketing program. **Implementation** is the stage in the management process during which an organization attempts to carry out its strategic plan. At the end of an operating period (or even during the period), management should conduct an **evaluation** of the organization's performance. This stage involves determining how well the company or division is achieving the goals set forth in its strategic planning and then, as necessary, preparing new or modified plans.

After studying this chapter, you should be able to explain:

- The role of implementation in the management process.
- Organizational structures used to implement marketing programs.
- Warranties and other postsale services as means of assuring customer satisfaction.
- The nature of a marketing audit.
- The meaning and effects of misdirected marketing effort.
- The steps comprising the evaluation process in marketing.
- Analyses of sales volume, market share, and marketing costs.
- How findings from sales and cost analyses can be used by managers.

Implementation in Marketing Management

There should be a close relationship among planning, implementation, and evaluation. Without strategic planning, a company's operational activities—its implementation tactics—can go off in any direction, like a team without a game plan. As stressed a few years ago, "Implementation . . . is a critical link between the formulation of marketing strategies and the achievement of superior organizational performance."[2]

Sparked by management consulting firms, there was tremendous interest in strategic planning a couple of decades ago. Then disenchantment set in, because many companies realized that strategic *planning* alone was not enough to ensure success. These plans had to be *effectively implemented*. Experience has shown that good planning cannot offset poor implementation, but effective implementation sometimes can overcome deficient planning.

In recent years, therefore, much attention has been devoted to implementing a company's strategies. Consider airlines and hotels that set objectives and then develop strategies related to prices. These enterprises are likely to be interested in the degree of price competition, the percentage of seats or rooms sold, and total revenue. Computer programs can assist service firms in this area of yield management. Omni Hotels Corp., for example, developed a program called OmniCHARM (Centralized Hotel Automated Revenue Management) to estimate demand on the basis of historical sales patterns. The demand estimates, along with data about the number of unsold rooms for different dates, help in setting specific prices that coincide with the firm's pricing objectives and strategies.[3]

In this ad, the Principal Financial Group stresses that it assembles a set of financial products to meet the specific needs of an individual customer rather than the same "cookie cutter" solution for everyone. Effective implementation will be challenging for the company, however. In particular, Principal will need to recruit, hire, and train representatives who can—as the ad promises—"analyze your current situation and arrive at smart business solutions."

Implementation comprises three activities:

- *Organizing the marketing effort.* The relationship between marketing and the other functions of the firm must be defined. Once a company has developed its strategic marketing plan, an early activity is to organize the people within the marketing department who will implement it.

- *Staffing the organization.* For plans to produce the intended results, a company or a nonbusiness concern needs skilled, dedicated employees to carry them out well. Thus selection of people is all-important, whatever the type of organization. A college coach's success depends greatly on his or her ability to recruit the right players. According to one article, the most common reason for failure among top executives is not putting the right people in the right jobs. Thus a CEO who intends to be successful should adopt the motto, "People first, strategy second."[4] Likewise, a sales manager's success depends in great measure on the people who are selected for selling positions.

- *Directing the execution of marketing plans.* In this third phase of implementation, revenues are generated by carrying out the firm's strategies and tactics. To do so, management needs to oversee the work of the people who have been selected and organized as the marketing team. Success in this phase depends to a large extent on four important aspects of managing employees—delegation, coordination, motivation, and communication.

Detailed discussion of staffing and directing an organization can be found in management textbooks. However, in this text, it is appropriate to consider how organizational structures are used to implement marketing programs.

Organizing for Implementation

Organizational structures receive considerable attention because executives in both American and foreign companies recognize that yesterday's arrangements may hinder operations in today's dynamic environment.[5] Traditional structures isolate different business functions and have many managerial layers between customers and decision makers. That runs counter to satisfying customers profitably, which requires talking with and listening to customers. Teamwork across business functions such as marketing and production is also essential.

AN ETHICAL DILEMMA?

A big question for numerous companies is how best to implement a marketing effort aimed at college students, who typically are very busy and are besieged by various forms of communication. A General Motors manager has one answer, "There's no better way to reach this market than through their peers."

Thus some firms involve students in devising *and* carrying out marketing programs, often paying them for doing so. In some cases, the students also receive college credit for their endeavors.

Examples of recent on-campus student-focused sales programs follow:

• At a major state university, marketing students designed and carried out a promotion to put the spotlight on Honda's Element model that is aimed at younger drivers.

• A growing number of companies (such as Citigroup Credit Services) "sponsor" classes, providing funds for class projects in which students develop and implement marketing activities for a firm's products.

Is it ethical or unethical for businesses to pay students and/or to sponsor classes with the intention of selling or at least promoting the companies' goods and services to the college market? Do you see any ethical problems in university departments receiving some compensation in conjunction with this type of project?

Sources: Teresa F. Lindeman, "Citigroup, Others Encourage College Students to Pitch Peers, Offer Free Pizza," *Knight Ridder Tribune Business News,* Apr. 20, 2004, no page given; Kate Fitzgerald, "Honda Goes to School with Ad Campaign," *Automotive News,* June 23, 2003, p. 24; and Cora Daniels, "If It's Marketing, Can It Also Be Education?" *Fortune,* Oct. 2, 2000, p. 274.

Kimberly-Clark, Intel, General Motors, Siemens (the huge German electronics concern), and Donna Karan International (the clothing maker) are among many firms that have made significant organizational changes. In some cases, traditional vertical structures are being replaced by horizontal organizations.[6] Several specific trends are noteworthy:

www.enterprise.com/about

www.ritzcarlton.com

• *Fewer organizational levels.* The intent is to aid communication among executives who develop strategic plans, the employees who have continuing contact with the market, and customers.

• *Employee empowerment.* Granting more authority to middle-level executives in decentralized locations can stimulate innovation and generate faster responses to market shifts. And empowering customer-contact personnel can boost both customer satisfaction and repeat business. With that in mind, Enterprise Rent-A-Car allows an employee to take special actions to satisfy a customer. Likewise, any staff member at a Ritz-Carlton hotel is empowered to spend up to $2,000 on a solution to a customer's problem.[7]

• *Cross-functional teams.* By having personnel from various departments work on a project, not only are barriers among functions broken down but the best combination of expertise and experience is dedicated to an assignment. Among the believers is a vice president of Nestlé USA, who stated, "Cross-functional teams in almost every instance will come up with a better solution than an individual." This type of team is strongly recommended for developing new products, particularly in high-technology industries.[8]

Revising an organizational structure is challenging, because employees must give up long-standing, comfortable arrangements. But the results often justify the effort. Modicon, a manufacturer of automation-control equipment that is now part of Schneider Electric, once considered product development strictly an engineering task. The company eventually decided to switch this important responsibility to a 15-person team representing marketing, manufacturing, and finance in addition to engineering. Under the revised arrangement, the time required to develop software packages was cut by two-thirds.[9]

Company-Wide Organization

In Chapter 1 we stated that one of the three components of the marketing concept is to coordinate all marketing activities. In product-oriented or sales-oriented firms, marketing activities are likely to be fragmented. The sales force is separate from advertising, and sales training may be under the human resources department. In a market-oriented enterprise, all marketing activities are coordinated under one executive, as shown in Figure 21.1. The marketing chief, who usually is a vice president, reports directly to the president, and is equivalent to top executives in finance, production, and other major functions.

Another aspect of organizational coordination is to establish effective working relationships between marketing and the other major functional areas. Marketing can help production, for example, by providing accurate sales forecasts. Production can return the favor by providing defect-free finished products precisely when needed to fill customers' orders. Marketing and finance specialists can work together to establish pricing and credit policies.

Sales Organization within a Marketing Department

The selling function within a marketing department may account for a significant share of resources, especially in large firms. Thus, a sales force frequently is specialized in some organizational fashion. The intent is to effectively implement the company's strategic marketing plan. Most often, the sales force is specialized in one of three ways—by geographic territory, product line, or customer type. Sometimes a hybrid form is created by combining the best features of two forms.

Geographic Specialization   Perhaps the most widely used method of specializing selling activities is on the basis of **geographic specialization.** Each sales person is assigned a specific territory in which to sell. Several sales people representing contiguous territories are placed under a district or regional sales manager. As shown in Figure 21.2A, these territorial supervisors report directly to the general sales manager.

FIGURE 21.1

**Company
Organization
Embracing the
Marketing Concept.**

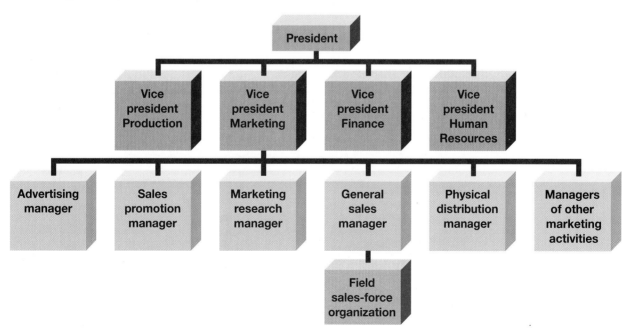

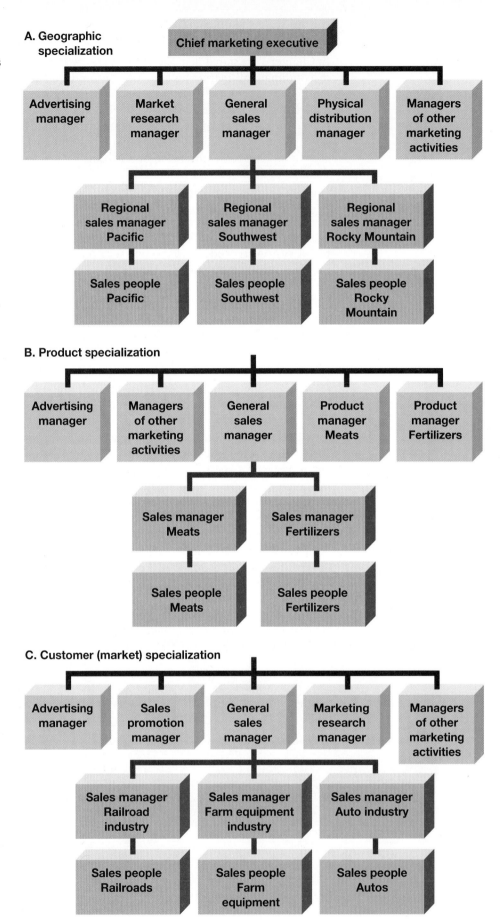

FIGURE 21.2

Major Forms of Sales Organization.

A. Geographic specialization

Chief marketing executive

- Advertising manager
- Market research manager
- General sales manager
- Physical distribution manager
- Managers of other marketing activities

- Regional sales manager Pacific
  - Sales people Pacific
- Regional sales manager Southwest
  - Sales people Southwest
- Regional sales manager Rocky Mountain
  - Sales people Rocky Mountain

B. Product specialization

- Advertising manager
- Managers of other marketing activities
- General sales manager
- Product manager Meats
- Product manager Fertilizers

- Sales manager Meats
  - Sales people Meats
- Sales manager Fertilizers
  - Sales people Fertilizers

C. Customer (market) specialization

- Advertising manager
- Sales promotion manager
- General sales manager
- Marketing research manager
- Managers of other marketing activities

- Sales manager Railroad industry
  - Sales people Railroads
- Sales manager Farm equipment industry
  - Sales people Farm equipment
- Sales manager Auto industry
  - Sales people Autos

A geographic organization is supposed to result in excellent implementation of sales strategies in each local market and strong coordination of the sales force. The underlying premise is that customers can be serviced quickly and thoroughly, and local sales reps can respond better to competitors' actions in a given territory.

As its major drawback, a geographic organization does not provide the product expertise or other specialized knowledge that some customers may want. To address that problem, the Kimberly-Clark Corp. decided to move away from a reliance on regions comprised of adjacent countries. The company switched to two divisions: developed markets such as the U.S. and Europe, and developing markets including various countries in Asia and Latin America. The rationale for the reorganization was that the two kinds of markets have distinct attributes. According to the company's CEO, the overriding issue in developing markets is how to devise and carry out innovative, yet cost-effective strategies. In contrast, a major issue in developed markets is sustaining good (and profitable) working relationships with huge retailers such as Carrefour and Wal-Mart.[10]

Product Specialization
Another basis for organizing a sales force is **product specialization,** as illustrated in Figure 21.2B. A company such as a meat packer may divide all of its products into two lines—meat products and fertilizers (made from the by-products of meat packing). One group of sales reps sells only meats and another group sells the fertilizers. Each group reports to its own product sales manager who, in turn, reports to the general sales manager.

This type of organization is especially well suited for companies that are marketing:

- Complex technical products, such as a variety of electronic products.
- Unrelated or dissimilar products, such as a mix of luggage, folding tables and chairs, and toy building blocks.
- Thousands of items, such as hardware.

The main advantage of a product-focused sales organization is the attention each line can get from its sales force. A drawback is that more than one sales rep from a company may call on the same customer. This duplication not only is costly but also may irritate customers. In 2000, FedEx Corp. converted to a unified sales force for its airfreight and ground-delivery services. The move was made to reduce duplication and to facilitate cross-selling of the distinct services. Several years after switching its sales force to customer specialization, the Eastman Kodak Co. adopted a product-focused arrangement for the entire company. The intent was to give executives more flexibility in managing product groups.[11]

Customer Specialization
In recent years, many companies have divided their sales departments on the basis of **customer specialization.** In this arrangement, customers are grouped by type of industry or by channel of distribution. An oil company may categorize its markets by industry, such as railroads, auto manufacturers, and farm-equipment producers, as shown in Figure 21.2C. A firm that specializes its sales operations by channel of distribution may have one sales force selling to wholesalers and another dealing directly with large retailers.

Companies that fully implement the marketing concept turn to the customer-focused type of organization. This arrangement is consistent with the customer-oriented philosophy that underlies the marketing concept. That is, the organizational emphasis is on markets and customers rather than on products. One author maintains that an organization must be structured around customer groups if integrated marketing communications is to be effective.[12]

A variation of customer specialization is the **major accounts organization.** Companies adopt this structure in order to deal with large, important customers. A major accounts organization usually involves team selling, a concept introduced in Chapter 18. Under this arrangement, a selling team—consisting perhaps of a sales rep, a technical specialist, a financial executive, and a manufacturing liaison—negotiates with a buying team from a customer's organization. Procter & Gamble, for example, established a series of selling teams, each specializing in a broad category (such as cleaning products) to better service key accounts, including Wal-Mart. A P&G sales team, now up to 300 people, has its office near Wal-Mart's headquarters in Bentonville, Arkansas.[13]

Postsale Follow-Through

It is shortsighted to think that marketing ends when a sale is made. In line with the marketing concept, a firm should be committed to ensuring that customers are fully satisfied. If that is accomplished, organizational objectives (including the desired level of profits) probably will be achieved. In addition, it's likely that loyal customers will be created, thereby contributing to the future vitality of the company.

Some specific elements of a marketing program are implemented largely after a sale is made. We will now consider important aspects of warranties and other desired postsale services.

Warranties

The purpose of a **warranty,** which we use interchangeably with *guarantee,* is to assure buyers they will be compensated if the product does not perform up to reasonable expectations. American companies decide on the terms and length of their product warranties. In contrast, the countries comprising the European Union agreed jointly that the length of guarantees must be at least two years. EU members that stipulate longer mandatory lengths (six years in the United Kingdom, for example) can keep such requirements.[14]

Years ago, courts seemed to recognize only an **express warranty,** which is one stated in written or spoken words. Usually this form of reassurance was quite limited in its coverage and seemed mainly to protect the seller from buyers' claims. As a result, the following caution was appropriate: "Caveat emptor," which means "Let the buyer beware."

But times change. Numerous complaints led to a governmental effort to protect consumers in many areas, including product warranties. Courts and government agencies have broadened the scope of warranty coverage by recognizing **implied warranty.** This means a warranty was *intended,* although not actually stated, by the

An automaker can differentiate its particular brand in various ways—through styling and/or fuel economy, for example. In 1999, seeking a differential advantage, Hyundai announced the longest warranty in the auto industry. The firm's "bumper-to-bumper" warranty was extended two years or 24,000 miles beyond the norm. Following the change, Hyundai's sales rose substantially. A related issue is the cost associated with the more generous warranty.

www.hyundaiusa.com/
global/warranty.asp

seller. Furthermore, producers are being held responsible, even when the sales contract is between a retailer and a consumer. Now the caution is: "Caveat venditor," or "Let the seller beware."

Product Liability   Passage of the Consumer Product Safety Act in 1972 reflected a changed attitude regarding product liability and injurious products. This federal legislation created the Consumer Product Safety Commission (CPSC), which has the authority to mandate safety standards for many consumer products not covered by separate laws or other agencies. The CPSC publishes information regarding injurious products, naming brands and producers. It can ban the distribution of these products without a court hearing. In turn, offending companies and the individuals leading them may face criminal, not just civil, charges. For example, a $4 million penalty was levied against Graco Children's Products for not notifying the CPSC that millions of units of its products had defects that had caused hundreds of injuries. The most common incidents were children falling out of a Graco high chair, stroller, or carrier. Hamilton Beach/Proctor-Silex Inc. was fined $1.2 million for unreported problems with its countertop appliances such as toasters.[15]

Product liability is a legal action asserting that an illness, accident, or death resulted from the named product because it was harmful, faulty, or inadequately labeled. Basically, liability results from one or more of three problems: a flaw in product design, a defect in production, or a deficiency in warning the customer about proper use and potentially harmful misuse of the product.[16]

In the past 25 years, some product-liability claims involved entire categories of *goods*, including asbestos insulation and breast implants. Other cases focused on specific brands of toys, tampons, pharmaceuticals, birth-control devices, tires, automobiles, acne medication, and chain saws, among others. For instance, claims were brought against the makers of the Ford Explorer sport-utility vehicle and Firestone tires, alleging liability in numerous rollover accidents. Claims have also been filed against firms offering *services* such as auto repairs and weight loss programs. According to critics, some product-liability suits are groundless or lack compelling evidence. For example, a law professor stated recently, "Asbestos litigation today is, for the most part, a massively fraudulent enterprise."[17]

In many product-liability cases, juries have granted enormous settlements to the plaintiffs—sometimes tens *or hundreds* of millions of dollars. Significant recent cases have involved the tobacco industry, with some lawsuits going in favor of the tobacco companies and others ending with awards to the plaintiffs. Cigarette makers were concerned about potentially catastrophic judgments from lawsuits filed on behalf of a large group of harmed smokers. Thus they accepted marketing restrictions and made huge special payments to the government in exchange for some limits on

Since beginning operations in 1973, the mission of the Consumer Product Safety Commission (CPSC) has been to keep people safe by reducing the risk of injuries and death associated with consumer products. The CPSC's jurisdiction covers more than 15,000 kinds of items. Other categories, such as alcoholic beverages and automobiles, fall under the purview of different federal agencies. Besides issuing recalls of unsafe products, the CPSC works with industries on voluntary safety standards and communicates with consumers about product-safety issues.

www.cpsc.gov

product-liability lawsuits. In 1998, tobacco companies agreed to pay a total of over $200 *billion* to the states over 25 years. In return, the industry received protection at the state level. By mid-2005, no similar arrangement had materialized at the federal level, although the tobacco industry and the government were discussing a much smaller settlement.[18]

Thousands of product-liability claims are filed every year in the U.S. Thus this issue is of great consequence to companies because of the financial risk as well as the adverse publicity connected with damage claims. It has proven to be difficult to write a federal law that (1) curbs lawsuits related to allegedly defective products and (2) is considered fair and acceptable by groups on both sides of the issue. Recently, Congress enacted a law that will require large class-action lawsuits to be tried in a federal court, which may curb product-liability lawsuits being filed in some state venues that have been "plaintiff friendly" in past verdicts.[19]

Lawsuits charging harm from defective products occur around the world. To mention just two examples, a group of British consumers sued three drug companies over adverse side effects from oral contraceptives, and Japanese consumers sought restitution from a milk products company because they fell ill after consuming a tainted product. In 2002, South Korea enacted product-liability legislation, joining more than 30 other major countries with such laws. Product-liability problems are likely to increase for companies marketing in western Europe. European laws now provide compensation to consumers in cases of demonstrated bodily injury or property damage from products, even when there has been no negligence on the part of the seller.[20]

To ward off product-liability claims, many manufacturers place expanded labels on their goods, telling consumers to not misuse the product and informing them of almost every conceivable danger associated with using it. Such **warning labels** go so far as to state: "Shin pads cannot protect any part of the body they do not cover." Or: "Do not iron clothes while on body." And, believe it or not, on a chain saw: "Do not attempt to stop chain with hands or genitals." Producers hope such blatant, seemingly obvious warnings protect them against charges that they did not properly inform consumers about a product's use, misuse, and potential dangers.[21]

Benefits versus Costs Deficient warranties and warning labels that do not protect companies from product-liability claims can be extremely expensive. In another sense, warranties can be very costly if numerous buyers must be compensated when a product fails or is unsatisfactory. Perhaps for that reason, some companies with powerful brands, including Dell Computer, Sony, and DaimlerChrysler have shortened the length of their warranties.[22]

Rather than considering only costs, some firms see marketing benefits in warranties. Many sellers, for example, promote their warranties in order to stimulate first-time *and* repeat purchases by reducing consumers' risks. With that in mind, more companies are making their warranties understandable and comprehensive— and, therefore, customer-friendly. Further, "underdog" firms, such as computer maker Atlas Micro, are seeking an advantage by offering longer warranties. The Korean manufacturer Hyundai offers a 10-year or 100,000–mile (whichever comes first) warranty on its cars' engines and transmissions and 5-year, 60,000-mile coverage on the rest of the vehicles.[23]

It is common practice among manufacturers, retailers, and especially service firms (given the intangible nature of services) to offer a full refund of the purchase price to a dissatisfied buyer. A number of hotel chains, for example, give cash, discounts, or even a free night's stay to any customer who reports a problem. In another field, Harry and David, which sells fresh fruit through catalogs and now online, offers the following assurance: "We guarantee your complete satisfaction. If you are not satisfied with this product, just let us know and we'll make it right with either an appropriate replacement or a refund." Occasionally, a customer may abuse a full-

www.harryanddavid.com

Which postsale services can be outsourced, perhaps to foreign firms?

Many enterprises contract with firms in other countries to carry out business functions. For example, Salton, Inc. relies on Chinese firms to manufacture its products, including George Foreman grills. Pharmaceutical makers such as Eli Lilly work with biotechnology organizations in Asia in an effort to reduce the cost of developing new drugs.

The outsourcing trend is also evident in marketing. A growing number of companies pay foreign firms to design and/or test products. For instance, Philips, Motorola, and Dell use creative agencies in Asia to design cell phones, flat-panel TVs, and digital cameras. As another example, at a facility in Hong Kong, technicians employed by Swiss-owned SGS test the fire resistance of products such as pajamas and Halloween masks.

The most frequently outsourced marketing activity is probably customer service. A prerequisite for an offshore "call center," a facility that receives and responds to inquiries from customers, is English-language proficiency. Thus India is often chosen as the site of a call center. Sometimes the facility is run by the U.S. firm, employing local workers, or it may be operated by an Indian company. Call centers are also arising in Caribbean countries. The advantages of this area are familiarity with American culture (partly from hosting tourists) and geographic proximity, which facilitates visits from executives in U.S.–based headquarters.

Some companies worry that investors may think that reliance on outsourcing means a lack of in-house capabilities in critical functions. Or, with or without legitimate reason, customers may resent foreign-made products or dealing with a company representative on the other side of the globe. In fact, a General Electric division retreated from Indian call centers when surveys revealed that health-care professionals "prefer to work with local, U.S.–based customer services."

A powerful driver of outsourcing is lower costs. For example, call-center workers in developing countries earn in the range of $3,000 to $8,000 annually compared to about $27,000 in the U.S. Outsourcing of marketing tasks such as customer service is likely to continue so long as companies judge that the benefits outweigh the costs.

Sources: Jay Solomon and Kathryn Kranhold, "Western Exposure: In India's Outsourcing Boom, GE Played a Starring Role," *The Wall Street Journal*, Mar. 23, 2005, pp. A1+; "Dell Inc.," *The Wall Street Journal*, Mar. 22, 2005, p. 1; Pete Engardio and Bruce Einhorn, "Outsourcing Innovation," *Business-Week*, Mar. 21, 2005, pp. 94+; Doreen Hemlock, "Caribbean Call Centers Booming," *South Florida Sun-Sentinel*, Mar. 6, 2005, p. 1E; and Matt Pottinger, "Outsourcing Safety Tests," *The Wall Street Journal*, Nov. 26, 2004, p. B1, B3.

refund guarantee (by exaggerating the magnitude of a problem with a hotel room, for example), but the benefits in terms of avoiding customer dissatisfaction and building customer loyalty are compelling.[24]

Customer-friendly warranties are absolutely vital in the online environment. According to one study, offering a money-back guarantee is the biggest step an Internet merchant can take in order to reduce the risk that consumers associate with online shopping.[25]

Other Postsale Services

www.kone.com/en

Many companies must provide **postsale service,** notably maintenance and repairs, to fulfill the terms of their warranties. Other firms offer postsale services to fully satisfy their customers or even to gain a differential advantage over competitors. Some businesses use postsale services to augment their revenues. For instance, Otis and KONE Corp., both of which sell elevators, rely on service contracts for a portion of their revenues *and* profits.

With more complex products, increasingly demanding and vocal consumers, and now the Internet environment, postsale service has become essential. There are distinctive challenges in attaining both efficiency and effectiveness when providing such services. To illustrate, brief profiles of several postsale activities follow.

Merchandise Returns The best approach is to minimize the need for returns by selling a satisfying product to a customer and, in situations where delivery is involved, getting the shipment to its destination on time. Even under the best of circumstances, however, some customers want or need to return their purchases. According to one estimate, 4% to 6% of all items purchased at the retail level are returned. Other recent research found that easy return or exchange of merchandise was the third most important consideration for online shoppers of luxury goods, such as expensive shoes and watches.[26]

Recognizing the importance and the cost of returns, a firm should consider how stringent or generous its conditions for accepting merchandise returns will be. Stringent conditions may curtail costs but are unlikely to gain favor with customers; the opposite is true for generous conditions. Looking for ways to improve their financial positions, a number of well-known retail firms have tightened their return policies. Target, for instance, announced that a purchase receipt must accompany any return request and that a "restocking fee" will be charged on some products in the electronics area. Other retailers, ranging from Staples to Limited Express, are using software to monitor customers' return patterns in order to minimize costly excesses and fraudulent refunds.[27]

Merchants that sell over the Internet and also operate retail stores or wholesale branches must decide whether or not to accept returns at the physical outlets. If a firm prohibits its bricks-and-mortar outlets from accepting returns of online purchases, it forfeits a built-in advantage it has over strictly online competitors. Thus the trend among "bricks-and-clicks" middlemen is to accept returns at their outlets.

Online-only companies are discovering that making the return process convenient for customers is a special challenge. Typically, customers are asked to send the returns to a warehouse or office operated by the company or to a separate business that handles fulfillment of orders for the online firm. On the basis of its studies, a research agency recommended that one of the top three ways of improving online service is to establish a simple return process. As with many matters, that's easier said than done.[28]

Maintenance and Repairs A recurring concern is that manufacturers and retailers do not provide adequate maintenance and repair services for the products they sell. A manufacturer can transfer the primary responsibility for such services to middlemen, compensate them for their efforts, and possibly even train their technicians and customer-contact staff members. This approach is evident in the automobile and personal computer industries. Or a manufacturer can establish regional factory service centers, staff them with well-trained technicians, and strive to make

Many, probably most, online marketers now realize that the quality of customer service is at least as important as website design, product assortment, and competitive prices in attracting and then keeping buyers. Further, many online customers strongly prefer to interact with an actual person. Companies that sell on the Internet can provide this type of customer service on their own or they can outsource this task to a vendor such as LivePerson. Timpani is LivePerson's "online customer sales and support" offering.

www.liveperson.com

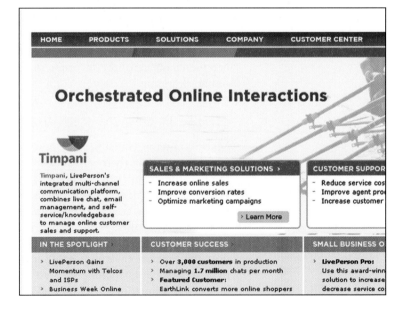

MARKETING IN THE INFORMATION ECONOMY

Can online customer service be personal—and pleasing?

Recognized as an important factor in closing sales and pleasing shoppers after a transaction is made, customer service in cyberspace is receiving more and more attention. Consequently, many, probably most, organizations are seeking the optimal way of dealing with questions and comments from prospects who are considering a purchase as well as customers who are unhappy for some reason. As in other business endeavors, an optimum would be the most efficient way of achieving a level of effectiveness that is consistent with the company's goals.

Numerous, perhaps most, online enterprises encourage input via e-mail and/or via a toll-free telephone line. A drawback of e-mail, besides any delayed response, is the lack of actual human interaction. As far back as 1999 (which is a long time ago given the rapid development of the Internet), research indicated that 90% of online customers want to interact with a real person—now.

A relatively new technology allows real-time electronic dialogue between an online visitor and a firm's customer service agent. The consumer initiates the "chat," typically through an icon on the website that has a label such as "Live Help." Then one or more e-mail iterations ensue. The online agent can even synchronize screens with the customer so they are looking at the same images or information. Typically, an agent is expected to chat with several customers at the same time. Of course, effectiveness and customer satisfaction may drop as a result of this attempt at boosting efficiency.

More and more enterprises are outsourcing the task of providing online, real-time personal assistance to firms such as LivePerson, Inc. Neiman Marcus Group's online retail division and the Intuit software company are among LivePerson's clients. A live chat allows a firm to provide a measure of personal service to online shoppers and customers. At the same time, this approach affords the opportunity to collect a variety of useful data regarding consumers' interests (about product features, for example) and concerns (about matters such as navigating around the website).

Another new technology has the capability of combining a live chat and a toll-free telephone call. Using voice-over-IP (the "IP" stands for Internet protocol), an online shopper whose computer has a built-in microphone clicks an icon to initiate a telephone call to a customer service rep. The same telephone line is used for Internet access and the call. The audio quality of voice-over-IP is still being refined so as to be suitable for widespread usage—and easy communication between a customer and a customer service rep.

Effective realtime customer service will be essential for *online* firms if they are to establish and maintain a differential advantage over traditional businesses *and* their online competitors. Providing pleasing postsale service via the Internet is also increasingly important for firms that operate primarily in physical space. Many customers expect to go online to obtain service ranging from technical information about products to guidance regarding merchandise returns or repairs. Technology-aided service is more efficient than the old-fashioned method, namely a telephone conversation between a customer and a company employee. It's estimated that a customer-service phone call costs $6 to $7 compared to about $2 for an online chat. Thus, like it or not, online, real-time customer service—with or without a personal element—is likely to become prevalent.

Sources: Erika D. Smith, "Online Chat Could Help to Keep Customers Smiling," *St. Louis Post-Dispatch,* June 28, 2004, p. E1; Bruce Horovitz, "Whatever Happened to Customer Service?" *USA Today,* Sept. 26–28, 2003, pp. 1A, 2A; Mary Ellen Podmolik, "Companies Chatting Up Customers," *Crain's Chicago Business,* Nov. 18, 2002, p. SR4; Peter Fuller, "A Two-Way Conversation," *Brandweek,* Feb. 25, 2002, p. 26; "Online Customer Service: Guiding Consumers through the Maze," *Financial Service ONLINE,* November 1999, pp. 24–27+; and Bill Meyers, "Service with an E-Smile," *USA Today,* Oct. 12, 1999, pp. 1B, 2B.

maintenance and repairs a profit-generating activity. This approach is found in the appliance industry. Or service or at least the first point of contact can be provided centrally. To process requests for various forms of customer service, Otis established a center that handles over 1.7 million calls a year, responding to situations ranging from a broken escalator to people trapped in an elevator.[29]

Some manufacturers of costly computers, office machines, and medical diagnostic equipment have developed "smart" products. With built-in sensors and microcomputers, such products diagnose themselves and/or allow a technician to conduct a diagnosis from a distance by means of either wired or wireless telecommunications.

www.otis.com

These innovative machine-to-machine (M2M) technologies expedite repairs and, by so doing, cut aggravating "downtime" for valuable products. Further, to the extent that labor costs associated with repairs are reduced, the manufacturer's profit margin on service contracts is improved.[30]

Complaint Handling The most common gripes among consumers, as determined by one study, are deficient product quality, deceptive sales methods, and poor repair work. Based on a compilation of over 400,000 complaints, the industries that cause headaches for the largest numbers of consumers are home improvements, auto sales, auto repairs, and credit. Consumers become particularly aggravated if they cannot voice their complaints and get their problems solved. According to research, "A majority of consumers are dissatisfied with the way their complaints are resolved." Ignored or mishandled complaints can have dire consequences with respect to lost business and/or negative word-of-mouth communication.[31]

Prompt, effective handling of complaints can increase or, if necessary, restore a customer's confidence in a firm, irrespective of whether it operates in physical space or cyberspace. Furthermore, "effective complaint handling can have a dramatic impact on customer retention rates, deflect the spread of damaging word of mouth, and improve bottomline performance." Perhaps with that in mind, a producer typically provides customers with a toll-free telephone number, an e-mail address for its customer service department, and ensures that incoming messages are handled by well trained, customer-oriented personnel. Research indicates that about 85% of phoned-in complaints are satisfied in a single call; less than 35% of complaints conveyed by e-mail or another electronic means are resolved so readily.[32]

Postsale follow-through, like more visible elements of the marketing mix, can be either a differential advantage or a disadvantage. Thus the various forms of follow-through certainly should be on the list of matters that managers monitor constantly.

Evaluating Marketing Performance

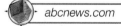

Soon after a firm's plans have been set in operation, the process of evaluation should begin. Without evaluation, management cannot tell whether a plan is working or which factors are contributing to its success or failure. Evaluation logically follows planning and implementation. A circular relationship exists, as illustrated in Figure 21.3. Plans are made, they are put into action, the results of those actions are evaluated, and new plans are prepared on the basis of this evaluation. To illustrate, the Walt Disney Co. launched an Internet portal, Go.com. However, after two years, the giant entertainment firm abandoned the effort because it could not draw viewers from other portals such as Yahoo. Instead, Disney refocused its Internet endeavors on the websites of its core brands, such as ABC News and ESPN along with the Disney online store.[33]

Previously we discussed evaluation as it relates to individual parts of a marketing program—the product-planning process, the performance of the sales force, and the effectiveness of the advertising program, for instance. Now let's look at the evaluation of the *total marketing effort*.

The Marketing Audit

A marketing audit is an essential element in a thorough evaluation. An audit implies an assessment of some activity, such as an enterprise's finances. Thus a **marketing audit** is a comprehensive review and evaluation of the marketing function in an organization—its environment, philosophy, goals, strategies, organizational structure, human and financial resources, and performance.[34]

FIGURE 21.3

The Circular Relationship among Management Tasks.

As suggested by Figure 21.3, the results of any evaluation—including a marketing audit—represent vital input to an organization's planning. In advocating the value of marketing audits in the banking industry, one writer stressed, "Simply stated, a [strategic] marketing plan should only be written after the completion of an intensive, objective marketing audit."[35]

A complete marketing audit is an extensive, difficult project. That's why it is conducted infrequently, perhaps every several years. However, a company should not delay a marketing audit until a major crisis arises.

The rewards of a marketing audit can justify the effort. By reviewing its strategies, the firm is likely to keep abreast of its changing business environment. Management can identify problem areas in marketing. The audit can spot, for instance, lack of coordination in the marketing program, outdated strategies, or unrealistic goals. Successes can also be analyzed, so the company can capitalize on its strong points. Furthermore, an audit should anticipate future situations. It is intended for "prognosis as well as diagnosis. . . . It is the practice of preventive as well as curative marketing medicine."[36]

Misdirected Marketing Effort

One benefit of evaluation is that it helps correct **misdirected** (or misplaced) **marketing effort.**

The 80–20 Principle
In most firms, a large proportion of the total orders, customers, territories, or products accounts for only a small share of total performance. Conversely, a small proportion produces a large share of most performance outcomes. This relationship has been characterized as the **80–20 principle.** That is, the large majority (say, 80%) of the orders, customers, territories, or products contribute only a small fraction (say, 20%) of sales or profit. One professor said, rather harshly, that customers in this group "nag you, call you, and don't add much revenue."[37] On the other hand, a relatively few of the selling units account for the large majority of the volume or profit.

The 80–20 figure is used to highlight the misplacement of marketing effort. In reality, of course, the percentage split varies from one situation to another. To give a couple of hypothetical examples, just 5% of customers might provide 90% of an organization's sales, or 70% of a service firm's clientele might lodge just 3% of all complaints (which means, of course, that the other 30% submit the remaining 97%).

The basic reason for the 80–20 or similar split is that almost every marketing program includes misdirected effort. Marketing endeavors and costs are proportional to the *numbers* of territories, customers, or products, rather than to their actual sales volume or profit. For example, approximately the same order-filling, billing, and delivery expenses are involved whether a $500 suit *or* a $25 necktie is sold in a Dillard's department store. A manufacturer such as Xerox may assign one sales person to each territory. Yet usually there are differences in the actual sales volume and profit among the territories. In each example, the marketing expense is not in line with the actual return.

Reasons for Misdirected Effort
Frequently, executives cannot uncover misdirected effort because they lack sufficient information. The **iceberg principle** is an analogy that illustrates this situation. Only the small tip of an iceberg is visible above the water's surface, and the huge submerged part represents the hidden danger. The figures representing total sales or total costs on an operating statement are like an iceberg tip. The detailed figures representing sales, costs, and other performance measures for each territory or product correspond to the dangerous submerged part.

Total sales or cost figures are too general to be really useful in evaluation; in fact, they often are misleading. A company's overall sales and profit figures may be satisfactory. But when these totals are subdivided by pertinent factors such as geographic territories, products, or time periods, serious weaknesses often are discovered. A manufacturer of audio equipment showed an overall increase of 12% in sales and 9% in net profit on one product line in one year. But in looking below the "tip of the iceberg," executives found that the sales change within territories ranged from an increase of 19% to a decrease of 3%. Profit rose as much as 14% in some territories, but was down 20% in one.

A more basic cause of misplaced marketing effort is that executives must make decisions based on inadequate knowledge of the exact nature of costs. Too often, management lacks useful information about (1) the disproportionate dispersion of marketing effort, (2) reliable standards for determining what should be spent on marketing, and (3) the results that should be expected from these expenditures.

As an illustration, a company may spend $2.5 million more on advertising this year than last year. But management ordinarily cannot state how much sales or profit should rise as a result of the added expenditures. Also, the executives do not know what would have happened if they had spent the same amount on (1) new-product development, (2) sales incentives for middlemen, or (3) some other aspect of the marketing program.

The Evaluation Process

Irrespective of whether a complete marketing audit or only an appraisal of individual components of the marketing program is being carried out, the evaluation process involves three steps:

1. Find out *what* happened. Compile the facts, compare results with goals and budgets to determine where they differ.
2. Find out *why* it happened. Determine, to the extent possible, which specific factors in the marketing program caused the results.
3. Decide *what to do* about it. Plan the next period's program so as to improve on unsatisfactory performance and capitalize on the aspects that worked out well.

To evaluate a total marketing program, we need to analyze results. Two tools are available to do this—sales volume analysis and marketing cost analysis. We'll discuss both tools using the Great Midwest Company ("the other GM")—a firm that markets office furniture. The company's 14-state market is divided into four sales districts, each with over 60 sales people, a district sales manager, and one or two assistants. The firm sells to office equipment wholesalers and directly to large business users. GM's product mix is divided into four groups—desks, chairs, filing equipment, and office accessories (wastebaskets and desk sets, for example). During the past 10 years, GM shut down its own manufacturing plants and now contracts with other firms to make the products that carry GM's brands.

Analyses of Sales Volume and Market Share

Management should analyze its sales volume in total and by relevant subdivisions such as geographic territories and product lines. The sales figures also should be examined against company goals. But that's not enough. A firm needs to measure its sales against the entire industry in which it competes. Each of these methods is described now.

Sales Volume Analysis

We start with an analysis of Great Midwest's total sales, as shown in Table 21.1. A **sales volume analysis** is a detailed study of the *net sales* section of a company's profit and loss statement (operating statement). Annual sales doubled from $180 million to $360 million during the 10-year period ending with fiscal year 2005. Furthermore, sales increased each year, with the exception of 2002. In most years, sales goals were met or surpassed. Thus far in our analysis, the company's situation is encouraging.

A study of total sales volume alone is usually insufficient and may even be misleading. Remember the analogy of an iceberg! To learn what is going on in the "submerged" parts of a market, we need to analyze sales volume by other relevant dimensions, such as territories.

Table 21.2 is a summary of the goals and actual results in Great Midwest's four districts. A key measurement is the *performance index* for each district—that is, actual sales divided by sales goal. An index of 100 means that the district did exactly what was expected. From the table we see that Great Lakes and Heartland did better than expected, and Delta surpassed its goal by a wide margin, but High Plains was quite a disappointment.

So far in our evaluation, we know a little about *what* happened in GM's districts. Now management has to figure out *why* it happened and *what should be done* about it. These are the difficult steps in evaluation. In the High Plains district, the problem may lie in some aspect of the marketing program, or competition may be especially strong in that district. If possible, GM's executives also should identify the reasons for Delta's success, and whether this information can be used to benefit other districts.

This brief examination of two aspects of sales volume analysis shows how this evaluation tool can be used. However, for a more useful evaluation, GM's management should dig deeper. They should analyze their sales volume by individual territories within districts and by product lines. Then they should carry their territorial analysis further by examining volume by product line and customer group *within* each territory. For instance, even though Delta did well overall, the iceberg notion may apply here. Despite the fine *total* performance in this district, there may be hidden weaknesses in an individual product line or territory.

| TABLE 21.1 | **Annual Sales Volume of Great Midwest Company, Industry Volume, and Company's Share in 14-State Market** | | |

Year	Company Volume (in millions of dollars)	Industry Volume in Company's Market (in millions of dollars)	Company's Percentage Share of Market
1996	180	3,600	5.0
1997	218	4,500	4.8
1998	225	4,650	4.8
1999	245	5,100	4.8
2000	280	6,000	4.7
2001	317	7,050	4.5
2002	304	6,660	4.6
2003	331	7,650	4.3
2004	347	8,250	4.2
2005	360	9,000	4.0

TABLE
21.2

District Sales Volume in Great Midwest Company, 2005

District	Sales Goals (in millions of dollars)	Actual Sales (in millions of dollars)	Performance Index (actual ÷ goal)	Dollar Variation (in millions)
Delta	$110	$125	114	+17
Great Lakes	93	96	103	+ 6
Heartland	76	77	101	+ 1
High Plains	86	62	72	−24
Total	$365	$360		

Market-Share Analysis

Comparing a company's sales results with its goals is a useful evaluation, but it does not indicate how a company is doing relative to competitors. A **market-share analysis** compares a company's sales with the industry's revenues. A company's share of the market should be analyzed in total, as well as by product line and market segment.

Probably the major obstacle in market-share analysis is obtaining industry sales information in total and in sufficient detail. Trade associations and government agencies are possible sources for sales volume statistics in many industries.

The Great Midwest Company situation illustrates the value of market-share analysis. Recall from Table 21.1 that GM's total sales doubled over a 10-year period, with annual increases in nine of those years. But, during this span, the annual sales for all competing firms in this geographic area increased from $3.6 billion to $9 billion (a 150% increase). Thus the company's market share actually *declined* from 5% to 4%. Although GM's annual sales increased 100%, its market share declined 20%.

The next step is to determine *why* Great Midwest's market position shrank. The number of possible causes is quite large, and this is what makes management's task so difficult. A weakness in almost any aspect of GM's product line, distribution arrangements, pricing structure, or promotional program may have contributed to the loss of market share. Or the culprit might have been competition. There may be new competitors in the market that were attracted by the rapid growth rates. Or competitors' marketing programs may be more effective than Great Midwest's.

Marketing Cost Analysis

An analysis of sales volume is helpful in evaluating a company's marketing effort. However, management needs to proceed further and assess costs to determine the relative profitability of its territories and product lines. In the words of one researcher, "As corporate profits turn down and stocks take a plunge, leading companies are looking at marketing cost analysis to lift their bottom lines [profits]." If marketers' expenditures are not worthwhile, their budgets may be reduced; in fact, they should be reduced.[38]

A **marketing cost analysis** is a detailed study of the *operating expenses* section of a company's profit and loss statement. As part of this analysis, management should examine any variations between budgeted and actual costs.

Types of Marketing Cost Analysis

A company's marketing costs may be analyzed:

- As they appear in its ledger accounts and profit and loss statement.
- After they are grouped into activity classifications.
- After these activity costs have been allocated to territories or products.

Analysis of Ledger Expenses The simplest, least expensive approach is a study of the *object of expenditure* costs as they appear in the profit and loss statement. These figures come from the company's accounting ledger records. The simplified operating statement for the Great Midwest Company on the left side of Table 21.3 is the model we will use in this discussion.

The procedure is to analyze each cost item, such as salaries and media space, in detail. We can compare this period's total with the totals for corresponding periods in the past, and observe the trends. In addition, we can examine actual costs against budgeted amounts. We should also compute each expense as a percentage of net sales. Then we should compare these expense ratios with industry figures, which are often available through trade associations.

Analysis of Activity Costs Total costs should be allocated among the various marketing activities such as advertising or warehousing. Then management can analyze the cost of each activity.

This procedure entails identifying the major activities and then allocating each ledger expense among those activities. As indicated in the expense distribution sheet on the right side of Table 21.3, we have decided on five activity cost groups in the Great Midwest example. Some items, such as the cost of media space, can be apportioned entirely to one activity (advertising). Other expenses must be spread across several activities. So management must decide on a reasonable basis for allocation among these activities. For example, property taxes may be assigned according to the proportion of total floor space occupied by each activity. Thus the warehouse

| TABLE 21.3 | **Profit and Loss Statement and Distribution of Natural Expenses to Activity Cost Groups, Great Midwest Company, 2005** |

Profit and Loss Statement (in $000)			Expense Distribution Sheet (in $000)				
Net sales		$360,000	**Activity (Functional) Cost Groups**				
Cost of goods sold		−234,000					
Gross margin		126,000	Personal Selling	Advertising/ Promotion	Warehousing and Shipping	Order Processing	Marketing Administration
Operating expenses:							
Salaries and commissions	$41,680		→ $27,060	$ 1,920	$ 4,200	$ 2,800	$ 5,700
Travel and entertainment	14,400		→ 10,400				4,000
Media space	11,760		→	11,760			
Supplies and services	4,400		→ 600	350	2,400	700	350
Property taxes	1,300		→ 160	50	600	300	190
Freight out	35,000		→		35,000		
Total expenses		− $108,540	$38,220	$14,080	$42,200	$ 3,800	$ 10,240
Net profit		17,460					

accounts for 46% of the total square feet of floor space in the firm, so the warehousing and shipping activity is charged with $600,000, which is 46% of the property taxes.

An analysis of marketing costs gives executives more information than they can get from an analysis of ledger accounts alone. Also, an examination of activity expenses in total provides a starting point for management to evaluate costs by territories, products, or other marketing units.

Analysis of Activity Costs by Product or Market   The third and most beneficial type of marketing cost analysis is a study of the expenses and profitability of specific components of a product assortment or total market. This type of analysis breaks out a product assortment by lines or individual items or divides up a market by territories, customer groups, or order sizes.

By combining a sales volume analysis with a marketing cost study, an executive or a staff member can prepare an operating statement for each product or market segment. These statements can then be assessed to determine how individual products or segments affect the total marketing program. Cost analysis by product or market enables management to pinpoint trouble spots much more effectively than does an analysis of either ledger account expenses or activity costs.

The procedure for a cost analysis by product or market is similar to that used to scrutinize activity costs. The total cost of each activity (the right side of Table 21.3) is allocated on some basis to each product or market segment being studied. Let's consider an example of a cost analysis, by sales districts, for the Great Midwest Company, as shown in Tables 21.4 and 21.5.

First, for each of the five GM activities, we select a reasonable basis for assigning the cost of that activity among the four districts. These bases are shown in the top part of Table 21.4. Then we determine the number of allocation "units" that

TABLE 21.4

Allocation of Activity Costs to Sales Districts, Great Midwest Company, 2005

Activity	Personal Selling	Advertising/ Promotion	Warehousing and Shipping	Order Processing and Billing	Marketing Administration
			Allocation Basis		
Allocation basis	Direct expense per district	Number of ad pages	Number of orders shipped	Number of invoice lines	Equally among districts
Total activity cost	$38,200,000	$14,080,000	$42,200,000	$3,800,000	$10,240,000
Number of allocation units		704 pages	105,500 orders	1,266,667 lines	4 districts
Cost per allocation unit		$20,000	$400	$3	$2,560,000
			Allocation of Costs		
Delta district < units	—	216 pages	33,000 orders	460,000 lines	—
Delta district < cost	$10,730,000	$4,320,000	$13,200,000	$1,380,000	$2,560,000
Great Lakes district < units	—	152 pages	28,500 orders	330,000 lines	—
Great Lakes district < cost	$10,001,000	$3,040,000	$11,400,000	$990,000	$2,560,000
Heartland district < units	—	176 pages	23,000 orders	266,667 lines	—
Heartland district < cost	$8,911,000	$3,520,000	$9,200,000	$800,000	$2,560,000
High Plains district < units	—	160 pages	21,000 orders	210,000 lines	—
High Plains district < cost	$8,578,000	$3,200,000	$8,400,000	$630,000	$2,560,000

make up each activity cost, and we find the cost per unit. This completes the allocation method, which tells us how to allocate costs to the four districts:

- Personal selling poses no problem because it is a direct expense, chargeable to the district in which it occurs.

- Advertising and promotion costs are allocated on the basis of the amount of advertising run in each district. GM realizes this method of allocation is flawed because it disregards various promotion costs, such as trade shows and dealer contests, but likes its simplicity (which should not overrule logic). GM purchased the equivalent of 704 pages of advertising during the year, at an average cost of $20,000 per page ($14,080,000 ÷ 704).

- Warehousing and shipping expenses are apportioned on the basis of the number of orders shipped. Because 105,500 orders were sent out during the year at a total activity cost of $42,200,000, the cost per order is $400.

- Order-processing expenses are allocated according to the number of invoice lines keyed in during the year. Because there were 1,266,667 lines, at a total activity cost of $3.8 million, the cost per line is $3.

- Marketing administration is a totally indirect expense. Thus it is divided equally among the four districts, with each district being allocated $2,560,000.

The final step is to compile the amount of each activity cost to be allocated to each district. The results are shown in the bottom part of Table 21.4. We see that $10,730,000 of personal selling expenses were charged directly to Delta, for example. Regarding advertising, the equivalent of 216 pages of advertising was run in Delta, so that district is charged with $4,320,000 (216 pages × $20,000 per page). In the case of warehousing and shipping expenses, 33,000 orders were shipped to customers in the Delta district, at an allocated cost of $400 per order, for a total cost of $13,200,000. To allocate order-processing expenses, management determined that 460,000 invoice lines went to customers in the Delta district. At $3 per line (the cost per allocation unit), Delta is charged with $1,380,000.

After activity costs have been allocated among the four districts, we can prepare a profit and loss statement for each district. These statements are shown in Table 21.5. Sales for each district are known from the sales volume analysis (Table 21.2). Cost of goods sold and gross margin for the respective districts are obtained by assuming that the company's gross margin of 35% ($126,000,000 ÷ $360,000,000) was maintained in each district.

TABLE 21.5

Profit and Loss Statements for Sales Districts (in $000), Great Midwest Company, 2005

	Total	Delta	Great Lakes	Heartland	High Plains
Net sales	$360,000	$125,000	$96,000	$77,000	$ 62,000
Cost of goods sold	−234,000	81,250	62,400	50,050	40,300
Gross margin	126,000	43,750	33,600	26,950	21,700
Operating expenses:					
Personal selling	38,220	10,730	10,001	8,911	8,578
Advertising/promotion	14,080	4,320	3,040	3,520	3,200
Warehousing and shipping	42,200	13,200	11,400	9,200	8,400
Order processing and billing	3,800	1,380	990	800	630
Marketing administration	10,240	2,560	2,560	2,560	2,560
Total expenses	108,540	32,190	27,991	24,991	23,368
Net profit in dollars	$ 17,460	$ 11,560	$ 5,609	$1,959	$ (1,668)
Net profit as percentage of sales	4.85%	9.25%	5.8%	2.5%	−2.7%

Table 21.5 subdivides Great Midwest's total results into operating statements for each of the four districts. For example, we note that net profit in the Delta area was 9.25% of sales ($11,560,000 ÷ $125,000,000). In sharp contrast, performance in the High Plains was poor, with a loss of 2.7% of sales ($1,668,000 ÷ $62,000,000).

At this point in our performance evaluation, we have completed the *what happened* stage. The next stage is to determine *why* the results are as summarized in Table 21.5. As mentioned earlier, this question is difficult to answer. In High Plains, for example, the sales force obtained only about two-thirds as many orders as the Delta force did (21,000 versus 33,000 as shown in Table 21.4). Was this because of poor selling, inadequate sales training, stiffer competition in High Plains, or some other reason among a multitude of possibilities?

After a performance evaluation has determined why district results came out as they did, management can move to the third stage in the evaluation process. That final stage is, *what should management do about the situation?* This stage will be discussed briefly after we review two major challenges in marketing cost analysis.

Challenges in Cost Analysis

If done thoroughly, marketing cost analysis takes substantial effort and thus is costly. In particular, the task of allocating costs is often quite difficult.

Allocating Costs
The challenge is associated with apportioning certain types of activity costs among individual territories, products, or other marketing units. Operating costs can be divided into direct and indirect expenses. **Direct costs,** also called *separable expenses,* are incurred totally in connection with one marketing unit such as a sales territory. Thus salary and travel expenses of a sales rep in the Delta district are direct expenses for that territory. The cost of newspaper space to advertise the company's lines of office furniture is a direct cost of marketing that product. Allocating direct expenses is straightforward. They can be charged entirely to the marketing unit that incurred them.

The challenge arises in allocating **indirect costs,** also called *common costs* or *overhead.* These expenses are incurred jointly for more than one marketing unit. Therefore, they cannot be charged totally to a single unit.

Within the category of indirect costs, some expenses are *variable* and others are *fixed.* (These two types of costs were introduced in Chapter 12.) Order processing and shipping, for example, are largely variable. They would *decrease* if some territories or products were eliminated; conversely, they would *increase* if new products or territories were added. Marketing administrative expenses are relatively fixed. The cost of the chief marketing executive's staff and related costs would remain about the same, whether or not the number of territories or product lines was changed. Of course, if a significant increase or decrease in scale occurs (for example, sale of one-half of a company's product lines to another firm), then marketing administration should be adjusted to reflect its scope of responsibilities.

Two common methods for allocating *indirect* expenses are to divide these costs (1) equally among the marketing units being studied (territories, for instance) or (2) in proportion to the sales volume in each marketing unit. But each method gives a different result for the total costs for a marketing unit and, as such, may mislead management.

Full Cost versus Contribution Margin
In a marketing cost analysis, two means of allocating expenses are (1) the contribution-margin (also called *contribution-to-overhead*) method and (2) the full-cost method. A controversy exists regarding which of these approaches is better for purposes of evaluation.

In the **contribution-margin approach,** only direct expenses are allocated to each marketing unit being analyzed. These costs presumably would not be incurred if that unit, such as a product or sales territory, were eliminated. When direct expenses are deducted from the unit's gross margin, the remainder is the amount that unit is contributing to cover total indirect expenses (or overhead).

In the **full-cost approach,** all expenses—direct and indirect—are allocated among the marketing units under scrutiny. By allocating *all* costs, management can estimate the net profit of each territory, product, or other unit.

For any specific marketing unit, these two methods can be summarized as follows:

Contribution Margin	Full Cost
Sales $	Sales $
less	*less*
Cost of goods sold	Cost of goods sold
equals	*equals*
Gross margin	Gross margin
less	*less*
Direct expenses	Direct expenses
equals	*less*
Contribution margin (the amount	Indirect expenses
available to cover indirect expenses	*equals*
plus a profit)	Net profit

Contribution-margin proponents contend that it is not possible to logically allocate indirect costs among products or market segments. Furthermore, these costs (such as the salary of the vice president of marketing or the expenses associated with a marketing research department) are not all related to a single territory or product, but rather pertain to the entire organization. Therefore, the marketing units should not bear any of these costs. Supporters of the contribution-margin approach also say that a full-cost analysis may show a net loss for a product or territory, but this unit may be contributing something to overhead. If the unprofitable unit is eliminated, its contribution to overhead would have to be borne by other units. With the contribution-margin approach, there would be no question about keeping this unit as long as there is no better alternative.

Proponents of the *full-cost* approach contend that a marketing cost analysis is intended to determine the net profitability of the units being examined. They believe that the contribution-margin method does not fulfill this purpose and may be misleading. A specific territory or product may show a contribution to overhead. Yet, after indirect costs are allocated, this product or territory may actually have a net loss. In effect, say the full-cost supporters, the contribution-margin approach is the iceberg notion in action. That is, the visible tip (the contribution margin) looks good, whereas the submerged part may contain a net loss.

Use of Findings from Volume and Cost Analyses

So far we have dealt with the first two stages of marketing performance evaluation—finding out what happened and why it happened. Now we should consider some examples of how management might use the results from a combined sales volume analysis and marketing cost analysis to improve performance.

Territories

Knowing the net profit *or* contribution to overhead of territories in relation to previously established expectations gives management several possibilities for action. If territorial problems stem from weaknesses in the distribution system, changes related to this component of the marketing mix may be needed. Firms that use manufacturers' agents may find it advisable to establish their own sales forces in growing markets, for instance. Or, a firm may decide that it would be more economical to substitute agents for its own sales people in all or some territories. Technology may be applied to bring about automatic replenishment and/or reordering via the Internet. If intense competition is the cause of unprofitable volume in some districts, modifications in the promotional program may be necessary. Finally, management may decide to adjust (expand or contract) territories in order to obtain greater cost efficiencies.

Of course, a losing territory might be shut down completely. An abandoned region may have been contributing something to overhead, however, even though a net loss was shown. Management must recognize that this contribution must now be carried by the remaining territories.

Products

When the profitability of each product or group of products is known, unprofitable models, sizes, or colors can be eliminated. Sales people's compensation plans may be altered to encourage the sale of high-margin items. Channels of distribution may be changed. For instance, instead of selling all of its products directly to business users, a machine tools manufacturer shifted to industrial distributors for standard products of low unit value. The company thereby improved the profitability of these products.

Management may decide to discontinue a losing product. But it should not do so without first considering the effect this decision will have on other items sold by the company. Often a low-volume or unprofitable product must be carried simply to round out the product assortment. Supermarkets, for example, carry salt and sugar even though these generate very little if any profit for a store. If they are not available at one store, that seller will lose business, because shoppers will go to other stores that do carry a full complement of groceries.

Customer Classes and Order Sizes

By combining a sales volume analysis with a cost study, executives can determine the profitability of each group of customers.[39] If one market segment is unprofitable or generates too little profit, then changes may be required in the pricing structure when selling to these customers. Or perhaps customers that have been sold to directly by a producer's sales force should be turned over to wholesaling middlemen. A manufacturer of air conditioners made just such a move when it found that direct sales to individual building contractors were not profitable; hence, this firm switched from its own sales staff to several manufacturers' agents.

A difficulty that afflicts some firms is referred to as the **small-order problem.** That is, many orders are below the break-even point. Revenue from each of these orders is actually less than allocated expenses. This problem occurs because several costs, such as billing or direct selling, are essentially the same whether the order amounts to $10 or $10,000. However, the problem extends beyond small orders to any customers who are unprofitable to the firm for one or more of various reasons. For example, a client may actually place relatively large orders but then be so demanding following the sale that the seller's cost of servicing the account is inordinately high.

Management's immediate reaction to the small-order problem may be that no order below the break-even point should be accepted. Or small-volume accounts should be dropped from the customer list. Such decisions may be harmful, however. Some of those small-order customers may, over time, grow into large, profitable accounts.

Management should deal with unprofitable customers, including those whose orders are too small, through a two-step process:

- Determine if troublesome accounts can be made profitable, either by motivating them to place larger orders, pruning discounts available to them, charging them higher prices or special fees, and/or reducing the level of service provided to them. Sometimes, proper handling can turn a losing account into a satisfactory one. For example, a small-order handling charge, which some customers would willingly pay, might improve the profit picture.

- If all else fails, cease doing business with unprofitable customers. This might be done, preferably gently, by "encouraging" customers to take their business elsewhere. Steps toward that end would include eliminating services they had been receiving and/or by not retaining the account when a purchase contract expires.[40]

Summary

The management process in marketing consists of the planning, implementation, and evaluation of the marketing effort in an organization. Implementation is the stage in which an enterprise takes steps to carry out its strategic planning. If it is not implemented effectively, strategic planning is virtually useless.

Implementation includes three activities: organizing, staffing, and directing. In organizing, the company should first coordinate all marketing activities into one department overseen by a top executive who reports directly to the president. Then, for the selling function within the marketing department, the company should choose a form of organizational specialization based on geographic territories, products, or customer types.

Some underappreciated components of a marketing program, namely warranties and other postsale services, are implemented largely after a sale is made. Warranties require considerable management attention these days because of consumer complaints and governmental regulations. Product liability is an issue of great consequence to companies because of the significant financial risk associated with consumers' claims of injuries caused when using a firm's product.

Many companies provide postsale service—such as merchandise returns, maintenance and repairs, and complaint handling—to fulfill the terms of their warranties and/or to augment their revenues. To promote customer satisfaction, a number of firms are striving to improve their methods of inviting and responding to consumer complaints.

The evaluation stage in the management process involves measuring performance results against predetermined goals. Evaluation enables management to determine the effectiveness of its implementation and to plan corrective action where necessary. A marketing audit is a key element in a marketing evaluation program.

Most companies are victims of at least some misdirected marketing effort. That is, the 80–20 and iceberg principles are at work in many firms because marketing costs are expended in relation to the number of marketing units (territories, products, customers), rather than in relation to their profit potential. Too many companies do not know how much they should spend for marketing activities, or what results they should get from these expenditures.

The financial results of marketing endeavors should be analyzed in terms of sales volume, market share, and marketing costs. One challenge in marketing cost analysis is allocating expenses, especially indirect costs, to the marketing units. Given detailed assessments, management can study sales volume and marketing costs by territories, product lines, categories of customer, and/or order sizes. The findings from these analyses can guide decisions regarding a company's marketing program.

More about **Zara**

The Inditex Group, Zara's parent company, has over 2,300 stores in more than 55 countries. The firm's combined annual revenues were 5.67 billion euros (equivalent to $7.34 billion) for the fiscal year that ended in early 2005. Collectively, Inditex's eight divisions sell well over 100 million garments yearly.

Zara accounts for the large majority (about 70%) of Inditex's total sales. The fashion-forward clothing chain has about a 5% market share in its native Spain; international sales account for over 50% of Zara's revenues. Profit margins have been steady at 10%, which compare favorably to the best in the industry.

Zara is especially well known in Europe, the Middle East, and South America. It has more than

750 stores in over 50 countries, but only 20 or so outlets in the U.S. Its present expansion is centered in Europe, especially Italy, although more U.S. stores remain a possibility.

Zara's success to date can be attributed to all three stages of the management process—planning, implementation, *and* also evaluation. Regarding this last stage, careful monitoring of marketing performance ensures that the stores are stocked with clothing that consumers want and that managers are confident will sell quickly. Store managers and salespeople, in fact, play a huge role in determining what is stocked in Zara stores. As they work, they carry personal digital assistants (PDAs) to record customer comments, requests, and likes and dislikes.

"The role of the store manager goes way beyond that of Gap and H&M [a Swedish competitor]," says one industry analyst. Managers' design suggestions are backed by the research of trend spotters who travel around the world looking for inspiration and ideas.

Typically, managers in every Zara store around the world submit their orders for new merchandise on a daily basis. Equally important, store managers use PDAs to send information about trends and customer preferences to the home office. Then the company's 300 designers evaluate the input about styles and colors, decide what new ideas will be appealing and what current designs need to be tweaked or even dropped, and consult the company's specialists about fabrics, production, and pricing. In turn, the designers create patterns that are transmitted to computers in the company's highly automated manufacturing plants. Customer needs and wants, gauged on a real-time basis, are thus largely responsible for the details of Zara's 11,000 new designs a year.[41]

1. Does Zara carry out a systematic evaluation process? That is, does the chain assess what happened, why, and what to do about it?

2. What measures should Inditex use in evaluating Zara's marketing performance?

Key Terms and Concepts

Planning (584)
Implementation (584)
Evaluation (584)
Geographic specialization (587)
Product specialization (589)
Customer specialization (589)
Major accounts organization (589)
Warranty (guarantee) (590)
Express warranty (590)

Implied warranty (590)
Product liability (591)
Warning label (592)
Postsale service (593)
Marketing audit (596)
Misdirected marketing effort (597)
80–20 principle (597)
Iceberg principle (597)

Sales volume analysis (599)
Market-share analysis (600)
Marketing cost analysis (600)
Direct costs (604)
Indirect costs (604)
Contribution-margin approach (604)
Full-cost approach (605)
Small-order problem (606)

Questions and Problems

1. "Good implementation in an organization can overcome poor planning, but good planning cannot overcome poor implementation." Explain, using examples from business periodicals, such as *Business Week*, *Forbes*, *Advertising Age*, *Brandweek*, and *The Wall Street Journal*.

2. Give some examples of companies that are likely to organize their sales forces by product groups.

3. A manufacturer of small aircraft designed for executive transportation, Cessna for example, has decided to implement the concept of a selling center. Who should be on this company's selling teams? What problems might this manufacturer encounter when it uses team selling?

4. Explain the relationship between a warranty on small electric appliances, such as a Toastmaster waffle maker, and the marketer's distribution system for these products.

5. a. Should the primary role of postsale services be to assure customer satisfaction or to generate added revenues for the firm?

   b. Would the way in which postsale services are carried out vary depending on the role given to this element of marketing by the firm's executives?

6. a. What are several ways in which providing postsale services would vary between an e-tailer and a retailer that has physical stores?

   b. Do online-only firms have any advantages with respect to carrying out postsale services?

7. A sales volume analysis by territories indicates that a manufacturer's sales of roofing materials increased 12% a year for the past three years in a territory comprising South Carolina, Georgia, and Florida. Does this statistic indicate conclusively that the company's sales volume performance is satisfactory in that territory?

8. A manufacturer found that one product accounted for 35% to 45% of the company's total sales in all but 2 of the 18 territories. In each of those two territories, this product accounted for only 14% of the company's volume. What factors might explain the relatively low sales of this item in the two districts?

9. What effects might a sales volume analysis by product have on training, supervising, and compensating a company's sales force?

10. Should a company stop selling to an unprofitable customer? Why or why not? If not, then what steps might the company take to make the account a profitable one?

Interactive Marketing Exercises

1. Interview a sales executive (a) in a manufacturing company and (b) in either a securities brokerage or a real estate brokerage firm to find out how they motivate their sales forces. As part of your report, give your evaluation of each motivational program.

2. Interview a marketing executive to find out how total marketing performance is evaluated in that particular company. As part of your report, include your appraisal of this firm's evaluation program.

Chapter 22

"Bezos realized that the value of any technology is in the benefits it provides to the customer."

Marketing and the Information Economy

Can **Amazon** Keep the Sales Flowing?

Should a business with losses of more than $3 billion in eight years be viewed as a model that could revolutionize the way many products are sold to consumers? If that business is called Amazon, maybe it should be.

Amazon began as an online bookstore in 1995. The founder, Jeff Bezos, noticed the growing use of the Internet by businesses and felt it offered some advantages over traditional retail stores. For example, an online retailer is open for business 24 hours a day, seven days a week. Also, with an online catalog and most orders shipped directly from suppliers to the customers, the merchandise offered is not constrained by the physical limits of the four walls of a store. And customers have the convenience of shopping from home or any place with an Internet connection.

But unlike many other Internet businesses, Bezos looked beyond the technology for a differential advantage. According to an analyst, "Jeff Bezos was the first one to figure out what the power of the Internet was for selling." Bezos realized that the value of any technology is in the benefits it provides to the customer. As a result, he used the Internet to make shopping easier, faster, and more personalized than many traditional retailers. For example, at Amazon, shoppers receive customized recommendations based on their past purchases and other buyers' similar choices, notification of new releases on subject matter they specify, and the opportunity to provide book reviews that are posted online.

Amazon has expanded far beyond its original offerings of books, CDs, and DVD to become a virtual one-stop shopping site. At last count there were 32 categories of merchandise available on its website (called "stores" by Amazon), ranging from staples such as health and beauty aids and pet supplies to more exotic items such as gourmet food and jewelry.

Other Amazon customer-focused innovations that make use of technology include the "Gold Box"—an icon at the top of the home page signaling an item on special offer for an hour; "Bottom of the Page Deals"—bargains on staple goods available for a single day; and "Search Inside the Book," which allows shoppers to select and read several pages of a book for free before they buy it. This last feature required that 120,000 books be digitally scanned and indexed.

With over 43 million active customers, it certainly appears that the blend of technology and customer orientation is working. As for the future, Bezos believes that almost anything can be sold over the Internet. And who is going to argue with a man who had the vision to name his company after the world's largest river to reflect the potential flow of products to consumers?[1]

Is Amazon's use of technology an end in itself or a means to an end?

www.amazon.com

Information has always played a major role in marketing. Today, both the quantity and quality of information is increasing at the fastest rate in history. Much of this growth is due to improvements in information technology and the ability of marketers to find creative ways to make use of it. The result is that marketers are entering an information economy in which new ways of doing business are being designed and some existing ways are being reconfigured. Some analysts even predict that instead of bricks and mortar (and inventory) defining a business, information and how it is used will be the key attributes of success in the near future.

The company described in the chapter-opening case is a good example. Despite losing $3 billion, Jeff Bezos didn't lose sight of his dream that information technology could be used to better serve customers. Not satisfied with only using the Internet to make shopping more convenient, he found creative ways to make it friendly and fun. And by encouraging and posting book reviews, he even created an online community in which customers can assist one another. Bezos has embraced information technology while recognizing that ultimately its usefulness is determined by how much value it provides customers.

In this chapter the goal is to examine the role of marketing in this emerging information economy. More specifically, we will look at how information technology is creating new opportunities and challenges and some of the ways marketers are trying to seize these opportunities. After studying this chapter you should:

Chapter Goals

- Appreciate the role of information in marketing.
- Be familiar with the importance of information technology and electronic networking.
- Understand how the Internet has changed how markets function.
- Appreciate some of the ways the Internet is affecting marketing strategy.
- Recognize challenges and opportunities marketers are addressing as they enter the information economy.

The Importance of Information in Marketing

The Industrial Revolution, beginning in the second half of the 19th century, marked the beginning of the widespread application of technology to business. Steam and electric power made it possible to operate large machinery and equipment, conveyors moved products along assembly lines and then into and out of inventory, and individual workers were taught to perform specialized tasks very efficiently. As a result, businesses began to experience substantial improvements in manufacturing productivity. However, the impact of manufacturing technology on marketing was not nearly as dramatic. Although it did result in lower costs and therefore lower prices, the job of the marketer remained largely unchanged, requiring considerable personal interaction before, during, and after most sales.

Significant increases in marketing productivity required a different kind of technology. The job of marketing is to direct the organization in how to most effectively satisfy customers. Providing direction entails learning as much as possible about the customer, and using that information to design need-satisfying strategies. For example, sellers must learn what buyers like and dislike by monitoring their behavior, asking them questions, and inviting their comments. And all marketers must gather data on current or potential markets to determine their status and to anticipate how they are likely to change. In short, marketing is driven by information.

The effective utilization of information improves the performance of marketing in ways that have been discussed throughout this book. For example, it results in:

- *Better products.* A refined understanding of the buyer allows a marketer to develop products that more closely fit the buyer's needs, requiring fewer compromises and greater satisfaction.

- *Better prices.* What customers are willing to pay for a product depends on how much they value it. Knowing how important a product is to a customer and what resources the customer has available to purchase it helps sellers set attractive prices.

- *Better distribution.* The likelihood of having a product available when and where a customer wants to find it is enhanced if the seller knows the shopping habits and preferences of the buyer.

- *Better promotion.* A product and its benefits can be communicated in many ways. Both the form and the content of advertisements and other promotions can be improved if the marketer understands the buyer's motivations and expectations.

- *Better implementation.* Quicker feedback on marketing programs permits managers to assess their performance and make adjustments before losses mount up or opportunities are missed. Today the response of customers to price changes and promotion programs can be monitored in real time rather than days or weeks after they are introduced.

But recognizing the importance of information and using it effectively are two different things. Except in the smallest businesses, utilization requires technology. In the case of marketing, gathering, analyzing, and storing large amounts of data about markets, competitors, media, distribution, and customer behavior wasn't practical before the widespread availability of computers.

Consider, for example, a supermarket chain with several stores, each with 30,000 different items on its shelves. Without computers, keeping track of the performance of each item, deciding which to keep and which to drop, and determining when and how much to reorder would be an enormous task. However, by today's standards, a relatively small computer can compile a record of all the transactions made at every checkout lane for each store. Utilizing predetermined programs, the computer can use the data to signal when individual items need to be reordered, given more or less shelf space, or even dropped.

Computers can also be used to carry out very complex tasks. Recall the example in Chapter 7 of data mining by Harrah's casinos. The firm profiles gamblers on the basis of their behavior and uses the information to design and target its promotional efforts. Sophisticated analytical techniques and powerful computers allow Harrah's and other firms to sift through millions of bits of consumer-related data and discover patterns that wouldn't be apparent to human observers no matter how much time and effort they invested. Thus the marriage of information and technology has become a fact of life in marketing.

Information Technology in Marketing

Numerous technological developments have had a significant impact on marketing. Certainly television (which provides advertisers access to many consumers at one time), household telephones (which permit easy interaction between buyers and sellers), and personal computers (which increase individual productivity of marketing managers) are examples. Rather than try to discuss all the information technology that is used in marketing, our discussion will focus on recent network applications. We will begin with a brief introduction to the Internet, the backbone of many of these tools, followed by an overview of several levels of electronic networking systems. Then we will return to the Internet for a more complete discussion of how it impacts marketing.

The Internet

In the early 1970s the **Internet** was created as part of a U.S. government project. Its original purpose was to link researchers at many different sites and allow them to exchange information. The procedure for using the Internet served the purposes of the researchers, but it was too cumbersome for broad commercial applications. Then, in 1989 the **World Wide Web** (now simply referred to as the Web) was developed. The Web provides access to a portion of the larger Internet (though the terms are now used interchangeably), making it possible for users to share a full range of communications from text to graphics and audio messages. Any individual or organization can create and register a **website,** a collection of Web files beginning with a home page, that is accessible through a unique address. Thus, as we will see, the Web has become the lynchpin for much of the communication that takes place between businesses and between businesses and consumers today.

Electronic Networking

Networks are individuals or organizations linked together to share data, exchange information and ideas, and perform tasks. Some networks are simple, requiring no technology. People have social networks, professional networks, and work group networks. You've probably been advised to develop personal networks and use them when looking for a job. **Electronic networks** are created when the individuals or organizations are linked via some form of telecommunications.[2]

In business, when the personal computers of individuals in a company or department are linked together a local electronic network or **intranet** is created. For example, at an appliance manufacturer, an intranet of designers, engineers, and marketers may be created to share input as a new product is developed. The power of these networks is expanded when they include a server, which is a central, more powerful

Communication technology is changing the ways we communicate. The lead designer of the first cell phone, Rudy Krolop, is shown here with his creation the DynaTAC8000X (standing on the table). Introduced by Motorola in 1983, it weighed in at 2 pounds, sold for $3,995, and required recharging after about a half-hour of use. Resting on the original is the Razr, one of Motorola's latest models. In contrast to the original, it is one-half inch thick, weighs 3.3 ounces, and has a battery life of seven hours.

 www.motorola.com

computer that can store large databases and perform sophisticated analyses. With access to the server through their PCs, the participants in a network can perform tasks not possible on individual PCs. Several levels of electronic networking exist in the information economy.

Electronic Data Interchange

When electronic networking moves outside the firm, it is known as **electronic data interchange (EDI),** which is a proprietary system in which data are exchanged between trading partners, to be used for standardized, preapproved transactions. For example, Kmart stocks Procter & Gamble's Tide detergent in its stores. When the inventory of Tide reaches a predetermined level in Kmart's distribution center, its computer automatically transmits an order to P&G's computer. The P&G computer confirms the order and sets in motion the activities to fill it. Transactions similar to this are carried out thousands of times daily between firms and their suppliers. Doing it electronically saves time, minimizes order-processing expenses, and reduces clerical errors.

Early EDI made use of long-distance telephone lines that allowed the computer in one firm to dial up and "talk" to a supplier's computer. More recent versions utilize the Web. EDI is limited to large firms because of the costs involved in implementation. Because it cannot quickly adjust to price or product availability changes, it is also somewhat inflexible.

Electronic Information Transfer

The Web ushered in another level of networking for marketers. Called **electronic information** (or e-information), this form of networking involves creating a corporate website and posting information on it. Firms are able to make vast amounts of information available on their websites. Typical examples include product descriptions, invitations to suppliers to submit bids on planned purchases, product operating instructions, and information about contacting sales personnel. Some e-information websites are open—that is, freely accessible to anyone. Others are restricted—that is, accessible only to those in possession of a password. By applying restrictions, a firm can make the information on its website available selectively to customers, distributors, and/or suppliers.

Many consumer product manufacturers and retailers view an e-information website as a necessary form of communication—like an ad with much more information than possible with traditional media. These sites often include special inducements to attract visitors, such as electronic coupons and contests. For business-to-business marketers, e-information reduces the need for paper-based communication and lowers the costs of working with suppliers and serving distributors because much of the information a customer or supply chain member needs is available 24 hours a day, seven days a week. As a result, e-information has become the most common use of the Internet for business-to-business marketers.

The postings on an e-information website typically fall into five categories:

- *Background and general information*—primarily the company's history, its mission, corporate philosophy, and general orientation. This category includes financial performance and investor information, the structure of the firm if it is global or has several divisions, and profiles of top managers. Employment opportunities with the firm also are frequently posted here, as are recent press releases. Background and general information pages would be accessible to anyone visiting the site.

- *Current business operations*—for existing and potential business partners. This category typically has information for suppliers (how to contact corporate buyers, invitations to bid on planned purchases, payment terms and conditions, delivery requirements) and customers (product descriptions, dealer contact information, credit terms). Because some of this information is considered confidential, access may be restricted and require a password.

- *Links*—connections to other related sites. For example, a furniture manufacturer's site might make it possible for consumers to link to the website of a retailer located in their area that carries the manufacturer's products. By simply clicking on an icon that describes the related site, the visitor is transferred to it.

- *Attraction and entertainment features*—tools and techniques for engaging site visitors. Attempts to attract and hold visitors to a site often involve weaving the desired promotional message into entertaining features. For example, McDonald's website includes an electronic coloring book, visual tours of McDonald's restaurants around the world, special promotion and contest information, nutrition information, overviews of the firm's environmental efforts, and many more attractions. Entertainment is much more common on the websites of consumer product marketers than on those of business-to-business marketers, but all sites must be attractive and easy to navigate to hold visitors' attention.

- *Contact point*—providing an e-mail link for visitors that allows them to ask questions or make comments. This opportunity for interaction is a major distinguishing feature for Internet communications compared to traditional media advertising. It also requires a high level of attention on the part of the site owner because unanswered inquiries or form letter responses can create substantial ill will.

The benefits marketers are seeking through a website depend on the nature of the organization. The primary benefit to business-to-business firms is greater efficiency in dealing with suppliers and customers. *If* current and potential suppliers and customers can be convinced to search a firm's website, answers to many of their routine questions can be answered without human interaction. For example, many websites include a "frequently asked questions" (FAQ) page.

www.kelloggs.com

www.whirlpool.com

A website (or portion of a business website) designed for final consumers is intended to build goodwill and strengthen relationships. It is comparable to brand-building advertising, except the opportunity exists to provide much more content and to interact with individual site visitors through e-mail. Virtually all large consumer packaged-goods firms such as Kellogg's, Coca-Cola, and Procter & Gamble maintain e-information sites, as do durable-goods manufacturers such as Whirlpool and Ford Motor Co.

A firm typically attracts visitors through ads placed in other media and by publicizing its website address (called its URL) on its letterhead and on executives' business cards. For both business and consumer marketers, websites offer flexibility, because their content can be changed as frequently as desired, and they have broad geographic reach, because anyone in the world with access to the Internet is potentially reachable.

Electronic Transactions   Note that e-information sites provide information but they are not designed to make transactions. Creating the capability of making purchases directly from a firm's website is known as **electronic transactions** (or e-transactions), the next higher level of electronic networking. E-transactions involve more interaction and feedback than e-information. Both consumer product marketers and business-to-business sellers make use of e-transactions. The average annual growth rate in online consumer sales has exceeded 20% every year since the U.S. Department of Commerce began reporting the results in 1999, amounting to over $117 billion in 2004.[3] Despite this rate of growth, consumer purchases on the Web account for only about 3.3% of total U.S. retail sales.

It may surprise you that the dollar volume of B2B (business-to-business) online transactions dwarf B2C (business-to-consumer) sales online. According to the U.S. Department of Commerce, business online purchasing is 16 times greater than consumer purchases.[4]

There are two categories of firms that conduct transactions over the Web: (1) new businesses seeking an effective way to reach the market, and (2) existing businesses expanding their access to the market or replacing their current channel. This is an important distinction because the Web has allowed new business models to be created that would be impossible using traditional channels. For example, eBags, an online luggage retailer, offers a selection of over 12,000 items, nearly 50 times the inventory a typical specialty store would stock, because its sales are shipped directly to customers from distributors and manufacturers.[5] Online auctions such as eBay, and the reverse auctions organized by Ariba are additional examples of new business models made possible by the Web.

www.ebags.com

www.ebay.com

www.ariba.com

www.silverfallsseed.com

The other category consists of existing firms, both small and large, that want to expand their market access. For example, Silver Falls Seed Company, a wildflower seed and plant company in Silverton, Oregon, could reach only a local clientele prior to going online. Now the firm sells seeds and plants (and provides gardening tips, an online newsletter, and some homespun advice on a variety of topics) to a much larger audience. In less than two years its website had nearly 100,000 visitors. Large firms are moving to the Internet as well. Here we find businesses of all types including business services providers such as Maritz, industrial goods suppliers such as W. W. Grainger, and cosmetics firms such as Avon. Wal-Mart, Toys R Us, Allstate, and Office Depot are just a few of the other well-known firms that have broadened their marketing reach through websites designed for e-transactions.

Some firms with e-information sites have avoided moving to e-transactions because of the negative impact selling directly can have on their existing channel members. Auto manufacturers are an example. Another reason for avoiding e-transactions is that even if one or more levels of distribution are removed from a channel, the functions must still be performed. Thus many firms opt to stick with their existing arrangements rather than create the necessary processing, shipping, and customer service required to deal with large numbers of individual orders.

Red Envelope, an upscale gift e-tailer, exemplifies firms that have benefited from electronic commerce. The firm shifted its promotional efforts from traditional mass media advertising to e-mail. A half-million biweekly e-mails direct prospects to the firm's printed catalog and website. The result has been increased exposure, lowered ordering costs, and increased sales.

 www.RedEnvelope.com

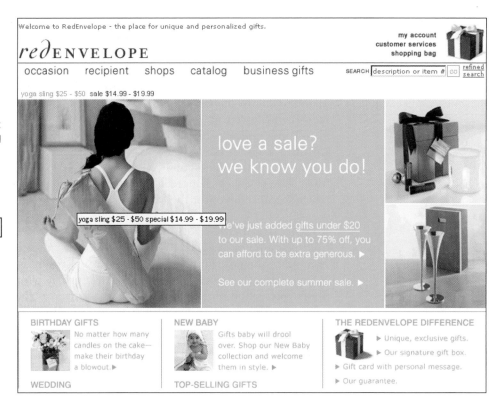

Electronic Commerce When a firm reconfigures its marketing operations around interactions with its value chain made possible by its Web connections, it is engaging in **electronic commerce** (or e-commerce). This is a sophisticated network that can link a large number of firms at different levels of a distribution channel in what is called an **extranet.** For example, Dow Chemical is linked with over 8,000 customers in 35 countries through an exchange it has created.[6] Customers can review their purchase histories, monitor their orders, and check on the availability of Dow products. In turn, Dow can monitor the customers' purchase patterns and inventory levels and adapt its production and sales efforts accordingly.

Depending on the firm, an extranet might also involve suppliers in the design of products on the website, monitor orders from the time they are taken until the finished products are delivered, and permit customers to examine and make suggestions about the firm's production schedule. Because extranets allow business partners access to highly sensitive data as well as future plans, they require strong relationships and a high level of trust. In return, they speed up decision making with the result that products get to market more quickly and at a lower cost.

The Impact of the Internet on Markets

Transforming the Web into a marketing tool was made possible by several important developments. The most basic is the Web browser. A **browser** provides an Internet visitor with the necessary application program to look at and interact with individual websites. Among the best known browsers are Netscape Navigator, Microsoft's Internet Explorer, and Apple's Safari.[7] Because a browser acts as a visitor's starting point on any visit to the Web, it has a significant influence on the subsequent sites a Web surfer will visit.

As the number of websites grew, it became apparent that an electronic **directory** (similar in concept to a phone book) was needed. What has become one of the largest and best-known directories was initiated by two graduate students who began compiling a list of sites organized by topics and subtopics. They called it Yahoo!. (The letters in the name stand for "Yet another hierarchical officious oracle," reflecting the youthful exuberance of the founders!) It now consists of hundreds of thousands of websites and millions of Web pages. Another popular directory is Google, which offers a search index containing over 8 billion pages.

Even with directories, finding your way around the Web can be difficult. To assist Web visitors, the browser developers and others have created gateway or portal websites. A **portal** is an entrance and a guide to the rest of the Web. In order to attract visitors, most browsers also serve as portals. Besides a directory of websites, they typically offer a search engine to look for information, and access to e-mail service, news, weather forecasts, and other information. Some of the better-known portals are Netscape, Lycos, Excite, and America Online. Browsers, directories, and portals permit easy access to the Web for virtually anyone with a PC and a telephone line connection.

Use of the Internet by businesses and consumers has grown very rapidly. Virtually all of the major firms in the U.S. now have some type of Internet presence, which means that in order to do business with them, their customers and suppliers must also have access.

Among U.S. consumers, access to the Web grew from 14% in 1996 to over 68% in 2005.[8] Usage also has increased. The number of times per month people log on is increasing, and the amount of total time they are logged on is going up (from 17.5 hours per month to 20.5 hours).[9] Several implications of this phenomenon on how markets operate are described below.

Control of Interactions

The traditional model of marketing communication has the seller largely in control of the information flow. When an advertiser uses traditional media, such as radio or television, a portion of the consumers exposed to the message are not particularly involved with it. However, advertisers believe that with repetition at least some part of the message is likely to make an impression on these passive recipients.

In the online environment the interactions are controlled by the recipient. It is the Internet user who must sit down at the computer, search out a website, and decide what pages to examine or ignore. Since an Internet site does not have any passive or incidental exposure, it must be sufficiently interesting to attract visitors and hold their attention. One approach is to permit a site visitor to personalize the message content. For example, by clicking on an object in the online video ad for General Motors' new Cadillac STS, a visitor can learn as much or as little about its design development, components, appearance, and climate control feature as desired. This new hyperlink technology, called *hotspotting*, permits an almost infinite number of visitor-designed messages.[10]

www.cadillac.com

More Complete and Timely Information

One of the features of the Internet is easy access to more complete and timely information. Customers of FedEx can track the location of a shipment at every stage of its journey because every package is bar-coded and scanned between 15 and 20 times between pickup and delivery. Likewise, consumers can acquire information previously available only to sellers. For example, knowing what a car dealer pays for a particular make of car and the cost to the dealer for specific options can be valuable negotiating tools for a consumer. In 1966, Edmund's began publishing such information in its automobile and truck buyers' guides and selling them in bookstores. However, not many consumers knew about the guides, they quickly became outdated, and consumers had to purchase them. Then Edmund's went online. Now

www.edmunds.com

Websites designed to allow consumers to compare the prices of a number of sellers for the same product have become so plentiful that many now specialize in a particular category or industry. For example, PriceFarmer.com focuses on books. Price searching websites also exist for new and used automobiles, airline reservations, apparel, perfume, home appliances, and many other products. The eventual result will be fewer fixed prices and more negotiation for all manner of consumer goods and services.

www.pricefarmer.com

free access to constantly updated information about new cars is as close as a mouse click, and 200,000 consumers a day take advantage of it.

Clearly the ability to make comparisons on the Internet forces online firms to be aware of and responsive to the offerings, including prices of other marketers. Customers can now gather comparison information from the Internet and use it in negotiations. In the past, many firms had a "geographic monopoly" because they had little or no local competition, and customers were uninformed about the cost of the same product elsewhere. Now there is no reason why a small firm buying printing services or a consumer buying a car should approach the purchase without comparative information.

Fewer Fixed Prices

Fixed prices are the norm in consumer markets, with only a few exceptions. In business-to-business marketing, negotiated prices are more common, but many prices are fixed there as well. This is likely to change. As the Internet makes real-time auctions possible, fixed prices for business and consumer sales may become rarities. eBay, the dominant firm in consumer and small business Internet auctions, has over 140 million registered users bidding on more than 430 million items. Products as diverse as a retired Russian submarine and Barbie dolls are offered on the eBay site.

The reverse auction is also increasing in popularity. In this situation, the buyer specifies what is desired and prospective sellers make offers, bidding the price down. Reverse auctions are expected to expand beyond standard, commodity items purchased by businesses to include a wide variety of consumer goods.

Traditional online auctions expand the market, giving sellers access to many more potential buyers. Reverse auctions also give buyers access to more sellers. In both scenarios, prices are determined in real time by the interactions of buyers and sellers.

Restructured Channels

In a traditional arrangement, a manufacturer produces a product and sells it to the next level in the distribution channel (possibly a wholesaler or a retailer). As was described in Chapter 14, firms further down the channel maintain an inventory of the product, promote it locally, possibly provide credit to buyers, take and process orders, distribute the product in smaller quantities to other firms or consumers, and provide a variety of services to the buyers. Many of these activities are related to filling orders, and are captured by the term **fulfillment.**

When a firm sells on the Web and therefore skips one or more channel levels, it must create the systems to provide fulfillment. Even a traditional retailer that adds a Web channel must arrange to process orders and get the product to the buyer. One

One criticism of online retailing is that it does not offer consumers the specialized services that a traditional retail store can provide. Though that may be true in many cases, marketers are finding ways to differentiate e-tailing. For example, consumers can customize Nike athletic shoes, Timbuk2 backpacks, and M&M candies (shown here) online. Even General Mills has explored the idea of allowing consumers to create their own ideal dry cereal blends from a list of 100 ingredients.

www.shopmms.com

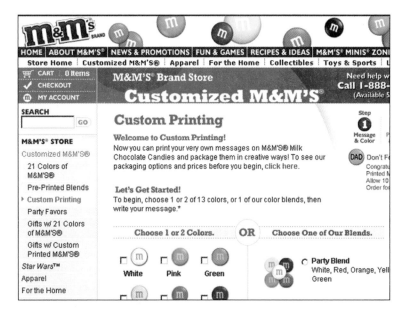

option is to perform these tasks internally. For example, a manufacturer that formerly shipped truckloads of products to wholesalers might start packaging and shipping individual units to consumers. Another option is to outsource fulfillment. Outsourcing may simply involve delivering the purchased product to the customer, or it may include everything from processing the order to postpurchase service issues and everything in-between. For example, JCPenney sells CD players in its stores and on its website, but it sells CDs online through Handleman Company. Handleman, because it fills orders for a number of retailers, can maintain the necessary inventory of music titles (estimated to be at least 200,000) to do this profitably.

www.handleman.com

Buyer Communication

Marketers recognize word-of-mouth communication as a potent force because it is seen as an assessment by an objective third party with nothing to gain or lose from a purchase decision. Of course, word of mouth can be negative as well as positive. Thus, firms go to considerable effort to encourage positive word of mouth and to resolve unfavorable impressions that might lead to negative word of mouth.

The Internet has magnified both the speed and the reach of word of mouth. Forums, chat rooms, and weblogs provide a nearly unlimited source of opinions about products and experiences.[11] Even if none of your friends has taken a Carnival cruise, purchased from an L. L. Bean's catalog, or stayed in a hotel in London, you can quickly gather opinions and recommendations from people who have.

Amazon created a forum for word of mouth by inviting its customers to offer reviews and ratings of the books they purchased online. The evaluations are then reproduced on the site for other customers. It is not clear how much influence word-of-mouth reactions from a stranger have on behavior, but their popularity is reflected in the fact that there is at least one site, www.complaints.com, dedicated entirely to negative word of mouth.

www.complaints.com

The Impact of the Internet on Marketing Strategy

The Internet has created many opportunities. New businesses were created to provide portals and servers to increase access to the Web. Other businesses, such as

Amazon and eBay, utilize the technology to serve customers in new ways. In addition to creating new businesses, the Web has changed existing ways of doing business. Firms at all levels of distribution have created their own websites to communicate with other businesses and consumers and to conduct transactions. As discussed above, the objectives of these sites are to reduce costs, generate revenue, or both. For example, the Internet has made it possible for national and regional fashion retailers to adjust prices on seasonal inventory based on demand in specific markets; allowed customers to easily reload gift cards, which speeds up purchases and strengthens loyalty; and caused almost all firms to reconsider their advertising media mixes.[12]

It's clear the Internet is having a broad impact on business. Next we will explore some specific strategic marketing implications.

Market Research

Like all good marketers, firms making use of the Internet want to segment markets and then concentrate on selected targets. Gathering data about website visits and visitors and relating that data to other information about visitors is a useful place to begin. Online research firm comScore Networks illustrates this approach. It monitors the Internet activities of a panel of 1.5 million Web users. Combining data on panel members' Web browsing with information on what they buy online, how often, and from what sites provides both general and specific insights into the impact of the Internet. For example, comScore's found that during the last 3 months of 2004 over 17 million American consumers visited online pharmacies located in the U.S. and abroad, and despite more than half having concerns about safety, 40% indicated they would buy drugs online if they were effective.[13]

Traditional marketing research techniques, including surveys and focus groups, are being conducted on the Web.[14] Clearly using the Web for research doesn't eliminate all the problems of more conventional methods. For example, just as in a mail survey, the researcher can't be sure who completed an Internet survey. But it does offer some unique opportunities. For example, the graphics now possible on the Internet allow respondents in a focus group or survey to look at visual images of a product in motion and from many different angles. Probably the biggest advantages of conducting research over the Internet are the speed with which it can be completed, the comparatively low cost, and the geographic reach. The biggest drawback is that many households in the U.S. do not have Internet access, so researchers must take care to ensure that respondents represent the group of interest.

There are other research techniques to identify segments that involve gathering data through electronic observation of site visitors. One approach, called **clustering**, tracks the pages visited, the amount of time at a page, and the items purchased by individuals while they navigate a site. It then creates groups or clusters of visitors with very similar patterns. When subsequent visitors display behavior similar to a particular cluster, they can be steered in real time to content or merchandise they are most likely to buy.

Amazon developed a similar technique called **collaborative filtering** that allows it to recommend books or tapes to an individual based on a comparison of the person's selections and the purchases of previous visitors. So, for example, assume that a number of visitors who purchased books on gardening from Amazon.com also examined books on home repairs. When you click on home repairs, in addition to giving you that information, the site would suggest some popular gardening titles.

Product

Internet capabilities allow marketers to reconsider how they segment and target markets. For example, product customization has been relatively common in business-to-business marketing, although it is generally limited to "big-ticket" purchases with high margins. On the other hand, nearly all consumer products are highly standardized. The primary reason for the difference is quite simple—the flow of information. Getting the customization details from the buyer to the seller, arranging to have suppliers provide the necessary parts, and sharing the information internally with manufacturing and other functions took too much time. The Internet speeds up that flow and makes customization not only possible but practical. Ford and General Motors have joined Toyota in a commitment to provide customized cars within five days of receiving an order. And the expectation is that customization will quickly spread to consumer electronics and appliances.[15]

One of the advantages of customization is drastically reducing the investment in inventory. Imagine an automobile dealership with only enough cars and trucks on its lot to permit test-drives. In the auto industry, studies indicate that increased efficiency in production, decreased inventories of parts and finished products, and lower transportation costs as a result of shifting from mass to customized production and marketing could reduce the prices of vehicles by as much as 30%.

Rather than competing on price, services marketers are learning to use Internet technology to improve products. For example, General Motors added an Internet link to its Onstar system, which combines a car phone and global-positioning equipment to offer travel information and emergency help. The added feature allows a driver to listen to an individually designed mix of news, customized traffic reports, and personal e-mail messages.

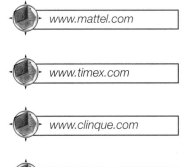

www.onstar.com

www.mattel.com

www.timex.com

www.clinique.com

www.sony.com

www.kodak.com

Channel Relationships

The attraction of the Web for manufacturers is a closer link with the final customer. By selling over the Web and eliminating middlemen, both business and consumer product makers are able to decide which of their products to present, how they will be presented, and what level of service will accompany them. Equally important, the direct connection of the Internet permits manufacturers to obtain unfiltered feedback from the buyers who actually use their products. Firms as diverse as Mattel, Timex, Clinique, Sony, and Kodak are using websites to sell their products.

For an established firm (other than a retailer), selling on the Web usually means bypassing one or more channel members or even a manufacturer's own sales force. In most instances, this is a source of tension. For example, when General Motors floated the idea of selling cars via the Web, there was an immediate negative response from its dealers. Closer to home, a firm's own sales force can be affected by Web sales. When Merrill Lynch announced it would offer online trading to its existing clients, its brokers were quick to ask how their commissions would be affected.

The issue is simple. Changing the way a product is sold and distributed has an impact on the individuals and organizations currently selling the product. Anticipating their reaction and ensuring they are treated fairly is not as obvious. By moving some of its sales to the Web, a firm risks losing the loyalty and commitment of its existing channel. W. W. Grainger dealt with this by guaranteeing its sales people commissions on all sales made on the Web by customers in their territories. However, paying commissions to sales people or distributors not actually involved in a sale eliminates at least some of the cost savings of selling on the Web.

Because the majority of sales for most manufacturers are still made through traditional channels, the risk of alienating important business partners has affected Web strategies. Some of the approaches used by manufacturers to avoid Internet-related channel conflict are:

- *Use the Web as a lead generator only.* Some manufacturers, notably makers of large consumer durables such as appliances and automobiles, use their websites to collect sales leads, and then direct potential customers to dealers located near them.

- *Offer different products online.* Mattel offers collectibles online that are not available in stores.

- *Involve middlemen in online sales.* When Amway started selling online, it devised a plan to engage and protect its 3 million independent sales representatives. Representatives are encouraged to sign up customers for Amway's website. The sales person then gets a commission for any online purchases made by customers they have registered.

- *Target a different market segment.* Clinique, which offers customized cosmetics and hair-care products on its website, targets consumers who avoid the cosmetics counters in department stores.

Middlemen have devised strategies of their own to add value to their positions in the supply chain. One approach is to take over the final assembly role for products purchased online. The manufacturer ships the product to the distributor in semifinished form, and the distributor completes the assembly and, if appropriate, tests the product before delivery. Called **channel assembly,** this approach allows products to be customized for customers and at the same time shortens the delivery time because many manufacturers, preferring not to disrupt their production processes, postpone custom projects. Another strategy, termed **co-location,** has employees of the distributor stationed at the manufacturer's site to arrange shipment of the finished product to the customer. Because the product is handled fewer times, co-location shortens delivery time.

The roles of some intermediaries commonly found in traditional channels have been adapted for online selling. For example, as many as 30% of Internet-only retailers use a variation of a business-to-business drop shipper to fill consumers' orders.[16] (See Chapter 16 for the description of a drop shipper.) That is, the retailer accepts the customer's order online, then forwards it to a distributor who ships the purchased product directly to the customer with the retailer's name on it. This relieves the Internet retailer of maintaining an inventory as well as the tasks associated with handling, packaging, and transporting the product.

The Internet has also created a new breed of electronic middlemen. These firms make or facilitate transactions through the Internet, but their only investment is a website. The model for this type of operation was created by eBay, the online auction. It has since been copied, modified, and extended to insurance, travel, long-distance phone calls, home repair services, and other industries.[17]

One thing is clear. When a firm uses the Internet for transactions, it has an impact on channel relationships. The resulting channel adjustment may be moderate (redefining the role of middlemen) or drastic (eliminating middlemen).

The Internet has spawned a new breed of B2B intermediaries. This site, usbid.com, specializes in electronic components. It boasts access to over 12 million parts from various suppliers and offers home pages in English, German, Spanish, and Chinese. Businesses wishing to buy or sell items can tap a global marketplace to check prices, request bids, or conduct auctions. Such sites have resulted in more choices for buyers and more prospects for sellers.

www.usbid.com

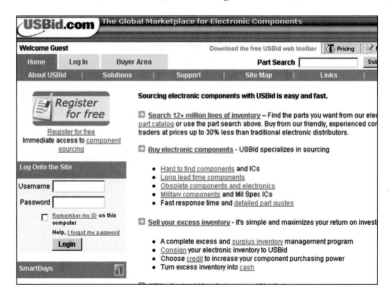

Price

www.proflowers.com

A major attraction of selling via the Internet is a reduction in overhead expenses that often translates into lower prices. For retailers, inventory is reduced or eliminated because most orders can be shipped directly from the manufacturer to the consumer. ProFlowers, an online florist, has reduced the distribution costs and shortened the time it takes for flowers to arrive at their destination by 50% by having them shipped directly from the growers.[18]

Unlike most traditional retailers, online merchants can gather considerable information about shoppers. Though they may never meet them face-to-face, they can track how often individual shoppers visit a site, how long they stay on a visit, what pages they examine, as well as what, how often, and how much they buy. Using this information and sophisticated computer programs, an online retailer can predict the best price to offer. Then when a consumer logs on the site, the program instantaneously selects the price at which to offer the product. This variable pricing strategy is considerably different than what consumers experience in most product categories, and a recent study found that many consumers resent it.[19]

Promotion

A website without visitors is a waste of money. Equally ineffective is a site without the right visitors—the organization's target audience. Part of the problem is simply the number of websites and the fact that the search engines can't keep track of them all. Imagine going to a mall with thousands of stores and looking for a particular one using an incomplete directory.

Another complicating factor was explained earlier. Visits to websites are always initiated by the visitor—a customer, supplier, or even a competitor. These characteristics of the Internet have resulted in some adjustments in how website promotion is carried out.

The first issue is *attracting* the right audience to a website. Several approaches are being used:[20]

- *Banner ads on other websites.* A **banner ad** is a boxed-in promotional message, often appearing at the top of a Web page. A site visitor who clicks on a banner ad is transported to the advertiser's home page. As Web visitors become familiar with banner ads, they tend to ignore them and their effectiveness diminishes. Banner ads are also the least targeted ads. Despite these shortcomings, they remain popular with advertisers due to their relatively low cost.

- *Pop-ups and pop-unders.* This is an ad format that creates a new browser window, either atop the browser the visitor to a site is viewing (pop-up) or behind the site currently being viewed (pop-under). Pop-unders fill the screen when the visitor closes a browser. These formats have generated considerable criticism from consumers because they are so intrusive.

- *Portal search arrangements.* For a fee, portals give a site a prominent position when a visitor undertakes an appropriately directed search. For example, if Sears Roebuck has a portal arrangement with Yahoo!, a consumer who uses Yahoo!'s search engine to find toy marketers will find Sears at or near the top of the list.

- *Sponsorship.* For a sponsorship fee, an advertiser is given a permanent place on the host's site. For example, iVillage, a site targeted at women, has a sponsor list that includes magazines, health and beauty aids, food products, home furnishings, and entertainment items. Each sponsor has special offers and advice for the target audience.

- *Targeted e-mail.* With this method, a firm directs e-mail to current or potential customers, inviting them to visit its site. When this approach is not properly targeted, it becomes electronic junk mail, or **spam,** and can create ill will among the recipients.

- *Affiliate promotion.* Under this approach, a firm includes on its site a link to related sites, usually in exchange for a commission on any sales the arrangement produces. For example, a site selling sporting goods might have as affiliates a sports magazine, a camping equipment site, and a sports memorabilia site. Affiliates are typically identified as such on the site.

Utilizing all of these methods, the volume of Web advertising increased from $2.8 billion in 1999 to $9.6 billion in 2004.[21] Although this is an impressive growth rate, it is important to keep in mind that it still amounts to less than 4% of total advertising expenditures.

Attracting visitors is only half the battle. The second objective of promotion is *holding* visitors once they click on a site. Internet users are generally viewed as impatient—not surprising, because speed and convenience are major attractions. With a simple mouse click, they can disappear as quickly as they arrived. Thus Internet marketers look for ways to make their sites "sticky."

www.cherrycoke.com

The holding power of a site is measured in terms of time spent per visit. For example, when Coca-Cola Co. found that visitors spent only an average of 90 seconds at cherrycoke.com, it redesigned the site.

There is still much to learn about attracting visitors to online sites and about marketing to them once they arrive. As firms gain experience and more research is conducted, they will develop more savvy about online efforts. In the meantime, some online marketers are willing to go to almost any length to attract customers. For example, in order to build market share, more.com, an online drugstore, allowed customers to lock in the price of an item forever as long as they purchased the item at least once a year. Unfortunately for the company, the tactic didn't build profits along with market share so more.com no longer exists.

Issues and Opportunities in the Information Economy

The information economy and the Internet pose major challenges for marketers. Not only are some traditional strategies and tactics obsolete or quickly becoming so, but entirely new issues are frequently discovered. As always, the firms that find ways to overcome these obstacles are likely to be the most successful in the long run.

Information Quality and Quantity

The Internet demonstrates how valuable information can be. A prospective car buyer who can compare the prices of several sellers has an advantage in negotiations. Similarly, a component supplier to a manufacturer kept informed of the manufacturer's production schedule can minimize inventory costs. However, as the Internet grows, the issues of the quality and quantity of the information provided is becoming a larger issue.

For a little as $75, anyone can register a Web address and create a website. As a result, exclusive of business and government websites, there are over 9 million personal websites or weblogs in existence and over 40,000 new ones are registered every day.[22] Visiting the Web is equally easy, requiring only access to a PC and a willingness to pay a monthly connection fee. The problem is that Web users are in danger of being buried by the onslaught of information, and websites risk being lost in the clutter. For example, do consumers want to sift through the terms and conditions of over 300 insurance providers, even if the information is conveniently provided on one website?

Another information issue is quality. There is very little regulation of the Internet and virtually no standards except voluntary guidelines set by professional orga-

nizations such as the Interactive Advertising Bureau (IAB) and the American Marketing Association. As a result, fraud is quite common. According to the results of a study by the research firm Experian, 97% of online retailers in England have experienced fraud. Furthermore, the reach of the Internet has made this a global problem. Online security experts that monitor chat rooms frequented by credit card thieves report that 5,000 credit card account numbers can be purchased in bulk for as little as $1,000 with guarantees that the numbers are valid![23]

The Web also creates instant critics. Anyone with a website can offer a critique of a company, a product, a book, or anything else, and there is nothing to ensure the credentials of the reviewer or the accuracy of the comments. Some evaluations are given credibility by the sites on which they appear. For example, Amazon has professional critics who review and recommend books and compact discs.

The challenge for marketers using the Internet is to understand their target markets well enough to provide them with the right amount of useful information. Doing any less will frustrate customers in the short term and possibly alienate them in the long run.

Customer Service

Infatuated with the technology and the ability to conduct transactions, some online marketers overlook the importance of service. Presale information, operating instructions, and postsale problem resolution frequently receive too little attention.

Many thought the Web could replace retail stores for consumers or the sales people for business-to-business customers. However, experience indicates that it is difficult to eliminate the services provided by these middlemen. Thus online marketers must address challenges such as returned merchandise, payment problems, and performance complaints. For example, when Amazon began its auction site, it offered a customer satisfaction guarantee. Even though the transactions are between the buyers and sellers, and Amazon only brings them together, Amazon is attempting to avoid the problems eBay experienced when customers were dissatisfied and had nowhere to turn.

Providing service may be the single biggest hurdle for firms contemplating a move to the Internet. Many of the more successful Internet retailers have found that combining stores with online access is the best formula.[24] Consumers can visit the store to see merchandise firsthand or to return merchandise. Alternatively, consumers can shop from home or use Internet kiosks in the store to obtain detailed information about products or to search for items that are not on the store's shelves. In effect, these retailers are offering the best of both worlds to their customers.

Security and Privacy

As many as 90% of consumers with Web access have never made an online purchase. The two major reasons are security and privacy. After years of being advised to guard against having credit card numbers stolen, consumers are now asked to freely give those numbers to strangers over the Internet. At the same time, publicity about hackers breaking into the databases of banks and other credit-granting organizations to steal account numbers has made many wary.[25] In addition, efforts by both federal agencies and state legislators to regulate the behavior of Web advertisers and sellers indicate to consumers that problems exist.[26]

Creating a climate of trust on the Internet is difficult. The challenge is compounded by its newness and intangibility. Without stores or employees to talk to face-to-face, consumers' hesitancy to share personal or financial information is not surprising. Online security systems, which involve encryption, digital certification, authentication, virtual account numbers, and other sophisticated technology are not likely to be understood by consumers. However, what they can understand is the assurance of the seller. To overcome the fears of potential customers, online buying must develop a reputation as being safe. That means the customers must perceive the system over which they make the transaction and the seller as trustworthy.

The Internet has opened new geographic markets to sellers and allowed buyers access to products and brands frequently unavailable from their local retailers. For example, of the approximately $2 billion in online sales made by Latin American retailers in 2004, more than one-third were made to consumers in the U.S. LaCarretica.com, based in Costa Rica, is one of those firms finding a receptive market among Costa Rican immigrants to the U.S.

www.lacarretica.com

www.landsend.com

A seller can create an image of legitimacy in several ways. One approach is to transfer an existing reputation earned in another selling format to electronic commerce. For example, Lands' End, with a proven record as a catalog retailer, makes this statement on its website about the safety of credit card transactions, "Our commitment in this regard is total and unconditional. It's Guaranteed. Period." Another approach is to create associations with trusted brands or firms. For example, a less-well-known firm can increase its credibility and trust by selling only well-established brands on its site. Finally, by having a well-known partner or recognizable sponsors, an unknown online merchant can give its site legitimacy.

Privacy concerns focus on how data about Internet visitors are collected and used. Data about Web visitors are gathered in several ways. Some data are provided by visitors when they register on a website. Registration is frequently required in order to gain access to specialized information, games, contests, and other attractive features. Consumers also provide information at the time of a purchase. In addition to some demographic data, the information requested to register on a site or make a purchase often includes a short survey with questions about activities, interests, and other purchase behavior. Data are also gathered without the direct involvement of the visitor. An online firm does this by using a **cookie**, a file placed on the hard drive of the visitor's computer that automatically records where the person goes online, the frequency of visits to a site, and the duration of each visit.

Internet marketers collect the data to better understand their current and potential markets. However, there are indications that consumers are increasingly uncomfortable with the data gathering. For example, 50% of Web surfers report removing cookies from their computer hard drives.[27] Among the other consumer protection concerns that have been raised are:

- *Gathering information.* Should marketers ever gather information without the express consent of the consumer? Even if permission is granted, should there be limits on the information considered appropriate to gather? Recognizing that children are especially vulnerable, Congress passed the Children's Online Privacy Protection Act, which requires that commercial websites obtain consent from a parent before asking children under 13 years of age for their names, addresses, telephone numbers, or other identifying information. Another challenging question is whether customers should be compensated for the information they provide because it obviously has value to the organizations collecting it.

- *Using information.* Once consumer information is gathered, should its application be constrained? For example, Amazon uses a consumer's profile to suggest

Marketers know that the difference between success and failure often hinges on how well they understand customers. As a result, there is a scramble to gather, analyze, and interpret customer data from a variety of sources. Some data the customers cannot control. For example reports of births, deaths, marriages, bankruptcies, and building permits are pubic records available to anyone. Other data are voluntarily provided when, for example, consumers participate in surveys, fill-out warranty cards, or allow cookies to be placed on their computer hard drives. Still other data are gathered surreptitiously. For example:

- The station a car radio is tuned to is determined by measuring the electric radiation emitted as the car passes monitoring equipment along the side of the road. Combined with a license plate number, this information can be linked to an individual or household.

- Radio frequency identification tags are placed in gambling casino chips to electronically track the betting, winning, and losing of individual gamblers.

- Utilizing global positioning system (GPS) satellites, an auto rental company can monitor the speed a vehicle is driven and where it goes without the renter's knowledge.

- Closed-community stored-value systems (often called smart cards), designed to permit commuters to speed through highway toll booths, make it possible to track where and when individuals travel and even how fast they go.

Individuals may have little control over the gathering of such data. As pointed out by Scott McNealy, Chairman of Sun Microsystems, "You already have zero privacy. Get over it." However, some contend since the data apply to the consumer it should not be used, shared, or sold without permission. Others argue that once it is organized into a database it belongs to the organizer, and for a business the first priority is to the owners. Do firms with access to such data have an ethical responsibility with regard to how it is used?

Sources: Will Wade, "EZPass Tries Where Others Have Failed," *American Banker*, Apr. 1, 2004, pp. 1+; David Whelan, "Google Me Not," *Forbes*, Aug. 16, 2004, pp. 102+; Matthew Maier, "Finding Profits in the GPS Economy," *Business 2.0*, April 2005, pp. 21–22; Rebecca Jarvis, "Casinos Bet Big on RFID," *Business 2.0*, April 2005, p. 26; Lucas Conley, "At 1600 Pennsylvania Avenue, of Course, It's 'Rush Limbaugh,'" *Fast Company*, February 2005, p. 29.

books, which few people find objectionable. But should a search engine, assumed by most users to be an objective directory, tailor its recommendations to a searcher's demographics or past purchases? In the U.S. there are few regulations; but in the European Union consumers must be given explicit explanations about how any information they provide will be used.

- *Selling, exchanging, or combining information.* Is it acceptable for a website that has gathered information legitimately to sell it to another firm? For example, an online investment broker or insurance agency would find information about an online bank's customers very valuable. What about combining catalog purchase behavior with online shopping behavior, as several research firms are planning to do? Although these profiles will initially be anonymous, as marketers search for patterns of behavior and target segments, there are questions about what might happen in the future when individuals can be specifically identified.

Marketers prefer self-regulation. However, there are calls for the government to provide greater control of Internet security and privacy.

International Markets

Theoretically, electronic commerce knows no boundaries. A customer in Taiwan can use the Internet to make a purchase from a Chicago-based firm as easily as can a customer in Milwaukee. The only physical constraint is delivery, and that has been greatly simplified by shipping companies. However, a variety of other issues must be overcome as marketers expand globally.

The model for Web-based marketing has been created in the U.S., relying on the infrastructure that's in place, but many parts of the world lack one or more critical components that have contributed to the rapid growth of online marketing. For example, three countries—the U.S., China, and Japan—account for over 40% of the world's Internet usage,[28] but China does not have a national credit card system. As a result, without a convenient method of paying, Chinese consumers account for a relatively small portion of online purchases.

And there's the issue of PC ownership. In countries where per capita income is only a few thousand dollars or less, few people can afford a PC. In some countries, notably Brazil, entrepreneurs are trying to reduce this problem by making the Web accessible in supermarket kiosks for consumers who lack computers.

There are also cultural barriers to the rapid expansion of the Internet. Although English is the standard language for business-to-business transactions, many small-business people are able to communicate only in their native languages. In terms of consumers, local Internet portals have been more successful than larger imported counterparts such as AOL because they provide a rich mix of local content.

Specific legal restrictions imposed by individual governments have added complications to international e-commerce. For example, there is a French requirement that all contracts be written in French, a ban in Finland on mentioning speed as a feature of a car, and a restriction in Sweden on advertising directed at children under 12 years of age. Another complication is sales tax. The European Union has decreed that purchases made by customers in its member countries are subject to sales tax, and government agencies in the U.S. and elsewhere are considering similar legislation.

In a somewhat surprising turn of events, laws designed to protect domestic businesses by creating artificially high prices have actually encouraged international online sales. For example, German consumers find it's cheaper to buy books from websites in Great Britain, and British consumers can get better deals on cars purchased from online dealers in Belgium.

The Future

Clearly the information economy has arrived. What is yet to be determined is how it will impact each individual industry and business. The challenge for marketers is to deter-

A GLOBAL PERSPECTIVE

What happens when high technology products meet low technology infrastructure?

Much of the world is unable to take advantage of technology because essential infrastructure support, such as a reliable source of electricity, is unavailable.

Recognizing the problem a British–South African firm, Freeplay Energy, develops products with simplified technology that operate on alternative power sources. For example, the firm is famous for its hand-cranked radios that bring news and other important information to six million people in underdeveloped countries. Other crank-powered products from Freeplay are a flashlight and a cell phone charger.

Recently the firm has designed four pieces of medical equipment powered by handcranks, foot pedals, or solar panels. The devices include instruments to measure oxygen in the blood, administer small doses of medication on a timed schedule, separate blood components, and monitor fetal heart rate. All are likely to improve diagnoses and treatment in areas where the infant mortality rates are 30 times that of developed countries.

Reengineering a high-tech product so it can reliably perform its essential function utilizing an alternative energy source can be a difficult task. However, Freeplay has shown there are not only markets for such products, but there is also a substantial benefit to society.

Sources: Ann Grimes, "Charge On," *The Wall Street Journal*, Feb. 24, 2005, p. B4; "Human-Powered Health Care," *The Economist*, Dec. 4, 2004, p. 14+.

mine how information can be most effectively utilized to meet the needs of the customer and satisfy the objectives of the organization. Not surprisingly, determining its value brings us back once again to the marketing concept. In the business-to-business sector, electronic networking has added to efficiency and contributed to bottom-line performance. It has been less successful in generating profits for firms that sell to consumers.

Thus far, the most successful Internet marketing sites deal in information. An interesting example is Ancestry.com, a profitable site that helps people track down their living and deceased family members using a large, searchable database. Because all aspects of a transaction are conducted over the Internet, maximum benefits are achieved. Next in line are the sites that market services such as airline seats or hotel rooms. These marketers have an inventory that becomes obsolete at a definable time—for example, when a plane takes off. The challenge is to develop a yield-management program that adjusts fares over time to fill the largest number of seats at the highest possible price. The most challenging Internet businesses are those handling physical goods that must be inventoried, stored, and distributed. Examples are online marketers of groceries, clothing, furniture, and automobiles. The logistics problems in these businesses consume much of the gains achieved from the online transactions.

Despite its expanding impact, electronic commerce is unlikely to replace traditional marketing as we know it. In 1999, Jeff Bezos, the founder of Amazon.com and one of the leaders of the e-commerce movement, predicted that Internet sellers could attract at most 15% of the world's retail sales. He explained that stores will always be around because people enjoy the interaction shopping provides, and some needs must be met more quickly than is possible over the Internet.[29] Time will tell if Bezos is correct or if a combination of technology and ingenuity will someday prove his prediction to be very conservative.

Summary

Information has always played a major role in marketing. The effective utilization of information leads to better products, prices, distribution, and promotion. Technology combined with information is especially powerful.

Although many forms of technology have influenced marketing, the Internet is currently having a major—perhaps unprecedented—impact.

Electronic networks are created when individuals or organizations are linked via some form of telecommunications. Internal electronic networks are called intranets. There are several types of external electronic networks, including electronic data interchanges, electronic information transfer, electronic transactions, electronic commerce, and extranets. All of these now make use of the Internet.

Internet marketing changes the dynamics in markets. The commercial application of the Internet required the development of the World Wide Web and several tools to make it accessible, including browsers, directories, and portals. Now the Web is available to virtually anyone with a PC. Customers gain greater control of interactions with businesses and have the opportunity to compare products and prices. More products are customized, and fewer prices are fixed. New ways are developed to deliver products to buyers, and buyers share more information. The Internet influences all areas of marketing, in particular marketing research, product design, channel relationships, pricing, and promotion.

The information economy poses both challenges and opportunities for marketers. Among the most significant are managing the quality and quantity of information, providing customer service, ensuring the security of transactions and the privacy of customers, and developing international electronic commerce.

The Internet will continue to grow and evolve. At this point companies dealing in information are best able to take advantage of the economies provided by the Internet, whereas those selling goods face the most challenges. Although its impact will be felt by all businesses, it's not likely that the Internet will entirely replace traditional marketing.

More about **Amazon**

After eight years of losses, Amazon generated its first full year of profit in 2003, and in 2004 it had $588 million in profits on sales of almost $6 billion. There are several reasons it took Amazon so long to become profitable. First, the company was selling to consumers on the Internet before it was a widely accepted channel. Early on, the majority of consumers did not have Internet access and many who did were uncomfortable giving out their credit card information. Second, Bezos is a firm believer in pricing below the competition. As a result, he constantly looks for ways to reduce his customers' outlays. For example, Amazon regularly offers reduced shipping charges even though critics said it would be too costly. Third, Amazon undertakes customer-oriented strategies such as alerting customers who may have forgotten and accidentally ordered items they already bought from Amazon years ago. Finally, in order to give customers more options, Amazon allows third parties to sell new and used products on its site, often at prices below its own. All of this is to fulfill the mission formulated by Bezos: "To create the world's most customer-centric company, the place where you can find and buy anything you want online."[30]

1. How has Amazon blended information technology with a customer-orientation?

2. If Amazon can sell to consumers at lower prices than conventional "brick and mortar" retailers, how can traditional retailers hope to survive?

Key Terms and Concepts

Internet (614)
World Wide Web (614)
Website (614)
Networks (614)
Electronic networks (614)
Intranet (614)
Electronic data interchange (EDI) (615)

Electronic information (615)
Electronic transactions (617)
Electronic commerce (618)
Extranet (618)
Browser (618)
Directory (619)
Portal (619)
Fulfillment (620)

Clustering (622)
Collaborative filtering (622)
Channel assembly (624)
Co-location (624)
Banner ad (625)
Spam (625)
Cookie (628)

Questions and Problems

1. Two examples of information technology that have had a significant impact on marketing are radio and television. How does the Internet differ from these breakthroughs as a marketing tool?

2. Examine the e-information sites of a fast-food restaurant and a traditional manufacturer (such as Whirlpool or Ford Motor Co.). Using the five categories of information described in the chapter, compare the sites.

3. What key strategic issues are faced by traditional "bricks-and-mortar" retailers such as Wal-Mart, Kmart, and Office Depot when they go online to sell products?

4. Describe one possible marketing implication of each of the following effects of the Internet:
   a. Interaction controlled by customers
   b. More and better information
   c. Fewer fixed prices
   d. New product-delivery methods
   e. More buyer communication

5. Why should firms such as Mattel, Timex, and Sony be concerned about their existing channels when they begin selling products to consumers via the Web?

6. Go to one of the Web portals (Netscape, Alta Vista, Lycos) and click through several links. Note the banner ads on each link. What appears to be the objective of the banner ads? What are some factors that may make them effective or ineffective?

7. Providing customer service appears to be one of the primary challenges for Internet marketers. What implications does this have for their "bricks-and-mortar" competitors?

8. There are concerns about Internet marketers using cookies to gather data about online customer behavior. Is this different than observing customers as they shop in retail stores?

Interactive Marketing Exercises

1. Interview five students who have shopped on the Web within the last week. Gather the following information:
   a. Why did they choose the Web as a place to shop?
   b. Did they make a purchase? Why or why not?
   c. In the process of shopping, did they make any unplanned site or page visits?
   d. How long did their shopping "trip" take?

   On the basis of this information as well as your own experiences, what do you see as the strengths and weaknesses of the Web as a marketing tool?

2. Talk to the owner or manager of a retail store in a category where online marketing is growing (such as books, recorded music, groceries, videos, or toys). Determine how serious a threat the person considers online marketing to be, and what changes have been made or are planned in response.

Cases for Part 7

McDonald's

Implementing a New Recipe for Success

When Ray Kroc opened his first McDonald's in 1955, he kept the format simple so it could be duplicated easily by franchisees with little or no restaurant experience. The company with the Golden Arches featured a menu of hamburgers, french fries, and soft drinks. The food was inexpensive, consistent in quality, and served speedily from nearly identical establishments that were pleasant and clean.

Over the ensuing 50 years, Kroc's initial vision led to the establishment of McDonald's as one of the world's best-known brands and the largest global restaurant chain, with revenues of $19 billion in 2004. Along the way, McDonald's introduced products that have remained perennial favorites, such as the Big Mac and the Egg McMuffin. And of course there's the Happy Meal, which is beloved by kids as much for the food as for the toy that comes with it.

But McDonald's has experienced its share of growing pains as well. While it has remained a popular destination for children, in recent years many adults began to eschew the fast-food chain in favor of alternatives such as Subway, the sandwich chain, and Panera, a "fast casual" bakery-cafe that features soups, salads, and sandwiches. To counteract the slip in popularity, McDonald's brought in a new chief marketing officer, Larry Light. Following an analysis of the situation, Light observed, "Consumers were embarrassed to say 'I ate at McDonald's.' People were saying things like, 'I have fond memories of McDonald's, but I've grown up and the brand hasn't grown with me.' It wasn't that customers weren't coming. They were coming but only because we were convenient and economical."

One of the reasons McDonald's had become so convenient was the company's aggressive expansion strategy, both in the U.S. and abroad. In 1995, the company added 1,100 new locations throughout the world, and it continued to maintain that breakneck pace through the year 2000. Between 1996 and 2002, the number of locations in Asia, Africa, and Latin America doubled. By October 2004, there were 9,000 restaurants operated by the McDonald's corporation, and an additional 22,000 franchised units owned by individuals (franchisees). The number of outlets created resentment among some McDonald's franchisees who charged that the company's newer outlets were cannibalizing the sales of existing restaurants. One store owner in Brazil watched 14 new McDonald's restaurants open near his location, and complained, "With every store that opened, I lost more sales."

Indeed, revenues in 2001 were down 1.3% compared to the previous year in locations that had been open at least a year, and in 2002, they had decreased another 2.1%. The company as a whole reported a net loss in January of 2003, its first since the year it began.

Confronting Some Super-Sized Problems

As McDonald's celebrated its 50th anniversary in 2005, it was benefiting from a catchy global advertising campaign that had its patrons all over the world humming "Bada ba ba baaaa . . . I'm lovin' it!" More important, the corporation has been re-examining and revising several of Kroc's fundamental policies. For example, it has slowed its rate of expansion and added new, nonburger food items to its menu. The company is also improving the ambience of its existing outlets.

For many years a fundamental component of McDonald's strategy for success was to grow sales by expanding its operations through new restaurant additions. Now McDonald's has slowed its rate of expansion considerably, in some cases closing restaurants with substandard levels of service, cleanliness, and decor. In 2004, it opened 432 new restaurants throughout the world, and the year before that, it unveiled only 21. Some areas actually experienced a net decrease in McDonald's outlets in the year 2003, including Asia and Latin America.

McDonald's has also had to confront the issue of Americans' ever-expanding waistlines. In 2000, about 300,000 Americans died of ailments attributed to being overweight, resulting in healthcare costs of $117 billion. Increasing concerns about health and nutrition, a low-carbohydrate dieting craze, and rising levels of juvenile obesity have led some consumers to move away from fried and grilled fast foods to fresh sandwiches and subs.

The chain's fattening food was highlighted in an award-winning documentary called *Supersize Me*, which followed the film's maker, Morgan Spurlock, as he ate exclusively at various McDonald's restaurants for 30 days. Spurlock gained 25 pounds and began suffering from a variety of highly publicized medical ailments. Adding to the negative picture, several consumers have sued McDonald's for contributing to their obesity problems. The cumulative effect was a barrage of bad publicity directed at McDonald's, resulting in the company's announcement that it would no longer offer super-sized portions.

Taking a Bite out of Big Mac

One fast-food company that has embraced a health-oriented position is Subway. In January 2000, it hired a young man named Jared to be its spokesperson. Jared had lost almost 250 pounds, simply by eating the same two low-fat Subway sandwiches every day for almost one year, and his story was told countless times on television commercials and talk-show appearances. In 2002, Subway surpassed McDonald's in total number of U.S. outlets. On a global level, Subway now operates more than 21,000 franchises in 75 countries, and reported sales of $6.8 billion in 2004, about one-third as much as McDonald's. "Our size doesn't begin to approach the global bigness of McDonald's, but it still feels pretty darn good to beat them on their home turf," commented a Subway spokesperson.

While Subway has been positioning itself as the wholesome fast-food alternative, other chains are attempting to appeal to the heaviest (no pun intended) fast-food eaters by developing menu items that taste great but in no way can be called healthy. In November 2004, Hardee's introduced its Monster Thickburger, which features two beef patties, four strips of bacon and three slices of American cheese. This carnivorous concoction weighs in with 1,418 calories and more than 100 grams of fat. McDonald's most indulgent burger, by comparison, is the Double Quarter Pounder with Cheese, with half as many calories and 40 grams of fat. Same-store sales at Hardee's had risen by 7% a year after the huge burger's introduction.

A new category of restaurants, dubbed "fast casual," has been steadily growing over the past several years. Customers at these establishments still place their orders at counters, but the atmosphere is cozier, and the ingredients are fresher than those found at traditional fast-food restaurants. According to one industry analyst, fast-casual restaurants, such as Panera, are able to charge a premium to people who "want to move beyond fast food, but still

need food fast." By the end of 2004, Panera had 741 bakery-cafes throughout the U.S., and revenues of almost half a billion dollars—a 31% increase over 2003.

As McDonald's began losing market share to the new crop of fast-casual establishments, it began investing in fast-casual chains, such as Pret A Manger, Chipotle Mexican, Rotisserie Grill, and Boston Market. The firm's plan to expand these chains throughout the U.S. and overseas pleased many existing franchisees, who were excited at the prospect of being able to operate these new restaurants. However, only a few years after purchasing Donato's Pizzera and Fazoli's, McDonald's divested itself of these underperforming units, reportedly to concentrate more on its flagship restaurants.

Cooking Up New Strategies for the Future

As McDonald's has decreased its number of new-store openings, it has begun to devise ways to reconnect with adults. One of the first steps was to develop appealing new menu items. Not since Chicken McNuggets made their debut in 1983 has the company had a successful, major new-product launch. Hoping to reverse that trend, the company introduced a line of premium salads, threw in a bottle of water and a pedometer, and marketed them as "Go Active Happy Meals" for adults. Since then, it has also developed a fruit and walnut salad, all-white meat chicken strips, and has begun offering apple slices and juice as alternatives to french fries and soda in Happy Meals.

To stimulate more breakfast traffic, McDonald's premiered the McGriddle in June 2003. Composed of two syrup-coated pancakes, eggs, cheese, and meat, the McGriddle cannot be termed healthy, but it was an instant success. And the company is intent on building on that momentum. As coffee has become ever more popular during the past ten years, McDonald's coffee sales have been ground down by 36%. The company is now experimenting with premium coffee, in an effort to take business back from Starbucks and Dunkin' Donuts, both of which sell twice as much coffee as the Golden Arches. "Younger folks are looking for that robust taste, and McDonald's coffee has pretty much stayed the same," commented one McDonald's franchisee.

To help it compete against the sandwich chains both at home and abroad, McDonald's is testing a line of toasted deli-style sandwiches called "Oven Selects." "Sandwiches outsell hamburgers by ten to one," commented Russ Smyth, president of McDonald's Europe. "So there is a great opportunity here."

Most of these new products also come with the advantage of an increased price tag, which will raise the average check size and boost restaurant sales. However, McDonald's has also stayed committed to providing value to its customers, and features the Pound Saver Menu in the United Kingdom, the Amazing Value Menu in Asia, and the Dollar Menu in the U.S.

To further improve the experience for its customers, McDonald's has been upgrading its physical locations and service. It has imposed stricter quality control standards and has a number of ways to monitor whether individual outlets are conforming to them, including consumer surveys and mystery shoppers. Mystery shoppers pose as regular customers and take notes on everything related to quality and service, including whether they were greeted with a smile, how long it took to get their food, and if their order was filled correctly.

After customers complained about long lines at the drive-through window, McDonald's began beefing up its staff and decreased the amount of wait time by as much as 12% since 2001. In addition, most McDonald's locations are now accepting debit and credit cards, and wireless Internet access is available in more than 6,500 of its establishments.

Beyond the menu, perhaps McDonald's most visible change has been the new promotional strategy it adopted under the guidance of Larry Light. When he came on board in 2002, he pulled the plug on more than 20 disparate advertising campaigns that were running all over the world. Light challenged the company's ad agencies to come up with a coherent message that could be used on a global scale. The eventual winner was a German firm with the tag line, "I'm Lovin' It," set to an addictive melody. Light then allowed each market to customize its own ads around the tag line and it has become nearly ubiquitous throughout the world.

The new campaign began running in the fall of 2003, and the first television ads had a hip-hop feel, which many felt gave the tired brand new energy. One franchisee extolled the benefits of the new campaign when he said, "After 37 years, I've had the opportunity to see many different campaigns, and ups and downs in advertising, but this positioning is a breathtaking turnaround." In 2004, *Advertising Age* magazine proclaimed McDonald's "Marketer of the Year."

Elsewhere on the promotional front change is underway. McDonald's long-standing, exclusive association with Disney ended in 2005. For 10 years, McDonald's was the only fast-food restaurant with promotional ties to Disney, and enjoyed riding the waves of Disney's success when it was pumping out animated hits, such as *The Lion King*. To replace Disney, McDonald's has signed a two-year pact with DreamWorks that will begin with promotions tied to *Shrek 3* in 2007. The new arrangement also gives McDonald's the flexibility to partner with other studios.

Separating from Disney and entering a non-exclusive contract with DreamWorks are indications that McDonald's wants to broaden its market focus. Another sign is the aggressive pursuit of teens and young adults with "Big Mac Meal Tracks," a limited-time promotion that gave customers the opportunity to download one song from Sony with the purchase of every Big Mac meal. According to one Sony executive, "In my 30 years in business, I never saw a more effective marketing machine than the program we did with McDonald's. Their ability to execute the program was damn near flawless and that's across six countries."

That's music to Light's ears, the man behind such promotional strategies. According to him, "The brand has to be constantly evolved to remain fresh and contemporary to meet consumer desires. There is no finish line." Certainly Ray Kroc would agree. Visionaries recognize change is the only constant. The challenge is anticipating the direction and responding with the correct strategy.

Questions

1. Describe several examples from the case that likely reflect strategic marketing planning and several others that represent strategic company planning at McDonald's.

2. Where would you place McDonald's traditional fast-food restaurants on the three planning models presented in Chapter 20? What implications would you draw from the placements?

3. How does the number of McDonald's outlets affect implementation of its marketing efforts?

www.mcdonalds.com

Preserving Its Status as Market Leader

Originally an expensive novelty, cellular phones were used primarily by business executives who felt the need to be accessible at all times. Throughout the 1990s, these mobile phones grew in popularity and affordability, and eventually many business people had them. By the end of the decade they also had attracted many consumers who appreciated their convenience for personal use.

The next revolution in wireless communication was pioneered by Research in Motion (RIM), a small company based in Waterloo, Canada. It introduced a compact personal digital assistant (PDA) with an easy-to-use design that could send and receive e-mail from almost anywhere. Called a BlackBerry, it attracted a core base of fanatical users, primarily executives, who saw it as an indispensable business accessory. Oprah Winfrey proclaimed the BlackBerry one of her "Favorite Things" in 2003. An official at the Environmental Protection Agency (EPA) gushed, "I think it's the greatest technical innovation. A lot of people complain about new systems, but BlackBerrys are almost universally raved about." There was even a word coined to describe the addictive nature of the device—CrackBerry.

Inevitably, other companies began developing their own handheld e-mail units, some with a number of added features, such as a cellular phone and even music-playing capability. After ruling the corporate PDA market for several years, RIM reached a crossroads. The firm was forced to decide whether to stay the course and continue to concentrate on business users or to expand its focus and also target the consumer market with additional functionality. This decision became even more critical when the biggest name in desktop computing software, Microsoft, decided to enter the wireless e-mail market.

Developing a Sweet New Product

Like so many other technology companies that sprang up in the late-20th century, RIM started with a college defection. In 1984, Mike Lazaridis, an electrical engineering student, left school to develop teleprompting software. After awhile, he became interested in the notion of sending information from corporate computers to wireless paging networks, and saw the Internet and the proliferation of e-mail as his opportunity to make it possible. He brought in Jim Balsillie, a graduate of Harvard's MBA program, and together they sold Lazaridis's idea to investors.

The first BlackBerry hit the market in 1998, and featured a tiny QWERTY keyboard that replicated the placement of the alphabetical keys on a full-sized computer keyboard. The device was comparable in size to a pager, and operated exclusively on BellSouth's pager data network. E-mail directed to a home or work computer was immediately forwarded to the recipient's BlackBerry. Owners became quite adept at manipulating their thumbs to tap out e-mail messages on these handheld devices, with the heaviest users contracting what became known as "BlackBerry Thumb."

RIM marketed the first BlackBerrys to top-level corporate executives who quickly became hooked on the ability to receive and send e-mail virtually anywhere, anytime. This led many of them to require that their staffs become BlackBerry users as well—a movement that has been met with a mixed response. While many business people appreciate being able to stay in contact with work on a constant basis, some resent feeling tied to the office by their BlackBerrys. "I still believe the premise that someone in my position is entitled to some personal time," commented an employee with the Defense Department. "I've had guys say they'd kill for one, but I don't like the fact that I am electronically tethered 24 hours a day, seven days a week." A vice president with the United States Postal Service explained that many spouses of his male managers also have complained. "They say their husbands pay more attention to their BlackBerrys than to [them] at dinner."

However, most users extol the benefits of their BlackBerrys. For instance, when employees go on vacation, there is less of a need to assign someone to cover for them, since they can regularly check in by using the device. BlackBerrys also help users manage the amount of work they will have once they return from vacation or business trips. "I do a fair amount of traveling, and this way I don't come into the office to a tidal wave of information," stated another Defense Department worker. In addition, it provides workers with more flexibility because they can wirelessly update their schedules without phoning into the office or setting up their laptops.

Tapping into Fruitful New Markets

More than 3 million people were thumbing through their e-mail via BlackBerrys by May of 2005, with the majority of them being corporate users. RIM had been particularly successful targeting financial companies, healthcare and pharmaceutical firms, legal enterprises, and real estate businesses. The government also has been a large-volume purchaser, representing almost 10% of RIM's client base in late-2004. "I picked up this thing, understood how it worked, and realized that it would change the lives of executives at the EPA—and frankly that's how it turned out," stated the EPA's deputy director of information analysis. To help information technology departments manage their employees' BlackBerry use, RIM also developed software that resides on an organization's server.

To try to broaden its appeal to a wider audience, RIM introduced a BlackBerry in 2002 that added a phone and a Web browser to the e-mail capability. However, the added functionality created operating problems, and even BlackBerry's usually exceptional e-mail service suffered. Newer models attempted to solve these problems, culminating in the BlackBerry 7100 series. For $199 and a monthly subscription fee of about $60, the 7100 "smartphone" features a generous screen and a keypad/dialing pad that condenses the entire alphabet into 14 buttons, with two characters sharing one key. To help users navigate this setup and reduce the amount they actually have to type, RIM developed SureType software, which automatically recognizes words as they are being formed and helps with spelling and grammar.

"The new 7100 opens them up to a wider audience of individuals instead of just companies," observed an industry analyst. "They're still not at a point where they can truly get to the soccer moms and dads . . . but what's attractive is widening Black-Berry's appeal." According to RIM, its strategy with the 7100 wasn't necessarily to appeal to the average consumer, but to try to reach out to the "prosumer" which it defined as an individual purchaser, probably a professional or business person. It also began more aggressively targeting smaller and mid-sized companies for multiple unit sales.

Initially, RIM sold BlackBerrys directly to users and provided them with airtime by purchasing it from cellular carriers. Eventually, it shifted to using the cellular carriers as the primary distribution channel for the device. And as RIM widened its focus beyond corporate clients to also target end users, the carriers did the same. For instance, AT&T Wireless started out by exclusively selling BlackBerrys through its direct corporate sales force, but soon began offering them in its retail locations and through its website.

By 2005, BlackBerrys were being sold by 95 different carriers in 40 countries at more than 50,000 retail locations. RIM reported sales of $1.35 billion, and net income in excess of $210 million; only two years earlier, the company had announced a net loss of $130 million. Almost 80% of its sales originated in North America, with the majority of the rest being generated in Europe. RIM's hopes of expanding its operations into Japan and South Korea were constrained by a technological barrier. In those countries, different cellular service standards make the Black-Berry incompatible with local cellular networks.

In an attempt to further expand its customer base and increase revenues, RIM began selling BlackBerry software to other handheld manufacturers. Companies such as Motorola, Nokia, and Siemens have incorporated the BlackBerry technology into their own devices, thereby competing directly with RIM's handsets. However, some of these manufacturers exhibited a bit of reluctance regarding this strategy. "We'll try to work with RIM," insisted a general manager for Nokia. "But someone who buys a RIM phone isn't buying one of ours. And we want to be the preferred mobile e-mail handset provider."

Getting into a Competitive Jam

Such partnerships and licensing agreements complicate an increasingly competitive environment in an industry that grew almost 17% in 2004 to $4.3 billion in sales. More than 12.3 million PDA's were sold throughout the world, with smartphones making the biggest gains. A smartphone is a handheld device that combines the functionality of a PDA with a mobile phone. In the U.S., RIM has a 42% share of the smartphone market, followed by Palm with 26%. Palm's latest product in this category, the Treo 650, was met with critical praise for its full keyboard, its camera, and its optional memory card that transforms the Treo into an MP3 player capable of storing 300 songs. For users who crave a gadget with gee-whiz appeal, the Treo 650 has it in abundance. "When I put the Treo next to the BlackBerry, no one is going to take the BlackBerry," stated the executive director at a law firm who was responsible for deciding whether to switch his employees from the Black-Berry to the Treo. However, its larger size and initial $499 price tag was seen as a drawback by many who felt the powerful device would remain out of reach of a good portion of the potential market. Anticipating that business users would probably comprise the majority of the Treo's buyers, Palm assembled a sales force to help its cellular carriers target potential corporate clients.

T-Mobile tried to keep pace with its smartphone entry, the Sidekick II, which is geared more toward the casual user and marketed to a younger audience. Its e-mail and voice capabilities were criticized for not being as functional as BlackBerry's, but the device was praised for its user-friendly keyboard and camera. The Sidekick II lacked an MP3 player, however, which may lessen its appeal to the hipsters T-Mobile is targeting.

But RIM is facing attacks on two fronts, as a couple of heavyweights get more serious about wireless e-mail. On the hardware side, Dell has been considering the possibility of modifying its Axim line of electronic organizers to compete with the BlackBerry. The new Axim smartphones would feature software by Good Technology, the same company currently partnering with Palm on the Treo 650. "Dell can offer the hardware component at a far lower price (than Black-Berry), which is the Dell model," commented an industry analyst. With hardware making up almost 70% of RIM's sales, this is undoubtedly a threatening situation for the BlackBerry maker.

At the same time, the world's largest and most successful software developer has been refining its wireless e-mail capabilities. "Microsoft aims to kill BlackBerry," bluntly stated one industry insider. To do this, Microsoft has been updating its Windows Mobile software, and has been busily licensing it to a number of different hardware developers. In addition, it has developed software that it will provide free of charge to clients who purchase a Microsoft Exchange e-mail server. (A server is a computer that provides information or software to other computers linked to a network.) This makes it possible for a client to forward e-mail from its Microsoft Exchange server to its employees' wireless handhelds. This will no doubt help the sales of the wireless e-mail devices Microsoft powers. And Microsoft has a built-in advantage in that many people are already comfortable using its software, such as Microsoft Excel and Windows, both of which will be incorporated into Windows Mobile. "Microsoft-based PDAs have gained favor mostly due to their affinity with the Windows PC market and Microsoft's ability to attract more than 30 licensees around the globe," explained an industry analyst.

But RIM's CEO doesn't sound worried and has expressed the utmost confidence in his BlackBerry devices and software. "The complexity is masked by this very simple, user-friendly device," stated Lazaridis. "This is a solution that has evolved and developed, and gone through trial by fire. Any competitor is going to have to go through that. We've done it right, we have the brand, we know how to make these devices. It's a very high standard to try to match." A

marketing vice president with T-Mobile agreed, "It's addictive. You give one to people and they don't want to give it back. Nobody does e-mail better than Black-Berry."

Questions

1. What appears to be RIM's organizational mission. Has it changed over the life of the BlackBerry?

2. Describe the product-market growth strategies RIM has pursued with BlackBerry. What adjustments has the firm made in its marketing mix as its strategy changes?

3. How would you position the BlackBerry 7100 series in the marketplace? How would you distinguish it from competitors?

4. What measures of marketing performance should be used for BlackBerry? For Microsoft's Windows Mobile?

Sources

Case 1: McDonald's www.mcdonalds.com, accessed June 30, 2005; www.subway.com, accessed June 30, 2005; www.panera.com, accessed June 30, 2005; Merissa Marr and Steven Gray, "McDonald's Woos New Partners as Disney Pact Nears End," The Wall Street Journal, June 6, 2005, p. B1; Steven Gray and Deborah Ball, "McDonald's Sees Rivals Bite Into Breakfast," The Wall Street Journal, Apr. 8, 2005, p. B1; Steven Gray, "For the Health-Unconscious, Era of Mammoth Burger Is Here," The Wall Street Journal, Jan. 27, 2005, p. B1; Michael Copeland, "Ronald Gets Back In Shape," Business 2.0, January/February 2005, p. 47; "Big Mac's Makeover," The Economist, Oct. 16, 2005, pp. 63+; Kenneth Hein, "Shaking Up a Sleepy Giant," Brandweek, Oct. 11, 2004, p. 5; Bruce Horovitz, "By Year's End, Regular Size Will Have to Do," USA Today, Mar. 4, 2004, p. 3B; Pallavi Gogoi, "Saving Mickey D's Bacon," BusinessWeek, Aug. 25, 2003, p. 46; "Can McDonald's Shape Up?" Time, Sept. 30, 2002, pp. 54–57; Julie Forster, "Thinking Outside the Burger Box," BusinessWeek, Sept. 16, 2002, pp. 66–67; Shelly Branch, "As Obesity Concerns Mount, Companies Fret Their Snacks, Drinks May Take the Blame," The Wall Street Journal, June 13, 2002, pp. B1+; Jennifer Ordonez, "Crunch Time," The Wall Street Journal, Jan. 16, 2001, p. A1; Miriam Jordan, "McDonald's Heats Up Tempers with Growth in Brazil," The Wall Street Journal, Oct. 4, 2000, p. A23; and Merissa Marr and Steven Gray, "McDonald's Signs Marketing Deal with DreamWorks," The Wall Street Journal, July 28, 2005, p. B3.

Case 2: BlackBerry www.blackberry.com, accessed July 6, 2005; www.palm.com, accessed July 6, 2005; www.windowsmobile.com, accessed July 6, 2005; George Stephanopoulos, "BlackBerry Guys," Time Canada, Apr. 18, 2005, p. 56; Paula Rooney, "BlackBerry Killer?" CRN, Apr. 4, 2005, p. 6; Victoria Murphy, "BlackBerry Jam," Forbes, Mar. 28, 2005, p. 52; "Attack of the BlackBerry Killers?" The Economist, Mar. 19, 2005, p. 68; "Gartner: PDA Revs Up 17%," Electronic News, Feb. 21, 2005, p. N; Ginny Parker, "Japan Begins to Ask for BlackBerrys," The Wall Street Journal, Dec. 16, 2004, p. B8; Beth Snyder Bulik, "BlackBerry's Latest Offers Taste to Regular Consumers," Advertising Age, Nov. 15, 2004, p. 8; Daniel Roth, "Can Anyone Topple BlackBerry," Fortune, Nov. 15, 2004, p. 48; Stephen Baker, "Thumbthing for Everyone," BusinessWeek, Nov. 8, 2004, p. 118; Alina Tugend, "BlackBerry Jam," Government Executive, Nov. 1, 2004, p. 40; Erick Schonfeld, "Back Berry Season," Business 2.0, October 2004, pp. 132–140.

Notes and References

Chapter 1

1. Trader Joe's website: *www.traderjoes.com*; Jeff Meyer, "Small Natural-Food Stores Feel Pinch of Whole Foods," *Christian Science Monitor,* Sept. 15, 2003, p. 15; Irvin Speizer, "The Grocery Chain that Shouldn't Be," *Fast Company,* February 2004, p. 31; Jena McGregor, "Leading Listener Winner: Trader Joe's," *Fast Company,* October 2004, pp. 82–83; Larry Armstrong, "Trader Joe's: The Trendy American Cousin," *BusinessWeek Online,* Apr. 26, 2004; Bob Quick, "Groceries Brace for Trader Joe's," *Free New Mexican,* Aug. 8, 2004.

2. The American Marketing Association revised its definition of *marketing* in 2004. The latest version is: "Marketing is an organizational function and a set of processes for creating, communicating, and delivering value to customers and for managing customer relationships in ways that benefit the organization and its stakeholders." Lisa M. Keefe, "What Is the Meaning of 'Marketing'?" *Marketing News,* Sept. 15, 2004, p. 17.

3. Robert J. Keith, "The Marketing Revolution," *Journal of Marketing,* January 1960, pp. 35–38, at p. 36.

4. Geraldine E. Williams, "High-Performance Marketing: An Interview with Nike's Phil Knight," *Harvard Business Review,* July–August 1992, pp. 91–101, at p. 92.

5. Tony Jackson, "Reflections of a Knowledge Worker," *Financial Times,* Apr. 27, 1999, p. 12.

6. The following market-oriented definitions are extracted from the websites and publications of the respective companies. Kodak: We help people share moments and share lives; Amazon.com: We make buying the fastest, easiest, and most enjoyable shopping experience possible; Hewlett-Packard: We engineer and deliver technology solutions that drive business value, create social value, and improve the lives of our customers; McGraw-Hill: Our mission is to provide essential information and insight that help individuals, markets, and societies perform to their potential; Steelcase: We help people work more effectively while helping organizations use space more efficiently; Caterpillar: We help our customers build the world's infrastructure and transport its resources.

7. Sarah Ellison, "Colgate's Fight for Market Share Will Likely Erode Profits," *The Wall Street Journal,*" Dec. 13, 2004, p. C1.

8. Sonya S. Hamilton, "You Don't Say," *Sales & Marketing Management,* October 1994, pp. 111–112.

9. Christopher W. Hart and Michael D. Johnson, "Growing the Trust Relationship," *Marketing Management,* Spring 1999, pp. 9–24; Eric Almquist, Carla Healon, and Nick Hall, "Making CRM Make Money," *Marketing Management,* May/June 2002, pp. 16– 21.

10. Harley-Davidson website: *www.harleydavidson.com,* February 2005.

11. John Deere and Company website: *www.johndeere.com,* February 2005.

12. Melanie Wells, "Have It Your Way," *Forbes,* Feb. 14, 2005, pp. 78+.

13. Frederick E. Webster, Jr., "Defining the New Marketing Concept," *Marketing Management,* vol. 2, no. 4, 1993, pp. 22–31.

14. Wells, op. cit., p. 84.

15. Kevin Lane Keller, *Strategic Brand Management,* 2nd ed., Prentice-Hall, Upper Saddle River, NJ, 2003.

16. "Business Ethics' 100 Best Corporate Citizens," Business Ethics website: *www.business-ethics.com.*

17. You may wonder how Fannie Mae ranks so highly given the scandals that rocked the firm in late 2004 (Bethany McLean and Oliver Ryan, "The Fall of Fannie Mae," *Fortune,* Jan. 24, 2005, pp. 122+). First, the five-year average is based on 2000 to 2004 performance, before the accounting problems were uncovered. Second, Fannie Mae has an excellent record of helping minorities, unmarried women, and native Americans gain access to home mortgages.

18. For a more complete discussion of ethics in marketing see: Patrick E. Murphy, Gene R. Laczniak, Norman E. Bowie, and Thomas A, Klein, *Ethical Marketing,* Pearson Prentice Hall, Upper Saddle River, NJ, 2005.

19. Patrick E. Murphy, *Eighty Exemplary Ethics Statements,* University of Notre Dame Press, Notre Dame, IN, 1998.

20. As an example, the American Marketing Association's code of ethics can be found at *www.marketingpower.com.*

21. An excellent review of the role marketing plays in our lives can be found in William L. Wilkie and Elizabeth S. Moore, "Marketing's Contribution to Society," *Journal of Marketing,* vol. 63, Special Issue, 1999, pp. 198–218.

22. Wells, loc. cit.

23. Trader Joe's website: *www.traderjoes.com*; Jena McGregor, "Leading Listener Winner: Trader Joe's," *Fast Company,* October 2004, pp. 82–83.

Chapter 2

1. "iTunes May Own the Market, but that Doesn't Stop Rivals' Trash Talk," *FinancialWire,* Jan. 5, 2005, p. 1; "It's Sno Napster," *Red Herring,* Dec. 3, 2004; Byron Acohido, "Now Playing: Stands for Microsoft Music," *USA Today,* Sept. 2, 2004, p. 6B; Nick Wingfield, "Online Music's Latest Tune," *The Wall Street Journal,* Aug. 27, 2004, pp. B1, B2; Walter S. Mossberg, "New Web Music Stores Offer Unique Features, and One Is a Winner," *The Wall Street Journal,* Apr. 1, 2004, p. B1; Nick Wingfield, "Shakeout May Mute Some Music-Downloading Services," *The Wall Street Journal,* Mar. 23, 2004, p. B1; "Product of the Year: Apple iTunes Music Store," *Fortune,* Dec. 22, 2003, p. 188; Devin Leonard, "Songs in the Key of Steve," *Fortune,* May 12, 2003, pp. 53–56+; Dawn C. Chmielewski, "Napster Returns Today as Subscription Music Service," *San Jose Mercury News,* Jan. 10, 2002, p. 1.

2. Kendra S. Albright, "Environmental Scanning: Radar for Success," *Information Management Journal,* May/June 2004, pp. 38+. Six "waves of change" (trends) are discussed in Steven T. Goldberg, "Trend Spotting," *Kiplinger's Personal Finance,* February 2002, pp. 34–39.

3. Ram Subramanian, Nirmala Fernandes, and Earl Harper, "Environmental Scanning in U.S. Companies: Their Nature and Their Relationship to Performance," *Management International Review,* Vol. 33, No. 3 (1993), pp. 271–286.

4. Melanie Wells, "Iced Coffee Market May Get Steamy," *USA Today,* Apr. 24, 1996, p. 2B.

5. Christine Bittar, "Act Two from the Purple Pill," *Brandweek,* Oct. 11, 2004, pp. M54+.

6. Michelle Conlin, "UnMarried America," *BusinessWeek,* Oct. 20, 2003, pp. 106+.

7. The population projections are based on data drawn from *www.census.gov/ipc/www/usinterimproj/natprojtab01a.pdf,* accessed on Feb. 19, 2005. The buying-power projections are taken from Jeffrey M. Humphreys, "The Multicultural Economy 2003: America's Minority Buying Power," *Georgia Business and Economic Conditions,* Second Quarter 2003, pp. 6, 10.

8. "Hispanics in the United States: Different Origins, Different Needs," *Chronicle of Higher Education,* Nov. 28, 2003, p. A10; "Hispanics Outnumber Blacks as Largest U.S. Minority, Data Show," *St. Louis Post-Dispatch,* Jan. 22, 2003, p. A2; and Gary L. Berman, "The Hispanic Market: Getting Down to Cases," *Sales & Marketing Management,* October 1991, p. 66.

9. "Ever-Elusive Inflation," *The Economist,* June 19, 1999, p. 24.

10. Margaret Popper, "Inflation's Gone. That's a Good Thing, Right?" *BusinessWeek,* Mar. 4, 2002, p. 60. For an essay that describes price deflation in retailing and recommends strategies for coping with deflation, see Walter K. Levy, "Beware, the Pricing Genie Is Out of the Bottle," *Retailing Issues Letter,* November 1994, pp. 1–4.

11. Molly Prior, "TRU Conversions Almost Complete," *DSN Retailing Today,* June 24, 2002, pp. 3, 37; and Monica Roman, "No Fun and Games at Toys 'R' Us," *BusinessWeek,* Feb. 11, 2002, p. 46.

12. James R. Hagerty, "Carpet Makers Confront Era That Extols Wood Floors," *The Wall Street Journal,* Mar. 31, 1998, p. B1.

13. Christina Cheddar Berk, "P&G Will Promote 'Green' Detergent," *The Wall Street Journal,* Jan. 19, 2005, p. B3B; Eric Johnson, "Opinion: Hydrogen Car Offers Mighty Smooth Ride," *Knight Ridder Tribune Business News,* May 3, 2004, p. 1; and *www.reclamere.com/our_services_recovery.htm,* accessed on July 16, 2002.

14. Geoffrey A. Fowler, "'Green' Sales Pitch Isn't Moving Many Products," *The Wall Street Journal,* Mar. 6, 2002, pp. B1, B4; and Laura Litvan, "Going 'Green' in the '90s," *Nation's Business,* February 1995, p. 31.

15. The contradiction between attitudes and buying behavior was reported in C. Mitchell Adrian and Michael D. Richard, "An Examination of Purchase Behavior versus Purchase Attitudes for Environmentally Friendly and Recycled Consumer Goods," *Southern Business Review,* Spring 1995, pp. 1–15. The plastic cup example was described in Stephen Budiansky, "Being Green Isn't Always What It Seems," *U.S. News & World Report,* Aug. 26, 1996, p. 42.

16. Peter Stisser, "A Deeper Shade of Green," *American Demographics,* March 1994, p. 28.

17. Thomas Russell, "Driving Women to Buy," *Furniture Today,* Dec. 13, 2004, p. 1.

18. The statistic regarding working women comes from John Merli, "Working Women Use Radio Heavily," *Broadcasting & Cable,* Aug. 3, 1998, p. 34. The advertising agency study was reported in Stephanie Thompson, "Spin City: 18–49 Women," *Brandweek,* May 10, 1999, pp. S16–S18.

19. Thompson, loc. cit.; and Teri Agins, "Many Women Lose Interest in Clothes, to Retailers' Dismay," *The Wall Street Journal,* Feb. 28, 1995, p. A1.

20. Diane Crispell, "The New World of Men," *American Demographics,* January 1992, pp. 38–43.

21. Martin Peers, "Buddy, Can You Spare Some Time?" *The Wall Street Journal,* Jan. 26, 2004, pp. B1, B3.

22. Vanessa O'Connell, "Campbell Decides Its IQ Health Meals May Be Ahead of the Curve for Foods," *The Wall Street Journal,* Apr. 27, 1998, p. B2.

23. Thomas Lee, "Cutting-Edge Rivalry Goes to Court," *St. Louis Post-Dispatch,* Dec. 25, 2003, pp. E1–E2.

24. Melanie Warner, "Oracle and Siebel's Software Hardball," *Fortune,* Oct. 16, 2000, pp. 391+.

25. "iTunes May Own the Market . . . ," loc. cit.; "It's Sno Napster," loc. cit.; and Acohido, loc. cit.

Chapter 3

1. IKEA website: *www.ikea.com;* David Dunne, "Branding the Experience," *Marketing Magazine,* Nov. 22, 2004, p. 11; Fiona Haley, "Fast Talk," *Fast Company,* December 2003, pp. 57+; Cora Daniels, "Create IKEA, Make Billions, Take Bus," *Fortune* May 3, 2004, p. 44; Mark Dickens, "Enter the Dragon," *Brand Strategy,* October 2004, pp. 34+; Paula M. Miller, "IKEA with Chinese Characters," *China Business Review,* July/August 2004, pp. 36+.

2. *International Trade Statistics 2004,* World Trade Organization, Lausanne, Switzerland, accessed at *www.wto.org.*

3. *Statistical Abstract of the United States, 2004–2005,* 124th ed., U.S. Bureau of the Census, Washington, DC, 2004, p. 811.

4. "International Trade," *Small Business Poll, 2004,* National Federation of Independent Business, vol. 4, no. 1, p. 1.

5. Douglas A. Blackmon and Diane Brady, "Just How Hard Should a U.S. Company Woo a Big Foreign Market?" *The Wall Street Journal,* Apr. 6, 1998, pp. A1+.

6. Miriam Jordan, "Pillsbury Presses Flour Power in India," *The Wall Street Journal,* May 5, 1999, pp. B1+.

7. Benjamin Fulford, "Japan: The American Revolution," *Forbes,* Apr. 12, 2004, p. 85; Naoya Chida, "Japan's Seiyu Reinventing Itself Using Wal-Mart Best Practices," *DSN Retailing Today,* Dec. 13, 2004, pp. 65+.

8. Mark Lasswell, "Lost in the Translation," *Business 2.0,* August 2004, pp. 68–70.

9. "World Development Indicators Database," World Bank, September 2004. Accessed at *www.worldbank.org,* March 2005.

10. World Trade Organization website: *www.wto.org.* Accessed March 2005. Commercial services are not included in the exports because figures are not available for many countries.

11. Joseph A. McKinney, "NAFTA Turns Ten," *Baylor Business Review,* Spring 2004, pp. 34–39.

12. Amazon 2004 performance, accessed at *www.amazon.com,* March 2005.

13. *Statistical Abstract of the United States, 2004–2005,* op. cit., pp. 805, 807.

14. Ginny Parker and Robert Guy Matthews, "Carrefour Retreat Points Up Pitfalls of Flying Solo into Japanese Market," *The Wall Street Journal,* Oct. 13, 2004, p. A14.

15. Nigel Burton, "$2bn Divorce May Be the Best Deal General Motors Ever Made," *Northern Echo,* Mar. 1, 2005, p. 19.

16. Leigh Gallagher and Melanie Wells, "Bad Fit," *Forbes,* Jan. 8, 2001, p. 210.

17. Leslie T. Chang, "Nestle Stumbles in China's Evolving Market," *The Wall Street Journal,* Dec. 8, 2004, p. A10.

18. Richard Johnson, "Crossovers Could Be World Cars, Says Ford Product Boss," *Automotive News Europe,* Jan. 28, 2002, p. 10.

19. Dexter Roberts, Wendy Zellner, and Carol Matlack, "Let the Retail Wars Begin," *BusinessWeek*, Jan. 17, 2005, pp. 44–45.

20. Greg Harris and Suleiman Attour, "The International Advertising Practices of Multinational Companies: A Content Analysis Study," *European Journal of Marketing*, vol. 37, no. 1 and 2, 2003, pp. 154–159.

21. Craig Simons, "Marketers Woo China's Real Masses," *The Wall Street Journal*, Aug. 29, 2003, p. A6.

22. IKEA website: *www.ikea.com*; David Dunne, "Branding the Experience," *Marketing Magazine*, Nov. 22, 2004, p. 11; Fiona Haley, "Fast Talk," *Fast Company*, December 2003, pp. 57+; Cora Daniels, "Create IKEA, Make Billions, Take Bus," *Fortune*, May 3, 2004, p. 44; Mark Dickens, "Enter the Dragon," *Brand Strategy*, October 2004, pp. 34+; Paula M. Miller, "IKEA with Chinese Characters," *China Business Review*, July/August 2004, pp. 36+.

Chapter 4

1. Song website: *www.song.com*; Nicole Harris, "Can Delta's Song Attract 'Discount Divas'?," *The Wall Street Journal*, Apr. 11, 2003, pp. B1+; Mike Beirne, "Song Takes Off, Hits the Right Notes," *Brandweek*, Mar. 22, 2004, p. R10; Rich Thomaselli, "Delta Takes Low-Key Approach to Low-Cost Carrier," *Advertising Age*, May 5, 2003, p. 4+; Wendy Zellner and Michael Arndt, "Cute New Planes, Same Old Problems," *BusinessWeek*, Mar. 1, 2004, p. 42; Rana Foroohar, "A 30,000-Foot Club," *Newsweek*, Sept. 20, 2004, p. E42.

2. Unless otherwise noted, the demographic statistics in this chapter come from *Statistical Abstract of the United States: 2004–2005*, 12th ed., Bureau of the Census, Washington, DC, 2004.

3. Jonathan Black, Bobbie Gossage, and Mike Hofman, "Inner City 100," *Inc Magazine*, May 2004, pp. 93+.

4. Family life-cycle models and their marketing implications are discussed in Charles M. Schaninger and William D. Danko, "A Conceptual and Empirical Comparison of Alternative Household Life Cycle Models," *Journal of Consumer Research*, March 1993, pp. 580–594; Robert E. Wilkes, "Household Life-Cycle Stages, Transitions, and Product Expenditures," *Journal of Consumer Research*, June 1995, pp. 27–42.

5. Michael J. Weiss, "Inconspicuous Consumption," *American Demographics*, April 2002, pp. 30–39.

6. Alison Stein Wellner, "The Census Report," *American Demographics*, January 2002, pp. S3–S6.

7. Ibid., p. 55.

8. "Total Expenditures, All Media, 2000–2004," compiled from data provided by Universal McCann advertising agency and reported in *Marketing News*, July 15, 2004, p. 15.

9. Gerry Khermouch and Jeff Green, "Buzzzz Marketing," *BusinessWeek*, July 30, 2001, pp. 50–56.

10. Richard P. Coleman, "Continuing Significance of Social Class to Marketing," *Journal of Consumer Research*, December 1983, pp. 265–280.

11. "Special Report: Ever Higher Society, Ever Harder to Ascend—Meritocracy in America," *The Economist*, Jan. 1, 2005, pp. 35 +.

12. Jennifer Edson Escalas and James R. Bettman, "You Are What They Eat: The Influence of Reference Groups on Consumers' Connections to Brands," *Journal of Consumer Psychology*, vol. 13, no. 3, 2003, pp. 339–348.

13. Rebecca Gardyn, "I'll Have What He's Having," *American Demographics*, July 2000, p. 22.

14. You may want to go to *www.whymilk. com* to see the number and variety of celebrities who have appeared in the "Got Milk?" advertisements for the American Dairy Farmers and Milk Processors.

15. Katy Kelly and Linda Kulman, "Kid Power," *U.S. News & World Report*, Sept. 13, 2004, pp. 46+.

16. A. H. Maslow, *Motivation and Personality*, Harper and Row, New York, 1954, pp. 80–106. Other motivation schemes are presented in most basic psychology texts.

17. Steven Reiss and Susan M. Havercamp, "Toward a Comprehensive Assessment of Fundamental Motivation: Factor Structure of the Reiss Profile," *Psychological Assessment*, June 1998, pp. 97–106.

18. Yumiko Ono, "Marketers Seek the 'Naked' Truth in Consumers' Psyches," *The Wall Street Journal*, June 30, 1997, p. B1.

19. This classic definition is from Gordon W. Allport, "Attitudes," in C. A. Murchinson, ed., *Handbook of Social Psychology*, Clark University Press, Worcester, MA, 1935, pp. 798–844.

20. "Songs in the Key of Flee," *Brandweek*, Feb. 16, 2004, pp. 17–19.

21. Michael Rowland, "As the Saying Goes: Follow the Money," *Brandweek*, Feb. 21, 2005, p. 20.

22. Diane Cole and Marc Silver, "Coffee, Tea, or Exercise?," *U.S. News & World Report*, June 7, 2004, p. 60+; Michael Arndt, "Flying Budget, But in Style," *BusinessWeek*, Mar. 15, 2004, p. 114; Brian Grow, "Can Delta's Song Carry a Tune?," *BusinessWeek*, Aug. 2, 2004, p. 80+; Sally B. Donnelly, "Friendlier Skies," *Time*, Jan. 26, 2004, p. 39+

Chapter 5

1. Boeing website: *www.boeing.com*; Sara Kehanlani Goo, "Airbus to Take on Boeing's Dreamliner," *The Washington Post*, Dec. 11, 2004, p. E01; J. Lynn Lundsford, "Behind Slide in Boeing Orders: Weak Sales Team or Firm Prices?," *The Wall Street Journal*, Dec. 23, 2004, pp. A1+.

2. Statistics on the business market cited in this chapter come from U.S. Census Bureau publications. A particularly useful source is the *Statistical Abstract of the United States*, available online at *www.census.gov*.

3. Wayne Wenzel, "Guidance Systems for Profit," *Farm Industry News*, July/August 2004, p. 21; Wayne Wenzel, "Farming on the Edge," *Farm Industry News*, December 2004, pp. 30+; Wayne Wenzel, "Autosteering Is Here," *Farm Industry News*, February 2004, p. N.

4. *Statistical Abstract of the United States, 2004–2005*, 124th ed., U.S. Bureau of the Census, Washington, DC, 2004, pp. 665, 668.

5. Andrew Park, "Texas Instruments Inside?," *BusinessWeek*, Dec. 6, 2004, p. 48.

6. Timothy Aeppel, "For Caterpillar, Commodity Boom Creates a Bind," *The Wall Street Journal*, Jan. 4, 2005, pp. A1+.

7. More information on NAICS (pronounced "Nakes") is available in *North American Industry Classification System–United States, 1997*, U.S. Government Printing Office, Washington, DC, 1997, and at the website *www.census.gov*.

8. For a review of buying center research see Richard G. Jennings and Richard E. Plank, "When the Purchasing Agent Is a Committee: Implications for Industrial Marketing," *Industrial Marketing Management*, November 1995, pp. 411–419.

9. This section is based on Lawrence A. Crosby and Sheree L. Johnson, "Technology: Friend or Foe to Customer Relationships?" *Marketing Management,* November/December 2001, pp. 10–11.

10. Robert J. Samuelson, "The Airbus Showdown," *Newsweek,* Dec. 13, 2004, p. 39; Carol Matlack and Stanley Holmes, "Look Up in the Sky—It's a Dogfight," *Business Week,* Oct. 25, 2004, p. 44.

Chapter 6

1. Dunkin' Donuts website: *www.dunkin donuts.com;* Daniel McGinn, "Oh, Sweet Revenge," *Newsweek,* Sept. 29, 2003, pp. E4+; Daniel McGinn, "Mr. Coffee—Not," *Newsweek,* Sept. 29, 2003, p. E8; William C. Symonds, David Kiley, and Stanley Homes, "A Java Jolt for Dunkin' Donuts," *Business Week,* Dec. 20, 2004, pp. 61+.

2. Kenneth Hein, "Got a Thrilla in the Mist," *Brandweek,* Jan. 19, 2004, pp. 16+.

3. Social class and family life cycle are described in all contemporary consumer behavior texts, for example J. Paul Peter and Jerry C. Olson, *Consumer Behavior and Marketing Strategy,* 7th ed., Homewood, IL: McGraw-Hill/Irwin, 2005.

4. From the *www.polo.com* website, March 2005.

5. Pallavi Gogi, "The Hot News in Banking: Bricks and Mortar," *Business-Week,* Apr. 21, 2003, pp. 83–84.

6. Gary McWilliams, "Analyzing Customers, Best Buy Decides Not All Are Welcome," *The Wall Street Journal,* Nov. 8, 2004, pp. A1+.

7. You may want to go to the website *www.candhsugar.com* to read how the company differentiates between sugar made from cane and sugar from beets.

8. Dennis Adair, "The Harley-Davidson V-Rod," *Design Engineering,* June 2004, pp. 26+.

9. Deborah Ball, Sarah Ellison, and Janet Adamy, "Probing Shoppers' Psyche," *The Wall Street Journal,* Oct. 28, 2004, pp. B1+.

10. Daniel de Vise, "Maryland Is Hailed for Education Gains," *The Washington Post,* Mar. 17, 2005, p. AA03.

11. Dunkin' Donuts website: *www.dunkindonuts.com;* Linda Tischler, "It's Not about the Doughnuts," *Fast Company* website exclusive, December 2004; Linda Tischler, "Creme of the Crop," *Fast Company* website exclusive, December 2004; Daniel McGinn,

"Mr. Coffee—Not," *News-week,* Sept. 29, 2003, p. E8.

Chapter 7

1. U.S. Department of Agriculture website: *www.usda.gov;* Etta Saltos, "The Food Pyramid-Food Label Connection," *FDA Consumer,* June, 1993, pp. 17+; Lisa van der Pool "USDA Seeks PR Shop for Food Pyramid," *Adweek,* June 14, 2004, p. 10; Nicholas Zamiska, "Food Pyramid Frenzy," *The Wall Street Journal,* July 29, 2004, p. B1; Douglas Quenqua, "USDA Begins Hunt for Agency to Tout New Food Pyramid," *PRWeek,* June 28, 2004, p. 3: Sara Schaefer Munoz, "Rebuilding the Pyramid," *The Wall Street Journal,* Jan. 27, 2005, pp. B1+.

2. Jack Honomichl, "Honomichl Top 50," *Marketing News,* June 15, 2004, special section, pp H1+.

3. Jack Honomichl, "A Tough Year," *Marketing News,* June 10, 2002, p. H3.

4. Carol Hymowitz, "CEOs Use Technology to Gather Information, Build Customer Loyalty," *The Wall Street Journal,* Oct. 26, 2004, p. B1.

5. Joe Ashbrook Nickell, "Welcome to Harrah's," *Business 2.0,* April 2002, pp. 48–54; Danielle Sacks, "2004 Fast Company Customers First Awards: High Tech Achievers," *Fast Company,* October 2004, pp. 79+.

6. Chana R. Schoenberger, "The Internet of Things," *Forbes,* Mar. 18, 2002, pp. 155–159.

7. Jeff Hall, "Objective Customer Feedback a Mystery," *DSN Retailing,* Oct. 25, 2004, p. 18. For a dissenting view on the use of mystery shoppers as a research method, see Scott Ahlstrand, "Why Spy?" *Gallup Management Journal,* Winter 2001, pp. 4–6. Other interesting research articles can be found at *www.gallupjournal.com.*

8. Market researchers are constantly looking for more effective methods for understanding behavior. For some examples of approaches being used see Thomas Mucha, "Why the Caveman Loves the Pitchman," *Business 2.0,* April 2005, pp. 37–40; Emily Nelson, "Focus Groups: P&G Keeps Cincinnati Busy with All Its Studies," *The Wall Street Journal,* Jan. 24, 2002, pp. A1+; Suzanne Vranica, "Some Focus Groups Use Mensa Members," *The Wall Street Journal,* Feb. 21, 2002, p. B6.

9. Michael Fielding, "Damage Control," *Marketing News,* Sept. 15, 2004, pp. 19+.

10. Fielding, ibid. For more information on counterintelligence efforts visit the websites of Integrated Strategic Information Services (*www.isisglobal.com*) and Knowledge Keepers, Ltd. (*www. knowledgekeepers.com*).

11. Lisa van der Pool "USDA Seeks PR Shop for Food Pyramid," *Adweek,* June 14, 2004, p. 10; Nicholas Zamiska, "Food Pyramid Frenzy," *The Wall Street Journal,* July 29, 2004, p. B1; Douglas Quenqua, "USDA Begins Hunt for Agency to Tout New Food Pyramid," *PRWeek,* June 28, 2004, p. 3: Sara Schaefer Munoz, "Rebuilding the Pyramid," *The Wall Street Journal,* Jan. 27, 2005, pp. B1+; Sara Schaefer Munoz, "The Food Pyramid Gets Personalized," *The Wall Street Journal,* Apr. 20, 2005, pp. D1+; Raymond Sokolov, "A Pain in the Cheops," *The Wall Street Journal,* Apr. 21, 2005, p. A16; Sonia Reyes, "Weighting the New Building Blocks," *BrandWeek,* May 2, 2005, pp. 24+.

Chapter 8

1. *www.imaginatik.com,* accessed on Mar. 20, 2005; Anne Fisher, "Get Employees to Brainstorm Online," *Fortune,* Nov. 29, 2004, p. 72; "How Their Garden Grows," *CFO IT,* Nov. 15, 2004, no pages given; "Belgacom Standardizes on Imaginatik's Idea Central Global to Foster Culture of Innovation," *Business Wire,* Oct. 19, 2004, no pages given; Christina Torode, "Imaginatik Puts Software under New Management," *Mass High Tech,* Aug. 23, 2004, p. 4; and Mark Hollmer, "Imaginatik Gives Suggestion Box a High-Tech Treatment," *The Boston Business Journal,* July 18, 2003, p. 19.

2. Bruce Horovitz, "Fast-Food Giants Hunt for New Products to Tempt Consumers," *USA Today,* July 3–4, 2002, pp. 1A, 2A.

3. For a different classification scheme that provides strategic guidelines for management by relating products and prices, see Patrick E. Murphy and Ben M. Enis, "Classifying Products Strategically," *Journal of Marketing,* July 1986, pp. 24–42. Also see Ernest F. Cooke, "The Relationship between a Product Classification System and Marketing Strategy," *Journal of Midwest Marketing,* Spring 1987, pp. 230–240.

4. Jeff Daniel, "It's So Cool, the Owners' Club Is Still Small," *St. Louis Post-Dispatch,* Nov. 15, 2004, pp. D1, D4; and Christine Bittar, "Kimberly-Clark Adds Cheeky Exposure to Ms. Cottonelle Toilet Paper Rollout," *Brandweek,* May 7, 2001, p. 8.

5. Durk Jager, as quoted in Katrina Brooker, "Can Procter & Gamble Change Its Culture, Protect Its Market Share, and Find the Next Tide?" *Fortune,* Apr. 26, 1999, p. 149.

6. Craig Smith, "Jaguar Workers Are Paying for Brand Failure," *Marketing,* Sept. 22, 2004, p. 30; "Changing Brands," *Marketing Week,* June 10, 2004, pp. 22+; Sarah Ellison, "Kraft's Stale Strategy," *The Wall Street Journal,* Dec. 18, 2003, pp. B1, B6; and Stuart Elliott, "The Famous Brands on Death Row," *The New York Times,* Nov. 7, 1993, p. 1F.

7. Barton G. Tretheway, "Everything New Is Old Again," *Marketing Management,* Spring 1998, p. 7.

8. K. C. Crain, "LaNeve: Cadillac's Coming Back, but Job Isn't Done," *Automotive News,* Jan. 19, 2004, p. 35; Nanette Byrnes, "Brands in a Bind," *BusinessWeek,* Aug. 28, 2000, pp. 234–236+; and Geoffrey Colvin, "How Rubbermaid Managed to Fail," *Fortune,* Nov. 23, 1998, pp. 32–33.

9. Respectively, Cliff Edwards, "Where Have All the Edsels Gone?" *Pittsburgh Post-Gazette,* May 25, 1999, p. F-7; Tretheway, loc. cit.; and Kuczmarski & Associates, as described in Christopher Power, "Flops," *BusinessWeek,* Aug. 16, 1993, pp. 76–77.

10. The reasons for failure are drawn from the "1995 Innovation Survey," conducted by Group EFO Limited of Weston, CT. The Starship example is drawn from Alan Farnham, "It's a Bird! It's a Plane! It's a Flop!" *Fortune,* May 2, 1994, pp. 108–110.

11. Kevin J. Clancy and Peter C. Krieg, "Surviving Innovation," *Marketing Management,* March/April 2003, p. 17; and Paul Lukas, "The Ghastliest Product Launches," *Fortune,* Mar. 16, 1998, p. 44.

12. Jerry Useem, "*Sold!* Elvis Impersonator for $61.23 an Hour," *Fortune,* Aug. 16, 1999, p. 36.

13. John Simons, "Greed Meets Terror," *Fortune,* Oct. 29, 2001, pp. 145–146.

14. Evan Ramstad, "Products Go Digital . . . Whether They Are or Not," *The Wall Street Journal,* Sept. 7, 1999, p. A11A.

15. Kenneth Cole, "Electric Cars Unlikely to Take Center Stage," *The Detroit News,* Dec. 21, 1998, p. F15.

16. As stressed by a consultant, Philip Himmelfarb, in Roberta Maynard, "The Heat Is On," *Nation's Business,* October 1997, pp. 16, 18.

17. These benefits and a "stage gate system" for new-product development are described in Robert G. Cooper and Elko J. Kleinschmidt, "Stage Gate Systems for New Product Success," *Marketing Management,* Vol. 1, No. 4, 1993, pp. 20–29. For an approach for managing multiple new-product development projects, see Steven C. Wheelwright and Kim B. Clark, "Creating Project Plans to Focus Product Development," *Harvard Business Review,* March–April 1992, pp. 70–82.

18. For a report on the criteria used in making "go–no go" decisions in the product-development process, see Ilkka A. Ronkainen, "Criteria Changes across Product Development Stages," *Industrial Marketing Management,* August 1985, pp. 171–178.

19. The information about customers, suppliers, and franchisees comes, respectively, from "Study: Launching New Products Is Worth the Risk," *Marketing News,* Jan. 20, 1992, p. 2; Neal Templin and Jeff Cole, "Manufacturers Use Suppliers to Help Them Develop New Products," *The Wall Street Journal,* Dec. 19, 1994, pp. A1, A6; and Jeffrey A. Tannenbaum, "Role Model," *The Wall Street Journal,* May 23, 1996, p. R22.

20. For more on the first two stages, termed *opportunity identification,* see Linda Rochford, "Generating and Screening New Product Ideas," *Industrial Marketing Management,* November 1991, pp. 287–296.

21. Faye Rice, "Secrets of Product Testing," *Fortune,* Nov. 29, 1994, pp. 166–171.

22. Jennifer Lach, "Meet You in Aisle Three," *American Demographics,* April 1999, pp. 41–42.

23. Cooper and Kleinschmidt, op. cit., pp. 22–23.

24. Development times are discussed in Pamela Buxton, "Time to Market Is NPD's Top Priority," *Marketing,* Mar. 30, 2000, p. 35. For an in-depth look at the development of the Frito Pie, see Emily Nelson, "Product Development Is Always Difficult; Consider the Frito Pie," *The Wall Street Journal,* Oct. 25, 1999, pp. A1, A22.

25. The omission of market tests was described in "Study: Launching New Products Is Worth the Risk," loc. cit. One automaker's acceleration efforts are summarized in "Norihiko Shirouzu, "Ford Aims to Speed Up Process of New-Vehicle Development," *The Wall Street Journal,* Feb. 20, 2003, p. B8.

26. Robert G. Cooper and Scott J. Edgett, "Critical Success Factors for New Financial Services," *Marketing Management,* Fall 1996, pp. 26–37; and Howard Schlossberg, "Services Development Lags Behind New Products," *Marketing News,* Nov. 6, 1989, p. 2.

27. For foundations of diffusion theory and a review of landmark studies on diffusion of innovation, see Everett M. Rogers, *Diffusion of Innovations,* 3rd ed., Free Press, New York, 1983.

28. Robert A. Guth and Khanh T. L. Tran, "The Geeks' Secret: Buying Gadgets Direct from Japan," *The Wall Street Journal,* Sept. 4, 2002, pp. D1, D4.

29. "GPS Offers Security," *Columbia Daily Tribune,* Aug. 25, 2002, p. 13A.

30. Denise Smith Amos, "Are You an 'Influential'? Advertisers Want You," *St. Louis Post-Dispatch,* Aug. 6, 1995, pp. E1, E9.

31. Rogers, loc. cit. A new perspective, termed *use diffusion,* which combines post-adoption usage and the characteristics affecting adoption rate, is tested in Chuan-Fong Shih and Alladi Venkatesh, "Beyond Adoption: Development and Application of a Use-Diffusion Model," *Journal of Marketing,* January 2004, pp. 59–72.

32. Tara Parker-Pope, "P&G Puts Two Cleaning Products on Its New Marketing Fast Track," *The Wall Street Journal,* May 18, 1999, p. B6; and Yumiko Ono, "Novel P&G Product Brings Dry Cleaning Home," *The Wall Street Journal,* Nov. 19, 1997, p. B1.

33. The quote about brand managers being an "endangered species" is drawn from Rance Crain, "Brand Management's Decline May Haunt GM," *Advertising Age,* Nov. 6, 1995, p. 16. The shifting arrangements are reported in David Welch, "GM Brand Managers Get the Boot," *BusinessWeek,* Apr. 22, 2002, p. 14; Jolie Solomon and Carol Hymowitz, "P&G Makes Changes in the Way It Develops and Sells Its Products," *The Wall Street Journal,* Aug. 11, 1987, pp. 1, 12; and Raymond Serafin, "Ford Taps Insiders as Brand Managers," *Advertising Age,* Jan. 1, 1996, p. 3.

34. Various arrangements are discussed in Eric M. Olson, Orville C. Walker, Jr., and Robert W. Ruekert, "Organizing for Effective New Product Development: The Moderating Role of Product Innovativeness," *Journal of Marketing,* January 1995, pp. 48–62. The favorable comment comes from Steve McDougal and Jeff Smith, "Wake Up Your Product Development," *Marketing Management,* Summer 1999, pp. 24–30.

35. *www.imaginatik.com,* accessed Mar. 20, 2005; "How Their Garden Grows," loc. cit.; and Jennifer Esty, "Those Wacky Customers!" *Fast Company,* January 2004, p. 40.

Chapter 9

1. *www.kodak.com,* accessed on Mar. 24, 2005; Dave Gussow, "Fading Away," *St. Petersburg Times,* Feb. 26, 2005, p. 1D; "Kodak Leads U.S. in Digital Cameras," *The Wall Street Journal,* Feb. 3, 2005, p. B4; James Bandler, "Ending Era, Kodak Will Stop Selling Most Film Cameras," *The Wall Street Journal,* Jan. 14, 2004, p. B1; James Bandler, "Kodak Shifts Focus from Film, Betting Future on Digital Lines," *The Wall Street Journal,* Sept. 25, 2003, pp. A1, A12; Faith Keenan, "Big Yellow's Digital Dilemma," *Business-Week,* Mar. 24, 2003, pp. 80–81; and Seth Mendelson, "Feuding on Film," *Supermarket Business,* July 15, 2000, pp. 85+.

2. Christopher Lawton, "Anheuser Tries Low-Carb Beer to Tap Diet Buzz," *The Wall Street Journal,* Sept. 13, 2002, pp. B1, B2.

3. David Welch, "Will These Rockets Rescue Saturn?" *BusinessWeek,* Jan. 17, 2005, p. 78; and Kate Maddox, "Brand Gives Intel Inside Track," *B to B,* Oct. 25, 2004, p. 25.

4. Michael Goldstein, "Few Leagues of Their Own," *BusinessWeek,* Jan. 18, 1999, pp. 74–76.

5. Scott McCartney, "How Discount Airlines Profited from Their Bigger Rivals' Woes," *The Wall Street Journal,* Aug. 12, 2004, pp. A1–A2; and Shawn Tully, "Airlines: Why the Big Boys Won't Come Back," *Fortune,* June 14, 2004, pp. 101–102+. For more on positioning in relation to a competitor, see Jack Trout and Al Ries, "*Don't Follow the Leader,*" *Sales & Marketing Management,* February 1994, pp. 25–26.

6. Laura Bird, "Romancing the Package," *Adweek's Marketing Week,* Jan. 21, 1991, pp. 10–11, 14.

7. Patricia Sellers, "'It Was a No-Brainer,'" *Fortune,* Feb. 21, 2005, pp. 96–98+; "Procter & Gamble Co.: Sunny Delight, Punica Brands Sold to Private-Equity Firm," *The Wall Street Journal,* Apr. 2, 2004, p. B4; and "J. M. Smucker Acquires Jif, Crisco Brands from P&G," *Nation's Restaurant News,* Oct. 29, 2001, p. 100.

8. James R. Hagerty, "Gilding the Drill Bit? Hardware Giants Go High-End," *The Wall Street Journal,* July 28, 1998, pp. B1, B7.

9. Peter Burrows, "Apple's Bold Swim Downstream," *BusinessWeek,* Jan. 24, 2005, pp. 33–34+; and Bianca Riemer and Laura Zinn, "Haute Couture That's Not So Haute," *BusinessWeek,* Apr. 22, 1991, p. 108.

10. Louise Lee, "Williams-Sonoma Tries a New Recipe," *BusinessWeek,* May 6, 2002, p. 36; and Lee Gomes, "H-P to Create a New Subsidiary to Sell Cheap 'Apollo' Brand of Ink-Jet Printers," *The Wall Street Journal,* Jan. 6, 1999, p. B4.

11. Hagerty, loc. cit.

12. William C. Symonds, "Would You Spend $1.50 for a Razor Blade?" *BusinessWeek,* Apr. 27, 1998, p. 46; and Mark Maremont, "Gillette Finally Reveals Its Vision of the Future, and It Has 3 Blades," *The Wall Street Journal,* Apr. 14, 1998, p. A1, A10.

13. Cliff Edwards, "Shaking Up Intel's Insides," *BusinessWeek,* Jan. 31, 2005, p. 35.

14. For an alternative perspective on the product life cycle, see Peter N. Golder and Gerard J. Tellis, "Cascades, Diffusion, and Turning Points in the Product Life Cycle," Report No. 03-120, Marketing Science Institute, Cambridge, MA, 2003. The criticisms are summarized in Geoffrey L. Gordon, Roger J. Calantone, and C. Anthony diBenedetto, "Mature Markets and Revitalization Strategies: An American Fable," *Business Horizons,* May–June 1991, pp. 39–50. Alternative life cycles are proposed in Edward D. Popper and Bruce D. Buskirk, "Technology Life Cycles in Industrial Markets," *Industrial Marketing Management.* February 1992, pp. 23–31; and C. Merle Crawford, "Business Took the Wrong Life Cycle from Biology," *The Journal of Product & Brand Management,* Winter 1992, pp. 51–57.

15. Sarah McBride, Phred Dvorak, and Don Clark, "Why HDTV Hasn't Arrived in Many Homes," *The Wall Street Journal,* Jan. 5, 2005, p. B1; and Elliot Spagat, "Hit Show of the Season: The Revival of Digital TV," *The Wall Street Journal,* Aug. 1, 2002, pp. D1, D3.

16. Neil Gross and Peter Coy, "The Technology Paradox," *BusinessWeek,* Mar. 6, 1995, p. 77.

17. Michael Booth, "Olestra, Where Art Thou?" *Denver Post,* Mar. 19, 2002, p. F-1.

18. Sal Ruibal, "Livestrong shows solidarity of 50m," *USA Today,* May 13–15, 2005, p. 1A; and Grace Aduroja, "Wristbands Promoting Causes Become Must-Have for Chicago-Area Teens," *Chicago Tribune,* Jan. 14, 2005, p. 1.

19. Eric Adler, "The Walkman at 20: Portable Stereo Has Changed the World," *St. Louis Post-Dispatch,* Sept. 2, 1999, p. G1.

20. Wailin Wong, "DVD-Audio Format Hasn't Caught On," *The Wall Street Journal,* Aug. 14, 2003, p. B4. The examples in this paragraph and the following one are drawn from "After the Compact Disc," *FT.com,* May 8, 2002; and Sarah Bryan Miller, "In Home Tech, 'Permanent Investments' Have a Short Life Span," *St. Louis Post-Dispatch,* July 7, 2002, pp. F1, F13.

21. Scott Leith, "Bottled Coffee Looks for Jolt," *The Atlanta Journal-Constitution,* Jan. 22, 2005, p. F1.

22. Kevin Maney, "Impregnable 'First Mover Advantage' Philosophy Suddenly Isn't," *USA Today,* July 18, 2001, p. 3B. For a discussion of three ways in which pioneers can be "dumb movers," see Gary Hamel, "Smart Mover, Dumb Mover," *Fortune,* Sept. 3, 2001, pp. 191–192+.

23. For a study of the effects of interrelated products on the survival of pioneers in a product category, see Raji Srinivasan, Gary L. Lilien, and Arvind Rangaswamy, "First In, First Out? The Effects of Network Externalities on Pioneer Survival," *Journal of Marketing,* January 2004, pp. 41–58. The concept of "pioneer advantage" and the historical study of the 50 product categories are described in Gerard J. Tellis and Peter N. Golder, "Pioneer Advantage: Marketing Logic or Marketing Legend," *USC Business,* Fall/Winter 1995, pp. 49–53.

24. Geoff Keighley, "Sony's Trojan Horse," *Business 2.0,* March 2005, pp. 41–43.

25. Ten distinct strategies are described in Joel R. Evans and Gregg Lombardo, "Marketing Strategies for Mature

Brands," *Journal of Product & Brand Management,* vol. 2, no. 1, 1993, pp. 5–19. For a discussion of four strategies—recapture, redesign, refocus, and recast—that are particularly applicable to *business* products, see Paul C. N. Michell, Peter Quinn, and Edward Percival, "Marketing Strategies for Mature Industrial Products," *Industrial Marketing Management,* August 1991, pp. 201–206.

26. Nicholas Shields, "U.S. Mint Hopes Collectors Will Flip for New State Quarter," *Los Angeles Times,* Feb. 1, 2005, p. B3; and Mike Vogel, "The Clouds Part," *Florida Trend,* July 1, 2004, p. 52.

27. Sandra Dolbow, "Meet Lycra's New Face," *Brandweek,* Apr. 24, 2000, pp. 1, 89; Becky Ebenkamp, "Lycra Streeetches," *Brandweek,* July 5, 1999, p. 3; and Monica Roman, "How Du Pont Keeps 'Em Coming Back for More," *BusinessWeek,* Aug. 20, 1990, p. 68.

28. Dana James, "Rejuvenating Mature Brands Can Be Stimulating Exercise," *Marketing News,* Aug. 16, 1999, p. 16.

29. Hardy Green, "The Last Word in New Words," *BusinessWeek,* Aug. 30, 1999, p. 6.

30. Bill Saporito, "How to Revive a Fading Firm," *Fortune,* Mar. 22, 1993, p. 80.

31. Joel Dreyfuss, "Planned Obsolescence Is Alive and Well," *Fortune,* Feb. 15, 1999, p. 192[P].

32. Lauren Goldstein, "Urban Wear Goes Suburban," *Fortune,* Dec. 21, 1998, pp. 169–170+.

33. For an example of producing multiple variations of a style, see Riemer and Zinn, loc. cit.

34. Fran Daniel, "All Business: Suits Making Comeback at Office," *Winston-Salem Journal,* Sept. 30, 2004, p. D1; Wendy Bounds, Rebecca Quick, and Emily Nelson, "In the Office, It's Anything Goes," *The Wall Street Journal,* Aug. 26, 1999, pp. B1, B4; and Teri Agins, "Many Women Lose Interest in Clothes, to Retailers' Dismay," *The Wall Street Journal,* Feb. 28, 1995, pp. A1, A8.

35. Veronica Chambers and Alisha Davis, "Direct from Paris . . . to the Mall," *Newsweek,* Apr. 13, 1998, pp. 64–65.

36. *www.kodak.com,* accessed on Mar. 24, 2005; Matthew Boyle, "Digital Deal Pits Xerox against Kodak," *Fortune,* Nov. 29, 2004, pp. 48, 52; and Bandler, "Kodak Shifts . . . ," loc. cit.

Chapter 10

1. *www.gm.com/company/corp_info/ history,* accessed on Apr. 2, 2005; Holman W. Jenkins, Jr., "GM Pulls into the Slow Lane," *The Wall Street Journal,* Apr. 13, 2005, p. A19; John K. Teahen, Jr., "Cadillac Keeps 'True Luxury' Title," *Automotive News,* Feb. 14, 2005, p. 10; Karen Lundegaard, "Adding Glitz to Graying Models; Buick, Cadillac, Mercury Boost Horsepower, Sound Systems to Attract Younger Buyers," *The Wall Street Journal,* Feb. 9, 2005, pp. D1+; David Welch, "The Second Coming of Cadillac," *BusinessWeek,* Nov. 24, 2003, pp. 79–80.

2. Adapted from Peter D. Bennett, ed., *Dictionary of Marketing Terms,* American Marketing Association, Chicago, 1988, p. 18. The incorrect usage is pointed out in John F. Gaski, "Some Troublesome Definitions of Elementary Marketing Concepts—Have You Ever Looked at It This Way?" in D. W. Stewart and N. J. Vilcassim, eds., *1995 AMA Winter Educators' Conference: Marketing Theory and Applications,* American Marketing Association, Chicago, 1995, pp. 425–429.

3. "World's Three Major Intellectual Property Offices Streamline Trademark Registration Process," *US Fed News,* June 3, 2004, no page given. For a description of changes in trademark law and court decisions on trademarks as well as their marketing implications, see Dorothy Cohen, "Trademark Strategy Revisited," *Journal of Marketing,* July 1991, pp. 46–59.

4. "Wrestling Federation Puts the Tag on a New Name," *Brandweek,* May 13, 2002, p. 16; and "Settlement Reached in Gateway Trademark Lawsuit," *Associated Press Newswires,* June 20, 2001.

5. Rodney Ho, "Brand-Name Diamonds: A Cut Above?" *The Wall Street Journal,* June 1, 1998, p. B1; and Betsy Morris, "The Brand's the Thing," *Fortune,* Mar. 4, 1996, pp. 72–75+.

6. "Nikhil Deogun, Charles Forelle, Dennis K. Berman, and Emily Nelson, "P&G to Buy Gillette for $54 Billion," *The Wall Street Journal,* Jan. 28, 2005, pp. A1, A5; and Thomas Kamm, "Rivalry in Luxury Goods Heats Up as Gucci and LVMH Unveil Deals," *The Wall Street Journal,* Nov. 16, 1999, p. A22.

7. Al Ries, "What's in a Name?" *Sales & Marketing Management,* October 1995, p. 36. This article also discusses eight attributes of a desirable brand name.

8. Jerri Stroud, "Disaster Sweeps Away Company's Old Name," *St. Louis Post-Dispatch,* Apr. 19, 2005, p. D2; Gwendolyn Bounds, "Brands Bearing Name 'Tsunami' Ponder Change," *The Wall Street Journal,* Jan. 18, 2005, pp. B1, B3. Material in this paragraph and the following one are drawn from Suein L. Hwang, "Picking Pithy Names Is Getting Trickier as Trademark Applications Proliferate," *The Wall Street Journal,* Jan. 14, 1992, p. B1.

9. For more about morphemes, see Teresa Pavia and Janeen A. Costa, "The Winning Number: Consumer Perceptions of Alpha-Numeric Brand Names," *Journal of Marketing,* July 1993, pp. 85–98; and Casey McCabe, "What's in a Name?" *Adweek's Marketing Week,* Apr. 16, 1990, p. 22.

10. Alex Frankel, "The New Science of Naming," *Business 2.0,* December 2004, pp. 53–55. For a good discussion of the special opportunities and challenges associated with services branding, see Vicki Clift, "Name Service Firms for the Long Haul," *Marketing News,* Dec. 6, 1993, p. 10. Some of the examples in this section are drawn from Leonard L. Berry, Edwin F. Lefkowith, and Terry Clark, "In Services, What's in a Name?," *Harvard Business Review,* September–October 1988, pp. 28–30.

11. Tom Davis, "Protecting U.S. Innovations from Intellectual Property Piracy," *Federal Document Clearing House Congressional Testimony,* Sept. 23, 2004, no page given; "Largest Counterfeit Software Seizure in U.S. History," *PR Newswire,* Nov. 16, 2001; and David Stipp, "Farewell, My Logo," *Fortune,* May 27, 1996, p. 130.

12. An excellent summary of this challenge and a list of safeguards are contained in Maxine S. Lans, "On Your Mark: Get Set or It May Go," *Marketing News,* Sept. 26, 1994, p. 12.

13. Jack Alexander, "What's in a Name? Too Much, Said the FTC," *Sales & Marketing Management,* January 1989, pp. 75, 78.

14. Matthew Dick, "Why You Must Never Sellotape® a Xerox® into Your Filofax®," *Journal of Brand Management,* July 2004, pp. 509+; and Carrie Goerne, "Rollerblade Reminds Everyone That Its Success Is Not Generic," *Marketing News,* Mar. 2, 1992, p. 1.

15. Patricia Sellers, "Brands: It's Thrive or Die," *Fortune,* Aug. 23, 1993, p. 53.

16. For an excellent discussion of the nature and benefits of this strategy, see

Dale Buss, "Joining Forces," *Sales and Marketing Management*, January 2005, pp. 38+.

17. Jeff Green, "Hold On—What Make of Alternator Is That?" *BusinessWeek*, Nov. 13, 2000, pp. 203–204.

18. Anne D'Innocenzio, "Big Retailers Steer Brand-Name Makers to Private Labels," *St. Louis Post-Dispatch*, June 2, 2002, p. E8.

19. Greg Burns, "A Froot Loop by Any Other Name," *BusinessWeek,* June 26, 1995, p. 72.

20. The study was conducted by Raj Sethuraman of the University of Iowa, and reported in Richard Gibson, "Store-Brand Pricing Has to Be Just Right," *The Wall Street Journal*, Feb. 14, 1992, p. B1. The second study was summarized in Stephen J. Hoch, "Private Label a Threat? Don't Believe It," *Advertising Age*, May 24, 1993, p. 19.

21. Thomas Lee, "Saving with Private Labels," *Star Tribune* (Minneapolis, MN), Nov. 14, 2004, p. 1D; Matthew Boyle, "Brand Killers," *Fortune*, Aug. 11, 2003, pp. 88–90+; and Clyde H. Farnsworth, "Quality: High. Price: Low. Big Ad Budget? Never," *The New York Times*, Feb. 6, 1994, p. F10.

22. The estimated share of store brands in several types of retail stores is from the Store Brands Today page on the Private Label Manufacturers Association website, *www.plma.com*, accessed on July 23, 2002. The proportion of retailers intending to place more emphasis on such products comes from Susan Zimmerman, "A Rosy Future," *Progressive Grocer*, November 1998, pp. 45–52. The $100 billion estimate was made by Destination Products International, as reported in Stephanie Thompson, "The New Private Enterprise," *Brandweek*, May 3, 1999, pp. 36+. The estimate of volume in 1995 is based on statistics in Emily DeNitto, "Back into Focus," *Brandweek*, May 29, 1995, pp. 22–26.

23. Boyle, loc. cit. Recommendations as to how manufacturers can sustain their brands are presented in Susan R. Ashley, "How to Effectively Compete against Private-Label Brands," *Journal of Advertising Research*, January–February 1998, pp. 75+.

24. Scheherazade Daneshkhu, "Awareness Becomes the Name of the Game," *Financial Times*, Sept. 9, 1999, p. II; and Paul Beckett and Suzanne Vranica, "Citigroup Spotlights Its Member Brands," *The Wall Street Journal*, June 25, 1999, p. B2.

25. There are potential disadvantages as well as advantages to introducing new products under the family brand. For more on this, see Barbara Loken and Deborah Roedder John, "Diluting Brand Beliefs: When Do Brand Extensions Have a Negative Impact?" *Journal of Marketing*, July 1993, pp. 71–84.

26. Norton Paley, "Back from the Dead," *Sales & Marketing Management*, July 1995, pp. 30+.

27. Cathy A. Enz, "Multibranding Strategy: The Case of Yum! Brands," *Cornell Hotel and Restaurant Administration Quarterly*, February 2005, pp. 85+; and D. C. Denison, "Ingredient Branding Puts Big Names in the Mix," *The Boston Globe*, May 26, 2002, p. E2.

28. This definition is drawn from the comprehensive examination of brand equity in Peter H. Farquhar, "Managing Brand Equity," *Journal of Advertising Research*, August/September 1990, pp. RC-7–RC-12. For more on brand equity, see David A. Aaker and Erich Joachimsthaler, *Brand Leadership*, The Free Press, New York, 2000; and Don E. Schultz, "Understanding and Measuring Brand Equity," *Marketing Management*, Spring 2000, pp. 8–9.

29. The quote is from Roger Baird, "Asset Tests," *Marketing Week*, Oct. 1, 1998, pp. 28–31.

30. The Kellogg's example was described by Farquhar, "Managing Brand Equity," op. cit., p. RC-7. The study of personal computers was summarized in Jim Carlton, "Marketing Plays a Bigger Role in Distributing PCs," *The Wall Street Journal*, Oct. 16, 1995, p. B4.

31. David Welch, "Firestone: Is This Brand Beyond Repair?" *BusinessWeek*, June 11, 2001, p. 48; and Christopher Carey, "TWA Boasts Best On-Time Record," *St. Louis Post-Dispatch*, Oct. 7, 1999, p. C2.

32. Farquhar, "Managing Brand Equity," op. cit., pp. RC-8–RC-10.

33. Morris, op. cit., p. 84.

34. The efforts of Oil of Olay to capitalize on its strong brand equity by introducing a new line are described in Tara Parker-Pope, "P&G's Cosmetics Make-over," *The Wall Street Journal*, Apr. 12, 1999, pp. B1, B3. For more on the rationale for the Marquis by Waterford line, see Judith Valente, "A New Brand Restores Sparkle to Waterford," *The Wall Street Journal*, Nov. 10, 1994, p. B1.

35. Statistics in this paragraph come from "Research: The US Licensing Market,"

Brand Strategy, Sept. 15, 2004, p. 38. Other material is drawn from David Kiley, "A Calorie-Conscious Sponge-Bob," *BusinessWeek*, Feb. 28, 2005, p. 16; "New York Unveils Licensing Program," *Adweek.com*, Feb. 9, 2005, online; and "Fashion Plays in Licensing," *Discount Store News*, June 7, 1999, pp. A6–A7.

36. Gerry Khermouch, "'Whoa, Cool Shirt.' 'Yeah, It's a Pepsi,'" *BusinessWeek*, Sept. 10, 2001, p. 84.

37. Dale D. Buss, "Hot Names, Top Dollars," *Nation's Business*, August 1995, p. 17.

38. Eliot Schreiber, "Retail Trends Shorten Life of Package Design," *Marketing News*, Dec. 5, 1994, p. 7.

39. Catherine Arnold, "Way Outside the Box," *Marketing News*, June 23, 2003, p. 14.

40. Ibid.; Matthew Boyle, "25 Breakout Companies," *Fortune*, May 16, 2005, p. 158; and Paul Lukas, "If It Ain't Got Glass, It Ain't Got Class," *Fortune*, Apr. 12, 1999, p. 40. For recommendations on managing the packaging aspect of a company's marketing mix, see Richard T. Hise and James U. McNeal, "Effective Packaging Management," *Business Horizons*, January–February 1988, pp. 47–51.

41. For further discussion of package-design strategies that can boost sales and profit, see Sue Bassin, "Innovative Packaging Strategies," *Journal of Business Strategy*, January–February 1988, pp. 38–42.

42. Betsy McKay, "Thinking inside the Box Helps Soda Makers Boost Sales," *The Wall Street Journal*, Aug. 2, 2002, pp. B1, B4.

43. Schreiber, loc. cit.

44. David Leonhardt, "The Hip New Drink: Milk," *BusinessWeek*, Feb. 16, 1998, p. 44.

45. Laura Bird, "Romancing the Package," *Adweek's Marketing Week*, Jan. 21, 1991, p. 10.

46. The history of food labeling in the U.S. is summarized concisely in "Highlights of Food Labeling," *Marketing News*, Mar. 15, 2004, p. 14. Information about the Nutrition Labeling and Education Act is drawn from the Food and Drug Administration website: *http://vm.cfsan.fda.gov/,dms/fdnewlab.html.*

47. John Sinisi, "New Rules Exact a Heavy Price as Labels Are Recast," *Brandweek*, Dec. 7, 1992, p. 3. For a study that examines the impact of the NLEA

on consumers' processing of nutrition information, see Christine Moorman, "A Quasi Experiment to Assess the Consumer and Informational Determinants of Nutrition Information Processing Activities: The Case of the Nutrition Labeling and Education Act," *Journal of Public Policy & Marketing,* Spring 1996, pp. 28–44. This issue of the journal contains several other articles examining various aspects of nutrition labeling.

48. Eleena de Lisser, "Is That $5 Gallon of Milk Really Organic?" *The Wall Street Journal,* Aug. 20, 2002, pp. D1, D4.

49. Laura M. Litvan, "Sizing Up Metric Labeling Rules," *Nation's Business,* November 1994, p. 62.

50. Bruce Nussbaum, "Is In-House Design on the Way Out?" *BusinessWeek,* September 1995, p. 130. For an overview of how IKEA, the Swedish-based furniture retailer, has made design an integral part of its marketing program, see Lisa Margonelli, "How IKEA Designs Its Sexy Price Tags," *Business 2.0,* October 2002, pp. 106–112.

51. David Rocks and Moon Ihlwan, "Samsung Design," *BusinessWeek,* Dec. 6, 2004, pp. 88–89+; and Bruce Nussbaum, "The Best Product Designs of the Year: Winners 2002," *BusinessWeek,* July 8, 2002, pp. 82–89+.

52. Rebecca Smith, "Beyond Recycling: Manufacturers Embrace 'C2C' Design," *The Wall Street Journal,* Mar. 3, 2005, pp. B1, B3; "Business Bulletin," *The Wall Street Journal,* July 13, 2000, p. A1; and Bruce Nussbaum, "What Works for One Works for All," *BusinessWeek,* Apr. 20, 1992, pp. 112–113.

53. Bradford Wernle, "VW Says Microbus Is Just for Europe," *Automotive News,* Jan. 17, 2005, p. 36. The Beetle's comeback was described in Paul Tharp, "VW's Hippie Bus Now for Yuppies," *New York Post,* June 12, 2002, p. 37; and Bill Vlasic, "Bug-Eyed over the New Beetle," *BusinessWeek,* May 25, 1998, p. 88. The figure pertaining to cost of design comes from Brian Dumaine, "Design That Sells and Sells and . . . ," *Fortune,* Mar. 11, 1991, pp. 86, 88.

54. Nancy Arnott, "Shades of Distinction," *Sales & Marketing Management,* June 1995, p. 20; Paul M. Barrett, "Color in the Court: Can Tints Be Trademarked?" *The Wall Street Journal,* Jan. 5, 1995, p. B1; and Junda Woo, "Rulings Clash over Colors in Trademarks," *The Wall Street Journal,* Feb. 25, 1993, p. B1.

55. Cindy Waxer, "Computer Couture," *Yahoo! Internet Life,* November 1999, pp. 144–145.

56. Sally Beatty, "Fashion's 'It' Colors," *The Wall Street Journal,* Feb. 4, 2005, pp. B1, B2.

57. Meera Somasundaram, "Red Packages Lure Shoppers Like Capes Flourished at Bulls," *The Wall Street Journal,* Sept. 18, 1995, p. A13B.

58. Scott Leith, "Drinks Try to Sustain the Buzz," *The Atlanta Journal-Constitution,* Oct. 30, 2004, p. G1; and Susan Carey, "More U.S. Companies Are Blue, and It's Not Just the Stock Market," *The Wall Street Journal,* Aug. 30, 2001, pp. A1, A2.

59. Ross Johnson and William O. Winchell, *Marketing and Quality Control.* American Society for Quality Control, Milwaukee, 1989, p. 2.

60. Scott McCartney, "Middling Quality as a Marketing Plus? Survey Finds a Link," *The Wall Street Journal,* May 16, 1994, p. B6.

61. "*Consumer Reports* New Car Preview 2005: Survey Predicts Reliability Problems with European Luxury Models," *U.S. Newswire,* Nov. 9, 2004, no page given. For a list of reasons why product quality is so important and for a discussion of the marketing function role in quality management, see Neil A. Morgan and Nigel F. Pierce, "Market Led Quality," *Industrial Marketing Management,* May 1992, pp. 111–118.

62. James B. Treece, "GM Hustles Compact into Production," *Automotive News,* Dec. 18, 2000, p. 36; "Buick to Lead Price Cuts for China's Auto Industry," *Xinhua News Agency,* Apr. 14, 2000, no page given; and T. S. Raghunathan, S. Subba Rao, and Luis S. Solis, "A Comparative Study of Quality Practices: USA, China and India," *Industrial Management & Data Systems,* May–June 1997, p. 192.

63. "Faster but Not Better," *Industry Week,* April 2004, p. 47.

64. "Lantronix® Receives ISO 14001 and ISO 9001 Certification," *PR Newswire,* Sept. 7, 2004, no page given; and Roger Mezger, "Industrial Seal of Approval," *Plain Dealer* (Cleveland, OH), Aug. 20, 2004, p. C1.

65. Mike Delpha, "ISO 9001:2000 Upgrade: Tips for a Smooth Transition," *Professional Safety,* July 2002, pp. 14, 17. ISO 9000 is covered in Ronald Henkoff, "The Hot New Seal of Quality," *Fortune,* June 28, 1993, pp. 116–118, 120.

66. Neal E. Boudette, "Cadillac Aims to Lure European Drivers with Compact Sedan" *The Wall Street Journal,* Feb. 17, 2005, p. D3; Jason Stein, "Cadillac Attacks Overseas Markets," *Automotive News,* Feb. 14, 2005, p. 3; and Normandy Madden, "GM Prepares for Cadillac in China," *Automotive News,* Oct. 4, 2004, p. 20.

Chapter 11

1. Zipcar website: *www.zipcar.com;* Brad Grimes, "Leaving the Driving to Zipcar," *PCMagazine,* Feb. 17, 2004, p. 60; Matt Palmquist, "Car-Sharing Moves into the Fast Lane," *Business 2.0,* December 2004, p. 40.

2. Statistics in the chapter related to the U.S. economy are from the *Statistical Abstract of the United States: 2004– 2005,* 12th ed., Bureau of the Census, Washington, DC, 2004.

3. Sean Callahan, "USPS to Break with U.S. Cycling Team." *B to B,* May 3, 2004, p. 5; Richard M. Vinoocur, "Print Council 'Discovers' the USPS," *American Printer,* May 2004, p. 49.

4. Valarie A. Zeithaml and Mary Jo Bitner, *Services Marketing,* 2nd ed., Burr Ridge, IL, Irwin McGraw-Hill, 2000.

5. Several excellent example of how services organizations focus on employees and customers can be found in Jena McGregor, "Customers 1st," *Fast Company,* October 2004, pp. 79+.

6. Melinda Ligos, "Mall Rats with a Social Conscience," *Sales & Marketing Management,* November 1999, p 115; Aja Whitaker, "Cause Marketing Gaining Ground," *Management Review,* September 1999, p. 8.

7. James Arndorfer, Jr., "Army Recruiting a Casualty of War," *Advertising Age,* Dec. 6, 2004, pp. 1+; Lev Grossman, "The Army's Killer App," *Time,* Feb. 28, 2005, pp. 43+.

8. Bree Fowler, "Congregation of Nuns Uses Internet, TV for Recruiting," *South Bend Tribune,* June 10, 2002, p. C3.

9. Satisfaction with services is based on a customer's perceptions of various types of convenience, most of which are controlled by the seller. Leonard L. Berry, Kathleen Seiders, and Dhruv Grewal, "Understanding Service Convenience," *Journal of Marketing,* July 2002, pp. 1–17, describes how the relationship may work.

10. "Quarterly Retail E-Commerce Sales, 4th Quarter 2004," U.S. Department of Commerce News, Economics and

Statistics Administration, U.S. Census Bureau, Feb. 24, 2005.

11. Zipcar website: *www.zipcar.com;* Daniel McGinn, "Pimp . . . My Rental," *Newsweek,* Dec. 20, 2004, p. 10; Mark Jewell, "Technology Makes Car-Sharing Road Easy," *South Bend Tribune,* Jan. 3, 2005, pp. C8+.

Chapter 12

1. *www.priceline.com,* accessed May 20, 2005; Avery Johnson, "Travel Web Sites Rethink the Bid-and-Bargain," *The Wall Street Journal,* Apr. 7, 2005, p. D2; Adam L. Freeman, "Priceline Discovers That Choice Really Does Matter," *The Wall Street Journal,* Apr. 21 2004, p. 1; Peter Grant, "Braddock Resigns As the Chairman of Priceline.com," *The Wall Street Journal,* Apr. 9, 2004, p. B3; Julia Angwin, "Hit by Travel Slump, Priceline Posts a Loss," *The Wall Street Journal,* Feb. 5, 2002, p. B5; Julia Angwin, "After Surviving Dog-Com Rout, Priceline Enters New Storm," *The Wall Street Journal,* Sept. 20, 2001, p. B9; Clay Shirky, "How Priceline Became a Real Business," *The Wall Street Journal,* Aug. 13, 2001, p. A12; Julia Angwin, "Priceline.com Posts a Profit, Crediting Stringent Cost Cuts, Escalating Demand," *The Wall Street Journal,* Aug. 1, 2001, p. A3; Peter Elkind, "The Hype Is Big, Really Big, at Priceline," *Fortune,* Sept. 6, 1999, pp. 193–194+; and Heather Green, "Priceline's Bid for the Big Time," *BusinessWeek,* Jan. 18, 1999, p. 43.

2. This list was suggested in part by John T. Mentzer and David J. Schwartz, *Marketing Today,* 4th ed., Harcourt Brace Jovanovich, San Diego, 1985, p. 599.

3. David Meer, "System Beaters, Brand Loyals, and Deal Shoppers: New Insights into the Role of Brand and Price," *Journal of Advertising Research,* May/June 1995, pp. RC2–RC7.

4. Stephen J. Hoch, Byung-Do Kim, Alan L. Montgomery, and Peter E. Rossi, "Determinants of Store-Level Price Elasticity," *Journal of Marketing Research,* February 1995, p. 28.

5. Frank R. Kardes, Maria L. Cronley, James J. Kellaris, and Steven S. Posavac, "The Role of Selective Information Processing in Price-Quality Inference," *Journal of Consumer Research,* September 2004, pp. 368+; and Roberta Maynard, "Taking Guesswork out of Pricing," *Nation's Business,* December 1997, p. 28. For

in-depth discussions of the relationship between price levels and perceived quality, see David J. Curry and Peter C. Riesz, "Prices and Price/Quality Relationships: A Longitudinal Analysis," *Journal of Marketing,* January 1988, pp. 36–51; and Valarie A. Zeithaml, "Consumer Perceptions of Price, Quality, and Value: A Means-End Model and Synthesis of Evidence," *Journal of Marketing,* July 1988, pp. 2–22.

6. David Meyer, "The 25 Most Influential Executives of the Business Travel Industry, 2004," *Business Travel News,* Jan. 17, 2005, pp. 1+; and Caroline Wilbert, "What Recession? Extended-Stay Hotels' Business Remains Sweet in a Sour Economy," *Atlanta Journal-Constitution,* Aug. 20, 2002, p. D1.

7. Dean Takahashi, "Little Caesar's Plans 'Big! Big!' Pizzas, while Keeping Price Structure the Same," *The Wall Street Journal,* Sept. 2, 1997, p. B6; and Rahul Jacob, "Beyond Quality and Value," *Fortune* (special issue), Autumn/Winter 1993, pp. 8, 10.

8. Gary H. Anthes, "The Price Had Better Be Right," *Computerworld,* Dec. 21, 1998, pp. 65–66.

9. Frank Alpert, Beth Wilson, and Michael T. Elliott, "Price Signaling: Does It Ever Work?" *Journal of Product & Brand Management,* vol. 2, no. 1, 1993, pp. 29–41.

10. For a list of 21 pricing objectives and a discussion of objectives as part of a strategic pricing program for industrial firms, see Michael H. Morris and Roger J. Calantone, "Four Components of Effective Pricing," *Industrial Marketing Management,* November 1990, pp. 321–329.

11. Greg Lamp, "Lower Prices for Roundup," *Corn & Soybean Digest,* Oct. 1, 2004, p. 5; and Robert Steyer, "Monsanto Slashes Roundup Prices," *St. Louis Post-Dispatch,* Sept. 2, 1998, p. C1.

12. Sam Nataraj and Jim Lee, "Dot-Com Companies: Are They All Hype?" *SAM Advanced Management Journal,* July 1, 2002, pp. 10+; and George Anders, "Buying Frenzy," *The Wall Street Journal,* July 12, 1999, pp. R6, R10.

13. "U.S. Automakers Rap Japan's Forex Intervention as Export Subsidies," *Knight Ridder Tribune Business News,* Apr. 30, 2005, p. 1.

14. For a discussion of new-product pricing, taking into account the product's perceived benefits and entry time, see

Eunsang Yoon, "Pricing Imitative New Products," *Industrial Marketing Management,* May 1991, pp. 115–125.

15. Maynard, op. cit., p. 27.

16. Greg Burns, "Even in Recovery, Factories Are Closing," *Chicago Tribune,* June 1, 2004, p. 9.

17. Imogen Wall, "It May Be a Dog-Eat-Dog World, but This Restaurant Won't Prove It," *The Wall Street Journal,* Dec. 11, 1998, p. B1.

18. For a report on how this is done in the business market, see Michael H. Morris and Mary L. Joyce, "How Marketers Evaluate Price Sensitivity," *Industrial Marketing Management,* May 1988, pp. 169–176.

19. George E. Cressman, Jr., "Snatching Defeat from the Jaws of Victory," *Marketing Management,* Summer 1997, p. 15.

20. Wendy Zellner, "Commentary: Waiting for the First Airline to Die," *BusinessWeek Online,* Jan. 24, 2005, no page given; and Trebor Banstetter, "Delta Sales Soar after Price Cuts," *Ft. Worth Star-Telegram,* Jan. 13, 2005, p. 3C.

21. Steve Hamm, "The Wild and Woolly World of Linux," *BusinessWeek,* Nov. 15, 1999, pp. 130, 134; James Aley, "Give It Away and Get Rich!" *Fortune,* June 10, 1996, pp. 90–92+; and Neil Gross and Peter Coy, "The Technology Paradox," *BusinessWeek,* Mar. 6, 1995, pp. 76–81, 84.

22. Tom Lester, "How to Ensure That the Price Is Exactly Right," *Financial Times,* Jan. 30, 2002, no pages given; and "Pricing Gets Easier (Sort Of)," *Inc.,* November 1993, p. 124.

23. Avraham Shama, "E-Coms and Their Marketing Strategies," *Business Horizons,* September 2001, pp. 14+; and Morris and Calantone, op. cit., p. 323.

24. The perspective that price dictates cost levels is presented in Christopher Farrell and Zachary Schiller, "Stuck!" *BusinessWeek,* Nov. 15, 1993, pp. 146, 148. The magnitude of Kodak's cost-cutting efforts is described in Chanoine Webb, "The Picture Just Keeps Getting Darker at Kodak," *Fortune,* June 21, 1999, p. 206.

25. For an approach to break-even analysis that includes semifixed costs and is of more practical value in situations typically faced by marketing executives, see Thomas L. Powers, "Break-even Analysis with Semifixed Costs," *Industrial Marketing Management,* February 1987, pp. 35–41.

26. G. Dean Kortge and Patrick A. Okonkwo, "Perceived Value Approach to Pricing," *Industrial Marketing Management*, May 1993, p. 134.

27. Dan Koeppel, "Fast Food's New Reality," *Adweek's Marketing Week*, Mar. 30, 1992, pp. 22–23.

28. Margaret Studer, "Patek Philippe Is Luxuriating in Independence," *The Wall Street Journal*, Dec. 11, 2000, p. B18; and Thomas T. Nagle, "Managing Price Competition," *Marketing Management*, vol. 2, no. 1, 1993, p. 41.

29. *http://cgi.pathfinder.com/cgi-bin/golfonline/instruction/teachers/2005/bin/top100.cgi*, accessed Feb. 12, 2005; and Mark Hyman, "The Coaches Are Cashing In," *BusinessWeek Online*, Aug. 16, 2004, no pages given.

30. Motoko Rich, "Big Hotel Chains to Sell Rooms on Priceline's Lowestfare.com," *The Wall Street Journal*, Mar. 19, 2003, p. D3; Matt Krantz, "Priceline Turns Its First Profit," *USA Today*, Aug. 1, 2001, p. 3B; Julia Angwin, "Priceline Founder Closes Online Bidding Sites for Gas and Groceries," *The Wall Street Journal*, Oct. 6, 2000, p. B1; and Nick Wingfield, "New Battlefield for Priceline Is Diapers, Tuna," *The Wall Street Journal*, Sept. 22, 1999, p. B1.

Chapter 13

1. *www.bose.com*, accessed May 22, 2005; Stephen Williams, "Test Drive: Newest Bose System Rides High on the Wave of Previous Success," *Newsday*, Oct. 31, 2004, p. E36; Joseph Palenchar, "Bose Boasts Main-Stereo Quality in Table Radio/CD," *TWICE*, Aug. 23, 2004, pp. 32+; Joseph Palenchar, "Dealers Cite Niche, Brand Exposure," *TWICE*, July 21, 2003, p. 25; Joseph Palenchar, "Untapped Niche, Demos Drive Bose Sellthrough," *TWICE*, July 21, 2003, p. 25; and Markkus Rovito, "Dealerscope Hall of Fame: Amar Bose," *Dealerscope*, January 2002, p. 70+.

2. Evan Perez and Nicole Harris, "Despite Early Signs of Victory, Discount Airlines Get Squeezed," *The Wall Street Journal*, Jan. 17, 2005, pp. A1, A8; and Scott McCartney, "How Discount Airlines Profited from Their Bigger Rivals' Woes," *The Wall Street Journal*, Aug. 12, 2004, pp. A1, A2.

3. Gary Strauss, "99¢ Only Started Trend," *USA Today*, June 22, 1998, pp. 1B, 2B. For an update, see Ann Zimmerman, "Behind the Dollar-Store Boom: A Nation of Bargain Hunters," *The Wall Street Journal*, Dec. 13, 2004, pp. A1, A10; and Robert Berner, "Out-Discounting the Discounter," *BusinessWeek*, May 10, 2004, pp. 78–79.

4. Don Clark, "Intel to Release Itanium 2 Chip—Company Hopes Entry Will Allow It to Charge High End of Computing," *The Asian Wall Street Journal*, July 9, 2002, p. A7.

5. Patricia Sellers, "Look Who Learned about Value," *Fortune*, Oct. 18, 1993, p. 75; and Bill Saporito, "Why the Price Wars Never End," *Fortune*, Mar. 23, 1992, pp. 68+.

6. Stratford Sherman, "How to Prosper in the Value Decade," *Fortune*, Nov. 30, 1992, p 98.

7. Anne Faircloth, "Values Retailers Go Dollar for Dollar," *Fortune*, July 6, 1998, p. 166.

8. Albert D. Bates, "Pricing for Profit," *Retailing Issues Newsletter*, September 1990, p. 1.

9. Robert Berner, "Race You to the Top of the Market," *BusinessWeek*, Dec. 8, 2003, p. 98. For three recommended forms of non-price competition for retailers, see Bates, op. cit., p. 4.

10. Sarah Ellison and Geoffrey A. Fowler, "Aisle 9 to Saks: P&G Brings Its $130 Skin Treatment to U.S.," *The Wall Street Journal*, Mar. 12, 2004, p. B1.

11. Michael Schuman, "Flat Chance," *Time*, Oct. 18, 2004, pp. 64+; and Sean O'Neill, "Eyes on the Price," *Kiplinger's Personal Finance*, September 2000, pp. 122–123.

12. Charles Forelle, "Do You Really Need a Turbo Toothbrush?" *The Wall Street Journal*, Oct. 1, 2002, pp. D1, D4; and Robert Berner, "Why P&G's Smile Is So Bright," *BusinessWeek*, Aug. 12, 2002, pp. 58–60.

13. Paul Roberts, "Trend Micro Gives Away Mobile Anti-Virus Software," *Network World*, Dec. 13, 2004, p. 20; and Neil Gross and Peter Coy, "The Technology Paradox," *BusinessWeek*, Mar. 6, 1995, pp. 76–77.

14. Reed K. Holden and Thomas T. Nagle, "Kamikaze Pricing," *Marketing Management*, Summer 1998, p. 39.

15. Dan Carney, "Caveat Predator?" *BusinessWeek*, May 22, 2000, pp. 116, 118; and Mike France and Steve Hamm, "Does Predatory Pricing Make Microsoft a Predator?" *BusinessWeek*, Nov. 23, 1998, pp. 130, 132.

16. Robert Steyer, "Monsanto Offers Discounts to Dairy Farmers," *St. Louis Post-Dispatch*, Oct. 22, 1995, p. 1E.

17. Dahleen Glanton, "Coupon Clippers Clean Up," *Chicago Tribune*, May 8, 2005, p. 1; Noreen O'Leary, "Dealing with Coupons," *Adweek*, Feb. 21, 2005, p. 29; and Roger O. Crockett, "Penny-Pinchers' Paradise: E-Coupons Are Catching on Fast—and Companies Are Learning to Use Them," *BusinessWeek e.biz*, Jan. 22, 2001, p. EB12.

18. Cherie Jacobs, "Taking the Bait," *Tampa Tribune*, Aug. 31, 2003, p. 1; and William M. Bulkeley, "Rebates' Secret Appeal to Manufacturers: Few Consumers Actually Redeem Them," *The Wall Street Journal*, Feb. 10, 1998, pp. B1, B6.

19. Leo Jakobson, "Coupons on the Go," *Incentive*, February 2005, p. 16; Crockett, loc. cit.; and Geoffrey A. Fowler, "Click and Clip," *The Wall Street Journal*, Oct. 21, 2002, p. R8.

20. For more about this approach, see Hermann Simon and Robert J. Dolan, "Price Customization," *Marketing Management*, Fall 1998, pp. 10–17.

21. "Another Cry of Price Discrimination," *Chain Store Age*, December 2004, p. 149; and William C. Smith, "Keeping Cases in Racing Trim," *National Law Journal*, Apr. 7, 2003, p. A9.

22. Douglas A. Blackmon, "FedEx Is to Adopt Rate Structure Based on Distance Package Travels," *The Wall Street Journal*, Jan. 23, 1997, p. B4.

23. For further discussion of pricing strategies and policies, see Gerard J. Tellis, "Beyond the Many Faces of Price: An Integration of Pricing Strategies," *Journal of Marketing*, October 1986, pp. 146–160.

24. For a theoretical model of flexible pricing and discussion of its managerial implications, see Kenneth R. Evans and Richard F. Beltramini, "A Theoretical Model of Consumer-Negotiated Pricing: An Orientation Perspective," *Journal of Marketing*, April 1987, pp. 58–73.

25. "Auto Report," *The Seattle Times*. Aug. 23, 2002, p. F1; and Joann Muller, "Old Carmakers Learn New Tricks," *BusinessWeek*, Apr. 12, 1999, pp. 116, 118.

26. Julia Angwin, "America Online Faces New Threat from Cut-Rate Internet Services," *The Wall Street Journal*, Feb. 3, 2003, pp. A1, A11; and Peter Coy, "Are Flat Rates Good Business?" *BusinessWeek*, Feb. 10, 1997, p. 108.

27. Strauss, loc. cit.

28. A study of the beneficial effects of odd pricing, if used on a very limited basis, is mentioned in "Why That Deal Is Only $9.99," *BusinessWeek,* Jan. 10, 2000, p. 36. Previously the effectiveness of odd pricing was described in Robert M. Schindler and Lori S. Warren, "Effects of Odd Pricing on Price Recall," *Journal of Business,* June 1989, pp. 165–177. Consumers' paying attention to just the first two digits in a price is examined in Mark Stiving and Russell S. Winer, "An Empirical Analysis of Price Endings with Scanner Data," *Journal of Consumer Research,* June 1997, pp. 57–67.

29. Eric Anderson and Duncan Simester, "Mind Your Pricing Cues," *Harvard Business Review,* September 2003, pp. 96–103.

30. Russell Gold and Ann Zimmerman, "Pumped Out: Wal-Mart's Defeat in Low-Cost Gas Game," *The Wall Street Journal,* Aug. 13, 2001, p. A14; and "Wal-Mart Wins Suit over Low-Price Strategy," *St. Louis Post-Dispatch,* Jan. 10, 1995, p. 7C.

31. Peter J. McGoldrick, Erica J. Betts, and Kathy A. Keeling, "High-Low Pricing: Audit Evidence and Consumer Preferences," *The Journal of Product and Brand Management,* 2000, pp. 316–331; G. S. Bobinski, D. Cox, and A. Cox, "Retail 'Sale' Advertising, Perceived Retailer Credibility and Price Rationale," *Journal of Retailing,* Fall 1996, pp. 291–306; and "Consumers' Reference Prices: Implications for Managers," *Stores,* April 1996, p. RR4.

32. Patrick J. Kaufmann, N. Craig Smith, and Gwendolyn K. Ortmeyer, "Deception in Retailer High-Low Pricing: A 'Rule of Reason' Approach," *Journal of Retailing,* Summer 1994, p. 151.

33. For an overview of how one chain, Family Dollar Stores, switched from high-low pricing to EDLP, see Michael Friedman, "A Contented Discounter," *Progressive Grocer,* November 1998, pp. 39–41. For information about other chains' use of EDLP, see Duke Ratliff, "Variations on the Theme," *Discount Merchandiser,* March 1996, pp. 24–25. The appearance of EDLP in Germany is covered in Jennifer Negley, "Jeden Tag Tiefpreise—Sprechen sie EDLP?" *Discount Store News,* June 8, 1998, p. 17.

34. Stuart Hirshfield, "The Squeeze," *Apparel Industry Magazine,* August 1998, pp. 60–64.

35. Tim Ambler, "P&G Learnt the Hard Way from Dropping Its Price Promotions," *Marketing,* June 7, 2001, p. 22.

36. Kathleen Seiders and Glenn B. Voss, "From Price to Purchase," *Marketing Management,* November/December 2004, pp. 38–43; and Stephen J. Hoch, Xavier Drpze, and Mary E. Purk, "EDLP, Hi-Lo, and Margin Arithmetic," *Journal of Marketing,* October 1994, pp. 16–27.

37. For a discussion of the legal status of resale price maintenance, plus some steps that manufacturers can take to avoid legal problems when establishing resale price maintenance programs, see Mary Jane Sheffet and Debra L. Scammon, "Resale Price Maintenance: Is It Safe to Suggest Retail Prices?" *Journal of Marketing,* Fall 1985, pp. 82–91.

38. Joel M. Cohen and Arthur J. Burke, "Antitrust: Supreme Court Acts on Maximum Pricing," *International Commercial Litigation,* December 1997/January 1998, p. 43; and Susan B. Garland, "You'll Charge What I Tell You to Charge," *BusinessWeek,* Oct. 6, 1997, pp. 118, 120.

39. "Nine West Settles State and Federal Price Fixing Charges," *M2 Presswire,* Mar. 7, 2000, no pages given.

40. Michael Selz, "Small Firms Use Variety of Ploys to Raise Prices," *The Wall Street Journal,* June 17, 1993, p. B1.

41. Thomas T. Nagle, "Managing Price Competition," *Marketing Management,* vol. 2, no. 1, 1993, p. 45.

42. Peter Burrows, "An Ear for Music," *BusinessWeek,* May 23, 2005, p. 50; Scott Kilman, "Diageo Says Industry Price War Is Crimping Its Burger King Sale," *The Wall Street Journal,* Nov. 8, 2002, p. A3; and Robert Weller, "Colorado Ski Resorts Give In to Need for Deep Discounts," *St. Louis Post-Dispatch,* Sept. 4, 1999, p. 33OT. The statement about price wars, made by a McKinsey consultant, was contained in David R. Henderson, "What Are Price Wars Good For? *Absolutely Nothing,*" *Fortune,* May 12, 1997, p. 156.

43. Andy Serwer, "Music Retailers Are Really Starting to Sing the Blues," *Fortune,* Mar. 8, 2004, p. 73. The description of price-war damages is from Andrew E. Serwer, "How to Escape a Price War," *Fortune,* June 13, 1994, pp. 82+.

44. *www.bose.com,* accessed May 22, 2005; Herbert Shuldiner, "Bose's Sound Strategy," *Chief Executive,* January/February 2005, pp. 34+; and Herb Shuldiner, "Bose Knows—Shocks?" *Ward's Auto World,* September 2004, pp. 26+.

Chapter 14

1. *www1.toysrus.com,* accessed on May 28, 2005; "Toys 'R' Us Reports 2004 Earnings Rise," *Bicycle Retailer and Industry News,* May 15, 2005, p. 9; Doug Desjardins, "Playtime Is Over for Toy Retailers," *DSN Retailing Today,* Feb. 7, 2005, pp. 14+; Joseph Pereira, Rob Tomsho, and Ann Zimmerman, "Toys 'Were' Us?" *The Wall Street Journal,* Aug. 12, 2004, pp. B1, B2; Joseph Pereira and Ann Zimmerman, "Toys 'R' Us Suppliers Pitch In," *The Wall Street Journal,* Nov. 10, 2004, pp. B1, B2; Doug Desjardins, "Toysrus.com Earns Title of Cyber World's Biggest Toy Store," *DSN Retailing Today,* June 7, 2004, pp. 22+; Anne D'Innocenzio, "Toy Wars," *St. Louis Post-Dispatch,* Feb. 19, 2004, pp. C1, C2; Abigail Goldman and Charles Piller, "Chronic Losses Take the Fun Out of EToys, Other Retailers," *The Miami Herald,* Jan. 29, 2000, pp. 1C, 3C; Katrina Brooker, "Toys Were Us," *Fortune,* Sept. 27, 1999, pp. 145–146+; and Betty Liu, "Toys R Us Set to Revamp 525 Stores," *Financial Times,* June 9, 1999, p. 17.

2. David Kirkpatrick, "How to Erase the Middleman in One Easy Lesson," *Fortune,* Mar. 17, 2003, p. 122; and "Merrill Lynch Shakes Up Industry by Going Online," *St. Louis Post-Dispatch,* July 22, 1999, p. B13. For a discussion of the contention that the Internet is the biggest influence on distribution since the Industrial Revolution, see Leyland Pitt, Pierre Berthon, and Jean-Paul Berthon, "Changing Channels: The Impact of the Internet on Distribution Strategy," *Business Horizons,* March/April 1999, pp. 19–28.

3. For insight regarding whether the Internet will eliminate middlemen in two industries, air travel and groceries, see Eric Clemons, "When Should You Bypass the Middleman?" *Financial Times,* Feb. 22, 1999, p. 14. The term *disintermediation* is explained further in "On-Line Commerce Business Trends," *The Wall Street Journal* Dec. 12, 1996, p. B4.

4. The concept of shifting activities, the possibility of manufacturers shifting some functions away from their firms, and the opportunity for small wholesalers to perform added functions to maintain their economic viability are

all discussed in Ronald D. Michman, "Managing Structural Changes in Marketing Channels," *The Journal of Business and Industrial Marketing,* Summer/Fall 1990, pp. 5–14. The distinctive ways in which electronic channel members carry out distribution-related activities are described in Robert D. Tamilia, Sylvain Senecal, and Giles Corriveau, "Conventional Channels of Distribution and Electronic Intermediaries: A Functional Analysis," *Journal of Marketing Channels,* vol. 9, nos. 3/4, pp. 27–48.

5. *www.coremark.com,* accessed on May 26, 2005.

6. *www.lotuslight.com,* accessed on May 26, 2005; and Julie Candler, "How to Choose a Distributor," *Nation's Business,* August 1993, p. 46.

7. *www.statefarm com/quote/ara.htm.* accessed on May 26, 2005; and Diane Brady, "Insurers Step Gingerly into Cyberspace," *BusinessWeek,* Nov. 22, 1999, p. 160.

8. Karen Roche and Bill O'Connell, "Dig a Wider Channel for Your Products," *Marketing News,* Nov. 9, 1998, p. 10.

9. For guidance on selecting channels for international markets, especially the decision of whether to use middlemen, see Saul Klein, "Selection of International Marketing Channels," *Journal of Global Marketing,* vol. 4, 1991, pp. 21–37.

10. The New Pig example is drawn from "Unconventional Channels," *Sales & Marketing Management,* October 1988, p. 38.

11. Milena Izmirileva, "Pfizer to Distribute Medicines Directly in Spain, As Farmaindustria Denies Supply Problems," *WMRC Daily Analysis,* Feb. 4, 2005, no pages given.

12. *www.marshallamps.com,* accessed on May 26, 2005.

13. An excellent discussion of distribution channels for business goods and services is found in Chapter 14 of Michael D. Hutt and Thomas W. Speh, *Business Marketing Management,* 8th ed., Thomson South-Western, Independence, KY, 2004.

14. Maricris G. Briones, "Resellers Hike Profits through Service," *Marketing News,* Feb. 15, 1999, pp. 1, 14; and Maricris G. Briones, "What Technology Wrought: Distribution Channel in Flux," *Marketing News,* Feb. 1, 1999, pp. 1, 15.

15. For an instructive discussion of this topic, see Donald H. Light, "A Guide for New Distribution Channel Strategies for Service Firms," *The Journal of Business Strategy,* Summer 1986, pp. 56–64.

16. Paul Cuckoo, "Airlines Join Forces to Cut Agent Commissions," *Knight Ridder Tribune Business News,* Feb. 15, 2005, p. 1; and George Anders, "Some Big Companies Long to Embrace Web but Settle for Flirtation," *The Wall Street Journal,* Nov. 4, 1998, p. A14.

17. Rowland T. Moriarty and Ursula Moran, "Managing Hybrid Marketing Systems," *Harvard Business Review,* November–December 1990, pp. 146–155.

18. For extensive discussion of this approach to serving distinct markets, see Wim G. Biemans, "Marketing in the Twilight Zone," *Business Horizons,* November/December 1998, pp. 69–76; and John A. Quelch, "Why Not Exploit Dual Marketing?" *Business Horizons,* January–February 1987, pp. 52–60.

19. Deborah Lohse, "Allstate to Launch Online Sales of Car and Home Insurance," *The Wall Street Journal,* Nov. 11, 1999, p. B18; Samuel Schiff, "Agency System Lives but Continued Survival Will Require Adapting to Changes," *Rough Notes,* February 1999, pp. 14–16; and "Dramatic Shift to Multiple Distribution Channels for Property-Casualty Insurance Industry," *Limra's Marketfacts,* March/April 1998, p. 6.

20. Katarzyna Moreno, "UnbeComing," *Fortune,* June 10, 2002, pp. 151–152; and Jim Edwards, "Carvel HQ Says Court's Decision Is Just Desserts," *Brandweek,* Oct. 25, 2004, p. 23.

21. The Scotts example comes from Valerie Reitman, "Manufacturers Start to Spurn Big Discounters," *The Wall Street Journal,* Nov. 30, 1993, p. B1. For further discussion of the advantages and disadvantages of multiple channels as well as ways to minimize conflict resulting from multiple channels, see Martin Everett, "When There's More than One Route to the Customer," *Sales & Marketing Management,* August 1990, pp. 48–50+.

22. "Ford Sells Oklahoma Dealerships," *Associated Press Newswires,* Apr. 4, 2002; Carol Matlack, "Swatch: Ready for Net Time?" *BusinessWeek,* Feb. 14, 2000, p. 61; Earle Eldridge, "GM Settles Argument with Dealerships," *USA Today,* Jan. 24, 2000, p. 2B; and Joann Muller, "Meet Your Local GM Dealer: GM," *BusinessWeek,* Oct. 11, 1999, p. 48.

23. For details about Kraft Foods' approach to coordinating (perhaps controlling) distribution activities, see Brandon Copple, "Shelf-Determination," *Forbes,* Apr. 15, 2002, pp. 130–132+.

24. Laura J. Hopper, "Sam's Town," *Regional Economist,* Oct. 1, 2004, p. 14. Wal-Mart's dominating power and increasing control in the area of distribution (and, more broadly, the economy and society as a whole), and some of the negative reactions it has received lately, are described in Ann Zimmerman, "Defending Wal-Mart," *The Wall Street Journal,* Oct. 6, 2004, pp. B1, B10; Jerry Useem, "One Nation under Wal-Mart," *Fortune,* Mar. 3, 2003, pp. 65–86+; Jim Hopkins, "Wal-Mart's Influence Grows," *USA Today,* Jan. 29, 2003, pp. 1B+; and Copple, op. cit., p. 140.

25. "Dynamic Shift to Multiple Distribution Channels . . . ," loc. cit.

26. Michael Selz, "More Small Firms Are Turning to Trade Intermediaries," *The Wall Street Journal,* Feb. 2, 1993, p. B2.

27. For more on the idea that market considerations should determine a channel structure, see Louis W. Stern and Frederick D. Sturdivant, "Customer-Driven Distribution Systems," *Harvard Business Review,* July–August 1987, pp. 34–41.

28. Anders, op. cit., pp. A1, A14.

29. Bert Rosenbloom and Trina L. Larsen, "How Foreign Firms View Their U.S. Distributors," *Industrial Marketing Management,* May 1992, pp. 93–101.

30. Felix Sanchez, " 'Famous Amos' Cookie Founder Rebounds with Upbeat Attitude, New Product Line," *Knight Ridder Tribune Business News,* Mar. 20, 2003, p. 1; and "Putting the Aim Back into Famous Amos," *Sales & Marketing Management,* June 1992, p. 31.

31. Reitman, op. cit., pp. B1, B2; and Christina Duff, "Nation's Retailers Ask Vendors to Help Share Expenses," *The Wall Street Journal,* Aug. 4, 1993, p. B4.

32. Gabriel Kahn, "Invisible Supplier Has Penney's Shirts All Buttoned Up," *The Wall Street Journal,* Sept. 11, 2003, pp. A1, A9.

33. For an in-depth discussion of differences in distribution intensity, as well as a study of this factor in the context of the consumer electronics industry, see Gary L. Frazier and Walfried M. Lassar, "Determinants of Distribution Intensity," *Journal of Marketing,* October 1996, pp. 39–51.

34. Patricia Sellers, "P&G: Teaching an Old Dog New Tricks," *Fortune,* May 31, 2004, pp. 166+.

35. *www.step2.com,* accessed on May 28, 2005; and Reitman, op. cit., pp. B1, B2.

36. Sara Nathan, "Defining the Seller in On-Line Market," *USA Today,* Aug. 26, 1999, p. 3B.

37. Mary Jo Feldstein, "Investigation into Buying at Saks Might Hit Close to Home," *St. Louis Post-Dispatch,* May 12, 2005, pp. C1, C3; and "Retailers' Defense: Chargebacks Spring from Non-Compliance," *HFN,* Oct. 8, 2001, pp. 11–12.

38. Stephane Farhi, "Eggs, Bread—and a Discount Daewoo," *Automotive News,* June 28, 1999, p. 46.

39. Thomas Lee, "A-B Watches from the Sidelines as Brewery Buyout Frenzy Unfolds," *St. Louis Post-Dispatch,* Apr. 21, 2002, p. E1; and Jakki J. Mohr, Robert J. Fisher, and John R. Nevin, "Communicating for Better Channel Relationships," *Marketing Management,* Summer 1999, p. 40.

40. *www.coleman.com,* accessed on May 28, 2005; and Teri Agins, "Apparel Makers Are Refashioning Their Operations," *The Wall Street Journal,* Jan. 13, 1994, p. B4.

41. Luisa Kroll, "Tough Guy," *Forbes,* Feb. 4, 2002, pp. 60–61; and Bill Saporito, "Cutting Out the Middleman," *Fortune,* Apr. 6, 1992, p. 96.

42. Rachel Melcer, "Graybar Grows out of Middleman Role," *St. Louis Post-Dispatch,* Sept. 1, 2002, p. E1.

43. Kevin Kelleher, "Giving Dealers a Raw Deal," *Business 2.0,* December 2004, pp. 82, 84.

44. Laura Bird and Wendy Bounds, "Stores' Demands Squeeze Apparel Companies," *The Wall Street Journal,* July 15, 1997, pp. B1, B12.

45. "Slotting Allowances in the Retail Grocery Industry: Selected Case Studies in Five Product Categories," Federal Trade Commission, Washington, DC, 2003, accessed at *www.ftc.gov/opa/2003/11/slottingallowancerpt031114.pdf;* Clayton Kale, "GAO Says Grocers Offered Little Help in Investigation," *St. Louis Post-Dispatch,* Sept. 15, 2000, p. C6; and Holman W. Jenkins, Jr., "We ♥ Slotting Fees," *The Wall Street Journal,* Sept. 22, 1999, p. A23.

46. Nichole L. Torres, "Examine Your Co-Op(tions)," *Entrepreneur,* July 2002, pp. 120, 128.

47. *www.truevalue.com,* accessed on May 28, 2005; Jeremy Mullman, "Competitors Squeeze TruServ," *Crain's Chicago Business,* Nov. 8, 2004, p. 3; and Jeff Bailey, "Co-Ops Gain as Firms Seek Competitive Power," *The Wall Street Journal,* Oct. 15, 2002, p. B5.

48. James E. Zemanek, Jr., and James W. Hardin, "How the Industrial Salesperson's Use of Power Can Affect Distributor Satisfaction: An Empirical Examination," *Journal of Marketing Channels,* vol. 3, no. 1, 1993, pp. 23–45.

49. An early description of the dominance of gigantic retailers and their demands on manufacturers can be found in Zachary Schiller and Wendy Zellner, "Clout!" *BusinessWeek,* Dec. 21, 1992, pp. 66–69+.

50. Wendy Zellner, "Wal-Mart Eases Its Grip," *BusinessWeek,* Feb. 16, 2004, p. 40; the Sutter situation was described in Candler, op. cit., p. 45. For a model showing a range of channel relationships, see John T. Gardner, W. Benoy Joseph, and Sharon Thach, "Modeling the Continuum of Relationship Styles between Distributors and Suppliers," *Journal of Marketing Channels,* vol. 2, no. 4, 1993, pp. 11+.

51. "Wal-Mart Expands Access to Product Sales History," *The Wall Street Journal,* Aug. 18, 1999, p. B8; and Myron Magnet, "The New Golden Rule of Business," *Fortune,* Feb. 21, 1994, pp. 60–64. For a discussion of attributes of successful alliances in channels, based on a study of computer dealers, see Jakki J. Mohr and Robert E. Spekman, "Perfecting Partnerships," *Marketing Management,* Winter/ Spring 1996, pp. 35–43.

52. Magnet, loc. cit. For more ideas on how to build a good producer-middleman relationship, see James A. Narus and James C. Anderson, "Distributor Contributions to Partnerships with Manufacturers," *Business Horizons,* September–October 1987, pp. 34–42.

53. Agins, loc. cit.

54. Hardy Green, "Selling Books Like Bacon," *BusinessWeek Online,* June 16, 2003, no page given; and Andrew Raskin, "Who's Minding the Store?" *Business 2.0,* February 2003, pp. 70+.

55. John R. Nevin, "Relationship Marketing and Distribution Channels: Exploring Fundamental Issues," *Journal of Marketing Channels,* vol. 23, no. 4, 1995, pp. 327–334.

56. Ellen Byron and Teri Agins, "When Exclusivity Means Illegality," *The Wall Street Journal,* Jan. 6, 2005, p. A11; and Ellen Byron, "Spitzer Charges Former CEO of Federated with Perjury," *The Wall Street Journal,* Jan. 5, 2005, pp. B1, B2.

57. "Federal Appeals Court Dismisses Antitrust Suit against Domino's," *Associated Press Newswire,* Aug. 27, 1997, no pages given; and Jeffrey A. Tannenbaum, "Franchisees Balk at High Prices for Supplies from Franchisers," *The Wall-Street Journal,* July 5, 1995, pp. B1, B2.

58. Byron and Agins, loc. cit.; Jennifer E. Gully, "Image Technical Services, Inc., v. Eastman Kodak Co.," *Berkeley Technology Law Journal,* 1998, pp. 339–353; and Wendy Bounds, "Jury Finds Kodak Monopolized Markets in Services and Parts for Its Machines," *The Wall Street Journal,* Sept. 19, 1995, p. A4.

59. Joseph Pereira, "Stride Rite Agrees to Settle Charges It Tried to Force Pricing by Retailers," *The Wall Street Journal,* Sept. 28, 1993, p. B5.

60. Doug Desjardins, "KKR Sweeps in to Save Toys 'R' Us—and U.S. Toy Business," *DSN Retailing Today,* Mar. 28, 2005, pp. 3+; Patricia L. Kirk, "Unhappy Toy Story," *Retail Traffic,* March 2005, pp. 10+; Desjardins, loc. cit.; and Pereira, Tomsho, and Zimmerman, loc. cit.

Chapter 15

1. *www.walgreen.com/about/history/default.jhtml,* Matthew Boyle, "Drug Wars," *Fortune,* June 13, 2005, pp. 79–80+; James Frederick, "At 104, Still Taking Competition by Storm," *Drug Store News,* Mar. 21, 2005, pp. 52+; James Frederick, "Riding the Wave of the Aging Population," *Drug Store News,* Mar. 21, 2005, pp. 68+; Antoinette Alexander, "Customer Loyalty Is in This Contender's Corner," *Drug Store News,* Mar. 21, 2005, pp. 60+; and Michelle L. Kirsche, "Service Is the Name of the Photo Game," *Drug Store News,* Mar. 21, 2005, p. 66.

2. *Statistical Abstract of the United States; 2004–2005,* 124th edition, U.S. Bureau of the Census, Washington, DC, 2004, pp. 656, 661.

3. As quoted in Lou Grabowsky, "Globalization: Reshaping the Retail Marketplace," *Retailing Issues Letter,* November 1989, p. 4.

4. Debbie Howell, "Ch. 11, M&As and Store Closings: Regionals and No.

Threes Feel the Heat," *DSN Retailing Today*, July 5, 2004, p. 20.

5. For specific ways in which small retailers can remain competitive, see Deborah Alexander, "Inventive Retailers Strut Stuff," *Omaha World-Herald*, Dec. 10, 2004, p. 1D; Lynda Edwards, "Ready, Set, Splurge," *The Arizona Daily Star*, Nov. 21, 2004, p. D1; and Joshua Hyatt, Julie Sloane, Ed Welles, and Maggie Overfelt, "Beat the Beast," *FSB: Fortune Small Business*, September 2004, pp. 42+.

6. *1992 Census of Retail Trade*, Subject Series, U.S. Bureau of the Census, Washington, DC, 1996, p. 2–7; and *1992 Census of Wholesale Trade*, Geographic Area Series—U.S., U.S. Bureau of the Census, Washington, DC, 1995, p. US-9. The 8% figure was calculated by multiplying the 11% representing wholesale operating expenses by 72%, the remainder after the 28% representing retailing operating expenses is subtracted from the 100% representing retail sales (or the consumer's dollar).

7. *www.7-eleven.com/about/history.asp*, accessed on June 1, 2005.

8. "5 Rules of Great Store Design," *Business 2.0*, March 2003, p. 47; and Bob Parks, "The Floor Plan with a Plan," *Business 2.0*, March 2003, pp. 48–49.

9. Joseph Weber, "How the Net Is Remaking the Mall," *BusinessWeek*, May 9, 2005, pp. 60–61; Kortney Stringer, "Abandoning the Mall," *The Wall Street Journal*, Mar. 24, 2004, pp. B1, B6; Dean Starkman, "The Mall without the Haul," *The Wall Street Journal*, July 25, 2001, pp. B1, B8; and Ellen Neuborne, "Stores Siphon Shoppers from Regional Malls," *USA Today*, June 13, 1995, p. 1B.

10. *www.mallofamerica.com/about_the_mall/mallfacts.aspx*, accessed on June 1, 2005; and "Mall of America Expansion," *Construction Bulletin*, March 2005, p. 6.

11. Eric Heisler, "Malls Try to Make a Lifestyle Change," *St. Louis Post-Dispatch*, Nov. 26, 2004, pp. B1, B8.

12. H. Lee Murphy, "Retail Revisions: Malls Seek Lifestyle Change," *Crain's Chicago Business*, Mar. 28, 2005, p. 36; Terry Pristin, "Shopping Malls Adopting New Strategies to Survive," *The New York Times*, Mar. 2, 2005, p. C7; and Leslie Zganjar, "Mall Makeovers," *The Business Journal*, Feb. 16–22, 2001, pp. 1, 9.

13. Barbara Thau, "Coming to a Mall Near You: Wal-Mart, Target and Costco?" *HFN*, Mar. 14, 2005, p. 4; Sheila Muto, "A Breath of Fresh Air for Troubled Malls," *The Wall Street Journal*, Aug. 4, 2004, p. B4; Chris Penttila, "Retaliatory Strike," *Entrepreneur*, December 2002, p. 122; and Pristin, loc. cit.

14. Andrew M. Carlo, "Ace's Urban Prototype Opens in Manhattan," *Home Channel News*, Sept. 30, 2004, pp. 3+; Matt Valley, "The Remalling of America," *National Real Estate Investor*, May 2002, pp. 18–24; and Gabrielle Solomon, "Striking Gold in the Nation's Urban Core," *Fortune*, May 10, 1999, p. 152[J].

15. *www.walmartstores.com*, accessed on Mar. 11, 2005; Gary McWilliams and Steven Gray, "Slimming Down Stores," *The Wall Street Journal*, Apr. 29, 2005, pp. B1, B4; and Mike Duff, "Home Depot Drops Villager's Hardware for New Concept," *DSN Retailing Today*, Apr. 22, 2002, p. 5.

16. The latest available statistics are found in *Statistical Abstract of the United States: 1995*, U.S. Bureau of the Census, Washington, DC, 1995, p. 783.

17. International Franchise Association website, *www.franchise.org/resourcetr/faq*, accessed on Apr. 1, 2005.

18. Anne Field, "Your Ticket to a New Career?" *BusinessWeek*, May 12, 2003, pp. 100–101; and Bernard Wysocki, Jr., "Start-Up with a Safety Net," *The Wall Street Journal*, Apr. 18, 2001, pp. B1, B6.

19. Kristi Arellano, "Sub Chain's Growth Takes Heat," *The Denver Post*, June 19, 2005, pp. 1k, 8k. Shirley Leung, "Be Your Own Boss with a Franchise—Not Quite," *The Wall Street Journal*, Dec. 9, 2003, p. A25; and Peter M. Birkeland, *Franchising Dreams*, University of Chicago Press, Chicago, 2002.

20. Jan Norman, "Franchising Growing as a Two-Way Street," *The Orange County Register*, May 12, 2005, p. 1; "Survey Reports 92 Percent of Franchisees Say They Are Successful," *Franchising World*, May/June 1998, pp. 34–36; and Geoff Williams, "Keep Thinking," *Entrepreneur*, September 2002, pp. 100+.

21. Growth areas for franchising are suggested in Richard Gibson, "Where the Buzz Is," *The Wall Street Journal*, Dec. 15, 2003, pp. R7, R9; and Virginia Brown Gilbert, "Franchising: It's Much More Than Fast Food Nowadays," *St. Louis Post-Dispatch*, Sept. 5, 2003, pp. C1, C15. Factors that have contributed to franchising's growth are outlined in Bruce J. Walker, "Retail Franchising in the 1990s," *Retailing Issues Letter*, January 1991, pp. 1–4.

22. Lorrie Grant, "Some Famous Store Names to Disappear," *USA Today*, July 29, 2005, p. 68; and Allison Linn, "Regional Store Names Become Casualties of Merger Madness," *St. Louis Post-Dispatch*, Mar. 4, 2005, p. C12.

23. Dave Carpenter, "Kmart Completes Buyout of Sears," *St. Louis Post-Dispatch*, Mar. 25, 2005, pp. D1, D14; Betsy Streisand, "Federated Buys Rival May to Create a Mammoth of the Mall," *U.S. News & World Report*, Mar. 14, 2005, p. 42; and Amy Merrick, Jeffrey A. Trachtenberg, and Ann Zimmerman, "Department Stores Fight an Uphill Battle Just to Stay Relevant," *The Wall Street Journal* Mar. 12, 2002, pp. A1, A17.

24. Streisand, loc. cit.

25. Ellen Byron, "New Penney: Chain Goes for 'Missing Middle,'" *The Wall Street Journal*, Feb. 14, 2005, pp. B1, B3; and Anne D'Innocenzio, "Department Stores Get Stylish Again," *St. Louis Post-Dispatch*, May 2, 2004, p. E2.

26. Doris Hajewski, "Kohl's Quarter Profits Rise 21%," *The Milwaukee Journal-Sentinel*, May 13, 2005, p. 1; Robert Berner, "Is Kohl's Coming Unbuttoned?" *BusinessWeek*, July 28, 2003, p. 44; and Thomas Lee, "Kohl's Keeps 'Em Coming In," *St. Louis Post-Dispatch*, Aug. 31, 2003, pp. E1, E8.

27. Patricia Corrigan, "The Bucks Stop Here," *St. Louis Post-Dispatch*, June 8, 2005, pp. E1, E4; and Anne D'Innocenzio, "What's in Store?" *St. Louis Post-Dispatch*, Nov. 18, 2004, pp. A1, A19.

28. *www.walmartstores.com*, accessed on Mar. 11, 2005; and Jason Roberson, "Supercenter on Horizon; When Wal-Marts Grow Up," *Dayton Daily News*, July 14, 2002, p. F1.

29. *shopping.discovery.com*; and "Sunglass Hut Expands Its Watch Retailing Operations," *Mergers and Acquisitions*, July 2000, pp. 10–11.

30. Maria Halkias, "Putting Baskets in the Big Apple," *The Dallas Morning News*, Jan. 29, 2005, p. 1D.

31. Becky Yerak, "Overgrowth Outlet Malls Thin Out, Slim Down and Swank Up," *Chicago Tribune*, July 24, 2005, p. 5-1. Doris Hajewski, "On Clearance: For Outlet Malls, It's Out with the Old, In with the New," *The Milwaukee–Journal Sentinel*, Mar. 27, 2005, p. D1; Sally

Beatty, "Paying Less for Prada," *The Wall Street Journal,* Apr. 29, 2003, pp. D1, D3; and Ray A. Smith, "Outlet Centers Go Upmarket with Amenities," *The Wall Street Journal,* June 6, 2001, p. B12.

32. "1982 to 1992: Clubs and Category Killers Arrive on the Scene," *DSN Retailing Today,* August 2002, pp. 21–25; and Babette Morgan, "Borders Enters Big Book-store Competition Here," *St. Louis Post-Dispatch,* Mar. 20, 1995, p. 3BP.

33. Michael V. Copeland, "Best Buy's Selling Machine," *Business 2.0,* July 2004, pp. 93–94+; Mike Duff, "IKEA Eyes Aggressive Growth," *DSN Retailing Today,* Jan. 27, 2003, pp. 1, 22; and "AutoNation Becomes Largest Retailer," *Automotive News,* Oct. 21, 2002, p. 47.

34. David Moin, "Category Killers' Concerns: Overgrowth and Extinction," *WWD,* Jan. 6, 2005, p. 17; Matthew Maier, "How to Beat Wal-Mart," *Business 2.0,* May 2005, pp. 108+; and William M. Bulkeley, "'Category Killers' Go from Lethal to Lame in the Space of a Decade," *The Wall Street Journal,* Mar. 9, 2000, pp. A1, A8.

35. Neil Currie, "UBS Q-Series Report: Do Supermarkets Have a Future?" *Progressive Grocer,* Apr. 15, 2005, pp. 62+; and Brian O'Keefe, "Meet Your New Neighborhood Grocer," *Fortune,* May 13, 2002, pp. 93–94, 96.

36. Robert Gorland, "Going Up against Goliath," *Progressive Grocer,* Apr. 15, 2005, pp. 68+; Ryan Matthews, "True Believers," *Progressive Grocer,* Apr. 15, 2005, pp. 80+; and Joel A. Baglole, "Loblaw Supermarkets Add Fitness Clubs to Offerings," *The Wall Street Journal,* Dec. 27, 1999, p. B4.

37. Elizabeth Esfahani, "7-Eleven Gets Sophis-ticated," *Business 2.0,* January/February 2005, pp. 93+; and Kortney Stringer, "Convenience Stores Turn a New Corner," *The Wall Street Journal,* June 1, 2004, p. B5.

38. Analisa Nazareno, "Upscale but Cheap, Costco May Be 'the Only Retailer Wal-Mart Fears,'" *Knight Ridder Tribune Business News,* Jan. 1, 2005, p. 1; Kortney Stringer, "Carving Out a Niche Pays Off," *The Wall Street Journal,* Nov. 3, 2004, p. B3; and Shelly Branch, "Inside the Cult of Costco," *Fortune,* Sept. 6, 1999, pp. 184–186+.

39. This estimate (perhaps better labeled a "guesstimate") of the total annual volume of nonstore retailing represents a sum of the estimates for the five types that are discussed in subsequent sections.

40. The sales figures are drawn from a compilation on the website of the World Federation of Direct Selling Associations: *www.wfdsa.* The estimated number of sales reps is from survey results on the website of the Direct Selling Association: *www.dsa.org/research/numbers.htm.*

41. Maria Puente, "Direct Selling Brings It All Home," *USA Today,* Oct. 28, 2003, p. 6D; and *www.dsa.org/research/numbers/htm.*

42. Rick Brooks, "A Deal with Target Put Lid on Revival at Tupperware," *The Wall Street Journal,* Feb. 18, 2004, pp. A1, A9; and Katarzyna Moreno, "UnbeComing," *Forbes,* June 10, 2002, pp 151, 152.

43. Michael McCarthy and Jayne O'Donnell, "FTC Idea Could Get Telemarketers to Stop Calling," *USA Today,* June 5, 2002, pp. 1B, 2B.

44. Dana Milbank, "Telephone Sales Reps Do Unrewarding Jobs That Few Can Abide," *The Wall Street Journal,* Sept. 23, 1993, pp. A1, A8. The estimated cost of telemarketing fraud is from Virgil Larson, "Telemarketing Scammers Try Double Dipping," *Omaha World-Herald,* Oct. 8, 2004, p. 1D.

45. "FTC Settles with Do Not Call Violators," *Computer and Internet Lawyer,* May 2005, pp. 24+; and Charles V. Gall and Margaret M. Stolar, "Federal and State Telemarketing Developments," *The Business Lawyer,* May 2004, pp. 1241+.

46. "The Vending Machine Is Back . . . ," *BrandPackaging,* August 2004, no page given.

47. "The Really Convenient Store," *Business 2.0,* March 2004, p. 38; Michael D. Sorkin, "Wrinkled Bills? No Problem for Today's Vending Machines," *St. Louis Post-Dispatch,* July 21, 2002, pp. A1, A11; and "Coke Machine Modems Send Distress Signals," *Marketing News,* Oct. 9, 1995, p. 2.

48. Donna Fuscaldo, "No Sale," *The Wall Street Journal,* Dec. 10, 2001, p. R10.

49. Nick Wingfield, "Online Merchants, as a Whole, Break Even," *The Wall Street Journal,* May 15, 2003, p. B4.

50. Mylene Mangalindan, "Online Retail Sales Are Expected to Rise to $172 Billion This Year," *The Wall Street Journal,* May 24, 2005, p. D5.

51. Timothy J. Mullaney, "The E-Biz Surprise," *BusinessWeek,* May 12, 2003, pp. 60–63+; and Katy McLaughlin,

"Back from the Dead: Buying Groceries Online," *The Wall Street Journal,* Feb. 25, 2003, pp. D1+.

52. Based on figures contained in the *Economic Impact: U.S. Direct & Interactive Marketing Today* study sponsored by the Direct Marketing Association, *www.the-dma.org/cgi/registered/research/libees-ecoimpact2.shtml,* and *www.the-dma.org/cgi/registered/research/charts/dmsales/medium/market.shtml,* accessed Nov. 27, 2002. The estimated sales refer only to direct orders, not to subsequent sales that were based on leads and store traffic generated by telemarketing. Although we considered it separately, telemarketing is sometimes included under the umbrella of direct marketing. Another term often associated with direct marketing, *mail order,* actually refers to the way an order is placed and/or delivered, whereas the types we describe focus on the way contact is made with consumers.

53. David Ranii, "Direct Mail Gains on Rivals," *The News & Observer* (Raleigh, NC), May 28, 2005, p. D1; and Chad Kaydo, "Planting the Seeds of Marketing," *Sales & Marketing Management,* August 1998, p. 73.

54. David Sharp, "Web-Sales Growth Doesn't Clip Catalogs," *St. Louis Post-Dispatch,* Dec. 4, 2004, p. 4BIZ; and Sherry Chiger, "Catalog Age 100: Behind the Numbers," Aug. 1, 2002, accessed at *catalogagemag.com* on Aug. 30, 2002.

55. *www.hsn.com* and *www.qvc.com,* both accessed on June 5, 2005.

56. A theory of institutional change, called the wheel of retailing, was first described in M. P. McNair, "Significant Trends and Developments in the Postwar Period," in A. B. Smith, ed., *Competitive Distribution in a Free, High-Level Economy and Its Implications for the University,* The University of Pittsburgh Press, Pittsburgh, 1958, pp. 17–18.

57. Donna Fuscaldo, "What's Woot," *The Wall Street Journal,* Apr. 25, 2005, p. R10l; Laura Heller, "Fine-Tuning the Right Formula for Success," *DSN Retailing Today,* Apr. 11, 2005, p. 31; Louise Lee, "There Goes the Gravy Train," *BusinessWeek,* Jan. 10, 2005, pp. 117, 118; and Maier, op. cit., pp. 112–113.

58. Andy Serwer, "The Malling of America," *Fortune,* Oct. 13, 2003, p. 229; Ann Grimes, "What's in Store," *The Wall Street Journal,* July 15, 2002,

p. R26; and Robert Berner and Gerry Khermouch, "Retail Reckoning," *Business Week,* Dec. 10, 2001, pp. 72–77.

59. Kavita Dasman, "E-tailing Strategies Still in Infancy," *WWD,* Mar. 9, 2005, p. 17B; Thomas J. Mullaney, "E-tailing Finally Hits Its Stride," *BusinessWeek,* Dec. 20, 2004, p. 36; and Julie Fishman-Lapin, "Online-Savvy Connecticut Shoppers Can Escape Black Friday Crowds at Malls," *The Stamford Advocate,* Nov. 25, 2004, no page given.

60. Jay A. Scansaroli and David M. Szymanski, "Who's Minding the Future?" *Retailing Issues Letter,* January 2002, pp. 1–8.

61. Boyle, loc. cit.; Michael Johnsen, "Aggressive Store-Growth Plan Ensures Future," *Drug Store News,* Mar. 21, 2005, pp. 56+; James Frederick, "For Walgreens, Mail Order Is Both Threat and Opportunity," *Drug Store News,* Mar. 21, 2005, pp. 72+; Laura Heller, "Orchestrating a Turnaround from Front End to Pharmacy," *DSN Retailing Today,* Sept. 6, 2004, p. 39; Dave Carpenter, "Walgreen Targets 12,000 Street Corners," *St. Louis Post-Dispatch,* May 9, 2004, p. E3; and Frederick, "At 104, . . . ," loc. cit.

Chapter 16

1. Company information and press releases at *www.grainger.com,* accessed June 5, 2005; Abrahm Lustgarten, "The List of Industry Champs: America's Most Admired Companies," *Fortune,* Mar. 7, 2005, pp. 85+; and Dale Buss, "The New Deal," *Sales & Marketing Management,* June 2002, pp. 24–30.

2. *www.pleion.com,* accessed June 7, 2005; Scott McMurray, "Return of the Middleman," *Business 2.0,* March 2003, pp. 53–54; Rich Sherman, "Wholesale Distribution—Back in the Chain Game," *Material Handling Management,* April 2001, pp. SCF12–SCF14; and "Making the Switch from Direct to Dealer Sales," *Nation's Business,* July 1996, p. 10.

3. *1992 Census of Wholesale Trade,* Subject Series—Miscellaneous Subjects, U.S. Bureau of the Census, Washington, DC, 1995, p. 42.

4. The terms *merchant wholesaler* and *wholesaler* are sometimes used synonymously with *wholesaling middleman.* This is not accurate, however. *Wholesaling middleman* is the all-inclusive term, covering the three major categories of firms engaged in wholesale trade, whereas *wholesaler* is more restrictive, applying to only one category, namely, merchant wholesaling middlemen.

5. Because manufacturers' sales facilities are owned by manufacturers rather than being truly independent, they could be viewed as a *direct* distribution channel, rather than as distinct middlemen used in indirect distribution. Although this view has merit, we treat manufacturers' sales facilities as a category of middlemen because the Census Bureau does and also because they are separate from manufacturing firms by location, if not by ownership.

6. Donald M. Jackson and Michael F. d'Amico, "Products and Markets Served by Distributors and Agents," *Industrial Marketing Management,* February 1989, p. 28.

7. For a comprehensive historical analysis of wholesaling, see Robert F. Lusch, Deborah Zizzo, and James M. Kenderine, *Foundations of Wholesaling: A Strategic and Financial Chart Book,* Distribution Research Program, University of Oklahoma, Norman, 1996.

8. Average operating expenses in this paragraph and the following one are based on the *1992 Census of Wholesale Trade,* Geographic Area Series—U.S., U.S. Bureau of the Census, Washington, DC, 1995, p. US-9; and the *1992 Census of Retail Trade,* Subject Series, U.S. Bureau of the Census, Washington, DC, 1996, p. 2–7. The 8% figure was calculated by multiplying the 11% representing wholesale operating expenses by 72%. The remainder after the 28% representing retail operating expenses is subtracted from the 100% representing retail sales (or the consumer's dollar).

9. *Statistical Abstract of the United States: 2004–2005,* 124th edition, U.S. Bureau of the Census, Washington, DC, 2004, p. 507.

10. *www.supervalu.com,* accessed June 7, 2005; and Leonard Klie, "Ringing in the Next 135 Years," *Food Logistics,* January/February 2005, p. 42.

11. Srisamom Phoosuphanusom, "Thai Mobile Phone Operator Cuts Out Middlemen in Bid to Get Closer to Retailers," *Bangkok Post,* Dec. 17, 2004, no page given; and Jeffrey A. Tannenbaum, "Cold War: Amana Refrigeration Fights Tiny Distributor," *The Wall Street Journal,* Feb. 26, 1992, p. B2.

12. Karen Jacobs, "Electronics Distributors Are Reporting Record Profits," *The Wall Street Journal,* July 13, 2000, p. B4. For recommendations on how wholesalers can compete effectively with chains of category-killer stores and warehouse clubs that tend to buy directly from manufacturers, see Robert F. Lusch and Deborah Zizzo, *Competing for Customers,* Distribution Research and Education Foundation, Washington, DC, 1995, pp. 80–108.

13. Faith Keenan, "Logistics Gets a Little Respect," *Business Week E.Biz,* Nov. 20, 2000, pp. EB114–EB115.

14. *1997 Economic Census,* Wholesale Trade, loc. cit.; and corresponding censuses from prior years.

15. U.S. Economic Census data for 1997, located at *factfinder.census.gov/servlet/ EconSectorServlet?_SectorId=42&_ lang=en.*

16. Kimberly Weisul, "Do You Dare Outsource Sales?" *Business Week Online,* June 18, 2001, no page given.

17. U.S. Economic Census Data for 1997, loc. cit. For more about manufacturers' reps, including a list of the advantages of using them, see the website of the Manufacturers' Agents National Association, *www.manaonline.org.*

18. Charles Shaw, "The Rep and the Future—Which Is Now," *Agency Sales,* January 2001, pp. 28–30; and Melissa Campanelli, "Agents of Change," *Sales & Marketing Management,* February 1995, pp. 71–75.

19. U.S. Economic Census data for 1997, loc. cit.

20. The Internet Auction List website, *www.internetauctionlist.com,* accessed March 11, 2005.

21. James A. Cooke, "The Two Faces of Globalization," *Logistics Management (2002),* July 2004, p. 28. The estimate of worldwide spending is from Bill Fahrenwald, "Supply Chain: Managing Logistics for the 21st Century," *Business Week,* Dec. 28, 1998, p. 45. The cost of logistics to an individual firm was estimated by the head of the North American Logistics Association, as reported in Francis J. Quinn, "Logistics' New Customer Focus," *Business Week,* Mar. 10, 1997, p. 54.

22. Jon Bigness, "In Today's Economy, There Is Big Money to Be Made in Logistics," *The Wall Street Journal,* Sept. 6, 1995, pp. A1, A9.

23. Bill Mcllvaine, "Going After Value—Logistics Providers Are Offering More Complex Services to Increasingly Demanding Customers," *EBN,* Feb. 25, 2002, pp. 27+. For a discussion of

how firms can achieve a differential advantage through superior physical distribution, see John T. Mentzer and Lisa R. Williams, "The Role of Logistics Leverage in Marketing Strategy," *Journal of Marketing Channels*, vol. 8, no. 3/4, 2001, pp. 29–48.

24. Bruce G. Posner, "Growth Strategies," *Inc.*, December 1989, p. 125.

25. Natalie Hope McDonald, "Under One Roof," *Dealerscope*, July 2002, p. 16. The quote is from George Anders, "Virtual Reality: Web Firms Go on Warehouse Building Boom," *The Wall Street Journal*, Sept. 8, 1999, pp. B1, B8. For more about online category managers, see Bob Sechler, "Behind the Curtain," *The Wall Street Journal*, July 15, 2002, p. R12; and Sandeep Dayal, Thomas D. French, and Vivek Sankaran, "The E-tailer's Secret Weapon," *The McKinsey Quarterly*, 2002, no. 2, no pages given, accessed at *www.mckinsey quarterly.com* on Dec. 8, 2002.

26. Karen Lundergaard, "Bumpy Ride," *The Wall Street Journal*, May 21, 2001, p. R21.

27. Fahrenwald, op. cit., p. 34; and Lundergaard, loc. cit.

28. The estimates of the extent of outsourcing are drawn from "Outsourcing of Logistics Is Globally Recognized as a Primary Business Strategy with Significant Value, According to New Study," *Business Wire*, Sept. 30, 2002, no page given; "Year of the 3PLs," *Journal of Commerce*, Feb. 18, 2002, p. 12; and McIlvaine, loc. cit.

29. Helen L. Richardson, "How to Maximize the Potential of 3PLs," *Logistics Today*, May 2005, pp. 19+; Benjamin Gordon, "Seven Mega-Trends That Will Reshape Logistics," *Traffic World*, Feb. 7, 2005, p. 1; McIlvaine, loc. cit.; and "Outsourcing to Drive Growth in Contract Logistics Market," *Logistics Focus*, September 1997, p. 16.

30. William Hoffman, "Vector SCM Shifts Gears," *Traffic World*, Feb. 28, 2005, p. 1; and Alorie Gilbert, "GM Joint Venture to Track In-Transit Inventory," *InformationWeek*, Dec. 18–25, 2000, p. 26.

31. The motives for contract logistics are drawn from Quinn, op. cit., p. 69. For more about contract logistics, see John Schultz, "7 Principles of a Successful 3PL Relationship," *Logistics Management (2002)*, March 2005, p. 39; Richardson, loc. cit.; and Gordon, loc. cit.

32. Cinda Becker, "An Industry Barometer," *Modern Healthcare*, June 18, 2001, pp. 80–84; and Tom Murray, "Just-in-Time Isn't Just for Show—It Sells," *Sales & Marketing Management*, May 1990, p. 64.

33. McIlvaine, loc. cit.

34. "Supply Chain Excellence," *Business-Week*, Apr. 25, 2005, p. 71.

35. Heidi Elliott, "Delivering Competition," *Electronic Business Today*, May 1997, pp. 34–36; and Ronald Henkoff, "Delivering the Goods," *Fortune*, Nov. 28, 1994, pp. 64+.

36. Richard Karpinski, "Wal-Mart Pushes Web EDI," *BtoB*, Oct. 14, 2002, p. 15; and Amy Zuckerman, "Should You Do EDI or Internet?" *Transportation & Distribution*, June 1999, pp. 40–42.

37. Jeff Bennett, "Compuware Acquires Covisint for $7 Million," *Detroit Free Press*, June 10, 2004, no page given; and Robert L. Simison, Fara Warner, and Gregory L. White, "Big Three Car Makers Plan Net Exchange," *The Wall Street Journal*, Feb. 28, 2000, pp. A3, A16.

38. Ian Mount, "Why EDI Won't Die," *Business 2.0*, August 2003, pp. 68–69.

39. Art Raymond, "Is JIT Dead?" *FDM*, January 2002, pp. 30–33. For further discussion of JIT, see Marvin W. Tucker and David A. Davis, "Key Ingredients for Successful Implementation of Just-in-Time: A System for All Business Sizes," *Business Horizons*, May–June 1993, pp. 59–65.

40. Philip Siekman, "Jeep Builds a New Kind of Plant," *Fortune*, Nov. 11, 2002, pp. T167[C]+.

41. Paulette Thomas, "Electronics Firm Ends Practice Just in Time," *The Wall Street Journal*, Oct. 29, 2002, p. B9; and William Atkinson, "Does JIT II Still Work in the Internet Age?," *Purchasing*, Sept. 6, 2001, pp. 41–42. Implications of JIT for channels are discussed in Steve McDaniel, Joseph G. Ormsby, and Alicia B. Gresham, "The Effect of JIT on Distributors," *Industrial Marketing Management*, May 1992, pp. 145–149.

42. Debbie Howell, "12 Hot Issues Facing Mass Retailing—6: Supply-Chain Management," *DSN Retailing Today*, May 20, 2002, p. 33; Jane Hodges, "Supply Chain CEOs," *Chief Executive*, January 2002, pp. 65–66; and Joseph Weber, "Just Get It to the Stores on Time," *BusinessWeek*, Mar. 6, 1995, pp. 66–67.

43. Brian Albright, "CPFR's Secret Benefit," *Frontline Solutions*, October 2002, pp. 30–35.

44. "Survey: Gap between SC Tech, Business Strategy," *Journal of Commerce Online*, Nov. 4, 2004, p. 1; Mohsen Attaran, "Nurturing the Supply Chain," *Industrial Management*, September/October 2004, p. 16; and John Verity, "Collaborative Forecasting: Vision Quest," *Computerworld*, Nov. 10, 1997, pp. S12–S14.

45. "Survey: Gap between SC Tech, Business Strategy," loc. cit.; and Rod Newing, "Industry Is About to Reinvent Itself," *Financial Times*, Dec. 15, 1999, p. 1.

46. "Supply Chain: Keeping It Moving," *Chain Store Age*, October 2002, pp. A26–A28.

47. Eric Heisler, "Unilever Packs Technology into Giant Distribution Center," *St. Louis Post-Dispatch*, Oct. 3, 2003, p. C6; Roger Huff, Jeff Levine, Gerald Moultry, David Rogers, and Gregg Schwerdt, "Up Close and Personal," *Transportation & Distribution*, August 2003, pp. 40+. For case studies about the design of distribution centers by two diverse companies, Jo-Ann Fabrics and Corporate Express, see Mary Aichlmayr, "Design Your Distribution Center Inside Out," *Transportation & Distribution*, November 2002, p. 30.

48. Nintendo's distribution center is detailed in "Nintendo Enhances Performance Conveyor Sortation," *Material Handling Management*, October 2001, pp. 47–51; and Michael Lear-Olimpi, "More than Just Games," *Warehousing Management*, September 1999, pp. 22–30.

49. Robert D. Hof, "What's with All the Warehouses?" *BusinessWeek e.biz*, Nov. 1, 1999, p. EB88.

50. Ann Keeton, "Sensors on Containers May Offer Safer Shipping," *The Wall Street Journal*, Mar. 31, 2005, pp. B4, B5; and Daniel Machalaba and Andy Pasztor, "Thinking Inside the Box: Shipping Containers Get 'Smart,'" *The Wall Street Journal*, Jan. 15, 2004, pp. B1, B6.

51. For research results indicating that perceptions of different modes vary across members of a buying center, see James H. Martin, James M. Daley, and Henry B. Burdg, "Buying Influences and Perceptions of Transportation Services," *Industrial Marketing Management*, November 1988, pp. 305–314.

52. Daniel Machalaba and Christopher J. Chipello, "Battling Trucks, Trains Gain Steam by Watching Clock," *The Wall Street Journal*, July 25, 2003, pp. A1, A16.

53. John Gallagher, "What Price Rail Relief?" *Traffic World,* Dec. 20, 2004, p. 1.

54. Anna Wilde Mathews, "More Firms Rely on 'One-Stop' Shipping," *The Wall Street Journal,* Apr. 29, 1997, p. A2.

55. The statement by the Yellow Corp. executive is from Haddad, "A Long Haul to Recovery?" *BusinessWeek,* Jan. 14, 2002, p. 118. Matthew Boyle, "Why FedEx Is Flying High," *Fortune,* Nov. 1, 2004, pp. 145–146+; Dean Foust, "Big Brown's New Bag," *BusinessWeek,* July 19, 2004, pp. 54+; and Kevin Kelleher, "Why FedEx Is Gaining Ground," *Business 2.0,* October 2003, pp. 56–57.

56. *www.grainger.com,* accessed June 5, 2005; Kate Maddox, "Growing Wiser," *B to B,* Sept. 9, 2002, pp. 1, 26; Douglas A. Blackmon, "Selling Motors to Mops, Unglamorous Grainger Is a Web-Sales Star," *The Wall Street Journal,* Dec. 13, 1999, pp. B1, B8; and Buss, loc. cit.

Chapter 17

1. Netflix website: *www.netflix.com;* Christopher Null, "How Netflix Is Fixing Hollywood," *Business 2.0,* July 2003, pp. 41–43; Michael Liedtke, "Netflix Pioneer Reed Hastings Has a Plan . . . ," *St. Louis Post-Dispatch,* Mar. 15, 2004, p. C4; Timothy J. Mullaney and Tom Lowry, "Netflix: Moving into Slo-Mo?" *BusinessWeek,* Aug. 2, 2004, p. 84; Kris Oser, "Netflix," *Advertising Age,* Nov. 1, 2004, p. S16.

2. Geoff Mulvihill, "Campbell's Earnings Slip Along with Business News," *Associated Press Business News,* Feb. 13, 2002, accessed at Lexis-Nexis, August 28, 2005.

3. Kenneth Hein, "Special Report—Soft Drinks," *Brandweek,* Apr. 25, 2005, p. SR28.

4. This is a condensed version of the definition offered by Don E. Shultz, "IMC Receives a More Appropriate Definition," *Marketing News,* Sept. 15, 2004, pp. 8+.

5. Jim Edwards, "Too Much of a Good Thing?" *Brandweek,* Aug. 9, 2004, pp. 20+; Becky Eberkamp, "Usher Says 'Yeah' to DVD Promo," *Brandweek,* Oct. 18, 2004, p. 10; Clare Armitt, "Nestlé to Launch New European Kids' Site with Shrek 2 Game," *New Media Age,* Oct. 7, 2004, p. 8.

6. Kerry A. Dolan, "The Soda with Buzz," *Forbes,* Mar. 28, 2005, pp. 126+.

7. Jerry Shriver, "No Need to Compare Apples and Grapes," *USA Today,* Apr. 22, 2005, p. 1D.

8. Mike Beirne, "South Africa Giving U.S. Travelers Big Picture," *Brandweek,* Apr. 18, 2005, p. 9.

9. To learn more about the legal battle between Papa John's and Pizza Hut over the slogan "Better Ingredients, Better Pizza," see Rene Sacasas, "The 'Pizza Wars,' " *Journal of the Academy of Marketing Science,* Spring 2001, pp. 205+; Jim Edwards, "Sour Dough: Pizza Hut v. Papa John's," *Brandweek,* May 21, 2001, pp. 26+.

10. Margaret Webb Pressler, "Use of Coupons Cuts Both Ways," *Washington Post,* Sept. 12, 2004, p. F01.

11. Steven Levy, "Flogging on a Blog," *Newsweek,* Mar. 10, 2003, p. 10.

12. An informative White Paper entitled "Guidance for Food Advertising Self-Regulation," produced by NARC in 2004, provides an excellent description of the history, procedures, and performance of this body. It can be found at *www.narcpartners.org.*

13. Holly J. Wagner, "Friendly Network for Netflix," *Video Store Magazine,* Dec. 5–Dec. 11, 2004, pp. 1+; Mylene Mangalindan, "Moving the Market—Tracking the Numbers," *The Wall Street Journal,* Dec. 29, 2004, p. C3; David Lieberman, "TiVo, Netflix Team to Deliver Internet Video-on-Demand," *USA Today,* Oct. 1, 2004, p. 4B.

Chapter 18

1. *www.cdw.com;* Michael Krauss, "CDW Exec Shares Sat Know-How," *Marketing News,* July 15, 2004, p. 6; Mary Ellen Podmolik, CDW Research Segments Audience Once, then Twice," *B to B,* Oct. 25, 2004, p. 10.

2. *Statistical Abstract of the United States: 2004–2005,* 12th ed., Bureau of the Census, Washington, DC, 2004.

3. William C. Moncrief, "Selling Activity and Sales Position Taxonomies for Industrial Salesforces," *Journal of Marketing Research,* August 1986, pp. 261–270.

4. Greg W. Marshall, William C. Moncrief, and Felicia G. Lassk, "The Current State of Sales Force Activity," *Industrial Marketing Management,* vol. 28, no. 1, 1998, pp. 87–98.

5. Michael V. Copeland, "Best Buy's Selling Machine," *Business 2.0,* July 2004, pp. 93–102.

6. Michele Marchetti, "What a Sales Call Costs," *Sales & Marketing Management,* September 2000, pp. 80+. The figures are derived from a study commissioned by *Sales & Marketing Management* magazine and are reported by type of sales approach, industry, size of company, and region.

7. The development and maintenance of buyer-seller relationships is conceptualized in an award-winning article by Barton A. Weitz and Kevin D. Bradford, "Personal Selling and Sales Management: A Relationship Marketing Perspective," *Journal of the Academy of Marketing Science,* vol 7, no. 2, Spring 1999, pp. 241–254.

8. For more information on the performance of business-to-business auctions see M. L. Emiliani and David J. Stec, "Business-to-Business Online Auctions: Key Issues for Purchasing Process Improvement," *Supply Chain Management,* 5 (4), pp. 176–186; M. L. Emiliani and David J. Stec, "Commentary on 'Reverse Auctions for Relationship Marketing' by Daly and Nath," *Industrial Marketing Management,* February 2005, pp. 167–171; Shawn P. Daly and Prithwiraj Nath, "Reverse Auctions and Buyer-Seller Relationships: A Rejoinder to Emiliani and Stec," *Industrial Marketing Management,* February 2005, pp. 173–176.

9. David Prater, "The Third Time's the Charm," *Sales & Marketing Management,* September 2000, pp. 101–104.

10. David Prater, "5 Steps to Salvaging a Failing SFA Program," *Sales & Marketing Management,* September 2000, p. 102; "Behind the Numbers," *Information World,* Jan. 10, 2005, p. 52.

11. Daniel Tynan, "CRM on the Cheap," *Sales & Marketing Management,* June 2004, pp. 36–40.

12. For a discussion of efforts to identify characteristics of successful sales people see Mark W. Johnston and Greg W. Marshall, *Sales Force Management,* 7th ed., Burr Ridge, IL: McGraw-Hill/Irwin, 2003, pp. 291+.

13. Julia Chang, "Role Reversal," *Sales & Marketing Management,* June 2004, p. 21; Julia Chang, "Selling in Action," *Sales & Marketing Management,* May 2004, p. 22; Kathryn Droullard, "Mind Your Manners, *Sales & Marketing Management,* January 2005, pp. 26–32.

14. Calabro, loc.cit.

15. Every issue of *Sales & Marketing Management* magazine contains a section devoted to motivation and sales force incentives. In addition, it is a frequent

subject of research in the *Journal of Personal Selling and Sales Management.*

16. John Taylor, "Program to Examine Kirby Sales Tactics," *Omaha World-Herald,* Apr. 4, 2002, p. 2D.

17. Information on current compensation practices in sales can be found in Christine Galea, "The 2004 Compensation Survey," *Sales & Marketing Management,* May 2004, pp. 28–34.

18. The use of performance measures is described in Sara Calabro, "Measuring Up," *Sales & Marketing Management,* March 2005, pp. 22–28.

19. Chuck Salter, "The Soft Sell," *Fast Company,* January 2005, pp. 72+; Brian Fonseca, "Rising from Ashes," *eWeek,* Nov. 29, 2004, p. 31.

Chapter 19

1. *www.nike.com;* Stanley Holmes, "The New Nike," *BusinessWeek,* Sept. 20, 2004, pp. 78+; Melanie Kletter, "Nike Does a Two-Step," *WWD,* Jan. 21, 2005, pp. 18+; R. Craig Endicott, "Top Marketers Spend $83 Billion," *Advertising Age,* Nov. 8, 2004, pp. 30+; Maureen Tracik, "Full-Court Press for LeBron," *The Wall Street Journal,* May 21, 2003, pp. B1+.

2. R. Craig Endicott, "Top Marketers Spend $83 Billion," *Advertising Age,* Nov. 8, 2004, pp. 30+.

3. R. Craig Endicott, "100 Leading National Advertisers," *Advertising Age,* June 27, 2005, pp. S1+.

4. Suzanne Varanica, "That Guy Showing Off His Hot New Phone May Be a Shill," *The Wall Street Journal,* July 31, 2002, pp. B1+.

5. Some blogs related to advertising you may find interesting are *www.adrants.com, www.ad-rag.com,* and *www.adverlab.blogspot.com.*

6. If you look at the ads in your local newspaper, you are likely to spot different retailers featuring the same items (supermarkets offering discounted Coke or Pepsi products, or sporting goods stores offering the same running shoe at a reduced price). These are very likely vertical cooperative ads in which the manufacturer has paid all or a portion of the cost.

7. Kathryn Kranhold, "Taco Bell Ads to Focus on Food, Not Dog," *The Wall Street Journal,* Oct. 11, 1999, p. B10.

8. "Broadcast Television," *Media Facts: A Guide to Competitive Media, 2004,* Radio Advertising Bureau, *www.*

9. "Cable TV," *Media Facts: A Guide to Competitive Media, 2004,* Radio Advertising Bureau, *www.rabmarketing.com,* accessed June 10, 2005.

10. "Direct Mail," *Media Facts: A Guide to Competitive Media, 2004,* Radio Advertising Bureau, *www.rabmarketing.com,* accessed June 10, 2005.

11. Ibid.

12. "Newspapers," *Media Facts: A Guide to Competitive Media, 2004,* Radio Advertising Bureau, *www.rabmarketing.com,* accessed June 10, 2005.

13. "2004–2005 Radio Marketing Guide and Fact Book," Radio Advertising Bureau, *www.rabmarketing.com,* accessed June 10, 2005.

14. "Yellow Pages," *Media Facts: A Guide to Competitive Media, 2004,* Radio Advertising Bureau, *www.rabmarketing.com,* accessed June 10, 2005.

15. "Magazines," *Media Facts: A Guide to Competitive Media, 2004,* Radio Advertising Bureau, *www.rabmarketing.com,* accessed June 10, 2005.

16. "Outdoor," *Media Facts: A Guide to Competitive Media, 2004,* Radio Advertising Bureau, *www.rabmarketing.com,* accessed June 10, 2005.

17. Jean Haliday, "Ford Finds E-Leads Productive," *Advertising Age,* Jan. 22, 2001, pp. 28+.

18. Betsy Spethman, "Trade Dollars Shift to Advertising," *PROMO Xtra,* Mar. 17, 2005, *www.promomarketing.com,* accessed June 10, 2005.

19. "Introduction: A Half-Full Glass," *PROMO 2002 Annual Report,* June 1, 2002, *www.promo.com/ar,* accessed Sept. 1, 2002.

20. Libby Estell and Jeanie Casison, "Sampling Sells: A Marketing Strategy that Motivates Consumers," *Incentive,* August 2002, p. 6.

21. Tim Parry, "Teaching Tools," *PROMO Magazine,* Apr. 1, 2005, *www.promomarketing.com,* accessed June 11, 2005.

22. Ibid.

23. Kathleen M. Joyce, "No Nickel and Dime," *PROMO Magazine,* Apr. 1, 2005, *www.promomarketing.com,* accessed June 11, 2005.

24. "IEG Sponsorship Report," *www.sponsorship.com,* accessed June 11, 2005.

25. "Product Placement Spending in Media 2005: Executive Summary" *PQ*

Media, March 2005, *www.pqmedia.com,* accessed June 11, 2005.

26. Jim Edwards, "Small Screen Gets Crowded as Brand Placements Double," *Brandweek,* May 9, 2005, p. 12.

27. *www.nike.com;* Mark Del Franco, "Nike Competes Now in the Mail," *Catalog Age,* January 2005, p. 10; Barry Janoff, "Mike and Spike Together Again," *Adweek,* Feb. 7, 2005, p. 7.

Chapter 20

1. Starbucks Corporation Fiscal 2004 Annual Report and other company information from *www.starbucks.com/aboutus,* accessed June 18, 2005; Steven Gray, "Coffee on the Double," *The Wall Street Journal,* Apr. 12, 2005, pp. B1, B7; Tom Van Riper, "McDonald's Brews Up Competition for Starbucks," *Daily News* (New York), Apr. 10, 2005, p. 13; Stanley Holmes, "For Starbucks, There's No Place Like Home," *BusinessWeek,* June 9, 2003, p. 48; Steven Gray, "Starbucks Brews Broader Menu," *The Wall Street Journal,* Feb. 9, 2005, p. B9; Julie Rawe, "Scoot Over, Starbucks," *Time,* Sept. 20, 2004, p. 49; Deborah Ball and Shirley Leung, "Latte Versus Latte," *The Wall Street Journal,* Feb. 10, 2004, pp. B1, B9; Noelle Knox, "Paris Starbucks Hopes to Prove U.S. Coffee Isn't 'Sock Juice,'" *USA Today,* Jan. 16, 2004, p. 3B; Stanley Holmes, "Planet Starbucks," *BusinessWeek,* Sept. 9, 2002, pp. 100–103+; Mark Pendergrast, "Starbucks Goes to Europe . . . with Humility and Respect," *The Wall Street Journal,* Apr. 9, 2002, p. B16; Helen Jung, "Starbucks' Card Smarts," *BusinessWeek,* Mar. 18, 2002, p. 14; "Making Customers Come Back for More," *Fortune,* Mar. 16, 1998, p. 156[L]; and Ingrid Abramovitch, "Miracles of Marketing," *Success,* April 1993, pp. 22–27.

2. Many writers and executives use the terms *control* and *evaluation* synonymously. We distinguish between them. To speak of control as only one part of the management process is too restrictive. Rather than being an isolated managerial function, control permeates virtually all other organizational activities. For example, management *controls* its operations through the goals and strategies it selects. Also, the type of organizational structure used in a marketing department determines the degree of *control* over marketing operations.

3. Derek F. Abell, "Strategic Windows," *Journal of Marketing,* July 1978, pp. 21–26.

4. *www.ecompanystore.com.*, accessed July 4, 2005; and Rodney Ho, "Forsaking Sentiment, Small Clients, a Business Grows," *The Wall Street Journal*, Jan. 3, 2000, pp. A11, A13.

5. *www.xerox.com/downloads/usa/en/n/nr_Xerox2005_2006FactBook.pdf*, accessed July 4, 2005.

6. *www.planethollywood.com,* accessed July 4, 2005; Jerry W. Jackson, "Hollywood Ending or Not?" *Orlando Sentinel*, May 15, 2002, p. C1; and Richard Gibson, "Fame Proves Fleeting at Planet Hollywood as Fans Avoid Reruns," *The Wall Street Journal*, Oct. 7, 1998, pp. A1, A6.

7. The survey results are reported in Ellen Neuborne, "Mad Ave: A Star Is Reborn," *BusinessWeek*, July 26, 1999, pp. 54–56+. For more on changing attitudes toward strategic planning, see John A. Byrne, "Strategic Planning," *BusinessWeek*, Aug. 26, 1996, pp. 46–52.

8. C. K. Prahalad, "Changes in the Competitive Battlefield," *Financial Times—FT.com*, Aug. 7, 2002, no pages given.

9. Michael A. O'Neil, "A Simple, Effective Approach to the Strategic Planning Process," *Supervision*, March 2001, pp. 3–5.

10. Dan Morse, "Many Small Businesses Don't Devote Time to Planning," *The Wall Street Journal*, Sept. 7, 1999, p. B2; and *Pulse of the Middle Market—1990*, BDO Seidman, New York, 1990, pp. 12–13.

11. For one approach to competitive analysis, see Bruce H. Clark, "Managing Competitive Interactions," *Marketing Management*, Fall/Winter 1998, pp. 8–20. For more about the consultants' recommended reflection process, see Michael Hammer and Steven A. Stanton, "The Power of Reflection," *Fortune*, Nov. 24, 1997, pp. 291+.

12. For more details, see Lili Vianello, "S.W.O.T. Analysis: Plan for Your Business to Be Successful," *Columbia Business Times*, Aug. 3–16, 2002, p. 36.

13. *www.radioshackcorporation.com,* accessed July 4, 2005; and Stephanie Anderson Forest, "Cable, Phone, Internet . . . Who Ya Gonna Call?" *BusinessWeek*, Mar. 1, 1999, pp. 64, 66.

14. Malcolm H. B. McDonald, "Ten Barriers to Marketing Planning," *The Journal of Business and Industrial Marketing*, Winter 1992, p. 15.

15. "An Old Formula That Still Works," *The Toronto Star*, Nov. 20, 2004, p. D24; and Joel A. Baglole, "Cough Syrup Touts 'Awful' Taste in U.S.," *The Wall Street Journal*, Dec. 15, 1999, p. B10.

16. Christopher Wanjek, "It's Not Easy Being Clean," *The Washington Post*, Oct. 3, 2000, p. Z6; and "Stacy Kravetz, "Dry Cleaners' New Wrinkle: Going Green," *The Wall Street Journal,* June 3, 1998, pp. B1, B15.

17. Differential advantage in the context of services and retail industries is examined in, respectively, Sundar G. Bharadwaj, P. Rajan Varadarajan, and John Fahy, "Sustainable Competitive Advantage in Service Industries: A Conceptual Model and Research Proposition," *Journal of Marketing*, October 1993, pp. 83–99; and Norman H. McMillan, "EST Retailing: How to Stay out of the Black Hole," *International Trends in Retailing*, Winter 1993, pp. 60–75.

18. Tom Daykin, "Midwest's Balancing Act," *The Milwaukee Journal Sentinel*, Jan. 16, 2005, no page given; and David Leonhardt, "Big Airlines Should Follow Midwest's Recipe," *BusinessWeek*, June 28, 1999, p. 40.

19. Marcia Stepanek, "How Fast Is Net Fast?" *BusinessWeek E.Biz*, Nov. 1, 1999, pp. EB52–EB54. One of many guidebooks for preparing an annual marketing plan is Roman G. Hiebing, Jr., and Scott W. Cooper, *The Successful Marketing Plan*, brief edition, NTC/Contemporary Publishing Group, Lincolnwood, IL, 2000.

20. For more about the contents of a marketing plan, especially the situation analysis, see Linda Lee and Denise Hayes, "Creating a Marketing Plan," *www.marketingpower.com/content1029.php#*, accessed July 9, 2005.

21. See H. Igor Ansoff, *The New Corporate Strategy*, Wiley, New York, 1988, pp. 82–85. In this updated discussion, Ansoff substituted the term *mission* for *market* in the matrix. We still prefer, and thus retain, the original term. For a critique of Ansoff's matrix and a revised version, see Randall L. Schultz, "A Note on the Product-Market Growth Matrix," working paper, University of Iowa, November 2004.

22. Jeff Bailey, "Reliance on a Few Big Customers Holds Risks," *The Wall Street Journal*, July 30, 2002, p. B5; and Martha Brannigan, "Cruise Lines Look to the Land to Get Boomers on Board," *The Wall Street Journal*, Dec. 6, 1999, p. B4.

23. Merissa Marr and Kim-Mai Cutler, "Fine Line on Wild Rides," *The Wall Street Journal*, July 1, 2005, pp. B1, B4; Sarah Ellison and Dennis K. Berman, "Wrigley to Buy Life Savers, Altoids," *The Wall Street Journal*, Nov. 15, 2004, pp. A3, A18; Janet Ginsburg, "Not the Flavor of the Month," *BusinessWeek*, Mar. 20, 2000, p. 128; and "Targeting Customer Needs Unveils New Opportunities," *Nation's Business*, September 1998, p. 12.

24. Bill Virgin, "Straying Too Far Can Make Diversification Fail," *The Seattle Post-Intelligencer*, Aug. 27, 2001, p. E1.

25. *www.lizclaiborne.com/company/default.asp*, accessed July 10, 2005; Julee Greenberg, "Claiborne Sets Brand Plan," *WWD*, May 20, 2005, p. 4; and Teri Agins, "Claiborne Patches Together an Empire," *The Wall Street Journal*, Feb. 2, 2000, pp. B1, B4.

26. Kate MacArthur, "Cannibalization a Risk as Coke Diet Brand Tally Grows to Seven," *Advertising Age*, Mar. 28, 2005, p. 3; and Mike Duff, "Strategy Looks to Grow Food and Minimize Cannibalization," *DSN Retailing Today*, Feb. 28, 2005, p. 44.

27. Rajesh K. Chandy and Gerard J. Tellis, "Organizing for Radical Product Innovation: The Overlooked Role of Willingness to Cannibalize," *Journal of Marketing Research*, November 1998, pp. 474+.

28. *The Experience Curve Reviewed: IV. The Growth Share Matrix of the Product Portfolio*, Boston Consulting Group, Boston, 1973.

29. Norihiko Shirouzu, "Lexus's Car Trouble; While Its SUVs Are a Big Hit, Sedan Sales Trail BMW's; New Models, Hybrids Coming," *The Wall Street Journal*, Mar. 18, 2005, p. B1; and Jay Palmer, "Taking Off the White Gloves," *Barron's*, Apr. 1, 2002, p. 19.

30. Sara Ellison and Suzanne Vranica, "Campbell Warms Campaign to Heal Soup Sales," *The Wall Street Journal*, Dec. 26, 2002, p. A10. William C. Symonds, "The Big Trim at Gillette," *BusinessWeek*, Nov. 8, 1999, p. 42.

31. "Netflix Makes It Big in Hollywood," *Fortune*, June 13, 2005, p. 34; Maria Halkias, "Weak Rentals Hurt Blockbuster," *Knight Ridder Tribune Business News*, Oct. 28, 2004, p. 1; and Stephanie Anderson Forest, "Blockbuster: The Sequel," *BusinessWeek*, Sept. 16, 2002, pp. 52–53.

32. Monica Gagnier, "How GM May Shrink Itself," *BusinessWeek*, Apr. 4, 2005, p. 46; and Alex Taylor III, "GM Hits the Skids," *Fortune*, Apr. 4, 2005, pp. 71+.

33. "A Fruit Revolution," *CSNews Online*, Mar. 28, 2005, no page given; and Nick Roskelly, "Balancing Act: Pursuing New Product Launches While Supporting Core Brands," *Beverage Industry*, October 2002, pp. 96+.

34. Discussed in Derek F. Abell and John S. Hammond, *Strategic Marketing Planning*, Prentice Hall, Englewood Cliffs, N.J., 1979.

35. Nanette Byrnes, "Xerox Is Dreaming in Color," *BusinessWeek*, Dec. 13, 2004, pp. 70, 74; and Lee Gomes, "Silicon Graphics Sets Designs to Ride High-End Computer Line to Turnaround," *The Wall Street Journal*, Nov. 15, 1999, p. B6.

36. Jeff Bailey, "What to Do When Your Hot Item Starts to Cool," *The Wall Street Journal*, Sept. 16, 2003, p. B10.

37. Pui-Wing Tam, "HP Looks Beyond Ink Sales for Growth," *The Wall Street Journal*, June 20, 2005, pp. B1, B5; and Peter Burrows, "Why HP Is Pruning the Printers," *BusinessWeek*, May 9, 2005, pp. 38–39.

38. Shirley Leung, "McDonald's to Shed Only 2 Brands," *The Wall Street Journal*, Dec. 16, 2003, p. B11.

39. Bob Garrison, "Building on Success," *Refrigerated & Frozen Foods*, April 2002, pp. 20+; Andrew Edgecliffe-Johnson, "Kraft Looks for More Purchases," *Financial Times—FT.com*, Sept. 3, 2001, no pages given; and Steven Lipin and Yumiko Ono, "Philip Morris's Bakery Unit Is for Sale; Asking Price Is Put at about $1 Billion," *The Wall Street Journal*, July 17, 1995, p. A3.

40. Improvements worth considering are suggested in the following articles: R. A. Proctor and J. S. Hassard, "Towards a New Model for Product Portfolio Analysis," *Management Decision*, vol. 28, no. 3, 1990, pp. 14–17; and Rick Brown, "Making the Product Portfolio a Basis for Action," *Long Range Planning*, February 1991, pp. 102–110.

41. Michael Treacy and Fred Wiersema, "How Market Leaders Keep Their Edge," *Fortune*, Feb. 6, 1995, pp. 88–90+; their ideas are fully described in Michael Treacy and Fred Wiersema, *The Discipline of Market Leaders*, Addison-Wesley, Boston, 1995.

42. For more about Nike's rebound and move into sporting goods, see Stanley Holmes, "The New Nike," *BusinessWeek*, Sept. 20, 2004, pp. 79–82; and Chuck Stogel, "It's Easier Being Green (If You're Nike)," *Brandweek*, Jan. 28, 2002, pp. 116–118+. For an overview of the strategic shift Juniper Networks Inc. had to make, see Ben Elgin, "Why Juniper Must Branch Out," *BusinessWeek*, July 1, 2002, pp. 95–96.

43. Company information from *www.starbucks.com/aboutus*, accessed June 18, 2005; Steven Gray and Ethan Smith, "At Starbucks, a Blend of Coffee and Music Creates a Potent Mix," *The Wall Street Journal*, July 19, 2005, pp. A1, A11; Stanley Holmes, "Strong Lattes, Sour Notes," *BusinessWeek*, June 20, 2005, pp. 58, 60; Stanley Holmes, "First the Music, Then the Coffee," *BusinessWeek*, Nov. 22, 2004, p. 66; Andy Serwer, "Hot Starbucks," *Fortune*, Jan. 26, 2004, pp. 61–64+; and Michael Krauss, "Starbucks Adds Value by Taking on Wireless," *Marketing News*, Feb. 3, 2003, p. 9.

Chapter 21

1. Inditex website, *www.inditex.com*, accessed June 8, 2005; "Business: The Future of Fashion; Inditex," *The Economist*, June 18, 2005, p. 63; Bob Evans, "If Speed Kills, Are You in Danger?" *InformationWeek*, Mar. 21, 2005, p. 86; Emily Scardino, "H&M Expands Reach in Manhattan," *DSN Retailing Today*, Nov. 22, 2004, pp. 5+; Kasra Ferdows, Michael A. Lewis, and José A. D. Machuca, "Rapid-Fire Fulfillment," *Harvard Business Review*, November 2004, pp. 104+; "H&M: Success in the U.S.," Sept. 20, 2004, p. 55; Erin White, "For Retailer Mango, Frenzied 'Fast Fashion' Proves Sweet," *The Wall Street Journal*, May 28, 2004, pp. B1, B2; Miguel Helft, "Fashion Fast Forward," *Business 2.0*, May 2002, pp. 61–66; Jane M. Folpe, "Zara Has a Made-to-Order Plan for Success," *Fortune*, Sept. 4, 2000, p. 80; and William Echikson, "The Mark of Zara," *BusinessWeek*, May 29, 2000, pp. 98–99.

2. Charles H. Noble and Michael P. Mokwa, "Implementing Marketing Strategies: Developing and Testing a Managerial Theory," *Journal of Marketing*, October 1999, pp. 57–73.

3. David Lewis, "Omni Maximizes Revenue," *Internet Week*, Nov. 26, 2001, p. 54; and Neal Templin, "Your Room Costs $250 . . . No! $200 . . . No . . .," *The Wall Street Journal*, May 5, 1999, pp. B1, B16.

4. Ram Charan and Geoffrey Colvin, "Why CEOs Fail," *Fortune*, June 21, 1999, pp. 69–72+.

5. Three developments that have affected organizational structures and, more broadly, the role of management are outlined in Ray Suutari, "Organizing for the New Economy," *CMA Management*, April 2001, pp. 12–13. For a discussion of two organizational forms—a marketing exchange company and a marketing coalition company—that are designed to cope with complex and dynamic business environments, see Ravi S. Achrol, "Evolution of the Marketing Organization: New Forms for Turbulent Environments," *Journal of Marketing*, October 1991, pp. 77–93.

6. For examples, see Brenda Paik Sunoo, "Redesigning the Company at Donna Karan," *Workforce*, July 1998, pp. 27+; Don Clark, "Intel Restructures into 5 Units, Putting Focus on Succession Issue," *The Wall Street Journal*, Jan. 18, 2005, p. A3; and Sarah Ellison, "Kimberly-Clark Is Set to Reorganize," *The Wall Street Journal*, Jan. 20, 2004, p. A3. Seven elements of a horizontal organization are described in John A. Byrne, "The Horizontal Corporation," *BusinessWeek*, Dec. 20, 1993, pp. 76–81.

7. Dana James, "Lighting the Way," *Marketing News*, Apr. 1, 2002, pp. 1, 11; and Evelyn Theiss, "Research Shows Good Service Is Getting Harder to Find," *St. Louis Post-Dispatch*, June 28, 1999, p. BP22.

8. "Cross-Functional Teams Flourish amid Today's Purchasing Evolution," *Supplier Selection & Management Report*, March 2002, no pages given; Avan R. Jassawalla and Hemant C. Sashittal, "Building Collaborative Cross-Functional New Product Teams," *The Academy of Management Executive*, August 1999, p. 50; and Donald Gerwin, "Team Empowerment in New Product Development," *Business Horizons*, July–August 1999, pp. 29+.

9. The Modicon example is from Byrne, op. cit., p. 80.

10. Ellison, loc. cit.

11. Hechinger, loc. cit.; and Rick Brooks, "FDX Plans Restructuring of Sales Force," *The Wall Street Journal*, Jan. 17, 2000, p. A3.

12. Don E. Schultz, "Structural Straitjackets Stifle Integrated Success," *Marketing News*, Mar. 1, 1999, p. 8.

13. Sarah Ellison, Ann Zimmerman, and Charles Forelle, "P&G's Sales Edge: The

Playbook It Honed at Wal-Mart," *The Wall Street Journal,* Jan. 31, 2005, pp. A1, A12.

14. Jennifer Hamilton and Ross D. Petty, "The European Union's Consumer Guarantees Directive," *Journal of Public Policy & Marketing,* Fall 2001, pp. 289–296; and Mike Smith, "Accord Reached on Product Guarantees," *The Financial Times,* Mar. 23, 1999, p. 2.

15. Elizabeth Wolfe, "Appliance Maker to Pay $1.2M Settlement," *Associated Press Newswires,* Mar. 30, 2005, no page given; and Christopher Conkey, "Safety Agency Takes Action on Baby Gear," *The Wall Street Journal,* Mar. 22, 2005, pp. D1, D4.

16. J. Joseph Muller, "Three Key Issues in Consideration of Product Liability," *Mid-Missouri Business Journal,* Feb. 16–29, 1996, p. 22.

17. For examples, see Karen Padley, "Ford Wins Appeal of Class Action," *National Post,* May 3, 2002, p. FP16; and Margaret Cronin Fisk, "Suit Probes Acne Drug's Possible Link to Depression," *Miami Daily Business Review,* Apr. 26, 2002, p. A12. The professor's quote was contained in Dan Ackman, "Asbestos Settlements Breaking Out All Over," *Forbes.com,* Dec. 12, 2002, no pages given.

18. Nanette Byrnes, "The Tobacco Suit That's Going Up in Smoke," *Business-Week,* June 27, 2005, p. 70; "Big Tobacco Cut Down to Size, Yet Again," *Economist.com/Global Agenda,* Mar. 27, 2002, no pages given; and "Tobacco Takes a Hit," *Time,* July 19, 1999, p. 34.

19. Arthur D. Postal, "Class-Action Reform Passed at Last, But Impact May Be Limited," *National Underwriter. P & C,* Feb. 21, 2005, pp. 6+. For the description of a simulation model of product liability costs, see Conway Lackman and John Lanasa, "Product Liability Cost as a Marketing Tool," *Industrial Marketing Management,* May 1993, pp. 149–154.

20. "Gov't to Encourage Industry Bodies to Set Up PL Centers," *The Korea Herald,* June 15, 2002, no pages given; and Carolyn Aldred, "Suit to Test Europe's Tort Rules," *Business Insurance,* Mar. 18, 2002, pp. 27+.

21. "Group Takes Note of 'Ridiculous' Warning Labels," *Columbia Daily Tribune,* Jan. 18, 2001, p. 6B; and "Seen 'n Heard," *Compliance Reporter,* Nov. 8, 1999, p. 8.

22. Jennifer Saranow, "DaimlerChrysler Goes in Reverse on Warranties," *The Wall Street Journal,* May 26, 2004, p. D4; and Jane Spencer, "Guaranteed to Last a Whole 90 Days," *The Wall Street Journal,* July 16, 2002, pp. D1, D5.

23. Spencer, loc. cit.; and Moon Ihlwan, "Hyundai: Kissing Clunkers Goodbye," *BusinessWeek,* May 17, 2004, p. 45.

24. For an example of an entire promotional campaign based on a service guarantee, see Stephanie Paterik, "Sheraton Plans to Pay Guests for Bad Service," *The Wall Street Journal,* Sept. 6, 2002, pp. B1, B4. For research in the context of services that recommends money-back guarantees, see Glenn B. Voss, A. Parasuraman, and Dhruv Grewal, "The Roles of Price, Performance, and Expectations in Determining Satisfaction in Service Exchanges," *Journal of Marketing,* October 1998, pp. 46+.

25. Dirk Van den Poel and Joseph Leunis, "Consumer Acceptance of the Internet as a Channel of Distribution," *Journal of Business Research,* July 1999, pp. 249–256. For other assurances valued by both traditional and online shoppers, see "Online Stores Beat Brick-and-Mortar in Customer Service," *CMP Tech Media,* Nov. 24, 2004, no page given.

26. Betty Lin-Fisher, "Stores at Point of No Return," *Akron Beacon Journal,* Dec. 14, 2004, p. D1; and Ann Zimmerman, "Keep It Simple," *The Wall Street Journal,* Apr. 15, 2002, p. R10.

27. Jane Spencer, "The Point of No Return," *The Wall Street Journal,* May 14, 2002, pp. D1, D2; and Fisher loc. cit.

28. "Business Bulletin," *The Wall Street Journal,* Jan. 20, 2000, p. A1; and Lorrie Grant, "Online Returns a Hassle, Even with a Storefront," *USA Today,* Oct. 28, 1999, p. 3B.

29. Information about annual number of calls handled was provided by OTISLINE via e-mail, Apr. 6, 2005. For more about Otis' commitment to customer service, see "J. Lynn Lunsford, "United Technologies' Formula: A Powerful Life from Elevators," *The Wall Street Journal,* July 2, 2003, pp. A1, A6.

30. Ian Barkin, "M2M: Creating a Connected World," *Telecommunications Americas,* October 2004, pp. 18+; Jagdish N. Sheth and Rajendra S. Sisodia, "Feeling the Heat," *Marketing Management,* Fall 1995, p. 22; and Scott McCartney, "PC Makers Cure Customer Ills with Virtual House Calls," *The Wall Street Journal,* Mar. 21, 1995, p. B10.

31. Kimberly Morrison, "Top 10 Consumer Complaints Include Telecom Frustrations, Contractor Complaints," *Knight Ridder Tribune Business News,* Feb. 11, 2005, p. 1; and William Flannery, "Too Many Firms Have Workers Who Think the Customer Isn't Always Right. Training Could Help," *St. Louis Post-Dispatch,* Apr. 18, 1999, pp. E1+. The quote is from Stephen W. Brown, "Service Recovery through IT," *Marketing Management,* Fall 1997, p. 25.

32. "Business Bulletin," *The Wall Street Journal,* Feb. 3, 2000, p. A1; and Stephen S. Tax, Stephen W. Brown, and Murali Chandrashekaran, "Customer Evaluations of Service Complaint Experiences: Implications for Relationship Marketing," *Journal of Marketing,* April 1998, p. 60. For useful recommendations, see Mary C. Gilly and Richard W. Hansen, "Consumer Complaint Handling as a Strategic Marketing Tool," *The Journal of Product and Brand Management,* Summer 1992, pp. 5–16.

33. Gary Gentile, "Disney Finds a Way to Make Profits on the Web," *St. Louis Post-Dispatch,* Nov. 12, 2002, pp. C1, C8.

34. For an overview of this technique, see Dennis W. Means, "A Marketing Audit Checklist," *Agency Sales Magazine,* October 1998, pp. 54+.

35. For guidelines about marketing audits, see "How to Kick Off or Pump Up Your Firm's Marketing Plan," *Accounting Office Management & Administration Report,* February 2002, no pages given; and Bill Merrick, "Marketing Committees Evolve as CUs Grow," *Credit Union Magazine,* December 2001, no pages given. The quote is from Dale Terry, "How Does Your Bank's Marketing Size Up?" *Bank Marketing,* January 1995, pp. 53–58.

36. For the original discussion of the marketing audit, see Abe Schuchman, "The Marketing Audit: Its Nature, Purpose, and Problems," in *Analyzing and Improving Marketing Performance: "Marketing Audits" in Theory and Practice,* American Management Association, New York, Management Report no. 32, 1959, p. 14.

37. Ravi Dhar, as quoted in Diane Brady, "Why Service Stinks," *BusinessWeek,* Oct. 23, 2000, pp. 118–122+.

38. The quote is from Daniel M. Hrisak, "Survey Respondents: Revenue Recognition Has Highest Priority," *Managing the General Ledger,* March 2001, p. 3. Also see John A. Weber, "Manag-

ing the Marketing Budget in a Cost-Constrained Environment," *Industrial Marketing Management,* November 2002, pp. 705–717.

39. For a method of determining the value of customers, see Roger Connell, "Calculating the Contribution of Customers—a Practical Approach," *Journal of Targeting, Measurement and Analysis,* September 2002, pp. 13+. For more about examining both sales volume and costs and their links to strategy, see Gordon A. Wyner, "Customer Profitability," *Marketing Management,* Winter 1999, pp. 8–9.

40. Will Morton, "The Unprofitable Customers," *The Wall Street Journal,* Oct. 28, 2002, p. R7.

41. Andrew McAfee, "Do You Have Too Much IT?" *MIT Sloan Management Review,* Spring 2004, pp. 18+; Inditex website, loc. cit.; "Business: The Future of Fast Fashion; Inditex," loc. cit.; Ferdows et al., loc. cit.; Helft, loc. cit.; Folpe, loc. cit.; and Echikson, loc. cit.

Chapter 22

1. Amazon website (*www.amazon.com*); Nick Wingfield, "Racing Barnes & Noble for Same-Day Delivery in New York," *The Wall Street Journal,* June 3, 2004, p. B1; Alan Deutschman, "Inside the Mind of Jeff Bezos," *Fast Company,* August 2004, pp. 52–58; Steven Levy, "Showtime at Amazon," *Newsweek,* Nov. 29, 2004, p. E6; Robert D. Hof, "The Wizard of Web Retailing," *BusinessWeek,* Dec. 20, 2004, p. 8.

2. The structure for this discussion of electronic networking is based on Ravi Kakakota, Ralph A. Oliva, and Bob Donath, "Move Over E-Commerce," *Marketing Management,* Fall 1999, pp. 22–31.

3. Barton Goldenberg, "The Consumer of the Future," *CRM Magazine,* May 2005, p. 22.

4. "E-Stats," U. S. Census Bureau, accessed at *www.census.gov,* June 24, 2005.

5. Timothy J. Mullaney and Robert D. Hof, "E-tailing Finally Hits Its Stride," *BusinessWeek,* Dec. 20, 2004, pp. 36+.

6. William Hoffman, Jennifer Keedy, and Karl Roberts, "The Unexpected Return of B2B," McKinsey Quarterly, no. 3, 2002, accessed at *www.mckinsey quarterly.com,* Oct. 7, 2002.

7. A website lists these and over 110 other browsers (*www.browser.evolt. org*).

8. Based on statistics derived from several sources and reported at *www.Internet WorldStats.com,* accessed June 21, 2005.

9. Catharine P. Taylor and Jeff Howe, "Web Disconnect," *Adweek,* Sept. 9, 2002, pp. 22+.

10. Matthew Maier, "Online Video Ads Get Ready to Grab You," *Business 2.0,* May 2005, pp. 25–26.

11. The most popular weblogs or blogs are indexed at several sites. Two of the best known indexes are *www.blogstreet. com* and *www.bloogz.com.*

12. Faith Keenan, "The Price Is Really Right," *BusinessWeek,* Mar. 31, 2003, pp. 62+; Rob Howe, "At Starbucks, the Future Is in Plastics," *Business 2.0,* August 2003, pp. 56+.

13. "Defying Governmental Opinions & Safety Concerns, Millions of Americans Turn to Non-Traditional Online Pharmacies," report by ComScore Networks found at *www.comscore. com,* "Press Release," accessed June 22, 2005.

14. The firm Socratic Technologies (*www. sotech.com*) offers interesting examples of the business and consumer research that can be conducted over the Internet.

15. The Covisint website (*www.covisint. com*) provides a demonstration of how the production of customized automobiles can occur.

16. "Can E-tailers Find Fulfillment?" *Knowledge@Wharton,* July 28, 2002, CNET news.com, accessed at *www. news.com,* Oct. 12, 2002.

17. Mylene Mangalindan, "Threatening eBay's Dominance, More Online Sellers Go It Alone," *The Wall Street Journal,* June 22, 2005, pp. A1+.

18. Bridget Finn, "A More Profitable Harvest," *Business 2.0,* May 2005, pp. 66–67.

19. Ted Bridis, "Online Stores Charge Different Prices Based on Shoppers' Surfing Habits," *The Wall Street Journal,* June 2, 2005, p. 4B.

20. The impact of the Internet on traditional media is described in Alan Deutschman, "Commercial Success," *Fast Company,* January 2005, pp. 74–79.

21. "IAB Internet Advertising Revenue Report," April 2005, Interactive Advertising Bureau, accessed at *www.iab.net,* June 24, 2005.

22. Stephen Blake and Heather Green, "Blogs Will Change Your Business," *BusinessWeek,* May 2, 2005, pp. 56+.

23. Matt Richtel, "Credit Card Theft Is Thriving Online as Global Market," *The New York Times,* May 13, 2002, p. A1.

24. Ann Grimes, "What's in a Store?" *The Wall Street Journal,* July 15, 2002, p. R6.

25. Kathy Chu, "Banks and Online Retailers Lose Customers to the Fear of ID Theft," *The Wall Street Journal,* Mar. 24, 2005, p. D2.

26. For information regarding online regulations to protect consumers visit *www.ftc.gov.*

27. Brian Morrissey, "Tech Cookies Are Crumbling," *Brandweek,* Mar. 21, 2005, p. 12.

28. "Top 15 Countries in Internet Usage, 2004," Information@Please Database, Pearson Education, Inc. accessed at *www.infoplease.com,* June 24, 2005.

29. Abaigail Goldman, "Father of Amazon.com Says E-tail Will Never Replace Mall," *The Idaho Statesman,* Dec. 27, 1999, p. 6B.

30. Deutschman, "Inside the Mind of Jeff Bezos," op. cit.; Levy, op. cit; Hof, op. cit.

Photo Credits

Chapter 1

p. 2 ©The McGraw-Hill Companies/Jill Braaten Photographer (DIL).
p. 4 ©Reuters/Corbis.
p. 6 Used with permission of Red Wing Shoe Company.
p. 14 Photo provided by Whirlpool Corporation.
p. 19 Chien Min Chung/OnAsia.
p. 22 Photo by Getty Images for T-Mobile.
p. 24 ©The McGraw-Hill Companies/Jill Braaten Photographer (DIL).

Chapter 2

p. 26 Photo by Justin Sullivan/Getty Images.
p. 31 Courtesy Air National Guard.
p. 34 ©Salesforce.com.
p. 36 ©M. Hruby.
p. 37 ©M. Hruby.
p. 41 Photo by Bill Pugliano/Getty Images.
p. 46 Photo by Justin Sullivan/Getty Images.

Chapter 3

p. 48 ©James Leynse/Corbis.
p. 51 ©Bob Krist/Corbis.
p. 55 ©Spencer Grant/PhotoEdit.
p. 57 These materials have been reproduced with the permission of eBay Inc. COPYRIGHT ©EBAY INC. ALL RIGHTS RESERVED.
p. 65 JIMIN LAI/AFP/Getty Images.
p. 72 AP Photo/Jan Pitman.
p. 74 ©James Leynse/Corbis.

Chapter 4

p. 84 Photo by Spencer Platt/Getty Images.
p. 88 ©2004 Mattel Inc. All Rights Reserved.
p. 96 ©Lee Blankenship.
p. 99 Photo by M. David Leeds/NBAE via Getty Images.
p. 102 AP Photo/Adam Rountree.
p. 106 ©Michael Keller/Corbis.
p. 108 Photo by Spencer Platt/Getty Images.

Chapter 5

p. 112 BOEING/AFP/Getty Images.
p. 115 ©Vittoriano Rastelli/Corbis.
p. 117 ©NASA/JPL/ZUMA/Corbis.

Chapter 6

p. 124 Photo by Pascal Le Segretain/Getty Images.
p. 129 Brand X Pictures/Getty Images.
p. 137 BOEING/AFP/Getty Images.

Chapter 6

p. 140 ©The McGraw-Hill Companies/Jill Braaten Photographer (DIL).
p. 143 ©The Loved Dog Company.
p. 146 Courtesy Deskey Associates Inc./New York.
p. 150 Photo by DaimlerChrysler AG/Getty Images.
p. 158 Russ Quakenbush Photography.
p. 165 ©The McGraw-Hill Companies/Jill Braaten Photographer (DIL).

Chapter 7

p. 168 (top) U.S. Department of Agriculture and the U.S. Department of Health and Human Services.
p. 168 (bottom) U.S. Department of Agriculture and the U.S. Department of Health and Human Services.
p. 174 Courtesy The Gillette Company.
p. 176 AP Photo/David Kohl.
p. 181 Courtesy U.S. Census Bureau.
p. 184 Courtesy of: TRU-Teenage Research Unlimited.
p. 189 Courtesy Society of Competitive Intelligence Professionals.
p. 194 (top) U.S. Department of Agriculture and the U.S. Department of Health and Human Services.
p. 194 (bottom) U.S. Department of Agriculture and the U.S. Department of Health and Human Services.

Chapter 8

p. 204 Courtesy Imaginatik.
p. 207 Courtesy Palm, Inc.
p. 210 Cole Haan is a trademark of Cole Haan and is used with permission. Photographs courtesy of Cole Haan. ©2002 Cole Haan.
p. 213 Courtesy Talon, Inc.
p. 215 Courtesy Colgate-Palmolive Company.
p. 216 AP Photo/Louis Lanzano.
p. 218 ©M. Hruby.
p. 221 Courtesy Goodyear Tire & Rubber Co.
p. 226 Malden Mills/AP Photo.
p. 229 Courtesy Imaginatik.

Chapter 9

p. 236 Courtesy Marriott International, Inc.
p. 237 Courtesy Kimberly-Clark.
p. 240 Photo by Robert Mora/Getty Images.
p. 245 Tim Sloan/AFP/Getty Images.
p. 247 Courtesy U.S. Mint.

Chapter 10

p. 256 www.ronkimballstock.com.
p. 260 Ad used with permission of Morton Salt; A Rohm and Haas Company.
p. 261 Used with permission of Nestlé Purina PetCare, ©Nestlé.
p. 262 Courtesy The Document Company Xerox Corporation.
p. 264 Greg Girard/Contact Press Images, Inc.
p. 265 Courtesy IBM Corporation.
p. 267 ©David Russell.
p. 269 Courtesy Con Agra Foods, Inc.
p. 274 Courtesy Dean Foods.
p. 277 Photo by: Ki Ho Park/Kirstone Photography.
p. 278 Courtesy Apple Computer, Inc.
p. 281 www.ronkimballstock.com.

Chapter 11

p. 284 Photo by Mario Tama/Getty Images.
p. 290 (left) Prudential Financial is a service mark of The Prudential Insurance Company of America.
p. 290 (right) Courtesy Allstate Insurance Company.
p. 291 ©Mark Muench/Corbis.
p. 295 ©2005 March of Dimes Birth Defects Foundation. Used by permission.
p. 301 Courtesy Red Lobster.
p. 305 Photo by Mario Tama/Getty Images.

Chapter 12

p. 316 ©The McGraw-Hill Companies/Jill Braaten Photographer (DIL).
p. 318 Courtesy Barter Business Unlimited, Inc.
p. 320 Courtesy Xerox Corporation.
p. 323 Courtesy Kroger Company.
p. 327 Hartz Mountain Corporation.
p. 339 Emmanuel Dunand/AFP/Getty Images.

Chapter 13

p. 341 ©The McGraw-Hill Companies/Jill Braaten Photographer (DIL).

p. 344 Courtesy Bose Corporation.
p. 347 Courtesy Dollar Tree Stores, Inc.
p. 350 ©Jonathan Nourok/PhotoEdit.
p. 352 Courtesy Monsanto.
p. 357 Courtesy FedEx.com.
p. 361 Courtesy Amazon.com.
p. 362 Courtesy Costco.
p. 366 Courtesy Bose Corporation.

Chapter 14

p. 376 Photo by Tim Boyle/Getty Images.
p. 379 Courtesy Timepieces International, Inc.
p. 381 Courtesy Aetna.
p. 387 ©Joe Heiner.
p. 396 ©Pasquini Cedric/Corbis Sygma.
p. 397 ©China Newsphoto/Reuters/Corbis.
p. 398 Courtesy IGA, Inc./Chicago, IL.
p. 404 Photo by Tim Boyle/Getty Images.

Chapter 15

p. 406 Photo by Tim Boyle/Getty Images.
p. 414 Courtesy ESI Design/Nathan Kirkman.
p. 417 Courtesy Winmark Corporation.
p. 420 ©James Leynse/Corbis/SABA.
p. 424 ©John Nienhuis.
p. 430 Photo by Tim Boyle/Getty Images.

Chapter 16

p. 434 Courtesy W.W. Grainger.
p. 442 ©Susan Van Etten/PhotoEdit.

p. 445 Courtesy GlobalNetXchange, LLC.
p. 449 Courtesy CNF, Inc.
p. 456 Mitch Kezar/Getty Images.
p. 459 Courtesy The Burlington Northern & Santa Fe Railway Company.
p. 460 Taxi/Getty Images.
p. 461 Courtesy W.W. Grainger.

Chapter 17

p. 472 AP Photo/Paul Sakuma.
p. 475 ©2005 BMW of North America, LLC. Used with permission. The BMW name and logo are registered trademarks.
p. 476 SPAM and SPAMMOBILE™ are trademarks of Hormel Foods, LLC and are used with permission by Hormel Foods Corporation.
p. 480 ©The Procter & Gamble Company. Used with permission.
p. 482 Courtesy Boise Office Solutions.
p. 485 Courtesy Volkswagen of America, Inc.; Agency: Arnold Worldwide, Inc.
p. 494 AP Photo/Paul Sakuma.

Chapter 18

p. 496 Courtesy CDW Corporation.
p. 501 Courtesy Netkey, Inc.
p. 505 Fisher-Thatcher/Getty Images.
p. 506 R.W. Jones/Corbis.
p. 513 Tom & Dee Ann McCarthy/Corbis.
p. 518 Courtesy CDW Corporation.

Chapter 19

p. 520 Photo by Tim Boyle/Getty Images.
p. 526 ©Beach 'N Billboard/Patrick Dori.

p. 528 The BURGER KING® trademark and Subservient Chicken are used with permission from Burger King Brands, Inc.
p. 535 The Gillette Company.
p. 536 Courtesy Roper-Starch Worldwide, ©Nestlé U.S.A.
p. 542 Courtesy CJ WORLDWIDE.
p. 547 Photo by Tim Boyle/Getty Images.

Chapter 20

p. 556 AP Photo/Ted S. Warren.
p. 559 Photo courtesy of eCompanyStore.
p. 560 Courtesy Lennox Int'l.
p. 565 Courtesy Windjammer-Barefoot Cruises, Ltd.
p. 569 ©The McGraw-Hill Companies.
p. 572 AP Photo/Rick Bowmer.
p. 578 AP Photo/Ted S. Warren.

Chapter 21

p. 582 Courtesy Inditex, S.A.
p. 585 Courtesy Principal Financial Services, Inc.
p. 590 Courtesy Hyundai Motor America.
p. 591 Courtesy U.S. Consumer Product Safety Commission.
p. 594 Courtesy LivePerson, Inc.
p. 607 Courtesy Inditex, S.A.

Chapter 22

p. 610 AP Photo/Richard Drew.
p. 615 AP Photo/M. Spencer Green.
p. 618 Courtesy Red Envelope, Inc.
p. 620 Courtesy Price Farmer, Inc.
p. 621 Courtesy Masterfoods USA.
p. 624 Courtesy of USBID, Inc. All Rights Reserved.
p. 632 AP Photo/Richard Drew.

Glossary

A

accessory equipment Business goods that have substantial value and are used in an organization's operations.

activity indicator of buying power A market factor that is related to sales and expenditures and serves as an indirect estimate of purchasing power.

administered vertical marketing system An arrangement that coordinates distribution activities through the market and/or economic power of one channel member or the shared power of two channel members.

adoption process The set of successive decisions an individual or organization makes before accepting an innovation.

adoption rate The speed or ease with which a new product is accepted.

advertising All activities involved in presenting to an audience a nonpersonal, sponsor-identified, paid-for message about a product or an organization.

advertising agency An independent company that provides specialized advertising services and may also offer more general marketing assistance.

advertising campaign All the tasks involved in transforming a theme into a coordinated advertising program to accomplish a specific goal for a product or brand.

advertising media The communications vehicles (such as newspapers, radio, and television) that carry advertising as well as other information and entertainment.

agent middleman A firm that never actually takes title to (i.e., owns) products it helps market but does arrange the transfer of title.

agent wholesaling middleman An independent firm that engages primarily in wholesaling by actively negotiating the sale or purchase of products on behalf of other firms but does not take title to the products being distributed.

agribusiness Farms, food-processing firms, and other large-scale farming-related enterprises.

AIDA A sequence of steps in various forms of promotion, notably personal selling and advertising, consisting of attracting *Attention*, holding *Interest*, arousing *Desire*, and generating buyer *Action*.

annual marketing plan A written document that presents the master blueprint for a year's marketing activity for a specified organizational division or major product.

arbitrage The purchase and sale of a product in different markets to benefit from the unequal prices.

Asia-Pacific Economic Cooperation forum (APEC) A trade pact among 21 Pacific Rim nations that seeks the elimination of major trade barriers.

Association of Southeast Asian Nations (ASEAN) An agreement creating a free-trade zone among Brunei, Cambodia, Indonesia, Laos, Malaysia, Myanmar, the Philippines, Singapore, Thailand and Vietnam.

attitude A learned predisposition to respond to an object or class of objects in a consistently favorable or unfavorable way.

auction company An agent wholesaling middleman that helps assembled buyers and sellers complete their transactions by providing auctioneers who do the selling and physical facilities for displaying the sellers' products.

automatic vending A form of nonstore retailing where the products are sold through a machine with no personal contact between the buyer and seller.

average fixed cost The total fixed cost divided by the number of units produced.

average fixed cost curve A graph of average fixed cost levels showing a decline as output increases because the total of the fixed costs is spread over an increasing number of units.

average revenue The unit price at a given level of unit sales. It is calculated by dividing total revenue by the number of units sold.

average total cost The total cost divided by the number of units produced.

average total cost curve A graph of average total costs, which starts high, then declines to its lowest point, reflecting optimum output with respect to total costs (not variable costs), and then rises because of diminishing returns.

average variable cost The total variable cost divided by the number of units produced.

average variable cost curve A graph of average variable cost levels, which starts high, then declines to its lowest point, reflecting optimum output with respect to variable costs (not total costs), and then rises.

B

baby boomers Americans born during the 20 years following World War II.

balance of payments The accounting record of all of a country's transactions with all the other nations of the world.

banner ad A boxed-in promotional message often appearing at the top of a Web page.

barter The exchange of goods and/or services for other products.

base price The price of one unit of the product at its point of production or resale. Same as *list price*.

BCG matrix See *Boston Consulting Group (BCG) matrix*.

behavioral segmentation Market segmentation based on consumers' product-related behavior, typically the benefits desired from a product and the rate at which the consumer uses the product.

blogs See weblogs.

Boston Consulting Group (BCG) matrix A strategic planning model that classifies strategic business units or major products according to market shares and growth rates.

boycott A refusal to buy products from a particular company or country.

brand A name and/or mark intended to identify and differentiate the product of one seller or a group of sellers.

brand equity The value a brand adds to a product.

brand label The application of the brand name alone to a product or package.

brand licensing See *trademark licensing*.

brand manager See *product manager*.

brand mark The part of a brand that appears in the form of a symbol, design, or distinctive color or type of lettering.

brand name The part of a brand that can be vocalized—words, letters, and/or numbers.

breadth The number of product lines offered for sale by a firm.

break-even analysis A method of calculating the level of output at which total revenue equals total costs, assuming a certain selling price.

break-even point The level of output at which total revenue equals total costs, assuming a certain selling price.

broker An agent wholesaling middleman that brings buyers and sellers together and provides market information to either party and that ordinarily neither physically handles products being distributed nor works on a continuing basis with those sellers or buyers.

browser A program that enables its users to access electronic documents included in the World Wide Web on the Internet.

business analysis One stage in the new-product development process, consisting of several steps to expand a surviving idea into a concrete business proposal.

business cycle The four recurring stages in an economy, typically prosperity, recession, depression, and recovery.

business format franchising An agreement, covering an entire method (or format) for operating a business, under which a successful business sells the right to operate the same business in different geographic areas.

business market The total of all business users.

business marketer A firm performing the activity of marketing goods and services.

business marketing The marketing of goods and services to business users rather than to ultimate consumers.

business product A product that is intended for purchase and resale or for purchase and use in producing other products or for providing services in an organization.

business services market The total set that deals in data and information such as marketing research firms, ad agencies, public utilities, and financial, insurance, legal, or real estate firms.

business-to-business advertising Advertising that is directed at businesses.

business-to-consumer advertising See *consumer advertising*.

business users Business, industrial, or institutional organizations that buy goods or services to use in their own organizations, to resell, or to make other products.

buy classes Three typical buying situations in the business market—namely new-task buying, modified rebuy, and straight rebuy.

buying center In an organization, all individuals or groups involved in the process of making a purchase decision.

buying motive The reason why a person or an organization buys a specific product or makes purchases from a specific firm.

buying roles The users, influencers, deciders, gatekeepers, and buyers who make up a buying center.

C

cannibalization Situation in which a firm introduces new products to stimulate sales but the profit comes at the expense of other products sold by that firm.

cartel A group of companies that produce similar products and act collectively to restrain competition in manufacturing and marketing.

cash discount A deduction granted to buyers for paying their bills within a specified period.

category-killer store A type of retail institution that has a narrow but very deep assortment, low prices, and few to moderate customer services. It is designed to "destroy" all competition in a specific product category.

category management A distribution practice in which a retailer allows a large supplier to manage an entire product category in a store or chain, with the supplier deciding which items will be placed on a retailer's shelves and in what quantities and locations.

cause-related marketing A source of promotion for nonbusiness organizations in which an alliance between a for-profit and a nonprofit organization helps to generate sales for the firm and publicity for the nonprofit organization.

change agent In the process of diffusion, a person who seeks to accelerate the spread of a given innovation.

channel assembly Strategy in which a distributor takes over the final assembly role, which allows products to be customized, thus shortening delivery time because manufacturers often delay custom projects so they don't disrupt their production processes.

channel conflict A situation in which one channel member perceives another channel member to be acting in a way that prevents the first member from achieving its distribution objectives.

channel control The actions of a firm to regulate the behavior of other companies in its distribution channel.

channel power The ability of a firm to influence or determine the behavior of another channel member.

chargeback A penalty that a retailer or wholesaler assesses to a vendor that actually or allegedly violates an agreed-upon distribution policy or procedure.

client market Individuals and/or organizations that are the recipients of a nonprofit organization's money or services. Same as *recipient market*.

clustering Electronic research technique that tracks the pages visited, the amount of time at a page, and the items purchased by individuals as they navigate a site.

cobranding Agreement between two separate companies, or two divisions within the same company, to place both of their respective brands on a particular product or enterprise; also called dual branding.

collaborative filtering Electronic research technique that compares a person's selections and the purchases of previous visitors and enables a site to recommend current products that may be of interest to the visitor.

collaborative planning, forecasting, and replenishment (CPFR) Method by which a producer or wholesaler and a customer, ordinarily a retail chain, jointly and interactively develop sales forecasts through a shared website and design marketing plans.

co-location Employees of a distributor are stationed at the manufacturer's site to arrange shipment of the finished product to the customers.

Combined Statistical Area (CSA) An urban area that consists of an adjacent metropolitan area (at least 50,000 residents) and a micropolitan statistical area (between 10,000 and 50,000 residents).

commercial information environment As contrasted with the social information environment, all communications directed to consumers by organizations and individuals involved in marketing.

Common Market of the South (MERCOSUR) An agreement between Argentina, Brazil, Paraguay, and Uruguay that allows 90% of trade among these countries to occur tariff free.

communication The verbal or nonverbal transmission of information between someone wanting to express an idea and someone else expected or expecting to get that idea. The four elements are a message, a source of the message, a communication channel, and a receiver.

company sales branch See *manufacturer's sales branch*.

comparison advertising A form of selective-demand advertising in which an advertiser either directly (by naming a rival brand) or indirectly (through inference) points out the differences among competing brands.

competitive intelligence The process of gathering and analyzing publicly available information about the activities and plans of competitors.

concentration strategy See *single-segment strategy*.

consumer advertising Advertising that is directed at consumers.

consumer buying-decision process The series of logical stages, which differ for consumers and organizations, that a prospective purchaser goes through when faced with a buying problem.

consumer product A product that is intended for purchase and use by household consumers for nonbusiness purposes.

Consumer Product Safety Act Federal legislation that created the Consumer Product Safety Commission (CPSC), which has authority to establish mandatory safety standards for many consumer products.

containerization A cargo-handling system in which shipments of products are enclosed in large metal or wood receptacles that are transported unopened from the time they leave the shipper's facilities until they reach their destination.

contract logistics An arrangement under which a firm outsources various business tasks to one or more independent firms.

contract manufacturing An arrangement in which a firm in one country arranges for a firm in another country to produce the product in the foreign country.

contracting A legal relationship that allows a firm to enter a foreign market indirectly, quickly establish a market presence, and experience a limited amount of risk.

contractual vertical marketing system An arrangement under which independent firms—producers, wholesalers, and retailers—operate under contracts specifying how they will operate in order to improve their distribution efficiency and effectiveness.

contribution-margin approach In marketing cost analysis, an accounting method in which only direct expenses are allocated to each marketing unit being analyzed.

convenience goods A category of tangible consumer products that the consumer has prior knowledge of and purchases with minimum time and effort.

convenience store A type of retail institution that concentrates on convenience-oriented groceries and nonfoods, typically has higher prices than other grocery stores, and offers few customer services.

cookie An inactive data file placed on a computer's hard drive after the user connects to a particular website; used to record the visitor's activities while connected to the site.

cooperative advertising Advertising promoting products of two or more firms that share its cost.

corporate chain An organization of two or more centrally owned and managed stores that generally handle the same lines of products.

corporate vertical marketing system An arrangement under which a firm at one level of a distribution channel owns the firms at the next level or owns the entire channel.

correlation analysis A statistical refinement of the direct-derivation method, an approach to demand forecasting that takes into account how close the association is between potential sales of the product and the market factor affecting its sales.

cost per thousand (CPM) The media cost of gaining exposure to 1,000 persons with an ad.

cost-plus pricing A major method of price determination in which the price of a unit of a product is set at a level equal to the unit's total cost plus a desired profit on the unit.

countertrade An arrangement under which domestically made products are traded for imported goods.

C2C design "Cradle to cradle" product design that seeks to recycle parts and components as much as possible.

culture A complex set of symbols and artifacts created by a society and handed down from generation to generation as determinants and regulators of human behavior.

cumulative discount A quantity discount based on the total volume purchased over a specified period.

customer relationship management (CRM) An ongoing interaction between a buyer and a seller in which the seller continuously improves its understanding of the buyer's needs, and the buyer becomes increasingly loyal to the seller because its needs are being so well satisfied.

customer specialization One method of organizing selling activities in which each sales person is assigned a specific group of customers, categorized by type of industry or channel of distribution, to which to sell. Same as *market specialization*.

D

database A set of related data that are organized, stored, and updated in a computer.

data mining Method used to identify patterns and meaningful relationships in masses of data that would be overlooked or unrecognizable to researchers.

data warehouse A collection of data from a variety of internal and external sources, compiled by a firm for use in conducting transactions.

decision support system (DSS) A procedure that allows a manager to interact with data using various methods of analysis to integrate, analyze, and interpret information.

decline stage The fourth, and final, part of a product life cycle during which the sales of a generic product category drop and most competitors abandon the market.

Delphi method A forecasting technique, applicable to sales forecasting, in which a group of experts individually and anonymously assesses future sales, after which each member has the chance to offer a revised assessment as the group moves toward a consensus.

demand forecasting The process of estimating sales of a product during some defined future period.

demographic segmentation Subdividing markets into groups based on population factors such as size, age, and growth.

demographics The characteristics of human populations, including such factors as size, distribution, and growth.

department store A large-scale retail institution that has a very broad and deep product assortment, tries not to compete on the basis of price, and offers a wide array of customer services.

depth The relative variety of sizes, colors, and models offered within a product line.

descriptive label The part of a product that gives information about its use, construction, care, performance, and/or other pertinent features.

desk jobber See *drop shipper*.

differential advantage Any feature of an organization or brand perceived by customers to be desirable and different from those of the competition.

differential disadvantage Any feature of an organization or brand perceived by customers to be undesirable and different from those of the competition.

diffusion A process by which an innovation spreads throughout a social system over time.

direct costs Separate expenses that are incurred totally in connection with one market segment or one unit of the sales organization. Same as *separable expenses.*

direct-derivation method An approach to demand forecasting that directly relates the behavior of a market factor to estimated demand.

direct distribution A channel consisting only of producer and final customer, with no middlemen providing assistance.

direct foreign investment A method through which a company can build or acquire production or distribution facilities in a foreign country.

direct investment The actions of a company to build or acquire its own production facilities in a foreign country.

direct marketing A form of nonstore retailing that uses advertising to contact consumers who, in turn, purchase products without visiting a retail store.

direct selling A form of nonstore retailing in which personal contact between a sales person and a consumer occurs away from a retail store. Sometimes called *in-home selling.*

direct tests Measuring or predicting the sales volume attributable to a single ad or an entire advertising campaign.

directory Collection of lists of websites organized by topics and subtopics.

disintermediation The replacement of some traditional intermediaries in a process due to the growth of Internet-based sales.

discount retailing A retailing approach that uses price as a major selling point by combining comparatively low prices and reduced costs of doing business.

discount store A large-scale retail institution that has a broad and shallow product assortment, low prices, and few customer services.

distribution center A facility that has under one roof an efficient, fully integrated system for the flow of products—taking orders, filling them, and preparing them for delivery to customers.

distribution channel The set of people and firms involved in the transfer of title to a product as the product moves from producer to ultimate consumer or business user.

drop shipper A merchant wholesaler that does not physically handle the product being distributed, but instead sells merchandise for delivery directly from the producer to the customer. Same as *desk jobber.*

dumping The process of selling products in foreign markets at prices below the prices charged for these goods in their home markets.

dynamic pricing A form of price adjustment that occurs instantly and frequently in accordance with what the market will bear.

E

early adopters A group of consumers that includes opinion leaders, is respected, has much influence on its peers, and is the second group (following the innovators) to adopt an innovation.

early majority A group of fairly deliberate consumers that adopts an innovation just before the "average" adopter in a social system.

economic environment A set of factors, including the business cycle, inflation, and interest rates, that affect the marketing activities of an organization.

economic order quantity (EOQ) The optimal quantity for reorder when replenishing inventory stocks, as indicated by the volume at which the sum of inventory-carrying costs and order-processing costs are at a minimum.

80–20 principle A situation in which a large proportion of the total orders, customers, territories, or products account for only a small share of the company's sales or profit, and vice versa.

elasticity of demand A price-volume relationship such that a change of one unit on the price scale results in a change of more than one unit on the volume scale.

electronic commerce The buying and selling of goods and services through the use of electronic networks.

electronic data interchange (EDI) Computer-to-computer transmission of orders, invoices, or other business information.

electronic information A form of networking involving the creation of a corporate website to post information about the firm.

electronic networks Individuals or organizations linked via some form of telecommunications.

electronic transactions Purchases made directly from a firm's website.

enterprise resource planning (ERP) systems Strategy in which the various business functions of sales, manufacturing, purchasing, distribution, financial management, and human resources are integrated through the use of computer programs; also called enterprise software.

environmental monitoring The process of gathering information regarding a company's external environment, analyzing it, and forecasting the impact of whatever trends the analysis suggests. Same as *environmental scanning.*

environmental scanning See *environmental monitoring.*

ethics The rules and standards of moral behavior that are generally accepted by a society.

European Union (EU) A political and economic alliance among most of the countries of Western Europe that seeks to liberalize trade among its members.

evaluation The stage of the management process during which an organization determines how well it is achieving the goals set in its strategic planning.

everyday low pricing (EDLP) A pricing strategy that involves consistently low prices and few, if any, temporary price reductions.

exchange The act of voluntarily providing a person or organization something of value in order to acquire something else of value.

exclusive dealing The practice by which a manufacturer prohibits its dealers from carrying products of its competitors.

exclusive distribution A strategy in which a supplier agrees to sell its product only to a single wholesaling middleman and/or retailer in a given market.

exclusive-territory policy The practice by which a producer requires each middleman to sell *only* to customers located within an assigned territory.

executive judgment A method of sales forecasting that consists of obtaining opinions regarding future sales volume from one or more executives.

expected price The price at which customers consciously or unconsciously value a product—what they think the product is worth.

experiment A method of gathering primary data in which the researcher measures the results of changing one variable in a situation while holding all others constant.

export agent A middleman that operates either in a manufacturer's country or in the destination country and that negotiates the sale of the product in another country and may provide additional services such as arranging for international financing, shipping, and insurance on behalf of the manufacturer.

export merchant A middleman operating in a manufacturer's country that buys goods and exports them.

exporting The activities by which a firm sells its product in another country, either directly to foreign importers or through import–export middlemen.

express warranty A statement in written or spoken words regarding restitution from seller to customer if the seller's product does not perform up to reasonable expectations.

extranet A network that links a large number of firms at different levels of a distribution channel.

F

fabricating materials Business goods that have received some processing and will undergo further processing as they become part of another product.

fabricating parts Business goods that already have been processed to some extent and will be assembled in their present form (with no further change) as part of another product.

face-to-face interview A face-to-face method of gathering data in a survey.

fad A product or style that becomes immensely popular nearly overnight and then falls out of favor with consumers almost as quickly.

family A group of two or more people related by blood, marriage, or adoption living together in a household.

family branding A strategy of using the company name for branding purposes.

family life-cycle stage The series of life stages that a family goes through, starting with young single people, progressing through married stages with young and then older children, and ending with older married and single people.

family packaging A strategy of using either highly similar packages for all products or packages with a common and clearly noticeable feature.

fashion A style that is popularly accepted and purchased by successive groups of people over a reasonably long period of time.

fashion-adoption process A series of buying waves by which a style becomes popular in a market; similar to diffusion of an innovation.

fashion cycle Wavelike movements representing the introduction, rise, popular acceptance, and decline of the market's acceptance of a style.

fashion obsolescence See *style obsolescence.*

Federal Trade Commission Act A federal law, passed in 1914, prohibiting unfair competition and establishing the Federal Trade Commission.

first-mover advantage Strategy of entering a market during the introductory stage of a product in order to build a dominant position; also called pioneer advantage.

fixed cost A cost that remains constant regardless of how many items are produced or sold.

flat-rate pricing Arrangement where a purchaser pays a stipulated single price and then can consume as much or as little of the product as desired.

flexible-price strategy A pricing strategy under which a seller charges different prices to similar customers who buy identical quantities of a product. Same as *variable-price strategy.*

FOB (free on board) factory pricing A geographic pricing strategy whereby the seller quotes the selling price at the point of production and the buyer selects the mode of transportation and pays all freight costs. Same as *FOB mill pricing.*

FOB mill pricing See *FOB factory pricing.*

focus group A preliminary data-gathering method involving an interactive interview of 6 to 12 people.

forecast demand The process of estimating sales of a product during some future period. Same as *demand forecasting.*

foreign exchange Trading the currency of one country for the currency of another country.

for-profit services firms Those that sell to consumers or other businesses with profitable operations as a primary goal.

franchising A type of contractual vertical marketing system that involves a continuing relationship in which a franchiser (the parent company) provides the right to use a trademark plus various management assistance in return for payments from a franchisee (the owner of the individual business unit).

freight-absorption pricing A geographic pricing strategy whereby the seller pays for (absorbs) some of the freight charges in order to penetrate more distant markets.

freight forwarder A specialized marketing institution that serves firms by consolidating less-than-carload or less-than-truckload shipments into carload or truckload quantities and arranging for door-to-door shipping service.

fulfillment The act of packing and shipping orders to customers.

full-cost approach In marketing cost analysis, an accounting method in which all expenses—direct and indirect—are allocated to the marketing units being analyzed.

full-service wholesaler An independent merchant middleman that performs a full range of wholesaling functions (from creating assortments to warehousing).

functional discount See *trade discount.*

functional obsolescence See *technological obsolescence.*

G

GE business screen See *General Electric (GE) business screen.*

General Agreement on Tariffs and Trade (GATT) See World Trade Organization (WTO).

General Electric (GE) business screen A planning model developed by General Electric that classifies strategic business units or major products based on two factors—market attractiveness and business position.

Generation X Those people in the U.S. who were born between approximately 1966 and 1976. Also called *baby busters, twentysomethings,* or *boomerangers.*

Generation Y Those people in the U.S. who were born between 1977 and 1994. Also called *echo boomers,* or *millennium generation.*

geographic segmentation Subdividing markets into groups based on their locations.

geographic specialization One method of organizing selling activities, in which each sales person is assigned a specific geographic area—called a territory—in which to sell.

global sales teams A type of personal selling where a team of sales people is responsible for all of its company's sales to an account anywhere in the world.

global strategy A strategy in which essentially the same marketing program is employed around the world.

goal See *objective*.

government market The segment of the business market that includes federal, state, and local units buying for government institutions such as schools, offices, hospitals, and military bases.

grade label The part of a product that identifies the product's judged quality (grade) by means of a letter, number, or word.

gray marketing Practice of buying a product in one country, agreeing to distribute it in a second country but diverting it to a third country. Also called export diversion.

Green River ordinance Law that restricts door-to-door salespeople by requiring them to register and purchase a license.

growth stage The second part of a product life cycle during which the sales and profits of a generic product category rise and competitors enter the market, causing profits to decline near the end of this part of the cycle.

H

heterogeneity A characteristic of a service indicating that each unit is somewhat different from other units of the same service.

hierarchy of effects The stages a buyer goes through in moving toward a purchase, specifically awareness, knowledge, liking, preference, conviction, and purchase.

high-low pricing A pricing strategy that combines frequent price reductions and aggressive promotion to convey an image of very low prices.

horizontal business market A situation where a given product is usable in a wide variety of industries.

horizontal conflict A form of channel conflict occurring among middlemen (either of the same type or different types) at the same level of distribution.

household A single person, a family, or any group of unrelated persons who occupy a housing unit.

hypothesis A tentative supposition that, if proven, would suggest a possible solution to a problem.

I

iceberg principle A concept related to performance evaluation stating that the summary data (tip of the iceberg) regarding an activity may hide significant variations among segments of this activity.

implementation The stage of the management process during which an organization attempts to carry out its strategic plans.

implied warranty An intended but unstated assurance regarding restitution from seller to customer if the seller's product does not perform up to reasonable expectations.

import–export agent An agent wholesaling middleman that brings together sellers and buyers in different countries. Export agents work in the country in which the product is made; import agents work in the country in which the product will be sold.

import quota A limit on the amount of a particular product that can be brought into a country.

impulse buying A form of low-involvement decision making; purchases made with little or no advance planning.

independent retailer A company with a single retail store that is not affiliated with a contractual vertical marketing system.

indirect costs Expenses that are incurred jointly for more than one marketing unit and therefore cannot be totally charged to one market segment.

indirect distribution A channel consisting of producer, final customer, and at least one level of middlemen.

indirect tests Measuring or predicting the effects of advertising by using a factor other than actual behavior.

inflation A rise in the prices of goods and services.

informal investigation The stage in a marketing research study at which preliminary, readily available data are gathered from relevant people inside and outside the company—middlemen, competitors, advertising agencies, and consumers.

infrastructure The country's levels and capabilities with respect to transportation, communications, and energy.

in-home selling See *direct selling*.

innovation adopter categories Groups of people differentiated according to when they accept a given innovation.

innovators A group of venturesome consumers that are the first to adopt an innovation.

inseparability A characteristic of a service indicating that it cannot be separated from the creator–seller of the service.

inside selling Situation where the customer comes to the sales person; includes retail stores and telephone order takers.

installations Manufactured products that are an organization's major, expensive, and long-lived equipment and that directly affect the scale of operations in an organization producing goods or services.

institutional advertising Advertising that presents information about the advertiser's business or tries to create a favorable impression—build goodwill—for the organization.

intangibility A characteristic of a service indicating that it has no physical attributes and, as a result, is impossible for customers to taste, feel, see, hear, or smell before they buy it.

integrated marketing communications (IMC) A strategy in which each of the promotion-mix components is carefully coordinated.

intensity of distribution The number of middlemen used by a producer at the retail and wholesale levels in a particular territory.

intensive distribution A strategy in which a producer sells its product through every available outlet in a market where a consumer might reasonably look for it.

interest rates The percentage amounts either charged to lend money or paid to acquire money.

intermodal transportation The use of two or more modes of transportation to move a shipment of freight.

international market Sales, market potential, or sales potential in foreign (or nondomestic) areas.

international marketing The activities of an organization to market its products in two or more countries.

Internet Global network of networks linking millions of users; originally created to link researchers at many different sites and allow them to exchange information.

Internet selling The offering of goods or services to customers over the Internet.

Internet survey A method of gathering data by posting questionnaires on a firm's website or by e-mailing them to a sample of individuals.

intranet A local electronic network created by linking the personal computers of individuals in a company or department.

introduction stage The first part of a product life cycle during which a generic product category is launched into the market in a full-scale marketing program. Same as *pioneering stage.*

inverse demand A price-volume relationship such that the higher the price, the greater the unit sales.

ISO 9000 quality standards The International Organization for Standardizations certification to assure that firms conform to specific standards in processes, procedures, operations, controls, and management.

J

joint venture A partnership arrangement in which a foreign operation is owned in part by a domestic company and in part by a foreign company.

just-in-time (JIT) A form of inventory control, purchasing, and production scheduling that involves buying parts and supplies in small quantities just in time for use in production and then producing in quantities just in time for sale.

K

kinked demand A condition in which total revenue declines when a product's price is increased or decreased in relation to the prevailing market level.

L

label The part of a product that carries information about the product and the seller.

laggards A group of tradition-bound consumers who are the last to adopt an innovation.

Lanham Trademark Act A federal law passed in 1946 that made it illegal for organizations to make false claims about their own products.

late majority A group of skeptical consumers who are slow to adopt an innovation but eventually do so to save money or in response to social pressure from their peers.

leader In leader pricing, an item on which price is cut.

leader pricing A pricing and promotional strategy in which temporary price cuts are made on a few items to attract customers.

learning Changes in behavior resulting from observation and experience.

level of involvement The amount of effort that is expended in satisfying a need.

licensing A business arrangement whereby one firm sells to another firm (for a fee or royalty) the right to use the first company's brand, patents, or manufacturing processes.

lifestyle Behavior that relate to a person's activities, interests, and opinions.

limited-line store A type of retail institution that has a narrow but deep product assortment and customer services that vary from store to store.

line extension One form of product-mix expansion in which a company adds a similar item to an existing product line with the same brand name.

list price See *base price.*

local-content law A regulation specifying the proportion of a finished product's components and labor that must be provided by the importing country.

local operating laws A constraint on how, when, or where retailing can be conducted.

local strategy A strategy used to develop customized marketing programs for each distinct area.

logistics See *physical distribution.*

loss leader In leader pricing, an item on which price is cut to a level that is below the store's cost.

loyalty Faithfulness in a particular brand or retailer so that the consumer purchases that brand or from that retailer without considering alternatives.

M

mail survey A method of gathering data by mailing a questionnaire to potential respondents and asking them to complete it and return it by mail.

major accounts organization A variation of customer specialization that usually involves team selling to better service key accounts.

management The process of planning, implementing, and evaluating the efforts of a group of people working toward a common goal.

manufacturers' agent An agent wholesaling middleman that sells part or all of a manufacturer's product mix in an assigned geographic territory. Same as *manufacturers' representative.*

manufacturers' representative See *manufacturers' agent.*

manufacturer's sales branch A manufacturer's sales facility that carries a stock of the product being sold. Same as *company sales branch.*

manufacturer's sales facility An establishment that engages primarily in wholesaling and is owned and operated by a manufacturer but is physically separated from manufacturing plants.

manufacturer's sales office A manufacturer's sales facility that does not carry a stock of the product being sold.

marginal cost The cost of producing and selling one more unit; that is, the cost of the last unit produced or sold.

marginal cost curve A graph of marginal cost levels, which slopes downward until marginal costs start to increase, at which point it rises.

marginal revenue The income derived from the sale of the last unit.

market People or organizations with needs to satisfy, money to spend, and the willingness to spend the money. Alternatively, any person or group with whom an individual or organization has an existing or potential exchange relationship.

market-aggregation strategy A plan of action under which an organization treats its total market as a single segment—that is, as one mass market whose members are considered to be alike with respect to demand for the product—and thus develops a single marketing mix to reach most of the customers in the entire market. Same as *mass-market strategy* and *undifferentiated-market strategy.*

market factor An item or element that (1) exists in a market, (2) may be measured quantitatively, and (3) is related to the demand for a good or service.

market-factor analysis A sales forecasting method that assumes the future demand for a product is related to the behavior of certain market factors and, as a result, involves determining what these factors are and then measuring their relationships to sales activity.

market orientation The third stage in the evolution of marketing management in which companies identify what customers want and tailor all their activities to satisfy those needs as efficiently as possible.

market-penetration pricing A strategy in which the initial price of a product is set low in relation to the target market's range of expected prices.

market potential The total sales volume that all organizations selling a product during a stated time period in a specific market could expect to achieve under ideal conditions.

market-response system A form of inventory control in which a purchase by a final customer activates a process to produce and deliver replacement items.

market segmentation The process of dividing the total market for a good or service into several smaller groups, such that the members of each group are similar with respect to the factors that influence demand.

market segments Within the same general market, groups of customers with different wants, buying preferences, or product-use behavior.

market share The proportion of total sales of a product during a stated time period in a specific market that is captured by a single firm.

market-share analysis A detailed analysis of the company's share of the market relative to competitors in total as well as by product line and market segment.

market-skimming pricing A strategy in which the initial price of a product is set high in relation to the target market's range of expected prices.

market specialization See *customer specialization*.

market tests One stage in the new-product development process, consisting of acquiring and analyzing actual consumers' reactions to proposed products.

marketer Any person or organization that desires to stimulate and facilitate exchanges.

marketing A total system of business activities designed to plan, price, promote, and distribute want-satisfying products to target markets to achieve organizational objectives.

marketing audit A comprehensive review and evaluation of the marketing function in an organization—its environment, philosophy, goals, strategies, organizational structure, human and financial resources, and performance.

marketing concept A philosophy of doing business that emphasizes customer orientation and coordination of marketing activities in order to achieve the organization's performance objectives.

marketing cost analysis A detailed study of the operating expenses section of a company's profit and loss statement.

marketing information system (MkIS) An ongoing, organized procedure to generate, analyze, disseminate, store, and retrieve information for use in making marketing decisions.

marketing intermediary An independent business organization that directly aids in the flow of products between a marketing organization and its markets.

marketing mix A combination of the four elements—product, pricing structure, distribution system, and promotional activities—used to satisfy the needs of an organization's target market(s) and, at the same time, achieve its marketing objectives.

marketing research The development, interpretation, and communication of decision-oriented information to be used in the strategic marketing process.

markup The amount added to the cost of a product to cover expenses and provide a profit. Same as *markon*.

Maslow's needs hierarchy A structure of five need levels, arranged in the order in which people seek to gratify them.

mass customization Developing, producing, and delivering affordable products with enough variety and uniqueness that nearly every potential customer can have exactly what he or she wants.

mass-market strategy See *market-aggregation strategy*.

maturity stage The third part of a product life cycle during which the sales of a generic product category continue to increase (but at a decreasing rate), profits decline largely because of price competition, and some firms leave the market.

merchant middleman A firm that actually takes title to (i.e., owns) products it helps to market.

merchant wholesaler An independently owned firm that engages primarily in wholesaling and takes title to products being distributed. Sometimes called a *wholesaler*.

methods of sales-force compensation The three types of compensation plans are straight salary, straight commission, and a combination plan.

Metropolitan Statistical Area (MSA) An urban area in the U.S. with at least 50,000 residents.

micromarketing The concept of marketing to a small segment of consumers.

Micropolitan Statistical Area An urban area that has at least one cluster of 10,000 residents but less than 50,000 residents.

middleman A business firm that renders services directly related to the purchase and/or sale of a product as it flows from producer to consumer.

middleman's brand A brand owned by a retailer or a wholesaler.

misdirected marketing effort Marketing endeavors that do not produce results commensurate with the resources expended.

mission An organization's statement of what customers it serves, what needs it satisfies, and what types of products it offers.

mix extension One form of product-mix expansion in which a company adds a new product line to its present assortment.

modified rebuy In the business market, a purchasing situation between a new task and a straight rebuy in terms of time and people involved, information needed, and alternatives considered.

motive A need sufficiently stimulated to move an individual to seek satisfaction.

multinational corporation A truly worldwide enterprise in which the foreign and the domestic operations are integrated and are not separately identified.

multiple-brand strategy A strategy in which a firm has more than one brand of essentially the same product, aimed either at the same target market or at distinct target markets.

multiple correlation A more sophisticated form of correlation analysis that allows the inclusion of more than one market factor in the calculation.

multiple-distribution channels The use by a producer of more than one channel of distribution for reasons such as achieving broad market coverage or avoiding total dependence on a single arrangement.

multiple packaging The practice of placing several units of the same product in one container.

multiple-segment strategy A plan of action that involves selecting two or more different groups of potential customers as the firm's target markets.

N

net profit percentage The ratio of net profit to net sales. See Appendix A.

networks Individuals or organizations linked together to share data, exchange information and ideas, and perform tasks.

new product A vague term that may refer to (1) really innovative, truly unique products, (2) replacement products that are significantly different from existing ones, or (3) imitative products that are new to a particular firm but are not new to the market.

new-product department or team An organizational structure for product planning and development that involves a small unit, consisting of five or fewer people, and that reports to the president.

new-product development process A set of six stages that a new product goes through, starting with idea generation and continuing through idea screening, business analysis, prototype development, market tests, and eventually commercialization (full-scale production and marketing).

new-product strategy A statement identifying the role a new product is expected to play in achieving corporate and marketing goals.

new-task buying In the business market, a purchasing situation in which a company for the first time considers buying a given item.

niche marketers Sellers that pursue single segments within the total market.

niche marketing A strategy in which goods and services are tailored to meet the needs of small market segments.

niche markets A small, targeted segment.

nonadopters Those consumers that never adopt an innovation.

nonbusiness market The total set of churches, colleges and universities, museums, hospitals and other health institutions, political parties, labor unions, and charitable organizations that do not have profit-making as a primary objective.

noncumulative discount A quantity discount based on the size of an individual order of one or more products.

nonprice competition A strategy in which a seller maintains stable prices and attempts to improve its market position by emphasizing other (nonprice) aspects of its marketing program.

nonprofit organizations Those groups that provide services but do not have a profit or surplus objective.

nonstore retailing Retailing activities resulting in transactions that occur away from a retail store.

North American Free Trade Agreement (NAFTA) An agreement among the United States, Canada, and Mexico to eliminate tariffs between the countries.

North American Industry Classification System (NAICS) Coding system similar to the SIC, but has 20 rather than 10 industry sectors, to provide a more detailed and contemporary classification scheme.

not-for-profit services organizations (N-F-P) Those groups that have a profit goal because growth and existence depend on generating revenue in excess of costs.

nutrition labeling The part of a product that provides information about the amount of calories, fat, cholesterol, sodium, carbohydrates, and protein contained in the package's contents.

O

objective A desired outcome. Same as *goal.*

observation method A method of gathering primary data by observing the actions of a person without direct interaction.

odd pricing A psychological pricing strategy that consists of setting prices at uneven (or odd) amounts, such as $4.99, rather than at even amounts, such as $5, in the belief that these seemingly lower prices will result in larger sales volume.

off-price retailer A type of retail institution, often found in the areas of apparel and shoes, that has a narrow and deep product assortment, low prices, and few customer services.

oligopoly A market structure dominated by a few firms, each marketing similar products.

one-price strategy A pricing strategy under which a seller charges the same price to all similar customers who buy identical quantities of a product.

one-stop shipping A transportation firm offers multiple modes of transportation of goods to its customers.

online category manager A distributor that handles e-commerce fulfillment in a particular product area for manufacturers and conventional retailers.

online retailing Electronic transactions made over the Internet in which the purchaser is the ultimate consumer.

operating supplies The "convenience" category of business goods, consisting of tangible products that are characterized by low dollar value per unit and a short life and that aid in an organization's operations without becoming part of the finished product.

organizational strategies Broad plans of action by which an organization intends to achieve its goals and fulfill its mission. These plans are for (1) the total organization in a small, single-product company or (2) each SBU in a large, multiproduct or multibusiness organization.

outside selling The kind of personal selling group in which sales people go to the customers, making contact by mail, telephone, or face-to-face.

P

package-delivery firms Companies that specialize in the delivery of small packages and high-priority mail.

packaging All the activities of designing and producing the container or wrapper for a product.

past sales analysis A method of sales forecasting that applies a flat percentage increase to the volume achieved last year or to the average volume of the past few years.

patronage buying motives The reasons why a consumer chooses to shop at a particular store.

perception The process carried out by an individual to receive, organize, and assign meaning to stimuli detected by the five senses.

perceptual map A visual representation of positioning that locates a brand or organization relative to alternatives.

perfect competition A market structure in which product differentiation is absent, buyers and sellers are well informed, and the seller has no discernible control over the selling price.

perishability A characteristic of a service indicating that it is highly transitory and cannot be stored.

personal interview See *face-to-face interview.*

personal selling The personal communication of information to persuade somebody to buy something. Alternatively, the direct (face-to-face or over-the-phone) presentation of a product to a prospective customer by a representative of the organization selling it.

personal selling process The logical sequence of prospecting, preapproach, presenting, and postsale services that a salesperson takes in dealing with a prospective buyer.

personality An individual's pattern of traits that influences behavioral responses.

physical distribution All the activities involved in the flow of products as they move physically from producer to consumer or industrial user. Same as *logistics.*

physical distribution management The development and operation of processes resulting in the effective and efficient physical flow of products.

physical facilities The building—including its location, size, design, and layout—that serves as a store for a retail firm.

piggyback service See *intermodal transportation.*

pioneering stage See *introduction stage.*

planned obsolescence   A strategy that is intended to make an existing product out of date and thus to increase the market for replacement products. There are two forms: technological and style.

planning   The process of deciding now what to do later, including when and how to do it.

political and legal forces   A set of factors, including monetary and fiscal policies, legislation, and regulations, that affect the marketing activities of an organization.

portal   An entrance and guide to the World Wide Web.

position   The way a product, brand, or organization is viewed in relation to the competition by current and prospective customers.

positioning   A product's image in relation to directly competitive products as well as other products marketed by the same company. Alternatively, a firm's strategies and actions related to favorably distinguishing itself from competitors in the minds of selected groups of consumers. Same as *product positioning.*

postage stamp pricing   See *uniform delivered pricing.*

postpurchase cognitive dissonance   The anxiety created by the fact that in most purchases the alternative selected has some negative features and the alternatives not selected have some positive features.

postsale service   Maintenance and repairs as well as other services that are provided to customers in order to fulfill the terms of a firm's warranty and/or to augment the firm's revenues.

predatory pricing   Driving competitors out of the marketplace by giving away products or charging a far-below-the-market price.

price   The amount of money and/or other items with utility needed to acquire a product.

price competition   A strategy in which a firm regularly offers products priced as low as possible, usually accompanied by few, if any, services.

price customization   Method of establishing prices based on how much different people value a product.

price differential   The difference in prices of an identical brand from one area to another.

price discrimination   A situation in which different customers pay different prices for the same product.

price lining   A pricing strategy whereby a firm selects a limited number of prices at which it will sell related products.

price war   A form of price competition that begins when one firm decreases its price in an effort to increase its sales volume and/or market share, the other firms retaliate by reducing prices on competing products, and additional price decreases by the original price cutter and/or its competitors usually follow.

pricing above competition   One form of market-based pricing in which price is set above the prevailing market level.

pricing below competition   One form of market-based pricing in which price is set below the level of your main competitors.

pricing objective   The desired outcome that management seeks to achieve with its pricing structure and strategies.

pricing to meet competition   A pricing method in which a firm ascertains what the market price is and, after allowing for customary markups for middlemen, arrives at its own selling price.

primary data   New data gathered specifically for the project at hand.

primary-demand advertising   Advertising that is designed to stimulate demand for a generic category of a product.

Printer's Ink statutes   State legislation intended to punish "untrue, deceptive, or misleading" advertising.

private warehouse   A warehouse that is owned and operated by the firm whose products are being stored and handled at the facility.

producer's brand   A brand that is owned by a manufacturer or other producer.

product   A set of tangible and intangible attributes, which may include packaging, color, price, quality, and brand, plus the seller's services and reputation. A product may be a good, service, place, person, or idea.

product abandonment   A decision and subsequent action by a firm to drop a product that has insufficient and/or declining sales and lacks profits.

product advertising   Advertising that focuses on a particular product or brand.

product alteration   A strategy of improving an existing product.

product and trade name franchising   A distribution agreement under which a supplier (the franchiser) authorizes a dealer (the franchisee) to sell a product line, using the parent company's trade name for promotional purposes.

product color   The hue(s) given to a particular product, including its packaging.

product counterfeiting   The unscrupulous placement of a brand name on a product without the legal right to do so.

product design   The arrangement of elements that collectively form a good or service.

product differentiation   A strategy in which a firm uses promotion to distinguish its product from competitive brands offered to the same aggregate market.

product liability   A legal action alleging that an illness, accident, or death resulted from the named product because it was harmful, faulty, or inadequately labeled.

product life cycle   The aggregate demand over an extended period of time for all brands comprising a generic product category.

product line   A broad group of products intended for essentially similar uses and having similar physical characteristics.

product manager   An organizational structure for product planning and development that makes one person responsible for planning new products as well as managing established products. Same as *brand manager.*

product-market growth matrix   A planning model that consists of four alternative growth strategies based on whether an organization will be selling its present products or new products to its present markets or new markets.

product mix   The set of all products offered for sale by a company.

product-mix contraction   A strategy in which a firm either eliminates an entire line or simplifies the assortment within a line.

product-mix expansion   A strategy in which a firm increases the depth within a particular line and/or the number of lines it offers to consumers.

product orientation   The first stage in the evolution of marketing management, in which the basic assumption is that making a good product will ensure business success.

product-planning committee   An organizational structure for product planning and development that involves a joint effort among executives from major departments and, especially in small firms, the president and/or another top-level executive.

product positioning   See *positioning.*

product quality   See *quality.*

product specialization   One method of organizing selling activities so that each sales person is assigned one or more product lines to sell.

promotion The element in an organization's marketing mix that serves to inform, persuade, and remind the market of a product and/or the organization selling it in the hope of influencing the recipients' feelings, beliefs, or behavior.

promotion mix The combination of personal selling, advertising, sales promotion, and public relations that is intended to help an organization achieve its marketing objectives.

promotional allowance A price reduction granted by a seller as payment for promotional services performed by buyers.

promotional budgeting methods The means used to determine the amount of dollars allocated to promotion in general and/or to specific forms of promotion.

provider market Individuals and/or organizations that contribute money, labor, or materials to a nonprofit organization.

psychoanalytic theory Freudian theory that argues people have subconscious drives that cannot be satisfied in socially acceptable ways.

psychographic segmentation Subdividing markets into groups based on personality dimensions, life-style characteristics, and values.

psychological obsolescence See *style obsolescence*.

public relations Communications efforts that are designed to favorably influence attitudes toward an organization, its products, and its policies.

public warehouse An independent firm that provides storage and handling facilities for individuals or companies for a fee.

publicity A special form of public relations that involves any communication about an organization, its products, or its policies through the media that is not paid for by the sponsoring organization.

pull strategy Promotional effort directed primarily at end users so they will ask middlemen for the product.

push strategy Promotional efforts directed primarily at middlemen that are the next link forward in the distribution channel for a product.

Q

qualitative evaluation bases In sales-force evaluation, subjective criteria for appraising the performance of sales people.

quality The degree to which a product meets the expectations of the customer. Same as *product quality*.

quantitative evaluation bases In sales-force evaluation, specific, objective criteria for appraising the performance of sales people.

quantity discount A deduction from a seller's list price that is offered to a buyer when a large quantity of the product is purchased.

R

Radio Frequency Identification (RFID) An alternative to barcoding that involves placing a tag in or on an object that emits a signal that can be read and interpreted by a receiver.

raw materials Business goods that become part of another tangible product prior to being processed in any way.

rebate A discount on a product that a customer obtains by submitting a form or certificate provided by the seller.

recipient market See *client market*.

reference group A group of people who influence a person's attitudes, values, and behavior.

refusal to deal A situation in which a producer that desires to select and perhaps control its channels declines to sell to some middlemen.

regional strategy A strategy used to market a product to different regions by recognizing distinctions in climate, custom, or taste.

relationship marketing See *customer relationship management (CRM)*.

relationship selling An attempt by a sales person or organization to develop a deeper, longer-lasting relationship built on trust with key customers—usually larger accounts.

repositioning Reestablishing a product's attractiveness in the target market.

resale price maintenance A pricing policy whereby a manufacturer seeks to control the prices at which middlemen resell their products.

research objective Specification of what the research is intended to accomplish.

reseller market One segment of the business market, consisting of wholesaling and retailing middlemen, that buys products for resale to other organizations or to consumers.

retail scanners The electronic devices at retail checkouts that read the bar code on each item.

retail trade See *retailing*.

retailer A firm engaged primarily in retailing.

retailer cooperative A type of contractual vertical marketing system that is formed by a group of small retailers who agree to establish and operate a wholesale warehouse.

retailing The sale, and all activities directly related to the sale, of goods and services to ultimate consumers for personal, nonbusiness use. Same as *retail trade*.

return on marketing investment A way for firms to measure profit gain from marketing expenditures.

Robinson-Patman Act A federal law passed in 1936 that was intended to curb price discrimination by large retailers and the granting by manufacturers of proportionally unequal promotional allowances to large retailers or wholesalers.

S

sales-force automation (SFA) Strategy of equipping sales people with laptop computers, cellular phones, fax machines, and pagers to give them access to databases, the Internet, and e-mail to help them manage accounts more effectively.

sales-force composite A method of forecasting sales that consists of collecting from all sales people estimates of sales for their territories during the future period of interest.

sales forecast An estimate of probable sales for one company's brand of a product during a stated time period in a specific market and assuming the use of a predetermined marketing plan.

sales orientation The second stage in the evolution of marketing management, in which the emphasis is on using various promotional activities to sell whatever the organization produces.

sales potential The portion of market potential that a specific company could expect to achieve under ideal conditions.

sales promotion Demand-stimulating devices designed to supplement advertising and facilitate personal selling.

sales team See *selling center*.

sales volume analysis A detailed study of the net sales section of a company's profit and loss statement.

scrambled merchandising The main source of horizontal channel conflict, a strategy under which a middleman diversifies by adding product lines not traditionally carried by its type of business.

seasonal discount A deduction from the list price that is offered to a customer for placing an order during the seller's slack season.

secondary data Available data, already gathered for some other purpose.

selective-demand advertising Advertising that is intended to stimulate demand for individual brands.

selective distribution A strategy in which a producer sells its product through multiple, but not all possible, wholesalers and retailers in a market where a consumer might reasonably look for it.

selective perception The process of screening all the marketing stimuli to which an individual is exposed on a daily basis.

self-concept The way a person sees himself/herself. Same as *self-image*.

self-image See *self-concept*.

selling agent An agent wholesaling middleman that essentially takes the place of a manufacturer's marketing department by marketing the manufacturer's entire output.

selling center A group of people representing a sales department as well as other functional areas in a firm (such as finance, production, and research and development) that work cooperatively to achieve a sale. Sometimes called a *sales team* or *team selling*.

separable expenses See *direct costs*.

services Identifiable, intangible activities that are the main object of a transaction designed to provide want-satisfaction to customers.

service encounter In services marketing, a customer's interaction with any service employee or with any tangible element, such as a service's physical surroundings.

service quality The degree to which an intangible offering meets the expectations of the customer.

shopping center A planned grouping of retail stores that lease space in a structure that is typically owned by a single organization and that can accommodate multiple tenants.

shopping goods A category of tangible consumer products that are purchased after the buyer has spent some time and effort comparing the price, quality, perhaps style, and/or other attributes of alternative products in several stores.

single-price strategy An extreme variation of a one-price strategy in which all items sold by a firm carry a single price.

single-segment strategy A plan of action that involves selecting one homogeneous segment from within a total market to be the firm's target market. Same as *concentration strategy*.

single-source data A data-gathering method in which exposure to television advertising and product purchases can be traced to individual households.

situation analysis The act of gathering and studying information pertaining to one or more specified aspects of an organization. Alternatively, a background investigation that helps in refining a research problem.

situational influence A temporary force associated with the immediate purchase environment that affects behavior.

slotting fee A fee that some retailers charge a manufacturer in order to place its product on store shelves. Same as *slotting allowance*.

small-order problem A situation confronting many firms, in which revenue from an order is less than allocated expenses because several costs, such as billing and direct selling, are essentially the same regardless of order size.

social and cultural forces A set of factors, including lifestyles, social values, and beliefs, that affect the marketing activities of an organization.

social class A division of, or ranking within, society based on education, occupation, and type of residential neighborhood.

social information environment As contrasted with the commercial information environment, all communications among family members, friends, and acquaintances about products.

societal marketing concept A revised version of the marketing concept under which a company recognizes that it should be concerned about not only the buyers of its products but also other people directly affected by its operations and with not only tomorrow but also the long term.

spam Electronic junk mail.

specialty goods A category of tangible consumer products for which consumers have a strong brand preference and are willing to expend substantial time and effort in locating and then buying the desired brand.

specialty store A type of retail institution that has a very narrow and deep product assortment (often concentrating on a specialized product line or even part of a specialized product line), that usually strives to maintain manufacturers' suggested prices and that typically provides at least standard customer services.

stages in the adoption process The six steps a prospective buyer goes through in deciding whether to purchase something new.

standards and certification A requirement that a product contain or exclude certain ingredients or that it be tested and certified as meeting certain restrictive standards.

stimulus-response theory The theory that learning occurs as a person (1) responds to some stimuli and (2) is rewarded with need satisfaction for a correct response or penalized for an incorrect one.

straight rebuy In the business market, a routine, low-involvement purchase with minimal information needs and no great consideration of alternatives.

strategic alliance A formal, long-term agreement between firms to combine their capabilities and resources to accomplish global objectives.

strategic business unit (SBU) A separate division for a major product or market in a multiproduct or multibusiness organization.

strategic company planning The level of planning that consists of (1) defining the organization's mission, (2) analyzing the situation, (3) setting organizational objectives, and (4) selecting appropriate strategies to achieve these objectives.

strategic marketing planning The level of planning that consists of (1) conducting a situation analysis, (2) developing marketing objectives, (3) determining positioning and differential advantage, (4) selecting target markets and measuring market demand, and (5) designing a strategic marketing mix.

strategic planning The managerial process of matching a firm's resources with its market opportunities over the long run.

strategic window The limited amount of time in which a firm's resources coincide with a particular market opportunity.

strategy A broad plan of action by which an organization intends to reach its objectives.

style A distinctive manner of presentation or construction in any art, product, or endeavor.

style obsolescence A form of planned obsolescence in which superficial characteristics of a product are altered so that the new model is easily differentiated from the previous model and people become dissatisfied with it.

Same as *fashion obsolescence* and *psychological obsolescence*.

subculture Groups in a culture that exhibit characteristic behavior patterns sufficient to distinguish them from other groups within the same culture.

suggested list price A pricing policy whereby a manufacturer recommends to retailers a final (retail) price that should provide them with their normal markups.

supercenter A combination of a discount house and a complete grocery store.

supermarket A type of retail institution that has a moderately broad and moderately deep product assortment spanning groceries and some nonfood lines, that offers relatively few customer services, and that ordinarily emphasizes price in either an offensive or defensive way.

supermarket retailing A retailing method that features several related product lines, a high degree of self-service, largely centralized checkout, and competitive prices.

suppliers The people or firms that supply the goods or services that an organization needs to produce what it sells.

supply chain management The combination of distribution channels and physical distribution to make up the total marketing system.

survey A method of gathering primary data by interviewing people in person, by telephone, by mail, or via the Internet.

survey of buyer intentions A form of sales forecasting in which a firm asks a sample of current or potential customers how much of a particular product they would buy at a given price during a specified future period.

SWOT assessment Identifying and evaluating an organization's most significant strengths, weaknesses, opportunities, and threats.

systems approach to physical distribution The unification of individual physical distribution activities.

systems selling Providing a total package of related goods and services to solve a customer's problem (needs).

T

tactic A specific means by which a strategy is implemented.

target market A group of customers (people or organizations) for whom a seller designs a particular marketing mix.

tariff A tax imposed on a product entering a country.

team selling See *selling center*.

technological obsolescence A form of planned obsolescence in which significant technical improvements result in a more effective product. Same as *functional obsolescence*.

technology Applications of science for industrial and commercial purposes.

telemarketing A form of nonstore retailing in which a sales person initiates contact with a shopper and also closes the sale over the telephone.

Telephone Consumer Protection Act Federal law that requires telemarketers to keep a "do-not-call" list of consumers who request that they not receive telephone solicitations, it restricts the indiscriminant use of automatic telephone dialing systems, and it prohibits marketers from sending advertising to a facsimile machine without first obtaining the recipient's permission.

telephone survey A method of gathering data by interviewing people over the telephone.

test marketing A method of demand forecasting in which a firm markets its new product in a limited geographic area, measures the sales, and then—from this sample—projects the company's sales over a larger area. Alternatively, a marketing research technique that uses this same approach to judge consumers' responses to a strategy before committing to a major marketing effort.

total cost The sum of total fixed cost and total variable cost for a specific quantity produced or sold.

total cost concept In physical distribution, the recognition that the best relationship between costs and profit must be established for the *entire* physical distribution system, rather than for individual activities.

total fixed cost The sum of all fixed costs.

total quality management (TQM) A philosophy as well as specific procedures, policies, and practices that commit an organization to continuous quality improvement in all of its activities.

total variable cost The sum of all variable costs.

trade balance In international business, the difference between the value of a nation's imports and the value of its exports.

trade barriers Created by governments to restrict trade and protect domestic industries, these are the most common legal forces affecting international marketers.

trade (functional) discount A reduction from the list price that is offered by a seller to buyers in payment for marketing functions the buyers will perform. Same as *functional discount*.

trademark A brand that has been adopted by a seller and given legal protection.

trademark infringement Act of manufacturing products with names and packaging similar to well-known goods in order to achieve sales.

Trademark Law Revision Act A federal law, passed in 1988, that broadened the Landham Trademark Act to encompass comparisons made in promotional activity.

trademark licensing A business arrangement in which the owner of a trademark grants permission to other firms to use the owner's brand name, logotype, and/or character on the licensee's products in return for a royalty on sales of those products. Same as *brand licensing*.

trading down A product-line strategy wherein a company adds a lower-priced product to a line to reach a market that cannot afford the higher-priced items or that see them as too expensive.

trading up A product-line strategy wherein a company adds a higher-priced product to a line in order to attract a broader market and, through its added prestige, helps the sale of its existing lower-priced products.

trend analysis A statistical method of forecasting sales over the long term by using regression analysis or over the short term by using a seasonal index of sales.

trickle-across theory In fashion adoption, a fashion cycle that moves horizontally and simultaneously within several socioeconomic levels.

trickle-down theory In fashion adoption, a fashion cycle that flows downward through several socioeconomic levels.

trickle-up theory In fashion adoption, a fashion cycle in which a style first becomes popular with lower socioeconomic levels and then flows upward to become popular among higher levels.

truck distributor See *truck jobber*.

truck jobber A merchant wholesaler that carries a selected line of perishable products and delivers them by truck to retail stores. Same as *truck distributor*.

tying contract The practice by which a manufacturer sells a product to a middleman only under the condition that the middleman also buy another (possibly unwanted) product from the manufacturer.

U

ultimate consumers People who buy goods or services for their own personal or household use in order to satisfy strictly nonbusiness wants.

undifferentiated-market strategy See *market-aggregation strategy.*

unfair-practices acts State laws intended to regulate some forms of leader pricing that are intended to drive other products or companies out of business. Same as *unfair-sales acts.*

unfair-sales acts See *unfair-practices acts.*

uniform delivered pricing A geographic pricing strategy whereby the same delivered price is quoted to all buyers regardless of their locations. Same as *postage stamp pricing.*

universal design The design of products in such a way that they can be easily used by all consumers, including disabled individuals, senior citizens, and others needing special considerations.

unsought goods A category of consumer tangible products that consists of new products the consumer is not yet aware of or products the consumer is aware of but does not want right now.

utility The attribute in an item that makes it capable of satisfying human wants.

V

value The ratio of perceived benefits to price and any other incurred costs.

value added The dollar value of a firm's output minus the value of the inputs it purchased from other firms.

value chain The combination of a company, its suppliers, and intermediaries, performing their own activities, to add value to a product.

value creation Meeting customers' desires through improved information and technology.

value pricing A form of price competition in which a firm seeks to improve the ratio of a product's benefits to its price and related costs.

values Intangible principles that are a reflection of people's needs, adjusted for the realities of the world in which they live.

variable cost A cost that changes directly in relation to the number of units produced or sold.

variable-price strategy See *flexible-price strategy.*

vertical business market A situation where a given product is usable by virtually all the firms in only one or two industries.

vertical conflict A form of channel conflict occurring among firms at different levels of the same channel, typically producer versus wholesaler or producer versus retailer.

vertical marketing system (VMS) A tightly coordinated distribution channel designed to improve operating efficiency and marketing effectiveness.

viral marketing Strategy of spreading positive information about a company from one person to another, often utilized by smaller firms.

voluntary chain A type of contractual vertical marketing system that is sponsored by a wholesaler who enters into a contract with interested retailers.

W

warehouse club A combined retailing and wholesaling institution that has a very broad but very shallow product assortment, very low prices, few customer services, and is open only to members. Same as *wholesale club.*

warning label The part of a product that tells consumers not to misuse the product and informs them of almost every conceivable danger associated with using it.

warranty An assurance given to buyers that they will be compensated in case the product does not perform up to reasonable expectations.

Weblogs Personalized websites that are frequently updated and linked to other sites. Same as *blog.*

website A collection of Web files, beginning with a home page, that is accessible through a unique address.

Wheeler-Lea Amendment A federal law, passed in 1938, that amended the Federal Trade Commission Act by strengthening the prohibition against unfair competition, especially false or misleading advertising.

wholesale club See *warehouse club.*

wholesale trade See *wholesaling.*

wholesaler See *merchant wholesaler.*

wholesaling The sale, and all activities directly related to the sale, of goods and services to businesses and other organizations for resale, use in producing other goods and services, or the operation of an organization.

wholesaling middleman A firm engaged primarily in wholesaling.

wholly owned subsidiary A business arrangement in foreign markets in which a company owns the foreign operation in order to gain maximum control over its marketing program and production operations.

World Trade Organization (WTO) Replaced GATT in 1995 as the governing body of global commerce, consisting of 148 member countries and accounting for 97% of world trade.

World Wide Web Collection of hyperlinked multimedia databases stored all over the world and accessible via the Internet.

Z

zone-delivered pricing A geographic pricing strategy whereby a seller divides its market into a limited number of broad geographic zones and then sets a uniform delivered price for each zone.

Name Index

A

A. C. Nielsen, 96, 469
A. G. Edwards, 466
A&W, 65, 269, 416
A9 (search engine), 78
Aaker, David A., 647
Aamco, 408
ABB Automation, 401
ABB Ltd., 321
Abbott Laboratories, 324
ABC, 310
ABC News, 596
Abell, Derek F., 659, 661
Abercrombie & Fitch, 198
Abramovitch, Ingrid, 659
Accenture consulting, 346
Ace Hardware, 389, 414, 416, 484
Achrol, Ravi S., 661
Ackman, Dan, 662
ACNielsen, 187
ACNielsen's Retail Measurement
    Services, 171
Acohido, Byron, 313, 640
Acosta, 384
Adair, Dennis, 643
Adams Aircraft, 127
Adamy, Janet, 555, 643
adidas America, 53, 56, 66, 326, 397,
    481–483, 486
adidas-Salomon AG, 66
Adler, Eric, 645
Adolf Coors, 15
Adrian, C. Mitchell, 641
Aduroja, Grace, 645
Advantage, 327
Advertising Age, 182, 552, 636
Advertising Slogan Hall of Fame, 489
AdWords, 77, 78
Aeppel, Timothy, 642
Aetna, 381
Affiliates, 473
Agins, Teri, 251, 470, 641, 646, 653,
    660
Ahead, 155
Ahlstrand, Scott, 643
Ahold, 429, 571
Aichlmayr, Mary, 657
Air Berlin, 137
Air National Guard, 31
AirAsia, 370
Airborne Inc., 201
Airbus, 113, 137
AirTran airlines, 79
Alaska Airlines, 262
Albertson's, 3, 151, 175, 379, 411, 422,
    454, 566
Albright, Brian, 657
Albright, Kendra S., 640
Alcoa, 322

Aldi, 3, 338
Aldred, Carolyn, 662
Alexander, Antoinette, 653
Alexander, Deborah, 654
Alexander, Jack, 646
Aley, James, 649
Alias, 543
Alibaba.com, 445
All My Children, 492
Alliance Entertainment, 448
Allied Domecq PLC, 141
Allied Van Lines, 262
Allport, Gordon W., 642
Allstate Corp., 387, 617
Almega Corp., 160
Almquist, Eric, 640
Alpert, Frank, 649
Altria Group, Inc., 569
AM General Corporation, 118, 549–551
AM PM stores, 423
Amana Refrigeration, 246, 441
Amazon.com, 9, 33, 56, 63, 78, 182–183,
    392, 426, 428, 456, 562, 577,
    610–612, 621, 622, 627, 628–629,
    631, 632
Ambler, Tim, 651
America Online, 76, 206, 359, 427,
    619, 630
America West, 317, 370
American Airlines, 85, 214, 270, 299,
    317, 339, 369, 370
American Basketball League (ABL), 235
American Can Company, 135
American Cancer Society, 5, 206, 288
American Community Survey (ACS), 181
American Eagle, 197
American Electric Power, 524
American Express, 33, 145, 290, 299
American FactFinder website, 180
American Girl, 404
American Heart Association, 276, 288
American Idol, 543, 554
American Marketing Association, 18, 182,
    192, 288, 493, 627
American Medical Association, 288
American Red Cross, 296
America's Army, 300
Ameritrade, 573
Amos, Denise Smith, 644
Amos, Wally, 391
Amway, 424, 624
Anaheim Angels, 309
Ancestry.com, 631
Anders, George, 392, 649, 652, 657
Anderson, Diane, 103
Anderson, Eric, 651
Anderson, James C., 653
Angwin, Julia, 649, 650
Anheuser-Busch Companies, 64, 235, 259,
    396–400

Animal Kingdom Lodge, 308
Ann Taylor, 117, 271, 498
Ansoff, H. Igor, 660
Anthes, Gary H., 649
Appel, David, 242
Apple Computer Inc., 26–28, 46, 47,
    133, 206, 220, 240, 246, 278,
    464, 497, 618
Apprentice, The, 492, 543
Arbitron, 183
Arby's, 207
Archer Daniels Midland, 545
Arco, 423
Arena Football, 480
Ariba, 118, 123, 136, 337, 617
Arizona State University, 486
Arkansas Supreme Court, 360
Arkinson, William, 657
Arm & Hammer, 258, 527
Armani, 210
Armitt, Clare, 658
Armor All Products, 268
Armstrong, David, 131
Armstrong, Lance, 288, 543
Armstrong, Larry, 640
Arndorfer, James, Jr., 648
Arndt, Michael, 642
Arnold, Catherine, 103, 477, 647
Arnott, Nancy, 648
Arrow Electronics, 401
Ashley, Susan R., 647
Askt, Daniel, 294
Aston, Adam, 82
AT&T Corp., 15, 328, 503, 508
AT&T Wireless, 638
ATA Airlines, 371
Atari, 311
Athlete's Foot, 414, 416
Athletic Store, 359
Atlas Micro, 592
Attaran, Mohsen, 657
Attour, Suleiman, 642
Au Bon Pain, 262
Auction Drop, 392
Autoliv, 448
AutoNation, 359, 422
Autozone, 355
Avis, 297, 486
Avon Breast Cancer Crusade, 300
Avon Products, 15, 299, 387, 390, 392,
    424, 500, 527, 573, 617

B

Babies "R" Us, 404
babyGap, 196
Bachelor, Beth, 151
Back to the Future, 543
BackRub, 76
Baglole, Joel A., 655, 660

E.T., 543
eToys, 38, 246, 377, 456
ETrade, 562
Eureka, 299
Euro Disney, 309
European Union (EU), 19, 20, 36, 42,
    59–60, 61, 190, 258, 280, 340, 383,
    590, 629, 630
Evans, Bob, 661
Evans, Joel R., 645
Evans, Kenneth R., 650
Eveready, 529
Everett, Martin, 652
Evian, 156
Ewing, Jack, 348
Excite, 619
Executive Gateway to the Internet, 182
Exline Inc., 570
Expedia, 317, 343
Express, 117
ExxonMobil, 120, 260, 322, 545

F

Fahey, Jonathan, 178
Fahrenwald, Bill, 656
Fahy, John, 660
Fairchild Semiconductor, 311, 450
Faircloth, Anne, 650
Fairfield Inns, 240
Fairlamb, David, 340
Fairmont chains, 340
Family Dollar Stores, 347, 349, 361, 420
Famous-Barr, 267, 419
Fannie Mae, 15
Fanning, Shawn, 27, 46
Fantastic Sams, 416
FAO Schwarz, 404
Farhi, Stephane, 653
Farnham, Alan, 644
Farnsworth, Clyde H., 647
Farquhar, Peter H., 647
Farrell, Christopher, 649
FastShip Inc., 457
Fatsis, Stefan, 82
Fazoli's, 576, 635
Federal Communications Commission
    (FCC), 79, 80, 491, 538
Federal Deposit Insurance Corporation
    (FDIC), 492
Federal Express (FedEx), 10, 22, 38, 54,
    199–202, 289, 303, 357, 450, 457,
    460, 461, 543, 589, 619
Federal Trade Commission (FTC), 135,
    182, 191, 196, 276, 356, 364, 399,
    425, 490–491, 492, 525
Federated Department Stores, 402,
    419, 564
Feldstein, Mary Jo, 653
Fendi, 340
Ferdows, Kasra, 661, 663
Ferguson, Stacey, 535
Fernandes, Nirmala, 640
Ferrari, 155, 340

Fiat, 66
Field, Anne, 654
Fielding, Michael, 643
50 Cent, 80
FindMRO.com, 462
Finn, Bridget, 663
Firestone, 389, 591
First Data, 160
Fisher, Anne, 643
Fisher, Donald, 196
Fisher, Robert J., 653
Fisher-Price, 88
Fishman-Lapin, Julie, 656
Fisk, Margaret Cronin, 662
Fitzgerald, Kate, 586
Flammang, Jim, 555
Flannery, William, 662
Flexcar, 305
Flint, Jerry, 238
Flint, Joe, 313
Flint, Perry, 374
Flores, Andrea Isabel, 392
Flores, Chris, 566
Florsheim, 258
Fluke Manufacturing, 248
Fogdog Sports, 426
Foley's, 419
Folpe, Jane M., 661, 663
Fonseca, Brian, 659
Food and Drug Administration (FDA),
    129, 276, 491
Food Marketing Institute, 180, 238
Ford Motor Company, 68, 79, 96, 99,
    104, 120, 135, 215, 222, 228, 236,
    257, 270, 299, 388, 389, 449, 523,
    525, 534, 591, 617, 623
Forelle, Charles, 646, 650, 661
Forest, Stephanie Anderson, 660
Formica Corporation, 264
Formula One, 483
Foroohar, Rana, 642
Forrester Research, 183, 477
Forster, Julie, 639
Fortune, 200, 369, 373, 435, 466, 518
Foss, Brad, 374
Four Seasons Hotels, 351
Foust, Dean, 202, 555, 658
Fowler, Bree, 648
Fowler, Geoffrey A., 263, 538, 641, 650
Fram, 527
France, Mike, 650
Franco, Mark Del, 659
Frankel, Alex, 646
Frazier, Gary L., 652
Frederick, James, 653, 656
Fred's Friendly Hardware, 395
Freeman, Adam L., 649
FreeMarkets, 123, 136
Freeplay Energy, 630
Freightliner, 136, 145
French, Thomas D., 657
FreshDirect, 38
Freud, Sigmund, 104
Friday's restaurants, 147

Friedman, Michael, 651
Friedman, Wayne, 531
Friends, 473
Frito-Lay International, 12, 220, 221,
    553, 554
Frontier, 85, 109, 235
Frontline, 327
Froogle, 78, 427
Fuji Photo Film, 57, 233, 332, 477
Fuld & Co., 182
Fulford, Benjamin, 127, 313, 641
Fuller, Peter, 595
Furniture Medic, 416
Furniture.com, 426
Fuscaldo, Donna, 655
Futon Factory, 333–334

G

Gagnier, Monica, 661
Galea, Christine, 659
Gall, Charles V., 655
Gallagher, John, 658
Gallagher, Leigh, 641
Gallup Poll, 182
Ganesan, Vasantha, 571
Gap Inc., 117, 158, 196–198, 350, 608
GapBody, 198
GapKids, 196
Garden.com, 246
Gardner, John T., 653
Gardyn, Rebecca, 642
Garland, Susan B., 651
Garrison, Bob, 661
Gartner Inc., 429
Gaski, John F., 646
Gates, Bill, 49
Gateway, 258, 373
Gellman, Gila E., 263
General Electric, 123, 125, 126, 209, 268,
    270, 388, 453, 552, 575, 593
General Foods, 216, 227
General Mills, 12, 37, 239, 525, 552, 621
General Motors Corp., 66, 79, 104, 118,
    153, 155, 215, 218, 228, 235, 236,
    256–257, 266, 270, 279, 281, 359,
    383, 388, 449, 542, 549, 550, 551,
    574, 586, 619, 623
General Services Administration, 118
Gentile, Gary, 662
Gentry, Connie Robbins, 573
Georgia-Pacific, 205
Gerber, 42
Gerwin, Donald, 661
Get Fit Foods, 486
Giannulli, Mossimo, 464, 465
Giant, 429
Gibson, Richard, 647, 654, 660
Gilbert, Alorie, 657
Gilbert, Jennifer, 507
Gilbert, Virginia Brown, 654
Gillette Company, 39, 67, 72, 174,
    239, 241–242, 260, 265, 267, 347,
    535, 574

Gilly, Mary C., 662
Gimbel, Barney, 374
Ginsburg, Janet, 660
Giorgio Armani, 240
Glanton, Dahleen, 650
Glaser, Rob, 27
GlaxoSmithKline, 477
Global Exchange Services, 452
GlobalNetXchange (GNX), 445
GMail, 77, 78
GNC, 418
Goerne, Carrie, 646
Goetzl, David, 531
Goff, Clare, 477
Gogoi, Pallavi, 639, 643
Goizueta, Robert, 553
Gold, Russell, 651
Gold, Stanley, 310
Goldberg, Steven T., 640
Goldenberg, Barton, 663
Golder, Peter N., 645
Goldman, Abigail, 651, 663
Goldstein, Lauren, 646
Goldstein, Michael, 645
Golf Magazine, 341
Gomes, Lee, 645, 661
Goo, Sara Kehanlani, 642
Good Housekeeping, 493
Good Technology, 639
Goodfellows, 464
Goodwill Industries, 299
Goodyear, 205, 221, 347, 382, 386, 388,
    389, 398, 477
Google Catalog Search, 78
Google Inc., 76–78, 261, 265, 427,
    534, 619
Google News Headlines, 77
Google PhoneBook, 77
Google Toolbar(tm), 77
Googleplex, 76
Gordon, Benjamin, 657
Gordon, Geoffrey L., 645
Gorland, Robert, 655
Gossage, Bobbi, 642
Grabowsky, Lou, 653
Grace Performance Chemicals, 205
Grace Performance Systems, 229
Graco Children's Products, 591
Grainger.com, 462
Grant, Lorrie, 662
Grant, Peter, 649
Graves, Michael, 464
Gray, Steven, 639, 654, 659
Graybar Electric, 397
Great Britain, 71
Great Midwest Company, 598–604
Great Wall Computer, 64
Green, Hardy, 646, 653
Green, Heather, 82, 454, 649, 663
Green, Jeff, 642, 647
Green Giant, 258
Greenberg, Julee, 660
Greene, Jay, 313
Greenpeace, 42
Gregory, Stephen, 222
Gresham, Alicia B., 657

Grewal, Dhruv, 648, 662
Grimes, Ann, 10, 630, 655, 663
Grimes, Brad, 648
Grimm, Matthew, 149
Gross, Bill, 78
Gross, Neil, 645, 649
Grossman, Lev, 313, 648
Group Danone, 571
Grover, Ronald, 313
Grow, Brian, 555, 642
GSI Commerce, 448
Gubernick, Lisa, 365
Gubor, 67
Gucci, 53, 264, 340
Gucci Group, 260
Guiness, 64
Gully, Jennifer E., 653
Gundlach, Gregory T., 399
Gurley, J. William, 374
Gussow, Dave, 645
Guth, Robert A., 314, 644
Gymboree, 198

H

H. J. Heinz, 215
H&M, 608
H&R Block, 417
Häagen-Dazs, 220, 271, 393
Habitat for Humanity, 14, 545
Haddad, Charles, 658
Hagenbaugh, Barbara, 365
Hagerty, James R., 641, 645
Hain Celestial Group, Inc., The, 143
Hajewski, Doris, 654
Hakim, Danny, 555
Haley, Fiona, 641, 642
Haliday, Jean, 659
Halkias, Maria, 654, 660
Hall, Jeff, 643
Hall, Nick, 640
Hallmark, 149, 516
Hamel, Gary, 645
Hamilton Beach/Proctor-Silex Inc., 591
Hamilton, David P., 337
Hamilton, Jennifer, 662
Hamilton, Sonya S., 640
Hamm, Steve, 313, 649
Hammer, Michael, 660
Hammer, Susanna, 299
Hammond, John S., 661
Hampton Inn, 159
Handleman Company, 621
Hank's, 491
Hansen, Richard W., 662
Hardee's, 635
Hardin, James W., 653
Harley-Davidson, 11, 156, 158, 271
Harley Owners Group (HOG), 11
Harper, Earl, 640
HarperCollins Publisher, 401
Harrah's Entertainment, 176
Harris, Greg, 642
Harris, Nicole, 642, 650
Harris poll, 269
Harry and David, 592

Hart, Christopher W., 640
Hartman luggage, 388
Hartz, 327
Hasbro Inc., 377
Hassard, J. S., 661
Hastings, Reed, 473
Havercamp, Susan M., 642
Hawaii Visitors Bureau, 206
Hawkins, Lee, Jr., 555
Hayes, Denise, 660
HD Radio, 81
Head and Shoulders shampoo, 157–158
Healey, James, 555
Healon, Carla, 640
Hear Music Coffee Houses, 578–579
Heavenly Ham, 416
Hedgpeth, Dana, 392
Hein, Kenneth, 313, 555, 639, 643, 658
Heineken, 455
Heinz, 42, 215, 270
Heisler, Eric, 654, 657
Helen's Arts and Craft, 574
Helft, Miguel, 661, 663
Heller, Laura, 470, 655
Helyar, John, 82, 470
Hemerling, Jim, 483
Hemlock, Doreen, 593
Henderson, David R., 651
Henkoff, Ronald, 648, 657
Henredon, 114
Herman Miller, 15
Hershey Foods Corporation, 67, 128,
    129, 220, 237, 269, 270
Hertz Car Rental, 79, 296, 297
Hewlett-Packard Co., 9, 15, 53, 233,
    240, 253, 270, 323, 372, 373, 374,
    497, 576
Hiebing, Roman G., Jr., 660
Higgins, John M., 531
Higgins, Michelle, 555
Hillblom, Larry, 200
Hillerich, 118
Hilton, 342
Himelstein, Linda, 38
Himmelfarb, Philip, 644
Hinnant, Lori, 324
Hirshfield, Stuart, 651
Hise, Richard T., 647
Ho, Rodney, 646, 660
Hoch, Stephen J., 647, 649, 651
Hodges, Jane, 657
Hof, Robert D., 337, 657, 663
Hoffman, William, 657, 663
Hofman, Mike, 642
Holden, Reed K., 650
Holiday Inn, 159, 235, 240, 268, 388
Hollmer, Mark, 643
Holmes, Stanley, 470, 643, 659, 661
Home Depot, 156, 190, 240, 391, 395,
    411, 413, 414, 422, 492
Home Instead, 418
Home Shopping Network, 428
Homes, Stanley, 643
Homestead House, 508
Honda Motor Company, 12, 32, 35, 67,
    79, 127, 178, 235, 270, 324, 498, 586

Hong Kong Disneyland, 309
Hong Kong Economic Times, 309
Honnomichl, Jack, 643
Hopi Nation, 410
Hopkins, Jim, 652
Hopper, Laura J., 652
Horovitz, Bruce, 595, 639, 643
Horowitz, Jed, 573
House Doctors Handyman Service, 418
Hout, Thomas, 483
Howe, Jeff, 663
Howe, Rob, 663
Howell, Debbie, 470, 653, 657
Hrisak, Daniel M., 662
Huang, Patricia, 127
Huck International, 121
Hudson's, 419
Huff, Roger, 657
Huli tribe (of New Guinea), 51
Humana, 303
Hummer, 118, 549–551
Humphreys, Jeffrey M., 641
Hunt-Wesson, 237
Hutt, Michael D., 652
Hwang, Suein L., 646
Hyatt Hotels, 342, 505
Hyatt, Joshua, 654
Hyman, Mark, 650
Hymowitz, Carol, 151, 643, 644
Hyundai, 58, 65, 79, 590–591, 592

I

IBM, 15, 52, 64, 120, 122, 123, 135, 265,
  270, 277, 312, 313, 372, 373, 454,
  486, 497, 500, 504, 516, 552
iBOT Mobility System, 41
IBP Inc., 566
Idea Central, 205, 229
Idea Central Global, 205
Idea Chain, 229
Idealab, 78
Idus-Howard Inc., 559
IGA, 388, 398, 416
Iger, Robert, 310
Iglesias, Enrique, 99
Ihlwan, Moon, 648, 662
IKEA, 48–50, 74, 422, 429
Imaginatik, 205–206, 229
Inditex Group, 583, 607
Information Resources, Inc. (IRI), 172, 177
Inside Radio, 79
Intel Corp., 15, 134, 235, 242, 270, 347,
  373, 586
Intelligent Quisine, 39
Interactive Advertising Bureau (IAB), 627
Interbrand-*BusinessWeek*, 269
InterContinental Hotels Group, 235,
  268, 342
International Association of Amusement
  Parks and Attractions, 124
International Council of Shopping
  Centers, 413
International Franchise Association, 416
International Mineral and Chemical
  Company, 116

Internet Explorer, 618
InTown Suites, 321
Intuit software company, 595
INVISTA, 265
Isaac Mizrahi, 524
Isdell, E. Neville, 553
iSoldIt, 392
iTunes Music Store, 27–28, 46–47
iVillage, 625
Izmirileva, Milena, 652
Izod, 239
iZone, 573

J

J. B. Hunt Transport, 459
J. C. Penney Corp., 58, 259, 267, 299,
  361, 391, 419, 454, 465, 500, 572,
  621
J. Crew, 429
J. D. Power, 257
J. Jill Group, 583
J. L. Hudson Company, 464
J. M. Smucker Co., 239
J. P. Morgan Chase, 293
Jackson, Donald M., 443, 656
Jackson, Jerry W., 660
Jackson, Kathy, 555
Jackson, Tony, 640
Jacob, Rahul, 649
Jacobs, Cherie, 650
Jacobs, Karen, 656
Jaffee, Michelle Koidin, 32
Jager, Durk, 644
Jaguar, 215, 257
Jakobson, Leo, 650
James, Dana, 646, 661
James, LeBron, 100, 521
Janeville, 198
Janoff, Barry, 659
Japan Center for Information and Cultural
  Affairs, 190
Japsen, Bruce, 324
Jarvis, Rebecca, 629
Jassawalla, Avan R., 661
Jayasankaran, S., 374
Jell-O, 237
Jenkins, Holman W., Jr., 646, 653
Jennings, Richard G., 642
JetBlue Airways, 79, 85, 109, 235, 278,
  296, 327, 370, 371
Jewell, Mark, 649
Jiffy Lube, 303
Joachimsthaler, Erich, 647
Jobs, Steve, 27–28, 310
John, Deborah Roedder, 647
John Deere, 116, 500
Johnsen, Michael, 656
Johnson, Avery, 649
Johnson, Eric, 641
Johnson, Michael D., 640
Johnson, Richard, 641
Johnson, Ross, 648
Johnson, Sheree L., 643
Johnson, Walter E., 156
Johnson & Johnson, 37, 41, 129, 237, 268

Johnson Controls, 266
Johnston, Mark W., 658
Jones, Quincy, 81
Jordan, Miriam, 639, 641
Joseph, W. Benoy, 653
Joyce, Kathleen M., 659
Joyce, Mary L., 649
Juan Valdez cafés, 557
Jumbo Sports, 422
Jung, Helen, 660
Juniper Networks, 577
JVC, 210

K

Kahn, Gabriel, 652
Kaikati, Andrew M., 96
Kaikati, Jack G., 96
Kaiser Permanente, 303
Kakakota, Ravi, 663
Kale, Clayton, 653
Kaltenheuser, Skip, 567
Kamen, Dean, 41
Kamm, Thomas, 646
Kamprad, Ingvar, 49
Kandra, Anne, 303
Kanter, James, 20
Karan, Donna, 240
Kardes, Frank R., 649
Karmazin, Mel, 80
Karpinski, Richard, 657
Kaufmann, Patrick J., 651
Kaydo, Chad, 655
Kaytes, Dave, 12
Kazaa, 46
KB Toys, 377, 404, 410
Keaten, Jamey, 313
Keebler, 266
Keedy, Jennifer, 663
Keefe, Lisa M., 640
Keeling, Kathy A., 651
Keenan, Faith, 645, 656, 663
Keeton, Ann, 657
Keighley, Geoff, 313, 645
Keith, Robert J., 640
Kelkoo, 427
Kellaris, James J., 649
Kelleher, Herb, 49, 369, 370
Kelleher, Kevin, 202, 653, 658
Keller, Kevin Lane, 640
Kellner, Tomas, 535
Kellogg Company, 23, 144,
  208, 220, 236, 268, 270, 391, 529,
  617
Kelly, Gary, 370, 371
Kelly, Katy, 642
Kemp, Ted, 337
Kenderine, James M., 656
KFC, 62, 64, 65, 68, 269, 489
Kharif, Olga, 127, 192
Khermouch, Gerry, 454, 470, 642,
  647, 656
Kia, 236
Kids "R" Us, 377
Kiley, David, 614, 643, 647
Kilman, Scott, 566, 651

Malcolm Baldrige National Quality
Award, 302
Malden Mills, 226
Mall of America, 413
Manchester United, 521
Mandese, Joe, 531, 535
Maney, Kevin, 645
Mangalindan, Mylene, 38, 294, 313, 655,
658, 663
Mango, 571
March of Dimes, 295
Marchetti, Michele, 658
Marcus, Bernie, 190
Marcus, Stanley, 409
Maremont, Mark, 645
Margonelli, Lisa, 648
Maritz, 617
Market Facts, Inc., 172
Marketing Tracks, 182
Marlboro, 270, 278
Marr, Merissa, 313, 639, 660
Marriott Corp., 22, 240, 258, 271, 289,
292, 321, 342, 524
Mars Inc., 220
Marshall, Greg W., 658
Marshall amplifiers, 384
Marshall Field's, 382, 411, 419, 464
Martha Stewart Living (MSL)
Omnimedia, 80
Martin, James H., 657
Martin, Justin, 273
Martin's, 491
Mary Kay, 424
Maryvale Hardware, 395
Maslow, Abraham, 100–101, 642
MasterCard, 33
Masterfoods USA, 102
Mateschitz, 483
Mathews, Anna Wilde, 658
Mathews, Robert Guy, 544
Matlack, Carol, 313, 642, 643, 652
Mattel Inc., 377, 623, 624
Matthews, Robert Guy, 641
Matthews, Ryan, 655
Mauborgne, Renee, 190
May Department Stores, 402, 419, 464
Maynard, Roberta, 644, 649
Mayo Clinic, 114
Maytag Corporation, 128, 265, 562
McAfee, Andrew, 663
McBride, Sarah, 82, 645
McCabe, Casey, 646
McCarthy, Michael, 82, 313, 555, 655
McCartney, Scott, 374, 645, 648, 650, 662
McDaniel, Steve, 657
McDonald, Malcom H. B., 660
McDonald, Natalie Hope, 657
McDonald's, 19, 49, 53, 64, 68, 72, 120,
161, 166, 186, 215, 220, 262, 270,
271, 298, 304, 416, 525, 529, 535,
543, 557, 576, 634–636
McDonnell Douglas, 113
McDougal, Steve, 645
McGinn, Daniel, 643, 649
McGoldrick, Peter J., 651

McGraw-Hill, 9, 569
McGregor, Jena, 640, 648
MCI, 525
McIlvaine, Bill, 656
McKay, Betsy, 555, 647
McKinney, Joseph A., 641
McKinsey, 321, 575
McLaughlin, Katy, 566, 655
McLean, Bethany, 640
McMillan, Norman H., 660
McMurray, Scott, 656
McNair, M.P., 655
McNeal, James U., 647
McNealy, Scott, 629
McNeil Specialty Products, 129
McQuivey, James, 183
McShane, Margot, 198
McWilliams, Gary, 374, 470, 643, 654
Means, Dennis W., 662
Mecca-Cola, 552
Medical Center Pharmacy, 570–571
Meer, David, 649
Melcer, Rachel, 454, 653
Mele, Jim, 447
Melilo, Wendy, 293
Mendelson, Seth, 645
Menlo Worldwide, 449
Men's Wearhouse, 361
Mentzer, John T., 649, 657
Meow Mix, 541
Mercedes-Benz, 55, 155, 237, 257, 551
Merck, 324, 500
Merisant Co., 129
Merli, John, 641
Merrick, Amy, 202, 470, 654
Merrick, Bill, 662
Merrill Lynch, 290, 295, 378, 392, 623
Mervyn's, 411, 419, 464
Method, 465
Metro, 70
Metrojet, 109
Metropolitan Opera, 297
Meyer, David, 649
Meyer, Jeff, 640
Meyers, Bill, 595
Mezger, Roger, 648
MGM Studios, 309
Michaels, Daniel, 374
Michelin, 529
Michell, Paul C. N., 646
Michman, Ronald D., 652
Mickelson, Phil, 99
Micron Technology, 134
Microsoft, 20, 23, 27, 46, 64, 78, 247,
248, 249, 270, 312, 313, 351, 365,
373, 497, 534, 552, 618, 637, 639
Midas Muffler, 303, 388, 389, 416, 417
Midwest Airlines, 567
Mighty Ducks of Anaheim, 309
Milbank, Dana, 655
Miller, Paula M., 641, 642
Miller, Sarah Bryan, 645
Miller, Scott, 42
Miller Brewing Company, 215, 525
Ming, Jenny, 198

Mirage resorts, 118
Mississippi Tourism Commission, 190
Mitsubishi, 65, 243, 523
Mizner Park, 414
Mizrahi, Isaac, 198, 464, 465
Mobil, 423
Mobiltrak, 183
Modernista!, 550
Modicon, 586
Modine Manufacturing, 15
Mohr, Jakki J., 653
Moin, David, 655
Mokwa, Michael P., 661
Molina, Julie, 468
Moltenbrey, Karen, 477
Monaco Coach, 152
Moncrief, William C., 658
Monsanto Co., 129, 324, 352, 353
Monster.com, 217
Montgomery, Alan L., 649
Montgomery Elevator, 135
Montgomery Ward, 414, 419
Moore, Elizabeth S., 640
Moorman, Christine, 648
Moran, Ursula, 652
more.com, 626
Moreno, Katarzyna, 652, 655
Morgan, Babette, 655
Morgan, Neil A., 648
Moriarty, Rowland T., 652
Morris, Betsy, 646, 647
Morris, Michael H., 649
Morrison, Kimberly, 662
Morrissey, Brian, 663
Morse, Dan, 660
Morton International, 259, 260
Morton, Will, 663
Mossberg, Walter S., 640
Motel 6, 292, 296
Mothers Against Drunk Driving (MADD),
300
MotoPhoto, 220
Motorola, 15, 593, 638
Moultry, Gerald, 657
Mount, Ian, 514, 657
Mr. Goodcents, 416
Mr. Rooter, 416
Mr. Transmission, 416
MROverstocks.com, 462
MSN, 206, 534
MSN Music, 46
MSN Search beta, 78
MTV, 531, 538
Mucha, Thomas, 643
Mullaney, Timothy J., 655, 656, 658, 663
Muller, J. Joseph, 662
Muller, Joann, 650, 652
Mullman, Jeremy, 653
Mulvihill, Geoff, 658
Munoz, Sara Schaefer, 643
Munsingwear, 215
Murphy, H. Lee, 654
Murphy, Patrick E., 640, 643
Murphy, Victoria, 639
Murrieta, Ed, 566

Pfizer Inc., 384
Phelan, Mark, 555
Phelps Dodge, 325
Philips, 66, 593
Phillips-Van Heusen, 397
Phoosuphanusom, Srisamom, 656
Pierce, Nigel F., 648
Pierre Cardin, 271–272
Pilkington Libbey-Owens-Ford, 459
Piller, Charles, 651
Pillsbury, 7, 54, 227, 237, 238, 529
Pioneer Research Inc., 79, 444
Pitney Bowes, 15
Pitt, Leyland, 651
Pixar, 310
Pizza Hut, 65, 69, 99, 218, 262, 269
Planet Hollywood, 561
Plank, Richard E., 642
Playboy Channel, 80
Pleion Corp., 437
Plymouth, 215
Podmolik, Mary Ellen, 595, 658
Poel, Dirk Van den, 662
Polaroid Holding Co., 41
Polo Ralph Lauren, 149, 271, 299, 389,
    398, 421, 583
Pope, Justin, 239
Popeyes, 416
Popper, Edward D., 645
Popper, Margaret, 641
Porter Novelli, 194
Posavac, Steven S., 649
Posner, Bruce G., 657
Postal, Arthur D., 662
Pottery-Barn.com, 337
Pottinger, Matt, 593
Power, Christopher, 644
Powers, Kemp, 470
Powers, Thomas L., 649
Prahalad, C. K., 660
Prater, David, 658
Pratt & Whitney, 120, 127
Premier Industrial, 340
Pressler, Margaret Webb, 658
Pressler, Paul, 196, 197, 198
Pret A Manger, 635
Price Club, 466–467
Price, Sol, 466
PriceFarmer.com, 620
PriceGrabber.com, 427
Priceline.com Inc., 58, 296, 316–317, 337,
    341–342, 343
PriceScan.com, 427
PricewaterhouseCoopers, 205
Prince, 220
Principle Financial Group, 585
Printers' Ink, 492
Printwear Xpress, 416
Prior, Molly, 641
Pristin, Terry, 654
Procter & Gamble Company, 10, 15, 35,
    36, 68, 72, 77, 93, 120, 144, 145, 159,
    172, 174, 190, 214, 226, 227, 228,
    239, 260, 268, 270, 271, 340, 350,
    351, 362, 389, 393, 399, 456, 505,
    522, 535, 542, 571, 590, 615, 617

Proctor, R. A., 661
Professional Pricing Society, 331
ProFlowers, 625
PROMO Magazine, 539
Prudential Insurance, 290, 296, 508
Prystay, Chris, 374, 483
Publix supermarkets, 408, 422
Puente, Maria, 655
Pur, 93
Purk, Mary E., 651

Q

Qantas, 258
Qibla-Cola, 553
Quaker Oats, 186, 270, 553
Quaker State, 220
Qualitex Company, 278
Quality Inns, 159
Quelch, John A., 652
Quenqua, Douglas, 643
Quick, Bob, 640
Quick, Rebecca, 646
Quinn, Francis J., 656
Quinn, Peter, 646
Quirk's Marketing Research Review, 182
QVC, 107, 428

R

RadioShack Corp., 486, 564
Raghunathan, T. S., 648
Rainbow International, 416
Rainwater, 98
Ralph's, 3
Ralston Purina, 261
Ramada Inn, 240
Ramstad, Evan, 644
Rand Corporation, 164
Rangaswamy, Arvind, 645
Ranii, David, 655
Rao, S. Subba, 648
Rapid Transmissions, 399
Raskin, Andrew, 653
Rasmusson, Erika, 313
Ratliff, Duke, 651
Rave, 197
Rawe, Julie, 659
Raymond, Art, 657
Re/Max, 303, 508
Reagan, Michael, 80
Reagan National Airport, 371
RealNetworks, 27, 364
RealPlayer, 27
ReCellular, Inc., 114
Reclamere, Inc., 36
Red Bull, 482, 483
Red Cross, 288, 304
Red Envelope, 618
Red Hat Inc., 234, 328
Red Lobster, 301
Red Roof Inn, 206
Red Wing Shoe Company, 6, 505–506
Reda, Susan, 38
Reebok, 326, 390, 488
Reed, Dan, 374

Reese's, 237, 543
Reidy, Chris, 239
Reinhardt, Andy, 192, 313, 429
Reiss, Steven, 642
Reitman, Valerie, 652, 653
Remy International, 53
Renault, 66
Republican Party, 206
Research in Motion (RIM),
    637–639
Residence Inn, 292, 321
Revell, Janice, 374
Revlon, 299
Reyes, Sonia, 643
Reynolds Metals, 266
Rice, Faye, 644
Rich, Motoko, 650
Richard, Michael D., 641
Richardson, Helen L., 657
Rich's, 419
Richtel, Matt, 663
Riell, Howard, 566
Riemer, Bianca, 645, 646
Ries, Al, 645, 646
Riesz, Peter C., 649
Riper, Tom Van, 659
Rite Aid, 407
Ritz-Carlton, 302, 340, 586
Roberson, Jason, 654
Roberts, Dexter, 365, 429, 642
Roberts, Johnnie, 313
Roberts, Karl, 663
Roberts, Paul, 650
Roche, Karen, 652
Rochford, Linda, 644
Rocks, David, 648
Rockwell Automation, 456
Rogers, David, 657
Rogers, Everett M., 644
Rolex, 264, 339, 340, 389
Rollerblade Inc., 265, 575
Rollins, Kevin, 373, 374
Rolls-Royce, 155
Roman Catholic Church, 237
Roman, Monica, 641, 646
Ronkainen, Ilkka A., 644
Rooney, Paula, 639
Rosenberg, Bill, 141
Rosenberg, Daniel, 566
Rosenbloom, Bert, 652
Roskelly, Nick, 661
Ross Dress for Less, 421
Rossi, Peter E., 649
Roth, Daniel, 639
Rotisserie Grill, 635
Rovito, Markkus, 650
Rowland, Michael, 642
Royal Caribbean Cruise Line,
    290, 570
Royal Crown Cola, 65, 215
Rubbermaid Inc., 215, 326
Ruehl, 198
Ruekert, Robert W., 645
Russell, Thomas, 641
Ryan, Oliver, 640
Ryanair, 370

XM Satellite Radio, 578
XM Satellite Radio Holdings Inc., 78–81

Y

Yahoo!, 78, 364, 427, 534, 596, 619, 625
Yang, Catherine, 82, 363
Yankelovich Monitor, 182
Year-round consumption, 2–4
Yellow Pages, 296
Yellow Roadway Corp., 461
Yerak, Becky, 654
YMCA, 296
Yoon, Eunsang, 649

Yoplait, 299
Young, Lauren, 374
Yum! Brands, 65, 269
Yves Saint Laurent, 251

Z

Zachery, G. Pascal, 160
Zamiska, Nicholas, 643
Zamzam Cola, 553
Zane's Cycles, 428
Zany Brainy, 404
Zara, 582–584, 607–608
ZDS (Zenith Data Systems), 118
Zeithaml, Valarie A., 648

Zellner, Wendy, 374, 470, 566, 642, 649, 653
Zemanek, James E., Jr., 653
Zenith, 243
Zganjar, Leslie, 654
Zimmerman, Ann, 470, 650, 651, 652, 653, 654, 661
Zimmerman, Susan, 647
Zingo, 303
Zinn, Laura, 645, 646
Zipcar, 284–286, 305–306
Zizzo, Deborah, 656
Zoots, 298
Zuckerman, Amy, 657
Zuckerman, Gregory, 82

Subject Index

components of, 116–120
determinants of demand in, 123–127
nature and scope of, 114–115
Business position, 575
Business services market, 118
Business-to-business advertising, 524
Business-to-consumer advertising, 524
Business users, 114, 145
Buy classes, 130
Buyer-seller relationships, 132–133
Buyers, 132
Buying behavior, services marketing and, 292; see also Business buying behavior; Consumer decision making
Buying centers, 131–132, 503, 505
Buying motives, 130
Buying roles, 132
Buzz marketing, 96

C

Call centers, 593
Can-Spam Act, 40
Cannibalization, 572, 573
Careers, in marketing, 6, 23
Cartel, 70
Cash cows, 574
Cash discounts, 353–354, 528
Catalog retailing, 428, 429
Category killers, 377, 418, 419, 421–422
Category management, 401
Cause-related marketing, 299, 300
Cell phones, 488, 507, 538, 637
Central American Free Trade Agreement (CAFTA), 35
Change agent, 225
Channel assembly, 624
Channel conflict, 395
Channel control, 400
Channel power, 400
Channels of distribution; see Distribution channels
Chargeback, 395
Charter schools, 157
Chat rooms, 96
Children, 149, 492, 493
Children's Online Privacy Protection Act, 628
Children's Television Act, 40
Churn, 473
Cigarette Labeling and Advertising Acts, 40
Clayton Antitrust Act, 40, 356, 401
Clicks-and-modem retailers, 408
Client market, 292
Clipping services, 190
Closed-community stored-value systems, 629
Clustering, 622
Co-location, 624
Cobranding, 269
Collaborative CRM, 133
Collaborative filtering, 622
Collaborative planning, 401
Collaborative planning, forecasting, and replenishment (CPFR), 454–455
Combination plan, 515

Combined Statistical Area (CSA), 87
Commerce Business Daily, 118
Commercial information environment, 95–96
Commercialization, 221
Commissions, 514–515
Common costs; see Indirect costs
Common Market of the South (MERCOSUR), 60
Communication
   defined, 481
   personal/nonpersonal, 5
   promotion and process of, 481–483
Company sales branches, 63–64
Comparison advertising, 524–525
Compatibility, 226, 227
Compensation, sales force, 513–515
Competition, 33–34
   external macroenvironment and, 30, 33–34
   federal regulation and, 490–491
   integrated marketing communication (IMC) and, 480
   international marketing and, 57
   legislation affecting marketing and, 40
   market research and, 171
   new-product development process and, 221
   physical distribution and, 449
   positioning and, 235
   pricing and, 297–298, 325, 326–327, 330, 336–341, 346–350, 355, 356, 364
   promotion and, 474, 475, 490, 539
   retailers and, 411, 419
   Walgreen Company and, 430–431
Competitive intelligence, 171, 189–191, 239
Complaint-management process, 304
Complaints, 596, 621
Complexity, 226, 227
Computers, 613, 614–615; see also Internet; Software
Concentration strategy; see Single-segment strategy
Concept test, 178
Consultative sales person, 500–501
Consumer Credit Protection Act, 40
Consumer decision making, 91–107
   buying-decision process, 91–95
   information/purchase decisions, 95–97
   psychological factors and, 100–106
   situational influences and, 106–107
   social influences and, 97–100
Consumer Goods Pricing Act of 1975, 363
Consumer goods/products, 208–211, 384–385, 438–439
Consumer market, 86–90
Consumer Product Safety Act, 40, 591
Consumer Product Safety Commission (CPSC), 492
Consumer Product Warranty Act, 40
Consumer promotions, 539
Consumer protection, 40, 60
Consumer Reports, 104

Containerization, 456–457
Contract logistics, 449
Contract manufacturing, 64
Contracting, 64
Contractual vertical marketing system, 389, 412, 415–418
Contribution-margin method, 604, 605
Convenience centers, 413
Convenience goods, 208–209
Convenience samples, 188, 190
Convenience stores, 418, 422–423
Conviction stage, of buying readiness, 486
Cookies, 182, 183, 191, 628, 629
Cooperative advertising, 527–528
Coordination, 10, 45
Copy test, 178
Copycat packaging, 273
Copyright laws, 68
Corporate chains, 415
Corporate vertical marketing system, 388–389
Correlation analysis, 162–163
Corruption Perception Index, 18
Cost per thousand (CPM), 530
Cost-plus pricing, 69, 296, 330–333
Counter intelligence, 191
Counterfeit products, 263–264
Countertrade, 69
Coupons, 354, 539, 540, 541–542
Credit cards, 12, 107
Cross-functional teams, 228, 586
Cultural preferences, sales and, 503
Cultural/social forces, 34–39
   fashion-adoption process and, 249
   international marketing and, 54–55
   Internet and cultural barriers, 630
Culture, 54–55, 97
Cumulative discounts, 352–353
Customer equity, 14
Customer intimacy, 577
Customer relationship management (CRM), 11, 133, 455, 507
Customer satisfaction, 178, 516–517
Customer service
   complaints and, 596
   Internet and, 594, 595, 627
   inventory control and, 453
   outsourcing and, 593
   physical distribution and, 449–450
   W. W. Grainger, Inc. and, 435
Customer specialization, 588, 589–590
Customer support, personal selling and, 500
Customer(s)
   defined, 5
   expectations and international marketing, 53
   orientation, 10, 11–12
   quality and, 12
Customization, 11–12, 20, 486–487
Customs, 55, 66

D

Data collecting, 187, 188
Data mining, 176, 193
Data sources, 177

Est dimensions, 565
Ethical dilemma
    on "copycat" packaging, 273
    on advocacy research, 192
    on bookstores/warehouse clubs, 423
    on business buying, 134
    on college students, 586
    on competitive intelligence, 239
    on Corruption Perception Index, 18
    on genetically modified (GM) food, 42
    on gray marketing, 446
    on healthy food, 293
    on information gathering, 629
    on invention-promotion firms, 222
    on marketing plans, 567
    on marketing to children, 149
    on media content and advertising, 492
    on paid experts, 529
    on pharmaceutical companies, 324
    on sales person changing jobs and
        shifting clients to new employer, 515
    on slotting fees, 399
    on store-controlled electronic
        systems, 363
    on word-of-mouth communication, 96
Ethics, 17–18, 191–192, 493
Ethnic markets; *see* Race/ethnicity
Evaluation, 558, 563, 584, 596–607
    advertising and, 534–536
    annual marketing plan and, 568
    customer classes/order sizes and,
        606–607
    integrated marketing communication
        (IMC) and, 479–480
    market share analysis and, 600
    marketing cost analysis, 600–605
    of marketing performance, 596–598
    products and, 606
    sales person's performance and,
        516–517
    sales volume analysis and,
        598–600, 605
    territories and, 605–606
Event marketing, 542–543
Everyday low pricing (EDLP), 361–362
Exchange, 5
Exclusive dealership, 394
Exclusive dealing, 402
Exclusive distribution, 393, 394
Exclusive distributorship, 394
Exclusive-territory policy, 403
Execution, 529
Executive judgment, 164, 326
Executive summary, 568
Expanding the line, 294–295
Expected price, 325, 326
Experiment, 181, 185–186
Export agents, 63, 64
Export diversion; *see* Gray marketing
Export merchant, 63
Exporting, 63–64
Express warranty, 590
External macroenvironment, 29–42
    competition, 30, 33–34
    demographics, 30–32
    economic conditions, 32–33

political/legal forces, 39–41
    social/cultural forces, 34–39
    technology, 41–42
External microenvironment, 42–44
Extranet, 618
Eye cameras, 182

F

Fabricating materials/parts, 212, 213
Facilitating organizations, 43
Factory outlets, 421
Fads, 244, 245
Fair Packaging and Labeling Act, 40, 276
Fair-trade laws, 363
False representation, 192
Family
    branding, 268
    defined, 99
    international marketing and, 54
    life cycle, 88–89, 148
    packaging, 273
    size/structure, 100
    two-income families, 97
Fashion, defined, 249
Fashion-adoption process, 249–250
Fashion cycle, 250
Fashion industry, 14, 115, 248–252
Fashion obsolescence; *see* Style
    obsolescence
*FedBizOpps/Commerce Business
    Daily,* 118
Federal regulation, 490–492
Federal Trade Commission Act, 40, 401,
    490–492
Feedback, 482, 483
Field experiments, 186
Financial schedules, 568
Finished goods, 446
First-mover advantage, 246
Fishyback service, 459
Fixed costs, 328, 329, 604
Fixed prices, 620
Flat-rate pricing, 359
Flexible-price strategy, 297, 358–359
FOB factory pricing/FOB mill pricing,
    356, 357, 358
Focus groups, 67, 184, 185, 197, 622
Food, Drug and Cosmetics Act, 40
Food pyramid, 168–170, 194
For-profit services firms, 287, 288
Forecast demand, 16
Forecasting, 160–164, 186, 251, 401
Foreign Corrupt Practices Act, 71
Foreign exchange, 69
Form utility, 21
4PL, 449
Franchise system, 416
Franchisee, 416
Franchising, 64, 416–418
Franchisor, 416
Free standing inserts (FSI), 541
Freight-absorption pricing, 358
Freight forwarders, 460
Frequent shopper programs, 177
Frugging, 192

FTC Improvement Act, 40
Fulfillment, 447–448, 462, 620–621
Full-cost method, 604, 605
Full nest I life-cycle stage, 89
Full nest II life-cycle stage, 89
Full-service wholesalers, 441–442
Functional discounts; *see* Trade discounts

G

Gambling casinos, 106, 107
Gatekeepers, 132
GE business screen, 575–576, 577
Gender roles, 36–37, 97
General Agreement on Tariffs and Trade
    (GATT), 58–59
Generation X, 32
Generation Y, 32
Generic names, 263–264
Genetically modified (GM) food, 42
Geodemographic clustering, 148
Geographic pricing strategies, 356–358
Geographic segmentation, 146–147, 152
Geographic specialization, 587–589
Global perspective; *see also* International
    marketing
    on brands, 259, 483
    on cell phones, 538
    on China, 571
    on competition and trade
        agreements, 35
    on consumer markets, 93
    on consumer protection, 20
    on containerization, 457
    on cultural preferences and
        sales, 503
    on currency, 340
    on exporting, 119
    on fashions, 251
    on First Data, 160
    on global services growth, 303
    on gray marketing, 383
    on high technology products/low
        technology infrastructure, 630
    on market research of auto
        manufacturers, 178
    on new-product ideas, 220
    on postsale services, 593
    on promotion, 483
    on retailers, 429
    on Wal-Mart, 348
Global positioning system (GPS),
    303, 629
Goals; *see* Objectives
Government market, 117–118
Government reports, 190
Governmental relationships with
    industries, 39
Grade label, 275
Gray marketing, 70–71, 383, 384, 446
Green River ordinance, 492–493
Grocery retailing, online, 38
Gross national income (GNI), 56
Growth stage, product life cycle, 241–242,
    243, 246, 247
Guarantees; *see* Warranties

H

Haptics, 131
Harvest strategy, 576
Health, social/cultural forces and, 39
Heterogeneity, 291
Hierarchy of effects, 485
High-low pricing, 361–362
Hispanics, 31, 55, 90, 220
Horizontal business markets, 126
Horizontal conflict, 395–396
Horizontal cooperative advertising, 528
Hotspotting, 619
Households, 99, 100
Hypothesis, 179–180, 181, 184

I

Iceberg principle, 597–598
Ideal self-concept, 105
Image utility, 21
Imitative products, 217–218
Implementation, 558, 563, 568,
    584–590, 613
Implied warranty, 590–591
Import-export agents, 445
Import quota, 58
Impulse buying, 92
Incentives, 301, 514
Income, consumer demographics and,
    89–90
Independent retailers, 415
Indirect-action advertising, 525
Indirect costs, 605
Indirect distribution, 384
Indirect tests, 536
Industrial Design Excellence Awards
    (IDEA), 277
Industrial distributors, 385, 439
Industrializing countries, 56
Inflation, 33
Influencers, 132
Infoimaging, 253
Infomercials, 428
Informal investigation, 180
Information; see also Information
    economy, marketing in the
    in business marketing, 122–123
    economy, 626–631
    importance of, 612–613
    purchase decisions and, 95–97
    technology, 613–618
    utility, 21
Information economy, marketing in the
    on bots, 427
    on credit cards, 12
    on electronic data gathering, 151
    on electronic technology and sales, 507
    on haptics, 131
    on Internet, 294
    on Internet and cannibalizations, 573
    on Internet and middlemen, 392
    on Internet pop-up ads, 103
    on new products (digital video
        recorders), 217
    on offshore call centers, 53

on online customer service, 595
on online grocery retailing, 38
on passive observation, 183
on permission marketing, 488
on pricing, 337
on television advertising audience
    measurement, 537
on tracking systems, 447
Infrastructure, 56
Initial public offering (IPO), 77
Initiative for a Competitive Inner City
    (ICIC), 88
Innovation adopter categories, 224
Innovative products, 217
Innovators, 224, 251
Inseparability, 291, 293
Inside order taker, 500
Inside Radio, 81
Inside selling, 499
Installations, 212, 213–214
Institutional advertising, 525
Intangibility, 290, 293, 295
Integrated marketing communication
    (IMC), 478–480
Intellectual property rights, 229
Intensive distribution, 393–394
Interactive media, 533–534
Intercity/intracity shipping, 457–458
Interest, personal selling process and, 509
Interest rates, 33
Intermediaries, 117, 380–381
Intermodal transportation, 459, 460
Internal forces, 44–45
Internal marketing, 300
International marketing, 49–82, 119–120;
        see also Global perspective
    attraction of, 52–53
    competition and, 30
    FedEx and, 201
    global sales teams, 504
    Idea Central Global and, 205
    IKEA and, 48–50, 74
    intermodal transportation and, 459
    Internet and, 629–630
    language and, 55, 63
    marketing information systems and,
        173–174
    marketing mix and, 67–73
    organization structures for, 63–67
    significance of international trade,
        50–52
    strategic planning for, 53–62
    summary of, 73
    test marketing and, 187
    UPS and, 201
    warehouse clubs and, 469
Internet; *see also* E-mail; Websites
    advertising and, 525–526
    appliances, 534
    auctions, 123, 136, 445, 506–507,
        617, 620, 624
    banking service, 145
    benefit segmentation and, 150–151
    bots, 95, 337, 427
    brokers and, 118

business market segmentation and, 153
business markets buying practices
    and, 136
cannibalization and, 573
chat rooms, 96
competitive intelligence and, 191
cookies, 182, 183, 191
coupons and, 542
customer relationships and, 11
customer service and, 594, 595, 627
Dell Inc. and, 372
digital-music services, 26–28, 46–47
direct mail and, 532
direct marketing and, 428
distribution and, 298, 378, 381, 384,
    387, 391, 395, 396, 398, 447,
    449, 456
e-tailers, 38, 408, 412, 426, 429, 454
elasticity of demand and, 121
electronic bulletin boards, 136
electronic commerce, 618
electronic date interchange (EDI)
    and, 452
electronic information transfer,
    615–616
electronic networking, 614–615, 617
electronic transactions, 617
executive judgment and, 164
exporting and, 63
fashion trends and, 251
Federal Trade Commission and, 491
fulfillment and, 448
future of information economy and,
    630–631
Idea Central and, 205
IKEA and, 49
impact of, on markets, 618–621
impact on marketing strategy, 621–626
information and, 123
information quality/quality and,
    626–627
intangibility and, 290
as interactive media, 533–534
internal forces and online retailers, 44
international marketing and, 57, 68,
    72, 119–120, 629–630
introduction to, 614
kiosks, 429, 501, 627
local operating laws and, 58
market-response systems and, 453
marketing to children and, 149
mass customization and, 12
merchandise returns and, 594
middlemen and, 392
Netflix and, 473, 494
online music stores, 26–28
package-delivery firms and, 460
patronage motives and, 94–95
percentage of retail sales, 302
personal selling and, 499
place utility and, 21
pop-up ads, 103
pricing and, 296, 337, 365, 370
promotion and, 477
regulation of, 492

resellers and, 117
rural population and, 87
sampling and, 188, 541
Sam's Club and, 469
satellite radio and, 79, 81
security/privacy and, 627–629
selling, 506–507
services marketing and, 300, 303
shipping suppliers and, 199
spamming, 532
Starbucks and, 578
suppliers and, 43
supply chain management and, 448
surveys, 185
television advertising and, 531
video games and, 312
W. W. Grainger, Inc. and, 435, 462
warranties and, 593
weblogs, 488, 526, 621, 626
wholesaling and, 437
Interstate trade, 355
Interviews, 183–184, 188
Intranets, 614
Intrastate trade, 355
Introduction stage, product life cycle,
241–242, 243, 246
Intrusiveness, 191
Invention, 68
Invention-promotion firms, 222
Inventory
control, 446, 448, 450, 451, 452–455
location and warehousing, 455–456
W. W. Grainger, Inc. and, 462
Inverse demand, 326
Invest strategy, 576
ISO 9000, 280

J

Jobbers, 439
Joint ventures, 64–65, 66
Just-in-time (JIT) production/delivery,
135, 453, 460

K

Kefauver-Harris Drug Amendments, 40
Key accounts, 123
Kinked demand, 337–338, 339
Knowledge stage, of buying readiness, 485

L

Labeling, 68, 272, 275–276
Laboratory, 185–186
Laggards, 225
Lanham Trademark Act, 40, 258, 262,
278, 490, 491
Late adopters, 224, 251
Late majority, 225
Laws, 39–40, 191
Layout, 413
Leader pricing, 360
Leaders, 360
Learning, 103–104
Leasing, 135–136

Less developed countries (LDCs), 56
Less-than-truckload (LTL), 200
Level of involvement, 92
Licensing, 64
Life-long learning, 28
Lifestyle, 149, 320
Lifestyle centers, 413, 414
Liking stage, of buying readiness,
485–486
Limited-line stores, 418, 420–422
Line extensions, 237, 238, 239, 271
Links, 616
List of values (LOV), 150
List price; see Base price
Lobbying, 545
Local-content law, 58
Local operating laws, 58
Local strategy, 54
Location, 412–414
Logistics; see Physical distribution
Logo, 258
Long-range planning, 561–562
Loss leader, 360
Lower-lower class, 99
Lower-middle class, 98
Loyalty, 92, 132

M

Macroenvironmental forces, 28, 29
Magazines, 530, 533, 541
Mail-in rebates, 354
Mail-order pharmacies, 430–431
Mail surveys, 185
Maintenance, repair, and operations
(MRO) products, 435
Maintenance/repairs, 594–596
Major accounts organization, 589–590
Mall intercept interview, 184
Management, defined, 558
Manufacturer's agents, 443–444, 451
Manufacturer's representatives, 443–444
Manufacturer's sales branch, 439–440
Manufacturer's sales facility, 439
Manufacturer's sales office, 439, 440
Marginal analysis, 330, 335–336
Marginal cost, 329, 336
Marginal cost curve, 330
Marginal revenue, 335, 336
Market, defined, 5, 15, 42–43
Market-acceptance stage, product life
cycle; see Growth stage, product
life cycle
Market-aggregation strategy, 154–155
Market attractiveness, 575
Market demand, 222
Market factor, 160–161
Market-factor analysis, 162, 164
Market orientation, 8–9
Market-penetration pricing, 351
Market potential, 161
Market research, 16, 168–195, 480, 622;
see also Marketing research
procedure
competitive intelligence and, 189–191

databases/data warehouses/data
mining and, 175–177
decision support systems (DSS) and,
174–175
defined, 171
ethical issues in, 191–192
food pyramid and, 168–170, 194
Gap Inc. and, 196–198
international marketing and, 67
marketing information systems (MkIS)
and, 172–174
scope of activities, 171–172
status of, 192–193
uses of, 170–171
Market-response systems, 453–455
Market segmentation, 142–154
behavioral segmentation, 150–151
benefits of, 143–144
business markets and, 152–154
defined, 143
demographic segmentation, 147–148
geographic segmentation,
146–147, 152
marketing planning and, 565–566
personal selling process and, 508
process of, 144–145
psychographic segmentation, 147,
148–150, 320
segmentation studies, 178, 197
services marketing and, 292
ultimate consumers/business users and,
145–146
Market segments, 15–16, 142
Market share, 160, 324, 575
Market-share analysis, 178, 600
Market-skimming pricing, 350
Market tests, 220–221
Marketing
concept, 9–15
cost of, 20
defined, 5–6
evolution of, 6–9
expenditures, 14
importance of, 18–23
nature and scope of, 4–6
programs, company's, 15–16
top executive in, 8
Marketing audits, 596–597
Marketing communications
manager, 480
Marketing cost analysis, 598,
600–605, 606
Marketing information system (MkIS),
171, 172–174, 193
Marketing intermediaries, 43–44
Marketing mix, 16–17
channels of distribution and, 381
geographic segmentation and, 147
integrated marketing communication
(IMC) and, 478
international marketing and, 50, 53,
67–73
market research and, 170–171
market segmentation and, 142
physical distribution and, 449

Security/privacy, Internet, 627–629
Segmentation; *see* Market segmentation
Selective attention, 102
Selective-demand advertising, 524
Selective distortion, 102
Selective distribution, 393, 394
Selective perception, 102
Selective retention, 102, 103
Self-concept, 105
Selling agents, 445
Selling centers, 503, 505
Separable expenses; *see* Direct costs
Service encounter, 300
Service mark, 258
Service quality, 301–302
Services; *see also* Services marketing
 defined, 286–287
 distribution of, 386
 managing service quality, 301–302
 market, 118
 marketers, 22
 nature and importance of, 286–288
 scope of, 287–288
Services marketing, 22, 289–301; *see also*
 Services
 characteristics of services, 290–292
 development of, 289
 distribution system and, 298–299
 future of, 302–304
 pricing structure and, 296–298
 product planning and, 293–296
 promotional program and, 299–301
Sherman Antitrust Act, 40, 401
Shipping rates, 451
Shopping centers, 413
Shopping goods, 209–221
Shopping robots (bots), 95, 337, 427
Short-range planning, 562
Simulated test market, 186–187
Single parents life-cycle stage, 89
Single-price strategy, 359
Single-segment strategy, 154
Single-source data, 177
Situation analysis, 179–180, 562,
 564, 568
Situational influences, consumer decision
 making and, 106–107
Slogans, 72, 296, 489
Slotting fees/allowances, 398–399
Small-order problem, 606–607
Smart box, 457
Smart cards, 629
Social class, 98–99, 148, 292
Social/cultural forces; *see* Cultural/social
 forces
Social influences, consumer decision
 making and, 97–100
Social information environment, 96
Social legislation/regulations, 39
Social mobility, 98
Social responsibility, 200, 277, 319
Social-responsibility report, 197
Societal marketing concept, 14–15
Software, 34, 53
South Asian Association for Regional
 Cooperation (SAARC), 61

Spamming, 532, 625
Specialty goods, 209, 210–211
Specialty stores, 418, 421
Sponsorships, 542–543, 625
Sports, extreme, 22
Sports drinks, 144
Stabilizing prices, 325
Staggers Rail Act, 40, 447
Standard Industrial Classification (SIC)
 system, 125
Standard Metropolitan Areas
 (SMAs), 125
Standards/certification, 58
Stars, 573–574
State/local regulation, 492–493
State Unfair Trade Practices Acts, 40
Stealth marketing, 32
Stimulus-response theory, 103–104
Straight-commission plan, 515
Straight rebuy, 130
Straight salary, 514
Strategic alliances, 65–66
Strategic business units (SBU), 569–570,
 573–577
Strategic company planning,
 562–563, 569
Strategic marketing planning, 562,
 563–567, 569, 587
Strategic window, 559
Strategy, defined, 346, 561
Streaming services, 27
Style, defined, 249
Style obsolescence, 249
Subcultures, 97–98
Subsidized industries, 52
Substitute products, 34
Suburban population, 88
Suggested list price, 363
Sugging, 192
Supercenters, 420
Supermarket, 422
Supermarket retailing, 422
Supermarkets, 418
Suppliers, 43, 229
Supply chain, 132
Supply chain management (SCM),
 448–449, 452, 454, 455
Supply chain optimization, 455
Surplus, 51
Survey(s), 181, 183, 190, 197
 of buyer intentions, 163, 326
 Internet, 185, 622
 mail, 185
 telephone, 67, 184–185, 191
SWOT assessment, 564
Syndicated research, 172
Syndicated services, 171
Systems selling, 503–504

T

Tactics, 561, 568
Target audience(s), 480
 advertising and, 524, 527, 529, 530
 integrated marketing communication
 (IMC) and, 478

Internet and, 625
promotion and, 475, 483,
 484–485, 540
Target-market strategies, 154–157
Target market(s), 16, 142
 channels of distribution and, 390
 marketing planning and, 565–566
 retailers and, 411
 services marketing and, 292
Target return, 322
Tariffs, 58
Taxes, 52
Team selling, 503, 590
Technological obsolescence, 249
Technology, 41–42, 52, 303; *see also*
 Internet
Teens, 184
Telemarketing, 425, 505–506
 business market segmentation
 and, 153
 manufacturer's agents and, 444
 personal selling and, 502, 509
 services marketing and, 300
 state/local regulation and, 492
 Telephone Consumer Protection Act of
 1991 and, 491
Telephone Consumer Protection Act of
 1991, 491
Telephone surveys, 67, 184–185, 191
Televised shopping, 428
Television, 538, 613
 advertising, 11, 528, 530, 531–532,
 535, 537
Terms of purchase, 107
Territories, 605–606
Test marketing, 163, 186,
 220–221, 326
Third-party logistics (3PL); *see* Contract
 logistics
Time, 37–38, 97, 106
Time utility, 21, 450
Timetables, 568
Total cost, 329
Total cost concept, 448
Total fixed cost, 328, 329, 335
Total quality management (TQM), 13,
 279–280
Total variable cost, 328, 329
Tracking systems, 447
Trade agreements, 58–62
Trade balance, 51
Trade barriers, 52, 58
Trade deficit, 51
Trade discounts, 353, 356
Trade intermediaries, 390
Trade promotions, 477, 539
Trade secret laws, 191
Trade shows, 543
Trade surplus, 52
Trademark Law Revision Act, 258
Trademark(s)
 brand names and, 264
 defined, 258
 international marketing and, 68
 licensing, 271–272
Trading down, 240–241, 483

Trading up, 240–241, 483
Transportation, 129, 446, 447, 448, 449, 450, 457–460
Trend analysis, 163
Trialability, 226
Trickle-across, theory of fashion adoption, 250
Trickle-down, theory of fashion adoption, 250
Trickle-up, theory of fashion adoption, 250
Truck distributors, 442
Truck jobbers, 442
Tying contracts, 402–403

U

Ultimate consumers, 86, 145
Undifferentiated-market strategy; *see* Market-aggregation strategy
Unfair-practices acts/unfair-sales acts, 360–361
Uniform delivered pricing, 357
Uniform resource locators (URLs), 4
Uninvolveds, 320
Unit value, 486–487
Universal design, 277
Unsought goods, 211
Upper class, 98
Upper-lower class, 98
Upper-middle class, 98
Urban population, 87
USA Today, 78
Usage rate, 151, 153–154
Users, 132
Utility, 20–21, 318

V

Value, 5, 13, 44, 320, 321
Value added, 114–115

Value chain, 43–44, 229, 378
Value creation, 13
Value disciplines, 577
Value pricing, 347, 348–349
Values, 150
Variable costs, 328, 335, 604
Variable-price strategy; *see* Flexible-price strategy
Vertical business markets, 125–126
Vertical conflict, 396–400
Vertical cooperative advertising, 527–528
Vertical marketing system (VMS), 388–389, 398, 442
Video games, 300, 311–314
Viral marketing, 96, 488, 526
Virtual coupons, 354
Visualization, 290
Voice-over-IP, 595
Voluntary chains, 416

W

Wants; *see* Needs/wants
Warehouse clubs, 418, 423
Warehousing, 446, 450, 455–456
Warning labels, 592
Warranties, 584, 590–593
Webb-Pomerene Act, 70
Weblogs, 488, 526, 621, 626
Websites, 3, 614, 616, 617, 619, 623, 626; *see also* Internet; World Wide Web
Wheeler-Lea Act, 40
Wheeler-Lea Amendment, 490–491
Wholesalers, 379, 409, 412, 416
    advertising and, 524, 527
    business markets and, 115, 116
    collaborative planning, forecasting, and replenishment (CPFR), 454–455

Computer Discount Warehouse Corporation (CDW), 497
    convenience goods and, 209
    discounts and, 353
    market-response systems and, 453
    merchant, 385, 439, 440, 441–443, 451
    new products and, 223
    personal selling and, 499, 500
    promotion and, 484
    Robinson-Patman Act and, 491
    W. W. Grainger, Inc. as, 434–436
Wholesaling
    agent wholesaling middlemen, 443–445
    middlemen, 436, 437, 439–440, 444
    nature and importance of, 436–440
Wholly owned subsidiaries, 66
Women, changing role of, 36–37
Word-of-mouth (WOM) communication, 96, 225, 525–526, 596, 621
World Wide Web, 534, 614; *see also* Internet; Websites

Y

Year-round consumption, 450
Yellow pages, 533
Young married life-cycle stage, 89

Z

Zone-delivered pricing, 357